Egon Ronay's MLC Guide 1992

Pubs

Including the Best of British Meat Dishes

Over 1750 establishments in Great Britain

D1400085

In association **with**

Sponsored by the Meat
and Livestock Commission

Egon Ronay's Guides
35 Tadema Road
London SW10 0PZ

Editor **Andrea Gillies**

Cover Illustration
© **Leo Duff**

Distributed by
AA Distribution Services Ltd
Dunhams Lane
Letchworth Hertfordshire

ISBN 1-871784-20-4

Typeset in Great Britain
Dorchester Typesetting Group Ltd
Dorchester, Dorset

Printed in Great Britain
The Grosvenor Press Ltd
Portsmouth, Hampshire

*All establishments are inspected anonymously
by Egon Ronay's Guides' team of professional
inspectors. Inspectors may reveal their
identities at establishments in order to check
facilities. The Guide is independent in its
editorial selection and does not accept
advertising, payment or hospitality from
listed establishments.*

Contents

FOREWORD

British Meat Catering Service is delighted to be sponsoring the 1992 edition of Egon Ronay's Pub Guide at a time when meat-based meals are becoming more popular than ever in pubs.

Pubs have developed a reputation for providing a wide selection of wholesome and delicious meat dishes ranging from traditional home-cooked favourites such as steak and kidney pie and succulent Sunday roasts, to more exotic flavours such as pork stir-fry, marinated lamb with garlic and Mexican spicy beef.

Not only is meat favourite with customers – recent independent surveys show that 97% of the population eat meat. When eating out they are also increasingly looking for quality and variety.

To satisfy this demand more and more publicans are buying British. In recognition of this, the British Meat Catering Service is working closely with brewers and individual publicans providing advice and guidance on all aspects of British meat and meat meals.

Brian Kilkenny,
Head of Home Marketing
Meat and Livestock Commission

A Short Guide To The Guide

Egon Ronay's MLC Pub Guide 1992 has a new size and format. As will be instantly apparent when you flick through the pages, pubs are now listed by county in England, Scotland and Wales and by island in the Channel Islands and Isle of Man sections. You'll find Isle of Wight under I, Greater London under L, Greater Manchester (with Merseyside) under M, and West Midlands under W.

Within each county chapter, there are two sorts of entry: first, the full inspectors' reports on selected pubs; second, short listings in alphabetical place-name order. Don't assume that a pub accorded only a short entry is automatically less worthwhile than a fully reported place. If a pub has reliably good food or accommodation or both we say so unambiguously in the course of a short entry; equally, some of the long reports we publish here are freely critical in tone.

Symbols at the top of a report offer a succinct reference as to what inspectors feel is notable about a pub. Top prize is the star symbol for outstanding food, and for that certain indefinable 'something' that makes a good pub special. Other awards are for good food (good, but not of star quality), bed and breakfast (not necessarily for luxury, but for a basic standard of comfort and cleanliness, and good value for money), for excellent cheeses, good wines by the glass, outdoor seating (a good summer pub, in other words), and for children's facilities.

★	outstanding
FOOD	good food
🍖	Best of British meat
🧀	British Farmhouse cheeses
🍷	good wines by the glass
B&B	good bed and breakfast
☼	good summer pub
☺	good family facilities

The very cream of this crop are our Pubs of 1992.

HOURS

If a listing doesn't mention Sunday opening hours, specifically, you can assume the standard ones (12-3, 7-10.30) are kept. If special Sunday lunchtime hours only are listed (say 12-2.30), then you can assume Sunday evening hours are standard. We say if a pub is closed during standard opening hours – many Welsh pubs are still closed on Sundays, and this is also still true in some areas of Scotland. Other Scottish pubs stay open all day, even on Sunday, but the usual Scottish Sunday hours are probably 12.30-2.30, 6.30-11. On the Channel Islands, pubs only open on Sunday if they are serving food; Jersey Sunday hours are 11-1, 4.30-11.

BAR SNACKS

The phrase 'bar snacks', refers to sandwiches, ploughmans lunches and other light snacks, and not bar meals, irrespective of how a particular pub describes its bar food.

TYPICAL DISHES

The 'typical dishes' list typically includes a home-made soup, one other starter, three main courses and a home-made pudding. We list bar meals first and (where applicable) restaurant dishes second. We specify vegetarian meals where they are available, and generally offer an example.

CHILDREN'S MENU/PORTIONS

'Children's Menu' usually means a short list of things with chips - beefburgers, fishfingers, baked beans, though it's sometimes more adventurous. 'Children's Portions' means smaller portions of ordinary adult meals, at smaller prices. It doesn't usually apply to everything on the menu, though.

CHEESE

Cheese means that a selection of better-than-average cheeses is served.

BEER

Beer means real, cask-conditioned traditional draught beers. We name the breweries and/or their beers, listed in brewery-alphabetical order. To the untutored eye, this can look a little illogical: it results in lists like 'Ruddles, Webster's; Thwaites', because Ruddles and Webster's belong to the same brewery empire; note that beers belonging to the same brewery are separated by a comma, those of different breweries, by a semi-colon.

WHISKY

Whisky means that the pub offers an interesting variety of, or unusually high number of Single Malts.

CIDER

A rare appearance in the listings: **Cider** refers to real, cask-conditioned cider, also known as Farmhouse Cider (though mostly these days it's commercially made in purpose-built plants).

FAMILY ROOMS

A family room is legally defined as any room in a pub that doesn't have a bar counter in it; some pubs have several rooms which fit this description, others none. It's entirely at the discretion of the licensee as to whether accompanied under-age children are allowed into the pub at all, however, as well as which, if any, of the legally usable rooms are designated family rooms. Sometimes they are less comfortable and appealing rooms than the rest of the pub, quite often doubling as pool or games rooms, for instance. If a pub doesn't have a family room as such, but still allows children into the pub for meals, we say so.

ACCOMMODATION

Christmas and New Year closure are not mentioned specifically; phone to check. Room prices are quoted for a double room (the all-inclusive price for two people, with breakfast), followed by the single room (or single occupancy) price. If there's just one price quoted, it's for a double room. If there are both standard and en suite rooms available, the price is likely to be for the standard one. There may be variations in price according to room size and season; check before booking. Children not catered for unless specifically mentioned.

All details and prices are up-to-date at the time of going to press.

Introduction

Ask any foreign tourist what it is that makes Britain British and chances are they'll include the public house on their list. Overseas visitors have a quaint and rosy vision of the Great British Pub, often spoiled when they visit them in person. Nasty soulless modernisation, loud music, lager louts and the worst food in the world, can be their impression of our great national institution. Extreme perhaps, but not unusual. What should have been a routine inspection of a well-known, creakily ancient and atmospheric old inn on the tourist trail turned into an ordeal for one of our inspectors this summer. Happily and comfortably seated in the creakily ancient and atmospheric old bar of said establishment, a decent pint of ale in hand, the time came to consult the bar meals menu. From the simple but appetising list of 'good home cooking' came a mushroom soup, unmistakeably out of a well-known tin, and not thinned enough, but with an undeniably fresh raw mushroom prettily sliced and arranged on top; and an avocado and prawn salad (£5.75), which turned up as a plateful of lettuce, pungent onion slices, raw peppers and the like, with a small cluster of soggy defrosted prawns in a marie-rose sauce (from a jar), and, pièce de résistance, a quarter of a rock-hard avocado fanned on top, its flesh more black than green. The manager was summoned; he was sorry, but it was the only avocado they had left. When the time came to pay, 45 pence had been deducted from the bill, in reparation for the avocado. Judging from our postbag, experiences like this are not uncommon.

It's a time of change in the Great British Pub, with an astonishing number of new licensees and owners to report this year. There's a lot of selling off and swapping going on. Redevelopment is rife. Partly this is due to the Monopolies and Mergers Commission report on the tied house system; it's also to do with growing ambitions in what others might call The Food Sector, still the fastest growing source of pub profits. The old-fashioned public house is an increasingly precarious survivor; not many millions to be made from a simple, foodless country alehouse where locals slump over their beers for hours on end, after all. Modern pub marketing is now a big business, and it's facility crazy: plush refurbishments for added comfort, play areas for children, space games and video juke boxes for the youth. But cheap and easy food in generous portions, that's the most profitable facility of them all, hence the all too familiar scampi and chips pub, which has no use for a cook at all, but employs a kitchen technician to oversee the microwave, fryer and deep freeze.

There's a widespread myth that good food is necessarily expensive food. It's not a surprising myth, however. Unlike, say, the French, we have no cheap and decent café culture, we don't think it normal and everyday to go out for lunch; going out to eat, in the happy expectation of eating decently, is still a great treat here. But a new generation of pub cooks is cutting right across this syndrome. A home-made pie (one with a proper pastry crust, and not a dollop of filling with a pre-cooked pastry puff square plonked on top), a homely, warming bake or layer, a simply cooked piece of quality meat or fish, with properly cooked fresh vegetables: these and other dishes like them are beginning to appear at prices which can match, even undercut, the kitchen fryer menu. From the top end of the scale, meanwhile, the influences of smart cuisine, at once exotic and exquisitely simple, are filtering visibly into the tradition too, and not only in expensive pub restaurants either, but also on mainstream lounge bar menus at comparatively bargain prices. Good news then, but not all good news. There are still too many licensees who can't be bothered, who lack imagination, and who hide behind the twin defence lines of the deep fryer menu: 'it's what the people want', and 'anything else is too expensive'. Too many previously good pubs have been submerged in vinegar bottles and frozen peas. It's getting harder to find a pub which offers no food at all; one of the most recent trends is towards over-ambition and something you might call Fake Gourmet. At the cheap end there's 'home cooking' which turns out to be home assembly of packet ingredients, or dressing up the convenience dish with a few little extras. In the medium price range, many apparently interesting menus are in fact supplied en masse by the increasingly sophisticated pub catering industry; companies who bulk produce and supply dishes like chicken with leeks and stilton, duck à l'orange, plaice stuffed with prawns, fish pie, or vegetarian meals like the now ubiquitous mushroom and nut fettuccine. Just because it's not a scampi and chips menu doesn't mean it's not bought in. At the top end of the market, the post-nouvelle modern cooking is now making real inroads into evening menus. Some of this is remarkably proficient and unbeatably cheap; but, there are an awful lot of badly handled filo pastry parcels and juliennes of leek and reduced stocks about as well.

But these are subtle and survivable problems when compared to the brash high street carvery and steakhouse empires, or The Chains, as they're commonly known. These have earned themselves a reputation for family value and traditional English cooking (of the roast beef and mixed grill with onion rings sort), which is, on inspection, rarely deserved. More worrying is the way Chain philosophy is spreading into pub catering: pizza parlours, 'brasseries' and farmhouse pantries abound.

There were over 65,000 pubs in Britain at the last count. Most communities have one at least. What a potential there is for simple, honest home cooking, unpretentious, good value, reliably edible, to become familiar and sociable, and, before too long, as traditional as deep frozen deep-fried orange-breadcrumbed scampi is now.

For an even more favourable view
of California wines,
just ask the wine waiter.

Wines of the Californias

COULD THIS BE THE MOST PERFECT PLACE ON EARTH TO MAKE WINE?

AMERICAN EXPRESS IS PROUD TO SUPPORT THE BEST OF BRITISH PUBS

American Express has long been associated with excellence. And the pubs in this year's Guide definitely fall into the "excellent" category.

Of course, particular congratulations are in order for the Pubs of the Year, shown opposite. But all the pubs featured offer more than just an extensive drinks menu.

Most serve food of a standard comparable with that of fine restaurants and offer very good value. Furthermore, the majority of proprietors have paid close attention to decor and atmosphere, from "olde worlde" to modern "designer" interiors. Some even offer excellent accommodation.

All this means that a pub featured in this Guide is more than just a place to begin an evening out. This is why many of the publicans have decided to welcome the American Express Card – a particular benefit to those who want more than a quick drink or two.

After all, as Cardmembers will already know, the American Express Card is far more convenient to carry than large amounts of cash.

And it's more flexible. If you're enjoying an evening in a pub but don't have a great deal of money with you, there's no need to move on to a restaurant, make a trip to the nearest cash dispenser or cut the evening short – you simply pay with The Card.

If you carry the American Express Card, you can add 3,000 British pubs to the long list of establishments where you'll already be accustomed to using it – like restaurants, hotels and a huge variety of shops. If you don't carry one, perhaps you should consider applying. Just call 0273 696933 for an application.

OUR 1992 PUBS OF THE YEAR

1992 PUB OF THE YEAR:
ROEBUCK, BRIMFIELD, HEREFORD & WORCESTER
The grand and overall winner of our prestigious title, Egon Ronay's Pub of the Year for 1992, is the Roebuck, for its individual style, excellent food in both the superb restaurant and characterful bar, its lovely bedrooms and breakfasts, and last, but by no means least, for its licensees, John and Carole Evans, who work so hard to ensure that not only is this one of the most interesting pubs in Britain to dine in, but also, beneath and behind all its many achievements, a real pub of traditional pub character.

1992 NEWCOMER OF THE YEAR:
WOMBWELL ARMS, WASS, NORTH YORKSHIRE
This part of Yorkshire is already well provided for with lovely old country inns, but the Wombwell Arms impressed us very much this year, with its meteoric rise from nowhere to one of the best in the north of England, thanks to imaginative rejuvenation from a previously very ordinary local. For its stylish refurbishment, delicious but pleasingly informal bistro-style food, impressive bedrooms and jovial hosts, the Wombwell Arms is our 1992 Newcomer of the Year.

1992 BRITISH MEAT PUB OF THE YEAR:
SUN INN, WINFORTON, HEREFORD & WORCESTER
Innovative cooking by the tremendously talented landlady here, described as "inspirational" by our visiting inspector, brings an enthusiastic and individualistic approach to all sorts of delicious meat meals, from eastern influenced dishes like lamb in coriander and lime, to popular and robustly traditional pies like the celebrated Piggy In The Orchard. For her eclectic and international approach to cooking good British meat, Wendy Hibbard wins for the Sun Inn at Winforton the title 1992 British Meat Pub of the Year.

The Bell at Stilton, Cambs is commended for its cooking of British lamb; The Rose and Crown at Romalkdirk, Co. Durham serves some of the best British pork, and British beef finds one of its happiest homes at the Royal Oak, Over Stratton, Somerset.

1992 BED AND BREAKFAST PUB OF THE YEAR:
GRIFFIN, LLYSWEN, POWYS
By no means new to the winner's podium, the Griffin is still a hard pub to beat for a pampering but properly pubby weekend getting away from it all. One of the best things that can be said about it is that it's nothing like a home from home: everything is always just so, the furnishings deep and welcoming, the log fire lit, the flowers fresh, the beams original; the food delicious, the greeting friendly...even the bedrooms are lovely. In recognition that a memorable bed and breakfast is about more than a clean and comfortable room and good morning meal, but also about the atmosphere of the whole surroundings, the Griffin at Llyswen is our 1992 Bed and Breakfast Pub of the Year.

1992 FAMILY PUB OF THE YEAR:
DOUBLE LOCKS, EXETER, DEVON

The Double Locks isn't easy to find, and that's part of its secret. Prettily set by the canal, the pub has lots to offer the whole family, and good children's pubs should also be places their parents look forward to visiting! So here the food is excellent, the interior nicely informal and relaxing, with several rooms open to families, and the outdoor facilities designed to keep even the most boisterous child happy: a large lawn, swings and a scramble net, even a volleyball court. There's Monopoly and other games indoors for less clement weather, and an atmosphere that genuinely welcomes children, rather than merely tolerating them.

1992 SUMMER PUB OF THE YEAR:
LAMB, GREAT RISSINGTON, GLOUCESTERSHIRE

Also an outstanding place to stay, with its excellent food and delightful bedrooms, the Lamb is an ideal place to be on a warm summer's day. It has the lot: landscaping, views, a summerhouse and aviary, a lazy English garden atmosphere, and the added and not inconsiderable bonus of a swimming pool for residents' use. All of this makes the Lamb at Great Rissington the clear winner of the title 1992 Summer Pub of the Year.

1992 WINE PUB OF THE YEAR:
GRIFFIN, FLETCHING, EAST SUSSEX

Aside from inspiring our inspector to call it 'everything a village pub should be', and offering good home-made food, the 16th century Griffin Inn has a very modern interest in good wines at reasonable prices: it's an excellent list, owing much to family connections with the celebrated Ebury Wine Bar in London; well-chosen, well-kept and well-presented, with a thoughtful range selected for drinking by the glass, and lots of half bottles.

1992 CHEESE PUB OF THE YEAR:
ROYAL OAK, DIDSBURY, GREATER MANCHESTER

Often overlooked simply because it has held the position of most interesting cheese pub in Britain for so long now, the Royal Oak has an unrivalled passion for good cheeses of every kind, even going to the lengths of scouring the Paris markets for new and exciting varieties. Beyond the sheer scale of the enterprise is an equally impressive dedication to service; every cheese can be tasted before choosing, and accompanying bread and pickles are first rate. There have been many imitators, but the Royal Oak at Didsbury is still the cheese pub of any year.

STAR-RATED PUBS 1992

Here is a complete list of the cream of the crop, those pubs which have most impressed our inspectors this year:

ENGLAND
Harrow, West Ilsley, Berks
Royal Oak, Yattendon, Berks
Queen's Head, Newton, Cambs
Pheasant, Higher Burwardsley, Cheshire
Maltsters Arms, Chapel Amble, Cornwall
Masons Arms, Cartmel Fell, Cumbria
Double Locks, Exeter, Devon
Old Rydon, Kingsteignton, Devon
Rose and Crown, Romaldkirk, Durham
Green Dragon, Cockleford, Gloucs
Lamb, Great Rissington, Gloucs
Wykeham Arms, Winchester, Hants
Roebuck, Brimfield, Hereford & Worcester
Sun Inn, Winforton, Hereford & Worcester
Harrow, Ightham Common, Kent
Plough, Ivy Hatch, Kent
Alma, Wandsworth, London
White Horse, Parsons Green, London
Hare Arms, Stow Bardolph, Norfolk
Old Coach House, Ashby St Ledgers, Northants
Warenford Lodge, Warenford, Northumbs
Notley Arms, Monksilver, Somerset
Royal Oak, Over Stratton, Somerset
Crown, Southwold, Suffolk
Wombwell Arms, Wass, North Yorks
Three Acres, Shelley, West Yorks

SCOTLAND
Hoffmans, Kirkcaldy, Fife
Kilberry Inn, Kilberry, Strathclyde

WALES
Blue Anchor, East Aberthaw, South Glamorgan
Griffin Inn, Llyswen, Powys

PUBS AROUND BRITAIN

WELCOME THE

AMERICAN EXPRESS CARD

Don't leave home without it

TALES FROM THE FRONT LINE

Our roving team of professional inspectors aren't always to be envied. Certainly, when the planets are favourable, and all the pubs they visit turn out to be either as good as ever they were, a predictable treat, or that even more exciting thing, the genuine new discovery, then it's rather a wonderful way to make a living, touring from one gourmet supper and feather bed to another. But it's not often like that; as the wise old saying goes, you have to kiss an awful lot of frogs before you find your prince.

Eating for a living can be a decidedly unpleasant experience. "Home made soup to their own recipe, it says: their recipe is to take a packet of minestrone and add whatever vegetables are left over from the previous day." It could be worse: "My plaice fillets in lemon sauce are fine, but are accompanied by mixed tinned peas and sweetcorn, jus-rol croquette potatoes and oven chips". They seem to have particularly unfortunate experiences with pies: "the crust is made of sage and onion stuffing mix, some sort of instant oats and margarine, all browned together under the grill; disgusting". And advertising can mislead: an eagerly anticipated lunch at an elsewhere-recommended establishment produced "grey-green beans, and micro-heated mashed potato, solid with a watery sheen and no taste whatsoever, save for the black bits, which are pepper". Sometimes, though, the signs are all too obvious from the first: "I arrived in the bar just in time to overhear the entire lunch menu being read out over the phone as an order to a frozen food company . . ." In another case, "the landlord had to put on the lights specially for me in the dining room, on a Saturday night . . . a popular pub this is not". "It was scarcely an auspicious start," bemoans another inspector, in the course of not recommending a pub for lunch, "trays of ready-cook chilli and steak and kidney pie filling were defrosting in the kitchen window when I arrived." Sometimes illumination comes by accident: "I put my head round the kitchen door to ask a question of the chef, who is at that precise moment defrosting a frozen gammon steak under the hot tap". But perhaps the most unenviable of all visits begins thus: "I crunch over fag ends to reach the bar, consider requesting a nose-peg to visit the loos . . . it's 1.30pm, and the chef is already well into the Carlsberg Special; I ask for a menu and am cheerfully told "sorry, no real food, it's all crap today". . . it says 'fresh roast kitten' on the specials board . . ." Sometimes the tales of woe from the front line are almost too unbearably detailed, but others are more succinct in their awarding of the downward thumb: "the à la carte features six ways to spoil a chicken", or "it's Tuesday and still Sunday roast beef and yorkshires on the specials board". These are some of the pubs that didn't make it.

m

eat to

live

Great British Meat

Good cooking is all about ingredients, and value for money is the key ingredient in the resurgence of good pub cooking. The reason that many pub car parks are brim-full, perhaps at the expense of the restaurant down the road, is that more and more people are discovering that within their doors, good, traditional food is affordably priced and served in a pleasantly informal environment. Another great attraction is the revival of regional dishes, made with fresh local ingredients: a really good steak and kidney pie, home-made, with tender meat, a rich gravy and a proper pastry crust is hard to beat, or a flavoursome, old fashioned toad in the hole, made with Cumberland or Lincolnshire sausage, and a fresh Yorkshire pudding; a simple, warming Lancashire hotpot or a succulent Sunday roast with freshly cooked vegetables. Slices of Wiltshire cured, York or Suffolk ham, teamed with real English cheese and home-baked bread makes that humblest of pub meals, the ploughman's lunch, a feast fit for anyone, particularly when accompanied by a fine pint of local beer. At its best, the Great British pub is one of the last bastions of authentic local cuisine.

In recognition of all this, the Meat and Livestock Commission has established the British Meat Catering Service (BMCS) to advise and guide our national, regional and local brewers, researching old recipes and developing new ones to make the most of our good British beef, pork, lamb and bacon.

Good juicy steaks are still the people's favourite, the most-ordered treat from the evening bar meals menu. At lunchtime, an old-fashioned cottage pie is making a comeback, though chili con carne is still so widely found as to be often referred to as traditional pub

Fillet of Herefordshire Beef, with pickled walnuts and garlic on a red wine and shallot sauce.

food! More and more often pubs are installing barbecues for al fresco summer dining; one of the simplest but most sophisticated barbecue dishes is a marinated British beef forequarter steak, doused in garlic; easy to make, quick to cook, delicious to eat. Even a humble home-made burger can be a gourmet treat, certainly in comparison to the blander high-street kind.

FILLET OF HEREFORDSHIRE BEEF WITH PICKLED WALNUTS AND GARLIC ON A RED WINE AND SHALLOT SAUCE

(serves 4)
Four 5-6 oz Herefordshire fillet steaks
4 tblsp clarified butter
2 shallots, chopped
4 pickled walnuts, halved
16 cloves of garlic
10 fl oz good red wine
10 fl oz strong beef stock
salt and pepper
knob of butter to finish sauce

THE ROEBUCK
Brimfield, Hereford & Worcester
1992 Pub of the Year

1. Prepare the garlic by breaking open the bulbs and carefully trimming the cloves. Place in a pan of boiling, lightly salted water, cook for 5 minutes, then change the water and repeat the process at least 4 times, so the garlic is not too strong; it should be just soft.

Drain and reserve until needed.

2. Put the clarified butter in a medium-sized heavy frying pan, and heat to sizzling. Seal each end of the steaks, and then brown the middle. Place in ovenproof dish and roast in a hot oven (220C, 400F, Gas Mark 6) for 8-12 minutes, depending on taste (rare or well done). At the end of the cooking time, it is important to let the fillets rest in a warm place for 5 minutes so that the juices set. Pour off any excess fat from pan.

3. Into the hot pan pour the red wine and reduce by half. Add the beef stock and the chopped shallots, and reduce again until the sauce is quite syrupy. Add the knob of butter, the juice from the dish the fillets have been resting in, and the pickled walnuts. Season to taste.

4. Place the garlic in a small tin foil parcel and place in oven to reheat.

5. Slice each fillet into five medallions and keep warm. Sauce each plate and arrange slices of fillet in half-moon shape, garnishing with the pickled walnut halves and hot garlic.

BRITISH BEEF IN BLACK BEAN SAUCE

(serves 6)
5 lb British braising steak
5 tblsp black eyed beans (soaked overnight)
1 jar black bean sauce
1 tsp sesame oil
1 tsp crushed garlic
1 tsp Garam Masala
1 tsp roasted curry powder
1-2 tsp oil
3½ pints home-made beef stock
Seasoned plain flour

THE SUN INN
Winforton, Hereford & Worcester
1992 British Meat Pub of the Year

1. Slice steak into large pieces and trim off any excess fat. Toss in seasoned flour; fry gently in shallow pan in the oil, until sealed (turning meat over once).

2. Put into casserole dish with all the other ingredients and cover with a tight lid. Cook in the oven at 150C (300F, Gas Mark 2) for 2-2½ hours. If necessary, thicken sauce with arrowroot before serving.

BRITISH STEAK, MUSHROOM AND 'OLD PECULIER' PIE

(serves 4)
1 lb best British stewing steak, diced
1 large onion, chopped
2 oz mushrooms, sliced
1 tblsp tomato purée
2 oz plain flour
10 fl oz Theakstons Old Peculier ale
10 fl oz beef stock or water
1 oz beef dripping or lard
Seasoning

Shortcrust pastry made with lard and plain flour

THE ROSE & CROWN HOTEL
Romaldkirk, Co. Durham

1. Seal the stewing steak in the fat; add chopped onions and cook a further 5 minutes.

2. Stir in flour and tomato purée thoroughly and add Old Peculier ale and stock; bring to the boil, then reduce heat immediately to a gentle simmer for 2 hours or until tender, adding the mushrooms after the first hour. Season and allow to cool.

3. Put into a large pie dish (or four individual ones) and cover with shortcrust pastry. Bake at 220C (425F, Gas Mark 7) for 20 minutes until golden brown.

BRITISH LAMB
IT'S SO EASY TO BE CREATIVE. SLAM IN THE LAMB.

New ideas for making more of our home-produced lamb are now materialising on the more imaginative pub menus: perhaps Valentine steaks, a boneless butterfly-shaped steak, or a marinated boneless leg steak, in addition to the ever-popular carvery roast. Or think laterally, and ring the changes by trying lamb (rather than the usual beef) in red wine casserole: diced lamb with onions and mushrooms in a red wine gravy, accompanied by steamed new potatoes and courgettes. Ring them again with a lamb and haricot bean pie, in a rich reduced stock, with onion and garlic in a simple shortcrust pastry.

LEG OF BRITISH LAMB WITH CRAB STUFFING

Serves 6
1 large boned leg of British lamb
carrots and onions, roughly chopped
(sufficient to cover bottom of casserole dish)
1 stick of celery, sliced
1 tsp curry powder
10 fl oz dry white wine
10 fl oz lamb stock (made from the bone)
5 fl oz double cream

For the stuffing:

8 oz white crab meat
4 oz brown crab meat
half tsp curry powder
1 tblsp fresh chopped mint
3 egg yolks
seasoning

THE SUN INN
Winforton, Hereford & Worcester
1992 British Meat Pub of the Year

1. Mix all stuffing ingredients together, fill the leg, and sew it up.

2. Layer carrot and onion in roasting tin, add celery and half the curry powder and place lamb on top; cover with tight lid, or foil if your roasting tin is lidless.

Fillet of British Lamb with ginger and rosemary.

3. Cook in a moderate oven (180C, 350F, Gas Mark 4) for about 2 hours.

4. Remove from oven and transfer the lamb to another ovenproof dish; return it to the oven to brown.

5. Pour wine and stock over vegetables remaining in roasting tin and bring to the boil on top of the stove; simmer and reduce for 5 minutes, then strain into a sauceboat, skimming off any impurities on the surface. Add the other half tsp curry powder and the cream. Pour sauce round vegetables to serve.

FILLET OF BRITISH LAMB WITH GINGER AND ROSEMARY

(serves 4)
1½ lb British lamb loin fillet
2 shallots, finely chopped
½ inch fresh ginger root, grated
2 tblsp clear honey
2 sprigs fresh rosemary
15 fl oz lamb stock
2 measures brandy
1 oz clarified butter

THE BELL
Stilton, Cambridgeshire

1. Cut the lamb fillet into four 6 oz pieces. Pan-fry in the hot butter until pink, and leave to rest in a warm place.

2. Add the shallots to the pan and cook until clear; flame in brandy and add the grated ginger, rosemary, honey and lamb stock. Reduce this sauce by half and check the seasoning.

3. Slice the lamb and arrange it on a serving plate. Strain the sauce over and garnish with fresh sprigs of rosemary.

LEAN ON
BRITISH
PORK

For many pubs, pork still means an option on the Sunday roast menu, with apple sauce, stuffing, roast potatoes and crackling. But others have discovered how versatile the meat is: on the barbecue, in kebabs, in a pork and cider casserole, or in pork and apple burgers, perhaps accompanied by a spicy barbecue sauce. Or dress it up in the evening: take a pork loin steak, stuff it with a herby minced pork filling and wrap the whole in a seasoned coating: delicious.

The star of the pub buffet counter, a cold honey-roasted ham, is still the favourite salad centrepiece. The York style is dry salt-cured and lightly smoked for a gentle flavour, and the Wiltshire cured style similar, while the Suffolk variety tends to be smokier in taste, and prepared in molasses for extra sweetness and contrast.

The BLT is now so well known that its initials hardly need explaining, but the bacon, lettuce and tomato sandwich is firmly entrenched at the top of the hot snack league. What few people realise when they're eating one is that cooked bacon is richer in three group vitamins than many fruits, vegetables, fish or cereals. It's also superb as a flavoursome pizza topping.

Increasingly, the humble mass-produced banger is being rivalled in the frying pan by more unusual, regional varieties, as more and more publicans take the trouble to organise supplies from local

Sauté of British Pork with sherry and fresh pasta.

makers. In Scottish pubs, it's the beef sausage that scores highest with pub customers; in Wales, lamb sausages; in East Anglia, the good old Lincolnshire model, made with chopped pork, seasonings and sage; while in the north, the Cumberland sausage is king; the Yorkshire variation being to add tomatoes for extra savoury flavour. When a sausage is this good, it's a shame to relegate it to the morning fry-up. Some pubs have solved this by simply offering an "All Day Breakfast", an idea that's taking off. Others pop regional varieties into the classic sausage sandwich, or hugely popular jumbo roll; good quality bangers and mash is making a comeback even in the smarter establishments, and sausages are also making guest appearances in old-fashioned casseroles and pies.

SAUTÉ OF BRITISH PORK WITH SHERRY AND FRESH PASTA

12 oz trimmed British pork fillet
1 oz clarified butter
Flour for dredging
4 fl oz Oloroso sherry
10 fl oz double cream

THE ROSE & CROWN HOTEL
Romaldkirk, Co. Durham

1. Trim the pork fillet so that you have pure lean meat; slice the fillet lengthwise into two pieces. Take one half of the fillet and, using a cook's knife, cut thin slices on a slant. Dust with flour.

2. Heat the butter in a pan and seal the pork; remove from pan and

keep warm. Deglaze the pan with the sherry, and reduce by half. Add the stock and reduce again by half. Add the cream and bring to a gentle simmer. Return the sealed meat to the pan and cook for only 5 minutes, until the meat is cooked and shows clear juices.

3. Season and serve with a dusting of chopped parsley or other fresh herbs. Delicious with fresh pasta tossed in butter, and a salad bowl.

BRITISH PORK TENDERLOIN WRAPPED IN PARMA HAM, WITH A MUSTARD SAUCE

(serves 4)
2 British pork tenderloins, trimmed (about 1lb 12oz)
6-8 prunes, stoned and cut in half lengthways
4 slices Parma ham
Small amount of caul (you may need to order this in advance from your butcher)

For the mustard sauce:

10 fl oz strong chicken stock, reduced to 5 fl oz
1 tblsp Pommery mustard
4 fl oz double cream
A dash of brandy
salt and pepper
watercress or parsley to garnish

THE ROEBUCK
Brimfield, Hereford & Worcester
1992 Pub of the Year

1. Make an incision with a small sharp knife along the full length of the tenderloins. Roll up the meat and push the prunes through the centre of the tenderloin.

2. Coat the base of a small frying pan sparingly with oil and heat until smoking. Seal the meat on all sides, remove from pan and allow to cool. When cool, roll the tenderloin up neatly in the slices of Parma ham.

3. Have the caul in warm water ready to use. Take a small amount and spread out on a work surface – you will be surprised how far it will stretch. Place the ham-wrapped tenderloin on the caul and cover it completely: this is not only to secure the ham but to baste the pork while cooking.

4. Cook in the oven for 20 minutes at 220C (425F, Gas Mark 7) and let it stand for a further 10 minutes.

5. To make the mustard sauce, add the mustard to the chicken stock in a small pan, bring to the boil and simmer for a few minutes. Add cream, bring back to the boil and reduce to a good creamy consistency, adding a touch of brandy. Season to taste.

6. To serve, carve each tenderloin into two and arrange on top of the sauce on warmed plates. Garnish with a sprig of watercress or parsley.

THE ART OF THE STOLEN KISS.

Timing is everything. Having chosen the right moment, an impulsive show of passion should always be followed by a tender embrace. Not unlike the world's most refined cognac.

MARTELL

COGNAC. L'ART DE MARTELL.

SINCE 1715.

MAP SECTION

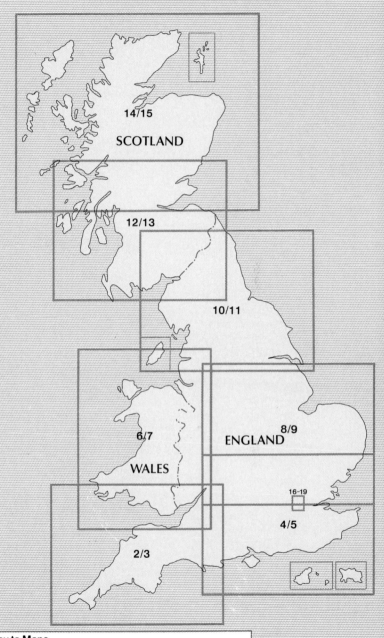

14/15

SCOTLAND

12/13

10/11

6/7

WALES

8/9

ENGLAND

2/3

16-19

4/5

Key to Maps

●━━━	Motorways
━━━	Primary Routes
───	'A' Roads
───	Link Roads
─·─·─	County Boundaries

Guide Establishments

o   Joyford

O   **Oswestry**

O   **Worksop**

© Alfresco Leisure Publications PLC   Designed and Produced by Euromap Ltd, Pangbourne, Berkshire.

1

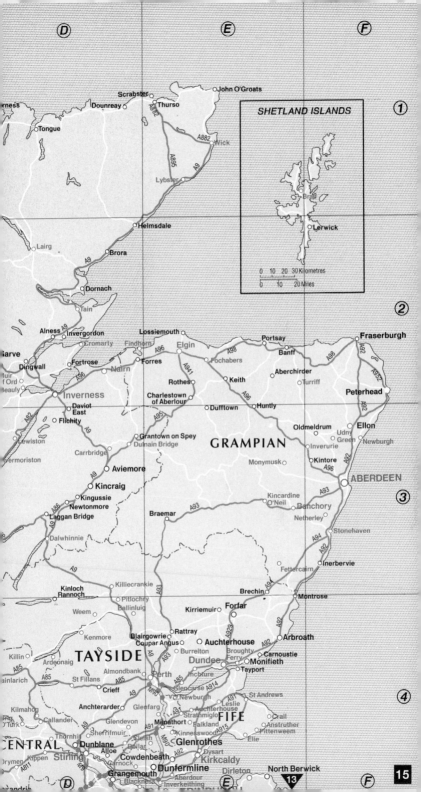

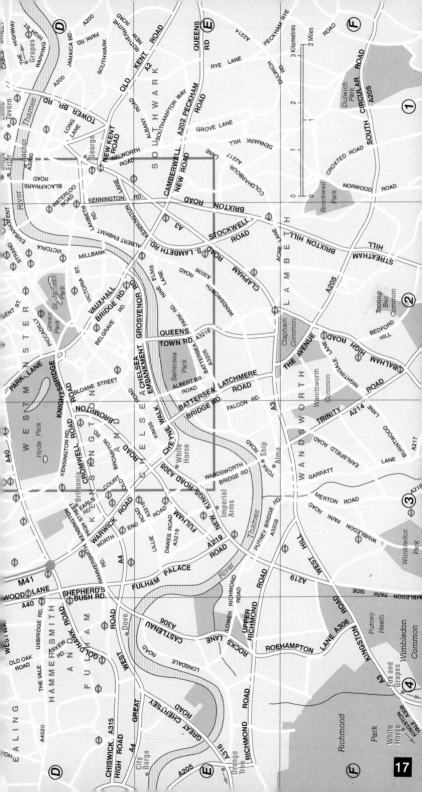

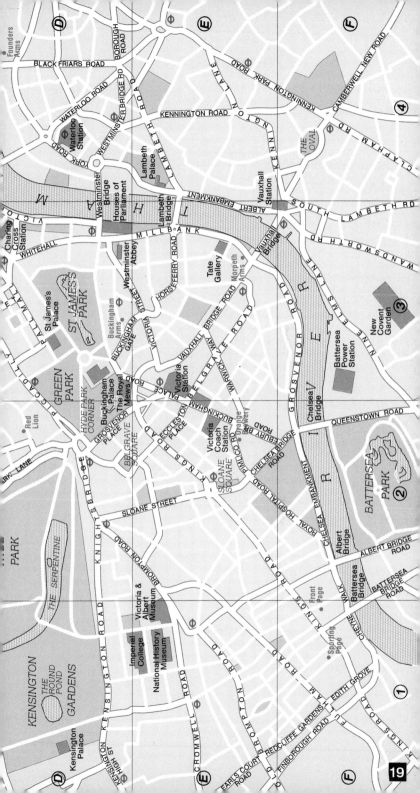

COUNTY ORDER

England

AVON

ABBOTS LEIGH   George Inn

Pill Road (A369), Bristol BS8 3RP   ▼
Tel: (0275) 372467
Open: 11.45-2.30, 6 (7 winter Sat)-11
Licensees: Michael and Elaine Meredith

One long bar with warming log fires in winter, agricultural bric-a-brac on the walls, and tables surrounded by cushioned pews.

Bar Meals: 12-2.15, 6.30-9 (not weekend eves); **Typical Dishes:** *Singapore laksa soup, marinated baby squid, garlic chicken en croute, natural smoked haddock Romany, Venus clams with samphire, chocolate and rum pithivier (main courses from around £5) Vegetarian Meals: stilton, leek and mushroom puff* `Cheese` `Beer` *Courage beers; Exmoor Gold; Fullers London Pride; Whitbread Boddingtons Bitter Children Allowed in Bar to Eat Garden Outdoor Eating* **No Credit Cards**

AUST   Boars Head

Main Road (just off M4) BS12 3AX
Tel: (04545) 2278
Open: 11-2.30, 6-11
Licensee: D R Poole

Characterful village pub with lots of small rooms, exposed stone walls, old winged settles, big country tables and rugs. 18 guest beers are rotated.

Bar Meals: 12-2, 7-10; bar snacks both sessions **Typical Dishes:** *paté £2, vegetable soup £1.10, steak and kidney pie £4.30, lasagne verdi £4.20, Yorkshire pud with sausage £3.95, bread and butter pudding £1.50 Vegetarian Meals: vegetarian lasagne £4.10 Children's Portions* `Beer` *Courage Best, Directors Family Room Outdoor Play Area Garden Outdoor Eating* **Credit Cards:** *Visa*

BACKWELL New Inn, 86 West Town Road Tel: (027 546) 2694: Wide and varied fish and seafood menu, plus a variety of steaks and grills. Bar meals lunch and evening; dining room open evenings only. Children allowed in bar to eat. Garden. Courage and Smiles beers.

BATHAMPTON   George Inn

Mill Lane BA2 6TR
Tel: (0225) 425079
Open: 11-2.30, 6-11
Licensees: Walter and Peter Hall

Creeper-clad 15th century pub by the Kennet and Avon canal. Several wood-beamed and cosy lounge areas to choose from.

Bar Meals: 12-2, 6.30-9.30; bar snacks both sessions **Typical Dishes:** *home-made soup £1.20, garlic mushrooms £2, baked ham with cauliflower cheese £5.20, chicken with apricot and brandy sauce £6.50, salmon quiche £4.50, crepes £1.90 Vegetarian Meals: vegetarian pancake £4.90* `Beer` *Courage beers Family Room Outdoor Play Area Garden*

BATHFORD   Crown

2 Bathford Hill BA1 7SL
Tel: (0225) 852297
Open: 1-2.30, 6.30-11 (10.30 winter Mon-Thur)
Licensees: Gregg and Angela Worrall

Eminently civilised old pub with a pleasingly informal, relaxing feel. Various rooms
are decorated in various ways, from conservatory simplicity to country house style.
Polished wood floors with rugs, nicely decorated walls, newspapers and magazines to
read, cafetière coffee and a nice wine list.

Bar Meals: 12-2 (not Mon), 7-9.30 (10 Fri/Sat); bar snacks both sessions **Typical**
Dishes: *stilton and white wine soup £2.30, garlic mushrooms £2.75, steak, mushroom and
ale pie – three sizes £5.10/£7.10/£11.50, Thai chicken and brown rice £7.45, smoked
haddock and prawn lasagne £5.95, bread and butter pudding with clotted cream £2.85
Vegetarian Meals: spicy lentil and vegetable pancake £4.25   Children's Menu/Portions*
`Cheese`　`Beer` *Draught Bass; Ruddles Best Bitter; Ushers Best   Family Room
Outdoor Play Area   Garden   Outdoor Eating* **Credit Cards:** *Access, Amex, Diners, Visa*

BATHFORD Swan, Kingsdown: Nice hillside pub in pretty countryside. Popular
for food; go for the specials. Gibbs Mew beers.

BRISTOL   Highbury Vaults

164 St Michael's Hill, Ringsdown BS2 8DE
Tel: (0272) 733203
Open: 12-11
Licensees: J S Payne and L Fricker

Nostalgically simple, pre-war style pub, convincingly put together in the late 1980s,
with no fruit machines or other modern intrusions. Generally busy front bar, and
series of quieter enclaves leading off. An emphasis on good beer and good value
cheap, filling food, which however avoids things with chips. Popular with students.

Bar Meals: 12-2, 5.30-8.30 (weekend eves); bar snacks lunchtime **Typical Dishes:** *beef
and beer stew with dumplings, chilli, pasta with ratatouille sauce (from £2)   Vegetarian
Meals: cheese and spinach lasagne* `Beer` *Brains SA; Smiles* `Cider` *Long Aston
Garden   Outdoor Eating* **No Credit Cards**

BRISTOL   Old Castle Green

46 Gloucester Lane BS2 0DP
Tel: (0272) 550925
Open: 11.30-11 (12-3, 7-11 Sat)
Licensees: David Legg and Heather Murphy-Mills

Traditional old pub in the centre of the city, with a business district philosophy –
food is guaranteed to be quickly presented; unlike some such establishments,
however, all meals are prepared daily from only fresh ingredients. A nice touch – all
hot dishes of the day come with either dauphinoise potatoes or basmati rice – a
blessed change from the usual 'chips or jackets'. Chicken Neapolitan is a house
speciality. Also stuffed Nan bread (lots of good Indian dishes) and fresh pasta. Always
two vegetarian specials. No juke box or fruit machines.

Bar Meals: 12-15-10.45, all opening hours weekends; bar snacks lunchtime **Typical**
Dishes: *onion bhaji £1.65, chicken Neapolitan £2.50, chilli con carne £2.50, chicken
dhansak £2.50, apple crumble   Vegetarian Meals: ratatouille* `Beer` *Marston Border*

Mild; Owd Rodger; Pedigree Bitter   *Children Allowed in Bar to Eat*   *Outdoor Play Area*
Garden   *Outdoor Eating*   **No Credit Cards**

CHURCHILL Crown, Skinners Lane (off A38) Tel: (0934) 852995: Listed for its
atmosphere and good beer, a characterful old cottage pub in a quiet lane, usually
busy. Real fire, no music, simple snack lunches, small garden. Butcombe, Cornish,
Cotleigh, Exmoor beers. Open 11-3, 6-11.

COMBE HAY   Wheatsheaf

near Bath BA2 7EG   `FOOD`
Tel: (0225) 833504   ☼
Open: 11-3 (2.30 winter), 6.30-11
Licensees: M G and Sue Taylor

Narrow twisting lanes lead to this charming village, hidden away in a fold of hills to
the south of Bath. Perched on a hillside looking across a small valley, the Wheatsheaf
dates back to the 17th century and is as pretty as a picture, its black and white facade
smothered in flowers and pierced with the entrances to dovecots, built into the walls
and still inhabited. Well spaced rustic tables and benches in the large sloping garden
make the best of the views, an ideal spot for summer eating and drinking. Inside,
there are rough stone walls, massive solid wooden tables, and also a huge blackboard
menu: food is important here. There is something to suit just about every taste, from
a home-cooked Wiltshire ham salad to more adventurous and sophisticated dishes,
monkfish with root ginger and spring onion cream sauce, or breast of chicken filled
with smoked salmon mousse and wrapped in pastry among them. Deep-fried
mushrooms filled with brie make a good starter, the hot filling spilling out to blend
with surrounding provencale sauce. Real ales like Hook Norton are drawn direct
from the barrel. There is no background music as such, but a good deal emanates
from the kitchen where, to judge by the singing, they are clearly happy in their
work.

*Bar Meals and Restaurant: 12-2, 6.30-9 (9.30 Fri/Sat); 11-2, 7-9 Sun; bar snacks
both sessions* **Typical Dishes BAR:** *leek and potato soup £2.25, garlic bread £1.25,
marinated pigeon breast £5.50, tagliatelle in ham, mushroom, cream and wine £5.25,
lasagne £4.25, home-made banoffee pie £2.75* **RESTAURANT:** *king prawns in garlic
and wine £6.50, chicken breast stuffed with salmon mousse £7.50, wild duck breast in black
cherry sauce £7.75, Aberdeen Angus sirloin in green pepper sauce £9.50, fresh fruit salad
£2.25 Vegetarian Meals: vegetable crepe in provencale sauce £4.40 Children's Portions*
`Beer` *Ash Vine; Courage Garden Outdoor Eating* **No Credit Cards**

COMPTON MARTIN   Ring O' Bells

Main Street BS18 6JE
Tel: (0761) 221284
Open: 11.30-2.30 (3 Sat), 7-11
Licensees: David and Jane Hunt

Rambling, well-balanced village pub, with a busy locals' bar, comfortable lounge
with open fire, nice family room, and large garden. Children are very well catered
for: five high chairs, toys, a rocking horse, and decent miniature meals. The highly
traditional bar menu is spiced up with offbeat daily specials, and seafood in summer,
home made pies in winter.

*Bar Meals: 12-2, 7.30 (7 Fri/Sat)-10 (9.30 Sun and winter Mon-Thur); bar snacks both
sessions* **Typical Dishes:** *carrot and tarragon soup £1.30, creamy mushrooms £3, goulash
£5.10, Cumberland sausage £3.50, grilled Wiltshire ham and eggs £4.10, bread and
butter pudding £1.65 Vegetarian Meals: mozzarella pasta penne Children's Menu*

Beer Bass; Butcombe; Wadworth   Family Room   Outdoor Play Area   Garden
Outdoor Eating   **No Credit Cards**

DUNDRY   Dundry Inn

Church Road BS18 8LH   ❢
Tel: (0272) 641722
Open: 11-3, 6-11
Licensee: D C Beck

Self-styled family pub opposite a famous church tower built as a landmark for
approaching shipping. Spectacular views across Bristol, Somerset, even Wales on a
good day, from the large garden. Huge menu.

Bar Meals: 12-2, 7-10.15 (9.45 Sun); bar snacks both sessions **Typical Dishes:** *soup of
the day £1.55, crispy potato skins, veal schnitzel £5.95, oggies (large filled puff pastries)
£6.15, jacket potato with prawns and asparagus, home-made lemon cheesecake Vegetarian
Meals: vegetarian oggie £5.95 Children's Portions* **Cheese** **Beer** *Courage Best;
Smiles Bitter; Wadworth 6X; Whitbread Boddingtons Bitter* **Whisky** *Family Room
Garden Outdoor Eating Summer Barbecue* **Credit Cards:** *Access, Amex, Diners, Visa*

HINTON CHARTERHOUSE   Rose & Crown

Hinton Charterhouse BA3 6AN
Tel: (0225) 722153
Licensee: Bryan Shelley

Late Victorian oak-panelled pub in quaint village not far from Bath. Friendly and
relaxed. Separate cellar restaurant.

Bar Meals: 12-2.30; also bar snacks **Restaurant:** *12-2 (Sun only), 7.30-10* **Typical
Dishes BAR:** *tomato and mint soup £1.10, whitebait £2.10, steak and kidney pie
£3.40, fish pie £3.25, treacle pudding £1.50* **RESTAURANT:** *lentil and bacon soup
£2.40, melon and orange with spicy dressing £2.95, steak en croute with stilton and garlic
£8.50, devilled kidneys £7.50, rack of lamb with port and redcurrant £9.75, banana and
Tia Maria gateau £2.40 Vegetarian Meals (bar): vegetarian casserole £2.30 Children's
Portions* **Beer** *Draught Bass; Marston Burton Bitter, Pedigree; Wadworth 6X*
Whisky *Children Allowed in Bar to Eat Garden* **Credit Cards** *(Restaurant): Access,
Visa*

HINTON CHARTERHOUSE Stag: Exposed stone walls, log fire, unusual and
often pricey bar food. Children allowed in dining area. Tables outside. Bunces,
Gibbs Mew, Marston, Smiles beers. Open all day at very busy times.

KELSTON   Old Crown Inn

near Bath BA1 9AQ
Tel: (0225) 423032
Open: 11.30-2.30, 5 (5.30 Winter)-11
Licensees: Richard Jackson and Michael Steele

Old coaching inn with stone floors, wood panelling, settles; one room once served
as a mortuary for bodies washed up by the Avon; upstairs was used as a magistrate's
court. Trollope's restaurant is named after a celebrated former landlord, Ted
Trollope.

Bar Meals and Restaurant: 12-2 (not Sun); restaurant only 7.30-9, Thur-Sat **Typical**

Dishes BAR: home-made soup £1.35, avocado and tuna fish £2.10, beef and Guinness casserole £5.20, cottage pie £3.95, smoked mackerel pie £3.95, rhubarb crumble £2.35 *RESTAURANT:* vegetable gratin £2.70, casserole of lamb £8.95, fillet steak £10.20, salmon steak with spicy seafood sauce £8.40   Vegetarian Meals (bar): spicy vegetarian casserole £4.25   **Beer**   Draught Bass; Butcombe Bitter; Smiles Best Bitter; Wadworth 6X   **Cider**   Mendip Magic   Children Allowed in Restaurant   Garden   Outdoor Eating **No Credit Cards**

LITTLETON ON SEVERN White Hart: Tel: (0454) 412275: Extremely well extended 16th century country pub with lots of character and traditional hatch servery. No music other than live jazz on Wednesdays. Recommended by locals for bar meals, lunch and evening. Real fires, family room, garden with boules. Smiles, Wadworth beers. Open all day Saturday.

MAYSHILL New Inn: On A432: Stone-built pub popular for friendly service and tasty imaginative bar food.

MIDFORD Hope & Anchor: On B3110 Tel: (0225) 832296: Freehouse near the Somerset Coal Canal. Opened-out bar is part 17th century; also restaurant and small family room. Food lunchtime and evening ranges from a single sausage to the landlord's favourite curries. Garden. Bass, Butcombe, Marston, Wadworth beers. Open 11.30-2.30, 6.30-11.

MONKTON COMBE   Wheelwrights Arms

Monkton Combe BA2 7HD
Tel: (0225) 722287
Open: 12-2.30, 6-11
Licensee: Roger Howard

Midford Valley inn with characterful old bar, cosily warmed by a huge log fire in cold weather, and modern accommodation in the converted barn. Just three miles from Bath.

Bar Meals and Restaurant: 12-2, 7.30-9.30; bar snacks both sessions   **Typical Dishes** *BAR:* home-made soup £1.30, prawn cocktail £2.95, steak and kidney pie £3.95, lasagne £3.40, chili con carne £3.95, apple pie (all home-made)   *RESTAURANT:* similar starters, salmon steak £8.20, local trout £8.30, swordfish £7.45   Vegetarian Meals Children's Portions   **Beer**   Adnams Southwold; Butcombe Bitter; Wadworth 6X Garden   Outdoor Eating   *Accommodation:* 8 bedrooms, all en suite, from £46 (single £38)   Children Welcome Overnight (minimum age 14)   Check-in: all day   **No Credit Cards**

NIBLEY   Swan

Badminton Road BS17 5JF
Tel: (0454) 312290
Open: 11-11
Licensee: G Dangerfield

Lively, pleasant one-bar pub with an exciting garden for children, which features not only climbing frames, a trampoline and rabbits, but also a pair of genuine two-berth cruisers, dry-docked as ingenious play equipment. There's also a punch and judy show and barbecue on clement summer Sunday evenings. Indoors, children are only allowed in the dining area.

Bar Meals: Mon-Sat lunchtimes; dining area evenings/Sun   **Typical Dishes:** home-made soup £1.35, home-made paté £1.95, liver in brandy sauce £4.45, mixed grill £8.95, fisherman's pie £3.95, bread and butter pudding £1.75   Vegetarian Meals: home-made

vegetable pie   Children's Menu ▮Beer▮ *Benskins Best; Courage Best; Directors;*
Wadworth 6X   Outdoor Play Area   Garden   Outdoor Eating   Summer Barbecue **Credit**
Cards: *Access, Visa*

OLD SODBURY Dog Inn, Badminton Road Tel: (0454) 312006: Village
Whitbread house, open all hours, with a long and wide menu, ranging from an open
prawn sandwich to a £20-for-two paella. Cheap bed and breakfast in adjacent Yew
Tree Cottage; cook-your-own breakfasts supplied on request. On the Cotswold
Way.

OLDBURY ON SEVERN   Anchor Inn

Church Road BS12 1QA   ▮
Tel: (0454) 413331
Open: 11.30-2.30, 6.30-11 (11.30-3, 6-11 Sat)
Licensees: Michael Dowdeswell and Peter Riley

Traditionally furnished two bar village pub, very popular both for dining and
drinking, thanks to its excellent range of beers. Food is beginning to look interesting
too, from a daily changing typed menu of just the right length. No chips, no soups
except occasionally in winter, no starters unless chosen from the separate cold food
menu. Book for the dining room. There are cribbage, bridge and fishing teams in
the public bar, and a boules pitch at the top of the garden.Good log fire in winter;
good local walks – only five minutes stroll to the Severn estuary, and views of the
bridge. Dogs are allowed inside, except for the dining room. No music.

Bar Meals: 11.30-2, 6.30 (6 Sat)-11; bar snacks both sessions **Typical Dishes:**
Somerset pork in cider £4.50, lamb in mustard sauce £5.25, local pork and garlic sausages
£4.65, chicken Beaujolais £4.35, charcoal grills (evenings), pineapple upsidedown pudding
£1.65   Vegetarian Meals: leek and potato bake £3.75   Children's Portions (some)
▮Beer▮ *Draught Bass; Butcombe; Marston; Theakston* ▮Whisky▮ ▮Cider▮ *Bland's*
Children Allowed in Dining Room to Eat   Garden   Outdoor Eating **Credit Cards:**
Access, Visa

PAULTON   Somerset Inn

Bath Road BS18 5PS   ▮FOOD▮
Tel: (0761) 412828   ✆
Open: 12-2.30 (3 Fri/Sat), 7-11   ☼
Licensees: Ian and Yvonne MacFarlane   🍖 ▮

Described by landlord Ian MacFarlane as "buried alive in the country near Hook
Norton", the Somerset is an inn which quietly and quickly grows on you. Maybe
it's the Mozart and Scarlatti tapes which ease the mood. Just as likely it's the pub's
surprising lack of space which necessarily and immediately instills a kind of pleasant
intimacy between its customers. At the bar are half a dozen stools, and in front of it
a similar number of smallish bar tables sharing the warmth of an open fire, while
tucked away around the corner is a single larger dining table. Failing pre-booked use
of this particular table, families with young children must fear relegation to the
garden. Four years ago, this was a male-oriented darts-and-dominoes pub; today it's
South Avon's honeypot for the food-minded. Yvonne's dedication to her food is
total, and from nearby Radford Mill farm come free-range eggs, organic vegetables,
garlic and herbs, plus meats, when available, from its organically reared herd. The
only thing you'll find fried, from her menu, is an egg – on top of the ever-popular
Somerset breakfast. The blackboard menu exhibits a much wider range of skills and
eclectic influences, for instance Spanish pork, Zorba's surprise (roast beef in a chilli-
tomato sauce served with pitta bread and a Greek salad), or a traditional style yokel

pie of ham, potato and cheese under a crispy short-crust pastry. Vegetarians are equally well cared for: perhaps a bean and lentil stew, or tortellini di ricotta served with generous heaps of salad. These are all substantial meals for one; alternatively, the baked trout cooked in white wine and served with prawns (£13.50) is plattered up with fresh vegetables and offered as a meal for two. Sandwiches, too, arrive doorstep size, with wonderful local fresh bread and generous fillings of tuna, cooked meats or cheese, perfectly accompanied by a glass of Ian's particularly well-kept Courage Best. To follow, the blackberry and apple pie features fresh blackberries from the pub's garden, while the sweeter "pudding pie" is made from apples soaked in Somerset cider, with walnuts and sultanas. The laid-back, unhurried atmosphere continues to draw its fair share of local trade – fishermen and farmers – while Wednesday evening's acoustic guitar session encourages (cajoles, even) regulars into turning up with their own guitars and compositions.

Bar Meals: 12-2, 7-9; bar snacks lunchtime **Typical Dishes:** *carrot soup £1.95, garlic mushrooms with stilton, Zorba's surprise £5.10, yokel pie £5.10, seafood lasagne £5.75, yokel pudding pie £2.35 Vegetarian Meals: ricotta pasta £5.10 Children's Portions* `Cheese` `Beer` *Courage Best; Eldridge Pope Royal Oak; Wadworth 6X* `Cider` *Taunton Traditional Outdoor Play Area Garden Outdoor Eating* **No Credit Cards**

RIDGEHILL Crown: Popular weekend pub with bar meals and separate restaurant; food lunch and evening. Log fires, cosy country views, small rear garden. Wadworth beers.

STANTON WICK	**Carpenters Arms**

Pensford, Bristol BS18 4BX   ♥
Tel: (0761) 490202   `B&B`
Open: 11-3, 6-11
Licensee: Nigel Pushman

Converted from a row of 17th century miners' cottages in the tiny hamlet of Stanton Wick, which overlooks the Chew valley, the Carpenters Arms is all one would expect of a country inn, complete with roses clambering up the walls and tubs of colourful flowers. Inside, there are low oak beams, natural stone walls and warming log fires; at one end of the building is a restaurant for formal eating, at the other, the less formal Coopers Parlour. The printed menu here includes grills, pies and a good choice of vegetarian dishes on a varied menu ranging from salade niçoise to Welsh rarebit. Daily specials on the short blackboard menu are not always what they seem, though: you might reasonably expect Lancashire hotpot to involve lamb and slices of potato, but here it turns out to be pork chops in tomato sauce. This is the Australian version apparently, from whence comes the chef. Whatever its origins, it's good to eat. Apple and blackcurrant crumble is less surprising but equally good, with a nice crumbly wholemeal topping; it's displayed in a cold cabinet along with other traditional English puddings. There are some ten wines available by the glass from a good, realistically-priced wine list and a handful of real ales to wash down the eats. Immaculate bedrooms are appropriately cottagey in style, with pine furniture and pretty coordinating fabrics and wall coverings. Modern conveniences are not forgotten and there are smart, modern carpeted bathrooms.

Bar Meals: 12-2, 7-10; bar snacks both sessions **Restaurant:** *12-2 (not Mon), 7-10 (not Sun eve)* **Typical Dishes BAR:** *home-made soup £1.50, goujons of sole £3.55, trio lamb cutlets £6.25, steaks from £8.90, fish pie £5.95, treacle tart* **RESTAURANT:** *home-made soup £2.35, avocado and smoked chicken £3.75, rack of English lamb £12.75, steaks from £12.75, grilled Dover sole £13.95 Vegetarian Meals: tagliatelle with asparagus £4.25 Children's Portions* `Cheese` `Beer` *Draught Bass; Butcombe Bitter; Theakston Bitter; Wadworth 6X* `Whisky` *Macallan 15, 20, 25 yr Family Room Patio/terrace Outdoor Eating* **Accommodation:** *12 bedrooms, all en suite, from £49.50 (single £42.50) Children Welcome Overnight (minimum age 10) Check-in: all day* **Credit Cards:** *Access, Visa*

TOCKINGTON   Swan Inn

Tockington Green BS12 4NJ
Open: 11-3, 6-11
Licensee: David Heenan

Pleasant, spacious pub in sleepy village.

Bar Meals: 12-2, 6-10 (not Sun eve); bar snacks both sessions   *Typical Dishes: French onion soup £1.25, garlic prawns £3.05, dragon pie £4.25, Persian lamb £4.40, barbecued chicken £4   Vegetarian Meals   Children's Portions*   Beer   *Courage Best Bitter, Directors*   Cider   *Taunton Traditional   Garden   Credit Cards: Access, Amex, Visa*

TORMARTON   Compass Inn

By junction 18, M4 GL9 1JB
Tel: (045 421) 8242
Open: 11-11 (2.30 close Sun lunch)
Licensees: Mr and Mrs Monyard

Busy creeper-clad former coaching inn, now a dining pub with a pleasant conservatory. Good-sized bedrooms in two modern extensions.

Bar Meals: 11-10.30 (12-2, 7-10 Sun); bar snacks both sessions **Restaurant:** 7-9.30
Typical Dishes BAR: home-made soup of the day £1.65, lasagne £5.10, seafood cassolette £5.30, ratatouille au gratin £4.80, local ice-cream £2.45   RESTAURANT: French onion soup £2.45, stuffed orange £3.75, 8 oz rump steak £8.95, pork stroganoff £9.95, salmon en croute £9.95, home-made puddings £2.45   Vegetarian Meals Children's Menu   Beer   *Archers Village Bitter; Draught Bass; Smiles Best Bitter*
Whisky   *Family Room   Outdoor Play Area   Garden   Accommodation: 31 bedrooms, all en suite, from £64.95 (single £49.95),   Children Welcome Overnight   Cots Available Check-in: all day   Credit Cards: Access, Amex, Diners, Visa*

UPTON CHEYNEY   Upton Inn

Brewery Hill BS15 6LY
Tel: (0272) 324489
Open: 11-2.30, 6.30 (6 Fri/Sat)-11
Licensees: P and M Hall

Village pub with creeper-clad exterior, elegant interior with wall-hangings, and separate restaurant. They aim to provide "excellent food in opulent surroundings at realistic prices". No children under 14.

*Bar Meals and Restaurant:*12-2, 7-10 (not Sun eve; restaurant closed Mon); bar snacks both sessions (except Fri/Sat pm)   *Typical Dishes BAR: home-made soup £1.40, beef casserole with horseradish £6.50, grilled breast of chicken in brandy and apricot sauce £6.50, smoked haddock with cucumber sauce £5.50, home-made damson and apple sorbet £2 Vegetarian Meals: vegetable crepe*   Beer   *Draught Bass; Wadworth   Patio/terrace Outdoor Eating   No Credit Cards*

WEST HARPTREE Blue Bowl: On B3314: Slickly run rural dining pub with various rooms, reserveable tables, large menu particularly strong on puddings. Family room; outdoor eating in child-friendly garden. Courage beers.

WICK Rose & Crown: High Street (A420) Tel: (027 582) 2198: 17th century inn with period atmosphere. Routine bar food (one or two specials though) and interesting restaurant, with low ceiling, oak beams and exposed stone walls; children allowed in here. Strong on steaks and fish; no food Sunday evening. Courage and Wadworth beers. Open: 11.30-2.30, 5.30-11.

WORLE Nut Tree, Ebdon Road Tel: (0934) 510900: Open-plan ex-farmhouse with relaxed, informal atmosphere. Large, varied menu with home-made dishes; food lunch and evening. Real fire, no music, family room, garden. Brains, Theakston and Wadworth beers. Open: 11-3, 5.30-11 (all day Friday and Saturday).

BEDFORDSHIRE

BEDFORD Bedford Arms, 2 Bromham Road Tel: (0234) 60113: Particularly good sandwiches plus a home-cooked hot dish of the day, Monday-Saturday lunchtimes. Charles Wells beers.

BIDDENHAM   Three Tuns

57 Main Road
Tel: (0234) 54847
Open: 11.30-2.30, 6-11
Licensees: Alan and Tina Wilkins

Stone-built village pub, modernised but attractive, with a comfortable low-beamed lounge and noisy public bar. Food is simple but fresh and home-cooked; the usual pub repertoire is varied by dishes like an old-fashioned chicken casserole, and supplemented by interesting specials. Children are allowed in the dining area.

Bar Meals: lunchtime and evening (not Sun) **Typical Dishes:** *home-made soup and sandwich £1.75, chilli, steak and kidney pie, lasagne (main courses around £3.50) Vegetarian Meals   Children's Menu*   **Beer**   *Greene King IPA, Abbot Ale   Outdoor Play Area   Garden*

BROOM   Cock Inn

23 High Street SG18 9NA
Tel: (0767) 314411
Open: 12-3, 6-11
Licensees: Jackie and Peter Little

Stretching back from the only street of a village with no middle, no shops and a postage stamp sized post office in the postmistress's front room, the Cock is a conversion of three interlinked Victorian cottages, its three panelled sitting areas furnished with bench seats and varnished tables, and a games room complete with the locally popular chair-skittles table. Look inside the two front rooms and find a novel collection of metallised tobacco adverts and shelves of aged beer and medicine bottles. The bar, central to everything here, is unchanged for over a century, its cellar down four wooden steps, where the Greene King IPA and Abbot ales are drawn direct from the cask. Things are on the move, though, since Jackie and Peter Little arrived. The present kitchen is being relocated to the end cottage, thus adding a 30-seat dining room for rather more relaxed eating; menus are expanding and evening cooking is being reintroduced, with an emphasis on Jackie's country-style dishes – pork and beef pinwheel, lamb and apricot pie, a mushroom stroganoff, or the dependable steak, mushroom and Guinness pie. But the Cock's tradition for cheeses carries on: local Stilton, mild, mature and farmhouse Cheddars, Lancashire, Wensleydale, red Leicester and double Gloucester all make for a fine ploughman's with salad, fresh pickles and a local cottage cob, baked exclusively for the pub. Also particularly popular – and meals in themselves – are the Vienna rolls filled with hot beef or gammon and the home-made paté used in the vegetarian ploughman's. Children are now made equally welcome and offered smaller portions of almost anything. The greatest bonus for families this year has been the neatly cleaned-up garden, which has plenty of picnic tables and parasols, and a secure tots' play area.

Bar Meals: 12-2, 6.30-9; bar snacks both sessions **Typical Dishes:** *stilton soup £1.50, egg mayonnaise £1.50, steak, kidney and mushroom pie £4.25, chilli with garlic bread £3.25, hot beef sandwich £2.95, pear and raspberry pie £1.75* *Vegetarian Meals: vegetable paté ploughmans £2.95* *Children's Portions* Beer *Greene King IPA, Abbot Ale* Whisky *Family Room Outdoor Play Area Garden Outdoor Eating Summer Barbecue* **No Credit Cards**

CARLTON Fox, High Street Tel: (0234) 720235: 18th century thatched village inn with bar and restaurant meals lunch and evening (not Sunday evening nor Mondays). No music. Garden. Adnams and Charles Wells beers. Open: 10.30-2.30, 6-11.

HARLINGTON   Carpenters Arms

Sundon Road LU5 6LS
Tel: (05255) 2384
Open: 12-2.30, 5.30-11 (11-11 Sat)
Licensees: P R Edwards and H Edwards

Early 17th century pub with beamed bars and separate upstairs restaurant, and a fine inglenook fireplace. All food is home-made from fresh local produce. Canapés provided with aperitifs upstairs are among the thoughtful touches here.

Bar Meals: 12-2, 6.30-9.30 (not Sun eve) **Restaurant:** *12.30-2.30 (12-2.15 Sun, closed Sat lunch), 7-9.15 Tue-Sat* **Typical Dishes BAR:** *stilton and celery soup £1.50, homemade paté £1.75, beer and beef pie £4.95, ham pancakes £3.95, home-cooked ham, egg and chips £4.45, bread and butter pudding £1.75* **RESTAURANT:** *3 courses and half-bottle of wine £14.65: carrot and orange soup, smoked mackerel and scrambled egg on buttered crumpet, oriental chicken and prawns, garlic pork pastry parcel, poached salmon with watercress sauce, apple and strawberry crumble* *Vegetarian Meals: curried vegetable parcels* Beer *Ruddles Bitter; County; Webster's Yorkshire Bitter Outdoor Play Area Garden Outdoor Eating Summer Barbecue* **Credit Cards:** *Access, Visa*

HOUGHTON CONQUEST   Knife and Cleaver

The Grove MK45 3LA
Tel: (0234) 740387
Open: 12-2.30, 7-11 (closed Sun eve)
Licensees: David and Pauline Loom

Set opposite the church in a peaceful village; popular with locals. Pleasant interior featuring Jacobean panelling; delightful conservatory dining area. Cooking uses all fresh produce, and they make their own ice-cream and pasta. Note that weekend bar food may be jeopardised if the restaurant is especially busy, particularly on Saturday evenings and Sunday lunchtimes.

Bar Meals: 12-2.30, 7-9.30 (weekday eves); bar snacks both sessions **Restaurant:** *12-2.30 (not Sat), 7-9.30 (not Sun)* **Typical Dishes BAR:** *courgette and coriander soup £1.65, smoked salmon mousse with spicy crab mayonnaise £4, home-made steak and kidney pie £4.95, moules marinière £4, home-made fish pie £4.95, chocolate torte £1.50* **RESTAURANT:** *home-made fish soup £2.60, wild mushroom and smoked ham pie £4.50, Cajun chicken £11.75, local venison with filo purse of apricots £12, loin of lamb on potato and garlic galette £12, summer pudding £3.25* *Vegetarian Meals: leek and orange roulade £4.95* *Children's Portions* Cheese Beer *Batemans XB; Banks & Taylor Shefford Bitter* Whisky *Garden Outdoor Eating* **Accommodation:** *9 bedrooms, all en* *suite, from £53 (single £41)   Children Welcome Overnight   Cot available   Check-in: all day   **Credit Cards:** Access, Amex, Visa*

KEYSOE   Chequers Inn

Pertenhall Road MK44 2HR
Tel: (0234) 708678
Open: 11-2.30 (12-2.30 Sun), 6.30-11 (closed Mon except bank hols)
Licensee: Jeffrey Kearns

Charming and comfortable, with an unusual pillared fireplace; log fires in cold weather. Very busy at lunchtime, get here early.

*Bar Meals: 12-2, 7-9.45 (9 Sun); bar snacks both sessions   **Typical Dishes:** courgette and parsley soup £1.75, mushrooms in home-made savoury sauce £2.75, steak in mustard cream sauce £9.50, chicken stuffed with stilton and chives £7.50, home-made Southwold steak pie £5.75, coffee nut pudding £2   Vegetarian Meals: parsnips Molly Parkin   Children's Menu/Portions   Beer   Batemans Bitter; Hook Norton Best Bitter; Marston Pedigree; Theakston Old Peculier   Family Room   Outdoor Play Area   Garden   Outdoor Eating   **Credit Cards:** Visa*

LITTLE ODELL   Mad Dog

212 High Street MK43 7AR   ▼
Tel: (0234) 720221
Open: 11-2.30 (12-2.30 Sun), 6-11
Licensees: Ken and Jean Parry

Thatched pub close to the Harrold-Odell country park. Real fire in inglenook, no music, and a roundabout for the children in the garden (though they are not allowed indoors). The name comes from a supposed cure for the bite of mad dogs which an 18th century landlord took in payment of a debt.

*Bar Meals: 12-1.45, 7-9.30 (12-1.30, 7-9.15 Sun); bar snacks both sessions   **Typical Dishes:** mushroom soup, breaded mushrooms with dip, home-made steak and kidney pie, home-made chilli, beef, mushroom and Guinness pie, apple and blackcurrant crumble   Vegetarian Meals: wheat and walnut casserole   Beer   Greene King IPA; Abbot Ale; Rayments Bitter   Outdoor Play Area   Garden   Outdoor Eating   **Credit Cards:** Access, Visa*

ODELL   Bell

Horsefair Lane MK43 7AG   FOOD
Tel: (0234) 720254   ✳
Open: 11-2.30 (12-2.30 Sun), 6-11   ☺
Licensee: D W Scott

There's great virtue in being content with serving the very simplest of pub food when the circumstances demand it, and at the tiny Bell Inn they've got it just about right. From the front, it's a mellow stone thatched house, and the original two front rooms, connected by a single bar servery, can still be clearly seen. Round the back, a brick extension has brought a succession of little rooms at varying levels, their low tables and stools adding to the almost miniature feel of the place. Old beams and original mantels, framing a cast iron range at one end, are hung with a collection of old brass beer taps; less traditional but rather more hygienic stainless steel engines are in active service now. Doreen Scott's stock-in-trade, in circumstances where the pub never appears less than full, is her single-dish flans of bacon or vegetables, pissaladière and pizza, omelettes and vegetable pie, which come with salad or chips or both, and appear designed to be eaten with fork only, in a confined space. Which they are. Otherwise, there are cold platters, toasties and sandwiches (with commendable hand-sliced bread) and a ploughmans which comes with a crock of home-made pickle. Added to these is a section honestly labelled "deep-fried" for lovers of scampi and other such things, and a routine dessert list with cheesecake, chocolate fudge and Danish pastry. But this is not all. A blackboard menu also materialises, offering steak and kidney pie, pork paprika or stuffed haddock pancakes, followed by pecan pie or crème caramel – a positively prodigious output from space so confined. It gets extremely busy, overflowing on summer days into the garden and under trees down on the banks of the river.

Bar Meals: 12-2 (1.30 Sun), 7-9.30 **Typical Dishes:** *mango chicken £4.95, lasagne £4, creamy fish pie £3.45, tarte Montmartre £1.45* Vegetarian Meals: *vegetable pie £3.35* Children's Menu `Beer` Greene King IPA; Rayments Bitter; Abbot Ale Family Room Outdoor Play Area Garden Outdoor Eating **No Credit Cards**

RADWELL   Swan Inn

Felmersham Road MK43 7HS   ❦
Tel: (0234) 781351
Open: 12-2.30, 7-11
Licensee: Terence Ian Naysmith

Quiet 17th century thatched country pub with rustic charm and real fire, in delightful village.

Bar Meals and Restaurant: 12-1.45 (not Sun), 7-9.45 (not Tue); *bar snacks lunchtime* **Typical Dishes BAR:** *carrot and orange soup £1.60, tuna and kiwi fruit £1.75, Cumberland lamb £8.15, home-made steak and kidney pie £4.95, medallions of pork £6.75, lemon pudding* **RESTAURANT:** *home-made salmon bisque £1.75, brochettes d'escargot £2.95, two fillets, two sauces £7.95, calves liver £8.75, peppered salmon steak £7.85* Vegetarian Meals: *vegetable stroganoff* Children's Portions `Cheese` `Beer` Charles Wells Bombardier, Eagle Bitter Family Room Outdoor Play Area Garden Outdoor Eating **Credit Cards:** *Access, Visa*

RISELEY Fox & Hounds, High Street: 16th century pub with beamed restaurant, popular for its traditionally hung and grilled steaks.

SHEFFORD White Horse, Deadman's Cross (A600) Tel: (023 066) 634: Roadside pub with a good local reputation for food, and a welcoming lounge bar with bookcases, armchairs and an open fire. Separate attractive restaurant. Bar Meals: lunch and evening; not Mon; Children's Menu; Banks & Taylors beers; family room garden; open: 12-3 (2.30 winter), 5.30 (7 Sat and winter)-11; 7.30 opening Sun eve.

STEPPINGLEY   French Horn

5 Church Road MK45 5AU   ❦
Tel: (0525) 712051
Open: 12-3 (not Mon), 6-11
Licensee: Eric Gilliland

Old and attractive inn, family-run, and now divided into a pool-table dominated public bar, L-shaped lounge with exposed 17th century timbers, and popular restaurant. Decent bar food, and they don't possess a microwave oven: look to the daily changing blackboard bar menu, strong on home-made pies, seafood and robust meat dishes. Real fire, no music.

Bar Meals and Restaurant: 12-2.30, 7-10 (9.30 restaurant); no food Sun/Mon eve; no bar meals Sat eve; bar snacks both sessions   **Typical Dishes BAR:** *home-made soup £1.95, home-made chicken liver pate £1.95, 7 oz rump steak £5.95, Barnsley chop £5.95, grilled Hoki fillets £5.95, crème caramel*   **RESTAURANT:** *lunch menu £12.95; dinner menu £17.95, or a la carte: smoked venison and Waldorf salad £4.35, quail financière £10.50, tournedos Helder £12.95, char-grilled halibut steak £12.95   Vegetarian Meals: stir-fry with garlic and rice   Children's Portions* Beer *Bass; Tetley; Wadworth   Children Allowed in Bar to Eat   Garden   Outdoor Eating*   **Credit Cards:** *Access, Amex, Diners, Visa*

TODDINGTON Oddfellows Arms, Conger Lane Tel: (05255) 2021: Attractive old pub on the village green. Three bars including a tiny public and smart Croft Bar with its gallery seating area, popular with local business types for lunches: lots of old-fashioned meat dishes (no food evenings). Roaring fire and friendly efficient service. Pavement drinking area. Ind Coope, Tetley beers. Open: 11-3, 6-11.

TURVEY   Three Cranes

High Street loop road MK43 8EP
Tel: (023 064) 305
Open: 11-3, 6-11
Licensee: David Alexander

300 year old stone pub renovated by the Victorians, in a pretty stone-built village, with an interesting church and abbey. Same menu in dining room.

Bar Meals: 11.30-2.30, 6-10 (12-2.30, 7-9.30 Sun); bar snacks both sessions *Restaurant:* 12-2.30 (Sun only), 6-10 **Typical Dishes BAR:** *curried parsnip soup £1.50, breaded mushrooms in garlic butter £1.95, steak, mushroom and ale pie £4.50, mixed grill £6.50, daily specials from £4.25, lemon crunch £1.65   Vegetarian Meals: home-made nut cutlets £4.25   Children's Portions* Beer *Adnams Best; Fullers London Pride; ESB; Hook Norton Best Bitter* Whisky *Children Allowed in Bar to Eat Outdoor Play Area   Garden   Outdoor Eating*   **Accommodation:** *3 bedrooms, 1 en suite, from £40 (single £30)   Children Welcome Overnight (minimum age 12)   Check-in: by arrangement*   **Credit Cards:** *Access, Visa*

WHIPSNADE Old Hunters Lodge: On B4540: Pleasant cosy little pub with separate restaurant, food lunch and evening from snacks to full meals; families welcome.

WOBURN   Magpie

Bedford Street (A418)
Tel: (0525) 290219
Open: 12-2.30 (3 Sat), 6-11
Licensee: Maurice McLaren

Little lounge, larger, basic but pleasant public bar, and separate restaurant in this 16th century former coaching inn near Woburn golf club. The licensee's dedication to fresh vegetables extends to growing his own in poly tunnels.

Bar Meals and Restaurant: daily lunch and evening; bar snacks both sessions **Typical Dishes BAR:** *home-made steak and oyster pie, venison pie, fresh tuna, cod and plaice (main courses from £4)* Beer *Ruddles, Webster's   Children Allowed in Bar to Eat   Garden* **Credit Cards:** *Access, Amex, Diners, Visa*

WOOTTON Chequers, Hall End: Popular, friendly and atmospheric 15th century pub with restaurant.

BERKSHIRE

ALDWORTH   Four Points

on B4009
Open: 11-2.30, 5.30-11
Licensees: John and Audrey Gillas

Simple home-cooked food in generous portions, at this attractive and relaxing
thatched pub: one bar with a tiled floor and open fire, another carpeted area leading
off, and simple, low key furnishings. Good sandwiches and salads. The garden is
across the road.

*Bar Meals: lunch and evening   Typical Dishes: moussaka, lasagne, rabbit pie – main
courses around £4 Vegetarian Meals*   **Beer**   *Courage; Morlands; Wadworth   Children
Allowed in Bar to Eat   Outdoor Play Area   Garden*

BINFIELD   Stag & Hounds

Forest Road (B3034) RG12 5HA   ❦
Tel: (0344) 483553
Licensee: B Howard

Built as a royal hunting lodge in the heart of Windsor Great Forest some 600 years
ago or more, and listed for its atmosphere: blackened beams, low ceilings, open fires
and five cosy little bars with nice old furnishings, as well as a pleasant lounge
adorned with a thimble collection. The remains of the ancient elm which once
marked the very centre of the forest are in the garden. Food, in the rather more
modern wine bar/bistro, is secondary here, but avoids the usual pub cliches.

Bar Meals: lunch and evening   Vegetarian Meals   Childrens Menu   **Beer**   *Courage
Family Room   Garden   Credit Cards: Access*

BOXFORD   Bell

Lambourn Road RG16 8DD   ❦
Tel: (048 838) 721
Open: 11-3, 6-11
Licensee: Paul Lavis

Mock-Tudor pub at a country crossroads not far from Newbury.

*Bar Meals and Restaurant: 11.30 (12 Sun and restaurant daily)-2, 7-10; bar snacks both
sessions   Typical Dishes BAR: carrot and coriander soup £1.80, port and stilton paté
£2.95, Cumberland sausage with onion sauce £4.95, Singapore chicken £5.45, rump steak
£8.50, rhubarb and orange sponge £2.25   RESTAURANT: leek and stilton soup
£2.65, smoked chicken Waldorf £3.65, lamb Madeira £10.95, fillet steak harlequin
£13.95, devilled veal £11.95, brandy baskets with exotic fruits £3.50   Vegetarian Meals:
fusille and mushrooms   Children's Menu/Portions*   **Beer**   *Courage Directors; Whitbread
Best, Boddingtons Bitter, Flowers Original   Children Allowed in Bar to Eat Patio/terrace
Accommodation: 11 bedrooms, all en suite, from £68 (single £56)   Children Welcome
Overnight   Cot Available   Check-in: all day   Credit Cards: Access, Amex, Diners, Visa*

COOKHAM DEAN Jolly Farmer, Church Lane: Low-beamed cottage pub
opposite the church, and owned by locals who are keen to preserve its 18th century
charm. Restaurant and garden. Courage beers.

CRAZIES HILL　　　　　　　　　　　　　　Horns

Signposted off A321, near Wargrave
Tel: (0734) 403226
Licensee: Mary Wheeler

Plain, unpretentious 400 year-old little pub in Windsor Forest, probably once a hunting lodge. Both traditional English and exotic Malaysian/Thai cooking, the latter can be surprisingly good; children allowed in to eat, in the small bistro/dining area, lunchtime and early evening. Limited food on Sunday and Monday evenings.

Bar Meals and Restaurant: daily lunch and evening;　bar snacks both sessions **Typical Dishes:** *beef in beer casserole, Nasi Goreng, shepherds pie, Nepalese chicken korma Vegetarian Meals* **Beer** *Brakspears　Patio/terrace* **No Credit Cards**

CURRIDGE Bunk Arms: Off B4009 Tel: (0635) 200400: Cosy pub with a real fire, no music, unhurried atmosphere, and restaurant extension. Home cooked food lunch and Monday-Saturday evenings. Garden. Adnams, Arkell's, Morlands and Theakston beers. Open: 11-2.30, 6-11.

EAST ILSLEY　　　　　　　　　　　　　　Swan

High Street (A34) RG16 0LF
Tel: (063 528) 238
Open: 10.30-2.30, 6-11
Licensees: Michael and Jenny Connolly

Lovely old village pub which has belonged to local brewers Morlands for over 150 years. The opened-out, refurbished interior still retains lots of nooks and crannies, different areas with different styles and customers, and the fruit machine and piped music don't intrude on the civilised mood too much.

Bar Meals and Restaurant: 11.45-2, 6.15-9.45; bar snacks both sessions **Typical Dishes BAR:** *paté with hot wholemeal bread and herb butter £3.50, local wild rabbit pie £4.40, pork ribs in port wine £4.40, large whole plaice £6.50, strawberry pancakes £2.20 Vegetarian Meals: macaroni cheese £3.50　Children's Menu/Portions* **Beer** *Morlands Family Room　Outdoor Play Area　Garden　Outdoor Eating* **Accommodation:** *10 bedrooms, 8 en suite, from £49 (single £33)　Children Welcome Overnight　Check-in: all day* **Credit Cards:** *Access, Visa.*

ETON Crown & Cushion, High Street Tel: (0753) 861531: Well-heeled 15th century pub, busy for its home-cooked food, particularly lunchtimes, when it's especially good value. Last meal orders 8pm; no food Sunday. Real fire, no music, garden. Courage beers. They also do bedrooms. Open: 11-3, 5.30-11 (all day Sat, and Fri in summer).

FRILSHAM   Pot Kiln

on Yattendon-Bucklebury road
Tel: (0635) 201366
Open: 12-2.30, 6.30-11
Licensee: Mrs Gent

Remote country pub, delightful in summer in the pretty little garden with its
soothing woodland views. The name derives from this being the site of old brick
kilns, abandoned after the war, and the building is, appropriately, of attractive redbrick
construction. Inside is distinctively old-fashioned, with simple wooden furnishings
(take a cushion), a warming open fire, and a good, relaxing atmosphere, with a
successful mix of locals and passing ramblers. There's live folk music on Sunday
evenings; otherwise, peace. Food is secondary to the atmosphere, but decent enough.

Bar Meals: lunch and evening (not Sun, nor Mon eve) bar snacks both sessions ***Typical Dishes:***
*home-made soup, steak, vegetarian curry, spinach and mushroom lasagne (main courses from around
£3)* **Beer** *Arkell's, Morlands, Ringwood   Family Room   Garden   Outdoor Eating*

HAMSTEAD MARSHALL   White Hart Inn

near Newbury RG15 0HW   FOOD
Tel: (0488) 58201   B&B
Open: 12-2.30, 6.30-11 (closed Sun)
Licensee: Nicola Aromando

The splendid herbaceous borders around the neat lawn at the front of this 16th century
inn are very English, and the pride and joy of Dorothy Aromando, but inside the Latin
influence of husband Nicola predominates in the White Hart's Italian menu. A few old
beams, mingling with some newer ones, give clues to the age of the building, but the
decor is basically simple: red plush in the bar, red cloths on the tables of the restaurant
leading off it. The same handwritten menu serves for both bar and restaurant meals, a
sensibly brief selection of pasta and meat dishes. A generous plateful of deep-fried squid,
cooked quickly and properly tender, serves equally well as a bar meal or restaurant
starter; in our case, as a prelude to some excellent mozzarella-filled minced lamb
meatballs that went particularly well with green noodles served in a creamy sauce.
Amongst the home-made puddings, crème caramel was outstanding, freshly cooked
and with the topping caramelised to just the right degree. An old barn to the rear of the
pub has been converted into six uncluttered bedrooms with pine furniture and good
cotton bedding. All have neat en suite bathrooms with showers over their bathtubs. Get
one of the two large rooms under the eaves, if you can, which have sloping ceilings and
exposed timbers, as well as an extra bed for family use. The two single rooms are very
compact. Good freshly cooked breakfasts set one up for the day ahead.

Bar Meals: 12-2, 7-10 ***Typical Dishes:*** *leek and courgette soup £3, bresaola £4.50,
pollo sorpresa £8.50, fritelle £8.50, salmone Genovese £9.50, rich almond tart £3.50
Vegetarian Meals: ricotta and spinach pancake* **Beer** *Hall & Woodhouse; Wadworth
Garden* ***Accommodation:*** *6 bedrooms, all en suite, from £50 (single £40)   Children
Welcome Overnight   Check-in: by arrangement* ***Credit Cards:*** *Access, Amex, Visa*

HARE HATCH   Queen Victoria

Blakes Lane RG10 9TA
Tel: (0734) 402477
Open: 11-3, 5.30-11
Licensee: C R Rossington

The constantly changing bar menu here is varied and adventurous, and the pub a
convivial, low-ceilinged 17th century two-roomed village local with a fruit machine
and video game, as well as a good selection of more traditional pursuits. Real fire,
no music.

Bar Meals: 11-2.45, 6-10.45; bar snacks both sessions   **Typical Dishes:** *fresh minestrone
£1, seafood garni with anchovy bread £2.80, beef, orange and Guinness casserole £4.15,
lamb masala with wild rice £4.50, chicken supreme in mushroom and tarragon sauce £4.25,
apple and blackberry crumble   Vegetarian Meals: cheese and vegetable bake £3.65
Children's Portions*   **Beer**   *Brakspears Mild, Bitter, Special, Old Ale   Children Allowed
in Bar to Eat   Garden   Outdoor Eating*   **No Credit Cards**

HOLYPORT Rising Sun, Forest Green Row Tel: (0628) 23639: Delightful two
bar pub converted from a pair of little cottages, popular with locals for lunch
(weekdays only). Friendly atmosphere, real fire, no music. Garden. Morlands beers.
Open: 11-2.30 (3 Fri/Sat), 5-11.

HURLEY   Dew Drop

**Go west from Hurley on A423, left up Honey Lane, right at postbox
after the farm, right again after hamlet.**
Open: 11.30-2.30, 6-11
Licensee: Michael Morris

Go for the home-made pies, casseroles and curries, all at around £4.50, and the
good traditional puddings, at this well-loved, tucked-away, genuinely unpretentious
cottage pub. Food is very much secondary to the atmosphere and rural peace; the
garden's delightful in summer, and it's a real hideaway of a place in winter, when
the twin log fires in the main bar are crackling. No children indoors.

Bar Meals: lunch and evening (no food Sun eve/all day Mon); bar snacks both sessions
Beer   *Brakspears   Outdoor Play Area   Garden*

HURLEY Black Boy, Henley Road Tel: (062 882) 4212: 16th century single bar
pub with a wood-burning stove and a dining emphasis. Home-cooked food
lunchtime and evening. No music. Garden. Brakspears beers. Open: 11-2.30 (3 Sat),
6-11.

HURST Castle: Rather distinguished old village inn opposite the church, with
old-fashioned country pub atmosphere, real fires, and two bars plus a dining area.
Outdoor tables overlook the green.

INKPEN   Swan Inn

Lower Inkpen, near Newbury RG15 0DX   **FOOD**
Tel: (04884) 326
Open: 11.30-2.30 (not Tue), 6.30-11; closed all day Mon
Licensee: John Scothorne

Colourful window boxes and hanging baskets of flowers adorn the front of this long,
low, white-painted 17th century country pub. Inside, there are lots of old beams and

timbers, some of them salvaged from a nearby barn, pew seating at one end and pink-clothed tables in the restaurant area at the other. After his return from 14 years out east, landlord John Scothorne thought Singaporean cooking and real ales would go well together; four years on, the experiment has proved a great success, and pints of good English bitter have proved fine partners for dishes like spicy lamb keema or sweet and sour fish, from a fairly extensive menu available in both the bar and, more formally, the restaurant at night. Mock chicken drumsticks made from chicken wings seasoned in sherry, crushed garlic and honey make particularly good, if rather sticky, finger food. For those with less exotic tastes, a traditional 'pub grub' menu at lunchtime features ploughmans, cottage pie and the like. The house wines are all bottled by a friend of John's (who also happens to be his partner in a French hotel) at his chateau just east of Bordeaux. The range includes an Entre Deux Mers, a Bordeaux Supérieur and a sweet dessert wine called Cadillac, while the nine other listed wines include a New Zealand Chardonnay, Australian Shiraz, Spanish Rioja and low alcohol American wine, plus champagne from the widow Clicquot if you are in celebratory mood, or experimenting with bold new accompaniments to Singaporean cooking.

Bar Meals: 12-1.45, 7-9.30; bar snacks lunchtime **Typical Dishes:** *thom yam koon soup £3.25, drunken prawns £3.75, Szechuan chicken £5.65, weeping tiger £8.50, pork tenderloin £6.50 Vegetarian Meals: crunchy spring vegetables £4.75* **Beer** *Arkells; Brakspears; Fullers; Whitbread* **Cider** *Addlestones Children Allowed in Bar to Eat Patio/terrace Outdoor Eating* **Credit Cards:** *Access, Visa*

KINGSCLERE   Swan Hotel

Swan Street RG15 8PP
Tel: (0635) 298314
Open: 11-2.30, 5.30-11
Licensee: Mr McLarin

Previously a star-rated entry in our guide, the Swan is now in new hands, and first reports suggest it's still worth a visit; the menu certainly looks interesting. Pleasant bar, and very nice bedrooms, with floral fabrics and fine period furnishings.

Bar Meals: 12.30-2, 7.30-9.30; bar snacks both sessions **Restaurant:** *7.30-9* **Typical Dishes BAR:** *courgette and cream soup £2.75, spinach and ricotta tortellini £3.95, veal in wine sauce £7.90, lamb Marengo £3.95, poached salmon steak £5.85, bread and butter pudding £3.75* **RESTAURANT:** *gazpacho £3.80, mussels in cream and saffron £4.25, supreme of chicken in mushroom sauce £9, lamb steak in madeira £8.75, monkfish with brandy £11.20, treacle sponge £3.75 Children's Portions* **Beer** *Gibbs Mew; Tetley; Theakston, Younger Accommodation: 10 bedrooms, all en suite, from £50 (single £45) Children Welcome Overnight Cots Available Check-in: all day* **Credit Cards:** *Access, Visa*

KINTBURY   Dundas Arms

Station Road (access via Halfway, past Kintbury turnoff from Hungerford-bound A4) RG15 0UT
Tel: (0488) 58263
Open: 11-2.30 (inc Sun), 6-11
Licensee: D A Dalzell-Piper

Well-loved, reliable old-fashioned waterside inn, by the Kennet and Avon canal, run by the Dalzell-Pipers since the 1960s. The civilised bar has a striking display of blue patterned plates entirely covering one wall. The riverside patio is very popular on summer lunchtimes. Nice bedrooms in a converted stable block, with French windows opening onto a quiet private terrace, where garden furniture is provided for each room. Cooking is reliably good.

Bar Meals: 12-2, 7-9; bar snacks both sessions   **Restaurant:** 12.30-1.30, 7.30-9.30 **Typical Dishes BAR:** home-made soup £2.50, crab au gratin £3.90, steak and kidney pie £5.95, fresh pasta with pesto £4.25, brie and broccoli pie £5.30, summer pudding £2.95   **RESTAURANT:** 3-course set price meals from £25 Vegetarian Meals Children's Portions   Cheese   Beer   Eldridge Pope Hardy Country Bitter; Fullers London Pride; Morlands OB   Whisky   Springbank 20 yr   Children Allowed in Bar to Eat Riverside Patio/terrace   Outdoor Eating   **Accommodation:** 5 bedrooms, all en suite, from £70 (single £60)   Children Welcome Overnight   Check-in: by arrangement   **Credit Cards:** Access, Amex, Diners, Visa

---

KNOWLE HILL   Seven Stars

Bath Road (A4)
Tel: (062 882) 2967
Open: 11-3, 5.30-11

Large 16th century coaching inn, popular for wedding receptions. Beyond the Georgian frontage is a series of comfortable panelled rooms with warming open fires; good for families – children are welcome until 9pm, and there are tree houses in the large garden. A recent change of hands has brought a smartening up. Bar food is simple, from snacks to steaks. No music.

Bar Meals: lunch and evening (not Mon); bar snacks both sessions   Vegetarian meals Children's Menu   Beer   Brakspears   Family Room   Outdoor Play Area   Garden **Accommodation:** 3 bedrooms, from £40.

OLD WINDSOR Oxford Blue, Crimp Hill (off A308) Tel: (0753) 861954: Good value, old-fashioned lunchtime food (also evening meals) in this cheery, popular 17th century pub; one bar with lots of aircraft memorabilia; pleasant garden room extension. They also do bedrooms. No music. Garden. Ind Coope, Tetley beers. Open all day.

REMENHAM   Little Angel

Remenham Lane (A423) RG9 2LS
Tel: (0491) 574165
Open: 11-2.30 (12-2 Sun), 6-10.30 (11 Fri/Sat)
Licensee: Ashley St John Bundock

Well-heeled dining pub with a menu strong on fresh fish, a striking red and black decorated main bar, Garden Room and Champagne Garden terrace (floodlit at night). Something vegetarian can be provided if there's nothing on the menu; children's portions are available on request.

Bar Meals and Restaurant: 12-2.30, 7.30-10.30; bar snacks both sessions   **Typical Dishes BAR:** chicken and leek soup £3, garlic mushrooms and prawns on toast £4.50, grilled (huge) plaice £8.50, steak and oyster pie £6.50, cannelloni £6, bread and butter pudding £3   **RESTAURANT:** carrot and coriander soup £3, salad supreme £6.50, grilled (huge) lemon sole £15, rack of lamb £14.50, fillet steak £16.50   Beer Brakspears   Garden   Outdoor Eating   **Credit Cards:** Access, Amex, Diners, Visa

SONNING   Bull

High Street RG4 0UP
Tel: (0734) 693901
Open: 10-2.30, 5.30-11
Licensee: Dennis Catton

Quintessentially southern English traditional pub, its ancient black and white exterior covered with plants and flowers – you can sit out here and admire them – while in its two linked rooms there are sturdy old beams, gleaming brass, quarry tiles, barrel chairs and an inglenook fireplace, alive with logs in winter, ablaze with flowers in summer. Very simple but decent lunchtime bar food centres on the cold buffet table. Bedrooms are stylishly old-fashioned, with white walls, beams and solid free-standing furniture; most overlook the church and courtyard. There's also a restaurant where children are permitted.

Bar Meals: 12-2; bar snacks both sessions **Typical Dishes:** *Traditional pies and quiches with salad, around £4; hot chicken dish, steak and kidney pie, home-made cheesecake Vegetarian Meals* `Cheese` `Beer` *Marston; Whitbread Patio/terrace* **Accommodation:** *5 bedrooms, sharing a bathroom, from £65 (single £35) Check-in: by arrangement*

STANFORD DINGLEY   Bull

Reading RG7 6LS   ⚱
Tel: (0734) 744409
Open: 12-3 (not Mon), 7-11
Licensees: Pat and Trudi Langdon

A tranquil village and a 15th century redbrick pub, one bar staunchly traditional with its quarry tiling, barrel seats, window settle and big black beams, the other a more modern, plainer saloon with plush banquettes. Reliably good home cooking.

Bar Meals: 12-2.30, 7.30-10; bar snacks both sessions **Typical Dishes:** *stilton soup £2.25, prawns à la crème £2.30, shepherds pie £3.95, beef stroganoff £5.95, scampi provencale £6.60, chocolate roulade £1.90 Vegetarian Meals: lasagne £4.20* `Beer` *Bass; Brakspears Family Room (until 8.30) Garden* **No Credit Cards**

STANFORD DINGLEY   Old Boot

near Bradfield RG7 6LS
Tel: (0734) 744292
Open: 11-2.30, 6-11
Licensee: Tony Howells

Increasingly popular for its home-cooked bar food, this relaxing village pub has old style furnishings, some well-chosen pictures and an open fire in the bar; there's also a charming little restaurant.

Bar Meals: 12-2, 6-10; 12-1.30, 7-9.30 Sun; bar snacks both sessions **Typical Dishes** *BAR: home-made soup £1.60, home-made half pound beefburgers £3, smoked salmon with scrambled eggs £3.50, chicken and stilton roulade £4, puddings from the restaurant trolley Vegetarian Meals Children's Menu/Portions* `Cheese` `Beer` *Brakspears; Eldridge Pope; Whitbread Children Allowed in Bar to Eat Garden Outdoor Eating* **Credit Cards:** *Access, Visa*

WARGRAVE   Bull

High Street   ❢
Tel: (0734) 403120
Open: 11-3, 6-11
Licensee: Noel Harman

Delightful 17th century brick-built village pub, with low beams, a pleasantly modernised interior – original timbers and huge fireplace remaining – and a local following for its home-cooked food, simple at lunchtimes (go for the specials), more interesting in the evening. There's also a restaurant, specialising in smart fish dishes. No music.

Bar Meals: *lunch and Mon-Sat evening; bar snacks both sessions* **Typical Dishes BAR:** *home-made soup £1.95, smoked pork sausages, steak and kidney pie, tortellini, pork spare ribs (main courses around £4 lunch, £7 evening) Vegetarian Meals Children's Menu* **Beer** *Brakspears Children Allowed in Bar to Eat Garden* **Accommodation:** *5 bedrooms from £35 (single £20)*

WEST ILSLEY   ★   Harrow

Newbury RG16 0AR   FOOD
Tel: (063 528) 260   ☻
Open: 11-3, 6-11   ☼
Licensee: Heather Humphreys

"Very unpretentious, in fact slightly tatty" read one of the inspector's notes on our last but one visit to the ever popular Harrow Inn. All this has changed now, in a recent programme of extension and refurbishment, wihch has whisked away the old dividing wall between the little bar and old dining rooms, and created a dining area proper behind the central fireplace. Antique furniture and several country settles have also arrived, creating a smartly rustic atmosphere, but still simple and old-fashioned, and friendly as ever. A new toilet block's been built too, with access from the bar. All this means there's now more space in which to relax, enjoy an excellent pint of Morlands beer (who founded their brewery in this village in 1711, but are now based in Abingdon), and a delicious lunch or supper. The food is as good as always; we've star-rated the Harrow for three consecutive editions, and the consistency of approach and cooking is admirable. Perhaps the general tone of the menu has risen a little (with prices in tandem), in keeping with the general smartening up of the place, but old favourites remain, at outstanding value for money, like the exceptional rabbit pie (£3.95) which wraps tender pieces of fresh rabbit with lemon and herbs in a puff pastry crust, accompanied by good al dente vegetables like properly cooked cabbage, potatoes, and a savoury side dish of leeks in a tomato sauce. The range of dishes, chosen from the seasonally changing handwritten menu and daily changing specials board, is wide enough to suit all tastes and pockets, from a simple home-made hamburger to a hearty three course meal. Soups, salads, bread and puddings are reliably good, the home-made puddings especially, and a fine selection of constantly varying British cheeses puts the seal on a splendid bill of fare. Portions are generous and decidedly non-nouvelle, and vegetarians are thoughtfully catered for: all in all a properly pubby combination of the imaginative and homely, which keeps people coming back. There are other reasons to visit too, like the village green setting, complete with lazy ducks on the pond, and a good garden for children with playthings and animals. It's on the edge of the Berkshire Downs, and just a mile from the Ridgeway footpath. But note that the accommodation experiment has now been abandoned – they no longer offer bedrooms.

Bar Meals: *12-2.15, 6-9.16; bar snacks both sessions* **Typical Dishes:** *mushroom and* *hazelnut soup £1.95, warm salad of mushrooms and bacon £2.50, rabbit pie with lemon and herbs £3.95, walnut and herb-crusted loin of lamb with redcurrant sauce £7.75, Somerset chicken breast poached with cider and apples £6.95, steamed marmalade sponge with orange sauce £2.25 Vegetarian Meals: savoury walnut roulade £4.75 Children's Portions* `Cheese` `Beer` *Morland Original, Old Masters, Old Speckled Hen Children Allowed in Bar to Eat Outdoor Play Area Garden **Credit Cards:** Access, Visa*

WINDSOR Carpenters Arms, 4 Market Street Tel: (0753) 863695: Good value home cooking, roast meats with all the trimmings and traditional pies a speciality, in a busy tourist area, opposite the castle. Food lunchtimes only; children allowed in to eat (no garden). Bass beers. Open: 11-3, 6-11; all day Friday, Saturday and in summer.

WINKFIELD   Olde Hatchet

Hatchet Lane SL4 2EE
Tel: (0344) 882303
Licensee: Christine Mace

Charming black and white country pub with conifers and umbrella-topped tables at the front and a garden to the side. Straightforward, enjoyable food is served in the low-beamed bar; nice service and presentation. Piped pop music can be intrusive.

*Bar Meals: 12-2.30, 7-9.30 (not Sun eve); bar snacks both sessions **Typical Dishes BAR:** smoked salmon hoagie, sausage ploughmans, barbecued spare ribs, smoked chicken salad (main courses around £4)* `Cheese` `Beer` *Bass Garden Outdoor Eating* **Credit Cards:** *Access, Amex, Visa*

WOKINGHAM Crooked Billet, Honey Hill (off B3430) Tel: (0734) 789256: Characterful, extended country pub in a peaceful spot about two miles south east of the town. Home cooking lunchtime and evening; very busy at lunchtimes. Real fires, no music, garden. Brakspears beers. Open all day.

WOOLHAMPTON   Angel Inn

Bath Road (A4)
Tel: (0734) 713307
Licensees: Roger and Lyn Jarvis

Attractive ivy-covered pub near the Kennet and Avon canal. The interior is festooned with bric-a-brac of every kind, collected by the landlord; it's lovely to sit out by the pond with its little bridge in good weather. The routine bar menu is enlivened by some unusual daily specials, and vegetables are mostly fresh; there's also a restaurant. They have a popular skittle alley, and offer conference facilities. Some of the bedrooms are in a neighbouring annexe.

*Bar Meals and Restaurant: daily lunchtime and evening; bar snacks both sessions **Typical Dishes BAR:** home-made soup, chicken and ham pie, beef and smoked oyster pie, stew with dumplings, tandoori and Chinese dishes (main courses around £4.50) Vegetarian Meals Children's Portions* `Beer` *Brakspears; Marston; Whitbread Children Allowed in Bar to Eat Garden **Accommodation:** 7 bedrooms, 5 en suite, from £45 (single £27) Children Welcome Overnight **Credit Cards:** Access, Amex, Diners, Visa*

YATTENDON ★ Royal Oak

near Newbury RG16 0UF
FOOD
Tel: (0635) 201325
Open: 12-2, 6-10
Licensees: J E G Huff and O R W Williams
B&B

Richard and Kate Smith have left the Royal Oak to concentrate on their other business, the Beetle and Wedge at Moulsford, Oxfordshire, but the new regime (an established one really, as there's been a management buy-out) has taken over the reins with confidence and flair; this is still a star-rated, detour-worthy pub. The interior retains its rustically refined appeal, the main lounge snugly welcoming, with plump-cushioned seats, rug-covered parquet floors, impressive floral displays, and blazing open fires; the quaint beamed and panelled bar is equally relaxing. The new broom has been sweeping, though, with some refurbishment of both public rooms and bedrooms planned in readiness for the 1992 season. You still don't have to opt for formal restaurant dining to enjoy spectacular food here: even in the bar, the choice is always spoiling, with a daily list of around 30 starters and mains combined, and a separate menu of around 10 sumptuous puddings. Start, perhaps, with a deliciously subtle creamy pea soup, a salad of noodles and seafood, marinated trout fillet, or a robust grilled kidney and black pudding confection draped in green mustard sauce. Middle with grilled lambsteak accompanied by flageolet beans in red wine, supreme of chicken – its sauce deliciously curried and dotted with wild mushrooms, or roast monkfish with a fondue of leeks and crayfish in a saffron sauce; vegetarians are also properly catered for with imaginative and delicious vegetable dishes a world away from the ubiquitous lasagne. Finish with a meltingly fresh beignet soufflé in hot lemon sauce, gooseberry tart, a tulipe of home-made sorbets, or a homely but wonderful apple and raspberry crumble topped with clotted cream. Prices have perhaps nudged up a little higher, and this is a grand occasion venue for most of us, with bar meal main courses routinely hitting £10, £15-£18 in the restaurant, even the ploughman's lunch is £5.50! – but the expense is well worthwhile. Bedrooms are particularly enjoyed, not just for the king-size beds and good en suite bathrooms (the two non-en suite have baths just across the hall), but for their general sense of style – all different – and thoughtful little extras of the quality toiletries, deep-pile towels, magazines and mineral water sort.

Bar Meals: 12-2, 7-10; bar snacks both sessions **Typical Dishes:** *creamy pea soup £3.25, crispy duck and salade frisée £4.90, medallions of pork with spinach and green pepper sauce £10.75, poached skate £8.95, ragout of fish with saffron sauce £10.50, hot lemon sponge with clotted cream £4.25* **Vegetarian Meals:** *fricassee of artichoke with fresh noodles £7.15* **Children's Portions** Cheese Beer *Adnams Bitter; Hall & Woodhouse Tanglefoot; Wadworth 6X* Family Room Outdoor Play Area Garden Outdoor Eating **Accommodation:** *5 bedrooms, all with private bathroom (3 en suite), from £70 (single £50)* Children Welcome Overnight Cots Available Check-in: all day **Credit Cards:** *Access, Amex, Diners*

BUCKINGHAMSHIRE

AMERSHAM King's Arms

High Street, Old Amersham HP7 0DJ
Tel: (0494) 726333
Open: 11-11
Licensee: John Jennison

The licensee, who also does the cooking here, using fresh local produce. A nice pub too, originally 15th century, with plenty of beams and character.

Bar Meals: 12-2.15, 6.30-9; bar snacks both sessions *Restaurant:* 12-2, 7-9.30; closed Sun eve and all day Mon **Typical Dishes BAR:** home-made soup £1.35, garlic mushrooms £2.50, steak and kidney pie £3.95, chicken curry £3.50, ham salad £3.70, home-made puddings **RESTAURANT:** chilled cucumber and mint soup £2.75, smoked duck breast £4, best end of lamb £15, veal Zurich style with rosti £14.50, monkfish in sesame seeds £15, puddings £4 Vegetarian Meals Cheese   Beer Ind Coope; Greene King Children Allowed in Bar to Eat Outdoor Play Area Garden **Credit Cards:** Access, Amex, Diners, Visa

AYLESBURY   Bottle & Glass

Gibraltar; by A418 just west of the town HP17 8TY
Tel: (0296) 748488
Open: 11-2.30, 6-11
Licensee: R Stevens

The usually raved-about Bottle and Glass faces an uncertain future as the guide goes to press. Since the Berrys sold the pub back to the brewery two years ago there has been a succession of managers here, and now new tenants in the shape of two couples are about to take over at this delightful old thatched inn. As of August 1991 it was unclear whether the chef would be kept on or not by the new regime; the rest of the staff, some of whom have been here twenty years, have been served redundancy notices by the brewery. Let's hope the high catering standards and unspoilt interior of the Bottle and Glass survive unscathed. The character of the pub alone makes it worth a visit, despite the fact that we are unable to give a rating on much else this year.

Bar Meals: 12-2, 7-9.30; bar snacks lunchtime *Typical Dishes:* asparagus soup £1.95, smoked mackerel terrine £3, Scotch fillet steak with green pepper sauce £9.50, best end of lamb with redcurrant and port sauce £6, poached rainbow trout Miranda £7.50, home-made caramel soufflé £2.50 Vegetarian Meals: fresh vegetable lasagne £3.50   Beer Adnams; Hook Norton; Tetley; Wadworth Children Allowed in Bar to Eat Garden Outdoor Eating **Credit Cards:** Access, Diners, Visa

BEACONSFIELD   Old Hare

41 Aylesbury End HP9 1LU   ❗
Tel: (0494) 673380
Open: 11-2.30, 5.30-11
Licensees: Andrew Reed and Leslie Chamberlain

Rambling, nicely chaotic multi-roomed dining pub, busy but well-organised. A simple, short menu concentrates on good old-fashioned bakes and pies, with a few new-fangled touches, as well as the usual sandwiches, burgers and salads. There's one addition in the evening: a green peppercorn steak in red wine (£8.25); note that puddings are served Monday-Saturday only.

Bar Meals: 12-2, 7.30-10; bar snacks both sessions *Typical Dishes:* broccoli and almond soup £1.95, deep-fried brie with crab apple jelly £3.25, chicken, ham and leek pie £3.95, rump steak £7.95, chilli spiced prawns and cod £4.25, lemon and kiwi fruit pavlova £1.95 Vegetarian Meals: leek and potato gratin £3.75 Children's Portions   Beer Benskins Bitter; Ind Coope Burton Ale; Tetley Bitter Whisky Garden Outdoor Eating Summer Barbecue **Credit Cards:** Access, Visa

BELLINGDON   Bull

Bellingdon Road
Open: 11-2.30, 6-11
Licensees: Jeff and Sue Steers

Delightful little redbrick cottage on the north side of the village; be early for the
bow window table. Attractive furnishings, beams, bric-a-brac displays and an
inglenook fireplace.

Bar Meals: lunch and evening; bar snacks both sessions   **Typical Dishes:** *home-made
soup £1.40, mushrooms in cider £1.95, beef, Guinness and mushroom pie £3.75, sauteed
kidneys in red wine £5, pork stroganoff £6, treacle tart £1.95   Vegetarian Meals* `Beer`
Benskins, Ind Coope; Greene King `Cider` *Addlestones   Garden   Outdoor Eating*

BLEDLOW Lions of Bledlow, From B4009, Bledlow Ridge road, then first right
Tel: (08444) 3345: Well-loved, historic old Chiltern pub with tiled floors, nice
furnishings, log fires, lovely views and garden. Home-cooked food lunch and
Monday-Saturday evening, also restaurant. Family room. Courage, Wadworth,
Youngs beers. Open: 11-3, 6-11.

BOLTER END   Peacock

Lane End HP14 3LU
Tel: (0494) 881417
Open: 11-2.30, 6-11
Licensee: Peter Hodges

New floor coverings and soft furnishings should be in place for Christmas 1991 in
this popular, much modernised old pub, which is however traditional enough to
prohibit gaming machines and piped music. There are no starters on the menu, and
three daily-changing specials plus pudding of the day are listed separately. Freshly
squeezed orange juice. No children indoors.

Bar Meals: 12-2, 7-10 (not Sun eve); bar snacks both sessions   **Typical Dishes:** *steak and
kidney pie with suet pastry, freshly griddled marinated breast of turkey, cod and prawn mornay
(main courses from £4), syrupy spotted dick   Vegetarian Meals: kidney bean and mushroom
provencale* `Beer` *ABC Bitter; Draught Bass   Garden   Outdoor Eating* **Credit
Cards:** *Access, Amex, Diners, Visa*

BUCKINGHAM New Inn, 18 Bridge Street Tel: (0280) 815713: Nice little pub
which specialises in home-cooked Sri Lankan curries, daily lunchtime and Monday-
Saturday evening; also a choice of traditional English or eastern breakfasts from
10am. Vegetarian meals. Family room. Greene King beers. Open: 10am-11pm.

CHENIES   Red Lion

Off A404 WD3 6ED
Tel: (0923) 282722
Open: 11-2.30, 5.30-11 (7.30-10.30 Sun eve)
Licensee: Michael Norris

A printed menu of rather down-market design misleads at the Red Lion, where
fresh, home-made food is the order of the day and chips are banned. The home-
produced pies are particularly fine. There's a tiny family room, and equally cramped
outdoor eating space. The comfortably modernised and refurbished L-shaped bar has
a separate dining area to its rear. No music or machines.

Bar Meals: 12-2, 7-10; bar snacks both sessions   **Typical Dishes:** chicken and lettuce soup £1.95, ham, stilton and walnut baskets £3.50, Chenies lamb pie £4.95, spicy meatballs £4.50, chicken Wellington £7.95, chocolate roulade £1.95   Vegetarian Meals: vegetarian pancakes £3.95   `Cheese`   `Beer`   Benskins Best Bitter; Ind Coope Burton Ale; Tetley Bitter; Wadworth 6X   Family Room (tiny)   Outdoor Eating   **Credit Cards:** Access, Visa

---

CHESHAM   Black Horse

Chesham Vale HP5 3NS
Tel: (0494) 784656
Open: 11.30-2.30, 6-11
Licensee: Roger Wordley

Much extended village alehouse, its cosy black-beamed original bar featuring a vast inglenook fireplace, and nice country furniture in the newer bar, plus a converted barn to take the overspill (as does the large rear garden). Home-made pies are the star of the menu. Children can come inside to eat 'by appointment only'.

Bar Meals: 12-2, 6-9.30; bar snacks both sessions   **Typical Dishes:** leek and potato soup £1.25, prawn fritters with lime dip £2.95, Scotch sirloin steak £5.95, wild rabbit and tarragon pie £4.75, venison sausages £3.95   Vegetarian Meals   Children's Portions   `Beer`   Adnams; Benskins; Ind Coope; Rayments   `Cider`   Addlestones   Outdoor Play Area   Garden   Summer Barbecue   **No Credit Cards**

COLESHILL   Red Lion

Village Road HP7 0LN
Tel: (0494) 727020
Open: 11-3.30, 6-11 (11-11 Fri/Sat)

Picturesque village pub in delightful spot close by the pond and church.

Bar Meals: 12-2.30, 7-9.30; bar snacks both sessions   **Typical Dishes:** watercress soup £1.30, dressed crab £2.20, fillet of pork stroganoff £5.25, baked ham with parsley sauce £4.95, fishermans pie £4.75, chocolate trifle £1.70   Vegetarian Meals: vegetable and pasta bake £4.25   Children's Portions   `Beer`   Ansells Mild; Benskins Best; Tetley Bitter   Children Allowed in Bar to Eat   Garden   Summer Barbecue

---

CUDDINGTON   Crown

Aylesbury Road HP18 0BB   `FOOD`
(signposted off A418 between Thame and Aylesbury)   `B&B`
Tel: (0844) 292222
Open: 12-2.30, 6-11
Licensee: B M Jones

The cooking is solely in the hands of the landlady at the Crown, so the daily menu, written up on a blackboard at one end of the bar, is kept short and pleasingly unpretentious. The choice could include Cumberland sausages, salmon roulade, tagliatelle carbonara, or a vast, crisp, filled Yorkshire pudding. Salads are crisp and fresh, and puddings simple, like fudge cake or ice cream. This is real pub home-cooking, honest, tasty, and always good value. The pub itself is welcoming and white-painted, in the centre of a picturesque and tranquil village, and has managed to preserve the friendly charm of a real country local. Inside, one long room is dominated by a long central bar counter with, to the left a carpeted lounge end, to the right a red tiled public bar area. Rustic roundback chairs surround solid wood tables topped with little vases of fresh flowers, and two huge inglenook fireplaces, one at each end, are topped by a fine old beam. In winter, open fires warm the room, while in kinder weather dried flower displays and other bits and pieces decorate the fireplace. You can also sit outside if it's fine. It's quietish at lunchtime, busier in the evening, and can positively heave at weekends. The licensees' springer spaniel lives up to its name in a particularly springy way. Overnight accommodation consists of just one cosy, twin-bedded room, spotlessly kept, with creaking floorboards, sloping ceilings and period furnishings. Books, magazines and a small black and white television are provided. You share the licensees' neat bathroom.

Bar Meals: 12.30-2, 7.30-9.30 (Wed-Sat eves); bar snacks lunchtime   **Typical Dishes:** *stilton and celery soup £2.10, gravadlax £3.55, home-made steak, kidney and Guinness pie £6.90, home-made lasagne £5.30, prawn salad £5.50, raspberry meringue £1.90 Vegetarian Meals: vegetarian pie £4* **Beer** *Fullers Chiswick Bitter; London Pride; ESB Children Allowed in Bar to Eat   Patio/terrace   Outdoor Eating* **Accommodation:** *1 bedroom, using separate bathroom, from £38.50 (single £19.25)   Check-in: by arrangement*

FAWLEY   Walnut Tree

Fawley Green RG9 6JE   `FOOD`
Tel: (049 163) 360   `B&B`
Open: 11-3 (2.30 winter), 6-11
Licensees: Geoffrey and Diana Knight

Unless you're a walker, or very lost, the Walnut Tree isn't a pub you're likely to just come across by accident. Tucked away in a quiet village, about a mile from the A4155, the pub only dates from 1958, when some enterprising local farmers, keen to have their own local, offered Brakspears brewery the land to build a pub on. The name comes from a couple of walnut trees which grow in the pub's large gardens, and the surrounding countryside is lovely, though the pub itself could hardly be said to be full of character. The public bar, to the right of the entrance, has simple furniture, a juke box and fruit machines; the main bar is papered in off-white anaglypta, and has upholstered bench seating, and leading off from this room is a recently opened conservatory with large picture windows and red tiled flooring. Out in the garden there's plenty of outdoor furniture to take the overspill, while a small children's play area features a swing, slide, sandpit, and a more than usually friendly house goat. Apart from its splendid setting, the great attraction at the Walnut Tree is the food, and the pub is often filled with diners, especially at weekends. There are not one but two blackboards, one for traditionalists, featuring good old-fashioned meat dishes like steak and kidney pie or beef stroganoff among its list; the other offering daily specials like kiwi mussels with garlic, calves liver with mushrooms, duck breast with honey and thyme, or a lovely, perfectly cooked piece of fresh salmon with a delicious beurre blanc. Prices are a little higher than most pubs, but standards are notably higher than most pubs too. In addition, on Thursday, Friday and Saturday evenings, an a la carte menu is presented in the simply-appointed dining room. Above the bars are two neat and attractively decorated bedrooms, each with a good sized double bed and quality pine furniture, plus soft-coloured curtains and bedspreads in a contemporary pattern. Each has its own, compact but good quality, shower room (the old shower-less third bedroom has now been turned over to staff use). Each room has thoughtful little extras like magazines and a bowl of fruit, as well as fine rural views. First class housekeeping. This is a fine pub for family excursions, but doesn't welcome children as overnight guests.

Bar Meals and Restaurant: 12-2, 7-10 (12-2.30, 7-9.30 Sun); bar snacks both sessions **Typical Dishes BAR:** *home-made soup £2.10, pan-fried whole prawns £4.95, duck breast with a honey and thyme sauce £8.95, salmon fillet with beurre blanc £7.95, grilled Dover sole £10.45, zucotto £2.20   Vegetarian Meals: cheese, leek and wine pancake Children's Portions* **Beer** *Brakspears Bitter; Special* **Whisky** *Children in Bar to Eat*

*Outdoor Play Area   Garden   Outdoor Eating Accommodation 2 bedrooms with en suite showers, from £50 (single £45)   Check-in: all day   **Credit Cards:** Access, Visa*

FINGEST   Chequers Inn

Fingest RG9 6QD
Tel: (0491) 63335
Open: 11-3, 6 (7 winter)-11
Licensee: Bryan Heasman

Charming 15th century redbrick village pub, traditionally furnished inside, and with French windows opening onto a delightful garden. Roaring log fires in winter. The restaurant has its own stylish bar area. All home-cooking, with no frozen food used.

Bar Meals and Restaurant: 12-2.30, 6.30 (7 Restaurant)-9.30; bar snacks both sessions Typical Dishes BAR: spicy leek and potato soup £1.95, egg and prawn Marie Rose £2.75, steak, kidney and mushroom pie £5.95, chicken and game pie, grilled trout almondine, Danish chocolate refrigerator cake   RESTAURANT: cornets of smoked salmon filled with prawns Marie Rose £6.50, roast duck in rum and honey sauce, beef Wellington, sirloin steak with melted stilton and port, medallions of port in mustard sauce £12.50, lemon meringue sponge   Vegetarian Meals: spinach and mushroom lasagne Beer *Brakspears Pale Ale, Special Bitter, Old Ale   Family Room   Outdoor Play Area   Garden   Outdoor Eating   Credit Cards: Access, Amex, Visa*

FORD   Dinton Hermit

near Aylesbury HP17 8XH
Tel: (0296) 748379
Licensees: John and Jane Tompkins

15th century stone cottage pub named after John Briggs, clerk to one of the judges who condemned Charles I to death. Two bars: a modernised log-fire warmed lounge, and characterful public bar; pretty garden for sunny days. Hearty home cooking draws the crowds; cheery waitress service helps.

Bar Meals: 12-2, 7-9.30 Tue-Sat   Typical Dishes: home-made vegetable soup, saucy mushrooms, gammon with cauliflower cheese, pork chop in cider and apples, fish dishes, fruit pie (main courses from around £5) Cheese Beer *Allied and Bass beers   Outdoor Play Area   Garden*

FORTY GREEN   Royal Standard of England

Beaconsfield HP9 1XS
Tel: (0494) 673382
Open: 11-3, 5.30-11
Licensees: Alan Wainwright and Philip Eldridge

Famous old pub, named by the decree of Charles II after he had been given sanctuary in the high rafters of what is now the food bar. Tremendous interior with superb array of collectors' items, now overlaid by a cheap and cheerful food operation lunchtime and evening, and huge crowds including coach parties. Go in winter. They sell at least 30 different English and other cheeses.

Bar Meals: 12-2.30, 6-10; bar snacks both sessions   Typical Dishes: home-made soup £1.50, avocado with crabmeat £1.50, home-made beef and oyster pie £4.95, home-made venison pie £4.95, plaice stuffed with prawns and crab £4.95, Bramley apple dumplings £1.50

Vegetarian Meals: quiche £4.75   Children's Menu/Portions `Cheese` `Beer` *Eldridge Pope; Marston* `Whisky` *Family Room   Garden   Outdoor Eating* **No Credit Cards**

FRIETH   Yew Tree

near Marlow RG9 6RJ   `FOOD`
Tel: (0494) 882330
Open: 10-2.30, 5.30 (6 winter)-11
Licensee: Franz AitzetMuller

Turn off the B482 just north west of Marlow and a drive through fine countryside brings you to the village of Frieth, and its 16th century red brick pride and joy, the Yew Tree. The pub is fronted by a pretty flower garden complete with furniture and a topiary. Inside, one long original-beamed bar features inglenook fireplaces at either end, over which hang collections of guns and brasses. Cupboard space is filled with china and glassware, while sporting prints line the walls, and simple wooden tables are surrounded by upholstered bench seating and wheelback chairs. Owner Franz AitzetMuller is Austrian, and also the chef, so that alongside the traditional steak and kidney pie, home-made sausages and the like you might also find pork schnitzel or weiner bruthuhn (spring chicken) among the daily-changing blackboard list in the bar. The menu changes according to what is fresh and plentiful, and the policy of insisting on the best quality ingredients is flattered further by deftness and flair at work in the kitchen. It's highly enjoyable, simple, delicious bar food, and at around £5 for a main course, not bad value either. The bar is generally teeming with diners at lunchtime; at weekends, and in the evenings, the smart but rustically styled Yew Tree restaurant is also busy. Here you will be offered more complicated, fussier dishes featuring meat, fish and game festooned with sauces and seasonings, alcohols and cream, from a largish menu of around ten starters and sixteen mains: allow £50 for two. Good value set menus offer a £13 lunch or £16 dinner. Service, by smartly dressed staff, is polished, but perhaps overly so. We found it a touch too regimented for a country pub: are bow ties really necessary when serving food to guests in the garden on a hot summer's day? (A delightful setting for lunch by the way). A decent array of wines by the glass is balanced by a good selection of draught beers and some intriguing fruit punches.

Bar Meals: 11.30-2.30, 6-10.30; bar snacks both sessions   Restaurant: 12-2.30, 7-10 Typical Dishes BAR: Portuguese fish soup £2.05, mushrooms on garlic bread £2.95, ham and mushroom strudel £4.15, bratwurst and sauerkraut £4.50, tagliatelle Milanaise £3.95   RESTAURANT: casserole of snails £5.95, fillet of beef Nelson £12.95, halibut with lobster and prawns £12.95, Dover sole £12.95   Vegetarian Meals: vegetarian pancake £2.95   Children's Portions `Beer` *Ringwood Old Thumper; Ruddles County, Webster's Yorkshire Bitter   Children Allowed in Bar to Eat   Garden   Outdoor Eating* **Credit Cards:** *Access, Amex, Visa*

GREAT HAMPDEN   Hampden Arms

near Great Missenden HP16 9RQ
Tel: (0494) 488255
Open: 12-2.30 (inc. Sun), 7-11 (closed winter Sun)
Licensees: Terry and Barbara Matthews

Two-roomed pub on a corner of Hampden common. Long and varied bar menu, and friendly service from popular newish licensees.

Bar Meals: 12-1.45, 7-9.30; bar snacks both sessions   Typical Dishes: home-made soup £1.85, misty Blue Mountain cocktail £2.85, home-made chicken and bacon pie £6.75, avocado filled with diced curried chicken £7.95, hot smoked mackerel in cheese sauce £5.25,

mille feuilles £2.95   Vegetarian Meals: fresh vegetable curry £5.50   Children's Portions
Beer *Ansells, Tetley; Greene King   Children Allowed in Small Side Bar to Eat*
*Garden   Outdoor Eating   **Credit Cards:** Access, Visa*

GREAT MISSENDEN   George

94 High Street HP16 0BG
Tel: (02406) 2084
Open: 11-2.30 (3 weekends), 6-11
Licensee: Guy Smith

A listed ancient monument, its 15th century timbers intact: there are a dozen foot-thick beams on the bar parlour ceiling alone. The most attractive room is upstairs, a spacious chamber complete with huge Gothic oak arch. Pleasant surroundings and service.

*Bar Meals: 12-2, 7-9.45; bar snacks both sessions   **Typical Dishes:** home-made soup £1.40, onion bhajis £2.75, Leicestershire chicken £8.40, steak £8.50, pasta £4.35, fruit crumble £1.95   Vegetarian Meals: avocado bake   Children's Menu/Portions   **Beer** ABC Best Bitter; Fullers London Pride; Greene King IPA; Wadworth 6X   Children Allowed in Bar to Eat   Outdoor Play Area   Garden   **Credit Cards:** Access, Visa*

HAMBLEDEN   Stag & Huntsman

Henley-on-Thames RG9 6RP
Tel: (0491) 571227
Open: 11-2.30 (3 Sat), 6-11

Unassuming three bar pub in delightful village; real fires; nice garden. Home cooking in bar and restaurant. No children.

*Bar Meals: 12-2, 7-9.30 (not Sun eve); bar snacks both sessions   **Restaurant:** 7-9.30 (Fri/Sat only)   **Typical Dishes BAR:** tomato and orange soup £2.50, Greenland prawns £3.60, steak and kidney pie £4.95, chilli Nachos £3.40, prawn pancakes £4.95, treacle tart £2.25   **RESTAURANT:** escargots £3.50, sirloin steak £9.50, salmon with dill sauce £8.50, smoked trout £4.50, hazelnut meringue £2.25   Vegetarian Meals: tagliatelle pesto   **Beer** Brakspears; Wadworth   Garden   **Accommodation:** 3 bedrooms, all en suite, from £48.50 (single £42.50)   Check-in: by arrangement   **Credit Cards:** Access, Visa*

HARTWELL Bugle Horn, Off A418 Tel: (0296) 748209: 17th century country pub with a pretty garden; home-cooking including pies and casseroles plus an interesting variety of baked potato fillings in the bar lunchtime and evening; also restaurant. Children allowed in to eat. Tetley Bitter. Usual credit cards.

LANE END   Old Sun

Church Road HP14 3HG   ❢
Tel: (0494) 881235
Open: 11-2.30, 6-11 (11-3, 5.30-11 Fri/Sat)
Licensee: Malcolm Raven

The huge old ex-fireplace in this cosy, relaxing pub was once a bakery, and now seats eight people around its large table. There are three inter-connected rooms with wall benches, private recesses, and plenty of distinctive bric-a-brac. Two real fires in winter. An enormous garden has lots of play equipment and good views.

Bar Meals: 12-2, 6-9 (Tue-Sat eves); bar snacks both sessions   **Typical Dishes:** *squire's gammon £4.75, chicken goujons £4, Scottish rarebit £2.50   Children's Portions*   `Beer` *Brakspear's Special; Greene King Abbot Ale; Marston Pedigree; Whitbread Flowers Original   Children Allowed in Bar to Eat   Outdoor Play Area   Garden   Outdoor Eating   Summer Barbecue*   **No Credit Cards**

LEY HILL   Swan

near Chesham HP5 1UT
Tel: (0494) 783075
Open: 11-2.30, 5.30-11
Licensees: Matthew and Theresa Lock

16th century pub overlooking the golf course, village cricket ground and common land. Fairly new, enthusiastic licensees are keen to encourage families: the Cygnets Menu offers a better than average selection of child-sized dishes, for instance. For adults, a rambling bar of character, with wall and window seats, an old cooking range, and no smoking area.

Bar Meals and Restaurant: 12-2, 7-9 (not Sun eve); bar snacks lunchtime   **Typical Dishes:** *pea and ham soup £1.55, smoked turkey breast, steak and kidney pudding, fillet steak with green peppercorn and brandy sauce, salmon steak with lemon cream sauce (main courses from £4), chocolate rum mousse   Vegetarian Meals: mushroom, sour cream and paprika pie*   `Cheese`   `Beer`   *Benskins Best; Ind Coope Burton Ale; Tetley Bitter; Youngs Special*   `Cider`   *Addlestones   Family Room   Outdoor Play Area   Garden   Outdoor Eating   Summer Barbecue*   **Credit Cards:** *Access, Visa*

LITTLE HAMPDEN   Rising Sun

Tel: (0494) 488393
Open: 11.30-2.30, 6.30-11 (not Sun eve; 7-10.30 Tue/Wed); closed Mon
Licensee: Rory Dawson

Fairly smart, refurbished dining pub in sleepy village lane. The plushly upholstered, opened-out interior is warmed by a woodburning stove in cold weather; food is interesting and avoids the usual pub cliches, and there's a monthly-changing table d'hote in the evenings. Traditional roast lunches only on Sunday. Good local walks, but muddy shoes and boots are frowned upon.

Bar Meals: lunch and Mon-Sat eve; no food Mon; bar snacks both sessions   **Typical Dishes:** *home-made soup £1.85, tandoori chicken £3.75, battered pork in sweet and sour sauce £6.25, home-made puddings   Vegetarian Meals*   `Beer`   *Adnams, Eldridge Pope, Marston*   `Cider`   *Garden*

LITTLE MISSENDEN   Red Lion

off A413
Tel: (02406) 2876
Open: 11-2.30 (12-2 Sun), 5.30-11

Unspoilt village local, simply furnished, with old kitchen range, nice coal fire, and no music. Friday and Saturday evenings bring a singalong by the piano, and the traditional pub game Shut the Box is also keenly played. There's a small riverside garden and there are plans for a big car park, reflecting the pub's growing reputation for unpretentious home-cooking. The Allied beers are joined by guest ales.

Bar Meals: lunchtime and evening   Children's Menu   **Beer**   Benskins, Ind Coope
Family Room   Garden

LITTLEWORTH COMMON Blackwood Arms, Common Lane Tel: (02814)
2169: Common-side pub popular with summer walkers; real fire, no music; large
menu includes home-cooked dishes, food served until 8.30, but more interesting for
its superb selection of beers. Garden. Open: 11-2.30, 5.30-11.

LONG CRENDON   Angel Inn

Bicester Road HP18 9EE   ▼
Tel: (0844) 208268
Open: 12-3, 6-12 (closed Sun June-Aug)
Licensee: M E Jones

Nicely refurbished, immaculately kept dining pub, "15th century with very modern
facilities" with one or two imaginative things on the daily changing blackboard
menu; good fresh fish and seafood. The dining room has the same menu. One of the
bedrooms has a ghost.

Bar Meals: 12-2.30, 7-10.15; bar snacks both sessions   **Typical Dishes:** scallop chowder
£2.50, rillettes of pork, rack of lamb £9.25, venison sausages £5.50, bouillabaisse
£13.95, spotted dick   Vegetarian Meals: fresh tagliatelle with tomatoes and chives £5.95
Cheese   **Beer**   Brakspears; Whitbread   **Whisky**   Patio/terrace   Summer Barbecue
Accommodation: 4 bedrooms, all en suite, from £45 (single £35)   Children Welcome
Overnight   Cot Available   Check-in: all day   **Credit Cards:** Access, Amex

MEDMENHAM   Olde Dog & Badger

Henley Road SL7 2HE
Tel: (0491) 571362
Open: 11-11 (11-3, 5.30-10.30 winter); 12-10.30 summer Sun
Licensees: William and Beryl Farrell

Quaint white-painted 16th century cottage pub with glorious hanging baskets in
summer. Indoors is much modernised, but retains low beams and an open fire.
Generally bustling. Good bar food, especially the pies.

Bar Meals and Restaurant: 12-10 (12-2.30, 6-10 winter), 7-10; bar snacks both sessions
Typical Dishes BAR: beef and vegetable soup £2.25, chef's paté £2.45, steak and kidney
pie in Guinness £4.95, chicken and ham pie £4.95, haddock au gratin £5.25, spotted dick
RESTAURANT: salmon surprise £3.90, rack of lamb £9.85, casserole of pheasant
£7.95, salmon in fennel £7.50   Vegetarian Meals: savoury nut burgers   Children's
Portions   **Beer**   Brakspear's Bitter; Wadworth 6X, Whitbread Flowers Original
Children Allowed in Bar to Eat   Patio/terrace   **Credit Cards:** Access, Amex, Diners, Visa

NEW BRADWELL New Inn: Grand Union Canal-side pub with waterside tables
and a routine bar menu enlivened by one or two more interesting dishes. Charles
Wells beers.

NEWTON BLOSSOMVILLE Old Mill Burnt Down: Busy riverside pub with
decent home cooking lunchtime and Monday-Saturday evening, from the usual
things to smarter, restauranty fare. Home-made game pie. Family room. Adnams,
Marston beers.

NORTH MARSTON   Bell

25 The High Street MK18 3PD
Tel: (029 667) 635
Open: 11-3, 6-11
Licensees: Vic and Sue Hinde

Split-level, comfortable pub with original fireplace and lots of timber.

Bar Meals: 12(12.30 Sun)-2.30, 7-10 (not Sun eve); bar snacks both sessions **Typical Dishes:** *brown onion soup £1.50, cheese paté £1.50, mixed grill £8, chicken Marengo £3.75, prawn lasagne £5, sherry trifle £1.50* **Vegetarian Meals:** *tomato and herb lasagne* **Children's Portions** [Beer] *ABC Best Bitter, Draught Bass; Wadworth 6X* **Children Allowed in Bar to Eat** *Outdoor Play Area* **Garden** *Outdoor Eating* **Credit Cards:** *Access, Visa*

PENN STREET   Hit or Miss

Penn Street HP7 0PX   ♥
Tel: (0494) 713109
Open: 11-3.30, 6-11
Licensee: David Fennell

Cricket-mad pub with its own team and ground, and lots of memorabilia in the comfortably modernised low-beamed bar and spacious restaurant. Real fire; no music.

Bar Meals: 11-2, 6-10; bar snacks both sessions **Restaurant:** *12-2, 7-10* **Typical Dishes BAR:** *French onion soup £1.90, deep-fried king prawns £3.75, penne Mexicana £4.75, steak and onion butty £3.95, meringue Monte Carlo £1.80* **RESTAURANT:** *asparagus soup £1.90, mushrooms in tarragon and garlic £2.50, char-broiled leg of lamb (for 2) £14.50, veal Alpine £5.75, salmon en croute £7.50, nougat glace £2* **Vegetarian Meals:** *vegetable stroganoff* **Children's Portions** [Beer] *Marston Pedigree; Ruddles Best; County; Webster's Yorkshire Bitter* **Garden** *Outdoor Eating* **Credit Cards:** *Access, Amex, Visa*

SAUNDERTON Golden Cross, Wycombe Road (A4010) Tel: (024 024) 2293: Roadside pub with peaceful garden where petanque is played; no music, real cider. Decent home cooking lunchtime and Tuesday-Saturday evening. Ind Coope Burton Ale. Open: 12-2.30, 5.30(6.30 Sat)-11.

SKIRMETT   Old Crown

High Street
Tel: (049 163) 435
Open: 10.30-2.30, 6-11
Licensees: Liz and Peter Mumby

Characterful old pub with a local reputation for excellent food; non-bookers will probably be disappointed. Two linked rooms have dining tables, beamed ceilings and open fires; there's also a real old-fashioned tap room, and all available space is cluttered with a vast collection of bric-a-brac. The separate restaurant (closed Monday) permits nice well-behaved children over ten; children under ten aren't even allowed in the garden.

Bar Meals: lunchtime and evening; bar snacks both sessions **Typical Dishes:** *home-made soup £2.40, steak and kidney pie £5.75, chicken breast stuffed with cream cheese and asparagus £7.25, home-made puddings* **Vegetarian Meals** [Beer] *Brakspears beers* **Garden** *Outdoor Eating* **Credit Cards**

SKIRMETT Kings Arms, Fingest Road: Attractive, traditional bar and modern extension in peaceful country pub with a mix of standards and specials on the lunchtime and Monday-Saturday bar menu; children allowed in to eat. There's also a small separate restaurant. Garden. Brakspears and Whitbread beers.

SPEEN   Old Plow

Flowers Bottom Lane HP17 0PZ
Tel: (0494) 488300
Open: 12-2.30 (inc Sun), 6.30-10.30; closed Sun eve/all day Mon
Licensees: Malcolm and Olivia Cowan

17th century ex-forge with low-beamed ceilings and tiled floors, well-cared for, with some good food. The main emphasis is on the restaurant, but bar meals are interesting in their own right.

Bar Meals: 12-2, 7-9; bar snacks both sessions   Restaurant: 12-2, 7.30-9.30   Typical Dishes BAR: leek, lamb and barley broth £2.95, smoked salmon paté £3.50, mussels £4.95, crispy duck legs in plum and ginger sauce £5.95, rabbit with winter vegetables £5.95, plum and peach crumble £2.95   RESTAURANT: provencale shellfish soup £4.95, smoked goose, chicken, avocado and French bean salad £8.95, lamb with ratatouille tartlets £15.95, sea bass with wild mushrooms £16.95, bouillabaisse £15.50, hot apple tart with ice-cream and raspberry coulis £5.50   Vegetarian Meals: pasta £5.50   Children's Portions ■Beer■ *Adnams Bitter; Brakspears Bitter; Greene King Abbot Ale   Children Allowed in Bar to Eat   Garden   Outdoor Eating   Credit Cards: Access, Amex, Visa*

THE LEE   Cock and Rabbit

Near Great Missenden
Tel: (024 020) 540
Open: 12-3, 6-11
Licensee: Franko Parollo

Restauranty but friendly and informal Italian-owned pub with a refreshingly different menu featuring lots of delicious home-made pasta at around £4, as well as more expensive, dinnerish dishes.

Bar Meals and Restaurant: 12-3, 6-10.30 (11 restaurant); bar snacks both sessions   Typical Dishes BAR: carrot and tarragon soup £1.60, garlic mushrooms £2.65, baby chicken £5.95, veal £6.45, lasagne £4.95, summer pudding £2   RESTAURANT: minestrone £2.65, seafood crepe £4.25, calves liver £7.50, salmon in raspberry cream £9.50, gnocchi £6, tivamisu £3   Vegetarian Meals: stuffed aubergines   Children's Portions ■Beer■ *Fullers London Pride; Marston Pedigree; Whitbread Flowers Original* ■Whisky■ *Children Allowed in Bar to Eat   Garden   Outdoor Eating   Credit Cards: Access, Amex, Visa*

THORNBOROUGH   Lone Tree

Buckingham Road MK18 2DZ
Tel: (0280) 812334
Open: 11.30-2.30, 6.30-11
Licensee: Martin Lister

Popular thatched pub on the A421, about four miles east of Buckingham – note the working Victorian post box in the wall. Theme eating nights are prominently advertised, and a supplementary blackboard menu lists fancier dishes (changing daily) than those on the printed table menus. Steaks are excellent – the fillet au poivre is recommended – and a steak and kidney pie generously filled, though the pastry can be a little on the soggy side. Fresh vegetables or salads and reasonable chips; puddings are a mixture of home-made and bought in.

Bar Meals: 12-2, 7-9.30; bar snacks both sessions **Typical Dishes:** *wild rice soup £1.95, Chinese tartlets £2.25, lamb steak with apricot and green peppercorns £6.95, chicken Versailles £6.95, blue marlin steak with hazelnut butter £8.50, little sticky toffee puddings £2.50 Vegetarian Meals: courgette Tian £4.50 Children's Menu/Portions* `Cheese` `Beer` *ABC Best Bitter, Draught Bass* `Whisky` *Longmorn 15 yr Children Allowed in Bar to Eat Outdoor Play Area Garden Outdoor Eating Summer Barbecue* **Credit Cards:** *Access, Amex, Visa*

TURVILLE   Bull and Butcher

Turville RG9 6QU
Tel: (049 163) 283
Open: 11-3, 6-11
Licensees: Anne and Peter Hanson

Pretty black and white timbered pub with real village local atmosphere. New licensees and a different menu since our last edition.

Bar Meals: 12-2, 6.45-9.45 (12-2, 7.30-9.30 Sun); bar snacks lunchtime **Typical Dishes:** *pumpkin soup £1.50, stilton and walnut paté £2.50, Bull and Butcher pie £4.95, sirloin steak £ 6.50, bobotie £4.95, sticky toffee pudding £2.25 Vegetarian Meals: mushroom stroganoff £3.50* `Beer` *Brakspears Pale Ale, Special Bitter, Old Ale Garden Outdoor Eating* **No Credit Cards**

WEST WYCOMBE   George & Dragon

London Road HP14 3AB
Tel: (0494) 464414
Open: 11-2.30 (12-2.30 Sun), 5.30-11 (11-11 Sat)
Licensees: Sonia Heath and Phillip Todd

Substantial 15th century inn with plenty of ghosts, in this attractive National Trust village. Surviving features include the cobbled archway entrance, heavy oak beams, ancient settles and open fireplaces; copper topped tables and wall seating are among the more modern influences. Reliably good food and local popularity mean the rambling bar is generally bustling. Bedrooms are suitably creaky and antique-laden, but tend to be on the small side.

Bar Meals: 12-2 (1.30 Sun), 6-9.30 (not Sun eve); bar snacks both sessions **Typical Dishes:** *fish soup £1.75, smoked salmon £4.25, beef Wellington, venison, beef and mushroom pie, seafood platter, hazelnut meringues (main courses from around £4) Vegetarian Meals: spinach and blue cheese pancakes* `Beer` *Courage Best Bitter; Directors; Gales HSB Family Room Outdoor Play Area Garden Outdoor Eating* **Accommodation:** *10 bedrooms, all en suite, from £50 (single £40) Children Welcome Overnight Cots Available Check-in: all day* **Credit Cards:** *Access, Amex, Visa*

WHITCHURCH   White Swan

10 High Street HP22 4JT
Tel: (0296) 641228
Open: 11-2.30 (12-2 Sun), 6-11
Licensee: Rex Tucker

Partly-thatched, 500 year old building which has been an inn since the mid 17th century, and still has the unspoilt atmosphere of an old-fashioned country pub. There's piped music, but no nasty modern gaming machines. The two bars are named after the house dogs, Charlie and Sam. Nice old furnishings and fresh flowers.

Bar Meals: 12-2 (1.45 Sun), 6-9.45   *Typical Dishes:* home-made soup £1.25, spare ribs £3, farmhouse pie £4.50, chicken tikka £4.50, seafood au gratin £4.50, cheese omelette £3.65   Vegetarian Meals: lasagne £4.50   Children's Portions   **Beer**   Fullers Chiswick Bitter; London Pride, ESB   **Whisky** Cragganmore   Family Room   Outdoor Play Area   Garden   Outdoor Eating   **No Credit Cards**

WOOBURN COMMON   Chequers Inn

Kiln Lane HP10 0JQ
Tel: (0628) 529575
Open: 11-11
Licensee: Peter Roehrig

FOOD
! ⊛
B&B

This red brick cottage had spent a few years as a private house when it was taken over by Peter Roehrig in 1976, who immediately set about re-converting it into a pub. Continuous expansion and refurbishment in the intervening years has resulted in a popular pub-cum-hotel. The bar retains much of its original 17th century character, though its style and atmosphere are now distinctly wine bar-ish. There are well-trodden floorboards, darkened ceiling and upright beams, exposed brickwork, and an open fireplace, flower-filled in summer, log-burning in the darker months. Handsome furnishings include solid settles, round-back chairs and very comfortable sofas in soft shades of peach. Rustic tables are topped with small vases of fresh flowers, and other plants and flower arrangements placed around the room. At lunchtimes the bar fills with businessmen from the nearby industrial estates, and the daily changing blackboard menu offers imaginative freshly cooked dishes like pasta twirls with tomato, bacon and basil, poached salmon with a cucumber sauce, or an escalope of veal with mushrooms and green peppercorns. The choice varies according to what's seasonal and fresh, and cooking is reliable. In the evenings, only sandwiches are available in the bar, when the restaurant takes over (also open lunchtimes and very popular). It's an appealing room with exposed floorboards, clothed tables, an exposed brick wall hung with old advertising posters, and lots of parlour plants, and the daily changing table d'hote and seasonal à la carte are interesting and well handled. Crisply deep-fried king prawns come on a syrupy sweet and sour sauce, and noisettes of lamb are cooked pink with a complementary rosemary and Meaux mustard sauce. Good fresh vegetables, and good puddings too. 17 bedrooms, each (bar the larger honeymoon suite) uniform in size and furnishings, have small floral print wallpapers and duvets, and free-standing stripped pine furniture. What they lack in personality they make up for with modern facilities. Rurally set, yet only ten minutes from both the M4 and M40, the Chequers is a very busy establishment and its car park is often filled with very choice motors. Accompanying customers can also be on the loud and expensive side. Peter Roehrig has recently opened a second establishment at nearby Cookham Dean.

Bar Meals: 12-2; bar snacks lunchtime   *Restaurant:* 12-2, 7-9.30   *Typical Dishes*
BAR: cream of courgette soup £2.20, supreme of chicken in sherry and grain mustard sauce

£5.65, red bream with herb butter £5.65, jacket potato with prawns and seafood £4.15 Vegetarian Meals: vegetarian Wellington with tomato and basil sauce `Cheese`   `Beer` *Eldridge Pope Dorchester Bitter, Thomas Hardy Bitter, Royal Oak   Garden   Outdoor Eating   Summer Barbecue* **Accommodation:** *17 bedrooms, all en suite, from £77.50 (single £72.50)   Children Welcome Overnight   Cot Available   Check-in: all day* **Credit Cards:** *Access, Amex, Visa*

WORMINGHALL   Clifden Arms

Worminghall HP18 9JR
Tel: (0844) 339273
Open: 11.30-3, 6(7 winter)-11
Licensees: Robert and Gwen Spencer

Quaint timbered and thatched old pub on the edge of the village, with lots of beams and a big fireplace where logs roar in the winter. Lots of old-fashioned, homely style in the main bar, also a lino-floored public and pool room, plus a restaurant, where families are permitted. A large, attractive garden has lots to interest children, including domestic birds and animals. A good pub for summer. The village is delightful, too.

Bar Meals: *12-2, 7-10; bar snacks both sessions* **Typical Dishes:** *stockpot soup £1.95, paté £2.95, chicken Kiev £6, sirloin steak £10.25, fishermans platter £4.50, blackberry and apple pancakes £1.55   Vegetarian Meals: mushroom and nut fettuccine   Children's Menu/Portions* `Beer` *Hook Norton Bitter; Morrells Varsity; Tetley Bitter   Family Room   Garden   Outdoor Eating   Summer Barbecue* **No Credit Cards**

CAMBRIDGESHIRE

BARNACK Millstone, Millstone Lane Tel: (0780) 740296: Traditional local with exposed stone and solid old timbers. Good value bar menu includes vegetarian and children's options, daily lunchtime, Tuesday-Saturday evening. Family room. Adnams, Everards beers. Open: 11-3, 6-11

BARRINGTON   Royal Oak

31 West Green CB2 5RZ
Tel: (0223) 870791
Open: 11.30-2.30, 6-11
Licensee: R E Nicholls

Timbered and thatched country favourite on the large village green. Seemingly always busy; a strong local reputation for good bar food means the car park is generally packed. Inside, rambling, traditionally furnished rooms, and a slick dining operation. Well worth a visit.

Bar Meals: *12-2, 6.30-10.30; bar snacks both sessions* **Typical Dishes:** *cream of vegetable soup £2.35, deep-fried mushrooms £2.80, steak and kidney pie £4.85, pork with ham and cheese stuffing £5.55, beef curry with saffron rice £4.70, raspberry pavlova £2.75 Vegetarian Meals: hazelnut, pineapple and pepper pancakes £5.65   Children's Portions* `Beer` *Adnams Bitter, Greene King IPA, Abbot Ale; Whitbread Flowers IPA   Family Room   Outdoor Play Area   Garden   Outdoor Eating* **Credit Cards:** *Access, Visa*

BARTLOW   Three Hills

near Linton B1 6PW   ▼
Tel: (0223) 891259
Open: 11.30-2.30, 6.30-11
Licensees: Sue and Steve Dixon

The Dixons have created a welcoming atmosphere here, aided by fresh flowers, polished brasses and an inglenook fireplace. Reliably good food.

Bar Meals: 12-1.45, 7-9.30; bar snacks lunchtime **Typical Dishes:** *curried parsnip soup £1.55, pear and stilton filo parcels £2.75, beef Wellington £12.75, supreme of chicken with lime and garlic butter £8.35, grilled sole topped with king prawns £9.35, raspberry Paris-Brest £2.40* *Vegetarian Meals: vegetable strudel £5.95* ▐ Beer ▌ *Greene King Garden* *Outdoor Eating* **Credit Cards:** *Access, Visa*

BOTTISHAM White Swan: Straightforward pub, now very popular for its cooking, with some unusual dishes. Paines beer.

CAMBRIDGE   Cambridge Blue

85/87 Gwydir Street CB1 2LG
Tel: (0223) 61382
Open: 11-3, 5.30-11
Licensee: Nicholas J Winnington

Rowing-mad, cosy little pub in a row of terraced houses. Quiet and traditional in feel (apart from a nasty modern quiz machine), with open fires and solid old furniture. Three rooms include a tiny snug and another reserved for non-smokers. A nicer garden than you might expect in the backstreets of a city features a boules pitch. No children indoors.

Bar Meals: 12-2, 6-9.30 (not Sun) **Typical Dishes:** *cauliflower soup £1.30, beef in beer, chilli con carne, various curries (main courses around £3)* *Vegetarian Meals: Mexican bean stew* *Children's Portions* ▐ Beer ▌ *Banks & Taylors beers* ▐ Cider ▌ *Westons Garden* *Outdoor Eating* **No Credit Cards**

CAMBRIDGE   Free Press

Prospect Row CB1 1OU
Tel: (0223) 68337
Open: 12-2.30, 6-11
Licensees: Chris and Debbie Lloyd

Tiny, highly atmospheric rowing-mad pub tucked away behind the police station, close to the city centre. Simply furnished, unspoilt interior, the snug also being used as the dining area, and rowing photographs everywhere. It gets extremely busy; be early. Simple, hearty home cooking is of the sort to defrost a cold-numbed oarsman.

Bar Meals: 12-2, 7-9 bar snacks both sessions **Typical Dishes:** *carrot and orange soup £1.20, turkey and cranberry pie with salad £3.95, bacon with peach curry sauce £3.50, lemon chicken £3.75, treacle tart £1.50 Vegetarian Meals* ▐ Cheese ▌ ▐ Beer ▌ *Greene King* *Children Allowed in to Eat* *Patio/terrace*

CAMBRIDGE   Tram Depot

Dover Street
Tel: (0223) 324553
Open: 11-3, 5-11 (11.30-11 Saturday).

Sister-pub of the celebrated Victoria at Earl Soham (q.v.), brilliantly converted from
the old Cambridge Street Tramway Company stables, in classic alehouse style. No
music. Food is beginning to look interesting; lots of vegetarian options too.

Bar Meals: lunchtime and Sun-Fri evening; bar snacks both sessions **Typical Dishes:**
*home-made soup, corned beef hash, pork chops in cider and apples, courgette roulade, treacle
tart (main courses from around £3.50) Vegetarian Meals Children's Menu* **Beer** *Earl
Soham Children Allowed in to Eat Patio/terrace*

CAXTON   Caxton Gibbet Inn

Ermine Street (A14/A45 roundabout)
Tel: (09544) 8855
Open: all day
Licensee: Iris Stewart

A three and a half acre smallholding provides free range eggs, goat's milk, vegetables
and herbs, and the cooking is done by the landlady's brother and son. Bar food is
routine, restaurant cooking (Tuesday-Saturday evenings) more ambitious. A modern
pub built in traditional style, highly recommended for its bed and breakfast: two of
the comfortable and stylish bedrooms have balconies, one a four-poster bed, and all
have remote control television and hairdryers. Double glazing helps cut out the
noise from the busy junction outside. You can still see the old gibbet, a few yards
away from the pub on the roadside.

Bar Meals: all day; bar snacks Children's Menu **Beer** *Adnams Bitter Children
Allowed in to Eat Garden* **Accommodation:** *4 bedrooms, all en suite (2 shower only),
from £50 Check-in: all day* **Credit Cards:** *Access, Diners, Visa*

COTON Plough: Tel: (0954) 210489: Attractive, well-kept country pub at the
edge of the village, accessible from Cambridge on the Wimpole Way footpath. The
original front bar is now the restaurant; the bar has moved into a rear extension. Bar
food cheap; served lunchtime and evening, children allowed for meals. Piped music;
nice service; pretty garden. Whitbread beer. Open: 11-2.30, 5-11.

DULLINGHAM Kings Head, Station Road: Popular dining pub by the village
green, where there are seats; wide-ranging menu; family room; Tolly Cobbold beer.

DUXFORD   John Barleycorn

Moorfield Road CB2 4PP
Tel: (0223) 832699
Open: 12-2.30, 6.30-11
Licensee: Henry Sewell

A new thatch has just been proudly installed at this well-kept pub, which is glorious
with hanging baskets, tubs and borders in high summer. Softly lit main bar with
country furniture; additional seating in a converted barn.

Bar Meals: 12-2, 6.30-10; bar snacks lunchtime **Typical Dishes:** *hot garlic prawns
£4.10, venison and vegetable pie £5.75, spiced beef and vegetables with suet dumplings
£5.75, evening grills £8.60, apple and blackcurrant crumble £3* **Beer** *Greene King
Mild, IPA, Abbot Ale Garden Outdoor Eating* **No Credit Cards**

ELSWORTH   George & Dragon

41 Boxworth Road CB3 8JQ
Tel: (09547) 236
Open: 11-2.30, 7-11
Licensee: M G Brownlie

Attractive, unusual pub with a panelled bar and separate dining area.

Bar Meals: 12-2, 7-10   **Typical Dishes:** *home-made soup £1.65, deep-fried mushrooms £2.65, chicken moussaka £4.95, chicken Normandy £6.75, veal with wild mushroom sauce £7.95, crème caramel   Vegetarian Meals: nut cutlets £4.95   Children's Menu* [Beer] *Greene King; Whitbread   Family Room   Outdoor Play Area   Garden   Outdoor Eating*   **Credit Cards:** *Access, Amex, Diners, Visa*

ELTON Crown, 8 Duck Street Tel: (0832) 280232: Listed village green pub rebuilt in 1985 after a devestating fire. Large bar, conservatory and restaurant; varied food lunch and evening; garden. Greene King, Marston beers. Open: 11.30-2.30, 6-11.

FEN DRAYTON   Three Tuns

High Street CB4 5SJ
Tel: (0954) 30242
Open: 11-2.30 (2 Sun lunch), 6.30-11
Licensee: Michael Nugent

Characterful timbered old pub, probably originally the local trade or guild hall. The present bar is outwith the original building, but brims with atmosphere: heavy moulded beams, inglenook fireplaces (one usually lit), oak furnishings, and lots of quality bric-a-brac. It gets extremely busy.

Bar Meals: 12-1.45, 7-9.30; bar snacks both sessions   **Typical Dishes:** *spicy lentil soup £1.80, pie of the day £4.05, macaroni ham and cheese special £3.75, breaded plaice fillet £4, hot treacle and almond tart £1.40   Vegetarian Meals: vegetable lasagne £3.90 Children's Portions* [Beer] *Greene King IPA; Rayments, Abbot Ale* [Whisky] *Family Room   Outdoor Play Area   Garden   Outdoor Eating*   **Credit Cards:** *Access, Visa*

FENSTANTON   King William IV

High Street PE18 9JF
Tel: (0480) 62467
Open: 11-3, 5.30-11
Licensee: J Shonfeldt

Attractive white-painted roadside inn, once three separate houses, next to the old clock tower, and very much the hub of village life. Its popularity is such that a glass roof has just been fitted to the patio area adjoining the restaurant, to provide more all-weather table space. The original bars are still reserved for drinkers, with newer extended areas for diners. Capability Brown is buried in the village churchyard.

Bar Meals and Restaurant: 11.30-2.15 (12-2 Sun), 7-10 (not Sun eve); bar snacks both sessions   **Typical Dishes BAR:** *home-made soup £1.65, mushrooms with garlic dip £2.10, venison and walnut pie £5.25, ham, egg and chips £3.50, fresh plaice rolled in oats £6.25, treacle and walnut pie £2   RESTAURANT: chicken tikka £3.65, breast of chicken Picasso £6.55, rib eye steak £8.75, fresh sole £9.75, gateau £2.50   Vegetarian Meals: broccoli and cheese crumble £4.50   Children's Portions* [Beer] *Greene King Mild, IPA, Rayments, Abbot Ale Children Allowed in Bar to Eat   Patio/terrace*   **Credit Cards:** *Access, Diners, Visa*

FOWLMERE
Chequers

High Street SG8 7SR
Tel: (0763) 208369
Open: 11.30-2.30, 6-11
Licensee: Norman Rushton

The Chequers was already a popular travellers' halt when Samuel Pepys stayed the night in 1659. There's still plenty of period charm, and the pub is still noted in many a diary as a good place to pause for refreshment. It's comfortably furnished, with a civilised, relaxing atmosphere, and eating, whether in bar or restaurant, is very much the thing. Food is reliably good. The newly built Archer Room is an attractive conservatory extension big enough to house a small wedding party.

Bar Meals and Restaurant: 12-2 (2.30 Sun), 7-10 (9.30 Sun); bar snacks both sessions *Typical Dishes BAR: guinea fowl and tarragon soup £2.40, stilton and walnut paté £2.90, Vietnamese style chicken £5.75, poached trout in orange sauce £5.60, summer pudding £2.40* **RESTAURANT:** *shrimp bisque £2.80, Barbary duck £11.60, rib eye amoureuse £12.30, bourride £12.70, strawberries in cinnamon batter £2.60 Vegetarian Meals: stuffed aubergines Children's Portions* **Beer** *Tollys Original, Bitter* **Whisky** *Family Room Children Allowed in Bar to Eat Garden Outdoor Eating* **Credit Cards:** *Access, Amex, Diners, Visa*

FOWLMERE
Queens Head

Long Lane SG8 7SZ
Tel: (0763) 208288
Open: 12-2.30, 6-11 (12-4, 7-11 Sat and hols)
Licensee: Howard Gascoyne

Thatched white-painted pub with half a dozen picnic tables in the garden. Inside, black painted beams, formica topped tables, and a lino floored lounge, but refurbishments are apparently under way. The speciality of the house is twenty or so varieties of cheese; the continental and unpasteurized varieties commanding the higher price, and all served with cottage cob or other local bread, salad garnish and pickles.

Bar Meals: 12-2 (2.30 weekends, holidays) *Typical Dishes: stilton and onion soup £1.55; jacket potatoes with various fillings in winter; cheese lunches £2.60/£3.35 Childrens Menu/Portions* **Cheese** **Beer** *Greene King IPA, Abbot Ale Children Allowed in Bar to Eat Garden Outdoor Eating* **No Credit Cards**

GREAT EVERSDEN
Hoops

High Street (off A603)
Tel: (0223) 262185
Open: 12-2.30, 7-11 (longer hours in summer)
Licensee: Alan Hawkins

17th century village local with a Jacobean fireplace, original timbers and a stone-flagged floor; there's also a simpler, noisy public bar. Food is usually of a simple, hearty sort, with lots of traditional dishes like cottage or fish pie; regular theme cooking evenings provide more exotic, international fare. More notable for its clean, good value bed and breakfast in a popular tourist area. The garden is large and child-friendly.

Bar Meals: lunchtime and evening; no food Sun; bar snacks both sessions *Children's Menu*

Beer *Mansfield; Charles Wells Children Allowed in to Eat Garden*
*Accommodation: 6 bedrooms, from £35 **No Credit Cards***

HAIL WESTON Royal Oak, High Street Tel: (0480) 72527: Attractive thatched
village inn with a real fire, games-equipped family room, garden, and home-cooked
food lunchtime and Tuesday-Saturday evening. Adnams, Mansfield, Charles Wells
beers. Open: 11-2.30 (3 Sat), 6-11.

HEYDON   King William IV

Chishill Road SG8 8PW
Tel: (0763) 838773
Open: 12-3, 6-11
Licensee: Mary Kirkham

Unremarkable on the outside, but an Aladdin's Cave within, overflowing to an
almost oppressive degree with agricultural oddities and equipment, including a
plough, as well as giant bellows, cast iron cauldrons, stuffed animals in glass cases,
lamps, casks, plates, – even a copper font with a gothic style wooden top. Other
more traditional features include heavy beams and rustic tables, some of them
suspended by chains from the ceiling; also not so traditional piped music and fruit
machines. Lots of animals in the garden. Chips-with-everything bar food is very
much a secondary attraction.

Bar Meals: 12-2.30, 7-10 (10.30 weekends); bar snacks both sessions ***Typical Dishes:***
*farmhouse soup £1.75, King William mushrooms £2.75, steak and mushroom pie £4.25,
half char-grilled chicken £5.50, home-made apple pie Vegetarian Meals: lasagne £4.50*
Beer *Batemans; Greene King Family Room Garden Outdoor Eating Summer
Barbecue **Accommodation:** 3 bedrooms, 2 en suite, from £55 (single £30) Check-in: by
arrangement **Credit Cards:** Access, Visa*

HISTON   Red Lion

27 High Street CB4 4JD
Tel: (0223) 232288
Open: 11.30-2.30, 5.30-11 (11.30-4, 6-11 Sat)
Licensees: David Heald and Elaine Hyland

Well-run pub with an enthusiasm for genuine home-cooking, freshly prepared by
the landlady daily. No chips.

Bar Meals: 12-2 Mon-Fri; also bar snacks ***Typical Dishes:*** *leek and potato soup £1.60,
ham and asparagus pancakes £3.35, minted Turkish meatballs £3.35, ham and sweetcorn
bake £3.35, rum bananas Vegetarian Meals: quiche* **Beer** *Adnams Bitter; Draught
Bass; Taylor Landlord; Sam Smith Old Brewery Bitter Children Allowed in Bar to Eat
Outdoor Play Area Garden Outdoor Eating **No Credit Cards***

HOLME Admiral Wells, Station Road: The lowest pub in England, almost three
metres below sea level. Good soups and specials, lunchtime and evening in bar,
conservatory and restaurant. Family room. Petanque courts and play area in large
garden. Ind Coope, Tetley beers.

HOLYWELL   Olde Ferryboat

Huntington PE17 3TG
Tel: (0480) 812333
Open: 11-3, 6-11
Licensee: Richard Jeffrey

A thousand years of history at this delightful thatched and wisteria–draped riverside inn, originally a monastic ferry house. Particularly charming panelled alcove off the main bar, and good views from the sun terrace. £100,000 has been spent by newish (1989) owners; there's a new kitchen and two more bedrooms since our last edition. Haunted by Juliet, a young victim of unrequited love; don't go on March 17th unless you want to join the ghost-hunters.

Bar Meals: 12-2, 6.30-10; bar snacks lunchtime **Typical Dishes:** *chunky chicken and tarragon soup £1.99, home-made stilton paté £2.99, grilled Scotch sirloin steaks in sauces £8.95, home-made traditional pies £4.95, rolled trout fillets in whisky £6.95, summer pudding £1.99 Vegetarian Meals: hot spicy vegetarian pancake £5.75 Children's Menu/Portions* **Beer** *Adnams; Bass; Hook Norton Family Room Riverside Garden Outdoor Eating Summer Barbecue* **Accommodation:** *7 bedrooms, all en suite, from £49.50 (single £40) Children Welcome Overnight Cot Available Check-in: by arrangement* **Credit Cards:** *Access, Amex, Diners, Visa*

HORNINGSEA   Plough & Fleece

High Street CB5 9JG
Tel: (0223) 860795
Open: 11.30-2.30 (2 Sun), 7-11
Licensees: Mr and Mrs Grimes

FOOD

A grade II listed building, built in the Dutch style so popular in the East Anglia of the late 18th century, when Dutch engineers came to advise on the draining of the fenlands. The generally very busy Plough & Fleece attributes its great popularity to a reputation for delicious home cooked food, and in particular for its enthusiasm for old-fashioned regional cooking, which is often given a modern interpretation. Come here for homely, comforting hotpots, buttery bakes, cottage pie and cockles, as well as more contemporary treatments of dinner partyish food, like honey-roast guinea fowl, or a perfect poached salmon. Puddings are suitably gorgeous and cream-laden; the Northamptonshire chocolate pudding in particular has an informal international fan club. All this means the pub can get crowded, and a new dining room extension has been built to take the strain, providing a welcome haven for non-smokers. Another innovation for the 1992 season is a more extensive Sunday menu. The atmosphere of the whole pub is homely and traditional in feel, especially so in the unspoilt public bar, with its ancient settles, tiled floor, elm tables and custard coloured walls. The lounge is comfortable rather than characterful, and invariably packed with bar meal diners. Arrive early at lunchtime to beat the scrum. No children indoors.

Bar Meals and Restaurant: 12-2 (1.30 Sun), 7-9.30; no food Sun/Mon eves; bar snacks lunchtime **Typical Dishes:** *beef and barley soup £1.50, baked mushrooms £2.45, Suffolk ham hotpot £4.25, Romany rabbit £6.75, Welsh fish pie £5.15, Northamptonshire chocolate pudding Vegetarian Meals: eggstravaganza (asparagus, eggs, cheese and almonds)* **Beer** *Greene King IPA, Abbot Ale Garden Outdoor Eating* **Credit Cards:** *Access, Visa*

HUNTINGDON Victoria, Victoria Square, off Ouse Walk: Tucked-away back street pub, its one long bar nicely divided up into distinct areas; wide variety of food lunchtime and evening. Real cider, garden, fire. Camerons, Tolly Cobbold beers. Open: 11.30-2.30, 6-11.

KEYSTON   Pheasant Inn

The village loop road PE18 0RE ♥
Tel: (08014) 241
Open: 12-3, 6-11
Licensees: Nicholas Steiger and John Hoskins

Thatched and white-painted country pub, formerly in part the village smithy. The extended main bar is plain but civilised in style, and given over almost entirely to dining during meal-serving hours; even some of the outdoor tables are laid with cloths. A really rather marvellous wine list is supplemented by a regular programme of tutored tastings with accompanying three course lunches, popular with the well-heeled regular clientele. The pub is one of Ivo Vannocci's successful little chain of Poste Hotels.

Bar Meals and Restaurant: 12-2, 6 (7 restaurant)-10   Typical Dishes BAR: leek and potato soup £1.75, Paris mushrooms £3.25, steak and kidney pie £6.95, chicken chasseur £6.95, penne all'avvabbiate £5.95, chocolate truffle cake £2.95   RESTAURANT: smoked salmon strudel £4.25, lamb and herb crepinettes £12.95, lobster ravioli £12.95, grilled stuffed salmon £12.95, burnt Cambridgeshire cream £3.75 Vegetarian Meals (bar): mushroom risotto   Children's Portions   Cheese   Beer   Adnams Bitter; Batemans; Felinfoel Double Dragon   Children Allowed in Bar to Eat Patio/terrace
Credit Cards: Access, Amex, Diners, Visa

MILTON   Jolly Brewers

5 Fen Road CB4 6AD
Tel: (0223) 860585
Open: 11.30-2.30, 6-11(12-3, 7-11 Sat)
Licensees: Chris and Ange Costard

Appealingly unpretentious, with low-beamed ceilings, pine and darkwood tables and jugs of fresh flowers, as well as a liking for international cooking of an informal sort, particularly Dutch dishes. Good, reliable food; no chips. Pork satay is the house speciality. No children indoors, except by special dispensation on weekend lunchtimes.

Bar Meals: 12.15-1.45 (12.30-2 weekends), 7.30-11 (not Sun/Mon eves); bar snacks lunchtime   Typical Dishes: Dutch vegetable and noodle soup £1.35, chicken liver paté £2.25, Indonesian Satay £5.50, Thai chicken £5.95, layer sauerkraut £5.95, Dutch treat £2.50 Vegetarian Meals: vegetarian hotpot £4.50   Beer   Camerons Traditional Bitter; Courage Best, Directors; Tolly Cobbold Best Bitter   Garden   Outdoor Eating   No Credit Cards

NEWTON   ★ Queen's Head

Cambridge CB2 5PG
Tel: (0223) 870436
Open: 11.30 (11 Sat)-2.30 (2 Sun), 6-11
Licensee: David Short

Adequate proof, if proof were needed, that a brilliant sandwich is enough to win the pub food laurels. Those on offer here were described in our last guide as "probably the best pub sandwiches in Britain", and they still are; indeed the Shorts have been doing things this way for almost 30 years now. Simplicity and freshness are the keynotes: superb sandwiches, warming country soups, baked potatoes, and, in the evenings and weekends, platters of cold roast meats and cheeses, all of first-rate quality. The pub itself is delightful, too, traditionally furnished, warmly welcoming, and attracting a loyal following which ranges from Cambridge dons to local farmers. Belinda, the notorious resident goose, died in March 1991, but has now been stuffed and will return for the autumn season!

Bar Meals: 12-2.15, 6-10   Typical Dishes: home-made soup £1.65, beef, paté, smoked salmon, cheese sandwiches (£1.30-£1.90)   Children's Portions `Cheese` `Beer` *Adnams Bitter; Broadside, Old Ale (winter)* `Cider` *Crones Cider   Family Room (Games Room)   Patio/terrace   Outdoor Eating* **No Credit Cards**

ST NEOTS   Chequers Inn

St Mary's Street, Eynesbury PE19 2TA
Tel: (0480) 72116
Open: 10.30-3 (2.30 Sun lunch), 7-11
Licensee: David Taylor

Lovely old country pub, its main bar resplendent with old darkwood furniture and open fires, and the 'middle room', which leads to the restaurant, possessed of alluringly squashy chairs and sofas. Very good food, too.

Bar Meals: 12-2, 7-10; bar snacks both sessions   Restaurant: 12-1.45, 7-9.30 Typical Dishes BAR: home-made soup £1.65, leek and chicken pasta £3.95, home-made steak and mushroom pie £4.55, liver, bacon and onions £4.40, raspberry pavlova £2.25 **RESTAURANT:** *deep-fried brie béarnaise £5.85, pork tenderloin, mushrooms and peppercorns £11.20, Chequers fillets £14.95, large fillet of fresh plaice £14.60, crepe gateau £2.55 Vegetarian Meals   Children's Portions* `Beer` *Batemans XB   Children Allowed in Bar to Eat   Outdoor Play Area   Garden* **Credit Cards:** *Access, Amex, Diners, Visa*

SAWSTON University Arms, 84 London Road: Basic pub popular for its constantly changing range of beers. Home cooking, frequently oriental; home-made bread and wide vegetarian choice. Family room; patio area. Bar and restaurant food daily 12-2.30, 7-10.

SOTHOE Bell, Great North Road Tel: (0480) 810981: 18th century pub on the A1, with à la carte restaurant, and bar meals daily lunchtime and evening.

STILTON   Bell Inn

Great North Road PE7 3RA   `FOOD`
Tel: (0733) 241066
Open: 12-2.30, 6-11
Licensees: L A and M J McGivern   `B&B`

Transformation at the Bell! Reputedly the oldest coaching inn on the Great North Road, the Bell Inn boasts a Roman well in its courtyard and an impressive stone frontage, parts of which date from the 15th century; the 16th century inn sign, made of heavy copper plate with ornate wrought iron brackets, together said to weigh two and three-quarter tonnes, was recently restored. Beyond this, transformation begins in earnest, starting with the stone courtyard arch, over which are inscribed distances to Huntingdon (12), Stamford (14) and London (74), which is now glassed in to form the entrance to reception and hotel services, the 1990 additions. Discreetly concealed from the road are two wings of en suite bedrooms whose 20th century trappings include telephones, satellite television and whirlpool baths, while tokens of the past are confined to the odd four-poster bed. This is a pity, as the rest of the building is simply splendid. The village bar retains its stone-flagged floor and cosy alcoves huddled round the great log fire: this is where the original Stilton cheese was sold to travellers in the 1720s. Today it's served with plum bread and a Normandy soup of cider and onions; wash these down with a pint of Ruddles or Pedigree for the very simplest of pub lunches. Amongst other cheesy offerings on the bar snack menu, you'll find stilton and walnut paté, avocado with prawns and cheese, and melted cheese on the gammon steaks. Posted on the specials board are items for the less single-minded: egg hongroise with a salad (£1.95), turkey escalopes with wine and mushrooms (£5.95), steak, kidney and Murphy's in a crusty pie (£5.95), dressed crab (£4.50) or a daily roast (£4.95), with perhaps coconut flan or mandarin charlotte russe to follow. More serious food is on offer in the restaurant above, in which linen-covered tables are widely spaced in two sections under gnarled oak beams and a vaulted ceiling with original exposed rafters. A galleried cocktail lounge nestles right under the recently renovated roof space. In addition to an extensive a la carte, there's a weekly table d'hote dinner menu at £12.50 which offers perhaps the best value: smoked salmon salad or deep-fried brie preceding fillet of lamb with ginger and rosemary jus, a seafood panache poached in wine and dill, or rump steak 'café de Paris'. The stilton with plum bread, this time with a glass of late bottled port makes a further, welcome appearance at the end.

Bar Meals: 12-2, 6-9.30 (7-9 Sun); bar snacks both sessions   *Restaurant:* 7-9.30
Typical Dishes BAR: stilton and celery soup £1.65, terrine of smooth stilton and hazelnut paté £2.95, grilled lamb kidneys, liver and bacon £4.95, ham hock £5.25, salmon fillet £5.75, creme brulée   *RESTAURANT:* consommé Celestine £3.50, warm halloumi cheese salad £4.25, lavender lamb £11.75, king prawn and Glenmorangie scampi £13.50, wild salmon dumpling £13.75   *Vegetarian Meals:* stir-fry vegetables   *Children's Portions*
Beer   Burton Bridge; Marston Pedigree; Ruddles County; Tetley Bitter   *Children Allowed in Bar to Eat   Outdoor Play Area   Garden   Outdoor Eating   Summer Barbecue*
Accommodation: 19 bedrooms, all en suite, from £72 (single £57)   Children Welcome Overnight   Cots Available   Check-in: all day   *Credit Cards:* Access, Amex, Diners, Visa

---

SUTTON GAULT   Anchor Inn

Bury Lane CB6 2BD   ▼
Tel: (0353) 778537
Open: 12-2.30, 6.30-11 (may close Sun eves Nov-March)
Licensee: Robin Moore

350 year old riverside ferry inn with extensive views over the Ouse washes. Gaslit at night, and always full of atmosphere, with old tiled floors, panelled walls and antique pine furnishings. Robin and Heather Moore, formerly of the well-liked Eight Bells, Saffron Walden, have now purchased the Anchor, and the future looks extremely promising. The menu changes daily, and there's a 90 strong wine list. Definitely one to watch.

Bar Meals: 12-2, 6.30-9.30 (6.30-10 Fri/Sat, 7-9 Sun); bar snacks lunchtime   *Typical Dishes:* home-made soup £2, grilled dates in bacon on mild mustard sauce £3.70, duck with Chinese spice sauce £9.50, filo pastry stuffed with celery, fresh basil and cream cheese £5.75, Lowestoft seafood pie £6.95, sticky toffee pudding £2.60   *Vegetarian Meals:* curried nut loaf with tomato and basil sauce £5.75   Children's Portions   **Beer**   Tolly Cobbold Original   Family Room   Riverside Patio/terrace   Outdoor Eating   *Credit Cards:* Access, Visa

SWAVESEY   Trinity Foot

Huntingdon Road CB4 5PD
Tel: (0954) 30315
Open: 11-2.30, 6-11
Licensee: H J Mole

Fairly modern pub, named after Trinity College's hunt, or rather, specifically, its
horse-less followers.

Bar Meals: 12-2, 6-10; bar snacks both sessions **Typical Dishes:** *home-made soup
£1.75, oysters £5, rack of lamb £6.75, hot garlic prawns £6, steak Diane, various fresh
fish, summer pudding £1.80* *Vegetarian Meals: fresh vegetables au gratin £3.75
Children's Portions* Beer *Ruddles; Whitbread* *Children Allowed in Bar to Eat
Outdoor Play Area* *Patio/terrace* *Outdoor Eating* **Credit Cards:** *Access, Visa*

UFFORD   Ye Olde White Hart

Main Street PE9 3BH near Stamford   ▼
Tel: (0780) 740250
Open: 11-2.30, (12-2 Sun) 6-11
Licensees: Chris and Sally Hooton

17th century farm, a pub since 1800. Open fires, four acres of garden and goat-filled
paddock, fresh vegetables and a sunken patio which seats 100, used for Sunday
morning jazz. Nice to vegetarians.

Bar Meals: 12-2 (restaurant also), 7-9.15 (Tue-Sat); bar snacks lunchtime **Typical
Dishes BAR and RESTAURANT:** *home-made soup £2, Molly Malone cockles, mussels
and prawns au gratin £3.75, fillet beef stuffed with stilton in a port and herb sauce £9.50,
supreme of chicken in a lobster and prawn sauce £6.50, saute of monkfish £8, blotto
blackcurrant sundae* *Vegetarian Meals: mushroom and asparagus hotpot £4.50* Beer
Theakston Best Bitter, Old Peculier *Family Room* *Children Allowed in Bar to Eat
Outdoor Play Area* *Garden* *Outdoor Eating* *Summer Barbecue*

WARESLEY Duncombe Arms: Popular bar in re-fashioned, originally Tudor
building, usually bustling. One or two interesting dishes on lunchtime and evening
bar menu. Greene King beers.

WESTON COLVILLE Fox and Hounds, Weston Green: Pleasant pub with
unusual Portuguese specials on the bar menu. Children allowed in bar to eat.
Garden and outdoor eating; summer barbecue. Live music from the keyboard and
piano, but no pool or jukebox. Bar meals lunchtime weekends, 7-10.30 Tues-Sat.

CHESHIRE

ASTON Bhurtpore, Wrenbury Road: Eastern and other unusual dishes in
extensively refurbished and remodelled dining pub. Real ales.

BEESTON   Beeston Castle Hotel

Bunbury Heath, on A49 near Tarporley CW6 9NJ   ❢
Tel: (0829) 260234
Open: 11-3, 5.30-11 (11-11 Fri/Sat)
Licensee: N A Smith

Close to the Shropshire Union Canal, and next door to Beeston Smithfield market
(market days Wednesday and Friday). The basic menu is supplemented by daily
specials.

Bar Meals: 11-2, 6.30-9.30 (12-2, 7-9 Sun); snacks only Tue eve   **Typical Dishes:**
*beer and cheese soup £1.50, tandoori wings £2.75, braised steak and onions £4.45, roast
beef (choice of three meats every day) £4.95, Madras prawn curry £6.50, hot chocolate
fondue £3.95 Vegetarian Meals   Children's Menu/Portions*   Beer   *Draught Bass,
Stones Bitter; Robinsons Old Tom   Family Room   Outdoor Play Area Patio/terrace
Outdoor Eating   Summer Barbecue   Credit Cards: Access, Visa*

BICKLEY MOSS   Cholmondeley Arms

Cholmondeley SY14 8BT   FOOD
Tel: (0829) 720300
Open: 11-3, 6.30 (6 Sat, 7 winter)-11   ☼   B&B
Licensees: Julian and Ginney Harrison, Guy and Carolyn Ross-Lowe ☺

Standing beside the A51 trunk road hard by the entrance to Cholmondeley Castle
and gardens, the Harrisons' unique roadhouse exists primarily to provide upmarket
pub food in surroundings more than a little unusual. This they achieve in staggering
quantity (up to 200 diners on some Saturday nights), so book if you're able to. It's a
Victorian brick building, with steep, white-painted gables and an octagonal bell
tower, originally the village school. Enter a T-shaped hall, and the pine-built bar,
which has desks and blackboards mounted on a gallery over it, is flanked on each
side by high-roofed halls of salmon pink hue, with well-spaced tables in stripped
pine, assorted pews and former chapel chairs with hymnbook racks. Someone's
interest in serious French food is indicated by a gallery of framed Parisian menus.
The old blackboards are put to good use, listing the daily specials – pick of the food
on offer – and an impressive house wine selection which includes a good Sauvignon,
house claret and Cotes du Rhone. Soups and pies change daily; courgette and
tomato perhaps, then steak and kidney, or chicken and parsley. Look a little further
and, typically, there's chicken korma with rice, lamb kidneys with sherry and parsley
sauce, vegetable-stuffed aubergine and a generously sauced portion of salmon and
spinach lasagne served with salad. Puddings on the board might well include
strawberry pavlova, bread and butter pudding and a hot jam sponge in keeping with
school traditions. The unchanging printed menu offers an even wider, if plainer,
choice. 'The School Lunch' is a hot spicy sausage in a baguette, "The
Cholmondeley Open" an open prawn sandwich with egg, tomato, cucumber and
mayonnaise. A word of warning, though, to parents of young families: despite a safe
garden and play area, lots of outdoor seating in fine weather and plenty of high
chairs indoors, a children's portion of chicken nuggets or fishfingers with chips
should never cost £3.30 a go. Across the car park are four bright, cottagey
bedrooms (three double and one family) in the old schoolhouse building. All have
bath or shower, television, telephone, clock radio, tea tray and hair dryer. Report
back to the classroom next morning for a slap-up breakfast.

Bar Meals: 12-2.15, 6/6.30-10 (9.30 Sun); bar snacks lunchtime   **Typical Dishes:**
*stilton soup £1.85, hot crab paté £3.50, chicken piri piri £6.90, kidneys in sherry and
parsley £6.95, salmon fishcakes and hollandaise £5.90, Grand Marnier soufflé £3
Vegetarian Meals: stuffed aubergine £5.25   Children's Menu*   Beer   *Marston Pedigree;*

*Ruddles County; Whitbread Boddingtons Bitter, Flowers IPA   Children Allowed in Bar to Eat   Outdoor Play Area   Garden   Outdoor Eating   **Accommodation:** 4 bedrooms, all en suite, from £40 (single £30)   Children Welcome Overnight   Cots Available   Check-in: by arrangement   **Credit Cards:** Access, Visa*

BOLLINGTON   Church House Inn

Church Street SK10 5PY
Tel: (0625) 574014
Open: 12-3, 5.30-11
Licensee: Stephen Robinson

Friendly, typical village local with two open fires and agricultural bric-a-brac.

*Bar Meals: 12-2, 6.30-9.30; bar snacks lunchtime   **Typical Dishes:** courgette soup £1.20, dim sum £2.45, steak Diane, home-made steak and kidney pie, poached salmon (main courses from £4), almond torte   Vegetarian Meals   Beer   Marston Bitter; Tetley Bitter; Theakston Bitter; Whitbread Boddingtons Bitter   Whisky   Family Room   Outdoor Play Area   Patio/terrace   Summer Barbecue   No Credit Cards*

BOTTOM OF THE OVEN   Stanley Arms

near Wildboarclough, Macclesfield Forest SK11 0AR
Tel: (02605) 2414
Open: 11.30-3, 7-11
Licensee: Alan Harvey

Remote moorland pub of unspoilt charm. Two drinking rooms with black woodwork, discreetly floral fabrics, wall seating and copper topped tables, plus attractive dining room. Open fires, good rural views, and a very popular pub for lunch (be early in summer). They specialise in fresh fish dishes, though meat-eaters are also remarkably well catered for.

*Bar Meals and Restaurant: 12-2.30 (2 restaurant), 7-10; bar snacks lunchtime   **Typical Dishes BAR:** chicken and mint soup £1.55, smoked salmon and scrambled egg on toast £3.80, liver and onions £4.95, duckling à l'orange £8.95, halibut steak £7.75, lemon soufflé £2   **RESTAURANT:** mushrooms in garlic £3.10, fillet au poivre £11.95, casserole of rabbit £8.30, fresh salmon in filo pastry £12.50, banoffee pie £2   Vegetarian Meals: vegetable cutlet £5.95   Children's Menu   Beer   Marston Burton Best, Pedigree Family Room   Garden   Outdoor Eating   Credit Cards: Access, Visa*

BRERETON GREEN   Bears Head

near Sandbach CW11 9RS   FOOD
Tel: (0477) 35251
Open: 11-3, 6-11
Licensees: R F and M Tarquini

A celebrated roadhouse alongside the A50, the Bear has expanded into a collection of buildings, fronted by the original half-timbered inn which dates from 1615, if not earlier. Panels of wattle and daub, carefully preserved and displayed in the bar, are evidence of the building's longevity and, despite the many more recent extensions, its inglenook fireplaces and oak beams hung with horse brasses still have lots of old-fashioned charm. Today's pub, run by the Tarquini family for some 30 years, is divided into cosy alcoves by means of cleverly placed original timbers and panels, and is full of the fragrance of ubiquitous fresh flowers. Burtonwood Bitter and Bass are the bonuses for beer drinkers, but the intrusive noise of pop classics may be less appreciated by those seeking more intimate conversation. Lunchtime and evening bar food is both stylish and substantial, ranging from open sandwiches (£3.75-£5.50) with salad to satisfying hot dishes like garlic buttered lamb chops (£4.95) with seasonal vegetables, or a Scotch salmon salad (£5.90); daily specialities typically feature moules marinière (£4.35), liver and onions (£5.25), baked haddock mornay (£5.50) or the house speciality, black pudding with whisky and mustard sauce (£4.95). By night the restaurant evokes the stuff of dinner dates and anniversaries, tinged with more than a hint of deja-vu: spumantes and pink champagnes are popped in discreetly hidden corners, while steak Diane and veal marsala sizzle lovingly (if over-long) on flickering lamps. Mammoth desserts arrive by trolley, typified by fruit and cream-soaked pastries, or fruits served in cream, or pastries soaked in fruit – for though many will say how much the food world has changed, not everyone here appears aware of it. And so to bed, where practical considerations for the business traveller generally take precedence over romance, with formica-topped, dual-purpose dressing tables and work spaces, television, radio, dial-out phones and trouser presses. Fully half the bathrooms have a shower only, and in general they are rather cramped and poorly lit.

Bar Meals: 12-2, 7-10; bar snacks both sessions **Restaurant:** *12.30-2, 7.30-10* **Typical Dishes BAR:** *home-made soup £1.55, paté £3.50, moussaka £3.95, ravioli £4.25, lamb chops £4.95, home-made puddings £1.95* **RESTAURANT:** *smoked salmon £8.95, T-bone steak £10.95, tournedos Prague £13.95, home-made puddings £3.25 Vegetarian Meals: baked avocado* Beer *Draught Bass; Burtonwood Best Bitter* Whisky *Children Allowed in Bar to Eat Outdoor Play Area Patio/terrace Outdoor Eating* **Accommodation:** *24 bedrooms, all en suite, from £50.50 (single £27.50) Children Welcome Overnight Check-in: all day* **Credit Cards:** *Access, Amex, Visa*

BUGLAWTON Church House, Buxton Road Tel: (0260) 272466: Spacious pub with steak pie and moussaka style bar meals, plus a more interesting daily special, lunch and evening (12-2, 6-9). Real fire, two family rooms, garden, outdoor eating. Robinsons beers. Open: 11.30-3, 6-11.

CHESTER   Albion Inn

2 Park Street CH1 1RN

Tel: (0244) 340345

Open: 11.30-3 (2.30 Sun), 5.30-11; 11.30-3.45, 6-11 Sat

Licensee: Michael Mercer

The last unspoilt Victorian corner pub in Chester, or so they say. Good home-cooking of a resolutely old-fashioned kind, entirely fitting for a pub dedicated to the memory of World War One. No chips or modern fried convenience options, and no irritating little plastic sachets of sauces either. There are plans to expand the evening menu, and start doing regional, traditional puddings, too.

Bar Meals: 12-2, 6-9 (Fri/Sat eves); bar snacks both sessions **Typical Dishes:** *green pea and lentil soup £1, home-made steak and kidney in Guinness, home cooked gammon and pease pudding, beef and barley stew (main courses around £3) Vegetarian Meals: curry* Beer *Greenalls Mild, Bitter, Thomas Greenalls Original* Whisky *Bowmore Children Allowed in Bar to Eat* **Credit Cards:** *Access, Visa*

CHESTER   Ye Olde Kings Head

48/50 Lower Bridge Street CH1 1RS
Tel: (0244) 324855
Open: 11-11
Licensee: M Perrin

Pristine black and white timbered 16th century inn with overhanging upper storey.
Pity about the rather downmarket sign announcing the entrance to "Mrs B's
Farmhouse Pantry", with lots of pine and pink and floral wallpaper in evidence
inside. Bars are hotelly but retain much of the original woodwork. Bedrooms are
attractive and well-equipped; part-refurbishment of some of them is now under
way.

Bar Meals: 12-2.30; also bar snacks *Restaurant: 12-2, 6-10 (12-9.30 Sun)* ***Typical
Dishes BAR:*** *tomato, chicken and ham soup 99p, beef in Guinness, shepherd's pie,
moussaka £3.25, bread and butter pudding £1.50* ***RESTAURANT:*** *vegetable soup
95p, bacon ribs £2.35, Somerset pork £6.95, lamb steak £6.25, pantry platter £4.50,
banoffee pie £1.50* *Vegetarian Meals: vegetable lasagne* *Children's Menu/Portions*
[Beer] *Davenports Bitter; Thomas Greenalls Original* *Family Room* **Accommodation:**
8 bedrooms, all en suite, from £49 (single £39.90; 4-poster £59) *Children Welcome
Overnight* *Cots Available* *Check-in: all day* **Credit Cards:** *Access, Amex, Diners, Visa*

DELAMERE Fishpool: Delightful country pub with a traditional layout and lots
of real fires, near Delamere Forest. Varied bar menu. Greenalls beers.

DISLEY   Dandy Cock Inn

Market Street SK12 2DT
Tel: (0663) 763712
Open: 11.30-11
Licensees: Bill and Helen Whitney

Spick and span family-run village pub with restaurant and tremendous views across
the neighbouring valley.

Bar Meals and Restaurant: 12-3, 6-10 (12-2.30, 7-9.30 Sun); restaurant closed Mon
Typical Dishes BAR/RESTAURANT: *chilli soup £1.10, mushrooms in stilton
£2.50, beef cooked in Guinness £4.95, sirloin steak, pink peppercorns, brandy and cream
£8.50, fresh Welsh lobster thermidor £14.50* *Vegetarian Meals: wild rice risotto*
Children's Portions [Beer] *Robinsons Mild, Best Bitter, Old Tom* *Family Room*
Patio/terrace *Outdoor Eating* **Credit Cards:** *Access, Visa*

FULLERS MOOR   Copper Mine

Nantwich Road, Broxton CH3 9JH
Tel: (0829) 782293
Open: 11.30-3, 6.30-11
Licensees: Geoff and Linda Aldridge

A conservatory with six additional tables has just been added to this civilised,
spacious country-style pub, whose bars are littered with copper mining memorabilia.
Spacious grounds, open fires, and a dining room with the same menu.

Bar Meals: 12-3, 7-9.30; bar snacks both sessions ***Typical Dishes:*** *turkey and vegetable
broth £1.50, crispy jacket fries with savoury dip £1.50, spicy chicken tikka with creamy
mint dressing £5.95, steak Medici £7.95, mushroom and stilton pancakes £3.95, bread
and butter pudding with Grand Marnier* *Vegetarian Meals: vegetarian lasagne* *Children's*

Menu   `Beer`   *Draught Bass; Burtonwood Bitter*   *Children Allowed in Bar to Eat*
Outdoor Play Area   *Garden*   *Outdoor Eating*   **Credit Cards:** *Access, Visa*

GOOSTREY   Crown

111 Main Road
Tel: (0477) 32128
Open: 11-3, 5.30-11
Licensee: Peter McGrath

Handsome 16th century pub in popular village, with an attractively furnished
double-room lounge, traditional tap room, rear dining room-cum-bistro, and
upstairs overspill dining room (when not booked by private parties). Extremely
popular for its food, light and snackish at lunchtime, with excellent sandwiches and a
hot daily special (around £3.50), and old-fashioned dinner dishes of the steak, duck
and rack of lamb sort (around £6), for which booking is essential at weekends. This
is the nearest pub to Jodrell Bank Radio Telescope. No music, real fires.

Bar Meals: *lunch and Mon-Sat eve; no food Mon*   **Restaurant:** *Mon-Sat eve; bar snacks*
lunchtime   `Beer`   *Marston*   *Children Allowed in Bar to Eat*   *Patio/terrace*
Accommodation: *Bedrooms from £25*   **Credit Cards:** *Access, Visa*

GREAT BUDWORTH   George & Dragon

High Street CW9 6HF
Tel: (0606) 891317
Open: 11.30-3.30, 6-11
Licensee: Malcolm Curtin

Picturesque local at the heart of a delightful village, opposite the church. Cosy,
rambling, wood-panelled lounge; lively public bar, and upstairs 'restaurant', which
has the same menu, and where families are welcome.

Bar Meals: *12-2.30, 6.30-9.30; bar snacks both sessions*   **Restaurant:** *12-2.30 (Sun*
only), 7-9.30 (weekends)   **Typical Dishes:** *home-made soup £1.15, dim sum £2.80,*
beef bourguignon £4.45, peppered rump steak £7.75, grilled swordfish £5.25   *Vegetarian*
Meals: vegetable curry   *Children's Menu*   `Beer`   *Tetley Bitter, Ind Coope Burton Ale*
`Whisky` *The Balvenie, Dalwhinnie*   *Children Allowed in Bar to Eat (lunch)*   *Patio/terrace*
Outdoor Eating   **Credit Cards:** *Access, Amex*

HIGHER BURWARDSLEY   ★   Pheasant

near Tattenhall CH3 9PF   `FOOD`
Tel: (0829) 70434
Open: 11-3, 7-11   `B&B`
Licensee: David Greenhaugh

Tucked into the hillside amongst the Peckforton hills, the Pheasant is best located by
following signs to the candle factory from the A534. It's plain to see, on arrival, that
the place was once a farm, and the more surprising, therefore, to find that there has
been a pub here since the 17th century. The oldest part, a half-timbered sandstone
farmhouse, is the venue for the bar, which claims to house the largest log fire in
Cheshire. The adjacent Highland Room, generally known as the Bistro, was once
the kitchen and retains the old cast-iron range. The most recent addition is an
imposing conservatory of striking modernity, which overlooks a tiered patio and,
beyond this, right across the Cheshire plain towards North Wales. The old barn,

formerly the centre of village life with its regular weekend barn dances, has now been skilfully converted into six very comfortable bedrooms, equipped to the highest pub standards, with televisions, clock radios, hair dryers, mini-bars and roomy – if poorly lit – bathrooms. Stonework interiors are eye-catching, and nights tranquil. Two further bedrooms, housed in the pub proper, boast original beams and brighter bathrooms, as well as memorable views. There are three quite distinct aspects to the food operation. A self-service counter in the conservatory is useful for a quick lunch, perhaps of chicken provencale, mushroom stroganoff or a Sunday plate of roast beef and Yorkshires (all at under £5), with half portions offered to children, and extended hours at weekends. In the bar, blackboards display a daily changing list for those requiring a little more comfort and exclusivity: vegetable soup, grilled lamb chops, lamb curry or beef and Guinness pie typify the offerings here. The Bistro, meanwhile, comes into its own at night (and for Sunday lunch in winter). A further elaboration of the other menus, it offers more substantial fare, with more vegetables and fewer chips, in an informal and intimate setting. Space is limited; booking is advised. Landlord David Greenhaugh has an unusual and passionate interest, in his prize-winning herd of pedigree Highland cattle. It's not surprising, therefore, to find a certain bias towards meat dishes, amongst which the steaks are outstanding, especially when one of "the family" is on offer! The winter menu offers dishes of equal merit, including pheasant casserole, roast haunch of venison and a recent, prize-winning, chicken and stilton roulade, wrapped in bacon. Amongst the home-made 'to follows', the bread and butter pudding and banoffee pie come out tops; so, too, do a friendly bunch of staff who go out of their way to be pleasant and helpful.

Bar Meals: 12-2, 7-10; *bar snacks both sessions*   *Restaurant:* 7-10   *Typical Dishes* *BAR:* *pumpkin soup, brie pancake £2.25, grilled lamb chops £4.50, rump steak £6, shark steak £4.20, bread and butter pudding £1.80*   *Restaurant:* *rack of lamb £8.50, duck £8, chicken roulade £7.50, halibut £7.80*   *Vegetarian Meals: mushroom stroganoff £4.20* *Children's Portions*   ▪ Beer ▪   *Draught Bass* ▪ Whisky ▪ *Family Room*   *Garden*   *Outdoor Eating*   *Accommodation: 8 bedrooms, all en suite, from £60 (single £40)*   *Children Welcome Overnight*   *Cot Available*   *Check-in: all day*   *Credit Cards: Access, Amex, Diners, Visa*

KNUTSFORD White Lion, 94 King Street Tel: (0565) 2018: Lunchtime food pub strong on cheese and paté ploughmans', Monday-Saturday. Real fire, no music. Hydes and Tetley beers. Open: 11-3, 5.30-11 (all day summer Saturday).

LOWER PEOVER   Bells of Peover

The Cobbles WA16 9PZ   ▼
Tel: (056 572) 2269
Open: 11.30-3, 5.30-11
Licensee: David Barker

Recommended primarily for its atmosphere: a lovely, creeper-covered old pub by the church, at the end of a cobbled lane off the B5081. Toby jugs of all sizes and styles make amusing company in the snug, where the bar counter is to be found; the barless main room has a motley collection of old tables and chairs, copper and brass, and decorative blue plates. The evening bar menu is different to the lunch list shown here, with a few more expensive dishes, like a £6 turkey escalope. Children are allowed in the restaurant.

Bar Meals: 12-2, 6.30-8.30; *bar snacks both sessions*   *Restaurant:* 12-2, 7-9.30 *Typical Dishes BAR:* *celery and stilton soup £1.35, deep-fried mushrooms £2.45, home-made steak and kidney pie £4.75, half roast chicken £4.95, fresh plaice £5.25, lemon soufflé £2.35*   *RESTAURANT:* *set lunch menu £9.50: game terrine, beef stroganoff, lamb cutlets, halibut, raspberry pavlova*   *Vegetarian Meals*   ▪ Beer ▪   *Greenalls* *Patio/terrace*   *Outdoor Eating*   *Credit Cards (restaurant): Visa*

MACCLESFIELD   Sutton Hall

Bullocks Lane, Sutton SK11 0HE

FOOD

Tel: (02605) 3211

B&B

Open: 11-11

Licensee: Robert Bradshaw

Proprietors Robert and Phyllida Bradshaw see Sutton Hall as pub (first and foremost), restaurant and hotel, in that order, and their priorities, thus set, are significant. Central to the building, a wood and stone-built 16th century mansion in use as a nunnery until just 30 years ago, is the pub itself, which has a really stunning interior. The black oak beams, gnarled and knotted, which frame the bar are certainly of much older origin than the rest of the structure, there having been a manor house on this site since 1093, and a unique atmosphere is created by the combination of oak panelling, exposed stonework, leaded windows and two large log-burning fireplaces, one of them guarded by a medieval knight in armour. The fiercely traditional bar menu is thus much in keeping with its surroundings. Starters and snacks are of the French onion soup, avocado with prawns, and home-made chicken liver paté, while the main dishes – veal cordon bleu, steak and kidney pie topped with oysters, and perhaps a lasagne, all served with salad, chips or boiled potatoes – weigh in at quite respectable prices. Vegetarians are offered dishes like mushroom stroganoff, spinach pancakes filled with ratatouille, or home-made vegetable terrine. The adjacent restaurant, kitted out in flock wallpaper with polished mahogany tables, takes itself a little more seriously, with a weekly three-course lunch at £9.75 (£10.75 on Sunday, including a soup course) and a nightly four-course dinner at serious prices. Main courses of individual beef Wellington, half duckling with orange sauce, or veal à la crème are decidedly substantial, as are the cold desserts dispensed from the inevitable sweet trolley. Bedroom conversion by the present owners has seen the installation of bathrooms throughout, and modern-day amenities like remote control televisions, and trouser presses. The antique flavour, however, is well preserved in lace-covered four-poster beds and deep leather easy chairs, although (a penalty of antiquity) there's a distinct shortage of natural daylight through their leaded Gothic windows, further dimmed by heavily overhanging eaves. The Hall's immediate environs, backing on to a working farm at the rear, appear so close to ramshackle as to cause some initial concern, but the warmth of the interior and the casual tomfoolery between landlord, staff and regulars suggest that such imperfection and incompleteness are not, perhaps, entirely accidental.

Bar Meals and Restaurant: 12-2.30, 7-10; bar snacks both sessions **Typical Dishes** *BAR: home-made soup £1.45, chilled melon gondola with Parma ham £4.25, steak and kidney pie with oysters £5.25, supreme of chicken £5.25, veal cordon bleu £5.25 RESTAURANT: dinner menu £17.95: gravadlax, sorbet, beef Wellington, sirloin steak, goujons of hake, puddings or cheese Vegetarian Meals: spinach pancakes £5.25* Beer *Bass; Marston* Whisky *Family Room (weekend lunch) Garden Outdoor Eating* **Accommodation:** *10 bedrooms, all en suite, from £80 (single £65) Children Welcome Overnight Cots Available Check-in: all day* **Credit Cards:** *Access, Amex, Visa*

MARBURY   Swan Inn

Whitchurch SY13 4LS

Tel: (0948) 3715

Open: 12-3 (not Mon), 7-11

Licensees: George and Ann Sumner

Real, home-made chips are a famous local speciality at the Swan Inn, in a small pretty Cheshire village which regularly wins 'best kept' awards. In addition to the menu there are at least four specials every day; fresh vegetables. Food is unremarkable but decent enough of its kind, from the standard printed menu. Puddings are usually of the banana splittish sort.

Bar Meals and Restaurant: 12-2, 7-9.30; *bar snacks both sessions*   **Typical Dishes** *BAR/RESTAURANT: home-made soup £1.30, chef's paté £2.35, prawn cocktail £3, Persian lamb £5.25, pork Dijonnaise £5.25, fish pie £5.25, summer pudding £1.80 Vegetarian Meals: vegetable quiche £4.25   Children's Portions* `Cheese` `Beer` *Greenalls Mild, Bitter; Stones Bitter* `Whisky` *Children Allowed in Bar to Eat   Outdoor Play Area   Garden   Outdoor Eating* **No Credit Cards**

MOBBERLEY   Bird In Hand

on B5085 WA16 7BN
Tel: (0565) 873149
Open: 11-3, 5.30-11 (all day Sat)
Licensee: Andrew Towers

English village pub, complete with its original series of small wood-panelled drinking rooms leading off from a central servery, and now likely to be brimming with foreign tourists – Manchester airport is just ten minutes away. Open fire; fruit machine. The pub has changed hands since our last edition.

Bar Meals: 12-2 (2.30 Sun), 7-9.30; *bar snacks both sessions*   **Typical Dishes:** *home-made soup £1.50, paté £3, home-made steak and onion pie £4.40, giant Yorkshire pudding filled with spicy sausage £4.75, Welsh rarebit £4.40, treacle tart £1.95 Vegetarian Meals: vegetable lasagne   Children's Portions* `Beer` *Samuel Smith Old Brewery Bitter, Museum Ale   Family Room Patio/terrace   Outdoor Eating* **Credit Cards:** *Access, Visa*

OLLERTON   Dun Cow

Chelford Road (A537)
Tel: (0565) 3093
Open: all day
Licensee: Geoffrey Tilling

Delightfully atmospheric old pub, long a favourite for its character and good simple home cooking, but which has now changed hands. The low-ceilinged lounge has two open fires, some nice pieces of furniture, and a little snug leading off; there's also a small tap room.

Bar Meals: 12-2, 6.30-9.30 (Wed-Sat eves); *bar snacks both sessions*   `Beer` *Greenalls Children Allowed in Bar to Eat   Patio/terrace* **No Credit Cards**

OVERTON Ring o' Bells, Bellemonte Road: 17th century multi-roomed pub of character, with an old-fashioned hatch servery and decent lunchtime hot specials. Children allowed. Greenalls beers.

RAINOW   Highwayman

on A5002, north of Rainow
Tel: (0625) 573245
Open: 11.30-3, 7-11
Licensee: Frank Jones

The bar food is routine stuff on the whole, aside from a decent range of home-made pizzas, but this is a characterful pub and a very popular one, with tremendous views across the Cheshire Plain, and an old-fashioned interior, its various little rooms all warmed by a real fire. The beer's reliably good too. Get here early for a seat.

Bar Meals: daily lunchtime and evening; bar snacks both sessions   `Beer`   *Thwaites Bitter Family Room   Patio/terrace.*

TARPORLEY   Rising Sun

High Street (A49)
Tel: (0829) 732423
Open: 11-2.30, 5.30-11
Licensee: Alec Robertson

Another fine Cheshire village pub, of such unspoilt charm that ordinary food is almost forgivable. Various low-ceilinged, quaint little rooms ramble about, warmed by a trio of fires, and with ancient settles among its nice decorative touches like a series of old Worthington brewery mirrors. Bar food is cheap and cheerful at lunchtime, perhaps steak and kidney pie, or ham and eggs; the evening list is more three-coursey, with chicken, steaks and mixed grills leading the field (main courses around £6). It gets incredibly busy at weekends, especially when the local cricketers move in.

Bar Meals: 12-2, 6-9.30 (not Sun eve); bar snacks both sessions   `Beer`   *Robinsons Best Mild, Best Bitter   Children Allowed in Bar to Eat*

TUSHINGHAM   Blue Bell Inn

Bell o' the Hill, Whitchurch SY13 4RS
Tel: (0948) 2172
Open: 11-2.30 (not Mon), 6-11
Licensee: Mark Sumner

Probably the only pub in this guide haunted by a ghostly duck; the full story is explained on the bar wall. A remarkable old building, opposite a farm, just off the A41, the Blue Bell has massive oak doors, an original multi-roomed layout, heavy beams and old-fashioned hatch serveries, but also modern plush wall seating.

Bar Meals: 12-2 (not Mon), 6.30-10; bar snacks both sessions   **Typical Dishes:** *watercress and almond soup £1.50, deep-fried feta cheese £1.95, beef olives, chicken sunnyside, fresh plaice stuffed with prawns and mushrooms, fresh fruit pavlova (main courses from £4)   Vegetarian Meals: spinach and peanut pancake with stilton sauce   Children's Menu/Portions*   `Cheese`   `Beer`   *Greenalls Bitter; Thomas Greenalls Original*   `Cider` *Symonds Drystone   Family Room   Outdoor Play Area   Garden   No Credit Cards*

WALKER BARN Setter Dog, on A537: Simple moorland pub with good views, real fire and separate restaurant. Marston beers.

WESTON   White Lion Inn

Main Road, near Crewe CW2 5NA
Tel: (0270) 500303
Open: 11-3, 6.30 (7 winter)-11
Licensee: Alison Davies

The original Tudor farmhouse pub, complete with appropriately atmospheric beamed bar, now has a modern hotel with a businesslike atmosphere (and features) grafted onto the back. Piped music, smartly turned out staff, and 'le diner menu' (sic), French with English explanations, is high price and over-long. They do conference packages. Hotel accommodation we found a bit self-consciously upmarket and stuffy. The bar meals menu (which packs them in), is short and dominated by light snacks.

Bar Meals: 12-2 (1.45 Sun), 7-9.30; bar snacks both sessions   *Restaurant:* 12-1.30, 7-9.30   *Typical Dishes BAR:* home-made soup £1.35, mushrooms in garlic butter £2.75, gammon steak £4.50, roast of the day £3.95, local Dee salmon £5.95, chocolate roulade   *RESTAURANT:* home-made soup £2.20, moules mariniere £4.95, canard roti £9.95, chateaubriand (for 2) £23.50, turbot en croute £10.95, trifle   *Vegetarian Meals Children's Portions* **Cheese** (restaurant) **Beer** Ind Coope Burton Ale; Tetley Bitter **Whisky** *Family Room Garden Outdoor Eating* **Accommodation:** 17 rooms, all en suite, from £55 (single £45) Children Welcome Overnight Cot Available Check-in: all day **Credit Cards:** Access, Amex, Diners, Visa

WILLASTON Pollards, Wistaston Road: Interesting old ex-farmhouse with a nice interior, the original 14th century building with a modern garden room extension, and large lawns. Bar food lunchtime and evening; also restaurant.

WILMSLOW   Farmers Arms
Chapel Lane
Tel: (0625) 532443
Open: all day

Very simple but honest home-made food, at this bustling town-centre local pub. Steak and kidney pie, curries, fresh fish from Grimsby, and a daily vegetarian special, as well as one or two adventurous foreign dishes, and home-made chutney. Chips with everything; low prices. The pub itself is attractively old-fashioned, with various little rooms, lots of bric-a-brac, fine etched windows, and a family room decked out with cartoons. Real fire; no music.

Bar Meals: Mon-Sat lunchtime; bar snacks boths sessions *Vegetarian Meals   Children's Menu* **Beer** *Whitbread   Family Room   Garden*

WYBUNBURY   Swan
on B5071
Tel: (0270) 841280
Open: 12-3, 7-11
Licensee: Richard Staveley

An attractive little two-roomed pub, which has lots of agricultural and other bric-a-brac and pretty decorative touches, as well as a cheering winter fire.

Bar Meals: lunchtime and Mon-Sat eve; bar snacks both sessions   *Typical Dishes:* home-made soup, garlic mushrooms, Mexican pork, rack of lamb, moussaka (main courses from around £4) *Vegetarian Meals: lasagne   Children's Menu* **Beer** McEwan, Theakston, Younger *Children Allowed in to Eat   Outdoor Play Area   Garden* **Accommodation:** Bedrooms from £35

CLEVELAND

EGGLESCLIFFE Pot & Glass, Church Road: Historic, attractive rural pub with cheap home cooked food at lunchtime, a family room and garden. No music. Draught Bass. Open: 11-3, 5.30-11

HARTBURN Stockton Arms, Darlington Road Tel: (0642) 580104: Pleasant and friendly pub in a smart Stockton suburb, with good value decent bar snacks and separate dining room, where children are allowed; menus feature one or two imaginative dishes.Good value en suite bedrooms. Draught Bass. Open all day.

HIGH LEVEN Fox Covert, Low Lane (A1044): Attractive old farm building conversion, with a comfortable open plan interior style. The lunchtime and evening bar menu includes one or two interesting options. Vaux beers. Open: 11-3, 5-11.

HILTON   Falcon Inn

Just off A19 TS15 9LB
Tel: (0642) 592228
Open: 11.30-3, 6.30-11.30
Licensee: Kenneth Holm

Spacious, chintzily civilised dining pub serving the Middlesbrough business community, among others.

Bar Meals: 11.30-2, 6.30-10 (12-2, 7-9.30 Sun); bar snacks both sessions **Typical Dishes:** *vegetable soup £1.55, granary mushrooms £2.95, pork parmesan, chicken and broccoli lasagne, orange and Cointreau basket (main courses from around £4)* *Vegetarian Meals: cheese and broccoli quiche* *Children's Menu/Portions* *Family Room* *Garden* *Outdoor Eating* **Credit Cards:** *Access, Amex, Diners, Visa*

LONGNEWTON Vane Arms, Darlington Road: Refurbished village pub with simple home cooking lunchtime and evening, a real fire, garden and no music. Draught Bass. Open: 11.30-3, 7-11.

MOORSHOLM Jolly Sailor: on A171: Stone-built moorland pub, comfortably modernised, with a mix of standards and specials on the lunchtime and evening menu – go for the fresh haddock or home-made steak and kidney pie; family room and children's menu; garden tables. Open: 11.30-3, 6-11 (all day Saturday).

NEWTON Kings Head: on A173: Refurbished old pub, popular for food; dining room, terrace and good local walks. Courage beer.

YARM Ketton Ox, 100 High Street Tel: (0642) 788311: Attractively opened-out and refurbished, locally famous old coaching inn, once a popular cock-fighting pub – walled-up oval windows betray the site of the former cock pit. Busy lunchtime and evening food trade, Thursday-Sunday (book). Vaux beers. Open: 11-2.30, 5.30-11 (all day Saturday and summer).

CORNWALL

BOSCASTLE   Napoleon

Top of the village
Tel: (0840) 250204
Open: 11-3, 5.30-11 (noon-3, 7-11 winter)

One of three good pubs in a quaintly steep old fishing village (the Wellington also has its fans), with a glorious miniature harbour owned by the National Trust. A pretty little inn with polished slate floors and various cosy rooms. A short (very short at quiet times) menu features some interesting home-cooked options, and beer is reliably good.

Bar Meals: daily lunch and evening bar snacks both sessions   `Beer`   Draught Bass; St
Austell Family room   Garden

CALSTOCK Boot: Busy free house in pretty Plymouth commuter village.
Routine bar food, and more interesting upstairs restaurant; bedrooms.

CHAPEL AMBLE   ★   Maltsters Arms

Chapel Amble PL27 6EU   `FOOD`
Tel: (0208) 812473   ☻
Open: 11-3, 6-11   ▼
Licensees: Jeffrey and Vivienne Pollard

This rambling pub isn't outstanding for its character, but the cooking is well above
average. A central bar, warmed by a large open fire, has three rooms leading off; one
of these is officially the dining area, but tables aren't laid until a food order is made.
There are no frills, no tablecloths even, but taped Gilbert and Sullivan music creates
a civilised and jolly atmosphere and, despite the non-restauranty decor, it's the kind
of pub where most customers come to eat. Owner Jeff Pollard does the cooking,
while Vivienne runs the bar. Fine fresh ingredients, with a particular emphasis on
fish and seafood. Start with good home-made soups ($£1.95$), progress through
delicious starters like a grilled goats cheese on salad leaves ($£3.10$), followed perhaps
by three tender pieces of steamed turbot fillet served with a light hollandaise and
sautéed sliced asparagus ($£11.75$) or a superb monkfish bourguignon ($£9.25$).
Carnivores aren't neglected either: try the home-made raised pork pie with their
own onion chutney ($£3.95$), lambs liver sautéed with bacon and onions ($£4.50$),
home-made sirloin meatballs with a piquant tomato sauce ($£4.50$) or a char-grilled
Aberdeen Angus steak with peppercorn and ginger wine sauce ($£9.15$), all from the
delightfully varied lunchtime menu. A properly made vegetarian nut roast with
chestnut stuffing and a red wine sauce ($£5.10$) and a good selection of ploughmans
with excellent local cheeses also feature here. The evening menu allows for choice
in style and price too: pork terrine with an orange preserve ($£3.95$) and whole
langoustines ($£7.95$) are typical starters, and the main courses allow for both a
budget supper – home-made lasagne al forno with Italian cheeses and mortadella at a
very reasonable $£5.50$ – and a real blow-out treat, perhaps choosing the $£19.50$
shellfish platter, featuring fresh lobster direct from their own tanks. Puddings are
good too, a down-to-earth selection of favourites like bread and butter, and treacle
tart, for around $£2$. There's a good range of bottled beers in addition to the rather
ordinary draught selection, and Australian wines are now very popular on a notably
ungreedy wine list. It's very busy indeed in summer, pretty quiet in winter, when
the summer crowds have gone and the seasonal-based menu is more limited in
scope.

Bar Meals: 12-2.30, 7-9.30; bar snacks lunchtime   **Typical Dishes:** stilton and celery
soup $£1.95$, home-made taramasalata $£3.40$, chicken breast stuffed with lobster $£9.15$,
paella (cooked to order) $£14.50$, saltimbocca $£8.55$, bread and butter pudding with clotted
cream $£1.90$ Vegetarian Meals: agnolotti pasta $£5.95$ Children's Menu   Children's
Portions (some)   `Cheese`   `Beer`   Ruddles County, Ushers Best Bitter   Children
Allowed in Bar to Eat   Garden   Outdoor Eating   **Credit Cards:** Access, Visa

---

CHARLESTOWN   Rashleigh Arms

near the harbour PL25 3NJ
Tel: (0726) 73635
Open: 11-11

Large Georgian pub–hotel in charming Cornish port. Three bars plus a newish
dining room, with the same menu and prices.

Bar Meals: 12-2, 7-10; bar snacks both sessions   **Typical Dishes:** *beef and tomato soup £1.40, home-made paté £2.25, roast of the day £4.45, steak and kidney pie £3.75, fish pie £3.75, fruit pies £1.50   Vegetarian Meals: oaty cauliflower and broccoli gratin Children's Menu* ▮Beer▮ *Draught Bass; Ruddles County; St Austell Tinners Bitter; Wadworth 6X   Family Room   Outdoor Play Area   Garden   Outdoor Eating   Summer Barbecue   **Accommodation:** 5 bedrooms, all en suite, from £40 (single £25)   Children Welcome Overnight (minimum age 10)   Check-in: by arrangement   **Credit Cards:** Access, Visa*

CONSTANTINE   Trengilly Wartha Inn

Constantine TR11 5RP   ▼
Tel: (0326) 40332
Open: 11-3 (2.30 Sun and winter), 6-11
Licensees: Nigel Logan and Michael Maguire

Really rather smart country inn and restaurant, a mile from the village in a gloriously pretty area, and with six acres of its own grounds. The bars are a delight, unspoilt and simple, with exposed stone and beams, traditional furnishings, and a good mix of locals and visitors. The dining room aims to echo the atmosphere of a family-run French hotel, the cooking modern, but the breakfasts resolutely traditional English.

Bar Meals: 12-2.15 (2 Sun and winter), 6.30-9.30; bar snacks both sessions
Restaurant: 7.30-9.30   *Typical Dishes BAR: courgette and almond soup with home-made bread £1.50, smoked haddock paté £2.50, Trengilly cassoulet £5, venison sausages £3, fresh tagliatelle with hot tomato sauce £4.40, pear and almond tart £1.70* **RESTAURANT:** *£16 set menu (8 choice): chicken and plum terrine, fillet of beef in pastry, honey profiteroles   Vegetarian Meals: leek and black-eyed bean pie £4   Children's Menu/Portions* ▮Cheese▮ ▮Beer▮ *Courage Directors; Exmoor Ale; St Austell HSD; Theakston XB* ▮Whisky▮ *Lagavulin 16 yr* ▮Cider▮ *Proper Job (local farm), Taunton Traditional   Family Room   Outdoor Play Area   Garden   Outdoor Eating* **Accommodation:** *6 bedrooms, 5 en suite, from £41 (single £32)   Children Welcome Overnight   Cots Available   Check-in: all day   **Credit Cards:** Access, Amex, Visa*

GOLDSITHNEY   Crown

Fore Street (B3280)
Tel: (0736) 710494
Open: 11-3, 6-11

Relaxing and informal village pub with a Cornish flavour in the traditionalist bar menu; stars of the show are the vast home-made pasties, flanked by a good beef pie, and much use of local free range meats. Real clotted cream on the puddings, and low prices throughout; the pub is busy with hungry locals when not mobbed by summer tourists. There's also a restaurant featuring smarter fare, particularly strong on fish, and just one double room available for overnight stops.

Bar Meals: daily lunchtime and evening; bar snacks lunchtime   *Children's Menu* ▮Beer▮ *St Austell   Garden   **Credit Cards:** Access, Visa*

HELFORD   Shipwrights Arms

near Helston TR12 6JX   ❢
Tel: (032 623) 235
Open: 11-2.30, 6-11
Licensees: Brandon Flynn and Charles Herbert

Stunningly located on the banks of the Helford estuary, its approach road so narrow that in summer it's restricted to pedestrian use only. But it's the worth the effort, particularly in the busy summer months, when barbecues are held in the magical terraced gardens. The interior is quite special too, staunchly traditional, with lots of nautical bits and pieces, and lots of yachting types swapping unlikely stories too. The simple lunchtime bar food and smarter, fishier evening fare is also reliably good; it gets extremely busy.

Bar Meals: 12-1.30, 7-9 *(not Sun nor Mon eves winter); bar snacks lunchtime* **Typical Dishes:** *home-made soup £1.75, garlic mushrooms £2.50, steak and kidney pudding £4.25, local crab salad £6, beef bourguignon £6, lobster from £9 home-made puddings from £2 Vegetarian Meals   Children's Portions* Cheese Beer *Cornish Original Children Allowed in to Eat   Garden*

HELSTON   New Inn

Wendron TR13 0EA
Tel: (0326) 572683
Open: 12-3, 7-11
Licensee: Gloria Standcumbe

Plush red carpets, varnished pine, and lots of brass and other agricultural bric-a-brac on display in both the lounge and traditional public bar. Lovely hanging baskets in summer. Recommended for bed and breakfast.

Bar Meals and Restaurant: 12-2, 7-10; *bar snacks both sessions* **Typical Dishes:** *Parma ham and melon £3.20, beef bourguignon £7, T-bone steak £7.50, swordfish steak £6.95, apple tart and clotted cream   Vegetarian Meals: vegetarian chilli   Children's Portions* Beer *Cornish Original; Newquay Steam Bitter; Whitbread Flowers IPA   Children Allowed in Bar to Eat   Outdoor Play Area   Garden   Outdoor Eating* **Accommodation:** *2 bedrooms, sharing a bathroom, from £40 (single £20)   Check-in: by arrangement* **No Credit Cards**

HESSENFORD   Copley Arms

near Torpoint PL11 3JH
Tel: (05034) 209
Open: 11-2.30, 6-11 (all day summer)
Licensee: E Chidzoy

This boxy white-washed roadside pub is utterly transformed in summer, when the window boxes, hanging baskets and pavement flower tubs are a riot of pinks and reds, front and back, and the paved riverside drinking terrace really comes into its own.

Bar Meals: 12-2, 7-9.15; *bar snacks lunchtime* **Typical Dishes:** *garlic mushrooms en croute £2.50, Mexican chicken £4.95, fish pie £4.95, trout £5.60, chocolate rum mousse £1.50   Vegetarian Meals: cauliflower florets with garlic dip   Children's Menu/Portions* Beer *St Austell   Family Room   Outdoor Play Area   Riverside Garden   Outdoor Eating   Summer Barbecue* **Accommodation:** *6 bedrooms, sharing 2 bathrooms, from £30* *(single £15)   Children Welcome Overnight (minimum age 5)   Check-in: all day*   **Credit Cards:** *Access, Visa*

LANNER Coppice Inn: on A393 Tel: (0209) 216668: Decent pub; lunchtime and evening bar food; enormous gardens; family room. Ind Coope, Tetley beers. Open: 11-3, 6-11.

LISKEARD Fountain Hotel, The Parade Tel: (0579) 42154: Modernised, comfortable town centre coaching inn with a family room, lounge with dining area leading off, and decent lunchtime and evening food. Also bedrooms. Courage beer. Open: 11-3, 5.30-11.

LONG ROCK   Mexico Inn

Penzance TR20 8JL   `FOOD`
Tel: (0736) 710625
Open: 12-2.30, 6-11
Licensee: Pat and Bob Owen

The name comes from one Bill Trewarthan, a mining engineer who returned from the silver mines of Mexico in 1794 to open a silver mine nearby the present pub. The mine flooded in 1799, but the Mexico Inn is still here, a typical Cornish terrace pub, originally the counting house where Trewarthan paid his miners and for which he obtained a license to sell beer, a brilliant tactical move which both kept the workers happy and recouped most of the wages he had just paid out. It's a friendly, characterful place with rough granite walls, wheelbacked chairs around scrubbed wooden tables, and exposed joists and ceiling boards – the floorboards of the upper floor, painted black and red. Although the bar is small, the menu is anything but, a long and eclectic list that ranges from burgers to chopped squid, as well as traditional Mexican chillied chicken with chocolate. Long menus do not usually bode well for standards, but virtually everything here is home-cooked, including the particularly succulent ham generously sliced into wholemeal bread sandwiches. Vegetarians are well looked after too, with the likes of nutty stuffed mushrooms, and cauliflower and almond au gratin. It's not a pub for children – there's no indoor family area and no children's menu – although a small corner of the car park at the rear has been screened off and furnished with a few rustic tables and benches.

Bar Meals: *12-2.30, 6-9.30; bar snacks both sessions*   **Typical Dishes:** *minestrone £1.75, camembert and garlic stuffed mushrooms £2.50, sirloin steak with various sauces, from £8, chicken pizzaiola £5.50, Indian lamb curry £5.50, home-made pistachio ice cream £1.95   Vegetarian Meals: Mexican pancakes £5   Children's Portions*   `Beer` *Bass   Garden   Outdoor Eating*   **No Credit Cards**

LOSTWITHIEL   Royal Oak

Duke Street PL22 1AO
Tel: (0208) 872552
Open: 11-3, 5.30-11
Licensees: Malcolm and Eileen Hine

13th century inn just off the main road in the original capital of Cornwall. There are two bars, the lounge being given over entirely to dining at mealtimes; the saloon is the local meeting place. Cooking by the landlady, using fresh local produce.

Bar Meals: *12-2, 6.30-10 (7-9.30 Sun); bar snacks both sessions*   **Typical Dishes:** *French onion soup £1.50, prawn cocktail £2.50, Mrs Hine's cow pie £3.75, Barbary duck £9.50, Fowey scallops £6.95, treacle tart £1.35   Vegetarian Meals: broccoli and cream* *cheese pie   Children's Menu*   **Beer**   *Draught Bass; Fullers London Pride; Marston Pedigree; Whitbread Flowers Original   Family Room   Garden   Outdoor Eating* **Accommodation:** *6 bedrooms, all en suite, from £42 (single £24.50)   Check-in: all day* **Credit Cards:** *Access, Amex, Diners, Visa*

MANACCAN   New Inn

Tel: (0326) 623323   **FOOD**
Open: 11-3, 6-11   ☼
Licensee: Patrick Cullinan

Visitors are welcome at this thatched, cottagey pub deep in Daphne Du Maurier country (the original Frenchman's Creek is nearby), but the atmosphere is very much that of the locals' village pub. The actual age of the New Inn isn't clear, but it certainly predates Oliver Cromwell, to whose soldiers it was quite specifically placed out of bounds during the Civil War. The interior, with boarded walls and exposed ceilings, isn't much changed in a hundred years, and Paddy the landlord aims to keep it that way. The air of tradition extends to pub games: shove ha'penny, chess, backgammon and cards among them, which all help the regulars while away the long winter evenings. As does the range of well-kept beers, still drawn direct from the barrel on a rack behind the bar. This isn't really a pub for children, but there are plenty of tables outside in the extensive garden for summer family meals. A short blackboard menu offers robustly cooked typical pub dishes like cottage pie at lunchtime, together with some inventive soups, like cheese and calabrese or carrot and tarragon, the latter more like a thin puree of vegetables than a soup, all served with great wedges of wholemeal bread. The evening menu has a wider horizon: garlic prawns, chicken fricassée with pasta, plus oysters and lobsters, if given prior notice. Good puddings come generously accompanied by wonderful thick clotted cream; the chocolate strawberry roulade is particularly unmissable. To walk it off, take a stroll up to the village church, where a remarkable 200 year old fig tree is literally growing out of the wall. Its other claim to fame, incidentally, is that Captain Bligh was imprisoned in the vestry for a time, mistaken for a French spy when he landed here after being cast adrift from the Bounty. Manaccan was put firmly on the world map for a time when a mineral (manaccanite) was discovered nearby which in its heyday enjoyed a monopoly as an additive for strengthening metal alloys.

Bar Meals: *12-2, 6.30-9.30 (12.30-1.45, 7-9 winter); bar snacks lunchtime* **Typical Dishes:** *fresh vegetable soup £1.50, crab £3.50, duck breast in various sauces £6, casseroles £3.50, fresh fish £4.50-£6, treacle tart £2   Vegetarian Meals: ratatouille   Children's Portions* **Beer** *Cornish Original; Marston Pedigree   Children Allowed in Bar to Eat Outdoor Play Area   Garden   Outdoor Eating* **No Credit Cards**

METHERELL   Carpenters Arms

Callington PL17 8BJ
Tel: (0579) 50242
Open: 12-2.30, 7-11
Licensees: Douglas and Jill Brace

A 15th century pub with food, successfully resisting the temptation to turn into a restaurant. The bar oozes character, with its heavy stone walls and floors, little windows, low beams, high-backed settles, and lots of plants, though the more modern lounge is less inspiring. They no longer offer overnight accommodation.

Bar Meals: *12-1.45 (1.30 Sun), 7-9.30; bar snacks both sessions* **Typical Dishes:** *home-made soup £1.60, mixed grill £8.50, home-made chicken, ham and mushroom pie £4.75, fresh plaice £3.95, spicy pudding £1.60   Vegetarian Meals: Chinese bean casserole*

£3.95   Children's Menu   ▬Beer▬   *Draught Bass; Wadworth 6X; Wiltshire Old Grumble; Whitbread Flowers Original   Family Room   Outdoor Play Area   Patio/terrace   Outdoor Eating*   **No Credit Cards**

MEVAGISSEY Ship, Fore Street Tel: (0726) 843324: Smartened up Elizabethan inn near the harbour, with a nautical interior theme. Avoid high spring tides when the bar's likely to be under water. Welcoming to families. Lunchtime and evening bar food features good local fish; children and vegetarians also catered for. Bedrooms. St Austell beers. Open: 11-3, 5.30-11 (all day summer).

MITHIAN   Miners Arms

St Agnes TR5 0QF
Tel: (0872) 552375
Open: 11-3 (2 winter), 6-11
Licensee: Peter Andrew

Characterful old pub, refurbished and improved (not a euphemism in this case), and now extended by the addition of what was the village shop. Low ceilings, wonky walls, a wood block floor and attractive bits of bric a brac, as well as a fascinating wall painting of Elizabeth I. The gardens and car park have recently been landscaped.

Bar Meals: 11-2, 6-10 (12-2, 6-9 winter); bar snacks both sessions   **Typical Dishes:** *garlic wild mushrooms £1.75, crab bake with walnut bread £3.50, Cornish pie (lamb, apple and onion) £4.95, fish and spinach pie £4.95, aduki bean cottage pie £4.55, fresh fig crumble £1.50   Vegetarian Meals: vegetarian cannelloni £4.65   Children's Menu*
▬Beer▬   *Marston; Whitbread   Family Room   Outdoor Play Area   Garden   Patio/terrace*
Credit Cards: *Access, Visa*

MORWENSTOW   Bush

Crosstown
Tel: (028 883) 242
Open: 12-2.30, 7-11; closed winter Mon
Licensee: J H Gregory

After a romantic walk along the cliffs, where the eccentric 19th century local vicar, the Reverend Hawker, built a little shack from which to contemplate the sea and the greater questions (and now the smallest building in National Trust hands), the simple, traditional Bush, a genuinely ancient pub with a Celtic piscina set into one wall, makes the perfect resting place. Food is simple and traditional too: delicious home-made soup, pasties, steak and kidney pie or warming winter stew, all at very low prices; the excellent ploughmans, with good bread, cheese and home-made pickle, makes an ideal post-ramble snack. No children.

Bar Meals: Mon-Sat lunchtime   ▬Beer▬   *St Austell   Patio/terrace*

MOUSEHOLE   Ship Inn

Penzance TR19 6QX
Tel: (0736) 731234
Open: 10.30-3, 6-11 (all day summer)
Licensee: Michael Maddern

Delightfully unassuming little fishing pub in a beautiful coastal village, friendly, simply furnished, uncarpeted, and with an open fire.

Bar Meals: 12-3, 6-9.30; bar snacks both sessions   *Typical Dishes:* crab chowder £1.80, local seafood crepes, peppered steaks, lamb kebabs, baked fish gratin (main courses from under £4), blackcurrant cheesecake Vegetarian Meals   Children's Portions   **Beer**   St Austell beers Family Room Patio/terrace   Outdoor Eating   *Accommodation:* 3 bedrooms, all en suite, from £40 (single £30)   Children Welcome Overnight   Check-in: all day   **No Credit Cards**

PADSTOW   London Inn

Lanadwell Street PL28 8AN   ⚐
Tel: (0841) 532554
Open: 11-4, 6-11
Licensee: M C Lean

Three old fisherman's cottages, merged into a pub in 1802, the London is plainly decorated and furnished, full of nautical atmosphere, and often busy, with a thriving local trade. An old fashioned pub "for mature drinkers", they say; children are only allowed in the restaurant. Discreet improvements are being made: showers are being installed in bedrooms in time to greet the 1992 season.

Bar Meals and Restaurant: 12-2.30, 7-10; bar snacks lunchtime   *Typical Dishes* *BAR:* home-made soup £1.30, paté £2, chicken curry £3.75, ocean pie £4 *RESTAURANT:* rump steak £9.50, fresh farm chicken £8.50, gammon steak £6.20 Vegetarian Meals: vegetarian lasagne   Children's Menu/Portions   **Cheese**   **Beer**   St Austell Bosuns Bitter; Tinners Bitter, HSD   **Whisky**   Singleton, Aberlour   Children over 14 Allowed in Bar to Eat   *Accommodation* (closed Christmas): 3 bedrooms, all with showers, from £35 (single £25)   Children Welcome Overnight   Cot Available   Check-in: by arrangement   **No Credit Cards**

PENZANCE   Turks Head Inn

Chapel Street TR18 4AF
Tel: (0736) 63093
Open: 11-3, 5.30-11
Licensees: Bill and Veronica Morris

Popular terraced side-street local, a lot older than it looks; the present main bar at the front was originally the medieval inn's courtyard. The old cellar is now the dining room, where the old smugglers' tunnel to the harbour, later used as secret access to first floor priest holes, can still be seen. Usually busy, popular for lunches, and lively with young locals in the evening. Piped music.

Bar Meals: 11-2.30, 6-10 (12-2.30, 7-10 Sun); bar snacks lunchtime   *Typical Dishes:* bacon and lentil soup £1.20, smoked salmon medley £4.10, steak and kidney pie £4.50, Mexican hotpot £3.95, mariners pie £5.95, apple suet dumpling   Vegetarian Meals: cauliflower and vegetable gratin   Children's Portions   **Beer**   Cornish; Whitbread   Family Room   Garden   Outdoor Eating   *Credit Cards: Access, Visa*

PENZANCE Mount's Bay Inn, Werrytown Tel: (0736) 63027: Cheering, friendly pub with real fire, no music, decent lunchtime and evening bar meals. Draught Bass. Open: 11-2.30, 5.30-11.

PERRANUTHNOE   Victoria Inn

Penzance TR20 9NP
Tel: (0736) 710309
Open: 11.30-2.30, 6.30-11
Licensees: Chris and Julia Martin

Superb little pub just off the A394. Officially described as a safe house for the clergy, but equally welcoming to families and dogs. Lots of maritime memorabilia. The landlady's cooking is sound and homely, from the fairly standard printed menu to plain, traditionally pubby daily specials.

Bar Meals: 12-2, 6.30-9; bar snacks both sessions **Typical Dishes:** *vegetable soup £1.90, garlic bread 95p, chicken curry, sirloin steak, gammon steak (main courses from £4) Vegetarian Meals: nut rissoles in pepper sauce   Children's Menu/Portions* **Beer** *Courage; John Smith   Family Room   Garden   Outdoor Eating   Summer Barbecue* **Accommodation:** *2 bedrooms, both with showers, from £20 (single £10) (no breakfast) Children Welcome Overnight   Check-in: all day* **No Credit Cards**

PHILLEIGH   Roseland Inn

Philleigh TR2 5NB
Open: 11-2.30 (inc Sun), 6-11 (11.30-2.30, 7-11 winter)
Licensee: Desmond Sinnott

17th century cob-built Cornish treasure, run with enthusiastic panache and never less than spotless. The front terrace is delightfully floral, and indoors there are old-fashioned seats, a lovely old settle, worn slate floors, fresh flowers, low beams and a welcoming winter fire.

Bar Meals: 12-2, 6.30-9 (summer eves only) **Typical Dishes:** *home-made soup, curry, lasagne, seafood mornay (main courses £4), bread and butter pudding* **Beer** *Cornish Original;   Whitbread Flowers IPA   Family Room   Patio   Outdoor Eating* **No Credit Cards**

POLPERRO   Blue Peter

The Quay
Tel: (0503) 72743
Open: all day
Licensees: Terry Bicknell, Jennie Craig-Hallam, Tim Horn

Unspoilt little fishing pub in a very touristy village; it's a good ten minute walk down from the public car park at the top to the quaint little harbour and its popular little pub. Head for the main bar, and be early: it's traditional, authentically seafaring in mood, with nice old furnishings, and soothing views – but there are also modern games machines and piped music. Families can use the less atmospheric family room upstairs. Decent food is crowned by the freshest possible local fish and seafood.

Bar Meals: 12-2.30, 6-9.30; bar snacks both sessions **Typical Dishes:** *home-made soup £1.30, crab platter £4, chicken curry £4, home-cooked pizzas £3* **Beer** *St Austell* **Cider** *Family Room   Patio/terrace*

POLPERRO   Three Pilchards

The Quay PL13 2QZ
Tel: (0503) 72233
Open: 11-11 (11-3, 7-11 winter)
Licensee: Ennis Jones

Polperro's oldest pub, plain and simple, popular with fishermen and walkers. Simple menu too, but good home cooking.

Bar Meals: 12-2, 7-9.30 (all day until 10 summer)   ***Typical Dishes:*** *half chicken £3.75, home-made beef in ale £3.50, plaice and chips £3.75   Vegetarian Meals: curry Children's Menu/Portions*   `Beer`   *Courage Best, Directors*   `Cider`   *local scrumpy (summer)   Garden   Outdoor Eating*   **No Credit Cards**

PORTHLEVEN   Ship Inn

Porthleven TR13 9JS
Tel: (0326) 572841
Open: 11.30-3, 6.30-11 (11.30-2.30, 7-11 winter)
Licensee: Colin Oakden

Small harbourside pub, romantically set in the cliffside and reached by a flight of stone stairs. Superb sea views from the window seats, and good log fires in winter, in the year-round upstairs bar; the family room is to the rear of this, while the ground floor 'cellar bar' is used only in summer. No chips.

Bar Meals: 12-2.30, 7-9.30; bar snacks both sessions   ***Typical Dishes:*** *mussels £2.95, sirloin steak £7.95, smoked haddock £6.95, fish pie £4.95, Dorset apple cake   Vegetarian Meals: curry £4.95   Children's Portions*   `Beer`   *Courage Best; Directors; John Smith's Bitter   Family Room   Garden   Outdoor Eating*   **No Credit Cards**

PORT ISAAC   Port Gaverne Hotel

Port Gaverne PL29 3SQ
Tel: (0208) 880244
Open: 11-3, 5.30-11
Licensees: Frederick and Marjorie Ross

Charming 17th century inn beautifully located in a sheltered little cove, in the same friendly and competent hands for well over 20 years. Recommended for bed and breakfast: the best of the cheerful en suite rooms have dormer windows and pretty sea views, and extras include a welcome cup of morning tea and the newspaper delivered to your door. Residents have their own bar and balconied lounge. Bars are nice too: the first decorated with old photographs and nautical bits and pieces, and two cosy little slate-floored snugs leading off at the rear; roaring open fires are blissful after a wuthering winter walk. Bar food is simple: nice sandwiches, a few home-made dishes like cottage or steak and kidney pie; in summer it's a cold buffet at lunchtime, and on Sundays all year. The smarter restaurant also does set Sunday roast lunches. Families are welcome, but rules quite specific – children are allowed in the restaurant or 'captain's cabin' (book), under sixes until 8pm only.

Bar Meals: 12-2, 7-10; bar snacks both sessions   `Beer`   *St Austell; Whitbread Children Allowed in to Eat   Garden*   ***Accommodation*** *(closed mid Jan-end Feb): 19 bedrooms, from £80 (single £40)   Check-in: all day*   **No Credit Cards**

PORTLOE Lugger: Another delightful cove-set pub, at the end of twisting lanes; pretty and well-run, with decent bar food.

RESTRONGUET PASSAGE   Pandora

Mylor Bridge, Falmouth TR11 5ST
Tel: (0326) 372678
Open: 12-2.30, 6.30-11 (all day summer inc Sun)
Licensees: Roger and Helen Hough

The Pandora's reputation grows and grows, not just for its delicious bar food, but because of its unrivalled position, a quaint old thatched pub right by the creek, with a patio and pontoon for fine weather. It gets absolutely packed with people in summer. Indoors is attractive and old fashioned, in its three cosy bars: polished flagstones, snug little alcoves, sometimes dangerously low wooden ceilings, a kitchen range and log fire. Local fish dominates the menu.

Bar Meals: 12-2, 7-9.30 (10 Fri/Sat); 12-2.30 (teas 3.30-6), 6.30-10 summer; bar snacks both sessions **Restaurant:** *7-10* **Typical Dishes BAR:** *mushroom and watercress soup £1.80, seafood hors d'oeuvre £3.75, chicken and asparagus pie £4.25, moules marinière £4.30, crab thermidor £5.50, lemon meringue pie £1.95* **RESTAURANT:** *Cornish crab soup £2.75, fresh salmon and prawns £4.50, roast duck and apricot sauce £11.95, seafood medley £13.75, local turbot with saffron and chive sauce £13.75, chocolate marquise £2.50* *Vegetarian Meals: lasagne* *Children's Menu/Portions* **Beer** *Bass; St Austell* *Children Allowed in Parts of Bar to Eat* *Riverside* *Outdoor Eating* **Credit Cards:** *Access, Visa*

ST AGNES   Driftwood Spars Hotel

Trevaunance Cove TR5 0RT
Tel: 087 255) 2428
Open: 11-11 (11.30 Fri/Sat)
Licensees: Gordon and Gill Treleaven

Tempting oasis of a place, on the edge of one of Cornwall's best beaches. Built in the 17th century, of local stone and slate, and using enormous ship's timbers and spars – hence the name. Two attractive bars, a friendly atmosphere, a new restaurant-cum-dining-room (with a similar menu at slightly higher prices), and simply furnished but well-maintained bedrooms with pine beds and stripey wallpaper.

Bar Meals: 12-2.30, 6.30-9.30 (all day July/Aug); bar snacks both sessions **Restaurant:** *7-9.30* **Typical Dishes BAR:** *curried cauliflower soup £1.45, mussels in cider and cream £2.65, casserole of lamb £4, pork chops in sour cream £4, sole and smoked salmon in filo pastry £4.50, blackberry and apple pie with clotted cream £1.60* *Children's Menu* **Cheese** **Beer** *Draught Bass; Ind Coope Burton Ale; Palmers IPA; Tetley Bitter* **Whisky** *Springbank* **Cider** *Addlestones* *Family Room (summer)* *Outdoor Eating* **Accommodation:** *10 bedrooms, all with showers, 7 fully en suite, from £50 (single £25)* *Children Welcome Overnight* *Cots Available* *Check-in: all day* **Credit Cards:** *Access, Amex, Diners, Visa*

ST CLEER   Stag Inn

Liskeard PL14 5DA
Tel: (0579) 42305
Open: 11-3, 6.30-11
Licensees: Donald Gardner and Donald Parker

Traditional village local with a cosy atmosphere, on the edge of Bodmin Moor. Go for the local dishes and specials: meat pies and casseroles, plus three varieties of lasagne: standard, vegetarian and, somewhat quaintly, ladies' portion, all of which are home prepared.

Bar Meals: 12-2.30, 7-9.30; bar snacks both sessions   **Typical Dishes:** *minestrone £1, egg mayonnaise £1.30, local farm duckling £6, beef, kidney and mushroom pie £3.50, chicken curry and rice £3.50, puddings £1.50   Vegetarian Meals: lasagne   Children's Menu   Children's Portions (Sun lunch)* Beer *Draught Bass; St Austell; Whitbread* Cider *Stonehouse   Patio/terrace   Outdoor Eating* **No Credit Cards**

ST DOMINIC Who'd Have Thought It: Handsome stone roadside pub with a red turkey-carpeted, pleasant interior; lunchtime and evening bar food includes steak and kidney pie, salmon en croute, chicken curry – prices from around £4.50. Bass, St Austell beers. Open: 11.30-2.30 (12-2.30 Sun), 7-11.

ST MAWES   Rising Sun

The Square TR2 5DJ   ❦
Tel: (0326) 270233
Open: 11-2.30, 6-11
Licensees: Brian Davies and Stephen Busby

Lively little hotel with delightful harbour views, a locally popular main bar, plain but with a much-coveted window seat, and a cane-furnished conservatory bar. Bar snacks and more pubby food (hot dishes from around £3.50) are also available, in addition to the more ambitious dishes listed here. Now owned by the St Austell brewery.

*Bar Meals: 11-2.30, 7-9; bar snacks both sessions   **Restaurant:** 12.30-2 (Sun only), 7.30-9   **Typical Dishes:** celery and stilton soup, wild woodland mushrooms, roulade of veal stuffed with shellfish mousse, rack of lamb, king scallops, crème brulée   Vegetarian Meals: cabbage strudel   Children's Menu/Portions* Beer *St Austell Bosuns Bitter, HSD* Whisky *Children Allowed in Bar to Eat   Patio/terrace   Outdoor Eating   Summer Barbecue   **Accommodation** (closed Jan/Feb): 12 bedrooms, 10 en suite   Children Welcome Overnight (minimum age 6)   Check-in: all day   **Credit Cards:** Access, Visa*

ST NEOT London Inn, off A38 Tel: (0579) 20263: Popular village inn next to the church; lunchtime and evening bar food in carpeted lounge dining area; some home-cooked dishes on the menu. Family room. Garden. Ruddles, Ushers beers.

SCORRIER   Fox & Hounds

Redruth TR16 5BS
Tel: (0209) 820205
Open: 11-2.30 (2 Sun), 6.30 (6 Mon-Thur)-10.30 (11 Fri/Sat)
Licensee: David Halfpenny

Well-liked, usually busy dining pub complete with smartly uniformed waitresses. One long bar is broken up by partitions; seating is modern red plush, tables copper-topped, and walls adorned with foxhunting prints; good log fires in winter; a small front extension is reserved for non-smokers. The food is reliably good, and it gets busy early.

*Bar Meals and Restaurant: 12-2 (1.30 Sun), 7-10 (9.30 restaurant; no food Mon eves); bar snacks both sessions   **Typical Dishes BAR:** Armenian soup £1.90, Lebanese lamb £4.05, steak and kidney pie £3.95, Hawaiian surprise £3.25, Lockshen pudding £1.75   **RESTAURANT:** mushroom and tarragon soup £1.90, Thai chicken satay £2.75, Highland steak £8.95, local trout in mushroom sauce £5.95, pavlova £1.75   Vegetarian Meals* Beer *Cornish Bitter, JD Dry Hop; Whitbread Flowers IPA   Children over 14 Allowed in Bar to Eat   Garden   Outdoor Eating* **No Credit Cards**

SENNEN COVE   Old Success Inn

off A30, by Whitesands Bay
Tel: (0736) 871232
Licensee: Mr F Carroll

Just a mile north of Land's End, an originally 17th century inn refurbished in smart
modern country hotel style, lots of plain white plaster, pine panelling, old
photographs, and smartly-dressed staff. The location is glorious, right beside a great
sweep of sand, with tremendous views; a good place for a winter getaway.
Recommended for bed and breakfast: comfortable en suite bedrooms, many with
inspiring prospects from their windows, all with solid pine furnishings (one four-
poster bed), attractive fabrics and all the usual facilities. The resident's lounge is
spacious and stylish. Bar food is fairly routine, but local fish and seafood shine.
There's also a restaurant.

Bar Meals: *daily lunchtime and evening* `Beer` *Draught Bass   Family Room   Garden*
Accommodation: *11 bedrooms, all en suite, from £50   Children Welcome Overnight*
Cots Available   Check-in: all day   **Credit Cards:** *Visa*

TREGADILLET   Eliot Arms

off A30, near Launceston PL15 7EU
Tel: (056 677) 2051
Open: 11-2.30 (inc Sun), 6-11
Licensee: John Cook

Also known as the Square and Compass, the pretty, creeper-covered Eliot Arms was
built in 1626, modernised in 1840, and contains a collection of some 66 clocks, as
well as a host of other memorabilia, littered across every square inch of wall. Lots of
little rooms ramble about, and nice old furniture is freely and successfully mixed
with modern seating. Tremendous character and varied food.

Bar Meals: *12-2 (1.30 Sun), 7-9.30; bar snacks both sessions*   **Typical Dishes:**
*mushroom soup £1.25, curried prawn cocktail £2.95, home-made vegetarian moussaka
£4.50, oriental-style special £7.95, fresh seafood platter £7.25, hazelnut pavlova
Vegetarian Meals   Children's Portions (some)* `Beer` *Cornish Best; Whitbread Flowers
IPA   Family Room   Outdoor Play Area   Garden   Outdoor Eating*   **Accommodation:** *2
bedrooms, from £30 (single £16)   Children Welcome Overnight   Cot Available   Check-
in: by arrangement*   **No Credit Cards**

TRELEIGH   Inn For All Seasons

Tel: (0209) 219511
Open: 11-3, 5.30-11
Licensees: John Milan and Frank Atherley

Now run full-time by the people who used to be at the Rising Sun at St Mawes,
and already looking promising for its food and accommodation. The bar is large and
attractively decorated, and much used for dining; service is friendly and welcoming.
There's an evening restaurant, where traditional roast Sunday lunches are also served.

Bar Meals: *daily lunchtime and evening; bar snacks both sessions*   **Typical Dishes:** *home-
made soup £1.65, lentil and wild mushroom terrine £2.95, home-cooked ham salad £4,
monkfish £4.75, game casserole £5.50, sticky toffee pudding £1.75   Vegetarian Meals
Children's Portions* `Beer` *Wadworth   Children allowed in Bar to Eat   Patio/terrace*
Accommodation: *Bedrooms, all en suite, from £50   Children Welcome Overnight*   **Credit
Cards**

UPTON CROSS Caradon Inn, on B3254: Pleasant roadside pub with a bustling friendly atmosphere, lots of locals, and a lunch and evening bar menu encompassing the routine and delicious – good home-made steak and kidney, and seafood pies. Garden. St Austell, Wadworth, Whitbread beers. Open: 11-3, 5.30-11.

CUMBRIA

ALSTON Angel, Front Street Tel: (0434) 381363: Handy for the Pennine Way, a lively, cosy old one bar pub with a splendid fire, excellent sandwiches, decent lunch and evening home cooking; children allowed in to eat. Bedrooms. McEwan, Tetley beers. Open: 11-4, 7-11.

APPLEBY   Royal Oak

Bongate CA16 6UN ❢
Tel: (07683) 51463
Open: 11.30-3, 6-11
Licensees: Colin and Hilary Cheyne

Ancient black and white coaching inn, dating back to the year 1100 in parts. Outside, leaded windows, flowers in tubs and hanging baskets; inside, a comfortable and popular meeting and eating place. A cosy tap room features oak panelling and an open fire; theres a relaxing, beamed lounge, and a little snug encloses the bar counter. The separate dining room, candlelit at night, has the same menu as the bar; in both, the evening menu is slightly different to the lunchtime list, and a nice wine list offers lots of half bottles. The homely little beamed and unevenly floored bedrooms have been refurbished (the whole inn is involved in a constant improvement programme). A pleasant resident's lounge looks out towards Appleby Castle.

Bar Meals and Restaurant: 12-2, 6.30 (7 Sun)-9; bar snacks lunchtime **Typical Dishes BAR and RESTAURANT:** *fishy, meaty canapes £4.45, marinated herrings £2.95, local lamb cutlets £4.45, coriander chicken £4.95, seafood mornay £5.45, chocolate hazelnut meringue Vegetarian Meals: leek and cheese sausages £3.75 Children's Menu* Cheese Beer *Draught Bass; Theakston Bitter; Yates Bitter* Whisky *Ardbeg, Longmorn Children Allowed in Bar to Eat Patio/terrace Outdoor Eating* **Accommodation:** *9 bedrooms, all 7 doubles en suite, from £50 (£30 single) Children Welcome Overnight Cot Available Check-in: all day* **Credit Cards:** *Access, Amex, Diners, Visa*

ASKHAM   Punch Bowl

Penrith CA10 2PF
Tel: (09312) 443
Open: 11-3, 6-11 (12-3, 7-11 winter)
Licensee: David Riley

Traditionally furnished village pub, prettily situated by the green, on the edge of the Lowther estate.

Bar Meals: 12-2, 7-9; bar snacks lunchtime **Typical Dishes:** *home-made soup £1.85, stilton fries with Cumberland sauce £3.20, turkey bake £4.85, smoked chicken £5.05, Riggindale pot £5.75, treacle and coconut tart Vegetarian Meals: mushroom and tomato lasagne Children's Menu* Beer *Whitbread Family Room Outdoor Play Area Garden* **Accommodation:** *4 bedrooms, sharing 2 bathrooms, double room from £37 (£18.50 per person; £10 per child under 10 years) Children Welcome Overnight Cots Available Check-in: by arrangement* **Credit Cards:** *Access, Visa*

BARBON   Barbon Inn

via Carnforth LA6 2LJ
Tel: (046 836) 233
Open: 12-3, 6.30-11
Licensee: Lindsey MacDiarmid

In a peaceful spot just off the A683 Sedburgh-Kirby Lonsdale road (signposted), this is a long and rangy, cream-painted coaching inn with a Georgian feel. Enter through the creaking iron gate into a pretty garden with outdoor furniture, and into the inn itself, which is immediately striking for its genteel and civilised air. Given this build-up, we found the actual accommodation disappointing, having been given a room only just large enough for two people to move about in, plain and unappealing in style, with a washbasin, wardrobe and view of the car park. The carpet was also a little past its best, but linen spotlessly clean. A windowless bathroom is functional rather than luxurious. Downstairs, things improve dramatically. An extremely pleasant bar with comfortable little rooms leading off is friendly and relaxing, with a nice crowd of regulars. Bar meals are very popular. But the dining room is the star here: it has real coaching inn character, is spaciously laid out, with good glass and silver, fresh flowers, and windows overlooking the garden. A small adjoining drinking area serves as a diners' bar. The set five-course dinners ($£14.95$) here are a popular feature. Home-made carrot soup was excellent and a piece of melon in elderberry champagne beautifully presented. Steak was a bit disappointing, being on the small side, tough and lukewarm, though accompanying vegetables were first rate, carrots, new potatoes and cauliflower, served in separate dishes. Trout was very good, hot and perfectly done, and puddings a varied bunch. Perhaps it might be wisest to stick with the good, reliable bar food, which features dishes like home-cooked steak and kidney pie, home-baked ham and Cumberland sausage. Service is hospitable and hard-working. Despite some reservations, this is a handsome and atmospheric place to visit for a meal, in a romantic rural area of great beauty.

Bar Meals: 12-2, 7-9; bar snacks both sessions **Restaurant:** *12.30-1.30 Sun only, 7.30-9* **Typical Dishes BAR:** *vegetable soup £1.35, garlic mushrooms £2.95, steak and kidney pie £4.95, Cumberland sausage £3.75, sirloin steak £8.50, chocolate fudge cake £1.75* **RESTAURANT:** *5-course menu £14.95* *Vegetarian Meals: mixed bean casserole £4.95* *Children's Portions* ■Beer■ *Theakston* ■Whisky■ *Children Allowed in Bar to Eat* *Outdoor Play Area* *Garden* *Outdoor Eating* **Accommodation:** *10 bedrooms, sharing 4 bathrooms, from £50 (single £26)* *Children Welcome Overnight Cots Available* *Check-in: all day* **Credit Cards:** *Access, Visa*

BASSENTHWAITE   Sun

off A591
Tel: (059 681) 439
Open: 11-3, 6-11 (12-2.30, 6.30-11 winter)
Licensees: Giuseppe and Josephine Scopelliti

Popular country inn at the top of a little village two miles from the lake. Two traditional bars with plenty of nooks and crannies, beyond the monumental bar counter. Very popular for its food, which, like its licensees, marries the Cumbrian and Italian together. Nice views from the front terrace.

Bar Meals: 12-1.30, 6.30-8.30 (not Sun eve) *bar snacks both sessions* **Typical Dishes:** *home-made meat or vegetable lasagne with garlic bread £4.75, Cumberland sausage, game or steak and kidney pie £4.25, honey and walnut tart £1.70* *Vegetarian Meals* ■Beer■ *Jennings* *Family Room* *Patio/terrace*

BASSENTHWAITE LAKE   Pheasant Inn

Bassenthwaite Lake CA13 9YE
Tel: (07687) 76234
Open: 11-3 (12-2 Sun), 5.30-10.30
Licensee: Barrington Wilson

Originally a farm, the Pheasant has been a hotel since 1826, and has a genuinely unspoilt atmosphere still wonderfully suggestive of the Victorian country inn. Its inimitable style occupies the place at which country house hotel and farmers' pub meet and converge. The bar has a smoky patina of age, in enfolding tones of terracotta, and simple country furniture; the lounge is more country house, with prettily patterned easy chairs gathered round a roaring log fire, and there are also two residents' lounges. Old-fashioned values extend to the banning of television on the premises. The dining room is non-smoking. Bedrooms are all prettily furnished and well-equipped, though true escapists may find some of them more modern in style than they might expect in so nostalgic a place. They will not be disappointed in the surrounding countryside, though.

Bar meals: 11.30-2; also bar snacks   Restaurant: 12.30-2, 7-8.30   Typical Dishes BAR: potato and watercress soup £1.35, smoked Scotch salmon £5.60, smoked Herdwick lamb £3.85, seafood platter £4.65   RESTAURANT: carrot and orange soup £1.20, potted Silloth shrimps £3, breast of chicken £5.10, steak and kidney pie £4.90, grilled lamb cutlets with redcurrant jelly £6.30, home-made fruit pie £2.10   Vegetarian Meals: blackeye bean bake £4.40   Children's Portions   Cheese (restaurant)   Beer Theakston Best; Draught Bass   Whisky   Family Room (not Sun)   Outdoor Play Area   Garden Outdoor Eating   Accommodation: 20 bedrooms, all en suite, from £82 (single £45) Children Welcome Overnight (minimum age 8)   Check-in: all day   No Credit Cards

BOOT   Burnmoor Inn

Eskdale CA19 1TG
Tel: (09467) 23224
Open: 11-3, 4.45-11
Licensees: Tony and Heidi Foster

In the same family for close on 40 years, the Burnmoor is an attractive gabled and white-painted hotel in glorious hill scenery at the foot of Scafell. The bar is basic rather than quaint, and the beamed ex-stable dining room rather starkly white, but softened by evening lighting; it has a similar menu to the bar, at slightly higher prices. They grow their own vegetables and fruit, and keep pigs and hens, so produce is assured of freshness. Mrs Foster brings an Austrian influence to the menu and wine list.

Bar Meals: 11-2, 6-9; bar snacks lunchtime   Restaurant: 7-8   Typical Dishes BAR: Wiener Schnitzel £5.40, Cumberland game pie £4.90, poached rainbow trout £5, apple strudel £1.40   RESTAURANT: similar menu, slightly higher prices   Vegetarian Meals: Spanish quiche £3   Children's Portions   Beer Jennings Bitter   Family Room Outdoor Play Area   Garden   Outdoor Eating   Accommodation (closed first 3 weeks Nov): 8 bedrooms, 6 en suite, from £36.80 (single £18.40)   Children Welcome Overnight (minimum age 6)   Check-in: by arrangement   Credit Cards: Access

BOOT   Woolpack Inn

Eskdale CA19 1TH
Tel: (09467) 23230
Open: 11-3, 6-11
Licensee: Gordon Fox

Recommended for bed and breakfast: a 17th century inn at the head of Eskdale valley in good walking country. Convivial public bar and attractive exposed-stone-walled lounge. Bright, traditional bedrooms come equipped with teamakers, electric blankets and cosy candlewick bedspreads. Four have their own shower cabinets; all share a neat public bathroom. Chintzy residents' lounge.

Bar Meals: 12-2, 6.30-9; bar snacks lunchtime **Restaurant:** *6.30-8.30* **Typical Dishes BAR:** *vegetable soup £1.10, steak and kidney pie £4.35, chilli £3.45, fishermans pie £4.50, sherry trifle £1.50* **RESTAURANT:** *garlic and lentil paté £2.45, venison pie £5.75, pork in cider £4.45, chicken and asparagus pie £4.45, peach and brandy gateau £1.75* *Vegetarian Meals: lasagne £3.95* *Children's Menu/Portions* **Beer** *Theakston* **Whisky** *Children Allowed in Bar to Eat* *Outdoor Play Area* *Garden Outdoor Eating* **Accommodation:** *8 bedrooms, 4 with showers, from £36 (single £18) Children Welcome Overnight* *Cot Available* *Check-in: all day* **Credit Cards:** *Access, Visa*

BOWLAND BRIDGE   Hare & Hounds

Grange-over-Sands LA11 6NN
Tel: (04488) 333
Open: 11.30-3, 5.30-11
Licensee: Peter Thompson

Truly rural, good-looking old inn owned by an ex-international soccer player. The red turkey-carpeted bar successfully blends ancient and modern, with its rough stone walls, discreet farming bric-a-brac and simple wooden furniture; open fires in winter weather. The dramatically high-ceilinged dining room is for residents only; the residents lounge is rather over-chintzified, and clashes a bit with the same red turkey carpeting. Bedrooms are immaculately kept, beamy and floral, but inspectors have commented on their small size. Delightful garden.

Bar Meals: 11.50-2, 6.50-9 (6.15-9.30 Sat); bar snacks both sessions **Typical Dishes:** *home-made soup £1.20, prawn platter £3.50, chicken Kiev £5.25, beef stroganoff £4.95, fillet steak £8.75* *Vegetarian Meals: vegetarian lasagne* *Children's Portions* **Beer** *Tetley Bitter* *Children Allowed in Bar to Eat* *Outdoor Play Area* *Garden* **Accommodation:** *16 bedrooms, 13 en suite, from £38 (single £29)* *Children Welcome Overnight* *Cots Available* *Check-in: all day* **Credit Cards:** *Access, Visa*

BROUGHTON-IN-FURNESS   Black Cock Inn

Princes Street L20 6WQ
Tel: (0229) 716529
Open: 11-3, 6-11
Licensee: Kevin Howarth

16th century street-side coaching inn. The renovated lounge bar has beams, a real fire and piney country furniture; the dining room seats 20, and has the same menu. Bedrooms are simple.

Bar Meals: 12-2, 6.30-9.30; bar snacks both sessions **Typical Dishes:** *home-made soup £1.20, garlic mushrooms £1.95, steak and kidney pie £4.25, venison £5.50,*

Cumberland sausage £4.25   Vegetarian Meals: vegetable lasagne   Children's Menu
Beer   *Ruddles Best Bitter, County; Webster's Choice   Family Room   Garden   Outdoor Eating*   **Accommodation:** *4 bedrooms, sharing 2 bathrooms, from £28 (single £14) Children Welcome Overnight   Cot Available   Check-in: all day*   **No Credit Cards**

BUTTERMERE   Bridge Hotel
Buttermere CA13 9UZ
Tel: (059 685) 252
Open: 10.30-11 (winter closed 3-6)
Licensee: D C McGuire

Handsome roadside stone-built hotel, with a quietly civilised country hotel interior – the bar is distinctly unpubby, but certainly relaxing (and is to be refurbished in January '92) ; the sitting room offers a successful clash of florals, with good squashy sofas and an open fire. Free afternoon teas are served to guests here, an admirable tradition. There's no television (poor reception), and vinegar is banned on the premises, for fear it will infect the beer.

Bar Meals: 12-2.30, 6-9.30; bar snacks both sessions   **Restaurant:** *7-8.30*   **Typical Dishes BAR:** *tomato and orange soup £1.75, deep-fried brie £1.75, spicy Cumberland sausage £4.50, beef and real ale pie £4.75, Cumbrian tatie-ash and beetroot £4.50, chocolate fudge cake £1.75*   **Restaurant:** *set price menu £15.75   Vegetarian Meals: mild bean curry £4.25   Children's Menu*   **Cheese**   **Beer**   *McEwan 80; Theakston Best Bitter, XB, Old Peculier; Younger Scotch   Children Allowed in Bar to Eat   Patio/terrace Outdoor Eating*   **Accommodation:** *22 bedrooms, all en suite, from £64 (single £39.50) Children Welcome Overnight   Cots Available   Check-in: from 3*   **No Credit Cards**

CARTMEL FELL   ★   Masons Arms
Strawberry Bank LA11 6NW   **FOOD**
Tel: (04488) 486   ☼
Open: 11.30-3, 6-11   !
Licensee: Helen J Stevenson

The only problem with the perfect pub is that too many people know about it, and so it is with the justifiably famous, well-loved Masons Arms, a prototype classic if ever there was one. The setting is glorious – perched on the hillside at Strawberry Bank with lakeland views in all directions, and the interior is equally inspiring, a series of quaint, unspoilt little farmhouse rooms. In the main bar are polished old flagstones, a big open fire, sagging ceiling beams, simple country furniture and well-chosen pictures. Several cottagey anterooms offer old pews, odd bits of furniture, a sideboard, an old stove, and a curious little cupboard set into the wall. Tiny thickset windows frame pretty valley views; rough stone walls are freshly whitewashed. Aside from excellent bar food, there's the widest choice of drinks to be found anywhere – including their own three homebrews, and, in edition II of their comprehensive bottled beer list, well over 200 interesting international names, including Kriek and Weizenthaler. The blackboard menu offers a pleasing variety of home-made dishes – though how they turn out such a volume of fresh food in such cramped conditions to so many people remains a mystery – including half a dozen or so vegetarian dishes. Simple country casseroles and hotpots are the star of the list, and pies are good too: the chicken and mushroom beautifully balanced, tender and chunky, with an excellent buttery pastry. Other choices might typically feature gravadlax, a French style fish soup, fennel and cashew nut crumble, delicious chicken or beef burritos, and creamy peppered kidneys. Puddings, mostly of the good old fashioned sort, are also good. Simple well cooked food tastes outstandingly fine in such splendid surroundings; be early for a seat on the terrace in summer. Four self-catering apartments converted from an old stone barn offer good holiday accommodation, let by the week. The Masons gets almost unbearably busy in summer; go in winter if you can.

Bar Meals: 12-2, 6-8.45; bar snacks both sessions   **Typical Dishes:** *home-made soup £1.95, barbecued spare ribs £5.95, Cumberland sausage and cider casserole £6.25, salmon and hake hotpot £5.95, banoffee pie £2.50   Vegetarian Meals: cashew nut and okra curry £4.95   Children's Portions*   Beer   *Lakeland beers (brewed here)*   Cider   *Weston's Family Room   Patio/terrace*   **No Credit Cards**

CASTERTON   Pheasant

Kirkby Lonsdale LA6 2RX   ♥
Tel: (05242) 71230   B&B
Open: 11.30-2.30, 6-11
Licensees: David and Sally Hesmond Halgh

This extremely well-maintained pebbledash building is at the heart of the village, next to the A683. Although roadside, it enjoys some fine views to the rear over open country to the hills beyond. At the front, a paved patio is furnished with rustic tables and bench seating. The entrance leads in through the Garden Room, a small summery lounge full of parlour plants and cane couches. Beyond this, the main bar area consists of three clean, well-lit adjoining rooms, a bar counter with ornate carved panelling central to them all. In the two main rooms, either side of the counter, there's plushly upholstered banquette seating in deep burgundy tones, polished wood tables topped with fresh flowers, and Pheasant dining mats, while aerial photos of the pub and countrified pictures dress the walls. The third room has a large mellow stone fireplace, gold-upholstered seating and magazines to read. The same menu applies both in bar and restaurant, the latter a long room, part panelled, with candlelight in the evenings, and waitress service, which can be frustratingly slow and lacks polish. Safe old standards like gammon, steaks and roast duck are capably if not excitingly done. While by no means luxurious, the rooms are certainly comfortable and well-kept, a number of them with fine antique furniture (including one four-poster), the rest with less impressive white fitted units. The nicest rooms have views over open land to the rear, and welcome little extras include mineral water and sweets.Compact bathrooms – one with shower only – lack natural light and are modestly appointed, though clean and well stocked with towels. There's a homely first floor residents lounge. Breakfasts are adequate, with good bacon.

Bar Meals: 12-2, 6.30-9.15 (also restaurant eves); bar snacks both sessions   **Typical Dishes:** *cream of celery, stilton and apple soup £1.85, home-smoked salmon, home-made beefsteak and kidney pie £6.25, veal chop £8.50, poached local salmon, sticky toffee pudding   Vegetarian Meals: pasta £4.75   Children's Portions*   Beer   *Theakston Old Peculier   Family Room   Garden   Outdoor Eating*   **Accommodation** *(closed Jan): 10 bedrooms, all en suite, from £52.50 (single £37.50)   Children Welcome Overnight   Cot Available   Check-in: all day*   **Credit Cards:** *Access, Visa*

CONISTON   Ship

Bowmanstead LA21 8HB
Tel: (05394) 41224
Open: 11-3, 5.30-1 (11-11 summer Sat)
Licensees: Derrick and Linda Freedman

Easily missed, standing above the A593 on the Coniston side of Bowmanstead, reached up a narrow unmarked track. Near a large campsite.

Bar Meals: 12-2, 5.30-9.30; bar snacks both sessions   ***Typical Dishes:*** *home-made soup £1.20, steak and Guinness pie £4, Cumberland sausage £3.70, grilled Coniston char (seasonal) £5.25, sticky toffee pudding £1.50   Vegetarian Meals: veggieburgers £3.60 Children's Menu* ■ Beer ■ *Hartleys XB   Family Room   Patio/terrace   Outdoor Eating **Accommodation:** 3 bedrooms, sharing a bathroom, from £26 (single £16)   Children Welcome Overnight   Cot Available* **No Credit Cards**

DALTON-IN-FURNESS   Brown Cow

Goose Green (off A590) LA15 8LQ
Tel: (0229) 62553
Open: 11-3, 6-11 (11-11 Sat, 12-10.30 Sun)
Licensees: C L and P Bell

Atmospheric, resolutely traditional country pub in the town, a surprisingly sleepy, village-like part of it, with a delightful garden. Go for the home-made dishes on the typed and photocopied menu.

Bar Meals: 12-2, 7-9.30 (12-9.30 Sun); bar snacks both sessions   ***Typical Dishes:*** *cauliflower soup £1.10, garlic mushrooms, home-made chicken curry, mixed grill, lemon sole cordon bleu, blackcurrant cheesecake (main courses from around £3.50)   Vegetarian Meals: home-made vegetable curry* ■ Beer ■ *Matthew Brown Bitter; Theakston Best Bitter, XB Family Room   Outdoor Play Area   Garden   Outdoor Eating* **No Credit Cards**

DENT   Sun

Main Street LA10 5QL
Tel: (05875) 208
Open: 11-2.30, 7-11 (all day summer)
Licensee: Martin Stafford

Delightfully old-fashioned village inn, pretty inside and out, with original timbers, comfortable furniture and a warming winter fire. They set up their own little brewery, a couple of miles down the road, in 1990, and now supply some other pubs in the area. Soup is the only starter offered.

Bar Meals 12-2, 6.30 (7 winter)-8.30;   bar snacks both sessions   ***Typical Dishes:*** *minestrone £1, home-made steak and kidney pie £3.15, home-made pastie £2.55, rump steak £4.35, mandarin cheesecake £1.50   Vegetarian Meals: lasagne £3   Children's Menu/Portions* ■ Beer ■ *Dent beers; Theakston, Youngers   Family Room   Garden Outdoor Eating **Accommodation:** 3 bedrooms, sharing a bathroom, from £27 (single £13.50)   Children Welcome Overnight   Cots Available   Check-in: all day* **Credit Cards:** *Access, Visa*

ELTERWATER   Britannia Inn

Ambleside WA22 9HP
Tel: (09667) 210
Open: 11-11
Licensee: David Fry

Well-loved old Lakeland perennial, white-painted and inviting, in a glorious spot, and very popular with walkers. The little beamed bar is simple to the point of spartan, in keeping with farming and rambling traditions, with other drinking rooms leading off; the atmosphere is informal and relaxed, particularly in winter when the crowds have subsided, and the log fires are crackling. Head for the new outdoor drinking area on a sunny day. There's a chintzy, comfortable resident's lounge and dining room. Bedrooms are clean, bright and pretty, with charming views.

Bar Meals: *12-2, 6.30-9; snacks 2-5*   **Restaurant:** *7.30 pm (Fri/Sat only in winter)* **Typical Dishes:** *soup of the day £1.15, home-made paté £1.75, Cumberland sausage £4, Cumberland pie £4.35, plaice stuffed with prawns £4.65, bread and butter pudding £1.75 Vegetarian Meals (bar): vegetable bake   Children's Menu/Portions* **Beer** *Jennings Mild, Bitter; Marston Pedigree; Mitchells Bitter* **Whisky** *Cragganmore, Linkwood   Children Allowed in Bar to Eat   Patio/terrace   Outdoor Eating* **Accommodation:** *9 bedrooms, 6 en suite, from £35 (single £17.50)   Children Welcome Overnight   Cots Available Check-in: all day* **Credit Cards:** *Access, Visa*

ESKDALE GREEN   Bower House Inn

Holmrook CA19 1TD
Tel: (09467) 23244
Open: 11-3, 5.30-11
Licensee: D J Connor

A perennial favourite, this unspoilt country inn, built as a farmhouse in the 17th century, has the advantage of a location in perfect and unimproved peace, in good walking country. There's also a warm welcome in the cosy beamed bar, with its polished darkwood furnishings and open log fire, and the separate pretty restaurant. Good food, and good accommodation too: best bedrooms are in the converted barn and garden cottage annexes, modern and well-equipped, with excellent bathrooms. Older, simpler, non-en suite rooms in the main building. Comfortable residents' lounge.

Bar Meals: *12-2, 6.30 (7 Sun)-9.30; bar snacks both sessions*   **Restaurant:** *7-9* **Typical Dishes BAR:** *home-made soup £1.40, home-made paté £2.50, steak and kidney pie £4.75, lasagne, grilled plaice £4.50, sticky toffee pudding £2* **RESTAURANT:** *smoked salmon paté, wild duck, halibut   Vegetarian Meals: spicy bean casserole   Children's Portions* **Cheese** **Beer** *Hartleys; Ruddles; Youngers   Children Allowed in Bar to Eat Outdoor Play Area   Riverside Garden   Outdoor Eating* **Accommodation:** *22 bedrooms, all en suite, from £53.50 (single £35)   Children Welcome Overnight   Cots Available Check-in: all day* **Credit Cards:** *Access, Visa*

FAR SAWREY   Sawrey Hotel

B5285,1 mile from Windemere car ferry LA22 0LQ
Tel: (05394) 43425
Open: 11-3, 5.30-11
Licensee: D D Brayshaw

Attractive white-painted 18th century rural inn, the main bar converted from the old stable block, with bedrooms above. We list 1992 room prices.

Bar Meals: *11.30-2.30; bar snacks lunchtime*   **Restaurant:** *12-2, 7-8.45*   **Typical Dishes BAR:** *turkey and rice broth £1, chicken liver paté £2.20, sirloin steak £5.90, Cumberland sausage £3.20, Esthwaite trout £4.20, raspberry cream puffs £1.50* **RESTAURANT:** *table d'hote dinner £12.95: carrot and coriander soup, roast local chicken, ham and asparagus mornay, poached halibut, chocolate pudding   Vegetarian Meals: savoury quiche   Children's Portions* **Beer** *Jennings Bitter; Theakston Best, Old Peculier* **Whisky** *Cragganmore   Family Room   Outdoor Play Area   Garden   Outdoor Eating* **Accommodation** *(closed fortnight over Christmas): 17 bedrooms, 13 en suite, from £43 (single £21.50)   Children Welcome Overnight   Cots Available   Check-in: all day* **No Credit Cards**

FAUGH   String of Horses

Faugh CA4 9EG   `B&B`
Tel: (0228) 70297
Open: 11.30-3, 5.30-11
Licensee: Anne M Tasker

White-painted L-shaped substantial old inn, with a beamed and panelled lounge complete with food servery (but no real ale because there's no cellar), and a second, 'Cocktail' bar, also oak panelled, but now reserved for restaurant diners. White-painted bedrooms, well-maintained rather than stylish, have modern prints, carpets and floral fabrics, although three have four-posters and exciting bathrooms. A swimming pool and sauna for residents' use add to the attraction of staying here.

Bar Meals and Restaurant: 12-2.30, 6.30 (7 restaurant)-10; bar snacks lunchtime *Typical Dishes BAR:* broccoli soup £1.25, eggs Benedict £3.95, pork calypso £5.50, steak and oyster pie £4.95, chicken Madras £4.75, bread and butter pudding with brandy custard £1.95   **RESTAURANT:** French onion soup £2.50, veal scaloppine £12.75, lamb in port £11.25, sautéed beef Funchal £12.95   *Vegetarian Meals:* celery and cashew nut risotto   *Children's Menu/Portions*   `Cheese`   *Children Allowed in Bar to Eat Patio/terrace   Outdoor Eating   **Accommodation:** 14 bedrooms, all en suite, from £65 (single £58)   Children Welcome Overnight   Cots Available   Check-in: all day   **Credit Cards:** Access, Amex, Diners, Visa*

GARRIGIL George & Dragon: 17th century village pub with lots of exposed stone and wood in bar and dining room.

GREAT BROUGHTON Broughton Craggs: Tel: (0900) 824400: Country hotel in attractive grounds half a mile to the east of the village. Extensive views from elegant lounge bar, home-cooked meals daily, lunch and evening; also restaurant à la carte. Bass, Jennings, Theakston beers.

GRIZEBECK Greyhound, on A595 Tel: (0229) 89224: Comfortable roadside inn at the foot of Kirkby Fell, with local slate floors, real fires, a family room and garden. Especially popular at weekends for lunch and evening bar meals; decent home cooking. John Smith's Bitter. Open: 12-3, 6-11.

HAWKSHEAD   Drunken Duck Inn

Barngates, 2 miles north of Hawkshead; follow Barngates   `FOOD`
signs from B5286 LA22 0NG   `B&B`
Tel: (05394) 36347
Open: 11.30-3, 6-11
Licensees: Peter and Stephanie Barton

There are fabulous views towards Ambleside from this white pebbledash pub which stands in splendid isolation in glorious Lakeland countryside, the perfect peace spoilt only by the occasional low-flying military jet. Despite its seclusion, the pub is extremely popular with walkers and tourists, and weekends can get especially hectic. In good weather, they spill out onto the rustically furnished small front patio, and the grass over the narrow road. The country-style interior, a main bar and three adjoining rooms, features original beams, open fires, stripped settles, ladderback chairs and lots of landscape and sporting prints. Main bar walls are covered with snarling fox heads, displays of fishing flies (the pub has its own trout-filled tarn), deer skulls and other local memorabilia. Justly popular bar food, blackboard-listed in the bar, has a bistro-style feel, changes daily, and makes good use of fresh local produce. A good selection of pates precedes dishes like beef and vegetable braise, courgette risotto, game casserole, Mediterranean pasta or Dijon lamb casserole – decent pieces of lamb in a creamy Dijon mustard sauce with potatoes and vegetables, served with a chunk of good granary bread. Sponges like chocolate and cherry (bit heavy), and almond and walnut are typical of the sturdy pudding choice. It's reasonably priced, reasonable cooking. Ten excellent en suite bedrooms are all individually designed using Laura Ashley style wallcovering and fabrics in soft, restful shades. Furniture varies from room to room, stripped wood and units in some, antique pieces in others. All the usual modern creature comforts include impeccable bathrooms with fluffy towels and good lighting. Service is young, willing and friendly.

Bar Meals: 12-2, 6.30 (7 Sun)-9; bar snacks lunchtime **Restaurant:** *8 pm Fri/Sat* **Typical Dishes BAR:** *cauliflower and sweetcorn soup £1.50, venison paté £2.95, lamb and potato curry £4.95, crispy duck £5.25, tuna and chilli in filo pastry £4.95, sticky toffee pudding* **RESTAURANT:** *4-course set dinner £18 Vegetarian Meals: lentil and peanut bake £4.75* Beer *Jennings; Marston; Theakston; Yates* Whisky *Family Room Outdoor Play Area Patio/terrace Outdoor Eating* **Accommodation:** *10 bedrooms, all en suite, from £59.50 (single £40) Children Welcome Overnight Cots Available Check-in: all day* **Credit Cards:** *Access, Visa*

HAWKSHEAD   Queen's Head Hotel

Hawkshead LA22 0NS
Tel: (09666) 271
Open: 11-5, 6-11
Licensee: Tony Merrick

Pretty white-painted Elizabethan inn in an attractive village street. Bigger than it appears from the outside, opening out into two panelled bar areas, comfortable rather than characterful, and a neat rear dining room. Low beams and simple furnishings characterise the main house bedrooms; cottage rooms are all en suite and the two newest ones have Beatrix Potter-inspired decor. Plushly comfortable residents lounge.

Bar Meals: 12-2.30, 6.15-9.30; bar snacks both sessions **Restaurant:** *6.15-9.30* **Typical Dishes BAR:** *broccoli and stilton soup £1.40, Queen's crunchy mushrooms, tandoori chicken, Queen's Head Yorkshire pudding, cod, chips and mushy peas (main courses from around £4.50), sticky toffee pudding £2.25 Vegetarian Meals Children's Portions* Beer *Hartleys; Robinsons Family Room Patio/terrace Outdoor Eating* **Accommodation:** *13 bedrooms, 10 en suite, from £44 (single £28.50) Children Welcome Overnight Check-in: all day* **Credit Cards:** *Access, Amex, Visa*

HELTON Helton Inn on Haweswater road Tel: (09312) 232: Basic end-terrace pub; home cooking lunch and evening, real fire, no music, lovely views from garden. Theakston beer. Open: 12-3, 6-11 (closed winter lunch; 8-11 Tue-Sat eve).

HAWKSHEAD Kings Arms The Square Tel: (09666) 372: Attractive interior, delightful terrace overlooking Elizabethan square, fruit machine and piped music. Bar food lunch and evening; old-fashioned bedrooms at reasonable prices. Nice children tolerated. Theakston beers. Open all day.

HESKET NEWMARKET   Old Crown

A mile south east of B5299 at Caldbeck
Tel: (06998) 288
Open: 11.30-3, 5.30-11

Friendly little fell-side pub, unspoilt to the point of needing a little cheering up. The simple main bar has assorted tables, a little counter, and old floor coverings, lots of books, and beam-hung mugs. Country café style dining room. Their own home-brewed beers, and decent home cooking (the curries are particularly fancied) are a big draw: but note they might only offer soup and a roll some lunchtimes. Worth a visit just for the delightful village.

Bar Meals: *lunch and evening; bar snacks both sessions*   ▀Beer▀   *own brews; Thwaites Family Room   Garden*

HEVERSHAM   Blue Bell Princes Way Tel: (05395) 62018. Extended, pristine black and white inn, traditionally styled inside. Some home-made, simple dishes on the good value bar menu. Family room. Bedrooms. Garden. Sam Smiths beers. Open: 11-3, 6-11.

KESWICK   Pheasant
Crosthwaite Road CA12 5PP
Tel: (07687) 72219
Open: 11-3, 5.30-11
Licensees: David and Marion Wright

Homely little inn just off the A66, about a mile from the town centre. A nice old-fashioned bar, its walls decorated with colourful cartoons. The menu may look ordinary but it's all local and fresh. Bedrooms are neat and simple.

Bar Meals and Restaurant: *12-2, 5.30-8; bar snacks both sessions*   **Typical Dishes:** *main courses £4.50-£7.50: local sirloin and T-bone steak, ham and eggs, Cumberland sausage, lemon meringue   Children's Portions*   ▀Beer▀   *Jennings Bitter   Children Allowed in Bar to Eat   Patio/terrace   Outdoor Eating*   **Accommodation:** *3 bedrooms, sharing a bathroom, from £30 (single £18)   Children Welcome Overnight   Cot Available   Check-in: all day*   **No Credit Cards**

KESWICK George, St John's Street Tel: (07687) 72076: Hotel coaching inn in town centre; no music, open fires, popular with walkers; home cooked food lunch and until 8.30. Theakston, Yates beers. Open all day.

KIRKBY LONSDALE   Snooty Fox Tavern
Main Street LA6 2AH
Tel: (05242) 71308
Open: 11-3, 6-11
Licensees: Andrew Walker and Jack Shone

An excellent breakfast served in civilised style in your own bedroom is one of the pleasures of staying at the Snooty Fox, a pristine white-painted town centre Jacobean inn. Bars are traditional, with lots of wood, stone and bric-a-brac, and the dining room, with its country furniture, lovely fireplace and charmingly eclectic collectables dotted about is a welcoming place to eat (same menu throughout the pub).

Bar Meals: *12-2.30, 7-10 (10.30 dining room, 9.30 Sun); bar snacks both sessions*   **Typical Dishes BAR:** *venison and redcurrant soup £1.65, prawn and ginger filo parcels £3.10, Lakeland bacon, apple and sage crusty pie £4.90, fresh fettucini stir fry with chicken and vegetables £4.25, monkfish £8.95, Key lime pie £2*   **RESTAURANT:** *similar menu and prices   Vegetarian Meals: Corsican pancake £3.15   Children's Portions*   ▀Beer▀   *Hartleys XB   Family Room   Outdoor Play Area   Garden   Outdoor Eating*   **Accommodation:** *3 bedrooms, all en suite, from £45 (single £25)   Children Welcome Overnight   Cots Available   Check-in: all day*   **No Credit Cards**

KIRKBY STEPHEN   Kings Arms Hotel

Market Street CA17 4QN
Tel: (0930) 71378
Licensees: Jenny Reed and Keith Simpson

Small convivial hotel bar, with open fire and panelled walls, as well as simple bar
food like steak and kidney or shepherds pie. The lunchtime dining room is probably
a better bet, prettily laid and decorated, with fresh fish, steaks, roasts and salads, and
good cheeses to follow. Booking essential for the traditional Sunday lunch.
Bedrooms are also recommended, traditional in style with lacy bedspreads and solid
period furniture.

Bar Meals and Restaurant: 12-1.45, 7-8.45; bar snacks `Cheese` `Beer` *Whitbread*
Children Allowed in Bar to Eat   Garden **Accommodation:** *9 bedrooms, 3 en suite, from*
£50   Children Welcome Overnight   Check-in: all day **Credit Cards:** *Access, Visa*

LANGDALE   Old Dungeon Ghyll Hotel

100 yards off B5343 at head of valley
Tel: (09667) 272
Licensee: Neil Walmsley
Open: 11-11

Cosy and attractive walkers' bar, with coveted window seats cut into the
monumental stone walls, a warming open fire, and good views, in a popular inn
spectacularly set in excellent fell-walking country. Simple home cooking; need to
book for a proper evening meal. They now have a pizza oven.

Bar Meals: 12-2, 6-8.30 **Typical Dishes:** *venison soup £1.30, home-made pizzas,*
Cumberland sausage, chilli con carne (main courses from around £4)   Children's Menu
`Beer` *Marston; Theakston; Yates   Children Allowed in Bar to Eat   Garden*
Accommodation: *10 bedrooms, 4 en suite (showers), from £40   Children Welcome*
Overnight **Credit Cards:** *Access, Visa*

LITTLE LANGDALE   Three Shires

Ambleside LA22 9NZ
Tel: (09667) 215
Open: 11-11 (12-3, 8-10.30 winter)
Licensee: Ian K Stephenson

Appealingly plain, slate-floored walkers' bar, where bar meals are served (you can
also eat out by the stream); other public rooms are less enchanting. Bedrooms are
modern, with white laminate furniture and floral curtains, light and bright if not
romantic, but with pretty views through their sash windows. Delightful countryside.

Bar Meals: 12-2, 6.30-9; bar snacks both sessions **Restaurant:** *7.15-8* **Typical**
Dishes BAR: *chicken and sweetcorn soup £1.35, mushrooms in cream and garlic £2.70,*
steak and kidney pie £4.60, game pie £5.20, local baked trout £5.60, strawberry pavlova
RESTAURANT: *set price dinner £15.50   Vegetarian Meals: vegetable stroganoff*
Children's Menu/Portions `Beer` *Ruddles County; Webster's Yorkshire Bitter* `Whisky`
Milton Duff   Family Room   Garden   Outdoor Eating **Accommodation** *(closed Jan): 11*
bedrooms, 7 en suite, from £61 (single £37.50)   Children Welcome Overnight   Cot
Available   Check-in: all day **No Credit Cards**

METAL BRIDGE   Metal Bridge Inn

Floriston CA6 4HG
Tel: (0228) 74206
Open: 11-3, 5.30-11
Licensee: Paul Ockleford

A change of licensee at this popular, picturesque bed and breakfasting inn on the Esk.

*Bar Meals: 12-2, 5.30-9.30; bar snacks both sessions   Restaurant: 7-9.30   **Typical Dishes BAR:** home-made soup £1.20, home-made paté £1.85, steak pie £4.25, Cumberland sausage £3.95, home-made lasagne £3.95   **RESTAURANT:** paté £2.45, rump steak £8.95, chicken supreme £6.95, salmon steak £7.95   Children's Menu/Portions   Family Room   Riverside Garden   **Accommodation:** 3 bedrooms, all en suite, from £45 (single £30.50)   Children Welcome Overnight   Cot Available   Check-in: by arrangement   **Credit Cards:** Access, Amex, Diners, Visa*

NEWBY Newby Bridge Inn on A590 Tel: (05395) 31222: By the river, in its own grounds, with tables on the lawn. Children welcome. Bar and restaurant meals daily; lunch and evening. Wide-ranging menu. Bedrooms. Youngers beer.

OXEN PARK   Manor House

Two miles off A590 LA12 8HG   ❢
Tel: (0229) 861345
Open: 11-3, 6-11
Licensees: Kevin and Jennifer Pyne

Roadside inn set in a small hamlet on the edge of Grizedale Forest; spick and span, original beams, nice open fire. Purpose built (screened) caravan facility.

*Bar Meals and Restaurant: 12-2, 6.30-9.30 (7-9 Sun); bar snacks both sessions   **Typical Dishes BAR and RESTAURANT:** farmhouse mushroom soup £1.20, local potted shrimps £3.25, home-made Hungarian goulash £4.95, local Esthwaite trout £5.65, scampi provencale £6.95, apple pie £1.50   Vegetarian Meals: stilton, broccoli and mushroom quiche   **Beer**   Hartleys XB   Children Allowed in Bar to Eat   Outdoor Play Area Patio/terrace   Outdoor Eating   Summer Barbecue   **Accommodation:** 4 bedrooms, sharing one bathroom, from £39 (single £26)   Children Welcome Overnight   Cots Available   Check-in: all day   **No Credit Cards***

PENRITH Agricultural Hotel, Castlegate Tel: (0768) 62622: Characterful market town pub with an impressive Victorian bar. Popular with farming community and offering a menu of cheap wholesome home cooking to match. Live jazz on Thursday evenings. Lunch and evening bar meals. Children allowed in to eat; patio/terrace. Modest bedrooms. Marston beer. No Credit Cards.

RAVENSTONEDALE Kings Head off A65: Refurbished throughout, but beamed bar, log fires, lunch and evening meals.

SCALES   White Horse

On A66, near Threlkeld CA12 4SY   FOOD
Tel: (07687) 79241
Open: 11.30-2.30, 6.30-11 (12-2, 7-11 winter)
Licensees: Laurence and Judith Slattery

Set back from the A66 between Keswick and Penrith, the whitewashed White

Horse is surrounded by stunning Cumbrian countryside and is within easy reach of splendid walking country. Immaculately kept, the interior has a strong hunting and sporting theme, its uneven whitewashed walls covered with horsey prints, photographs of local meets, and caricatures, while a large hanging backs up the white horse theme. The low beamed ceiling, slate fireplace (customers put coins between the gaps, later collected for charity), well-polished copper pans, stuffed birds and animals, and lots of plants all add to the rustic atmosphere. Old banquettes upholstered in deep red surround well-polished tables topped with small vases of flowers. There are also a couple of small panelled ante-rooms, one of them turned into a cosy little snug. Local produce features strongly on the short lunchtime bar menu, including Woodall of Waberthwaite's excellent dry-cured ham, served with free-range eggs and their delicious Cumberland sausages. There might also be a fresh soup, potted shrimps or a ploughmans with two cheeses, apple and oatcake. Delicious sticky toffee pudding to finish. Evenings bring candlelight and a more restauranty menu; booking is essential, as it gets extremely busy. Starters like a garlic mushroom tart with brioche, followed by poached rainbow trout with lemon and parsley butter, pork fillet with sherry and mushroom sauce or breast of chicken with a mild curry sauce all testify to first-rate fresh produce. Prices are fair: expect to spend in the region of £30 for two for a three course meal with coffee.

Bar Meals: *12-2, 7-8.30; bar snacks lunchtime*   **Typical Dishes:** *home-made soup £1.50, garlic mushroom tart £1.95, Cumberland sausage with apple sauce and port jelly, chicken breast with curry cream sauce, Scottish salmon with dill mayonnaise (lunchtime main courses from £5), brown bread and honey ice-cream*   *Vegetarian Meals: spinach-stuffed pancakes with blue cheese sauce   Children's Portions* Cheese   Beer   *Marston* Whisky   *Children Allowed in Bar to Eat   Patio/terrace*   **Credit Cards:** *Access, Visa*

SEATHWAITE   Newfield Inn

Duddon Valley, Broughton in Furness LA20 6ED
Tel: (0229) 716208
Open: 11-3, 6-11
Licensee: Andrew Burgess

Sensitively modernised, genuinely unspoilt old country inn in good walking area which sidesteps the main tourist routes. Wordsworth wrote 34 sonnets about the Duddon Valley. 16th century bar with oak beams and original slate floors. Dining room with same menu (wider choice in the evening).

Bar Meals: *12-2.30, 6-9; bar snacks both sessions*   **Typical Dishes:** *herrings in Madeira sauce £1.75, 10 oz sirloin steak £8.50, home-made steak pie £3.75, Cumberland sausage £3.75, pear and chocolate crumble £3.75   Vegetarian Meals: vegetarian moussaka £3.75 Children's Portions* Beer   *MeEwans; Theakston* Whisky *Lavagulin 16 yr   Family Room   Outdoor Play Area   Garden   Outdoor Eating   Summer Barbecue* **Accommodation:** *two self-catering holiday flats, £130-£170 a week (also short breaks in winter)*   **No Credit Cards**

SEDBERGH   Dalesman

Main Street LA10 5BN
Tel: (05396) 21183
Open: 11-3, 6-11
Licensee: Barry Garnett

Well-kept old market town inn with spartan public bar (no juke box), popular buttery, and pavement tables.

Bar Meals and Restaurant: 12-2, 6-9.30; bar snacks both sessions   **Typical Dishes**
BAR and RESTAURANT: *home-made soup £1.50, prawn cocktail, steak, gammon,
venison, sherry trifle Vegetarian Meals: vegetable lasagne Children's Menu/Portions*
Beer *Dalesman Bitter; Ind Coope Burton Ale; Tetley Mild, Bitter; Younger No. 3
Family Room Children Allowed in Bar to Eat Patio/terrace Outdoor Eating*
Accommodation: *6 bedrooms, 4 en suite, from £38 (single £27) Children Welcome
Overnight Check-in: all day **Credit Cards:** Access, Visa*

TALKIN   Blacksmiths Arms

near Brampton CA8 1LE
Tel: (06977) 3452
Open: 11-3.30, 6-11
Licensees: T and P Bagshaw

Home cooking by landlady Pat Bagshaw, in 19th century smithy conversion; a
recent kitchen extension has geared them up for the 1992 season. Dishes listed here
are at the top end of the all-purpose menu; simpler bar meals include liver and
onions and steak and kidney pie.

Bar Meals: 12-2, 7-9; bar snacks both sessions **Typical Dishes:** *home-made soup
£1.35, deep-fried camembert £2.45, venison in red wine and blackcurrant sauce £6.25,
paté-filled fillet steak chasseur £8.95, fillet of salmon poached in white wine £6.50, apple
pie Vegetarian Meals: lasagne Children's Menu/Portions* **Beer** *Theakston;
Whitbread Boddingtons Family Room Patio/terrace* **Accommodation:** *5 bedrooms, all
en suite, from £40 (single £28) Children Welcome Overnight Cot Available Check-in:
all day* **Credit Cards:** *Access, Visa*

TALKIN Tarn End, Talkin Tarn: Lakeside farmhouse pub, very popular for food
and nice bedrooms; boats for residents.

ULVERSTON   Bay Horse

Canal Foot LA12 9EL
Tel: (0229) 53972
Open: 11-3, 6-11
Licensee: Robert Lyons

Very popular, well-regarded dining pub, decidedly restaurauty in emphasis, but they
have also been offering not too extravagantly priced informal food in the bar at
lunchtimes for the last year or two. The pub itself is charming and traditional, and
owned by the same people who have the Miller Howe hotel on Windermere.

Bar Meals: 12-2 (not Mon); bar snacks **Restaurant:** 12-1.30, 7-9; restaurant closed
Mon lunch and all day Sun **Typical Dishes BAR:** *home-made soup £1.35, savoury
terrine with cranberry and ginger puree £3.95, bobotie £5.50, ham and mushroom
macaroni £5.50, cod, courgette, apple and water chestnut bake £6.25, home-made
puddings £2.50* **RESTAURANT:** *chilled mango and lime soup £1.80, smoked duck
breast £4.25, steak in sour cream, brandy and paprika on tagliatelle £11.25, medallions of
Lakeland lamb on a damson cheese and parsley crouton £11.95, fresh salmon stuffed with a
lemon sole and pistachio mousse £11.25, summer pudding £3.50 Vegetarian Meals:
mushroom and onion paté-stuffed apple £5.25* **Beer** *Mitchells Children Allowed in
Bar to Eat Riverside Patio/terrace* **Accommodation** *(from March 1992): 6 bedrooms, all
en suite, from £55 Children Welcome Overnight (minimum age 12) Check-in: by
arrangement* **Credit Cards:** *Access, Visa*

WASDALE HEAD   Wasdale Head Inn

Signposted from Gosforth CA20 1EX
Tel: (09467) 26229
Open: 11-11 (12-10.30 Sun); mid-Nov to mid-March 6-11 Fri, 11.30-3,
5.30-11 Sat, 12-3 Sun
Licensee: Jaspar Carr

Famous walkers' and climbers' pub in splendid isolation with steep fells by way of
backdrop, a setting of romantic grandeur. Ritson's bar, named after its first landlord
(the world's biggest liar) has high ceilings, a polished slate floor, wood-panelling, and
cushioned old settles. There's a residents bar and relaxing lounge. Bedrooms are
comfortable and unfussy.

Bar Meals: 11-3, 6.30-10; bar snacks both sessions   Restaurant: 7.15 for 7.30
Typical Dishes BAR: home-made vegetable soup £1.40, garlic mushrooms £2.75,
Cumberland sausage £5.75, steak and kidney pie £4.10, Cumberland tatie pot £5.75,
hedgerow crumble £2.25   RESTAURANT: 5 courses £16: love apple and claret soup,
smoked breast of duck, chicken and stilton roulade, roast lamb pauillac, beef fillet with madeira
and Dijonnaise sauce, baked apples with honey and Calvados   Vegetarian Meals: vegetable
goulash `Cheese` *(restaurant)* `Beer` *Jennings Bitter; Theakston Bitter, Old Peculier;*
Yates Bitter `Whisky` *Glendronach, Tamnavulin   Family Room   Riverside Garden*
Outdoor Eating Accommodation (closed mid-Nov–28 Dec and mid-Jan–mid-March): 10
bedrooms, all en suite, from £96 (single £48.50) dinner included   Children Welcome
Overnight   Cots Available   Check-in: all day   Credit Cards: Access, Visa

DERBYSHIRE

ACRESFORD   Cricketts Inn

on A444
Tel: (0524) 760359

Old coaching inn on the Leicestershire border. Try the hot daily specials; home-
cooked meat sandwiches are also very popular.

Bar Meals: lunch and evening; bar snacks both sessions   Typical Dishes: home-made soup,
chicken casserole, local trout, lamb Shrewsbury (main courses from £4) `Cheese` `Beer`
Draught Bass   Children Allowed in Bar to Eat (lunchtime)   No Credit Cards

APPERKNOWLE Yellow Lion 45 High Street Tel: (0246) 413181: Stone-built
village house, lots of character in comfy lounge; decent bar food lunchtime and
evening, from snacks to restaurant meals; children allowed in dining room. Garden.
Bass, Tetley beers. Open: 12-2 (3 Sat), 5-11.

ASHFORD-IN-THE-WATER   Ashford Hotel

near Bakewell DE4 1QB
Tel: (0629) 812725
Open: 11-11
Licensee: John Dawson

Pleasant, well-kept roadside hotel with local stone exterior and a bar "that meets today's requirements of the discerning drinker", or so they say. Red patterned carpets, lots of brass nick–nacks, chintzy curtains and mint green plush-topped stools. Separate dining room cum restaurant with pink cloths. Nice bedrooms.

*Bar Meals: 12-2, 6.30 (7 Sun)-9   Restaurant: 12-2 (Sun only), 7-9.30   **Typical Dishes BAR:** broccoli and almond soup with amaretto, avocado with prawns, filled Yorkshire pudding, home-made lasagne, cidered pork with sage and apple, treacle sponge (main courses from around £4)   **RESTAURANT:** seafood special, Derbyshire lamb steak with mint and thyme butter, goujons of chicken with lemon, beef Wellington (main courses from £10 up) Vegetarian Meals: cheese, nut and vegetable crumble   Children's Menu/Portions* `Cheese` `Beer` *Draught Bass* `Whisky` *Family Room   Outdoor Play Area   Garden   Outdoor Eating   **Accommodation:** 7 rooms, 2 with 4-poster beds, all en suite, from £65 (single £50)   Children Welcome Overnight   Cot Available   Check-in: all day   **Credit Cards:** Access, Amex, Diners, Visa*

ASHFORD-IN-THE-WATER Black Bull: Refurbished lounge much used for dining; one or two interesting things on the menu.

ASHOVER Black Swan, Church Street: Single room Bass pub with dining area; lunchtime and evening bar meals. Pretty village. **Red Lion**: Handsome pub with decent food, real ales.

BIRCH VALE   Sycamore

Sycamore Road
Tel: (0663) 42715
Open: 12-3, 6-11; all day weekends
Licensees: Malcolm and Christine Nash

Downstairs drinking bar with indoor fountain, and upstairs dining bar, so popular that a "queuing board" has been introduced. Hot stone cooking a speciality. Beware the weekend discos (not Saturday night).

*Bar Meals: 12-2.30, 7-10; bar snacks both sessions   **Typical Dishes:** home-made soup £1.40, all-day breakfast, steak and mushroom pie £3.75, marinated chicken breast £4.95, hot stone steaks from £6.50, home-made puddings £1.75   Vegetarian Meals   Children's Menu* `Beer` *Bass; Wards   Family Room   Outdoor Play Area   Garden   Outdoor Eating   **Accommodation:** bedrooms, all en suite, from £50 (single £35)   Children Welcome Overnight*

BIRCHOVER   Druid Inn

Main Street DE4 2BL   `FOOD`
Tel: (0629) 650302
Open: 12-3, 7-12
Licensees: Brian Bunce and Nigel Telford

Climb the long hill from the B5056 signposted Stanton Moor Stone Circle, and be sure not to miss a glimpse of Row Tor, high above the pub, where extraordinary fissures and passageways through the rock suggest (rather than prove) very early occupation by man; hence the Druid's unusual name. Proprietor Brian Bunce this year marks his first decade at the Druid by seeking ways to expand the menus, extend the seating and improve the service here. It's an egalitarian sort of place, frequented in about equal numbers by both county types and country walkers; Range Rovers and Transits rub tyre tracks in the car park. From portal to chimney pot it's entirely ivy-covered, with a terrace in front and, to one side, a restaurant area on two floors, connected by a tiled umbilical passageway. There's no bar at which to stand, except when ordering food, and not much in the way of good beer either, but it's the food they all come for. The menu fills four blackboards, including a complete vegetarian selection from almond and sultana risotto through vegetable and fruit curry to tagliatelle alla Scala. Main dish favourites span the globe: Shangri-La stir-fry, Pacific lamb with ginger and pineapple, before heading home again via beef with Guinness and mushrooms to Row Tor medieval chicken with raisins, apricots and cinnamon. A dish of lamb rogan served with nuts and fruit, partnered by an onion bhaji and mint yoghurt is a feast for one, and practically sufficient for two. Steak is variously sauced or comes in pies with mussels or mushrooms, and there's plenty of fish, steamed salmon, baked trout or seafood pasta, all partnered by an above average range of good value wines by single glass or whole bottle.

Bar Meals and Restaurant: *12-2, 7-9.30 (9 winter)*   ***Typical Dishes BAR and RESTAURANT:*** *cream of cauliflower soup £1.70, prawns in hot garlic butter with apple and celery £3.85, Old English beef stew with dumplings £5.10, Cantonese chicken £6.50, poached trout with Russian walnut sauce £8.20, Bakewell pudding £2.30   Vegetarian Meals: tagliatelle with stilton, walnuts and mushrooms £3.80   Children's Portions* Beer *Marston Pedigree* Whisky *Children Allowed in Bar to Eat   Patio/terrace* ***Credit Cards:*** *Access, Amex, Diners, Visa*

BRASSINGTON   Olde Gate

Well Street DE4 4HJ
Tel: (062 985) 448
Open: 12-2.30 (3 Sat), 6-11
Licensees: Paul and Ellen Burlinson

17th century pub built of local stone and oak timbers salvaged from the Armada. No music, no fruit machines or space games. Very traditional and attractive inside, with open log fires in winter; simple wooden furnishings and oak panelled dining room.

Bar Meals: *12-1.45, 7-9 (not Sun/Mon eve); bar snacks lunchtime*   ***Typical Dishes:*** *home-made soup £1.50, smoked salmon £3.95, ragout of lamb £5.95, steak, kidney and mushroom pie £5.50, seafood tagliatelle £6.25, apple pie £1.75   Vegetarian Meals: lasagne £5.25* Beer *Marston   Children over 10 Allowed in Bar to Eat   Garden Outdoor Eating   Summer Barbecue* ***No Credit Cards***

CASTLETON   Nags Head

Castleton S30 2WH
Tel: (0433) 620248
Open: 11-3, 6-11
Licensee: C J Walker

17th century coaching house built of severe grey local stone, in a tiny village at the head of Hope Valley, under the hilltop site of Peveril Castle. Bar meals are served both lunchtime and evening, but the emphasis is very much in the elegant two-tiered restaurant at night. Bedrooms are also elegant, and furnished in a handsome period style; three with four-posters, all well-equipped. The most expensive offer spa baths; the cheapest shower and toilet only. A bright first floor residents' lounge is done out in chintz and bamboo.

Bar Meals: *11.30-3.45, 6-10.45 (12-3.45, 7-10.15 Sun); bar snacks both sessions*
Restaurant: *12-2 (2.30 Sun), 7-10*   **Typical Dishes BAR:** *minted pea and ham soup*
£1.55, deep-fried paté-filled mushrooms £2.85, home-made steak and kidney pie £4.95,
fresh codling in parsley sauce £4.95, hot dressed crab with garlic breadcrumbs £4.95,
chocolate and hazelnut meringue £2.20   **RESTAURANT:** *creamy chicken and smoked*
salmon soup £2.50, asparagus and ham pancake mornay £5.95, chicken and scampi in
lobster sauce £10.75, veal mozzarella £10, turbot champagne £13.75 Vegetarian Meals
Children's Portions ▪ Beer ▪ *Draught Bass* **Accommodation:** *8 bedrooms, all en suite,*
from £52 (single £42)   Children Welcome Overnight   Cot Available   Check-in: all day
Credit Cards: *Access, Amex, Diners, Visa*

DERBY   Dolphin Inn

6/7 Queen Street DE5 1NR
Tel: (0332) 297741
Open: 10.30-11
Licensee: N Barker

The oldest pub in Derby, dating from the 16th century, in a conveniently central
spot. No juke box or machines. Simple no-frills pub food.

Bar Meals: *until 7; also bar snacks*   **Typical Dishes:** *vegetable soup £1.20, steak and*
kidney pie £3.40, Worcester sausages £3.30, grilled rainbow trout £3.60   Vegetarian
Meals: vegetables au gratin £2.95   Children's Menu/Portions ▪ Beer ▪ *Draught Bass,*
Highgate Mild ▪ Cider ▪ *Addlestones   Children Allowed in Bar to Eat   Garden   Outdoor*
Eating   **No Credit Cards**

DERBY Alexandra, 203 Siddals Road Tel: (0332) 293993: One of the Tynemill
pubs, which profess to be green in policies – real meat, organic vegetables. Bar meals
lunchtime; not Sunday. Daily specials, nice cheese. Patio/terrace. Bateman, Marston
beers. Open: 11-3, 4.30 (6 Sat)-11.

DRONFIELD   Old Sidings

91 Chesterfield Road S18 6XE
Tel: (0246) 410023
Open: 12-11
Licensees: Anne and Bill Stanaway

The extensive menu features an 11-strong vegetarian list at this popular dining pub,
now run by the experienced Stanaways, previously at the Red House in Sheffield.

Bar Meals: *12-2.30, 6-8.30 (not Sun eve); bar snacks both sessions*   **Restaurant:** *12-5*
Sun only, 7-9.45 (not Sun)   **Typical Dishes BAR:** *vegetable soup £1.25, home-made*
giant Yorkshire pudding with onion gravy £1.45, beef curry £2.85, gammon steak £3.85,
stuffed giant Yorkshire pudding £2.85, treacle sponge £1.45   **RESTAURANT:** *stilton*
and celery soup £1.45, smoked mackerel paté £2.35, rack of lamb with tarragon and
cucumber sauce £6.75, fur and feather pie £4.55, salmon steak in a raspberry vinegar and
pink peppercorn sauce £6.25, bread and butter pudding £1.45   Vegetarian Meals: home-
made fruit and vegetable curry   Children's Menu/Portions ▪ Beer ▪ *Bass; Marston;*
Whitbread   Family Room   Children Allowed in Bar to Eat   Patio/terrace   **Credit Cards:**
Access, Visa

EDNASTON Yew Tree: Four rooms served from a central servery; decent bar
meals lunch and evening. Draught Bass.

EYAM   Miners Arms

Water Lane S30 1RG
Tel: (0433) 30853 (630853 from spring '92)
Licensees: Mr and Mrs Cook

Run by the Cooks for almost 30 years, pleasant 17th century picturesque village inn
with original leaded light windows, mock Tudor beams and open fires. Refurbished
bars. Some of the simply appointed bedrooms are in an annexe.

Bar Meals: 12-2.30; bar snacks Restaurant: 12-2.30, 7-9.30 Typical Dishes BAR:
vegetable broth £1.50, smoked chicken and melon £2.25, chopped steak with onion gravy
£3.50, fillet of pork in apple and Calvados sauce £5, cod mornay £4, chocolate roulade
Children's Portions `Cheese` *Children Allowed in Bar to Eat   Garden Outdoor Eating*
Accommodation: 5 bedrooms, 1 en suite, from £30 (single £25)   Children Welcome
Overnight   Cots Available   Check-in: all day   No Credit Cards

EYAM   Rose & Crown

Main Road S30 1QW
Tel: (0433) 30858
Open: 12-3 (not Mon), 7.30-11.20
Licensees: D G and L Mason

Beautifully situated in the romantic 'plague village' of Eyam, in the National Park.
The spartan modernised bar, with woodchip walls and dralon banquettes, is about to
be refurbished as we go to press. Modest overnight accommodation at modest
prices.

Bar Meals and Dining Room: 12-2, 7.30-9; bar snacks both sessions Typical Dishes
BAR: vegetable soup £1.45, sirloin steak £8.60, home-made steak and kidney pie £3.35,
seafood platter £4.35, treacle tart £1.40   DINING ROOM: similar menu and prices
Children Allowed in Bar to Eat   Outdoor Play Area   Patio   Outdoor Eating
Accommodation: 3 bedrooms, all with showers, from £34 (single £25)   Children Welcome
Overnight (minimum age 10)   Check-in: all day   No Credit Cards

FARNAH GREEN   Bluebell

Hazelwood, Belper DE5 2UP
Tel: (0773) 826495
Open: 12-3, 7-11
Licensees: Frederick and Winifred Silver

Smartened up dining pub with a separate restaurant which is redolent of a well-
heeled city Indian restaurant in decor.

Bar Meals and Restaurant: 12-2, 7-9.30 (no food Mon, Sun eve; restaurant food only on
Sat eve/Sun lunch)   Typical Dishes BAR: soup £1.25, mushroom pancake £3.95, steak
and kidney pie £4.35, bacon and black pudding brunch £4.15, Sloppy Joe £3.95, bread
and butter pudding £1.70   RESTAURANT: soup £1.45, Bluebell smokies £4.95,
duckling à l'orange £10.50, carré d'agneau roti £10.75, fresh lobster £17.50, bread and
butter pudding £2.95   Vegetarian Meals: vegetables en croute   Children's Portions
`Cheese` `Beer` *Draught Bass* `Whisky` *Knockando 16 yr   Family Room   Garden*
Outdoor Eating   Credit Cards: Diners, Visa

FOOLOW   Lazy Landlord

Foolow S30 1QR
Tel: (0433) 30873
Open: 11.30-3, 6-11
Licensees: D W, M D and K Holden

Old beamed Peak District pub, in a scenic village complete with duck pond, village green and old stone cross. Reliably good food from a menu that combines old English favourites with more modern cooking. Exciting specials and perfectly cooked vegetables. A second room has a more relaxed atmosphere than the often bustling main bar, with a variety of seats, a high ceiling, and open fire. There's also a dining room (same menu).

Bar Meals and Dining Room: 11.30-2, 6-10 (12-2, 7-9.30 Sun); bar snacks both sessions   *Typical Dishes:* mushroom and coriander soup £1.65, goat's milk cheesecake £2.75, steak and kidney pie £4.85, chicken supremes £6.50, trout with prawns £6.75, summer pudding £1.80   Vegetarian Meals: vegetable crumble   Children's Menu   `Cheese`   `Beer`   Ward Sheffield Best Bitter; Darley Thorne Dark Mild   Children Allowed in Bar to Eat   Outdoor Eating   **No Credit Cards**

GREAT HUCKLOW Queen Anne off B6049 Tel: (0298) 871246. Tiny tap room and dining lounge in friendly, family-run village pub, decent and often interesting bar meals, weekend lunchtime and daily evening. Real fires, no music; freshly squeezed orange juice; garden. Tetley beers. Open: 12-3 (not winter weekdays), 7-11.

GRINDLEFORD   Maynard Arms

On B6521 north of village   S30 1HP
Tel: (0433) 30321
Open: 11-3, 5.30-11 (all day Sat)
Licensees: Robert Graham and Helen Siddall

Tastefully refurbished early Victorian inn, with comfortable and spacious bedrooms, three of them 'superior', two with four-posters, the rest attractive with decent laminate furnishings. Two relaxing bars and charming lounge.

Bar Meals: 12-2, 5.30-9.30; bar snacks both sessions   *Typical Dishes:* filled Yorkshire puddings £3.50, fish and chips £3, steak, kidney and mushroom pie £3.95, curries £3.50, home-made puddings £1   Vegetarian Meals: lasagne £3.75   Children's Menu   `Beer`   Stones   Children Allowed in Bar to Eat   Garden   *Accommodation:* 13 bedrooms, from £60 (single £50)   Children Welcome Overnight   Check-in: all day   **Credit Cards:** Access, Amex, Diners, Visa

HOLLINGTON   Red Lion

near Ashbourne DE6 3AG
Tel: (0335) 60241
Open: 12-2.15 (not Mon), 7-11
Licensees: Ken and Rosemary Price

One for ardent curry fans; the smell can get quite overpowering otherwise! But they do English dishes, with fresh vegetables (no chips) too. Central bar serves two little eating areas; village pool room bar at rear. Lino floors, bentwood chairs, formica table tops, ketchup bottles – café-style and very popular.

Bar Meals: 12-1.30, 7-9.30   bar snacks lunchtime   *Typical Dishes:* vegetable and

*chicken soup £1.20, sirloin steak, home-made beef, chicken and vegetable curries, lamb chops
in blackcurrant, mint and wine sauce, drunken bread and butter pudding   Vegetarian Meals:
giant pastie* **Beer** *Marston Pedigree   Family Room   Outdoor Play Area   Garden
Outdoor Eating   Summer Barbecue* **No Credit Cards**

HOPE   Poachers Arms

Castleton Road S30 2RD
Tel: (0433) 20380
Open: 12-3, 6-11
Licensee: Gladys Bushell

Copper-topped tables, beams, plaster walls, and a pair of stuffed fox heads, in this
Peak District National Park pub. Reliably good bar food. Bedrooms are variously
sized, some very large; white woodchip or patterned walls, furniture utilitarian
laminate or cheap reproduction, with the odd antique mixed in.

*Bar Meals: 12-2, 6-10; bar snacks both sessions   **Restaurant:** 12-1, 7-9.30   **Typical
Dishes BAR:** rich game soup £1.25, roast of the day, game casserole, steak and kidney pie
(main courses from £4.80), lemon cheesecake   Vegetarian Meals: vegetable duet £4.90*
Beer *Courage Directors; John Smith's Bitter   Family Room   Children Allowed in Bar
to Eat Patio   Outdoor Eating   **Accommodation:** 6 bedrooms, all en suite, from £52
(single £39)   Children Welcome Overnight   Cot Available   Check-in: all day   **Credit
Cards:** Access, Visa*

ILKESTON Durham Ox, Durham Street Tel: (0602) 324570: Back-street local.
Cheap and cheerful bar lunches, always featuring real ale beef casserole. Wards beers.
Open: 11-4, 6-11 (11-11 Sat).

KINGS NEWTON Hardinge Arms: Characterful bar with smart dining area
leading off and splendid carved counter. Children welcome.

LITTLE LONGSTONE   Packhorse

off B6465, near Monsal Head
Tel: (062 987) 471
Open: 11-3, 5-11 (all day Sat)
Licensees: Sandra and Mark Luthgoe

18th century village cottage tavern, full of old-fashioned charm, very popular with
walkers. Real fires, no music, animals in the steep little garden. Beef dripping
sandwiches a local favourite.

*Bar Meals: lunchtime and evening; bar snacks both sessions   **Typical Dishes:** home-made
soup £1.25, spare ribs £2, steak and kidney pie £3.65, chilli £3.65, duck with
Cumberland sauce £5.70, home-made puddings £1.50   Children's Menu* **Beer**
Marston   Children Allowed in Bar to Eat (until 9 pm)   Garden

---

LITTON   Red Lion

Litton SK17 8QU
Tel: (0298) 871458
Open: 12-2 (weekends), 7-11
Licensees: M, N and PM Hodgson

16th century country dining pub overlooking the village green. Open coal and log
fires, oak beams, stone walls, fresh flowers, and a strong local following. Country
restaurant cooking with a strong French influence.

Bar Meals: 12-1.15 *(weekends only), 7-9; bar snacks lunchtime* **Typical Dishes:** *broccoli and stilton soup £1.40, French onion tart, venison casserole, half chicken with nut stuffing, fresh halibut (main courses from £4), brown bread and butter pudding* Vegetarian Meals: *aubergine layer* Children's Portions Cheese Beer *Theakston Bitter; Whitbread Boddingtons Bitter* Children Allowed in Bar to Eat Outdoor Play Area **Credit Cards:** Access, Visa

MARSTON MONTGOMERY Crown: Warming fires and well-presented food.

MELBOURNE White Swan: Popular for Sunday lunch; ambitious bar food all week. Children welcome. Garden. Marston Pedigree.

OAKERTHORPE   Anchor Inn

Chesterfield Road DE5 7LP
Tel: (0773) 833575
Open: 11.30-3, 7-11
Licensees: S W Henshaw and J R Flint

Pleasant roadside pub with exposed stone, real fires, red turkey carpeting and large bow windows providing lots of light. A simple lunchtime menu is supplemented by specials, more so in the evening. Three tables in the bar are designated for family mealtime use.

Bar Meals: 12-2.30 *(2 Sun); bar snacks lunchtime* **Restaurant:** *12-2, 7-9.30 (12-1.30, 7-9 Sun)* **Typical Dishes BAR:** *home-made soup of the day £1.25, prawn cocktail £2.95, home-made steak and kidney pie £3.95, baked gammon with apricot and ginger stuffing £4.95, grilled cod fillet with parsley sauce £4.50, two chocolate cheesecake £1.40* **RESTAURANT:** *similar menu, higher prices pm* Vegetarian Meals: *mushroom stroganoff* Children's Portions (some) Beer *Draught Bass; Marston Pedigree* Children Allowed in Bar to Eat (3 tables for family use at mealtimes) Outdoor Play Area Garden Outdoor Eating **No Credit Cards**

OVER HADDON   Lathkil Hotel

near Bakewell DE4 1JE
Tel: (0629) 812501
Open: 11.30-3, 6-11
Licensee: R P Grigor-Taylor

FOOD
B&B

Signposted from the B5055 White Peak scenic route, just two miles from Bakewell, the Lathkil scores with residents and visitors alike with its unparelleled views of the Peak National Park and spectacular Lathkil Dale several hundred feet below. A pub since at least 1813, and in the same hands for the last ten years, the spelling of Lathkil, we are told, "is extremely voluntary", a sentiment which could equally well be applied to the clientele – who carefully leave muddy walking boots in the hallway – and to the service, which is always friendly without ever truly pampering. Extensions in the 1930s created a Victorian style bar whose use of miniature-sized tables and chairs gives an illusion of space; there's also a post-war dining room extension with huge picture windows for making the most of the view. Local landscape photographer Ray Kenning has contributed a stunning set of portraits of Derbyshire's great houses, Haddon, Chatsworth, Hardwick and Kedleston among them. Lunch is served buffet-style from a hot and cold counter to the rear: soup or paté served with rolls, steak and kidney pie, beef and mushroom casserole, lasagne and quiche are all self-served with vegetables or salads (never fewer than seven). Puddings are home-made and frequently change at peak times: cheesecake, walnut flan and treacle tart giving way to fruit crumble, Bakewell pudding or lemon meringue. Dinner à la carte, and Sunday lunches (reservations only) produce garlic mushrooms (£1.95), smoked salmon, and mussels vinaigrette (£2.30), grilled Lathkil trout (£7.50), sole stuffed with crabmeat (£7.95), and scallops and chicken with leeks and stilton (£7.75). Four bedrooms, converted to include bathrooms some five years ago (one a single with shower only), may be limited in space, but are comprehensive in facilities: all have colour television, clock radios, telephone and a personal bar and fridge. The best two, at the front, look across the dale to Youlgrave and the original village of Nether Haddon, now part of the Haddon estate. From the rear rooms, there are less edifying views, of fellow-patrons' wheel-hubs in the car park!

Bar Meals: 12-2; bar snacks lunchtime **Restaurant:** *7-9 Mon-Sat* **Typical Dishes** **BAR:** *watercress soup £1, paté de campagne £2, steak and kidney pie £4.10, beef and mushroom casserole £4.10, lasagne £3.90, lemon meringue pie £1.50* **RESTAURANT:** *smoked salmon £2.85, chicken Hartington £7.75, half a duck £9.95, grilled whole lemon sole £9.95, banoffee pie £2* *Vegetarian Meals: brie and broccoli pithiviers* *Children's Portions* *Family Room (lunchtime only)* *Patio/terrace* *Outdoor Eating* **Accommodation:** *4 bedrooms, all en suite, from £60 (single £32.50)* *Children Welcome Overnight* *Check-in: all day* **Credit Cards:** *Access, Diners, Visa*

SHARDLOW   Malt Shovel

The Wharf
Tel: (0332) 792392
Open: 11.30-3, 5.30-11
Licensees: Peter and Gillian Morton-Harrison

Trent and Mersey Canal-side pub, dating from 18th century and originally a busy maltings; the conversion is successful, spacious and pubby; be early for a window seat. Plain bar menu enlivened by home-cooked daily specials, but all good value and very popular.

Bar Meals: Mon-Sat lunchtime; bar snacks **Typical Dishes:** *home-made soup £1, beef casserole £2.75, chilli £2.65, salmon and prawn pie £3.75, Elizabethan pork £4.25* *Vegetarian Meals* *Children's Portions* **Beer** *Marston* *Children Allowed in Bar to Eat* *Patio* **No Credit Cards**

SPARROWPIT Wanted Inn: Cosy, friendly old stone pub in glorious countryside. Home-cooked food.

STANTON Gate Inn: Woodlands Road (A444) Tel: (0283) 216818: Popular local with dining area leading off bar. Lunch and evening meals Monday-Saturday. Garden. Marston Pedigree. Open: 11-3, 6-11.

TIDESWELL   George

Commercial Road (B6049)
Tel: (0298) 871382
Open: 11-3, 7-11

18th century market town coaching inn. Small snug, traditional locals' (noisy) tap room, dining lounge and dining room proper. Eclectic menu includes good steak and kidney pie; cheap and generous garlic bread. Good value bedrooms.

Bar Meals: 12-2, 7-9 **Typical Dishes:** *steak and kidney pie, poachers pie, local stuffed trout (main courses from £4)* *Vegetarian Meals: mung bean and mushroom biryani* **Beer** *Hardys & Hansons* **Accommodation:** *5 bedrooms, from £35* *Children Welcome Overnight* **Credit Cards:** *Access, Visa*

WARDLOW   Bulls Head

near Tideswell, Buxton SK17 8RP
Tel: (0298) 871431
Open: 11-3 Sat (closed Tue/Thur lunchtime, and some Mon/Wed/Fri lunchtimes!), 6.30-11
Licensee: Selina Wetherall

Unassuming-looking but very popular village dining pub. Note peculiar, ad hoc lunchtime hours; Friday lunchtime is usually a safe bet; otherwise join the evening crowds.

Bar Meals: 12-2.15 (see opening hours note), 6.30 (7 Sun)-9.30 **Typical Dishes:** *leek and onion soup £1.25, home-made chicken liver paté £1.95, lasagne al forno £4.25, steak and kidney pie £4.25, seafood mornay £4.25, apple and blackberry crumble £1.95 Vegetarian Meals: vegetable lasagne £4.50 Children's Portions* Beer *Mansfield; Wards Family Room Outdoor Play Area Garden Outdoor Eating* **Accommodation:** *2 bedrooms, sharing a bathroom, from £35 Children Welcome Overnight Cot Available Check-in: all day* **No Credit Cards**

WARDLOW Three Stags Heads, Wardlow Mires. Delightfully rustic cottage pub with pottery business, and home-made food, often unusual/Italianate. Worth a look. Theakston, Younger beers. Open, and food served, all day.

WOOLLEY MOOR   White Horse

White Horse Lane DE5 6FG   FOOD
Tel: (0246) 590319
Open: 11.30-2.30 (3 weekends), 6.30-11
Licensees : Bill and Jill Taylor

The White Horse could justifiably be called a "find", were it not for the fact that hundreds of regulars have already homed in on the Taylors' smart, friendly pub over the last five years. Approached from the A61 at Stretton, it's scarcely on the beaten track, being in a tiny hilltop hamlet above the river Amber at the point where it flows into Ogston reservoir. The large paddock and garden borders the memorial sports field; a sandpit, swings, and small adventure playground help keep the youngsters happy. There are at least two dozen trestle tables outside: bag one for a summer lunch, but remember the number before going inside to order. Within, there's restaurant seating for around 60 people, and it fills up quickly, so booking is recommended. This dining area, reached through a stone archway, was originally the pub lounge, a cottagey, carpeted area in two sections, with large picture windows and attractive lace-clothed tables. On the printed menu, meals with chips include grilled gammon, and steak pie, as well as straightforward, unrepentant chip butties, large or small. For more interesting eating, look to the specials board: crispy cauliflower with a yoghurt dip, deep-fried potato skins, a sole fillet stuffed with crab and scallops, vegan bulgar wheat chilli, vegetarian potato and sweetcorn flan, turkey and broccoli crumble, Riber farm pork and chestnut sausage (with broccoli and tomatoes, topped with cheese), all these constitute pub fare with a difference. It's substantial stuff, nicely cooked and presented and, above all, tasty. Meanwhile, the Smoke Room still remains the village local, with its quarry-tiled floor, red leather banquettes, Britannia tables and prominent dartboard; Monday night dominoes are played in a seriously competitive spirit. This is where a good drop of ale comes in. In addition to Draught Bass, a healthy rotation of guest beers is publicised well in advance, a good proportion of them from independent breweries. Piped music, when playing, is of the restful kind. This is a smart and impressive pub, professionally managed, and it runs like clockwork.

Bar Meals and Restaurant: 11.30-2 (2.15 Sun), 6.45-9 (6.30-9.30 Fri/Sat); restaurant closed Sun eve; bar snacks both sessions   **Typical Dishes:** *seafood chowder £1.05, crispy courgettes with yogurt and sour cream dip £1.75, venison sausage bake £4.25, turkey and broccoli crumble £4.50, home-made game pies £3.40, treacle and walnut pie £1.40 Vegetarian Meals: bean goulash £3.95   Children's Menu/Portions* `Cheese` `Beer` *Draught Bass   Outdoor Play Area   Garden   **No Credit Cards** (under review)*

DEVON

AXMOUTH   Ship

on B3172 EX12 4AF   ♛
Tel: (0297) 21838
Open: 11-2 (2.30 summer), 6-11
Licensees: Jane and Christopher Chapman

Comfortable village pub with a large collection of dolls, a real fire, decent bar food, and a large interesting garden with birds from Newbury Wildlife Hospital recouperating in it.

Bar Meals: 12-2, 7-9 (10 summer); bar snacks both sessions   **Typical Dishes:** *home-made soup £1.50, steak, kidney and Guinness pie £4.95, whole local plaice £4, vegetarian special £2.50-£3.50, blackcurrant sponge £1.75 Vegetarian Meals   Children's Portions* `Beer` *Devenish; Whitbread   Family Room   Outdoor Play Area   Garden   Outdoor Eating   **No Credit Cards***

BANTHAM   Sloop Inn

near Kingsbridge TQ7 3AJ   ♛
Tel: (0548) 560489
Open: 11-2.30 (12-2.30 Sun), 6-11
Licensee: Neil Girling

16th century landlord John Widdon was a notorious smuggler, and the atmospheric flagstoned interior of the Sloop still has a strongly nautical atmosphere, and lots of old seagoing memorabilia. Recommended for bed and breakfast: good-sized rooms, modern furnishings, and good value. Just 300 yards from the sea.

Bar Meals: 12-2, 7-10; bar snacks both sessions   **Typical Dishes:** *turkey broth £1.40, garlic prawns £3.10, local lamb steak £6.30, fresh skate wing £7.40, giant cod fillet £6.55, summer pudding £1.95   Vegetarian Meals: vegetable pasta £4.80* `Beer` *Bass; Ruddles; Ushers* `Whisky` `Cider` *Churchwards   Family Room   Patio/terrace   Outdoor Eating   **Accommodation** (closed Dec-Feb): 5 bedrooms, 4 en suite, from £22.50 Children Welcome Overnight   Cots Available   Check-in: by arrangement   **No Credit Cards***

BEER   Anchor Inn

Fore Street EX12 3ET
Tel: (0297) 20386
Open 11-11 (11-2.30, 5.30-11 winter)
Licensee: David M Boalch

A fresh fish pub, offering not only local haddock, cod and sole, but also brill, monkfish, salmon and a pleasing variety of seafood in season, including lobsters. They're also nice to vegetarians. The cliff-top garden overlooks the sea.

Bar Meals and Restaurant: 12-2, 7-9.30 (9 winter); bar snacks both sessions **Typical Dishes BAR** *and* **RESTAURANT:** *chicken and sweetcorn soup, main courses mostly local fish, wide variety of prices Vegetarian meals Children's Menu (limited)* Beer *Wadsworth 6X* **Credit Cards:** *Access, Visa*

BLACKAWTON   Normandy Arms

Chapel Street TQ9 7BN
Tel: (080 421) 316
Open: 11.30-3, 6-11 (12-2.30, 7-11 winter)
Licensees: Jonathan and Mark Gibson

15th century modernised and well-run village pub of great popularity. The Normandy Landings theme is much in evidence. Reliably good food, all home-made using local produce, and four comfortable and attractive bedrooms.

Bar Meals: 12-2, 7-9.30 (10 Sat, 9 Sun); bar snacks both sessions **Typical Dishes:** *cream of mushroom soup £1.60, prawns £3.85, Blackawton steak £8.25, Devonish pork £7.75, trout Cleopatra £8.25, tipsy cake £2.50 Vegetarian Meals Children's Menu/Portions* Beer *Draught Bass; Blackawton Bitter, Gold (summer), 44 Special (winter); Ruddles Best Bitter Family Room Outdoor Play Area Garden* **Accommodation:** *4 bedrooms, all en suite, from £46 (single £30) Children Welcome Overnight Cot Available Check-in: all day* **Credit Cards:** *Access, Visa*

BROADCLYST New Inn, Whimple Road: Warm and friendly farmhouse conversion full of equestrian bric-a-brac. Home cooking includes their own bread.

BROADHEMBURY   Drewe Arms

Broadhembury EX14 0NF
Tel: (040 484) 267
Open: 11-3, 6-11
Licensee: Kerstin Burge

Quaint little thatched pub, in a similar Tudor village unique in its preservation. The pub was built in 1298 to house masons working on the local church; the delightful interior, with its romantic mullion windows, features some 15th century linenfold panelling. Reliably good food since the Burges took over a couple of years ago; local fish a speciality. Nice garden.

Bar Meals and Restaurant: 12-2, 7-10; bar snacks both sessions **Typical Dishes** **BAR:** *home-made soup £2.25, seafood selection £4.95, bobotie £5.95, fresh codling £5.25, fresh mussels £5.65, home-made puddings £2.25* **RESTAURANT:** *similar starters and puddings; fillet of turbot £11.95, sea bass £13.95, John Dory £10.95 Vegetarian Meals: mushroom stilton and garlic bake Children's Portions* Cheese Beer *Bass; Cotleigh Children Allowed in Bar to Eat Garden Outdoor Eating Credit Cards: Access, Visa*

BUTTERLEIGH   Butterleigh Inn

On the hill road from Tiverton to Cullompton, EX15 1PN   �
Tel: (0884) 855407
Open: Mon-Fri 12-2.30 (3 Sat), 6 (5 Fri)-11
Licensees: Mike and Penny Wolter

Unspoilt farming pub in glorious countryside, just three miles from junction 5 of the M5 motorway. The two-part main bar is half lounge, half public end with simple

wooden furnishings; a tiny snug takes just four intimate tables. Inglenook fireplace
and old fashioned pub games. Good home-made food, getting smarter all the time;
good value B&B. No children indoors, and over-14s only for overnight stays.

Bar Meals: 12-2, 7-9.45 (9.30 Sun); bar snacks lunchtime   *Typical Dishes: carrot and
apple soup £1.95, potted cheese reserve £2.25, grilled quail with port and redcurrant sauce
£5.95, Devon farmhouse pie £3.50, spinach and mushroom pancake £3.50, chocolate rum
pot £1.95   Vegetarian Meals: mushroom and almond croustade £3.50*   Beer Cotleigh
Harrier, Tawny, Old Buzzard; Mitchells Best Bitter   Cider   *Outdoor Play Area
Garden   Outdoor Eating   **Accommodation:** 2 bedrooms, sharing a bathroom, from £30
(single £20)   Check-in: after 6 pm   **No Credit Cards***

CHARDSTOCK George: Tel (0460) 20241: Quaint thatched pub; smartly rustic
interior; outdoor tables, restaurant, and bedrooms. Wide-ranging menu. Whitbread
beers.

CHERITON BISHOP   Old Thatch Inn

Exeter EX6 6JH
Tel: (0647) 24204
Open: 12-3, 7 (6.30 summer, 6 Sat all year)-11
Licensee: Brian Bryon-Edmond

Outstanding for good old-fashioned English alehouse food, featuring exciting use of
fresh offal, alongside newer-fangled fare, prepared by an enthusiastic chef-proprietor.
A nice old pub, too, in the Dartmoor National Park: a useful detour from the A30
route. No children.

Bar Meals: 12-2.15, 6.30-9.30; bar snacks both sessions   *Typical Dishes: tomato, onion
and herb soup £1.10, sautéed kidneys £1.95, braised oxtail £3.95, Thatch mixed grill
£4.60, duck bigarade £6.95   Vegetarian Meals: leek and aubergine bake*   Beer
*Furguson Dartmoor Best, Ind Coope Burton Ale; Wadworth 6X   **Accommodation** (closed
1-14 Nov): 3 bedrooms, all en suite, from £41 (single £29)   No children overnight
(minimum age 14)   Check-in: by arrangement   **Credit Cards:** Access, Visa'*

CHILLINGTON   Chillington Inn

near Kingsbridge TQ7 2JS
Tel: (0548) 580244
Open 12-2.30, 6-11

The front door of this white-painted 16th century inn opens directly onto the main
road through the village, with no pavement in between, so take care when leaving
after a convivial evening. Inside, the unpretentiously snug bar (complete with its
handsome collection of banknotes from around the world) offers a wide variety of
French bread and wholemeal sandwiches plus snacks like omelettes and spare ribs
with French fries. For more substantial meals, a small restaurant, displaying a
collection of decorative plates around the walls, provides a short menu of home-
cooked dishes ranging from hearty soups and steaks to hot smoked mackerel with
gooseberry sauce and baked trout with hazelnuts and fennel. Good puddings come
with thick clotted cream. A tiny garden to the rear is home to a pair of rabbits, a
great attraction for children, who are made most welcome here. Two charming
bedrooms have matching wallpaper and fabrics in a pretty trellis pattern with
bedhead drapes, and ruffled blinds at the windows. Each room has its own bathroom
across the corridor, decorated to match the rooms, but bring your own soap as none
is provided. Breakfasts are continental, not English. The pub is closed on weekday
lunchtimes. Parking is difficult.

Bar Meals: 12-2, 7-10; bar snacks both sessions   **Typical Dishes:** *home-made soup £2.25, salade nicoise £3.90, fillet steak £11.95, rack of lamb £8.50, skate with black butter £8.50, treacle tart   Vegetarian Meals: pasta   Children's Portions* ▐ Beer ▌ *Palmers; Whitbread   Children Allowed in Bar to Eat   Outdoor Play Area   Garden   Outdoor Eating* **Accommodation:** *3 bedrooms, all en suite, from £30 (single £20)   Children Welcome Overnight   Cots Available   Check-in: all day* **Credit Cards:** *Access, Amex, Visa*

CHURCHSTOW   Church House Inn

On A379, near Kingsbridge TQ7 3QW
Tel: (0548) 852237
Open: 11-2.30 (12-2 Sun), 6-11
Licensee: Nick Nicholson

13th century former Benedictine monks' house, complete with modern spin-offs like the 'Friar's Carvery', but lots of medieval atmosphere also remains, in the deep window seats and heavy stone walls, huge dark beams and enormous open fireplace. The long bar has lots of cushioned settles, and food from a screened-off servery at one end. There's also a conservatory style bar at the back.

Bar Meals: 12-1.30, 6.30-9; bar snacks both sessions   **Typical Dishes:** *potato and stilton soup £1.50, prawn cocktail £2.25, steak and kidney pie £3.75, devilled chicken £3.75, haddock and chips £3.25, hot chocolate fudge cake £1.75   Vegetarian Meals: vegetarian lasagne £2.25   Children's Portions* ▐ Beer ▌ *Draught Bass; Ruddles County, Ushers Best Family Room   Patio/terrace   Outdoor Eating* **No Credit Cards**

COCKWOOD   Anchor Inn

Starcross EX6 8RA   ¶
Tel: (0626) 890203
Open: 11-2.30 (12-2.30 Sun), 6-11 (11-11 summer)
Licensees: H C Barnes and P G Keyte

Large old harbourside pub, extended over the years but still admirably traditional in spirit. The main bar divides into three areas, with a comfortable little snug at one end dominated by a welcoming coal fire. Black panelling, low ceilings and lots of private little alcoves lend intimacy to a rambling space. Bar food favours the fishy.

Bar Meals and Restaurant: 12-2, 7-10; bar snacks both sessions   **Typical Dishes:** *home-made soup £2.35, home-made paté, fillet steak, shellfish selection, poached fresh salmon (main courses around £5), bread pudding   Vegetarian Meals: ratatouille   Children's Menu/Portions* ▐ Cheese ▌ ▐ Beer ▌ *Draught Bass; Eldridge Pope Royal Oak; Whitbread Flowers Original Children Allowed in Bar to Eat   Riverside Patio/terrace* **Credit Cards:** *Access, Visa*

COCKWOOD   Ship EX6 8PA Tel: (0626) 890373. Harbourside dining pub; waitress service and good local fish; food served 12-2, 7-10. Garden. Courage beers.

COLEFORD   New Inn

Coleford EX17 5BZ
Tel: (0363) 84242
Open: 11.30-2.30, 6-11
Licensee: Paul Bott

Pretty thatched inn with a characterfully rambling interior in which ancient and modern blend successfully: fitted red carpets, fresh white walls, heavy beams, simple wooden furniture and settles, and a discreet variety of attractive brass and bric-a-brac. Food is a big thing, and can appear to take over the place at busy times. There's a stream-side patio..

Bar Meals: *12-2, 7-10; bar snacks both sessions*   **Typical Dishes:** *carrot and orange soup £1.90, stilton and walnut paté £2.95, hot beef Creole £6.50, chicken breast in tarragon sauce £7.95, lamb cutlet and onion sauce £7.95, caramel and hazelnut tart £2.10 Vegetarian Meals: tagliatelle £4.25   Children's Portions* `Cheese` `Beer` *Wadworth 6X; Whitbread Flowers Original, IPA   Family Room   Patio/terrace   Outdoor Eating* **Accommodation:** *3 bedrooms, 1 en suite, from £34 (single £20)   Children Welcome Overnight   Check-in: all day*   **Credit Cards:** *Access, Amex, Visa*

COMBEINTEIGNHEAD Wild Goose Tel: (0626) 872241: Eclectic interior and menu, including vegetarian choice; separate restaurant. Garden. Cotleigh, Exmoor, Wadworth beers. Open: 11-2.30, 6-11

CORNWORTHY   Hunters Lodge

Off A381
Tel: (080 423) 204
Open: 11.30-3, 6.30-11 (11-3, 6-11 Sat)
Licensee: Robin Thoms

Unspoilt, simply refurbished country local, with a cosy low-ceilinged bar and attractive dining room, nice in winter when the log fire's burning. Splendid bar food; good fresh vegetables.

Bar Meals: *12-2, 7-10; bar snacks both sessions*   **Typical Dishes:** *grilled sardines £1.95, stuffed mushrooms £3.50, garlic prawns £4, steak and kidney pie £4.50, pheasant £7.50 Vegetarian Meals   Children's Portions* `Beer` *Blackawton; Ushers* `Cider` *Children Allowed in Bar to Eat   Outdoor Play Area   Garden   Summer Barbecue*

CULLOMPTON   Manor House Hotel

Fore Street EX15 1JL   `B&B`
Tel: (0884) 32281   ☺
Open: all day
Licensee: Seven Hardaker

Built as the town house for a rich wool merchant, part of this hotel-cum-inn dates back to 1603, and fine old casement windows jut out from the freshly-painted black and white facade. Inside has an attractive mix of styles, the knotty pine bar Victorian in feel (aside from the pair of fruit machines) and the several rooms that together form the restaurant distinctly Georgian and decidedly smart with well-chosen fabrics, crisply clothed tables and most comfortable high-backed upholstered dining chairs. In between bar and restaurant is the informal Veryard's Carvery, its roasts housed under large stainless steel domes, with a display of traditional English puddings and a motley collection of well spaced out dining tables and chairs. The same menu serves all areas, from ploughmans and sandwiches through a routine burgers, fish'n'chips and steaks list, to the makings of full three course meals. Blackboard daily specials supplement the printed menu. A certain lack of finesse and care in the cooking (grilled pork chops come with a heavy, almost overpowering, stilton sauce) is compensated for by generosity of portion and the fact that almost everything is home-made. Although there is no special menu for children, they can always find fish-fingers, baked beans or the like, and will happily provide half portions of other dishes, baby food proper, and highchairs. The appealing bedrooms are all individually decorated, with stylish coordinating fabrics, nicely framed botanical prints, and good free-standing furniture in mahogany or an orangey pine finish. All the usual modern comforts. Carpeted bathrooms have wooden toilet seats, good thermostatically controlled showers over the baths, and nice touches like cottonwool balls and pot pourri. Most rooms are at the front of the building facing the main road; double glazing helps to reduce the traffic noise, and one of the two quieter rooms to the rear has a pair of bunk beds for families.

Bar Meals: 12-2.30, 7-9.30; bar snacks both sessions   *Restaurant:* 7-10   *Typical Dishes BAR:* game and cherry soup £1.40, cretts (egg, cream, smoked fish) £3.25, steak, mushroom and whisky pie £9.50, venison, pheasant and pigeon pie £5.95, fish and chips £4.60, steamed treacle pudding £1.95   *RESTAURANT:* tomato, carrot and orange soup £1.60, mushroom and bacon feuilleté £2.75, chicken in tarragon and chervil sauce £7.95, venison medallions in Grand Marnier £9.95, sea bass in lemon and capers £9.25, crème brulée £2.25   *Vegetarian Meals:* pasta £4.25   *Children's Portions*   **Beer**   Bass; Theakston   *Family Room   Patio/terrace   Outdoor Eating   **Accommodation:** 9 bedrooms, all en suite, from £42.50 (single £35)   Children Welcome Overnight   Cots Available   Check-in: all day   **Credit Cards:** Access, Visa*

DALWOOD   Tuckers Arms

Off A35 EX13 7EG
Tel: (040 488) 342
Open: 12-2, 6 (6.30 winter)-11
Licensees: David and Kate Beck

Picture-book pretty thatched pub in a delightful Axe Valley village, beside the Corry Brook. Originally a manor house, parts of which date back 700 years; the refurbished, relaxing interior has a mix of chairs, original flagstoned floors, beams aplenty and a large inglenook fireplace. The bedrooms were added in 1989. Food is reliably good.

Bar Meals: 12-2, 7-10; bar snacks both sessions   *Typical Dishes:* broccoli and stilton soup £1.65, potato skins with stilton and port £3.80, rack of lamb £7.55, fresh local trout £6.25, salmon and asparagus tiddy £6.95, apple pie with clotted cream £1.95   *Vegetarian Meals:* moussaka £5.25   *Children's Menu*   **Beer**   Marston Pedigree; Wadworth 6X Whitbread Boddingtons Bitter, Flowers Original   **Whisky**   *Family Room   Garden Outdoor Eating   **Accommodation:** 5 bedrooms, all en suite, from £40 (single £25) Children Welcome Overnight   Check-in: all day   **Credit Cards:** Access, Visa*

DARTINGTON   Cott Inn

Dartington TQ9 6HE   ❢
Tel: (0803) 863777
Open: 11-2.30 (12-2 Sun), 6-11
Licensees: Mr and Mrs Stephen Culverhouse

A delightful 14th century thatched, stone and cob-built inn, continuously licensed since 1320, and severely damaged by fire in 1989 (they only closed for two days), but now fully restored. The English oak trusses newly replaced in the roof came courtesy of the great Kent hurricane. Now protected by the latest fire detection systems, and probably the safest thatched pub in England, as well as one of the longest, at 183 feet long. Lunch is a hot and cold buffet; listed dishes are from the evening menu. No children except in the dining room (by arrangement); no children overnight.

Bar Meals: 12-2.15, 6.30-9.30 (7-9 Sun/Mon); bar snacks lunchtime   *Restaurant:* 12-2.15, 7 pm or 9 pm sittings   *Typical Dishes:* hot and cold buffet at lunchtimevenings: cauliflower and stilton soup £2.25, camembert fritters with cranberry sauce £3.25, loin of port in Devon cider £5.95, guinea fowl £11.50, monkfish Cott style £10.95, raspberry

pavlova £2.30   Vegetarian Meals: vegetable pancake £5.95   Children's Portions (some)
Beer   *Blackawton 44 Special*   **Whisky**   *Glenkinchie 10 yr, Lagavulin 16 yr*   **Cider**
*Churchwards Farmhouse   Garden   Patio/terrace   Outdoor Eating   **Accommodation:** 6
bedrooms, 5 en suite, from £45 (single £40)   Check-in: all day   **Credit Cards:** Access,
Amex, Visa*

DARTMOUTH   Cherub

13 Higher Street TQ6 9BB
Tel: (0803) 832571
Open: 11-3, 5-11
Licensees: John and Janet Hill

Grade I listed 14th century fishing pub with an extraordinary timbered exterior and
busy, table-crammed small bar inside. The upstairs restaurant has a good reputation;
bar food is excellent at a fraction of the price.

*Bar Meals and Restaurant: 12-2, 7-10; bar snacks both sessions   **Typical Dishes BAR:**
carrot and courgette soup £1.50, Cherub smokie £2.95, smoked chicken and ham £5.25,
thatched pie £3.75, seafood pasta £5.25, bread and butter pudding £2.25
RESTAURANT: French onion soup £1.60, smoked whole prawns £4.25, steaks from
£9, sole roulade £10.95, salmon in orange sauce £9.95   Vegetarian Meals: pasta
Margarita* **Cheese**   **Beer**   *Blackawton Bitter; Ind Coope Burton Ale; Whitbread
Flowers Original* **Whisky**   *Children Allowed in Bar to Eat   Outdoor Play Area
Riverside Garden   Outdoor Eating   Summer Barbecue   **Credit Cards:** Access, Visa*

DODDISCOMBSLEIGH   Nobody Inn

Doddiscombsleigh EX6 7PS   **FOOD**
Tel: (0647) 52394
Open: 12-2.30, 6 (7 winter)-11
Licensee: N Borst-Smith

According to legend, a previous owner of this delightful old inn closed and locked
the door against the knocking of weary travellers, pretending that there was nobody
in, and it has remained the 'Nobody Inn' ever since. Today one can be sure that
somebody's in, and of a warm welcome within its mellow bars. The mood is
enhanced by a wealth of old beams, ancient settles and a motley collection of
antique tables; horse brasses and copper pots and pans decorate the inglenook
fireplace, and a real fire burns in winter. The varied bar menu includes a smooth
paté made from local Devon crab, served with an excellent malted wholemeal bread,
and the special Nobody soup, made with chicken stock, vegetables and fruit,
resulting in a dark, consommé-like broth with a slightly sweet, spicy flavour. In the
characterful restaurant, offerings range from Devon-cured venison and mussels from
the Exe to snails bourguignon and fillet of beef with tarragon sauce, and for the
sweet-toothed, home-made puddings come with great dollops of real clotted cream.
But ensure you leave a space for possibly the best collection of Devonshire cheeses
to be found anywhere. Six different cheeses can be chosen from a selection of more
than two dozen, including cow's, goat's and ewe's milk cheeses, many of them
unpasteurized, with wonderfully evocative names like Devon Garland, Ticklemoor,
St Nectar and Toatley. Even more impressive is the globetrotting wine list, which
features over 700 bins and is particularly strong in the Loire. Sixteen of them are also
offered by the glass at any one time and there are no less than 230 different whiskies
to choose from. Four of the modestly comfortable bedrooms are in the inn itself,
two with en suite shower and toilet, as well as teasmades and a drinks tray bearing
full bottles of brandy, gin and whisky – charged up by consumption, at bar prices.
Three larger en suite rooms are in a small early 17th century Manor House about

150 yards away, next to the church. These are traditionally furnished with old rather than antique pieces, and a ready-to-serve continental breakfast is provided in the fridge. Alternatively, stroll up to the inn for one of their excellent cooked breakfasts. Though the Nobody Inn isn't really geared up for children, they can be accommodated in the Manor House, and there's a small patio with tables in the pub's very pretty garden with its incongruous 'keep off the grass' sign.

Bar Meals: 12-2, 7-10; bar snacks both sessions **Restaurant:** *7.30* **Typical Dishes** **BAR:** *Nobody soup £1.50, home-made duck paté £2.60, beef in beer £3, duck and orange pie £3.20, hot smoked mackerel £2.90, spiced bread pudding £1.80* **RESTAURANT:** *avocado and prawn £3.88, roast duck £8.68, chicken Kiev £6.33, plaice £7.10, crème brulée £2.24* *Vegetarian Meals: chilli* `Cheese` `Beer` *Draught Bass; Eldridge Pope Royal Oak; Whitbread Flowers IPA* `Whisky` `Cider` *Grays, Inch's Stonehouse* *Patio/terrace* *Outdoor Eating* **Accommodation** *(closed 12-19 Jan): 7 bedrooms, 5 en suite, from £44 (single £28)* *Check-in: all day* **Credit Cards:** *Access, Visa*

EAST BUDLEIGH   Sir Walter Raleigh. Tel: (03954) 2510. Attractive local meeting place in glorious village. Decent lunchtime and evening bar food includes lots of local fish; middling prices; worth trying. Modest bedrooms. Cornish beers. Open: 11-3, 6-11.

EAST DOWN   Pyne Arms

Off A39 EX31 4LX
Tel: (0271) 850207
Open: 11-2.30, 6-11
Licensees: Jurgen and Elisabeth Kempf

Little pebbledash pub, one of four 'Exmoor Inns', which share a common menu, long and varied, with lots of seafood as well as a strong meat list featuring four sorts of English veal. Traditional interior with lots of nooks and crannies, plus a small galleried loft area.

Bar Meals: 12-2, 7-10; bar snacks both sessions **Typical Dishes:** *home-made paté £2.65, snails £2.70, German veal sausage £3.45, steak Diane £8.30, poached trout £5.35, green figs and fresh cream £1.65* `Beer` *Whitbread Flowers IPA* *Patio/terrace* **Credit Cards:** *Access, Visa*

EXETER   ★ Double Locks

Canal Bank EX2 6LT   `FOOD`
Tel: (0392) 56947
Open: 11-11
Licensee: Jamie Stuart

The Double Locks isn't easy to find but it's well worth the effort. First find the Marsh Barton trading estate and drive through it to the council incinerator – don't worry, the pub is some way yet – until you reach the plank canal bridge, which is made for vehicles, although it may not appear to be. Once across, turn right, and a single track road will bring you to the red brick Georgian Double Locks. Equally popular with business people and students, this is the perfect summer pub: there are swans on the canal next to the eponymous lock, a large garden shaded by huge pine trees, a bare earth handball court, swings and a scramble net for the children, and a barbecue both lunchtime and evening in summer, weather permitting. There's even a small marquee in which to shelter from errant showers. Inside is very informal. Several rooms have black and white tiled floors, draw-leaf domestic dining room tables and lots of posters advertising local events. Chess, draughts, Monopoly,

Scrabble and bar billiards are all keenly played. A huge blackboard displays the day's offerings, featuring almost as many options for vegetarians as carnivores. The lentil soup, full of tomato, thick with vegetables and partnered by a large wholemeal roll, is almost a meal in itself. The steak and kidney pie, full of tender chunks of meat, comes with a proper pastry top, cooked on top of the pie. Breakfasts here mean a traditional fry-up, either meat or vegetarian, plus a pint of the beer of your choice, at the all-in price of £4. There is no special children's menu but most things also come in smaller portions at smaller prices, and several rooms can be used by families, who are made genuinely welcome.

Bar Meals: 11-10.30 (12-10 Sun); bar snacks both sessions   **Typical Dishes:** soup of the day £1.25, mushrooms on toast £2.50, steak and kidney pie £4.20, beef chilli £3, turkey and mushroom pie £4.20, Bourneville chocolate ice-cream £1.70   Vegetarian Meals: vegetable beanie £3   Beer   Adnams Broadside; Greene King Abbot Ale; Wadworth 6X   Cider   Grays, Inch's   Family Room   Outdoor Play Area   Riverside Garden   Outdoor Eating   Summer Barbecue   **No Credit Cards**

FRITHELSTOCK   Clinton Arms

off Bideford Road EX38 8JH
Tel: (0805) 23279
Open: 11.30-3, 6-11 (12-2.30, 7-11 winter)

Diners' and family pub with a jolly atmosphere, its front lawn, also the village green, a perfect spot for relaxing summer meals. The priory ruins are opposite, in this sleepy affluent village. Children can be safely let off the leash in the walled rear garden.

Bar Meals: 12-2.30, 7-10 (9.30 Sun); bar snacks both sessions   **Typical Dishes:** home-made soup £1.75, prawns in garlic butter, half duckling in orange sauce, peppered fillet steak, whole plaice, apple and sultana sponge (main courses from around £5)   Vegetarian Meals: harvester pie   Children's Menu/Portions   Beer   Draught Bass   Cider   Family Room   Outdoor Play Area   Garden   Outdoor Eating   **Accommodation:** 4 bedrooms, 1 en suite, from £30 (single £15)   Children Welcome Overnight   Cot Available   Check-in: all day   **Credit Cards:** Access, Visa

---

HARBERTON   Church House Inn

near Totnes TQ9 7SF
Tel: (0803) 863707
Open: 11.30 (12 winter)-3, 6-11
Licensees: Mr and Mrs D S Wright

Tucked away by the village church, and originally a chantry house for monks, one of whom is said to be still lurking on the premises, the Church House didn't pass out of clerical hands until 1950. The carefully removed plaster of centuries has revealed ancient fluted oak beams, a magnificent medieval oak screen, a Tudor window frame and 13th century glass. The open plan bar and restaurant area, which share a common menu, were once the great chamber, and are now furnished with old pews and settles.

Bar Meals and Restaurant: 12-2, 7-9.30   **Typical Dishes:** home-made tomato and fresh herb soup £1.50, deep-fried brie in bacon with redcurrant sauce £3.25, roast guinea fowl £7.95, chicken breast filled with crab and prawns £7.50, fresh grilled plaice filled with prawns and cheese £6.95, ginger ice-cream with brandy snap and clotted cream £2.25   Vegetarian Meals: tortellini ricotta £4.95   Children's Menu/Portions   Beer   Courage Best Bitter, Directors; Draught Bass; Wadworth 6X   Family Room   Children over 14 Allowed in Bar to Eat   **No Credit Cards**

HATHERLEIGH   George Hotel

Market Street EX20 3JN
Tel: (0837) 810454
Open: 11-3, 6-11 (10.30-11 Mon/Tue)
Licensees: Veronica Devereux and John Dunbar-Ainley

Cob and thatch inn, originally a monks' retreat. The main bar is in the converted brewhouse, with an extended area reserved for non-smokers. The inn's original bar, atmospherically laden with original beams, heavy stone walls, an enormous open fire and a pleasing variety of comfortable seats and sofas, is now largely confined to residential use. The market bar across the way is opened on Tuesdays only, and there's a fine cobbled courtyard drinking area. A good place to stay. They have an outdoor swimming pool.

Bar Meals: 12-2, 6 (7 Sun)-9.30; bar snacks both sessions **Restaurant:** *7-9.30* **Typical Dishes BAR:** *home-made soup £1.60, moules mariniere £2.60, steak and kidney pie £3.75, local steaks £7.25, tagliatelle carbonara £3.30, raspberry and apple crumble £1.85* **RESTAURANT:** *crespolini £2.90, sirloin of beef Glenfiddich £9, duck mish-mish £9.50, Dover sole, peach and amaretto brulée £2* *Vegetarian Meals: spinach and mushroom roulade Children's Menu/Portions* `Cheese` `Beer` *Draught Bass; Whitbread Boddingtons Bitter, Castle Eden Ale* `Whisky` *Lagavulin 16 yr* `Cider` *Inch's* *Family Room* *Patio/terrace Outdoor Eating* **Accommodation:** *11 bedrooms, 9 en suite, from £42 (single £32)* *Children Welcome Overnight* *Cots Available* *Check-in: from midday* **Credit Cards:** *Access, Visa*

HATHERLEIGH   Tally Ho

14 Market Street EX20 3JN
Tel: (0837) 810306
Open: 11-2.30 (12-2 Sun), 6-11.30; all day Tue
Licensees: Gianni and Annamaria Scoz

A regenerated old pub, 'discovered' in 1983 by its present Italian owners, and gradually improved in the intervening years. Nice old furnishings, a partly exposed brick floor, warming working stoves, and relaxing touches like candles in bottles. The bar menu is very simple, and there's a charming little dining room for a blow-out authentic Italian dinner.

Bar Meals: 11.30-2, 7-9.30; also restaurant in evenings; bar snacks lunchtime **Typical Dishes BAR:** *minestrone £2.50, Devon devilled crab £3.95, sirloin steak £8.75, chicken cacciatora £4.95, fritto misto £7.95, Devon apple in-and-out £1.75* **RESTAURANT:** *onion soup £3.15, filetto al carpaccio £4.95, valdostana £12.25, scaloppine romagnola £11.75, scampi provencale £10.65, cassata £2.75 Vegetarian Meals (bar): spinach omelette £2.85* `Cheese` `Beer` *Tally Ho Brewery Beers* `Whisky` `Cider` *Inch's* *Children Allowed in Bar to Eat* *Outdoor Play Area* *Garden* *Outdoor Eating* *Summer Barbecue* **Accommodation:** *3 bedrooms, all en suite, from £38 (single £25)* *Children Welcome Overnight (minimum age 8)* *Check-in: all day* **Credit Cards:** *Access, Visa*

HAYTOR VALE   Rock Inn

Haytor Vale TQ13 9XP
Tel: (0364) 66130
Open: 11-3, 6.30-11
Licensee: Christopher Graves

Sturdy old pub in tiny, wuthering Dartmoor village; a characterful traditional interior, complete with lovely old furnishings and open fires, and reliably good bar food, with a particularly strong list of light meals and snacks, and the promise of fresh local vegetables.

Bar Meals: 11-2, 7-9.30; bar snacks both sessions **Restaurant:** *7.30-9* **Typical Dishes BAR:** *woodland mushrooms £3.95, Haytor rabbit surprise £4.25, beef and venison pie £4.95, mild lamb and mint curry £4.75, red mullet with mustard butter £7.95, treacle and walnut tart £1.55* **RESTAURANT:** *set menu £17.95: tomato and onion soup, fresh mussels, venison in real ale, local duck, whole grilled brill, local ice-creams* **Vegetarian Meals:** *spicy vegetable chilli £4.55* **Cheese** *(restaurant)* **Beer** *Draught Bass; Eldridge Pope Best, Thomas Hardy Country, Royal Oak* **Family Room** **Garden** **Outdoor Eating Accommodation:** *10 bedrooms, all en suite, from £55 (single £37.50)* **Children Welcome Overnight** **Cots Available** **Check-in: all day** **Credit Cards:** *Access, Amex, Visa*

HOLNE Church House. Tel: (03643) 208. Grade II listed medieval inn with fine Dartmoor views; good local walks; traditional pub home-cooking from fresh ingredients. Blackawton Bitter, real cider. Bedrooms. Open: 12-2.30 (3 Sat), 6.30-11; close slightly earlier winter.

HORNDON   Elephants Nest

Off A386 at Mary Tavy Inn PL19 9NQ
Tel: (0822) 810273
Open: 11.30-2.30 (12-2.30 Sun), 6.30-11
Licensees: Nick and Gill Hamer and Peta Hughes

Named after a landlord of great size and/or possessed of a great nest of a beard (the mythology is a little confused). Growing popularity has led to expansion of the eating and drinking space, into the cellar. Window seats, old rugs and flagstones and an open fire make this a good pub for winter weather. The food appears to be getting smarter.

Bar Meals: 11.30-2, 7-10 (12-2, 7-9.45 Sun); bar snacks both sessions **Typical Dishes:** *home-made soup of the day £1.20, giant cheesy mussels £2.80, beef and stilton pie £4.50, braised venison with orange and juniper sauce £4.85, fresh Tavy trout with almonds; chocolate and brandy crunch cake £1.70* **Vegetarian Meals:** *vegetable goulash £3.30* **Children's Portions** **Beer** *Palmers IPA; St Austell HSD; Webster's Yorkshire Bitter; Whitbread Boddingtons Best* **Family Room (2 rooms)** **Garden** **Outdoor Eating Accommodation:** *2 bedrooms, sharing a bathroom, from £28* **Children Welcome Overnight** **Cot Available** **Check-in: by arrangement** **No Credit Cards**

HORSEBRIDGE   Royal

near Tavistock   PL19 8PJ
Tel: (082 287) 214
Open: 12-2.30, 7-11
Licensees: Terry and June Wood

Three excellent reasons for a detour to Terry Wood's informal pub: to look at the ancient Tamar Bridge, to sample their own home-brewed ales, and to try the landlady's cooking, including herby home-made bread with the ploughman's. Imaginative salads; no chips. The interior is marvellously relaxing, too.

Bar Meals: 12-2, 7.15-9.30 (not Sun eve); bar snacks both sessions **Typical Dishes:** *beef and oyster pie £3.25, chilli/curry/moussaka £2.50, duck à l'orange £4.95, good home-made puddings £1.50* **Vegetarian Meals:** *nut roast £3.25* **Cheese** **Beer** *own home-brew; Bass; Greene King; Marston* **No Credit Cards**

IDDESLEIGH   Duke of York

Winkleigh EX19 8BG   FOOD
Tel: (0837) 810253   ※
Open: 11.20-3 (2.30 winter), 6.30-11; closed Mon
Licensees: John and Trish Colvill

Originally built to house the stone masons working on the 13th century church next door, the thatched Duke of York is the ideal village pub, with real food, real ale and a real welcome from John and Trish (when she is not busy working in the kitchen) Colvill. Scrubbed wooden tables sport fresh flowers and candles in wax encrusted bottles, and an open log fire burns, even in summer unless it's a really warm day. The blackboard-listed menu offers the usual home-made soup and ploughmans, the latter with either West Country cheeses or home-cooked ham plus wonderful granary bread, as well as more unusual items like spicy merguez sausages in pitta bread, grilled sardines or a cheese and lentil loaf. It's worth leaving a little space for the home-made puddings, which come with real, thick, yellow, farmhouse clotted cream. From Wednesday to Saturday evenings, a short, fixed-price menu is also on offer in the beamed dining room, featuring dishes like duck liver gateau and escalope of salmon with watercress hollandaise. Children are made welcome and provided with smaller portions at smaller prices. In addition, nursing mothers are offered the use of one of the four neat white-painted bedrooms, which have simple white melamine furniture and floral duvets. Just one has an en suite bathroom, the others share. The pub is closed Monday and Tuesday lunchtimes in winter. The cottage garden is very pretty.

Bar Meals: 12-2.30, 7-9.30; bar snacks both sessions   *Restaurant:* 7.30-9.30 (booking essential)   *Typical Dishes BAR:* lettuce and bacon soup £2, grilled sardines £3, breast of chicken £5, lamb and potato curry £5, salmon and prawn pie £5, sticky toffee pudding £2.25   *RESTAURANT:* dinner menu £19.50: Mediterranean fish soup, scallop and red pepper kebab, rack of lamb, braised guinea fowl with fresh chanterelles, monkfish with mustard sauce, tortoni with mango purée   Vegetarian Meals: hot spinach mousse   Children's Portions   Cheese   Beer   Cotleigh Tawny Bitter; Palmers IPA; Smiles Best; Wadworth 6X   Cider   Inch's   Family Room   Outdoor Play Area   Garden   Outdoor Eating   *Accommodation* (closed Christmas/New Year): 4 bedrooms, 1 en suite, from £45 (single £20)   Children Welcome Overnight   Cot Available   Check-in: all day   *No Credit Cards*

KINGSBRIDGE   Ashburton Arms

On A379, West Charleton TQ7 2AH
Tel: (0548) 531242
Open: 12-2.30, 6-11
Licensees: Elizabeth and Brian Saunders

Steak on the rocks – a great slab of local beef cooked to order on a hot stone – is the speciality of the house, in a light, bright, carpeted and piney roadside pub on the Torcross road. Fresh local crabs are a summer favourite. They have a non-smoking dining room.

Bar Meals: 12-1.45, 7-9.30; bar snacks both sessions   *Typical Dishes:* home-made soup of the day £1.60, grilled sardines £2, steak on the rocks (£7.20-£11.50), lemon sole £7.50, fresh fish, pavlova £2   Vegetarian Meals: fresh vegetable, apricot and scrumpy bake   Children's Menu/Portions   Beer   Draught Bass, Dartmoor Best   Cider   Luscombe   Family Room (small)   Patio/terrace   *Accommodation:* 4 bedrooms, sharing a bathroom, from £31 (single £17)   Children Welcome Overnight (minimum age 10)   Check-in: by arrangement   *Credit Cards:* Access, Visa

KINGSKERSWELL   **Barn Owl**

Aller Mills TQ12 5AN
Tel: (0803) 872130
Open: 11.30-2.30 (12-2.30 Sun), 6.30-11
Licensees: Derek and Margaret Warner

The A380 into Torquay is best avoided in summer, but if you find yourself stuck in the perennial traffic jam which passes Newton Abbot, look out for a sign to the Barn Owl Inn, which offers decent food, even better bedrooms and a friendly welcome. Lovingly restored by the Warners over the last six years, the original 16th century farmhouse has a neat if unremarkable exterior which makes its characterful interior even more of a surprise. Old beams, rough stone walls and flagstoned floors have been uncovered, and real log fires warm each of the three bars in winter. One room features an inglenook fireplace, another an ancient blackleaded range, while in the largest bar, oak panelling and an ornate plasterwork ceiling are rather grander than might be expected of a modest farmhouse – a tribute to the prosperity and aspirations of a former owner, perhaps. Fresh flowers on all the tables add to the general charm of the surroundings. A printed bar menu offers a good range of steaks, fresh fish, hot jacket potatoes and sandwiches with fillings including some excellent home-boiled ham carved off the bone, in good granary bread. In addition, a blackboard menu lists the dishes of the day, perhaps a salmon bake with large flakes of fresh salmon layered with slices of potato, hotpot style. There's always a vegetarian dish on the list. Remember to bring your appetite; portions are generous. In the evenings, the French-inspired à la carte is offered in a converted barn restaurant. Six newly-created bedrooms within the original farmhouse combine considerable charm with modern conveniences like television and direct dial phones. The renovations included an extensive sound-proofing programme, which effectively eliminates any noise from the bars below. Rooms are cottagey in style, with black beams, white plaster walls, dark-stained pine furniture locally made in solid country style, and their own individual floral fabrics, perhaps red poppy, honeysuckle or sweet pea. This 'signature' design is also used above dados in the bathrooms and in panels on the doors, the outsides of which are covered with old floor boards, thus cunningly concealing the modern fireproof doors within. Bowls of fruit and mineral water add the final homely touch. No children under 14 are permitted in either bars or bedrooms, but they are tolerated in the small garden.

Bar Meals: 12-2, 7-10; bar snacks both sessions **Restaurant:** *12-2 (Sun only), 7-9.45* **Typical Dishes BAR:** *chicken and sweetcorn soup £1.50, garlic mushrooms £3.25, chicken auberge £5.50, navarin of lamb £5.25, salmon koulibiac £5.75, chocolate fudge gateau £1.95* **RESTAURANT:** *crab bisque £2.95, melon with lemon sorbet and raspberries £3.65, fillet steak £12.75, guinea fowl £10.95, casserole of fish £11.25, zuccotto £2 Vegetarian Meals: hazelnut and mushroom pie* Beer *Ind Coope Burton Ale* Whisky *Cragganmore Garden Outdoor Eating* **Accommodation:** *6 bedrooms, all en suite, from £60 (single £47.50) Check-in: all day* **Credit Cards:** *Access, Visa*

KINGSTEIGNTON   ★   **Old Rydon**

Rydon Road TQ12 3QG FOOD
Tel: (0626) 54626
Open: 11-2.30, 6-11
Licensees: Hermann and Miranda Hruby

Hermann Hruby is still producing some of the best pub food in the south west, and in that respect little has changed since the Hrubys bought the Old Rydon in 1978. But there has been one other significant development since our last edition, the building of a splendid, and large, heated conservatory, leafy with vines, jasmine, bougainvillea and other plants, which opened in March 91, and allows for indoors al fresco eating all year. This has brought much-needed additional space to the previously very cramped little bar, where reputation had brought an ever-growing number of fans, despite its slightly out of the way location. (To find the pub, take Longford Lane off the A381, and Rydon Road's on the right). It's a Grade II listed former farmhouse, converted in the 1960s, with an original old cider loft forming an attractive part of the bar, previously the farm stables. Underneath the plank and beam ceiling adorned with pewter mugs is a raised log fire; the whitewashed stone walls hung with antlers and horns. Tables here are drinking style, too small and cramped for relaxed dining, many of the seats converted barrels. Separate from the bar, a comfortable diners' lounge leads through to the little restaurant: this is the oldest part of the building, with original wood screens. The whole is full of character and charm, run in a friendly and personal style, but most visitors come for the delicious and interesting food, chosen from a globetrotting menu, with confidently handled eastern dishes like nasi goreng, as well as staunchly English specialities like beef, mushroom and stilton pie – both of these old favourites. The blackboard specials menu embraces the exotic and the plain – thick, warming country soups, an old-fashioned rabbit casserole, pork in Malayan peanut sauce, and a quite superb fish salad: fish, seafood and local game feature prominently in their season. In addition to which there are imaginative side salads, starters that make good lunchtime snacks on their own (though they don't serve sandwiches) and first rate accompaniments like boulangère potatoes and al dente green vegetables. Succulent puddings come with real clotted cream. Aside from the new conservatory, the sheltered walled garden makes an ideal summer venue for lunch.

Bar Meals: 12-2, 7-10; *bar snacks both sessions*   *Restaurant:* 7-9.30   **Typical Dishes** **BAR:** *vegetable, lentil and lovage soup £1.25, red bean dip £1.95, beef and mushroom pie in port and stilton sauce £4.95, Viennese chicken £4.95, nasi goreng £4.95, tiramisu* **RESTAURANT:** *tomato, orange, bacon and tarragon soup £2.35, mixed seafood hors d'oeuvre £4.85, noisettes of lamb with green peppercorn and sorrel sauce £10.95, pork tenderloin charcoal-grilled with roast pepper sauce and cashew nuts £10.95, choux ring with fresh fruit and cream £2.35 Vegetarian Meals: fettuccine £3.95   Children's Menu Children's Portions (restaurant)* `Cheese` *(restaurant)* `Beer` *Draught Bass; Wadworth 6X Family Room   Outdoor Play Area   Garden   Outdoor Eating* **Credit Cards:** *Access, Amex, Diners, Visa*

KNOWSTONE   Masons Arms

Knowstone EX36 4RY   ❢
Tel: (03984) 231
Open: 11-3 (possible 2.30 winter), 7-11
Licensees: Elizabeth and David Todd

Thatched 13th century inn in the sort of truly tranquil spot where dogs fall asleep in the middle of the road. A good place for a drink and the food's not at all bad either: soups and puddings are particularly good. Overnight accommodation cannot be recommended, however; we had an unfortunate experience with a bed held up at one corner by a pile of books in a room in which the only cupboard space was a collection of coathangers on a hook on the back of the door (which, incidentally, had no lock).

Bar Meals: 12-2, 7-9.30 (12.30-2, 7-9 Sun); *bar snacks both sessions*   *Restaurant:* Sun *lunch 12.30-2, and 7-9 (not Sun or Tue)*   **Typical Dishes BAR:** *minestrone £1.40, salade nicoise £2.95, home-made pies £3.60, quail Masons Arms £6.95, speciality curries £4.60, Danish apple cake £1.65 RESTAURANT: set meals £11.25 Vegetarian Meals: red bean moussaka £3.60   Children's Portions* `Cheese`   `Beer`   *Cotleigh Tawny Bitter; Hall & Woodhouse Badger Best Bitter* `Whisky` *Family Room   Garden* **Accommodation:** *5 bedrooms, 2 en suite, from £35 (single £26)   Children Welcome Overnight   Cots Available   Check-in: all day* **No Credit Cards**

LOWER ASHTON   Manor Inn

near Christow EX6 7QL
Tel: (0647) 52304
Open: 11.30-2.30 (12-2.30 Sun), 6-11; closed Mon
Licensees: G W and C M S Mann

Traditional Teign Valley local, keen on pub games. Good unfussy honest home-made food prepared by the landlady. Ice-cream from a local farm.

Bar Meals: *12-1.45, 7-9.45; bar snacks both sessions*   **Typical Dishes:** *tomato and orange soup £1.40, chilli £3.65, lamb ragout £4.35, blackcurrant pie £1.75*   *Vegetarian Meals: ratatouille* **Beer** *Draught Bass; Cotleigh Tawny Bitter; Wadworth 6X*   *Garden Outdoor Eating*   **No Credit Cards**

LYDFORD   Castle Inn

Okehampton EX20 4BH
Tel: (082 282) 242
Open: 11-3, 6-11
Licensees: M and C G Walker

Pink-washed, with wisteria entangled in its small front verandah, the Castle is certainly a pretty little pub, but it's not until you go inside that you realise how old it is. Much is 12th century, with various later additions, and it just oozes atmosphere, with its slate floor and low sagging ceilings turned a deep amber colour by time and smoke. The place is literally crammed with bits and pieces collected by landlords over the years, includings several marvellous old high backed settles (some with little roofs), dozens of decorative plates, numerous old photos, handbills and a fine collection of Hogarth prints. At least one former owner was a strong royalist to judge by the many commemorative plates; there's even an illuminated speech, made by Elizabeth I to her troops at Tilbury in 1588. Seven of only 31 remaining Lydford pennies minted by Ethelred the Unready in the 10th century are on display too, the rest being held by the British Museum. Mo and Clive Walker took over here only a short while ago, but it's already clear that the Castle's reputation for good food and a friendly welcome is safe in their hands. A blackboard bar menu covers the usual ground plus the odd surprise like a sardine loaf, and all the fish, for the seafood risotto for example, comes fresh from Plymouth three times a week. At lunchtime, this menu applies throughout the inn, but at night it's limited to the smaller bar and snug, when the main bar becomes a restaurant. Here, an à la carte menu features the likes of thick cut local salmon cutlets and pork Dijonnaise (with a delicious and perfectly balanced stilton and Dijon mustard cream sauce), and there's a particularly good value table d'hote. Notable amongst the puddings is a lovely soft, almondy treacle tart. Booking is advisable. Eight mostly antique-furnished bedrooms are decorated in a variety of somewhat less than stylish floral wallpapers, with unco-ordinated polycotton duvets. Nevertheless, the rooms have a certain charm, and Mo has yet to get to work on them. Half the rooms are en suite (one with a plastic shower cubicle and WC), while the others share a perfectly acceptable bathroom. There is quite a lot to see in the vicinity of the pub. Immediately next door is the castle with its rather gruesome history; local folklore has it that even to this day the birds, sensing its evil, will not go near the place. Rather more welcoming, the church boasts some fine wood carving on no less than 69 pew ends, featuring all manner of birds, fish, flowers and animals, as well as a very fine rood screen. Just a short walk away is the famously picturesque Lydford gorge and its wooded walks.

Bar Meals: *11-2.30, 6.30-9.30; bar snacks both sessions*   **Restaurant:** *6.30-9.30*
Typical Dishes BAR: *leek and asparagus soup £1.95, steak and kidney pie £4.50, liver Italienne £4.25, chilli lamb in coconut sauce £4.50, sticky toffee pudding £2.25*

RESTAURANT: *German vegetable soup £2.50, smoked salmon £4.95, lamb romarin £10.95, tournedos chasseur £13.50, lemon sole £9.95, grape Alaska £2.25 Vegetarian Meals: nut loaf   Children's Menu/Portions* ▐ Beer ▌ *Ind Coope Burton Ale; Wadworth 6X   Family Room   Outdoor Play Area   Garden   Outdoor Eating* **Accommodation:** *8 bedrooms, 4 en suite, from £35 (single £25)   Children Welcome Overnight   Cots Available   Check-in: all day*   **Credit Cards:** *Access, Amex, Visa*

MILTON COMBE   Who'd Have Thought It

near Yelverton PL20 6HP
Tel: (0822) 853313
Open: 11.30-2.30 (3 Sat), 6.30-11
Licensees: Keith Yeo and Gary Rager

Tiny village romantically located in a steeply wooded hollow. Three rooms, each with its own style: lots of period touches in the main bar, with ancient settles, foxes heads, and exposed stone. A fairly routine printed menu is supplemented daily by a blackboard list of around five starters and puddings, and 10–15 main course specials. No children indoors.

Bar Meals: *12-2, 7-9.30; bar snacks both sessions*   **Typical Dishes:** *turkey, ham and lentil soup £1.75, garlic prawns £3.25, home-made steak and kidney pie £3.75, chicken in cider £4.50, home-made 'dinner plate' pasties £1.90, apple pie and clotted cream £1.60 Vegetarian Meals: vegetarian crumble £3.50   Children's Portions* ▐ Beer ▌ *Blackawton Headstrong; Eldridge Pope Royal Oak; Exmoor Bitter; Wadworth 6X* ▐ Cider ▌ *Outdoor Play Area   Riverside Garden   Outdoor Eating*   **No Credit Cards**

NORTH BOVEY   Ring of Bells

North Bovey TQ13 8RB
Tel: (0647) 40375
Open: 11-3, 6-11
Licensee: Anthony P Rix

Accomplished thatched 13th century pub in a delightful village. The main bar is carpeted and opened up, with lots of heavy beams and a splendid inglenook fireplace. Fruit machine and piped music. Good value bed and breakfast.

Bar Meals and Restaurant: *12-2, 6.30 (7 restaurant)-9; bar snacks both sessions* **Typical Dishes BAR:** *home-made soup £1.95, farmhouse paté £2.75, steak and kidney pie £4.75, lasagne verdi £3.95, chilli con carne £3.95, treacle tart £2.50* **RESTAURANT:** *mussels provencale £3.50, entrecote chasseur £8.25, chicken supreme Devonshire £7.25, local trout £7.50, seasonal fruit crumble £2.50   Vegetarian Meals: pasta provencale au gratin £3.75   Children's Menu/Portions* ▐ Beer ▌ *Ind Coope Burton Ale; Marston Pedigree; Wadworth 6X* ▐ Cider ▌ *Addlestones; Grays   Family Room Outdoor Play Area   Garden   Outdoor Eating* **Accommodation:** *3 bedrooms, all en suite, from £40 (single £25)   Children Welcome Overnight   Cots Available   Check-in: all day* **No Credit Cards**

PARRACOMBE Fox & Goose off A39: Friendly local with far-too-long blackboard menu; lots of game and fish. Whitbread beers.

PETER TAVY   Peter Tavy Inn

Off A386 PL19 9NN
Tel: (0822) 810348
Open: 11.30-2.30 (3 Sat), 6.30-11
Licensees: Philip and Janice Hawkins

Atmospheric, popular old pub, now very popular for its food. Marvellous in winter, with its series of heavy-beamed, low-ceilinged, snug little bars, and roaring fire. They opened the restaurant in 1990, and rebuilt the kitchen, to cope with the increasingly foodie emphasis of their trade. Not as wholemeal as they used to be, but still better to vegetarians than most.

Bar Meals and Restaurant: 12-2, 7-9.30 (9.45 restaurant); bar snacks both sessions
Typical Dishes BAR: home-made vegetable soup £1.30, scallop wrapped in bacon £4.25, lasagne £4.35, chilli £4.35, cottage pie £3.20, mixed fruit crumble £1.10
RESTAURANT: similar starters, steak au poivre £9.15, seafood steak £14, stuffed lemon sole £10.50, chocolate fudge cake £1.75   Vegetarian Meals: vegetable moussaka £4.25
Beer *Butcombe Bitter; Eldridge Pope Royal Oak: Exmoor Gold   Outdoor Play Area Garden   Outdoor Eating   Credit Cards: Access, Visa*

PLYMOUTH Brown Bear, Chapel Street Tel: (0752) 564663: Seafarers' pub, very lively in the evenings. Usually busy with diners; seafood-led menu, showing signs of ambition (weekday lunches; Tue-Sat evenings). Courage beers. Open: 11-3, 5.30-11.

PLYMPTON Bovingdon Hall Tel: (0752) 346837: Renovated Elizabethan manor house with popular restaurant. Not cheap. Also bar meals daily. Children welcome. Whitbread beers.

RATTERY   Church House Inn

South Brent TQ10 9LD
Tel: (0364) 42220
Open: 11-2.30, 6 (6.30 winter)-11
Licensees: B and J J Evans

Originally an 11th century monastic resting house and hostel for the masons working on the nearby church: the list of vicars since 1199 is displayed in the bar. Though opened up into an elongated lounge, the massive oak screen and beams, great open fireplaces and spiral stone staircase remain. Friday evenings are candlelit.

Bar Meals: 12-2.30, 7-9.30; bar snacks both sessions   Typical Dishes: tomato and beef soup, melon and sorbet £2.35, roast duck £5.95, steak and kidney pie, salmon steak £6.75, lemon meringue pie £1.90   Vegetarian Meals: vegetable risotto £4.25   Children's Menu/Portions **Cheese** **Beer** *Ind Coope Burton Ale, Dartmoor Best, Tetley Bitter* **Whisky** *Cragganmore, Dalwhinnie* **Cider** *Luscombe   Family Room (snug area) Outdoor Play Area   Patio/terrace   Outdoor Eating   Credit Cards: Access, Diners, Visa*

RINGMORE   Journey's End Inn

Ringmore TQ7 4HL
Tel: (0548) 810205
Open: 11.30-3, 6.30-11
Licensee: Richard Sully

Charming, ancient village inn which has long been reliable for food and accommodation – but which was about to change hands as we went to press, so the following details may, of course, change.

Bar Meals: 12-2.15, 7-10; bar snacks both sessions   ***Typical Dishes:*** *home-made French onion soup £1.50, beef casserole £4.50, home-made curry £4.90, steaks £5.75-£10.50, treacle tart with clotted cream £1.90   Vegetarian Meals: lasagne £3.75   Children's Menu/Portions* Beer *Butcombe Bitter; Exmoor Bitter; Greene King Abbot Ale; Marston Pedigree   Family Room   Outdoor Play Area   Garden   Outdoor Eating   Summer Barbecue   **Accommodation:** 4 bedrooms, 2 en suite, from £36 (single £20)   Check-in: all day   **Credit Cards:** Access, Visa*

SANDY PARK Sandy Park Inn Tel: (06473) 3538. Thatched white pub, furnished in simple country local style; decent lunchtime and evening food, more choice in evenings. Modest bedrooms. Eldridge Pope, Marston, Palmers beers. Open: 11-3, 5-11 (all day summer).

SIDMOUTH Old Ship, Old Fore Street Tel: (0395) 512127: Old smuggling pub with panelling and beams. Real fire; no music. Upstairs restaurant earning a reputation for good local fish. Simpler bar meals lunch and evening. Cornish, Marston, Whitbread beers. Open: 11-2.30, 6-11.

SILVERTON   Three Tuns

14 Exeter Road EX5 4HX
Tel: (0392) 860352
Open: 11.30-2.30, 5.30-11

Pleasantly upgraded 15th century thatched inn in a large village-cum-small town, popular for its food with locals, tourists and business lunchers. Window seats and log fire.

Bar Meals and Restaurant: 12-2, 6.30-10; bar snacks both sessions   ***Typical Dishes:*** *home-made soup £1.25, home-made paté £1.35, venison steak £8.95, escalope of pork £6.25, breast of chicken £7.25, treacle tart £1.95   Vegetarian Meals: nut roast with wine and mushroom sauce £5.25   Children's Portions* Beer *Courage Directors, John Smith's Bitter; Fullers London Pride; Ruddles County   Patio/terrace   Outdoor Eating   **Accommodation:** 5 bedrooms, all en suite, from £40 (single £30)   Children Welcome Overnight   Cot Available   Check-in: all day   **Credit Cards:** Access, Amex, Visa*

SOUTH ZEAL   Oxenham Arms

South Zeal EX20 2JT
Tel: (0837) 840244
Open: 11-2.30 (12-2.30 Sun), 6-11
Licensee: James Henry

Village centre, ancient inn, romantically fronted and creeper-covered. Genuinely unspoilt inside too, with worn flag floors, vast open fires, original beams, rough plaster walls, spooky passageways, solidly traditional drinking areas, and a relaxingly clubbish lounge. Nice, old-fashioned bedrooms offer discreet modern comforts; a delightful place to stay.

Bar Meals: 12-2, 7-9.30; bar snacks both sessions   *Restaurant:* 12.30-1.30, 7.30-9   ***Typical Dishes BAR:*** *potato and leek soup £1.25, mushrooms in garlic butter £2.25, steak, kidney, Guinness and mushroom pie £3.95, cold roast beef platter £4.25, salmon and broccoli mornay £3.95, chocolate, brandy and biscuit gateau £1.75*   **RESTAURANT:** *lunch £8.40, dinner £14.50; main courses might include: roast Devonshire duckling with bigarade sauce, grilled 10 ounce sirloin steak garni, poached fresh salmon with watercress sauce   Vegetarian Meals: vegetarian curry £3.25   Children's Portions* Beer *Draught Bass; St Austell Tinner's   Family Room   Outdoor Play Area   Garden   Outdoor Eating   **Accommodation:** 8 bedrooms, 7 en suite, from £40 (single £32.50)   Children Welcome Overnight   Cots Available   Check-in: all day   **Credit Cards:** Access, Amex, Diners, Visa*

SOUTHPOOL   Millbrook Inn

near Kingsbridge TQ7 2RW
Tel: (0548) 531581
Open: 11-3, 5.30-11 (longer hours summer)
Licensees: the Spedding family

Customers arrive at this small pub close to Salcombe estuary by boat when the tide is high, and Millbrook stream flows past the sunny little terrace. Two welcoming, comfortable bars within. New licensees since our last edition.

Bar Meals: 12-2, 6.15-9 (later summer); bar snacks both sessions **Typical Dishes:** *home-made leek and potato soup £1.40, smoked mackerel £2.75, cottage pie £3, fishermans pie £3.15, fresh crab salad £5.35, Devon apple cider cake with clotted cream £1.25 Vegetarian Meals: stilton and broccoli quiche £3.25 Children's Portions* **Beer** *Draught Bass* **Cider** *Churchwards   Children Allowed in Bar to Eat   Patio/terrace   Outdoor Eating* **No Credit Cards**

STOCKLAND   Kings Arms

Stockland EX14 9BS
Tel: (040 488) 361
Open: 12-3, 6.30-11
Licensees: Heinz Kiefer and Paul Diviani

A tremendous range of island malt whiskies is just one of the lures at the Kings Arms; the last exciseman at Lagavulin distillery was also the landlord's father! An inn since the early 18th century at least, it's grade II listed, though considerably renovated and extended a few years ago. Best book to eat. A marvellously unspoilt interior, both in the dining lounge and flagstoned stone-walled bar.

Bar Meals: 12-1.45; also bar snacks **Restaurant:** *12-1.45, 6.30-9.30; no food Sun lunch* **Typical Dishes:** *home-made soup £1.50, garlic mushrooms £2.50, chicken tikka masala £6.50, sirloin of beef roulade £8.50, sole fillets in white wine cream and dill sauce with crab £9.50, apple and cinnamon strudel £2 Vegetarian Meals: vegetable curry £4.50 Children's Portions* **Beer** *Exmoor Ale; Hall & Woodhouse Badger Best Bitter; Ushers Best* **Whisky** *Family Room   Outdoor Play Area   Patio/terrace   Outdoor Eating Summer Barbecue* **Accommodation:** *3 bedrooms, all en suite, from £30 (single £20) Children Welcome Overnight   Check-in: all day* **No Credit Cards**

THELBRIDGE   Thelbridge Cross Inn

near Witheridge EX17 4SQ   ❢
Tel: (0884) 860316
Open: 11.30-3, 6.30-11
Licensees: W G and R E Ball

Attractive old inn, recently extended. Views across to Dartmoor and good local walks. Owner-managed, with a cosy bar, and simple pretty bedrooms. No live music, juke box or pool table. 'Lorna Doone' stagecoach brings extra Sunday lunch trade.

Bar Meals and Restaurant: 12-2, 7-9.30; also bar snacks both sessions **Typical Dishes BAR:** *leek and potato soup £1.50, mussels with garlic and herb butter, brandied fillet of beef, honey-glazed rack of lamb, grilled whole lemon sole, gateaux Vegetarian Meals: ratatouille bake   Children's Menu/Portions* **Beer** *Draught Bass; Butcombe Bitter;*

Wadworth 6X **Whisky** *Lavagulin 16 yr* **Cider** *Inch's Harvest, Wassail   Family Room   Outdoor Play Area   Garden   Outdoor Eating*   **Accommodation:** *8 rooms, all en suite, from £45 (single £30)   Children Welcome Overnight   Cots Available   Check-in: all day*   **Credit Cards:** *Access, Visa*

THROWLEIGH Northmore Arms Tel: (064 723) 428: In hamlet of Wonson, up lane by post office. Usually busy. Bar food Monday–Saturday lunch and evening. Garden. Whitbread beers; local cider.

TORCROSS   Start Bay Inn

on A379
Tel: (0548) 580553
Open: 11.30-2.30, 6-11
Licensee: Paul Stubbs

Busy thatched dining pub by Slapton Ley lake; be early for a seat inside. Fresh fish is the house speciality, particularly the fried cod or haddock, in three sizes from average to plate-sized. Excellent value. No children under 14.

Bar Meals: *11.30-1, 6-10; bar snacks both sessions*   **Typical Dishes:** *cod/haddock £3/£3.50/£4.50, seafood platter £6.25, steaks from £7   Vegetarian Meals: lasagne £3.25*   **Beer** *Marston; Whitbread* **Cider**

TUCKENHAY   Maltster's Arms

Tuckenhay TQ9 7EQ   **FOOD**
Tel: (0803) 732350   ▼
Open: 11-3, 6-11
Licensees: Keith Floyd and John Pitchford

Keith Floyd has lavished much time and hard cash carefully un–modernising the Maltster's, and it's now stylishly simple, with various individually decorated rooms, the best of which is the riverside restaurant, flooded with light at lunchtime through large picture windows. Cheap it ain't, but everything's home-made and carefully prepared; the menu displaying a typically Floydian combination of delicate seafoods and sausages and chips.

Bar Meals: *11-2, 6-9.30; bar snacks both sessions*   **Restaurant:** *12-2, 6.30-9.30*   **Typical Dishes BAR:** *home-made soup £2.50, smoked salmon £5.50, sirloin steak £9.75, sausages and chips £4.50, prawns £5.50, gooseberry pie £3.50*   **RESTAURANT:** *baked avocado with bacon and walnuts £5.80, breast of duck £16.50, lobster £22.50, scallops in bacon £18.50, lemon tart £5.50   Children's Portions*   **Cheese**   **Beer** *Draught Bass; Blackawton Bitter; Exmoor Ale* **Whisky** *Family Room   Riverside Summer Barbecue*   **Credit Cards:** *Access, Amex, Visa*

UGBOROUGH Anchor Inn Lutterburn Street Tel: (0752) 892283. Italian–run local with good fresh food; many ingredients supplied by locals, including fish, game and vegetables. Italian dishes in restaurant; food lunchtime and evening. Family room. Bass, Cornish, Ruddles, Wadworth beers.

WIDECOMBE-IN-THE-MOOR   Old Inn

Widecombe-in-the-Moor TQ13 7TA
Tel: (03642) 207
Open: 11-2.30, 6.30 (6 Sat, 7 winter)-11
Licensees: Alan and Susie Boult

14th century Dartmoor inn, which sits beneath the 120 foot tower of the St Pancras church, 'cathedral of the moors'. A devastating fire in the 1970s means much of the Old Inn is actually pretty new, though original stonework and fireplaces and two ghosts remain.

Bar Meals: 11-2.30, 6.30-10 (11-2, 7-10 winter); 12-2.30, 7-9.30 Sun all year; bar snacks both sessions **Typical Dishes:** *potato and watercress soup £1.50, smoked mackerel paté £2.50, roast lamb with gin sauce £4.75, rump steak and stilton pie £4.95, Mediterranean fish casserole £4.95, zabaglione trifle £2 Vegetarian Meals: celery nut roast with chilli sauce Children's Portions* **Beer** *Ushers Best Bitter; Widecombe Wallop* **Whisky** *Macallan 1971* **Cider** *Grays Family Room Outdoor Play Area Garden Outdoor Eating* **No Credit Cards**

YARDE DOWN   Poltimore Arms

South Molton EX36 3HA
Tel: (0598) 710381
Open: 11.30-2.30 (12-2 Sun), 6.30-11
Licensees: R M and M A Wright

Lovely pub in a tiny hamlet which can nonetheless boast its own cricket team (just about everybody's in it). A rustic setting and a charmingly down at heel country interior.

Bar Meals: 11.30-2, 6.30-9.30; bar snacks both sessions **Typical Dishes:** *home-made soup £1.10, prawn cocktail £1.35, home-made turkey or steak and kidney pie £3.50, rump steak £5.80, plaice and prawns in white wine sauce £4.50, mud pie £1.20 Vegetarian Meals: cheese and nut croquettes £2.75 Children's Menu/Portions* **Beer** *Cotleigh; Ruddles* **Cider** *Inch's Family Room Outdoor Play Area Garden Outdoor Eating* **No Credit Cards**

DORSET

ANSTY   Fox Inn

Ansty DT2 7PN
Tel: (0258) 880328
Open: 11-3, 6-11
Licensees: Gary and Kathryn Witheyman

Deep in Thomas Hardy territory, lost in narrow country lanes, this well-known pub has managed to keep something of a farming pub atmosphere, despite the dizzying scale of the food operation in its various bars. There are original nooks and crannies, simple furnishings, lots of beams, and flattering deep reds and blues, as well as vast plate collections in the Platter Bar, and toby jugs (almost 800 of them) in the Toby Bar. A modern extension housing the family room is less inspiring. The Platter Bar is home to the carvery, with 14 cold meats and perhaps as many as 30 salads; there are also jacket potatoes in the Spud Bar, and a barbecue chargrill indoors and out. Bedrooms are clean and comfortable; those in the extension are lighter and airier.

Bar Meals: 12-2, 7-9.30; bar snacks both sessions **Restaurant:** *7-10* **Typical Dishes** **BAR:** *vegetable soup £1.10, prawn cocktail £2.95, pork chop £5.50, spare ribs £5, swordfish steak £5.50, treacle pudding £1.95* **RESTAURANT:** *carrot and orange soup £1.60, frogs' legs provencale £3.95, Abbotts bag steak £11.50, chicken princess £7.65,*

*poached halibut £7.95, spotted dick £2.25   Vegetarian Meals: vegetable lasagne
Children's Menu/Portions* **Beer** *Eldridge Pope Best Bitter, Royal Oak; Hall &
Woodhouse Badger Best Bitter; Wadworth 6X* **Whisky** **Cider** *Addlestones   Family
Room   Outdoor Play Area   Garden   Outdoor Eating   Summer Barbecue*
Accommodation: *14 bedrooms, all en suite, from £48 (single £38)   Children Welcome
Overnight   Cots Available   Check-in: all day   **Credit Cards:** Access, Amex, Visa*

ASKERSWELL   Spyway Inn

Askerswell DT2 9EP
Tel: (0308) 85250
Open: 10-2.30, 6-11
Licensees: Don and Jackie Roderick

Charming pub in popular tourist area; be early in summer. Various cosy little rooms
have old-fashioned furniture, some window seats, and pretty oddments of
countryware. The menu is on the routine side, but reliable enough. The garden is
delightful.

Bar Meals: *12-2, 6.45-9.15; bar snacks lunchtime   **Typical Dishes:** vegetable soup
£1.20, egg and prawn mayonnaise £2.95, sirloin steak £7.50, pork rib steak £4.25,
seafood crepe £3.25, bread and butter pudding £1.40   Vegetarian Meals: savoury quiche
Children's Portions* **Beer** *Ruddles County, Ushers Best Bitter, Webster's Yorkshire
Bitter* **Whisky** *Bruichladdich, Old Fettercairn   Family Room   Outdoor Play Area
Garden   **Credit Cards:** Access, Visa*

BOURTON   White Lion

High Street SP8 5AT
Tel: (0747) 840866
Open: 10.30-2.30, 6-11
Licensee: Christopher Frowde

Popular, friendly, genuinely unspoilt old pub run by the same licensee for ten years.
All the traditional features: beams, flagstones, nice old furnishings, real fires, plus
interesting, reliable home-cooking. Pretty garden.

Bar Meals: *11-1.45, 6.15-9.30; bar snacks both sessions   **Restaurant:** 11-1.45, 6.30-
9.30   Typical Dishes BAR: home-made soup £1.60, home-made paté-stuffed mushrooms
£2.95, beef in red wine £4.35, home-cooked ham salad £4.50, stuffed trout £4.95, jam
roly poly   Vegetarian Meals   Children's Menu/Portions* **Beer** *Ash Vine; Ruddles,
Ushers   Family Room   Outdoor Play Area   Garden   Outdoor Eating   Summer Barbecue
Credit Cards: Access, Visa*

BRANKSOME PARK   Inn In The Park

Pinewood Road BH13 6JS   ▼
Tel: (0202) 761318
Open: 11-2.30, 5.30-11 (11-3, 6-11 Sat)
Licensees: Alan and Paula Potter

On the road to Branksome Chine and the sea, this looks from the outside like a
substantial Victorian guest house, but the bar is pubbier than first impressions
suggest. It's also welcoming to all comers, and has a growing reputation for fine bar
food, offering produce from Dorset Harvest, a local farmers and growers
consortium. Attractive dining room and bright, simple bedrooms.

Bar Meals: 12-2.30; also bar snacks lunchtime   *Restaurant:* 7-9.30 (not Sun)   **Typical Dishes BAR:** *steak and kidney pie £3.95, beef olives £3.95, local fish pie £3.95, cheesecakes £1.75*   **RESTAURANT:** *local fish soup £1.75, spinach and mushroom parcels £2.45, fillet of pork in cream and calvados £7.25, chicken avocado £7.25, fresh local fish and shellfish £6.50, trifles £1.75 Vegetarian Meals   Children's Menu/Portions* | Cheese | | Beer | *Adnams Southwold Bitter; Draught Bass; Wadworth 6X* | Whisky | *Glenfarclas   Family Room (lunchtime)   Patio/terrace   Outdoor Eating   **Accommodation:** 5 bedrooms, all en suite, from £39 (single £27)   Children Welcome Overnight   Cot Available   Check-in: all day   **Credit Cards:** Access, Visa*

BRIDPORT   George Hotel

4 South Street DT6 3NQ
Tel: (0308) 23187
Open: 10-11
Licensee: John Mander

Delightfully eccentric pub in a handsome Georgian building. Consistently reliable food, excellent snacks, fresh fish direct from the quay, and civilised touches like freshly squeezed fruit juices. An old-fashioned local in style, with young staff and perhaps loud jazz in the bar; the dining room is quieter. Non-residents can get a continental breakfast from 8.30am. Bedrooms are modest.

Bar Meals: 12-3, 6.30-11; no food Sun; bar snacks both sessions   **Typical Dishes:** *cream of calabrese soup £1.30, smoked fish mousse £2.75, entrecote steak £7.35, lamb cutlets £4.25, whole grilled trout £4.75, fresh raspberry tart £3.25   Vegetarian Meals: fettuccine verdi £3.25* | Cheese | | Beer | *Palmers Bridport Bitter, IPA, Tally Ho   Family Room* **Accommodation:** *4 bedrooms, sharing a bathroom, from £37 (single £18.50)   Children Welcome Overnight   Check-in: all day   **Credit Cards:** Access, Visa*

BUCKLAND NEWTON   Gaggle of Geese

Buckland Newton DT2 7BS
Tel: (03005) 249
Open: 12-3, 6.30-11
Licensees: Trevor and Jan Marpole

Civilised and attractive main bar in tranquil village pub with pretty garden complete with pond. A routine menu has its fans. Planning permission has been granted for five self-contained motel units.

Bar Meals and Restaurant: 12-2.30, 6.30-10.30; bar snacks both sessions   **Typical Dishes BAR:** *mushroom and garlic soup £1.60, smoked mackerel £2.75, home-cooked ham, egg, beans and chips £3.25, gammon steak and pineapple £5.50, breaded scampi £4.25, treacle tart and custard £1.75*   **RESTAURANT:** *country vegetable soup £1.60, avocado with prawns £2.95, sirloin steak £7.50, whole plaice stuffed with prawns £3.95, roasts (on Sunday) £4.25, apple and blackcurrant pie £1.75   Vegetarian Meals: macaroni cheese £2.95   Children's Menu/Portions* | Beer | *Draught Bass; Hall & Woodhouse Badger Best Bitter; Marston Pedigree; Wadworth 6X   Family Room   Outdoor Play Area   Garden   Outdoor Eating   **No Credit Cards**

CERNE ABBAS — New Inn

14 Long Street DT2 7JF
Tel: (0300) 341274
Open: 11-2.30, 6-11; 11-11 Sat
Licensee: Paul Edmunds

A typical Dorset setting and a splendid old inn, a listed 15th century ex monastic resting house, complete with original stone roof. There's a priest hole by the fireplace, charming window-seats with High Street views, an excellent wine list and reputable food (despite the rather off-putting style of the menu). The ubiquitous scampi, burgers and the like are balanced by hot daily meat and fish specials, plus several interesting perennials. Simple bedrooms have sloping floors and plenty of character.

Bar Meals: 12-2, 6.30-9.30; bar snacks both sessions **Typical Dishes:** *home-made soup of the day £1.85, Dorset paté £3.75, rump steak £9.15, grandmother's omelette £4.60, pan fried trout £6.55 Vegetarian Meals: savoury vegetable nut strudel Children's Portions* **Beer** *Eldridge Pope Dorchester Bitter, Thomas Hardy Country Bitter, Royal Oak* **Whisky** *Family Room Outdoor Play Area Garden Outdoor Eating* **Accommodation** *(closed Christmas week): 5 bedrooms, sharing 2 bathrooms, from £40 (single £25) Check-in: all day* **Credit Cards:** *Access, Diners, Visa*

CERNE ABBAS — Red Lion

Long Street DT2 7JF
Tel: (0300) 341441
Open: 11.30-2.30, 6.30-11
Licensee: Christopher J Grey

Ancient, Grade II listed pub with a Victorian facade, thanks to a late 19th century fire. There's also a beautiful 16th century fireplace, crackling with logs in winter, a five star ladies toilet, and a sheltered south facing cottage-planted garden. The food is beginning to attract attention.

Bar Meals: 11.45-2, 6.45-9.30 (12-2, 7-9 Sun); bar snacks both sessions **Typical Dishes:** *sweet pepper and courgette soup £1.60, garlic mushrooms £2.60, venison, pork and apricots in Guinness pie, Dorset lamb, lemon and mint casserole, tuna and vegetable bake (main courses from around £4), apple and apricot crumble Vegetarian Meals: asparagus pancakes Children's Portions* **Cheese** **Beer** *Adnams Southwold; Ringwood Best Bitter; Smiles Best Bitter; Wadworth 6X Family Room (for children over 5) Outdoor Play Area Garden Outdoor Eating* **No Credit Cards**

CHEDINGTON — Winyards Gap

near Beaminster DT8 3HY
Tel: (0935) 891244
Open: 11-3, 6.30-11 (11-2.30, 7-11 winter)
Licensees: Clive and Pam Martin

Ancient inn on unique site on the edge of the Dorset Downs, with views across the Axe valley. Pleasantly modernised inside; busy, with a well-organised food operation; home-made deep dish pies the house speciality. Self-catering cottage flats in converted barn, from £15 a night.

Bar Meals: 12-2, 7-9.30 (9 Mon-Wed winter); bar snacks both sessions **Typical Dishes:** *tomato and courgette soup £1.40, crispy mushrooms with garlic dip £2.50, Colonel Napier's deep filled pie £5.50, Dorset cream chicken £5.50, smoked salmon and scrambled eggs*

£5.75, spotted dick   Vegetarian Meals: ratatouille   Children's Menu   Children's Portions (some)   **Beer**   Exmoor; Marston; Whitbread   **Cider**   (summer)   Family Room   Outdoor Play Area   Garden   Outdoor Eating   **No Credit Cards**

CHESIL   Cove House Inn

Chesil Beach, Portland DT5 1AW
Tel: (0305) 820895
Open: 11-2.30 (or later), 6.30-11
Licensees: Pat and Debbie Jackson

Gloriously positioned, beach-side pub with a bar and dining room of subtle, simple, fishing pub atmosphere. They specialise in fresh local fish, listing the day's catch on the blackboard menu; prices are a little higher, and the food a little more fancy, in the evenings. You can eat outside, by the sea wall; wonderful sunsets. No children in the bar.

Bar Meals and Restaurant: 12-2, 7-9 (not Sun eve); bar snacks both sessions   **Typical Dishes:** home-made soup of the day £1.50, home-made smoked mackerel paté £2.75, steak and kidney pie £6.75, local lamb cutlets £6.25, whole scampi tails £4.75, brown bread ice-cream £2   Vegetarian Meals: sweetcorn and mushroom crumble £5.75   Children's Menu (limited, restaurant)   **Beer**   Cornish Royal Wessex, Greene King Abbot Ale; Marston Pedigree; Wadworth 6X   Patio/terrace   Outdoor Eating   **No Credit Cards**

CHURCH KNOWLE   New Inn

near Wareham BH20 5NQ   ♥
Tel: (0929) 480357
Open: 11-3, 6-11 (7-10.30 winter)
Licensee: Maurice Estop

Overlooking the Purbeck Hills, a partly thatched, very popular pub with a stylish public bar and comfortable lounge.

Bar Meals: 12-2.15, 6.30-9.15; bar snacks both sessions   **Restaurant:** Sun lunch, 7-9.30 (not Mon)   **Typical Dishes BAR:** Dorset blue vinny soup £1.45, moules marinière £4, beefsteak and kidney pie in Guinness £4.60, Dorset lamb and aubergine pie £7.50, fresh battered plaice £5.85   **RESTAURANT:** grilled sardines £4, melon with prawns £4, fillet of beef stroganoff £8.50, lamb in orange and ginger £8.75, foil-baked sea bass £11.50   Vegetarian Meals: moussaka   Children's Menu   **Beer**   Marston; Whitbread   Children Allowed in Bar to Eat   Outdoor Play Area   Garden   Outdoor Eating   **Credit Cards:** Access, Visa

---

CORFE CASTLE   Fox

West Street (off A351)
Tel: (0929) 480449
Open: 11-2.30, 7 (6 summer)-11
Licensee: A L Brown

Unspoilt 16th century inn, with a snug (very snug) little front bar and slightly less enchanting larger lounge. Simple bar food of the quiche/salad/pie/old-fashioned pudding sort; very low prices. The dining pub in Corfe Castle is the Greyhound (see below). The Fox is the one for summer, though, and its mature, pretty garden has views of the famous ruin.

Bar Meals: lunchtime   **Beer**   Whitbread   Garden   Outdoor Eating

CORFE CASTLE Greyhound on A351: Popular, traditional old pub at the foot of the castle, with a family room and good local seafood amongst the lunchtime and evening bar meals. Whitbread beers. Open: 11-3, 6 (6.30 winter)-11.

CORSCOMBE   Fox Inn

Corscombe DT2 0NS
Tel: (0935) 891330
Open: 12-2.30, 7-11
Licensees: Mr and Mrs Lee

"Real Ale, Country Cooking, No Chips or Microwaves" it says on the postcard, showing a pretty little thatched pub of stone and cob, built in 1620. Equally neat and appealing inside, the small entrance lobby is decorated with a wild flower and ivy mural painted directly onto the walls. Beyond are two bars, one, with its hunting prints, reflecting landlord Martyn Lee's favourite pastime, and the other prettily furnished with blue gingham curtains, table cloths, banquette seat covers, – even the fabric covering the barrel stools. A huge old stone fireplace boasts a real log fire in winter, while behind the bar a collection of plates, copper and pewterware is displayed. All is overseen by an array of stuffed owls in glass cases. It's still very much a local's pub, complete with local cricket team; fairly few tourists seem to find their way to this quiet backwater. Most Friday nights and Sunday lunchtimes a blues pianist entertains in a separate, newly opened stable conversion. Foodwise, it's all down to Martyn's mother, who works alone in her microwave-free kitchen. The menu is, sensibly, not overlong and largely the same lunch and evening, too, except that sandwiches and ploughmans are dropped at night and a couple of fish dishes added. The beef stew which comes in Yorkshire pudding at lunchtime is transmogrified into an evening meal by putting it into a pie dish, and serving it up with fresh vegetables. Fox's Favourite – a generous quantity of chicken with peppers in a cream sauce – lives up to its name, although the apple pie doesn't, being in reality a roundle of undercooked puff pastry slapped on top of a base of stewed apple just before serving.

Bar Meals and Restaurant: 12-2, 7-9; *bar snacks both sessions*   **Typical Dishes:** *home-made soup of the day £1.80, home-made country paté £2.50, beef stew £5.25, chicken in cream sauce £5.25, casserole £5.25, apple charlotte £1.75   Vegetarian Meals: macaroni cheese £3.25*   **Beer** *Exmoor Ale; Hook Norton* **Cider**   *Family Room   Outdoor Play Area   Garden   Outdoor Eating* **No Credit Cards**

CRANBORNE   Fleur de Lys

5 Wimborne Street BH21 5PP
Tel: (07254) 282
Open: 10.30-2.30, 6-11
Licensee: Charles T Hancock

Historical connections are many at the Fleur de Lys: Thomas Hardy visited when writing Tess of the D'Urbervilles, Rupert Brooke wrote a poem on the premises, and Hanging Judge Jeffreys stayed the night. The pub itself is modernised and pleasant, with period features remaining. The upgrading programme will be extended to the bedrooms in 1992, some of which have original beams, all of which are clean and simply-furnished. Bar food is reliably good, and puddings outstanding.

Bar Meals and Restaurant: 12-2, 7-9.30 (10 *restaurant*); *bar snacks both sessions*
Typical Dishes BAR: *chicken and vegetable soup £1.70, devilled whitebait £3.30, home-made steak pie £4.75, carbonade of beef £5.55, whole lemon sole £7.75, raspberry pavlova £1.90   RESTAURANT: watercress soup £1.95, boozy melon and grapes £3.40, gammon, venison and mushroom pie £7.45, medallions of pork fillet £9.45, poached salmon*

*with prawn and tarragon sauce £8.75   Vegetarian Meals: cream cheese and spinach
cannelloni £4.85   Children's Portions*   **Beer**   *Hall & Woodhouse Badger Best Bitter,
Tanglefoot*   **Cider**   *Taunton Traditional   Family Room   Garden   Outdoor Eating*
Accommodation: *8 bedrooms, 7 en suite, from £36 (single £25)   Children Welcome
Overnight   Cot Available   Check-in: all day*   **Credit Cards:** *Access, Visa*

EAST LULWORTH   Weld Arms

on B3070 BH20 5QQ
Tel: (092 941) 211
Open: 11-3, 5.30-11 (11.30-2.30, 6.30-11 winter)
Licensees: Peter and Alix Crowther

Distinctive and relaxing thatched old pub with a welcoming fire, a mix of attractive
furnishings including large country kitchen tables, and nautical memorabilia, thanks
to the yachtsman licensee. Lovely garden.

Bar Meals: *12-2, 7-9; bar snacks lunchtime*   **Restaurant:** *7-9.30 (not Sun)*   **Typical
Dishes BAR:** *watercress soup £1.40, baked avocado £3.20, fidget pie £4.40, Wiltshire
plait £4.40, fish Wellington £4.40, treacle tart £2*   **RESTAURANT:** *duck breasts with
lavender sauce £8, game pie £8, salmon en croute £8.40   Vegetarian Meals: layered
savoury pancakes   Children's Menu*   **Cheese**   **Beer**   *Whitbread Best Bitter   Family
Room   Children Allowed in Bar to Eat   Outdoor Play Area   Garden*   **Accommodation:**
*3 bedrooms, sharing a bathroom, from £28 (single £16)   Children Welcome Overnight
Cot Available   Check-in: by arrangement*   **No Credit Cards**

HINTON ST MARY   White Horse

off B3092 DT10 1NA
Tel: (0258) 72723
Open: 11.30-2.30 (3 Sat), 6-11
Licensee: A C Thomas

Attractively extended and modernised pub in lovely village. They specialise in steaks
and homely, traditional dishes.

Bar Meals: *12-2, 6.45-9.15; bar snacks both sessions*   **Typical Dishes:** *home-made soup
£1.50, steaks £6.25-£10.25, home-made rabbit pie £4.25, local trout £4.95, pavlova
£1.50   Vegetarian Meals: pasta and mushrooms with garlic sauce £3.95   Children's
Portions*   **Beer**   *Wadworth 6X   Children Allowed in Bar to Eat   Outdoor Play Area
Garden   Outdoor Eating   Summer Barbecue*   **No Credit Cards**

HORTON   Horton Inn

near Wimborne BH21 5AD
Tel: (0258) 840252
Open: 11-2.30, 6-11
Licensees: Nicholas and Ivan Caplan

Attractively refurbished 18th century country inn at a crossroads on the B3078, in
downland countryside. Proprietor-run with enthusiasm; good eating in the convivial
bar, or garden in summer. Bedrooms are bright and fresh, and extremely spacious;
all feature comfy easychairs, and two have their own roomy, well-equipped
bathrooms. First floor residents' lounge.

Bar Meals and Restaurant: 12-2 (2.30 Sun), 7-10; *bar snacks both sessions* **Typical Dishes RESTAURANT:** *asparagus soup £3.95, vermouth-flavoured mushrooms with béarnaise sauce, medallions of beef fillet au poivre, rack of lamb with Cumberland sauce, whole Poole plaice (main courses around £13), hazelnut meringue* *Vegetarian Meals: broccoli and cream cheese pie* *Children's Portions* Beer *Courage; Ringwood; Wadworth* Whisky *Family Room* *Outdoor Play Area* *Garden* *Outdoor Eating* **Accommodation:** *5 bedrooms, 2 en suite, from £45 (single £30)* *Children Welcome Overnight* *Cot Available* *Check-in: all day* *Credit Cards: Access, Visa*

IBBERTON Crown Tel: (0258) 817448: Quiet, pretty country local with real fire, family room and outdoor drinking. Bar meals daily lunch and evening. Draught Bass. Open: 11-2.30, 6-11.

LYME REGIS   Pilot Boat Inn

Bridge Street DT7 3QA
Tel: (02974) 443157
Open: 11-3, 6-11 (11-2.30, 7-11 winter)
Licensee: Bill Wiscombe

Commendable straightforwardness and honesty earns gold stars at the Pilot Boat, whose menu openly admits which dishes are bought in (not many, as it happens) and which home-made. The front bar is modernised in blue plush but still very much a fishing haunt; a lounge at the back overlooks the river. The food is reliably good.

Bar Meals: 12-2.15, 6-10 (7-9.30 winter); *bar snacks both sessions* **Typical Dishes:** *rich crab paté £3.50, vegetable samosas £3.75, steak and kidney pie in Palmers Bitter £4.95, pork and cider casserole £5.95, Lyme Bay skate wing £6.95* *Vegetarian Meals: cheese and lentil loaf with peanut sauce £5.25* *Children's Menu* Beer *Palmers Bridport Bitter, IPA, Tally Ho* *Children Allowed in Bar to Eat* *Patio/terrace* *Outdoor Eating* **Credit Cards:** *Access, Visa*

MILTON ABBAS   Hambro Arms

near Blandford Forum DT11 0BP
Tel: (0258) 880233
Open: 11-2.30, 6.30-11
Licensee: Ken Baines

Thatched 18th century inn in picturesque village street. Open fires in winter; good bed and breakfast. No children in the bar.

Bar Meals: 12-2, 7-9.30 (9 Sun); *bar snacks both sessions* **Typical Dishes:** *beef and vegetable soup £2.25, local Dorset paté £2.25, home-made steak and mushroom pie £6.95, roast pheasant £6.95, beef Wellington £8.95, home-made apple pie* *Vegetarian Meals: mushroom and broccoli mornay* Beer *Whitbread Flowers IPA* *Outdoor Play Area Patio/terrace* **Accommodation:** *2 bedrooms, both en suite, from £50 (single £30)* *Children Welcome Overnight ('by arrangement')* *Check-in: by arrangement* **Credit Cards:** *Access, Visa*

NORTH WOOTTON   Three Elms

North Wootton DT9 5JW   ♥
Tel: (0935) 812881
Open: 11-2.30, 6.30 (6 Fri/Sat)-11
Licensees: Howard and Eileen Manning

Simple old-fashioned local with a country coffee shop feel in one bar, more pubby
in the other. A collection of around 900 model cars provides a focal point. A long,
fairly routine menu is joined by a daily specials board running to around 10 home-
cooked dishes; go for these.

Bar Meals: 12-2, 6.30-10; bar snacks both sessions   **Typical Dishes:** *two soups of the
day, each £1.85, home-made duck liver paté £2.85, individual steak pie £4.85, rabbit and
swede crumble, landlord's braised steak in beer, almond meringue £1.85   Vegetarian Meals:
mushroom brioche £4.85   Children's Menu/Portions* **Beer** *Fullers London Pride;
Greene King Abbot Ale; Smiles Best Bitter; Wadworth 6X* **Whisky** **Cider**
*Addlestones, Burrow Hill   Children Allowed in Bar to Eat   Outdoor Play Area   Garden
Outdoor Eating* **Accommodation:** *3 bedrooms, sharing a bathroom, from £32 (single
£25)   Children Welcome Overnight   Check-in: by arrangement* **Credit Cards:** *Access,
Visa*

PEACEMARSH   Dolphin Inn

Peacemarsh SP8 4HB   ♥
Tel: (0747) 822758
Open: 11-2.30, 6.30 (7 Mon)-11
Licensees: Tim and Ann-Marie Gould

Creeper-covered ex-farmhouse where the landlord also does the cooking. Two
attractively plain, old-fashioned rooms; an open log fire in the lounge.

Bar Meals: 12-2, 7-9.30 (9 Sun); bar snacks both sessions   **Typical Dishes:** *leek and
potato soup £1.50, green lipped mussels £3.80, hedgerow pork £4.90, Highland fling
£5.10, traveller's trio £4.70, date and walnut pudding   Vegetarian Meals: Gloucester pie
Children's Menu/Portions* **Cheese** **Beer** *Hall & Woodhouse Badger Best Bitter,
Tanglefoot* **Cider** *Taunton Traditional   Children Allowed in Bar to Eat   Outdoor Play
Area   Garden   Outdoor Eating   Summer Barbecue* **Credit Cards:** *Access, Amex,
Diners, Visa*

PIDDLEHINTON   Thimble Inn

Piddlehinton DT2 7UE
Tel: (03004) 270
Open: 12-2.30 (seven days), 7-11
Licensees: N R White and V J Lanfear

Creeper-covered, picturesque thatched old pub with intimate, cosy interior, nice
wooden furnishings, thimble collection.

Bar Meals: 12-2, 7-9; bar snacks both sessions   **Typical Dishes:** *mushroom soup £1.35,
home-made paté £2.70, steak and oyster pudding £4.95, beef and venison pie £4.95, beef
curry £4.65, chicken a la king £4.65, lemon meringue pie £1.80   Vegetarian Meals:
vegetable bake £4.50* **Beer** *Eldridge Pope Thomas Hardy Ale; Hall & Woodhouse
Badger BB, Tanglefoot* **Whisky** *Glenkinchie, Tamdhu   Family Room   Outdoor Play
Area   Riverside Garden   Outdoor Eating* **No Credit Cards**

PLUSH   Brace of Pheasants

off B3134 DT2 7RQ
Tel: (03004) 357
Open: 11.30-2.30, 7-11
Licensees: Jane and Geoffrey Knights

Characterful ex-row of village cottages in a pretty rural spot. The bar is lovely in winter, with its stove at one end, log fire at the other.

*Bar Meals and Restaurant: 12-2, 7-10; bar snacks both sessions **Typical Dishes BAR:** mushroom and stilton soup £1.75, crab savoury £2.95, liver, bacon and onion £5.85, home-made game pie £7.75, lemon and tarragon chicken £5.75, Tia Maria cheesecake £2.35 **RESTAURANT:** tomato, sherry and apple soup £1.75, chicken livers £3.25, pigeon breast £7.95, fillet steak £12.25, Vegetarian Meals: vegetable stir-fry £5.75 Children's Menu/Portions* **Beer** *Greene King Abbot Ale; Ind Coope Burton Ale; Wadworth 6X; Whitbread Flowers Original* **Cider** *Addlestones Family Room Outdoor Play Area Garden **Accommodation:** 4 bedrooms, all en suite, from £40 Children Welcome Overnight Cots Available Check-in: by arrangement **Credit Cards:** Access, Visa*

POWERSTOCK   Three Horseshoes Inn

Powerstock DT6 3TF   ▼
Tel: (030 885) 328
Open: 11-3, 6-11
Licensee: Pat Ferguson

Reliable old favourite, rebuilt in 1906 after a devastating fire, but solidly old-fashioned in style, with its stone and thatch, simple country furnishings and open fires. But people come here for the bar food; not cheap, certainly, but fresh and delicious, specialising in fish. Main courses listed below come in at around £8-£12, though cheaper, less restauranty options are also on the menu; pancakes, pasta, and less luxurious fish dishes. Note that they now only let two bedrooms; both large and traditionally styled, with nice bathrooms and lovely views. Delightful garden.

*Bar Meals and Restaurant: 12-2, 7-10 (10.30 restaurant); bar snacks both sessions **Typical Dishes:** red lentil soup £2.50, mussels £5.50; fillet of sea bass on a julienne of vegetables with garlic sauce, pan-fried wing of skate, John Dory deauvillaise; sticky toffee pudding Vegetarian Meals: spinach roulade on tomato sauce Children's Portions* **Cheese** **Beer** *Palmers Bridport Bitter, IPA Children Allowed in Bar to Eat Outdoor Play Area Garden Outdoor Eating Summer Barbecue **Accommodation:** 2 bedrooms, both en suite, from £60 Children Welcome Overnight Cots Available Check-in: by arrangement Credit Cards: Access, Amex, Visa*

SANDFORD ORCAS   Mitre

Tel: (096 322) 271
Open: 11.30-2.30, 7-11
Licensees: Philip and Brenda Hayes

Lots of animals, old flagstones, an open fire, wall benches and a separate dining room in this white-painted old village pub. Their own sheep and local deer on the menu.

*Bar Meals: 12-2, 7-10; bar snacks both sessions **Typical Dishes:** home-cooked ham and eggs £3.50, steak and kidney pie £4.25, rack of lamb/venison specials, sticky toffee pudding £1.85 Vegetarian Meals: curry £3.95 Children's Portions* **Beer** *Butcombe Bitter* **Cider** *Children Allowed in to Eat Garden*

SHAVE CROSS   Shave Cross Inn

Marshwood Vale DT6 6HW
Tel: (0308) 68358
Open: 12-3, 7-11 (closed Mon)
Licensees: Bill and Ruth Slade

Charming cob and flint old inn in beautiful Marshwood Vale, once a busy resting place for pilgrims on their way to Whitchurch, as well as monastic visitors, who frequently had their tonsures trimmed while staying, hence the name. Stone floor, inglenook fireplace, beamed ceiling, rustic furnishings, and a delightful suntrap garden. Popular with the local caravan site on wet summer days.

Bar Meals: 12-2, 7-9.45; bar snacks both sessions **Typical Dishes:** *Dorset paté £2.40, half-dozen oysters £3.45, chicken, ham and leek pie £3.75, kebabs £5.50, char-grilled sirloin steak £7.75, local ice-cream £1.30 Vegetarian Meals: spinach and mushroom lasagne £3.75 Children's Menu* Beer *Draught Bass; Eldridge Pope Royal Oak; Hall & Woodhouse Badger Best Bitter* Cider *Taunton Traditional Family Room Outdoor Play Area Garden Outdoor Eating Summer Barbecue* **No Credit Cards**

SHERBORNE Antelope, Green Hill: Bar and restaurant popular for homely food in big helpings. **Skippers**, on A352: More interesting menu, with something to suit all tastes; good range of beers, and cider in summer. Bass, Butcombe, plus guests. Open: 11.30-2.30, 5.30 (6.30 Sat)–11.

SHROTON   Cricketers

Just off A350 DT11 8QD
Tel: (0258) 860421
Open: 11-3, 7-11
Licensees: Robert and Sarah Pillow

Secluded village pub beneath Hambledon Hill, popular with walkers and HQ for the local cricket team.

Bar Meals and Restaurant: 12 (12.30 Sun restaurant)-2, 7-9.45; restaurant closed Sun eve/all day Mon; bar snacks both sessions **Typical Dishes BAR:** *leek and potato soup £1.35, jumbo sausage and chips £2, lasagne £3.85, veal, ham and leek pie £4.45, treacle tart £1.90* **RESTAURANT:** *watercress soup £1.40, mushrooms with cheese and spinach in filo pastry £2.65, chicken breast stuffed with ham and pineapple £7.45, medallions of fillet steak in brandy sauce £7.90, wild salmon with herb butter £7.90, brandy and coffee gateau £1.90 Vegetarian Meals: vegetable pancake rolls £2.65 Children's Portions* Cheese Beer *Courage Best; Fullers London Pride; Greene King IPA; Samuel Smith Old Brewery Bitter Children Allowed in Bar to Eat Outdoor Play Area Garden Outdoor Eating* **Credit Cards:** *Access, Visa*

STOKE ABBOT   New Inn

off A3066
Tel: (0308) 68333
Open: 12-2.30, 7-11
Licensee: Graham Gibbs

As the name doesn't suggest, the New Inn is very old, thatched and cobbled without, simply modernised within. A huge collection of horse brasses, and pictures of birds spotted in the garden. Children are allowed in the separate dining room.

Bar Meals: *lunchtime and evening; bar snacks both sessions*   ***Typical Dishes:*** *steak and kidney pie £4.25, stilton flan £3.75, pizza £3.50, chicken cacciatore £4.50*   *Vegetarian Meals*   *Children's Menu*   Beer   *Palmers*   *Outdoor Play Area*   *Garden*
Accommodation: *3 bedrooms, sharing a bathroom, from £30 (single £15)*   *Children Welcome Overnight*   ***Credit Cards:*** *Access, Visa*

STUDLAND Bankes Arms Hotel, Manor Road Tel: (092 944) 225: Cliff-top inn with fine beach below; old smugglers' haven; impressive views. Wide-ranging menu of home-made food; bed and breakfast. Children welcome. Marston, Whitbread beers.

STURMINSTER NEWTON Bull Tel: (0258) 72435: 16th century inn with thatched roof, real fire, family room and garden. No piped music. Fish-led menu, lunch and evening. Hall & Woodhouse, Charles Wells beers. Open: 11-2.30, 6-11.
Red Lion: Homely, cosy pub with real fire, home cooking and nice atmosphere.

SUTTON POYNTZ   Springhead

Sutton Poyntz DT3 6LW
Tel: (0884) 32281
Open: 11-2.30, 6-11
Licensees: Jim and Julie White

The village pub was formerly in one of the old stone cottages across the pretty duck-filled stream from the rather more substantial late Victorian inn in this most charming of Dorset villages. The pub takes its name from the nearby spring and waterworks, which actually incorporates one of the funnels from Brunel's steamship, the Great Eastern. Owned by Devenish, the interior of the inn is largely the work of brewery designers, with its high shelves of contrivedly casual piles of old books and bottles, and various framed displays of clay pipes, brass plates and shotgun cartridges, but managers Tim and Julie White have successfully individualised things with the help of a bar billiards table, magazines, and the daily papers to read, and their own relaxed friendliness. Instead of a regular real ale there's a changing selection of at least three guest beers, but they are equally happy if all you want is a pot of tea or coffee. The food side is down to Julie, who cooks everything herself in winter and gets in help in summer, when the blackboard menu reflects the tastes and experience of the assistant; at the time of writing, a Thai chef has contributed specials like beef in oyster sauce with ribbon noodles, but the menu still mostly consists of rather more conventional dishes like steak and kidney pie or chicken chasseur. Light lunchers will find the vegetable soup particularly nice, with lots of firmly cooked diced vegetables in a milky stock, plenty of sandwiches (good ham), ploughmans, jacket potatoes and salads. For children there are fish-shaped fishcakes or jumbo sausages, and they will always boil an egg. They're looked after in the garden, too, where an extensive play area has rustic swings, a slide and a climbing frame; as well as splendid views of the Dorset Downs and the huge chalk-cut figure of a mounted George III. One of the pub's outbuildings has been turned into a shop where genuinely locally made craft goods and pictures by local artists are on sale throughout the summer and at weekends in winter.

Bar Meals: *12-2, 7-9; bar snacks both sessions*   ***Typical Dishes:*** *tomato and orange soup £1.70, garlic mushrooms £3.95, steak and kidney pie £5.25, lamb curry £5.25, chicken in root ginger £5.65, caramel brown bread ice-cream £2*   *Vegetarian Meals: vegetable pilaff £4.95, Children's Menu/Portions*   Beer   *Brakspears; Butcombe; Greene King; Whitbread*   Whisky   *Family Room*   *Outdoor Play Area*   *Riverside Garden*   *Outdoor Eating*   *Summer Barbecue*   ***Credit Cards:*** *Access, Visa*

TRENT   Rose & Crown

Trent DT9 4SL   ♥
Tel: (0935) 850776
Open: 12-2.30, 6.30 (7 winter)-11
Licensees: Charles and Nancy Marion-Crawford

A 40-seat conservatory restaurant has been newly added to this unspoilt country
pub, initially two separate thatched cottages. Refreshingly unpretentious within,
simply furnished, with a rug-strewn stone floor and roaring log fires in winter. No
pub games, fruit machines or music. A great emphasis on good fresh food, though,
making good use of local gardens and farms, and especially liked for its excellent
local cheeses.

Bar Meals: 12-2, 7-9.30 (10 Fri/Sat); bar snacks both sessions **Typical Dishes:** *local
wild game soup £1.75, fresh crab mornay £3.25, venison steak with gin and juniper £6.25,
chicken supreme with two pepper sauces £5.75, Cajun style swordfish £7.50, Georgia pecan
pie   Vegetarian Meals: pasta conchiglie with provencale sauce   Children's Menu/Portions*
`Cheese`   `Beer` *Brakspears Bitter; Hook Norton Bitter; Oakhill Bitter; Wadworth 6X*
`Cider` *Family Room Garden   Outdoor Eating* **Credit Cards:** *Access, Visa*

UPLODERS   Crown Inn

Uploders DT6 4NU
Tel: (030 885) 356
Open: 11-3, 6.30-11
Licensees: Bob and Kay Renshaw

Enthusiastic young licensees have extended the Crown into the adjoining stable, and
furnished it attractively in a winning country style. Good home-made traditional
puddings, from a microwave-less kitchen.

Bar Meals and Restaurant: 12-2, 6.30-9.30 (10 bar); bar snacks both sessions **Typical
Dishes BAR:** *various soups of the day £1.25, eggs Jacqueline £3.45, jagar schnitzel
£6.50, ham and asparagus cheese £3.45, home-made steak and kidney pie £4.45*
RESTAURANT: *cheese beignets, pork fillet £9.95, zrazi Nelson £11.95, baked salmon
£9.95   Vegetarian Meals: Eastern feast Children's Menu* `Beer` *Palmers Bridport Bitter
Family Room   Outdoor Play Area   Garden   Outdoor Eating   Summer Barbecue* **Credit
Cards:** *Access, Visa*

WEST BEXINGTON   Manor Hotel

Beech Road DT2 9DF   ♥
Tel: (0308) 897616
Open: 11-11
Licensees: Richard and Jayne Childs

Old manor house just a short walk from Chesil Bank. Stone-walled cellar bar, leafy
conservatory, residents' lounge. Books, magazines and dried flower arrangements
add a homely, welcoming touch to simply furnished but well-equipped bedrooms.
They offer a £9.65 set Sunday lunch, and a special £6.65 three course children's
menu. Readers have written in praise of the food, in response to our last edition's
singleminded praise of the bed and breakfast here.

Bar Meals: 12-2, 6.30-10 (cold food all day); bar snacks both sessions **Restaurant:** *12-
1.30, 7-9.30* **Typical Dishes BAR:** *lentil and tarragon soup £1.55, crab and asparagus
pancake £4.65, duck à l'orange £6.35, fish thermidor £9.45, grilled hake provencale*

£7.95, sticky toffee pudding £2.25   **RESTAURANT:** set dinner £17.95: roast quail, avocado and pear with prawns, noisettes of lamb, sirloin steak Bordelaise, scallop and monkfish kebabs   *Vegetarian Meals: vegetarian tagliatelle   Children's Menu* [Cheese] [Beer] *Palmers Bridport Bitter, Royal Oak; Wadworth 6X   Family Room   Outdoor Play Area Garden   Outdoor Eating   **Accommodation:** 13 bedrooms, all en suite, from £68.50 (single £40.50)   Children Welcome Overnight   Cots Available   Check-in: after 2 pm* **Credit Cards:** *Access, Amex, Diners, Visa*

WEST KNIGHTON New Inn: Friendly, refurbished pub with restaurant, family room and garden. Cornish beers.

WEST LULWORTH   Castle Inn

Main Road   BH20 5RN
Tel: (092 941) 311
Open: 11-2.30 (12-2.30 Sun), 7-11
Licensees: G B and P J Halliday

Quaint 17th century roadside pub with a heavy thatch and country style bars (mind your head on the hanging pewter tankards). Homely bedrooms vary greatly in size, but all have thoughtful extras. Attractive terraced rose garden.

Bar Meals: *11-2, 7-10.30; bar snacks both sessions*   **Restaurant:** *12-2.30 (Sun only), 7.30-9.30*   **Typical Dishes BAR:** *home-made soup £1.20, mussels £2, venison pie £4.80, liver and bacon £4, swordfish £4.90, plum duff £1.20*   **RESTAURANT:** *similar starters, duck £9.80, spicy lamb £8.50, cheesecake £1.75   Vegetarian Meals: veggie sausages   Children's Menu/Portions* [Beer] *Cornish Royal Wessex; Marston Pedigree; Whitbread Best, Flowers Original* [Cider] *Bulmers Traditional   Children Allowed in Bar to Eat   Outdoor Play Area   Garden   Outdoor Eating   Summer Barbecue* **Accommodation:** *14 bedrooms, 9 en suite, from £33 (single £20)   Children Welcome Overnight   Cots Available   Check-in: all day*   **Credit Cards:** *Access, Amex, Diners, Visa*

WEST STAFFORD   Wise Man Inn

West Stafford DT2 8AG
Tel: (0305) 263694
Open: 11-2.30 (12-2.30 Sun), 6.30-11
Licensees: Mike and Pauline Denkins

The nearest pub to Thomas Hardy's birthplace at Bockhampton; a poem hymning the virtues of ale, attributed to Hardy, appears on the front wall: "health lies in the equipoise", apparently. Thatched, pleasant two-bar pub, tidy and well-run.

Bar Meals and Restaurant: *12-2, 6.45-9 (7-8.30 summer Sun); bar snacks both sessions*   **Typical Dishes:** *celery and stilton soup £1.25, garlic mushrooms on fried bread £2.50, home-made steak and kidney pie £3.75, home-made lamb Madras curry £3.95, home-made leek and ham cheesy bake £3.25, treacle tart £1.50   Vegetarian Meals: vegetable and lentil curry £3.50   Children's Portions* [Beer] *Cornish Royal Wessex; Whitbread Flowers IPA* [Whisky] *Cragganmore, Singleton* [Cider] *Taunton Traditional   Children Allowed in Bar to Eat   Outdoor Play Area   Garden*   **Credit Cards:** *Access, Visa*

WINTERBORNE ZELSTON   Botany Bay

On A31 DT11 9ET
Tel: (092 945) 227
Open: 11-2.30, 5.30-11 (12 restaurant); all day Fri/Sat
Licensees: Chris and Bev Massey

Well-regarded locally for its decent food, especially the home-made pies.

*Bar Meals and Restaurant: 11.30-2.30, 6-10 (12-2.30, 7-10 Sun restaurant); bar snacks both sessions   **Typical Dishes BAR:** home-made soup £1.40, moules marinière £3.75, sauté of beef Botany Bay £7.25, home-made pies £3.95, various lasagnes £4.25, spotted dick £1.75   **RESTAURANT:** beef Wellington £9.75, chicken stuffed with lobster £8.75, tiger prawns £11.95   Vegetarian Meals: nut stroganoff £4.95   Children's Menu/Portions   Beer   Ringwood Bitter; Ruddles Best; Whitbread Boddingtons Bitter, Flowers Original   Children Allowed in Bar to Eat   Outdoor Play Area   Patio/terrace Outdoor Eating   Summer Barbecue   **Credit Cards:** Access, Visa*

DURHAM

COATHAM MUNDEVILLE   Stables Bar

Hall Garth Country House Hotel
Darlington DL1 3LU
Tel: (0325) 300400
Open: 11-3, 5.30-11
Licensee: John Forbes

Unusual bar converted, as the name suggests, from the hotel's old stables; airy, high-ceilinged, and in a useful spot for travellers, though the menu is routine enough.

*Bar Meals: 12-2, 7-10; bar snacks both sessions   **Typical Dishes:** home-made soup £1.20, prawn cocktail £2.65, steak and mushroom pie £3.65, gammon steak £4.95, lasagne £3.50, fruit crumble £1.60   Vegetarian Meals: vegetable lasagne £3.85 Children's Menu   Beer   Draught Bass; N Yorks Brewery Flying Herbert; Theakston Best Bitter, XB   Family Room   Outdoor Play Area   Garden   Outdoor Eating **Accommodation:** 10 bedrooms, all en suite, from £80 (single £60)   Children Welcome Overnight   Cots Available   Check-in: all day   **Credit Cards:** Access, Amex, Diners, Visa*

CORNSAY   Blackhorse Inn Main Street. Smart rural pub overlooking Gladdow valley. Bar food in separate dining area, Sunday lunchtime and daily evening; no music; garden. Camerons beers. Open: 12-3 (Sun only), 7-11.

COTHERSTONE   Fox & Hounds

Cotherstone DL12 9PF   `FOOD`
Tel: (0833) 50241   `B&B`
Open: Mon-Sat 11.30-2.30, 6.30-11
Licensees: Patrick and Jenny Crawley

North of Barnard Castle, on the B6277, the village of Cotherstone stands in an area of outstanding natural beauty, where the Tees and Balder rivers meet. The Fox and Hounds is back from the main road, overlooking a small village green; a coaching inn for over 200 years, it's been run for just the last five of those by the ever enthusiastic and amiable Crawleys. A stripped-stone entrance hall leads into the main bar, which has heavily beamed ceilings and rough painted walls. A brick fireplace is hung with polished brasses; in summer it boasts fine dried flower displays and polished copperware, in winter a fire that warms the whole room. Window sills are crammed with pot plants and walls hung with mainly hunting prints. Rustic benches and wheelback chairs surround well-used wooden tables. Adjoining the bar, a small dining area has polished ready-laid tables and pretty, cottagey curtains, while at the other side of the entrance is a second eating area, again with heavy beams and rustic style furnishings. Quality bar food produced with real enthusiasm by Patrick Crawley draws in the crowds. In addition to a standard menu featuring steaks, lamb cutlets and steak and kidney pie, a specials board of more interesting dishes allows him to use what's best from the markets. Meat and vegetables come from local suppliers, and fish arrives daily from Hartlepool. Fish is a particularly strong point here: perhaps fresh haddock, either deep-fried or poached, simply grilled fillets of lemon sole or a beautifully poached fillet of excellent salmon with an interesting sauce of orange and spring onion. Quality local meat finds a showcase in medallions of beef with a mushroom and madeira sauce, or the pub's own invention, chicken Cotherstone, served with ham, Cotherstone cheese and a white wine sauce. Vegetables are fresh and well cooked, salads fresh and crisp. Added to all of which, puddings are a must! A wonderful hot treacle sponge with custard is extremely popular, and a rich but wonderful white chocolate and Bacardi crunch matches it (if only in calories). Naturally the dining areas get very busy, especially at weekends. Bedrooms show a similar eye for detail as the cooking. Designed and appointed by Jenny Crawley, and named after local dales, the two doubles and single twin are furnished in country style with fine pine furniture or solid period pieces, balanced by light fresh furnishings and decor. Homely touches include ornaments, mineral water and respectable local watercolours. Beds are firm and comfortable, sheets crisp. Each room is en suite (one with shower), with carpets and practical fittings, though extractor fans are noisy. Rooms are priced on a dinner, bed and breakfast rate. A homely residents' lounge with exposed floorboards and big comfy armchairs is also home to the family parrot.

Bar Meals: 12-1.45, 7-9; bar snacks lunchtime   ***Typical Dishes:*** *beef and vegetable broth £1.95, smoked haddock and prawn mousse with home-made walnut toast £3.45, Teesdale lamb and apricot casserole £6.95, breast of chicken £8.95, poached fresh salmon with orange, ginger and spring onion sauce £9.45, treacle sponge £2.45   Vegetarian Meals: vegetable crumble   Children's Menu/Portions* **Cheese**   **Beer** *John Smith's Bitter, Magnet   Children Allowed in Bar to Eat   **Accommodation:** 3 bedrooms, all en suite, from £70 (single £47.50); prices include dinner   Children Welcome Overnight (minimum age 9)   Check-in: all day   **Credit Cards:** Access Visa*

CROXDALE Coach and Horses Low Butcher Race (A167) Tel: (0388) 814484. Spacious diners' roadhouse – food lunchtime and evening – with home-made specials, fresh pizzas from proper oven; frozen fish, but own free-range eggs. Children welcome for meals. Vaux, Woods beers.

DURHAM Swan & Three Cygnets: Riverside pub with decent cold lunches. Door policy in evening, when gets young and noisy.

EASTGATE Horsley Hall off A689: Manorial pub with ordinary bar and delightful unspoilt restaurant; lovely views.

EGGLESTON	**Three Tuns**

Eggleston DL12 0AH
Tel: (0833) 50289
Open: 11-3, 7-11
Licensee: Peter John Kirkman

Get here early for one of the coveted window seats in the Teesdale Room, with splendid views across the valley. The traditionally furnished, civilised bar has old oak settles and an open fire. Booking is essential for Sunday lunch. Eggs come from their own free-range hens.

Bar Meals: 12-2, 7-9 (9.30 Sat); bar snacks lunchtime   **Typical Dishes:** *home-made soup £1.25, avocado with prawns £2.30, home-made steak and kidney pie £3.95, half roast duckling with orange sauce £6.25, fresh salmon steak £4.95, Dutch apple pie £1.60 Vegetarian Meals: three-egg omelette   Children's Menu/Portions   Children Allowed in Bar to Eat   Outdoor Play Area   Garden   Outdoor Eating* **No Credit Cards**

ESH HILL TOP Board Inn Tel: (091) 372 1237: Multi-roomed pub; warming fires; free from piped music; family room. Popular, value for money bar meals, lunch and evening. McEwan, Theakston beers. Open:12-11.

FIR TREE   Duke of York

On A68, near Crook DL15 8DG   FOOD
Tel: (0388) 762848
Open: all day summer; 10.30-3, 6.30-11 winter
Licensee: Ray Suggett

This large white-painted 18th century inn by the A68 has been in the same family for five generations, and when Ray Suggett inherited the pub in 1966, he was working as a scientist for the UN in Africa. He initiated a restoration programme and installed managers from afar, before returning to take over personally in 1984. Today the Duke of York is a very popular stop-off for both locals and tourists, especially at weekends, and a new kitchen is the latest of the continuing improvements. Both an interesting collection of stone-age flints and letters from celebrity visitors hang on one wall of the entrance, leading into two bar areas. One, to the right of the entrance, is furnished with round back chairs, bench seating and solid wooden tables; its beamed ceiling and walls hung with horsey pictures, plates and bottles on high shelves. The other bar is more homely, with wing chairs, curtains and stools, all tapestry-upholstered. African mementoes include fearsome spears, hunting rifles and photographs, grouped around the stone fireplace, and a juke box stands alongside the bar counter. Adjoining this area is an unfussy dining room with rough white walls and polished ready-laid tables. Blackboards in each bar list the food on offer. The top bar tends to be more bar-foody, the bottom one restaurany – but often the two converge and overlap. Prices are a little above the average for the area, but the cooking (in the hands of Marilyn Suggett) is reassuringly good. Fish is fresh and meat all comes from a dependable local butcher. The choice is wide, from salads and open sandwiches to more elaborate classical dishes like tournedos Rossini, beef bourguignon, lemon sole, lamb Reform or (every pub's favourite) steak and kidney pie. A delicious pork zaccharoff had tender chunks of pork in a sauce of madeira, ham, peppers and cream. All dishes come with a selection of crisp, fresh potatoes and vegetables. Puddings are also good. Smartly uniformed staff are polite and quietly efficient but on busy days can look a little overstretched. To the rear is a pleasant garden, bordered by trees, and a paddock.

Bar Meals and Restaurant: 12-2 (cold food 3 pm), 6-10; bar snacks both sessions
Typical Dishes BAR: *celery and stilton soup £1.95, chicken liver paté £1.95, home-made steak and kidney pie £4.95, chicken chasseur £7.25, fresh Aberdeen cod £4.75, sherry trifle £1.95*   **RESTAURANT:** *carrot and mint soup £1.95, garlic king prawns £5.95, pork zaccharoff £7.75, beef stroganoff £7.95, Arctic chicken with prawns £7.95, chocolate mousse £2.25   Vegetarian Meals: mushroom and pepper stroganoff £6.25   Children's Menu/Portions* Beer *Draught Bass* Whisky *Port Ellen   Children Allowed in Bar to Eat   Outdoor Play Area   Garden   Outdoor Eating* **Credit Cards:** *Access, Visa*

GREAT STAINTON   Kings Arms

The Green TS21 1NA
Tel: (0740) 30361
Open: 1.30-3, 6-11
Licensee: Thomas W Plews

Large, comfortable saloon and busy locals' bar.

Bar Meals: 11.30-2, 6-9.45; bar snacks both sessions   **Restaurant:** 12-2, 6.30-9.45
Typical Dishes RESTAURANT: cream of lettuce soup £1.70, smoked salmon and
prawns £2.95, liver, sausage and gammon strips in red wine £8.45, fillet steak in red wine,
onions and mushrooms £10.65, king prawns in garlic or cheese sauce £9.45   Vegetarian
Meals: lasagne   Children's Portions   ▮Beer▮   Marston Pedigree; Whitbread Castle Eden
Ale, Flowers Original   Family Room   Children Allowed in Bar to Eat   Outdoor Eating
Credit Cards: Access, Amex, Diners, Visa

GRETA BRIDGE   Morritt Arms Hotel

Greta Bridge DL12 9SE
Tel: (08330) 27232
Licensees: David and John Mulley

Old-fashioned peace and quiet are promised in the Dickens Bar of this well-loved
old coaching inn, so named because the novelist stayed here while researching
Nicholas Nickleby in 1838. A substantial and imposing building, run personally by
its proprietor twin brothers, the interior has a homely, unashamedly unmodernised
feel, particularly evident to residents. The bar (there's also a quite separate, and quite
different public bar) has high ceilings, traditional furnishings, and views out over the
lawn. Open fires in winter. Bedrooms vary: many are quite modestly furnished,
though others have brass bedsteads and one sports a four-poster. A good base for the
north country tour. Vegetarians need to give prior notice of their needs.

Bar Meals: 11-2 (3 pm cold food); restaurant 12-1.30 (Sun only), 7-8.45; bar snacks both
sessions   **Typical Dishes BAR:** chicken and sweetcorn soup £1.50, home-made steak and
mushroom pie £5.50, noisettes of lamb with curried fruity sauce £7, medallions of pork,
peach and brandy sauce £7, cod and chips £4.50   **RESTAURANT** dinner menu £21:
mulligatawny soup, fillet of beef Marsanne, poached fresh salmon, grilled whole lemon sole,
summer pudding   Children's Portions   Children Allowed in Bar to Eat   Outdoor Play
Area   Garden   Outdoor Eating   **Accommodation:** 17 bedrooms, all en suite, from £73
(single £48)   Children Welcome Overnight   Cots Available   Check-in: all day   **Credit
Cards:** Access, Amex, Diners, Visa

HEIGHINGTON STATION Locomotion One Heighington Lane, Newton
Aycliffe Tel: (0325) 320132. Extraordinary local landmark, a former railway station
sucessfully converted into a traditional drinkers' pub. Wide selection of beers; very
simple food. Open: 11-3, 5.30-11 (all day Sunday).

HETT Hett Village Inn: Pleasant, opened-out village pub; family room; garden.
Bar meals daily, lunch and evening. Theakston, Youngers beers. Open: 12-2 Sat,
7-11.

LANCHESTER   Queens Head

Front Street DH7 0LA
Tel: (0207) 520200
Open: 11-3.30, 6.30-11.30
Licensee: Joan Gray

Grade II listed pub at the heart of the village. Welcoming and warmed by open fires. Menu prices higher in the evening; children allowed in the dining room.

Bar Meals: 12-2, 7-9.30; bar snacks both sessions **Typical Dishes:** *home-made broth £1, garlic mushrooms £2.10, home-cooked steak and kidney pie £2.95, liver and sausage casserole £2.95, fresh cod or haddock £2.95, fruit pies £1.50 Vegetarian Meals: lasagne Children's Portions* ▮Beer▮ *Vaux Double Maxim Outdoor Eating* **Accommodation:** *3 bedrooms, sharing a bathroom, from £30 (single £17) Children Welcome Overnight Check-in: all day* **No Credit Cards**

MIDDLETON IN TEESDALE Teesdale, Market Place: Well-kept, central pub with decent Bar Meals and smart restaurant. Bedrooms. Courage, Tetley beers.

MIDDLETON ONE ROW Devonport, The Front Tel: (0325) 332255: Popular for light eating and good views. Bar meals lunchtime and evening, menu includes some interesting dishes and vegetarian options. Bedrooms. Theakston beers. Open all day.

NEASHAM   Newbus Arms

Neasham DL2 1PE
Tel: (0325) 721071
Open: all day
Licensee: John Abel

A Best Western hotel, with features like a Frequent Visitors Loyalty Discount. The menu promises that your word is the chef's command – an intoxicating promise of consumer power. It's a stunning white building, in part dating from 1610 but more reminscent of a high Edwardian country house, complete with crenellated top at the rear. Lovely grounds. Hardly a pub by any definition but they do offer good value bar lunches and suppers and as such is worth knowing about. The bar is nicely pubby with distinguished old counter fittings, too.

Bar Meals: 12-2, 6.30-10; bar snacks both sessions **Restaurant:** *7-10* **Typical Dishes** **BAR:** *steak, kidney and mushroom pie £4.25, home-made Cumberland sausage £2.75, barbecued suckling ribs £3.95, cod in beer batter £4.95, fruit crumble £1.95* **RESTAURANT:** *two soups of the day, each £1.25, cold poached seafoods £3.95, lambs liver with onions and bacon £4.75, roast duck with sage and apple stuffing £10.95, grilled trout stuffed with almonds and grapes £5.50, sherry trifle £1.95 Vegetarian Meals: spinach and mushroom pancake £5 Children's Menu* ▮Beer▮ *Camerons Traditional Bitter, Strongarm Children Allowed in Bar to Eat Outdoor Play Area Garden Outdoor Eating* **Accommodation:** *15 bedrooms, all en suite, from £75 (single £49) Children Welcome Overnight Cots Available Check-in: all day* **Credit Cards:** *Access, Amex, Diners, Visa*

NEVILLES CROSS Duke of Wellington Tel: (091 384) 2735. Extensive, organised dining pub with long menu in bar and restaurant (lunchtime and evening); high proportion fresh ingredients; main courses around £4; £10 in the restaurant. Stones Best Bitter.

PIERCEBRIDGE   George

Piercebridge DL2 3SW
Tel: (0325) 374576
Open: all day
Licensee: John R Wain

Handsome white 16th century roadside coaching inn in the heart of the north east
tourist area. Three civilised and comfortable bars have at least five open fires
between them, old wooden furniture, and, in the lounge, overlooking the river
Tees, chesterfield sofas. Two brothers who died at the George, and their grandfather
clock which stopped at the same moment, prompted an 1850s American lyricist to
pen a well-known old song. The clock is still here. Fishing is free to overnight
residents.

Bar Meals and Restaurant: 11.30-2.30, 6.30-10; *bar snacks both sessions* ***Typical***
Dishes BAR: *home-made soup £1.65, tuna and cucumber savoury £1.65, pork in oyster
sauce with rice £5.75, cream of seafood in a filo pastry boat £5.50, cod in mushroom sauce
£4.50, lemon meringue pie £1.65* *Vegetarian Meals: Mexican vegetable fajhita £4.75*
Children's Portions **Beer** *Webster's Yorkshire Bitter* *Family Room* *Riverside Garden*
Outdoor Eating *Summer Barbecue* ***Accommodation:*** *35 bedrooms, all en suite, from*
£48 (single £38) *Children Welcome Overnight* *Cot Available* *Check-in: all day*
Credit Cards: *Access, Amex, Diners, Visa*

ROMALDKIRK   ★   Rose & Crown

Romaldkirk DL12 9EB   FOOD
Tel: (0833) 50213   ❢
Open: 11-3 (12-2 Sun), 5.30-11   B&B
Licensees: Christopher and Alison Davy

In an area of pretty villages, Romaldkirk must be one of the most picturesque, with
its attractive cottages and open greens. The Rose and Crown, an imposing 18th
century coaching inn, stands alongside the ancient village church, together
effectively dominating the village centre. Since taking over the inn five years ago,
Chris and Alison Davy have implemented many changes and undertaken
sympathetic upgrading. The main bar, dominated by a fine stone fireplace, has lots
of wood panelling, old black and white photos of the village, a grandfather clock
and some alarming-looking traps. Wrought iron legged tables are surrounded by
round back chairs or bench seating, and on the dining side of the room there are
exposed stone walls, beams and old farm implements. A part-panelled restaurant has
elegantly clothed tables and a civilised air, and the residents' lounge, heavily
endowed with more stripped stone and beams, features wing chairs and period
furniture, books, magazines and board games. Everywhere there are local
watercolours. The food under the new regime has also been revived, with regularly
changing bar menus (which differ lunch and evening) supplemented by a specials
board. Fresh local produce is combined to good effect to produce interesting and
imaginative dishes like baked mussels in a light cream sauce, glazed with the local
Cotherstone cheese. Tender strips of delicious pork fillet are served in a cream and
sherry sauce, accompanied by fresh pasta and a crisp, colourful salad. Good puddings
complete the picture, perhaps an apple and raspberry pie. Local fish is a strong point,
too: smoked eel with horseradish, deep-fried monkfish, halibut and river trout, and a
brace of herring with gooseberry puree are all typical of the repertoire. Service is
friendly and smiling. Meanwhile, in the restaurant, food is a five-course affair, again
with a local bias, using herrings, poussins and venison. Expect to spend about £40
for two here, for food carefully prepared with obvious knowledge and enthusiasm.
Bedrooms are slowly undergoing refurbishment: to date, five of the six main house
rooms have been given a facelift. Creaking floorboards, beams, stripped stone walls,

well-chosen antique furniture and contemporary fabrics are typical, and duvets can be swapped for sheets and blankets. Front facing views overlook the village green. All the en suite facilities are carpeted and fully tiled, though in a rather dated style. Housekeeping seems on the ball, though we don't like finding chambermaids in our room when we come back from breakfast! Five further rooms, in an outside annexe, are more uniform in size and design, with modern furniture and fittings.

Bar Meals: 12-1.30, 6.30-9.30 (7-9 Sun); bar snacks lunchtime   *Restaurant:* 12-1.30 (Sun only), 7.30-9 (not Sun eve)   *Typical Dishes BAR:* carrot, leek and lentil soup, fresh mussels with cream and local cheese £2.95, steak, mushroom and Old Peculier pie £4.25, escalope of veal £7.25, pink trout with chive hollandaise £5.50, sticky toffee pudding *RESTAURANT* menu £18: courgette and apple soup, crab and avocado mousse, loin of pork with walnut stuffing, apple and Calvados sauce, breast of woodpigeon with port and orange sauce, roast monkfish with lobster butter   *Vegetarian Meals:* fresh pasta with peppers and mushrooms   *Children's Portions*   Cheese   Beer   Theakston Best Bitter, Old Peculier; Youngers No. 3   Whisky   Children Allowed in Bar to Eat   Patio/terrace   Outdoor Eating *Accommodation:* 11 bedrooms, all en suite, from £63.50 (single £45)   Children Welcome Overnight   Cots Available   Check-in: all day   *Credit Cards:* Access, Visa

---

ROMALDKIRK   Kirk Inn

Barnard Castle DL12 9ED
Tel: (0833) 50260
Open: 12-3 (not Tue), 6-11
Licensee: Dennis Frampton

On the village green, also the local post office for two hours each morning, this is a real community local, but the increasing food trade has prompted a new kitchen and small new dining room this year. All meals are cooked by the landlord, who is very anti-fast food, and believes in piling his customers' plates with six or seven varieties of fresh vegetables.

Bar Meals: 12-2, 7.30-9 (also dining room evenings); no food Sun eve, nor all day Tue; bar snacks Mon-Sat lunchtime   *Typical Dishes:* chicken and mushroom soup £1.75, garlic mushrooms £2.50, medallions of pork in brandy and cream sauce £7.25, chicken breast fillet, mushroom sauce £6.25, fresh poached salmon with prawns £7.50, port and cherry cream cake £1.60   *Vegetarian Meals:* vegetarian wellie (fresh vegetables and paté in puff pastry)   *Children's Portions*   Beer   Whitbread Castle Eden Ale, Boddingtons Bitter Family Room   Garden   Outdoor Eating   *No Credit Cards*

SACRISTON Travellers Rest Tel: (091) 371 0458. *Bar Meals:* 12-2, 7-9.45; bar snacks both sessions. *Restaurant:* 12-2 Sun only, 7-9.30. Family room; garden, outdoor eating. Boules pitch. McEwans, Theakston, Younger beers. Open: 11-3, 6-11.

SHINCLIFFE Seven Stars: on A177 Tel: (091) 384 8454: Pleasingly unspoilt but smart farming pub just two miles from Durham city. Simple food in big helpings, lunch and evening. No music; outdoor drinking. Bedrooms. Vaux beers.

WHORLTON Bridge Inn, Tel: (0833) 27341: Cosy village pub with simple, genuine home-made food, including real chips; soups and pies at lunchtime (except Wed); fishy and meaty dinner dishes evenings Wed-Sat. Good home-made puddings. Children welcome. Courage beer. Open: 11-4 (not Wed), 7-11.

WOLSINGHAM   Bay Horse

Upper Town DU3 3EX
Tel: (0388) 527220
Open: all day
Licensee: Amanda Ellila

Neatly kept two-roomed inn on the edge of the town. Nice to children.

Bar Meals: 12-2, 7-10; *bar snacks both sessions*   **Typical Dishes:** *lentil soup 90p, garlic mushrooms £1.60, steak and kidney pie £3.50, lamb cutlets £4.50, venison sausages £3.95, home-made fruit pie   Vegetarian Meals: wheat casserole £3.75   Children's Menu/Portions*   Beer   *Tetley Bitter; Whitbread Boddingtons Bitter   Children Allowed in Bar to Eat   Patio/terrace*   **Accommodation:** *8 bedrooms, 5 en suite, from £30 (single £18)   Children Welcome Overnight   Check-in: all day*   **Credit Cards:** *Access, Visa*

ESSEX

ALTHORNE Huntsman & Hounds: Substantially extended, thatched cottage pub; low ceiling, real fires and rustic decorations. Garden. Greene King beers.

ARDLEIGH   Wooden Fender

Harwich Road CO7 7PA
Tel: (0206) 230466
Open: 11-3, 6-11
Licensee: Pauline Tyler

Surprisingly ancient inn, now a busy, modernised but pleasant roadside inn, named after a fence built to stop cattle falling into a nearby pond. We list dishes from the lunchtime bar menu here: it's slightly more expensive in the evening.

Bar Meals: 11.30-2, 6.30-9.30; *bar snacks both sessions*   **Restaurant:** 7-11   **Typical Dishes BAR:** *smoked haddock pasta £3.50, home-made cottage pie £3.05, home-made steak and kidney pudding £3.50, sweet and sour pork £3.90, home-made apple pie £1.30*   **RESTAURANT:** *soup of the day £2.20, breaded prawns with garlic dip £3.20, fillet steak Rossini £11.75, escalope of veal Marsala £11.25, lemon sole £9.75, puddings £2.15   Vegetarian Meals (bar): spinach and mushroom lasagne £3.40*   Beer   *Adnams; Courage; Greene King*   Whisky   *Children Allowed in Bar to Eat   Garden*   **Credit Cards:** *Access, Amex, Visa*

ARKESDEN   Axe & Compasses

Tel: (0799) 550272
Open: 11-2.30, 6-11
Licensee: Jenny Roberts

Superb 17th century village pub, handsomely furnished and notably relaxing. Regular dishes and roasts at lunchtime, and themed food nights each evening: Monday, it's vegetarian, Tuesday is fish, Wednesday the steak special, Thursday homely English, Friday and Saturday restauranty à la carte, and Sunday is pasta night.

Bar Meals and Restaurant: lunchtime and evening; no bar meals Mon eve; bar snacks both sessions   **Typical Dishes (lunch):** *home-made tomato soup £1.10, steak and kidney pie, fish and chips, hotpot (main courses around £4), lemon soufflé £2.25   Children's Menu*   Beer   *Greene King   Children Allowed in Restaurant   Patio/terrace   Summer Barbecue*

BIRDBROOK Plough: The Street Tel: (044 085) 336: Pretty village local with real fires, garden and restaurant. No piped music. Bar meals daily, lunch and evening; restaurant Wednesday-Saturday. Adnams, Greene King beers. Open: 11-2.30, 5.30-11.

BLACKMORE Prince Albert, The Green: Warm and friendly local with log fires. Bar menu includes vegetarian options. Draught Bass.

BRADWELL ON SEA Kings Head: Popular dining pub, well-run, nice to children; decent bar food.

BROOMFIELD   Kings Arms

295 Main Road CM1 5AU
Tel: (0245) 440258
Open: 11-2.30, 6.30-11
Licensees: Robin Moore and Amanda King

The resident ghost wears a feathered cavalier's hat and has been known to ring the bell for 'time' at this old black and white timbered pub on the corner of the main road and church green. The cavalier wouldn't recognise much of the interior, as apart from the heavily beamed ceiling little else that's original remains. There are tapestry-upholstered chairs around the good eating-height tables, some wrought iron above the bar counter, and fireplaces are 1920s brick. The room is divided into two halves, one of which is set up as a restaurant; the same daily changing typed menu is available throughout, with an additional blackboard list of lighter snacks in the bar at lunchtimes. Manager Mark Cook does the cooking and produces some really appetising dishes. Grilled dates wrapped in bacon with a creamy mustard sauce make an excellent and unusual starter or light snack, and the pork, mushroom and cider pie comes with a good short pastry crust enveloping a generous filling of tender pork. The menu is well-balanced: there's also a good selection of fish dishes, like grilled sardines with garlic mayonnaise, locally smoked Shetland salmon and various charcoal grills, vegetarian dishes and a few children's favourites (also half portions of most things); families can use the restaurant area. There is no garden, but some tables are provided out at the front for summer drinking. Regular teas and coffees are joined by hot chocolate with whipped cream, cappuccino, espresso, decaffeinated and liqueur coffees.

Bar Meals: 12-2, 6.30-9.30 (10 Sat); 7-9.30 summer Sun; bar snacks lunchtime
Typical Dishes: home-made soup £1.95, baked mushrooms in cream and garlic £3.95, steak, kidney and mushroom pie £5.95, fillet of lamb à la grecque £7.50, whole fresh lemon sole stuffed with crab, lemon and almond £8.25, pecan pie £2.50 Vegetarian Meals: vegetable pancakes £5.25 Children's Menu/Portions `Beer` *Adnams Bitter; Crouch Vale Bitter; Fullers London Pride; Mauldons Bitter* `Cider` *Coates Children Allowed in Bar to Eat Credit Cards: Access, Visa*

BURNHAM-ON-CROUCH   Olde White Harte Hotel

The Quay CM0 8AS
Tel: (0621) 782106
Open: 11-3, 6-11
Licensee: J G Lewis

Scenically located town-centre pub overlooking the yachting marina; the waterside terrace is lovely in summer. Two characterful wood-panelled bars have polished oak furnishings and a nautical atmosphere; there's also a small residents' lounge. There are four more bedrooms than in our last edition: ask for one with a window seat overlooking the estuary.

Bar Meals and Restaurant: 12-2.30 (2 restaurant), 7.30-9; bar snacks both sessions
Typical Dishes BAR: home-made soup 80p, whitebait £2, lamb chops, roast of the day,
lasagne (all at £3.30)   *Vegetarian Meals:* lasagne   *Children's Menu (restaurant)*   `Beer`
Adnams Bitter; Tolly Cobbold Bitter   Family Room   *Accommodation:* 15 bedrooms, 11
en suite, from £33 (single £18.70)   Children Welcome Overnight   Cots Available
Check-in: all day   *No Credit Cards*

CANFIELD END   Lion & Lamb

Canfield End CM6 1SR
Tel: (0279) 870257
Open: 11-3, 6-11
Licensees: Mr and Mrs Rasor

Popular family dining pub, with cold buffet, salad table, and large car park.

Bar Meals and Restaurant: 12-2, 6-10; bar snacks both sessions   *Typical Dishes BAR:*
mushroom, parsley and garlic soup £1.90, stilton mushrooms £3.25, steak and kidney pie
£4.95, barbecued spare ribs £4.95, broccoli and smoked haddock pancakes £4.50, banoffee
pie £2.10   *RESTAURANT:* similar starters and puddings; peppered sirloin steak
£10.50, noisettes of lamb £9.50, scampi thermidor £10.50   *Vegetarian Meals:* cheese and
vegetable pie £4.95   Children's Menu/Portions   `Beer`   Adnams; Ridleys   Children
Allowed in Bar to Eat   Outdoor Play Area   Garden   Outdoor Eating   Summer Barbecue
Credit Cards: Access, Visa

CLAVERING   Cricketers

near Saffron Walden CB11 4QT
Tel: (0799) 550442
Open: 10.30-2.30, 6.30-11
Licensee: Trevor Oliver

Very much a dining pub, with a cricketing theme and well-organised, amiable
service. Food is on the smartish side; salads look particularly expensive; after
ordering your meal, you're invited to help yourself from the self-service salad bar.
The printed menu is augmented by daily blackboard specials.

Bar Meals: 12-2, 7-10; bar snacks both sessions   *Typical Dishes:* veal, chicken and
pistachio terrine £3.50, ham and leek tartlet £2.75, char-grilled pork loin with stilton and
cream sauce £7.50, lambs kidneys with tarragon vinegar and tomato sauce £6.25, salmon
steak with chive butter £7.75   *Vegetarian Meals:* oyster mushroom, baby sweetcorn and
pepper pastry £7.75   Children's Menu   `Beer`   Whitbread   Family Room   Garden
Outdoor Eating   *Credit Cards:* Access, Visa

COGGESHALL Fleece, West Street: Very cheap, genuine home cooking lunch
and evening in village local next door to Paycockes House. Greene King beers.
White Hart, Main Street: Nicely furnished 15th century pub, going up in the
world with able young licensees. Home-cooked lunches. Adnams beers.

COLCHESTER   Foresters

Castle Road
Tel: (0206) 42646

Busy local near the castle and Roman wall; daily changing home-cooked food, no
printed menu. Fresh vegetables served al dente; good salads.

Bar Meals: lunchtime and evening   Typical Dishes: French onion soup, chicken satay, lamb and stilton pot, seafood pancake (main courses around £4)   Vegetarian Meals: hazelnut loaf with mushroom sauce **Beer** *Marston; Whitbread   Family Room   **No Credit Cards***

DEBDEN   Plough

High Street CB11 3LE
Tel: (0799) 40396
Open: 12-3, 6-11 (all day Sat)
Licensee: K M Egan

Nicely refurbished country local, just outside Saffron Walden; real fire; no music; good garden for families. The dining room has the same menu as the bar.

Bar Meals: 12-2, 7.30-10; bar snacks   Typical Dishes: breaded mushrooms with 4 different dips, chicken stuffed with prawns and lobster £6.95, ham, egg and chips £2.95, trout with roast almonds £6.25, home-made fruit puddings £1.30   Vegetarian Meals: lasagne £3.95   Children's Menu/Portions **Beer** *Greene King   Children Allowed in Bar to Eat   Outdoor Play Area   Garden   Outdoor Eating   Summer Barbecue   **No Credit Cards***

DEDHAM   Anchor

Heath Road
Tel: (0206) 323471
Open: 11-3, 6-11

Refurbished, peaceful pub with opened-out bar, new restaurant and a strong local following; the menu's a mixture of the mundane and the genuinely home-made; large beer garden.

Bar Meals: lunchtime and evening; bar snacks both sessions   Typical Dishes: cottage pie, beef and beer casserole, game pies (main courses from £3.50), baked apples   Vegetarian Meals   Children's Menu **Beer** *Adnams; Greene King   Children Allowed in Bar to Eat   Garden   **No Credit Cards***

DEDHAM   Marlborough Head Hotel

Mill Lane CO7 6DH   `FOOD`
Tel: (0206) 323250   `B&B`
Open: 11-2.30, 6-11
Licensee: B Wills

Surrounded by picturesque Constable country, Dedham is a charming village, and the Marlborough Head, which occupies that most traditional of sites, directly opposite the church, has been dispensing hospitality for over 550 years. Woodcarving is a speciality here, outside on the black and white timbered upper storey of the building, inside above a massive old fireplace in the entrance lobby, as well as a particularly fine carved oak fireplace, original to the inn and now found in the family/coach party room. Several other rooms and bars, one featuring a heavily beamed ceiling, are furnished with good eating-height tables and the odd copper or brass ornament. Food orders are made at a leather-topped desk, quoting the number painted on a little stone on your table, from a long menu that runs the gamut from a simple jacket potato to the likes of salmon with hollandaise sauce and Aga roasted back bacon steak with peaches. Not to be missed is the Marlborough soup, just bursting with flavour, made with vegetables and a proper beef stock. Try to leave room for a pudding too, a light chocolate roulade filled with raspberries, or perhaps a fresh plum crumble; all, except the cheesecake, home-made. Spacious bedrooms, one double and two singles, are modestly but pleasantly furnished with a variety of pieces from the antiqueish and old pine to more modern bedside tables. Each has a few old timbers and sloping floors, and candlewick bedspreads add a homely touch. Two have compact, lino-floored en suite shower rooms with toilets, and the double a proper bathroom.

Bar Meals: 12-2, 7-9.30 (10 Fri/Sat); bar snacks both sessions   ***Typical Dishes:*** *home-made soup £1.35, spicy smoked mackerel £2.50, English lamb chops with Cumberland sauce £5.50, pan-fried veal with vermouth sauce £6, fried lemon sole £5, sherry trifle £2.75   Vegetarian Meals: pine kernel risotto £4* Beer *Adnams; Benskins   Family Room   Outdoor Play Area   Garden   Outdoor Eating* ***Accommodation:*** *3 bedrooms, all en suite, from £47.50 (single £30)   Children Welcome Overnight   Check-in: by arrangement* ***Credit Cards:*** *Access, Visa*

ELSENHAM   Crown

High Street (B1051)
Tel: (0279) 812827
Open: 11-2.30, 6-11

The local cricket club headquarters; the menu an eclectic mix of the homely and the modern, but their own burgers are as popular as any of these. They also make their own bread, pickles and ice-cream.

Bar Meals and Restaurant: lunchtime and Tue-Sat evening; no food Sun   ***Typical Dishes:*** *home-made soup, asparagus tartlet, rack of lamb, steak and kidney pie, local trout (main courses from £4), home-made pavlova   Vegetarian Meals   Children's Portions* Beer *Benskins   Children Allowed in Bar to Eat   Garden* ***Credit Cards:*** *Access, Visa*

FULLER STREET Square & Compasses, The Green Tel: (0245) 361477: Cyclists, walkers and real ale fans' favourite; attractive isolated cottage pub, staunchly traditional, with simple home cooking lunch and evening. Live folk music once monthly. Garden. Ridleys IPA. Open: 12-3, 6-11.

GESTINGTHORPE Pheasant Tel: (0787) 61196: Another traditional Essex village local, with live folk music and lots of other lively social activities. Interesting restaurant with home-cooked specials; food lunch and evening; no chips. Family room, garden. Adnams, Batemans, Greene King, Mauldon, Nethergate beers. Open: 11-3, 6-11 (all day summer).

GREAT CHESTERFORD   Plough

High Street CB10 1PL
Tel: (0799) 30283
Open: 11-2.30, 6-11
Licensee: I Cooper

Delightful village pub with a traditional, unspoilt interior, a pleasant atmosphere, and increasingly smart looking bar food. Superb garden. No children indoors.

Bar Meals: 12-2, 7-9; bar snacks lunchtime   ***Typical Dishes:*** *home-made soup £1.50, venison, monkfish tails, prawns on spinach with hollandaise £5, fresh fruit salad   Vegetarian Meals: vegetable risotto* Beer *Greene King IPA, Abbot Ale, Rayments Special   Outdoor Play Area   Garden   Outdoor Eating* ***No Credit Cards***

GREAT CLACTON   Robin Hood

211 London Road CO15 4ED
Tel: (0255) 421519
Open: 11-3, 6-11
Licensee: John Taylor

Rolls and omelettes were all that was on offer when the Taylors took over ten years ago; the pub was a row of farm cottages until 1960 when Bass Charrington converted it. Cosy beamed local and, now, a popular, homely dining pub with two open fires.

Bar Meals and Restaurant: 12-2.15 (restaurant Sun only), 7.30-10; bar snacks both sessions   Typical Dishes BAR: vegetable soup £1.35, prawn cocktail £3.10, home-made steak and kidney pie £4, home-made beef curry £4.50, home-made Lancashire hotpot £4, apple pie £2   RESTAURANT: French onion soup £1.35, fresh melon and passion fruit sorbet £2.60, peppered 8 oz sirloin steak £8.60, home-made steak and red wine pie £6, barbecued pork spare ribs £8.50, bread pudding £2   Vegetarian Meals: vegetable chilli Children's Menu/Portions   `Beer` *Adnams; Bass   Family Room   Outdoor Play Area Garden   Outdoor Eating   Credit Cards: Access, Visa*

GREAT HENNY   Henny Swan

near Sudbury CO10 7LS
Tel: (0787) 269238
Open: 11-3, 6-11
Licensee: P A Underhill

Ex-barge house by a weir on the river Stour, once called simply the Swan. There's a pleasant dining lounge, and a Victorian style conservatory which extends from the restaurant and leads onto a patio/barbecue area; hog roasts are popular. The bar menu's similar, but topped and tailed with snacks and salads.

Bar Meals and Restaurant: 12-2, 7-9.30 (10 Fri/Sat; no food Sun eve); bar snacks Typical Dishes RESTAURANT: soup of the day £1.60, Greek salad with feta cheese £2.10, 16 oz T-bone steak £9.95, guinea fowl with redcurrant and sherry sauce £8.25, fresh trout with almonds £7.50, pancakes with coffee ice-cream and maple syrup £2.10 Vegetarian Meals   `Beer` *Greene King   Riverside Garden   Outdoor Eating   Summer Barbecue   No Credit Cards*

HADSTOCK King's Head: Simple, friendly pub in old village. Wide-ranging menu. Closed Monday lunchtime.

HASTINGWOOD COMMON   Rainbow & Dove

Hastingwood Common CM17 9JX
Tel: (0279) 415419
Open: 11.30-2.30, 6.30-11
Licensee: A R Bird

Charming old rose-covered 16th century pub very close to junction 7 of the M11 motorway, its name a reference to Noah's Ark (and it gets almost as crowded inside). Food is very simple and cheap at lunchtime.

Bar Meals: 12-2.30, 7-9.30 (Wed-Sat eves); bar snacks lunchtime   Typical Dishes: mushroom soup, whitebait, steaks, Braughing sausages, Rainbow grill (main courses around £4), treacle pudding   Vegetarian Meals: pizza   Children's Menu/Portions   `Beer` *Tetley Bitter   Children Allowed in Bar to Eat   Outdoor Play Area   Garden   Outdoor Eating   Summer Barbecue   No Credit Cards*

HATFIELD BROAD OAK Dukes Head: Handy for Stanstead Airport; decent bar meals; popular, attractive dining pub.

HIGH RODING   Black Lion

High Roding CM6 1NP
Tel: (0371) 872847
Open: 10.30-3, 6-11
Licensee: T D Redley

Black and white timbered Tudor roadside pub. Intimate bar full of old beams, brick-built bar counter, and cosy rustic atmosphere; a second bar is less atmospheric, with pool table and fruit machine, and doubles as a family room. Blackboard menu, changing every six weeks or so: Italian specialities are the big draw.

*Bar Meals: 12-2, 7-9.30; bar snacks both sessions   **Typical Dishes BAR:** meat and vegetable soup £1, garlic mushrooms £2.50, grilled gammon £5.90, seafood pancake £5.90, home-made apple pie £1.40   **RESTAURANT:** scallops skewer £4.50, beef Wellington £5.90, duckling in Grand Marnier £9   Vegetarian Meals: vegetarian pancake £7.50   Children's Portions   Beer   Ridleys   Children Allowed in Bar to Eat   Outdoor Play Area   Garden   Outdoor Eating   **Credit Cards:** Access, Visa*

HORNDON ON THE HILL   Bell

High Road SS17 8LD
Tel: (0375) 673154
Open: 11-2.30, 6-11
Licensee: N S B Vereker

A hot cross bun is nailed to a ceiling beam at the Bell every Good Friday, and the collection of shrunken, fossilised old buns is now pretty spectacular. A sporty, friendly community pub, free from music, gaming machines and pool tables, it has an opened-up bar, lots of old wood and stone, and an attractive garden. They need notice for vegetarian needs in the restaurant. The accommodation is located next door.

*Bar Meals: 12-1.45, 6.30-9.45; bar snacks both sessions   **Restaurant:** 12.15-1.45, 7.15-9.45   **Typical Dishes BAR:** leek and potato soup £1.95, marinated lamb steak £5.25, loin of pork, mushroom sauce £4.95, cod in pastry with herb sauce £4.95, home-made apple pie £1.80   **RESTAURANT:** cream of lettuce soup £2.10, smoked salmon and vegetable strudel £4.20, lamb in pastry with haggis £11.25, fillet of beef with lentils and smoked bacon £13, grilled halibut with mustard crust £12.25, trio of chocolate pudding £2.50   Vegetarian Meals: vegetable quiche   Children's Portions   Cheese   (restaurant)   Beer   Draught Bass, Charrington IPA   Children Allowed in Bar to Eat   Patio/terrace   Outdoor Eating   Summer Barbecue   **Accommodation:** 10 bedrooms, all en suite, from £45 (room charge, no single rate)   Children Welcome Overnight   Cots Available   Check-in: all day   **Credit Cards:** Access, Amex, Diners, Visa*

LAMARSH   Red Lion

Back road from Bures to Sudbury
Tel: (0787) 227918
Open: 11-3, 6-11
Licensees: John and Angela O'Sullivan

Best in winter when the log fire's lit, a tiled little Essex pub, comfortably
modernised, originally timbered, and much used by locals. The restaurant's in the
old barn.

Bar Meals: daily lunchtime and evening; bar snacks both sessions **Restaurant:** *Thur-Sat
evenings and Sun lunch* **Typical Dishes:** *home-made soup £1.20, ham and eggs,
spaghetti, rump steaks (main courses from £3.50)* Beer *Adnams; Greene King
Children Allowed in Bar to Eat until early evening Outdoor Play Area Garden*

LITTLE BRAXTED   Green Man

Kelvedon Road
Tel: (0621) 891659
Open: 11-3, 6-11
Licensee: Eion MacGregor

Secluded, unspoilt little brick and tiled pub with comfortable lounge and traditional
public bar. Good for summer dining, though the bar menu is routine. Substantial
French bread sandwiches.

Bar Meals: 12-2, 7.30-10.15; bar snacks both sessions **Typical Dishes:** *beef curry,
lasagne, chilli (around £3)* Beer *Ridleys IPA Garden*

LITTLEBURY   Queens Head

High Street CB11 4TD   ⚥
Tel: (0799) 22251
Open: 11.30-2.30, 5-11 (12-11 Sat)
Licensees: Deborah and Jeremy O'Gorman

A popular, enthusiastically-run dining pub which even produces its own quarterly
newsletter to a mailing list of 600 fans. Special events are a big thing here, any
excuse welcome for a theme eating evening; they follow the social calendar quite
closely, and on the international side, Creole weekends have been a big hit. A new
kitchen extension has just been finished. The menu's the same in bar and dining
room.

Bar Meals: 12-2, 7-9; bar snacks lunchtime **Typical Dishes:** *home-made soup £1.80,
baked avocado with stilton butter £2.80, fillet steak au poivre with raspberries £8.15, lamb
cutlets with herbs and redcurrant sauce £5.90, trout with marjoram and wine £5.40, treacle
and walnut tart £2 Vegetarian Meals: stir-fry with egg noodles £4.40 Children's
Menu/Portions* Cheese Beer *Adnams; Everards; Marston; Nethergate Children
Allowed in Bar to Eat Outdoor Play Area Garden Outdoor Eating* **Accommodation:**
*6 bedrooms, all en suite, from £39 (single £30) Children Welcome Overnight Cot
Available Check-in: by arrangement* **Credit Cards:** *Access, Visa*

MALDON Blue Boar Hotel, Silver Street Tel: (0621) 852681: Splendid old
coaching inn, busy and friendly; real fires; quiet corners; decent bar food lunch and
evening. Bedrooms, Adnams beers. Open: 11-3, 6-11. **White Horse**: Also worth
trying for interesting food.

MASHBURY   Fox Inn

Fox Road   ▼
Tel: (0245) 31573
Open: 12-3, 6.30-11
Licensee: Mario Balshaw

Remote country pub run by a Swiss-trained chef, particular about details. Daily
changing blackboard menu genuinely depends on fresh produce availability.
Traditional pub dishes in modern dress a speciality.

Bar Meals: lunchtime and evening (no food Tue); bar snacks lunchtime   ***Typical Dishes:***
boozy beef and seafood casseroles, stuffed chicken breast, fresh salmon with lemon sauce (main
courses from £5)   Children's Portions   Beer   *Ridleys   Garden*

MILL GREEN   Viper

Highwood Road
Tel: (0277) 352010
Open: 11-2.30 (3 Sat), 6-11
Licensee: Fred Beard

Very popular, idyllically-set little country pub, best enjoyed after a wander through
the surrounding woods – but beware the mosquitoes. Food is secondary to the
charm of the environment (lovely gardens) and traditional interior, and secondary to
the life of the pub; just snacks of the soup/sandwiches/ploughmans and chilli sort.

Bar snacks lunchtime   Beer   *Ruddles Best, County   Garden*

MORETON Moreton Massey: Refurbished open-plan dining pub popular for
bar meals; interesting beers and wine list. Restaurant. **White Hart**: Farmers' local
with separate restaurant. Good beers. Open: 10.30-2.30, 6-11.

NORTH FAMBRIDGE Ferryboat, The Quay: Delightful little riverside cottage
pub, quaint interior, lovely for a summer drink. Yachting types in summer. Bar
meals. Tetleys beers.

PELDON Plough: Simple weather-boarded and tiled village local with strong
seafood menu.

RICKLING GREEN   Cricketers' Arms

Rickling Green CB11 3YE
Tel: (079 988) 322
Open: 11-3, 6-11
Licensees: Jo and Tim Proctor

Mellow redbrick pub, nicely set by the village green, though not very special inside,
except for its enormously hospitable hosts; nothing is too much trouble, and
friendliness almost intrusive.

Bar Meals and Restaurant: 12-2, 6.30-10 (12.15-2 (3 restaurant), 7.15-9.30 Sun); bar
snacks both sessions   ***Typical Dishes BAR:*** *mushroom soup £1.30, soft roes and toast*
£2.25, mussels (3 sorts) £3.50-£4.75, sirloin steak £6.95, lambs liver and bacon £4.25,
banoffee pie £1.75   **RESTAURANT:** *set menus £15.50 and £17.50: leek and stilton*
soup, oeufs en cocotte, saffron lamb, fillet Rossini, pineapple Romanoff   Vegetarian Meals:
vegetable stroganoff £3.50   Children's Menu/Portions   Beer   *Tolly Cobbold Mild,*
Original   Family Room   Patio/terrace   Outdoor Eating   Summer Barbecue

Accommodation: 7 bedrooms, all en suite, from £45 (single £40)   Children Welcome
Overnight   Cot Available   Check-in: all day   **Credit Cards:** Access, Amex, Diners, Visa

---

SAFFRON WALDEN   Eight Bells

18 Bridge Street CB10 1BU   ❢
Tel: (0799) 22790
Open: 11-3, 6-11

Solidly traditional bar, partitioned by ancient wall timbers into two smaller rooms,
complete with old furniture, mellow cream walls, exposed timbers and brick. An
apparently unchanging bar menu offers reliably good food, though not at old-
fashioned prices. Note they no longer offer bedrooms.

Bar Meals: 12-2.30, 6.30-9.30 (10 Sat); 12-3, 7-9.30 Sun; bar snacks both sessions
*Typical Dishes BAR: cheese and onion soup £1.70, prawn and sweetcorn parcel £4.35,
saffron chicken £6.10, steak, kidney and mushroom pie £5.95, baked salmon in wine and
mushrooms £7.45, chocolate and brandy pot RESTAURANT: menus £13-£20: celery
and ham soup, stuffed courgettes, Thaxted duckling with honey and apricots, sirloin steak
stuffed with paté, monkfish and prawn kebabs Vegetarian Meals   Children's Menu/Portions*
Beer *Adnams Bitter; Greene King IPA   Children Allowed in Bar to Eat   Outdoor
Play Area   Garden   **Credit Cards:** Access, Amex, Diners, Visa*

SAFFRON WALDEN   Saffron Hotel

High Street CB10 1AY   ❢
Tel: (0799) 22676
Licensees: Craddock family

Good honest home cooking by the landlord at this friendly town centre pub, with
its smartly spruced-up dining bar. Generous helpings; excellent snacks; crisp-leaved
salads. Some bedrooms are attractively modernised, with full en suite bathrooms; the
rest have showers.

Bar Meals: 12-2, 7-9.30 (no food Sun)   *Typical Dishes: home-made soup, moules
marinière, steak, kidney and Guinness pie, chicken escalope in cream and paprika, liver and bacon,
bread and butter pudding (main courses from around £5) Vegetarian Meals* Cheese   Beer
*Courage; Greene King   **Accommodation:** 21 bedrooms, all en suite, from £50   Children
Welcome Overnight   Cots Available   Check-in: all day   **Credit Cards:** Access, Visa*

SOUTH FAMBRIDGE Anchor Hotel, Fambridge Road Tel: (0702) 203535:
River Crouch-side pub popular with weekend sailing types. Good home-made pies
in the bar and rather smart restaurant (steaks a speciality); food daily lunch and Mon-
Sat evenings. Children allowed in to eat. Seafood in summer. Garden. Adnams,
Greene King, Marston beers. Open: 10-2.30, 7 (6 Fri/Sat)-11.

STOCK   Hoop

21 High Street CM4 9BD
Tel: (0277) 841137
Open: all day
Licensee: Albert Kitchin

Unspoilt, simple, cosy beer-lovers' favourite in equally unspoilt Essex village. Bar
food, more interesting than it used to be, is pleasingly traditionalist in style, in
keeping with this well-heeled London commuter area. May Day weekend features a
100-brand name beer festival.

Bar Meals: 10 am-10.30 pm; *bar snacks all day*   **Typical Dishes:** *home-made soup £1, whitebait £2.50, steak and kidney pudding £3.50, braised oxtail with dumplings £3.50, fish pie with trout and prawn £4.50, blackcurrant and apple pie £1.50   Vegetarian Meals: home-made vegetable pie £3.50*   **Beer**   *Adnams Bitter; Crouch Vale Bitter; Nethergates Bitter; Wadworth 6X*   **Cider**   *Outdoor Play Area   Garden   Outdoor Eating   Summer Barbecue*   **No Credit Cards**

STOCK Bear Inn: The Square Tel: (0277) 840232: Another popular haunt in this well-heeled multi-pub commuter village. Smart, modern cooking by the chef-licensee in the restaurant and bar, where the traditional and nouvelle meet. Cater well for vegetarians. Children allowed in to eat. Garden. No bar food Sat night/Sun lunch. Adnams, Ind Coope beers.

THAXTED   Farmhouse Inn

Monk Street CM6 2NR   ❦
Tel: (0371) 830864
Open: 11-11
Licensees: Max Conde and Michael Horn

Popular ex-farmhouse hotel.

Bar Meals and Restaurant: 12-2.30, 6.30-9.30; *bar snacks both sessions*   **Typical Dishes BAR:** *home-made soup £1.75, melon £1.35, chicken Kiev £8.95, pasta with broccoli £5.95, fillet of plaice £5.65, home-made apple pie £1.95*   **RESTAURANT:** *stilton mushrooms £3.75, steak Diane £10.95, mushroom stroganoff £6.50, brill princess £9.50, summer pudding £2.95   Vegetarian Meals: vegetable curry £4.95   Children's Portions*   **Beer**   *Adnams Bitter; Greene King IPA   Children Allowed in Bar to Eat   Outdoor Play Area   Garden   Outdoor Eating   Summer Barbecue*   **Accommodation:** *11 bedrooms, all en suite, from £50   Children Welcome Overnight   Cots Available   Check-in: all day*   **Credit Cards:** *Access, Amex, Visa*

TILLINGHAM   Cap & Feathers

8 South Street
Tel: (0621) 779212
Open: 11-3, 6-11 (12-10.30 Sun)
Licensees: Robin Walster and Colin Bocking

Delightfully unspoilt, imaginatively preserved and run, classic weather-boarded Essex village inn, in a sleepy village. Warm, woody interior with eclectic mix of traditional furnishings, board floors, real fire; several distinct areas ramble about; ancient bar billiards table still operates on shillings. Excellent bar meals; try something from their own garden smokery.

Bar Meals: 12-2, 7-9.30;   *bar snacks both sessions*   **Typical Dishes:** *home-smoked fillet steak £2.75, home-made beef and ale pie £3.95, home-made game pie £4.25, home-smoked trout £4.60, apple and cider crumble £1.50   Vegetarian Meals: home-made vegetable sausages £3.95   Children's Menu/Portions*   **Beer**   *Crouch Vale*   **Cider**   *Family Room   Garden   Outdoor Eating   Summer Barbecue*   **Accommodation:** *4 bedrooms, sharing a bathroom, from £30 (single £15)   Children Welcome Overnight   Cot Available   Check-in: by arrangement*   **No credit cards**

TOOT HILL   Green Man

near Ongar CM5 9SD   ¶
Tel: (037 882) 2255
Open: 11-3, 6-11
Licensee: Peter Roads

Many years an award winner for its floral courtyard. Promising bar food and wine list; no children under 10.

Bar Meals: 12-2, 6.30-10; bar snacks both sessions **Restaurant:** *lunch Sun only, 7-9.30 Tue-Sat* **Typical Dishes BAR:** *home-made soup £1.80, mushrooms with garlic and bacon £2.50, wild rabbit with herb dumplings £5.90, chicken breast with stilton sauce £5.50, lamb hotpot £4.90, rhubarb crumble* **RESTAURANT:** *set-price 4-course dinner £20* *Vegetarian Meals: avocado with hot cheese sauce* **Beer** *Adnams; Ruddles; Webster's* *Children over 10 Allowed in Bar to Eat* *Outdoor Play Area* *Garden Outdoor Eating* **No Credit Cards**

WALTHAM ABBEY Volunteer: On the Loughton road, at the edge of Epping Forest; huge, rambling roadhouse, attractively done. Good Chinese specials.

GLOUCESTERSHIRE

AMBERLEY   Black Horse

Left by Amberley Inn, then immediate right GL5 5AD
Tel: (0453) 872556
Open: 11.30-3, 6-11
Licensee: Evert Abendanon

200 year old country pub with lovely views over a neighbouring hillside, a pleasantly modernised, carpeted bar, and a new licensee, producing some interesting-sounding bar food. Walk it all off with a stroll on nearby Minchinhampton Common.

Bar Meals: 12-2, 6.30-10.30; bar snacks both sessions **Typical Dishes:** *home-made soup £1.70, spinach pancake £3.25, charcoal-grilled meats from £5.25, pork, beef and kidney casserole £4.25, fresh whole plaice £5.50, fresh pears in red wine £2.25* *Vegetarian Meals: baked mushrooms in cumin* *Children's Portions* **Beer** *Greene King Abbot Ale; Hook Norton Bitter; Tetley Bitter; Wadworth 6X* *Family Room* *Outdoor Play Area* *Garden* *Outdoor Eating* *Summer Barbecue* **Credit Cards:** *Visa*

AMPNEY CRUCIS   Crown of Crucis Hotel

On A417 GL7 5RS   ¶
Tel: (0285) 851806
Open: 11-3, 5.30-11 (all day summer)

The original roadside inn, charmingly built of local stone, has a modern, gabled bedroom extension, all grouped around an open courtyard. The bar is pleasantly modernised rather than especially atmospheric, but hotel public rooms are creamy and chintzily relaxing, and the whole is certainly well-cared for and managed. A busy food pub at weekends, with a loyal local trade.

Bar Meals and Restaurant: 12-2.30, 6 (7 restaurant)-10; bar snacks both sessions **Typical Dishes BAR:** *home-made soup £1.10, paté £2, steak and kidney pie £4.55,* *cauliflower, bacon and tomato mornay £3.95, salmon and asparagus pancakes £4.75, banoffee pie £1.75* **RESTAURANT:** *asparagus soup £2.25, warm scallop, mushroom and bacon salad £3.20, brace of roast quail £9.60, tournedos Rossini £9.95, red mullet with tomato and tarragon £6.50, sherry trifle £2* Vegetarian Meals: herb pancakes with mushroom, spinach and nuts   Children's Menu/Portions   `Cheese`   `Beer`   Archers Village Bitter; Marston Pedigree; Tetley Bitter   Children Allowed in Bar to Eat   Outdoor Play Area   Riverside Garden   Outdoor Eating   **Accommodation:** 26 bedrooms, all en suite, from £58 (single £47)   Children Welcome Overnight   Cots Available   Check-in: all day   **Credit Cards:** Access, Amex, Visa

---

BARNSLEY   Village Pub

On A433 GL7 5EF
Tel: (0285) 740421
Open: 11-3, 6-11
Licensee: S Stevens

Very popular drive-out-to-eat pub on the Cirencester to Burford road. Communicating rooms are pleasantly modernised, low ceilinged still, with some settles and stripped stone walls, and with tasteful agricultural memorabilia; log fires in winter.

Bar Meals: *12-2, 7-9 (9.30 Fri/Sat); bar snacks both sessions* **Typical Dishes:** *home-made soup £1.75, beef in Guinness £5.45, Gloucester sausage £4.60, steak and kidney pie £4.35* Vegetarian Meals: lentil and nut cutlet   Children's Portions   `Beer` Wadworth 6X; Whitbread Flowers IPA   `Cider`   Blands   Family Room   Outdoor Play Area   Patio/terrace   **Accommodation:** 6 bedrooms, 4 en suite, from £43 (single £28.75) Children Welcome Overnight   Check-in: all day   **Credit Cards:** Access, Visa

---

BIBURY   Catherine Wheel

Bibury GL7 6DJ   ☼
Tel: (028 574) 250
Open: 11-3, 6-11
Licensee: William May

Pear trees grow against the wall at each side of the entrance to this 500 year old stone pub, run in friendly, relaxed style by Bill May and his son Michael. Inside, the three small rooms have the mellow atmosphere of an unpretentious, unspoilt local. Most of the drinking is done in the first bar, which has a log fire in winter and ceiling beams taken from old wooden ships, when they were broken up in Gloucester docks – an example of 15th century recycling. Most of the eating takes place in the other two rooms, both with woodburning stoves and one with red plush upholstery. A handwritten menu covers the regular dishes like sandwiches (the home-cooked ham is first rate), ploughmans, steaks and salads, while a blackboard menu displays the specials of the day, perhaps salmon with herb butter, ratatouille au gratin or chilli con carne. There are usually several excellent home-made soups on offer; the well-balanced celery and stilton is recommended. Walk off lunch, or build an appetite for dinner, with a stroll around this pretty village; the trout farm welcomes visitors and there's a rustic museum in Arlington Mill. For overnight guests, there are two modest bedrooms, furnished with cheap modern white melamine furniture, although both have remote control television and tea and coffee kit. The larger room has three beds to accommodate families. A shared bathroom has a separate shower cubicle in addition to the tub. It's not pristine, but perfectly acceptable. Massive cooked breakfasts challenge the healthiest of appetites.

Bar Meals: *12-2, 7-10 (9.30 Sun); bar snacks both sessions* **Typical Dishes:** *mushroom soup £1.75, chicken liver paté £2.50, steak in Guinness £4.95, Chinese chicken £4.95,*

halibut in prune sauce £5.30, bread pudding £1.50   Vegetarian Meals: ratatouille £4.50
Children's Portions   Beer   *Courage*   Whisky   *Family Room   Children Allowed in Bar*
to Eat   Garden   Outdoor Eating   **Accommodation:** *2 bedrooms, sharing a bathroom, from*
£30   Children Welcome Overnight   Check-in: all day   **No Credit Cards**

BLEDINGTON   Kings Head

The Green; near Kingham OX7 6HD
Tel: (0608) 658365
Open: 11-2.30 (12-2 Sun), 6-11
Licensees: Michael and Annette Royce

Cotswold village pub on the Oxfordshire border, in a gloriously unspoilt spot by the
green and brook, complete with ducks all known by name. The original bar is
charming, with a smoky patina of age, ancient settles, simple wooden furnishings
and an open fire, as well as tapestry-topped stools and other modern touches. A
lounge (overlooking the garden) and dining room are less quaint, but attractive
enough; there's also a locals' public bar. Well-known for its food, the pub gets very
busy at peak periods. A good place to stay, at the heart of the Cotswold tourist belt.

Bar Meals and Restaurant: 12-2 (1.30 Sun), 7-9.30; bar snacks lunchtime   **Typical**
Dishes BAR: *home-made soup £1.50, black pudding with apple and bacon £2.25, braised*
kidneys £4.25, pan fried avocado £4.25, courgette and prawn bake £3.95, toffee and
walnut flan £1.25   **RESTAURANT:** *chip beef £2.95, local duck with sage and plum*
puree £9.50, stuffed veal £8.95, brace of quail with apricot and spinach £8.95, treacle tart
£1.50   Vegetarian Meals: spiced bean casserole £4.25   Children's Menu/Portions
Beer   *Hook Norton Bitter; Tetley Bitter; Wadworth 6X*   Whisky   *Family Room*
Outdoor Play Area   Garden   **Accommodation:** *6 bedrooms, all en suite, from £45 (single*
£27)   Children Welcome Overnight   Cot Available   Check-in: all day

BLOCKLEY   Crown Inn and Hotel

High Street GL56 9EX
Tel: (0386) 700245
Open: 11-3, 6-11
Licensees: Jim and Betty Champion

Smartened up, well-heeled Cotswold village inn of mellow golden stone. Original
bar fittings, comfortable traditional chairs, pretty carpeting, flashes of exposed stone,
attractive light fittings, and the general air of a market town hotel lounge all
characterise the public drinking and bar meal areas. The excellent Coach House
Restaurant is pink and piney; the Grill Room more masculine, in a plain pubby
dining room style. Comfortable, carpeted bedrooms feature co-ordinating modern
fabrics as well as the odd original beam and some nice pine furniture. Lots of
supplements bounce up the cost of a bargain-looking dinner menu.

Bar Meals and Restaurant: 12-2 (2.30 Sun), 7-9.30; bar snacks lunchtime   **Typical**
Dishes BAR: *home-made soup £1.95, chicken provencale, bowl of chilli, seafood lasagne*
(main courses around £5), raspberry mousse £1.95 **RESTAURANT** *dinner menu*
£16.95: fish terrine, Parma ham (+£3), local rack of lamb (+£2.50), fillet of beef bearnaise
(+£4), salmon steak (+£3)   Vegetarian Meals: lasagne   Beer   *Butcombe Bitter;*
Courage Directors, John Smith's Bitter; Wadworth 6X   Children Allowed in Bar to Eat
Patio/terrace   Outdoor Eating   **Accommodation:** *21 bedrooms, all en suite, from £67.94*
(single £50.57)   Children Welcome Overnight   Cots Available   Check-in: after 1 pm
Credit Cards: *Access, Amex, Visa*

BOURTON ON THE WATER Duke of Wellington: Bistro-style dining
operation in nice pub avoids the usual bar menu cliches. Garden.

BROAD CAMPDEN   Bakers Arms

Chipping Campden GL55 6UR
Tel: (0386) 840515
Open: 11.30-3, 5.30-11
Licensees: Carolyn and Tony Perry

This old village granary makes a delightful country pub, with its Cotswold stone walls and oak beams, splendid old bar counter and good mix of furnishings, a framed hand-woven rug picture of the inn, and large open fire where logs crackle in winter. A good base for a walk and light lunch; its gets very busy. Let them know if you are intending to leave your car in the car park while off on an extended ramble.

Bar Meals: 12-2.30, 5.30-9.45 (12-2, 7-8.45 Sun); bar snacks both sessions **Typical Dishes:** *herby tomato soup £1.15, prawn cocktail £2.55, cottage pie £2.75, chicken Madras £3.25, smoked haddock bake £3.15, fresh fruit pavlova £1.75   Vegetarian Meals: mushroom and nut fettuccine   Children's Menu   Children's Portions (some)*   `Beer` *Beer Engine; Jolly Roger; Theakston; Wadworth   Children Allowed in Bar to Eat   Outdoor Play Area   Garden   Outdoor Eating* **No Credit Cards**

BROCKHAMPTON   Craven Arms

off A436 by river Colne
Tel: (0242) 820410
Open: 11-3, 6-11

Family-run, extended, modernised and immaculately kept 17th century pub with several rooms, some pine and other furnishings, an open fire and a thriving bar meals trade. Home cooking from fresh ingredients, simple at lunchtime (see list), and of the order of duck, salmon and steaks in the evenings. Very popular for Sunday lunch.

Bar Meals: daily lunch and Mon-Sat eve **Typical Dishes:** *home-cooked ham salad, steak and kidney pie, chicken and mushroom crumble, sticky toffee pudding (main courses around £4) Vegetarian Meals* `Beer` *Butcombe; Hook Norton; Wadworth   Children Allowed in Bar to Eat   Garden   Outdoor Eating* **No Credit Cards**

CHEDWORTH   Seven Tuns

Chedworth GL54 4AE
Tel: (0285) 720242
Open: 12-3, 6.30-11 (closed Mon lunch winter)
Licensee: Brian Eacott

Cottagey and atmospheric old alehouse, lost in winding country lanes. Period charm, complete with original settles, hunting prints and log fire in the main bar; simpler public and family room has a games area attached. The lounge is "for adults only"; locals and visitors mix well. They specialise in steaks. There's a pretty walled garden across the lane.

Bar Meals: 12-2.15, 7-9.15; bar snacks both sessions **Typical Dishes:** *lentil soup £1.15, patés £1.85, steak and kidney pie £3.60, spinach and mushroom lasagne £3.50, old-fashioned stews (winter), fruit crumble £1.20   Vegetarian Meals: cauliflower cheese £2.40   Children's Menu* `Beer` *Courage Best, Directors, John Smith's Bitter   Family Room   Garden   Outdoor Eating* **No Credit Cards**

CHIPPING CAMPDEN Kings Arms, Main Street: Nice little hotel in this beautiful village, popular with tourists for bed and breakfast. The historic old **Noel Arms** is also rated as an overnight stop, though its bar food is extremely routine.

COCKLEFORD ★ Green Dragon Inn

Cowley, Cheltenham GL53 9NW
Tel: (024 287) 271
Licensee: B Hinton

A wealth of good things awaits patrons of the Green Dragon, which stands in deep countryside just off the A435. It dates from the 17th century,and started life as a cider house. Beer drinkers today will appreciate the traditional service of fine real ales direct from the cask: there may be Hook Norton, Bass, Wadworth, Archers and Theakstons on any given day. Equally, even the most regular of diners will not tire of Donald Campbell's weekly changing menus. Start, for instance, with a rich bouillabaisse soup, coronation mushrooms or prawns Alabama, and proceed to a steak, kidney and oyster pudding, halibut hollandaise, or mushroom and almond pasanda. Round it all off with baked jam roll, banoffee pie, or the intriguing Tracy's Tipsy Drizzle. For those of lesser appetites, there's granary bread and cheese, various quiches, honey glazed ham, and a wide choice of cheese for ploughmans lunching. The central bar serves as the fulcrum of much activity, with dining room style seating at the upper level (book at weekends, when there's waitress service), and a lower bar with rather more appeal to Cotswold Way walkers. The old farriers building, which once housed a skittle alley, has been restored to create a function suite, which is pressed into service on Sundays for a popular carvery lunch. Its pebbled patio – a lovely summer setting – overlooks a trout stream and Cowley lake. Immensely popular all year round, those in the know come early for the best fireside seats in winter, or the pick of the summer spots on a flower-bedecked patio. Service cannot be faulted here either, and there's always a cheery welcome for strangers and regulars alike from Sue and Barry Hinton.

Bar Meals: 11.15-2, 6.15-10 (12-2; 2.30 carvery; 7.15-10 Sun); bar snacks both sessions Typical Dishes BAR: mussel and onion soup £1.50, prawn and Guinness paté £2.50, beef and beetroot £4.75, mustard-glazed lamb £4.50, sea bream bonne femme £4.75, grape and Irish cream cheesecake £1.75 Vegetarian Meals: winter vegetable casserole Children's Portions (on request) **Beer** *Archers Golden; Butcombe Bitter; Hook Norton Best Bitter* **Cider** *Riverside Garden Outdoor Eating No Credit Cards*

COLESBOURNE Colesbourne Inn

near Cheltenham GL53 9NP
Tel: (024 287) 376
Open: 11-11 (11-3, 6-11 Sat)
Licensees: Eric and Mary Bird

Cotswold country pub by the main A435; the 200 year old inn is the same age as the road, built to service the increasingly fashionable spa town tourist trade. Panelled bars feature open fires and reliable bar food which is beginning to show signs of ambition. There's also Brambles Restaurant, and ten bedrooms in a converted stable block, with a mix of furniture, and well-equipped, with good en suite facilities.

Bar Meals: 12-3, 6.30 (7 Sun)-10; bar snacks both sessions Typical Dishes: tomato and sweetcorn soup £1.75, home-made paté with orange sauce £3.25, white devil chicken £7.75, home-made steak, Guinness and mushroom pie £6.95, hot smoked lamb fillet with pink berry sauce £8.25, summer pudding £1.95 Vegetarian Meals: vegetable stroganoff £5.50 Children's Portions **Cheese** **Beer** *Wadworth beers Family Room Outdoor Play Area Garden Outdoor Eating Accommodation: 10 bedrooms all en suite,*

from £50 (single £30)   Children Welcome Overnight   Cot Available   Check-in: all day
Credit Cards: *Access, Amex, Diners, Visa*

DYMOCK   Beauchamp Arms

Dymock GL18 1LP
Tel: (035 185) 266
Open: all day
Licensee: K Forde

Pretty garden and popular for lunchtime bar food. Dymock single Gloucester cheese
is worth sampling.

Bar Meals: *12-3*   **Restaurant:** *6.30-9.30*   **Typical Dishes BAR:** *home-made soup
£1.45, garlic mushrooms £2.75, Italian style braised rabbit, Chinese style chicken, roast
partridge with braised red cabbage, chilled lemon soufflé   Vegetarian Meals: sweet and sour
stuffed peppers   Children's Portions* ▉Beer▉ *Marston; Whitbread; Wye Valley* ▉Cider▉
*Weston's   Children Allowed in Bar to Eat   Outdoor Play Area   Garden   Summer
Barbecue*   **No Credit Cards**

EWEN   Wild Duck Inn

Drakes Island GL7 6BV   ▼
Tel: (0285) 770310
Open: all day
Licensees: Brian and Tina Mussell

Lovely Cotswold village pub near the Water Park. The dimly-lit Post Horn bar is
nicely poised between traditional and smartened up; the restaurant has red walls,
candles in bottles, and simple pine furniture, and bedrooms (particularly the two
four-poster ones in the oldest part of the building) are decent, though the extension-
housed remainder might seem surprisingly modern in style. The Grouse Room
residents lounge, a haven of peace overlooking the pretty gardens, is also open to
diners.

Bar Meals: *12-2, 7-9.45; bar snacks both sessions*   **Typical Dishes:** *home-made soup
£2, Portuguese style chicken breast piri piri £7.25, stilton and bacon-stuffed fillet steak
£11.95, parrot fish £8.95, bread and butter pudding £2.50   Vegetarian Meals: cabbage
and mushroom bake £5.25   Children's Portions* ▉Beer▉ *Draught Bass; Theakston XB,
Old Peculier; Wadworth 6X   Family Room   Garden   Outdoor Eating   Summer Barbecue*
Accommodation: *10 bedrooms, all en suite   Children Welcome Overnight   Cots Available
Check-in: all day*   **Credit Cards:** *Access, Visa*

FORD   Plough

On B4077, Temple Gutting
Tel: (0386) 73215
Open: 11-3, 5-11

Long a favourite of Cotswold ramblers and lovers of the traditional English pub
everywhere, the interior of the idyllic little 13th century Plough has all the
atmosphere you could wish for. But it's also about to change hands, so food and
other details will probably be subject to change from late 1991.

Bar Meals: *12-2, 7-9.30; bar snacks lunchtime*   **Typical Dishes:** *game soup £1.75,
garlic mushrooms £2.45, game pie £4.75, steak and kidney pie £4.75, mixed grill £6.25,
banoffee pie £1.75   Vegetarian Meals: fusille colbuco with aubergine and wine sauce*

Children's Menu/Portions Cheese Beer *Donningtons BB, SBA* Cider *Coates Children Allowed in Bar to Eat   Garden   **Accommodation:** 4 bedrooms, sharing a bathroom, from £30 (single £15)   Children Welcome Overnight   Cot Available   Check-in: all day*

FOSSEBRIDGE Fossebridge Inn: on A429 Tel: (028 572) 310: Long a favourite for its food and airy overnight accommodation, the Fossebridge Inn has now passed into new hands.

FOSSE CROSS   Hare & Hounds

near Chedworth GL54 4NW
Tel: (0285) 720288
Open: 11-3, 6-11
Licensee: Michael Turner

Family dining pub, 300 years old, built of Cotswold stone, and with warming log fires. Caravan site next door.

Bar Meals: *12-2.15, 7-10; bar snacks both sessions* ***Typical Dishes:*** *home-made soup £1.50, stilton paté £2.25, steak and kidney cooked in stout with dumplings £4.50, fresh pan-fried trout £4.50, fresh pasta with basil, tomato and cream sauce £3.95, treacle tart £1.50   Vegetarian Meals: cheesy potato pie   Children's Menu/Portions* Beer *Hook Norton; Theakston; Wadworth* Cider *Blands   Children Allowed in Bar to Eat Outdoor Play Area   Garden   Outdoor Eating* ***Credit Cards:*** *Access, Amex, Diners, Visa*

GREAT BARRINGTON   Fox

A mile off A41 (signs)
Tel: (04514) 385
Open: 11.30-2.30, 6.30-11
Licensees: Pat and Bill Mayer

Genuinely unspoilt little Cotswold pub, run by the same people for many years; its charm is of the simple alehouse sort, and not tweely countrified, take note. Low ceilings, stone walls, rustic furnishings, open fires, a skittle alley, and outdoor tables by the pretty river Windrush. Food is very much secondary, but good beer very much to the fore. They also offer unpretentious bedrooms; popular with walking types. No music.

Bar Meals:: *lunch and evening (no food Sunday)* Beer *Donnington* Cider *Garden* ***Accommodation:*** *5 bedrooms, from £35 (single £18)*

GREAT RISSINGTON   ★ Lamb

Great Rissington GL54 2LP   FOOD
Tel: (0451) 20388   B&B
Open: 11.30-2.30, 6.30-11
Licensee: Richard Cleverly

Originally a farmhouse, the oldest part of the Lamb dates back nearly 300 years, the newest just a couple of years. That it is difficult to tell the difference is a tribute to the skill and craftsmanship of the appropriately named landlord Richard Cleverly, formerly a builder, who has done all the most recent work himself. The charming restaurant, for instance, with its candles and lacy tablecloths, is housed in a new extension, but makes imaginative use of old timbers and stonework. It fits in well with the stone-walled bar, where, incidentally, hangs a plaque to the memory of the airmen who died when their Wellington bomber crashed in the garden here during the second world war; part of a propeller is displayed above the wood-burning stove. Kate Cleverly is no less talented than husband Richard, taking justifiable pride in the fact that everything on the menu is genuinely home-made; even the chicken en croute is cooked to order, starting from scratch with a raw chicken breast. The daily changing blackboard bar menu carries starters like freshly baked stilton puffs – stilton cheese in a light puff pastry pillow, which also makes a good substantial snack when served with salad. Steak and duck pie is another favourite, and the treacle tart made by Kate's mother is almost mandatory. The restaurant menu also applies in the bar, giving an even wider choice, and they can usually find some fishfingers or baked beans on toast for children with a hankering for convenience foods. Richard and Kate's skills have combined in the creation of charming bedrooms; his renovations include built-in wardrobes made with salvaged timbers, and a splendid four-poster bed, testifies to his skills as a wood carver. Kate's contribution is the pretty decor, each room highly individual in style, with coordinating fabrics and wall coverings. Most of the furniture is antique and all but two rooms, which share a shower room, have en suite bathrooms (five with showers rather than baths). They make a virtue out of not having television or radios in the rooms but addicts will find them in the cosy residents' lounge, as well as in the best guest room, a quite luxurious suite. A heated indoor swimming pool in the delightful garden, which also boasts an aviary, summer house and play area, is a luxury all residents can share in the summer months.

Bar Meals: *12-2, 7-9 (9.30 weekends); restaurant evenings only; bar snacks both sessions* **Typical Dishes BAR:** *home-made soup £2.25, garlic and cream mushrooms, steak and duck pie, rack of lamb with honey and garlic sauce, fresh grilled salmon steaks (bar main courses around £5), lemon cheesecake* **RESTAURANT:** *potted shrimps £3.50, beef Wellington £10.50, spicy chicken £7.95, grilled sardines £6.50 Vegetarian Meals: vegetables en croute Children's Menu* Cheese Beer *Draught Bass; Hook Norton Bitter; Wadworth 6X Family Room Garden Outdoor Eating* **Accommodation:** *12 bedrooms, 10 en suite, from £34 (single £30) Children Welcome Overnight Cots Available Check-in: all day* **Credit Cards:** *Access, Visa*

GRETTON   Royal Oak

near Winchcombe GL54 5EP
Tel: (0242) 602477
Open: 11-2.30, 6-11
Licensees: Robert and Kathryn Willison

Excellent for people with children in tow, the Royal Oak has a particularly large, safe garden for small people to explore, with a proper play area. At the bottom of the garden runs the GWR steam railway, which runs from Toddington a few miles away, and brings a lot of trade. The pub itself is a mixture of ancient and modern, with flagstone floors, beams, stripped oak, pine tables and a conservatory dining room, and visitors are equally diverse, a mix of locals, holidaymakers and daytrippers, enjoying varied bar food from a long blackboard list and proper pub restaurant dishes. Live folk music on Wednesday evenings.

Bar Meals: *12-2, 7-9.30; bar snacks both sessions* **Typical Dishes:** *cheddar and potato soup £1.75, baked crab and mushroom pot £2.75, lamb and apricot curry £4.25, rack of lamb with wine and cranberry sauce £7, grilled salmon steak £5.50, chocolate fruit'n'nut biscuit cake £1.70 Vegetarian Meals Children's Portions* Beer *Courage Best, John Smith's Bitter; Eldridge Pope Thomas Hardy Country Bitter; Wadworth 6X* Whisky *Family Room Children Allowed in Bar to Eat Outdoor Play Area Garden Outdoor Eating* **Credit Cards:** *Access, Visa*

GUITING POWER   Olde Inne

Winchcombe Road GL54 5UX
Tel: (0451) 850392
Open: 11.30-2, 5.30-11
Licensees: Ken and Paula Thouless-Meyrick

Frikadeller is a minced pork rissole, just one of the enterprising Scandinavian
specialities the still fairly-new owner licensees of this splendid old village pub have
introduced to an otherwise straightforward menu. Well worth a visit.

Bar Meals and Restaurant: 12-2, 7-9 (9.30 restaurant weekends)   ***Typical Dishes***
BAR: *home-made soup £2.25, steak and kidney pie £2.75, frikadeller £4.50, coffee fudge
pudding £1.75*   ***RESTAURANT:*** *gravadlax £3.75, chicken and stilton roulade £7.25,
rump steak £7.75, pork steak Dijon £6.50   Vegetarian Meals: butterbean bake £4.50
Children's Menu* ▆Beer▆ *Hook Norton Bitter; Theakston BB, Old Peculier* ▆Whisky▆
▆Cider▆ *Thatcher's   Children Allowed in Bar to Eat   Outdoor Play Area   Garden
Outdoor Eating* **No Credit Cards**

HARTPURY   Canning Arms

Gloucester Road
Tel: (0452) 70275
Open: 12-2.30 (not Mon), 7-11
Licensees: John and Jeanne Ashton

Newish licensees are making friends at this comfortable family pub.

*Bar Meals: 12-2, 7-9.30; bar snacks both sessions   **Typical Dishes:** stock-pot soup
£1.35, various home-made patés, rump steak, lamb with rosemary, chicken and peach curry,
banoffee pie (main courses from £4)   Vegetarian Meals: broccoli and cream cheese pie
Children's Menu/Portions* ▆Beer▆ *Draught Bass; Ind Coope Burton Ale; Marston
Pedigree; Theakston Old Peculier* ▆Cider▆ *local scrumpy   Children Allowed in Bar to Eat
Outdoor Play Area   Garden   Outdoor Eating* **No Credit Cards**

JOYFORD Dog & Muffler off B4432/B4228 Tel: (0594) 832444: Secluded
country pub with oodles of character and popular bar meals, lunch and Mon-Sat
eve; no food Monday. Garden, no music. Samuel Smith beers. Open: 11-2.30,
6-11.

KILKENNY Kilkenny Inn on A436: Promising new licensees of wide and
reputable experience in pub catering, at this cosy country pub; food lunch and
evening.

KINGSCOTE   Hunters Hall Inn

Kingscote GL8 8XZ
Tel: (0453) 860393
Open: 11-3, 6.30-11
Licensee: David Barnett-Roberts

Unusually spacious, comfortably genteel old inn, continuously licensed since the
15th century. High ceilinged, connecting rooms hold a pleasing variety of furniture,
both squashy and elegant, exposed stone walls and open fires. An upstairs Gallery
(families can use) takes more diners, and there's also a quite separate, quite different,
low-ceilinged locals' public bar. Bar food is buffet-servery style, with hot dishes
listed on a blackboard, simple and reliably good. Recommended for family
expeditions.

Bar Meals: 12-2, 7-9.45; bar snacks lunchtime   *Restaurant:* 7.30-9.45 (Tue-Sat)
Typical Dishes BAR: courgette and lemon soup £2, seafood pancake £2.95, home-made
steak and kidney pie £4.90, barbecued ribs £4.90, seafood lasagne £5.20, lemon meringue
£2   *RESTAURANT:* farmhouse broth £2.30, fillet of lamb £9.90, pigeon breasts
£8.50, venison £9.90, apple and walnut pie £2.30   *Vegetarian Meals:* hot vegetable
pancake   Children's Menu/Portions   Cheese   (restaurant)   Beer   Draught Bass; Hook
Norton Bitter; Uley Old Spot; Wadworth 6X   Whisky   Family Room   Outdoor Play
Area   Garden   Outdoor Eating   Summer Barbecue   *Accommodation:* 12 bedrooms, all
en suite, from £54 (single £44)   Children Welcome Overnight   Cots Available   Check-
in: all day   *Credit Cards:* Access, Amex, Diners, Visa

LITTLE WASHBOURNE   Hobnails

Little Washbourne GL20 8NQ
Tel: (0242) 620237
Open: 11-2.30 (12-2.30 Sun), 6-11
Licensee: Stephen Farbrother

The licensee's family have run the Hobnails for almost 250 years, which must be
some kind of record. The front bar is simply and traditionally furnished, with a
quarry-tiled floor and low beams; there's also a modernised, carpeted rear lounge. A
printed menu features a vast selection of intriguingly filled baps, as well as home-
made puddings. A separate menu carries a short list of good hot home-made specials.

Bar Meals and Restaurant: 12-2, 7-10.30 (9.30 restaurant); bar snacks both sessions
Typical Dishes: oxtail soup with sherry £1.95, duck pâté £2.80, steak and onion £5.90,
home-made lamb casserole £5.60, macaroni, gammon and sweetcorn cheese £4.50, dark
chocolate and fresh lemon pie £2.40   *Vegetarian Meals:* filo parcels with Swiss cheese and
leeks   Beer   Wadworth 6X; Whitbread; Flowers Original, IPA   Cider   Family
Room   Outdoor Play Area   Garden   Outdoor Eating   *Credit Cards:* Access, Visa

---

LOWER SWELL   Golden Ball

Stow-on-the-Wold GL54 1LF
Tel: (0451) 30247
Open: 11-2.30 (12-2.30 Sun), 6.30-11
Licensees: S J and V J Aldridge

Simple, friendly two-room village pub, with a real fire and traditional pub games.
Vegetarians need to make their presence known, and something will be rustled up;
bar food is traditionally meaty, with lots of pies and bakes. No children under 14
inside or overnight.

Bar Meals: 12-2, 7-9; bar snacks lunchtime   *Typical Dishes:* home-made soup £1.75,
garlic prawns £2.95, home-made beef and pigeon pie £4.75, home-made chicken crumble
£4.50, home-made fish pie £4.75, home-made apple pie £1.75   Children's Menu
Beer   Donnington BB, SBA   Cider   Weston's   Outdoor Play Area   Garden
Outdoor Eating   *Accommodation* (closed mid-Jan to mid-Feb): 2 double bedrooms, neither
en suite, from £32   Check-in: by arrangement   *No Credit Cards*

LOWER WICK — Pickwick

near Dursley GL11 6DD
Tel: (0453) 810259
Open: 11-3, 6-11
Licensees: Colin and Jane Pickford

Totally refurbished 18th century pub with open fires and a large car park, close to the M5 motorway link.

Bar Meals: *12-2.15, 6-10; bar snacks both sessions* ***Typical Dishes:*** *chicken breast with apricot and walnut stuffing £5.25, garlic lamb with pilaff rice £4.95, salmon filo parcels with citrus sauce £5.95, black cherry brulée £1.75 Vegetarian Meals: tagliatelle with cream and stilton sauce £4.25* **Beer** *Draught Bass; Butcombe Bitter; Theakston Best* **Cider** *Blands, Black Jack Children Allowed in Bar to Eat Outdoor Play Area Garden Outdoor Eating* ***No Credit Cards***

MORETON IN THE MARSH — Redesdale Arms Hotel

High Street GL56 0AW **B&B**
Tel: (0608) 50308
Licensees: Michael Elvis and Patricia Seedhouse

Popular for its stylish bedrooms, which include six in an annexe and three luxury suites with patios; good facilities in all. The Archway Bar, with its Queen Anne panelling, a good open fire and a handsome flagged floor, is a civilised setting for drinks; nice residents' conservatory; most recent reports on the bar food suggest it's on the up, though certainly not cheap.

Bar Meals: *lunch and evening Children's Portions* **Beer** *Bass; Courage Children Allowed in Bar to Eat* ***Accommodation:*** *20 bedrooms, all en suite, from £60 (single £39) Children Welcome Overnight* ***Credit Cards:*** *Access, Visa*

NEWLAND — Ostrich Inn

Coleford GL16 8NP
Tel: (0594) 33260
Open: 11.30-3, 6-11
Licensees: Richard and Veronica Dewe

Mercifully unmodernised Forest of Dean pub with 13th century origins. There's a dining room with the same menu and prices. No children.

Bar Meals: *12-2, 7-9.30; bar snacks lunchtime* ***Typical Dishes:*** *home-made soup £1.50, stilton and walnut paté £2, steak and oyster pie £5, turkey Creole £5, roast rack of lamb £5.50, bread and butter pudding £2 Vegetarian Meals: nut roast £5* **Cheese** **Beer** *Exmoor Ale; Greene King Abbot Ale; Marston Pedigree; Whitbread Boddingtons Bitter* **Whisky** *Garden* ***Accommodation:*** *2 bedrooms, sharing a bathroom, from £30 (single £15) Check-in: all day* ***No Credit Cards***

NORTH CERNEY   Bathurst Arms

near Cirencester GL7 7BZ   ¥
Tel: (028 583) 281
Open: 11-2.30, 6-11
Licensees: Freddie and Caroline Seward

17th century coaching inn alongside the A435, not far from Cotswold Water Park, and the end of a terrace of charming old cottages. Rustic unspoilt bar with flagged floor, good reliable food from an ever-changing blackboard selection, and light pretty bedrooms, each rather tweely named after an English flower. Restaurant main courses are £6-£12.

Bar Meals and Restaurant: 11.45-2.30, 6.15-9.30; bar snacks lunchtime **Typical Dishes BAR:** *tomato and basil soup, deep-fried whitebait, sirloin steak garni, fillet of pork stroganoff, fish dishes like fresh whole crab (main courses £4-£6), banoffee pie* *Vegetarian Meals: spinach and mushroom lasagne* *Children's Portions* `Cheese` `Beer` *Archers Best Bitter; Courage Best; Hook Norton Bitter* *Family Room* *Riverside Garden* *Outdoor Eating* *Summer Barbecue* **Accommodation:** *6 bedrooms, 4 en suite, from £45 (single £35)* *Children Welcome Overnight* *Cot Available* *Check-in: before 3 or after 6* **Credit Cards:** *Access, Visa*

NORTHLEACH   Wheatsheaf Hotel

West End GL54 3EZ
Tel: (0451) 60244
Open: 10.30-3, 6-11
Licensee: Sheila E Reeves

Old roadside coaching inn, fairly quietly situated in an old Cotswold wool town, famous for its 15th century church.

Bar Meals: 12-2, 6.30-9.30; bar snacks both sessions **Restaurant:** *12.30-2, 7-9.30* **Typical Dishes BAR:** *carrot and orange soup £2, home-made paté £3.50, steak and ale pie £4.65, chicken tikka masala £5.50, grilled cod in smoked butter £3.75, raspberry caprice £2.50* **RESTAURANT:** *stilton and celery soup £2.50, salmon and dill mousse en choux £3.75, duckling breast £9.85, fillet of pork £8.95, local trout £7.95, coffee Renoir pudding £3.50* *Vegetarian Meals: egg noodles with blue cheese sauce £3.85* `Cheese` `Beer` *Theakston Best; Wadworth 6X* *Outdoor Play Area* *Garden* *Outdoor Eating* **Accommodation:** *8 bedrooms, all en suite, from £65 (single £35)* *Children Welcome Overnight* *Cots Available* *Check-in: all day* **Credit Cards:** *Access, Visa*

PAINSWICK   Royal Oak

St Mary's Street
Open: 11-3, 6-11
Licensee: Mr Morris

Busy, friendly pub in the centre of this quaint and affluent little town. The modernised lounge, partitioned by an enormous open fireplace, has exposed stone and a beautiful old oak door; there's a second bar and little sun lounge room too. Go for the daily changing home-made dishes (around £5) like haddock with poached eggs; there are also good sandwiches, snacks and ploughmans.

Bar Meals: lunch and early evening (not Sun); bar snacks both sessions `Beer` *Whitbread* *Family Room* *Patio/terrace*

PRESTBURY Plough, Mill Street Tel: (0242) 244175: Most attractive half-timbered and thatched village pub with a delightfully old fashioned rear bar; real fire; no music; bar food. Garden. Whitbread beers. Open: 10.30-2.30, 6-11.

ST BRIAVELS   George

High Street (opposite Castle)
Tel: (0594) 530228
Open: 11-3, 6-11 (all day sometimes)
Licensees: Maurice and Cherry Day

Three connecting rooms with nice furnishings, beams and a big open fire, popular with all comers and often very busy. Routine bar food is pepped up by home-made sausages, local trout and the house speciality: the made-for-four Oriental Steamboat, a dish of meat, fish, quails eggs and exotic fruits (two days' notice required). Piped music; garden chess.

Bar Meals: 12.30-3 (2.30 Sun), 7.30-9.30; bar snacks both sessions   Children's Menu
Beer *Hall & Woodhouse; Marston; Wadworth   Children Allowed in Bar to Eat (until 9 pm)   Garden   Outdoor Eating* **Accommodation:** *Bedrooms from £40 (single £30)*

SHUTHONGER   Crown

on A38 GL20 6EF
Tel: (0684) 293714
Open: 11-3, 6-11
Licensee: Mark Thomas

Not an entirely foodie pub by any means; there's a thriving, loyal real ale trade here. But there's also a restaurant, which keeps the same hours and where children are welcome.

Bar Meals: 12-2, 7-10 (not Sun/Mon eve Oct-May); bar snacks both sessions **Typical Dishes:** *chicken, leek and potato soup £1.75, paté campagne £2, home-made steak and kidney pie £4.95, escalope of veal in mushroom sauce £7.50, poached salmon in asparagus sauce £7.50, jam roly poly £2   Vegetarian Meals: mushroom stroganoff £4.95 Children's Menu/Portions* Beer *Banks's Bitter; Draught Bass, Charrington IPA* **Credit Cards:** *Access, Amex, Diners, Visa*

SIDDINGTON   Greyhound

Ashton Road (off A419)
Tel: (0285) 653573
Open: 11.30-2.30, 6.30 (7 Mon/Sat)-11
Licensee: Elaine Flaxman

Interesting furnishings of eclectic taste, lots of brass and copperware, beams, two open fires and a woodburning stove in this successfully extended old village pub; no music in the lounge. Food is beginning to look promising, with interesting specials, fresh local produce and real vegetables, plus their own eggs. Very popular locally, usually busy and friendly to strangers. No children indoors, though.

Bar Meals: 11.30-2, 7-10.30; bar snacks both sessions **Typical Dishes:** *home-made soup £1.95, garlic prawns £3.25, lamb and aubergine pie, salmon, sorrel and spinach pie, lasagne (main courses from around £4.50), jam roly poly   Vegetarian Meals* Beer *Hall & Woodhouse; Wadworth   Garden* **No Credit Cards**

TWYNING Village Inn: Just what it says it is. Decent, if slightly expensive, bar food; menu limited early in the week.

UPPER ODDINGTON   Horse & Groom

Moreton-in-Marsh GL56 0XH
Tel: (0451) 30584
Open: 11-2.30 (12-2.30 Sun), 6 (6.30 winter)-11
Licensees: R and S Gainford

Golden stone village inn with two delightfully rustic bars, lots of exposed stone, a cheering open fire, solid old furnishings, and flagstoned floors. A separate cosy dining room has less charm, but the garden is huge and full of features, a stream, fishpond, little bridge, and aviary amongst them. Bedrooms are simple and modernised, with white walls and modern fabrics and fittings.

Bar Meals and Restaurant: 12-2, 6.30-10; bar snacks both sessions   **Typical Dishes**
BAR: *stilton and broccoli soup £1.50, deep-fried brie with cranberry and orange sauce £2.75, steak, Guinness and mushroom pie £4.70, beef cobbler £4.95, fresh local trout with garden herbs £5.25, cornflake and treacle tart £1.95*   **RESTAURANT:** *chilled watercress soup £2, avocado with smoked salmon and prawns £4.75, jugged hare with sausagemeat balls £7.45, sirloin steak glazed with stilton and cider £9.95, poached salmon with orange and mint sauce £8.25, summer pudding £2.25   Vegetarian Meals: broccoli and macaroni bake   Children's Menu/Portions*   Beer   *Hook Norton Bitter, Old Hooky; Wadworth 6X*   Cider   *Taunton   Family Room   Outdoor Play Area   Garden   Outdoor Eating*
Accommodation: *8 bedrooms, all en suite, from £45 (single £22.50)   Children Welcome Overnight   Cots Available   Check-in: by arrangement*   **Credit Cards:** *Access, Amex*

WATERLEY BOTTOM   New Inn

North Nibley, Dursley GL11 6EF
Tel: (0453) 543659
Open: 12-2.30, 7-11
Licensee: Ruby Sainty

Large, friendly modernised pub at the end of winding country lanes to the east of North Nibley, in a pretty and secluded valley. The beamed lounge, mercifully devoid of canned music, and warmed by an open fire, has old settles, Windsor chairs, and picture windows with views across the garden. It's a keen real ale pub, littered with breweriana. The food is routine bar meal stuff, but this is a good (and incredibly popular) place to stay, being cheap, attractive accommodation in a good touring area.

Bar Meals: 12-2 (1.30 Sun), 7-9.30; bar snacks both sessions   **Typical Dishes:** *home-made soup £1.50, paté £2.40, steak and onion pie £3.70, lasagne £3.80, chilli £3.50, peach and banana crumble £1.20 (all dishes home-made)   Vegetarian Meals: home-made quiche*   Beer   *Cotleigh Tawny Bitter; Greene King Abbot Ale; Smiles Best Bitter; Theakston Old Peculier*   Whisky   Cider   *Inch's   Outdoor Play Area   Garden*
Accommodation: *2 bedrooms, sharing a bathroom, from £35 (single £17.50)   Check-in: by arrangement*   **No Credit Cards**

WHITMINSTER Old Forge: Attractive, beamy old pub with a separate restaurant.

WOODCHESTER   Ram Inn

South Woodchester, near Stroud GL5 5EL
Tel: (0453) 873329
Open: 11-3, 6-11
Licensees: Michael and Eileen McAsey

An attractive blend of ancient and modern, plus three open fires in the L-shaped bar makes this a good spot for a winter lunch, and in summer the terrace is equally delightful, with wonderful views across the valley. A small dining room is cosy in the evenings, bistro-simple, with candles and blackboard specials. Fresh vegetables are properly cooked. Families are allowed in here.

Bar Meals: 12-2, 6.30-9.30; bar snacks both sessions   **Typical Dishes:** *potato and stilton soup £1.65, lamb and apricot pie £4.95, cauliflower and haddock au gratin £4.95, crab thermidor £6.25, chocolate roulade £2.25   Vegetarian Meals: spinach and stilton pie Children's Portions*   **Beer**   *Archers Village Bitter; Hook Norton Old Hooky; Uley Old Spot; Whitbread Boddingtons Bitter   Patio/terrace   Outdoor Eating*   **Credit Cards:** *Access, Visa*

WOOLASTON COMMON Rising Sun off A48, through Netherend village Tel: (059 452) 282: Good country pub in a pretty spot; home-cooked curries very popular – they also do take-aways (no food Wednesday). Garden. Hook Norton, Marston, Theakston beers. Open: 12-2.30 (not Wed), 6.30-11.

HAMPSHIRE

BATTRAMSLEY Hobler on A337: Very popular dining pub, with some unusual and restauranty dishes among the usual bar meals; tables are often reserved in the evening. Pleasant interior; large garden; play area and summer bar. Whitbread beers. Open: 10.30-2.30, 6-11.

BEAUWORTH   Milbury's

near Cheriton, Alresford SO24 0PB   ☀
Tel: (0962) 771248   ☺
Open: 11-2.30 (3 Fri/Sat), 6-11
Licensees: L G and J Larden

The South Down Way passes by the front door of this old tile-hung pub. It's set on a hill just to the south of the village, the site of some bronze age burial mounds or barrows, and the pub's name is actually a corruption of Mill-Barrow, the name of the last remaining mound just 150 yards away. The main bar boasts old brickwork, a flagstone floor and rough hewn three-legged tables, but the most fascinating feature is an enormous treadmill, within which a poor donkey once walked to raise water from a 300 foot well. For the price of a donation to the Guide Dogs for the Blind, you are invited to drop an ice-cube down the well and count the nearly eight seconds it takes to splash in the water far below. The bar menu runs the gamut from home-made soup and ploughmans served with great wedges of granary bread to pints of Norwegian prawns and grilled tuna steak, plus various grills, salads and home-made puddings. For more formal eating, there's a pretty, pink, dado-panelled restaurant with a French-inspired menu. Children are made positively welcome, with their own small section on the menu and swings out in a large garden carved from one corner of a field. Three newly-created bedrooms offer overnight accommodation: one of them a proper suite with a separate sitting room and en suite bathroom, while the other two rooms, in the older, more characterful part of the building, share a large bathroom with separate shower cubicle.

Bar Meals: *12-2, 7-10; bar snacks both sessions* ***Restaurant:*** *12-1.30, 7.15-9.30* ***Typical Dishes BAR:*** *chicken and mushroom soup £1.40, breaded mushrooms with garlic mayonnaise £3.10, beefsteak and Guinness pie £4.35, stuffed pancake with spinach, prawns and cottage cheese £4.10, grilled tuna steak £6.95, hazelnut meringues £1.25 Vegetarian Meals: pasta and avocado salad £3.50 Children's Menu/Portions* **Beer** *Courage Directors, John Smith's Bitter; Gales HSB; Ruddles County Family Room Outdoor Play Area Garden Outdoor Eating Summer Barbecue* ***Accommodation:*** *3 bedrooms, 1 en suite, from £32.50 (single £16.75) Children Welcome Overnight Cot Available Check-in: by arrangement* ***Credit Cards:*** *Access, Amex, Visa*

BENTLEY Star, London Road (A31): Old fashioned wood-panelled one bar local; decent home cooking lunchtime and evening. No music. Courage beers. Open: 11-3, 6-11.

BENTWORTH — Sun

Sun Hill (Alton Road)
Tel: (0420) 62338
Open: 11.30-3, 6-11
Licensee: Jeremy McKay

Lovely, unspoilt old country pub, with two linked low-beamed bars, one brick-floored, one board; nice furnishings, prints and decor and twin woodburning stoves.

Bar Meals: *12-2, 6-9.30; bar snacks both sessions* ***Typical Dishes:*** *ham and eggs, cottage pie, lasagne, fish (main courses around £4) Vegetarian Meals* **Beer** *Bass; Bunces; Gales; Marston Garden*

BOLDRE — Red Lion

Lymington SO41 8NE
Tel: (0590) 673177
Open: 11-3, 6-11 (11-11 summer)
Licensees: John and Penny Bicknell

Delightful old pub, dating from around 1650 and mentioned as an alehouse in the Domesday Book. Outside, an old cart is strewn with flowers, and hanging baskets and troughs are a riot of colour in summer. Inside, four charming, black-beamed rooms each have their own country style, with real fires, a mix of old furnishings, hunting prints, a chamber pot collection, tapestries and man-traps. The same menu applies in the dining room. Most meals come with chips.

Bar Meals: *11-2.30, 6-10.15 (12-2.15, 7-10.15 Sun); all day summer; bar snacks both sessions* ***Typical Dishes:*** *farmhouse soup £1.70, smoked trout £4.10, half duckling £5.90, gammon and eggs £5.90, beef in Guinness with dumplings £5.90, home-made apple pie £2.40 Vegetarian Meals: vegetable casserole £4.10* **Beer** *Eldridge Pope Dorchester Bitter, Royal Oak Garden Outdoor Eating* ***Credit Cards:*** *Access, Visa*

BOTLEY — Bugle Inn

The Square SO3 2EA
Tel: (0489) 783773
Open: 11-11
Licensee: M J Grattan

Pleasant dining pub specialising in steak and chicken.

Bar Meals: *12-2.15, 6.30-10.15; bar snacks both sessions*   **Restaurant:** *12-2, 7-10*
Typical Dishes BAR: *carrot soup £1.75, moules marinière £3.65, lasagne £4.95, beef,
ale and mushroom pie £4.95, lobster thermidor £8.50, chocolate brandy crunch £2.35*
RESTAURANT: *stuffed green-lipped mussels £4.25, chicken supreme stuffed with
seafood, fillet steak Diane £11.95, grilled seafood platter £10.50, fresh fruit meringue nests
£2.50   Vegetarian Meals: baked avocado   Children's Portions*   `Beer`   *Marston;
Whitbread   Patio/terrace   Outdoor Eating*   **Accommodation:** *3 bedrooms, sharing a
bathroom, from £35 (single £20)   Children Welcome Overnight   Check-in: all day*
Credit Cards: *Access, Visa*

BRAMDEN   Fox

On A272 SO24 0LP   ♥
Tel: (096 279) 363
Open: 10.30-2.30 (3 Sat), 6-11
Licensee: Jane Inder

Attractive old white weatherboard pub set back from the main road. Inside is
extensively modernised, and very much dining oriented, but well-kept and comfy.
Good lunchtime bar food is simpler than the evening list (below), with dishes like
steak and kidney pie, and cauliflower cheese, around £5.50. Enclosed patio and
delightful lawn with good play area.

Bar Meals: *12-2, 7-9.30; bar snacks both sessions*   **Typical Dishes:** *home-made soup
£2.40, stuffed mushrooms £3, beef stroganoff, noisettes of lamb, lemon and almond chicken
(main courses from around £7)   Vegetarian Meals*   `Cheese`   `Beer`   *Marston   Garden*

BURITON   Five Bells

High Street, near Petersfield GU31 5RX
Tel: (0730) 63584
Open: 11-3, 5.30-11
Licensee: John Ligertwood

Nicely refurbished 16th century pub which became a free house in early 1991.
400 yards from the start of the South Downs Way walk; four large open fires are
cheering to cold-numbed ramblers. A varied food operation includes a fresh fish
board, a special healthy living menu (no added sugar, salt or fat), a spicy dish list for
curry fans, as well as pancakes, pasta, vegetarian and steaks. Prior permission needed
for children indoors. They'll have accommodation by March 1992 (no details
available).

Bar Meals and Restaurant: *12-2, 6.30 (7 restaurant)-10; bar snacks both sessions*
Typical Dishes BAR: *watercress soup £2, asparagus and brie bake £3.75, rabbit in
mustard and cider £5.95, trout in mushroom and sour cream sauce £6.95, beef in beer
£4.95, treacle tart £1.95*   **RESTAURANT:** *menu £13.75: mussels, pork tenderloin,
venison, monkfish, chocolate and brandy slice   Vegetarian Meals: vegetable goulash £4.25
Children's Portions*   `Beer`   *Ballards Best; Ind Coope Burton Ale; Hall & Woodhouse
Tanglefoot; Tetley Bitter*   `Cider`   *Addlestones   Garden   Outdoor Eating   Summer
Barbecue*   **Credit Cards:** *Access, Visa*

BURSLEDON   Jolly Sailor

Lands End Road, Old Bursledon SO3 8DN
Tel: (0703) 40555
Open: 11-2.30, 6-11 (11-11 summer Sats)
Licensee: Ronald May

Harbourside pub, a retreat for yachtsmen since Nelson and immortalised on
television as a set for Howard's Way. Lovely position, with outdoor drinking
overlooking the river and its many boats. Nautical front bar with good views, and
flagstoned back bar, both notably well-kept and managed.

*Bar Meals: 12-2, 6-9.30 (12-2.30, 7-9 Sun); bar snacks both sessions   Restaurant: 7-
9.30 (not Sun)   Typical Dishes BAR: garlic mushrooms £3.25, beef and mushroom pie
£4.95, rib eye steak £7.95, fish and chips £4.75, treacle sponge   RESTAURANT:
moules marinière £4.50, chateaubriand (for 2) £29.50, veal escalopes with apricots £11.25,
king prawns with garlic £12.95, jam roly poly   Vegetarian Meals: vegetable lasagne
Children's Menu   Beer   Everards Old Original; Gales HSB; Hall & Woodhouse Badger
Best Bitter, Tanglefoot; Wadworth 6X   Children Allowed in Bar to Eat   Riverside Garden
Outdoor Eating   Summer Barbecue   Credit Cards: Access, Amex, Visa*

CRAWLEY   Fox & Hounds

Crawley SO21 2PR   ▼
Tel: (0962) 72285
Open: 11.30-2.30, 6.30-11
Licensees: Luis and Doreen Sanz-Diez

Splendid Tudorbethan style turn of the century pub, its red brick exterior beautifully
kitted out with convincing beams and overhanging upper storeys, in a well-heeled,
pretty village. Cosy main bar with simple home-made food and good fresh fish;
main courses £7-£9 in the more ambitious restaurant. Three pristine bedrooms are
now all en suite, attractively decorated, with light wood furnishings and soothing
colours.

*Bar Meals and Restaurant: 12-2, 7-9.30; bar snacks lunchtime   Typical Dishes BAR:
leek and stilton soup £1.75, trio of fish terrine £2.95, steak and kidney pie £5.95, seafood
pancake £5.95, deep-fried stuffed mushrooms £5.95, blackcurrant bombe   Vegetarian
Meals: pancake   Children's Portions   Beer   Gales BB, Wadworth 6X   Whisky
Children Allowed in Bar to Eat   Outdoor Play Area   Garden   Outdoor Eating
Accommodation: 3 bedrooms, all en suite, from £55 (single £45)   Children Welcome
Overnight   Cot Available   Check-in: all day   Credit Cards: Access, Visa*

DAMERHAM Compasses on B3078 Tel: (07253) 231: Lively village local; the
lounge is quietest. Live jazz on Friday evenings; large garden with play area; real fire.
Varied bar menu, including vegetarian choices. Bedrooms. Ind Coope, Wadworth
beers. Open: 10.30-2.30, 6-11.

DOWNTON   Royal Oak

on A337
Tel: (0590) 642297
Open: 11-2.30, 6-11 (10.30 winter weekdays)
Licensee: Audrey Eveleigh

In the same family for 130 years, and traditionally run: no juke box, no fruit
machines, no chips, just home-cooked food from fresh ingredients. Bars are

immaculately kept, one of them no-smoking, and there's a ramp for disabled access. Three open fires in winter; cream teas in summer.

Bar Meals: lunchtime and evening; bar snacks both sessions   **Typical Dishes:** *steak and Guinness pie, smoked haddock pie, bacon and mustard pancakes, steamed treacle pudding Vegetarian Meals: macaroni and broccoli bake*   **Beer**   *Whitbread   Family Room   Garden* **No Credit Cards**

DROXFORD   Hurdles Inn

Station Road (B2150) SO3 1QU
Tel: (0489) 877451
Open: 11-3, 6-11
Licensees: Pamela and Ian Mulle

Well known food pub, cheap, cheerful, and usually packed with diners. A mix of routine bar food (the soup isn't home-made) and daily specials in the café-like bar – where tables are shared – and £5/£6 more restaurany main courses in the separate dining room (over 14s only). Book for weekend visits.

Bar Meals: 12-2.30, 7 (6.30 Sat)-10; bar snacks both sessions   **Restaurant:** *7-10 Mon-Sat*   **Typical Dishes:** *home-made paté £2.20, home-made steak and kidney pudding £3.30, home-made steak and mushroom pie £3.65, home-made lasagne £3.70, Hurdles special sundae £1.55   Vegetarian Meals: home-made nut loaf £3.30*   **Beer**   *Courage; Gales; Marston   Patio/terrace   Outdoor Eating*   **No Credit Cards**

DUNDRIDGE Hampshire Bowman, Dundridge Lane, off B3035: Secluded Downland, one bar, brick-floored pub, an ex-slaughterhouse. Real fire, no music, and good plain home cooking; also outdoor tables in large garden. Children allowed in to eat. Archers, Courage, Gales beers. Open: 11-2.30, 6-11 (maybe afternoons summer).

ELLISFIELD   Fox

Green Lane RG25 2QW   ♥
Tel: (0256) 381210
Open: 11.30-2.30, 6.30-11
Licensees: Ray Bull and Glenys Dickenson

Excellent village pub, at the end of a tangle of quiet country lanes. Enjoyably honest, unpretentious cooking; real fire; no music. No children indoors.

Bar Meals: 12-1.45, 7-9.30 (not Mon eve); bar snacks lunchtime   **Typical Dishes:** *stilton and celery soup £1.95, paté £2.75, Oriental beef £5.95, lamb and orange casserole £5.95, chilli £4.25, home-made apple pie £1.95   Vegetarian Meals: cheesy vegetable hotpot £4.25*   **Beer**   *Bunces Bitter; Gales HSB; Marston Pedigree Bitter; Theakston Best, Old Peculier   Garden   Outdoor Eating*   **Credit Cards:** *Access, Visa*

EMERY DOWN   New Forest Inn

Emery Down SO43 7DY   ♥
Tel: (0703) 282329
Open: 11-2.30 (12-2 Sun), 6-11 (10.30 winter)
Licensees: Mr and Mrs N Emberley

Prettily set in woodland, the building of the inn was the result of the first successful establishment of squatters' rights on Crown land, in the early 18th century. Much extended since, it has a big, busy open-plan bar and fairly modern seating and style, with effective country touches and real fires. Food takes a country theme too, with lots of game, as well as "dishes stolen from all over the world". A pub known for its genuine welcome.

Bar Meals: 11-2, 6-9.30 (12-1.30, 7-9 Sun); *bar snacks both sessions* **Typical Dishes:** *clam chowder £2.25, loaded potato skins £3.75, supreme of chicken in stilton sauce £7.25, pork in green peppercorn sauce £7.25, country casseroles, steaks to £9.25, apple and cider pudding £2.25 Vegetarian Meals: nut roasts with korma sauce Children's Portions* Beer *Marston Pedigree; Wadworth 6X; Whitbread Flowers Original, Strong Country Bitter Family Room Garden Outdoor Eating* **Accommodation:** *4 bedrooms, all en suite, from £50 (single £25) Children Welcome Overnight Check-in: by arrangement* **Credit Cards:** *Access, Visa*

FACCOMBE   Jack Russell Inn

near Andover SP11 0DS   ☼
Tel: (026 487) 315
Open: 12-2.30, 7-11
Licensees: Paul Foster and David Harbottle

Faccombe is a tiny, out-of-the-way village owned by the 'big house' it surrounds, and almost entirely occupied by estate workers. The story goes that when the new estate owner decided to renovate the old village pub, it just fell down, so he had to rebuild it. In any event, the present simple red brick building dates from 1983, but is quickly being mellowed by a spreading Virginia creeper and hanging baskets of flowers. The modest bar boasts a few rural artefacts and has already developed the yellow patina of eight years of cigarette smoke on walls and ceiling. The best place to eat is in the large conservatory, which looks out onto the garden, where a rustic climbing frame is provided for children, who are tolerated rather than encouraged; in winter the few children's meals disappear from the menu altogether. A blackboard lists the mostly home-made dishes which offer a good varied choice, from home-cooked ham and eggs to curry. The individual steak and kidney pudding with accompanying freshly steamed vegetables can't fail to satisfy the largest appetite; if it should, and apple pie can be managed for afters, ask them to serve it cold as microwave re-heating ruins an otherwise good pastry. The food trade is highly organised: when ordering food at the bar, you are given a little plastic table number so that the waitress can find you easily, and booking is advisable, particularly at weekends and for the traditional Sunday lunch. Three simple bedrooms, just one with en suite bathroom, offer good clean accommodation with functional melamine furniture, poly-cotton bedding and the usual tea and coffee making kit. There are televisions, but no telephones.

Bar Meals: 12-2, 7-9.30; *bar snacks both sessions* **Typical Dishes:** *potato and watercress soup £1.25, home-made pork and liver paté £1.80, home-made steak and kidney pudding £4.50, fresh salmon in lemon and parsley sauce £5.75, home-made trawlerman's pie £4.75, spotted dick £1.25 Vegetarian Meals: spaghetti Children's Menu/Portions* Beer *Palmers IPA Children Allowed in Bar to Eat (over 5) Garden* **Accommodation:** *3 rooms, 1 en suite, from £40 (single £25) Check-in: by arrangement* **Credit Cards:** *Access, Visa*

HAMMER VALE Prince of Wales: Take Bulmer Hill road off A3, then right at the junction, for an atmospheric country pub at the meeting point of three counties. Real fire, garden, live music Sunday evening; decent bar food lunchtime and Monday-Saturday evening. Gales beers. Open: 11.30-2.30, 6-11.

HORTON HEATH   Lapstone

Botley Road (B3354)
Tel: (0703) 692377
Open: 11-3, 6-11
Licensee: P O'Brien

A relaxing pub with fresh flowers and a charity bookstall, as well as locally popular home-cooked food, prepared by a landlady with a passion for good curries. Also a good vegetarian selection, and more traditionally English food like beef in stout casserole.

Bar Meals: lunchtime and evening; bar snacks both sessions Typical Dishes steak and mushroom pie, chilli, beef dupiaza, six cheese pie (main courses from £3.50) Vegetarian Meals   Children's Menu   `Beer`   *Marston; Whitbread   Children Allowed in to Eat Outdoor Play Area   Garden*   **No Credit Cards**

HURSTBOURNE TARRANT George & Dragon, The Square (A343): Classic coaching inn, originally Elizabethan, with Georgian extensions. Home cooking lunchtime and Monday-Saturday evenings; real fire; garden. Courage, Wadworth beers. Open 10-2.30, 5-11.

LANGSTONE Ship on A3023: Large seaside pub in attractive setting; food lunchtime and evening; real fire. Gales beers.

LINWOOD   High Corner Inn

Ringwood BH24 3QY
Tel: (0425) 473973
Open: 11-3 (2.30 Sun), 6-11 (all day Sat)
Licensees: Roger G Kernan and Amanda Robertson

Early 18th century inn set in seven acres of the New Forest: bar food, carvery, restaurant, stable room, barbecue area, public squash court, Lego room and bedrooms. All happily back in working order after the devastating 1989 fire. A quiet hideaway in winter, mobbed in high summer.

Bar Meals: 12-2, 7 (6.30 summer Sat)-10; bar snacks both sessions   **Restaurant:** *7-10*
***Typical Dishes BAR:** home-made soup £1.45, whitebait £2.85, steak, kidney and mushroom pie £5.35, High Corner grill £9.25, smoked fish crumble £4.45, crème caramel £1.60*   **RESTAURANT:** *soup £1.65, stilton fritters £3.35, noisettes of venison £8.25, roast rack of lamb £6.95, breast of Barbary duck £7,95, banana beignets £2.65 Vegetarian Meals: crisp mushroom fritters £3.35   Children's Menu/Portions*   `Cheese` `Beer`   *Wadworth 6X; Whitbread Flowers Original, Winter Royal   Family Room (three rooms)   Outdoor Play Area   Garden   Outdoor Eating   Summer Barbecue*
***Accommodation:** 8 bedrooms, all en suite, from £66 (single £45.50)   Children Welcome Overnight   Cots Available   Check-in: all day*   **Credit Cards:** *Access, Amex, Diners, Visa*

LOWER FROYLE   Prince of Wales

off A31
Tel: (0420) 23102
Open: 11-2.30, 6-11

Extremely popular, usually bustling Edwardian village pub, with reliably good home-cooked food which makes extensive use of local organic produce. The daily blackboard menu is strong on traditional dishes like corned beef hash and bubble and squeak, or a real chicken Kiev, but the main dining emphasis is on the £12.50

three course suppers, which are more restaurant in style. Book for the huge set Sunday lunch.

Bar Meals: daily lunchtime and evening; bar snacks lunchtime Vegetarian Meals Children's Portions **Beer** *Courage, Theakston Children Allowed in Bar to Eat Garden*

LOWER WIELD   Yew Tree Inn

Alresford SO24 9RX
Tel: (0256) 389224
Open: 12-3, 6-11
Licensees: Michael and Ann Ferguson

Cosy whitewashed pub off the B3046 at Preston Candover, in a remote rural spot opposite the cricket ground; Sunday matches are taken very seriously. A short but interesting menu features both the simple and homely and the extravagantly restauranty.

Bar Meals: 12-2.15 (1.45 Sun), 7-9.45; not Sun eve, nor all day Mon; bar snacks every lunchtime and Tue-Thur eves **Typical Dishes:** *French onion soup £2.30, avocado, tomato and crispy bacon salad £3.35, steak and kidney pie £5.35, tournedos of beef with mustard and herb crust £13.25, gateau of salmon, turbot and mushrooms £11.95, steamed dark orange pudding £2.95 Children's Portions* **Cheese** **Beer** *Bunces Best; Exmoor Ale; Marston Pedigree Children Allowed in Bar to Eat Outdoor Play Area Garden Outdoor Eating* **Credit Cards:** *Access, Visa*

MARCHWOOD Pilgrim Inn, Hythe Road (off A326): Delightful thatched old pub with lovely garden and a host of hanging baskets. Home cooking at lunchtime; vegetarians and children also catered for. Real fire; no music. Bass beers. Open: 11-2.30, 6-11.

NEWTOWN   Travellers Rest

Church Road (off B2177)
Tel: (0329) 833263
Open: 11-3, 6-11
Licensee: Peter Redman

The fairly routine bar menu is enlivened by an often exciting hot daily special, usually gamey in winter, fishy in summer; get there on the right day and a real bargain pheasant or lobster lunch might be on offer. The pub itself is a mid 18th century cottage with two simply furnished old bars and a pretty garden. Occasional live folk music.

Bar Meals: 12-2, 7.30-10.30; bar snacks both sessions **Typical Dishes:** *bacon pudding, ham and eggs, roast quail, fried plaice, fresh crab (main courses from around £3), home-made fruit flans Vegetarian Meals* **Beer** *Gibbs Mew Garden*

OVINGTON   Bush Inn

off A31 SO24 0RE
Tel: (0962) 732764
Open: 11-2.30, 6-11
Licensee: Robert Middleton

A new licensee since our last edition has perfectly maintained the wonderfully unspoilt atmosphere of the Bush, and also introduced some more interesting food, home-made soups, steak and kidney pie and mussels among them (main courses from £5). Lost down a winding, wooded lane in the Itchen valley, this rose-covered cottage has rustically furnished, softly lit bars, often crammed with people. Nice riverside walks. Children are allowed in the dining room.

Bar Meals: lunchtime and evening; bar snacks both sessions   Children's Menu   Beer
Gales; Wadworth; Whitbread   Patio/terrace   Outdoor Eating

PENNINGTON Chequers, Ridgeway Lane: Stylishly spartan yachting pub with old alehouse atmosphere; bar food fresh and unusual; children allowed in dining area; garden. Gales, Wadworth, Whitbread beers.

PETERSFIELD   Good Intent

40/45 College Street GU31 4AF
Tel: (0730) 63838
Open: 11.30 (11 Sat)-2.30 (12-2.30 Sun), 6-11; closed Mon
Licensees: J A and L Marechal

16th century free house with a beamy single bar and a Swiss licensee chef. Vegetarians need to give warning of their needs.

*Bar Meals: 12-2, 6.30-9; bar snacks both sessions   **Restaurant:** 7-9   **Typical Dishes**
BAR: home-made soup £1.95, whitebait £2.95, veal cordon bleu £7.50, home-cooked beef ploughmans £4.50, meringues £1.50   **RESTAURANT:** similar starters, peppered steak £9.50, escalope of veal £8.50, halibut mornay £8.50, lemon royale £1.75
Children's Portions*   Beer   *Ballards Bitter; Draught Bass; Fullers London Pride; Hall & Woodhouse Tanglefoot   Children Allowed in Bar to Eat   Patio/terrace   Outdoor Eating
Credit Cards: Access, Visa*

PRIORS DEAN   White Horse

near Petersfield GU32 1DA   ♈
Tel: (0420) 58387
Open: 11-2.30 (3 Sat), 6-11
Licensees: Jack Eddleston and Andrew Lathom

Also called the Pub with No Name; there is no sign. Fiendish to get to: leave Petersfield on the A272 Winchester-bound, turn right towards Steep, then after about four miles, take the East Tisted road at the crossroads, then immediate right down the second gravel track. It's worth the effort, for this is a quite wonderful, genuinely unspoilt by modernity, 17th century farmhouse pub of utterly simple (uncomfortable, some would say) charm. First world war poet Edward Thomas wrote his first published work, Up in the Wind, about the pub; it's 750 feet up on top of the Downs, with peaceful views on every side. There are 26 country wines. No children indoors.

*Bar Meals: 11.30-2, 8-9.30; bar snacks lunchtime   **Typical Dishes:** thick country soup (winter) £2, beef and venison pie £5.25, Norfolk pie £5, fishermans pie £4.50
Vegetarian Meals: spinach and mushroom lasagne £4.50*   Beer   *Ballards Best Bitter; Eldridge Pope Royal Oak; Ringwood Fortyniner   Outdoor Play Area   Garden   Outdoor Eating   **No Credit Cards***

ROTHERWICK   Coach & Horses

The Street RG27 89BG
Tel: (025 676) 2542
Open: 11-2.30, 5-11
Licensee: Terry Williams (Mrs)

Winter fires, beamed ceilings and a motley collection of furniture in two little rooms leading off the separate hatch servery in this creeper-covered part 16th century village dining pub, very popular with locals for lunch. Reliably good food ranges from the simple and snackish to steaks and fish; carvery on Sundays. A huge range of real ales.

Bar Meals: 12-2, 7-10 (9.45 Sun); bar snacks both sessions **Typical Dishes:** *paté £2, pizzas £3, ham and eggs £4.50, steaks from £6.50* `Cheese` `Beer` *Ansells; Bunces; Eldridge Pope; Palmers   Children Allowed in Bar to Eat   Patio/terrace* **No Credit Cards**

SOBERTON   White Lion

Off A32 past Wickham, taking the second Soberton turning SO3 1PF
Tel: (0489) 877346   ▼
Open: 11-2.30 (3 weekends), 6-11
Licensees: Rod and Joanie Johnson

Extremely lively 17th century country pub, with two slightly worn looking bars and lots of theme events; as they cheerfully admit, "we'll celebrate anything, even Mexican Independence Day". Barbecues and pig roasts a speciality.

Bar Meals and Restaurant: 11.30-2.30 (12-2.15 restaurant), 6-10.30; bar snacks both sessions **Typical Dishes BAR:** *stilton and courgette soup £1.50, mushrooms provencale £2.75, home-made beef curry £4.25, spaghetti marinara £4.25, monkfish provencale £7.50, bread and butter pudding £1.75* **RESTAURANT:** *stilton-stuffed mushrooms £4.25, kidneys in sherry £6.95, avocado and tomato bake £5.50   Vegetarian Meals: pasta   Children's Menu/Portions* `Beer` *Marston Pedigree; Wadworth 6X; Whitbread Flowers Original   Family Room   Outdoor Play Area   Garden   Outdoor Eating   Summer Barbecue* **Credit Cards:** *Access, Visa*

SOUTHSEA Wine Vaults, Albert Road (opposite theatre), Tel: (0705) 864712: Stylishly basic real ale pub, a genuine free house, with a large, busy wood-panelled main bar and quieter snug. The new attic restaurant specialises in wholefood cooking. Huge range of beers. Open: 11.30-3, 5.30-11 (all day Fri/Sat).

SPARSHOLT   Plough

Main Road SO21 2NW
Tel: (096 272) 353
Open: 11-3, 6.30 (6 Fri/Sat)-11
Licensee: Michael Miles

Originally a Whitbread pub, now in the Wadworth stable, and completely refurbished since new licensees arrived in January 1991. £17,000 has been spent on the kitchen alone. Blackboard listed food only, no printed menus, in an old ex-farmhouse in pretty countryside, popular with walkers. Fresh vegetables from their own garden, and two acres of lawn.

Bar Meals: 12 (12.30 Sun)-2, 6.30-8.30 Wed-Sat eve; no food Mon; bar snacks lunchtime **Typical Dishes:** *farmhouse hotch potch £1.50, garlic mushrooms £2.75, chicken and pepper curry £4.25, pork chops in cider £5.50, jam roly poly £1.50*

Vegetarian Meals: vegetarian stroganoff   Children's Menu/Portions `Cheese`   `Beer`
Hall & Woodhouse Tanglefoot; Wadworth beers   Family Room   Garden   Outdoor Eating
No Credit Cards

STEEP   Harrow Inn

Steep GU32 2DA
Tel: (0730) 62685
Open: 11-2.30 (3 Fri/Sat), 6-11
Licensee: Edward McCutcheon

Somewhere between 400 and 500 years old, the Harrow is a modest little pub
tucked down a sleepy country lane that dwindles into a footpath by a little stream.
The tenancy has been in the same family since 1929 and in recent years the landlord
has been engaged in constant battles with the brewery, who wanted to modernise.
Edward McCutcheon finally won the war this year, when he managed to buy the
inn; he can now keep it very much as it must have been in the last century (earlier,
even). Two small rooms have boarded walls, an old brick inglenook fireplace,
scrubbed wooden tables and a hatch-like bar, behind which barrels of beer sit on
racks, with bundles of drying flowers hanging above. There's a small cottagey garden
to one side, and some old sloping rustic benches and tables out at the front. Toilets
are in a separate brick building on the other side of the lane. The food is limited to a
few wholesome snacks: a split pea based soup full of fresh vegetables (spoilt only by
the dried parsley sprinkled on top) served with great chunks of bread; a few salads
and sandwiches of beef, cheese or home-cooked ham (Ellen cooks about 20
gammons a week); Scotch eggs, most of the eggs coming from their own hens, and
perhaps a meat loaf or marrow filled with mince and topped with cheese. Apart
from the beers, there's a good selection of fruit wines.

Bar Meals: 12-2, 6.30-9.30 or 10   Typical Dishes: home-made split pea and ham soup
£2, shepherd's pie £4.50, lasagne £4.50, marrow stuffed with ham and topped with cheese
£4.50   Vegetarian Meals: cauliflower cheese £4.50 `Beer` *Whitbread   Garden*
Outdoor Eating **No Credit Cards**

STEEP   Cricketers

1 Church Walk (off A325) GU32 2DW
Tel: (0730) 61035
Open: 11.45-2.30, 5.45-11
Licensee: W T Turnbull

Pleasant pub at the foot of 'Little Switzerland', popular with ramblers. Twenty old
English fruit wines. A minimum age of 14 for overnight stays.

Bar Meals: 12-2, 6.45-9.15; bar snacks both sessions   Typical Dishes: tomato soup
£1.85, melon with Parma ham £2.45, lamb and apricot pie £3.95, home-made lasagne
£3.95, lemon sole mornay £4.25, apple pie £2   Vegetarian Meals: spaghetti bake
`Beer` *Gales beers* `Whisky` *Children Allowed in Bar to Eat   Outdoor Play Area*
Garden   Outdoor Eating   Accommodation: 3 bedrooms, 2 with shower, from £32 (single
£26)   Check-in: by arrangement   Credit Cards: Access, Amex, Visa

---

STUCKTON   Three Lions

Fordingbridge SP6 2HF   ▼
Tel: (0425) 652489
Open: Tue-Sat
Licensees: Karl and June Wadsack

The previously star-rated Three Lions is much more of a "serious restaurant with bar" than a pub these days, although it's still nominally of free house status, and they do get lunchtime customers who pop in for a drink and a snack (of a superior sort – no sandwiches, ploughmans or chips). These high–class light meals we list as 'bar meals' here; full meals, both lunch and evening, appear under restaurant typical dishes. Over 14s only.

Bar Meals: 12.15-1.30   Restaurant: 12.15-1.30, 7.15-9   Typical Dishes BAR: fresh asparagus soup £2.80, duck liver paté £4.20, smoked chicken, bacon and quails egg salad £5.10, Swedish soused herrings with Jersey Royal potatoes £5.25, baked Devon scallops, each £2.75, home-made ice-cream £3.75   RESTAURANT: clear seafood soup £4.20, hot seafood au gratin £5.30, half English farm duck with apricot and hazelnut stuffing £11.70, Wiener schnitzel £12.50, sea bass with lemon and saffron sauce £12.70, hot French lemon tart £3.75   Vegetarian Meals: fresh spinach and Edam strudels £3.60 `Cheese` `Beer` *Ind Coope Burton Ale; Wadworth 6X* `Whisky` *Credit Cards: Access, Visa*

TANGLEY   Fox Inn

Tangley SP11 0RU
Tel: (026 470) 276
Licensees: John and Gwen Troke

Remote, smartish country pub off the A343 with a welcoming atmosphere in its tiny bars. Reliably good food from the landlady cook.

Bar Meals and Restaurant: 12-2 including Sun, 6-10 (not Sun eve); bar snacks both sessions   Typical Dishes BAR: onion and stilton soup £1.15, home-made chicken liver paté £2, chicken and mushroom pie £4.15, lamb and apricot curry £3.60, mushroom and prawn pot £3.60, sticky toffee pudding   RESTAURANT: similar starters and puddings, roast venison in citrus wine sauce £8.50, breast of chicken with prawns and sherry £6.75, Royal Oak beef £7.25   Vegetarian Meals: chilli vegetable bean pot £2.60   Children's Portions `Beer` *Draught Bass; Courage Best; Eldridge Pope Royal Oak   Children Allowed in Bar to Eat   Patio/terrace   Outdoor Eating   Accommodation: 2 bedrooms, en suite facilities, from £40 (single £32)   Check-in: all day   No Credit Cards*

TESTCOMBE   Mayfly

Stockbridge SO20 6AZ
Tel: (0264) 860283
Open: 11-11 (2.30 closing Sun lunch)
Licensee: Barry Lane

Quaintly traditional bar and bright conservatory, and a riverside beer garden for sunnier weather. Simple home-cooked bar food and a delicious variety of mainly French cheeses.

Bar Meals: 12-2, 7-9   Typical Dishes: home-made soup £1.50, smoked chicken £4.50, tandoori chicken £3.60, steak and vegetable pie £3.95, home-made puddings £2   Vegetarian Meals: quiche `Cheese` `Beer` *Whitbread   Family Room   Garden   Outdoor Eating   Credit Cards: Access, Visa*

TICHBORNE   Tichborne Arms

Tichborne SO24 0NA
Tel: (0962) 733760
Licensees: Peter and Chris Byron

Despite its quiet location, in an Itchen Valley hamlet, this is a pub much driven out to for lunch and supper. Red brick and thatched, it has an unspoilt panelled room on the right, and a larger, noisier room on the left with fruit machine et al. Reliably good cooking, with especially tempting puddings. No children indoors.

Bar Meals: 12-1.45, 6.30-9.45 (12-1.30, 7-9.30 Sun); bar snacks both sessions
Typical Dishes: *basil and tomato soup £1.50, liver and bacon nibbles £2, beef cobbler £4.65, bolognaise pancakes £4.15, local pink trout £5.95, fudge and walnut flan Vegetarian Meals: stilton and broccoli quiche* **Beer** *Courage Best, Directors; Wadworth 6X* **No Credit Cards**

UPTON GREY   Hoddington Arms

near Basingstoke RG25 2RL
Tel: (0256) 862371
Open: 11-2.30 (12-2.30 Sun), 6-11; 11.30-2.30, 7-11 Sat
Licensee: Ian W Fisher

Fairly smart local in well-heeled village, warm and welcoming. Cooking by the licensees. Nice garden.

Bar Meals: 12-2, 7.30-9.30; bar snacks both sessions   **Restaurant:** *7.30-9.30*   ***Typical Dishes BAR:*** *home-made soup £1.65, garlic-stuffed mushrooms £2.15, braised lambs kidneys £3.65, pork fillet en croute £4.25, sea bream fillet with herb sauce £4, sherry trifle £2*   **RESTAURANT:** *moules marinière £3.50, roast guinea fowl with cucumber and sorrel sauce £7.95, roast rack of lamb £7.50, whole Dover sole £11, gooseberry fool £2 Vegetarian Meals: stuffed peppers   Children's Menu/Portions* **Cheese**   **Beer** *Morland beers   Family Room   Outdoor Play Area   Garden   Outdoor Eating* **Credit Cards:** *Access, Visa*

VERNHAM DEAN   Boot Inn

Littledown, near Andover SP11 0EF
Tel: (0264) 87213
Open: 12-2.30, 7-11 (12-3, 6-11 summer); closed Mon
Licensee: Neale Baker

There's a routine basket meals-style printed menu and much more interesting specials board at this charming old thatched pub, 15th century with a 16th century extension. Originally a cobbler's, who doubled as an ale maker, the tiny white-panelled bar is still fetchingly homely; there's also a conservatory and family room, but it's nicest out of doors on sunny days in the two acres of grounds.

Bar Meals: 12-2, 7-9.30 Mon-Sat; bar snacks both sessions   ***Typical Dishes:*** *oxtail soup £1.95, crab paté £2, rump steak £7, wings of fire £3.75, grilled trout £5.25, treacle tart £1.75   Vegetarian Meals: vegetable pie £4.50   Children's Menu* **Beer** *Hall & Woodhouse Badger Best; Hook Norton Old Hooky; Marston Burton Best Bitter; Wadworth 6X* **Whisky** *Family Room   Outdoor Play Area   Garden   Outdoor Eating   Summer Barbecue* **Credit Cards:** *Access, Visa*

WELL   Chequers

near Odiham RG25 1TL
Tel: (0256) 862605
Open: 11-3, 5.30-11
Licensees: C Phillips and H Stanford

Low-ceilinged, panelled, beamed, old-fashioned pub, half-transformed into a bistro
(it used to be French-run). The menu changes daily and all food is prepared on the
premises by an Anglo-Australian team, which allows for a great variety of influences.
The vine-covered patio is lovely in summer.

Bar Meals: 12-2.30, 7-10 (9.30 Sun); bar snacks both sessions   *Restaurant:* 7.30 (one
sitting)   *Typical Dishes:* home-made soup £1.95, roasted aubergine dip with crudites,
scrambled egg with smoked salmon, Thai style chicken or seafood (main courses from £3.50),
banoffee pie   Vegetarian Meals: warm brie salad with almonds   Children's Portions
Cheese   Beer   Wadworth 6X, Whitbread Boddingtons Bitter, Flowers Original
Family Room (lunchtime)   Outdoor Play Area   Garden   Outdoor Eating   Summer
Barbecue   *Credit Cards:* Access, Visa

WEST MEON Thomas Lord, High Street: Pleasant village pub, cricket-mad,
with decent home cooking lunchtime and evening. Whitbread beers.

WINCHESTER   ★   Wykeham Arms

75 Kingsgate Street SO23 9PE   FOOD
Tel: (0962) 853834
Open: 11-11
Licensee: Graeme Jameson   B&B

Tucked away in the narrow back streets of Winchester, hard by the cathedral close,
Graeme and Anne Jameson have turned the mellow, red brick, 250 year old 'Wyk'
into one of the finest hostelries in the land. The main bar, which is mostly for
drinkers, has old fashioned school room desks with integral seats, some authentically
carved with the initials of inattentive pupils from years gone by. Collections of hats,
mugs and fascinating old prints and cartoons adorn the bar and no less than six other
interconnecting rooms, all set up for eating. The old pine, candle-lit dining tables
each have a brass money slot to collect donations for the upkeep of the cathedral; at
present the pub is trying to raise £60,000 to endow the "Wykeham Lay Clerkship"
which will support at least one Lay Clerk (paid chorister) in perpetuity. Much
patronised by the Dons from Winchester College, and barristers attending the local
courts (amongst many others), this is probably the best place to eat in town, and
booking is essential. A blackboard menu changes daily, offering unusual, but
invariably successful, combinations of flavours like ginger mousse with chicken
breast, thyme and horseradish sauce with rack of lamb, or their renowned stilton and
quince paté; an excellent bearnaise sauce would alone put many more pretentious
restaurants to shame. Twenty names on the well-chosen wine list are also available
by the glass, and for summer eating and drinking there is a neat walled garden.
Individually decorated bedrooms have stylish matching bedcovers and curtains and
mostly honeyed pine furniture. All have mini-bars, television and telephones, plus
homely extras like fresh flowers, books, magazines and pot pourri. Modern en suite
bathrooms, all with showers over tubs, boast quality Woods of Windsor toiletries.
First rate cooked breakfasts, with freshly squeezed orange juice, are served in a
charming period breakfast room on the first floor.

Bar Meals and Restaurant: 12-2.30, 6.30-8.45; bar snacks lunchtime (no food Mon eve,
nor all day Sun)   *Typical Dishes BAR:* home-made soup £1.95, stilton and quince paté
£2.95, cottage pie £4.25, chicken and sweet pepper casserole £5.25, fresh pasta carbonara

£4.50, cinnamon and apple crumble £2.95   **RESTAURANT:** *home-made soup £2.25, hot potted smoked trout £3.25, breast of chicken in filo pastry £8.75, beef and venison casserole £7.25, fillet of Scottish smoked salmon £9.25   Vegetarian Meals: wholemeal cheese and chive tart* `Cheese` █ `Beer` █ *Eldridge Pope   Garden   Outdoor Eating* **Accommodation:** *7 bedrooms, all en suite, from £69.50 (single £59.50)   Check-in: all day*   **No Credit Cards**

WINCHESTER   Old Vine

8 Great Minster Street SO23 9HA   ❢
Tel: (0962) 854616
Open: 11-11
Licensee: James Rawling

Attractive cottage pub opposite the main cathedral gates, with newish licensees who have brought a dining emphasis, besides a total refurbishment. The menus are a mix of old standards and inviting home-made specials; the landlady's proper home-made chicken Kiev has been winning fans. The menu's much simpler and shorter at lunchtimes.

Bar Meals: *12-2.15, 7-9.15; bar snacks both sessions*   **Typical Dishes:** *hot and spicy chicken wings £2.50, deep-fried camembert £2.75, Barnsley chop £6.50, home-made chicken Kiev £5.25, steak and kidney pie £3.95   Vegetarian Meals: nut cutlets £3.45 (lunch)   Children's Menu/Portions* █ `Beer` █ *Courage Best, Directors; John Smith's Bitter Family Room   Children Allowed in Bar to Eat   Patio/terrace* **Credit Cards:** *Access, Visa*

WOLVERTON COMMON   Hare & Hounds

near Basingstoke RG26 5RW
Tel: (0635) 298361
Licensees: Donald and Bernice Wilson

Busy 17th century pub just off the A339, personably run with a homely style. Simple but good home cooking of the shepherds pie sort is supplemented by imaginative offerings like aubergine and ricotta bake with herbs and yoghurt, lamb cutlets with parmesan; a restaurant offers full à la carte.

Bar Meals: *11.30-2, 6-10 (12-2, 7-10 Sun); bar snacks lunchtime   Vegetarian Meals* `Cheese` █ `Beer` █ *Wadworth; Whitbread   Family Room* **Credit Cards:** *Access, Amex, Diners, Visa*

HEREFORD & WORCESTER

BELBROUGHTON   Queens Hotel

near Stourbridge DY9 0DU
Tel: (0562) 730276
Open: 11.30-2.30, 5.30-11 (11.30-3, 6-11 Sat)
Licensee: Marmaduke Ferguson

Popular pub in pretty village. Stream and old millstones by car park.

Bar Meals: *lunch daily; suppers Mon-Fri; bar snacks both sessions*   **Typical Dishes:** *home-made soup £1.10, garlic mushrooms £2.15, cheese, ham and onion pie £3.85, chilli £3.85, salmon with parsley sauce £5.85, Bakewell tart £1.85   Vegetarian Meals: quiche* █ `Beer` █ *Marston Burton Best Bitter, Pedigree   Family Room   Patio/terrace* **No Credit Cards**

BEWDLEY   Black Boy

Kidderminster Road DY12 1AG
Tel: (0299) 402199
Open: 11-3, 6-11
Licensee: Alastair Wilson

Solidly built 17th century inn with two pleasantly traditional beamed bars, one devoted to displays of regimental insignia of the British army. Lunchtime bar meals from a small menu with daily changing additions, carefully and enjoyably prepared. Best bedrooms are in the Georgian annexe, bright, homely and comfortable; residents have the use of three lounge areas, including a delightfully chintzy Georgian one.

Bar Meals: 11.30-2; bar snacks both sessions   ***Typical Dishes:*** *carrot and coriander soup, baked ham with parsley sauce, Bakewell tart   Family Room*   ***Accommodation:*** *20 bedrooms, from £43 (single £29)   Check-in all day*   ***Credit Cards:*** *Access, Amex, Visa*

BEWDLEY   Little Packhorse

31 High Street DY12 2DH
Tel: (0299) 403762
Open: 11-3, 6-11
Licensee: Peter D'Amery

Atmospheric old-fashioned pub, early 17th century, and one of the popular "Little Pub Co." chain, of Desperate Dan Pie fame. Lots of bric-a-brac. Cheap, cheerful and friendly. The back room has recently been refurbished.

Bar Meals: 12-2, 6-10; bar snacks lunchtime   ***Typical Dishes:*** *home-made soup £1.60, half pint of prawns £3.25, Desperate Dan pie £4.65, meat lasagne £3.55, Severn shark steak £5.45, spotted dick £1.60   Vegetarian Meals: lasagne   Children's Portions*
Beer   *Ind Coope Burton Ale; Lumphammer (brewed here)   Family Room*   ***Credit Cards:*** *Access, Visa*

BRETFORTON   Fleece Inn

The Cross WR11 5JE
Tel: (0386) 831173
Open: 11-2.30 (12-2.30 Sun), 6-11
Licensee: Norman J Griffiths

National Trust-owned timewarp of a pub with 19th century and older atmosphere and a museum-like array of beautiful things, many of them extremely valuable and rare – note especially the priceless collection of Stuart pewter. Still, they say, run on the lines the pre-1977 owner, the redoubtable Miss Taplin, insisted upon: no crisps or nuts allowed, though they do offer a chips with everything type menu.

Bar Meals: 12-2, 7-9 (not Mon eve); bar snacks both sessions   ***Typical Dishes:*** *steak and kidney pie £3.80, Gloucester sausage £2.90, plaice £3.45   Vegetarian Meals: ratatouille lasagne £3.50   Children's Portions*   **Beer**   *Burton Bridge Bitter; Hook Norton Best Bitter; Jolly Roger Shipwrecked; Uley Pigs Ear*   **Cider**   *Weston's   Family Room Outdoor Play Area   Garden   Outdoor Eating   Summer Barbecue*   ***No Credit Cards***

BRIMFIELD ★ Roebuck

Brimfield SY8 4NE
Tel: (058 472) 230
Open: 12-2.30 (inc Sun), 7-11 closed Mon
Licensee: John Evans

FOOD
B&B

There's no more individual a pub in these parts than the Roebuck, and no finer pub restaurant than this one, Poppies. With his background in the brewing trade, landlord John Evans didn't need convincing that, catering plans notwithstanding, Brimfield's only pub should still be accessible to the locals. For her part, Carole, the daughter of a Welsh farmer, was undeterred in her desire to cook, and as her command of the kitchen grew, so did the style and atmosphere that were to become Poppies. Diners entering the lounge bar, a characterful room with a 15th century beamed ceiling and dark oak panels, sometimes think they are already in the restaurant, and it's delightful to instead be ushered into a bright and cheery room with parquet floor and cane-back chairs, a fine start to what turns out to be a splendid meal. Yet the Roebuck isn't simply about fine dining, as Carole's food can also be enjoyed in the lounge at a fraction of the restaurant price. Her command of composition and subtle blends of colour and flavour are frankly bewildering for one who is, it also turns out, self-taught: the savoury bread and butter pudding with pine kernels and tomato custard is unique. Marinaded fillets of red mullet, ratatouille terrine with basil sauce, chicken breasts with tarragon butter filling and cream sauce; all these have featured recently in the bar menu at £7.50 or less. Meanwhile, in the restaurant, diners were enjoying spinach soufflé with anchovy hollandaise, and Herefordshire beef fillet with roast garlic and pickled walnuts for around £22. Either way, there's a comprehensive list of hot and cold desserts to follow, and some sixteen cheeses from local St Anne's goat's cheese to faraway Cashel Blue, listed on a separate cheese menu. And then, if you're wise enough to choose to stay, there are three lovely cottage bedrooms (two doubles with showers and a twin with full bathroom) to choose from. A wonderful country breakfast, including Herefordshire apple juice, local honey, and Carole's home-made sausages, will set you up for the day and set the seal on a memorable stay.

Bar Meals and Restaurant: 12-2, 7-9.30 Tue-Sat   Typical Dishes BAR: home-made soup with Roebuck rolls £2.70, crab pot £4.50, chicken in Dunkertons cider pie £5.70, savoury baked beefsteak tomato with home-made pasta £5.70, lemon sole with lime and capers £8.50, bread and butter pudding with apricot sauce and Guernsey cream £4.50 RESTAURANT: soup of the day £3.90, baked queen scallops with mushroom and garlic £6, Herefordshire beef with pickled walnuts, roast garlic and red wine sauce £15.50, pan-fried calves liver, Dubonnet and orange sauce £15, grilled Cornish lobster £22, fresh lemon tart £4.70   Vegetarian Meals: spinach and pine kernel pie £5.20   Cheese   Whisky Dalwhinnie 15 yr, Glenkinchie 10 yr   Cider   Children Allowed in Bar to Eat Patio/terrace   Outdoor Eating   Accommodation (closed a week in Oct, fortnight in Feb): 3 bedrooms, all en suite, from £60 (single £35)   Children Welcome   Overnight (minimum age 8)   Check-in: all day   Credit Cards: Access, Visa

BROADWAY Crown & Trumpet

Church Street WR12 7E
Tel: (0386) 853202
Open: 11-3, 5.30-11 (11-2.30, 6-11 winter)
Licensee: Andrew Scott

Picturesque village inn just off the green. Food is all home-made and seasonal in approach.

Bar Meals: 12-2.30, 6-9.30 (12-2, 6.30-9 winter); bar snacks both sessions   **Typical Dishes:** home-made soup £1.65, Worcestershire pie £3.95, country chicken in cider pie £4.25, cheese and asparagus flan £3.95, various local fruit puddings £1.85   Vegetarian Meals: home-made vegetable gratin £3.95   Children's Portions   Beer   Whitbread Children Allowed in Bar to Eat   Patio/terrace   **Accommodation:** 3 bedrooms, sharing a bathroom, from £35 (single £17.50)   Children Welcome Overnight   Cot Available Check-in: by arrangement   **No Credit Cards**

BROMYARD Crown & Sceptre, 7 Sherford Street Tel: (0885) 48244: Plain, popular market town pub: large inglenook, old maps and adverts, real home cooking, good and varied pies. Meals lunchtime and evening (not Sun/Wed evenings). Banks's, Hook Norton, Whitbread, Wood's beer. Open: 11-2.30 (3.30 Sat), 6.30-11.

BROUGHTON HACKETT March Hare on A422: Basically furnished, methodically-run, popular pub with some interesting bar food (lunchtime and evening) and steakhouse restaurant. Garden with play equipment. Hook Norton, Ruddles, Whitbread beers.

CAREY   Cottage of Content

Good signs from Hoarwithy; by the Wye bridge
Tel: (043 270) 242
Open: 12-2.30 (not winter Mon/Tue), 7 (6 summer)-11
Licensee: Mike Wainford

Aptly named, idyllic little 15th century cottage pub, off the beaten track enough to be a haven of peace at lunchtimes despite its fame. A warren of tiny oak-beamed rooms, with open fires and ancient settles. Recommended for its bed and breakfast, in three delightful bedrooms brimming with creaky character; modern comforts include simple carpeted bathrooms, tea makers and television.

Bar Meals: lunchtime and evening; bar snacks both sessions   **Typical Dishes:** home-made soup £1.50, garlic mussels £2.25, home-made pies £4, vegetable crumble £3.25, steak £7.75 Vegetarian Meals   Beer   Hook Norton; Marston   Cider   Family Room Garden   **Accommodation:** 3 bedrooms, all en suite, from £40   Children Welcome Overnight   **Credit Cards:** Visa

CLIFFORD Castlefield Inn on B4350: Truly peaceful, in a pretty spot on the Wye; simple lunchtime bar food.

CROWLE   Old Chequers

Crowle WR7 4AA
Tel: (090 560) 275
Open: 12-2.30, 7-11
Licensees: I M and J S Thomas

Extended, smartened-up country dining pub; by no means cheap but with a competent menu and wine list. Interesting specials. No children indoors.

Bar Meals: 12-1.45, 7-9.45 (not Sun eve); bar snacks both sessions   **Typical Dishes:** leek and chicken soup £1.95, baked egg, smoked salmon and cream cheese £3.80, chicken boursin £7.50, medallions of beef with tomato and mozzarella £8.25, fresh salmon with herb butter £7.50, double chocolate mousse £2.50   Vegetarian Meals: vegetable bake £4.95   Children's Portions (some)   Beer   Ansells; Bass; Hook Norton   Garden Outdoor Eating   **No Credit Cards**

CUTNALL GREEN New Inn on A422 Tel: (029 923) 202: Decent lunchtime and evening food in bar and busy dining room, lots of home cooking in evidence; nice service; real fire; garden. Marston beers. Open: 11.30-3, 5.30-11.

DORSTONE   Pandy Inn

Signposted off B4348 Golden Valley HR3 6AN
Tel: (0981) 550273
Open: 12-3 (not winter Mon/Tue), 7-11
Licensees: Christopher and Margaret Burtonwood

12th century inn, creaking with age and atmosphere. A real community local as well as an increasingly popular dining pub; head for the original bar, with its solid medieval character and enormous open fire. A dining room has the same menu.

Bar Meals: 12-2, 7-9.45; bar snacks lunchtime   **Typical Dishes:** *carrot and coriander soup £1.40, hummous with hot pitta bread £2.50, wild rabbit pie £4.95, fresh pasta with herby tomato and pepper sauce £4.75, sea trout in mushroom and prawn sauce £7.50, chocolate mousse with crème de menthe £1.75*   *Vegetarian Meals: spicy lentil and vegetable pie £4.75*   *Children's Menu/Portions*   `Cheese`   `Beer`   *Draught Bass; Whitbread Boddingtons Bitter*   `Cider`   *Weston's*   *Children Allowed in Bar to Eat*   *Outdoor Play Area*   *Garden*   *Outdoor Eating*   **No Credit Cards**

EARDISLAND   White Swan

Main Road (formerly A44)
Open: 12-2.30, 6-11

Bargain home cooking, especially the renowned steak pie, and tempting puddings; it's very foodie at weekends especially, so be early (no bookings). A relaxing, pretty pub, traditionally styled, with real fires, and the daily papers laid out for customers in the low-beamed cosy lounge; basic, lively public bar. Glorious village.

Bar Meals: lunch and evening until 9; bar snacks both sessions   *Vegetarian Meals*   `Beer`   *Marston*   *Children Allowed in to Eat*   *Play Area*   *Garden*

FOWNHOPE   Green Man

Fownhope HR1 4PE
Tel: (0432) 860243
Open: 11-2.30, 6-11
Licensees: A F and M J Williams

Enormous, towering black and white Tudor inn recommended for its bed and breakfast, though the food is routine enough stuff. Inside is more modernised manorial than strictly pubby. Bedrooms are well kept (courtyard rooms are smaller); ask for one of the two oldest, in the main building. Afternoon tea on the gracious lawns in summer.

Bar Meals: 12-2, 6.30-10; bar snacks both sessions   **Restaurant:** *7.30-9*   **Typical Dishes BAR:** *home-made soup £1.40, paté £1.95, gammon platter £4.65, home-made steak pie £4.65, roast local chicken £3.10, banoffee pie £1.50*   **RESTAURANT:** *paté £2.55, fillet steak £8.75, lamb cutlets à l'orange £7.50*   *Vegetarian Meals: lasagne Children's Menu/Portions*   `Beer`   *Courage Best; Hook Norton Bitter; Marston Pedigree*   `Cider`   *Weston's*   *Family Room*   *Outdoor Play Area*   *Garden*   *Outdoor Eating*   **Accommodation:** *20 bedrooms, all en suite, from £44.50 (single £31.75)*   *Children Welcome Overnight*   *Cots Available*   *Check-in: all day*   **Credit Cards:** *Access, Amex, Visa*

HANLEY CASTLE Three Kings off B4211, next to church Tel: (06846) 2686: Classic village pub, half old timbered cottage, half Georgian extension, with various little rooms and a traditional hatch servery. Simple decent bar menu and imaginative specials, lunchtime and Mon-Sat evenings. Family room. Garden. Butcombe, Theakston, Wadworth beers. Open: 11-2.30, 7-11.

KIDDERMINSTER Little Tumbling Sailor, Mill Lane: One of the Little Pub Co. chain, with an all-consuming nautical theme. Lots of fish on the lunchtime and evening bar menu; children's menu; garden. Ind Coope and house beers. Open: 11-3, 5.30-11.

KNIGHTWICK   Talbot Hotel

Worcester WR6 5PH
Tel: (0886) 21235
Open: 11-11 (12-2, 7-10 Sun)
Licensees: John and Anne Clift

Prettily set, attractive white inn, originally 14th century. The old bar, with modern carpets and curtains, is dominated by its vast open fireplace; the oak-panelled dining room is romantically gloomy, warmed by a wood-burning stove. Food is imaginative and tempting, though, rather extraordinarily, there's a £2.50 supplement for non-residents in the dining room (same menu). Main building bedrooms are best, though three have no bathrooms attached; extension-housed rooms, all en suite, are simple and cottagey in style. The residents' lounge is comfortable and modern rather than quaint and beamy.

Bar Meals: 12-2, 6.30-9.30; bar snacks both sessions **Typical Dishes:** *avocado soup £1.50, basil and lemon oyster profiteroles £4.50, liver and bacon £5.50, stir-fried pigeon with spinach £7.50, pork with apricot and soya glaze £7.50, lemon roulade with fresh blackberries £3 Vegetarian Meals: lentil and courgette pasties £6.50 Children's Portions* `Beer` *Banks's Bitter; Draught Bass; Whitbread Flowers IPA* `Whisky` *Children Allowed in Bar to Eat Patio/terrace Outdoor Eating Summer Barbecue* **Accommodation:** *10 bedrooms, 7 en suite, from £39 (single £23) Children Welcome Overnight Cot Available Check-in: all day* **Credit Cards:** *Access, Visa*

LEDBURY   Feathers Hotel

High Street HR8 1DS   `FOOD`
Tel: (0531) 5266   `B&B`
Open: 10.30-11 (12-2, 7-10.30 Sun)

Midsummer is the best time to draw up in front of the Feathers, when the massive display of hanging baskets creates a blaze of colour against its black and white timbered frame. It was built around 1565 as a staging post on the Royal Mail route from Cheltenham to Aberystwyth, and it's residents who still get the best deal today: the stairs creak, the landing's crazily uneven and the beamed bedroom walls and ceilings are full of period character, while bathrooms have been carefully installed over the years, and new arrivals find fresh fruit in the room. Some-one even comes in to turn down the beds. The hotel's latest addition, "Fuggles", takes its name from the famous Herefordshire hop-producer, John Fuggle. It's brick-lined and beamed, hung heavily with hops, and has its own menu, supplemented by specials chalked up on a board. Connecting Fuggles to the main lounge, the hotel bar is a convivial spot, though the beer range doesn't usually inspire. There's also the Feather's main restaurant, which by comparison is rather disappointing and fares unfavourably in price. Take curried parsnip soup and a home-made burger in Fuggles at £6.60, against sautéed prawns with ginger and soy (a very small portion) and pepper-sauced Hereford sirloin at precisely £10 more in the restaurant, where, à la carte, three courses, coffee and a bottle of house vin (very) ordinaire routinely approaches £50 for two.

Bar Meals: 12-2, 7-10; bar snacks lunchtime **Restaurant: 7-9.30** **Typical Dishes BAR:** *home-made soup £1.90, mushrooms with bacon and cheese £2.50, lamb and butterbean casserole £4.95, Herefordshire sirloin steak £9.25, supreme of salmon with parsley butter £6.45, home-made treacle tart £2.10* **RESTAURANT:** *avocado mousse with crab £3.75, supreme of chicken stuffed with smoked salmon £12.95, escalope of veal £13.25, filo pastry parcel of scallops and prawns £13.95, bombe surprise £3.70 Vegetarian Meals: stilton and walnut terrine £4.75   Children's Portions* Beer *Banks's Bitter; Draught Bass; Felinfoel Bitter; Hook Norton Bitter* Cider *Weston's   Children Allowed in Bar to Eat   Patio/terrace   Outdoor Eating* **Accommodation:** *11 bedrooms, all en suite, from £78.50 (single £55.50)   Children Welcome Overnight   Cots Available Check-in: all day* **Credit Cards:** *Access, Amex, Diners, Visa*

LYONSHALL   Royal George Inn

Kington HR5 3JN   ▼
Tel: (05448) 210
Open: 12-2.30 (inc Sun), 7-11
Licensee: John Edward Allen

Originally 17th century one-storey pub with later upper floor extension. Cosy beamed lounge, public bar, games room and new country restaurant. Snug bedrooms are simply furnished.

Bar Meals: 12-2, 7-9.45; bar snacks both sessions **Typical Dishes:** *home-made soup £1.95, smoked salmon stuffed with prawns £4.50, Welsh lamb steaks with orange and mint sauce £8.95, paella £9.25, lemon sole stuffed with scallops and crabmeat £8.95, king size banana split £3.25   Vegetarian Meals: baked vegetables au gratin £3.95   Children's Menu/Portions* Beer *Whitbread Castle Eden Ale, Flowers IPA, Original   Family Room   Outdoor Play Area   Garden   Outdoor Eating* **Accommodation:** *2 bedrooms, sharing 2 separate bathrooms, from £38 (single £22)   Children Welcome Overnight Check-in: all day* **Credit Cards:** *Access, Amex*

MAMBLE   Dog & Duck

on A456
Tel: (029 922) 291
Open: lunchtime and Tue-Sat evening; closed all day Mon
Licensees: Pat and Peter Gully

Rejuvented old country pub, now run by the people who made the Crispin at Stourbridge in the Midlands so popular. Home cooking is always imaginative, and makes good use of local produce.

Bar Meals: Tue-Sun lunchtime, Tue-Sat evenings; bar snacks lunchtime **Typical Dishes:** *turnip soup, calves liver and bacon, stir-fried chicken and vegetables, paella, damson ice-cream (main courses from around £4)   Vegetarian Meals* Beer *Hook Norton   Family Room Garden* **Credit Cards:** *Access, Amex, Diners, Visa*

OMBERSLEY — Kings Arms

near Droitwich WR9 0EW
Tel: (0905) 620315
Open: 11-2.45, 5.30-11 (12-10.30 Sun)
Licensees: Chris and Judy Blundell

New owners at the Kings Arms have in fact been licensees here for thirteen years, every year of it listed in this guide, but have now bought the pub from Bass. Creakingly old and bent with age, the Kings Arms has half-timbering, three large open fires, and a brand new kitchen. A total refurbishment should be complete by Easter 1992.

Bar Meals: 12.15-2.15, 6-10 (12-10 Sun); bar snacks lunchtime   *Typical Dishes:* fennel soup £1.80, smokies £3.75, turkey pasta bake £4.95, steak and kidney pie £4.75, turkey and leek pie £5.75, treacle and nut tart £1.85   *Vegetarian Meals: vegetable crumble*   **Beer** *Draught Bass; Whitbread Boddingtons Bitter, Flowers IPA* **Whisky** *Tormore Children Allowed in Bar to Eat   Garden   No Credit Cards*

PEMBRIDGE — New Inn

Market Square HR6 9DZ
Tel: (05447) 427
Open: 11-3 (4 Sat), 6-11; 11-2.30, 6.30-11 winter
Licensee: Jane Melvin

A favourite for its modest but enjoyable, good value bed and breakfast, this atmospheric 14th century inn overlooking the tiny covered village market has bulging walls, heavy beams, sloping floors and lots of rustic character. Bar food avoids the usual with-chips cliche, and goes for deep-fried brie, and chicken in cider (£3.50) instead. The nicest bedroom is the big one at the front, with its own en suite shower.

Bar Meals: lunchtime and evening; bar snacks both sessions   Vegetarian Meals **Beer** *Marston; Whitbread   Children Allowed in to Eat   Patio/terrace   Accommodation: 6 bedrooms, 1 en suite, from £30   Children Welcome Overnight   Check-in: by arrangement No Credit Cards*

PENSAX — Bell Inn

near Abberley WR6 6AE
Tel: (0299) 896677
Open: 12-2.30, 6.30-11
Licensees: John and Christine Stronger

FOOD

Very much a country roadside pub, the Bell's attempts to be most things to all comers succeeds primarily because of what might be called, in marketing-speak, consistency of product. John Stronger's enthusiasm for his cellar brings a continually varying selection of real ales and guest beers: Hook Norton, Wood's Special and Pendle Witches Brew among them. Christine's approach to the food is pure dedication, involving early starts and invariably also late finishes, just to keep up with the demand for her beef in Guinness, steak and kidney (secret recipe), lasagnes (including vegetarian), bolognese and chilli. Plainer palates are equally catered for on a menu of some two dozen main dishes, as well as bar snacks of sausage, egg and chips, ploughmans various, and steak or sausage sandwiches, which are always on offer. Additional blackboards proclaim the guest beers on offer as well as listing the kitchen specials, perhaps lamb and apricot pie, spicy chicken casserole, and own-recipe mariner's pie, all at under £5.50. The Bell isn't instantly appealing, and needs tidying up outside, but its interior grows on you. There are bare boards and pews in the bar, odd refectory and Britannia tables and captains' chairs in the dining room – which has a fine view of the rolling Herefordshire countryside – and a fenestrated snug which once housed the old bar. But it is the licensees who make the place, highly personable people with an enthusiasm that becomes infectious.

Bar Meals: 12-2, 7-10 (9.30 Sun); *bar snacks both sessions*   *Typical Dishes: carrot and coriander soup £1.60, stilton and port paté £2.35, steak and kidney pie £4.50, chicken with orange and rosemary £5.40, beef in Guinness £5.40, hot walnut fudge pudding £1.85   Vegetarian Meals: broccoli and stilton quiche £4.50   Children's Menu* ▐Beer▌ *Cotleigh Tawny Bitter; Hook Norton Bitter; Moorhouse's Pendle Witches Brew; Taylor Landlord   Family Room   Patio/terrace   Outdoor Eating*

RUCKHALL COMMON   Ancient Camp Inn

near Eaton Bishop HR2 9QX   ▐FOOD▌
Tel: (0981) 250449   ❗ ☻
Open: 12-2.30 (inc. Sun; not Mon), 6-11 (closed Mon eve winter) ▐B&B▌
Licensees: David and Nova Hague   ⚔ ☼

The route from the A465 at Belmont Abbey to Ruckhall turns into a twist of narrow lanes. Once there, look carefully for signs to the Ancient Camp, so named because the site was once an Iron Age fort. Certainly, it must have been impregnable from the northern side, as the pub stands atop an escarpment overlooking a wide bend in the river Wye. In fair weather, there's a fine view across the fertile river valley from a front patio bordered by roses, the backdrop of the inn fronted by window boxes and hanging baskets. Interior conversions by the present owners, David and Nova Hague, have retained original stonework and flagstone floors wherever possible, and this results in an intimate atmosphere to which dried flowers and huge log fires add a special glow in winter. Doyenne of the kitchen is Nova, and her production is prodigious. Bar meals and some sandwiches are available at lunchtime (except Monday), and though bar food remains available in the evenings and may be booked in advance, much greater emphasis is placed on her evening restaurant menu. Start with home-made soup, or pears in roquefort and watercress salad, followed perhaps by boned quail stuffed with chestnut and apple, fillet steak, plain or with a choice of sauces, or a seafood bretonne with lobster sauce. Tempting home-made puddings include lemon syllabub and Flemish apple flan. It's not only the food that shines at the Ancient Camp: the inn's five-bedroomed accommodation is also quite special. At the rear are three neat bedrooms with en suite showers; to the front, two superb bedrooms, one with a private sitting room, the other's en suite bath elevated to maximise its river view. All are fully centrally heated, with telephone, television and bedside clock radio.

Bar Meals: 12-2, 7-9.30 (nor Sun eve nor all Mon)   *Restaurant:* 7-9 Tue-Sat   *Typical Dishes BAR: carrot and coriander soup £1.75, home-made taramasalata £3.25, Greek shepherds pie £5.25, garlic chicken £5.95, fresh pasta with cream and mushrooms £4.95, iced coffee soufflé £2.75   RESTAURANT: celery and apple soup £1.95, mushrooms à la grecque £3.25, fillet steak £12.25, stuffed quail £11.50, seafood bretonne £9.50, chocolate roulade £2.75   Vegetarian Meals: black-eyed bean casserole* ▐Cheese▌ ▐Beer▌ *Whitbread WCPA; Wood's Parish Bitter   Family Room (lunch)   Riverside Garden Outdoor Eating   Accommodation: 5 bedrooms, all en suite, from £45 (single £32) Children Welcome   Overnight (minimum age 8)   Check-in: all day   Credit Cards: Access, Visa*

ST OWENS CROSS New Inn Junction of A4137/B4521 Tel: (098 987) 274: Old country inn on busy road, traditionally furnished, with a garden, real fire and separate restaurant. Bar food lunchtime and evening. Double-glazed bedrooms. Bass, Courage, Hook Norton, Smiles beers. Open: 12-2.30, 6-11.

SELLACK   Loughpool Inn

Ross-on-Wye HR9 6LX
Tel: (098 987) 236
Open: 12-2.30 (12-2 Sun), 7-11
Licensees: Karen Whitford and June Fryer

Pretty Marches cottage pub with a genuinely unspoilt interior and interesting food. Beams, stone flags, nice old furnishings and two log fires in the main bar, with other attractive rooms leading off. Children are only allowed in the dining room.

Bar Meals and Restaurant: 12-1.45, 7-9.30; bar snacks both sessions   **Typical Dishes**
BAR: chive and potato soup £1.50, stuffed mushrooms £2.50, pork with apricots and brandy £5.75, courgette bake £4.75, tuna and pasta bake £5.25, rum pot £1.50
RESTAURANT: *tomato and orange soup £1.50, garlic chicken £5.75, moussaka £4.50, chicken curry £5, lemon syllabub £1.50 Vegetarian Meals   Children's Portions*
Beer *Draught Bass; Wye Valley Hereford Bitter* Whisky Cider *Weston's   Garden Outdoor Eating*   **No Credit Cards**

SHOBDON   Bateman Arms

near Leominster HR6 9LX
Tel: (056 881) 374
Open: 12-2.30, 7-11
Licensee: C R Williams

Imposing 15th century black and white pub, popular for its home-made food. Attractive interior with open fires, antiques and country charm. Daily specials board.

Bar Meals: 12-2, 7-10; bar snacks both sessions   **Typical Dishes:** *home-made soup £1.40, giant prawn puffs with garlic butter £3.25, steak and kidney pudding £5.50, supreme of chicken with cream, rosemary and lemon £6.50, fish crumble £5.50, bread and butter pudding £2   Vegetarian Meals: mushroom strudel £4.60* Cheese Beer
Wood's Parish Bitter   Children Allowed in Bar to Eat   Outdoor Play Area   Garden Outdoor Eating   **No Credit Cards**

SPETCHLEY   Berkeley Arms

Evesham Road WR7 4QL
Tel: (0905) 65269
Open: 11.30-3, 6-11
Licensee: Neil Griffin

Large popular roadside pub with a large function suite (watch out on Saturdays in summer) and home-cooked food.

Bar Meals: 12-2, 6-9.30; bar snacks both sessions   **Typical Dishes:** *minestrone £1.50, grilled sardines £2.75, beef in ale pie £4.50, chicken princess £5.25, char-grilled sirloin steak £6.95, fresh fruit pavlova £1.95   Vegetarian Meals: broccoli and mushroom mornay   Children's Menu/Portions* Beer *Benskins Bitter; Ind Coope Burton Ale; Tetley Bitter   Children Allowed in Bar to Eat   Outdoor Play Area   Garden   Outdoor Eating*
Accommodation: *3 bedrooms, 1 en suite, from £40 (single £25)   Children Welcome Overnight   Check-in: by arrangement*   **Credit Cards:** *Access*

STIFFORDS BRIDGE   Red Lion

on A4103, Cradley, near Malvern WR13 5NN
Tel: (0886) 880318
Open: 12-3, 6.30-11
Licensees: Andrew and Rachel Williams

Old oak-beamed inn with log fires in both lounges and fairly low-key piped music, but no juke box or pool.

Bar Meals: 12-2.30, 7-9.30 (12.30-2.30, 7-9 Sun, eves summer only); bar snacks both sessions **Restaurant:** *7.30-9.15 Wed-Sat* **Typical Dishes BAR:** *country vegetable soup £1.40, garlic mushrooms with mint £2.25, liver and bacon casserole £4.25, home-made pies £4.25, poached salmon with prawns £6.25, lemon meringue pie* **RESTAURANT:** *minestrone £1.40, stilton and port paté £1.80, noisettes of lamb £6.50, chicken stuffed with asparagus in puff pastry £7, roast breast of duck £8* **Vegetarian Meals:** *spinach, cheese and mushroom pancakes* **Children's Menu/Portions** | Cheese | | Beer | *Banks's Mild, Bitter; Ind Coope Burton Ale; Wood's Special Bitter* | Whisky | | Cider | *Knights* **Children Allowed in Bar to Eat** **Outdoor Play Area** **Riverside Garden** **Outdoor Eating** **Summer Barbecue** **Accommodation:** *2 bedrooms, sharing a bathroom, from £35 (single £20)* **Children Welcome Overnight** **Cot Available** **Check-in: all day** **Credit Cards:** *Access, Visa*

STOKE LACY Plough Inn on A465 Tel: (08853) 658: Unassuming pub next door to Symonds cider factory; nothing special aside from good, unusual bar meals of a traditionally English kind; simply-done game casseroles; food lunchtime and evening, 12-2, 6.30-10. Greenalls beers. Access, Visa.

STOURPORT ON SEVERN Steps Horse: Home-made food, traditional and exotic, in this town centre pub; meals lunchtime and Tue-Sat evenings; also evening restaurant. Children allowed in to eat. Bass. All credit cards.

ULLINGSWICK Three Crowns Tel: (0432) 820279: Half a mile east of the village, a secluded, traditional pub with hop garlands, tiled floors, simple furnishings, a real fire and no music. Bar food lunchtime and evening. Ind Coope, Tetley beers. Open: 12-2.30 (3.30 Sat), 7-11.

UPPER WYCHE Chase Inn, Chase Road: Malvern country pub with good views, limited but sometimes interesting bar food. Donnington beers.

UPTON UPON SEVERN Swan, Riverside Tel: (06846) 2601: Attractive, fairly smart dining pub with a lunchtime food bar and evening bistro. Good bakes and pies (no snacks); no children under 12. Bass, Butcombe, Wadworth beers. Open: 11.30-2.30, 6-11.

WEOBLEY   Olde Salutation Inn

Market Pitch HR4 8SJ
Tel: (0544) 318443
Open: 11-3, 7-11
Licensees: Christopher and Frances Anthony

Nice pub in picturesque village. Pleasantly modernised lounge has a real fire, with restaurant leading off; also public bar with machines and juke box. Babies can stay (by arrangement) though cots and linen aren't provided; otherwise over 14s only overnight.

Bar Meals and Restaurant: 12-2, 7-9.30 (9 restaurant; not Sun); bar snacks lunchtime **Typical Dishes BAR:** *mushroom soup £1.60, paté £1.85, Indonesian stir-fry £4.75, mushroom, ham and garlic au gratin £3.95, fresh whole plaice £5.75, fresh lemon tart*

£2.55   **RESTAURANT:** *stilton soup £1.95, quails eggs with avocado £3.45, roast guinea fowl £10.75, beef roquefort £11.95, salmon and brill lattice £11.95, coffee and pineapple meringue £2.70*   *Children's Portions*   Cheese   Beer   *Hook Norton Best Bitter; Marston Pedigree; Whitbread Boddingtons Bitter*   Whisky   Cider   *Symonds, Weston's*   *Family Room*   *Patio/terrace*   *Outdoor Eating*   **Accommodation:** *4 bedrooms, 2 en suite, from £30 (single £20)*   *Check-in: all day*   **Credit Cards:** *Access, Visa*

WHITNEY-ON-WYE   Boat Inn

Whitney-on-Wye HR3 6EH
Tel: (04973) 223
Open: 11-2.30, 7-11
Licensees: H and S Jordan

Roomy and always tidy riverbank pub, nicely furnished, with picture windows overlooking the water.

Bar Meals: *12-2, 7-9.45; bar snacks both sessions*   **Typical Dishes:** *home-made soup £1.95, mushrooms on toast £2.45, home-made steak and kidney pie £4.95, herb chops £4.95, home-made chicken and pineapple curry £4.95, pancakes with vanilla ice and maple syrup £1.95*   *Vegetarian Meals: vegetable curry*   *Children's Portions*   Beer   *Draught Bass; John Smith's Bitter*   *Children Allowed in Bar to Eat*   *Riverside Garden*   *Outdoor Eating*

WHITNEY-ON-WYE   Rhydspence Inn

On A438, a mile to the west of Whitney HR3 6EU
Tel: (04973) 262
Open: 11-2.30 (12-2.30 Sun), 7-11
Licensees: Peter and Pamela Glover

Well-loved, reliably entertaining old inn set in the heart of Kilvert country. Delightful timbered interior and two attractive bars, with real fires, old furniture and beams aplenty. Nice touches include magazines and newspapers, creating an atmosphere in keeping with the old library chairs. Charming dining room and new restaurant overlooking the garden. Five comfortable bedrooms have beams, sloping floors, plus an armchair at the least; some rooms are more romantic, others more modern in style. Good food includes an excellent choice of farmhouse cheeses.

Bar Meals and Restaurant: *11-2 (12-2 Sun and restaurant), 7-9.30; bar snacks both sessions*   **Typical Dishes:** *home-made soup £2.10, whitebait £3.95, beef curry £5.25, spare ribs £4.95, fish £4.95, marrons Mont Blanc £2.75*   *Vegetarian Meals*   *Children's Portions*   Cheese   Beer   *Draught Bass; Marston Pedigree; Robinsons Bitter*   Cider   *Dunkertons*   *Family Room*   *Garden*   *Outdoor Eating*   **Accommodation:** *5 bedrooms, all en suite, from £51.20 (single £25.60)*   *Children Welcome Overnight*   *Check-in: all day*   **Credit Cards:** *Access, Amex, Visa*

WILLERSEY Dormy House: Really a hotel but with a welcome for non-residents in its old ex-farmhouse bar; nice but pricey food lunch and evening.

WINFORTON ★ Sun Inn

On A438 HR3 6EA
Tel: (0544) 327677
Open: 11-3, 6.30-11
Licensees: Brian and Wendy Hibbard

`FOOD`
! ☺
☼

The Wye valley road, otherwise known as the A438, winds out of Wales past Hay-on-Wye, a popular tourist route to Hereford and points north. By following the road some three miles into England, Wendy and Brian Hibbard have become celebrated émigrés, and the numbers are growing of those who follow to sample Wendy Hibbard's inspirational cooking. A Jane Grigson fan, yet a fine innovator in her own right, her recent inclination towards spicy, eastern flavours has brought many new fans beating a path to the door. Thus Eastern Promise, a dish of lamb, coriander, lime and ginger; beef in black bean sauce, vegetable biryani with cashew nuts, and duck with an oriental plum sauce all make regular appearances. Lighter lunch treats might easily include devilled crab au gratin, oriental ribs or hot and spicy wings of fire. In addition to a flair for the cooking of foreign parts (so to speak), good old traditional English cooking is also well represented, often with a characteristic Wendy Hibbard twist in the tail: her popular pies and celebrated 'Piggy in the Orchard' are always assured of a place on the menu. For more adventurous evening diners, a salmon fillet is wrapped around laverbread and bacon, a leg of lamb is stuffed with crab, and veal à la grecque is served up with spinach sauce, always accompanied by generous portions of crunchy, flavourful vegetables. A little bit of room should still be reserved, however, for some unusual desserts, a nuts about nuts tart, or "Kilimanjaro", an ice-cream pudding topped with snowy meringue, or a boozy crème de cacao mousse. Throughout the menu, food is beautifully designed as well as cooked: Wendy takes pride in presentation, a skill which has evolved apace following her success in national pub food competitions. Yet we are still talking pub here. Brian Hibbard sees to that, overseeing proceedings from the bar with an avuncular eye, while dispensing Brains, from Cardiff, and Wood's, from Craven Arms; he's equally at home discussing the merits of a fine selection of cheeses for the ploughman's, where Shropshire blue, Orkney smoked and mature farmhouse cheddar rub shoulders with his native Merlin goat's cheese and a fine organic Pencarreg. Equally, the exposed stone walls studded with agricultural implements, wood-burning stoves and high settles, and the corner dart board (for occasional use), ensure that the surroundings remain essentially pubby, that the conversation is convivial and that the relaxed atmosphere remains conducive to the enjoyment of fine pub food.

Bar Meals: 12-2, 7-9.30 (9.45 weekends); bar snacks both sessions **Typical Dishes:** *marrow and savory soup £1.50, crab and spinach tart £2.50, oxtails braised in cider £6.99, Welsh chicken and leek pie £4.99, fillet of salmon with a bacon and laverbread sauce £7.99, nuts about nuts tart £2.50 Vegetarian Meals: vegetable and cashew nut biryani £4.99 Children's Portions* `Cheese` `Beer` *Brains Bitter; Whitbread Boddingtons Bitter, Flowers Original; Wood's Bitter* `Cider` *Weston's Children Allowed in Bar to Eat Outdoor Play Area Garden Outdoor Eating* **No Credit Cards**

WOLVERLEY Lock: Popular canalside dining pub; bar meals lunchtime and evening. Banks's beers.

WOOLHOPE Butchers Arms

Woolhope HR1 4RF
Tel: (0432) 860281
Open: 11.30-2.30, 7 (6.30 Fri/Sat)-11
Licensees: Charles Power and Nicholas Squire

Another old favourite on the Welsh Borders tour. It's a classically black and white timbered, part 14th century, and delightfully unpretentious old inn, lost down leafy lanes, and simply furnished in country style with good log fires in winter and lots of old-fashioned peace and quiet. Charming garden. New licensees.

Bar Meals: 11.30-2.15 (12-2 Sun), 7.30-10 (10.30 Fri/Sat); bar snacks both sessions **Restaurant:** *7-9 Wed-Sat* **Typical Dishes BAR:** *stilton and celery soup £1.40, leek and hazelnut terrine £2.35, rabbit, bacon and cider pie £4.95, lamb and cranberry casserole £5.25, rolled fillet of plaice with scallops and prawns £5.25, bread and butter pudding £1.75 Vegetarian Meals: mushroom, butterbean and basil stew £4.50 Children's Menu* ▉Cheese▉ ▉Beer▉ *Hook Norton; Marston* ▉Cider▉ *Weston's Children Allowed in Bar to Eat Garden Outdoor Eating* **Accommodation:** *3 bedrooms, sharing a bathroom, from £39 (single £25) Children Welcome Overnight Check-in: all day* **No Credit Cards**

WOOLHOPE   Crown Inn

Woolhope HR1 4QP
Tel: (0432) 860468
Open: 12-2.30, 6.30 (7 Sun and winter)-11
Licensees: Neil and Sally Gordon

Promising new entry in this guide, and packed with diners from early evening in summer. One menu is on offer in both the main bar (modernised and airy rather than quaint) and dining room, where tables can be reserved. Dining children must be guaranteed well behaved.

Bar Meals: 12-2, 7-10; bar snacks both sessions **Typical Dishes:** *home-made soup £1.40, home-made potted stilton and mushroom £2.20, grilled sirloin steak £7.50, lamb and cranberry casserole £4.15, fusilli with Shropshire Blue and port £3.95, Bailey's cheesecake £1.55 Vegetarian Meals: cauliflower and potato bake £3.95 Children's Menu* ▉Beer▉ *Draught Bass; Hook Norton Best Bitter; Smiles Best Bitter* ▉Cider▉ *Weston's Children Allowed in Bar to Eat Garden Outdoor Eating* **No Credit Cards**

WORCESTER   Farriers Arms

9 Fish Street WR1 2HN
Tel: (0905) 27569
Open: 11-11 (12-2.30, 7-10.30 Sun)
Licensee: Nona Petersen

Attractively modernised old city tavern, with a relaxing lounge and large public bar, as well as a summer terrace with its own hatch servery. No children indoors.

Bar Meals: 11.30-9 (except for 30 minutes 2.30-3); bar snacks all day **Typical Dishes:** *celery and stilton soup £1.25, smoked mackerel paté £2.20, beef and mushroom pie £3.25, chilli con carne £3.25, seafood pie £3.25, treacle tart £1.50 Vegetarian Meals: broccoli bake £2.50* ▉Beer▉ *Courage Best, Directors Patio/terrace Outdoor Eating* **No Credit Cards**

HERTFORDSHIRE

ABBOTS LANGLEY Compasses Good hot specials of a restauranty sort.

ALDBURY   Valiant Trooper

Trooper Road HP23 5RW
Tel: (044 285) 203
Open: 12-3, 6-11 (all day summer and winter Sat)
Licensee: D E O'Gorman

The only frozen food on offer here is the ice-cream. Otherwise it's all home-made.
Various rooms have various styles. Very cheap drinks. Good walking area.

Bar Meals: 12.30-2 (not Sun), 6.30-8.30 (Tue-Fri); bar snacks both sessions
Restaurant: 12.30-2 (not Sat), 7.30-9.30 (not Sun); restaurant closed all day Mon
Typical Dishes BAR: French onion soup £2, mixed grill £4.90, roast beef £4.70, grilled
local trout £4.70, fruit crumble £1.50   RESTAURANT: set lunch £7.50, dinner
£11.95: tomato soup, saucy pancakes, sirloin au poivre, kidneys Creole, grilled halibut
Brunoise, chocolate mousse   Vegetarian Meals: stuffed peppers   Children's Portions
`Beer` *Adnams; Fullers; Greene King; Marston   Family Room   Outdoor Play Area*
Garden   Outdoor Eating   Credit Cards: Access, Visa

ARDELEY   Jolly Waggoner

Tel: (0438) 861350
Open: 11.30-3, 6.30-11
Licensee: Darren Perkins

Delightfully rustic pub with a drinking bar of great charm and an eating bar which
has expanded into a neighbouring cottage. Same menu in both. Main courses have
fresh vegetables. Tempting puddings.

Bar Meals: 12-2.30, 7-10.30; bar snacks both sessions   Typical Dishes: home-made
soup £1.95, paté and cheese filo parcels £2.95, fillet steak £10.50, duck supreme £9.95,
chicken supreme £9.95, lemon posset   Vegetarian Meals: vegetable lasagne `Cheese`
`Beer` *Greene King IPA, Abbot Ale   Children Allowed in Bar to Eat   Garden*
Outdoor Eating   Summer Barbecue   No Credit Cards

ASHWELL   Bushel & Strike

Mill Street, opposite village green SG7 5LY   `FOOD`
Tel: (046 274) 2394   ☼
Open: 12-2.30, 6.30-11   ♥
Licensees: Tony and Sandra Lynch

It's in summer that the Bushel and Strike's pretty garden and patio really come into
their own: a peaceful retreat from the madness of the A1M, just four miles away
through pretty countryside. It's an unassuming white-painted building, standing
opposite the village church, but behind this typical local pub facade lies a frequently
hectic, thriving business well-versed in the rapid provision of bar meals. The
interior, comprising three adjoining rooms, is uncluttered, kitted out in Laura
Ashley style wallcoverings and rustic wooden furniture. You'll probably find all the
tables are laid with place mats and cutlery: at mealtimes, this is very much a dining
pub, not a drinking one. A pine table in one corner holds a couple of cold joints,
ham on the bone and beef perhaps, alongside which are about ten large pots of
different salads. The rest of the menu is displayed on a large wall-mounted board.
The choice is varied, even cosmopolitan: fresh mussels, herring roes or spring rolls
to begin with perhaps, followed by rabbit casserole, creole chicken or baked trout.
It's a long list, running to around 30 items, mainly priced at around £6. To follow,
perhaps fruit crumble or bread and butter pudding, or a Häagen-Dazs ice-cream. It

gets very busy, and at times can appear overstretched: a dish of Turkish lamb promised much, but arrived lukewarm and a little overdone. There was nothing wrong with the flavour though, good and spicy, and fruity, as it should be. Likewise the service, which starts out efficient and smilingly, can end up visibly harassed and uneven, but on the whole they cope pretty well with the demand. A separate restaurant, decorated with agricultural equipment and bric-a-brac has higher prices, and a slightly different menu. The Bushel and Strike has lost its 'local' feeling, but in its place is a tremendously popular dining house with a good local reputation which attracts a great variety of customers.

Bar Meals: 12-2, 7-9.30; bar snacks both sessions Restaurant: 12-2, 7.30-9.30 (not Mon) Typical Dishes BAR: leek and potato soup £2.25, baked soused herrings £3.50, Turkish lamb £5.50, rabbit pie £5.50, Creole gumbo £5.50, bread, butter and whisky pudding £2 RESTAURANT: fish soup £3.50, char-grilled venison steak £8.95, roast rack of lamb in herbs £8.95, monkfish in spring onions and ginger £8.50, honey fudge cake £2.75 Vegetarian Meals: pasta bake £4.95 Children's Portions Beer Adnams; Charles Wells Children Allowed in Bar to Eat Garden Outdoor Eating Summer Barbecue Credit Cards: Access, Visa

ASHWELL Rose & Crown, 69 High Street Tel: (046 274) 2420: Wholesome home cooking lunchtime and evening in pretty 15th century village pub; real fire; no music; garden; children's menu. Greene King beers. Open: 10.30-2.30 (12-2 Sun), 6-11.

AYOT ST LAWRENCE   Brocket Arms

near Welwyn AL6 9BT
Tel: (0438) 820250
Open: 11-3, 6-11
Licensee: C T Wingfield Digby

Splendid medieval pub in an equally splendid village, in unlikely proximity to the commuter belt, but even closer to Shaw's Corner, where GBS lived (and now National Trust-owned). The unspoilt interior has oak beams, an inglenook fireplace and usually tasteful piped music. Children in restaurant only.

Bar Meals and Restaurant: 12-2, 7.30-9.30 (not Sun eve); bar snacks both sessions Typical Dishes BAR: stilton and onion soup £1.50, steak and kidney pie £4.50, steak £4.50, summer pudding £1.50 RESTAURANT: soup £2.50, mushrooms in Dubonnet sauce £2.50, tournedos Rossini £8.50, sherry trifle £1.50 Vegetarian Meals (restaurant): vegetable nut dish £8 Children's Portions Beer Adnams; Greene King; Marston Pedigree; Wadworth 6X Cider Weston's Outdoor Play Area Garden Outdoor Eating Summer Barbecue Accommodation: 6 bedrooms, 2 en suite, from £40 (single also £40) Children Welcome Overnight (minimum age 8) Check-in: by arrangement Credit Cards: Access, Visa

---

BARLEY   Fox & Hounds

High Street (B1368)
Tel: (076 384) 459
Open: 12-2.30, 6-11
Licensee: Rita Nicholson

Pleasingly traditional village local, 15th century with rambling low-ceilinged rooms, splendid open fires and a separate dining area. The lively atmosphere occasionally teeters on the brink of chaos. A beer drinkers' favourite – good home-brew beers as well as favourites from around the country; keen on traditional pub games. Decent, mostly home–cooked bar food is prepared by the landlady's son. Sunday lunch carvery; theme food evenings.

Bar Meals: 12-2, 6.30-10; bar snacks both sessions **Typical Dishes:** *whitebait £2.50, steak and kidney pie, beef stroganoff, salmon with prawns, cassoulet (main courses from around £4) Vegetarian Meals Children's Portions* **Beer** *Barley Old Dragon, Flame Thrower; Brakspears; Marston; Wadworth* **Cider** *Children Allowed in to Eat Garden* **No Credit Cards**

CROMER HYDE   Crooked Chimney

off B653 AL8 7XE
Tel: (0707) 323832
Open: 11-2.30, 5.30-11
Licensee: Peter Lloyd

Named after its own distinctly crooked chimney – a useful landmark if lost and uncertain – a popular dining pub with a daily changing bar menu and a restaurant list that changes seasonally.

Bar Meals: 12-2, 6-10 (Sun 12-2.30, 7-9.30; eve summer only); bar snacks both sessions **Restaurant:** *12-2 (not Sat), 7-10 (12-2.30 Sun; closed Sun eve)* **Typical Dishes BAR:** *home-made soup £1.65, cider mushrooms £3.45, lasagne £4.50, prawn thermidor £4.45, seafood pie £4.95* **RESTAURANT:** *smoked salmon cornets £5.75, chicken stuffed with prawns and crabmeat in champagne sauce £8.95, fillet of beef in cream and brandy £17, Hertfordshire lamb £10.95, lemon syllabub Vegetarian Meals: vegetable moussaka £4.25 Children's Menu (bar)* **Beer** *Benskins, Ind Coope, Tetley Children Allowed in Bar to Eat Outdoor Play Area Garden Outdoor Eating* **Credit Cards:** *Access, Visa*

DATCHWORTH Horns Inn Bramfield Road, Bulls Green. Delightful country pub, lots of 15th century character remaining: timbers, brick floors, attractive rugs, good fire, decent lunches. Patio. Whitbread.

FLAUNDEN   Bricklayers Arms

Long Lane, Hog Pits Bottom HP3 0PH
Tel: (0442) 833322
Open: 11-2.30, 5.30 (6 winter)-11
Licensee: A P Power

Pretty village pub with a pleasant modernised interior and reminders of ancient origins, plus a good summer garden with mature trees. Massively popular locally for food, and a new restaurant shows definite signs of ambition. They offer set menus for parties of ten or over. There's a garden salad bar, weather permitting. Children allowed in restaurant.

Bar Meals and Restaurant: 12-2, 7-9 (not Sun eve); bar snacks both sessions **Typical Dishes:** *fresh asparagus soup £1.80, prawn stroganoff, beef and ale pie, peppered sirloin steak, grilled Dover sole (main courses £4 up), home-made treacle tart Vegetarian Meals: vegetable bake* **Beer** *Adnams; Brakspears; Everards; Fullers* **Cider** *Addlestones Garden Outdoor Eating* **Credit Cards:** *Access, Visa*

GREAT OFFLEY   Green Man

High Street SG5 3AR
Tel: (0462) 76256
Licensee: Raymond Scarbrow

Busy, rambling country pub with good views from the well–organised garden.

Bar Meals and Restaurant: 12-2.30, 7-10; cold food and snacks all day   ***Typical Dishes BAR:*** minestrone £1.25, prawn cocktail £2.80, large filled Yorkshire pudding £3.50, steak and kidney pie £4.10, lasagne £4.10, apple pie £2   ***RESTAURANT:*** smoked salmon £5.65, beef stroganoff £11.50, peppered steak £13.25, chicken Kiev £8.95, fruit salad £3   *Vegetarian Meals: vegetable pie £4.10   Children's Portions*   **Beer**   *Banks & Taylor Shefford Bitter, Greene King IPA, Abbot Ale, Whitbread Flowers Original   Children Allowed in Bar to Eat   Outdoor Play Area   Garden   Outdoor Eating*   ***Credit Cards:*** *Access, Visa*

GREAT OFFLEY   Red Lion

Kings Walden Road SG5 3DZ
Tel: (0462) 76281
Licensees: Colin and Eileen Bowett

Now properly known as the Red Lion and Lodge Hotel, an almost roadside red brick pub with a bar snack menu which includes a daily special dish. Both restaurant and bedrooms are modernised and well-kept.

Bar Meals and Restaurant: 12-1.45, 7-9.45; bar snacks both sessions   ***Typical Dishes RESTAURANT:*** set menu £18.75: French onion soup, mushrooms baked in cream and sherry, guinea fowl with wild mushrooms, scampi provencale, roast quail with ham and red wine sauce, sherry trifle   *Vegetarian Meals: vegetable curry   Children's Portions*   **Beer**   *Brakspears Bitter; Marston Pedigree; Whitbread Boddingtons Bitter, Castle Eden Ale   Family Room   Outdoor Play Area   Garden   Outdoor Eating   **Accommodation:** 5 bedrooms, all en suite, from £55   Children Welcome Overnight   Check-in: all day   **Credit Cards:** Access, Amex, Diners, Visa*

HERTFORD   Sportsman

117 Fore Street SG14 1AX
Tel: (0992) 551621
Open: 11.30-3, 5.30-11
Licensee: R Webster

Everything from substantial snacks to smart restauranty food in well-kept, smartened-up dining pub.

Bar Meals: 11.30-2.30, 5.30-9.30; bar snacks both sessions   ***Restaurant:*** 12-2.30, 7-9.30   ***Typical Dishes BAR:*** beef and tomato soup £1.50, prawn and pasta salad £2.30, minute steak £3.25, beef and mushroom pie £4.25, lasagne £4.50, apple sponge £2   ***RESTAURANT:*** melon with summer fruits £3.30, pork fillet with mushrooms and cream £9, salmon en croute £9.50, poached monkfish and scallops mornay £9.50, treacle tart £2   *Vegetarian Meals: vegetable quiche   Children's Portions*   **Beer**   *Adnams; Hall & Woodhouse; Marston; Ridleys   Children Allowed in Bar to Eat   **Credit Cards:** Access, Amex, Visa*

HERTFORD Woolpack Old Cross. McMullen brewery tap, bare wood floors and traditional alehouse style; decent lunches.

LITTLE HADHAM   Nags Head

The Ford SG11 2AX
Tel: (0279) 771555
Open: 10.30-3, 6-11
Licensee: M A Robinson

Built of old ships' timbers in around 1500, on the once busy old London to
Cambridge road, but now a reasonably quiet country local. Children in dining room
(same menu).

Bar Meals: 12-2, 6-9.30; bar snacks lunchtime **Typical Dishes:** *home-made soup*
£1.50, paté £2.25, sirloin steak £7.50, prawn thermidor £6.25, treacle tart *Vegetarian*
Meals: harvest pie *Children's Menu/Portions* Beer *Greene King IPA, Abbot Ale*
Patio/terrace *Outdoor Eating* **No Credit Cards**

MUCH HADHAM Bull High Street Tel: (027 984) 2668. Rambling, busy village
pub with decent lunches and suppers, children's portions, good summer garden.

OXHEY Haydon Arms 76 Upper Paddock Road Tel: (0923) 34834. Village
local, decent lunches, garden; Benskins, Ind Coope beers. Open all day (closed
3-5.30 Mon/Tue).

POTTERS BAR Chequers Coopers Lane: Very cheap home cooking of the
toad-in-the-hole sort, at comfortable locals' pub with garden. Courage beers. Open
all day.

PUCKERIDGE   White Hart

High Street SG11 1RR
Tel: (0920) 821309
Open: 11-2.30, 5.30-11
Licensees: Colin and Rita Boom

Small family-run business with a big menu, flexible about what's eaten when, and
strong on seafoody, fishy things. There's a 10% mandatory service charge on
(bookable) dining room meals (same menu). The cold seafood platter is famously
large. Nice, animal-laden garden for children.

Bar Meals and Restaurant: 12-2, 6.30-9.45 (7-9.30 Sun); bar snacks both sessions
Typical Dishes BAR: *turkey broth £1.70, Arbroath smokie £3.25, turkey and mushroom*
pie £5.25, moussaka £5.50, whole baked plaice £5.95, raspberry and hazelnut meringue
£1.70 **RESTAURANT:** *similar starters and puddings, potted shrimps £3, whole lemon*
sole £5.95, half lobster £8.95, crab and prawn mayonnaise £6.75 *Vegetarian Meals:*
tomato pancakes £5.25 *Children's Menu/Portions* Beer *Greene King; McMullen*
Children Allowed in Bar to Eat *Outdoor Play Area* *Garden* *Outdoor Eating* **Credit**
Cards: *Access, Diners, Visa*

ST ALBANS   Garibaldi

61 Albert Street AL1 1RT
Tel: (0727) 55046
Open: 11-3, 5-11 (11-11 Fri/Sat)
Licensees: Paul McFarlane and Valerie Doyle

Pleasant old pub with unexpected hidey-holes around its small island bar, and a piney,
dining café-style conservatory room leading off. Food can be eaten anywhere; queue
and collect at the dining end servery. Food's reliable, simple, home-cooked. No chips.

Bar Meals: 12-2, 6.30-9 (not Sun eve); bar snacks both sessions **Typical Dishes:** *carrot and coriander soup £1.50, fillet of lamb in a tart cranberry sauce £3.75, boozy bullock pie £4.20, mushroom stroganoff £3.25, rhubarb crumble £1.50 Vegetarian Meals: spicy vegetable couscous £3.25 Children's Portions* Beer *Fullers Chiswick, London Pride* Family Room Patio/terrace Outdoor Eating **No Credit Cards**

ST ALBANS   Rose and Crown

St Michaels Street AL3 4SG
Tel: (0727) 51903
Open: 11-2.30, 5.30-11 (11-3, 6-11 Sat)
Licensees: John and Paula Milligan

The Milligans hide out here when seeking refuge from their other pub, the tourist-swamped, much-photographed Falkland Arms, Great Tew (q.v., Oxon). This is a pleasingly simple, woody and traditional old pub down in St Michaels, near Verulamium Park; a little off the office-trade patch, so often a quiet gem at lunchtimes. Reliably nice, simple pub food. Unusual crisps and snuffs, and lots of country wines.

Bar Meals: 11.30-2.10; bar snacks lunchtime **Typical Dishes:** *leek and potato soup £1.50, beef and dumpling casserole £3.75, chicken with apricots in white wine sauce £4.50, cheese, potato and onion pie £2.50, rhubarb crumble £1.50 Vegetarian Meals: cheese and lentil bake Children's Portions* Beer *Adnams: Benskins Best; Greene King Abbot Ale; Tetley Bitter* Whisky Cider *Coombes, Great Oak* Patio/terrace Outdoor Eating **No Credit Cards**

SAWBRIDGEWORTH Market House Hotel 42 Knight Street Tel: (0279) 722807: 16th century inn hotel with a beamed inglenook, no fruit machines, a varied lunchtime and evening menu; Adnams, Greene King, Wadworth beers. Open 11-3, 5.30-11.

TEWIN   Plume of Feathers

57 Upper Green AL6 0LX   FOOD
Tel: (043 871) 7265
Open: 11-3, 6.30-11
Licensees: Barry Thornton and Jackie Watt

A prominent sign, which also doubles as a bus stop, is the first clue to the location of the Plume of Feathers, which is hidden behind tall bushes well back from the main road. Its white painted exterior is made pretty by splendid plant boxes and flower displays; at the back is a fair-sized garden with wooden furniture, its atmosphere spoilt slightly by a fence hiding the rear kitchen entrance. The Plume's interior is not large, but the bar has tremendous character, with low ceilings, intimate corners, exposed beams, uneven walls, old wooden and copper-top tables, period settles and a variety of roundback and spindle chairs. Pictures of horses and other rural scenes litter the walls, along with a cheerful clutter of horse brasses, stuffed fish and game birds and other rural paraphernalia, while a collection of ties hang over the bar counter, and vases of fresh flowers add a cheery, personal note. The second room is lighter and smaller, with less bric-a-brac, and less atmosphere. It's the food most people are drawn to, either in the bar or more expensive restaurant, which is evidently also doing a lot of trade, especially with the local business community, who also throng the bar at lunchtimes. Head for the main bar, but get there early. The daily changing menu, written up on blackboards, ranges from the comfortingly traditional to the daringly nouvelle. Hungarian lamb goulash is tender and spicy; other choices included breaded cheeses, deep-fried and served with blackcurrant dressing, American vegetable bake, or deep-fried cod in a beer batter. There are also toasted sandwiches. The cooking is better than competent, showing real respect for the produce and for flavour, and fair pricing won't break the bank. In contrast, the restaurant, with its more formal settings and service can see an average bill for two hit £50. Service is friendly and relaxed, by and large. This is a lovely village pub, popular with a wide range of people, including locals like Dame Barbara Cartland, and the standard of food on offer makes it well worth a detour.

Bar Meals and Restaurant: 12-2.30, 7-9.30 (not Sun eve)   *Typical Dishes BAR:* *home-made soup £1.95, curried banana wrapped in bacon £2.65, hot daily-changing specials £3.95-£5.95, treacle sponge £2.50* **RESTAURANT:** *boneless quail £5.75, Dover sole (varies), rack of lamb £10.75, magret duck £13.50 Vegetarian Meals: American Bake Children's Portions* **Beer** *Adnams; Benskins; Greene King; Youngs Children Allowed in Bar to Eat Garden Outdoor Eating* **Credit Cards:** *Access, Visa*

WALKERN   White Lion

High Street SG2 7PA
Tel: (0438) 861251
Open: 11.30-2.30, 7-11
Licensee: Michael Windebank

Pleasant old pub with alcoves and inglenook furniture, warm and welcoming. Sound home cooking.

Bar Meals: 12-2, 7-9.30; bar snacks both sessions   *Typical Dishes:* *home-made soup £1.50, garlic mushrooms £3.50, home-made steak and kidney pudding £5.50, breaded lamb cutlets with wine sauce £6.50, fresh fish (cod, skate, plaice) £4.75-£6.50, bread pudding Vegetarian Meals: vegetable curry Children's Menu/Portions* **Beer** *Greene King IPA, Abbot Ale Children Allowed in Bar to Eat Outdoor Play Area Garden Outdoor Eating* **Credit Cards:** *Access, Visa*

WALKERN Yew Tree: Popular for bar food and McMullens ales; particularly good steaks from ex-butcher landlord.

WATTON AT STONE   George & Dragon

High Street SG14 3TA   FOOD
Tel: (0920) 830285   ❢
Open: 11-2.30, 6-11
Licensee: Kevin Dinnin

It's possible that by the time this guide appears, the two separate bar and restaurant menus at the George and Dragon will have transmogrified into just one menu covering both eating areas: hopefully this doesn't mean they'll be trading up to restaurant status. The pub is popular with everyone, from OAPs to business class, and its well-balanced bar menu attracts a fair number of locals in, with perhaps Corsican fish soup, Alsace onion tart or skewered king prawns to start, pigeon and turkey in madeira sauce, pork stroganoff, or a fillet of red snapper with a walnut oil and thyme dressing to follow. Puddings include gooseberry crumble, or a very fine lemon meringue pie. The cooking is unfussy and reliable, but can suffer from the perils of bulk preparation; prices aren't bad, but portion size is variable. Reasonable house wines are available by the carafe. The bars are usually bustling with diners, some of whom travel some distance to eat here. The public bar is a locals' spot, though, with keen cribbage players, black and white photographs of the pub and village in days gone by, and furnishings similar to the main bar, in the oldest part of the building, which has a wonderfully homely atmosphere enhanced by jovial management and welcome touches like fresh flowers and the day's newspapers.

There are also exposed beams, open fireplaces, ochre stained walls hung with a mixture of framed oil and watercolour paintings, and two large bay windows admitting lots of natural light. Furnishings are a mixture of blue upholstered bench seating and simple wood chairs around oak tables topped with candles. There are a couple of modern regulations though: no credit cards are taken for bills under £10, and sleeveless shirts are prohibited in the bars. This is a difficult pub to miss, as it dominates the centre of the village, and is of pink-painted pebbledash. There's a small flower-filled garden and patio for kinder weather.

Bar Meals: 12-2, 7.15-10 (no food Sun); bar snacks both sessions   *Restaurant:* 12-2 Tue-Fri, 7.30-9.30 Tue-Sat   *Typical Dishes BAR:* home-made soup £1.30, Alsace onion tart £2.80, pigeon breasts with diced turkey £5.50, fillet of pork stroganoff £5, fillet of sole in wine and mushroom sauce £5.75, summer pudding £1.80   *RESTAURANT:* smokie £4.80, breast of duck in red wine, medallions of venison, halibut in white wine (main courses £15), strawberry romanoff £3.30   *Vegetarian Meals:* ratatouille crumble   **Beer** Greene King IPA, Abbot Ale   **Whisky**   *Garden   Outdoor Eating*   *Credit Cards:* Access, Amex, Diners, Visa

WESTMILL   Sword in Hand

near Buntingford SG9 9LQ
Tel: (0763) 71356
Open: 12-2.30 (3 weekends), 6-11
Licensees: David and Heather Hopperton

They've now got planning permission for six further bedrooms at this attractive pub in a charming village just off the A10. Carpeted bar with good log fire and black and white timbering.

Bar Meals: 12-2, 7-9.30 (9 Sun/Mon); bar snacks both sessions   *Typical Dishes:* French onion soup £1.75, garlic mushrooms £2.95, lamb with rosemary £4.50, mixed grill £7.95, chicken, gammon and mushroom pie £4.25, banoffee pie £2.25   *Vegetarian Meals:* lasagne £4.25   *Children's Portions*   **Beer**   *Greene King; Ind Coope   Children Allowed in Bar to Eat   Outdoor Play Area   Garden   Outdoor Eating   Summer Barbecue*   *Accommodation:* 1 bedroom, from £40 (single £30) Check-in: all day   *No Credit Cards*

WHITWELL   Maidens Head

67 High Street SG4 8AH
Tel: (0438) 871392
Open: 11.30-2.30, 5.30-11 (all day Sat)
Licensee: Michael Jones

Characterful old pub. No home-made soups or puddings. No children indoors.

Bar Meals: 12-2, 6.30-9; bar snacks both sessions   *Typical Dishes:* avocado with prawns, sirloin steak £7.25, rib steak £8.50, chicken in cream with pasta £4.25 Vegetarian Meals   **Beer**   *Courage Directors; McMullen AK Original, Country Bitter*   **Whisky**   *Outdoor Play Area   Garden*   *No Credit Cards*

WHITWELL Eagle & Child: Comfortably modernised, popular for bar food, with occasionally outstanding specials; Whitbread beers; large rear garden.

HUMBERSIDE

ALDBROUGH George & Dragon 1 High Street (B1242) Tel: (0964) 527230.
Smartened up coastal village pub, popular for lunchtime and evening bar meals,
though jukebox can be intrusive; accommodation offered in neighbouring cottages.
Youngers beers. Open 12-3, 7-11.

BARNETBY LE WOLD Station. Opposite the station, and full of railway
nostalgia; decent lunchtime and evening bar meals.

BARNOLDBY LE BECK   Ship Inn

Main Road (off A18) DN37 0BG   ❦
Tel: (0472) 822308
Open: 11-3, 5.30-11
Licensee: Charles Gillis

18th century village pub with a separate restaurant specialising in fish. Charles Gillis
was previously at the West Park Hotel, Harrogate. Real fire.

Bar Meals: 12-2, 7-10; bar snacks both sessions **Typical Dishes:** *home-made soup
£1.50, seafood crepe £1.95, home-made pies, sirloin steak, various fresh fish dishes, hot
chocolate and brandy fudge cake* *Vegetarian Meals: pasta dishes* *Children's Portions*
Beer *Children Allowed in Bar to Eat* **No Credit Cards**

BISHOP WILTON   Fleece Inn

Bishop Wilton YO4 1RU
Tel: (07596) 251
Open: 12-3, 6 (7 winter)-11
Licensee: Leslie Wells

Lovely village setting overlooking the green, the Norman church and the Wolds
beyond. A central bar divides lounge and public areas, with a breakfast/dining room
to the rear. Food is nothing special, but recommended for bed and breakfast. Four
bedrooms are in the original building, and three en suite rooms in a separate pantiled
block. Live country and western music on Friday evenings.

Bar Meals: 12-2, 7-9.30; bar snacks both sessions **Restaurant:** *7-9.30* **Typical
Dishes BAR:** *French onion soup 90p, steak pie, lasagne, cottage pie (low prices)*
RESTAURANT: *prawn omelette, farmhouse mixed grill, pepper steak, trout in wine and
mustard sauce* *Vegetarian Meals: lasagne* *Children's Menu/Portions* Beer *John
Smith's Bitter; Tetley Bitter* *Children Allowed in Bar to Eat* *Outdoor Eating*
Accommodation: *7 bedrooms, 4 en suite, from £38 (single £20)* *Children Welcome
Overnight* *Cot Available* *Check-in: all day* **No Credit Cards**

BRIGG White Horse, Wrawby Street Tel: (0652) 52242: Excellent home made
pork pies and other lunchtime and evening bar meals in friendly, busy old inn;
garden; Wards beers. Open: 11-2.30, 5-11.

BROUGHTON   Red Lion

High Street DN20 0HY
Tel: (0652) 652560
Open: 11-3, 6-11 (all day Fri/Sat)
Licensees: Melvyn and Denise Beniston

In an area distinctly lacking in good pubs, it's refreshing to find one as fine as the Red Lion, a part red brick, part pebbledash building dominating the main village street. There are two bars, one either side of the main entrance, the first a high-ceilinged locals' public, its well-trodden black and red tiling topped with modest furniture, and a masculine simplicity rather compromised by tasteful patterned wallcoverings in subtle tones of pink. The smaller, carpeted lounge is quieter and more intimate, its walls almost wholly panelled and decorated with assorted china and prints, the large window hung with pretty chintzy curtains. Food is in the hands of landlord Melvyn Beniston. Fresh produce is used and a good choice of butcher means meat is notably good: tender, pink-cooked lamb chops come with real chips, crisp and perfectly fried. Vegetables too are done with excellent care – none of your standard discoloured peas and overcooked mush here; instead, al dente carrots, fresh celery provencale and properly cooked broccoli. Daily changing specials (a larger choice at weekends when the pub's at its busiest) typically include brunch, poached smoked haddock, and liver and onions, while the standard printed menu begins with freshly made sandwiches, salads and omelettes and moves on to house specialities like kidneys Portuguese, chicken Hussar or fillet steak royale, all prepared and served with no little care and attention. Desserts are good too, perhaps a moist, flavoursome cherry Bakewell or a delicious strawberry shortcake. Set Sunday lunch offers a choice of roasts at highly competitive prices. It gets very busy.

Bar Meals: 12-2, 7.30-10 (not Sun eve); no food Mon; bar snacks both sessions **Typical Dishes**: *tomato and orange soup £1.15, prawns in Pernod with kiwi fruit £2.95, fillet Medici £7.95, steak and stout £4.25, salmon steak with prawns and cream £6.25, rum truffle cheesecake £1.55 Children's Portions* **Beer** *Mansfield beers* **Whisky** *Children Allowed in Bar to Eat   Outdoor Play Area   Garden   Outdoor Eating   Summer Barbecue* **No Credit Cards**

ELLERKER   Black Horse

Church Lane HU15 2DN
Tel: (0430) 423270
Open: 12-3, 6.30-12 (closed Mon and Tue lunch)
Licensee: Michael Kingston

Farmhouse cottage overlooking two village greens, and which aims for a continental bistro atmosphere. Quiet at lunchtimes early in the week, but booking is essential every evening. Main course prices include a half bottle of house wine; the menu changes daily.

Bar Meals and Restaurant: 12-1.30 (2 Sun), 6.30-10 (eves restaurant only); bar snacks lunchtime **Typical Dishes**: *asparagus soup £1.20, whole avocado with prawns £2.55, fresh roasted local chicken £7.45, fillet steak princess £10.40, local gammon steaks with hot peaches £7.10, raspberry and redcurrant pie £1.65 Vegetarian Meals: carrot and spinach paté £1.65 Children's Menu/Portions   Family Room (annexe)   Outdoor Play Area Patio/terrace   Outdoor Eating* **No Credit Cards** *(may change)*

FLAMBOROUGH Royal Dog & Duck Dog and Duck Square (junction B1255/B1229) Tel: (0262) 850206. Rambling, traditional pub which welcomes families; popular for food; bedrooms. Bass beers. Open: 11-4, 6.30-11.

GREAT KELK Chestnut Horse. Unspoilt cottage pub in farming area, popular for good value home-cooked food. No music; real fire; family room. Bass, Courage beers. Open all day.

HEDON   Shakespeare Inn

9 Baxtergate (off A1033)
Tel: (0482) 898371
Open: 11-11
Licensees: Alex and Susan Craig

Cosy, friendly one-roomed pub with 3000 beermats adorning the ceiling, in the formerly busiest port on the Humber, with 14th century origins. Keen real ale fans, and good food too: fresh haddock direct from Hull on Friday and Saturday lunchtimes, but otherwise homely, honest fare like local gammon with free range eggs, beef in red wine, steak and kidney pie, and maybe jam roly poly for pudding.

Bar Meals: 12-7 (12-3 Sun) `Beer` *Vaux; Wards   Family room   Patio/terrace* **No Credit Cards**

LANGTOFT   Old Mill
                                                                  ♥

Mill Lane YO25 0BQ
Tel: (0377) 87284
Licensee: C E Dawson

Now the Old Mill Country House Hotel and Restaurant, the latter with a longer, wider range and main courses from £9 up. Interesting bar menu specials. Bedrooms were built in 1990 in the old stables; no children under 14 overnight.

Bar Meals and Restaurant: 12-2, 6.30-10 **Typical Dishes BAR:** *mange-tout and watercress soup £1.95, home-made chicken and duck liver paté £3.45, sweet roast loin of pork £5.50, Szechuan hot fried crispy beef £7.75, medallions of monkfish and prawn Waleska £9.50, toffee vacherin £3.25   Vegetarian Meals: stir-fried Chinese vegetables* `Beer` *Tetley Bitter; Youngers Scotch* **Accommodation:** *9 bedrooms, all en suite, from £60 (single £40)   Check-in: all day* **Credit Cards:** *Access, Amex, Visa*

LANGTOFT   Ship Inn

Scarborough Road YO25 0TH
Tel: (0377) 87243
Open: 12-3, 7-11
Licensee: E M Tonks

By way of contrast to the Old Mill, a cosy village local with modest home-cooked bar meals.

Bar Meals: 12-2, 7-9.15; bar snacks both sessions **Restaurant:** *12-2.15 (Sun only), 7-9.30 Wed-Sun* **Typical Dishes BAR:** *home-made soup £1, garlic mushrooms £2.25, ham and eggs £4.95, home-made pie £3.25, home-made lasagne £3.25, trifle £1.50* **RESTAURANT:** *similar starters and puddings; ham and eggs £6.75, steak Diane £8.75, duck à l'orange £7.25   Vegetarian Meals: lasagne   Children's Menu/Portions* `Beer` *Camerons Traditional Bitter, Strongarm; Youngers Scotch* `Cider` *Children Allowed in Bar to Eat   Outdoor Play Area   Garden   Outdoor Eating* **Accommodation:** *4 bedrooms, all en suite, from £30 (single £20)   Children Welcome Overnight   Check-in: by arrangement* **Credit Cards:** *Access, Amex, Diners, Visa*

LITTLE DRIFFIELD   Downe Arms

Little Driffield YO25 7DX
Tel: (0377) 42243
Open: 12-2.30, 7-11
Licensee: Stuart Wood

Completely refurbished white corner pub, with some original beams and character intact. No music. The menu mixes scampi standards with more interesting specials, and restaurary dishes (which we've listed here).

Bar Meals: 12-2.30, 7-9.30; bar snacks lunchtime **Typical Dishes:** *home-made soup £1.35, seafood pancake £2.95, beef Wellington £10.80, veal £7.80, trout £9.60, apple crumble £1.95   Vegetarian Meals: Welsh rarebit   Children's Menu/Portions* `Beer`
*Tetley Bitter   Children Allowed in Bar to Eat   Garden   **Credit Cards:** Access, Visa*

LOW CATTON   Gold Cup Inn

Low Catton YO4 1EA
Tel: (0759) 71354
Open: 11.30-3.30 (not Mon), 7-11
Licensees: Raymond and Patricia Hales

An old favourite in the York area, much driven out to for lunches and suppers. Modernised but pleasant and relaxing, with two real fires in the rambling three-room lounge; there's also a noisier games room at the rear. Must book for Sunday lunches. The beer garden features lots of little farm animals to delight children, and access to the river bank.

*Bar Meals: 12-2, 7-10; bar snacks lunchtime   **Restaurant:** 7-10   **Typical Dishes** BAR: minestrone £1.30, grapefruit cocktail £1.30, steak and mushroom pie in Guinness £3.95, honey roast ham with scrumpy sauce £3.95, fishermans pie £4.25, pecan pie £1.60   RESTAURANT: cream of cauliflower soup £1.55, Parma ham and Waldorf salad £3.50, poached breast of chicken in creamy minted sauce £8.25, casserole of guinea fowl £8.75, grilled Barnsley chop £7.75, chocolate mousse £1.85   Vegetarian Meals: cashew nut, yogurt and pepper bake £3.95   Children's Menu/Portions* `Beer` *John Smith's Bitter; Tetley Bitter   Children Allowed in Bar to Eat   Outdoor Play Area Garden   Outdoor Eating   **No Credit Cards**

NORTH DALTON   Star Inn

Warter Road YO25 9UX
Tel: (0377) 81688
Open: 11-11
Licensee: Nick Cragg

Very popular with readers for its atmosphere, food and in particular its stable-conversion bed and breakfast, but we learned as we went to press that the Star is up for sale, so all the following details may change.

*Bar Meals: 12-2, 7-10 (9.30 Sun); bar snacks both sessions   **Typical Dishes:** home-made soup £1.35, brie fritters £3.25, rabbit pie £3.75, game casserole £6.95, tuna and sweetcorn conchiglie £3.95, hot sticky toffee pudding £1.75   Vegetarian Meals: broccoli and cheese bake   Children's Portions* `Beer` *John Smith   Children Allowed in Bar to Eat Garden   Outdoor Eating   **Accommodation:** 7 bedrooms, all en suite, from £55 (single £39.50)   Check-in: all day   **Credit Cards:** Access, Visa*

NORTH FRODINGHAM Star, Main Street (B1249): Friendly pub with decent evening bar meals; games area in modern extension; garden; Camerons beers. Open: Sun lunch; 7-11 all week.

SLEDMERE   Triton Inn

Sledmere YO25 0XQ
Tel: (0377) 86644
Open: 12-3, 7-11
Licensee: C E Emmett

Characterful old roadside inn on an ancient East Yorkshire estate. Worth trying for bed and breakfast. The residents' dining room is also used for popular Sunday lunches.

Bar Meals: 12-2, 7-9; bar snacks both sessions **Typical Dishes:** *home-made soup £1.45, paté £1.95, home-made steak and kidney pie, home-made cottage pie, chicken cordon bleu, rhubarb crumble Vegetarian Meals: lasagne verdi Children's Menu/Portions* Beer *Tetley Bitter Family Room Patio/terrace Outdoor Eating* **Accommodation:** *7 bedrooms, 3 en suite, from £40 (single £20) Children Welcome Overnight Check-in: by arrangement* **Credit Cards:** *Access, Visa*

SOUTH DALTON   Pipe & Glass

Beverley HU17 7PN
Tel: (0430) 810246
Open: 11.30-2.30, 7-11 (closed Mon)
Licensee: Malcolm Crease

Done up since our last edition, and now boasting a conservatory restaurant with views over the Dalton Estate. Otherwise, a Wolds village pub with an attractive traditional interior, leather seats, settles and log fires. The garden is lovely in summer. Reliable bar food.

Bar Meals: 12-2, 7-10; bar snacks both sessions **Typical Dishes:** *celery and stilton soup £1.65, prawn cocotte £2.95, chicken piri piri £4.25, home-made pheasant pie with apples and Calvados £6.75, seafood tagliatelle £4.75, sticky toffee pudding £2.35 Vegetarian Meals: mushroom stroganoff £3.95 Children's Menu/Portions* Cheese Beer *Ruddles Best; Whitbread Castle Eden Ale* Whisky *Springbank 15 yr Children Allowed in Bar to Eat Outdoor Play Area Garden Outdoor Eating* **Credit Cards:** *Access, Visa*

ULCEBY   Brocklesby Ox

Church Lane DN39 6TG
Open: 11-3, 6.30-11
Licensees: Neville and Anne Glover

Cheery old pub with very simple food; decent fish and chips.

Bar Meals: 12-2, 7.30-9.15; bar snacks both sessions **Typical Dishes:** *home-made soup 95p, prawn cocktail £2, steak and kidney pie £3.50, game sausage £4, fresh haddock £4, bramble and apple pie £1.50 Children's Portions* Beer *Bass Family Room Outdoor Play Area Garden Outdoor Eating* **No Credit Cards**

WESTWOODSIDE — Park Drain Hotel

Isle of Axholme
Tel: (0427) 752255
Open: 10.30-4, 6-11
Licensee: Nick Sutherton

Secluded, unusual Victorian pub, in Park Drain, about 400 yards off the B1396. Spacious public bar, comfortable lounge and separate restaurant; despite its out of the way spot, becoming popular for the chef-licensee's enthusiastic, traditional cooking; homely in the bar, smarter in the restaurant, where children are permitted.

Bar Meals and restaurant: *lunchtime and Tue-Sun evening* **Typical Dishes BAR:** *leek and potato soup, fish in beer batter, range of home-made curries, steak and mushroom pie* **Beer** *Courage* *Patio/terrace*

ISLE OF WIGHT

BONCHURCH — Bonchurch Inn

The Shute PO38 1NU
Tel: (0983) 852611
Open: 11-3, 6.30-11
Licensees: U and A G Besozzi

Bonchurch's only pub has an invigorating Italian flavour. Good nautical atmosphere, too: the public bar is cut into the rocks of the Shute. Solid fuel stove.

Bar Meals: *11-2.30, 6.30-10; bar snacks both sessions* **Restaurant:** *6.30-9.30*
Typical Dishes: *minestrone £1.20, antipasto £3.95, fillet steak Bonchurch, veal marsala, venison in port wine (main courses £4-£7), zabaglione £1.95* *Vegetarian Meals: cannelloni and spinach £3.80* *Children's Portions* **Beer** *Draught Bas; Burts VPA; Whitbread Flowers Original* *Family Room* *Outdoor Play Area* *Patio/terrace* *Outdoor Eating* **Accommodation:** *3 bedrooms, sharing a bathroom, from £35 (single £17.50) Children Welcome Overnight* *Cot Available* *Check-in: by arrangement* **No Credit Cards**

CHALE — Clarendon Hotel/Wight Mouse Inn

On B3399 PO38 2HA
Tel: (0983) 730431
Open: all day
Licensees: John and Jean Bradshaw

A perennial favourite, for its atmosphere, the energy with which it's run, the bed and breakfast and the genuine welcome to children: the Wight Mouse Inn was our 1990 Family Pub of the Year. Parents with children are treated like first class citizens both inside and out. There are decent home-made bar meals too, featuring delicious local fish and seafood, and an astonishing 365 whiskies. Nice bedrooms in the Clarendon next door (a 17th century coaching inn in its own right) successfully blend period and modern comforts, excellent family facilities and pretty views. One even has a waterbed. There's a new luxury family suite, and the hotel dining room has been extended this year.

Bar Meals and Restaurant: 11.30-10 (12-2.30, 7-9.30 Sun); bar snacks all day
Typical Dishes BAR: tomato and basil soup £1.40, prawn cocktail £2.80, giant
Clarendon mixed grill £6.50, crab and prawn mornay £5.90, vegetables au gratin £3.10,
home-made gateaux £1.60 *RESTAURANT:* carrot and coriander soup £1.40, smoked
mackerel paté £2.10, T-bone steak £9.40, fishermans platter £5.90, gravadlax £5.90,
home-made meringue nest £1.60   Vegetarian Meals: quiche of the day £3.30   Children's
Menu/Portions   **Beer**   Burts VPA; Marston Pedigree; Wadworth 6X; Whitbread
Boddingtons Bitter   **Whisky**   Glen Grant 1936, Old Pulteney 1961   Family Room (3
rooms)   Outdoor Play Area   Garden   Outdoor Eating   **Accommodation:** 15 bedrooms,
most en suite, from £54 (single £27)   Children Welcome Overnight   Cots Available
Check-in: all day   **No Credit Cards**

COWES Pier View 25 High Street. Well-run sailing pub with a considered,
occasionally unusual bar menu lunch and evening; decent house wines; children
allowed in to eat. Whitbread beers.

DOWNEND Hare & Hounds on B3056: Thatched, traditional country pub with
an original little bar and modern extension to the rear; and excellent island beer,
Burts.

FRESHWATER   Red Lion

Church Place PO40 9BP
Tel: (0983) 754925
Open: 11.30-3, 5.30-11 (11-4, 6-11 Sat)
Licensee: Bryan Farrant

Good country interior with flagged floors, rustic tables, reproduction settles.

Bar Meals: 11.30-2, 6.30-10 (12-2, 7-9.45 Sun)   *Typical Dishes:* stilton soup
£1.20, crab cocktail, chicken tikka masala £3.75, turkey fillets in onion and lemon sauce
£3.75, beef curry £3.95, trifle £1.10   Vegetarian Meals: macaroni cheese £2.50
Children's Portions   **Beer**   Gales HSB; Marston Pedigree; Whitbread Flowers Original
Family Room   Outdoor Play Area   Garden   Outdoor Eating   **No Credit Cards**

FRESHWATER Royal Standard Hotel School Green Road Tel: (0983)
753227: Afternoon tea and reasonable bar meals of a simple, home-cooked sort in
cheery little bar in village hotel. Bedrooms.

NEWPORT Castle Hotel 91 High Street. Ancient, stone-floored pub with
monumental end wall and more modern features; lunchtime and evening bar meals,
Marston, Whitbread beers and real cider. Open: 10.30-3, 6-11.

NEWPORT Wheatsheaf Hotel St Thomas Square Tel: (0983) 523865: 17th
century coaching inn with comfortable, traditional bar, casement clock and open
fire; family room; decent bar meals; refurbished bedrooms. Whitbread beers.

SEAVIEW   Seaview Hotel

High Street PO34 5EX   `FOOD`
Tel: (0983) 612711   `B&B`
Open: 10.30-3, 6-11
Licensee: Nicholas Hayward

Actually a small early Victorian seaside hotel, the bars at the Seaview are nonetheless
quite pubby and the bar meals are too good to miss. Just yards from the sea front

with its pebble beach and pretty assortment of sailing dinghies bobbing in the bay, the hotel has enormous charm, starting with the small front patio complete with flagpole, and the little central courtyard. Both bars have a nautical theme, one with photos of old ships and antique oak tables, the other more rustic in style, with its bare floorboards, dado pine panelling and, more unusually, part of an old ship's mast. Eat in the cosy restaurant under wicker lampshades at crisply-clothed tables, or choose from the bar menu; either way the emphasis is on seafood: perhaps warm prawn and mushroom salad with smoked Isle of Wight garlic and toasted pine kernels, or local crab blended with cream and fresh garden herbs, served hot with crusty wholemeal bread. There are also steaks, sandwiches and home-made puddings. Pretty, individually decorated bedrooms – blues and yellows are the favoured colours – are most appealing, with lots of pictures, books and objets d'art. The best, and largest, rooms feature antique furniture; others have simple white-painted built-in units. Two of the rooms have their own patios and on the top floor there's also a suite, its two bedrooms separated by a sitting room. Bathrooms are as spick and span as the bedrooms; toiletries come in little wicker 'swan' baskets, and towels are large and soft. Two cosy lounges are reserved for residents and restaurant diners, one of them for non-smokers.

Bar Meals and Restaurant: 12-2, 7-9.30; bar snacks both sessions   *Typical Dishes BAR:* home-made soup £1.95, blue cheese salad £2.95, plaice and chips £3.95, scampi and chips £5.95, lobster thermidor £7.95, meringues £2.95   *RESTAURANT:* crab £3.95, noisette of lamb £8.95, calves liver £12.95, fillet of beef £14.95, summer pudding £3.95 Vegetarian Meals   Children's Menu   **Beer**   Whitbread Flowers IPA, Original **Whisky** Auchentoshan, Bladnoch   Children Allowed in Bar to Eat   Patio/terrace *Accommodation:* 16 bedrooms, all en suite, from £65 (single £43.50)   Children Welcome Overnight   Cots Available   Check-in: all day   *Credit Cards:* Access, Amex, Visa

---

VENTNOR   Spyglass Inn

The Esplanade PO38 1JX   ☀
Tel: (0983) 855338   ☺
Open: 11-3, 7-11 (10.30 am- 11 pm summer)
Licensees: Neal and Stephanie Gibbs

Stephanie and Neal Gibbs are both native islanders (or Calk Heads, in the local vernacular) who have done a marvellous job of totally rebuilding the Spyglass Inn after the disastrous fire of just a few years ago. Wandering around the several interconnecting rooms, which include two reserved for non-smokers and several where children are welcome, it is difficult to believe that the pub is not hundreds of years old. The bar counter is built of old pews and the whole place full of old seafaring prints and photographs, as well as numerous nautical antiques, ranging from a brass binnacle and ship's wheel to old oars and model ships in glass cases. The setting for the pink-washed Spyglass Inn could not be better either, at one end of the seafront with a front terraced area stretching right to the edge of the sea wall. In winter, the waves break right over the wall and more than one customer has been known to get a soaking by mis-timing their exit from the pub. In summer, there's an outside bar and ice-cream kiosk, as well as a barbecue on occasions. The menu features standard pub fare like chilli, ploughmans and beefburgers; the thing to look out for is the local seafood: crab served out of its shell in generous bowlfuls with salad, and locally caught lobsters, kept live in their own tank. In winter, there are home-made soups and casseroles from a blackboard menu, and on Saturday nights a candlelit dinner, for which booking is advisable, complete with pianist. In the season, there is entertainment nightly (less frequently in winter), which might be live piano, a jazz trio or a skiffle group. One neat little flatlet with upholstered rattan furniture and a sea-facing balcony offers accommodation for up to two adults and two children; breakfast is served in the bar. A public car park is just 50 yards away, but check your brakes before venturing down here – the road to the seafront has hairpin bends and a gradient of 1 in 4.

Bar Meals: 12-2.15, 7-9.30; bar snacks both sessions **Typical Dishes:** *chicken and vegetable soup £1.95, crab cocktail £2.50, steak £7.50, lasagne £3.75, jacket potato £2.50, apple pie £1.95 Vegetarian Meals: vegetarian lasagne £3.75 Children's Menu/Portions* `Beer` *own beer; Gibbs New; Ind Coope Family Room Riverside Patio/terrace Outdoor Eating Summer Barbecue*

YARMOUTH   Bugle

The Square PO41 0NS
Tel: (0983) 760272
Licensees: Chris Troup and Rinaldo Perpetuini

Lively seaside pub, recommended for bed and breakfast, though ask for a room away from the above bar. Weekend entertainment from a singing duo, and good summer barbecues. Nautically themed bar features ship's planks, pennants and pictures aplenty. Routine bar food; try the seafood salad; also a restaurant. Bright bedrooms are unfussily modernised; all the usual facilities; parking spaces reserved for residents.

Bar Meals: lunchtime and evening Children's Menu `Beer` *Marston; Whitbread Family Room Garden* **Accommodation:** *10 bedrooms, 4 en suite, from £60 Children Welcome Overnight Check-in: all day* **Credit Cards:** *Access, Visa*

YARMOUTH George Hotel Quay Street Tel: (0983) 760331. Nautically themed, professionally staffed, newly done-up bar in popular hotel. Bar meals; bedrooms.

KENT

BARHAM   Dolls House

Elham Valley Road CT4 6LN   ▼
Tel: (0227) 831241
Open: all day
Licensees: Ernie and Lynne Tweedie

Flexible mix and match menus offer both snacks and dinnerish dishes all day in this refurbished 16th century building with a pretty old-fashioned garden featuring doves and life-like dolls. Inglenook fireplace in restaurant, plus piano: "musicians welcome".

Bar Meals: all open hours **Typical Dishes:** *carrot soup £1.95, home-made paté £2.25, Ingoldsby lamb pie £5.85, local rabbit and cider pie £5.85, duck with marmalade sauce £11.25, hot banana pancake £2.25 Vegetarian Meals: pecan and mushroom flan Children's Menu/Portions* `Beer` *King & Barnes Sussex Bitter; Shepherd Neame Master Brew Bitter; Wadworth 6X* `Cider` *Pilgrims, Theobalds Children Allowed in Bar to Eat Outdoor Play Area Garden Outdoor Eating* **Credit Cards:** *Access, Visa*

BENENDEN   King William IV

The Street TN17 5DJ   ♥
Tel: (0580) 240636
Open: 11-3, 6-11
Licensee: Allan Austin

16th century tile-hung pub, upmarket rustic in style, reflecting its well-heeled location. Fresh flowers on plain wooden tables, a log fire in the inglenook, exposed beams, and a relaxing, lived-in air: much used by locals, and some strangers have felt a bit unwelcome. Vigorously traditional home cooking recommended though: we particularly enjoyed the duck liver paté, and fish pie with red cabbage.

Bar Meals: 12-2 (not Sun), 7-9 Wed-Sat; bar snacks both sessions **Typical Dishes:** *stilton and celery soup £1.50, smoked salmon mousse, home-made sweet and sour pork or chicken, home-made pies, salmon steak with hollandaise (main courses from £4), steamed puddings Vegetarian Meals: home-made vegetable cobbler* **Beer** *Shepherd Neame Children Allowed in Bar to Eat Garden Outdoor Eating* **No Credit Cards**

BIDDENDEN   Three Chimneys

Ashford TN27 8HA
Tel: (0580) 291472
Open: 11-2.30 (12-2.30 Sun), 6-11
Licensees: C F W Sayers and G A Sheepwash

A recent visit revealed the much-loved Three Chimneys to be as good as ever. It has every natural advantage, being a classic country pub, its original, small-roomed layout and old-fashioned furnishings intact. Old settles, low beams, nice decor, warming open fires: glorious. Then there's the range of more than decent bar food; you can book tables in the family Garden Room, and the garden is lovely for summer eating. Don't, incidentally, look for three chimneys on the roof: the name comes from the pub's location at the meeting of three lanes, or Trois Chemins, as it was called by French prisoners of war kept near here in another century.

Bar Meals: 12-2, 7-10; bar snacks both sessions **Typical Dishes:** *chilled mint and stilton soup £2.15, spinach and ham mousse £2.80, cold honey-roasted chicken £6.25, sherried kidneys £5.35, fish lasagne £4.85, grape and banana pavlova £2.75 Vegetarian Meals: broccoli quiche £4.60* **Beer** *Adnams; Goachers; Harveys; Wadworth 6X* **Whisky** **Cider** *Biddenden Family Room Garden Outdoor Eating* **No Credit Cards**

BRASTED Bull, High Street (A25). Popular for bar meals under enthusiastic newish licensees; bat and trap game; garden. Shepherd Neame beers. Open: 10.30-2.30, 6-11 (all day Sat).

BRENCHLEY   Rose & Crown

High Street TN12 7NQ   ♥
Tel: (089 272) 2107
Open: 11-3, 6-11
Licensees: Rowland and Alison Hill

Pretty, typically Kentish 15th century inn, originally the stables and staff rooms for the old Palace of Brenchley opposite. Lots of exposed timber, a pretty little carpeted bar and civilised dining room with proper linens. Bedrooms are comfortable; two have four-posters.

Bar Meals: 12-2.30, 7-10; bar snacks both sessions   **Restaurant:** 7-10   **Typical Dishes**
BAR: *asparagus soup £2.50, garlic mushrooms £2.50, rabbit pie £4.15, spicy chicken and vegetable stir-fry £4.25, smoked chicken and bacon tagliatelle £4.15, treacle and orange tart £2*   **RESTAURANT:** *celery and stilton soup with walnuts £3.50, scallop, French bean and bacon salad £4.15, breast of French duck with raspberry and mango £11.95, lamb with honey, rosemary and almonds £9.95, fillet of beef stuffed with stilton £15.75, summer fruit pavlova £3*   *Vegetarian Meals: avocado risotto £3.95*   Children's Portions   Beer
Adnams; Harveys; Marston Pedigree; Wadworth 6X   Cider   Chiddingstone   Children Allowed in Bar to Eat   Outdoor Play Area   Patio/terrace   **Accommodation:** 10 bedrooms, all en suite, from £45 (single £35)   Children Welcome Overnight   Cot Available   Check-in: all day   **Credit Cards:** Access, Amex, Visa

---

BURHAM   Golden Eagle

80 Church Street ME1 3SD
Tel: (0634) 668975
Open: 11-2.30, 6.15-11
Licensee: V L T Forde

Rather dated-looking interior, but also original beams and a speciality for Malaysian and Chinese food; English options limited.

Bar Meals: 12-2, 7-10; bar snacks both sessions   **Typical Dishes:** *chicken and sweetcorn soup £1.30, spare ribs of pork £4.60, beef and peppers in black bean sauce £5.85, king prawns in sambal sauce £6, mee goreng £4.65, lychee meringue nests £1.50   Vegetarian Meals: wor-tip crispy corn £5.50*   Beer   Marston Pedigree; Wadworth 6X; Whitbread Flowers Original   Children Allowed in Bar to Eat   Patio/terrace   Outdoor Eating   **Credit Cards:** Access, Visa

---

CHARING   Old Oak Hotel

High Street TN27 0HU
Tel: (0233) 712307
Open: 11-11

Largish courtyard hotel in medieval North Downs village. The snug bar is properly pubby, and the upstairs restaurant is in the old malting room. Fresh meat, game and vegetables.

Bar Meals: 12-2.30, 7-9.30; bar snacks lunchtime   **Typical Dishes:** *stilton and onion soup £1.25, prawn and mushroom bake £2.50, half shoulder of roast lamb £10 (for 2), home-made steak and kidney pudding £4.50, dressed lobster salad £6.50, jam roly poly   Vegetarian Meals: spinach and mushroom bake*   Children's Portions   Beer   Brakspears; Shepherd Neame; Whitbread Boddingtons Bitter   Children Allowed in Bar to Eat   Summer Barbecue   **Accommodation:** 10 bedrooms, all en suite, from £45 (single £25)   Children Welcome Overnight   Cots Available   Check-in: all day   **Credit Cards:** Access, Visa

CHIDDINGSTONE CAUSEWAY Little Brown Jug, on B2027: Decent food, nice atmosphere, real ale; spacious garden with play area.

CHILHAM   Woolpack

High Street CT4 8DL
Tel: (0227) 730208
Open: 11-3, 6-11
Licensee: Glyn Ford

A new licensee at this well-liked 16th century pub has, kept things pretty much as they were. The bar is relaxing and traditional, with its mix of wall, dining and comfy seating. Lots of timbers and vast log-lit inglenook fireplace. Bar food is of the steak and kidney pie, beef stew, lasagne and salad sort, at reasonable prices; children are allowed in the restaurant. Some of the bedrooms are in the main building, some in converted outbuildings, and three in a stable block across the road, all pleasantly finished and decorated.

Bar Meals: lunchtime and evening; bar snacks both sessions   *Children's Menu*   `Beer`
*Shepherd Neame   Outdoor Play Area   Garden   **Accommodation:** 17 bedrooms, 14 en suite, from £50 (single £40)   Children Welcome Overnight   Check-in: all day   **Credit Cards:** Access, Amex, Diners, Visa*

CHILLENDEN Griffins Head Tel: (0304) 840325. Friendly, unpretentious village meeting place; attractive original bar with stone flags; beams and open fire. Decent lunchtime and evening bar food draws the crowds. Summer barbecue. Shepherd Neame beers. Open: 10-2.30, 6-11.

CLIFFE   Black Bull

186 Church Street ME3 7QD
Tel: (0634) 220893
Open: 12-3, 7-11
Licensees: Michael and Soh Pek Berry

Late Victorian pub on historic tavern site, perhaps with a secret tunnel leading to the local parish church, which happens to be the largest in England. The three bars and cellar restaurant specialise in Far Eastern cooking, mainly Malaysian, and share the same menu, much cheaper in the bar. Huge set meals at around £17.50 a head are the house speciality.

Bar Meals: 12-3, starters only in evening   **Restaurant:** 7-10   **Typical Dishes BAR:** soup of the day £1.95, satay £3.95, hokkein pork £5.10, kofta curry £5.35, king prawn sambal £5.75, kueh dada £2.75 Vegetarian Meals   `Beer`   Adnams Best; Batemans XXXB; Ringwood 4X; Wadworth 6X   Children Allowed in Bar to Eat   **Credit Cards:** Access, Visa*

DARGATE   Dove

Plum Pudding Lane (off A299)
Tel: (0227) 751360
Open: 11-3, 6-11
Licensees: Peter and Susan Smith

An idyllic summer pub, with its mature gardens and trees, dovecote, rockery and pool, and masses of cottage flowers. Inside is mellow and wood-panelled, attractively modernised, and with a good proportion of home-made dishes on the menu.

Bar Meals: lunchtime and Mon-Sat evenings; bar snacks both sessions   **Typical Dishes:** soup £1.35, lasagne £2.60, cauliflower and sweetcorn cheese £3.50, pork chop £6.50, *game in season   Vegetarian Meals   Children's Menu   ▐ Beer ▌   Shepherd Neame Master Brew Bitter   Family Room (lunchtime)   Outdoor Play Area   Garden   Outdoor Eating*

DUNGENESS Pilot: Popular weekend haunt, right on the shingle beach; fresh fish on the menu.

EASTLING   Carpenters Arms

near Faversham ME13 0AZ
Tel: (079 589) 234
Open: 11-4, 6-11
Licensees: Tony and Mary O'Regan

Tony and Mary O'Regan ran a pub in the centre of London for many years, so the move to deepest rural Kent, a few years ago, must have been quite a culture shock – Eastling doesn't even boast a village shop, and it's easy to get lost in the surrounding country lanes. The mellow red brick Carpenters Arms dates back to the 14th century and is teeming with character. An old inglenook fireplace in the brick floored restaurant has an old baking oven; corn dollies decorate the old timbers and beams, and a host of flowers and pot plants add a homely touch. The red carpet-tiled bar features lots of old photos, a collection of old bottles, and pew seating around draw-leaf dining room tables. The bar menu is not over long, featuring hearty home-made soups, burgers, ham and eggs, ploughmans and sandwiches. Steaks and simple fish dishes are to be found in the restaurant, served with a good selection of some six or seven fresh vegetables, along with surprises like snails in garlic and brandy amongst the starters. All is freshly cooked to order. Older children are only allowed inside if eating in the restaurant, but there are a few tables in the garden and small portions are available of suitable dishes. Meanwhile, next door in a typically Kentish white clapperboard house are four peaceful bedrooms, two of them rather on the small side, with shower cabinets and toilets en suite. The best room is much more spacious with a full en suite bathroom. All have the same floral curtains, which contrast rather oddly with abstract patterned duvets, as well as TVs and radio alarms. Good breakfasts are served in the restaurant.

Bar Meals and Restaurant: 12-2.30 (1.30 Sun), 6.30 (7 restaurant)-10.30 (no food Sun eve); bar snacks lunch and evening   *Typical Dishes BAR:* broccoli and stilton soup £1.50, garlic mushrooms £2.75, beef in ale pie £6.50, lamb and apricot pie £6.50, 8 oz burger £3.80, bread pudding and custard £2   *RESTAURANT:* garlic mushrooms £2.75, fillet steak £9.15, Barbary duck £8.95, Dover sole £10.50   Vegetarian Meals: pasta Children's Portions   ▐ Beer ▌   Shepherd Neame   ▐ Whisky ▌   Outdoor Play Area   Garden Outdoor Eating   *Accommodation:* 4 bedrooms, all en suite, from £35 (single £30) Check-in: all day   *Credit Cards:* Access, Amex, Visa

---

FORDWICH   Fordwich Arms

near Canterbury   CT2 0DB
Tel: (0227) 710444
Open: 11-2.30, 6-11
Licensees: Nigel and Patsy Thompson

New licensees at the popular Fordwich, but the food's looking similar in style to the previous regime. It's a solid Tudor-style village pub, with a rather handsome but not intimidatingly smart interior – standard enough furnishings, but a parquet floor, green hessian walls, and lovely arched windows. The terrace is also a civilised spot.

Bar Meals: 12-2, 6-10 Mon-Sat; bar snacks both sessions   *Typical Dishes:* home-made soup £1.50, bacon and onion pudding £4.40, seafood gratin £5.40, salads £4.25

Vegetarian Meals: lasagne £4 **Beer** *Marston; Whitbread   Children Allowed in to Eat Patio/terrace*

GOUDHURST Green Cross Inn Station Road (A262) Tel: Opened-out and refurbished friendly country inn-hotel, with home-cooked, robustly old-fashioned pub food, good value bedrooms. Exmoor Ale, Harveys beers. Open: 11-2.30, 6-11.

GREEN STREET GREEN   Ship

on B260, Darenth, Dartford DA2 8DP
Tel: (04747) 2279
Open: 11-2.30, 6 (5.30 winter)-11
Licensee: Denis E C Thompson

Cheap and cheerful home-cooking in popular two-bar pub.

Bar Meals: *12-2; bar snacks both sessions* ***Typical Dishes:*** *onion soup £1.50, avocado and prawns £3, steak and kidney pie £3.20, roast pork £3, prawns in breadcrumbs £2.75, bread and butter pudding £1.50   Vegetarian Meals: cauliflower cheese   Children's Portions* **Beer** *Courage; Youngs   Family Room   Outdoor Play Area   Garden   Outdoor Eating* ***No Credit Cards***

GROOMBRIDGE   Crown

on B2110
Tel: (089 286) 4742
Open: 11-2.30 (3 Sat), 6-11
Licensees: Bill and Vivienne Rhodes

Quaint Elizabethan Kentish tile-hung pub, rambling and characterful, with period square-panelling. Be early to get a seat in the cosy main bar; the dining room adjoining the food servery is rather cramped. Nice outdoor seating on the front terrace or village green.

Bar Meals: *lunchtime and Mon-Sat evening; bar snacks both sessions* ***Typical Dishes:*** *home-made soup £1.50, steak and mushroom pie £4.40, poached salmon £4.70, chicken curry £4   Vegetarian Meals* **Beer** *Brakspears; Harveys; Marston* **Cider** *Family Room   Patio/terrace* ***Accommodation:*** *bedrooms, half en suite, from £30 (single £20)*

HARRIETSHAM   Ringlestone Inn

between Harrietsham and Wormshill   ❢
Tel: (0622) 859900
Open: 11-3, 6.30-11
Licensee: Michael Millington-Burk

Splendidly atmospheric old inn, remotely tucked away by the Pilgrim's Way. Brick floors and walls, low beamed ceilings, intricately carved settles and a magnificent oak dresser. Choose freely from bar and restaurant menus, and sit anywhere to eat: tables are proper dining height in the restaurant, drinks height in the bar. Excellent choice and cheeses. There may be nine new bedrooms in the adjacent farmhouse for 1992: planning permission pending as we went to press.

Bar Meals and Restaurant: *12-2 (12.15-2.15 Sun), 7-9.30* ***Typical Dishes:*** *lunchtime buffet: lamb and coconut curry £3.95, chicken casserole £3.95, herrings in madeira £2.55, apple and sultana flan £2.75; evening menu: crab paté £3.75, game pie £6.25,* *pork loin steaks £7.95, chilli £4.95, summer pudding £2.85   Vegetarian Meals: vegetable pie £5.50   Children's Portions* 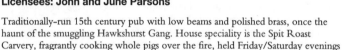 *Adnams Broadside; Batemans; Gales; Shepherd Neame* **Cider** *Biddenden, Theobalds   Children Allowed in Bar to Eat Garden   Outdoor Eating   **Credit Cards:** Access, Amex, Diners, Visa*

HAWKHURST   Oak & Ivy

Rye Road TN18 5DB
Tel: (0580) 753293
Open: 11-2.30, 6-11 (all day Sat)
Licensees: John and June Parsons

Traditionally-run 15th century pub with low beams and polished brass, once the haunt of the smuggling Hawkshurst Gang. House speciality is the Spit Roast Carvery, fragrantly cooking whole pigs over the fire, held Friday/Saturday evenings and Sunday lunch (booking advised).

*Bar Meals: 12-2, 6.30-9.30; bar snacks both sessions   **Typical Dishes:** soup of the day £2, prawn cocktail £3.75, home-made steak and mushroom pie £4.50, home-made chilli con carne £4.50, home-made steak and kidney pudding £4.50, spotted dick £1.75 Vegetarian Meals: lasagne £3.95   Children's Menu/Portions* **Beer** *Harveys PA; Whitbread Flowers, Fremlins   Family Room   Outdoor Play Area   Garden   Outdoor Eating   Summer Barbecue   **Credit Cards:** Access, Diners, Visa*

HILDENBOROUGH Gate Inn Tel: (0227) 86498. Rural local, good for simple snacks like local raised pies, ploughmans and interesting sandwiches, daily lunchtime and evening. Shepherd Neame beers.

ICKHAM   Duke William

The Street CT3 1QP
Tel: (0227) 721308
Open: 11-3 (not Mon), 6-11
Licensees: Alistair Robin and Carol Ann McNeill

Comfortable, welcoming old village pub close to A257. Full meals tend to be the restauranty sort – in fact it's restaurant meals listed below – with simple snacks in the front bar, all of reliable quality. Lots of fish, fresh vegetables: burgers and fishfingers are banned, even for children.

*Bar Meals: 12-2.30, 6-10; bar snacks both sessions   **Typical Dishes:** home-made soup £1.60, New Zealand mussels £4.50, veal escalope £12.95, fillet of lamb with redcurrant sauce £6.95, red mullet £7.50, apple and blackberry pie   Vegetarian Meals: pasta dishes Children's Portions* **Beer** *Adnams; Harveys; Shepherd Neame; Youngs* **Whisky** *Lagavulin 16 yr* **Cider** *Biddenden   Family Room   Outdoor Play Area   Garden Outdoor Eating   **Credit Cards:** Access, Amex, Diners, Visa*

IGHTHAM COMMON   ★   Harrow Inn

Common Road (off A25) TN15 9ER
Tel: (0732) 885912   **FOOD**
Open: 12-3, 6.30-11 (12-4, 7-10.30 Sun)
Licensee: Gerard Costelloe

Coloured lights around the door offer a welcome at this Virginia creeper-hung stone inn on a country lane. The small front bar is rather less salubrious, apparently denied sight of a paintbrush for several decades. A couple of stuffed birds in glass cases and old motor racing photos are mounted on the drab walls above dado pine panelling, and there's a pair of disreputable leather armchairs and a pool table in the room next door; the whole effect wobbles on the very fine line between characterful and seedy. Boxes of board games and newspapers laid out on a side table are a nice touch, and the new young landlord and his friendly staff soon dispel any doubts. Gerard Costelloe has an impressive catering background, and the cooking is excellent. Well-balanced soups arrive in large tureens from which one helps oneself, along with a whole freshly baked rye loaf on its own bread board. There are always a couple of pasta dishes, at least one of them vegetarian, as well as the likes of beef and sausage pie, which has good herby sausage and chunks of lean meat in rich gravy under a freshly baked pastry crust. It's worth saving a little space for pudding, like a classic summer pudding, properly made, its bread thoroughly soaked in the juice of soft fruits. The bars are not really suitable for children but they are welcome (particularly for Sunday lunch) in the cottagey restaurant, its conservatory extension complete with grape vine. The menu here tends to the somewhat more adventurous, a starter of avocado with coriander and red wine salad followed by John Dory with rhubarb and basil sauce typifying the style.

Bar Meals and Restaurant: *12-2.30 (2 pm bar, 3.30 restaurant Sun); restaurant closed Sun eve and all Mon; bar snacks both sessions* **Typical Dishes BAR:** *cabbage and marrow soup £1.95, kidneys and spinach £3.50, beef and stout pie £3.50, pasta Alfredo £4.95, baked trout and garlic £5.55, strudel £1.65* **RESTAURANT:** *leek and broccoli soup £2.10, mushrooms in sour cream £4, lamb fillet with lemon sauce £9.50, John Dory with rhubarb and basil £10.50, langoustines, lobster and prawns in cream £11, baked pears £2.85 Vegetarian Meals: tagliatelle* **Beer** *Elgoods; Shepherd Neame; Sussex Brewery Family Room (lunchtime) Garden Outdoor Eating* **Credit Cards:** *Access, Amex, Visa*

IVY HATCH   ★   Plough

Coach Road   TN15 0NL   `FOOD`
Tel: (0732) 810268
Open: 11-3, 6-11 (closed Sun eve)
Licensees: Keith Edwards and Gillian Ginzler

Quite apart from its outstandingly good cooking, the Plough is the kind of pub just about everyone would love to have as their local. A large mid 18th century roadside inn dominating this little hamlet, it's just enough off the beaten track, although well signposted. Within, it's peaceful and genuinely unspoilt, with dark pitch pine-lined walls and inky-dark polished furniture which glows mahogany in the light of a crackling log fire, and candlelight by night. By way of contrast, the conservatory dining extension, home to the justifiably well-regarded Le Chantecler restaurant, is light and fresh, with its soft pink linens, cane furniture and decorative greenery. But you don't have to opt for formal restaurant dining to enjoy excellent food at the Plough, because the bar food here is also a cut above the ordinary. From the blackboard listed menu, choose an excellently flavoured soup (the fish soup is particularly good), perhaps an airy, delicate flan with featherlight pastry- the mussel and asparagus tart especially memorable – or a mouthwatering pissaladière, finishing with a classic, tangy tarte au citron. Or stick patriotically to some good old English specialities: a broccoli and stilton soup, warming oxtail stew, game casserole, or liver and onions. Puddings, the same list shared by restaurant and bar, also cross the channel and back; perhaps a delicate crème brulée or, if the weather demands it, a richly satisfying baked Bramley apple. All show a lightness of touch and substantial skill. Tables can't be booked in the bar, so be early, or be patient. Note, too, that on Sunday lunchtimes the food choice may be very limited in the bar, while the restaurant is closed all day.

Bar Meals: *12-2.30, 7-10 (12-2 Sun, not Sun eve); bar snacks lunchtime* **Restaurant:** *12-2.30, 7-9.30 (no food Sun)* **Typical Dishes BAR:** *broccoli and stilton soup £2.50,* *smoked chicken and mango salad £4.95, venison casserole £8.95, whiting £7.50, avocado salad £5.95, tarte au citron* **RESTAURANT:** *bouillabaisse £4, smoked wild boar £4.50, roast mallard duck with oyster mushrooms, roast rack of lamb with rosemary and sage, paupiette of brill in dill sauce (main courses £12.50), baked Bramley apple £3.95 Vegetarian Meals: ratatouille Children's Portions* `Cheese` `Beer` *Brakspears; Marston; Whitbread Children Allowed in Bar to Eat Garden Outdoor Eating* **Credit Cards:** *Access, Visa*

IVY HATCH   Rose & Crown

Stone Street TN15 0LT
Tel: (0732) 810233
Open: 11.30-3, 6.30-12
Licensees: Luigi and Debbie Carugati

"We are not a stylish pub; people like it here because we are friendly, the atmosphere is comfortable, food is good and prices reasonable". It certainly gets very busy.

Bar Meals: *12-2, 7-9 (9.30 Fri/Sat); bar snacks both sessions* **Typical Dishes:** *home-made soup £1.30, smoked salmon £3.95, pasta of the day £3.50, escalope of veal £6.75, rack of lamb with Cumberland sauce £6.50, trifle £1.95 Vegetarian Meals: Mushroom piccant £2.75 Children's Portions* `Beer` *Harveys; Whitbread Children Allowed in Bar to Eat Outdoor Play Area Garden Outdoor Eating* **No Credit Cards**

KINGSGATE Fayreness Kingsgate Avenue: Gloriously set, right on the pretty beach, and gets very busy; worth being early for decent bar meals and tasty Youngs beers.

LAMBERHURST   Brown Trout

on B2169, near entrance to Scotney Castle   ❢
Tel: (0892) 890312
Open: 11-3, 6-11
Licensee: Joseph Stringer

Very well-known dining pub, loved for its fresh fish, bargain specials and relaxing atmosphere. Book well in advance for weekend treats; be early for a seat in the little bar, rather than the dining room extension. Lovely in summer.

Bar Meals: *11-2, 6-10* **Typical Dishes:** *moules marinière £3.20, Mediterranean garlic prawns £4.50, escalope of veal £5.80, crab and prawn pie £4.40, Dover sole £10, grilled trout £3.70 Vegetarian Meals Children's Portions* `Beer` *Marston; Whitbread Children Allowed in Bar to Eat Garden*

LARKFIELD Monks Head New Hythe Lane: 16th century, attractively old-fashioned pub just off the M20; a mix of the standard and special on the menu; Courage beers.

LINTON   Bull Inn

Linton Hill ME17 4AW
Tel: (0622) 743612
Open: 11.30-3, 6.30 (6 Thur-Sat)-11
Licensees: Pam and Dave Brown

If you love fresh fish, this is the pub for you. Delivered regularly from Rye, Hastings and Folkestone, the choice includes plaice, haddock, cod, brill and huss, whether grilled or fried in a good light batter. Other dishes on the menu include Scotch salmon, dressed crab, sautéed monkfish, fisherman's pie and skate wings. Lasagne, steak and kidney or shepherd's pie are on the menu for those who really don't want fish. Home-made apple crumble for pudding.

Bar Meals: 11.30-2.30, 7-9 (6.30-10 Thur-Sat); 12-2.15, 7-8.30 Sun   *Restaurant:* 12-2, 7-10.30 (no food Sun eve)   *Vegetarian Meals: mushroom stroganoff   Children's Portions*   **Beer**   *Whitbread   Children Allowed in Bar to Eat*   **Credit Cards:** *Access, Visa*

MARSHSIDE   Gate Inn
Chisley
Tel: (022 786) 498
Open: 11-2.30 (3 Sat), 6-11
Licensee: Christopher Smith

Delightfully set, with a duckpond in the garden. Indoors, it's rustic and wholly unpretentious, and prides itself on still being "a talkers's pub", in tandem with a thriving bar meal trade. Fresh, local produce is used to produce homely honest English fare, along with sandwiches, burgers and a famous black pudding. Free-range eggs and local vegetables are also sold over the bar. A good log fire in winter.

Bar Meals: all open hours; bar snacks   *Typical Dishes: home-made soup £1.10, prawns £1.40, sausage hotpot £3.25, home-boiled bacon ploughmans £2.50, bread pudding 95p   Vegetarian Meals: bean and pepper hotpot £3.25   Children's Portions*   **Beer**   *Shepherd Neame beers   Family Room   Outdoor Play Area   Riverside Garden   Outdoor Eating Summer Barbecue*   **No Credit Cards**

NEWNHAM   George Inn
44 The Street ME9 0LL   ❦
Tel: (079 589) 237
Open: 10.30-3 (12-2 Sun), 6-11
Licensee: Simon Barnes

Fine rugs on polished wood floors, exposed beams, open fires, evening candlelight, pretty flowers and a piano are a sample of the civilised ingredients at this lovely 16th century tile-hung pub, its large garden backing onto sheep pastures. The food is always imaginative and varied, and takes over the whole interior at mealtimes, as there's no separate dining or restaurant area. Children are "reluctantly" admitted for meals.

Bar Meals: 12-2 (1.30 Sun), 7.30-10 (no food Sun eve, nor all day Mon); bar snacks both sessions   *Typical Dishes: fish soup £2, baked avocado with smoked chicken au gratin £3.60, fillet steak with port and cream sauce £11.25, pot roast half shoulder of lamb with wine and redcurrant sauce £8.60, game pudding £6.25, well pudding £2.50   Vegetarian Meals: vegetable and stilton filo parcel £5*   **Beer**   *Shepherd Neame   Children Allowed in Bar to Eat   Outdoor Play Area   Garden   Outdoor Eating*   **No Credit Cards**

PLUCKLEY   Dering Arms
Station Road TN27 0RR   ❦
Tel: (023 384) 371
Open: 11-3, 6-11
Licensee: James Buss

Impressive manorial building, once the Dering Estate hunting lodge, with curving Dutch gables, rounded triple lancet 'Dering' windows, and a rather spooky grandeur. Within, many improvements are under way, and will continue well into 1992; let's hope the rustic simplicity will survive intact. Aside from the smart restauranty food listed here, there are one or two good homelier dishes like local trout and a daily pie.

Bar Meals: 12-2, 6.30-10; bar snacks both sessions **Typical Dishes:** *carrot, apple and chervil soup £1.85, avocado with stilton £2.25, chicken in port and green peppercorn sauce £8.45, monkfish with bacon and orange sauce £8.95, fillet of halibut meunière £8.95, chestnut and chocolate slice Vegetarian Meals: spinach and stilton pie £4.25 Children's Portions* Beer *Goachers; Shepherd Neame; Youngs* Cider *Biddenden Family Room Garden Outdoor Eating* **Accommodation:** *3 bedrooms, sharing a bathroom, from £36 (single £28) Children Welcome Overnight Check-in: by arrangement* **No Credit Cards**

PLUCKLEY Black Horse: Dering windows feature here too, at the cosy old village local, with settles, an open fire and generally well-heeled bar food; popular with business types at lunchtime. Marston, Whitbread beers.

ROCHESTER Greyhound 68 Rochester Avenue, Tel: (0634) 44120. Victorian back street local with chaises longues and a kitchen range in the saloon bar; also basic, noisy public. Homely snack food Mon–Sat lunchtime and evening: home-made pies, salads and ploughmans. Shepherd Neame Bitter. Open: 10–3, 6–11.

RUSTHALL   Red Lion

82 Lower Green Road TN4 8TW
Tel: (0892) 20086
Open: 11-3, 6-11
Licensees: Barry and Eileen Cooter

Licensed since 1415, with a characterful beamed bar and plush carpeted lounge. Very simple, good home cooking; less choice in the evening.

Bar Meals: 12.30-2, 7-10 (no food Sun); bar snacks both sessions **Typical Dishes:** *wild mushroom soup £1.25, garlic mushrooms with brandy and herb stuffing £1.75, savoury meat balls with hot curry sauce £2.50, gammon steak £3.55, goujons of plaice £3.50, chocolate nut sundae £1.50 Children's Portions* Beer *Marston Pedigree; Wadworth 6X; Whitbread Fremlins Bitter Children Allowed in Bar to Eat Garden Outdoor Eating* **No Credit Cards**

ST MARGARETS-AT-CLIFFE   Cliffe Tavern

High Street CT15 6AT
Tel: (0304) 852749
Open: 11-3 (flexible), 6-11
Licensee: C J Waring Westby

Long a favourite for its particular charm, the Cliffe Tavern is a 17th century series of Kentish clapboard buildings with a pretty walled garden, at the heart of the village. It's well liked for bed and breakfast particularly – most rooms are across the yard in cottages. Food is on the up now, with the introduction of a daily changing blackboard menu, and more imaginative dishes. Soups have come in for particular praise. An excellent stop-over on the way to Dover ferries.

Bar Meals: 12-2, 7-10; bar snacks both sessions **Typical Dishes:** *carrot, orange and coriander soup £1.90, spinach, garlic and brie puffs £2.70, chicken breast with tarragon and cream £5.90, chicken and mushroom pie £4.25, fresh lemon sole £8.50, home-made* *chocolate roulade £2.50   Vegetarian Meals: aubergine and bean goulash £4.95   Children's Portions*   **Beer**   *Adnams Bitter; Ruddles County; Shepherd Neame Master Brew Bitter Family Room   Garden   Outdoor Eating*   **Accommodation:** *12 bedrooms, all en suite, from £72 (single £45)   Children Welcome Overnight   Cot Available   Check-in: all day*   **Credit Cards:** *Access, Amex, Diners, Visa*

SANDGATE   Ship

65 High Street CT20 3AH
Tel: (0303) 48525
Open: 11-3, 6-11
Licensee: Stewart Whiffin

Attractive street-corner gabled local which looks as if it might be about to put to sea. Unchanged within since the early 1950s; good beer, popular home-cooked pies. No home-made puddings, though.

Bar Meals: *12-2.15, 6-9; bar snacks both sessions*   **Typical Dishes:** *home-made tomato soup £1.30, steak in ale pastry pie £3.95, fishermans pie £3.95, potato moussaka £3.50 Vegetarian Meals: cauliflower cheese £3.20*   **Beer**   *Ind Coope; Ringwood; Wadworth*   **Cider**   *Addlestones   Patio/terrace   Outdoor Eating*   **No Credit Cards**

SMARDEN   Bell

Bell Lane TN26 8PW   ❢
Tel: (0233) 77283
Open: 11.30-2.30, 6-11
Licensee: Ian Turner

Tiled and rose-covered medieval Kentish inn in peaceful countryside (take the road between the church and Chequers pub, then left at the junction). The usually very busy, rustic interior has hop-festooned oak beams and inglenook fireplaces in three flagstoned bars; candlelight in the evenings. Bar food is reliable. A narrow outside spiral staircase leads to four cottagey bedrooms furnished in solid period style. Continental breakfasts only, served in rooms.

Bar Meals: *12-2, 6.30-10; bar snacks both sessions*   **Typical Dishes:** *home-made soup £1.40, clam fries £2.10, Greek shepherds pie £3.15, chicken tikka salad £4.85, steak and kidney pie £4.45, chocolate crunch cake   Vegetarian Meals: home-made pizza Children's Portions*   **Beer**   *Fullers; Goachers; Harvey; Shepherd Neame*   **Cider**   *Biddenden   Family Room   Outdoor Play Area   Garden   Outdoor Eating*   **Accommodation:** *4 bedrooms, sharing 2 bathrooms, from £28 (single £18)   Children Welcome Overnight   Check-in: by arrangement*   **Credit Cards:** *Access, Visa*

SMARDEN   Chequers Inn

1 The Street TN27 8QA
Tel: (0233) 77217
Open: 10-2.30, 6-11
Licensees: Frank and Frances Stevens

14th century weatherboarded pub with real fires and ghosts, run by the Stevens family for 22 years. Decent bar food runs from the simplest snacks to things with chips and the restauranty dishes listed here. Fresh vegetables.

Bar Meals: *12-2.30, 7-10; bar snacks both sessions*   **Typical Dishes:** *home-made soup £1.95, terrine of smoked salmon £3.95, crispy roast duckling curacao £8.95, English lamb* cutlet with rosemary £8.75, baked red mullet with orange and anchovy £6.75, date and ginger pudding with toffee sauce £2.95   Vegetarian Meals: quorn provencale £5.75 Children's Portions   `Beer`   Courage Best, Directors, John Smith's Bitter   `Whisky` Children Allowed in Bar to Eat   Outdoor Play Area   Garden   Outdoor Eating **Accommodation:** 7 bedrooms, sharing 2 bathrooms, from £31 (single £19)   Children Welcome Overnight   Cots Available   Check-in: all day   **Credit Cards:** Access, Visa

---

SPELDHURST   George & Dragon

Speldhurst Hill, Tunbridge Wells TN3 0NN   ☻
Tel: (089 286) 3125
Open: 11-3, 6-11
Licensees: Iain Murray and Christopher Plumpton

New wine merchant owners of this well-loved ancient timbered landmark have put in newish managers, and the menu has changed; the stunningly attractive first floor restaurant, once extremely expensive and smart, is now looking fairly average in price (no reports on food, though). There's a new £10.50/£13.50 table d'hote. The wine list is, unsurprisingly, looking particularly strong.

Bar Meals: 12-2.15; 7-10; bar snacks both sessions   **Restaurant:** 12-2 (not Mon/Sat), 7-10 (not Sun)   **Typical Dishes BAR:** carrot, orange and ginger soup £1.95, grilled sardines £3.95, pork casserole £4.75, cottage pie £3.50, grilled plaice with prawns and capers £4.75, apple cake £2.50   **RESTAURANT:** seafood soup £3.50, quail's eggs £3.95, rack of lamb £8.95, mock wild boar £10.45, roast pheasant £11.25   Vegetarian Meals: terrine   `Beer` Fullers; Harveys   Family Room   Garden   Outdoor Eating   **Credit Cards:** Access, Visa

---

TUNBRIDGE WELLS   Sankeys at the Gate

39 Mount Ephraim TN4 8AA   ☻
Tel: (0892) 511422
Open: 12-3, 6-11 (closed Sun)
Licensee: Guy Sankey

Well-known Tunbridge Wells perennial, created by Guy Sankey from an old engineering works in a solid late Victorian house. The 'bar' is really more of an informal seafood restaurant; there's also a restaurant area proper, which will be entirely separate after 1992 remodelling, when the bar will also expand into the cellar. The menu changes daily. Good cheeses.

Bar Meals: 12-2, 7-10; bar snacks both sessions   **Typical Dishes:** Gate fish soup £3.50, smoked eel £3.50, seafood paella £10, cold salmon salad £5.50, monkfish roasted with garlic £11.50, home-made puddings £3.50   `Cheese`   `Beer`   Harveys PA   `Whisky` Children Allowed in Bar to Eat   Garden   **Credit Cards:** Access, Amex, Visa

---

ULCOMBE   Pepper Box

Fairbourne Heath ME17 1LP   `FOOD`
Tel: (0622) 842558   ☼
Open: 11-3, 6.30-11
Licensees: Geoff and Sarah Pemble

The Pepper Box is a cottagey pub with low eaves and white-painted stone walls, surrounded by fields of corn. Dating back to the 15th century, it was once the haunt of smugglers and takes its name (apparently unique) from their favourite weapon, the Pepper Box pistol. A three-piece suite takes pride of place in front of an inglenook fireplace in the beamed bar, and old pewter mugs – some belonging to regular customers – hang above the bar counter along with decorative hopbines. A Shepherd Neame–owned house, the tenancy has been in the same family since 1958 with Sarah and Geoff Pemble currently providing the hospitable welcome. Fresh fish is one of the highlights of a bar menu that also includes a creamy chicken curry in which a touch of sweetness nicely tames the spiciness, along with the likes of ham, egg and chips, and Kent Korker sausages. Bought-in puddings are displayed in a cold cabinet. The same menu is also available in the small dining room, with its oak tables and wood-burning Aga, by prior reservation. Children are not allowed inside the pub, but they are welcome in the large, pretty garden, which has swings and a tree house. There's a short but varied list of wines, and the Shepherd Neame ales are drawn direct from barrels behind the bar.

Bar Meals: 12-2, 7-10 (no food Sun); bar snacks lunchtime   *Typical Dishes: curried parsnip soup £1.50, port and stilton paté £3, poached salmon hollandaise £6, Somerset chicken pie £5, Oriental stir-fry £4.80, spicy bread pudding £1.80   Vegetarian Meals: lasagne £3.50   Children's Portions* **Beer** *Shepherd Neame beers   Outdoor Play Area Garden   Outdoor Eating* **No Credit Cards**

WARREN STREET   Harrow Inn
near Lenham, Maidstone ME17 2ED
Tel: (0622) 858727
Open: 11.30-2.30, 7-11
Licensees: Alan Cole and Sheila Burns

Once a rest-house for Canterbury pilgrims, now a converted and refurbished downland inn not far from the M2 motorway. Simple cushioned chairs and stools around little tables in the lounge bar, much used for dining, plus a separate restaurant overlooking the garden. Food is reliably good. Good bed and breakfast, too, some of the rooms being especially large and cluttered with comforts. All are now en suite, and 10 of them are 'family rooms'.

Bar Meals and Restaurant: 12-2, 7-10 (9.30 Sun); bar snacks both sessions   *Typical Dishes BAR: home-made soup £1.95, mushrooms in wine, stilton and cream £2.55, chicken with garlic, cucumber and cream £7.25, lamb fillet topped with banana in a light curry sauce £7.95, seafood pancakes in lobster and brandy sauce £7, mango bavarois £2.50* **RESTAURANT:** *chicken liver with apples, shallots and Calvados £2.95, magret of duck with black cherries and Tia Maria £12.95, fillet of salmon in orange and Cointreau sauce £10.25, trout stuffed with prawns and crabmeat £9.95, strawberry malakoff £3.25 Vegetarian Meals: vegetable stir-fry £6.75   Children's Menu/Portions* **Beer** *Ruddles County; Shepherd Neame; Wadworth 6X* **Cider** *Biddenden   Children Allowed in Bar to Eat   Outdoor Play Area   Garden   Outdoor Eating* **Accommodation:** *15 bedrooms, all en suite, from £58 (single £45)   Children Welcome Overnight   Cots Available Check-in: all day* **Credit Cards:** *Access, Visa*

WEALD   Chequer Tree
Scabharbour Road TN14 6WL
Tel: (0732) 463386
Open: 11.30-3, 6-11
Licensee: John Leonard Pocknell

Roomy, modernised, tidy country pub with a lovely and varied garden.

Bar Meals and Restaurant: 12-3, 7-10; bar snacks both sessions   *Typical Dishes BAR: home-made soup £1.50, grilled sardines £2.25, steak and kidney pie £4.50, lasagne £3.50, curry £4, gateau Diane* **RESTAURANT:** *similar starters; asparagus chicken £7.50, steaks from £7.75, skate in cider £7   Vegetarian Meals: cauliflower cheese*

Children's Portions   **Beer**   Ruddles Best, County; Webster's Yorkshire Bitter   Children
Allowed in Bar to Eat   Outdoor Play Area   Garden   Outdoor Eating   Summer Barbecue
Credit Cards: Access, Amex, Diners, Visa

WORTH   St Crispin Inn

The Street CT14 0DF
Tel: (0304) 612081
Open: 11-2.30, 6-11
Licensees: Randolph Tillings and Jefferey Lenham

Refurbished village pub with heavy timbers, brick walls, a big log fire and a pleasant
rear garden. The small dining room shares the bar menu; there's also a carvery and
char-grill. A new rear terrace has an all-weather retractable awning.

Bar Meals: 12-2.15, 6-9.30; bar snacks both sessions   **Typical Dishes:** tomato and
stilton soup £1.20, garlic mushrooms £2.95, chicken breasts in stilton sauce £5.95, char-

grilled halibut £4.95, char-grilled giant prawns £6.25   Vegetarian Meals: pasta £3.25
Children's Menu/Portions   **Beer**   Gales HSB; Marston Pedigree, Merrie Monk;
Shepherd Neame Master Brew Bitter   **Whisky**   **Cider**   Theobalds Barn   Children
Allowed in Bar to Eat   Outdoor Play Area   Garden   Outdoor Eating   Summer Barbecue
Accommodation: 7 bedrooms, all en suite, from £40 (single £28)   Children Welcome
Overnight   Check-in: by arrangement   **Credit Cards:** Access, Visa

LANCASHIRE

BAMBER BRIDGE   Olde Hob Inn

8 Church Road PR5 6EP
Tel: (0772) 36863
Open: 11.30-3, 5.30-11
Licensees: David and Evelyn Greenough

Family-run 17th century thatched coaching inn near junction 29 of the M6, and as
such a useful stop-off. Separate dining room/restaurant.

Bar Meals: 12-2, 6-9 (10 Sat; not Sun eve); bar snacks both sessions   **Typical Dishes:**
broth £1, garlic mushrooms £1.75, turkey steak biryani £3.50, chilli con carne £3.50,
rainbow trout £3.75, apple and blackcurrant pie   Vegetarian Meals: chilli vegetables
Children's Menu/Portions   **Beer**   Matthew Brown, Theakston   Family Room   Garden
Outdoor Eating   **Credit Cards:** Access, Visa

BILSBORROW   Owd Nells

Canalside, St Michaels Road (A6) PR3 0RS
Tel: (0995) 40010
Open: all day (inc. Sun)
Licensee: Roy Wilkinson

Part of an unusual mini leisure complex called Guy's Thatched Hamlet, which aims
its good value food and overnight accommodation at passing business traffic. A
nicely furnished, traditionally styled modern pub by the canal. Very generous
portions; it's fine just to pop in for a starter and a drink.

Bar Meals: 11-8.30 (snacks 8.30-10.30); bar snacks all day   **Restaurant:** 12-3, 6-12
(all day Sun and Bank Holidays)   **Typical Dishes BAR:** country broth £1.15, paté

£2.35, home-made steak and kidney pudding £3.95, hot roast beef sandwich £3, large fish and chips £3.95, apple pie £1.60   **RESTAURANT:** *minestrone £1.60, stilton fritters £2.75, sirloin on the bone £9.25, chicken à la creme £8.30, banana crepe £2.60 Vegetarian Meals: quiche   Children's Menu*   ~~Beer~~   *Fullers; Hartleys; Whitbread   Family Room   Outdoor Play Area   Canalside Garden   Outdoor Eating*   **Accommodation:** *32 bedrooms, all en suite, from £39.15 (single £34.65)   Children Welcome Overnight   Cots Available   Check-in: all day*   **Credit Cards:** *Access, Amex, Visa*

BLACKO   Moorcock Inn

Gisburn Road BB9 6NF   ▐ FOOD ▌
Tel: (0282) 64186   ☼
Open: 12-2.30, 7-12 (supper extension) 12-11 Sun
Licensees: Elizabeth and Peter Holt

Standing on its own, alongside the A682 north of Blacko, the whitewashed Moorcock Inn overlooks wonderful rolling countryside. Inside is unassuming and unpretentious. Two adjoining rooms have plain painted walls, simple prints, brass plates and a collection of china plates; stone fireplaces are topped with ornaments and brassware. All the tables are laid for dining, surrounded by upholstered bench seating and simple wooden chairs, a style continued in the large adjoining dining room. Large picture windows in both rooms offer lovely views over the surrounding landscape. Licensees Elizabeth and Peter Holt have built up an enviable reputation for good fresh food, and custom comes from far and wide. The printed menu is backed up by a daily changing specials board, where dishes could include a home-made game pie, seafood pasta, or fresh fillets of lemon sole, filled with crab meat and covered with a rich cheese sauce. The printed menu travels around the world: vegetable biryani alongside bratwurst with sauerkraut, schweinschnitzel and goulash. Beside these, the menu covers tried and trusted pub favourites like steak and kidney pie or lasagne, and a good selection of vegetarian dishes. Cooking is perfectly competent, without ever being spectacular; prices realistic, portions generous, service friendly and quick. The Moorcock's a useful resting place after a bracing morning on the moors; the Pendle Walk almost passes the door, and in sunny weather the garden is lovely.

Bar Meals: *12-2.30, 7-10.30; bar snacks both sessions*   **Typical Dishes:** *home-made soup and French bread £1.50, garlic prawns £3.75, whole spring chicken with barbecue sauce £4.25, whole ham shank in mustard sauce with sauté potatoes and sauerkraut £4.75, halibut mornay in shrimp sauce £5.25, apple and strawberry pie £1.75   Vegetarian Meals: stuffed peppers   Children's Portions*   ▐ Beer ▌   *Thwaites   Family Room   Garden*   **No Credit Cards**

BLACKSNAPE Red Lion. Popular dining pub on old Roman road; informal home cooking includes their own pizzas.

BOLTON BY BOWLAND   Coach and Horses

20 Main Street BB7 4NW
Tel: (02007) 202
Open: 11.30-3 (not Tue), 7-11
Licensees: Cliff and Sheila Ferguson

Pretty, well-run pub in glorious spot, with coal fires and simple home-cooking. Very busy summer weekends. Dining room.

Bar Meals: *12-2, 7.30-10; bar snacks both sessions*   **Typical Dishes:** *hot garlic prawns £3.95, Cumberland sausage £3.95, beef in ale £3.95, gammon special topped with cheese,* *pineapple and tomato £4.25, summer fruit trifle £1.95   Vegetarian Meals: stir-fry vegetables in a red pepper case   Children's Portions*   **Beer**   *Whitbread Boddingtons Mild, Bitter, Castle Eden Ale   Family Room   Patio/terrace   Outdoor Eating   **Accommodation:** 3 bedrooms, sharing a bathroom, from £30 (single £15)   Children Welcome Overnight Cot Available   Check-in: all day   **No Credit Cards***

CHORLEY Market Tavern, Cleveland Street: Characterful pub with four old fashioned little bars, real fire and no music. Local black puddings are the highlight of the lunchtime menu. Ind Coope beers. Open: 11-4, 7-11.

CHURCHTOWN   Punchbowl Inn

Church Street PR3 0HT
Tel: (0995) 603360
Open: 11.30-3, 6-11
Licensee: David Robert Singleton

Partly 15th century pub in pretty village. Coal and log fires in the several cosy bar areas. Aberdeen Angus beef is used in the meat pies. Specials board. Open all day for meals Sunday.

Bar Meals and Restaurant: 11.30-2, 6-10; bar snacks both sessions   Typical Dishes: beef and vegetable soup £1.25, garlic mushrooms £2.25, steak and kidney pie £5.25, Lincolnshire-style sausages £4.20, halibut steak £6.50, cranachan £1.85   Vegetarian Meals   Children's Portions   **Beer**   *Tetley Bitter; Whitbread Boddingtons Bitter   Family Room   Patio/terrace   Outdoor Eating   Credit Cards: Access, Visa*

CLITHEROE   Craven Heifer

Chipping Road BB7 3LX
Tel: (0254) 826215
Open: 12-3, 7-11
Licensee: Alan Wallbank

Well-organised Ribble Valley local. Same menu in dining room.

Bar Meals: 12-2, 7-9.30; bar snacks both sessions   Typical Dishes: home-made soup £1.50, ham and gruyère £3.75, sirloin steak £7.95, roast duckling £7.25, Chaigley pie £6.50, puddings (all home-made) £2   Vegetarian Meals: vegetable lasagne £4.95   Children's Portions   **Beer**   *Tetley Bitter*   **Whisky**   *Family Room   Credit Cards: Access, Visa*

DARWEN   Old Rosins Inn

Treacle Row, Pickup Bank BB3 3QD
Tel: (0254) 771264
Open: all day
Licensee: Bryan Hankinson

18th century inn set in open moorland with panoramic views.

Bar Meals: all day; also bar snacks   Restaurant: 12-2, 7-10   Typical Dishes BAR: country vegetable soup £1, garlic mushrooms £1.75, home-made chicken tikka £4, beef in Old Peculier £3.75, braised steak and onions £4, bread and butter pudding £1.60   RESTAURANT: stilton and celery soup £2.25, fresh game terrine £4.75, braised local lamb £9.75, trio of fillets (pork, beef, lamb) £11.95, parcels of brill fillet £8.95, home-made ice-cream £2.25   Vegetarian Meals: kebabs   Children's Menu/Portions   **Beer**

Theakston Old Peculier; Taylor Landlord; Whitbread Boddingtons Bitter, Flowers IPA **Whisky** *Outdoor Play Area   Patio/terrace   Outdoor Eating*   **Accommodation:** *15 bedrooms, all en suite, from £45 (single £35)   Children Welcome Overnight   Cots Available   Check-in: all day*   **Credit Cards:** *Access, Amex, Diners, Visa*

DOWNHAM   Assheton Arms

near Clitheroe BB7 4BJ
Tel: (0200) 41227
Open: 12-3, 7-11
Licensee: David Busby

The focal point of this unspoilt stone-built old estate village. An opened-up, red-carpeted bar has attractive furnishings and window seats. You can hire the holiday cottage next door by the week.

Bar Meals: *12-2, 7-10; bar snacks both sessions*   **Typical Dishes:** *ham and vegetable broth £1.45, deep-fried brie and Lancashire cheese £2.90, steak and kidney pie £4.50, pan-fried sirloin in garlic mushroom sauce £8.75, scampi provencale £9.25, spotted dick £1.75 Vegetarian Meals: cauliflower and mushroom provencale £4.50   Children's Menu/Portions* **Beer** *Marston Pedigree; Whitbread Bentleys, Castle Eden Ale   Children Allowed in Bar to Eat   Patio/terrace   Outdoor Eating*   **Credit Cards:** *Access, Visa*

EUXTON   Euxton Mills

Wigan Road PR7 6JD
Tel: (0257) 264002
Open: 11.30-3, 5.30 (6.15 Sat)-11
Licensees: Brian and Maureen Dowd

18th century low-beamed pub which buys most of its food locally. The five daily roasts are the biggest seller. A choice of freshly made chips/boiled/roasted/jacket potatoes and two fresh vegetables accompany all main course meals.

Bar Meals: *12-2, 6 (6.15 Sat)-9.30 (7-9 Sun); bar snacks both sessions*   **Typical Dishes:** *pea and ham soup 95p, local black pudding with fried onions £1.50, hot roast meat, huge mixed grill, deep-fried breaded plaice (main courses from £3), home-made apple pie Vegetarian Meals: quiche   Children's Portions* **Beer** *Burtonwood   Children Allowed in Bar to Eat   Patio/terrace   Outdoor Eating*   **No Credit Cards**

FLEETWOOD   North Euston Hotel

Esplanade FY7 6BN
Tel: (0253) 876525
Open: 11-3.30, 6-11
Licensee: T W Cowpe

Listed for its popular Fleetwood Fish and Chips (£3.10); there are also sandwiches, soup and bought-in puddings in the bar; £8.50 table d'hote or à la carte in the restaurant. It's a large pubby bar within this Victorian crescent hotel, by the Blackpool tram terminus. Good views of ships and Lake District hills; jazz band on Wednesdays.

Bar Meals: *12-2; bar snacks*   **Restaurant:** *12.30-2, 7-9.30 (8.30 Sun)   Children's Portions* **Beer** *Bass; Ruddles; Webster's* **Whisky** *Family Room*   **Accommodation:** *56 bedrooms, all en suite, from £58 (single £40)   Children Welcome Overnight   Cots Available   Check-in: all day*   **Credit Cards:** *Access, Amex, Diners, Visa*

GARSTANG Th'Owd Tithe Barn off Church Street: Ethnic Lancastrian, complete with waitresses in mob caps; an attractively converted barn, with farmhouse parlour style dining room. Decent if unexciting bar food; no real ale. Open: 11-3, 7 (6 Sat)-11; closed Mon.

GARSTANG Wheatsheaf. Locally very popular for its genuinely unspoilt, creaky cottagey atmosphere and often interesting lunchtime and evening food.

GISBURN   White Bull

Main Street BB7 4HE
Tel: (0200) 445233
Open: 11-3, 6-11
Licensees: Rosie and Clive Lee

18th century pub on A59, buy the foot of Pendle Hill, of Pendle Witches fame. Fish and seafood are the speciality in the restaurant.

Bar Meals: 11.30-2.30, 6.30-9; bar snacks both sessions **Restaurant:** *12-2, 7-10*
Typical Dishes BAR: carrot and lentil soup £1.95, crab paté £2.75, lamb rogan josh £4.95, steak and mushroom pie £4.25, fresh haddock and chips £3.65, bread and butter pudding **RESTAURANT:** *broccoli and bacon soup £1.95, sweet and sour tiger tail prawns £3.95, steak and stilton carpetbag £7.95, pollo gamberretti £6.95, spinach tagliatelle and king prawns £5.65 Vegetarian Meals: asparagus and stilton au gratin Children's Menu/Portions* **Beer** *Whitbread Boddingtons Family Room Children Allowed in Bar to Eat Outdoor Play Area Garden Outdoor Eating* **Credit Cards:** *Access, Visa*

GOOSNARGH   Bushells Arms

Church Lane PR3 2BH   FOOD
Tel: (0772) 865235
Open: 12-3, 6-11
Licensees: David and Glynis Best

Just 4 miles from Junction 32 of the M6, this modernised Georgian building offers a splendid alternative to the expensive plastic food of the motorway service areas. To reach the pub, follow the A6 North and turn onto the B5269; once in the village, take the left turn opposite the post office, and you'll find the Bushells Arms about a quarter of a mile along on the right. It's run by the experienced David and Glynis Best, who have written a book on the business side of pub catering, using much of their own experience. Certainly the food at the Bushells is first rate: cooking is in the hands of Glynis, who produces a long, wide and cosmopolitan selection of specials, blackboard-listed behind the food counter, as well as those on the distinguished printed menu . An interest in what she describes as other countries' peasant dishes might typically materialise in a South Indian egg and prawn curry, a rich Greek beef stew or Lebanese kaftka, a delicious dish of mince, spiced and heavily flavoured with mint, topped with tomato and glazed with cheese: basically very simple, but with strong and exotic combinations of flavours. British dishes aren't forgotten either: a steak, kidney and Murphy's pie and a liver, onion, sausage and bacon casserole are both admirably handled. There are fine accompaniments, too, like O'Brien potatoes, a delicious mix of diced potato with cream, peppers, spices, garlic and parmesan cheese. Great care and enthusiasm are evident throughout, and the short wine list is constantly being reviewed. The interior of the pub itself is cleverly divided into a number of alcoves and bays using effective wooden screens and exposed sandstone columns and walls. There's also lots of greenery, not all of it real. Seating is mainly on plush red upholstered button banquettes and stools, arranged around unfussy wooden tables, and a couple of the areas are non-smoking. Brasses and watercolours in a real mix of styles hang on the walls, and there's piped music. To the rear is a well-maintained garden with white plastic patio furniture, useful in summer when the pub gets extremely busy. Staff are noticeably welcoming and friendly. The village, incidentally, is pronounced Goozner.

Bar Meals: *12-2.30, 7-10; bar snacks lunchtime* **Typical Dishes:** *lovage soup £1, falafel £1.80, stifatho £5.50, chicken Olympus £5.50, luxury fish pie £5, 18th century chocolate and rum pie £1.75* *Vegetarian Meals: vegetable pastie £4* *Children's Menu* **Beer** *Whitbread Boddingtons Bitter* *Children Allowed in Bar to Eat* *Garden Outdoor Eating* **No Credit Cards**

GOOSNARGH Horns. Outside the village, close by Bleasdale Fell: warm and comfortable old pub; simple home cooking.

LANESHAW BRIDGE Alma Inn, Emmott Lane: Nice country inn half a mile from the village; home cooking lunch and evening; real fire; garden. Ind Coope, Tetley beers. Open: 11.30-3, 6.30-11; meals served all day Sunday.

LITTLE ECCLESTON   Cartford Country Inn & Hotel

Cartford Lane
Tel: (0995) 70166
Open: 12-3, 7-11 (opens a little earlier summer)

Prettily located on the river Wyre, and it makes the most of it in the balcony dining area. Lots of character and comfort within, and a hectic weekend food trade, as well as in the evening, when pizzas are popular. They also do bedrooms (no details).

Bar Meals: *lunchtime and evening; bar snacks both sessions* **Typical Dishes:** *leek and potato soup, home-made steak pie, lots of curries, seven sorts of pizza (main courses from £3.50)* *Vegetarian Meals: pizza/curry* *Children's Menu* **Beer** *Marston; Moorhouse's; Taylor; Whitbread* *Family Room* *Garden*

ORMSKIRK Buck i'th'Vine 35 Burscough Street, Tel: (0695) 72647. Simple home cooking (Tue-Sat lunchtime) of the chilli con carne sort, in historic, nook and cranny-filled pedestrian street pub, with a unique sweetshop window bar counter; family room; attractive garden. Walkers beers. Open: 11.30-3, 5.30-11 (all day Thur-Sat).

SLAIDBURN   Hark to Bounty

Slaidburn, just off B6478 BB7 3EP   `B&B`
Tel: (02006) 246   ☀
Open: all day
Licensee: Linda Smith

Inspiring countryside, seemingly untouched by progress, surrounds the picturesque village of Slaidburn, a solidly rural village full of stone buildings and narrow streets. Just off the main road, the Hark to Bounty dates back to the 13th century, built from the same sombre local stone. Its most interesting feature is an original first floor courtroom, for many years the main court between Lancaster and York, and still in use until 1937. Nowadays it's used as a function room, complete with old jury benches and witness box, now a bar counter. The main bar is, oddly, rather lacking in character. One long room, with rough-painted walls and rustic wooden tables and chairs, it's rather overly-spartan in style, but has an open fireplace adorned with polished brass and copperware, and a few heavy beams cross the ceiling. A standard bar menu offers dishes like

Cumberland sausage, quarter of roast duck with ginger, or Forest of Bowland casserole, a frankly disappointing dish of local venison, rabbit and pigeon (all overdone) in an overly rich, salty sauce. Daily changing specials are blackboard listed: perhaps roast guinea fowl, chicken chasseur, poached salmon or halibut. Foodwise, puddings are probably the highlight – a lemon and ginger crunch was nice – but overall, food is let down by careless cooking. There's also a small restaurant. Upstairs, seven en suite bedrooms (one with shower only) are cottagey in style, with floral curtains and bedspreads, creaking floorboards, exposed beams, and furniture which varies from modern fitted units to period pieces. Bathrooms are carpeted, but rather dimly lit; many baths also have showers. To the rear of the inn, a sheltered garden, with wooden tables and bench seating, leads down to the pretty little river.

Bar Meals and Restaurant: 12-2, 6 (7 restaurant)-9; bar snacks both sessions **Typical Dishes** *BAR: home-made soup £1.40, garlic mushrooms £2.60, Cumberland sausage £3.90, home-made steak and kidney pie £4, Forest of Bowland casserole £4.75, lemon and ginger crunch £1.90* **RESTAURANT:** *herb-marinated salmon £3.50, roast duckling £9, baked local ham £8, Bowland trout £7.50* **Vegetarian Meals:** *Yorkshire pudding with leek and mushroom sauce* **Children's Portions** ▮Beer▮ *Theakston* ▮Whisky▮ *Children Allowed in Bar to Eat   Outdoor Play Area   Riverside Garden   Outdoor Eating   Summer Barbecue* **Accommodation:** *8 bedrooms, all en suite, from £40 (single £20)* **Children Welcome Overnight   Cots Available   Check-in: all day** ***Credit Cards:*** *Access, Amex, Visa*

TARLETON   Cock & Bottle

70 Church Road PR4 6UP
Tel: (0772) 812258
Open: 11-3 (12-2.30 Sun), 5-11
Licensee: C Bayliff

Refreshingly, the licensees admit there's no historical interest on offer here – just decent food made from all fresh ingredients, with some unusual dishes included on the daily changing menu. Fresh fish delivered every day.

Bar Meals: 12-2, 6-10 (12-2.30, 5-10 Sun); bar snacks both sessions **Typical Dishes:** *tomato and basil soup £1.10, seafood noodles £3.45, beef stroganoff £8.95, various pasta dishes £4.50, various daily specials from £7.45, chocolate roly poly* **Vegetarian Meals:** *vegetable risotto* **Children's Menu/Portions** ▮Beer▮ *Thwaites Mild, Bitter* **Children Allowed in Bar to Eat   Outdoor Play Area   Garden   Outdoor Eating** ***Credit Cards:*** *Access, Visa*

THORNLEY Derby Arms Chipping Lane. Lovely views of Longridge Fell from this solidly stone-built and old-fashioned country pub; decent lunchtime and evening bar meals. Family room. Greenalls beers. Open: 11-3, 6-11.

TOCKHOLES Black Bull Brokenstones Road, Livesey. Views across fine walking country from popular dining pub; routine food includes home-cooked pizzas. **Rock Inn:** Cosy, countrified pub with good daily specials and other decent lunchtime and evening dishes (not Monday). Both pubs have Thwaites beers.

WEST BRADFORD   Three Millstones

Waddington Road BB7 5SX
Tel: (0200) 23340
Open: 12-3, 7-11

Old coaching inn close to the river Ribble, in a historic village. There's a view of Pendle Hill from the beer garden. Nice atmosphere; good hotpots.

Bar Meals: 12-2, 7-9.30; bar snacks both sessions   **Typical Dishes:** vegetable soup £1.10, herrings in curry sauce £1.95, home-made steak and kidney plate pie £4.60, spicy beef pot £4.25, fresh salmon steak £4.25, sticky toffee pudding £1.75   Vegetarian Meals: vegetable stroganoff   Children's Menu   ▣ Beer ▣   Theakston Best, Old Peculier   Family Room   Outdoor Play Area   Garden   Outdoor Eating   Summer Barbecue   **Credit Cards:** Access, Visa

---

WHITEWELL	Inn at Whitewell

Forest of Bowland BB7 3AT	FOOD
Tel: (02008) 222	☻
Open: 11-3, 6-11	❗
Licensee: Richard Bowman	B&B ☼

Well away from the hurly burly, the Whitewell Inn stands next to the village church, overlooking the river Hodder (and owns five miles of fishing rights) in the beautiful, unspoilt countryside of the little-known Forest of Bowland. Back in the 14th century, the inn was home to the keeper of the King's deer, and the Queen still owns the building as part of the Duchy of Lancaster. Inside, it's wonderfully relaxed, laid-back, even, some would say, mildly eccentric – with a haphazard arrangement of furnishings and bric-a-brac. In the main bar there are wooden tables, old settles, roundback chairs, a stone fireplace, log burning in cold weather, and heavy ceiling beams. An entrance hall has colourful rugs, more settles, even a piano, and a selection of magazines, papers and books for some serious loitering. A wide variety of pictures, dotted about the building, come from the inn's own art gallery space; there's also a small wine merchant business, as well as expensive sweaters and hunting gear in the shop. Food is served in both the bar and restaurant, which overlooks the river; the bar meal selection follows the tried and trusted steak sandwich/seafood pancake/steak and mushroom pie formula, from mostly fresh, local produce, and is decently rather than excitingly cooked. More ambitious cooking – sometimes overly so – is at work in the restaurant, where local ingredients include fish from this very river. Grilled king scallops, cooked a little too early, had hardened on top, but the fillet of Wensleydale wild boar, though a little tough, had good gamey flavour, with a splendid juniper sauce (not enough). Vegetables were disappointingly overdone, however. Calorific puddings like sticky toffee; a good wine list; casual service, rather too unhurried at times. Bedrooms have shrunk from eleven to nine, and are undergoing some impressive refurbishments, each room individually styled, with pretty fabrics, antique furnishings and a good mix of pictures. Unusual extras include video recorders and superb Bang and Olufson stereo systems, as well as books, magazines, and a set of binoculars: the best and largest rooms overlook the river and the country beyond. Bathrooms are also now given individual treatment, three of them with rather fine Victorian baths, as well as shower attachments. Everything is immaculately clean. On sunny days, the attractive rear lawn, furnished with simple benches, is an ideal spot to relax and soak in the view.

Bar Meals: 12-2, 7.15-9.30; bar snacks both sessions   **Restaurant:** 7.30-9.30   **Typical Dishes BAR:** watercress soup £1.30, duck liver paté £3.50, steak and kidney pie £5.20, Cumberland sausage £5, fishermans pie £5.60, bread and butter pudding £2   **RESTAURANT** dinner menu £18.50: potato and wild garlic soup, timbale of sole, smoked trout and saffron, fillet of Bowland lamb with a mint mousse, fillet of Wensleydale wild boar, pan-fried sea bass and scallops, summer pudding   Vegetarian Meals: leek and potato pie £4   Children's Portions   ▣ Cheese ▣   ▣ Beer ▣   Moorhouses Premier Bitter, Pendle Witches Brew   Family Room   Riverside Garden   Outdoor Eating   **Accommodation:** 9 bedrooms, all en suite, from £57 (single £43)   Children Welcome Overnight   Cots Available   Check-in: all day   **Credit Cards:** Access, Amex, Diners, Visa

WRIGHTINGTON BAR High Moor Inn, High Moor Lane: Popular dining pub; decent meals, fresh vegetables, practised service.

YEALAND CONYERS New Inn 40 Yealand Road, Tel: (0524) 732938. 17th century farmhouse pub, attractively unpretentious inside; simple home cooking – casseroles, pies and fresh fish dishes, Tue–Sun lunchtime. Family room. Hartleys beer.

LEICESTERSHIRE

BELTON   George Hotel

Market Place LE12 9UH
Tel: (0530) 222426
Licensee: H Houston

Modernised roadside hotel with a comfortable rather than attractive interior. Red plush banquettes line the bar walls, waiting room style, the centre of the room taken up by a free-standing brazier fireplace. Modern bedrooms.

Bar Meals: 12-2.15 (2 Sun), 7-10.45 (10.15 Sun); bar snacks lunchtime **Restaurant:** *12-1.45, 7-10.15 (12-2, 7-9.45 Sun)* **Typical Dishes BAR:** *home-made soup £1.45, home-made paté £2.75, steak and kidney pie £5.45, harvesters lunch £3.85* **Restaurant:** *similar starters at higher prices, pigeon breasts with port £10.35, carpetbagger steak £13.90, skate in black butter £8.95* *Vegetarian Meals: lasagne* *Children's Menu/Portions* Beer *Matthew Brown Home Mild, Bitter; Youngers Scotch* *Family Room* *Garden* *Outdoor Eating* **Accommodation:** *23 bedrooms, 16 en suite, from £44.90 (single £26.95)* *Children Welcome Overnight* *Cots Available* *Check-in: all day* **Credit Cards:** *Access, Amex, Diners, Visa*

BRANSTON Wheel Inn, Main Street. Popular and sometimes interesting bar food lunchtime and evening. Batemans and Courage beers.

BRAUNSTON   Old Plough

Church Street LE15 8QY   ❦
Tel: (0572) 722714
Open: 10-3, 6-11
Licensees: Amanda and Andrew Reid

Rejuvenated, stone-built old coaching inn just two minutes outside Oakham on the Leicester road; run by newish licensees, previously successful at the White Horse, Empingham. Decent food of wide variety and price in lounge, pretty dining conservatory or outdoors on two patios.

Bar Meals: 12-2, 7-10; bar snacks both sessions **Typical Dishes:** *home-made soup £1.65, mushrooms £3.50, home-made steak, kidney and ale pie £5.95, home-made lasagne £4.95, salmon filo £7.95, home-made lemon roulade £1.95* *Children's Menu/Portions* Beer *Courage; Theakston* *Children Allowed in Bar to Eat* *Outdoor Play Area* *Garden* *Outdoor Eating* *Summer Barbecue* **Credit Cards:** *Access, Amex, Diners, Visa*

BURROUGH-ON-THE-HILL   Stag and Hounds

near Melton Mowbray LE14 2JQ
Tel: (066 477) 375
Open: 12-2 Wed-Fri, Easter-Sept (12-3 weekends all year), 7-11
Licensees: Peter and Susan Lerston

Ordinary enough village local with very popular home-cooked food.

Bar Meals: 12-1.45 (2.30 weekends), 7-10; bar snacks both sessions   **Typical Dishes:**
*mushroom soup £1.45, smoked mackerel with stilton sauce £2.95, drunken bull (steak
chunks cooked in beer) £5.99, mixed grill £4.99, Huntingdon fidget pie (bacon, apples and
cider) £5.25, ice-cream sundae £2.99   Vegetarian Meals: vegetable pie £3.50   Children's
Portions* `Cheese` `Beer` *Bateman; Lloyds; Marston* `Cider` *Weston's   Family
Room   Outdoor Play Area   Garden   Outdoor Eating   No Credit Cards*

CATTHORPE Cherry Tree. Village pub, cheered-up under newish young
licensees; popular for lunch (Fri/Sat/Sun only). Closed Mon-Thur lunchtime. Bass
beer.

CROFT Heathcote Arms Hill Street, Tel: (0455) 282439. Hill-top traditional pub
overlooking river; informal and welcoming; simple honest home cooking lunchtime
and evening. Adnams, Everards, Moles beers. Open: 11-2.30, 5.30-11 (all day Sat).

EMPINGHAM   White Horse

2 Main Street (A606) LE15 8PR
Tel: (078 086) 221
Open: all day
Licensee: Roger Bourne

Popular dining pub close to Rutland Water. All home-made food, with freshly
cooked vegetables. The refurbished interior has plush wall-seats and armchairs, the
largest log fire in Rutland and pretty flowers. Half the bedrooms are in a successfully
converted stable block, with stripped pine furniture and pretty fabrics; all these are
en suite. Main house bedrooms are full of traditional character.

*Bar Meals: 12-2, 6.30-9.45 (12-2.15, 6.30-9.30 Fri/Sat)   Typical Dishes: soup of
the day £1.60, garlic hoagies with mozzarella £1.95, steak and kidney pie £4.85,
spaghetti carbonara £5.10, seafood kedgeree £5.95, home-made sherry trifle £2.30
Vegetarian Meals: pizza £4.40   Children's Portions* `Beer` *Courage Directors, John
Smith's Bitter, Magnet   Family Room   Garden   Accommodation: 13 bedrooms, 8 en
suite, from £35 (single £25)   Children Welcome Overnight   Cots Available   Check-in:
all day   Credit Cards: Access, Amex, Diners, Visa*

FLECKNEY Old Crown, High Street, Tel: (0533) 402223. Cleanly refurbished,
spick and span rather than quaint village pub with large lounge and little snug.
Lunchtime and evening home cooking. Adnams, Everards beers. Open: 12-2.30, 5-11.

GLASTON Monkton Arms. Popular foodie pub; prices in middling range, meals
lunchtime and evening; children's dishes. Theakston beers.

GLOOSTON — Old Barn

Main Street LE16 7ST

Tel: (085 884) 215

Open: 12-2.30, 7-11, closed Sun eve/Mon lunch

Licensees: Charles Edmondson-Jones and Stewart Sturge

`FOOD`
`B&B`

On the route of the old Roman road called the Gartree, the Old Barn stands at the centre of a tiny hamlet and just across the road from a picture postcard row of stone terraced cottages: the pub's 16th century frontage of tiny leaded windows framed by flowering boxes and hanging baskets also makes a summer picture. Within, the premises readily divide into two separate sections, a postage stamp size cocktail bar and restaurant to the front, its tables forming booths thanks to high-backed pews and brass-ringed curtaining, and, at a lower level to the rear, a cellar bar largely devoted to snacks and bar meals, in which stripped pine tables and kitchen chairs are gathered in front of a winter log-burning fire. Prominently displayed blackboard specials run from home-made soup through smoked salmon quiche to sole fillets in lobster sauce or roast poussin in rosemary gravy. Restaurant meals follow a more formal menu, changed fortnightly, which offers three courses at £13.50, and an à la carte added on Friday and Saturday nights. Mussels in hot apple sauce, sole with bananas and cream, steaks flamed in fresh basil and malt whisky, all make use of the freshest produce available; vegetarian dishes are specially prepared to order, and the puddings are home-made, crumbles and fruit flans coming from the kitchen of the lady next door. Bedrooms were added three years ago: two doubles and a twin, well fitted out with duvets, trouser press and hair dryer, small televisions and bedside radio. Owing to lack of space, the modular fitted shower rooms are a practical, if cramped, solution, but the towels could certainly be bigger. Host Charles Edmondson-Jones and chef/partner Stewart Sturge add a final ingredient of good service and genuine friendliness which many could learn from: the Old Barn is one of those pubs people keep coming back to.

Bar Meals and Restaurant: 12-1.30 (restaurant Sun only), 7-9.30; bar snacks both sessions   *Typical Dishes BAR:* home-made soup £1.75, herb mushrooms £3.50, hot beef sandwich £4.50, ham hock with mustard £5.50, sole fillet in lobster and prawn sauce £6.45   *RESTAURANT:* table d'hote: Sun lunch £8.45, evenings £13.75   Vegetarian Meals: vegetarian bake £5.20   Children's Portions   `Beer`   Adnams; Batemans; Jennings; Theakston   Children Allowed in Bar to Eat   Outdoor Play Area   Garden   Outdoor Eating   *Accommodation:* 3 bedrooms, all en suite, from £42.50 (single £37.50)   Children Welcome Overnight (minimum age 5)   Cot Available   Check-in: by arrangement   *Credit Cards:* Access, Visa

GRIMSTON — Black Horse

Melton Mowbray LE14 3BZ

Tel: (0664) 812358

Open: 12-2.30 (inc Sun), 7-11; closed Sun eve and all day Mon

The garden is the village green and the interior awash with cricket-abilia, including over 80 autographed bats. No children under 14.

Bar Meals: 12-1.30, 7.30-9.30; bar snacks both sessions   *Typical Dishes:* home-made soup £1.50, corn on the cob £1.95, steak pie £4.75, poussin £4.95, fresh haddock £4.65, home-made pavlova £1.70   `Beer`   Marston   Garden   **No Credit Cards**

HALLATON   Bewicke Arms

1 Eastgate LE16 8UB   `FOOD`
Tel: (085 889) 217   ♟
Open: 12-2.30, 7-11   `B&B`
Licensee: Neil Spiers   ☼ ☺

Sixteen years consistent performance, many of them recognised by this guide, is sufficient testimony to the style of the Bewicke and to Gail and Neil Spiers, who run it so well. Their 400 year old country inn, rethatched at enormous expense over the winter of 1989/90, stands above the Welland valley in the heart of fine Leicestershire countryside. Hallaton itself is locally renowned for the parish church's Norman tower, the conical butter cross on the village green – right across the road from the pub – and the tiny village museum which offers a unique insight into its rural past. Little has changed in the immediate landscape and at the Bewicke in the intervening years. One new development, however, is the offer of accommodation in a large luxury apartment, complete with self-contained kitchen and lounge/dining room, directly above the pub. It has four bedrooms and two bathrooms, and is available for weekly self-catering in its entirety; failing that, the bedrooms are let individually for bed and breakfast. The pub below is a cracking good local, though its range of beers is unexciting, and an equally predictable printed menu lists the usual steaks and grills, ploughmans and sandwiches, so look to the specials board for more adventurous options. Starters typically include garlic mushrooms, deep-fried camembert, and mussels baked in pastry, while top sellers among the main courses include a beery beef casserole, chicken boursin and Cromer crab salad. Vegetarians get a good look in, too, with risotto, lasagne and a cauliflower, courgette and mushroom bake topped with stilton crumble, and there's a fair choice of home-made puddings of the cheesecake, pavlova, and treacle sponge with custard genre. Wines offered by the bottle are more interesting than the house beers: a printed, largely European list is backed by a wines of the month board, typically featuring Australian and Chilean specials. The pub is consistently busy, and the more recently added Bottom Room, stone clad with a bow window, Austrian blinds and an effective library theme, opens when demand dictates. At weekends it's almost certain to be full, so better book.

Bar Meals: 12-2, 7.30-9.45; bar snacks both sessions   ***Typical Dishes:*** *help-yourself soup £1.65, baked mussels in pastry £3.20, chicken boursin £6.80, beery beef casserole £5.40, chilli con carne £4.80, treacle sponge £4.80   Vegetarian Meals: spinach and mushroom pancake £4.80   Children's Menu/Portions* `Beer` *Marston Pedigree; Ruddles Best, County, Webster's Yorkshire Bitter Family Room   Outdoor Play Area Patio/terrace   Outdoor Eating* ***Accommodation:*** *3 bedrooms, 2 en suite, from £39.50 (single £32.50)   Children Welcome Overnight   Cot Available   Check-in: all day* ***Credit Cards:*** *Access, Visa*

HOSE   Rose & Crown

Bolton Lane
Tel: (0949) 60424
Open: 11.30-2.30, 7-11
Licensees: Carl and Carmel Routh

An interesting, changing range of beers, and home-cooked food in this comfy, popular Vale of Belvoir pub; eat in the lounge or new upstairs dining area, which specialises in a cheap, steak-centred table d'hote.

Bar Meals: lunchtime and evening; bar snacks both sessions   ***Typical Dishes:*** *home-made pies £5, large crisp salads from £5, stilton-topped sirloins and other steaks from £6* `Beer` *five varying real ales   Children Allowed in Bar to Eat   Garden* ***Credit Cards:*** *Visa*

HUNGARTON Black Boy, Main Street, Tel: (053 750) 601. Large spartan public bar, small cosy lounge, home-cooked food lunchtime and evening Mon-Sat. Real fire; no music. Bass beers. Open: 11-2.30, 6-11.

KEGWORTH   Cap & Stocking

20 Borough Street DE7 2FF
Tel: (0509) 674814
Open: 11.30-3, 6-11
Licensees: W P Poynton and C A Poulter

Loved for its atmosphere rather than its food, which is fairly routine but always good value; look out for the home-made specials.

Bar Meals: 12-2.30, 6.30-8.30; bar snacks both sessions **Typical Dishes:** *minestrone 95p, home-made paté £1.95, chicken curry £2.95, beef carbonade £2.95, spaghetti bolognese £2.55, treacle sponge 95p Vegetarian Meals: spaghetti £2.55* **Beer** *Adnams Bitter; Draught Bass, Highgate Mild* **Cider** *Weston's Family Room Outdoor Play Area Garden Outdoor Eating* **No Credit Cards**

KIBWORTH BEAUCHAMP Coach and Horses, 2 Leicester Road (A6) Tel: (0533) 792247. Traditional coaching inn with beams and fires; popular for food, mostly home-cooked. Ind Coope, Tetley beers. Open: 11.30-3, 5-11 (all day Fri/Sat).

LEICESTER   Welford Place

9 Welford Place LE1 6ZH   FOOD
Tel: (0533) 470758
Open: 10.30-11
Licensees: Susan and Michael Hope

This striking Victorian building, designed by Joseph Goddard in 1876, stands at a convenient city centre intersection between the High Street, Cathedral, Castle Park and Granby Halls. Formerly home to the private members Leicestershire Club, Welford Place is operated by the Hope family, who have so succesfully run Lincoln's now-famous 'Wig and Mitre' (qv.) over the last twelve years. Their latest classy operation promotes itself both as a watering hole for the seriously intentioned and a haven of peace. There are no music noises and, they hope, no pretension, to a set-up which opens for breakfast and morning coffee, offers a Specials menu which purports to change twice daily, and promises its à la carte will be available all day throughout the premises until 11 pm. Thus, in the bar – a striking semi-circular room with high windows overlooking Welford Place itself and furnished with leather armchairs and glass-topped tables – a light, relaxing lunch might mean a bowl of fresh vegetable soup, a twice-baked cheese soufflé with smoked ham and salad, or various patés and sandwiches (all at under £5), with a creamy pint of Ruddles or a glass of chilled white wine. Those seeking a more substantial lunch may opt for a warm salad of boneless quail with mushrooms and bacon, braised beef with horseradish cream, or a large grilled plaice with chive butter sauce, and confidently expect change from £7.50, perhaps with coffee vacherin, bread and butter pudding or banana bavarois to follow. Across the grand parquet-floored hall, the restaurant, a stolid, square room in blues and russets, appears, perhaps, a little more formal than it's intended to be, with an à la carte menu extending to pan-fried pork with sultanas and pine kernels, or veal kidneys with basmati rice and tarragon mustard sauce (each around £10), and desserts of chocolate gateau or tiramisu. The new Welford Place adjoins the recently reconstructed Leicester magistrates courts, from which it appears destined to draw much trade, as a kind of glamorous lawyers' canteen.

Bar Meals and Restaurant: all day, also snacks   **Typical Dishes BAR:** *sweetbreads with mushrooms £4.50, cheese and ham soufflé £4.50, beef with red wine £5.25, chicken supreme on a sweetcorn pancake £10.50, salmon with hollandaise and broad beans £10.50, rich chocolate mousse £2.50   Vegetarian Meals   Children's Portions* `Cheese` `Beer` *Ruddles* `Whisky`   **Credit Cards:** *Access, Amex, Diners, Visa*

LOUGHBOROUGH   Swan in the Rushes

21 The Rushes (A6)
Tel: (0509) 217014
Open: 11-2.30, 5-11 (11-3, 6.30-11 Sat)
Licensees: Julian and Gillian Grocock

We rate this as the best of the Tynemill group of pubs, which makes a virtue of keeping things simple, fresh (organic where possible) and at old-fashioned prices. The refurbished two room interior is nothing remotely special, but the food is remarkably good value. The lamb casserole is recommended: full of flavour, and accompanied by generous fresh carrots, beans, cauliflower; new potatoes and mash.

Bar Meals: daily lunchtime and Mon-Sat evening; bar snacks both sessions   **Typical Dishes:** *spaghetti bolognese £1.95, lamb casserole £3.25, vegetarian curry £2.75, apple crumble and custard 95p   Vegetarian Meals   Children's Menu* `Beer` *Bateman; Marston; Tetley   Children Allowed in Bar to Eat (lunchtime)*   **Accommodation:** *4 bedrooms, 2 en suite, from £35 (single £20)*

LYDDINGTON   Marquess of Exeter Hotel

Main Street LE15 9LT near Uppingham
Tel: (0572) 822477
Open: 11.30-3, 6.30-11
Licensees: L S Evitt and R M Morrell

Nice old stone inn in prosperous village. Now a Best Western hotel targeting business traffic, and rather dull 'masculine taste' bedrooms reflect this. The main bar is pleasant enough, with exposed stone and red plush chairs and stools. They've got a new wine merchant.

Bar Meals: 12.15-2, 7.15-10; bar snacks both sessions   **Restaurant:** *12.30-2 (not Sat), 7.30-9.30 (not Sun)*   **Typical Dishes BAR:** *leek and potato soup £1.45, garlic mushrooms £2.85, spaghetti figadini £4.95, fricassee of salmon £5.20, cheesecake £1.65* **RESTAURANT:** *£15.35 menu: salmon/tuna roulade, beef olive bordelaise, pudding and coffee   Vegetarian Meals: mushroom and tomato bake   Children's Portions* `Beer` *Batemans XXXB; Ruddles Best Bitter, County; Theakston XB* `Whisky` *Family Room* **Accommodation:** *17 bedrooms, all en suite, from £67 (single £53)   Children Welcome Overnight   Cots Available   Check-in: all day*   **Credit Cards:** *Access, Amex, Diners, Visa*

MARKET OVERTON   Black Bull

Market Overton LE15 7PW
Tel: (087 283) 677
Open: 11-3, 6-11
Licensees: Valerie Owen

Having bought a semi-derelict, part-thatched ale-house in 1985, John and Val Owen set single-mindedly about planning the conversion work needed to create what they were really after – a relaxed local pub with good value dining. The bar's agreeable interior of blue banquettes, polished tables, poker-back chairs and background popular music (there are speakers everywhere, even in the loos!) creates a chatty, relaxed atmosphere in which to engage in banter with the landlord and enjoy the beer. Across a central area of original flagstone floor, the new dining room, converted from a former garage, opens seven nights a week and for Sunday lunch. A buffet stand takes care of cold starters and self-served vegetables; hot starters like moules marinière, and main dishes like the ever-popular rack of lamb, a salmon and seafood vol-au-vent, or kidneys Turbigo are ordered from prominent blackboard displays and waitressed to the table. Steaks can be fillet, sirloin or 16 oz T-bone; there are also lots of fish dishes, or perhaps a double chicken breast stuffed with stilton. Kitchen limitations, however, dictate a reliance on mainly bought-in puddings other than fruit salads and the occasional lemon meringue. Lunchtime bar food is rather simpler: ye olde English fish and chips (a great hit), Rutland sausages, steak, kidney and beer pie, tagliatelle with ham and cream sauce, or just ploughmans and sandwiches, all of consistent quality. Upstairs, one en suite double and a twin are equipped with televisions and a tea tray, whilst, in a mews row just off the village green, the Owens rent out their lovely stone-built country cottage (two up, two down) on a weekly self-catering basis but – sorry – please don't bring the children.

Bar Meals: 12-2, 7-10; bar snacks both sessions   **Typical Dishes:** *chicken and noodle soup £1.45, salmon and asparagus pancake £2.95, steak and kidney pie £4.95, venison and guinea fowl casserole £6.25, steak and chips £8.95, apple dumplings £1.75 Vegetarian Meals: mushroom stroganoff Children's Portions* **Beer** *Bass; Ruddles; Theakston Children Alowed in Bar to Eat Patio/terrace Outdoor Eating* **Credit Cards:** *Visa*

NORTH KILWORTH White Lion. Friendly, comfortable; decent bar food including robustly traditional English dishes. Marston's beers.

OAKHAM Wheatsheaf Northgate. 17th century two roomed local; real fire; garden; plain home cooking. Adnams and Everard beers. Open: 11-2.30 (3 Fri/Sat), 6-11.

OLD DALBY   Crown Inn

Debdale Hill, Melton Mowbray LR14 3LF
Tel: (0664) 823134
Open: 12-2.30, 6-11
Licensees: Lynne Strafford, Bryan and Salvatore Inguanta

Country pub, once a farmhouse. Rambling, rustic interior with real charm, lovely fabrics, open fires; the uniformed staff look a little out of place. Enjoyable, often ambitious cooking. Better be early.

Bar Meals: 12-1.45, 6-9.30; bar snacks both sessions **Restaurant:** *12-1.30, 7-9* **Typical Dishes BAR:** *red pepper, leek and celeriac soup £2.50, kromeskis £4.95, French duck breast £8.95, Chinese chicken £7.95, seafood brochette with seaweed £7.95, Sicilian trifle* **RESTAURANT** *lunch menu £16, dinner £21: Colston Bassett stilton and onion soup, rack of English lamb with orange, medallions of fillet beef with oyster sauce, fresh Dover sole in tarragon and lemon, strawberry filo Vegetarian Meals: stuffed pepper £6.50* **Cheese** **Beer** *Batemans; Fullers; Nethergate; Woodforde's* **Whisky** *Family Room Garden Outdoor Eating Summer Barbecue* **No Credit Cards**

PRESTON   Fox & Hounds

2 Cross Lane LE15 9NQ
Tel: (057 285) 492
Open: 11.30-3, 6.30-11 (12-2, 7-11 winter)

16th century pub in what estate agents describe as a "most sought-after village". Lots of beamy character remains. Unpretentious home cooking.

Bar Meals: 12-2, 7-9.30 (9 Sun/Mon); bar snacks both sessions **Typical Dishes:** *minestrone £1.45, farmhouse paté with port £2.50, steak and kidney pie £4.75, beef in ale £4.75, chilli con carne £3.95, raspberry cheesecake Vegetarian Meals: vegetable moussaka Children's Portions* ▇ Beer ▇ *Adnams; Marston; Theakston, Younger Children Allowed in Bar to Eat Outdoor Play Area Garden Outdoor Eating* **No Credit Cards**

SALTBY Nags Head 1 Back Street Tel: (0476) 860491. Beamed, wood-panelled bar, and unusual bar billiards room in 18th century stone-built pub with home cooking and four-poster beds. Greene King, Ruddles beers. Open: 12-2.30, 7-11.

SILEBY   White Swan

Swan Street
Tel: (050 981) 4832
Licensee: Theresa Wallace

A promising new entry, its menu brimming with home-cooked, varied dishes prepared by an enthusiastic landlady; comfy, refurbished book-lined dining lounge bar.

Bar Meals: Tue-Sat and Sun lunchtime; bar snacks both sessions **Typical Dishes:** *home-made soups, home-made spinach pasta with seafood sauce, roast guinea fowl, seafood casserole, walnut sponge with butterscotch sauce Vegetarian Meals: mushroom casserole Children's Portions* ▇ Beer ▇ *Ansells; Tetley; Marston Children Allowed in to Eat* **Credit Cards:** *Access, Visa*

SKEFFINGTON Fox & Hounds, Uppingham Road (A47). Busy roadhouse with campsite; surprisingly decent home-cooked specials – fish, Irish stew, butterfly prawns, as well as routine bar menu; Mon-Sat lunchtime and evening. Greenalls beers.

STRETTON Ram Jam Inn Great North Road. Extremely useful, more civilised than the Little Chef A1 stopping point; continental café-bar and modern lounge with buffet counter; restaurant; good value bedrooms. Ruddles beers.

SUTTON CHENEY Royal Arms Main Street: Sophisticated bar food; handsome village pub with upstairs restaurant and family room-conservatory. Garden. Marston's beers.

WALCOTE   Black Horse

Lutterworth Road LE17 4JU
Tel: (0455) 552684
Open: 12-2.30 (not Mon/Tue), 6.30 (5.30 Fri)-11
Licensee: Saovanee Tinker

A standard plush banquette refurbishment, but by no means ordinary food: everything on the menu is Thai, as is the landlady; delicious food at remarkably cheap prices. Also twenty fruit wines by the glass.

Bar Meals: 12-2, 6.30-9.30   *Typical Dishes:* pork phat khing, kaeng kai, khao mu deang, beef in garlic and chilli, Thai mixed grill (main courses from £3)   *Vegetarian Meals:* vegetarian stir-fry   Children's Portions   `Beer`   Burton Bridge Bitter; Hook Norton Best Bitter, Old Hooky; Taylor Landlord   `Cider`   Weston's   Family Room   Outdoor Play Area   Patio/terrace   Outdoor Eating   **No Credit Cards**

WALTON ON THE WOLDS   Anchor

2 Loughborough Road
Tel: (0509) 880018
Licensee: Pat Shutt

Not far from Melton Mowbray, and the landlady comes from a pie-making family, so it's not surprising that her speciality is hot water crust pies, using traditional moulds: game, pork and rabbit, or steak and kidney perhaps. Good vegetables too.

Bar Meals: lunchtime and evening; bar snacks both sessions   *Typical Dishes:* home-cooked ham and eggs, herby fish pie, chicken parisienne (main courses from £3.50), rummy bread pudding   `Beer`   Ind Coope   Family Room   Garden

WHISSENDINE White Lion Main Street, Tel: (066 479) 233. Welcoming local with traditional pub games, decent lunchtime and evening bar food, nice garden. Bedrooms cheap. Everards beers.

WHITWELL   Noel Arms

Main Street LE15 8BW   ❦
Tel: (078 086) 334
Open; 10.30-3, 6-11
Licensee: Sam Healey

Get here early for a seat in the tiny twin rooms at the front, the original alehouse. The overflow spills into a spacious rear extension of much less charm. The restaurant has a seafoody, fishy emphasis; they even have their own seawater tanks. All puddings are home-made.

Bar Meals: 12-2.30, 7-10; bar snacks lunchtime   *Restaurant:* 12-2, 7-9.30   *Typical Dishes BAR:* carrot and orange soup £2, home-made paté £2, home-made steak and kidney pie £5, home-made chicken Kiev £6.95, grilled halibut £7.95, pavlova   Vegetarian Meals: baked aubergine   Children's Menu/Portions   `Beer`   Allied beers; Marston Pedigree   `Whisky`   Children Allowed in Bar to Eat   Outdoor Play Area   Garden Summer Barbecue   *Accommodation:* 8 bedrooms, 4 en suite, from £38 (single £29) Children Welcome Overnight   Cot Available   Check-in: all day   *Credit Cards:* Access, Visa

WORTHINGTON Malt Shovel. Main Street, Tel: (0530) 222343: Mid-18th century two bar pub with a family room and animals in the garden; real fire; popular lunchtime and evening food; Marston's beer. Open: 12-2 (closed Mon), 7-11.

WYMONDHAM   Hunters Arms

4 Edmondthorpe Road LE14 2AD
Tel: (057 284) 633
Open: 11-2.30 (not Mon), 6.30-11
Licensee: Marcel Pierre Mascaro

Nice roadside village inn, bought by a pub-loving Frenchman in 1985; traditional
English pub food in the bar (but no home-made puddings), French à la carte in the
restaurant.

*Bar Meals: 12-2, 7-9.30 (no bar meals Sun/Mon)   **Restaurant:** 12-1.30 (Sun only),
Fri/Sat eves   **Typical Dishes BAR:** mushroom soup £1.30, home-made paté, steak and
kidney pie £3.95, lasagne £3.85, fishermans pie £4.25   **RESTAURANT:** dinner menu
£14.75   Vegetarian Meals: puff pastry parcels   Children's Portions* ▐Beer▌ *Draught
Bass; Greene King IPA, Abbots Ale   Children Allowed in Bar to Eat   Outdoor Play Area
Garden   Outdoor Eating   **Credit Cards:** Access, Visa (in restaurant only)*

LINCOLNSHIRE

ALFORD   White Horse Hotel

29 West Street LN13 9DG
Tel: (0507) 462218
Open: 11-2.30 (12-2.30 Sun), 6.30-11
Licensees: Jan and Sheila Laskowski

Successfully restored and refurbished 16th century town pub, popular for food.
Chintzy bedrooms.

*Bar Meals: 12-2, 7-10; bar snacks both sessions   **Typical Dishes:** home-made soup
£1.20, garlic mushrooms £2.25, minted lamb steak £3.75, lambs liver, onions, sausage
and sherry £3.80, pan-fried halibut with prawns and mushrooms £5.95, sherry trifle £2
Vegetarian Meals: stuffed peppers   Children's Portions* ▐Beer▌ *Bass; Batemans   Children
Allowed in Bar to Eat   **Accommodation:** 9 bedrooms, 7 en suite, from £34 (single £24)
Children Welcome Overnight   Check-in: by arrangement   **Credit Cards:** Access, Visa*

ALFORD Half Moon, 25 West Street: Handy for the craft markets; decent bar
meals and separate restaurant. Bass, Wards beers. Open: 10-3.30, 6-11.

ASWARBY   Tally Ho

near Sleaford NG34 8SA
Tel: (05295) 205
Open: 12-2.30, 6-11
Licensee: C Davis

Straightforward, home-made food at this mellow 18th century country inn, its two
rooms featuring exposed stone and brickwork aplenty, country prints, log fire and
woodburning stove. Bedrooms in the adjoining stable block are comfortable,
soothingly decorated and provide plenty of hanging and writing space. Timber
clambering equipment for children on the rear lawn.

*Bar Meals and Dining Room: 12-2, 7-9.45; bar snacks both sessions   **Typical Dishes**
home-made soup £1.25, mushrooms in garlic £2.70, steak £6.90, chicken Kiev £5.90,
haddock £3.90, lemon cheesecake £1.95   Children's Portions* ▐Beer▌ *Batemans Bitter;
Courage Directors; Greene King IPA   Children Allowed in Bar to Eat   Outdoor Play Area*

*Garden   Outdoor Eating   **Accommodation:** 6 bedrooms, all en suite, from £42 (single £28)*
*Children Welcome Overnight   Cot Available   Check-in: all day   **No Credit Cards***

BOSTON   Burton House Hotel

Wainfleet Road
Tel: (0205) 362307
Open: 10.30-3, 6-1

Hotel proper with pubby stable bar, spacious lounge overlooking garden, and simple
food; try the daily changing hot special. Fresh local vegetables.

Bar Meals: *12-1.45, 7-9.30; bar snacks both sessions   **Typical Dishes:** steak and kidney
pie £2.75, liver, kidney, sausage and pork casserole £3, chicken à la crème £3.50, treacle
tart* Beer *Bass; Batemans   **Credit Cards:** Access, Visa*

BOSTON Carpenters Arms Union Street Tel: (0205) 362840. Busy backstreet
pub, popular with all types; lunchtime menu includes some interesting specials; good
value brass bed B&B. Batemans beers. Open: 11-3 (4 Fri/Sat), 7-11.

BURGH LE MARSH White Hart, High Street (A158) Tel: (0754) 810321.
Attractive lounge with Crown Derby collection; lively juke box public bar;
Harts restaurant. Good value B&B. Families welcome. Batemans, Tetley beers.
Open: 11-3, 6-11.

CASTLE BYTHAM Castle Inn Friendly local with a local following for lunch
and evening bar meals; no food Tuesday.

CHAPEL ST LEONARDS Ship Sea Road Tel: (0754) 72975. Bustling local
popular with regulars and holidaymakers; lunchtime and evening bar meals in
summer; large garden has children's play area. Batemans beers. Open: 11-3, 7-11.

COLEBY   Bell

Far Lane, Lincoln LN5 0AH
Tel: (0522) 810240
Open: 11-3, 7-11
Licensee: M D Aram

Dining pub with three connecting carpeted bars, and open fires.

Bar Meals: *12-2, 7-10; bar snacks lunchtime   **Typical Dishes:** leek and stilton soup
£1.75, garlic mushrooms in tomato and basil sauce £2.50, roast rack of lamb with a claret
sauce £6.95, Napoli beef £6.95, chicken en croute with smoked salmon and prawns £7.95,
bread and butter pudding £2   Vegetarian Meals: broccoli and cauliflower crepes £4.45
Children's Menu/Portions* Beer *Courage Directors; Marston Pedigree   Family Room
Children Allowed in Bar to Eat   **Credit Cards:** Access, Diners, Visa*

CONINGSBY   Lea Gate Inn

Coningsby LN4 4RS
Tel: (0526) 42370
Open: 11.30-2.30, 7-11
Licensee: R B Dennison

Last of the once numerous Fen Guide Houses, places of safety on the treacherous
eastern marshes. Traditional features, brick and beams, three open fires in the lounge

areas, and garden room. The yew tree is the same age as the pub; the attractive garden also features a koi carp pond.

Bar Meals and Restaurant: 12-2, 7-10; *bar snacks both sessions*   ***Typical Dishes BAR:*** home-made soup £1.20, garlic mushrooms £1.70, steak and kidney pie £3.65, chilli £3.30, syllabub £1.65   ***RESTAURANT:*** *similar starters and puddings, duckling* £8.50, plaice £6   *Vegetarian Meals: lasagne*   Beer   *Marston Pedigree; Taylor Landlord; Whitbread Boddingtons Bitter, Castle Eden Ale   Children Allowed in Bar to Eat Outdoor Play Area   Poolside Garden   Outdoor Eating*   **No Credit Cards**

DONINGTON-ON-BAIN   Black Horse

Main Road LN11 9TJ
Tel: (0507) 343640
Open: 11.30-3, 7-11
Licensee: Anthony Pacey

On the Viking Way, as interior murals commemorate. A routine bar menu is supplemented by fresh cod or haddock on Friday and Saturday lunch, plus specials like beef olives, venison goulash and fresh salmon. The new 8-bedroomed motel opened in August 1991; cots should be available for 1992.

Bar Meals: 11.30-2, 7-10 (9.30 Sun); *bar snacks both sessions*   ***Typical Dishes:*** *home-made soup* £1.75, *paté* £1.75, *home-made steak and kidney pie* £3.95, *rump steak* £5.95, *scampi and chips* £3.25, *apple pie* £1.50   *Vegetarian Meals: courgette and tomato cheese bake* £4.35   *Children's Menu/Portions*   Beer   *Adnams Bitter, Broadside; Ruddles County, Webster's Yorkshire Bitter*   Whisky   *Family Room   Outdoor Play Area Garden   Outdoor Eating   Summer Barbecue*   ***Accommodation:*** *8 bedrooms, all en suite, from* £35 (single £25)   *Children Welcome Overnight   Check-in: by arrangement*   **No Credit Cards**

DYKE   Wishing Well Inn

Bourne PE10 0AF
Tel: (0778) 422970
Open: 10.30-3.30 (12-2.30 Sun),6.30-11
Licensee: G R Jones

Done-up, opened-out village inn, a relaxing venue with its candlelight, heavy beams, exposed stone and (natch) wishing well. Simple home cooking.

Bar Meals and Restaurant: 12-2, 7-9; *bar snacks both sessions*   ***Typical Dishes BAR:*** *home-made soup* £1.20, *home-made steak pie* £3.25, *home-made lasagne* £3.25, *lemon meringue pie*   ***RESTAURANT:*** *similar starters and puddings, rump steak* £6.60, *chicken supreme* £6.95   *Vegetarian Meals: lasagne   Children's Portions*   Beer   *Greene King Abbot Ale; Ind Coope Burton Ale, Tetley Bitter   Children Allowed in Bar to Eat   Outdoor Play Area   Garden   Outdoor Eating*   ***Accommodation:*** *7 bedrooms, 4 en suite, from* £27 (single £16.50)   *Children Welcome Overnight   Check-in: all day*   **No Credit Cards**

FRAMPTON Moers Arms Church End Tel: (0205) 722408. Rather smart dining pub with decent bar and restaurant meals; garden. Bass beers. Open: 10.30-3, 6.30-11.

GRANTHAM   Five Bells

79 Brook Street
Tel: (0476) 67152
Open: 11-2.30, 5-11
Licensee: Sandra Mills

Recently refurbished, and now offering bedrooms. Real (free-range) meats; varying home-cooked specials; good home-made skin-on chips. Opposite Kings School. Has been found closed at lunchtimes.

Bar Meals: lunchtime and evening; bar snacks both sessions **Typical Dishes:** *moules marinière, steak and kidney pie, chicken Parisienne, beef stew with herby dumplings (main courses from £4), hot Danish apple cake* *Vegetarian Meals* *Children's Portions* `Beer` *Greenalls, Marston* *Children Allowed in Bar to Eat* *Patio/terrace* **Credit Cards:** *Access, Visa*

GRANTHAM Beehive Castlegate Tel: (0476) 67794. Bar food, tends to the plain and homely, stylish renovated town centre alehouse; gets young and noisy. Mansfield beers. Open: 11-3, 5-11 (11-4, 7-11 Sat).

GREATFORD   Hare and Hounds

Village Street PE9 4QA
Tel: (0778) 560332
Open: 12-3, 6-11
Licensees: Olga and Ricky Payne-Podmore

Cheering, cosy little pub with decent meals. No frozen convenience food used: only fresh food from fresh ingredients. Close to Stamford and Burleigh House.

Bar Meals: 12-2 (not Sun), 7-9; bar snacks both sessions **Typical Dishes:** *tomato soup £1.20, Florida cocktail 95p, sirloin steak £8.75, pork in cream and Calvados £5.95, moules marinière £5.75, apple pie £1.25* `Beer` *Adnams; Mansfield; Charles Wells* *Children Allowed in Bar to Eat (lunchtime only)* *Garden* *Outdoor Eating* **Credit Cards:** *Access, Visa*

GREAT LIMBER   New Inn

High Street (A18)
Tel: (0469) 60257
Licensee: Colin Spencer

Spacious, popular pub dominating this estate village; Brocklesby Park, nearby, is the seat of the Earl of Yarborough, who still owns the New Inn. Traditional lounge free of music, electronic games, but with real fires and decent, plain home cooking. Modest accommodation.

Bar Meals: weekday lunchtimes `Beer` *Batemans; Tetley; Wards; Youngers* *Garden* **Accommodation:** *8 bedrooms, from £25*

GRIMSTHORPE   Black Horse Inn

Bourne PE10 0LY
Tel: (077 832) 247
Open: 11-2, 7.15-11 (closed Sun)
Licensees: Kenneth and Joyce Fisher

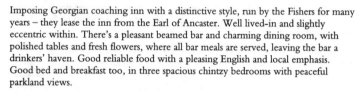

Imposing Georgian coaching inn with a distinctive style, run by the Fishers for many years – they lease the inn from the Earl of Ancaster. Well lived-in and slightly eccentric within. There's a pleasant beamed bar and charming dining room, with polished tables and fresh flowers, where all bar meals are served, leaving the bar a drinkers' haven. Good reliable food with a pleasing English and local emphasis. Good bed and breakfast too, in three spacious chintzy bedrooms with peaceful parkland views.

Bar Meals: 12-1.45, 7.30-9.30; bar snacks both sessions **Typical Dishes:** *home-made soup £1.99, stilton and herb paté £2.95, Mrs Beeton's beefsteak, kidney and mushroom pie £4.95, Lincolnshire lamb baskets £4.95, Fenland savoury pancake £3.95, Vegetarian Meals: Lincolnshire stovies £1.25* **Beer** *Camerons Traditional Bitter* **Accommodation:** *3 bedrooms, all en suite, from £52 (single £41) Children Welcome Overnight (minimum age 7) Check-in: by arrangement* **Credit Cards:** *Access, Amex, Visa*

HOUGH ON THE HILL Brownlow Arms Tel: (0400) 50234. Handsome old pub dominating quiet village, well refurbished in 1990, though a modern fridgeful of desserts is rather out of place in the middle of the main lounge. We found the bar meals very disappointing, but B&B is popular.

INGHAM Inn on the Green High Street. Refurbished village green pub with a varied, international bar menu; gets busy at weekends.

IRNHAM Griffin Inn Main Road Tel: (047 684) 201. Ancient inn, unchanged and unchanging, in romantic estate village in pretty countryside. No music. Bedrooms. Greene King beers. Open: 11.30-2.30, 7-11 (closed Monday).

KIRKBY LA THORPE Queens Head, Church Lane: Refurbished, comfortable village pub popular for lunch and supper; garden; Draught Bass. Open: 11.30-2.30, 6-11.

LINCOLN   Wig & Mitre

29 Steep Hill LN2 1LU   FOOD
Tel: (0522) 535190
Open: all day
Licensees: Valerie and Michael Hope

The Hope family's trendy city-centre pub is not the historic ale-house it purports to be, but is none-the-less a classic. Its really rather ordinary exterior, a glass shop front under a flower-laden cast-iron balcony, stands between the Lincoln Vintner and Chantilly's bridal shop; Lincoln cathedral is just a stone's throw away across cobbled streets where once the Roman *via principalis* ran, and its echoing hourly chimes are almost deafening. The pub's interior – which also has a rear access from Drury Lane – won a Business and Industry Award in 1978 for the meticulous restoration of its genuine Tudor timbers, between which sections of 13th century daub and wattle walls are still visible. Connected by three staircases, there's a warren of rooms in which to eat, two bars dispensing Sam Smith's Old Brewery bitter and oak-casked Museum ale, and a tiny rear patio, as well as a table from which you can pick up the day's papers for a browse. The menu encourages all comers to eat as little or as much as they'd like at any time throughout the premises, thus encompassing every taste and pleasing all pockets, and the catering is ambitious: breakfast starts at 8am and food's served through to 11 o' clock in the evening. There are two daily blackboard menus, one taking over from the other at around 4pm. From this, perhaps a broccoli soup (£1.75), lentil and garlic paté (£3.50), ratatouille with garlic bread (£3.55), and cheesy potato bake (£3.50), baked cod with a garlic crust (£6.95), beef braised in Sam Smith's beer (£5.25) or, stepping up a level, a steamed panaché of brill, monkfish, red mullet and scallops, at £12.90. In addition, an all-day à la carte extends the selection with a salad of sweetbreads and oyster mushrooms (£4.95), marinaded beef fillet with parmesan (£6.50), and pork fillet sautéed with Calvados and cream (£10.25) among them. Daily puddings are pretty universal: chocolate biscuit cake, raspberry parfait with fruit coulis, meringue nests with ice-cream and butterscotch or chocolate roulade. Nominated as a "courtesy enterprise" by the Polite Society in 1988, staff today are especially smart and courteous, and there are plenty of them in evidence even at the busiest times.

Bar Meals and Restaurant: 8 am-11 pm; bar snacks   **Typical Dishes BAR:** *watercress and mushroom soup £1.75, tuna and lemon paté £3.50, pork with bacon and green peppercorns £4.95, bowl of chilli £3.95, minced lamb and basil lasagne £4.25, rich chocolate parfait £2.50*   **RESTAURANT:** *warm salad of lamb's sweetbreads and oyster mushrooms £4.95, Swiss cheese soufflé with ham and cream £4.95, roast farm chicken £10.95, sautéed calves livers £10.95, medallions of beef fillet £13.50, daily puddings menu*   *Vegetarian Meals: broccoli and cheese bake £3.50*   **Beer**   *Samuel Smith Old Brewery Bitter, Museum Ale*   **Whisky**   *Patio/terrace   Outdoor Eating*   **Credit Cards:** *Access, Amex, Diners, Visa*

NAVENBY Kings Head. Attractive little pub with decent lunchtime and evening food; restaurant.

NETTLEHAM Plough The Green Tel: (0522) 750275. Cosy, low-beamed village pub with a warm welcome and good home-made pies, especially the rabbit; bar meals lunchtime only. Family room, garden. Batemans beers. Open: 11-3(4 Sat), 7-11 (all day Fri).

NEWTON	**Red Lion**

near Sleaford NE34 0EE
Tel: (05297) 256
Open: 11-3, 6-11
Licensee: C P Watkin

Long a favourite for its 17th century charm and remote rural position off the A52, the pub now has a new licensee, who's creating a popular food trade here with his imaginative cold carvery and 15 choice salads, all finished off with tempting puddings. Everything's roasted, cooked and chopped on site.

Bar Meals: 12-2, 7-10 (9.30 Sun); bar snacks lunchtime   **Typical Dishes:** *cold carvery 3 meat/fish choices £6.25, cold carvery 4 meat/fish choices £7.25, cold carvery unlimited choices £8.25, home-made pudding £1.65*   *Vegetarian Meals: quiche   Children's Portions*   **Beer**   *Batemans XXXB   Family Room   Outdoor Play Area   Garden   Outdoor Eating*   **No Credit Cards**

OASBY Houblon Arms Main Street Tel (05295) 215. Low-beamed town meeting place, lunch and evening food; real fire, no music. Batemans and Taylors beers. Open: 11-2.30, 7-11.

PARTNEY   Red Lion

near Spilsby PE23 4PG
Tel: (0790) 52271
Open: 11-2.30 (12-2.30 Sun), 7-11; closed Tue
Licensee: Derek Gamblin

Home-made main course bakes, pies and casseroles at a nice old pub; the landlady's
puddings are worth a try too. There'll be garden tables for the 1992 season.

Bar Meals: 12-2, 7-9.30; bar snacks lunchtime   **Typical Dishes:** *home-made paté*
£1.60, pheasant pie £5.75, beef in beer with a garlic crust £5.50, seafood lasagne £5.25,
bread and butter pudding £1.50   Vegetarian Meals: vegetable lasagne   Children's Portions
■ Beer ■ *Draught Bass; Batemans   Children Allowed in Bar to Eat   Garden   Outdoor*
Eating   **No Credit Cards**

RAITHBY BY SPILSBY   Red Lion

Main Street PE23 4DS
Tel: (0790) 53727
Open: 12-3 (weekends/hols only), 7-11
Licensee: Roger Smith

There are good home-made pizzas in the bar, but the main food emphasis rests in
the Victorian dining room. Everything's home-made and everything fresh except for
frozen peas. There are no chips. A 16th century listed village pub.

Bar Meals: during opening hours; bar snacks lunchtime   **Restaurant:** *Sun lunch and from*
7.30 Wed-Sat   **Typical Dishes BAR:** *range of home-made pizzas £1.50-£3*
Restaurant: *home-made soup £1.25, smoked salmon £1.95, baked lamb £6.75, breast of*
duckling £7.75, king prawn tails £8, spotted dick £1.50   Vegetarian Meals: fennel au
gratin   Children's Portions ■ Beer ■ *Home Bitter, Theakston XB, Younger IPA* ■ Cider ■
Children Allowed in Bar to Eat

SAXILBY Bridge on A57: Canalside pub with fresh trout and other bar food, and
decent restaurant; children allowed in to eat; garden; Marston, Ruddles beers.

SILK WILLOUGHBY   Horseshoes

Sleaford HG34 8NZ   FOOD
Tel: (0529) 303153
Licensee: Francisco Cunago

The Cunagos' red brick pub stands alongside the busy A15 at the heart of an
otherwise quiet village. Despite also recently acquiring the Carr Arms in nearby
Sleaford, they continue to run the Horseshoes in a polished and good-humoured
way. The large bar, divided up into distinct sitting areas, is homely and
unpretentious in decor and furnishings: bottle green banquettes, solid, simple
wooden tables with little vases of flowers, plants on windowsills and indoor hanging
baskets, twin brick fireplaces, and an eclectic mix of pictures, prints and splendid old
photographs on the walls. Large windows admit lots of natural light in the daytime;
it's rather gloomy in the evening. The piped music is a bit irritating. Blackboard
listed bar food, ever popular, features old standards of the lasagne, steak and kidney
pie and haddock sort; a second board lists more interesting daily specials: perhaps
chicken Argenteuil (white wine and asparagus), lamb's kidneys with sherry, or oxtail
braised with haricot beans. A fresh bream fillet was mildly overdone but served in a
classic white wine and tomato sauce; cooking is perfectly capable, but presentation
on the slapdash side, with dishes apparently dumped on the plate, school dinner

style. There's also a small restaurant, smartly turned out, its tables spaciously arranged, with a reasonably good value table d'hote as well as a seasonally changing à la carte. Dishes are of the old-fashioned sort – lobster thermidor, duckling Normande, fillet steak au poivre. The atmosphere throughout is unambiguously welcoming, with cheery staff, including the Cunagos' charming daughter who runs things in their absence. Note that 5 per cent is routinely added to bills paid by credit card.

Bar Meals and Restaurant: 12-2, 7-10; bar snacks both sessions **Typical Dishes BAR:** *home-made soup £1.50, paté £1.95, steak and kidney pie £4.95, chicken cacciatore £5.25, hake in prawn sauce £5.90* **RESTAURANT:** *lamb's kidneys £4.25, tournedos stilton £10.25, beef persillé £10.50, jumbo scampi £10.25 Vegetarian Meals: baked egg Florentine* ▪Beer▪ *Bass; Courage Directors, John Smith's Bitter Children Allowed in Bar to Eat Outdoor Play Area Garden Outdoor Eating* **Credit Cards:** *Access, Visa*

SKEGNESS Vine, Vine Road Tel: (0754) 610611 17th century former smugglers' haunt, now a comfortable refuge from the tourist track; plain and homely food; bedrooms. Batemans beers. Open: 10-3, 6-11.

SLEAFORD Marquis of Granby 65 Westgate. Cosy little one-room local, gets busy in the evening; regularly changing menu of homely home cooking, including vegetarian dishes, until 8pm. Garden. Ind Coope, Tetley beers. Open: 11-3, 6.30-11.

SOUTH RAUCEBY   Bustard Inn

Main Street NG34 8QG
Tel: (0529) 8250
Open: 12-2.30, 7-11
Licensees: Mike and Brenda Peterken

Honest home cooking at very sensible prices in this modernised, listed stone pub in an idyllic village setting. In winter, a good log fire; in summer, a lovely garden.

Bar Meals: 12-2, 7.30-10; bar snacks both sessions **Typical Dishes:** *home-made soup, home-made steak and kidney pie £2.75, Burgundy beef £2.75, seafood thermidor £3.25, pear and ginger crumble £1 Vegetarian Meals: vegetable goulash £2.25 Children's Portions* ▪Beer▪ *Ruddles Best, County Children Allowed in Bar to Eat Outdoor Play Area Garden Outdoor Eating* **No Credit Cards**

SPRINGTHORPE   New Inn

16 Hill Road DN21 5PY
Tel: (042 783) 254
Open: 12-2 (inc Sun), 7-11
Licensees: Maureen and Mike Nelson

Country pub in charming village, with a garden and a green for sunny days. The menu's a mixture of standards and specials prepared by the landlady cook.

Bar Meals and Restaurant: 12-2, 7-10 (Mon by booking only); bar snacks both sessions **Typical Dishes BAR:** *chicken and leek soup £1.25, prawn cocktail £2.60, beef in red wine casserole £4.40, home-made steak and onion pie £3.85, cheese cod bake £4.40, syrup sponge £1.60* **RESTAURANT:** *similar starters and puddings, roast beef with Yorkshire pudding £4.40, steak £8.75, large plaice £6.50 Vegetarian Meals: celery and walnut gratin Children's Portions* ▪Beer▪ *Batemans XXXB; Ruddles Children Allowed in Bar to Eat Garden Outdoor Eating* **No Credit Cards**

STAMFORD   Bull & Swan

High Street, St Martins PE9 2LJ
Tel: (0780) 63558
Open: 11-3, 6-11
Licensee: David John Wood

There's a new licensee at the Bull & Swan, usually recommended in this guide for
its bed and breakfast, as well as for its three cosy, traditional bars..

Bar Meals: 12-2.15, 6.15-10.15 (7-10 Sun); bar snacks both sessions **Restaurant:** *12-
2.15 (Sun only), 6.15-10.15 Thur-Sat* **Typical Dishes BAR:** *tomato soup 95p, seafood
pancake mornay £2.95, steak, kidney and mushroom pie £3.85, canelloni £3.85, trout
meunière £5.60, home-made apple pie £1.20* **RESTAURANT:** *dinner menu £12.50
Vegetarian Meals: ratatouille nicoise £3.25 Children's Portions* Beer *Camerons
Strongarm; Tolly Cobbold Original Family Room Children Allowed in Bar to Eat
Outdoor Eating Patio/terrace* **Accommodation:** *7 bedrooms, 5 en suite, from £38 (single
£28) Children Welcome Overnight Cots Available Check-in: all day* **Credit Cards:**
Access, Visa

STAMFORD   George Hotel

71 St Martins PE9 2LB   `FOOD`
Tel: (0780) 55171   ! ☻
Open: all day   `B&B`
Licensees: Chris Pitman and Ivo Vannocci   🐟 ✳

Arguably the finest of England's old coaching inns, the George is worth a visit at any
time. It's believed there's been a hostelry of sorts here since the Norman period,
originally as a stopping place for pilgrims on their way to the Holy Land, and a crypt
under what's now the cocktail bar is certainly medieval, while much of the present
building, which dates from 1597, remains in the veritable warren of rooms which
makes up the public areas. Facing the High Street, the oak-panelled London Suite
and York Bar were once waiting rooms for the "twenty up and twenty down"
stages which passed this way, but for the modern pub-goer this bar is probably the
least attractive, being solidly masculine in its appearance – and the guest beer has
(like some of the wayfarers of old) been known to hang around longer than is good
for it. The Garden Lounge, however, which is exotically bedecked in orchids, palms
and orange trees, provides a fine setting for informal eating throughout the day:
lunch including a fine cold buffet augmented by home-made pies, with which,
incidentally, up to 20 wines are offered by the glass. Next door, and by far the most
picturesque spot, is the enclosed courtyard. Surrounded by the ivy-covered hotel
buildings, hung with vast flowering baskets and illuminated by old street lamps, it
makes an ideal venue for morning coffee and afternoon tea, as well as barbecues on
mid-summer evenings. Restaurant dining, in an elegant, chandeliered hall sporting
silver urns, duck presses, and carving trolleys still in daily use, runs along more
classical – and comparatively pricey – lines. Plenty of modern touches shine through
in the food, though: spring onions and stem ginger with a ravioli of crab, perhaps; or
a duet of contrasting sauces, one of sweet onions, one of port wine, partnering a
generous tasty beef fillet. Accommodation at the George is strictly hotel, which is
fine if you're prepared to pay. A liveried porter shows you to the room and there's a
full, cosseting night service: not too many pubs today recall this part of our heritage!
But the comfort of plushly draped bedrooms, close-carpeted through to bathrooms
fitted out with bespoke toiletries, generous towels and rather wonky telephone

showers, is all quintessentially British and not to be sneered at. A morning tray of tea appears at the appointed time with folded daily paper, and a traditional English breakfast down in the Garden Lounge sets well-rested residents up for the day.

Bar Meals: all day, also bar snacks   ***Restaurant:*** 12.30-2.30, 7.15-10.30   ***Typical Dishes BAR:*** soup of the day £3.25, chicken liver paté £2.95, warm salad of duck £5.95, char-grilled kebab £6.75, Billingsgate fish and chips £6.95, puddings £3.65 ***RESTAURANT:*** soup of the day £3.75, terrine of baby leeks £6.45, local pigeon £13.45, pan-fried lemon sole £14.50, salmon in tomato and chive sauce £15.95, puddings £3.95   *Vegetarian Meals:* gruyère cheese fritters £6.95   *Children's Portions* `Cheese` `Beer` *Adnams Bitter; Ruddles Best* `Whisky` *Family Room   Patio/terrace   Outdoor Eating   Summer Barbecue* ***Accommodation:*** 47 bedrooms, all en suite, from £97.50 (single £66)   Children Welcome Overnight   Cots Available   Check-in: all day   ***Credit Cards:*** Access, Amex, Diners, Visa

---

TETFORD   White Hart

Tel: (065 883) 255
Open: 12-3 (not Mon), 7-11
Licensee: Stuart Dick

Original, simple village pub bar, with a tiled floor, wood tables, cushioned settles, and inglenook; also functional modern dining extension, and non-smoking snug. Hit and miss bar food includes good value grilled chops and fish; home-made puddings. In a good walking area.

Bar Meals: lunchtime and evening (not Mon); bar snacks both sessions   `Beer` *Batemans; Marston   Children Allowed in Bar to Eat   Outdoor Play Area   Garden* ***Accommodation:*** Bedrooms from £30 (£20 single)

WILSFORD   Plough

Main Road
Tel: (0400) 30304
Licensee: Isobel German

Enterprising country pub, locally very popular for its good home cooking. Real, fresh handcut chips in the bar; curry night on Wednesday, good value set Sunday lunches. In the restaurant, stuffed chicken breast, and various steaks in sauces.

Bar Meals and Restaurant: lunchtime and Tue-Sun evening   *Vegetarian Meals Children's Menu* `Beer` *Bass; Batemans, various guest beers   Children Allowed in Bar to Eat   Garden*

GREATER LONDON

Albion   Barnsbury N1

10 Thornhill Road
Tel: (071) 607 7450
Open: 11-3, 5.30-11 (11-11 summer)
Licensee: Michael Parish

Elegant Georgian building in genteel street, a tea house in the early 19th century, built by Thomas Albion Oldfield, who then ran it as a dairy until it became a tavern mid-century. Now 'Chef & Brewer'. The large and airy main bar has Victorian atmosphere and an enormous old bar counter; there's a dining area proper to the right, and a ramble of other wood-panelled drinking rooms. Large, pretty beer garden at the rear. Simple but reliably good food.

Bar Meals: 12-2.30, 7-9.30; bar snacks both sessions   ***Typical Dishes:*** *minestrone £1.30, smoked mackerel £3.30, steak and kidney pie £6.25, chicken in barbecue sauce £5.60, fishermans pie £5.10   Vegetarian Meals: leek and potato bake £4.35   Children's Portions*   Beer   *Ruddles Best Bitter, County; Webster's Yorkshire Bitter   Children Allowed in Bar to Eat   Garden   Outdoor Eating   Summer Barbecue   **Credit Cards:** Access, Amex, Diners, Visa*

Alma ★   Wandsworth SW18

499 Old York Road   FOOD
Tel: (081) 870 2537
Licensees: C C Gotto and D Madden
Open: 11-3, 5-11 (all day Sat)

The Alma brings a little bit of France to downtown Wandsworth. Opposite the railway station, this large Victorian pub has been transformed into a French café-bar, and not without a sense of humour they call it the Alma Hotel de la Gare. The exterior of the pub remains very English, in dark green tiling with lots of hanging baskets. Once inside, the French influence begins, done very much tongue in cheek, with a decidedly franglais feel. The spacious main bar has a slightly seedy charm and, oddly, it works, creating a splendidly informal atmosphere. An island bar counter dominates the centre of the room, around which are arranged high stools. In keeping with the French theme, there's a good selection of wines by the glass, and all spirits are poured direct from the bottle (no optics) in generous French measures, a fifth of a gill rather than a sixth. Large check flooring is topped with modest pieces of furniture; mahogany panelling features colourful painted mirrors and large pictures of French café-life adorn one wall. The room invariably has a lively buzz to it and often gets very busy. Only sandwiches are served in the bar; the real food is in the small adjoining dining room, its yellow-painted walls complete with restored frieze, and furnished in French style, with paper cloths over oilcloths. Walls are hung with French posters, while in the centre of the room, a monster piece of furniture is topped by large plants in terracotta pots and displays of fresh flowers. The standard menu, written in jokey French (with translations) is supplemented by a daily changing specials board. The printed menu lists dishes like croque-monsieur, French onion soup and half a pound of Toulouse sausages served with frites. There's also marinated brochette of beef or muffins Alma – hot muffins with smoked salmon and sour cream. The regularly changing board makes best use of what's fresh, including some particularly good fish. A beautiful piece of Cornish lemon sole was supremely fresh and simply pan-fried with lemon and capers, accompanied by a small mixed salad. Everything is handled with a confident hand. Alongside some exotic sorbets, the dessert choice is very English – what's more English than treacle sponge with custard!? Service is friendly and unhurried, and prices are very reasonable.

*Bar Meals: 12-3 Restaurant: 12-3, 7-10.30; bar snacks lunchtime **Typical Dishes** **RESTAURANT:** carrot and leek soup £1.95, feta and spinach filo parcels £3.15, steak and kidney pie £5.15, poached Scottish salmon £6.25, moules marinière £3.95, blackberry and apple pie £1.95 Vegetarian Meals: brazil nut roast en croute with herb and pine stuffing £4.85* `Cheese` `Beer` *Youngs*

Anchor   Southwark SE1

34 Park Street, Bankside
Tel: (071) 407 1577
Open: 11-11
Licensee: Brian Redshaw

Listed for atmosphere and position rather than food; there was a pub on this site during the Great Fire of London, though the present building is mid-18th century, refurbished in the 1960s. Lots of panelling, beams, four little rooms, leather seating and a waterside patio.

*Bar Meals: 11.30 (12 Sun)-3, 5 (7 Sun)-9; bar snacks both sessions **Restaurant:** 12-2.30, 6 (7 Sun)-10 **Typical Dishes BAR:** home-made soup £1.50, sweet and sour chicken £4.30, Cumberland pie £4.30, chilli £4.30, spotted dick **RESTAURANT:** leek and potato soup £2.50, surf and turf £15.95, rack of lamb £13.50, calves liver and bacon £11.25 Vegetarian Meals: vegetable bake Children's Portions* `Beer` *Courage Best, Directors; Larkins Best Bitter; Wadworth 6X Family Room Riverside Garden Outdoor Eating **Credit Cards:** Access, Amex, Diners, Visa*

Argyll Arms   Oxford Circus W1

18 Argyll Street
Tel: (071) 734 6117
Open: 11-11
Licensee: Mike Tayara

Still lots of traditional city tavern atmosphere at this large, rambling oasis opposite the side underground station exit at Oxford Circus. Quieter upstairs.

*Bar Meals: 12-9; bar snacks all day **Typical Dishes:** roast beef with Yorkshire pudding and roast potatoes, steak and kidney pie, shepherds pie (main courses around £4), apple pie Vegetarian Meals: home-made quiche Children's Portions* `Beer` *Marston Pedigree; Tetley Bitter; Wadworth 6X* `Cider` *Addlestones Children Allowed in Bar to Eat **No Credit Cards***

Black Friar   City EC4

174 Queen Victoria Street
Tel: (071) 236 5650
Open: 11.30-3, 4.30-9 (all day summer); closed weekends
Licensee: David McKinstry

Probably the most extraordinary public house in London; a Victorian wedge-shaped pub occupying the site of a medieval friary, and pre-occupied with these historic themes: friars disport themselves in various stages of drunkenness on the outside walls, and in the inner back room, Edwardian art-nouveau includes gaudy marble walls and fireplace, a mosaic ceiling, ornate seating and mirrors, bas-relief friezes of friars at play, and stern monastic mottoes. Food is rudimentary, but the daily specials (around £3.50) include dishes like coq au vin.

Bar Meals: weekday lunchtimes; bar snacks Mon-Thur eves   **Beer**   *Adnams; Bass; Tetley; Whitbread   Children Allowed in Bar to Eat   Patio/terrace*

Britannia   Kensington W8

1 Allen Street
Open: all day (11-3, 5.30-11 Sat)

Cheering and often surprisingly peaceful old pub just a few yards off Kensington High Street. At the front, public and saloon bars are divided by a partition, and share a horseshoe bar; wood panelling, settles and other seats, some in the bow windows. At the back, beyond the saloon, a spacious, modern and brightly furnished room has its own bar and food servery: simple buffet dishes, hot special at lunchtime. Head for the restaurant, for decent homely food like steak, kidney and Beamish pie.

Bar Meals: lunchtime   Restaurant: lunch and evening   **Beer**   *Youngs   Garden*

Brutons, 15 Bruton Lane, W1. Wine-bar-cum-pub of some style, just off Berkeley Square; simple traditional interior, waitress service, maybe loud piped music; seafood dishes. Courage and Websters beers.

Buckingham Arms, 62 Petty France, SW1. Busy Westminster pub with popular home-cooked food (lunch and evening), including beef in Youngs casserole, pork goulash, real burgers; good sandwiches. Close to Wellington barracks and the passport office. Youngs beers. Open: all day (11-3, 7-11 Sat, 12-2 Sun; closed Sun eve).

Cittie of York   Holborn WC1

22 High Holborn
Tel: (071) 242 7670
Open: 11-11(11-3, 5.30-11 Sat); closed Sun

High Victorian architecture on a medieval pub and 17th century coffee house site. The vast gothic style drinking hall has a vaulted ceiling and the longest bar counter in Britain, the gantry above it stacked with thousand-gallon wine vats, and a catwalk (for filling the now redundant vats) above that; lamps suspended from the rafters, and a coal-burning stove. Be early for a seat in one of the little booths; it gets extremely busy. Or head for the little wood-panelled room leading off, adorned with old York prints (patriotic references to Sam Smiths brewery ownership); lunchtime food counters are located in the main hall and downstairs cellar bar.

*Bar Meals: 12-2.30, 5.30-9.30 (not Sun); bar snacks both sessions   **Typical Dishes:** cold baked ham salad, chilli, lasagne, beef stew with dumplings (main courses from £3.50)*   **Beer**   *Sam Smiths   Children Allowed in Bar to Eat   **Credit Cards:** Access, Visa*

City Barge 27 Strand-on-the-Green, W4. Characterful 15th century riverside pub; charming original bar, modern extension and warm, bright conservatory. Now operating as a restaurant on weekday lunchtimes; pubbier in the evenings (no food then). Courage beers. Open: 11-3, 5.30-11 (all day Sat).

Compton Arms 4 Compton Avenue, off Canonbury Lane N1. Cosy old-fashioned alehouse in cobbled mews; lunchtime food a mix of the routine and occasionally special hot daily special. Little rear terrace.Greene King beers. Open all day.

Crockers — Maida Vale NW8

24 Aberdeen Place
Tel: (071) 268 6608
Open: all day
Licensee: David Toft

Extraordinary lavish, spacious and high-ceilinged folly, built in the belief that Marylebone Station was to be located on the site next door. It wasn't.

Bar Meals: *12-2.30, 6-10; bar snacks both sessions* ***Typical Dishes:*** *steak and kidney pie £3.50, lamb chops in mint £3.50, fish pie £3.50 Vegetarian Meals: vegetarian bake Children's Portions* Beer *Arkell; Brakspear; Marston Family Room Patio/terrace Outdoor Eating* ***No Credit Cards***

Dove — Hammersmith W6

19 Upper Mall
Tel: (081) 748 5405
Open: 11-11
Licensee: Brian Lovrey

Well-known, well-loved riverside pub. The tiny front snug is in the Guinness Book of Records; the main bar has leatherette seating and copper-top tables, and there's a quieter upper level with nicer furnishings and food servery, plus a very popular outdoor drinking area by the river. No children indoors.

Bar Meals: *12-3, 5.30-9.30; bar snacks both sessions* ***Typical Dishes:*** *chilli con carne, chicken, ham and leek pie, carbonade of beef, apple pie (main courses from around £3.50) Vegetarian Meals* Beer *Fullers London Pride, ESB Riverside Patio/terrace Outdoor Eating*

Eagle Tavern Shepherdess Walk, off City Road N1. Famous old pub, once part of the complex that included the Grecian Theatre, where Marie Lloyd and other household names once performed. Prints and posters in the large, modernised bar are all that remains. The cosy little side bar has more character. Lunchtime food features a hot daily special. Bass beers.

Flask 14 Flask Walk NW3. Atmospheric old Hampstead village pub, bursting to the gunnels most weekends and summer evenings; attractively simple and down at heel inside. Reputedly the local actors' hangout. Food is very much secondary. Attractive sun-trap garden.

Founders Arms — Southwark SE1

52 Hopton Street, Bankside
Tel: (071) 928 1899
Open: all day

Successfully designed modern Youngs pub, near Blackfriars Bridge. Its almost entirely glass walls at the rear make the most of the river frontage; eat on the large brick-floored terrace in fine weather, with its view of the City and St Pauls. Plain pubby food of the buffet sort; good raised pies; the little partitioned off restaurant area has more ambitious offerings, and is a popular business lunch venue. Unusually for the area, they also do set Sunday lunches.

Bar Meals and Restaurant: *11-9.30 bar snacks both sessions* Beer *Youngs Children in Restaurant Patio/terrace* ***Credit Cards****: Access, Amex, Diners, Visa*

Fox & Anchor   Smithfield EC1

115 Charterhouse Street
Tel: (071) 253 4838
Open: all day Mon-Fri; closed weekends
Licensee: John Hale

The meat is undeniably fresh at this highly traditional old Smithfield pub, where the market men gather for generous plates of English breakfast. The steak and kidney pie is recommended. Non-carnivores should visit on Wednesdays, when the Scottish smoked haddock joins the menu. There's a minimum £3 charge. (Note it closes for staff holidays in late August)

Bar Meals: *breakfast 7 am-10.30 am; lunch 12-2.30*   **Typical Dishes:** *breakfast £6.50, home-made soup £1.65, home-made steak and kidney pie £7, lamb/pork chops and other grills around £6.50, whole battered plaice*   **Beer**   *Ind Coope Burton Ale, Tetley Bitter; Youngs Bitter   Children Allowed in Bar to Eat*   **Credit Cards:** *Access, Visa*

Fox & Grapes   Wimbledon Common SW19

Camp Road
Tel: (081) 946 5599
Open: 11-3, 5.30-11
Licensees: John and Debra Baker

Once a gin shop, converted with the next door stables into a pub in 1956, fronting Wimbledon Common. All food is home-cooked, from locally bought produce, including patés and puddings. Lots of theme nights. Tapas bar. No children indoors.

Bar Meals: *12-2.30, 5.30-9; bar snacks both sessions*   **Typical Dishes:** *chicken and lobster strudel £4.75, Moroccan lamb £4.25, roast beef trencher £4.75, deep fiesta flan Vegetarian Meals: leek and potato pie £3.95*   **Beer**   *Courage Best, Directors, John Smith's Bitter, Magnet*   **Credit Cards:** *Access, Visa*

Front Page   Chelsea SW3

35 Old Church Street   **FOOD**
Tel: (071) 352 2908
Open: 11-3, 5.30 (6 Sat)-11
Licensees: Coghill, Phillips and Fowler

In a quiet residential area of Chelsea, just off the hustle and bustle of the Kings Road, stands the Front Page, on a prime corner site, its white-painted exterior decked with colourful hanging baskets and large attractive gaslamps. Inside is spacious, extremely light and airy, thanks to high ceilings and large windows which let in plenty of natural daylight. Rich navy blue curtains are matched by painted ceiling borders, and whirling ceiling fans help keep the room fresh. Part-panelled, it's furnished in informal rustic style with solid stripped wood tables, round-back chairs and long benches on well-worn floorboards; walls have minimal covering, save some Victorian style nudes. At either end of the bar, two large blackboards display the day's food choice, which is interesting and light in a bistro style: regular favourites include snacks like tuna paté or potato skins with sour cream and chives; as main courses, perhaps an asparagus and bacon gratinée, smoked salmon and scrambled egg, salmon fishcakes or a very flavoursome dish of Thai chicken, in which thin strips of moist chicken breast are served in a mild creamy curry sauce, noticeably laced (to its benefit) with coconut, and accompanied by rice and a small, fresh, colourful salad. Those traditionalists who crave a more solid English lunch are catered for with dishes the likes of sausage and mash. The cooking here will never win awards, but is reliable enough, and fresh produce is well handled. Young, friendly and keen staff provide good service, with a smile. This is a pub worth knowing about, just moments from the crush of the Kings Road and its array of noisier, busier, less welcoming places.

Bar Meals: 12-2.15, 7-10.15 **Typical Dishes:** *carrot and orange soup £2.50, chicken liver paté £3.50, sirloin steak sandwich £4.70, hot chicken, bacon and avocado salad £4.70, salmon fishcakes with hollandaise £5.70, baked bananas £3* *Vegetarian Meals: spinach and pepper roulade* **Beer** *Ruddles County, Webster's Yorkshire Bitter; Whitbread Boddingtons Bitter* **No Credit Cards**

George   Southwark SE1

77 Borough High Street
Tel: (071) 407 2056
Open: 11.30-11 (12-3, 6-11 Sat)
Licensee: John Hall

Former Elizabethan galleried inn, now National Trust protected, hidden away down an unpromising alley in a rather dismal part of town. The 'patio' is actually the original courtyard, lovely in summer, and used by families. Tremendously atmospheric interior, a honeypot for tourists. Bar meals come with two salads. No vegetarian dishes in bar.

Bar Meals: 12-2.30; bar snacks lunchtime **Restaurant:** *12-2, 6-9 (Tue-Thur eves)* **Typical Dishes BAR:** *shepherds pie £4, hot Cornish pastie £3.25, quiche £3.50, trifle £1.75* **RESTAURANT:** *soup £2, char-grilled sardines £3.25, pan fried pork with cider and sage £8.10, home-made steak and ale pie £7.60, fish of the day £7.95, spotted dick £2.80 Vegetarian Meals (restaurant: one choice, £6.80)* **Beer** *Fullers London Pride; Greene King Abbot Ale; Whitbread Boddingtons Bitter* *Patio/terrace* *Outdoor Eating* **Credit Cards:** *Access, Amex, Diners, Visa*

Grapes   Limehouse E14

76 Narrow Street   **FOOD**
Tel: (071) 987 4396
Open: 11.30-2.30; closed weekday evenings (12-2, 7-10.30 weekends)
Licensee: Linda Hubbard

Over 300 years old, the Grapes probably hasn't changed much since Dickens, a frequent visitor, used it as the model for the Six Jolly Fellowship Porters in 'Our Mutual Friend'. A n•rrow riverside pub, squeezed in between buildings that used to house ships' chandlers, block and tackle makers, barge builders and the like, it's easy to imagine Thames watermen drinking in the downstairs bar, with its bare floorboards and boarded, nicotine-stained ceiling. Prime position for watching the passing traffic is from the two tables on a (now glassed-in) verandah overlooking the river, whose murky water laps at the back wall of the building. Take the door marked 'Ladies' and the steep narrow staircase beyond to find the unpretentious first floor fish restaurant. Most things come either grilled, meunière or mornay, the latter not the most refined of sauces, but there are also scallops wrapped in bacon, skate au beurre noir, and an exceptionally creamy version of moules marinière. The great strength here is the quality of the fish – always fresh and never frozen; oysters and lobsters have to be ordered in advance. Book for a lunchtime visit, when it's likely to be busy with Dockland's newly arrived business community. Sandwiches and seafood snacks are available in the bar.

Bar Meals: 12-2, 6-9 *bar snacks both sessions* **Restaurant:** *12-2 (not Sat), 7-9 (not Mon)* **Typical Dishes RESTAURANT:** *moules marinière £3.25, sugar-glazed sea bass*

£9, lemon sole with sauteed prawns and coral butter £9.25, bread and butter pudding Vegetarian Meals: pancakes   Children's Portions   `Beer`   *Ind Coope Burton Ale, Tetley Bitter   Children Allowed in Restaurant to Eat*   **Credit Cards:** *Access, Amex, Diners, Visa*

Holly Bush   Hampstead NW3

Holly Mount, up steep alleyway off Heath Street
Tel: (071) 435 2892
Open: 11-3, 5.30-11 (11-4, 6-11 Sat)
Licensee: Hazel Dure

Be early for a seat in the original front bar, converted from stables in the 18th century: unpretentiously stylish, with its real gas lighting and old wooden settles; a more modern lounge leads off at the rear. Live jazz on Thursday evenings. Decent home cooking by the landlady.

Bar Meals: *lunchtime and evening Tue-Sat, Sun lunch*   **Typical Dishes:** *pea soup, sausage and apple pie, vegetable hotpot, white fish curry (main courses from around £4)*
`Beer`   *Benskins, Ind Coope, Tetley; Youngs   Children Allowed in Bar to Eat (until 8pm) Patio/terrace*

Imperial Arms   Chelsea SW6

577 Kings Road
Tel: (071) 736 9179
Open: 10-11 (10-3, 7.30-11 Sat)
Licensees: Suzanne and Cornelius O'Grady

The promising-looking menu includes a good sandwich list and daily specials, many at £4-£5; there's also a separate restaurant.

Bar Meals: *12-3 (breakfast 10-12), 7-11; bar snacks both sessions*   **Typical Dishes:** *home-made soup £2.50, sausages with onion gravy and mashed potatoes £4.25, entrecote steak £10.75, fresh pasta vongole £5.75, hot chocolate fudge cake £2.75   Vegetarian Meals: eggs Florentine £4.25   Children's Portions*   `Beer`   *Ruddles Best, County, Webster's Yorkshire Bitter   Children Allowed in Bar to Eat   Outdoor Play Area   Garden Summer Barbecue*   **Credit Cards:** *Access, Amex, Diners, Visa*

Kings Arms 68 Titchfield Street W1: City centre local, relaxing atmosphere, reliable moussaka/curry/pizza type lunches. Bass beers, pavement drinking area.

Lamb   Bloomsbury WC1

94 Lambs Conduit Street   ❢
Tel: (071) 405 0713
Open: all day
Licensees: Richard and Rosemary Whyte

A lovely old Victorian local, popular with Bloomsbury office and lecturer types for an excellent after-work pint of Youngs, and reliably plain food from the corner servery. The cosy, usually rather cramped bar winds around the splendid counter, complete with its original gantry and snob screens, from a quiet little anteroom down some steps at the top left, via leather wall benches, little wooden tables and stools, to a locals' public end at the right hand side. Sunday roast lunches.

Bar Meals: *12-2.30 (2.45 Sun); bar snacks both sessions*   **Typical Dishes:** *stilton and cider soup £1.50, prawn and melon £1.50, beef olives, Cumberland sausages, cheese, ham* *and leek pie (main courses from £3.50), home-made apple pie*   Vegetarian Meals: *macaroni cheese*   `Beer` *Youngs* `Whisky`   *Patio/terrace   Outdoor Eating*   **Credit Cards:** *Access, Amex, Diners, Visa*

Lamb & Flag   Covent Garden WC2

33 Rose Street (off Garrick Street)
Tel: (071) 237 4088
Open: all day
Licensee: Adrian Zimmerman

Behind the Georgian frontage is the only surviving example of a 17th century timber-framed building in the west end. The downstairs bar has changed little since Dickens described it; the upstairs Dryden Room is usually quieter (the poet was beaten up right outside the door). The major modern attraction is the excellent range of cheeses, including Somerset Brie, Sage Derby, Blue Cheshire and Blue Shropshire, as well as a range of patés, all served with French bread. There are also chilli/curry hot meals.

Bar Meals: *12-9.30 (not Sun); bar snacks* `Cheese` / `Beer`   *Courage*   **No Credit Cards**

Lamb Tavern   The City EC3

10-12 Leadenhall Market
Tel: (071) 626 2454
Open: 11-9.30; closed weekends
Licensee: D R S Morris

Right next to Richard Rodgers' ultra-modern Lloyds building is Leadenhall market, which is known for its Victorian cast iron and glass-covered cobbled lanes, as well as being home to the Lamb Tavern. It's tempting to describe it as a 'spit and sawdust' pub, except that there is no sawdust and the city gents, for this is a predominantly male preserve, would never dream of spitting; the red lino of the ground floor bar does tend to get covered in cigarette ends though. It's a characterful place, with engraved glass windows, cast iron pillars, a tiled picture panel depicting Dick Whittington, and a spiral staircase leading up to a mezzanine floor. The pub was used as a location for the filming of Branigan with John Wayne (as a photo of the 'Duke' together with landlady Linda Morris testifies) as well as a scene from the Winds of War with Robert Mitchum. Foodwise the thing to go for is the succulent hot roast beef sandwich; the wing-rib is carved to order and served in lengths of real French bread. There are other things available: various sandwiches in the tiled basement bar where the dart players congregate; some hot dishes of the day, like cottage pie and seafood mornay (mainly for staff meals according to the landlady) in the first floor bar, where there are also proper tables to sit at; but the beef is the best and by far the most popular choice. A delicious spin-off from all this beef-roasting is the dripping it generates, which can be had with a piece of French bread for just 50 pence. A real treat. About a dozen wines are listed on a blackboard with house wine and a Liebfraumilch available by the glass.

Bar Meals: *11-2.30; bar snacks* **Typical Dishes:** *hot roast beef on French bread £3.50, dishes of the day from £3.50* `Beer` *Youngs Bitter, Special* **Credit Cards:** *Access, Amex, Visa*

Marquess Tavern   Canonbury N1

32 Canonbury Street   ♥
Tel: (071) 354 2975
Open: all day
Licensees: Peter and Norman Footman

Splendid, spick and span 1850 corner pub, handsome outside and in, rather prettily
set in a sleepy affluent Islington mews, by the new canal walk. Comfortable and
plush inside, with distinguished features, elegant fireplaces, a fine bar counter and
swags and tails. Good hot servery food and excellent £4 specials. Picnic tables on
the pavement.

*Bar Meals: 11-11 (no food Sun)   **Typical Dishes:** home-made soup, prawns, corned beef
pie, steak and kidney pie, shepherds pie   Vegetarian Meals: cheese-stuffed mushrooms*
■ Beer ■ *Youngs   Patio/terrace   Outdoor Eating*   **No Credit Cards**

Monkey Puzzle   Paddington W2

30 Southwick Street   ♥
Tel: (071) 723 0143
Open: 11-3, 5.30-11
Licensee: C P Field

Home cooking, generous portions.

*Bar Meals: 12-2.30, 5.30-10; bar snacks both sessions   **Typical Dishes:** French onion
soup £1.45, garlic mushrooms and bacon, steak au poivre, chicken stuffed with cheese and
mushrooms, home-made steak, mushroom and Guinness pie, Normandy apple flan (main
courses from around £4)   Vegetarian Meals: home-made egg, spinach and stilton pie
Children's Menu/Portions* ■ Beer ■ *Arkells; Brakspears; Fullers; Greene King   Children
Allowed in Bar to Eat   Outdoor Play Area   Garden   Outdoor Eating*   **Credit Cards:**
Access, Visa

Morpeth Arms   Westminster SW1

58 Millbank   ♥
Tel: (071) 834 6442
Open: 11-11
Licensees: Peter and Pat Perfect

Purpose-built for the warders of the old Millbank prison, now very handy for visits
to the Tate Gallery.

*Bar Meals: 11-10; bar snacks all day   **Typical Dishes:** minestrone £1.95, spicy chicken
wings £1.95, chicken tandoori, veal with pasta, beef and Guinness pie (main courses all
£3.35), bread and butter pudding   Vegetarian Meals: chilli   Children's Portions* ■ Beer ■
Youngs   Children Allowed in Bar to Eat   Patio/terrace   Outdoor Eating   **Credit Cards:**
Access, Amex, Visa

Olde Cheshire Cheese Wine Office Court, off Fleet Street, EC4 Tel: (071) 353
6170. Literary London landmark, rebuilt after the Great Fire, and little changed
since the days of Dickens and his carousing chums, except that it's even busier.
Simple snacks in the bar; traditional English chop-house food in the popular upstairs
restaurant. Sam Smiths beers. Open all day; closed weekends.

Old Red Lion 418 St Johns Street, EC1. Informal theatre bar with decent home cooking, salt beef sandwiches, pies and bakes; fish on Fridays. Courtyard drinking area. Food weekday lunchtimes and evenings; cold snacks weekends. Bass beers.

Opera Tavern   Covent Garden W2

23 Catherine Street
Tel: (071) 836 7321
Open: 12-11 (closed Sun lunch)
Licensees: John Still and Michelle Herma Fouwler

Directly opposite the Theatre Royal, Drury Lane.

*Bar Meals: 12-8; bar snacks all day   **Typical Dishes:** leek and potato soup £1.75, paté £1.60, beef goulash, home-made steak and kidney pie, home-made lamb and apple pie, apricot and apple crumble   Vegetarian Meals: vegetable mornay   Children's Portions*
`Beer` *Ind Coope Burton Ale, Tetley Bitter; Youngs Bitter   Children Allowed in Bar to Eat (upstairs)   Patio/terrace   Outdoor Eating   **Credit Cards:** Access, Visa*

Orange Brewery   Pimlico SW1

37 Pimlico Road
Open: noon-11
Licensee: Bernadette Cloran

Good fruity home-brewed beers are a major attraction at this characterful old-fashioned pub, with woody alehouse style, tall stools around high tables, sofas and nice pieces of Victoriana. Food is served in the adjacent Pie and Ale shop: a café-like room with booth seating and a servery. Home-cooked pies £4.

Bar Meals: lunchtime and evening; bar snacks both sessions   `Beer`   *own range of beers   Children allowed in café   Patio/terrace*

Orange Tree, 45 Kew Road, Richmond, Tel: (081) 940 0944: Bustling traditional Victorian pub with well-known upstairs theatre. Excellent, imaginative sandwiches; basket meal style hot food; good value lunchtime restaurant buffet; vegetarian meals; smarter evening à la carte. Children welcome. Food all day (12-3.30 Sun). Patio. Youngs beers.

Princess Louise   Holborn W1

208 High Holborn   ♥
Tel: (071) 405 8816
Open: all day (12-3, 6-11 Sat)
Licensee: Ian Phillips

Bare wood floors, splendid etched mirors, ornate moulded ceilings and fin de siècle glazed tiles, in this opulent 1872-built pub, last refurbished at the turn of the century, and now generally packed with local office workers. The gents toilets are a listed building. Food is cheap and cheerful: snacks in the downstairs bar, chilli/lasagne and specials upstairs. A good range of ales, changing frequently, and champagne by the glass. Jazz on Saturdays. No children.

Bar Meals: lunchtime and evening; bar snacks both sessions   `Beer`   *Greene King; Vaux; Wards; Whitbread*

Red Lion   Mayfair W1

1 Waverton Street
Tel: (071) 499 1307
Open: 11.30-11 (11.30-3, 6-11 Sat)
Licensee: Raymond Dodgson

Mayfair pub with prices to match, but atmospheric and unspoilt, almost rural in feel.
Famous for displaying the day's Financial Times at eye level in the gents. Bar food
includes good sandwiches, game pie, nice quiches (around £4). All puddings home-
made.

Bar Meals and Restaurant: 12-3 (2.30 restaurant), 6-10; bar snacks both sessions
*Typical Dishes RESTAURANT: home-made soup of the day £3.50, duck and lobster
terrine £5.95, braised oxtail with shallots £10.95, steak and kidney pie £11.95, sautéed
lambs kidneys in madeira sauce £11.95 Children's Portions* `Beer` *Greene King IPA;
Ruddles Best, County; Webster's Yorkshire Bitter Children Allowed in Bar to Eat* **Credit
Cards:** *Access, Amex, Diners, Visa*

Rossetti   Maida Vale NW8

23 Queens Grove
Tel: (071) 722 7141
Open: 11-3, 5.30-11 (all day Fri/Sat)
Licensee: Franco Ferrer

A stylish dash of Italy in north west London. Built in the early 1960s, in honour of
the pre-Raphaelites, and kitted out in strong colours, wickerwork, smartly tiled
floors, and Roman statuary. A chef looks after the upper level restaurant, while the
cheery, chatty landlord runs the good, often interesting brasserie-style food in the
main bar. Italian style fish on Fridays; proper coffee.

*Bar Meals: Mon-Sat lunchtime and evening **Typical Dishes:** minestrone £1.30, pasta,
pizzas £3.25, chicken casserole £4 Children's Portions* `Beer` *Fullers Children
Allowed in Bar to Eat Patio/terrace **Credit Cards:** Access, Amex, Diners, Visa*

Salisbury   Covent Garden WC2

90 St Martins Lane WC2N 4AP   ♥
Tel: (071) 836 5863
Open: all day
Licensees: Kevin and Patsy Lee

The oldest theatre pub in London. Beautiful cut glass, carved mahogany fittings,
brass lamps, velvet curtains, and a theatrical atmosphere. Welcoming and cheery.
Pavement drinking.

*Bar Meals: 12-8; bar snacks all day **Typical Dishes:** country vegetable soup £1.75,
melon with ginger or port £1.75, steak and kidney pie with ale £4.75, shepherds pie
£4.50, roast beef and Yorkshire pudding £4.75, apple crumble £1.75 Vegetarian Meals:
pasta Children's Portions* `Beer` *Ind Coope; Webster's Family Room Patio/terrace
Outdoor Eating **Credit Cards:** Access, Amex, Diners, Visa*

Sekforde Arms Sekforde Street EC1. Refurbished, attractive pub specialising in
authentic home-cooked curries, plus casseroles and other traditional English
favourites; fresh vegetables. Also lunchtime restaurant: children in here. Bar meals
weekdays. Youngs beers. Open all day.

The Ship   Wandsworth SW18

41 Jews Row   FOOD

Tel: (081) 870 9667

Open: all day

Licensees: C C Gotto and P Lewis

Directions to find the Ship don't sound promising: drive past Wandsworth bus garage and you'll see the pub beside a ready-mix concrete plant. Once there, though, things immediately begin to look up. A delightful terrace, complete with rose-covered rustic trellis, stretches all the way to the riverside. The pub gets very busy in fine weather, when barbecues lunch and evening offer steaks, kebabs, burgers and fish alongside the likes of half lobsters, pastry-wrapped salmon stuffed with herby cream cheese, and well-kept cheeses from a cold cabinet. In less clement weather, the cold dishes are displayed on an old butchers block in the centre of the conservatory bar, where hot dishes can also be chosen from a blackboard menu. The setting is informal and the food very good. Individual dishes change often, according to what's seasonal: a half lobster with a couple of composite salads is a summer treat, and very affordable at just £4.50. Salads are fresh and chunky, the cheeses look ripe and appealing, and there's good French bread. The conservatory bar makes a pleasant venue, with its motley collection of old wooden tables, benches, chairs and pews; there's also a public bar, very much a locals' haunt, where simple filled rolls are also on offer. The Ship is a Young's pub, under a joint tenancy with the nearby Alma (see above), and now also the Coopers Arms in Chelsea – if this kind of quality can keep being duplicated in other parts of London, this is empire-building of the very best kind. The beer is good and there's a wine list of two dozen decent labels, with a choice of around eight by the glass, in addition. Note that when weather permits, the barbecue is very much the focal point of the pub, more or less replacing the indoor hot menu, apart from dishes that lend themselves to barbecueing.

Bar Meals *12-10 (lunch and evening Sunday); bar snacks lunchtime* **Typical Dishes:** *carrot and pumpkin soup £1.65, grilled goats cheese and tarragon salad £3.75, fresh New Forest sausages £4.95, Thai chicken £5.45, duck breast in port and raspberry sauce £6.50, chocolate roulade £1.65 Vegetarian Meals: brie and cambazola filo parcels in herby tomato sauce £3.25* Cheese Beer *Youngs Riverside Garden Outdoor Eating Summer Barbecue* **Credit Cards:** *Access, Amex, Visa*

Slug & Lettuce   Westbourne Grove W2

47 Hereford Road

Tel: (071) 229 1503

Open: 11-3, 5.30-11 (11-11 Fri/Sat)

Licensee: Rebecca Bennett

Polished woodwork and cosy corners, a warm and friendly atmosphere, and youthful regulars. A blackboard lists dishes of the day; vegetarians are better treated than usual. Large enclosed gardens to the front and rear, conservatory, and an elegant dining room.

Bar Meals: *12-2.30, 6.30-9.30* **Typical Dishes:** *cream of leek and potato soup £1.65, guacamole £2.95, skillet of Cumberland sausages £3.75, chicken supreme with avocado £5.65, Scotch salmon fish cakes with hollandaise £5.10 Vegetarian Meals: fresh vegetables in tikka masala sauce £4.05* Beer *Draught Bass; Ruddles, Webster's Yorkshire Bitter Children Allowed in Bar to Eat Garden Outdoor Eating Summer Barbecue* **Credit Cards:** *Access, Visa*

Spaniards Inn   Hampstead NW3

Spaniards Road
Tel: (081) 455 3276
Open: 11-11
Licensee: P A Rendall

Atmospheric whitewashed pub, once the home of the Spanish ambassador to James I. Dick Turpin, the Gordon rioters, Charles Dickens and John Keats were later sometime visitors; the garden and aviary are said to have prompted Ode to a Nightingale. Lovely old settles, open fires and intimate corners in the downstairs bar (very busy); quieter upstairs in the evenings.

Bar Meals: *12-3, 6 (7 Sun)-9.30 (10 Fri/Sat); bar snacks both sessions* **Typical Dishes:** *home-made soup £2.25, lasagne/moussaka £4.25, chicken chasseur £4.50, steak and kidney pie £4.75 Vegetarian Meals: chilli £3.50* **Beer** *Draught Bass; Fullers London Pride; Highgate Mild Family Room Garden Outdoor Eating* **Credit Cards:** *Access, Visa*

Sporting Page   Chelsea SW10

6 Camera Place, SW10 0BH   `FOOD`
Tel: (071) 352 6465
Open: 11-3, 5.30 (7 when Chelsea play at home)-11
Licensees: Christopher and Michael Phillips and Rupert Fowler

The former Red Lion was remodelled and renamed a couple of years ago, and now has the atmosphere of a wine bar, with a predominantly young clientele. There are dark blue walls above pale wood dado panelling, with decorative tiled panels depicting famous sporting events, the Boat Race among them, and sporting figures like W G Grace, while the seating is largely made up of upholstered benches around solid lightwood tables. The blackboard menu makes a nod towards traditional bar room stodge, listing dishes like bangers, mash and beans, contrasted wittily with more upwardly mobile delicacies like scrambled eggs with smoked salmon (nice soft egg over a generous helping of fish, and a salad garnish); chicken liver paté (over-fluffy, sort of semi-whipped, and a bit bland), salmon fishcakes with a hollandaise sauce, a vegetable and nut stir-fry, or tomato and bacon soup (a bit acidic). A chicken and mushroom pie had a rather over-baked top but plenty of filling with good white chicken flesh, though the sauce was over-thickened; it tasted all right though. A good vinaigrette dressing for the salad arrived separately in a jug and made an ideal dip – not that this was the original intention of course – for the good bread. All in all, a nicely varied menu of home-made dishes by most pub standards.

Bar Meals: *12-2.30, 7-10; bar snacks both sessions* **Typical Dishes:** *French onion soup £2.70, smoked mackerel paté £3.50, salmon fishcakes with hollandaise £5.75, smoked salmon and scrambled egg £5, banoffee pie Vegetarian Meals: ratatouille au gratin £3.25* **Beer** *Ruddles, Webster's; Whitbread Boddingtons Bitter Children Allowed in Bar to Eat (usually) Patio/terrace Outdoor Eating* **No Credit Cards**

Spread Eagle 141 Albert Street, NW1. Well-modernised, friendly Youngs pub on Parkway corner. Lunchtime food from wood-panelled anteroom: poachers pie, cauliflower cheese. Camden Town locals.

Unicorn 32 Duke Street, SW1. Popular cellar pub with decent and unusual food, seafood and European dishes particularly. Nice service. Handy for Fortnum & Mason. Real ales.

White Cross Hotel   Richmond

Water Lane, Riverside TW9 1TH   ❢
Tel: (081) 940 6844
Open: 11-11

Despite the loudly-proclaimed name WHITE CROSS HOTEL, there are no
bedrooms, and a properly pubby interior here, plus a superb Thames-side location,
overlooking Richmond Bridge. Real ale, real fires (three) and real food – a growing
reputation for delicious, simple English bar meals, all home-made. Proper herb
garden. Superb soups. 'Madly busy' in summer. No juke box or other music, nor
fruit machines.

*Bar Meals: 12-3.30 (snacks till 6), 6-8   Typical Dishes: carrot and coriander soup
£1.75, escargots £3, rabbit pie £3.95, beef in Beamish £4.20, tomato and fennel casserole
£3.95, apple charlotte £1.75   Vegetarian Meals: cashew and mushroom paella*   **Beer**
*Youngs Bitter, Special   Family Room   Riverside Patio/terrace   Outdoor Eating Winter
Barbecue and Brazier   Credit Cards: Access, Visa*

White Horse ★   Fulham SW6

1-3 Parson's Green   FOOD
Tel: (071) 736 2115   ☻
Open: 11.30-3, 5-11 (11-3, 7-11 Sat); open 11 am Sun for breakfast   ❢
Licensee: Sally Cruickshank   ☜ ☼

Fairly unremarkable premises, its interior Victorian and opened-up in style, with a
nicotine yellow ceiling, bentwood chairs around eating-height tables, and a few red
leather chesterfields for comfort, plays unexpected and slightly out of the way host
to a remarkable public house, in which food plays an important part. Despite the
popularity and quality of the catering, however, the indefatigable Sally Cruickshank
has pulled off the notoriously difficult trick of retaining the atmosphere of a real pub,
a pub with food, rather than a restaurant with a bar. Everything is home-made using
quality ingredients. At lunchtime, counter-served dishes might include a particularly
appetising-looking beef casserole, fresh asparagus quiche, sausages and cold meats
with interesting salads, like pearl barley with parsley. A good chicken and mushroom
vol au vent comes with buttery new potatoes doused in fresh mint. The one-price
lunchtime puddings, like apple crumble, summer pudding or bread and butter
pudding in various guises, are mostly made by Sally, with Pauline Fisher taking
charge of the main courses. At night, when table service takes over, and red check
cloths and candles appear on some of the tables, a pleasingly simple printed menu
offers cheering supper dishes just made for accompaniment with a good pint of beer
(of which more in a minute). Three Fine English Sausages, made in Fulham, come
with chutney or salad; there are Malaysian and game raised pies, and potato skins,
good and crispy, with a garlicky mayonnaise. Evening chef Louise Kay also offers a
blackboard of daily specials: more grown-up food like chow mein, moules
mariniere, fish in filo pastry, or deep fried brie with cranberry sauce. In addition to
the regular menu there is a traditional Sunday lunch, and on weekend lunchtimes a
notorious brunch guaranteed to contain at least 10 high cholesterol ingredients. The
White Horse has a particular and personal style, the fruits of ten years hard work by
the manager and her staff, and it can be hard to believe that this is in fact a Bass
brewery-owned pub. Apart from offering the best pint of Draught Bass in the whole
of London, there is a commendable commitment to beer in general, including a
menu of speciality bottled names from around the world. Try a Pilsener Urquell
with a plate of fine English cheeses, or a Liefman's Frambozenbier on it's own, as a
sort of liquid pudding. Additionally, a good, informative wine list offers a guide to
the relative sweetness of the whites and full-bodiedness of the reds, and there are a
couple of different wines available by the glass every week. At the first glimpse of

the sun, customers spill out onto the triangular pavement drinking area outside the pub, which has tables and chairs, and onto the green beyond.

Bar Meals: 12-2.45 (1-2.30 winter Sun), 6-10; bar snacks both sessions **Typical Dishes** **LUNCH:** *carrot and tarragon soup, home-cooked ham and paté salads, rabbit in mustard sauce £4.75, steak, pickled walnut and kidney pie £4.90, spinach and feta filo pie £5.20, various crumbles* **EVENING** *(wine bar area): wild mushroom pasta £5.50, pork chow shin £5.25, lamb in filo pastry £6.30, fish mille feuilles £6.15, summer pudding* **Vegetarian Meals** ▮Cheese▮ ▮Beer▮ *Adnams; Draught Bass, Highgate Mild* **Children Allowed in Bar to Eat** **Outdoor Play Area** **Patio/terrace** **Outdoor Eating** **No Credit Cards**

MANCHESTER AND MERSEYSIDE

AINSWORTH, Greater Manchester **Prince William**. Small and cosy with decent northern pub meals, separate dining room, pleasant atmosphere.

BARNSTON, Greater Manchester   **Fox & Hounds**

Barnston Road L61 1BW
Tel: (051) 648 1323
Open: 11.30-3, 5,30-11
Licensees: Ralph and Helen Leech

Three rooms, two bars, lots of bric-a-brac, no chips.

Bar Meals: 12-2 (not Sun); bar snacks **Typical Dishes:** *home-made soup 95p, speciality paté, various casseroles £3.25, pasta dishes £2.95, corned beef hash £2.95, bread and butter pudding £1.50 Vegetarian Meals: mushroom provencale* ▮Beer▮ *Ruddles Best, County; Webster's beers* ▮Whisky▮ **Family Room** **Outdoor Play Area** **Patio/terrace** **Outdoor Eating** **No Credit Cards**

BLACKLEY, Greater Manchester **Old House at Home** 52 Bottomley Side. Cottagey local in secluded spot; take path between Slack Road and Crumpsall Vale. Mon-Sat lunchtime food. Websters and Wilsons beers. Open: 12-4, 7-11.

BLACKSTONE EDGE, Greater Manchester   **White House**

on A58
Tel: (0706) 78456
Open: 11.30-3, 7-11
Licensee: Neville Marney

Moorland pub of local stone; walkers bar; sofa-strewn Pennine Room; plain third bar with picture window. Simple bar food and hot daily specials; cheap and cheerful.

Bar Meals: 11.30-2, 7-10; bar snacks both sessions **Children's Menu** ▮Beer▮ *Clarks; Exmoor; Moorhouse's; Robinwood* **Children Allowed in to Eat (until 9 pm)**

BURY, Greater Manchester   Church Inn

Castle Hill Road, Birtle BL9 6UH
Tel: (061) 764 2857
Open: 12-3 (not Sat), 7-11
Licensee: Terry Leyden

Family-run dining pub behind Birtle church. The original 17th century building is charming and much extended.

Bar Meals and Restaurant: 12-2 (restaurant Sun only), Tue-Sun eves; bar snacks both sessions **Typical Dishes BAR:** *vegetable soup £1.20, garlic mushrooms £2.20, Cumberland sausage £2.50, chilli con carne £2.95, tandoori spare ribs £2.75, apple pie* **RESTAURANT:** *Bury black pudding £1.65, lamb chops £5.25, chicken tarragon £5.75, poached salmon princess £7.90 Vegetarian Meals: nuthouse rissoles £2.75 Children's Menu/Portions* **Beer** *Theakston Best, Old Peculier Children Allowed in Bar to Eat (lunch only) Garden Outdoor Eating* **Credit Cards:** *Access, Visa*

DIDSBURY, Greater Manchester   Royal Oak

729 Wilmslow Road M20 0RH   `FOOD`
Tel: (061) 445 3152
Open: 11-3, 5-11 (11-11 Sat)
Licensee: Arthur Gosling

For lovers of cheese, the Royal Oak is a sort of paradise. Over the last 35 years (24 of them at the Royal Oak), cheese-loving landlord Arthur Gosling has continued to offer probably the largest choice of cheese in the country. A minimum of 50 are always on offer, often many more, and the pub has become so well-known that it's now part of the local tourist trail. Regular visitors find the selection is constantly evolving; one supplier even scours the cheese markets in Paris on behalf of the pub. Recently we found seven varieties of Gouda alone, in the great display to one side of the bar. If you find it difficult to choose, then the obliging staff are only too willing to cut as many tasters as you need, and once you've made your choice be prepared for a huge portion of about 1lb in weight. This is served with immense quantities of splendid fresh granary bread and, rather disappointingly, foil packet butters, as well as bowls of beetroot, pickled onions and cucumber. The price for whatever cheese you choose is a very reasonable £2.30. The pub itself is a rather unassuming red brick building at the end of a row of shops. Its interior is simple but oddly effective: flock wallpapers are covered with a fine collection of old theatrical posters, mainly from the 19th century, and the landlord's own large collection of porcelain casks (spirits and sherry), which he believes to be the largest in the world. Simple seating surrounds cast-iron framed tables complete with their old-fashioned brass anti-spill rims. In fine weather there are a few tables outside, overlooking the busy main road.

Bar Meals: 12-2 (weekdays) **Typical Dishes:** *bread and cheese £2.30; selection changes daily; soup in winter* `Cheese` **Beer** *Marston Dark Mild, Best Bitter, Pedigree* **No Credit Cards**

DIGGLE, Greater Manchester   **Diggle Hotel**

Station Houses OL3 5JZ   `B&B`
Tel: (0457) 872741   ☼
Open: 12-3, 7-11 (all day Sat)   ☺
Licensee: Gerald Mitchell

The village of Diggle is signposted off the A670; if approaching from the north,
you'll need to pass the junction and use the turning circle as left turns are prohibited.
Once through the village, watch out for signs for the Diggle Hotel (by the school).
The hotel itself, a dark stone building by the railway line, dates back to 1789, and is
close to the (disused) longest canal tunnel in Britain, some three and a quarter miles
long. The owners of the Diggle, Gerald and Barbara Mitchell and their daughter
Dawn, gave up running a newsagents in Leeds to take over this free house some
four years ago. The interior of the building is neat and unpretentious. The main
room (and adjoining small room where children can sit) is full of polished brass and
copperware, and the plain walls decorated with a number of 'country' pictures. One
wall has a display of bank notes and coins, both past and present – it's interesting to
see how the notes have shrunk (in size and value!) over the years. Over the bar itself
there's a collection of photos of locals. A standard selection of pub food is served
lunch and evening, ranging from ploughmans and sandwiches to steak and kidney
pie or farmhouse gammon. Upstairs there are three neat, unfussy double bedrooms,
two of them quite compact, the largest with views towards the village. Modern
fitted furniture is used in all rooms, as are duvets with pretty floral covers, and
washbasins. The shared and carpeted bathroom also has a separate shower unit. A
homely residents' lounge has fawn upholstered seating, books and games. The
Mitchells are friendly and charming hosts, and staff equally pleasant.

Bar Meals: 12-2 (2.30 Sun), 7-10; all day Sat; bar snacks both sessions   **Typical**
Dishes: home-made soup £1.05, paté £2.05, steak and kidney pie £3.35, sirloin steak
£7.20, breaded plaice £3.35, bread and butter pudding £1.05   Vegetarian Meals: cheese
and onion flan £3.15   Children's Menu   `Beer`   Taylor Landlord, Golden Best;
Whitbread Boddingtons Bitter   `Whisky`   Family Room   Outdoor Play Area   Garden
Outdoor Eating   **Accommodation:** 3 bedrooms, sharing a bathroom, from £35 (single
£25)   Children Welcome Overnight   Check-in: all day   **Credit Cards:** Access, Visa

---

HEATON NORRIS, Greater Manchester   **Nursery Inn**

Green Lane (off A6)
Tel: (061) 432 2044
Open: 11.30-3, 5.30-11 (all day Sat)
Licensee: Susan Lindsay

Suburban 1930s pub with a traditional layout: vault, smoke room, lobby, lounge;
wood-panelling, and a manicured bowling green at the rear. Fresh fish and fresh
vegetables available daily (limited menu on Saturdays).

Bar Meals: lunchtimes (not Sun); bar snacks both sessions   **Typical Dishes:** home-made steak
and kidney pie, local roast pork, Goan curries, cannelloni (main courses from £3.50)   Children's
Menu   `Beer`   Hydes   Children Allowed in Bar to Eat   Garden   **No Credit Cards**

HUYTON, Merseyside **Rose & Crown** 2 Archway Road: Spacious busy pub near
church; cheap lunchtime food; family room; garden. Walkers beers. Open all day.

LITTLE BOLLINGTON, Greater Manchester **Olde Number Three** Lymm
Road. Haunted old coaching stop, with good value lunchtime and evening meals in
hearty platefuls. Good quality steaks. No music; real fire; garden. Children allowed
for meals. Courage beers. Open: 11.30-3, 5.30-11.

LIVERPOOL, Merseyside   Philharmonic

36 Hope Street
Tel: (051) 709 1163
Open: 11.30-11 (11.30-3, 6-11 Sat)
Licensees: Phil and Carol Ross

Extraordinary cathedral of Victorian confidence and excess. Glorious tiling, carving,
panelling and etched glass: a social museum piece with food and drink available.
Modern intrusions (juke box, fruit machine), though. Remarkable toilets. Children
in dining room.

*Bar Meals: bar snacks lunchtime **Dining Room:** 11.30-2.30   **Typical Dishes:** home-
made soup 95p, egg mayonnaise, steak and kidney pie £2.95, curry £2.75, haddock
£3.20, home-made fruit pies   Vegetarian Meals: lasagne   Children's Portions* `Beer`
Jennings Bitter; Ind Coope Burton Ale, Tetley Mild, Bitter `Whisky`   **No Credit Cards**

MANCHESTER   Lass O' Gowrie

36 Charles Street M1 7DB
Tel: (061) 273 6932
Open: 11.30-11
Licensees: Joe and Vi Fylan

Simply furnished and decorated in a successful alehouse style, with bare brick walls,
hopsack-strewn high ceilings, wooden floors and genuine gas lighting. Good reliable
bar food of a similarly simple and traditional sort: cold dishes for eating with beer.

*Bar Meals: 12-2.30; bar snacks   **Typical Dishes:** cold dishes only: speciality pies, quiches
and cheeses   Vegetarian Meals: mushroom and spinach quiche* `Cheese` `Beer`
Whitbread and home-brewed beers `Cider`   *Family Room*   **No Credit Cards**

MANCHESTER   Mark Addy

Stanley Street, Salford, Manchester 3
Open: all day
Licensee: John Edwards

Deeply smart waterside pub with a distinctly unpubby smoked glass facade and
brick-bayed and boothed interior with an elegant modern air. Canalside drinking
area. Another of the growing band of cheese pubs – particularly popular in the north
west; a range of dozens, both British and continental, plus patés, with granary bread.
Outstanding value.

Bar snacks all day `Beer` *Marston; Whitbread   Children Allowed in Bar to Eat
Patio/terrace*   **No Credit Cards**

MANCHESTER   Mr Thomas's Chop House

52 Cross Street M2 7EA

Tel: (061) 832 2245
Open: 11-11 (11-3, 8-11 Sat); closed Sun
Licensees: Richard Tatlow and Richard Davis

Mr Thomas's Chop House (no-one knows how it got its name) is little changed
since it first opened its doors in 1867, thanks largely to co-owners Richard Davis
and Richard Tatlow, who re-opened the pub's splendid dining room after it had
spent long years of use as offices. Standing on one of Manchester's busy shopping
streets (close to the Arndale Centre), the pub has an unassuming and deceptively
small frontage. Thought to be the last surviving Victorian pub in the city, its small,
narrow front bar features fine oak panelling, a mosaic-tiled floor (which spreads
throughout) and Victorian-style lamps and decor. Walk through this room and an
apparently small space quite suddenly opens out into the splendid dining area. Here,
original and impressive wall tiles combine splendidly with the mosaic floor, and
pink-clothed tables bearing small vases of fresh flowers are well-spaced and
invariably full. The Chop House is extremely popular with business lunchers, who
regularly fill the place on weekdays, so be prepared to wait for a table. Freshly-made
sandwiches (made to order) are available in the bar, including a wonderful hot roast
beef one, the meat freshly roasted each day. But the dining room is where most
people eat. A printed menu offers a varied list, including recently-introduced tapas
dishes like fried monkfish, braised squid and beef meatballs. On the regular menu,
robustly prepared starters include black pudding with mustard sauce, deep-fried
mushrooms or king prawns in garlic butter. Follow these with a perfectly-cooked
Barnsley chop (superb meat), a northern mixed grill, grilled gammon or lamb's liver
with bacon and onions. Puddings are reassuringly traditional, with old favourites like
rice pudding, fruit crumble and bread and butter pudding. Expect to pay around
£30 for two for a full 3-course lunch, or opt for tapas or just a single dish and you
can spend a lot less. Service is friendly and informal. Weekends bring a younger and
noisier crowd, as well as loud music... the landlord makes sure he has weekends off.

Bar Meals: 11.30-3, 5-8 (not Sat eve; no food Sun); bar snacks both sessions
Restaurant: 11.30-4 (3 Sat, not Sun)   ***Typical Dishes BAR:*** *home-made soup, hot roast*
beef, selection of cold meats, cheeses and fish   ***RESTAURANT:*** *black pudding with*
mustard sauce, roast joint of the day, fillet of plaice with smoked trout mousse, game and
seafood (in season), bread and butter pudding   **Beer**   *Whitbread Boddingtons Bitter,*
Castle Eden Ale   ***Credit Cards:*** *Access, Visa*

MANCHESTER Smithfields 77 Shude Hill: Fairly recent bank-conversion next
door to Arndale Centre. Very cheap bar snacks, some surprisingly substantial, and
upstairs restaurant with ambitions (Thur-Sat). Jennings, Ind Coope, Tetley beers.
Open daily lunch and evening. Access and Visa taken.

MARPLE BRIDGE, Greater Manchester **Hare & Hounds** Ley Lane. Country
pub in pretty spot; open fire; decent lunchtime and evening bar food; garden.
Robinsons beers. Usual hours.

MELLOR, Greater Manchester **Devonshire Arms** Longhurst Lane. Charming
country local in Pennine village south of city; well-heeled regulars; decent bar meals.
Robinsons beers.

MIDDLETON, Greater Manchester   Olde Boars Head

Long Street
Open: 11.30-3, 5.30-11 (12-3, 7-11 Sat)
Licensee: Martin Reeves

Handsomely renovated early medieval inn, with Elizabethan refurbishments.
Rambling and individually styled rooms are full of ancient character and the cosy
parlour atmosphere of the 19th century. Plain and homely bar food, but other
options than things with chips. Piped pop.

Bar Meals: lunchtime; bar snacks   **Beer**   *Lees   Children Allowed in Bar to Eat (until*
8 pm)   Patio/terrace

MOTTRAM, Greater Manchester **Waggon Inn**: Rusticised dining pub, popular
for its hot specials, lunchtime and evening.

ROMILEY, Greater Manchester **Duke of York** Stockport Road (B6104). Tel:
(061) 430 2806: Historic old pub, comfortably refurbished, with various rooms
including popular rear vault; no music; decent lunchtime and evening bar and
restaurant meals; garden. Courage beers. Open: 11-3, 5.30-11.

RUSHOLME, Greater Manchester   Rampant Lion

17 Anson Road, Manchester M14 5BZ
Tel: (061) 224 1916
Open: 11.30-11
Licensees: Salvador and Gill Abalo

Formerly a private club with showbizzy members; a pub since 1984. Just five
minutes from Manchester city centre, with extensive grounds and parking.

Bar Meals: 12-2.30; bar snacks both sessions   **Typical Dishes:** *leek and potato soup*
£1.10, home-made paté £1.20, roast of the day £4, steak and mushroom pie £3, paella
£4, Manchester tart   Vegetarian Meals: vegetable pancake £2.20   Children's Portions
Beer   *Greenalls Original; Ind Coope Burton Ale, Tetley Bitter; Whitbread Boddingtons*
*Bitter   Family Room   Garden   Outdoor Eating   **Accommodation:** 3 bedrooms, all en*
suite, from £32.50 (single £27.50)   Children Welcome Overnight   Cots Available
*Check-in: all day   **Credit Cards:** Access, Amex, Diners, Visa*

SOUTHPORT, Merseyside **Herald Hotel** 16 Portland Street Tel: (0704) 34424:
Lunchtime bar food includes good home baking, hot daily specials, in cheery pub-
hotel in Victorian resort.   **Two Brewers** Kingsway. Varied bar food, smarter
restaurant, comfortable pub.

STALYBRIDGE, Greater Manchester   Hare & Hounds

Mottram Road SK15 2RF
Tel: (061) 338 4614
Open: 11.30-3, 5.30-11
Licensees: G and D Atkinson

Country pub-style city pub. Very simple menu but good home cooking.

Bar Meals:: 12-2.30, 5.30-7.30; bar snacks both sessions   **Typical Dishes:** *French onion*
soup £1.25, home-made paté £1.75, chicken kebab £4.95, pizza £3.50, deep-fried

haddock £3.50, fruit pie   *Vegetarian Meals: vegetarian chilli*   *Children's Menu/Portions*
Beer   Draught Bass   Family Room   Outdoor Play Area   Garden   Outdoor Eating
Credit Cards: *Access, Visa*

STOCKPORT, Greater Manchester   Bakers Vaults

Market Place SK1 1ES   ❢
Tel: (061) 429 8934
Licensees: Ian and Dorothy Brookes

No printed menu, just good honest home-made food from fresh local ingredients,
changing often. Eclectic tastes catered for – traditional English, Frenchified and the
comparatively exotic all rub shoulders on the long blackboard list. Prices very low.

Bar Meals: 12-2.30, 5.30-8.30 (Fri/Sat eve only); bar snacks lunchtime   **Typical**
Dishes: *cheddar cheese and broccoli soup, cheese and garlic stuffed deep-fried mushrooms, pork*
Parisienne £3.85, southern fried Cajun chicken £3.85, Dalmatian steak (entrecote in pink
peppercorns, blue cheese and cream) £4.65, raspberry strudel £1.25   Vegetarian Meals:
Cuban curry £3.25 **Beer** *Robinsons   Children Allowed in Bar to Eat* **No Credit**
Cards

Plough 82 Heaton Moor Road. Refurbished and antiqued, and popular for decent
bar food.

STOCKPORT, Greater Manchester   Red Bull

14 Middle Hillgate SK3 4YL
Tel: (061) 480 2087
Open: 11.30-3, 5-11
Licensee: Brian Lawrence

Modest pub with good home cooking. No home-made puddings, though.

Bar Meals: 12-2.15; bar snacks 5-7.30   **Typical Dishes:** *green pea and bacon soup*
£1.25, home-made paté £1.70, lamb and mushroom parcel £2.90, gammon and egg
£3.20, fish and chips £2.75   Vegetarian Meals: nut cutlets **Beer** *Robinsons Mild,*
Bitter   Children Allowed in Bar to Eat (lunch) **No Credit Cards**

THORNTON HOUGH, Merseyside   Seven Stars

Church Road (B5136)
Tel: (051) 336 4574
Open: 11.30-11 (11-3, 5-11 winter)
Licensee: C E Nelson

Cleanly refurbished, purposeful dining pub, with dining tables, cushioned kitchen
chairs and modern banquettes in its two communicating rooms, and waitress service.
The usual menu is highly routine, but on a lucky day the hot specials may be
rewarding. There'a a vegetarian dish of the day. Attractive terrace and garden area
for fine weather.

Bar Meals: lunchtime and evening; bar snacks lunchtime   **Typical Dishes** soup 95p,
gammon and eggs, hotpot, rabbit stew (main courses from £4)   Vegetarian Meals **Beer**
Whitbread   Garden

UPPERMILL, Greater Manchester   Cross Keys

Running Hill Gate (a mile off A670)
Tel: (0457) 874626
Open: 11-3, 6.30-11 (all day summer)
Licensee: Philip Kay

A bustling, lively 18th century local and magnet for visitors, its rambling interior has flagstone floors, low beams and ancient settles among the more modern seats; open fire; no music. The menu's a mix of scampi type 'convenience' and more interesting specials. It's the HQ of the Oldham Mountain Rescue Team. There's live jazz on Mondays, folk on Wednesdays.

Bar Meals: lunchtime and evening; bar snacks both sessions **Typical Dishes:** *spring rolls, liver and bacon casserole, chilli (main courses from £3), apricot crumble* *Vegetarian Meals* *Children's Portions* Beer *Lees* *Patio/terrace*

URMSTON, Greater Manchester **Manor Hey** 130 Stretford Road Tel: (061) 748 3896. Plain home cookikng at reasonable prices (including Sunday roast lunches) in popular hotel bar; children and vegetarians catered for. Theakston, Youngers beers. Open: 11.30-3, 7-11.

WIGAN, Greater Manchester **Old Pear Tree** Frog Lane. Beer drinkers' favourite, and not bad lunchtime food either; near the bus station. Burtonwood beers. Open: 12-3.30, 5.30-11.

WOODFORD, Greater Manchester **Davenport Arms** 550 Chester Road (A5102), Tel: (061) 439 2435. Very decent home-cooked lunches, including ploughmans with a choice of a dozen cheeses, in worth-a-detour classic country pub on suburban fringes. Real fire; no music; garden. Robinsons beers. Open: 11-3.30, 5.15-11.

NORFOLK

ATTLEBOROUGH   Griffin

Church Street NR17 2AH
Tel: (0953) 452149
Open: 10.30-2.30, 5.30-11
Licensee: Richard Ashbourne

Charming 16th century coaching inn with a wealth of period details, in the town centre. Sensitively refurbished. Open fires, lots of bric-a-brac, welcoming atmosphere. Go for fresh local fish in the bar; smarter food in the separate restaurant.

Bar Meals: 11.30-2, 6.30-9.30 (12-2, 7-9.30 Sun); bar snacks lunchtime **Typical Dishes:** *chicken and leek soup £1.25, whitebait £2.50, home-made steak and kidney pie £4.25, Griffin brunch £4.50, duck in black cherry sauce £9, tropical cheesecake* *Vegetarian Meals: tagliatelle Nicoise* Beer *Greene King; Marston; Whitbread* Cider *Children Allowed in Bar to Eat* *Patio/terrace* **Accommodation:** *8 bedrooms, sharing 3 bathrooms, from £30 (single £20)* *Children Welcome Overnight* *Cot Available* *Check-in: all day* **No Credit Cards**

BLAKENEY   Kings Arms

Westgate Street NR25 7NQ
Tel: (0263) 740341
Open: 11-11 (12-10.30 Sun for meals)
Licensee: John Howard Davies

Three pleasant knocked-through rooms in pretty Grade II listed cottage pub not far from the harbour. Ex-theatrical licensees. A self-contained flatlet is available for holiday lets (and perhaps a second for 1992).

Bar Meals: all day summer (12-2.30, 6-9.30 winter); bar snacks both sessions **Typical Dishes:** *seasonal fresh vegetable soup £1.60, fresh crab/local mussels £3, home-made meat pie £4.90, home-made curry £3.90, fresh cod £4, fruit crumble £2 Vegetarian Meals: vegetable curry £3.90 Children's Menu/Portions* ■Beer■ *Marston Pedigree; Ruddles County; Webster's Yorkshire Bitter Family Room Outdoor Play Area Garden Outdoor Eating* **Credit Cards:** *Access, Visa*

BLICKLING   Buckinghamshire Arms

off B1354, near Aylesham NR11 6NF
Tel: (0263) 732133
Open: 11-2.30, 6-11
Licensees: John and Judith Summers

Splendid 17th century inn which stands deferentially at the gates of the even more splendid Blickling Hall; both are now National Trust property. New licensees since our last edition have cheered up the bar meals, and introduced fresh fish and home-made pies. Also an excellent place to stay, two of the three bedrooms have dramatic evening views across to the floodlit hall; original features and four-posters plus a tidy shared bathroom with old-fashioned tub make this a characterful bed and breakfast stop. Children are allowed in the restaurant.

Bar Meals: lunchtime and evening ■Beer■ *Adnams; Greene King; Woodfordes Outdoor Play Area Garden Outdoor Eating* **Accommodation:** *3 bedrooms, sharing a bathroom, from £50 (single £40) Children Welcome Overnight Check-in: all day* **Credit Cards:** *Access, Visa*

BRANCASTER STAITHE   Jolly Sailors

Kings Lynn PE31 8BJ   ▼
Tel: (0485) 210314
Open: 11-3, 7-11 (11-11 summer)
Licensee: Alister Borthwick

Very popular country pub on the edge of a huge dune and salt flat area. Three rooms blend traditional and modern.

Bar Meals and Restaurant: 12-2.30, 7-9 (later Fri/Sat); all day July/Aug; bar snacks both sessions **Typical Dishes BAR:** *home-made soup £1.20, Staithe mussels in white wine £4.20, chicken and mushroom pie £4.60, seafood pancakes £5.30, fish pie £4.90, summer pudding £2.40* **RESTAURANT:** *crab mornay £3.50, pheasant casserole £7.40, sautéed lambs kidneys £8.70, smoked haddock in shellfish sauce £8.90, home-made puddings from £2.20 Vegetarian Meals: vegetarian lasagne Children's Menu* ■Beer■ *Greene King IPA, Abbot Ale* ■Cider■ *Suffolk Strong Family Room Outdoor Play Area Garden Outdoor Eating* **Credit Cards:** *Access, Diners, Visa*

BRISLEY   Bell

The Green NR20 5DW
Tel: (0362) 668108
Open: 11-3, 6-11
Licensees: C H Carter and J Ford

16th century pub with original beams, and winter log fires in its three inglenooks. In the small cottage to the rear, Richard Taverner translated the Bible from Latin into English in 1575. The Bell overlooks the largest common land in Norfolk, at some 200 acres; just 200 yards from the village centre.

Bar Meals: 12-2.30, 6-9.30; bar snacks both sessions **Restaurant:** *12-3 Sun, 7-10 Tue-Sat* **Typical Dishes BAR:** *home-made soup £1.55, moules marinière £2.95, home-made steak and kidney pie £3.75, fresh salmon hollandaise £4.50, smoked haddock mornay £4.25, home-made cherry cheesecake £1.70* **RESTAURANT:** *fresh turbot in shrimp sauce £12.55, fresh sea bass in cream and pepper sauce £12.50, fresh whole brill £11.95, home-made summer pudding £2.75 Vegetarian Meals: home-made tagliatelle £3.25 Children's Menu/Portions* **Beer** *Ind Coope, Tetley; Whitbread; Woodford's* **Cider** *Addlestones Children Allowed in Bar to Eat Outdoor Play Area Patio/terrace Outdoor Eating Summer Barbecue* **Credit Cards:** *Access, Visa*

CAWSTON   Ratcatchers Inn

Cawston NR10 4HA
Tel: (0603) 871430
Open: 12-2.30, 7-11
Licensees: Eugene and Jill Charlier

One to watch, with promising food, despite an over-long and rather difficult to read printed menu, which is backed up by an appetising list of blackboard specials with lots of fresh fish and perhaps breast of pigeon or duck, as well as a vegetarian dish. The word is certainly out locally; we found all 20 or so tables booked up the evening we dropped by, a good buzz about the place and cheery, helpful staff. It's probably the only pub called the Ratcatchers in the country, a pleasantly old fashioned free house in a rural spot just off the B1149. A charming balcony offers good sunset views. The pub is being extended, and overnight accommodation may follow.

Bar Meals: 12-2, 7-10.15 (12-1.45, 7-9.45 Sun); bar snacks both sessions **Typical Dishes:** *home-made soup £1.30, quails egg and crispy bacon salad £2.95, steak and kidney pie £4.35, guinea fowl £5.65, chicken and crab with vermouth sauce £5.95, treacle sponge and custard £1.75 Vegetarian Meals: spaghetti £4.95 Children's Menu/Portions* **Beer** *Adnams Best Bitter Children Allowed in Bar to Eat Garden Outdoor Eating* **No Credit Cards**

CLEY-NEXT-THE-SEA   George & Dragon Hotel

High Street NR25 7RN
Tel: (0263) 740652
Open: 11-2.30, 6-11
Licensee: Rodney Sewell

Extensively remodelled and redecorated, the previously low-key George & Dragon, a salt marsh and sea-side village hotel, is now aiming much higher with its facilities and food. Menus are looking promising, with lots of local seafood, fresh vegetables and local meat, as well as the favourite, pan haggerty, a comfortingly old-fashioned potato layer dish. The hotel is also hoping to become a major birdwatching centre. Same menu in the dining room. Bars are nicely pubby and used by locals.

Bar Meals: 12-2, 7-9; *bar snacks lunchtime and winter evenings* **Typical Dishes:** *home-made soup £1.60, Cley cider pickled herring £2.65, chicken divan £5.25, sauté of beef chasseur £6.95, pan haggerty £4.75, lemon meringue cheesecake £1.75 Vegetarian Meals: cauliflower cheese £3.75 Children's Menu/Portions* Beer *Greene King Abbot Ale, IPA, Rayments* Whisky *Family Room Garden Outdoor Eating* **Accommodation:** *9 bedrooms, 6 en suite, from £40 (single £30) Children Welcome Overnight Cots Available Check-in: by arrangement* **No Credit Cards**

COLKIRK   Crown

Fakenham NR21 7AA
Tel: (0328) 862172
Open: 11-2.30, 6-11
Licensee: Patrick Whitmore

Redbrick village centre pub with home-cooked food. What was the restaurant is now a dining room with the same menu as the bar.

Bar Meals: 12-1.45, 7-9.30; *bar snacks lunchtime* **Typical Dishes:** *broccoli soup £1.30, garlic mushrooms £2.10, home-made steak and kidney pie £3.95, home-made chicken fillet in stilton sauce £5.50, steak £9.25, bread and butter pudding £2.20 Vegetarian Meals: home-made cashew nut roast, tomato and herb sauce £3.80 Children's Portions* Cheese Beer *Greene King beers* Whisky *Children Allowed in Bar to Eat Patio/terrace Outdoor Eating* **Credit Cards:** *Access, Visa*

CROMER   Bath House

The Promenade
Tel: (0263) 514260
Open: 10-3, 5.30-11 (all day summer); closed mid-Jan to mid-March
Licensees: Ben and Barbara Wheston

Handsome Regency inn with pleasant and welcoming bar in this likeable Victorian resort; a good place for windy walks and long weekends. The famous local crabs are landed only yards away, and in season are the house speciality. Fresh vegetables and reliable homely cooking by the landlady. Most of the rooms, all on the first floor, have views of the sea; residents' lounge.

Bar Meals: lunchtime and evening; *bar snacks both sessions* **Typical Dishes:** *crab soup, steak and Guinness pie, fish bake, home-baked ham salad, spotted dick Vegetarian Meals Children's Menu* Beer *Bateman; Greene King* **Accommodation:** *7 bedrooms, all en suite, from £40 (single £20)* **Credit Cards:** *Access, Visa*

DERSINGHAM   Feathers Hotel

Manor Road PE31 6LN   B&B
Tel: (0485) 40207
Open: 11-2.30, 5.30-11
Licensees: Tony and Maxine Martin

Fine stone-built carrstone pub not far from Sandringham and close to gentle woodland rambles. Mellow oak-panelled main bar overlooks splendid garden with solid wooden tables for summer drinking; also a cheery horse-brassy public bar. Recommended for bed and breakfast.

Bar Meals: lunchtime and evening *Vegetarian Meals* *Children's Menu* **Beer**
Adnams; Bass *Children Allowed in Bar to Eat* *Outdoor Play Area* *Garden* *Summer
Barbecue* **Accommodation:** *6 bedrooms, sharing 2 bathrooms, from £50* *Children
Welcome Overnight* *Check-in: all day* **Credit Cards:** *Access, Visa*

DOCKING   Pilgrims Reach

High Street PE31 8NH
Tel: (0485) 518383
Open: 12-3 (12-2.30 Sun), 7-11; closed Tue
Licensee: Brian Bean

16th century pub once much used by passing pilgrims; the barn they used for B&B
is now the main bar area. All rooms have inglenook fireplaces. Only fresh produce,
local where possible, is used by the chef-proprietor.

Bar Meals: 12-2, 7-9; bar snacks both sessions **Restaurant:** *12-2.3-0, 7-9.30* **Typical
Dishes BAR:** *home-made soup £1.95, grilled sardines £3.95, chicken chasseur, home-
made steak pie, chilli con carne, apple and sultana pie* **RESTAURANT:** *steak au poivre,
chateaubriand, lemon sole Florentine, grilled bananas with Cointreau* *Vegetarian Meals:
lasagne* *Children's Portions* **Beer** *Adnams; Greene King* *Children Allowed in Bar to
Eat* *Outdoor Play Area* *Garden* *Outdoor Eating* **No Credit Cards**

DOWNHAM MARKET   Cock Tavern

43 Lynn Road PE38 9NP
Tel: (0366) 385047
Open: 11-2.30 (not Tue), 7-11
Licensees: Roger and Julia Hassell

Small, neatly-kept pub run with warmth and enthusiasm, often packed with fans of
the landlady's cooking. Sauté potatoes rather than the ubiquitous chips. No children
indoors.

Bar Meals: 12-1.45 (not Sun), 7-9.15; no food Tue; bar snacks both sessions **Typical
Dishes:** *carrot and potato soup with tarragon £1.80, six large snails £3.45, beef, prune and
Beamish casserole £4.95, bacon, cheddar and onion flan £3.95, mixed bean casserole
£3.95, honey and almond tart £1.95* *Vegetarian Meals: mushroom bake* *Children's
Portions* **Beer** *John Smith's Bitter; Whitbread Flowers Original* **Cider** *Outdoor
Play Area* *Garden* *Outdoor Eating* **No Credit Cards**

DOWNHAM MARKET   Crown Hotel

Downham Market PE38 9DH
Tel: (0366) 382322
Open: 11-2.30, 6-11 (all day Fri/Sat)
Licensee: John Champion

17th century coaching inn, worth trying for bed and breakfast.

Bar Meals: 12-2, 6-9; bar snacks both sessions **Typical Dishes:** *stilton and onion soup
£1.35, paté, steak and kidney pie, Somerset pork, fishermans pie, chocolate brandy gateau
(main courses from around £4)* *Vegetarian Meals: lasagne* *Children's Menu/Portions*
Beer *Draught Bass; Batemans; Greene King; Woodfordes* *Family Room* *Children
Allowed in Bar to Eat* *Patio/terrace* **Accommodation:** *10 bedrooms, 7 en suite, from
£36 (single £26)* *Children Welcome Overnight* *Cot Available* *Check-in: all day*
Credit Cards: *Access, Amex, Diners, Visa*

EAST HARLING Swan High Street. Cosy, characterful tile-floored and low-beamed village local; straightforward home cooking lunchtime and evening.

EAST RUSTON   Butchers Arms

Oak Lane NR12 9JG
Tel: (0692) 650237
Open: 12-3, 6-11

Friendly family-run free house which makes good use of local fish.

Bar Meals and Restaurant: 12-2.30, 6.30-10.30; bar snacks both sessions **Typical Dishes BAR:** *home-made soup £1.50, ham-stuffed peaches £2, roast of the day £3, steak and mushroom pie £3, sea shanties £2.50, fresh raspberry pie £2* **RESTAURANT:** *fresh crab £2.50, steak in whisky sauce £6.50, scampi and prawn provencale £6.50, fresh large plaice £4.50, chocolate and orange gateau £2* *Vegetarian Meals: vegetarian lasagne £3.75* *Children's Menu/Portions* ▊Beer▊ *Adnams; Tetley Bitter; Woodfordes* *Family Room* *Outdoor Play Area* *Garden* *Outdoor Eating* **No Credit Cards**

GILLINGHAM   Swan

Loddon Road NR34 0LD
Tel: (0502) 712055
Open: 7 am (breakfast)-11 pm; all day Sun for meals
Licensee: C F Ablitt

Full name the Swan Motel, on a roadside site with five acres of grounds. Modernised, airy and well-kept; plush and frilly-curtained bar and dining room; clean modern bedrooms.

Bar Meals and Restaurant: 11-2.30 (7-9 breakfast), 6-10; bar snacks both sessions **Typical Dishes BAR:** *mushroom soup £1.30, home-made paté £2.40, steak and kidney pie £3.95, beef in red wine £4.95, lasagne £3.95, plum pudding* **RESTAURANT:** *garlic mushrooms £2.40, sirloin steak £9.75, fresh salmon £6.80, lobster £16* *Vegetarian Meals: lasagne* *Children's Menu/Portions* ▊Beer▊ *Adnams Bitter, Broadside; Draught Bass; Marston Pedigree* *Family Room* *Outdoor Play Area* *Garden* *Outdoor Eating* *Summer Barbecue* **Accommodation:** *14 bedrooms, all en suite, from £38 (single £28) Children Welcome Overnight* *Cot Available* *Check-in: all day* **Credit Cards:** *Access, Visa*

GREAT BIRCHAM   Kings Head Hotel

Kings Lynn PE31 6RJ
Tel: (048 523) 265
Open: 11-2.30, 6.30-11
Licensee: I Verrando

An Italian landlord means the menu mixes Italian with traditional English dishes. It can close early on quiet lunchtimes.

Bar Meals: 12-2, 7-9.30; bar snacks lunchtime **Typical Dishes BAR:** *home-made soup £2, home-made steak and kidney pie £5.50, egg and vegetable bake £4.80, home-made fish cakes with crab sauce £5.50* **RESTAURANT:** *lobster thermidor £12.50, halibut £9.80, scallops in marsala £9.80, fruit of the forest pavlova* *Vegetarian Meals: vegetables and avocado mornay £4.50* *Children's Portions* ▊Beer▊ *Adnams Best; Draught Bass* ▊Whisky▊ *Family Room* *Outdoor Play Area* *Garden* *Outdoor Eating*

Accommodation: *5 bedrooms, all en suite, from £50 (single £43)   Children Welcome*
*Overnight   Check-in: all day   **Credit Cards:** Access, Visa*

HAPPISBURGH   Hill House

The Hill (off B1159)
Tel: (0692) 650004
Open: 11-3, 6-11 (11-2.30, 7-11 winter)

Next to a church with an elegant bell tower, the Hill House was a Tudor
stonemason's cottage, and still has lots of old-time character. The sea is just 500
yards away, so local fish is a speciality; also fresh local meat and vegetables, and their
own seasonal salads. Good daily home-cooked specials in the attractive restaurant:
casseroles, sauced steaks, fresh crabs, vegetarian dish of the day. They also let
bedrooms.

Bar Meals and Restaurant: *lunchtime and evening (not Sun eve nor all Mon in winter); bar
snacks both sessions* Beer *Adnams; Greene King; Woodford's   Children Allowed in Bar
to Eat   Garden   Credit Cards: Access, Visa*

HEMPSTEAD   Hare & Hounds

Holt NR25 6LD   ¶
Tel: (0263) 713285
Open: 12-3, 7-11
Licensee: J M D Hobson

Simple old country pub run by the owners with no extra staff. Popular with locals
all year, tourists in the season. All food is home-cooked: main courses all around
£4.50. The nice old-fashioned interior has tiled floors topped with rugs, a variety of
furnishings, cottage windows with deep sills, and a woodburning stove. No
machines or music. "No whisky drinkers", so no malts.

Bar Meals: *12.15-2.15, 7.15-9.15; bar snacks lunchtime*   ***Typical Dishes:*** *(no starters),
leek, bacon and potato bake, pheasant casserole, cassoulet, seasonal fruit pies   Vegetarian
Meals: green bean and lentil pie   Children's Portions* Beer *Family Room   Garden
Outdoor Eating   **No Credit Cards***

HETHERSETT Greyhound Henstead Road: Attractive village local with decent
bar meals, nice garden. Watneys beers. **Kings Head** 36 Old Norwich Road
(B1172): Imaginative cooking, lunchtime and Fri/Sat evenings. Pretty summer
garden. Ruddles, Webster's beers.

HOLKHAM Victoria Hotel near Holkham Hall on A149 Tel: (0328) 710469:
Victorian hotel on the coast road; good views from the bar bay windows; try local
fish on the otherwise routine menu. Eight reasonably priced bedrooms. Adnams
beers.

KINGS LYNN Tudor Rose St Nicholas Street Tel: (0553) 762824. Fresh home-
cooked meals in attractive oak-beamed bars and restaurant. No music; garden;
bedrooms. Adnams beers. Open 11-3, 5 (5.30 Sat)-11.

MUNDESLEY   Royal Hotel

30 Paston Road NR11 8BN
Tel: (0263) 720096
Open: 11-2, 6-11
Licensee: Michael Fotis

Little coastal town with good beach; the hotel is on the cliff-top, overlooking the
sea. Much modernised, but pleasant bar. Go for the specials and local seafood.

Bar Meals and Restaurant: 12-2, 7-10 (11 Sat); bar snacks both sessions **Typical**
Dishes BAR: *home-made soup £1, paté £1.95, roast pork £4.20, steak sandwich*
£3.95, deep-fried haddock £3.75 **RESTAURANT:** *similar starters and puddings,*
tournedos Rossini £10.95, duck à l'orange £9, Dover sole meunière £11.95 **Children's**
Portions Beer *Adnams; Greene King* Whisky *Family Room   Patio/terrace*
Outdoor Eating **Accommodation:** *42 bedrooms, all en suite, from £45 (single £29.95)*
Children Welcome Overnight   Cots Available   Check-in: all day **Credit Cards:** *Access,*
Diners, Visa

MUNDFORD Crown Crown Street Tel: (0842) 878233. Refurbished old
coaching stop in pretty village, with a welcome for strangers, and decent bar meals.
Bedrooms. Real ale.

NEATISHEAD   Barton Angler

Irstead Row NR12 8XP
Tel: (0692) 630740
Open: 11.30-2.30, 6.30-11
Licensees: Tim and Anne King

Boats available for hire. All aboard for the food too.

Bar Meals: 12-2, 7-9; bar snacks both sessions **Restaurant:** *7-9.30* **Typical Dishes**
BAR: *home-made soup £1.95, garlic mushrooms £2.75, chicken curry £4.95, steak and*
ale pie £5.25, lasagne £4.95, bread and butter pudding £1.95 **RESTAURANT:**
similar starters; beef Nelson £11.95, chicken Stanley £8.50, kidneys espagnole £8.50,
strawberry japonaise £3 Vegetarian Meals (bar): lasagne £4.95   Children's Menu/Portions
Beer *Greene King   Garden   Outdoor Eating   Summer Barbecue* **Accommodation:** *7*
bedrooms, 5 en suite, from £50 (single £25)   Children Welcome Overnight   Cot Available
Check-in: all day **Credit Cards:** *Access, Amex, Visa*

NORTH CREAKE   Jolly Farmers

1 Burnham Road NR21 9JW
Tel: (0328) 738185
Open: 11-3, 6-11
Licensee: Peter Whitney

Small local village pub, with an open log fire in the lounge, and a dining room
popular with parties. Daily specials include fresh local fish and seafood. Fresh
vegetables with all main courses. Sunday lunch is confined to traditional roasts.

Bar Meals: 12.15-1.45, 7-9.45; bar snacks lunchtime **Restaurant:** *7-9.45 (no food in*
bar or restaurant Mon) **Typical Dishes:** *leek and celery soup £1.55, stilton mushrooms*
£3.15, sirloin steak £7.50, duck breast and sweet pepper £7.95, salmon £6.50, fresh fruit
trifle £1.70 Vegetarian Meals: tagliatelle £4.95   Children's Portions Beer *Courage*
Best; Greene King Abbot Ale; Tolly Cobbold Bitter   Family Room   Outdoor Play Area
Garden **No Credit Cards**

NORWICH   Adam & Eve

Bishopgate   ▼
Open: all day
Licensee: Colin Burgess

The oldest pub in the city, part 13th century, and traditionally furnished with
ancient carved settles and benches, part-panelled walls, handsome parquet or tiled
floors. Bar food's a mix of the routine and more interesting; fewer of the latter, but
always good value. Decent sandwiches.

Bar Meals: lunchtime and evening; bar snacks both sessions **Typical Dishes:** *shepherds
pie, pork in cider, fish pie (main courses around £3.20), bread and butter pudding
Vegetarian Meal* ▮Beer▮ *Ruddles, Webster's   Children Allowed in Bar to Eat
Patio/terrace*

NORWICH   Reindeer

10 Dereham Road NR2 4AY   ▼
Tel: (0603) 666821
Open: 11-3, 5-11 (all day Sat)
Licensees: Wolfe Witnam and Andrew Howard

Popular home-brew pub – a window allows a view of the little brewhouse
operation – with traditional, no-frills alehouse atmosphere; young and trendy in the
evenings. Live folk music.

Bar Meals: 12-2.30, 5-9.30; bar snacks lunchtime **Typical Dishes:** *parsnip and apple
soup £1.90, dahl samput (aubergines and chillies) £2, lamb cassoulet £3.20, Malayan
chicken stew £4.50, spicy king prawn chow mein £5.30, local ice-cream £1.50   Vegetarian
Meals: lentil bake* ▮Beer▮ *own brews* ▮Cider▮ *Patio/terrace   Outdoor Eating* **No
Credit Cards**

POTTER HEIGHAM Falsgate Wroxham Road (A1065). Homely local worth
knowing for simple, cheap pasta dishes; a useful stop. Courage beers.

REEDHAM   Reedham Ferry Inn

Norwich NR30 5TX
Tel: (0493) 700429
Open: 11-3, 6.30-11 (11-2.30, 7-11 winter)
Licensee: David N Archer

Traditional back bar and less inspiring front bar in little riverside pub popular with
Norfolk Broad holidayers. Well-kept and thoughtfully run. A promising looking
menu advises all vegetables are fresh and served al dente.

Bar Meals: 12-2.15 (2.45 cold food), 7-10; bar snacks both sessions **Typical Dishes:**
*soup of the day £2.10, dim sum £3, char-grilled lamb chops £6, roast quail £6, home-
made steak and kidney pie £5.60   Vegetarian Meals: mushrooms en croute £5.30
Children's Menu* ▮Beer▮ *Adnams; Woodfordes* ▮Whisky▮ *Family Room   Riverside
Patio/terrace   Outdoor Eating* **Credit Cards:** *Access, Visa*

REEPHAM Old Brewery House Hotel Market Square Tel: (0603) 870881:
Creeper-clad redbrick hotel locally known as the Dial House (sundial above the
front porch). Characterful little bar and Georgian lounge with views over the square.
Routine bar food; decent B&B children welcome. Garden. Good range of beers.

RINGSTEAD   Gin Trap Inn

High Street
Tel: (048 525) 264
Open: 11.30-2.30, 7-11 (11.30-3, 6-11 summer)
Licensees: Brian and Margaret Haymes

Opened-up split level bar, clean and comfortable with attractive touches (be early for a window seat), and lots of bric-a-brac, including the notorious traps themselves. Seats are bookable in the little dining room on Saturday evenings. Decent bar food and delicious specials; free nibbles on Sunday lunchtime, a noble pub tradition. Petanque played in the garden.

Bar Meals: 12-2, 7-9.30 (10 Fri/Sat, not winter Sun); bar snacks both sessions **Typical Dishes:** *home-made steak and kidney pie, home-made lasagne, fish or Norfolk pie (main courses from £4) Vegetarian Meals Children's Menu* **Beer** *Adnams; Greene King; Ruddles; Woodforde's Nice children allowed in dining area Garden*

ROCKLAND ST MARY New Inn 12 New Inn Hill Tel: (05088) 395. Decent lunchtime and evening bar food, comfort and welcome; traditional pub games; boats moored over the road. Children welcome. Courage beers. Open: 11-2.30, 6.30-11 (12-2, 7.30-11 winter).

SALHOUSE Lodge Rectory Road Tel: (0603) 782828. Splendid ex rectory pub, converted 15 years ago; lovely grounds for summer drinking. Decent lunchtime and evening bar food too; children and vegetarians catered for. Greene King, Theakston, Woodforde's beers. Open: 11-2.30, 6-11.

SCOLE   Scole Inn

Norwich Road IP21 4DR
Tel: (0379) 740481   **B&B**
Open: 11-11
Licensee: Philip Hills

Good Bed and Breakfast. Glorious 17th century Dutch facade.

Bar Meals and Restaurant: 12-2.30, 6-10 (12-2, 7-9 Sun); bar snacks both sessions **Typical Dishes BAR:** *home-made soup £1.50, croissant filled with garlic and prawns £2.25, home-made steak and kidney pie £4.25, tagliatelle with diced chicken and bacon in spinach sauce £4.75, Cumberland sausages £3.25* **RESTAURANT:** *smoked Barbary duck with orange and walnut sauce £3.85, poached chicken breast with a wild mushroom sauce £9.25, guinea fowl with a cider and apple meat glaze £9.25, red mullet wrapped in smoked salmon £8.15 Vegetarian Meals: homity pie Children's Portions* **Beer** *Adnams Best, Broadside; Draught Bass* **Whisky** *Children Allowed in Bar to Eat Garden* **Accommodation:** *23 bedrooms, all en suite, from £63.50 (single £46) Children Welcome Overnight Cots Available Check-in: all day* **Credit Cards:** *Access, Amex, Diners, Visa*

SCOLE   **Crossways**

Ipswich Road IP21 4DP
Tel: (0379) 740638
Open: 11-11
Licensee: Peter Black

The Crossways' location at the crossing of the A140 with the A143 would be ideal were it not for incessant traffic hold-ups on the corner. Double glazing for the bedrooms works well enough, but the pub's exterior is not self-cleaning, and simply crossing the road is at times plain treacherous. This is not to detract in any way from Peter Black's unusual and idiosyncratic pub, which plays host to a good mix of generations and tastes with its admirably varied choice, first of food from pizzas and curries through to seafood or steaks, and second, of locations in which to relax and enjoy it. Central to the issue is the pub bar itself, which manages to capture all the trappings and atmosphere of a good local without resorting to darts and a pool table. Prominently displayed menu boards offer vindaloo, Madras, tikka and biryani curries (one always vegetarian), six varieties of pizza in 9 or 12 inch sizes (from £3.50 up), several traditional pies and grills, and house specials like seafood Catalana (£5.50), mushroom and stilton stroganoff (£4.50), and Singaporean mah-mee. Evenings add a weekly changing table d'hote at around £10 for three courses, as well as a varied à la carte menu. Eat either in an airy conservatory-style bistro or in the more formal dining room, where French windows open out onto a rear patio and large, enclosed garden. There's a strong showing of fresh fish from Lowestoft, and the first-class steaks come from locally-farmed herds. Savoury pancakes (£7.50), vegetable chilli (£7.50), Spanish paella, Dover sole (£14.95) and beef stroganoff (£9.25) are typical favourites from a much wider selection. In addition to a well-kept range of beers, amongst which the prize-winning Adnams is the star, the bar's new vacu-vin allows up to thirty wines to be served by the glass from an even more extensive list whose many bargains can also be purchased wholesale. The building is reputed to be 16th century and was still a private house until conversion in the 1950s, when original floorboards from the upper storey were used to panel the walls of what is now the pub lounge. Upstairs, the bedrooms have been carefully designed and neatly kitted out. Three have full en suite facilities, the remaining two sharing a bathroom. Meanwhile, below, Peter, his staff and many regulars await the 1992 construction of the Scole by-pass with singular sang froid.

Bar Meals: 11-2.15, 6-10; bar snacks both sessions   Restaurant: 12-2.15, 7-10
Typical Dishes BAR: *chicken and sweetcorn soup £1.25, fresh prawns with garlic dip £3.25, lamb and apricot pie £4.50, Singaporean mah-mee £6.95, mushroom and stilton stroganoff £4.25, chocolate and ginger trifle £1.95   **RESTAURANT:** shellfish in garlic butter £2.95, chicken breast with fresh lime sauce £8.25, half roast duck with wild berry sauce £9.50, paella £9.50, hot black cherries with brandy sauce £2.50   Vegetarian Meals: savoury pancake £3.95   Children's Portions   **Beer** Adnams Bitter   **Cider** Burnards Garden   Outdoor Eating   Summer Barbecue   **Accommodation:** 5 bedrooms, 3 en suite, from £35 (single £30)   Children Welcome Overnight   Cot Available   Check-in: all day   **Credit Cards:** Access, Amex, Diners, Visa*

SCOTTOW   **Three Horseshoes**

Tel: (069 269) 243
Open: all day

Keen real ale pub with a good, constantly changing range and August mini beer festival. Interesting food, too, including fresh local game in season, and a variety of pies, among the home-made section on the varied bar menu. Fish is mostly bought in. They also have bedrooms.

Bar Meals: lunchtime and evening; bar snacks both sessions   **Typical Dishes:** *poachers, steak and kidney, pork and apple pies, beef stroganoff, chilli (main courses from £3.50) Vegetarian Meals: vegetable curry with pilau rice   Children's Menu*   Beer   *Various Children Allowed in Bar to Eat   Garden*

SCULTHORPE Sculthorpe Mill on A148. Another pub run by the people who have the Lifeboat at Thornham (q.v.); a free-house restaurant in a converted 18th century water mill on the river Wensum. Bar meals seven days; restaurant Tue-Sat evenings.

SEDGEFORD King William IV Heacham Road (B1454) Tel: (0485) 71765. A useful detour off the busy coast road, and good home cooking, using local meat and vegetables; hotpots and casseroles and some ambitious specials, all at low prices. Food lunchtime and evening. Adnams, Bass, Greene King beers. Open: 11-3, 6.30-11.

SMALLBURGH   Crown

Smallburgh Hill NR12 9AD   ♥
Tel: (0692) 536314
Open: 11.30-2.30, 5.30-11 (12-4, 7-11 Sun)
Licensee: Carl Richard Hunter

Thatched, beamed 15th century building with barrel furniture and a large open fire. Menus are interchangeable; fresh vegetables always, daily changing menu. B&B from 1992 (no details available).

Bar Meals: 12-2, 6-9; bar snacks both sessions   **Restaurant:** *12-2 (Sun only), 7.30-9.30* **Typical Dishes BAR:** *tomato and plum soup £1.50, home-made paté £1.85, pigeon pie £4.95, beef and ale pie £3.95, Barnsley chops with rosemary £4.95, apple or rhubarb pie £1.60*   **RESTAURANT:** *grilled Mediterranean prawns £3.85, roquefort steak £9.50, madeira steak £9.50, fresh lemon sole £7.95   Vegetarian Meals: leek and lager pie £3.95 Children's Portions*   Beer   *Courage Directors; Greene King IPA; Whitbread Castle Eden Ale, Flowers IPA   Children Allowed in Bar to Eat   Outdoor Play Area   Garden Outdoor Eating*   **No Credit Cards**

SNETTISHAM   Rose & Crown

Old Church Road PE31 7LX
Tel: (0485) 541382
Open: 11-3, 5.30-11

Splendid white-painted 14th century free house inn, with old-fashioned stone-floored locals' public, traditional front bar with enormous fire, carpeted dining room and airy modern extension. Gets very busy. Food of every style and price, much of it routine bar meal style.

Bar Meals: 12-2, 6.30-10; bar snacks both sessions   **Typical Dishes:** *courgette soup £1.50, melon and prawns £2.95, king size mixed grill £9.50, half a barbecued chicken £6.50, fillet steak with blue cheese £10.50, home-made meringues £1.75   Vegetarian Meals: savoury pancakes £5.95   Children's Menu/Portions*   Beer   *Adnams; Draught Bass; Greene King IPA, Abbot Ale   Family Room   Outdoor Play Area   Garden Outdoor Eating   Summer Barbecue*   **Accommodation:** *3 bedrooms, 1 en suite, from £25 (single £15)   Children Welcome Overnight   Check-in: by arrangement*   **Credit Cards:** *Access, Visa*

STANHOE   Crown Inn

Kings Lynn PE32 4QD   ♥
Tel: (0485) 518330
Open: 11-3, 6-11

Quiet country pub specialising in home-made food, particularly game in season.
Fresh vegetables.

Bar Meals: 12-2, 7-9; no food Mon; bar snacks both sessions   **Typical Dishes:** *game soup*
£1.50, avocado and crab cocktail £2.80, breast of pigeon casserole £4.80, jugged hare
£4.80, Crown fish cakes £3.80, summer/autumn pudding £2   Vegetarian Meals:
vegetable lasagne   Children's Menu/Portions **Beer** *Elgoods beers   Children Allowed in*
Bar to Eat   Garden   Outdoor Eating   **No Credit Cards**

STOKESBY   Ferry Inn

Great Yarmouth NR29 3EX
Tel: (0493) 751096
Open: 11-3, 6.30-11
Licensees: Roger and Gloria Scott-Phillips

Plain, traditional waterside pub of spartan character. Busy with river folk in summer
(free moorings).

Bar Meals: 12-2, 7-9; bar snacks lunchtime   **Typical Dishes:** *garden vegetable soup £2,*
smoked mackerel £2.70, home-made beef and onion pie £4.25, rump steak £7.95, seafood
platter £5.40, summer pudding £1.75 Vegetarian Meals   Children's Menu **Beer**
Adnams Extra; Whitbread beers   Family Room   Outdoor Play Area   Riverside   Garden
Outdoor Eating   **No Credit Cards**

STOW BARDOLPH   ★   Hare Arms

Kings Lynn PE34 3HT   FOOD
Tel: (0366) 382229   ♥
Open: 11-2.30 (12-2.30 Sun), 6-11   ☺
Licensees: David and Patricia McManus

This regularly star-rated entry is a picturesque country pub in a delightful Norfolk
village just a few miles south of Kings Lynn. Inside is pleasantly refurbished and
immaculately run, with a cosy bar, elegant restaurant, popular conservatory
extension (also the family room) and an intriguing coach house in the garden for
children. The pub gets its name, not from the animal, but from a prominent local
family, still found in these parts; venture into the church, and a wax effigy of one
Sarah Hare is posted as a warning to others not to transgress the Sabbath – the
unfortunate Sarah pricked her finger while sewing on a Sunday and died of blood
poisoning. Cast such morbidity aside, and head straight for the cheery welcome and
excellent food at the Hare, where a fairly unexceptional printed menu of home-
made curries, lasagnes and grills is thrown into the shade by quite exceptional daily
specials. But be early, because this is by no means a secret. The star of the specials
board is the freshest local fish, perhaps a sole with a good crisp salad (£5.95), prawn
and mushroom stuffed plaice in a tangy lemon sauce (£5.50) or a grilled cod
mornay (£4.75), with fresh local crabs and lobsters in season. But meat eaters are by
no means neglected: lightly sauced chicken, a superb steak, oyster and Guinness pie,
spicy spare ribs, and a particularly memorable lamb steak with mint hollandaise
(£6.50), are typical of the daily meat specials. Winter brings game casseroles. It's not
really a pub for vegetarians, though one or two token dishes are offered. Nice wines
by the glass and a serious list of bottles.

Bar Meals: *12-2, 7-10; bar snacks lunchtime*   **Restaurant:** *7.30-9.30 (not Sun)*
Typical Dishes BAR: *stilton and bacon soup £1.50, chicken breast with tarragon £4.75, steak, oyster and Guinness pie £5.50, banoffee pie £2.25*   **RESTAURANT:** *stir-fried scallops £4.25, magret of duck in madeira £13.95, salmon en croute hollandaise £13.25, pork in roquefort £13.50, strawberry and fresh mint cheesecake £2.75   Vegetarian Meals: vegetable lasagne £4.75   Children's Portions* ▮Beer▮ *Greene King IPA, Abbot Ale, Rayments Bitter* ▮Whisky▮ *Family Room (conservatory)   Garden   Outdoor Eating* **No Credit Cards**

SWANTON MORLEY   Darby's

Dereham NR20 4JT
Tel: (0362) 637647
Open: 11-2.30, 6-11
Licensee: John Carrick

Converted from two cottages in 1986 by the licensee, a local farmer, after the local mega-brewery closed the village's last traditional pub. Now offering camping and caravan space.

Bar Meals and Restaurant: *12-2, 7-10; bar snacks both sessions*   **Typical Dishes BAR:** *cauliflower and stilton soup £1.65, garlic mushrooms £2.50, chicken and mushroom pie £3.75, fusilli £3.50, fishermans catch £3.95, cheesecake £1.65*   **RESTAURANT:** *French farmhouse platter £3.75, rump, sirloin, T-bone steaks £8.75-£12.50, seafood mixed grill £11.50, coquilles Saint Jacques £9.50   Vegetarian Meals: vegetable curry £3.25   Children's Menu/Portions* ▮Beer▮ *Adnams: Greene King Abbot Ale; Woodfordes Wherry* ▮Cider▮ *Family Room   Children Allowed in Bar to Eat   Outdoor Play Area   Garden   Outdoor Eating   Summer Barbecue* **Accommodation:** *4 bedrooms, sharing 2 bathrooms, from £29.50 (single £15)   Children Welcome Overnight   Cots Available   Check-in: all day*   **Credit Cards:** *Access, Visa*

THOMPSON Chequers Inn Griston Road Tel: (095 383) 360. Thatched village local in secluded spot; three unspoilt low-ceilinged bars, family room, good value home cooking and usually very busy. Garden. Adnams, Bass beers. Open: 11-3, 6-11.

THORNHAM   Lifeboat Inn

Ship Lane PE36 6LT
Tel: (048 526) 236
Open: all day
Licensee: Nicholas Handley

A perennial classic: the Lifeboat is a charming whitewashed 16th century ex-farm, ideally set for weekend escapes on the edge of an expanse of salt flats; wake to the sound of the sea, or of doves cooing in the cote. Even casual visitors can enjoy the characterful ramble of old rooms, low-ceilinged, small-doored, five-fired, rustically furnished and decorated. Food is good; hearty winter hot dishes, summer al fresco, autumn seafood, and a splendid little restaurant. Bedrooms have been dramatically increased in number since our last edition, from two to fourteen, and prices risen; new rooms are in a barn conversion.

Bar Meals: *12-3, 7-10 (all day summer); bar snacks both sessions*   **Restaurant:** *7-10*
Typical Dishes BAR: *calabrese soup £1.90, whole sardines in garlic £3.50, home-made pie of the day £5.25, sirloin steak £9.50, mussels in wine and cream £4.95, ginger sponge £1.75*   **RESTAURANT:** *lobster bisque £2.50, steamed scallops in lime butter sauce £6.50, medallions of beef fillet in mild mustard sauce £14.75, breast of duck with honey and thyme gravy £14.50, poached salmon with roquefort cheese £13.75, apple strudel*

£2.50 *Vegetarian Meals: spinach pasta Children's Menu/Portions* `Beer` *Adnams;
Greene King* `Cider` *Taunton Traditional Family Room Outdoor Play Area Garden
Outdoor Eating Summer Barbecue* **Accommodation:** *14 bedrooms, all en suite, from
£60 (single £35) Children Welcome Overnight Cots Available Check-in: all day*
Credit Cards: *Access, Amex, Diners, Visa*

Kings Head Church Street Tel: (048 526) 213. Village cottage pub with two cosy,
pretty bars; hearty home cooking. Greene King beers. Bedrooms.

TIVETSHALL ST MARY   Old Ram

Ipswich Road (A140) NR15 2DE
Tel: (0379) 608228 (tables)/676794 (accommodation)
Open: all day
Licensee: John Trafford

Five 'luxury' en suite rooms are now on offer at this popular roadside family dining
pub, where tables are often reserved. Try the daily fish specials. Good traditional
features and a warming fire in the main bar, which has other nice rooms leading off,
plus a dining room proper.

Bar Meals: *12-10; bar snacks* **Typical Dishes:** *chicken curry £5.50, steak and kidney
pie £5.75, jumbo plaice fillet £5.95, lemon chiffon cheesecake £2.25 Vegetarian Meals:
aubergine and mushroom bake £4.95 Children's Portions* `Beer` *Adnams; Greene
King; Ruddles, Webster's Family Room (coach house) Garden Outdoor Eating*
Accommodation: *5 bedrooms, all en suite, from £60 (single £40) Children Welcome
Overnight Check-in: all day* **Credit Cards:** *Access, Visa*

UPPER SHERINGHAM Red Lion on B1157 Tel: (0263) 825408. Home-
cooked fresh food on tiny daily menu; food can be very limited at lunchtimes
(Saturday especially, when preparing for a busy evening). Bedrooms are cheap
but also exceedingly modest. Adnams beers plus a guest ale. Open: 11-3,
6 (7 winter)-11.

WARHAM   Three Horseshoes

69 The Street NR23 1NL
Tel: (0328) 710547
Open: 11-2.30 (12-2.30 Sun), 6-11
Licensee: Ian Salmon

No chips, no baskets, and early last orders in the evening so that locals can enjoy a
traditional drinking environment. No curries or pasta dishes either – very much an
old-fashioned home-cooked English menu. A friendly, pleasantly spartan interior.
No under 14s overnight.

Bar Meals: *12-2.30, 7-8.30 (not Tue); bar snacks both sessions* **Restaurant:** *7-9 (Wed-
Sat)* **Typical Dishes BAR:** *crab and samphire soup £1.60, stewkey blues (local cockles in
cream and cider) £2.70, cottage roll savoury £4, Norfolk pastie £4, baked crab £4.50,
syrup sponge £1.75* **RESTAURANT:** *mackerel hotpot £3.50, roast duck £8, roast
lamb £7.50, pork and vegetable pie £7, Norfolk syllabub £2 Vegetarian Meals: baked
mushrooms Children's Portions* `Beer` *Greene King beers; Woodfordes Wherry Family
Room Outdoor Play Area Garden Outdoor Eating* **Accommodation:** *4 bedrooms, 1
en suite, from £33 (single £16.50) Check-in: all day* **No Credit Cards**

WELLS-NEXT-THE-SEA   Crown Hotel

The Buttlands NR23 1EX   `FOOD`
Tel: (0328) 710209   ❢
Open: 11-2.30, 6-11   `B&B`
Licensee: Wilfred Foyers   ☀

Outward appearances are sometimes deceptive, the facade of the Crown being a case
in point. It stands at the foot of a tree-lined village green, the Buttlands, where
medieval marksmen once practised their archery. Compared to the elegant Georgian
terraced houses which surround the green, the Crown's black and white painted
exterior (genuinely Tudor, as it turns out) has the rather care-worn look of a modest
town pub. But what a jewel it is inside! The bar progresses on three levels from
front to back, where a family-friendly conservatory of high-backed settles opens
onto the rear patio and stable yard. Within, there's an open log fire, high bar stools
and low copper-topped, barrel-shaped tables, the walls throughout covered with
portraits and memorabilia of Horatio Nelson – born in a nearby village and whose
sister reputedly lived on the Buttlands. The beer's good, and the bar menu is
extensive. Single course meals of curry, steak and kidney pie or vegetarian gougère
come in generous portions at £4.50 or less, there's a selection of pasta dishes and
omelettes at under £4, and grills from a mini "steakwich" through to a full mixed
grill at £11. Plenty of salads, sandwiches, and sausage-burger-fishfinger
combinations for the children complete the picture. The adjoining restaurant,
continuing the interior's Victorian theme, is neatly decked out with pink cloths and
fresh vased pinks, and offers more adventurous dining. Lunch is available daily
(booking essential on Sundays), and there's an evening choice of table d'hote or à la
carte, on which locally landed fish and shellfish feature prominently. Local mussels in
filo with provencale sauce and wild salmon hollandaise are prettily presented and
reveal much skill in their saucing, without the pretence of haute cuisine nor the
pretension of the "moderne". Gressingham duck breast, tournedos Rossini and
Wiener schnitzel are equally appealing, without taking any undue risks, and the
cream-heavy desserts carefully made. To describe the bedrooms as modest is not to
decry them: they are simply but adequately furnished and even the smallest offers a
view of the charming old town, across the Lion Yard where the London mail coach
once pulled in, and over pantiled roofs to the sturdy Norman church below. The
seal is set on an enjoyable stay by a tranquil night's rest in these evocative
surroundings, a hearty and enjoyable English breakfast, and the friendly service and
warm hospitality of the Foyers family and their youthful staff.

*Bar Meals and Restaurant: 12-2, 6.30 (7 restaurant)-9.30 (9 Sun and winter); bar
snacks both sessions*   ***Typical Dishes BAR:*** *home-made soup £1.60, chicken liver paté
£3, prawn and tomato gougère £3.95, seafood tagliatelle £4, goujons of white fish £4.25,
raspberry bavarois*   ***RESTAURANT:*** *chicken in champagne sauce £8, lambs kidneys in
sherry and cream £7.50, roast duck £8.75, pigeon breast in wild mushroom sauce £8.75,
plaice with prawn sauce £8*   *Vegetarian Meals: vegetarian gougère   Children's
Menu/Portions*   `Beer`   *Adnams Bitter; Marston Pedigree; Tetley Bitter   Family Room
Patio/terrace   Outdoor Eating*   ***Accommodation:*** *15 bedrooms, 10 en suite, from £54
(single £43)   Children Welcome Overnight   Cots Available   Check-in: all day*   ***Credit
Cards:*** *Access, Amex, Diners, Visa*

WEST WALTON King of Hearts School Road (off A47), Tel: (0945) 584785.
Locally very popular for good value home cooking, lunchtime and evening; children
and vegetarians catered for. Plush lounge; separate restaurant. Elgoods beers. Open:
11-2.30, 6.30-11.

WINTERTON-ON-SEA   Fisherman's Return

The Lane NR29 4BN   FOOD
Tel: (0493) 393305   B&B
Open: 11-2.30, 6 (7 winter)-11   ☼
Licensees: John and Kate Findlay   ☺

Small it may be, but this prettily-kept row of former fishermen's cottages is an ideal
hang-out for locals and visitors alike, be they fishermen or not. Built in traditional brick
and flint, the buildings are probably 16th century, and unaltered over the last quarter
century or more. The public bar is lined in varnished tongue-and-groove panelling and
hung with sepia photographs and prints of Lowestoft harbour, the Norfolk Broads and
the pub itself. Some of these, movie buffs will note, are not as old as they seem. Centre-
stage, the cast iron wood-burner opens up in winter to add a glow of warmth to an
already cheery atmosphere. A smaller and possibly older lounge, low ceilinged, with a
copper-hooded fireplace and oak mantel, is carpeted these days and ideal for a quick, if
cramped, snack. Families will more likely head to the "Tinho", a timbered rear
extension of pool table and games machines which leads mercifully quickly to a lovely
enclosed garden and adventure playground. The menu's pretty comprehensive.
Individual savouries and omelettes, generously garnished, are the popular choices:
taramasalata with hot pitta bread; fish and cottage pies; vegetarian, seafood and
Fisherman's omelettes, the latter with bacon, onion, mushrooms and cheese; steaks,
burgers and toasted sandwiches. Added to all of which, the daily blackboard weighs in
with home-made quiche and home-cured ham salads, pasta bolognese, cheese-topped
ratatouille, and blackberry and apple crumble. Overnighters, too, are in for a treat. A
tiny flint-lined spiral staircase leads up to four cosy bedrooms tucked under the eaves,
which share the house television (propped up on a seaman's trunk) and a pine-panelled
bathroom. The largest, family room also has a sitting area with its own television and
fridge. Modest comforts, maybe, but entirely adequate for a brief stay, a stone's throw
from the beach and long walks over the dunes. Visitors are made truly welcome by
John and Kate Findlay, and seen on their way with the heartiest of seafarer's breakfasts.
Unsurprisingly, not only fishermen return.

Bar Meals: 11-2, 6 (7 winter)-9.30; bar snacks both sessions **Typical Dishes:** *game and
vegetable soup £2.50, garlic mushrooms £2.50, char-grilled sirloin £9, seafood omelette with
prawns and smoked salmon £4.75, seafood platter £4.75, home-made cheesecake £1.60
Vegetarian Meals: vegetarian omelette £4.25   Children's Menu* ▐Beer▌ *Adnams; Ruddles,
Webster's* ▐Whisky▌ ▐Cider▌ *James White   Family Room   Outdoor Play Area   Garden
Outdoor Eating* **Accommodation:** *4 bedrooms, sharing a bathroom, from £40 (single £25)
Children Welcome Overnight   Cot Available   Check-in: by arrangement* **No Credit Cards**

WOLTERTON   Saracens Head

Norwich NR4 7LX
Tel: (0263) 768909
Open: 11-3, 6-11
Licensee: Robert Dawson-Smith

Refurbished, remodelled and re-opened in 1989. The old restaurant is now a linen-
less bistro with a blackboard menu. Fresh, mostly local produce. Monthly feasts.
Delightful walled garden and courtyard.

Bar Meals: 12-2.30, 6.30-10; bar snacks both sessions **Typical Dishes:** *home-made
soup £1.85, crispy-fried aubergine £2.65, local hare in raspberry sauce £4.75, lamb en
croute £5.95, grilled large local trout £5.85, brown bread and butter pudding £1.75
Children's Portions* ▐Beer▌ *Adnams Bitter, Broadside; Felinfoel Double Dragon
Children Allowed in Bar to Eat   Outdoor Play Area   Garden   Outdoor Eating*
Accommodation: *2 bedrooms, both en suite, from £45 (single £30)   Children Welcome
Overnight   Check-in: by arrangement* **Credit Cards:** *Access, Amex, Visa*

NORTHAMPTONSHIRE

ARTHINGWORTH Bulls Head: Well-run dining pub with log fires in winter and separate restaurant.

ASHBY ST LEDGERS ★ Olde Coach House Inn

3 miles from Junction 18, M1 CV23 8UN   `FOOD`
Tel: (0788) 890349
Open: 12-2.30 (inc Sun), 6-11
Licensees: Brian and Philippa McCabe

The traditional role of the local pub at the hub of community life is much the case here. A tiny, protected, village, Ashby St Ledgers is full of thatched houses and cottages clustered around the manor and 12th century church, and has a population of just one hundred. 98% of them we're told, drink here; the remaining two are doubtless just under age. An imposing rather than handsome ivy-clad exterior is today mostly reminiscent of the estate farmhouse it once was. Peering through the bow windows, you'll see a rather austere snug bar to one side and a sparsely furnished pool room to the other. But this frontage is very deceptive. Behind these is a cavernous structure incorporating small alcoves, huge log fires and oak beams, which progresses past the main interior bar and food buffet to an elevated, beamed restaurant beyond and, to the rear, a flat-roofed function and meeting room. Part of the adjoining old stables once housed the village post office, and today the stable yard makes a safe, enclosed area for bored youngsters to explore – as often as not with the McCabe children as resident playmates. The food operation is both thematic and diverse. Cold roast meats, salads, whole stilton and brie cheeses are displayed on the buffet, while daily kitchen specials like beef and beer pie with Guinness, and supreme of barbecued tandoori chicken are listed on an adjacent blackboard. Diverse fishes and cuts of meat are laid out by the nearby patio barbecue, cooked to order and brought out to diners at tables in the garden – quite the most popular of the Coach House's summer attractions. When the cooking and eating are confined to indoors, the kitchen steps in with a menu which runs, daily, through "all day breakfast", bangers and mash, vegetarian "Chinese meatballs", steak, fillets stuffed with stilton, or salmon poached with dill and white wine. Puddings, too, are all home-made and include chocolate mousse, bread and butter pudding, sherry trifle and lemon meringue pie. But the Olde Coach House Inn is equally a classic ale drinkers' pub; the four usual beers supplemented on any given day by three further guest beers from anywhere in Britain. Twice-yearly beer festivals add considerably to this number, and few British real ales are left untried. Once all the eating and drinking is done, half a dozen bedrooms are available, four with baths and shower, two shower only, and one sporting a rather splendid four-poster. That would about complete the picture, were it not for the sense of fun imbued by the resident landlords, Brian and Philippa McCabe, and their staff, who go out of their way to make overnighters welcome. Unsurprisingly, there are many non-Ashby regulars already, the most regular of whom end up virtually as honorary villagers.

Bar Meals: 12-2, 6-9.30; bar snacks both sessions **Typical Dishes:** *vegetable and stilton soup £1.50, Danish herring £3.25, all-day breakfast £4.25, bangers and mash £3.75, bread and butter pudding £1.75 Vegetarian Meals: pasta and broccoli bake £3.25 Children's Menu/Portions* `Beer` *Everards Old Original, Tiger; Whitbread Boddingtons Bitter, Flowers Original Family Room Garden Summer Barbecue* **Accommodation:** *6 bedrooms, all en suite, from £45 (single £38) Children Welcome Overnight Cots Available Check-in: all day* **Credit Cards:** *Access, Visa*

ASHTON   Old Crown

1 Stoke Road NN7 2JN
Tel: (0604) 862268
Open: 12-3.30, 6 (7 winter)-11
Licensees: Graham Dodds and Richard Harrison

15th century pub with lots of brass, weaponry and other bric-a-brac, an inglenook
fireplace and an old piano (sometimes pub singalongs). Puddings are bought in.
Children in dining room only.

Bar Meals: 12-2.30, 7-10; bar snacks lunchtime and weekday evenings   **Typical Dishes:**
*crab puffs £2.80, farmhouse longboats £2.25, steak parmigiana £7.95, 8 oz sirloin steak
£7.99, seafood elite £3.90   Vegetarian Meals: vegetarian nuggets £2.90   Children's
Menu*   Beer   *Charles Wells Eagle Bitter, Bombardier   Outdoor Play Area   Garden
Outdoor Eating   Summer Barbecue*   **Credit Cards:** *Access, Visa*

BARNWELL   Montagu Arms

near Oundle PE8 5PH
Tel: (0832) 273725
Open: 11.30-3 (4 Sat), 6 (7 winter)-11
Licensee: W M Davies

Named after Henry VIII's Chief Justice to the Court of the King's Bench, who lived
in Barnwell Castle; the inn also dates from about 1540. There's a tea room open on
Sundays in summer.

Bar Meals: 12-2.30, 7-10; bar snacks both sessions   **Typical Dishes:** *leek and potato
soup £1.45, mushrooms in garlic and sherry £1.95, Barnwell bake £4.95, braised lamb
chops with onion gravy £4.95, roast breast of chicken chasseur £4.95, sherry trifle £1.95
Vegetarian Meals: vegetable strudel £4.25   Children's Menu/Portions*   Beer   *Batemans;
Greene King; Hook Norton   Family Room   Children Allowed in Bar to Eat   Outdoor
Play Area   Garden   Outdoor Eating   Summer Barbecue*   **Accommodation:** *5 twin rooms,
all en suite, from £40 (single £25)   Children Welcome Overnight   Check-in: all day*
Credit Cards: *Access, Visa*

BLAKESLEY   Bartholomew Arms

High Street NN12 8RE
Tel: (0327) 860292
Open: 11-3, 6.30-11
Licensee: C A Hackett

Charming, welcoming pub with a model ship collection in the public bar, guns and
cricket memorabilia in the lounge. Good for bed and breakfast at the modest prices.
Simple, homely, well-kept bedrooms.

Bar Meals: 12-2, 6.30-9.30; bar snacks both sessions   **Typical Dishes:** *soup 80p,
lasagne £2.60, chilli con carne £2.80, tuna bake £3.10   Vegetarian Meals: broccoli and
cream cheese   Children's Portions*   Beer   *Marston Pedigree; Ruddles County*   Whisky
Children Allowed in Bar to Eat   Outdoor Play Area   Garden   **Accommodation:** *5
bedrooms, 1 en suite, from £35 (single £18)   Children Welcome Overnight   Cots
Available   Check-in: all day*   **No Credit Cards**

CLAY COTON Fox & Hounds: Traditional one-roomed pub in tiny hamlet, with a comfortable lounge end and stone-flagged public bar area. Popular with the local hunt. Real fires; no music; garden; decent home cooked lunches and suppers. Bateman, Hook Norton, Jennings, Wadworth beers. Open 12-2.30, 7-11.

EAST HADDON   Red Lion

Tel: (0604) 770223
Open: 11-2.30, 6-11
Licensee: Ian H Kennedy

Civilised little hotel of golden stone in a country location not far from the M1. Pleasant, relaxing lounge bar with a mix of furnishings, china and pewter; smaller, plainer public. Recommended for its cottagey, well-kept bedrooms.

Bar Meals and Restaurant: 12.30-2, 7-9.30; bar snacks both sessions   ***Typical Dishes*** *BAR:* stock-pot soup £2.25, Brussels paté £3.75, braised beef in red wine £5.25, ham and mushroom pancakes £4.75, grilled sardines £4.25   *RESTAURANT:* vichyssoise £2.95, fresh asparagus £4.75, tournedos Rossini £15.75, duckling in bitter orange sauce £14.75, rack of lamb £13.75, home-made puddings £3.25   *Vegetarian Meals:* three cheese and tomato quiche £4.75   *Children's Menu/Portions*   `Cheese`   `Beer`   *Charles Wells   Family Room   Garden   **Accommodation:** 5 bedrooms, sharing 2 bathrooms, from £48 (single £35)   Children Welcome Overnight   Cots Available   Check-in: by arrangement   **Credit Cards:** Access, Diners, Visa*

FARTHINGSTONE Kings Arms Popular old-fashioned pub with decent home cooking.

FOTHERINGHAY   Falcon Inn

Peterborough PE8 5HZ   `FOOD`
Tel: (08326) 254   ☆
Open: 10-3, 6-11   ❢
Licensee: Alan Stewart

The Falcon is a splendidly relaxed and relaxing country pub, which feeds its customers and looks after them very well. A pretty stone building, surrounded by tiny outhouses and a rambling farmyard, embellished with flowers and greenery, its colourful, carefully tended garden, complete with tables on its patio and lawn, and open-ended double conservatory are good omens for a summer lunch. Within, it's brightly painted and carpeted throughout. Prints of historic Fotheringay castle, a memorial to the ancient "College of the Blessed Virgin", and the wrought iron 18th century bell clappers from the village church all reflect the owners' interest in local folklore. A very popular food pub, the Falcon also remains a busy village local, with a populous public bar where personalised pewter pots hang, darts and dominoes are played, and contributions are invited to the church's floodlighting fund. The reason most people come, though is to eat, and after fifteen years' practice the Stewarts can make justifiable claims to be past masters. Each day the menu offers up to twenty starters, just as many main dishes and a dozen or more puddings, mostly cold and fruity in summer, hot and comforting on those long winter nights. This is prodigious production of fresh food, coming from a kitchen so small (with no microwaves and precious little use of the chip fryer) that three is a crowd. The need to book can't, therefore, be over-emphasised, but once you're seated and provided with menus, everything will proceed smoothly – if not always rapidly – from that point.

Bar Meals: 12.15-2, 6.30-9.30 (7-9 Sun); bar snacks both sessions   ***Typical Dishes:*** *beef broth £2.40, pear with stilton and walnut dressing £2.10, old English game pie*

£4.20, carbonade of beef £7.80, roast duckling with apple and rosemary stuffing £6.40, plum and hazelnut crumble £2   Vegetarian Meals: leeks and mushrooms in filo pastry £3 Children's Portions   Cheese   Beer   *Adnams; Elgoods; Greene King; Ruddles* Children Allowed in Bar to Eat   Garden   Outdoor Eating   **Credit Cards:** *Access, Visa*

GREAT OXENDON — George

Market Harborough LE16 8NA
Tel: (0858) 465205
Open: 11.30-3, 6.30-11 (closed Sun eve Oct-April)
Licensee: Allan Wiseman

Proprietor-run. Food cooked to order. Bedrooms have now adopted a 'bed in the wall system', allowing for conversion into a meeting room for 10 people. Sounds intriguing...

Bar Meals and Restaurant: *12-2 (not restaurant Mon), 7-10 (not Sun); bar snacks lunchtime*   **Typical Dishes BAR:** *home-made soup £1.35, Brixworth paté £1.75, chicken lasagne £4.25, beef and Guinness pie £4.75, smoked seafood platter £4.25, bread and butter pudding £1.75*   **RESTAURANT:** *soup £2.65, pigeon and bacon salad £3.95, venison escalope £10.65, piccata pork Milanaise £10.95, salmon and monkfish casserole £11.45, vegetarian special £8.95   Vegetarian Meals: courgette and mushroom crumble £3.35   Children's Portions*   Beer   *Adnams; Batemans; Marston; Samuel Smith* Family Room   Outdoor Play Area   Garden   Outdoor Eating   **Accommodation** *(from December 1991): 3 bedrooms, all en suite, from £47.50   Children Welcome Overnight Cot Available   Check-in: all day*   **Credit Cards:** *Access, Amex, Visa*

LAMPORT — Lamport Swan

Market Harborough Road NN6 9EZ
Tel: (060 128) 555
Open: 11-3, 5.30-11
Licensees: Frederick and Sylvia Jolliffe

Extremely popular, busy, extended pub enthusiastically owned and run by unflagging Canadians. What may look like mass catering of the usual big-car-park family pub sort is actually well-organised large scale catering of high standards. Plenty of unusual dishes among the old pub favourites. Bargain set menus, and excellent vegetarian dishes. Opposite Lamport Hall.

Bar Meals and Restaurant: *12-2, 6.30 (7 restaurant)-10; bar snacks both sessions* **Typical Dishes BAR:** *carrot and orange soup £1.25, ham and cheese pancake £1.95, steak and kidney pie £4.40, cauliflower and prawn bake £4.75, cod and broccoli mornay £4.25, bread and butter pudding £1.75*   **RESTAURANT:** *mushroom and almond soup £1.35, Oriental king prawns £2.95, beef bourguignon £6.50, medallions of pork chasseur £5.95, Whitby cod £8.75, pear belle Helene £1.95 Vegetarian Meals: farmhouse fritters £4.25   Children's Menu/Portions*   Beer   *Marston Pedigree; Whitbread Flowers IPA* Family Room   Children Allowed in Bar to Eat   Outdoor Play Area   Garden   Outdoor Eating   **Credit Cards:** *Access, Visa*

LOWICK   Snooty Fox

Lowick NN14 3BS
Tel: (08012) 3434
Open: 11.30-3, 6-12
Licensee: John Lewis

17th century long house inn with a nicely renovated double roomed lounge, oak beams, exposed stone walls, two open fires and an extraordinary carved bar counter. Children are genuinely welcome.

Bar Meals and Restaurant: 11.30-3, 6-12; *bar snacks lunchtime*   **Typical Dishes**
BAR: home-made soup £1.20, local asparagus £2.95, crispy garlic chicken half £5.95, moghal spiced fillet of lamb £4.95, grilled whole prawns £3.95 or £6.95
RESTAURANT: 24 oz T-bone steak £10.95, supreme of chicken, lamb dishes, from £6.95, halibut, fresh shellfish   Children's Menu Cheese   Beer *Adnams Bitter; Courage Directors; Marston Pedigree; Ruddles Best, County   Children Allowed in Bar to Eat   Outdoor Play Area   Garden   Outdoor Eating   **Credit Cards:** Access, Visa*

MARSTON TRUSSELL Sun Inn Tel: (0508) 465531. Interesting, very cheap restauranty bar food, dotted among the usual pies and fish; good soups. They also do bedrooms. Bass, Marston, Whitbread beers.

PYTCHLEY Overstone Arms: Smartly organised dining pub; try the home-cooked pies; pretty garden. Watneys beer.

ROCKINGHAM Sondes Arms: Locally well-known for atmosphere and decent home cooking; homely and honest. Charles Wells beers.

ROTHWELL   Red Lion Hotel

Market Hill
Tel: (0536) 710409
Open: 11-2.30, 5.30-11
Licensees: Jim and Anne Tibbs

Imposing Edwardian market place hotel, with four bars, a comfortable atmosphere, and a curiously Mexican look to the menu, particularly in the evening restaurant. The en suite bedrooms are in adjoining cottages. Live music Saturdays. Morning coffee.

Bar Meals: 11 am-10 pm; bar snacks lunchtime **Typical Dishes:** *English or Mexican breakfast; home-baked ham and eggs, game pies (main courses from £3)   Vegetarian Meals* Beer *Charles Wells* **Accommodation:** *12 bedrooms, 6 en suite, from £35 (single £20) Children Welcome Overnight* **Credit Cards:** *Access, Visa*

RUSHDEN King Edward VII Queen Street. Traditional corner local, a piano in the large public bar, cosy lounge, real fire; decent lunchtime and evening meals. Adnams, Charles Wells beers. Open: 10.30 am-11 pm.

SUTTON BASSETT — Queen's Head

near Market Harborough LE16 8HP
Tel: (0858) 463530
Open: 11.45-3, 6.30-11
Licensees: J U and N A Powell

The restaurant has a new sitting area of its own, and newly installed windows give pretty views over the valley.

Bar Meals: *11.45-2, 7-9.30 (10 Fri/Sat); bar snacks lunchtime* **Typical Dishes:** *stilton and celery soup £1.50, avocado and tuna fish paté, chicken Mississippi £6.10, potato skins supreme topped with chicken, mushrooms, chees and ham £4.95, spaghetti carbonara £4.05, home-made bread and butter pudding, Grand Marnier crème caramel Vegetarian Meals: broccoli and mushroom mornay £4.95 Children's Menu/Portions* ▪Beer▪ *Adnams; Batemans; Greene King; Marston Children Allowed in Bar to Eat Patio Outdoor Eating* **Credit Cards:** *Access, Visa*

THORPE MANDEVILLE — Three Conies

Tel: (0295) 711025
Open: 11-3, 6-11
Licensees: John and Maureen Day

17th century stone-built village pub with good home cooking at lunchtime (see list) and slightly smarter, different evening menu. Attractively modernised low-beamed lounge; pool table-dominated public bar; nice garden. The family homes of George Washington and John Dryden are close by.

Bar Meals: *lunchtime and evening; bar snacks lunchtime* **Typical Dishes:** *home-made soup £1.20, garlic and cream mushrooms £2, steak and kidney pie £3.50, chicken casserole £4, home-made ice-cream £1.95 Vegetarian Meals* ▪Beer▪ *Hook Norton Family Room Garden*

TOWCESTER — Plough

Market Square (A5)
Tel: (0327) 50738
Open: 10.30 am-11 pm

Pleasant two-roomed pub by the market place, with a formidable reputation for good home-made burgers, prepared and cooked by an enthusiastic chef-licensee. Real fire; no music.

Bar Meals: *lunchtime and evening; bar snacks both sessions* **Typical Dishes:** *crab and sweetcorn chowder, steak and kidney pie, curries, cold poached salmon salad (main courses from £3) Vegetarian Meals Children's Menu* ▪Beer▪ *Adnams; Charles Wells Children Allowed in to Eat* **Credit Cards:** *Amex*

TWYWELL   Old Friar

Lower Street NN14 3AH
Tel: (08012) 2625
Open: 11-2.30, 6-11
Licensee: David John Crisp

Dining pub with plain wood furnishings; beams and brick fireplaces have friar motifs. Good outdoor play area for children, with tree swings.

Bar Meals: 12-1.45, 7-9.45; bar snacks both sessions   ***Typical Dishes:*** *home-made soup £1.65, fresh melon and passion fruit sorbet £2.35, carvery (three meats) £6.95, fillet steak £10.95, whole trout with celery and walnut stuffing £8.45, syllabub £2.10   Vegetarian Meals: vegetable tikka £5.25   Children's Menu/Portions* `Beer` *Ruddles Best, County, Webster's Yorkshire Bitter   Children Allowed in Bar to Eat   Outdoor Play Area   Garden Outdoor Eating*   ***Credit Cards:*** *Access, Visa*

UPPER BENEFIELD   Wheatsheaf Hotel

Peterborough PE8 5AN
Tel: (08325) 254
Open: all day
Licensee: A J Levitt-Cooke

Well-heeled pub hotel.

Bar Meals and Restaurant: 12-2, 6.30 (7 restaurant)-10; bar snacks both sessions   ***Typical Dishes BAR:*** *French onion soup £1.95, cheese-stuffed mushrooms £2.45, rump steak au poivre £5.50, steak and ale pie £3.95, chicken Kiev £4.95, banoffee pie* ***RESTAURANT:*** *courgette and mint soup £2.95, melon fantasia £3.75, medallion of lamb £11.50, chateaubriand (for 2) £24.50, escalope of salmon £11.95, flambé puddings Vegetarian Meals: vegetable lasagne   Children's Portions* `Beer` *Adnams; Courage Best; Marston Pedigree; Whitbread Boddingtons Bitter   Outdoor Play Area   Garden   Outdoor Eating*   ***Accommodation:*** *12 bedrooms, all en suite, from £52.50 (single £42.50) Children Welcome Overnight   Cot Available   Check-in: all day*   ***Credit Cards:*** *Access, Amex, Diners, Visa*

WAKERLEY Exeter Arms Main Street Tel: (0572) 87817. Reputedly haunted pub near the woods; standard pub food including a decent steak and kidney pie (12-2, 6-9); children welcome. Adnams and Batemans beers. Open: 12-3 (not Mon), 6-11.

WEEDON Narrowboat Inn Stowe Hill (A5) Tel: (0327) 40536. Very popular, opened-out family pub by Grand Union Canal. Half-Chinese landlady makes exotic specials alongside lunchtime basket meals; good Cantonese restaurant. Children welcome. Charles Wells beers. Open: 11-2.30, 5.30-11 (all day Sat).

WESTON Crown. Cosy, traditional village pub with decent lunchtime and evening bar food. Hook Norton, Wadworth beers.

YARWELL Angel Main Street. Secluded, unspoilt village focal point; friendly, nice bar food, children welcome. Youngers beers.

NORTHUMBERLAND

ACOMB   Miners Arms

Main Street NE46 4PW
Tel: (0434) 603909
Open: 11-3, 5-11 (11-11 summer and winter Sats)
Licensee: K S Millar

So enthusiastic are they about their reputation for good real ales at the Miners Arms that the bar is to be altered to accommodate a staggering 14 beers and ciders. This is a charming, traditional village pub, built in 1745, with exposed stone walls, original beams and open fire.

Bar Meals: 12-2 (2.30 summer), 6.30-9 (10 summer); bar snacks both sessions   **Typical Dishes:** *country vegetable soup £1, Brussels paté £1.75, steak and mushroom pie £3.45, country taverners pork £4.25, 6 oz rump steak £5.50, rhubarb and apple crumble £1.20 Vegetarian Meals: vegetable moussaka   Children's Menu/Portions*   Beer   *Big Lamp Prince Bishop; Federation Best Bitter; Morrells Varsity; Old Mill Traditional Bitter   Family Room   Garden   Outdoor Eating   Summer Barbecue*   **No Credit Cards**

ALLENHEADS   Allenheads Inn

near Hexham NE47 9HJ
Tel: (0434) 685200
Open: 12-3, 7-11
Licensees: Peter and Linda Stenson

Pretty, remote village high in the North Pennines, a good walking area. The former home of Sir Thomas Wentworth, it now offers an Antiques Bar and Royal Room. Residents' sitting room, but no televisions in bedrooms.

Bar Meals: 12-2.30, 7-10; bar snacks both sessions   **Restaurant:** 7-9.30 (bookings only) **Typical Dishes BAR:** *white onion soup £1, mussels in garlic butter £1, steak and kidney pie £3.50, game pie £3.50, cottage pie £3, black velvet pudding £1.50* **RESTAURANT:** *steak £6, duckling £6, salmon £6 (3-course meal inc. coffee £8.50) Vegetarian Meals: chilli £3   Children's Portions   Family Room   Patio/terrace   Outdoor Eating*   **Accommodation:** *8 bedrooms, all en suite, from £40 (single £20)   Children Welcome Overnight   Cot Available   Check-in: all day*   **No Credit Cards**

ALNMOUTH   Red Lion

Northumberland Street
Tel: (0665) 830584
Open: 12-2.30, 7-11 (longer hours summer)
Licensee: Donald Hume

Cosy 16th century coaching inn with an enthusiastic cook-landlord; local white fish a speciality, and local seafood in the à la carte restaurant. No chips in either. They also let bedrooms.

Bar Meals: lunchtime; bar snacks   **RESTAURANT:** evenings   **Typical Dishes BAR:** *home-made soup 95p, steak, kidney and ale pie, Thai chicken curry, local lemon sole (around £3), banana fritters   Vegetarian Meals   Children's Menu*   Beer   *McEwan, Theakston; Tetley   Children Allowed in Bar to Eat   Garden*

ALNMOUTH   Schooner Hotel

Northumberland Street NE66 2RS
Tel: (0665) 830216
Open: 11-11
Licensee: John G C Orde

Large white–painted Georgian hotel dominating other buildings in the street.
Civilised, restful interior. Nice little seaside town, a good base for Northumbrian
breaks.

Bar Meals: 12-2.30, 7-9.30; bar snacks both sessions   *Restaurant:* 12-2.30 (Sun only),
7-10.30   *Typical Dishes BAR:* Northumbrian broth, garlic mushrooms £1.50, steak and
kidney pie £3.50, haddock and chips £3.50, fish salad £3.50, steamed treacle pudding
RESTAURANT: spinach and cauliflower soup, potted local crab, chicken cacciatora £4.95,
sirloin steak   Vegetarian Meals   Children's Menu/Portions   `Cheese`   `Beer`   Belhaven;
Marston; Theakston; Whitbread   `Whisky`   Family Room (conservatory)   Garden
Outdoor Eating   *Accommodation:* 23 bedrooms, all en suite, from £60 (single £30)
Children Welcome Overnight   Cots Available   Check-in: all day   *Credit Cards:* Access,
Amex, Diners, Visa

ALNWICK   Queens Head

Market Street NE66 1SS
Tel: (0665) 602442
Open: 11-11

Lively town hotel bar; families can use dining room for meals or even just for drinks.

Bar Meals: 12-2, 7-9; bar snacks lunchime   *Typical Dishes:* split pea and ham broth
£1.20, local kipper, sirloin steak au poivre £8, chicken curry £4.60, griddled trout with
fennel sauce £5.80, gooseberry crumble £1.80   Vegetarian Meals: red dragon pie £4.20
Children's Menu   `Beer`   Vaux Samson; Wards Sheffield Best Bitter   Patio/terrace
Outdoor Eating   *Accommodation:* 5 bedrooms, sharing one bathroom, from £30 (single
£15)   Children Welcome Overnight   Cots Available   Check-in: all day   *No Credit*
Cards

BAMBURGH   Lord Crewe Arms

Front Street NE69 7BL
Tel: (06684) 243
Open: 11-3, 6-11 (March-Oct eves)
Licensee: Brian Holland

Large old inn hotel with decent bar food, a mix of the homely home-made and
fresh seafood specials; The 'cocktail bar' is the pubbiest.

Bar Meals: 11.30-2.30, 6-10; bar snacks both sessions   *Restaurant:* 12-2, 6-9.30
Typical Dishes BAR: steak and kidney pie £4.95, fresh local fish £4.25, lobster tails
£5.25, fruit tarts   *RESTAURANT:* home-made soup £1.40, crabmeat cocktail £2.50,
sirloin steak garni £8, local pork sausages £4, seafood selection £8   Vegetarian Meals:
quiche   Children's Menu   `Beer`   Theakston Best   `Whisky`   Children Allowed in Bar to
Eat   Patio/terrace   Outdoor Eating   *Accommodation* (closed Nov-March): 25 bedrooms,
20 en suite, from £45 (single £32)   Children Welcome Overnight (minimum age 5)
Check-in: all day   *Credit Cards:* Access, Visa

BAMBURGH   **Victoria Hotel**

Front Street NE69 7BP
Tel: (06684) 431
Open: 11-11
Licensee: Robert Wright Goodfellow

Pleasant old inn at the centre of beautiful coastal village; a good port of call after a
bracing beach walk or a closer look at the enormous cliff-top castle.

*Bar Meals and Restaurant: 12-2 (restaurant Sun lunch only 12-1.30), 6-8.30 (9.30
Fri/Sat); bar snacks both sessions   Typical Dishes BAR: leek soup £1, seafood platter
£2.75, beefsteak and kidney pie £3.50, lambs liver and onions £3.95, fresh fish and chips
£3.50, fruit tarts £2 (all home-made)   RESTAURANT: butterbean and spinach soup
£1.30, fillet of smoked mackerel £2.75, brace of Cheviot lamb cutlets £7.25, oven-baked
breast of duckling in honey £8.25, poached Tweed salmon £8.50, coffee bavarois £2.50
Vegetarian Meals: vegetable lasagne   Children's Menu/Portions   Beer   Darlings
Longstone Bitter; Mitchells; Tetley Bitter   Family Room   Accommodation: 23 bedrooms,
16 ensuite, from £40 (single £25)   Children Welcome Overnight   Cots Available
Check-in: all day   Credit Cards: Access, Amex, Diners, Visa*

BELFORD   **Blue Bell**

Market Place NE70 7NE
Tel: (06683) 543
Licensees: Carl and Jean Shirley

Handsome, creeper-clad old inn dominating hamlet close by the A1. Stylishly
refurbished lounge with matching carpets and upholstery; newish public/family
room in former stables, and nice old-fashioned dining room overlooking garden.
Recommended for bed and breakfast: bedrooms are pretty and homely, with period
style furnishings, a couple of armchairs and lots of decorative ornaments; two are in
the annexe.

*Bar Meals: lunchtime and evening   Children's Menu   Beer   Theakston   Family Room
Garden   Accommodation: 15 bedrooms, all en suite, from £60   Credit Cards: Access,
Amex, Diners, Visa*

BELSAY Highlander, NE20 0DN, Tel: (0661) 881220. Locally popular for
reasonably priced bar food and £10 three-course table d'hote in dining room.
Children's menu and room; garden. Theakstons beers. Open: 11-3, 6-11.

BLANCHLAND   **Lord Crewe Arms Hotel**

near Consett DH8 9SP
Tel: (0434) 675251
Open: 11-6, 3-11
Licensees: A S Todd, P R and P A Gingell

The original building dates from 1235, when the inn was built as a monastic guest
house: you can still see the remains of the old monastery in the garden. The Derwent
Bar has settles and beams; the Crypt Bar is exactly what it says it is, its stone walls
curving into a remarkable barrel-vaulted ceiling. Given this pedigree, the restaurant and
some of the bedrooms are more modern than you might expect. A conference room
and business tariffs suggest the Lord Crewe Arms is popular with corporate trade.

*Bar Meals: 12-2; bar snacks lunchtime   Restaurant: 12-2 (Sun only), 7-9   Typical
Dishes BAR: home-made soup £1.50, pork and apple burgers £4.50, chicken with*

tagliatelle £4.75, grilled lamb kebabs £4.75, smoked salmon salad £7, pudding of the day £1.50 **RESTAURANT:** *4-course dinner £19.75-£23: quails with pecan nuts, smoked goose breast, mignons of pork fillet, sirloin steak with green peppercorns, lobster salad, hot apple torte Vegetarian Meals (restaurant) Children's Portions* `Cheese` `Beer` *Vaux Samson Family Room Outdoor Play Area Garden Outdoor Eating*
Accommodation: *18 bedrooms, all en suite, from £96 (single £71.50) Children Welcome Overnight Cots Available Check-in: all day* **Credit Cards:** *Access, Amex, Diners, Visa*

CARTERWAYHEADS   Manor House Inn

near Shotley Bridge DH8 9LX
Tel: (0207) 55268
Open: 11-3, 6-11
Licensees: Anthony, Jane and Elizabeth Pelly

Getting a strong local reputation for good bar meals. Plush comfortable lounge; simple woody public bar. The restaurant has its own sitting area.

Bar Meals: *12-2.30, 7-9.30 (9 Sun); bar snacks both sessions* **Restaurant:** *7.30-9.30 Tue-Sat (Thur-Sat Jan-March)* **Typical Dishes BAR:** *curried parsnip soup £1.80, chicken liver paté £3.50, lamb, orange and rosemary casserole £4.90, wild salmon with mint butter £6.75, courgette and mushroom pancake £4.25, sticky toffee pudding £1.90*
RESTAURANT: *fresh tomato and tarragon soup £2.75, prawn and scallop brochette with hazelnut sauce £4.25, noisettes of lamb with apricot sauce £10.25, marinated tandoori chicken breast £9.25, flamed escalope of venison with whisky £9.95, double chocolate berry tart £3 Vegetarian Meals: pasta au gratin £3.75 Children's Menu/Portions* `Cheese`
`Beer` *Fullers; Ruddles; Yates* `Whisky` *Children Allowed in Bar to Eat Garden Outdoor Eating* **Credit Cards:** *Access, Visa*

CHATTON   Percy Arms Hotel

Alnwick NE66 5PS
Tel: (06685) 244
Open: 11-3, 6-11
Licensee: K and P Topham

Popular, pleasantly modernised roadside country inn in sleepy village, excellent for anglers. Recommended for bed and breakfast: they now have seven rooms, all en suite.

Bar Meals: *12-1.30, 6.30-9.30; bar snacks both sessions* **Typical Dishes:** *vegetable soup £1.10, paté £1.95, steak and kidney pie £3.95, sirloin steak £7.35, fresh cod £3.60, chocolate brandy mousse £1.95 Vegetarian Meals: vegetable pasta bake £4 Children's Menu/Portions* `Beer` *Theakstons XB* `Whisky` *Family Room Children Allowed in Bar to Eat Garden Outdoor Eating* **Accommodation:** *7 bedrooms, all en suite, from £40 (single £20) Children Welcome Overnight Cots Available Check-in: all day* **No Credit Cards**

DUNSTAN   Cottage Inn

Alnwick NE66 3SZ
Tel: (0665) 576658   `B&B`
Open: 11-3, 6-11
Licensees: Lawrence and Shirley Jobling

A conversion of five cottages, white-painted and creeper-strewn, in a sleepy little village. Pleasant panelled lounge; public bar has pool, and film star cut-outs; also black and white tiled conservatory. Restaurant lunch menu looks promising but proves over-ambitious; bar meals of acceptable quality; more upmarket menu in restaurant evenings. Recommended for B&B: bedrooms neat, well maintained, with garden views, and well-lit en suite facilities have showers as well as baths. Eight acres of grounds: the garden is lovely for outdoor eating and completely safe for children.

Bar Meals: 12-2.30, 6-9.30 (7-9 Sun); bar snacks lunchtime   *Restaurant:* 12-2.30 (Sun only), 7-9.30   *Typical Dishes BAR:* *fresh vegetable soup £1.25, chicken liver paté £1.95, old English hotpot £3.95, braised liver and Cumberland sausage in beer sauce £4.50, Craster seafood platter £4.50, gooseberry and blackberry sponge £1.75* *RESTAURANT:* *set menu £11.95: pear and stilton soup, pigeon breast with horseradish and leek sauce, medallion of venison on wild berry sauce, roulade of seafood, cassoulet of game, Lindisfarne syllabub* *Vegetarian Meals: vegetable Malaysia* *Children's Menu/Portions* Cheese Beer *Ruddles* *Family Room* *Children Allowed in Bar to Eat* *Outdoor Play Area* *Garden* *Outdoor Eating* *Accommodation:* *10 bedrooms, all en suite, from £55 (single £35)* *Children Welcome Overnight* *Cots Available* *Check-in: all day* *Credit Cards: Access, Visa*

EGLINGHAM   Tankerville Arms

Alnwick NE66 2TX
Tel: (066 578) 444
Open: 11-3, 6-12
Licensee: George Heydon

Plush banquette-modernised stone-built village pub with two coal fires; they're planning a total refurbishment for the 1992 season. The restaurant features main courses like venison cordon rouge (£9.10).

Bar Meals and Restaurant: 11-2, 6-11 (12 restaurant); bar snacks both sessions   *Typical Dishes:* *home-made soup, salmon, sole, baked rainbow trout £4.60, home-made puddings* *Vegetarian Meals: asparagus and pine kernel parcels* *Children's Menu/Portions* Cheese Beer *Stones Bitter; Tetley Bitter* Whisky *Family Room* *Outdoor Play Area* *Garden Outdoor Eating* *Credit Cards: Access, Visa*

FALSTONE   Blackcock

Tel: (0660) 40200
Open: 11-3, 6-11 (all day Sat)

Useful stop when visiting Europe's largest man-made forest, not far from the equally superlative Kielder Water. Welcoming stone-built walkers' favourite with period coal fires and a Beatonette stove; handsome dining room. Grand piano in the residents' lounge; the modest bedrooms will probably all be upgraded to en suite status for 1992.

Bar Meals: *lunchtime and evening* Beer *Greenalls Original* Cider *Family Room* *Garden* *Accommodation:* *3 bedrooms, from £35 (single £18)* *Children Welcome Overnight* *No Credit Cards*

HALTWHISTLE   Grey Bull

Main Street NE49 0DL
Tel: (0434) 320298
Open: 12-3 (not Wed), 7-11 (12-11 summer)
Licensees: Max and Claire Heaviside

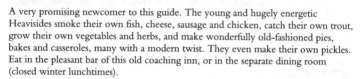

A very promising newcomer to this guide. The young and hugely energetic Heavisides smoke their own fish, cheese, sausage and chicken, catch their own trout, grow their own vegetables and herbs, and make wonderfully old-fashioned pies, bakes and casseroles, many with a modern twist. They even make their own pickles. Eat in the pleasant bar of this old coaching inn, or in the separate dining room (closed winter lunchtimes).

Bar Meals: 12-2, 7-9.30; bar snacks both sessions **Typical Dishes:** *leek and potato soup £1.50, seafood elite £2.45, Max's boozer's pie £5.95, pork in apple and cider £6, Victorian rabbit pie £5.95, Hadrian's apple pie £1.55 Vegetarian Meals: spicy vegetable casserole Children's Menu/Portions* `Cheese` `Beer` *Hadrian Centurion; Jennings; Marston Pedigree; Theakston Bitter Children Allowed in Bar to Eat Outdoor Play Area Garden Outdoor Eating Summer Barbecue* **Accommodation:** *6 bedrooms, sharing 2 bathrooms, from £30 (single £17) Children Welcome Overnight Check-in: all day* **Credit Cards:** *Access, Diners, Visa*

HALTWHISTLE   Milecastle Inn

Military Road NE49 9NN
Tel: (0434) 320682
Open: 12-2.30, 6.30-11
Licensees: Ralph and Margaret Payne

Perched high, overlooking Hadrian's Wall, a small, traditional 17th century country pub with a vast collection of brass and copper, good log fires and a separate restaurant. No music, machines or pool table. Good reliable food.

Bar Meals: 12-2, 6.30 (7 Sun)-9; bar snacks lunchtime **Restaurant:** *12-1.30 (Sun only), 6.30-9 (Tue-Sat)* **Typical Dishes BAR:** *spicy tomato and celery soup £1.20, garlic goujons £2.25, wild boar and duckling pie £5.85, turkey, ham and chestnut pie £5.85, venison sausage £4, hot treacle tart £1.60* **RESTAURANT:** *smoked salmon and crab bisque £1.75, home-made game paté £3.65, roast venison in game sauce £10.50, duckling in wild cherry sauce £10.95, king prawn provencale £11.75, hot sticky toffee pudding £2 Vegetarian Meals: vegetable pancakes Children's Portions* `Beer` *Ruddles; Theakston; Webster's; Youngers* `Whisky` *Children over 5 Allowed in Bar to Eat Garden Outdoor Eating* **Credit Cards:** *Access, Diners, Visa*

HAYDON BRIDGE   General Havelock

Ratcliffe Road NE47 6ER
Tel: (0434) 684376   `FOOD`
Open: 11.30-2.30 (12-2 Sun), 7-11; closed Mon/Tue
Licensees: Ian and Angela Clyde

The dark green exterior of the General Havelock certainly helps it stand out from neighbouring cottages. It was named after Sunderland-born General Henry Havelock, who relieved the Indian town of Lucknow in the late 1880s. The interior of the pub is also dark green. In the front bar area there are wrought-iron-legged tables, stripped wood and padded benches, and some brilliant wildlife photographs taken by a local photographer. The pub's main draw, though, is its dining room in the converted stables to the rear, a high-ceilinged room with exposed beams, natural stone walls, watercolours of local scenes and black and white photos of the landlady's grandparents. Polished tables are ready-set and button banquette seating runs the length of the room. The cooking is in the accomplished hands of self-taught chef Angela Clyde, who prides herself on using only fresh produce: meat comes from a local butcher in Hexham, and fish delivered twice a week from North Shields. The short lunchtime menu includes soup like stilton and onion or a home-made terrine amongst the starters, followed by a daily roast and a fish dish. In the evenings a set price three course menu has a more upmarket feel, roast duck with redcurrants perhaps, fillet of plaice with mozzarella or breast of chicken with spinach, ginger and garlic. Cooking is of a high standard, and the home-made puddings are also first class: dark chocolate mousse and a splendid plum tart (with very good pastry) are typical. Service is friendly, casual but efficient. To the rear of the dining room is a paved patio which runs down to a lawn and the River Tyne. Though the pub has its regulars who use the bar for a drink, this is really more of a dining pub, and people travel some distance to eat here. Weekends (including a popular Sunday lunch) can be very busy, so booking is advised. They close all day Monday and Tuesday.

Bar Meals: 12-2; bar snacks lunchtime   *Restaurant:* 12-2, 7.30-10   *Typical Dishes*
BAR: cream of celery soup £1.45, devilled crab £2.30, roast sirloin £5.70, fillet of plaice £5.40, broccoli and cheese quiche £5.10, apricot tart £2.40   *RESTAURANT:* 4-course set menu   Vegetarian Meals: spinach pancake   Children's Portions   ▮ Beer ▮ Tetley Bitter   Children Allowed in Bar to Eat   Riverside Garden   Outdoor Eating   *No Credit Cards*

LONGFRAMLINGTON   Granby Inn

on A697 NE65 8DP
Tel: (066 570) 228
Open: 11-3, 6-11
Licensee: Anne Bright

Cosy, attractively modernised little 18th century inn, recommended for bed and breakfast. Main building bedrooms are small, neat and modern, all but one of them en suite; garden chalets incorporate a small sitting area, fridge and bathroom, and standards of housekeeping are reliably high everywhere. Good breakfasts: try the kippers. The pub gets foody in the evening; children over 8 are allowed inside at lunchtimes.

Bar Meals: lunchtime and evening; bar snacks lunchtime   *Typical Dishes:* home-made soup £1.35, moules marinière £2.75, home-made steak and kidney pie £3.75, duckling à l'orange £7.75, chicken Kiev £6.35   Garden   *Accommodation:* 6 bedrooms, from £45 (single £23)   Children over 8 Welcome Overnight   *Credit Cards:* Access, Amex, Visa

Anglers Arms Wheldon Bridge. Rather gloomy pub, popular for fresh local fish; bar meals lunchtime; attentive service. Wards beers.

LONGHORSLEY   Linden Pub

Morpeth NE65 8XF
Tel: (0670) 516611
Open: 11-3, 6-11
Licensees: J M Moore and R W Tait

Part of the Linden Hall Hotel, or rather in a converted outbuilding behind it. A new granary restaurant has now opened in the pub itself, with all home-cooked food. Pricey accommodation in the hotel.

Bar Meals: 12-2, 6-8; bar snacks both sessions   *Restaurant:* 12-2, 7.30-9.30   **Typical Dishes RESTAURANT:** smoked peppercorn mackerel £2.60, breadcrumbed slices of pork £5.85, spinach tagliatelle with mushroom sauce £4.95, fillet of sole £6.20, summer pudding £1.95   Vegetarian Meals: vegetable lasagne   Children's Menu/Portions   `Cheese`   `Beer`   Ruddles; Theakston   Children Allowed in Bar to Eat   Outdoor Play Area   Garden   Outdoor Eating   Summer Barbecue   **Accommodation:** 45 bedrooms, all en suite, from £79.50 (single £69.50)   Children Welcome Overnight   Check-in: by arrangement   **Credit Cards:** Access, Amex, Diners, Visa

---

LOWICK   Black Bull

2/4 Main Street TD15 2UA
Tel: (0289) 88228
Open: 12-3, 6-11
Licensees: Tom and Anne Grundy

All main courses are prepared in their own kitchens, and all vegetables are fresh at this nice old village inn, popular with locals and as an off-the-A1 stopping point. Aside from the peaceful back snug and livelier locals' bar, there's a dining room seating 66, built and opened in 1988. The informally restauranty menu features a six-strong vegetarian list. You can hire a self-catering cottage next door to the pub March-October.

Restaurant: 12-2 (1.30 Sun), 6 (7 Sun)-9 (9.30 Sat); no food Mon Oct-Easter; bar snacks lunchtime   **Typical Dishes RESTAURANT:** minestrone £1.20, stuffed mushrooms £2.65, home-made steak and kidney pie £4.15, noisettes of lamb £5.25, orange tarragon chicken £5.10, apple pie   Vegetarian Meals: red dragon pie £4.65   Children's Menu/Portions   `Beer`   McEwans 70/-, 80/-; Theakston XB   `Whisky`   Children Allowed in Bar to Eat   Garden   Outdoor Eating   **Credit Cards:** Access, Visa

---

MATFEN   Black Bull

Matfen NE20 0RP
Tel: (0661) 886330
Open: 11-3, 6-11
Licensees: Colin and Michele Scott

Pretty creeper-covered stone-built roadside pub with open fires. Overlooks village green and river Pont.

Bar Meals and Restaurant: 12-2, 6.30 (7 restaurant)-9.30; bar snacks both sessions   **Typical Dishes BAR:** leek and celery soup £1.30, asparagus and ham pancake £3.25, steak, kidney and real ale pie £4.25, guinea fowl casserole £4.25, prawn and cod tagliatelle £3.95, sherry trifle £1.85   **RESTAURANT:** cauliflower soup £1.60, warm duck salad £4.95, beef fillet oriental style £8.95, rack of lamb with thyme sauce £8.25, turbot with herb crust, hot gingerbread £1.85   Vegetarian Meals: spicy vegetable chilli £3.50   Children's Portions   `Beer`   Theakston Best, XB; Youngers No.3   `Whisky`   Family Room   Patio/terrace   Outdoor Eating   **Accommodation:** 5 bedrooms, sharing 2 bathrooms, from £30 (single £18)   Children Welcome Overnight   Cot Available   Check-in: all day   **Credit Cards:** Access, Visa

NEWTON BY THE SEA Ship The Square, Low Newton. Spartan local in glorious and undiscovered setting close to beach; try the crab sandwiches. No real ale. Children welcome.

RENNINGTON   **Masons Arms**

Alnwick NE66 3RX
Tel: (0665) 577275
Open: 11.30-2.30, 6.30-11
Licensee: F J Sloan

Large 18th century coaching inn on the old Great North Road. No children under 14 overnight.

Bar Meals: 12-2, 7-9.30; bar snacks lunchtime   Restaurant: 7-9   Typical Dishes BAR: bean and tomato soup £1.05, chicken liver paté £1.95, lamb cutlets garni £4.25, royal game pie £4.50, seafood au gratin £3.95, tipsy toffee ice £1.75   RESTAURANT: broccoli and stilton soup £1.50, garlic cream mushrooms £3.95, salmis of duck £13.75, garlic king prawns £12.95, stilton chicken £9.95, cranachan £2.50   Vegetarian Meals: spinach and mushroom lasagne £4.95   Children's Menu/Portions Beer *McEwans 80/-; Theakston Best   Family Room   Patio/terrace   Outdoor Eating   Accommodation: 8 bedrooms, 4 en suite (annexe rooms), from £35.50 (single £18)   Check-in: all day Credit Cards: Access, Visa*

SEAHOUSES   **Olde Ship**

9 Main Street NE68 7RD   B&B
Tel: (0665) 720200   ✳
Open: 11-3, 6-11
Licensee: Alan C Glen

Perched above the small harbour with splendid sea views out to the Farne Islands, the Olde Ship began life as a farmhouse in 1745. It has been in present licensees Alan and Jean Glen's family since 1910, each generation, beginning with Alan's grandparents, introducing their own improvements. Behind the grey stone exterior there lies a real treasure trove of nautical paraphernalia collected over 80 years; the saloon bar is quite something and must be a nightmare to clean! The whole room is full of objects hanging from ceiling, walls and bar: a ship's figurehead, oars, diving helmet, brass lamps, ship's wheel, baskets, model boats, pictures, barrels, fishing gear and more besides. As well as all these objects there are some excellent black and white photos of old local fishermen, exposed floorboards, panelled walls and simple red bench seating. The smaller cabin bar has panelling, royal blue upholstered seating and even more collectibles, while a small area to the rear (where children can sit) features stuffed seabirds in cases. Upstairs the nautical theme continues, with a fine collection of large model boats in one of the first floor hallways. A blackboard displays the day's choice of bar food (lunch only), perhaps steak and kidney pie, lemon sole with shrimp sauce or liver and onions. Sandwiches are available too. Evenings bring a short choice, uncomplicated table d'hote menu. The bedrooms, including four in outside annexes, are clean, neat and unfussy, with plain painted walls and cottagey bedspreads; furniture varies from modern fitted units to more traditional free-standing pieces. Direct dial telephone, television (with satellite) and mineral water (local, of course) are standard, and every room is en suite, though half have shower only, and some are on the small side. The pub also has its own lawn and summerhouse overlooking the harbour and enjoying fabulous views. In the evenings, the bars fill with the locals and fishermen who mix well with outsiders.

Bar Meals: 12-2.30; bar snacks evening   Restaurant: 12-2, 7-8.30   Typical Dishes: crab soup £1.50, smoked mackerel, beef and rabbit pie, bosun's fish stew, fishermans pie (main courses around £3/£3.50), clootie dumpling   Vegetarian Meals: leek and cheese pie Children's Portions Beer *Theakston Best, XB* Whisky *Family Room   Outdoor Play Area   Garden   Outdoor Eating Accommodation (closed Dec/Jan): 12 bedrooms, all en suite, from £56 (single £28)   Check-in: all day   Credit Cards: Access, Visa*

SEATON SLUICE — Waterford Arms

Collywell Bay Road
Tel: (091) 237 0450
Open: 11-3.30, 6.30-11
Licensee: Patricia Charlton

Modernised pub with lots of delicious local fish – really local, from the nearby harbour.

Bar Meals: *12-2.15, 7.30-9.15* ***Typical Dishes:*** *home-made broth £1.35, home-made steak and kidney pie £4.65, leek pudding with mince and vegetables £4.35, fresh seafood platter £9.25, rice pudding with sultanas and maple syrup £1.25 Children's Portions* **Beer** *Vaux beers Family Room* ***Accommodation:*** *3 bedrooms, all with showers, from £45 (single £22.50) Children Welcome Overnight Check-in: all day* ***No Credit Cards***

STANNERSBURN — Pheasant Inn

Falstone NE48 1DD 🍷
Tel: (0434) 240382
Open: 11-3, 6-11 (12-2, 6.30-11 winter); closed Mon Jan-Feb
Licensee: W R C Kershaw

Old stone country inn a mile from Kielder Water. Beamed ceilings, open fires and home cooking.

Bar Meals: *12-2, 7-9; bar snacks both sessions* ***Restaurant:*** *12-2 (Sun only), 7-9 (not Sun)* ***Typical Dishes BAR:*** *home-made soup £1.40, sweet pickled herring £2.50, steak and kidney pie £4.75, home-made lasagne £4.75, home-cooked ham salad £4.25, banana fudge pie* ***RESTAURANT:*** *chicken breast with leek and stilton £7.25, cider-baked gammon with Cumberland sauce £7.25, fillet steak en croute with madeira sauce £10.50 Vegetarian Meals: vegetable lasagne Children's Menu Children's Portions (some)* **Beer** *McEwans 80/-, Theakston Best, XB, Youngers 70/-* **Whisky** *Children Allowed in Bar to Eat Outdoor Play Area Patio/terrace Outdoor Eating* ***Accommodation:*** *12 bedrooms, 7 en suite, from £38 (single £20) Children Welcome Overnight Check-in: all day* ***No Credit Cards***

WALL — Hadrian

near Hexham NE46 4EE
Tel: (043 481) 232
Licensees: Kevin and Helen Kelly

Warm and inviting foyer and lounge with deep luxurious armchairs, in handsome 16th century house with Jacobean features; a nice place to stay. Though only three of the bedrooms are fully en suite, the others have clean, functional shower units.

Bar Meals: *lunchtime and evening; bar snacks lunchtime* **Beer** *Vaux Samson, Lorimers Best Scotch Children Allowed in Bar to Eat* ***Accommodation:*** *9 bedrooms, 3 en suite, from £45* ***Credit Cards:*** *Access, Visa*

WARENFORD   ★   Warenford Lodge

near Belford NE70 7HY   `FOOD`
Tel: (0668) 213453
Open: 12-1.30, 7-11; closed Mon
Licensee: Ray Matthewman

There's a wonderfully eclectic range of good bar food on offer at the Warenford
Lodge, especially so for the otherwise deeply conservative north east (not a slur on
Northumbria, just the result of much experience). Menus change here twice yearly,
in spring and autumn, reflecting seasonal produce and appetite, but a random
selection of favourites might well feature Syrian lamb roll, English woodpigeon
casserole, Manx tanrogan (scallop and mushroom), or an Andalucian casserole with
mixed vegetables, butter beans, smoked sausage, garlic and ham, all perfectly
seasoned and partnered by a great wedge of brown bread. Equally unmissable are the
grilled herby mussels, plump and tender with a light breadcrumb, parsley and garlic
topping. Herbs are particularly skilfully used here, in a subtle leek and lovage soup,
say, or the unusual and delicious blackcurrant and mint pie. The unifying factor
behind it all, exotic or homely, is the instinctive, hearty cooking of Mrs
Matthewman, at work in the kitchen while Ray tends to the bar. It's been 12
successful years now, and you need to book for weekend evenings (or any time in
summer), such is their local reputation. The pub itself is a fairly unassuming roadside
building, on the village loop road off the A1 – keep your eyes peeled, incidentally,
as the sign's very easy to miss. Inside, however, it's a handsome old place, with
exposed thickset stone and a smartly modern air which blends well with the
atmosphere of an old-fashioned private house. There are little mullion windows,
polished light pine tables and cushioned benches in the split level bar, a big stone
fireplace in the lower part, and a woodburning stove in the upper area, which has
armchairs and sofas just made for relaxing.

Bar Meals: 12-1.30, 7-9.30; bar snacks both sessions   *Restaurant:* 7-9.30   *Typical
Dishes:* leek and lovage soup £1.50, grilled herby mussels £2.90, venison £5.70, deep-
fried lamb's kidneys £4.20, spinach and pasta casserole £4.20, blackcurrant and mint pie
£2   Vegetarian Meals: spicy vegetable casserole £3.75   Children's Portions   `Cheese`
Credit Cards: Access, Diners, Visa

WOOLER   Ryecroft Hotel

Ryecroft Way (A697)
Tel: (0668) 81459
Open: all day
Licensees: Pat and David McKechnie

Family-run, modern redbrick hotel with awnings, in a suburban street of a grey but
charming small Northumberland town, well-placed for a little gentle tourism. An
open fire, conservatory extension and warm welcome lend character to the interior,
and the Ryecroft has a strong local reputation for good home cooking. Bedrooms
are comfortable.

Bar Meals: lunchtime and evening; bar snacks both sessions   *Typical Dishes:* cheese soup,
fruits de mer, pork in cider casserole, smoked salmon quiche, home-made puddings   Vegetarian
Meals   `Beer`   Marston; Tetley; Yates   Children Allowed in Bar to Eat   Garden
Accommodation: 9 bedrooms, all en suite, from £55 (single £30)   Check-in: all day

NOTTINGHAMSHIRE

ARNOLD   Burnt Stump

Burnt Stump Hill (off A60)
Tel: (0602) 631508

Surrounded by some thirty acres of parkland, a popular pub and restaurant with an over-long menu (there are about twenty choices on the starters list alone), but an assurance that local fresh ingredients are used wherever possible. The garden is lovely in summer; no children indoors.

Bar Meals and Restaurant: 12-2, 7-10 (not Sun eve); bar snacks lunchtime   **Typical Dishes:** *vegetable broth, grilled sardines, veal cordon bleu, scampi kebabs, various steaks (main courses from £5)*   Beer *Mansfield Riding Bitter   Vegetarian Meals   Garden*   **Credit Cards:** *Access, Amex, Diners, Visa*

BLIDWORTH   Bird in Hand

Main Street
Tel: (0623) 792356
Open: 11-3 (4 Sat), 6-11

Genuinely friendly, cosy one-bar village local with an island bar and lovely views over Sherwood Forest; real fire; no music. Good lunchtime food of a simple, homely kind centres on their popular home-made pies; good sandwiches, too, including an open sirloin one on French bread: delicious.

Bar Meals: Mon-Sat lunchtime; bar snacks both sessions   **Typical Dishes:** *thick vegetable soups, steak and kidney pie, cottage pie, Cornish pasties (main courses from £3.50)*   Beer *Mansfield Riding Bitter, Old Baily   Children Allowed in Bar to Eat   Garden*   **No Credit Cards**

CAYTHORPE Black Horse, Tel: (0602) 663520. Characterful 18th century inn with decent home cooking lunchtime and evening, real fire, garden, no music. Greenalls beers. Open: 11.45-2.30 (12-2 Sun), 6-11.

CLAYWORTH   Blacksmiths Arms

High Street
Tel: (0777) 817348   ▼

A rather run down looking creeper-clad village pub from the outside, but clean and cottagey within, a stone-clad bar, fresh carpet tiling, and framed antique mirrors; piped music's not too intrusive. Interesting daily specials enliven an otherwise routine bar meals menu; the evening table d'hote and à la carte restaurant opened in June '91.

Bar Meals: lunchtime and evening   **Restaurant:** *evenings*   **Typical Dishes BAR:** *ragout of minted lamb £3.95, steak and mushroom pie £4.35, lemon chicken stir-fry £4*   **RESTAURANT:** *pork terrine £2.75, smoked duck £3.95, mixed grill £13.50, salmon steak £9.95, Dover sole £12.50   Children's Menu*   Beer *Bass; Tetley; Whitbread*

COSTOCK Generous Briton 14 Main Street, Tel: (0509) 852347. Home-cooked lunches Monday-Saturday; traditional roast on Sundays, at homely, unassuming village local with real fire, lounge and public. John Smith's Bitter. Open: 11-2.30, 6.30-11.

DRAKEHOLES   Griff Inn

near Bawtry
Tel: (0777) 817206
Open: 12-3, 7-11
Licensees: M P Edmanson

Less of a hamlet than a multiple road junction, where the A631 meets the B6045, Drakeholes marks a right-angle turn on the Chesterfield canal where it tunnels for 150 yards under the road system. Standing above the basin, fronted by a large patio and canalside picnic tables, the Griff (once known as the White Swan) is built in the same distinctive red brick which characterises the estate village (both shopless and publess) of nearby Wiseton Hall. The 18th century inn's interior echoes the grand style of an earlier age, with its marble-floored entrance foyer and bar, and intimate oak-panelled cocktail lounge. Grand eating is not, however, de rigueur, the extensive bar menu encompassing old fashioned pies like shepherd's, sausage and onion (£4.25), steak and ale, game (£6) or seafood (£5.75); country lentil crumble (£4.20) and stuffed peppers. There are also jacket potatoes (from £1.95), salads (£4.25 up), sandwiches (£1.95 up) and children's items (£2.35), plus a Sunday bar lunch (£4.25) and weekend carvery (£5.50). Separating the bar from the (non-smoking) restaurant, a bright breakfast room doubles as a gift shop, selling miniature pottery, pot pourri and hand-made candles. The restaurant itself, meanwhile, combines table d'hote (£14.50) and Sunday lunch (£9.25) with an ambitious à la carte, whose carefully cooked and neatly presented food struggles manfully to live up to some perhaps effusive descriptions. For instance, "prawn patties" (£4.60), baby vol-au-vents of prawns in mornay sauce; "Highland fling" (£11.60), salmon and pineapple in puff pastry with a Drambuie sauce; and "Sicilian fillet" (£11.60), which turns out to be an excellent steak overwhelmed by anchovy and capers with cheesy breadcrumbs. The service can tend to be similarly self-conscious. The Griff is certainly useful to know for a quiet country stay in the Eden valley. Bedrooms are neatly appointed in pastel shades and varnished pine, which create a cottagey effect without fuss or particular luxury. There are televisions but no phones. En suite bathrooms are spacious and airy with good, powerful showers for early morning invigoration prior to a substantial country breakfast.

Bar Meals and Restaurant: 12-2 (2.30 Sun), 7-10; bar snacks both sessions Vegetarian Meals Children's Menu/Portions **Beer** *Tetley; Whitbread Children Allowed in Bar to Eat Patio Outdoor Eating* **Accommodation:** *3 bedrooms, all en suite, from £50 (single £30) Children Welcome Overnight Cots Available Check-in all day* **Credit Cards:** *Access, Visa*

ELKESLEY   Robin Hood Inn

High Street, just off A1 DN22 8AJ
Tel: (077 783) 259
Open: 11-3, 6.30-11
Licensee: Alan Draper

Opposite the 13th century village church. Cooking by the licensee using fresh ingredients where possible: fresh fish twice a week. A wide variety of meals, from £2.50 bakes to saucy steaks. Pan-fried chicken with a mushroom cream sauce (£6.95) is a typical restaurant dish.

Bar Meals and Restaurant: 12-2, 7-9 (10 Fri/Sat); bar snacks both sessions **Typical Dishes:** *home-made soup, garlic and ginger mushrooms, pan-fried rump steak, cream and brandy sauce, mixed grill, grilled trout with prawns and capers, chocolate and rum dessert*

Vegetarian Meals: cheese and vegetable bake £2.45   Children's Menu/Portions `Beer`
Whitbread beers   Children Allowed in Bar to Eat   Outdoor Play Area   Garden   Outdoor
Eating   **No Credit Cards**

ELTON Manor Arms, Tel: (0949) 50272. Standard button-back dralon lounge
bar with juke box, pool table in public bar, conservatory and small garden; sausage
and tomato bake £4.25, steak and kidney pie £3.95; more restaurranty food Tue-Sat
evenings; £7.50 main courses. Courage beers.

EPPERSTONE Cross Keys Main Street (off A6097), Tel: (0602) 663033.
Charming village local with real fire and family room; lunchtime and evening bar
meals; gets busy weekends. Hardys and Hansons beers. Open: 11-2.30 (12-2.30
Sun), 6-11.

HAYTON Boat Inn, Main Street. Listed primarily for its canalside position; lovely
summer garden, with picnic tables under an awning, play equipment and barbecue.
Food's average though, from an over-long menu in the bar or 'Gallery' carvery;
there's also £15 a head accommodation.

HOVERINGHAM   Reindeer Inn

Main Street NG14 7JR
Tel: (0602) 663629
Open: 12-3 (not Mon), 5.30-11
Licensees: Lesley and Ashley Grice

Proprietor-run typical village pub where the landlady does the cooking. No chips,
and lots of international theme evenings. Separate small dining room. Sunday lunch
is the full roast meats job, in the bar as well.

*Bar Meals: 12-1.45; bar snacks lunchtime   **Restaurant:** 12-1.45 (Sun only), 7-9.30
Tue-Sat   **Typical Dishes:** parsley, potato and smoked bacon soup £2.50, calves liver in
orange juice and Dubonnet £4.95, fillet steak stuffed with apples and stilton £11.95,
chicken stuffed with sage, onion and bacon in provencale sauce £7, halibut in lemon cream
with prawns £8, raspberry meringue bombe £3   Vegetarian Meals: Yorkshire pudding filled
with cauliflower cheese £3* `Cheese` `Beer` *Marston Burton Best Bitter, Pedigree*
`Whisky` *Children Allowed in Bar to Eat   Patio/terrace   Outdoor Eating   Summer
Barbecue*   **Credit Cards:** *Amex, Visa*

HOVERINGHAM Marquis of Granby Main Street. Small free house, strong on
guest beers and local popularity, not so strong on food; things with chips, steaks at
night; a hot special on Saturday lunchtime. No food on Sundays. A short walk from
the river Trent.

KIMBERLEY   Nelson & Railway

Station Road NG16 2NR
Tel: (0602) 382177
Open: 11-3, 5-11 (all day Fri/Sat)
Licensees: Harry and Pat Burton

Popular old pub, friendly and family-run. Go for the home-made specials.

*Bar Meals: 12-3, 5-9; bar snacks both sessions   **Typical Dishes:** home-made soup 95p,
home-made paté £1.55, steak and kidney pie £3.95, grilled gammon £4.25, beef
bourguignon £4.50, gooseberry crumble £1.20   Vegetarian Meals: spinach and mushroom
lasagne £3.50   Children's Menu/Portions* `Beer` *Hardy & Hanson beers   Family*

*Room   Outdoor Play Area   Garden   Outdoor Eating   **Accommodation:** 2 bedrooms, sharing a bathroom, from £31 (single £18.50)   Children Welcome Overnight   Cots Available   Check-in: all day   **No Credit Cards***

KNEESALL Angel Inn. Comfortable, spacious connecting rooms, decent bar food lunchtime and evening.

LAXTON   Dovecote

near Newark NG22 0NU
Tel: (0777) 871586
Open: 11-3, 6.30-11
Licensees: John and Elizabeth Waters

Red brick village pub in England's last remaining open field village; visitors' centre behind the building. Pleasant interior, friendly and cosy. Set Sunday lunches are also served, at £6.85.

*Bar Meals: 12-2.15, 7-10; bar snacks both sessions   **Typical Dishes:** home-made soup £1.50, crudités £2.75, home-made steak and kidney pie £4.25, beef in Guinness £5.95, deep-fried seafood platter £4.95, home-made apple pie £1.60   Vegetarian Meals: macaroni cheese £4.95   Children's Menu/Portions   Beer Mansfield Old Baily; Whitbread Castle Eden Ale   Family Room   Outdoor Play Area   Patio/terrace   Outdoor Eating   **No Credit Cards***

MANSFIELD Talbot Nottingham Road. Refurbished, rather smart dining pub, attracts a young crowd, for decent home cooking, some restauranty dishes; quieter at lunchtime.

MAPPERLEY Travellers Rest Mapperley Plains, Tel: (0602) 264412. Family-oriented cheap dining pub-roadhouse; family room open 5-10.30 (12-3 weekends). Youngers beers. Open all day.

NEWARK Old Kings Arms 19 Kirkgate. One step up from spit and sawdust (with frankly grotty loos); a Tynemill pub, keen on the green and organic; home-made soup, local sausages, steak and mushroom pie with over-cooked fresh vegetables (main courses from £3.50). Food Tue-Sat. Marston's beers. Open: 10.30-3, 5.30-11. **Old Malt Shovel,** 25 Northgate: Pleasant, lively little town local with distinctly homely daily specials – perhaps a home-made half-pound burger with real chips, £3. Taylors and Wards beers.

NORTH MUSKHAM Muskham Ferry Ferry Lane. In a pretty spot by the river, a useful stop just off the A1; bar food, buffet and restaurant, lunch and evening.

NOTTINGHAM   Lincolnshire Poacher

161-163 Mansfield Road
Tel (0602) 411584
Open: 11-3, 5 (6 Sat)-11

Another of the Tynemill Group of 'green'-minded pubs, transformed from the former Old Grey Nags Head. Rather arty within, all bare boards, pine tables, banquette pews and low stools; also a tiny rear conservatory; there are picnic tables in the large rear yard. The toilets aren't as smart as the rest. Much of the food is filled rolls and cobs, and there are decent vegetarian choices, as well as homely old tavern favourites like sausage and mash.

*Bar Meals: Mon-Fri lunch and evening until 8; Sat lunch bar snacks both sessions   **Typical Dishes:** pea soup, sausage and mash, chicken korma, beef in ale (main courses from £3), rice*

pudding with peaches £1.50   *Vegetarian Meals   Children's Portions*   Beer   *Batemans;*
Marston   Children Allowed in Bar to Eat   Garden

NOTTINGHAM   Trip to Jerusalem

Brewhouse Yard, Castle Road NG1 6AD
Tel: (0602) 473171
Open: 11-3 (4 Sat), 5.30-11
Licensees: Brian and Janet Palethorpe

Bought by Hardys & Hansons brewery, who have installed new licensees. Originally
a brewhouse for Nottingham Castle, and built into the caves at the foot of its wall,
the Trip to Jerusalem (known as The Pilgrim in the 18th century) has been a pub
for 800 years, a habitual resting place for crusading knights on their way to bash the
heathen overseas. The present building is mainly 17th century; the unique rock-face
walls most apparent in the spooky upstairs bar, which is opened only when the pub
is busy. Downstairs has panelled walls, built-in cushioned settles, barrel tables, and
exposed-rock alcoves; visitors' banknotes and coins littering the beams. In fine
weather there are patios to the side and back, and extra seating in the cobbled yard
opposite. Food's distinctly secondary.

Bar Meals: lunchtime snacks   ***Typical Dishes:*** *brunch in a bun* £1.75, *'Grandma Batty's
pork/beef filled Yorkshire puddings'* £3.80, *liver and onions* £2.75   Beer   *Hardys &
Hansons; Marston   Patio/terrace.*

STAUNTON IN THE VALE Staunton Arms. Attractively refurbished, with a
mezzanine dining area, and decent bar meals. Marston, Tetley beers.

UPTON   French Horn

Main Street (A612)   ❢
Tel: (0636) 812394
Open: 11-3, 6.30-11
Licensees: Graham and Linda Mills

Opened-out, refurbished dining pub with the most crowded pub car park in Upton:
the interior's simple with cushioned leather chairs, banquettes and wooden tables,
and there's a large sloping rear garden with picnic tables to the rear. The smart
money heads for the upstairs brasserie, where there's more choice at the top end of
the scale (closed Sun eve).

Bar Meals: 12-2, 6.30-10;   bar snacks both sessions   ***Typical Dishes:*** *soup* £1.25, *stir-
fried pork* £3.50, *lamb cobbler* £5, *salmon with lime and herb butter* £5.85, *sticky toffee
pudding* £1.95   *Vegetarian Meals   Children's Portions*   Beer   *Courage   Children
Allowed in Bar to Eat   Garden*

WELLOW   Olde Red Lion

Eakring Road (off A616)
Tel: (0623) 861000
Open: 11.30-3, 5.30-11
Licensees: John and Carol Henshaw

Several small cosy bars in this popular old pub; refurbished, well-run and often
swamped with hungry locals at peak feeding times; good value food in generous
portions. Sunday lunch is particularly busy.

*Bar Meals: 12-2, 7.30-10;   bar snacks both sessions   **Typical Dishes:** home-made soup £1, garlic mushrooms £1.95, steak and kidney pie £3.25, tandoori chicken £4.50, hot pot £3.25   Vegetarian Meals   Children's Menu   **Beer**   Marston; Ruddles; Whitbread   Outdoor Play Area   Garden*

WEST LEAKE   Star Inn

Melton Lane LE12 5RQ
Tel: (0509) 852233
Open: 12-2.30, 7-11 (closed Sun)
Licensee: Frank Whatnall

Also known as the Pit House – cockfights were once popular here. Warm and welcoming, traditionally furnished interior. Very short daily list – just one hot dish – but honest home cooking.

*Bar Meals: 12.30-2 Mon-Fri; bar snacks   **Typical Dishes:** cold meats and wide range of salads on daily cold table £3.25, hot daily special, around same price, home-made puddings under £1   Vegetarian Meals: spinach quiche, salad bar   Children's Menu/Portions   **Beer**   Adnams Bitter; Draught Bass   Children Allowed in Bar to Eat   Outdoor Play Area   Patio/terrace   Outdoor Eating   **No Credit Cards***

WEST STOCKWITH Waterfront Inn Charming waterside pub with decent bar meals lunch and evening.

OXFORDSHIRE

BECKLEY   Abingdon Arms

High Street OX3 9UU
Tel: (086 735) 311
Open: 11.30-2.30, 6.30-11 (12-2.30, 8-10.30 Sun)
Licensee: Hugh Greatbatch

Beautifully positioned village pub with inspiring views from the pretty garden. Inside is nothing special, plainly furnished with cloth-covered wall seats in the lounge and a separate public bar, but people come here for the excellent food, which mirrors the seasons, with lots of delicious picnicky things in summer, cold poached salmon and chicken amongst them, and warming bakes, curries and other hot dishes in winter. No children indoors.

*Bar Meals: 12.15-1.45, 7.15-9.15 (not Sun), bar snacks lunchtime   **Typical Dishes:** home-made soup £1.95, blini £3.50, roast beef £6.25, chicken curry £5.25, salmon £6.40, ice-cream £1.85   Vegetarian Meals: stuffed aubergine £5.35   **Beer**   Adnams Bitter; Wadworth 6X   Garden   Outdoor Eating   **No Credit Cards***

BENSON   Farmers Man

Benson OX10 6LQ
Tel: (0491) 35405
Open: 11-11
Licensees: Mr and Mrs Robinson

Newish licensees have brought praise for the food and atmosphere here.

Bar Meals and Restaurant: 12-2, 7-10; bar snacks both sessions   **Typical Dishes:** *leek and potato soup £1.95, chicken and bacon salad £3.75, lamb with red wine, honey and mint £7.95, duck with raspberries and cognac £6.95, skewer of monkfish wrapped in bacon £7.50, meringue and strawberries £2.25   Vegetarian Meals: tagliatelle with tomato and artichoke hearts   Children's Portions* [Beer] *Brakspears   Family Room   Patio/terrace Outdoor Eating*   **Credit Cards:** *Access, Visa*

BICESTER   Plough Inn

63 North Street OX6 7NB
Tel: (0869) 249083
Open: 11-3, 5.30-11 (11-11 Fri/Sat)
Licensee: Per Egeberg

16th century town pub with beamed ceilings and open fires; food served in a set aside part of the horseshoe-shaped bar. Home cooking.

Bar Meals: 12-2.30, 6.30-9.15 (not Sun); bar snacks both sessions   **Typical Dishes:** *mushroom, onion and garlic soup £1.20, chicken satay £1.20, 8 oz rump steak £5.95, home-made pork in cider £3.85, home-made steak and Guinness pie £3.95, Dutch apple tart   Vegetarian Meals: spinach and mushroom lasagne £3   Children's Menu* [Beer] *Morrells Varsity   Children Allowed in Bar to Eat   Patio/terrace*   **Accommodation:** *5 bedrooms, 2 en suite, from £25 (single £20)   Children Welcome Overnight   Cot Available   Check-in: all day*   **No Credit Cards**

BRIGHTWELL BALDWIN   Lord Nelson

near Watlington OX9 5NP
Tel: (0491) 612497
Open: 11.30-3.30, 6.30-11.15
Licensees: Peter Neal and Richard Britcliffe

A pretty stone-built pub opposite the village church, with lots of Nelson memorabilia inside. Attractively modernised with a mix of chairs around dining tables, candles, lanterns and fresh flowers. New licensees since our last edition have kept up cooking standards; it's now possible to also order from the lunchtime restaurant menu in the bar. Children inside by arrangement only. Pleasant outdoor drinking on the verandah or lawn.

Bar Meals and Restaurant: 12-2, 7-10 (restaurant closed Sun eve and all Mon); bar snacks both sessions   **Typical Dishes:** *home-made soup £2.50, home-made duck liver and pork paté £2.95, roast guinea fowl with creamy cider and onion sauce £7.50, supreme of chicken with prawns and asparagus £7.75, blackcurrants in madeira   Vegetarian Meals: tagliatelle   Children's Portions (some)* [Beer] *Brakspears   Garden   Outdoor Eating*   **Credit Cards:** *Access, Amex, Diners, Visa*

BURCOT   Chequers

Abingdon Road OX14 3DP
Tel: (086 730) 7771
Open: 11-2.30, 6-11
Licensee: Michael Weeks

Originally a staging post for river Thames barges and their crews, until the now A415 road was built outside. Charming, part 16th century beamed and thatched building with unspoilt quarry-tiled bars. Same menu in the dining room; home-baked bread; piano music.

Bar Meals: 12-2, 6.30-9.30; bar snacks both sessions   **Typical Dishes:** *pepper and sweetcorn soup £1.50, deep-fried choux buns with ham and cheese £2.75, beef and fennel lasagne £4.50, spicy minced lamb £4.35, baby chicken provencale £4.85, Mary's disaster cake £1.75   Vegetarian Meals: Somerset casserole £4.25*   ▋Beer▋ *Ruddles County; Ushers Best   Children Allowed in Bar to Eat   Garden   Outdoor Eating*   **Credit Cards:** *Access, Visa*

BURFORD   Lamb Inn

Sheep Street OX18 4LR   ❦
Tel: (0993) 823155
Open: 11-2.30, 6-11
Licensees: Richard and Caroline de Wolf

Well-loved bed and breakfasting inn of great charm and unspoilt character, which contrives to be both upmarket and informal. Lovely public rooms with superior furnishings, rugs in the lounge, bare stone floors in the public bar. Log fires. Nice bedrooms; nice little suntrap garden.

Bar Meals: 12-2 (not Sun)   **Restaurant:** 12.30-1.45 (Sun only), 7.30-9   **Typical Dishes BAR:** *mushroom and brie soup £2.25, terrine of salmon and sole with cucumber and mint dressing £3.50, honey-glazed lamb cutlets £5.95, duck liver and bacon salad £4, tagliatelle carbonara £5.25, gateau Victoire with creme anglaise*   **RESTAURANT:** *dinner menu £19-£23: courgette and coriander soup, avocado and pepper tartlet, roast duckling with oyster mushrooms, cranberry and port sauce, escalope of veal with walnut and stilton cream, baked red mullet provencale, home-made puddings   Vegetarian Meals: pithivier of avocado, mushroom and walnuts on champagne cream   Children's Portions*   ▋Beer▋ *Wadworth beers   Family Room   Garden   Outdoor Eating*   **Accommodation:** *15 bedrooms, 14 en suite, from £70 (single £36)   Children Welcome Overnight   Cot Available   Check-in: all day*   **Credit Cards:** *Access, Visa*

BURFORD   Mermaid

High Street OX18 4QF
Tel: (099 382) 2193
Open: 10.30-11
Licensee: F J Titcombe

Reliably good food; the same menu in bar and dining room – hot meals start at about £5. Flagstoned, romantically gloomy bar of unspoilt charm; on sunny days the wide pavement's tables are the place to be. Children in dining room only.

Bar Meals: 12-2.30 (3 weekends), 6-10 (9.30 Sun); bar snacks lunchtime   **Typical Dishes:** *home-made soup £1.95, garlic mushrooms £4.50, black velvet chicken £7.95, fillet of beef Wychwood £14.95,   Cotswold trout £8.65, treacle tart   Vegetarian Meals: macaroni and broccoli cheese   Children's Portions*   ▋Beer▋ *Morlands   Patio/terrace   Outdoor Eating*   **Credit Cards:** *Access, Visa*

CHADLINGTON   Tite Inn

Mill End OX7 3NY   `FOOD`
Tel: (060 876) 475   ♼
Open: 12-2.30, 6.30 (7 winter)-11; closed Mon
Licensees: Michael and Susan Willis

From the outside, this warm Cotswold stone 16th century pub is as pretty as a
picture, complete with cottage roses clambering up the walls. Inside, the original
rough stone walls remain, but otherwise it is almost too neat and tidy, with its
modern carpeted floor and wheelback chairs. A table displaying newspapers and
magazines is a nice touch, though, and there is also a garden room which features
bunches of grapes hanging from a vine covering the roof. The origin of the unusual
name is uncertain but is thought to refer to the nearby springs which used to feed a
mill pond. Michael Willis behind the bar looks after the real ales, which include the
happily named Dr Thirstys Draught from the local Glenny's brewery, while Susan
looks after the kitchen. Hearty home-made soups and succulent gammon
sandwiches made with superior wholemeal bread are amongst the offerings listed on
the regularly changing blackboard menu, although bobotie (a hot sweet curry from
South Africa) is, by popular demand, a permanent fixture, and there are always
several vegetarian dishes available. At night, one end of the bar becomes a restaurant
with dishes ranging from chicken breast in a cider and honey sauce to steak and
kidney pie. The bar menu is a little shorter in the evening. Children are made
genuinely welcome and small portions are no problem.

Bar Meals: 12-2, 6.30-9 (12-1.30, 7-8.30 Sun)   *Restaurant:* Roast Sun lunches; 7-9
Mon-Sat   *Typical Dishes BAR:* celery and stilton soup £1.95, hot seafood cocotte £3.50,
braised lamb kidneys in port £5.95, boiled gammon with parsley sauce £5.50, chicken breast
in cider and honey sauce £6.25, apple and sultana crumble £1.95   Vegetarian Meals:
baked brie with salad £4.25   Children's Portions   `Beer`   Adnams Bitter; Glennys
Bitter; Hall & Woodhouse Tanglefoot; Wadworth 6X   `Cider`   Blands   Family Room
Garden   Outdoor Eating   **No Credit Cards**

CHINNOR   Sir Charles Napier

Spriggs Holly OX9 4BX   ♼
Tel: (0494) 483011
Open: 11.45-4, 6.30-12; closed Sun eve and all Mon
Licensee: Julie Griffiths

Even more restauranty than when we last reported on it, this distinctly unassuming-
looking country inn, the bar is simply furnished with bare floors and beams, and a
good fire in winter. Lunchtime during the week is the time to enjoy the
comparative bargain of a bar meal here; evenings and weekends are more formal,
and Sunday lunch particularly well-heeled (at around £50 for two, it ought to be);
evening meals can easily notch up twice the expense, but if you splash out, go on a
warm summer evening, when the tables on the terrace are candlelit.

Bar Meals: Tue-Sat lunch   *Typical Dishes:* cucumber and mint soup £3.20, shellfish
mariniere £4.70, braised Welsh lamb £8.70, baked ham with poached eggs £4.20
Children's Portions   `Cheese`   `Beer`   Wadworth   `Whisky`   Children Allowed in Bar to
Eat (lunchtime)   Garden   Outdoor Eating   **Credit Cards:** Amex, Diners

CLANFIELD   Clanfield Tavern

on A4095 OX8 2RG
Tel: (036 781) 223
Open: 11.30-2.30, 6-11
Licensees: Keith and Anne Gill

Charming 17th century pub of Cotswold stone, with uneven flagstoned floors, low-beamed ceilings and a large open fire. Routine bar food is enlivened by more interesting daily specials, perhaps game, fish or homely casseroles (around £5). Recommended for accommodation: three attractively furnished rooms have a mixture of traditional and modern pieces. Attractive views from the colourful small lawn.

Bar Meals: 12-2, 6-10; bar snacks both sessions *Children's Portions* `Beer` *Hook Norton; Morlands; Morrells Family Room Garden **Accommodation:** 3 bedrooms, sharing a bathroom, from £30 (20 single) Check-in: all day **Credit Cards:** Visa*

CLIFTON   Duke of Cumberland's Head

Deddington OX5 4PE
Tel: (0869) 38534
Open: 11.30-3, 6.30-11
Licensee: John Clark

Thatched old stone-built pub on the B4031, complete with beams and inglenook fireplace. Busy usually. No music, except for live jazz once a month.

Bar Meals and Restaurant: 12-2, 7-9.30 (not Sun); restaurant closed Mon; bar snacks lunchtime *Typical Dishes BAR:* broccoli and ginger soup £1.40, smoked salmon with horseradish mousse £2.50, steak and kidney pie £4.25, beef bourguignon £4.25, fresh grilled plaice £4.95, gratin of raspberries *RESTAURANT:* tomato and orange soup £1.50, deep-fried camembert £4.50, duck with peaches £8.95, fillet of beef Richelieu £19.90 (for 2) Vegetarian Meals: vegetable lasagne Children's Portions `Beer` Hook Norton; Jennings; Ruddles; Wadworth Children Allowed in Bar to Eat Garden Outdoor Eating **Accommodation:** 3 bedrooms, all en suite, from £32 (single £19) Children Welcome Overnight Check-in: by arrangement **Credit Cards:** Access, Visa*

CROWELL   Catherine Wheel

near Chinnor OX9 4RR
Tel: (0844) 51431
Licensees: Stuart and Lorraine MacKay

Good eating in a quaint old pub with an attractive country atmosphere, and an enthusiastic (and highly competent) amateur cook landlady.

Bar Meals: 12-2 (2.30 weekends), 7-9 (not Sun/Mon) *Typical Dishes:* tuna paté, crispy fried mushrooms, chicken Dijon, pork kebabs, swordfish in shrimp sauce (main courses from £4) `Cheese` Vegetarian Meals `Beer` ABC Bitter; Bass Family Room **No credit cards**

DORCHESTER ON THAMES   George Hotel

High Street OX10 7HA
Tel: (0865) 340404
Open: 11-3, 6-11
Licensees: Mark Stott and Brian Griffin

Smartly modernised, civilised old inn with a country hotel rather than inn-like feel. Originally built as a brewhouse for the Norman Abbey opposite. The bar is very attractive, with nice old chairs and tables, sofas and cushioned settles, all well-spaced and distinctly unpub-like, but bar food's available here nonetheless. Half the attractive bedrooms are in the main building, half in a converted stable block.

Bar Meals and Restaurant: 12-2, 7-9.30 (9.45 restaurant) **Typical Dishes BAR:** *mushroom soup £2.50, potted prawn and mushroom £3.50, calves liver and bacon £6, Cornish fish pie £5, hot daily specials £5, home-made puddings £2.50* **RESTAURANT:** *tomato and orange soup £3, salt and pepper tiger prawns, entrecote of veal with wild mushrooms, rack of lamb with a mustard and herb crust, seafood in a buttery court bouillon, iced ginger parfait with acacia honey caramel Vegetarian Meals: avocado and gruyere bake Children's Portions* Cheese Beer *Brakspears* Whisky *Family Room Garden* **Accommodation:** *18 bedrooms, all en suite, from £75 (single £62) Children Welcome Overnight Cot Available Check-in: all day* **Credit Cards:** *Access, Amex, Visa*

DORCHESTER ON THAMES Fleur de Lys. Timbered old coaching inn with decent bar food; morning coffee.

EYNSHAM   Newlands Inn

Newland Street   ❢
Tel: (0865) 881486
Open: 11-2.30, 6-11
Licensees: Nicholas and Caroline Godden

Nice old pub with traditional interior and their own smokery.

Bar Meals and Restaurant: 12-2, 7-9.30 (10 restaurant); bar snacks both sessions **Typical Dishes BAR:** *home-prepared gravadlax, baked brie and almonds, local organic lamb steaks, fresh local trout, pan-fried king prawns, creme brulee Vegetarian Meals: lasagne* Beer *Hook Norton; Tetley; Wadworth Children Allowed in Bar to Eat Outdoor Play Area Patio/terrace Outdoor Eating Summer Barbecue* **Credit Cards:** *Access, Visa*

FOREST HILL White Horse. Friendly village local, refurbished but with character touches; separate dining room, often imaginative home-cooked food, nice sandwiches. Morrells beers.

FYFIELD   White Hart

near Abingdon OX13 5LN
Tel: (0865) 390585
Open: 11-2.30, 6.30-11
Licensee: John Howard

500 year old ex-chantry house with a 30 feet high gallery and four family rooms. The landlord is also the cook.

Bar Meals: 12-2, 7-10; bar snacks both sessions **Typical Dishes:** *home-made soup £1.95, garlic mushrooms £2.75, steak and kidney pie £5.25, venison in red wine £6.95, chicken breast with mushrooms and paté £6.80, treacle tart £1.95 Vegetarian Meals:*

spinach and feta in filo £4.50   *Children's Portions*   **Beer**   *Hook Norton; Theakston;*
Wadworth; Whitbread Boddingtons Bitter   **Cider**   *Weston's   Family Room   Garden*
Outdoor Eating   **Credit Cards:** *Access, Amex, Visa*

GORING HEATH   King Charles Head

near Reading RG8 7RL   ▼
Tel: (0491) 680268
Open: 11-3, 6-11
Licensees: Bernard Morris and Richard Fay

Rambling, characterful old brick cottage in a romantic woodland setting. Several
rooms lead off the central bar; two real fires. A modern extension bar leads into two
and a half acres of lovely garden. Menus are flexible, both bar snacks and restaurant
meals are awarded table service; lots of good vegetarian dishes. No juke box or
background music.

Bar Meals: *12-2.30, 7-9.30 (not Sun eve); bar snacks both sessions* **Typical Dishes:**
chicken and vegetable soup £1.75, *venison sausages* £4.25,   *Cotswold chicken, lasagne*
£4.95, *home-baked apple pie* *Vegetarian Meals: stilton and cheddar croquettes* *Children's*
Portions **Beer** *Adnams; Gibbs Mew; Glenny; Theakston* *Children Allowed in Bar to*
Eat *Outdoor Play Area* *Garden* *Outdoor Eating* *Summer Barbecue* **No Credit**
Cards

GREAT MILTON Bell The Green (off A329) Tel: (0844) 269270. Welcoming
country pub, popular for genuine home cooking lunch and evening and good range
of well-kept beers. Real fires, garden, no music. Brakspears, Donnington, Marston,
Uley beers. Open: 12-2, 7-11.

GREAT TEW   Falkland Arms

Great Tew OX7 4DB   **B&B**
Tel: (060 883) 653   ☼
Open: 11.30-2.30 (not Mon; 12-2 Sun), 6-11
Licensees: John and Hazel Milligan

Great Tew must be one of the prettiest of Cotswold villages and has the inestimable
advantage of being a bit out of the way and not on the main tourist trail. Despite the
ambition implied by its name, it's actually rather a small place, with barely a score of
mostly thatched cottages, a small general store and, naturally, in its rightful place
opposite the church, the village inn. Dating back to the 16th century, the creeper-
clad Falkland Arms must be close to everybody's ideal country pub, with high-
backed settles, a flagstone floor and a prized collection of hundreds of jugs and mugs
hanging from the old beams. A pretty garden shaded by a large hornbeam tree is
complete with dovecote, whose occupants seem to spend most of the day perched
on the pub's stone tiled roof cooing to each other. As well they might. Hall &
Woodhouse Tanglefoot, Hook Norton, Donnington BB and Wadworth 6X are the
regular real ales, supplemented by an ever-changing selection of guest beers (some
250 in a full year). They also sell snuff, and even clay pipes ready-filled with
tobacco. Food is served at lunchtimes only from a short but varied blackboard menu
that changes daily but always includes a vegetarian dish (the landlord John Milligan
eats not of meat), along with ploughmans and perhaps a rook pie (well at least it
wasn't dove). Everything is home-made, from a clear-flavoured celery soup to an
apple pie clothed in soft short pastry. Four cottagey bedrooms, two with fourposter
beds and two with old iron bedsteads, are furnished with antiques and decorated
with pretty co-ordinating fabrics and wall coverings. The largest, under the eaves,
has a pitched ceiling, exposed timbers and its own en suite bathroom. Others have
showers and, all but one, their own toilets. Televisions and tea and coffee things are

standard, and you can help yourself to fresh milk from the kitchen. Breakfast is at 9 o'clock prompt (9.30 on Sundays) and they like the rooms vacated by 10.30 on day of departure. Bookings must be confirmed in writing with a 50% deposit: a policy they felt compelled to adopt as a result of an incident in which a party failed to turn up.

Bar Meals: *12-2 Tue-Sat; bar snacks*   **Typical Dishes:** *home-made soup £1.30, pork and stilton hotpot £5, steak and kidney cobbler £5, cod and prawn crumble £4.80, rhubarb crumble £1.50   Vegetarian Meals: vegetable hotpot £4.50   Children's Menu/Portions*   `Beer` *Donnington; Hook Norton; Hall & Woodhouse; Wadworth* `Cider` *Weston's   Children Allowed in Bar to Eat   Outdoor Play Area   Garden   Summer Barbecue*   **Accommodation:** *4 bedrooms, 3 en suite, from £40 (single £28)   Children Welcome Overnight   Check-in: by arrangement*   **No Credit Cards**

HANWELL   Moon & Sixpence

near Banbury OX17 1HW
Tel: (0295) 730544
Open: weekday lunchtimes, Mon-Sat eves
Licensees: Leonardo and Gillian de Felice

Describes itself as a restaurant with rooms rather than an inn, an emphasis further brought home this year with a remodelled restaurant seating up to 100 people, as well as a 'new improved' bar leading out onto a patio. Old bar meal favourites like steak and kidney pie are still available, though. Delightfully relaxing interior. Children are allowed in both dining areas.

Bar Meals: *12-2; bar snacks*   **Restaurant:** *12-2, 7-9.45*   **Typical Dishes BAR:** *home-made soup of the day £2, Ogen melon and strawberries £5.25, home-made steak and kidney pie £5.50, fresh pasta £5.50, whole grilled plaice £6.95, tiramisu £2.85*   **Restaurant:** *similar starters and puddings, avocado Leonardo £4.45, veal £9.55, venison with wild fruits £9.55   Vegetarian Meals: pasta Napoletana   Children's Portions*   `Cheese`   `Beer` *Whitbread Flowers* `Whisky` *Patio/terrace*   **Accommodation** *(closed August): 3 bedrooms, sharing a bathroom, from £48 (single £35)   Children Welcome Overnight   Check-in: all day*   **Credit Cards:** *Access, Visa*

HENLEY ON THAMES   Little Angel

Remenham Lane RG9 2LS
Tel: (0491) 574165
Open: 11-2.30, 6-10.30 (11 Fri/Sat)
Licensee: Ashley St John Bundock

A new licensee since our last edition has changed the menu, but the Little Angel is still well worth a visit. It's a fine old pub, just over the bridge on the A423. In addition, any wine on the list will be opened for a glassful on request; a barbecue is being built for 1992.

Bar Meals: *12-2, 7-10; bar snacks both sessions*   **Restaurant:** *12.30-2, 7.30-10*   **Typical Dishes BAR:** *carrot and coriander soup £3, garlic mushrooms and prawns on toast, farmers steak and mushroom pie, tagliatelle carbonara, grilled plaice tartare (main courses from £5), chocolate marquise with coffee bean sauce   Vegetarian Meals: tagliatelle   Children's Portions*   `Beer` *Brakspears   Children Allowed in Bar to Eat   Patio/terrace   Outdoor Eating*   **Credit Cards:** *Access, Amex, Diners, Visa*

Three Tuns, 5 Market Place   Tel: (0491) 573260.   Characterful town centre pub with small public and oak-beamed lounge with a large fireplace (and restaurant licence). Eccentric pricing system: lasagne costs precisely £3.34; small terrace dining area. Brakspears beers. Open all day.

HENTON   Peacock Inn

near Chinnor OX9 4AH
Tel: (0844) 53519
Open: 12-3, 6-11
Licensee: Herbert Good

Very pretty black and white timbered, thatched inn, some 600 years old, in a sleepy village just off the B4009. Peacocks roam the grounds; the bar is comfortably refurbished and immaculately kept. Some bedrooms are in an extension, which also houses the residents' lounge; eight new ones since our last edition. All are smart and well equipped: recommended for bed and breakfast.

Bar Meals: 12-2; bar snacks   *Restaurant:* 12-2, 7-10 (not Sun eve)   *Typical Dishes*
BAR: grilled fresh sardines £3.85, gammon steak and pineapple £5.95, roast beef salad £6.95, prawn omelette £5.45, fruit crumble £2.45   *RESTAURANT:* deep-fried brie with redcurrant sauce £3.85, roast half duck with orange £11.95, sirloin steak with melted stilton £10.90, grilled fresh plaice with garlic and parsley £8.25, sherry trifle £2.45
Vegetarian Meals: mushroom and aubergine lasagne £7.45   *Children's Menu*   `Beer`
Brakspears   *Children Allowed in Bar to Eat*   *Patio/terrace*   *Outdoor Eating*
Accommodation: 20 bedrooms, all en suite, from £52 (single £45)   *Children Welcome*
Overnight   *Check-in: all day*   *Credit Cards:* Access, Amex, Visa

LEWKNOR   Leathern Bottle

1 High Street OX9 5TH
Tel: (0844) 51482
Open: 11-2.30, 6-11
Licensee: M S Fletcher

Homely country pub with Cromwellian connections. Close to junction 6 of the M4 motorway.

Bar Meals: 12-2, 7-9.30; bar snacks lunchtime   *Typical Dishes:* Mediterranean fish soup £2.25, king prawns £2.75, home-made steak and kidney pie £4.50, spare ribs £5.90, seafood pasta bake £4.75, bread and butter pudding £1.60   *Vegetarian Meals:* lasagne
Children's Portions   `Beer`   *Brakspears*   *Family Room*   *Outdoor Play Area*   *Garden*
No Credit Cards

LITTLE MILTON   Lamb Inn

on A329 OX9 7PU
Tel: (0844) 279527
Open: 11-2.30, 6.30-11
Licensee: David Bowell

Thatched and golden stone pub with rustic, characterful bars (windows at stooping height), and good home cooking; a standard menu enlivened by more elaborate blackboard specials.

Bar Meals: 12-2, 7-10; bar snacks both sessions   *Typical Dishes:* beef and Guinness casserole, kidneys Dijonnaise, chicken in tarragon sauce (from £5.50), chocolate pot £1.95
Vegetarian Meals   `Cheese`   `Beer`   *Ind Coope, Tetley*   *Children Allowed in Bar to Eat*
Garden   *Credit Cards:* Diners

LITTLE MILTON   Plough

Thame Road OX9 7QD
Tel: (0844) 278180
Open: 11-11
Licensee: Patrick Dillon

17th century village pub of character, and a genuine local. Pig roasts in summer; restaurant main courses around £8.

*Bar Meals and Restaurant: 11-9; bar snacks both sessions   **Typical Dishes BAR:** steak and kidney in red wine, beef and Guinness pie, smoked haddock crumble (main courses around £4), spotted dick   Vegetarian Meals: lasagne   Children's Menu/Portions*   **Beer**   *Bass; Felinfoel; Morrells   Family Room   Children Allowed in Bar to Eat   Outdoor Play Area   Garden   Outdoor Eating   Summer Barbecue   **No Credit Cards***

LONG HANBOROUGH   Bell

115 Main Road OX8 2JX
Tel: (0993) 881324
Open: 10.30-3, 6.30-11
Licensees: Philip and Marise Fry

Unusual tree–stump furnishings and busy function room, the Waggoners, for mass dining.

*Bar Meals: 11.30-2.30, 6.30-10.30 (12-2.30, 7-10.15 Sun); bar snacks both sessions   **Restaurant:** 6.30 (7 Sun)-10   **Typical Dishes:** soup of the day £1.55, prawn and smoked salmon cocktail £2.70, beef Wellington £12.75, pork fillet stuffed with apricots in mead sauce £8.50, half a roast duckling with plum sauce £7.90; brandied chocolate mousse £1.75   Vegetarian Meals: tagliatelle with mushroom sauce   Children's Menu/Portions*   **Beer**   *Felinfoel; Morrells*   **Cider**   *Family Room   Patio/terrace   Outdoor Eating*   **Credit Cards:** *Access, Visa (from 1992)*

LONG WITTENHAM   Machine Man

Fieldside, off High Street OX14 4QP
Tel: (086 730) 7835
Open: 11-3, 6.30-11
Licensee: Gordon Lindsay

Cheery, popular local in conservation village. Very simple homely meals; slightly higher prices in the dining room. Look out for good bargain specials like a delicious game hotpot.

*Bar Meals: 12-2.30, 7-9.30   bar snacks both sessions   **Typical Dishes:** minestrone £1.60, garlic mushrooms £1.80, curries £3.25, lasagne £3.25, grills £7.25, home-made puddings £1.80   Vegetarian Meals   Children's Menu/Portions*   **Beer**   *Eldridge Pope; Exmoor Ales; Hook Norton*   **Cider**   *Addlestones   Children Allowed in Bar to Eat   Outdoor Play Area   Patio/terrace   Outdoor Eating   **Accommodation:** 4 bedrooms, 2 en suite, from £38 (single £24)   Children Welcome Overnight   Check-in: all day   **Credit Cards:** Access, Visa*

LOWER ASSENDON Golden Ball on B480. Locally popular for good home-made pies; characterful old pub; Brakspears beers.

LOWER WOLVERCOTE   Trout

95 Godstow Road
Tel: (0865) 54485

Simple bar snacks with more interesting hot specials in winter; stuffed or smoked trout, too, in this well-loved riverside pub, close by the abbey ruins, and with peacocks roaming its grounds. There's also a restaurant.

Bar Meals: *lunch and evening   bar snacks both sessions*   **Typical Dishes:** *home-made soup, home-made paté, smoked salmon sandwiches, chicken casserole (hot specials from £4)*
Beer *Bass   Garden   Credit Cards*

MAIDENSGROVE   Five Horseshoes

west of the village RG9 6EY   ❢
Tel: (0491) 641282
Open: 11.30-2.30, 6.30-11
Licensees: Graham and Mary Cromack

New kitchens and a brand new dining conservatory with rural views are scheduled to open March 1992 at this very popular dining pub; creeper-clad, 17th century, and alone in Chiltern countryside. Walkers use the public bar.

Bar Meals: *12-2, 7-9.30 (usually); bar snacks both sessions*   **Typical Dishes:** *home-made soup £2.20, avocado and walnut paté £4.50, stir-fried beef in tangy sherry sauce £6.95, chilli chicken, poached in wine and stuffed with brie £6.25, escalope of Scotch salmon on mustard, tomato and dill sauce £7.25, chocolate and orange meringue pie £2.50   Vegetarian Meals: asparagus, mushroom and cream cheese filo parcels £4.75   Children's Portions*
Beer *Brakspears* **Whisky** *Garden   Outdoor Eating Summer Eating*   **Credit Cards:** *Access, Visa*

MIDDLETON STONEY   Jersey Arms

Middleton Stoney OX6 8SE
Tel: (086 989) 234
Open: 11-11
Licensee: Donald Livingston

16th century Cotswold stone inn, now the 2 star Jersey Arms Hotel and Restaurant, well placed for Oxford. Unpretentious and cosy bars with a traditional feel; good large bedrooms, two of them with sitting areas, three suites proper. Similar dishes served in restaurant at higher prices.

Bar Meals: *12-2, 6-9; bar snacks lunchtime*   **Restaurant:** *12.30-2, 7.30-9.30*   **Typical Dishes BAR:** *home-made soup £2, paté £2.95, chicken £5.95, sirloin steak £10.75   Vegetarian Meals: vegetarian crepe* **Cheese** **Beer** *Youngers Scotch, IPA   Children Allowed in Bar to Eat   Outdoor Play Area   Garden   Outdoor Eating*   **Accommodation:** *16 bedrooms, all en suite, from £59.50 (single £49.50)   Children Welcome Overnight Cots Available   Check-in: all day*   **Credit Cards:** *Access, Amex, Diners, Visa*

MURCOTT   Nut Tree

near Kidlington OX5 2RE
Tel: (086 733) 253
Open: 11-3, 6.30-11
Licensees: Gordon and Diane Evans

Quaint white thatched pub with a duckpond and a reputation for good steaks and fish.

Bar Meals: 12-2, 6.30-9.30 Mon-Sat; bar snacks both sessions   **Typical Dishes:** *home-made soup £2.05, king prawns in garlic butter £3.10, steaks £10.50-£12.80, gammon with curried peach £6.65, fresh fish from £5.50   Vegetarian Meals: vegetarian pie*
Beer   *Draught Bass; Fullers London Pride; Wadworth 6X   Children Allowed in Bar to Eat   Garden   Outdoor Eating*   **No Credit Cards**

NUFFIELD   Crown

Henley on Thames RG9 5SJ
Tel: (0491) 641335
Open: 11-2.30 (3 Sat), 6-11
Licensee: Gerald Bean

Pleasantly refurbished pub with beams and inglenook. The menu changes seasonally; daily specials board; all food home-made by the licensees. No children in the evening.

Bar Meals: 12-2, 7-9.45 (9.30 Sun); bar snacks both sessions   **Typical Dishes:** *celery and stilton soup £2.25, Greek style pasta salad £3.75, home-made steak and kidney pie £5.25, local pork, honey and sage sausages £3.25, salmon steak £7.75, raspberry cheesecake £1.95   Vegetarian Meals: vegetable curry £4.95*   **Cheese**   **Beer**
Brakspears beers   Family Room   Garden   Outdoor Eating   **No Credit Cards**

OXFORD   Old Tom

101 St Aldgates
Tel: (0865) 243034
Open: 10.30-3, 5-11
Licensee: Rotraud Palmer

Promising new Oxford city centre entry, small but cosy, usually busy, and fast earning itself a reputation for genuine home cooking; no chips, guaranteed. The German chef-licensee has introduced a few new dishes to the usual pub repertoire. Good cold dishes too.

Bar Meals: lunch and evening   bar snacks both sessions   **Typical Dishes:** *steak and kidney pie, hotpot, Rhineland pie (main courses from £4)   Vegetarian Meals   Children's Portions*
Beer   *Morrells Bitter, Varsity   Children Allowed in Bar to Eat   Patio*   **Credit Cards:** *Access, Amex, Visa*

OXFORD Turf Tavern 4 Bath Place, off Holywell Street Tel: (0865) 243235. Famous medieval gem, tucked away by the old city wall, and usually very busy with students and tourists. Robust standard pub food of the lasagne/steak pie sort, but you don't come here for the cooking. Archers, Glenny, Whitbread beers. Open all day.

PYRTON   Plough

near Watlington OX9 5AP
Tel: (049 161) 2003
Open: 11.30-2.30 (not Mon), 6-11
Licensees: R Grogan and L Tuffin

17th century thatched village pub with large open log fires. No children indoors.

Bar Meals: 12-2, 7-10 (9 Sun); no food Mon; bar snacks lunchtime   **Typical Dishes:**
stilton and cauliflower soup £2.50, paté £3.25, braised beef in horseradish £5.65, chicken
supreme in lemon mustard sauce £8.95, roast duckling £9.75, apricot and amaretto soufflé
£2.50   Vegetarian Meals: stilton, leek and pasta bake   Children's Portions (some)
Beer   *Adnams Southwold; Fullers ESB   Patio/terrace   Outdoor Eating*   **Credit Cards:**
Access, Visa

ROKE   Home Sweet Home

near Benson OX9 6JD
Tel: (0491) 38429
Open: 11-3, 5.30-11
Licensees: P and I M Mountford and J Madle

Handsome 16th century dining pub, extremely popular for its bar meals and
restaurant. Cosy, characterful double-roomed main bar, carpeted sitting room, log
fires. Run by the same people who have the Old Boot, Stanford Dingley, Berks.

Bar Meals and Restaurant: 12-2, 5.30 (7 restaurant)-10; (7-9.30 Sun); bar snacks both
sessions   **Typical Dishes BAR:** *French onion soup £1.65, calves liver with bacon £5.95,*
chicken breast stuffed with garlic mushrooms £5.95, home-made pie of the day £4.60
RESTAURANT: *baked avocado with bacon and prawns, steak with Tia Maria £10.95,*
chicken and stilton roulade £6.40, salmon steak with chives and cream £7.70   Vegetarian
Meals: Glamorgan sausages   Children's Portions Beer *Brakspears; Fullers* Whisky
Garden   Outdoor Eating   **Credit Cards:** *Access, Visa*

RUSSELLS WATER   Beehive Inn

near Henley on Thames RG9 6ER
Tel: (0491) 641306
Open: 12-3, 7-11 (closed Mon/Tue)
Licensee: John Jenkins

Immortalised on celluloid in Chitty Chitty Bang Bang (the car drove through the
duck pond at the front): an early 17th century pub converted from a pair of little
cottages; original fireplaces and their bread ovens remain. Situated on an enormous
common – good for a post-pudding walk. Daily changing menu; tables can be
booked in the dining room (same food).

Bar Meals: 12-2.30, 7-9.30; bar snacks lunchtime   **Typical Dishes:** *potato, leek and*
parmesan soup £2, home-made wild game terrine £3.15, steak and mushroom pie £5,
calves liver with sage and onion confit £7.50, char-grilled fillet of wild salmon with tomato
and basil sauce £7.50, treacle, walnut and ginger tart £2.50   Vegetarian Meals: ratatouille
£3.50   Children's Menu/Portions Beer *Adnams; Hall & Woodhouse; Wadworth*
Family Room   Garden **No Credit Cards**

SATWELL   Lamb

off B481
Tel: (04917) 482
Open: 11-3, 6-11

Classic cottage pub, low-beamed and quaint, with a real fire in the inglenook and
spit roasts on Sundays.

Bar Meals: lunch and evening;   bar snacks both sessions   ***Typical Dishes:*** leek and potato
soup, beef and Guinness pie, lamb and leek pie, pork and ale casserole, cherry tart (main
courses from £4)   *Vegetarian Meals:* ratatouille lasagne   *Children's Menu*   `Beer`
Brakspears   *Children Allowed in Bar to Eat   Garden*

SHENINGTON   Bell

near Banbury OX15 6NQ
Tel: (0295) 87274
Open: 12-3, 7-11 (not Sun)
Licensees: Stephen and Jennifer Dixon

Delightful old golden-stone cottage in a pretty terrace. Heavy beams, wall and
window seats, and three simply modernised rooms. Tables at the front of the
building overlook the attractive green.

Restaurant: 12-3, 7-12; bar snacks lunchtime   ***Typical Dishes:*** carrot and tarragon soup
£1.95, mushrooms in cream and paprika, chicken in cumin, cider and apple £5.75, Goanese
beef £5.75, roast pork with apple, nut and celery stuffing £5.95, fresh apricot and brandy
trifle   *Vegetarian Meals:* vegetable and stilton crumble   *Children's Portions*   `Beer` Hook
Norton Best Bitter; Whitbread Boddingtons Bitter   *Children Allowed in Bar to Eat   **Credit
Cards:*** Access, Visa

SHIPTON UNDER WYCHWOOD   Lamb Inn

High Street OX7 6DQ   `FOOD`
Tel: (0993) 830465
Open: 11-2.30 (12-2.30 Sun), 6-11; closed Mon   `B&B`
Licensee: L Valenta

Tucked away down a quiet side road, the Lamb is a typical 17th century Cotswold
building, complete with honey-coloured stone walls and stone tiled roof, and its
neat little patio with parasol-shaded tables makes an ideal spot in summer. Inside, all
is equally immaculate. The beamed bar has a polished woodblock floor and mostly
antique furniture: a settle here, a pew there, and attractive old oak tables. At
lunchtimes, the cold buffet displayed in the bar offers cold cuts like fresh salmon,
ham and beef, a vegetarian tart and hot dish of the day. In the evening, an extensive
blackboard menu offers the choice of a full three-course meal or perhaps just a light
snack. Main dishes like guinea fowl or whole pan-fried Cornish plaice come in
generous portions with good simply-cooked fresh vegetables; as an added bonus,
someone in the kitchen has the cool, light hand needed to produce melt-in-the-
mouth pastry for the home-made fruit pies. For more formal dining there is a cosy
low-beamed restaurant. The owner's interest in wine is evident from a well-chosen
wine list, four or five of which are available by the glass. The Lamb's five bedrooms
are all as neat as a new pin, with cream coloured melamine furniture and spotless
modern bathrooms. Two of the rooms boast some old beams and these help lend a
little extra character. Televisions, radio alarms and tea and coffee making kit are
standard, with mineral water and bowls of fruit as welcoming extras. The convivial

hubbub from the bar below is quite audible in some rooms, which might be a problem if you want an early night. Good hearty cooked breakfasts are worth getting up for.

Bar Meals: 12-2, 7-10; *bar snacks lunchtime*   *Restaurant:* 7-9.30   *Typical Dishes:* stilton and parsnip soup £2, smoked mussel and bacon salad, roast garlic lamb, Wychwood chicken (with asparagus and ham), braised guinea fowl, treacle tart   *Vegetarian Meals:* vegetable stroganoff   *Children's Portions*   Beer   Hook Norton; Wadworth   Cider   Blands   Patio/terrace   Outdoor Eating   *Accommodation:* 8 bedrooms, all en suite, from £68 (single £48)   Check-in: all day   *Credit Cards:* Access, Amex, Visa

SHIPTON UNDER WYCHWOOD   Shaven Crown Hotel

High Street OX7 6BA
Tel: (0993) 830330
Open: 12-2.30, 7-11

Originally a 14th century hospice to Bruern Abbey, hence the monastic–sounding name (which doesn't really do this charming building any favours). A delightful courtyard garden, where you can eat in good weather, is the most unspoilt spot; residents' lounge in the old medieval hall, and more down to earth Buttery Bar. Bedrooms vary in size, some smaller than you might expect for the price.

Bar Meals: 12-2, 7-9.30; *bar snacks both sessions*   *Restaurant:* 7.30-9.30   *Typical Dishes BAR:* soup of the day £1.65, smoked haddock mousse £2.75, steak, kidney and mushroom pie £4.75, spinach and bacon lasagne £4.95, bobotie (curried meat loaf) £4.75, Duke of Cambridge tart £1.75   *RESTAURANT:* set price dinner £17.50: warm pigeon salad, creamed scallops, pork savoyarde, rack of lamb, orange chicken, blackberry bombe   *Vegetarian Meals:* mushroom and walnut pancake £3.95   *Children's Portions*   Beer   Hook Norton Best Bitter; Whitbread Flowers Original   Cider   Gordon Bland   Children Allowed in Bar to Eat   Garden   Outdoor Eating   *Accommodation:* 9 bedrooms, all en suite, from £67 (single £31)   Children Welcome Overnight   Cot Available   Check-in: by arrangement   *Credit Cards:* Access, Visa

SIBFORD GOWER   Wykham Arms

Colony Lane OX15 5RX
Tel: (029 578) 351
Open: 12-3 (not Mon), 6.30-11
Licensees: John and Carol Currington-Sivyer

Thatched pub with low-beamed lounge and a deep well, now made a feature of.

Bar Meals and Restaurant: 12-2, 7-9.30 (9 Sun); no food Mon; bar snacks both sessions   *Typical Dishes BAR:* home-made soup £1.65, sardines with crab butter £2.75, curry £4.75, home-cooked ham and eggs £4.75, poached plaice fillets £5.80   *RESTAURANT:* pan-fried whitebait £2.85, chicken stuffed with prawns £8.50, fillet steak with stilton £10.50, whole lemon sole £8.95   *Vegetarian Meals:* spinach and mushroom lasagne £4.50   *Children's Menu/Portions*   Beer   Draught Bass; Hook Norton Best Bitter; Whitbread Boddingtons Bitter; Flowers Original   Family Room   Outdoor Play Area   Garden   Outdoor Eating   *Credit Cards:* Access, Visa

SONNING EYE   Flowing Spring

Henley Road RG4 9RB   ♥
Tel: (0734) 693207
Open: 12-2.30, 5.30-11 (12-3, 6-11 Sat)
Licensees: Mick and Norma Whelan

A spring rises in the field next door to this cosy roadside pub which prides itself on a relaxing atmosphere. The huge garden is reached via a wrought iron staircase.

Bar Meals: 12-2, 7-9 (no food Sun, nor Mon/Tue eves); bar snacks lunchtime   **Typical Dishes:** *home-made soup £1.50, mushrooms in garlic butter £2.50, Cumberland sausage £3.25, beef and basil lasagne £3.50, steak and mushroom pie £3.25   Vegetarian Meals: red bean and green pepper lasagne £3.50   Children's Menu*   Beer   *Fullers   Garden Outdoor Eating*   **No Credit Cards**

SOULDERN   Fox Inn

Fox Lane OX6 9JW   ♥
Tel: (0869) 345284
Open: 11.30-3, 6-11
Licensee: Ian Robert Mackay

Traditional Cotswold village inn with a German landlady and thus an interesting mixture of a menu. Good value bed and breakfast.

Bar Meals and Restaurant: 12-2, 7-9.30 (not Sun eve); bar snacks both sessions   **Typical Dishes BAR:** *leek and potato soup £1.75, Matjes herring £2.55, Wiener schnitzel £6.25, Angus rump steak £6.30, gravadlax £5.25, rhubarb fool £1.95*   **RESTAURANT:** *similar starters and puddings, smoked boar £4.50, rack of lamb £6.90, peppered pork fillet £7.25, veal Holstein £6.95   Vegetarian Meals: tagliatelle   Children's Portions*   Cheese   Beer   *Bass; Hook Norton   Children Allowed in Bar to Eat Outdoor Play Area   Garden   Outdoor Eating   Summer Barbecue*   **Accommodation:** *4 bedrooms, 2 en suite, from £32 (single £19.50)   Children Welcome Overnight   Check-in: by arrangement*   **Credit Cards:** *Access, Visa*

STANTON ST JOHN   Star Inn

Oxford OX9 1EX
Tel: (086 735) 277
Open: 11-2.30 (12-2.30 Sun), 6.30-11
Licensee: Nigel Tucker

An 18th century ex butcher's: lots of period feel remains in the two original little bars, both low-beamed, one brick-floored, the other carpeted and furniture crammed. An answer to extreme popularity has been found in a successful extension; another follows, in Edwardian style and intended for families. A simple menu and reliably good food.

Bar Meals: 12-2, 7-10; bar snacks both sessions   **Typical Dishes:** *watercress soup £1.79, home-made chicken liver paté £2.95, beef and Guinness pie, mushroom and courgette tagliatelle, home-made curries (main courses £3.95-£4.25), blackberry and apple pie £1.95 Vegetarian Meals: broccoli and mushroom quiche   Children's Menu/Portions*   Beer   *Wadworth   Family Room   Outdoor Play Area   Garden   Outdoor Eating*   **No Credit Cards**

STEEPLE ASTON   Red Lion

off A423 OX5 3RY
Tel: (0869) 40225
Open: 11-3, 6-11
Licensee: Colin Mead

Quaint, comfortable little stone-built pub, with a splendid old settle, stone fireplace and fine prints. Low flying jets from Upper Heyford can rather shatter the peace of the little sun-trap garden though. Good plain cooking, blackboard listed.

Bar Meals: 12-2 (not Sun); bar snacks   **Typical Dishes:** *home-made soup, taramasalata £2.60, smoked salmon platter £4.20, beef casserole £3, fresh fish dishes   Vegetarian Meals* `Cheese`   `Beer` *Badger; Hook Norton; Wadworth   Garden*   **Credit Cards:** *Access, Visa*

STOKE ROW   Crooked Billet

Newlands Lane
Tel: (0491) 681048
Open: 12-2.30, 7-11
Licensee: Paul Clerehugh

Traditionally furnished, pleasingly rustic interior with three little rooms, real fires, and a three acre garden merging into Chiltern woods. One of the few remaining pubs without a bar counter: beer is drawn directly from barrels in a little cellar. Fresh home-cooked food (chef-proprietor) from a daily changing menu.

Bar Meals: 12-2.30, 7-10.30   **Typical Dishes:** *field mushroom soup with madeira £2.95, queen scallop and mussel tartlet £4.95, quails with a nutty sherry stuffing served in a nest with walnut sauce £9.95, medallions of lamb fillet £10.70, fresh fillet of sea bass £9.95, treacle tart with real custard £2.75   Vegetarian Meals: wild mushrooms with home-made noodles £8.95   Children's Portions* `Cheese`   `Beer` *Brakspears beers* `Cider` *Coates   Children Allowed in Bar to Eat   Garden*   **Credit Cards:** *Access, Visa (from 1992)*

STONOR Stonor Arms: Well heeled, revamped village dining pub; characterful with restaurant food.

SUTTON COURTENAY   Fish

Appleford Road, Abingdon OX14 4NQ
Tel: (0235) 848242
Open: 12-2.30, 7-11
Licensees: Bruce and Kay Buchan

Unassuming-looking late 19th century roadside pub behind which facade springs a catering operation of ambition and expertise. Not a place for shepherd's pie. Often busy with foodies and lunchers on expenses, in a pubby, informal interior. Bruce Buchan was formerly head chef at the Bear, Hungerford.

Bar Meals and Restaurant: 12-2.15, 7-9.30 (10 Fri/Sat); no food Tue eves; bar snacks lunchtime   **Typical Dishes:** *fish soup with aioli £4.50, crispy duck and five spice salad £4.95, sautéed veal kidneys with rosti and mustard £9.50, tian of squab pigeon and port sauce, fricassee of scallops and langoustines £11.95, brandy snap of summer fruits and almond ice-cream £3.95   Vegetarian Meals: bolognese of chanterelles and green noodles* `Beer` *Morland Original, Old Speckled Hen   Children Allowed in Bar to Eat*   **Credit Cards:** *Access, Amex, Visa*

SWALCLIFFE   Stags Head

near Banbury OX15 5EJ
Tel: (029 578) 232
Open: 12-2.30 (3 weekends), 6.30-11
Licensee: Keith Lainsbury

Thatched Cotswold stone inn in picturesque village. Oak settles and stools.

Bar Meals: 12-2, 7.30-10 (9 Sun); bar snacks lunchtime   *Typical Dishes:* broccoli soup
£1.80, stilton and port paté £2.50, chicken St Clements £5.50, beef and mushroom pie
cooked in damson wine £5.75, fresh salmon steak with hot cucumber sauce £7.25, plum
mousse £2   Vegetarian Meals: marrow casserole £5   Children's Menu/Portions   `Beer`
Hook Norton; Marston; Pedigree   Children Allowed in Bar to Eat   Outdoor Play Area
Garden   Outdoor Eating   Summer Barbecue   **No Credit Cards**

SWINBROOK Swan off A40 Tel: (099 382) 2165. Riverside ex-watermill with
traditional pub games, old-fashioned tap room and decent home cooking lunch and
evening. Morlands, Wadworth beers. Open: 11.30-2.30, 6-11.

THAME   Abingdon Arms

21 Cornmarket OX9 2BL
Tel: (084 421) 2969
Open: 11-3, 5-11
Licensee: Wayne Bonner

Friendly, imaginatively run little pub with an unspoilt interior; newspapers and
magazines provided for lazing with.

Bar Meals: 12-2, 6-10; bar snacks both sessions   *Typical Dishes:* cheese and celery soup
£1.25, garlic mushrooms £2.45, steak and Guinness pie, barbecued spare ribs, fresh pasta,
spotted dick   Vegetarian Meals: noodles in walnut sauce   `Beer`   Adnams; Ruddles;
Theakston; Wadworth   Children Allowed in Bar to Eat   Outdoor Play Area   Garden
Outdoor Eating   Summer Barbecue   **Credit Cards:** Access, Visa

TOWERSEY   Three Horseshoes

near Thame OX9 3QY
Tel: (084 421) 2322
Open: 12-3, 6-11
Licensees: Mary and Robert Worsdell

Redbrick, part 13th century pub, with a converted 12th century barn, now popular
for functions. Roaring log fire in winter. Food recommended.

Bar Meals and Restaurant: 12-2, 6.30-10 (7-9.30 Sun); bar snacks both sessions
Typical Dishes BAR: watercress soup £2, butterfly prawns £3.50, home-made lamb and
leek pie £4.85, 6 oz rump steak £6.60, home-made fishcakes in parsley sauce £5.10, jam
roly poly £2.25   **RESTAURANT:** table d'hote £12.75: clam chowder, crab claws, half
roast Gressingham duck, chicken princess, grilled halibut, treacle tart   Vegetarian Meals: pasta
parmigiana £4.85   Children's Portions (some)   `Beer`   Allied; Wadworth   Children
Allowed in Bar to Eat   Outdoor Play Area   Garden   Outdoor Eating   **Credit Cards:**
Access, Visa

WATLINGTON	Chequers

Love Lane OX9 5RA
Tel: (049 161) 2874
Open: 11.30-2.30, 6-11
Licensees: John and Anna Valentine

A useful stop, less than two and a half miles from junction 6 of the M40. It's a characterful, rambling old pub with a lovely summer garden; we were disappointed in the steak and kidney pie, though (rather ordinary helping of stew with a puff pastry square).

Bar Meals: all open hours; bar snacks lunchtime **Typical Dishes:** *chicken and leek soup £1.80, butterfly prawns in chilli dip £3.50, steaks from £9.50, various chicken dishes £7, veal Valdostana £8.80, crème brulée £2.50 Vegetarian Meals: spinach-filled cannelloni £4.50* ▇▇▇ Beer ▇▇▇ *Brakspears beers Garden Outdoor Eating* **No Credit Cards**

WOODSTOCK Feathers Hotel, Market Street. Stylish and smart hotel with interesting bar food; try it at lunchtime.

SHROPSHIRE

ASTON MUNSLOW Swan. Nice rambling old pub, open fires, decent food, garden.

BRIDGES Horseshoe Inn Ratlinghope Tel: (058 861) 260. Bar meals and snacks: 12-2. Family room, patio/terrace and outdoor eating. Adnams, Holdens, Marston's beers, and Westons cider. Open: 12-2.30, 6-11 (closed lunchtime Mon-Thur Jan-March).

BRIDGNORTH	Down Inn

Ludlow Road WV16 6HA FOOD
Tel: (074 635) 624 ❗ 🍴
Open: 11-2.30, 6.30-11 (not Sun eve) ☼
Licensees: Paul Millington and Bill Watson ☺

This is an atmospheric pub where food is taken fairly seriously but, according to licensees Paul and Beverley Millington, ably assisted by Beverley's father Bill Watson, nothing else need be. Previously known for 250 years as the Unicorn, the pub is on the B4363, some two and a half miles from Bridgnorth on the Ludlow road and, despite some development in the rather ponderous style of the 1960s, still aims to remain as traditional a pub as possible. Some modern innovations are more welcome, like fresh machine-squeezed-to-order orange juice. Most people would opt for one of the beers though, with national brands like Websters, Ruddles and Ansells appearing alongside the likes of Fullers ESB or Royal Oak in the three guest slots. Unsurprisingly, the food retains a similarly traditional feel: the ploughmans alone is available with up to fourteen English cheeses, there are plenty of steaks, and a traditional Sunday lunch is served throughout the bar and restaurant. The latter's menu has a seasonal bias, so that pheasant, venison and guinea fowl come into their own in autumn as the Down's celebrated fresh fish and garden produce become more scarce. Nonetheless a late summer specials board spoils for choice: shell-on prawns by the half pint (£2.50), home-potted shrimps (£2.95), plus whole plaice, trout (£6.85) and fresh salmon (£8.50) represented in various guises. Equally traditional, the bar menu lists braised steak in Murphys stout (£7.70), Olde English chicken pie (£5.70), and seafood crumble (£5.80), served with three fresh vegetables and a daily potato dish. Children's portions of any of these can be provided should young palates have risen beyond the (very fairly priced) fishfingers, baked beans and toasties. "Choccy rum pots", treacle and nut tart, apple Bakewell or fresh fruit vacherin (£2.50) weigh in at the end alongside cafetière or espresso coffees and half a dozen teas, while light opera and classical overtures play softly in the background.

Bar Meals and Restaurant: 12-2, 7-9.30 (not Sun eve); bar snacks both sessions
Typical Dishes BAR: home-made soup £1.65, chicken tikka £2.95, Murphy's pudding £7.50, venison casserole £8.60, spatchcock chicken £6.85, bread and butter pudding £2.50 **RESTAURANT:** baked seafood avocado £3.95, roast best end of Shropshire lamb £8.90, strips of fillet beef in spinach and tarragon sauce £10.50, stuffed lemon sole £9.50, choux swans with fresh strawberries £3 Vegetarian Meals Children's
Menu/Portions `Cheese` `Beer` Fullers; Ruddles; Wadworth; Whitbread `Whisky`
Family Room   Outdoor Play Area   Patio/terrace   Outdoor Eating   Summer Barbecue
Credit Cards: Access, Visa

BROCKTON   Feathers

near Much Wenlock TF13 6JR   `FOOD`
Tel: (074 636) 202   ☕
Open: 12-2.30 (inc Sun), 6.30-11 (closed Mon)   ❗
Licensees: Martin and Andrea Hayward   ☀

The historic Feathers stands at a crossroads on the B4378 Much Wenlock to Craven Arms road, signed left to Bridgnorth and right to Church Stretton. Deceptively small outside, it's half-timbered at one end and stone-clad to the rear, where the entrance leads via a picturesque patio through the conservatory. Inside, it divides into an intimate public bar where one corner table is formed by a huge bellows on legs, and three interconnecting rooms, on two levels, devoted largely to eating. Martin and Andrea Hayward's first two years here, after long experience in the wine bar and bistro trade, have signalled the arrival of some serious pub food, commendable both for its quality and diversity. A two-page handwritten menu is supplemented by an extensive range of blackboard specials: cheese-topped smokies (£3.65), baked avocado (£3.65), or a garlicky "crostini" (£2.25) topped with peppers and bubbling cheese, may serve equally as a starter or a single-course snack. Of more substantial stuff are main courses, ranging from steak, kidney and mushroom pie (£6.75) through chicken and broccoli mornay (£7.65) and vegetables au gratin (£5.95), to rack of lamb with rosemary and garlic crust (£7.95), grilled trout fillets with prawn garnish (£7.95), or a whole poussin provencale (£7.95). Traditional puddings (£2.45) are guaranteed to fill up every remaining corner; butterscotch and walnut fudge, treacle pudding or apple and raspberry tart are typical. Beer drinkers will enjoy a good pint of hand-pulled Banks's bitter; house wine comes by the bottle, glass or goblet, there are half a dozen each of named reds or whites by the bottle, and an excellent cup of coffee arrives in a cafetière. Andrea's kitchen hand-bell announces when each cooked-to-order dish is ready, ensuring prompt delivery to tables; salad garnishes are generous and Martin arrives equally promptly with the two-pint jug of home-made dressing.

Bar meals: 12-2.30, 6.30-9.30 (7-9 Sun) bar snacks both sessions *Typical Dishes:*
carrot and smoked bacon soup £2, baked avocado £33.65, chicken and broccoli mornay £7.65, rack of lamb £7.95, poussin provencale £7.95, bread and butter pudding £2.45
Vegetarian Meals: vegetables au gratin Children's Menu/Portions `Beer` Banks's Bitter
Family room   Patio/terrace   Outdoor Eating   **No credit cards**

BROSELEY   Cumberland Hotel

Jackson Avenue TF12 5NB
Tel: (0952) 882301
Licensees: Pat and Ivor Southorn

Handsome, family-run Victorian hotel in its own grounds, two miles from the famous Iron Bridge. Restaurant meals are eaten off Coalport china; bar meals are cheap and cheerful, made by the landlord's daughter.

Bar Meals and Restaurant: 12-3, 6.30-10; bar snacks both sessions   **Typical Dishes:** *home-made soup £1.25, melon with prawns, roast beef, steaks, lemon sole (main courses from £3), blackberry and apple pie   Vegetarian Meals: bean and vegetable hotpot   Children's Menu/Portions*   Beer   *Ansells; Bass; Ruddles; Webster's   Family Room   Outdoor Play Area   Garden   Outdoor Eating*   **Accommodation;** *14 bedrooms, all en suite, from £30   Children Welcome Overnight   Cots Available   Check-in: all day*   **Credit Cards:** *Diners, Visa*

CARDINGTON   Royal Oak

near Church Stretton SY6 7JZ
Tel: (06943) 266
Open: 12-2.30 (inc Sun), 7-11; closed Mon Nov-Easter
Licensee: John Seymour

Old country free house in a pretty spot. Pleasing, relaxing bar mixes traditional and modern, with a good log fire and nice decorative bits and pieces. There's also a noisy games machine bar upstairs. Bought-in puddings.

Bar Meals: 12-2, 7-8.30 (not Sun); bar snacks both sessions   **Typical Dishes:** *home-made soup £2, fidget pie £3.20, lasagne £3.75, chicken cobbler £5.35   Vegetarian Meals: cauliflower cheese £2.50   Children's Portions*   Beer   *Bass; Ruddles; Wadworth   Children Allowed in Bar to Eat   Patio/terrace   Outdoor Eating*   **Accommodation:** *1 bedroom, £33 (single £22)   Children Welcome Overnight   Check-in: by arrangement*   **No Credit Cards**

CLAVERLEY   Crown Inn

High Street WV5 7DY
Tel: (07466) 228
Open: 12-3, 7-11
Licensee: Leslie Stewart

Lovely old pub in glorious picture-book village; Tudor styling and heavy beams in three rooms. Good family garden.

Bar Meals: 12-2, 7-9 (Thur-Sat eve only)   **Typical Dishes:** *steak and kidney pie £2.95, gammon £3.25, fresh fish £3.50-£6.50 (Fri/Sat)   Children's Portions*   Beer   *Banks's Bitter, Hansons Mild*   Whisky   *Children Allowed in Bar to Eat (lunch)   Outdoor Play Area   Garden   Outdoor Eating*   **No Credit Cards**

HEATHTON   Old Gate Inn
Claverley WV5 7EB
Tel: (07466) 431
Open: 12-2.30, 7-11
Licensees: Jamie and Diane Atkins

Restored old pub in splendid rural setting. Real fire. No music.

Bar Meals: 12-2, 7-9; *bar snacks lunchtime* **Typical Dishes:** *char-grilled steaks £4.30-*
£7.85, char-grilled half chicken £4.80, home-made ocean pie £3.95, spotted dick
Vegetarian Meals: cheese and broccoli bake £4.30 Children's Menu/Portions [Beer]
Holts; Taylor Family Room Outdoor Play Area Garden Outdoor Eating Summer
Barbecue **Credit Cards:** *Access, Amex, Visa*

HENGOED   Last Inn
off B4579
Tel: (0691) 659747
Open: 12-3 (Sun only), 7-11
Licensees: Jean and Jim Heaton

Homely country pub with various room and a beer connoisseur dog. Homely food,
too, cooked by the former cookery teacher landlady.

Bar Meals: Wed-Mon eves, Sun lunch **Typical Dishes:** *beef in ale casserole £2.60, steak*
and kidney pie £2.60, chicken chasseur £3.20, orange sorbet [Beer] *Bass; Marston;*
Wood's Family Room Garden

HODNET Bear. Well-known, well-heeled old hotel, with decent meals in the
pubby bar. Opposite Hodnet Hall gardens.

HOPESGATE   Stables Inn
near Minsterley SY5 0EP   [FOOD]
Tel: (0743) 891344
Open: 11.30-2.30, 7-11; closed Mon
Licensees: Denis and Debbie Harding

Country lanes signposted from the A488 eventually lead to the Hardings' tiny
secluded pub, set in glorious countryside above the Hope valley. It's a distinctly
traditional pub, whose attractions in addition to the good food and beer are an
atmosphere in which good company can be enjoyed, in the absence of intruding
gaming machines or jukeboxes. The bar is L-shaped, its blackened oak beams hung
with pottery mugs, and the imposing open stone fireplace is log-burning in winter.
The mood is intimate and friendly; summer talk is largely of cricket, and the exploits
of the pub's new team. Four draught beers on handpumps include the local Wood's
Special, and in summer a choice of draught ciders. Lunchtime choices, posted on the
blackboard, range from cream of leek soup, broccoli and bacon quiche and
taramasalata through to spicy tandoori chicken and a cheesy tomato and aubergine
bake. Evening eating (Wednesday to Saturday only) is a mite more serious. Booking
is strongly advised: there are only four tables in the dining room, so diners usually
overflow into the adjacent snug. Debbie's cooking makes the best use of local
supplies and seasonal produce, skilfully combining Cumberland sauce with a roast
haunch of venison; bacon and Meaux mustard with sautéed lamb's liver, or in
bringing a ham, cheese and cider filling to an oven-baked chicken. They're
substantial eaters in these parts, so there's no shortage of takers for seconds: treacle

sponge with custard, the landlady's now celebrated bread and butter pudding, or a seasonal fruit crumble served with local farm ice-cream.

Bar Meals: 12-1.30; bar snacks   **Restaurant:** *7-8.30*   **Typical Dishes:** *curried apple soup £1.50, mushrooms and smoked salmon on toast £3, roast haunch of venison in Cumberland sauce £7.25, Spanish pork £5.50, mixed local sausages with cheesy potato bake £3.75, bread and butter pudding   Vegetarian Meals: Shropshire Blue and mushroom crumble £4.75   Children's Portions*   Beer   *Ind Coope Burton Ale; Marston Pedigree; Wood's Special*   Cider   *Addlestones, Weston's   Children Allowed in Bar to Eat Patio/terrace*   **No Credit Cards**

HOPTON WAFERS   Crown Inn

near Cledbury Mortimer DY14 0NB   FOOD
Tel: (0299) 270372   ♍
Open: 12-3, 6-11   B&B
Licensees: John Price and Tim Alexander   ☼

Two and a half miles from the peak of Clee Hill, nestling in a wooded valley, is the Norman hamlet of Hopton Wafers. The creeper-clad Crown is set in its own garden which slopes down to one of the many streams (crossed here by the A4117) which flow down to the Tewe valley. Bounded on three sides by terraces of tables with their colourful summer parasols, it's a splendid spot for al fresco eating, but parents with little ones should watch out for the duckpond, as perilous as it is picturesque. Inside, the Rent Room, where once local villagers came to pay their rents, houses an atmospheric and intimate bar where talk is frequently of the shootin' and fishin' sort over a glass of Boddingtons, Flowers Original or Bass. Snacks and bar meals have a strongly fishy emphasis: rollmops (£3.50), smoked mackerel (£3.50) and grilled sardines (£3.50) preceding whole grilled plaice (£6.50), poached halibut (£6.50) or seafood pancakes (£5.95). But meat eaters aren't forgotten, with hearty steak and mushroom pie (£5.50), or duck breast with oyster and chilli sauce (£6.50), which come with three fresh vegetables and a choice of potatoes. Nor are vegetarians neglected: decent meatless meals include celery and cashew risotto, or tagliatelle verdi with tomato and basil (£4.25), and children's portions of virtually anything for £2.50 will please many parents. Puddings, home-made daily (£1.95) include treacle tart, peach and apple pie, or a banana and rum trifle. Behind a central stone chimney, in which huge log fires burn at both sides in winter, the restaurant serves a three-course dinner (from Tuesday to Saturday) and Sunday lunch, for which you should book. Market-fresh fish, real escalopes flamed with Calvados, roast guinea fowl with redcurrant and orange sauce, and grilled steaks, with or without pepper sauce, are typical of Crown restaurant main courses. Recent reorganisation has increased to eight the bedrooms, whose decor and character are commendable, with central heating now installed for the coming winter. Unsuspecting overnighters are in for a treat of exposed rafters, sloping corridors and creaky floorboards – with which the automatic trouser press and bathroom telephone extensions seem faintly at odds; all, nonetheless, are assured a high degree of comfort, a warm welcome and the convivial company of a fine country inn.

Bar Meals: 12-2, 7-9.30; bar snacks both sessions   **Restaurant:** *7-10 Tue-Sat*   **Typical Dishes BAR:** *carrot and orange soup £1.75, prawns with garlic mayonnaise £4, game pie £6.25, medallions of beef £7.50, monkfish with lemon and lime sauce £6.95, Bakewell tart £1.95*   **RESTAURANT** *dinner menu £17.50: parsnip and ginger soup, bouchée of baby scallops, quail Normande with wild mushrooms, baked duck breast in honey and orange sauce, poached halibut, chocolate roulade   Vegetarian Meals: cashew nut and celery risotto Children's Menu/Portions*   Cheese   Beer   *Draught Bass; Whitbread beers*   Whisky   *Children Allowed in Bar to Eat   Riverside Garden   Outdoor Eating*   **Accommodation:** *8 bedrooms, all en suite, from £55 (single £35)   Children Welcome Overnight   Cots Available   Check-in: all day*   **Credit Cards:** *Access, Visa*

LINLEY BROOK   Pheasant Inn

Bridgnorth WV16 4RJ
Tel: (0746) 762260
Open: 12-2.30, 6.30-11
Licensees: Simon and Elizabeth Reed

Traditional country pub complete with honeysuckle round the door, and which aims to provide "good value basic food". Not a pub for families – very much an adult hideaway. Nor one for vegetarians. Real fires. No music.

Bar Meals: 12-2, 6.30-10; bar snacks both sessions **Typical Dishes:** *home-made soup £1, gammon and own eggs £4.95, rump steak £5.95, home-made lasagne £3.95, blackberry and apple pie £1.25* ▉Beer▉ *Holden; Hook Norton, Mitchells; Titanic* ▉Cider▉ *Weston's Garden Outdoor Eating* **No Credit Cards**

LITTLE STRETTON   Green Dragon

Ludlow Road SY6 6RE
Tel: (0694) 722925
Open: 11-3, 6-11
Licensees: Michele and Jim Greenough

New owners as of March 1991 are keen to expand the home cooking on the bar meals side here, and also have plans for building work in 1992; there may be bedrooms by the summer. Good walkers' pub, at the foot of the Long Mynd Hills; comfortably refurbished lounge with open fire and fine views.

Bar Meals: 11.30-2, 6.30-9 (9.30 summer); bar snacks both sessions **Typical Dishes:** *carrot and ginger soup £1.25, deep-fried king prawns £2.35, home-made steak and kidney pie £4.50, home-made beef in beer casserole £4.50, cheese and broccoli bake £4.50, apple pie Vegetarian Meals Children's Menu/Portions* ▉Beer▉ *Ruddles, Webster's; Wood's Children Allowed in Dining Room Garden Outdoor Eating* **No credit cards**

LLANFAIR WATERDINE   Red Lion Inn

near Knighton LD7 1TU
Tel: (0547) 528214
Open: 12-2 (inc Sun but not Tue), 7-11
Licensees: Mick and Judy Richards

Comforting little tap room and rambling lounge, at delightful riverside inn with lovely garden. Good value B&B; same menu in bar and restaurant; no children indoors or overnight.

Bar Meals and Restaurant: 12-1.30, 7-9 (9.30 Sat, 8.30 Sun); bar snacks lunchtime **Typical Dishes BAR:** *leek and potato soup £1.30, home-made chicken liver paté £2.85, beef in garlic, red wine and mushrooms £5.95, chicken madras £4.75, spaghetti bolognese £4, banoffee pie £2 Vegetarian Meals: vegetable curry £4* ▉Beer▉ *Ansells Mild; Marston Pedigree* ▉Cider▉ *Weston's Outdoor Play Area Garden Outdoor Eating* **Accommodation:** *3 bedrooms, 1 en suite, from £35 (single £20) Check-in: by arrangement* **No Credit Cards**

LLANYMYNECH   Bradford Arms

Oswestry SY22 6EJ   ▼
Tel: (0691) 830582
Open: 12-2.30 (inc Sun), 7-11; closed Mon and 3 weeks Oct/Nov
Licensees: Anne and Michael Murphy

Village pub with above-average food in its spotless, comfortably traditional bar. Very good puddings.

Bar Meals: 12-2, 7-10   Restaurant: 7-10   Typical Dishes BAR: leek and potato soup £1.50, cold curried eggs £2.25, chicken in garlic, bacon and cream sauce £4.75, lamb in tarragon sauce £4.95, fillet of salmon Florentine £4.95, gooseberry and honey cheesecake £1.85   RESTAURANT: French onion soup £1.75, stuffed mushrooms in red wine £2.75, calves liver Swiss style £11.25, fillet steak £11.95, fillet of salmon £10.95, redcurrant and almond pie £1.85   Vegetarian Meals: stuffed vine leaves £4.25   Children's Portions Cheese Beer *Marston Pedigree   Children Allowed in Bar to Eat Patio/terrace   Outdoor Eating   No Credit Cards*

LONGDEN Tankerville Arms. Varied food operation, including evening buffets and à la carte.

LUDLOW   Church Inn

Church Street, Buttercross SY8 1AW
Tel: (0584) 872174
Open: 11-11
Licensee: Stuart Copland

Pleasant rather than characterful old pub in the centre of this ancient Marches town, a good base for touring the Border country. All food is cooked from fresh ingredients. Bedrooms might be noisy: ask for one by the Walk.

Bar Meals and Restaurant: 12-2, 6.30-9 (9.30 Fri/Sat); bar snacks lunchtime   Typical Dishes BAR: home-made soup £1.30, steaks £6, home-made pies £4.50, fresh fish grills £4, home-made puddings   RESTAURANT: 3-course menu (5 choices) £10.75 Vegetarian Meals: vegetable pancakes   Children's Portions (some) Beer *Ansells, Ruddles, Webster's   Children Allowed in Bar to Eat (side area)   Accommodation: 9 bedrooms, all en suite, from £40 (single £28)   Children Welcome Overnight   Cots Available   Check-in: all day   Credit Cards: Access, Visa*

MARKET DRAYTON   Corbet Arms Hotel

High Street TF9 1PY
Tel: (0630) 652037
Open: 11-11
Licensee: Peter Stubbins

A new licensee and a recent full refurbishment at this creeper-clad, hotelly ex-coaching inn at the centre of the town. Modern facilities have been introduced and prices have risen. The bar menu's routine stuff, but we've recommended B&B here in the past, and freshly decorated bedrooms have spanking new facilities, while keeping lots of original character from their exposed beams and the like. The dining room is nice, but otherwise the Corbet's not very pubby.

Bar Meals and Restaurant: 12-2 (Sun only in restaurant), 6-9; bar snacks both sessions   Typical Dishes BAR: French onion soup £1.10, potato skins £2.10, spaghetti bolognese £3.65, sirloin steak £8.95, moules marinière £4.25, strawberry kiss £2.25

RESTAURANT: *supper menu £9.75: deep-fried mushrooms, lamb cutlets, lambs liver and onions, beef in ale pie, pears in wine Vegetarian Meals: October pie £3.55 Children's Menu/Portions* **Cheese** **Beer** *Whitbread Boddingtons Bitter Family Room* ***Accommodation:*** *11 bedrooms, all en suite, from £70 (single £49.50) Children Welcome Overnight Cots Available Check-in: all day* ***Credit Cards:*** *Access, Amex, Diners, Visa*

MUCH WENLOCK — George & Dragon

2 High Street TF13 6AA
Tel: (0952) 727312
Open: 11-2.30 (12-2.30 Sun), 6 (7 winter)-11
Licensee: Eve Nolan

Lively, bustling town pub, locally popular, with a particularly busy front bar featuring a vast collection of water jugs, as well as other collectibles, and more little rooms at the back, nicely old-fashioned in style. It's all still here, up and running, including Eve Nolan's bistro, despite being up for sale these past couple of years.

Bar Meals: *12-2, 6.30-9.30; bar snacks both sessions* ***Restaurant:*** *7-9.30 (Tue-Sat)* ***Typical Dishes BAR:*** *fresh tomato and orange soup £1.65, stilton and walnut paté £2.50, chicken in Shropshire mead and cream £5.25, rabbit in mustard and cider £5, fishermans pie £5, hot sticky toffee pudding* ***RESTAURANT:*** *2 courses £11, 3 courses £13.50: carrot and coriander soup, avocado and bacon salad, rack of lamb with redcurrant, orange and mint jelly, steak, Guinness and mushroom pie, monkfish roasted with garlic Vegetarian Meals: leek and mushroom bake Children's Portions* **Beer** *Burton Bridge; Hook Norton; Ruddles; Titanic Family Room* ***No Credit Cards***

MUCH WENLOCK — Talbot Inn

High Street TH13 6AA
Tel: (0952) 727077
Open: 10.30-2.30, 6.15-11
Licensee: Timothy Lathe

As well as the evening menu, from which items are listed below, there are dishes like spicy pancake, haddock in lemon sauce and interesting varieties of ploughman style picnic lunches at under £5 on the short lunchtime list. The civilised interior of this ancient inn (originally a 14th century abbot's hall) mixes original beams with plush-covered banquette seating; good open fires and nice touches like fresh flowers. There are also seats in the old courtyard. The Talbot offers the best bed and breakfast in Much Wenlock : bedrooms are divided between the inn and a recent malthouse conversion with its own breakfast room; rooms are simple, pristine and modern in style.

Bar Meals and Restaurant: *12-2, 7-9.30 (8.30 Sun); bar snacks lunchtime* ***Typical Dishes BAR:*** *sweetcorn and tuna soup £1.50, smoked haddock in cheese and cream sauce £2.50, beef goulash £7.45, chicken in a yoghurt, orange and mint sauce £7.25, scampi provencale £9.50, bread and butter pudding £1.95 Vegetarian Meals: red dragon pie £4.50* **Cheese** **Beer** *Ruddles Best, Webster's Yorkshire Bitter* **Whisky** *Children Allowed in Bar to Eat Patio/terrace* ***Accommodation:*** *6 bedrooms, all en suite, from £50 (single £30) Children Welcome Overnight (minimum age 12) Check-in: all day* ***Credit Cards:*** *Access, Visa*

MUNSLOW   Crown

near Craven Arms SY7 9ET
Tel: (058 476) 205
Open: 12-2.30, 6-11 (12-11 Sat)
Licensee: Victor Pocock

Traditional country pub with stone walls and floors, and lots of period features in its
opened-out, split-level lounge.

Bar Meals: 12-2 (2.30 Sun), 7-10; bar snacks both sessions **Restaurant:** *7-10 (Thur-*
Sun) **Typical Dishes BAR:** *red pimento soup £1.20, home-made paté £2.25, steak and*
kidney pie £4.25, lasagne £4.50, roast chicken £4.25, home-made apple pie £1.45
RESTAURANT: *fish soup £3.35, seafood St Jacques £3.95, piquant lamb £7.95,*
stuffed baby chicken £8.50, two fishes £7.35, crepes Suzette £3.75   Vegetarian Meals:
home-made savoury pie £4.25   Children's Menu/Portions ▮Beer▮ *Bass; Wadworth;*
Whitbread   Family Room   Outdoor Play Area   Garden   Outdoor Eating

---

NEWCASTLE   Crown

Craven Arms SY7 8QL
Tel: (05884) 271
Open: 12-3, 6-11 (all day Sat)
Licensees: Jeff and Yvonne Aldridge

Pleasant 17th century inn in the Clun Valley, formerly a drovers' inn serving the
route from mid-Wales to the industrial Midlands. Three more bedrooms planned for
1992.

Bar Meals: 12-2, 7-9.30; bar snacks both sessions **Typical Dishes:** *mushroom soup*
£1.20, breaded mushrooms £1.95, steak and kidney pie £4.20, chicken à la king £3.95,
marinated lamb kebab £4.90, hazelnut meringue £1.50   Vegetarian Meals: tagliatelle verdi
Children's Portions ▮Beer▮ *Bass; Whitbread   Family Room   Outdoor Play Area*
Garden   Outdoor Eating **Accommodation:** *2 bedrooms, both en suite, from £45 (single*
£27)   Children Welcome Overnight   Cot Available   Check-in: all day

NEWPORT Kings Head, Chetwynd End (A519). Home-made burgers and
other homely pub food, with more restauranty specials. A barbecue in the garden;
children allowed indoors for meals; Marston's beers. Open: 11.30-3, 6.30-11 (all day
Fri/Sat).

NORBURY Sun. Unspoilt ancient village alehouse; bar meals lunch and evening.

NORTON   Hundred House Hotel

On A442, Shifnal TF11 9EE   ▮FOOD▮
Tel: (0952) 71353   ▮ ⌾
Open : 11-11   ▮B&B▮
Licensees: Henry, Sylvia and David Phillips   ☺

A 14th century half-timbered, thatched-roofed listed building signals the approach
to the Phillips family's historic pub, in the old Hundred of Brimstree, beside what
later turned into the A442. This barn, for barn it be, for centuries housed the local
court, and remains of the old stocks and whipping post can still be seen in the yard.
The main inn is of Georgian origin, with quarry-tiled floors, exposed brickwork,
beamed ceilings and oak panelling. The original rafters, cast iron fire surrounds and
blackened kitchen implements are all embellished by the hand-dried flowers which
hang everywhere, and a persistent fragrance stems from the fresh-picked mint and

tarragon secreted among the table arrangements: diners are invited to pick them for garnish and to visit their hosts' extensive flower and herb gardens. Similar enthusiasm for freshness and quality pervades the food operation, which runs through from 7 am to 10 pm. Menu starters are generous enough to double as a bar snack: perhaps a savoury pancake topped with cheese (£3.25), char-grilled chicken wings (£2.95), or ratatouille (£2.75). A la carte, new chef David Campbell has brought a touch more imagination to the monthly changing menus. Tomato and tarragon soup (£3), gambas pil pil (£6.25) and wild mushroom mousse (£5.25) are followed by marinated Shropshire chevon (kid), roulade of wild rabbit (£10.25) or medallions of venison (£11.95) on a typical autumn menu, with a similarly diverse list of puddings, including port and plum pie (£3), rum flavoured chocolate truffle, butterscotch profiteroles, and mascarpone with Tia Maria and coffee sponge. Of special vegetarian appeal are a pan-fried cake of aubergine layered with tomato, basil and feta cheese, or a celeriac and potato casserole served with mushroom butter sauce. Unsurprisingly, the bedrooms are equally classy, returning to the garden for their inspirational names and colour schemes of rose-geranium, perhaps, or fennel and dill. Brass bedsteads and rocking chairs abound, and extra child beds in the larger rooms are provided free of charge. There are even padded swing seats hanging from the rafters to keep the little people amused, and it's for imaginative overnight facilities that we give our children's pub award. Bathrooms are fully en suite, housekeeping throughout little short of immaculate, and fresh flowers and pot-pourris make thoughtful extras.

Bar Meals and Restaurant: every lunch and evening; bar snacks lunchtime **Typical Dishes BAR:** calabrese and cream cheese soup £2.25, Shropshire Blue and bacon salad, local game pie, rack of lamb Shrewsbury, fillet of cod with herb butter, treacle tart **RESTAURANT:** fish minestrone £3, home-cured gravadlax £4.95, cannon of lamb with two sauces £8.95, loin of venison with blueberries and sage £11.95, pork with apple and calvados £8.95, chocolate truffle with raspberry coulis £3 *Vegetarian Meals:* vegetable and pinenut crumble **Beer** Heritage Bitter; Whitbread Castle Eden Ale, Flowers Original Garden Outdoor Eating **Accommodation:** 9 bedrooms, all en suite, from £69 (single £59) Children Welcome Overnight Cots Available Check-in: all day **Credit Cards:** Access, Visa

---

PICKLESCOTT   Bottle and Glass

Church Stretton SY6 6NR
Tel: (06945) 345
Open: 12-3, 7-11
Licensee: David West

17th century inn near Long Mynd, with an attractive garden for summer eating, and fine bordered front seating area. Two refurbished, carpeted bars, with oak beams and open fires; separate restaurant. There's a popular £7 Sunday carvery.

Bar Meals: 12-2.30, 7-9; bar snacks lunchtime **Typical Dishes** (lunchtime): stilton and onion soup £1.30, garlic and herb prawns £3.30, various grills from £4.15 (evening): chicken Kiev £6.10 *Vegetarian Meals:* lasagne Children's Menu/Portions **Beer** Marston; Whitbread Children Allowed in Bar to Eat Garden Outdoor Eating **Accommodation:** 2 bedrooms, both en suite, from £45 (single £30) Cots Available Check-in: all day **No Credit Cards**

PIPE GATE Chetwode Arms on A51. Refurbished and attentively-run dining pub; lunchtime bar meals, evening restaurant.

SHIFNAL   Star Hotel (Oddfellows)

Market Place TF11 9AU
Tel: (0952) 461517
Open: 12-3, 6 (5.30 Fri)-12
Licensee: David Brookes

Proprietor-run free house with a new conservatory. No separate dining room.

Bar Meals: 12-3, 7-10 (not Sun); bar snacks both sessions   **Typical Dishes:** *home-made soup £1.75, deep-fried squid with spicy cream sauce £2.95, pork with Calvados £5.95, chicken with coriander £5.95, duck with plum and Bacardi rum £7.25, bread and butter pudding £1.75   Vegetarian Meals: tortelloni with broccoli and cashews £3.25   Children's Portions* ▮Beer▮ *Bathams; Greene King; Morrels; Whitbread   Children Allowed in Bar to Eat   Patio/terrace   Outdoor Eating   Summer Barbecue* **Accommodation:** *4 bedrooms, all en suite, from £60 (single £30)   Children Welcome Overnight   Check-in: all day* **Credit Cards:** *Access, Amex, Diners*

SHIFNAL   White Hart

4 High Street TF11 8BH
Tel: (0952) 461161
Open: 12-2 (3 Sat, closed Mon), 6-11
Licensee: Roger Bentley

Tastefully refurbished 16th century coaching inn with exposed beams taken from old ships. As well as the house speciality, German food, there might be anything from best-selling home-made burgers to fresh fried fish. Fresh cobs with home-cooked meat fillings lead the snacks list.

Bar Meals: 12-2 Tue-Sat; bar snacks both sessions   **Typical Dishes:** *jaeger schnitzel £5.50, goulash £3.50, roast beef, pork or lamb £3.50, fresh fruit   Children's Menu/Portions* ▮Beer▮ *Ansells Mild, Bitter;Draught Bass; Ind Coope Burton Ale; Pitfield Dark Star* ▮Cider▮ *Addlestones, Weston's   Garden* **No Credit Cards**

SHREWSBURY Castle Vaults Castle Gates. Popular free house in the shadow of the castle; Mexican food a speciality. Door policy (no scruffs, in other words). Marston's, Ruddles beers. Open: 11-3, 6-11 (not Sun eve).

STIPERSTONES Stiperstones Inn Tel: (0743) 791327. Decent bar meals like poached salmon, Old Peculier casserole for under £4, plus steaks, interesting puddings, food available all day. Vegetarians and children catered for.

UPPER AFFCOT Travellers Rest on A49 Tel: (06946) 275 Unassuming, friendly free house; bar meals; four en suite bedrooms.

WENLOCK   Wenlock Edge Inn

Hill Top TF3 6DJ   ▮FOOD▮
Tel: (074 636) 403   ▮
Open: 11.30-2.30 (3Sat), 6-11   ❄
Licensee: Stephen Waring

It's well worth the drive some four miles up the B4371 from Much Wenlock just to enjoy the view from Wenlock Edge. Leave the car park opposite the pub and cross a sheep pasture to find Ippikin's rock, from where you can admire the three and a half miles of wooded escarpment which forms the National Trust park. The pub is owned by the Warings and run very much as a family affair. The menu, like the landlord, is on the chatty side: if there's no wedgie pie available, you can always ask if they're doing oink and apple instead. In addition to hand-written menus describing the delights of beef and mushroom pie (guaranteed no kidney), prawn salad and plaice, the latter served with fresh vegetables and boiled potatoes but absolutely never with chips, there are daily specials listed on illuminated boards in each of the two bars. Cream of mushroom soup or Galia melon, a piece of baked salmon or a chicken, ham and mushroom pie are typical offerings. But leave room, too, for the good home-made puddings, of which "the famous lemon pudding" (their description), summer fruit crumble and home-made blackcurrant sorbet are typical. The building itself is decidedly quirky, original stone at the front, but with brick extensions tacked on higgledy piggledy at the sides and rear, and access to a dilapidated farmyard. The far from spacious interior features pews and cushioned window seats, an odd assortment of tables, and a tiny extension which serves in the evenings as a restaurant-cum-parlour. As fellow diners may be almost rubbing shoulders, Stephen Waring plays host from the bar, breaking the ice between strangers with animated conversations which are not always to everyone's taste. A favourite talking point is the Chinese horoscope. There is still one twin bedroom in use for an overnight stay, but a cottage to the rear is now nearing completion, and more bedrooms will become available in due course.

Bar Meals: 12-2, 7-9; no food Mon   bar snacks both sessions   *Typical Dishes:* sweet red pepper and tomato soup £1.75, prawn salad £3.25, steak and mushroom pie £4.20, wedgie pie (venison and beef) £5.90, Harveys chicken (a tomato and sherry sauce) £5.90, lemon pudding £4.90   Vegetarian Meals   Children's Portions   Beer   Robinsons; Ruddles, Webster's   Whisky   Garden   Outdoor Eating   *Accommodation:* 5 bedrooms (for summer 1992; 1 room meanwhile), all with showers, £38 (single £28)   Children Welcome Overnight   Check-in: after noon   *No credit cards*

WISTANSTOW   Plough

Craven Arms SY7 8DG
Tel: (0588) 673251
Open: 11.45-2.30, 7-11
Licensee: Robert West

The home of Wood's brewery, a tiny independent concern. Airy, high-ceilinged lounge with a very modern carpet, leading downstairs to the original bar. Aside from evening bar food, listed here (prices around £6), there's simpler but reliable lunchtime fare with good home-made soups and pies.

Bar Meals: 12-1.45, 7-9 (9.30 Sat; not Sun/Mon); bar snacks lunchtime   *Typical Dishes:* leek and potato soup £1.55, local rabbit in white wine and cream, kidneys Creole, chicken with cream cheese and garlic en croute, hazelnut meringue   Children's Portions   Cheese   Beer   Wood's beers   Cider   Weston's   Patio/terrace   Outdoor Eating   *No Credit Cards*

SOMERSET

AXBRIDGE   Lamb Inn

The Square   ▾
Tel: (0934) 732253
Open: 11-2.30 (3 Sat), 6.30-11
Licensees: Simon Whitmore and Max Wigginton

Rambling, ancient town pub, romantically set opposite King John's hunting lodge. Real fire, bric a brac, beams and settles, as well as more modern intrusions. Bar food is largely routine; good homely specials.

Bar Meals: lunch and evening;   bar snacks both sessions   **Typical Dishes:** home-made soup £2, steak in ale pie £3.70, cottage pie £3, tripe and onions £2.50   Vegetarian Meals   Children's Menu   Beer   Butcombe   Cider   Children Allowed in Bar to Eat (until 9pm)   Garden   **Accommodation:** 3 bedrooms, 2 en suite, from £40 (£18 single)

BARRINGTON Royal Oak Tel: (0460) 53455. Attractive old pub in delightful village; real fire, decent lunch and evening bar meals and occasionally inspired specials, worth a try. Cotleigh beers. Open: 12–2.30, 6.30–11 (all day Sat).

BATCOMBE   Three Horseshoes

Shepton Mallet BW4 6HE
Tel: (074 985) 359
Open: 11-2.30, 6.30-11
Licensees: Peter and Jennifer Charlton

Very old coaching inn not far from the A359, in a quiet pretty village. Much renovated: newest facilities include a reception area, new toilets and cellar; log fires and old beams remain, however. Restaurant with minstrel gallery – same menu as bar, with a wide range of food.

Bar Meals: 12-2, 7-10; bar snacks both sessions   **Typical Dishes:** home-made smoked trout paté £2.35, avocado with prawns £2.85, home-made chicken curry £3.40, home-made steak and kidney pie £3.95, chestnut and herb-stuffed fillet steak with stilton and brandy sauce £9.95, profiteroles £1.95   Vegetarian Meals (all home-made): mushroom and broccoli bake £4   Children's Menu/Portions   Beer   Marston; Oakhill; Whitbread   Cider   Riches   Family Room   Outdoor Play Area   Garden   Outdoor Eating   Summer Barbecue   **Accommodation:** 2 bedrooms, both en suite, from £36 (single £22)   Children Welcome Overnight   Cot Available   Check-in: by arrangement   **Credit Cards:** Access, Amex, Visa

---

BRADLEY GREEN   Malt Shovel

Blackmoor Lane, Cannington TA5 2NE
Tel: (0278) 653432
Open: 11.30-2.30 (3 Sat), 6.30 (7 winter)-11
Licensees: Robert and Frances Beverley

Rangy white-painted roadside inn with a traditional interior: wooden settles and other furniture in the main bar, and there's also a tiny red-walled snug. Routine bar food (same menu in the dining room), but outstanding value, comfortable bedrooms.

Bar Meals: 12-2, 7-9.30 (9 Sun, summer only); bar snacks lunchtime   **Typical Dishes:** celery and potato soup £1.50, home-made paté £1.75, fillet steak £8.95, home-made steak and kidney pie £3.50, goujons of plaice £4, lemon chiffon pie £2   Vegetarian Meals: pasta and spinach mornay £3   Children's Menu   Beer   Butcombe Bitter; Wadworth 6X   Cider   Lanes, Riches   Family Room   Outdoor Play Area   Garden   Outdoor Eating   **Accommodation:** 4 bedrooms, 1 en suite, from £26 (single £17.50)   Children Welcome Overnight   Cot Available   Check-in: all day   **No Credit Cards**

BRUSHFORD Carnarven Arms Tel: (0398) 23302. Busy inn with good light snacks, more restauranty meals, and decent bedrooms.

BRUTON Castle High Street. Busy family pub with hearty helpings of good value food; authentic Indian specials.

BURNHAM ON SEA   Royal Clarence Hotel

The Esplanade TA8 1BQ
Tel: (0278) 783138
Open: 11-11
Licensees: Dennis and Paul Quintin Davey

Listed for its decent upstairs restaurant, with bracing views out over the estuary. Once a coaching inn, the Royal Clarence is now much modernised, with rather downmarket looking bars and drab beige bedrooms. But they do brew two interesting beers of their own, Clarence Pride and Regent.

Bar Meals: 11.30-2.30, 6-9.30 (12-2.30, 7-9 Sun); bar snacks both sessions *Restaurant:* 12-1.30, 7-8.30   *Typical Dishes BAR:* home-made soup £1.20, steak £6.50, fillet of plaice £3.25, scampi £4.55, fruit crumble £1.10   *RESTAURANT:* steak £7.50, carbonade of beef £7.75, duck a l'orange £7.50   *Vegetarian Meals Children's Menu*   **Beer**   Butcombe Bitter; Wadworth 6X   **Whisky**   **Cider** Addlestones   Family Room   Patio/terrace   Outdoor Eating   *Accommodation:* 19 bedrooms, 17 en suite, from £41 (single £26)   Children Welcome Overnight   Cots

---

BUTLEIGH   Rose & Portcullis

near Glastonbury BA6 8TQ
Tel: (0458) 50287
Open: 12-3, 6-11
Licensees: Paul Tuckett and David Gardner

Solid stone-built roadside pub, stylishly refurbished, with a good mix of furnishings and a large, attractive dining conservatory.

Bar Meals and Restaurant: 12-2, 7-10; bar snacks both sessions   *Typical Dishes BAR:* chicken and sweetcorn soup £1.25, whitebait £1.95, boozy beef £3.95, kidneys in red wine £4.25, cottage pie £3.95, lemon cheesecake £1.95   *RESTAURANT:* carrot and orange soup £1.25, avocado £3.15, chicken breast stuffed with stilton £6.95, steak Diane £9.25, duck à l'orange £8.50, sherry trifle £1.95   *Vegetarian Meals:* lasagne £3.95   *Children's Menu/Portions*   **Beer**   Courage; Wadworth   Family Room   Garden   Outdoor Eating Summer Barbecue   *Credit Cards:* Access, Visa

---

CASTLE CARY   George Inn

Market Place BA7 7AH
Tel: (0963) 50761
Open: 12-3, 7-10.30
Licensee: G D Sparkes

Town-centre, listed 15th century coaching inn, in part even older – the elm beam over the inglenook fireplace in the bar dates back a further 500 years. Smartly refurbished; rustic panelled restaurant with a fancy £16 table d'hote; individually decorated bedrooms.

Bar Meals: 12-2, 7-9; bar snacks both sessions   *Restaurant:* 12-2 (Sun only), 7.30-9.30 (not Sun)   *Typical Dishes BAR:* carrot and orange soup £1.60, whitebait £2.90, spaghetti carbonara, chicken fillet stuffed with ham and cheese, home-made steak and kidney pie (main courses around £5), bread and butter pudding £1.85   *Vegetarian Meals Children's Portions*   **Beer**   Butcombe; Wadworth; Webster's   Children Allowed in Bar to Eat   Patio/terrace   Outdoor Eating   *Accommodation:* 16 bedrooms, all en suite, from £57 (single £42)   Children Welcome Overnight   Cots Available   Check-in: all day *Credit Cards:* Access, Visa

CRANMORE   Strode Arms

West Cranmore (off A361)   ❢
Tel: (074 988) 450
Open: 11.30-2.30, 6.30-11
Licensees: Dora and Rodney Phelps

Mostly 15th century coaching inn, formerly a farmhouse, opposite the village pond.
Delightfully rustic within, and run with imagination; the daily papers laid out in the
bar are a particularly welcome feature. Vintage cars meet outside on the first
Tuesday of the month. Children allowed in the restaurant.

Bar Meals: lunch and evening (not winter Sun eve);   bar snacks both sessions   **Typical**
Dishes: *smoked duck breast £4.75, steak and kidney pie £3.75, scallops and bacon
£4.75, home-made ice creams   Vegetarian Meals   Children's Portions*   `Beer` *Bunces;
Oakhill; Wadworth*   `Cider`   *Garden*

CROSCOMBE   Bull Terrier

Wells BA5 3QJ   ❢
Tel: (0749) 343658
Open: 12-2.30 (inc Sun), 7-11
Licensees: Stan and Pam Lea

Lovely old pub with three bars: the Inglenook, a red carpeted lounge with
cushioned wall seats and pretty beams; the Snug, leading off, and the Common Bar,
as well as a family room. Owners of the eponymous dog tend to gather here, but
not usually in alarming numbers. Fairly routine printed menu plus daily specials.
Recommended for bed and breakfast. No under 16s overnight.

*Bar Meals: 12-2, 7-9.30 (10 Fri/Sat); 12-1.45, 7-9 Sun; not Sun eve nor all day Mon
Nov-April; bar snacks both sessions*   **Typical Dishes:** *soup of the day £1.75, tuna and egg
mayonnaise £2.95, Scotch fillet steak £10.25, chicken Maryland £5.75, Barnsley chop
£5.50, apple strudel   Vegetarian Meals: spinach and peanut pancakes £4.75   Children's
Portions (some)*   `Beer` *Butcombe; Charles Wells; Hall & Woodhouse; Palmers*   `Whisky`
`Cider`   *Wilkins   Family Room   Garden   Outdoor Eating*   **Accommodation:** *3
bedrooms, 2 en suite, from £42 (single £20)   Check-in: all day*   **Credit Cards:** *Access,
Visa*

DITCHEAT Manor House   Suitably manorial without, refurbished in the usual
pub style within; decent good value bar meals; nice garden; Butcombe Bitter.

DOWLISH WAKE   New Inn

Ilminster TA19 0NZ
Tel: (0460) 52413
Open: 11-2.30, 6-11
Licensees: D Smith and T A Boosey

Well-loved little gem of a country pub, small, stone-walled, with a pleasingly old-
fashioned air, a good mix of furniture and a wood-burning stove. Cooking by the
Swiss landlady (rosti fans take note) is always good: choose either from a deceptively
plain typed bar menu or a smarter a la carte, listed here under restaurant dishes but
in fact mixed and matched with the bar menu in the evenings. They specialise in
steaks of all sorts and sauces. A delightful village, also home to Perry's Cider Mill.

Bar Meals: 12-2, 6.30-9; bar snacks both sessions   **Restaurant:** *7.15-9.15*   **Typical**
Dishes BAR: *soft roes on toast £2.75, Bellew sausage with rosti £2.45, chilli £2.85, liver*

and bacon casserole £3.35   **RESTAURANT:** *paté £2, butterfly prawns £2.70, fillet steak fondue £6.95, rack of lamb £8.95, sirloin with mushroom and raclette £8.25 Vegetarian Meals: nut roast £3.35   Children's Menu* ▆Beer▆ *Butcombe Bitter; Wadworth 6X* ▆Whisky▆ ▆Cider▆ *Perry's   Family Room   Outdoor Play Area   Garden Outdoor Eating*   **No Credit Cards**

EAST HARPTREE Castle of Comfort on B3134 Tel: (0761) 221321. Secluded but popular old coaching inn with an atmospheric bar, comfortable annexe bedrooms and bar meals. Bass, Butcombe beers. Open: 11.30-2.30, 7-11.

EXFORD   Crown Hotel

near Minehead TA24 7PP
Tel: (064 383) 554
Licensee: P J Mohan

A favourite of the huntin', shootin' and fishin' set, the 17th century Crown stands by the green in a lovely Exmoor village. Lots of traditional charm in the comfortable lounge and rustic bar, and pretty bedrooms of varying sizes, individually furnished, with excellent modern bathrooms. Thoughtful touches range from fresh fruit and a welcoming glass of sherry to hot water bottles, tea-makers and hairdryers.

Bar Meals: *lunch and evening*   **Accommodation:** *17 bedrooms, all en suite, from £60 Children Welcome Overnight   Cots Available   Check-in: all day*   **Credit Cards:** *Access, Amex, Visa*

FRESHFORD Inn at Freshford. Varied and generous home cooking in countrified bar at this delightful three storey old stone inn; also restaurant; outdoor eating on peaceful rear lawn. Watneys beers.

FROME Sun Inn, 6 Catherine Street Tel: (0373) 73123: Lively, pleasant old town-centre coaching inn with an enormous inglenook fireplace, decent lunchtime bar food (not Sunday), also restaurant; cheap bed and breakfast; lots of interesting beers. Open: 11-3, 6-11 (all day Sat).

GLASTONBURY   Mitre Inn

27 Benedict Street BA6 9NE
Tel: (0458) 31203
Open: 11-2.30, 6-11
Licensees: John and Ann Cichowicz

There are always at least five hot specials available at this traditional, friendly urban local.

Bar Meals: *12-2.15, 6.15 (7 Sun)-9.15; bar snacks both sessions*   **Typical Dishes:** *cream of mushroom soup £1.30, prawn special £2.50, Somerset chop £3.75, beef cobbler £3.75, minced beef and dumplings £3.25, hot banana cake £1.30   Vegetarian Meals: vegetable crumble £3.25   Children's Menu/Portions* ▆Beer▆ *Courage Best Bitter; John Smith's Bitter* ▆Cider▆ *Roger Wilkins Farmhouse   Family Room   Outdoor Play Area Garden   Outdoor Eating*   **No Credit Cards**

GLASTONBURY George & Pilgrims, High Street Tel: (0458) 31146. Stunning exterior, plainly refurbished inside. Routine bar food, more interesting upstairs restaurant; good value bedrooms.

HARDWAY   Bull Inn

near Bruton BA10 0LN
Tel: (0749) 812200
Open: 11.30-2.30, 5.30-11
Licensees: Martin Smith and Paul Stanley

A regular finalist in the highly competitive Pub Caterer cookery competition, so
popular for its food that it really pays to get here at opening time – latecomers have
been disappointed. A remote and charming pub on the Somerset plains.

Bar Meals: 12-1.45, 6-9.30; bar snacks both sessions   ***Restaurant:*** *7-9.15*   ***Typical***
Dishes BAR: *leek soup £1.65, mushrooms with dip £3.25, beef in beer casserole £4.95,
mixed grill £6.25, haddock and prawn mornay £4.95, treacle tart £1.75*
RESTAURANT: *similar starters and puddings, warm salad of chicken and scallops £3.45,
pheasant £7.50, duck breast in honey £8.50, salmon and turbot plait £8.95   Vegetarian
Meals: almond and pepper tart £3.95   Children's Portions* ▪Beer▪ *Butcombe Bitter;
Wadworth 6X   Children Allowed in Bar to Eat   Outdoor Play Area   Garden   Outdoor
Eating   Summer Barbecue   **Credit Cards:** Access, Visa*

HASELBURY PLUCKNETT   Haselbury Inn

on A3066   ❦
Tel: (0460) 72488
Open: 12-2.30, 7-11; closed Mon
Licensee: James Pooley

Characterful pub with an unusual bar, half given over to a chintzy sitting area,
complete with television half traditionally furnished, its tables candle-lit at night.
Also stylish rear restaurant proper, busy at weekends. Food is reliably good, with
fresh vegetables; the restaurant menu is also available in the bar.

Bar Meals: lunch and evening.   bar snacks both sessions   ***Typical Dishes:*** *game soup
£1.60, home-made paté £3, goulash £4, lambs kidney and bacon fettucini £3.75, local
trout £8, home-made puddings £2.25 Vegetarian Meals* ▪Beer▪ *Butcombe; Exmoor;
Wadworth; Whitbread Garden   Outdoor Eating*

HAWKRIDGE Tarr Steps Hotel Tarr Steps. Very much a hotel, but with a
properly pubby bar, nice restaurant.

HENSTRIDGE   Virginia Ash

Templecombe BA8 0PL
Tel: (0963) 62267
Open: 11-2.30, 6.30-11
Licensees: Martin and Kris Shone

Homely, popular, energetically-run pub, welcoming to families, with hearty
helpings of more than decent home cooking.

Bar Meals: 11.30-2, 6.30-10 (12-2, 7-9.30 Sun);   bar snacks both sessions   ***Typical***
Dishes: *turkey soup £1.50, paté £1.50, turkey ham and leek pie, Caundle pie, pheasant
and smoked bacon casserole (main courses £5), steamed pecan sponge pudding with
butterscotch sauce £2.25   Vegetarian Meals   Children's Menu/Portions* ▪Beer▪
*Courage; Wadworth   Children Allowed in Bar to Eat   Outdoor Play Area   Garden
Outdoor Eating   **Credit Cards:** Access, Visa*

HINTON ST GEORGE   Poulett Arms

off A30
Tel: (0460) 73149
Open: 11.30-3, 7-11
Licensees: Ray and Diane Chisnall

Smartly plush dining pub, with original stripped stone walls and fireplace, heavy
timbers, and two little anterooms, plus a rear drinkers' public. They also do
bedrooms (around £40 a double room).

Bar Meals: lunch and evening; bar snacks both sessions **Typical Dishes:** *home-made
soup £1.30, steak and kidney pie £4, cottage pie £3, trout £5 Vegetarian Meals: nut
roast Children's Portions* ▮Beer▮ *Ruddles, Ushers Family Room Garden Outdoor
Eating*

HOLYWELL LAKE Holywell Inn. Appealing lunchtime buffet, plus hot specials
and rather smart evening menu, at attractively refurbished village dining pub;
garden.

KEINTON MANDEVILLE   Quarry Inn

near Somerton TA11 6DZ
Tel: (0458) 223367
Open: 12-3, 6.30 (7 Sat)-11
Licensees: Barry and Becky Goddard

As the name suggests, once the quarrymaster's residence, early Victorian and roomy,
if not exactly quaint. A separate dining room is welcoming. No television in
bedrooms.

Bar Meals: 12-2, 7-9.30; bar snacks both sessions **Typical Dishes:** *home-made soup
£1.30, prawn cocktail £2.50, mixed grill £5.50, home-made steak and kidney pie £4.25,
fresh fish (Thur/Fri) £5-£6, bread and butter pudding £1.75 Vegetarian Meals: savoury
pasta Children's Menu/Portions* ▮Beer▮ *Oakhill Bitter; Wadworth 6X Children
Allowed in Bar to Eat Outdoor Play Area Garden Outdoor Eating* **Accommodation:**
*3 bedrooms, sharing a bathroom, from £27.50 (single £17.50) Children Welcome
Overnight Check-in: by arrangement* **Credit Cards:** *Visa*

KILVE   Hood Arms

near Bridgwater TA5 1EA
Tel: (027 874) 210
Open: 10.30-2.30 (2 Sun), 6-11
Licensees: Robbie Rutt and Neville White

Pristine 17th century white village inn at the foot of the Quantock hills, a mile from
the sea. Modernised, comfortable interior, with wood-burning stove in carpeted
main bar, which is bistro-like in the evenings. Also smaller, cosy lounge. Pleasant
garden. Friendly, welcoming service.

Bar Meals: 12-2 (1.30 Sun), 6.30-10 (7.15-9.30 Sun); bar snacks both sessions
Restaurant: *7-9.30 Wed-Sat* **Typical Dishes BAR:** *chicken and leek soup £1.60,
aubergine bake £4.25, National Trust pie £4.25, haddock and prawn mornay £4.25,
apple, brandy and mincemeat crumble £1.50* **RESTAURANT:** *home-made paté £1.75,
escalope of veal £8, Somerset fillet steak £9, Dover sole £10, puddings £2 Vegetarian
Meals: cauliflower, celery and stilton bake* ▮Cheese▮ ▮Beer▮ *Whitbread Boddingtons
Bitter, Flowers Original* ▮Whisky▮ *Outdoor Play Area Garden Outdoor Eating*

Accommodation: 5 bedrooms, all en suite, from £56 (single £33)   Children Welcome
Overnight (minimum age 7)   Check-in: all day   **Credit Cards:** Access, Visa

---

KNAPP   Rising Sun

North Curry TA3 6BG
Tel: (0823) 490436
Open: 11.30-2.30, 6.30-11
Licensee: Tony Atkinson

Very much a dining pub, pretty, white-painted and cottagey, and totally refurbished,
though many original features remain in this typical Somerset longhouse. On the
edge of the Levels. Real fire, no music, reliably good bar food.

Bar Meals: 12-2; bar snacks   **Restaurant:** 7-9.30   **Typical Dishes BAR:** *home-made
soup of the day £1.75, half-pint of prawns £3.50, spicy pork sausages £2.90, rump steak
£6.50, cauliflower and bacon cheese £2.85, treacle tart £1.75* **RESTAURANT:** *spicy
fish soup £3, home-made liver paté £2.45, rack of lamb en croute £8.75, chicken Calcutta
£8.25, scallops thermidor £9.75, home-made puddings £2.85 Vegetarian Meals
(restaurant): nut roast £6.50* Children's Portions   Beer Bass; Exmoor Ale; Whitbread
Boddingtons Bitter   Family Room   Patio/terrace   Outdoor Eating   **Credit Cards:** Access,
Visa

LANGLEY MARSH   Three Horseshoes

off A361
Tel: (0984) 23763
Open: 12-2.30, 7-11
Licensee: J Hopkins

Handsome village inn with a stylish rear bar, complete with piano, and noisier locals'
public at the front with a fruit machine and music. Food is a hundred percent home
cooked, and reliably delicious; no chips or fried foods; fresh vegetables. Lovely in
summer, on the lawn or verandah.

Bar Meals: lunch and evening; bar snacks both sessions   **Typical Dishes:** *home-made
soup £1.70, game paté £2.20, spiced beef £4.95, Somerset fish pie £4.20, chicken
casserole £4.50, real cheescake Vegetarian Meals: leek croustade £3.95* Children's
Portions   Beer Badger; Butcombe; Eldridge Pope; Palmers   Cider   Family Room
Outdoor Play Area   Garden   Outdoor Eating

LONG SUTTON   Lime Kiln Inn

Langport TA10 9JH
Tel: (0458) 241242
Open: 11.30-3, 5.30-11
Licensee: Clive Williams

Bar Meals: 12-2, 7-10; bar snacks both sessions   **Restaurant:** 7-10   **Typical Dishes
BAR:** *tomato soup £1.75, breaded mushrooms £2.95, home-made steak, kidney and
Guinness pie £4.75, chicken Kiev £5.95, all-day breakfast £4.25, treacle and almond tart
£1.95* **RESTAURANT:** *celery soup £1.75, smoked duck breast £3.75, fillet steak
£9.25, sherried kidneys £6.25, salmon steak £8.50, crepes with poached fruits £2.25
Vegetarian Meals: vegetarian chilli £3.25* Children's Menu/Portions   Beer Draught
Bass; Cotleigh Tawny Bitter; Greene King IPA   Cider   Burrow Hill   Children
Allowed in Bar to Eat   Outdoor Play Area   Garden   Outdoor Eating   **Accommodation:**

*3 bedrooms, 2 en suite, from £38 (single £30)   Children Welcome Overnight   Cot
Available   Check-in: all day   **Credit Cards:** Access, Visa*

LUXBOROUGH   Royal Oak

near Dunster, Exmoor National Park TA23 0SH
Tel: (0984) 40319
Open: 11-2.30, 6 (7 Dec-Feb)-11
Licensees: Robin and Helen Stamp

Nestling by a stream at the bottom of a steep-sided valley, deep in Exmoor's
Brendon Hills, the Royal Oak is a truly rustic rural inn. No piped music, no fruit
machines, no posh fixtures and fittings have intruded here – and the partly thatched
roof is really rather mangy. In short, no attempt whatsoever to tart the place up for
the grockles (sorry! holidaymakers), which is perhaps why so many flock here during
the summer months. The several rooms have flagstoned or cobbled floors, low
beams, old kitchen tables and hardly a pair of matching chairs. Besides uncontrived
charm, there are a couple of other good reasons for a visit here. Firstly, the splendid
choice of well-kept real ales, with an ever-changing selection of guest beers to
supplement the regular names. The other big attraction is the food, prepared by
alumni from the local catering college. An extensive menu ranges widely, from
sandwiches and jacket potatoes to home-made soups, partnered by great wedges of
crusty bread, and substantial main dishes like beef and Beamish pie with tender, lean
meat in a rich gravy cooked beneath a square of toothsome pastry. There's always a
vegetarian dish, and the ubiquitous fishfingers are offered to children. Steaks and fish
and a few other extras appear for the additional evening menu. It's still very much a
locals' pub: Tuesday night is quiz night, and every Friday a folk club takes over the
back room, which has a pool table and sadly unworkable old harmonium. Two
bedrooms are available for overnight guests but, being above the bars, are probably
not suitable for families with children or others with an early bedtime. Rooms are
perfectly clean and respectable but this is not luxury accommodation: a bed and a
couple of sticks of old furniture is about it. The large shared bathroom is in good
order but there is no shower.

Bar Meals: *12-2, 7-10; bar snacks both sessions*   **Typical Dishes:** *tomato and chive soup
£1.60, port and stilton paté £2.85, beef and Beamish pie £3.95, lamb curry £3.95,
chicken and chips £4.25, bread and butter pudding   Vegetarian Meals   Children's
Menu/Portions*   **Beer**   *Cotleigh Tawny Bitter; Eldridge Pope Royal Oak; Exmoor
Gold*   **Cider**   *Riches   Children Allowed in Bar to Eat   Garden   Outdoor Eating   No
Credit Cards*

LYDFORD ON FOSSE Cross Keys. Immaculately run, with decent home
cooked lunch and evening bar food.

MIDDLEZOY   George Inn

42 Main Road TA7 0NN
Tel: (0823) 69215
Open: 12-3 (not Mon), 7-11
Licensees: Keith and Maureen Waites

Handsome old inn, used to house the militia in the Battle of Sedgemoor, the last to
be fought on English soil. Flagstoned, beamy public bar, and inglenook fireplaces
both here and in the lounge, which is overrun by diners at peak feeding times.

Bar Meals: *12-2, 7.15-9.45 (no food Tue); bar snacks both sessions*   **Typical Dishes:**
*stilton and celery soup £1.35, mushrooms in cream and garlic sauce £2.75, smoked chicken
bake with crab sauce £7.25, strips of sirloin in brandy, mustard and cream £8.25, whole*

*plaice topped with prawns and garlic sauce £5.95, treacle tart £1.75   Vegetarian Meals:
celery bake   Children's Menu/Portions*   Beer   *Cotleigh; Goldfinch; Ringwood;
Robinsons*   Cider   *Inch's   Children Allowed in Bar to Eat   Outdoor Play Area   Garden
Outdoor Eating   **Accommodation:** 2 bedrooms, sharing a bathroom, from £30 (single
£15)   Check-in: all day   **No Credit Cards***

MILBORNE PORT Queens Head High Street Tel: (0963) 250314. Traditional
village local with large courtyard, separate restaurant, and a piano in the bar; bar
meals lunch and evening, real ales and ciders; three comfortable bedrooms.

MONKSILVER   ★   Notley Arms

Taunton TA4 4JB   FOOD
Tel: (0984) 56217   ☺
Open: 11 (12 Sun)-2.30, 6.30-11
Licensees: Sarah and Alistair Cade

The experienced Sarah and Alistair Cade have brought inimitable flair to the white-
painted roadside Notley Arms and in just a few short years built up a formidably
good reputation at this previously distinctly undistinctive village pub. The interior is
charmingly simple: an L-shaped bar with plain wooden furniture, black and white
timbered walls, candles at night, and twin woodburning stoves; a small but bright
and cheery family room leads off, and there's a stream at the bottom of the trim
cottage garden. The big attraction here, though, is the bar food, which roughly
divides into three categories – the traditional, the eastern or exotic, and the
vegetarian – all given equal thought, the finest fresh ingredients, and cooked with
sure-handed skill. Old favourites and four or five daily hot specials are all chalked up
on the blackboard: start with an excellent home-made soup, like a well balanced
tasty lentil and vegetable, or subtle potato and dill. For a light but satisfying lunch,
choose one of the delicious pitta bread sandwiches with garlic butter, tender meats
and good crispy salad. Our own favourite, Chinese red roast pork, features well-
marinated cubes of meat in a soy, five spice and hoy sin sauce, with stir-fried
pimento and courgette: delicious. Their smoked haddock pancake and vegetable
croustade are equally fine, as are puddings, with light pastry and good local cream.
Try the delicately tangy and moreish lemon meringue, or a locally made ice-cream.
A few more heavyweight dinnerish dishes like good tender steaks and fresh local
trout are added to the evening menu. Despite the crowds at peak times, all runs
effortlessly smoothly and with good humour. Even dogs are welcome here.

*Bar Meals: 12-2 (1.45 Sun), 7-9.30 (9 Sun); bar snacks both sessions   **Typical Dishes:**
potato and dill soup £1.25, home-made paté £2.80, home-made tagliatelle with ham and
mushrooms £3.75, Chinese red roast pork £4.95, courgette and basil filo with pinenuts
£3.95, treacle tart £1.75   Vegetarian Meals: potato, tomato and coconut curry £3.75
Children's Portions*   Beer   *Ruddles; Theakston; Ushers   Family Room   Outdoor Play
Area   Riverside Garden   Outdoor Eating   **No Credit Cards***

MONTACUTE   Kings Arms

On A3088 Montacute TA15 6UU
Tel: (0935) 822513
Licensee: Simon Price

Plushly modernised lounge with the mood of a small market town hotel; people
dress up to come for Sunday lunch here. Weekend lunches are dominated by the
buffet. Pretty pink and white dining room with separate, restauranty menu.
Vegetarians need to make special request for something suitable for them; no routine
vegetarian options. Refurbished bedrooms are mostly on the compact side – except
for the two new honeymoon rooms.

Bar Meals: 12-2, 7.30-10 (9.30 Sun); bar snacks both sessions   *Restaurant:* 12-2,
7.30-9 (not Sun)   *Typical Dishes BAR:* cauliflower soup £1.25, baked egg Albert £2,
steak and kidney pie £4.90, ham and asparagus bake £4.90, sweet and sour pork £4.90
RESTAURANT: chicken and sweetcorn soup £1.55, avocado vol-au-vent with crab
mousse £2.95, medallions of wild boar £10.95, breast of pigeon £10.50, beef olives
£10.75   Children's Menu/Portions   Beer   Draught Bass   Children Allowed in Bar to
Eat   Patio/terrace   *Accommodation:* 11 bedrooms, all en suite, from £64 (single £46)
Children Welcome Overnight   Cot Available   Check-in: all day   *Credit Cards:* Access,
Amex, Diners, Visa

NORTON ST PHILIP   George Inn

6 miles south-east of Bath BA3 6LH
Tel: (0373) 834224
Open: 11-2.30, 6-11
Licensee: Michael Moore

Of great historical interest, the George was built in 1223, and has a remarkable
facade, a romantic film set of a little courtyard, and splendid medieval main bar, its
simple wooden furniture completely overwhelmed by the huge fireplace, copper-
strewn beams and mullion windows. There's also a panelled lounge, and a cellar bar
at very busy times. Food is secondary, but go for the daily specials.

Bar Meals: 12-2.30, 6.30-10; bar snacks both sessions   *Restaurant:* 12.30-2, 7-9.30
Typical Dishes BAR: home-made soup £1.20, lasagne £3.25, lamb cutlets £3.75, roast
chicken £3.75, mixed bean casserole £3.25, blackcurrant cheesecake £1.25
RESTAURANT: soup £2.20, goujons of plaice, steak £9.75, lemon sole £6.75, trout
£7.25, chocolate fudge cake £1.25   Vegetarian Meals: vegetarian lasagne £3.25
Children's Portions   Beer   Draught Bass; Wadworth IPA, 6X   Family Room   Garden
Credit Cards: Access, Amex, Diners, Visa

NUNNEY   George

11 Church Street BA11 4LW   ▼
Tel: (0373) 836458
Open: 11-3.15, 5.30-11
Licensee: D R Page

White-painted, street-fronting coaching inn, its sign stretched right over the road,
opposite the castle ruin. Real fire, no music.

Bar Meals: 12-2, 7-9 (6.30-10 weekends); bar snacks both sessions   *Restaurant:* 12-2,
7-9 (6.30-10.30 weekends); closed Mon   *Typical Dishes BAR:* home-made soup with
own bread £1.80, crispy mushrooms £2.35, Scotch roast beef £5.50, home-made lasagne
£3.95, grilled gammon steak £5.20, at least 8 home-made puddings   *RESTAURANT:*
soup £2.25, prawn cocktail £3.25, Scotch fillet steak £8.95, fresh salmon £8.95, or table
d'hote menu, changed weekly, £12.95   Vegetarian Meals: vegan nut roast   Children's
Menu/Portions   Beer   Moles; Ruddles; Ushers   Family Room   Garden   Outdoor
Eating   Summer Barbecue   *Accommodation:* 12 bedrooms, all en suite, from £52 (single
£42)   Children Welcome Overnight   Cots Available   Check-in: all day   *Credit Cards:*
Access, Visa

OVER STRATTON ★ Royal Oak

South Petherton TA13 5LQ

FOOD

Tel: (0460) 40906

Open: 12-2.30, 7 (6.30 Sat)-11

Licensee: Lyn Holland

Although now a pub, this row of three 400 year old thatched cottages still merges with its neighbours in the main street of the village and, but for the pub sign, it would be easy to miss the Royal Oak altogether. Cottage atmosphere is still the secret of an interior with a real sense of style. Original features like old beams, hamstone and flag floors (as well as a couple of stone pillars that look to have been there for ever but were actually salvaged from the cellars of a nearby house a couple of years ago) blend successfully with dark red rag-rolled walls, scrubbed wooden tables, a polished granite bar counter and extensive displays of dried flowers, hops and strings of garlic. The latter seem to work as there was not a vampire to be seen anywhere. A globe-trotting menu takes its inspiration from you name where: croissants from France, stuffed vine leaves from Greece, Hawaiian pineapple and prawns, Polynesian lamb kebabs, steak and kidney pie from Blighty and much else besides. Perhaps surprisingly, given its impressive scope, everything is genuinely home-cooked. Non-fans of McDonalds should give the Royal Oak's own home-made char-grilled burger a try; this is as good as a burger can be. Fat, moist, succulent and laced with onions, it comes with piquant barbecue sauce, a generous amount of varied salad and crisp, plump golden chips. Landlady Lyn Holland is not only charming but also full of good ideas, like the Booty Box on the children's menu, full of goodies including a wholemeal sandwich, cheese, fruit, crisps and a crunchy bar in a special box children can take away with them. The adult equivalent is a barbecue pack containing a pair of lamb cutlets, sausage, gammon steak and a chicken drumstick (along with salad and jacket potato) that, weather permitting, is cooked on the grill outdoors. Beyond the barbecue, there are swings, a junior assault course and no less than three trampolines to keep the kids amused.

Bar Meals: 12-2, 7-10; bar snacks both sessions **Restaurant:** *12-1.45, 7-9.45*
Typical Dishes: *home-made soup £1.75, deep-fried brie £2.95, lamb in Greek pastry £8.95, spring chicken with hollandaise £7.95, Neptune's platter £10.95, apricot dacquoise £2.25 Vegetarian Meals: vegetable pasta bake £3.95 Children's Menu/Portions*
Beer *Hall & Woodhouse; Wadworth* Whisky *Outdoor Play Area Garden Outdoor Eating Summer Barbecue* **Credit Cards:** *Access, Visa*

PRIDDY New Inn

near Wells BA5 3BB

Tel: (0749) 676465

Open: 11.30-2.30 (12-2.30 Sun), 7-11

Licensee: Douglas Weston

15th century farmhouse, unchanged until the 1970s, when bars and more bedrooms were added. In the heart of the Mendips, the highest pub in Somerset. A fairly standard menu: they specialise in steaks and traditional puddings.

Bar Meals: 12-2.30, 7-10 (9.30 Sun); bar snacks both sessions **Typical Dishes:** *French onion soup £1.25, home-made chicken liver paté £2.50, four lamb cutlets with redcurrant, orange and mint jelly £6.20, sirloin steak £7.25, jumbo jacket potato with choice of topping £2-£3.45, bread and butter pudding £1.45 Vegetarian Meals: Mendip hotpot £3.65 Children's Portions* Beer *Eldridge Pope; Marston; Wadworth* Cider *Wilkins Children Allowed in Bar to Eat Outdoor Play Area Garden Outdoor Eating*
Accommodation: *6 bedrooms, sharing 2 bathrooms, from £29.50 (single £18.50) Children Welcome Overnight Cot Available Check-in: by arrangement* **No Credit Cards**

STAPLE FITZPAINE   Greyhound Inn

Taunton TA3 5SP
Tel: (0823) 480227
Open: 11-2.30, 5-11
Licensees: Steven and Audrey Watts

Built as a hunting lodge by the local lord of the manor in 1640, the Greyhound has since been extended a number of times. The result is a series of connecting rooms, some with flagstone floors, some with old timbers or natural stone walls and stools made out of old barrels. The latest addition, just a couple of years old, has been aged with dark-stained board panelling and a high plate shelf above, helping it to blend happily with the older parts of the inn. This is now the restaurant area, with ready-laid tables, red paper napkins and waitress service, but the menu is the same throughout the pub. The other rooms, also much used for dining, have good eating-height solid wooden tables sporting little posies of flowers and candles in bottles. A blackboard menu combines standard pub stuff such as chilli, sandwiches or ploughmans (here called a woodcutter's lunch), with more out of the way offerings like chilled watermelon, avocado with cottage cheese and elderberries, plus several pasta dishes. Audrey Watts, who owns the pub with son Steven, takes personal charge of the puddings, and her plum and melon pie is a particularly successful, and unusual, combination, while the hot treacle tart with clotted cream is so popular that customers will not allow its removal from the menu. Children are welcomed with smaller portions at smaller prices, and a play area outside has a splendid rustic climbing frame and slide to keep them amused. A skittle alley with its own bar is set in a former cow shed and available to groups; booking required.

Bar Meals and Restaurant: 12-2, 7-10; bar snacks both sessions   *Typical Dishes:* tomato and tarragon soup £1.65, deep-fried brie £2.75, fettucine Alfredo £4.45, spicy chicken wings £4.25, fresh mussels and langoustines £6.95, summer pudding £1.95 *Vegetarian Meals:* broccoli thermidor £3.95   *Children's Portions* Cheese   Beer Exmoor Ale; Marston Pedigree; Whitbread Boddingtons Bitter, Flowers Original Whisky Balvenie, Talisker Cider Lanes Farmhouse Cider; Taunton Traditional   *Family Room Patio/terrace   Outdoor Eating   Credit Cards: Access, Visa*

STOGUMBER White Horse Inn. Charming village local, rustically furnished, with lunch and evening bar food, always decent, often more interesting; well-kept Cotleigh beers; cheap double rooms. Open 11-2.30, 6-11.

STOKE ST GREGORY   Rose & Crown

Woodhill TA3 6EW
Tel: (0823) 490296
Open: 11-2.30, 6.30-11
Licensees: Ron and Irene Browning

In the hamlet of Woodhill, the Rose & Crown is a 17th century cottage pub with a delightful patio and, indoors, a fairly subtle horsey theme, lots of nooks and crannies, timbers and brasses aplenty. Readers are still travelling miles for the famous scrumpy chicken, just one of their good home-made dishes. Bedrooms are modest with modern fittings.

Bar Meals and Restaurant: 12-2, 7-10; bar snacks both sessions   *Typical Dishes BAR:* home-made soup with own bread £1.50, deep-fried Somerset brie with redcurrant jelly £2.25, scrumpy chicken £4.95, lasagne £4.25, fresh grilled skate £4.95, chocolate mousse cake £1.75   *RESTAURANT:* set supper menu £10: salami salad, escargots (£2 supp.), grilled lamb cutlets, local trout, creme caramel   *Vegetarian Meals:* nut roast provencale £4.95 *Children's Portions* Beer Eldridge Pope; Exmoor Ale   *Family Room   Garden*

Outdoor Eating Summer Barbecue **Accommodation:** *3 bedrooms, sharing a bathroom, from £34 (single £18.50) Children Welcome Overnight Check-in: all day* **Credit Cards:** *Access, Visa*

TRISCOMBE   Blue Ball

West Bagborough TA4 3HE
Tel: (09848) 242
Open: 11-2.30, 6 (7 winter)-11
Licensee: Gary Little

Known as the Blue Ball ever since it was built in the 18th century – probably after the masses of wild wurtleberries which grow on the hills behind. It's thatched, cottagey and very busy in the summer.

Bar Meals: *12-2, 7-9.30 (9 Sun); bar snacks both sessions* **Typical Dishes:** *tomato and orange soup £1.50, deep-fried brie with mango chutney £1.95, lamb cassoulet, Somerset pork casserole, chicken provencale (main courses £3-£5), treacle tart Vegetarian Meals: cheese pancake Children's Portions* `Cheese` `Beer` *Cotleigh Tawny Bitter; Exmoor Ale; Ind Coope Burton Ale, Tetley Bitter Family Room Garden Outdoor Eating* **No Credit Cards**

TRUDOXHILL   White Hart

Frome BA11 5DP
Tel: (0373) 836324
Open: 12-3, 7-11
Licensee: R A Viney

The home of the splendid Ash Vine Brewery, which alone makes it worth a visit, but it's also a nice, relaxing pub, with a long, opened-out bar and two real fires.

Bar Meals and Restaurant: *12-3, 7-10 (not Sun eve restaurant); bar snacks both sessions* **Typical Dishes BAR:** *home-made soup £1.25, smoked mackerel £2.50, steak and mushroom pie £4.25, scrumpy pork £5.95, beef goulash £3.95, fruit pie £1.50* **Restaurant:** *crispy king prawns £3.50, chicken chasseur £6.50, duck à l'orange £8.50, treacle tart £1.75 Vegetarian Meals: stilton and celery pie £3.95 Children's Menu/Portions* `Beer` *Ash Vine Bitter, Challenger, Tanker; Draught Bass* `Cider` *Thatchers Children Allowed in Bar to Eat Garden Outdoor Eating* **Credit Cards:** *Access, Visa*

WATERROW Rock Inn on B3277 Tel: (0984) 23293. Rock-face built pub in attractive hamlet; open-plan interior has a public end, a lounge area, and restaurant leading off. Decent food lunchtime and evening; bedrooms. Cotleigh, Exmoor beers. Open: 11-2.30, 6-11.

WEST HUNTSPILL   Crossways Inn

Highbridge TA9 3RA   ♟
Tel: (0278) 783756
Open: 11-3, 5.30 (6 Sat)-11
Licensees: Michael Ronca and Tony Eyles

Proprietor-run 17th century inn with a simple old-fashioned interior, fairly modest but clean and comfortable bedrooms, and a delightful covered patio at the rear. There'll be five bedrooms by March 1992. Reliably good home cooking.

Bar Meals: *12-2, 6.30-9.30; bar snacks both sessions*   **Restaurant:** *7-10 Fri/Sat only*
Typical Dishes BAR: *chunky vegetable soup £1.60, mackerel paté £2.50, beefsteak and mushroom pie £4.50, fish pie £4.50, king prawn kebab £4.50, chocolate pecan pie £1.80*
RESTAURANT *set dinners from £8.50: curried parsnip soup, cannelloni with mushroom and basil sauce, cassoulet, citrus chicken, cod Véronique, heavenly pie   Vegetarian Meals: pasta and aubergine bake £3.80   Children's Menu   Children's Portions (some)*   Beer
Butcombe; Eldridge Pope; Whitbread Flowers   Cider   *Rich's   Family Room   Outdoor Play Area   Garden   Outdoor Eating   Accommodation: 3 bedrooms, all en suite, from £34 (single £24)   Children Welcome Overnight   Cots Available   Check-in: by arrangement   Credit Cards: Access, Visa*

WEST PENNARD   Red Lion

Glastonbury Road BA6 8NH
Tel: (0458) 32941
Open: 11.30-3, 5.30-11
Licensees: W G Buskin and L A Jessemey

New owners here, with ordinary-looking menus, but it's long been a popular bed and breakfast pub, with rooms in a converted barn across the way. No children unless residents.

Bar Meals: *12.30-2.30, 6.30-9.30 (12.30-2, 7.30-9 Sun); bar snacks lunchtime*
Typical Dishes BAR: *home-made soup £1.50, garlic bread £1.75, lasagne £3.95, steak and kidney pie £4.95, breaded cod £3.95, apple pie £1.95   RESTAURANT: prawn cocktail £3.25, chicken Kiev £7.50, veal £9.50, fresh salmon £8.50, meringue nests £1.95   Vegetarian Meals: lasagne £3.95   Children's Portions*   Beer   *Hall & Woodhouse; Oakhill; Thompsons*   Cider   *Inch's   Garden   Accommodation: 7 bedrooms, all en suite, from £45 (single £30)   Children Welcome Overnight (minimum age 2)   Check-in: after midday   Credit Cards: Access, Amex, Visa*

WILLITON Foresters Arms Hotel 55 Long Street (A39)   Tel: (0984) 32508.
17th century coaching inn with real fire, family room, beer garden, skittle alley and restaurant. Bar meals lunch and evening; bedrooms. Cotleigh, Hall & Woodhouse, Hook Norton beers. Open: 11–2.30, 5–11 (all day Sat and summer).

WINSFORD   Royal Oak

Exmoor National Park TA24 7JE
Tel: (064 385) 455
Open: 11-2.30, 6-11
Licensee: Charles Steven

A hotel in a sleepy Exmoor village resistant to street lighting and noise. Despite the hotel status, very much a village local, and a lovely old thatched inn. A pleasantly refurbished, semi-smart, relaxing interior, nice home-made food (we've previously praised presentation and service in the restaurant particularly), and well-equipped bedrooms with excellent breakfasts. Some of the rooms are in an annexe. The inn's also notable for its unusually good vegetarian choice – an entire menu of them in the restaurant. Children can eat in the back bar only.

Bar Meals: *12-2, 6.30-9.30; bar snacks both sessions   Restaurant: (12.30-1.30 Sun only), 7.30-9.30   Typical Dishes BAR: home-made soup £1.75, home-made paté £3.95, steak and kidney pie £5.75, chicken pie £5.75, fish pie £5.75, summer pudding £2.25*
RESTAURANT: *table d'hote menu £18, or a la carte: cascade of prawns £5.75, roast duck £14.50, escalope of venison £13.50, rack of lamb £14.60, pudding of the day £2.75   Vegetarian Meals   Children's Portions*   Cheese   Beer   *Whitbread Flowers Original, IPA   Children Allowed in Bar to Eat   Riverside Garden   Outdoor Eating   Accommodation: 14*

*bedrooms, all en suite, from £89.50 (single £59.50)   Children Welcome Overnight   Cots Available   Check-in: all day   **Credit Cards:** Access, Amex, Diners, Visa*

WOOKEY — Burcott Inn

near Wells BA5 1NJ
Tel: (0749) 673874
Open: 11.30-2.30, 6-11

Popular roadside country pub, pleasingly simple in style, with lots of guest beers and interesting daily specials. Same menu in dining room. Real fire. No music.

*Bar Meals: 12-2, 6-9.30; bar snacks both sessions   **Typical Dishes:** home-made soup £1.40, prawn cocktail £2.75, veal rustica £6.95, chicken princess £6.75, fillet Diana £11.25, apple and raspberry crumble £1.85   Vegetarian Meals: spaghetti Napoletana Children's Portions   **Beer**   Archers; Ash Vine; Butcombe, Fullers   Family Room Outdoor Play Area   Garden   Outdoor Eating   Summer Barbecue   **No Credit Cards***

WOOLVERTON — Red Lion

on A36 BA3 6QS
Tel: (0373) 830350
Open: noon-11
Licensee: Barry Lander

Fronted by neat lawns, and set back from the busy road, this smart pub has flagstone floors, exposed stone, and open fires within, and a pleasingly informal approach to good eating. Hearty portions of interesting salads, attractively presented, and unusually-filled baked potatoes dominate the bar menu; hot daily specials also feature. The garden is lovely for a summer lunch.

*Bar Meals: 12-2(2 Sun), 7-10   **Typical Dishes:** chicken korma salad £5.75, savoyard salad £3.50, prawn and avocado salad £3.85, seafood platter £5.80   Vegetarian Meals Children's Portions   **Beer**   Bass; Wadworth   Family Room   Garden   Outdoor Eating* ***No Credit Cards***

STAFFORDSHIRE

ALREWAS — George & Dragon

Main Street DE13 7AE
Tel: (0283) 791476
Open: 11-2.30 (12-2.30 Sun), 6-11
Licensee: John Clayton Greenway

The extremely long-serving Stanbrooks have now left the George & Dragon, a very popular old inn with three characterful bars opening off a central servery. Bedrooms are modern, in the adjoining Claymar Hotel.

*Bar Meals: 12-2, 7-9.30; bar snacks both sessions   **Typical Dishes:** beef and onion soup £1.25, chicken paté £1.80, Pedigree pie £3.25, roast meat meals £3.95, chicken paprecash £4.25, apple crumble £1.40   Vegetarian Meals   Children's Menu/Portions   **Beer**   Marston Pedigree   Children Allowed in Bar to Eat   Outdoor Play Area   Garden Accommodation: 16 bedrooms, all en suite, from £40 (single £30)   Check-in: all day   **Credit Cards:** Access, Visa*

ALSTONEFIELD — Watts-Russell Arms

Hopedale DE6 2GD
Tel: (033 527) 271
Open: 11.30-3, 6.30-11 (12-2, 7-11 winter)
Licensees: Stephanie and Alf Harrison

Stone-built estate pub in the Peak District National Park, in good walking country.

Bar Meals: 12-2, 7-9; bar snacks both sessions **Typical Dishes:** *oxtail soup £1.30, mushrooms in port £1.80, gammon £5, home-made chilli £3.85, all-day breakfast £3.75, sherry trifle £1.30 Vegetarian Meals: omelettes £3.75 Children's Menu* ■ Beer ■ *Mansfield Children over 5 Allowed in Bar to Eat Outdoor Play Area Garden Outdoor Eating* **No Credit Cards**

ALTON Bulls Head Hotel High Street Tel: (0538) 702307. Splendid 18th century village inn in conservation area, not far from Alton Towers. Decent home cooked restaurant food; also lunchtime bar meals; cheap bedrooms, all with showers. Burton Bridge, Tetley beers.

AMINGTON Gate Inn Tamworth Road. Extended and smartened-up dining pub with decent lunch and evening bar meals, conservatory family room, small garden by canal. Marston's beers.

BOBBINGTON Six Ashes on A458. Friendly pub with home cooked lunches, Banks's beers.

BURSTON — Greyhound

Stafford ST18 0PR
Tel: (08897) 263
Open: 11-3, 6.30-11
Licensee: Alan Jordan

Simple country pub with a plainly furnished, carpeted interior and 'playland' for children.

Bar Meals: 12-2, 7-10; bar snacks both sessions **Typical Dishes:** *minestrone 60p, prawn cocktail £2.18, steak pie £4.95, sirloin steak £6.50, salmon steak £5.95, cherry pie £1.40 Vegetarian Meals: lasagne Children's Menu* ■ Beer ■ *Burtonwood Bitter; Ind Coope Burton Ale, Tetley Bitter Family Room Outdoor Play Area Garden Outdoor Eating* **Credit Cards:** *Access, Visa*

BUTTERTON — Black Lion

opposite the church ST13 7ST
Tel: (05388) 232
Open: 12-3 (not Wed), 7-11
Licensee: Ronald Smith

Interesting enough old pub built of Derbyshire stone, with horse brasses, music and games machines in its four small, characterful rooms. Recent refurbishments are complete: bedrooms are now en suite, and patio areas created outdoors; B&B might be good for walkers. Let down by the food: blackboards repeated printed menus verbatim on our last visit (steaks, grills, fried fish); carvery restaurant.

Bar Meals 12-2, 7-9.30; bar snacks both sessions Vegetarian Meals: lasagne Children's Menu ■ Beer ■ *McEwan, Theakston, Youngers Family Room Garden Outdoor Eating*

Accommodation: 3 bedrooms, all en suite, from £40 (single £24)   Children Welcome
Overnight   Cot Available   Check-in: all day   **Credit Cards:** Access, Amex, Visa

---

CAULDON   Yew Tree

Cauldon Lane, Waterhouses ST10 3EJ
Tel: (0538) 308348
Open: 10-3, 6-11
Licensee: Alan East

Snacks like sausage rolls, pork pies, and quiches, all at very low prices, are the only
food available at this classic 17th century pub. But food is hardly the point here.
Instead, enjoy Alan East's vast collection of antiques and bric-a-brac, the Persian rugs
which overlay original quarry tiled floors, cast-iron copper-top tables, a working
pianola and giant Victorian music boxes, which still operate for just 2p. In summer,
a restored 1928 charabanc plies a regular Sunday trade between the pub and nearby
bus and railway stations. Sleepy and undiscovered it is not, but worth a visit
neverthless: go in the evening and hear the landlord performing on the pianola.

Beer   *Draught Bass; Burton Bridge   Family Room*   **No Credit Cards**

GRINDON   Cavalier

Tel: (0538) 8285
Open: 12 (11.30 Sat)-3.30 (not Mon), 7-11
Licensee: Lynda Blunden

Just a mile from the Manifold Valley, a partly-carpeted, partly-tiled, rustically
furnished and decorated old pub, a popular walkers' halt. Food is a mixture of the
routine and restauranty: good pies and casseroles from £4.50.

Bar Meals: *Tue-Sun lunch, daily evenings;   bar snacks both sessions   Vegetarian Meals
Children's Portions*   **Beer**   *Marston; Ruddles   Family Room   Outdoor Play Area
Garden*

HUDDLESFORD Plough, Huddlesford Lane (off A38) Tel: (0543) 432389:
Open-plan, pleasant pub by canal, popular for lunchtime and evening bar meals (not
Sunday, nor all day Monday). Garden. Ansells, Ind Coope beers. Open: 11-2.30, 6-11

LEEK Abbey Inn Abbey Green Road Tel: (0538) 382865. Comes into the 'useful
to know' category: a quiet country spot, with bedrooms in converted outhouses
(£40 a double); three drinking rooms leading off servery, one very pubby. Very
ordinary food though. Bass beers.

LICHFIELD Pig & Truffle Tamworth Street. Popular, immaculately-kept dining
pub, with a changing specials board, and attentive service.

LONGSDON Holly Bush Denford. Superb canalside location, with play area,
and good local walks; busy with ramblers and boating types in summer. Well-kept
Ind Coope Burton Ale, too, but food disappoints – generally of the scampi and chips
sort. For bar meals, try **The Wheel,** Leek Road, Longsdon: wide and varied menu
(too long), dishes like chicken marengo, and home-made chips; pleasant coal-fired
interior, with notable toby jug collection; patio. Bass, Tetley beers.

NEWCASTLE UNDER LYME Slug & Lettuce Hassell Street. Dependable Slug
and Lettuce standards and attractive piney interior; as the name suggests, particularly
attentive to vegetarians. Ind Coope beers.

ONECOTE   Jervis Arms

near Leek ST13 7RU
Tel: (0538) 304206
Open: 12-2.30, 7-11
Licensee: Robert Sawdon

17th century Peak District pub in a riverside spot, a little wooden bridge connecting car park to garden. Changed hands recently. There's a self-catering cottage for let by the week.

Bar Meals: 12-2, 7-10; bar snacks both sessions   *Typical Dishes:* Scotch broth £1, prawn cocktail £2, chicken masala £4, fillet steak £7.50, home-made cottage pie £2.95, home-made apple pie £1.50   *Vegetarian Meals:* savoury cheesecake £3.95   Children's Menu/Portions   **Beer**   Bass, Ruddles, Theakston, Webster's   Family Room   Outdoor Play Area   Riverside Garden   Outdoor Eating   **No Credit Cards**

PENKHULL   Greyhound

Manor Court Street
Tel: (0782) 48978
Open: 12-3, 6.30-11
Licensee: John Chadwick

Originally the local manor courthouse, with cells in what are now the pub cellars, but little of the 16th century original remains, though some materials were used in the 1936 rebuilding: one bar is smartly traditional, another distinctly post-war in style. Bar food's nothing special; opt for a more interesting hot daily special.

Bar Meals: lunchtime;   bar snacks   *Typical Dishes:* cottage pie, chicken casserole, hotpot (main courses from £2.50)   *Vegetarian Meals*   Childrens Menu   **Beer**   Ansells; Ind Coope; Tetleys   Children Allowed in Bar to Eat   Patio/terrace

PENKRIDGE Star. Opened-up, refurbished village local; lunchtime bar meals include a home-made steak and kidney pie. Banks's beers.

RAMSHAW ROCKS   Winking Man

Blackshaw Moor ST13 8UH   ▼
Tel: (0538) 34361
Licensees: Gary and Sue Sheldon

Named after a local rock formation, at the heart of the Peak District. Worth trying for lunch but probably best avoided in the evenings – three discos a week in the function room.

Bar Meals: 12-2, 7-10 (9.30 Fri-Sun); bar snacks both sessions   *Typical Dishes:* celery soup £1.10, farmhouse paté with port £1.45, home-made steak and kidney pie £3.95, goujons of chicken breast £3.95, T-bone steak £8.50, choux pastry swans £1.50   *Vegetarian Meals:* stilton mushrooms £3.95   Children's Portions   **Beer**   Draught Bass   Children Allowed in Bar to Eat (lunch)   Patio/terrace   Outdoor Eating   **No Credit Cards**

RUDYARD   Poachers

Tel: (053 833) 294
Open: 12-2.30, 7-11
Licensees: Anne and Graham Yates

Formerly the Station Hotel, recently taken over, with Whitbread brewery backing.
There's now a definite emphasis on food here, with lots of standard catering of the
chicken kiev and stuffed plaice sort on the menu, more interesting things on the
daily blackboard (listed below), and an evening/Sunday lunch "Kipling's" à la carte,
with more of the same, plus steaks and fish with fancy sauces, and sweets from the
trolley.

Bar Meals: lunch and evening **Restaurant:** *Wed-Sat eves, Sun lunch* **Typical Dishes:**
*celery and mushroom soup £1, lamb dinner, liver and onions, goujons of plaice, sugar-baked
ham, rum truffle cake (main courses from £4)* *Vegetarian Meals* *Children's Menu*
Beer *Marston; Whitbread* *Family Room* *Patio/terrace*

TATTENHILL   Horseshoe Inn

Main Street DE13 9SD
Tel: (0283) 64913
Open: 11.30-3, 5.30-11
Licensees: Michael and Maureen Bould

Pleasant cream-painted roadside village inn dating back to 1680. An interesting wine
list – the Beaujolais range is imported direct – but both bar and à la carte menus are
on the predictable side, with one or two interesting exceptions.

*Bar Meals and Restaurant: 12-2 (1.30 Sun), 5.45-9.15 (not Sun/Mon eve); bar snacks
both sessions* **Typical Dishes BAR:** *cream of leek and potato soup £1, garlic mushrooms
£2.05, home-made steak and kidney pie £3.60, filled Yorkshire pudding £3.10, fruit pie*
RESTAURANT: *lettuce soup £1.15, prawn and egg marie rose £2.90, chicken fillet with
stilton sauce £8.70, baked trout with amaretto £6.75, fresh salmon £8.75* *Vegetarian
Meals: nut roast* *Children's Menu/Portions* Beer *Marston Pedigree, Owd Rodger
(winter)* Whisky *Family Room* *Outdoor Play Area* *Garden* *Outdoor Eating* **Credit
Cards:** *Access, Visa*

TUTBURY   Olde Dog & Partridge

High Street DE13 9LS   FOOD
Tel: (0283) 813030   B&B
Open: 10.30-3, 6-11
Licensee: Yvette Martindale

There's a 500 year tradition of hospitality at the Dog and Partridge, and much of the
original 15th century building is still happily intact, its half-timbered frontage with
diamond leaded windows classic picture postcard material, bedecked with flower
tubs and hanging baskets in summer. In 1568, Mary Queen of Scots was detained in
nearby Tutbury castle – "sorrowed for freedom, not from love" – at which time the
inn was already a celebrated haunt for the aristocracy. The building was further
extended in the 18th and 19th centuries to cope with its new-found fame as a
coaching inn on the main Liverpool/London route, and over the last ten years has
been painstakingly renovated to achieve the levels of comfort expected in the 1990s.
Hotel reception apart, the entire ground floor has now been made over to dining. A
series of rooms with alcoves and olde worlde partitions manages to give the
impression of a collection of intimate spaces, despite the presence, when full, of

upwards of 150 diners; yet there's still room for the pianist, one of whose jobs it is to trot out Happy Birthday, virtually on call, several times a night. All sections, however, lead to the buffet and carvery, which is what they all come for. It's a catering operation of quality-numbing complexity, and you'll work hard to find – and be served – the quality bits (described as à la carte) when all around are single-mindedly set on quantity, amassing groaning plates of roasts and potatoes piled high with self-served vegetables. There are bars at each end whose sole contribution to olde worlde charm is their thatched awnings, but these are scarcely pubby, and once the clamour for food has abated, they revert to hotel residents' bars in all but name. Three original bedrooms remain in the main building, whose black and white panelling and creaking, uneven floors provide the kind of romance craved by honeymooners and Americans. The remainder, however, are housed in an adjacent Georgian property which contains a fascinating central spiral staircase, ascending to an ornate glass-domed roof. All individually decorated, these bedrooms offer comprehensive 20th century comforts from private bathrooms to satellite television and mini-bars.

Bar Snacks: 12-2 (not Sun) **Restaurant:** *12-2, 6.30-10 (9.30 Sun, 6.15-10.30 Sat)* **Typical Dishes:** *cold table: help-yourself roasts and salads £5.25-£7.25; a la carte: vegetable soup £1.10, dressed crab £3.95, roast beef and Yorkshire pudding £6.95, beef and Owd Rodger pie £4.95, champagne salmon £7.75, local ice-creams £2.75 Vegetarian Meals: stroganoff £5.50 Children's Portions* **Beer** *Marston Pedigree Family Room Garden* **Accommodation:** *17 bedrooms, all en suite, from £59.50 (single £49.50) Children Welcome Overnight Cot Available Check-in: all day* **Credit Cards:** *Access, Amex, Visa*

UTTOXETER Roebuck Inn, 37 Dovebank (A518). Characterful 17th century inn with quarry-tiling and real fires; lunchtime and evening meals cooked by the landlord; five modest bedrooms. Bass beers.

WARSLOW   Greyhound

on B5053
Tel: (0298) 84249
Open: 11.30-3, 6.30-11 (11.45 Sat)
Licensees: Bob Charlton and Colin Cook

Relaxing, nicely furnished old pub, with beams, quality furnishings, including one or two antique settles, and an open fire. Close to the Manifold Valley. Bedrooms are cheap and modest (around £30 a double); children are allowed in the games room or public bar until 9pm; no proper family room.

Bar Meals: 12-2.30, 6.30-10; bar snacks both sessions **Typical Dishes:** *home-made soup £1, chicken in cider, curried pork, treacle tart (main courses from £3.50) Vegetarian Meals* **Beer** *Bass Garden Outdoor Eating*

WETTON Olde Royal Oak. Stone-built village pub, part-traditional, part-contemporary in style, with a sun lounge at the rear leading to the garden. Standard enough bar food; home-made steak and kidney pie, roast Sunday lunches popular. Ruddles, Theakstons beers. Open: 11.30-2.30, 7-11; perhaps longer in summer.

WHITMORE   Mainwaring Arms

Open: 11-2.30 (3 Sat), 5.30-11
Licensee: Peter Slack

Delightfully unspoilt old pub, with a maze of old-fashioned little rooms, lots of oak beams, several open fires, and a mix of ancient and modern furnishings. Lovely in summer, when barbecues are held on the cobbled rear terrace, or for its front seating area, with a classically English view of the quaint old church.

Bar Meals: lunch and evening; bar snacks both sessions   **Typical Dishes:** home-made soup £1, steak and kidney pie, gammon and eggs, chicken casserole (main courses from around £3.50), trifle   Vegetarian Meals   Children's Portions   ▮Beer▮ Bass; Marston; Whitbread   Children Allowed in Bar to Eat (lunch)   Patio/terrace   Outdoor Eating

SUFFOLK

BARDWELL   Six Bells

The Green IP31 1AW   ▼
Tel: (0359) 50820
Open: 12-2.30 (inc Sun), 7-11
Licensees: Richard and Carol Salmon

Regional finalists in the Pub Caterer competition for the last few years. Eat in the warm and traditionally furnished bar, or the simple restaurant with its country tables and chairs. Bedrooms are converted from the old barn and stables, all with shower rooms and all on the ground floor. Nice wine list.

Bar Meals and Restaurant: 12-2, 7-9.30; bar snacks lunchtime   **Typical Dishes BAR:** carrot and coriander soup £1.95, hot and spicy mushrooms £1.95, steak and ale pie £5.25, tipsy roast lamb £5.95, fishermans bake £4.95, profiteroles   **RESTAURANT:** celery soup with stilton toast £1.95, stilton and bacon filo parcels £2.75, chicken with brandy and apricot sauce £8.95, peppered fillet steak £11.50, salmon thermidor £8.95, toasted lemon cream sorbet £2.45   Vegetarian Meals: crispy-coated vegetables £4.45   Children's Menu/Portions   ▮Beer▮ Adnams Best; Wadworth 6X   Children Allowed in Bar to Eat   Outdoor Play Area   Garden   **Accommodation:** 7 bedrooms, all en suite, from £50 (single £28)   Children Welcome Overnight   Cot Available   Check-in: all day   **Credit Cards:** Access, Visa

---

BLYFORD   Queens Head

Southwold Road IP19 9JY
Tel: (050 270) 404
Open: 11-3, 6.30-11
Licensee: A R Matthews

Traditional features at the family-run Queens Head include a huge log fire, low-beamed ceiling, secret passage, and a charming ghost. It's the smallest pub in the area, with the largest menu. Vintage cars meet outside. No juke box, no music, no gaming machines.

Bar Meals: 12-2.30; bar snacks   **Restaurant:** 7-9.30   **Typical Dishes BAR:** game soup with port £1.85, whole garlic prawns £3.50, steak, kidney and mushroom pie £5.25, fresh rabbit casserole £4.25, wholemeal cheese and onion quiche £3.65, bread and butter pudding £1.85   **RESTAURANT:** venison in red wine £7.10, duckling with peaches £7.75, chicken with stilton sauce £5.95   Vegetarian Meals: pasta £4.50   Children's Menu/Portions   ▮Beer▮ Adnams   Family Room   Outdoor Play Area   Garden   Outdoor Eating   Summer Barbecue   **No Credit Cards**

BLYTHBURGH   White Hart

Halesworth IP19 9LQ
Tel: (0502) 70217
Open: 11-2.30, 7-11 (all day summer)
Licensee: Don Williamson

16th century inn on a much older site; splendid Elizabethan and Stuart features, and lots of people, as it's on the A12; despite the roadside location, there are lovely views across the river and marshes. Volleyball and petanque are played on the lawn, and there are cream teas 2.30-5.30 in summer, as well as an all-day salad bar.

Bar Meals: 12-2, 6.30-9.30; *bar snacks both sessions* **Typical Dishes:** *spicy lentil soup £1.75, prawns in garlic butter, steak and kidney pie £4.50, peppered fillet of pork £5.50, fish pie £4.50, apple pie* *Vegetarian Meals: crispy mushroom layer* *Children's Portions* ▆Beer▆ *Adnams* *Family Room* *Outdoor Play Area* *Garden* *Outdoor Eating* **Credit Cards:** *Access, Visa*

BRADFIELD ST GEORGE Fox & Hounds Felsham Road. Cheery, if not exactly beautiful pub, popular for food, some of it ambitious. Greene King beers.

BRANDESTON   Queens Head

The Street IP13 7AD
Tel: (072 882) 307
Open: 11.30-2.30, 5.30 (6 Sat)-11
Licensee: A P Smith

Splendid country pub with lovely summer garden and a good family room; open fire; no music, and a drinks-only rear bar.

Bar Meals: 12-2, 7-9.30 (not Sun eve); *bar snacks both sessions* **Typical Dishes:** *beef and vegetable soup £1.50, shell-on prawns £2.95, home-made beef lasagne £3.95, sausage and onion pie £3.50, fresh fruit pavlova* *Vegetarian Meals: home-made mushroom and nut pancake £3.25* *Children's Menu/Portions* ▆Beer▆ *Adnams* ▆Cider▆ *Children Allowed in Bar to Eat* *Outdoor Play Area* *Garden* *Outdoor Eating* **Accommodation:** *2 bedrooms, sharing a bathroom, from £30 (single £15)* *Children Welcome Overnight* *Check-in: by arrangement* **No Credit Cards**

BROME   Oaksmere

near Eye IP23 8AJ
Tel: (0379) 870326
Licensee: Michael Spratt

16th century country hotel surrounded by 20 acres of grounds and parkland. Imaginative bar meals in the pubby, beamed Tudor Bar.

Bar Meals: 12-2, 7-10 **Typical Dishes:** *carrot and coriander soup, fettucine with cream and parmesan, scallop-stuffed chicken, stir-fried beef, plum crumble (main courses from £4.50)* *Vegetarian Meals* ▆Cheese▆ ▆Beer▆ *Adnams; Courage* *Garden* **Credit Cards:** *Access, Amex, Diners Visa*

BURES   Eight Bells

Colchester Road CO8 5AE
Tel: (0787) 227354
Open: 11-2.30, 6-11

Attractive pub which recently became a free house. Simple home cooking.

Bar Meals: 12-2, 7-10; bar snacks both sessions   ***Typical Dishes:*** *white onion soup £1.10, prawn cocktail £2, toad in the hole £2, lamb chops £2.75, mixed grill £3.25, bread and butter pudding £1.25   Vegetarian Meals: pizza £1.50   ▇Beer▇ Benskins; Greene King   Children Allowed in Bar to Eat   Patio/terrace   Outdoor Eating   **No Credit Cards***

BURY ST EDMUNDS   Masons Arms

Whiting Street IP33 1NX
Tel: (0284) 753955
Open: 11-11 (11-3, 5-11 winter)
Licensee: Chris Warton

Popular town centre pub with a routine pub grub menu of things with chips, and a much more interesting specials board offering fresh home-cooked and exceptional value food, especially so the fish, seafood and steaks.

Bar Meals: 12-2, 7-9.30 (12-9.30 summer); bar snacks both sessions   ***Typical Dishes:*** *gazpacho £1.30, deep-fried camembert £2.45, home-made steak and kidney pie £3.50, home-made lasagne £3.50, grilled fresh plaice £4.50, tipsy bread and butter pudding Vegetarian Meals: curry   Children's Portions   ▇Beer▇ Greene King   Children Allowed in Bar to Eat   Outdoor Play Area   Patio/terrace   Outdoor Eating   **No Credit Cards***

BUXHALL   Crown

Mill Road IP14 3BW
Tel: (0449) 736521
Open: 11.30-2.30, 6.30-11
Licensees: Robert and Caroline Mahon

The still fairly new Mahons were previously at the Oak in Surbiton and the Albany, Thames Ditton, Surrey, and so are very experienced at catering in popular dining pubs. All food is home-cooked; no chips available. This is a tucked-away 15th century cottage pub with original beams throughout.

Bar Meals: 12-2.30, 7-10 (not Mon eve); bar snacks both sessions   ***Typical Dishes:*** *curried parsnip soup, salmon mousse, pork Dijon, venison in red wine, leek and ham provencale, raspberry pavlova   Vegetarian Meals: vegetable and garlic pasta   Children's Portions   ▇Beer▇ Adnams; Felinfoel; Greene King   Children Allowed in Bar to Eat   Outdoor Play Area   Garden   Outdoor Eating   **Credit Cards:** Access, Visa*

CAVENDISH   Bull

High Street C010 8AX
Tel: (0787) 280245
Licensees: Lorna and Mike Sansome

Homely 500-year old village pub run with great style, its mellow atmosphere enhanced by wall timbers and beams, heavy settles and lolling dogs. Simple, honest food from a tiny menu. Also recommended for bed and breakfast: three decent-sized cottagey bedrooms, white-painted and white-wood furnished, with lots more original beams; morning tea brought to the room; ground floor residents' lounge.

Bar Meals: 12-1.45, 6-8.30 *(Thur-Sat only); bar snacks both sessions* **Typical Dishes:** *steak and kidney pie £3.60, lasagne £3.50, apple crumble Vegetarian Meals* `Cheese` `Beer` *Adnams Garden* **Accommodation:** *3 bedrooms, sharing one bathroom and one shower room, from £35 Children Welcome Overnight Check-in: by arrangement*

George Inn The Green (A1092) Tel: (0782) 280248. Handsome bow-windowed old pub overlooking the green; decent bar food lunch and evening and four modest bedrooms. Whitbread beers.

CHELSWORTH   Peacock Inn

The Street IP7 7HU
Tel: (0449) 740758
Open: 11-3, 6-11
Licensees: A F Marsh and L R Bulgin

Genuinely unspoilt cottage pub; it's easy to pass by and not realise it's a pub at all. Inside is oak-timbered, inglenooked, and attractive dotted with an eclectic mix of pictures, some of which are for sale. Everything is immaculately kept, including the cottagey bedrooms, which also have washbasins, and share a beamed bathroom.

Bar Meals: 12-2, 6.30-10.30; *bar snacks both sessions* **Typical Dishes:** *stilton soup £2, game paté £2.50, steak and mushroom pie £5.50, pasta dishes £4.75, grilled salmon cutlet £7, apple and bramble pie £2.50 Vegetarian Meals: vegetable curry £4.75* `Beer` *Adnams; Greene King; Mauldons Children Allowed in Bar to Eat Garden Outdoor Eating* **Accommodation:** *5 bedrooms, sharing a bathroom, from £42 (single £24) Check-in: all day* **No Credit Cards**

CHEVINGTON Greyhound Inn Tel: (0284) 850765. Authentic Indian cooking, both meaty and vegetarian, at an otherwise ordinary village pub run by curry enthusiasts; meals 12-2, 7-10; children allowed in to eat; garden; Greene King beers. Open: 12-2.30 (not Mon/Wed), 7-11.

CLARE   Bell Hotel

Market Hill CO10 8NN   ♥
Tel: (0787) 277741
Open: all day
Licensees: Brian and Gloria Miles

Developments at this imposing half-timbered 16th century posting house since our last edition have brought a successful conservatory extension, a new rear terrace and landscaping in the garden. Bars are beamed and convivial, with open fires and splendid carved furniture; bar food is fairly routine, with steaks, pasta and pizzas leading the field; there's also a restaurant. Bedrooms are stylish and comfortable, traditionally furnished and strikingly decorated in the courtyard annexe; cottagey and simple in the main building. All the courtyard rooms are en suite; main house ones are a mixture.

Bar Meals: 12-2, 7-9.30; *bar snacks both sessions* *Vegetarian Meals* `Beer` *Nethergate Family Room Garden Outdoor Eating* **Accommodation:** *21 bedrooms, most en suite, from £50 (single £33) Check-in: all day* **Credit Cards:** *Access, Amex, Diners, Visa*

COCKFIELD — Three Horseshoes

Stows Hill IP30 0JD
Open: 12-2.30, 6-11
Licensee: Gerard Beattie

Thatched 14th century cottage pub, originally part of a hall house and court, and an alehouse since the early 19th century. Period lounge and lively locals' public bar. The home of the Pudding Club, for lovers of suety, custard-covered English puds (Thursday evenings, book early).

Bar Meals and Restaurant: 12-2, 6-9   Typical Dishes BAR: lentil and bacon soup £1.25, beef in Abbot Ale, steak and kidney pie, chicken curry (main courses around £4), ginger pudding with rum sauce   RESTAURANT: crab au gratin £1.95, steak, Guinness and oyster pie £5.25, pork and pineapple hotpot £4.95, plaice stuffed with prawns £4.95 Vegetarian Meals: bean and pepper goulash **Beer** *Greene King beers   Children Allowed in Bar to Eat   Garden   Outdoor Eating   No Credit Cards*

DEBENHAM Cherry Tree Cherry Tree Green Tel: (0728) 860275. Spacious local on the edge of this fine, former market town, now shrunk to village size. Home cooking lunch and evening; real fire; Tolly Cobbold beers. Open: 11-2.30, 5.45-11.

DUNWICH — Ship Inn

St James Street IP17 3DT
Tel: (072 873) 219
Open: 11-3, 6 (7 winter)-11
Licensees: Stephen and Ann Marshlain

Well-loved old smugglers' inn, overlooking the salt marshes and sea. The delightfully unspoilt public bar offers nautical bric-a-brac, a wood-burning stove in a huge brick fireplace, flagged floors and simple wooden furnishings; there's also a plain carpeted dining room. A fine Victorian staircase leads to simple homely bedrooms, light and clean with pretty fabrics and period touches, but no televisions. Good simple food in generous portions, too: the restaurant menu list below applies throughout the pub in the evenings; bar meals menu lunchtime only.

Bar Meals: 12-2, 7.30-9.15 (restaurant menu eves)   Restaurant: 7.30-9.15   Typical Dishes BAR: carrot and sweetcorn soup £1.10, home-made paté £2, cottage pie £3, lasagne £3.50, plaice and chips £3.75, boozy bread and butter pudding £1.60 RESTAURANT: cheese and onion soup £2.25, garlic mushrooms £2.75, sirloin steak £7.25, ham with peach and brandy sauce £6.50, local fish from £7.25, chocolate meringue £2.20   Vegetarian Meals: macaroni cheese   Children's Portions **Beer** *Adnams; Greene King   Family Room   Outdoor Play Area   Garden   Outdoor Eating Accommodation: 3 bedrooms, sharing 1 bath and 1 shower room, from £38 (single £19) Children Welcome Overnight   Cots Available   Check-in: by arrangement   No Credit Cards*

EARL SOHAM — Victoria

Woodbridge IP13 7RL
Tel: (0728) 685758
Open: 11.30-2.30, 5.30-11
Licensee: John Bjornson

Superb little country pub with an Icelandic landlord well-known for his passion for good home-brewed beer – it's awfully good stuff too – and modest home-cooked food of the sort that accompanies a good pint well. Simple old-fashioned furnishings, lots of wood on floors and walls, open fires and Queen Victoria pictures.

Bar Meals: 12-2, 6-10; bar snacks both sessions   **Typical Dishes:** *home-made soup £1.35, garlic mushrooms £2.05, meat lasagne £4.15, beef in beer £4.15, sweet and sour beans £3.25, meringue surprise £1.40 Vegetarian Meals* Beer *Earl Soham Brewery (on premises)* Cider *James White   Children Allowed in Bar to Eat   Garden   Outdoor Eating*   **No Credit Cards**

EDWARDSTONE White Horse Mill Green Tel: (0787) 211211. Traditional Suffolk pub decorated with old enamel signs; real fire; no music; games include steel quoits. Snacks all week; full menu Thursday–Sunday; Sunday lunch very popular. Greene King beers. Open: 11.30-2(3 Sat), 6.30-11.

ERWARTON Queens Head. Simple 16th century local, traditionally furnished; good views over estuary; lovely garden. Home cooking.

FRAMLINGHAM   White Horse

27 Well Close Square IP13 9DT
Tel: (0728) 723220
Open: 11.30-3, 6.30-11
Licensees: R J Oakey and N A Boyle

Refurbished old coaching inn, with original timbers surviving; fresh food from local suppliers; generous portions. A new games and family room, and 24 seater restaurant opened in April 1991.

Bar Meals and restaurant: 12-2.30, 7-9.30   bar snacks both sessions   **Typical Dishes** *BAR: beef and vegetable soup £1.50, avocado cheese £2.50, steak and ale pie £4, moussaka £3.50, hotpot £3.50, jam roly poly £1.50 RESTAURANT: asparagus soup £1.75, scampi kebabs £3.25, plaice £8.25, fillet Napoli £8.25, morello duckling £9.25, golden pudding £2.25 Vegetarian Meals   Childrens Menu/Portions* Beer *Ruddles, Webster's   Family Room Outdoor Play Area   Garden   Outdoor Eating   Summer barbecue*   **No Credit Cards**

Hare & Hounds, Castle Street. Whitewashed, steep-roofed, with a ramble of rooms and traditional hatch servery; bare board or flagged floors, a raised brick fireplace, and old wall settles. Scampi and chips type menu, but also home-made curries and pies. Whitbread beers.

FRAMSDEN   Dobermann

The Street IP14 6HG   ❢
Tel: (0473) 890461
Open: 11.30-2.30, 7-11
Licensee: Susan Frankland

Once called the Greyhound, now renamed for reasons incautious customers may discover should they chance their arm over the bar, this is a relaxing, well-kept attractive thatched inn. Two rooms are divided by a central log fire, and there's a good mix of furnishings, as well as prizes and pictures of the owners' dogs. No children indoors.

Bar Meals: 12-2, 7-9.30 (8 Sun)   **Typical Dishes:** *home-made soup £2.25, home-made chicken liver paté £2.95, chicken breast St Etienne £7.75, rabbit pie £5.90, steak and mushroom pie £6.25, brandy cordon bleu cake £2.75 Vegetarian Meals: nut loaf in spicy tomato sauce £4.25* Beer *Adnams; Felinfoel; Greene King* Whisky *Outdoor Play*

Area   Garden   Summer Barbecue **Accommodation:** *1 bedroom, £25 (single £18)*
Check-in: by arrangement **No Credit Cards**

FRESTON Boot Inn Shotley Road. Freston Mummers' headquarters, and
appropriately unspoilt; decent bar food includes fresh fish on Fridays. Tolly Cobbold
beers. Open: 11.30-3, 5.30-11.

GLEMSFORD   Black Lion

Lion Road CO10 7RF
Tel: (0787) 280684
Open: 12-3, 6-11
Licensee: Michael Kelvin

Despite the unremarkable exterior, and a roof which the brewery has conspicuously
failed to maintain, the Lion turns out to have a treasure of a Tudor interior complete
with half-timbered walls and rehabilitated timbers, which today serve to frame and
support the bar. With this noble lineage is mixed decor of a distinctly Edwardian
feel: quarry-tiled floors, country prints, leather armchairs and bay-window seats, all
of which is at once both uncluttered and charming. Michael and Anna Kelvin
quickly came to prominence here with their imaginative cooking, and five years on
have sought to extend their initial range. The black lion himself now has a paw in
the personalised menu of "cub's mouthfuls, pride's choices, lion's shares and tail
ends"; exemplified typically by ham guacamole (£2.95), lightly curried kocouda (as
starter £3.95, or main course £5.50), chicken champagne (copied, we hear, from a
Roux brother) and dark chocolate bavarois (£2.20). Further extending the pun,
dishes of the day are the mane attraction: for starters, perhaps, shrimps in sour cream
(£3.95) or vegetarian paté (£2.95), followed by a lamb tikka with rice (£5.25),
Mediterranean crevettes in garlic butter (£8.95), or 8 oz venison steaks, (£8.95),
from the nearby Denham estate, the largest fallow deer farm in Europe. Finally, tail
off into Jamaican crunch, chocolate whisky cake or delicious Suffolk farmhouse ice-
creams – honey and almond, peach and brandy or pistachio. Among their collection
of uniquely devised recipes, the Kelvins have drawn national attention with their
lamb chops crème de menthe, and a secret recipe steak and kidney pie, and such
attention is deserved, for this is fine food cooked with flair. An accompanying pint
of Greene King ale is drawn direct from the cask, and the wine list is carefully
selected, half a dozen of them served by the glass, including a club claret and the
house fizz. In an interesting recent experiment, they've offered a lower-priced
lunchtime menu of "daily value dishes", making eating here very good value indeed.

Bar Meals: *12-2 (not Mon, except holidays), 7-10 (not Sun); bar snacks both sessions*
Typical Dishes: *crab soup £2.30, Suffolk snails £3.95, steak and kidney pie £7.50,
chicken champagne £8.80, fresh Portuguese sardines £5.75, chocolate whisky cake £2.25*
Vegetarian Meals: *vegetable cheese bake £4.60*   **Children's Portions**   ▉ Beer ▉   *Greene King*
Children Allowed in Bar to Eat   *Outdoor Play Area*   *Garden*   *Outdoor Eating*   **No
Credit Cards**

HAWKEDON   Queens Head

Main Street (off A143)
Tel: (028 489) 218

Foodie pub with eccentric touches, such as the Roo's Tours coach (an old jalopy),
which transports parties here and back – the pub is Australian-owned.
Accommodation is planned, but no sign yet.

Bar Meals: *lunch and evening (not Mon)*   **Typical Dishes:** *home-made soup, mussels,
wood pigeon salad, seafood tagliatelle, liver and bacon casserole (main courses from £4.50)*

Vegetarian Meals ▰Beer▰ *Greene King; Nethergate   Children Allowed in Bar to Eat*
Garden **No Credit Cards**

HORRINGER   Beehive

The Street IP29 5SD
Tel: (0284) 735260
Open: 11.30-2.30 (12-2 Sun), 7-11
Licensees: Gary and Dianne Kingshott

Genuine home-made food is served throughout the bar areas here, and tables can be
booked: the ratio of reservations to casual droppers-in is usually about 50/50. A
printed menu is much more imaginative than most, and a specials board with
delicious fresh fish specials makes the choice even more difficult. Rambling,
traditionally furnished little rooms radiate off a central servery, warmed by a wood-
burning stove. The toilets have just been totally refurbished.

Bar Meals: 12-2, 7-10 (not Sun eve); bar snacks both sessions **Typical Dishes:** *sorrel
soup £1.60, parfait of duck livers and orange £3.25, local venison sausages in rich onion
gravy £4.95, omelette Arnold Bennett £4.75, stir-fry of prawns £6.95, sticky brazil nut
tart £1.95 Vegetarian Meals: broccoli and cheese bake £3.95* ▰Beer▰ *Greene King
Children Allowed in Bar to Eat   Garden* **Credit Cards:** *Access, Visa*

HOXNE   Swan

Low Street
Tel: (037 975) 275
Open: 12-2.30, 5.30-11
Licensees: Tony and Frances Thornton-Jones

The village is pronounced Hoxon. The Swan, a Grade II listed 15th century inn was
built by the Bishop of Norwich as the guest quarters to his now defunct summer
palace, and has been a hostelry since at least 1619: the original part of the building
features high ceilings and fluted oak joists. So popular is the pub food that an
ingenious system has been adopted for garden dining in which order numbers
materialise on the roof. It's a lovely place to eat: large, walled and bordered by
mature trees. You can play croquet too. Sunday lunch in the restaurant consists of a
cold buffet in summer, hot roasts in winter.

Bar Meals: 12-2 (not Sun), 7-9 weekdays; bar snacks both sessions **Restaurant:** *12-2
(Sun only), 7-9 Wed-Sat* **Typical Dishes BAR:** *leek and potato soup £1.30, mussels in
garlic butter £3.25, pasta carbonara £3.75, cheese and mushroom pancake £3.25, cod and
prawn au gratin £4.95, sticky toffee pudding £2.25* **RESTAURANT:** *onion and
coriander soup £1.50, herby cheese parcels £2.25, lamb cutlets in garlic sauce £8.95, lambs
kidneys in mustard sauce £7.95, veal escalope with lemon and parsley £7.95, blackberry
mousse Vegetarian Meals: spinach and feta pie £2.75 Children's Portions* ▰Cheese▰
▰Beer▰ *Adnams; Greene King Abbot Ale   Children Allowed in Bar to Eat   Outdoor Play
Area   Garden   Outdoor Eating* **No Credit Cards**

ICKLINGHAM Plough Inn The Street (A1101) Tel: (0638) 713370. Open-plan
village local, converted from a pair of old cottages. Riverside garden; lunch and
evening bar food (not Mon eve), real fire. Adnams, Bateman, Greene King beers.
Open: 12 (11 Sat)-3, 7-11.

IXWORTH   Pickerel Inn

High Street IP31 2HH   ♥
Tel: (0359) 30398
Open: 11-2.30 (3 Sat), 6-11
Licensee: E Vella Galea

A new licensee at the Pickerel ; an interesting menu and four bedrooms are a new feature too. It's an atmospheric, rambling, old-fashioned pub in a village just off the A143.

Bar Meals and Restaurant: 12-2, 7-9.30; bar snacks both sessions **Typical Dishes:** *tomato and red pepper soup £1.25, venison paté £2.50, chicken parmigiana £5.95, flamed pork with apricots £4.80, swordfish £5.95, chocolate fudge cake £1.95 Vegetarian Meals: mushroom and hazelnut stroganoff £4.50 Children's Portions* `Beer` *Greene King Family Room Outdoor Play Area Patio/terrace Outdoor Eating* **Accommodation:** *4 bedrooms, all en suite, from £50 (single £40)* **Credit Cards:** *Access, Visa*

KEDINGTON White Horse Sturmer Road Tel: (0440) 63564. Extremely popular village pub near the famous Saxon church; decent home cooking lunch and evening; booking essential for Sunday lunch. Bedrooms. Garden. Greene King beers. Open: 11-3, 5-11.

LAVENHAM   Angel Inn

Market Place C010 9QZ   ♥
Tel: (0787) 247388
Open: 11-3, 6-11
Licensees: Roy Whitworth and John Barry

Newish tenants have revitalised this delightful early 15th century inn, overlooking the medieval marketplace and guildhall. The interior and gardens have been refurbished, and the bar opened-up, preserving, of course, the rare Tudor shop window uncovered in earlier renovations. Food is now the main thing – even the locals' bar billiard table doubles as a buffet surface at lunchtime; the menu changes twice daily, and favours fresh local produce, including vegetables; no chips. Live classical piano some lunchtimes and evenings. Nice bedrooms.

Bar Meals and Restaurant: 11.45-2.15, 6.45-9.15 (12-2, 7-9 Sun); bar snacks lunchtime **Typical Dishes BAR:** *carrot and lentil soup £1.95, fresh sardines £2.95, beef and ale pie £4.95, duck breasts with lime and ginger £7.95, fresh salmon steak poached in wine and herbs £7.75, raspberry pavlova £2.25 Vegetarian Meals Children's Portions* `Cheese` `Beer` *Nethergate; Ruddles, Webster's* `Whisky` *Family Room Outdoor Play Area Garden Outdoor Eating Summer Barbecue* **Accommodation:** *7 bedrooms, all en suite, from £45 (single £30) Children Welcome Overnight Cots Available Check-in: all day* **Credit Cards:** *Access, Visa*

LAXFIELD   Kings Head

Gorams Mill Lane IP13 8DW
Tel: (0986) 798395
Open: 11-3, 6-11
Licensee: E Macleod

Unspoilt, rethatched, repainted traditional old pub with a good mix of country furnishings and a real fire. Locals know it as the Lowhouse. There's no bar (too new-fangled a feature); instead beer is served from the barrels in the tap room. Some of the fine old settles are themselves listed and protected. Summer brings morris dancers and there's often live folk music. There's also a restaurant for which you have to book.

Bar Meals: 11.30-2.30, 6.30-10; bar snacks both sessions   Typical Dishes: Scotch broth £1.50, kipper £1.50, steak and kidney pie £3.60, pork and apple pie £3.60, lasagne £3.80, apple pie £1.50   Vegetarian Meals: macaroni cheese £2.85   Children's Menu/Portions   Beer   *Adnams; Bass, Hall & Woodhouse; Wadworth*   Cider   *Kingfisher   Family Room   Outdoor Play Area   Garden   Outdoor Eating   Summer Barbecue*   No Credit Cards

---

LIDGATE   Star Inn

The Street (B1063) CB8 9PP   ❦
Tel: (0638) 500275
Open: 12-2.30 (3 Sat), 7-11
Licensees: John and Pat Austin-Stone

Beware of ducks, when approaching this lively village local; they may be leisurely in crossing the road to the pond. It's a beamed old inn, keen on barbecues: indoor charcoal style on summer weekends, and spit-roast beef cooked over the open fire in winter; otherwise, the mixed menu includes convenience favourites, and much more interesting home cooking.

Bar Meals: 12-2.30, 7-10.30 (not Tue eve);   bar snacks both sessions   Typical Dishes: ham and pea soup £1.40, home-cured gravadlax £2.60, home-made creamy lamb korma £5.30, spicy chicken tikka £4.50, rainbow trout £4.60, summer pudding   Vegetarian Meals   Children's Portions   Beer   *Greene King   Children Allowed in Bar to Eat (lunch)   Outdoor Play Area   Garden   Outdoor Eating   Summer Barbecue*   No Credit Cards

---

LONG MELFORD   Crown Inn

Hall Street CO10 9JN
Tel: (0787) 77666
Licensees: Mr and Mrs Heavens

Historic inn, built in 1620, and recommended for bed and breakfast. Rooms in both the original building and converted coach house are individually decorated and furnished with smart darkwood pieces; one with a four-poster bed, all with the usual little comforts, including teamakers and hairdryers. The open-plan bar is refurbished in modern pastels, airy and comfortable.

Bar Meals: lunch and evening;   bar snacks both sessions   Vegetarian Meals   Children's Menu   Beer   *Adnams; Greene King   Family Room   Outdoor Play Area   Garden   Outdoor Eating   Accommodation: 12 bedrooms, all en suite, from £50   Children Welcome Overnight   Cots Available   Check-in: all day   Credit Cards: Access, Amex, Diners, Visa

---

MILDENHALL   Bell Hotel

High Street IP28 7EA
Tel: (0638) 717272
Licensee: J A Child

Family-run inn-hotel with a splendid interior of fire-blackened beams, uneven surfaces and old panelling. Recommended for bed and breakfast: rooms are unfussy, neat and comfortable, all furnished with phones, television and teamakers.

Bar Meals: lunch and evening   Vegetarian Meals   ▇Beer▇   Adnams; Greene King
Family Room   Patio/terrace   **Accommodation:** 17 bedrooms, most en suite, from £60
Check-in: all day   **Credit Cards:** Access, Amex, Diners, Visa

---

ORFORD   Kings Head

Front Street IP12 2LW   ¶
Tel: (0394) 450271
Open: 11-2.30, 6-11 (all day Sat)
Licensee: Alistair Shaw

Pleasantly modernised, very old inn with surviving Tudor details and a real fire.
Kitchen and toilets have just been refurbished. Children in restaurant only.

Bar Meals: 12-2, 6.30-9   **Restaurant:** 12-1.45, 7-9   **Typical Dishes BAR:** seafood
chowder £1.95, locally-grown samphire £3.85, chicken with pasta £5.35, hot seafood
platter £5.95, monkfish and lobster soufflé £5.95, hot ginger pudding £2.50
RESTAURANT: oysters 39p (each), dressed crab £4.95, Dover sole £9.25, fish pie
£6.05, turbot £8.95, fruit crumble £2.75   Vegetarian Meals: mushroom and garlic
tagliatelle   Children's Portions   ▇Beer▇   Adnams   Garden   Outdoor Eating
Accommodation: 6 bedrooms, sharing 2 bathrooms, from £36 (single £22)   Children
Welcome Overnight (minimum age 5)   Check-in: by arrangement   **Credit Cards:** Diners

ORFORD Jolly Sailor Quay Street Tel: (0394) 450243: Unspoilt quayside inn,
made of old ships' timbers; various rooms lead off an old-fashioned hatch servery;
unusual staircase, uncommon collectables. Simple pies, scampi, steak menu lunch
and evening until 8.45. Look out for fresh fish; local cod. Modest bedrooms.
Adnams beers. Open: 11-2.30 (12-2.30 Sun), 6-11.

PIN MILL   Butt & Oyster

Take signs for Chelmondiston off Shotley Road
Tel: (047 384) 224
Open: 11-2.30 (4 Sat), 7-11; all day summer
Licensees: Dick and Brenda Mainwaring

Classic riverside pub, chock-full of tourists when not with locals, all enjoying the
simple charm of its old settles, tiled floors and fine views: be early for a waterside
windowseat, or one of the sturdy wooden outdoor ones on the bank. The routine
bar menu is cheered up by home-cooked daily specials of the pies and casseroles
kind; few of them reach £4. Traditional pub games are popular when the crowds
have gone home.

Bar Meals: 12-2, 7-10;   bar snacks both sessions   Vegetarian Meals   Children's Menu
▇Beer▇   Camerons, Tolly Cobbold   Family Room   Patio/terrace

---

RATTLESDEN   Brewers Arms

Bury St Edmunds IP30 0RJ
Tel: (0449) 736377
Open: 12-2.30 (3 weekends, closed Mon), 7-11
Licensee: Ronald Cole

Attractive 16th century pub with a blackboard menu. All food is home-cooked on
the daily changing list.

Bar Meals: 12-2, 7-9 (not Sun eve); bar snacks lunchtime   **Typical Dishes:** *fresh tomato and tarragon soup £1.50, hot prawns in garlic and lemon £2.95, Goan chicken curry £5.20, Turkish lamb, rolled stuffed plaice with spinach and feta £5.50, bread and butter pudding £2.20 Vegetarian Meals   Children's Portions* Beer *Greene King   Children Allowed in Bar to Eat   Outdoor Play Area   Garden   Outdoor Eating*   **No Credit Cards**

REDE   Plough

Village off A143, Bury road IP29 4BE
Tel: (028 489) 208
Open: 11-3, 6.30-11
Licensees: B J and J K Desborough

Early 17th century pub in a peaceful and lovely spot by the village pond. Beams aplenty and a fine collection of teapots, as well as modern seating and occasional piped radio. Good daily specials.

Bar Meals and Restaurant: 12-2, 7-9.45; bar snacks both sessions   **Typical Dishes BAR:** *home-made soup £1.95, mussels £2.95, pork mustard £4.95, minty lamb £4.95, marlin with shellfish sauce £6.95* **RESTAURANT:** *veal in Dijon mustard and brandy £9.95, ocean chicken £9.50, Dover sole £10.95, game in season   Vegetarian Meals: mushroom stroganoff   Children's Portions* Cheese *Children Allowed in Bar to Eat Garden   Outdoor Eating*   **Credit Cards:** *Access, Visa*

RICKINGHALL   Hamblyn House

The Street IP22 1BN
Tel: (0379) 898292
Open: 10.30-3, 6.30-11
Licensees: David Robinson and George Wellings

Originally the home of one James Hamblyn, one of the founding fathers of the city of Chicago, and a fine building with strong Dutch architectural influence.
Traditional bars, and a splendid staircase sweeping up to the bedrooms; they've been refurbished in readiness for the 1992 season.

Bar Meals: 11-2.30, 6.30-9.30; bar snacks both sessions   **Restaurant:** 11-2, 7-9.30 (10.30 Sat)   **Typical Dishes BAR:** *home-made soup £1.30, prawn cocktail, steak and mushroom pie £5.75, baked halibut £7.25, salads from £3.75* **RESTAURANT:** *duck à l'orange £11.75, breast of chicken in hazelnut sauce £11.25, whole trout stuffed with prawns £9.75   Vegetarian Meals: vegetable pancake   Children's Menu/Portions* Beer *Adnams; Greene King   Family Room   Outdoor Play Area   Garden   Outdoor Eating* **Accommodation:** *6 bedrooms, 3 en suite, from £48 (single £25)   Children Welcome Overnight   Cot Available   Check-in: all day*   **Credit Cards:** *Access, Amex, Diners, Visa*

RUMBURGH Buck Inn Mill Road Tel: (098 685) 257. Unspoilt pub with flagged floors, panelled walls and ceiling in its ramble of little rooms, and a new dining room families can use. Bar Meals lunch and evening; Adnams, Greene King, Mauldon beers; real cider in summer. Open all day.

SNAPE   Golden Key

Priory Road IP17 1SQ
Tel: (072 888) 510
Open: 11-3, 6-11
Licensees: Max and Susie Kissick-Jones

Close to the Maltings concert hall, a delightful and tasteful pub with a tiled old-fashioned public end and a carpeted lounge end, a real fire at each, plus pretty furnishings and pictures. The menu is, as ever, simple but reliably good. No children indoors.

Bar Meals: 12-2.30, 6-9; bar snacks both sessions   **Typical Dishes:** *courgette and potato soup, smoked mackerel paté, steak and mushroom pie £5.95, roast beef £5.95, hot smoked haddock quiche £4.95, lemon cake £2.25   Vegetarian Meals: spinach and mushroom quiche* ▬Beer▬ *Adnams   Outdoor Play Area   Patio/terrace   Outdoor Eating* **No Credit Cards**

SNAPE Plough and Sail The Maltings: The concert hall local, traditionally stylish with alehouse decor, decent bar meals and separate restaurant. Adnams beers.

SOUTHWOLD   ★   Crown

High Street IP18 6DP
Tel: (0502) 722275
Open: 10.20-3, 6-11 (closed 2nd week Jan)
Licensee: Anne Simpson

FOOD
B&B

Local brewers, Adnams, take the credit for the stylish restoration of Southwold's central Georgian inn. While not without fault in attempting to be most things to all comers, the Crown is to be applauded for its success in bringing straightforward food, prime condition beers and excellent wines to the average spender. As the brewery's head offices happen to be housed upstairs, the nautically themed rear bar is naturally a showcase for their Mild, Bitter and Broadside ales; complete with binnacle and navigation lamps, the bar's curved and glassed-in rear panel gives the entirely fitting impression of being the flagship's bridge. To the front, facing the High Street, the Parlour serves as half lounge, half coffee shop, while the front bar and attendant restaurant, decked out with green-grained panelling and Georgian style brass lamps, has a refined air, yet is totally without pretension or stuffiness. Wines by the glass, from a list selected monthly by Simon Loftus, are kept in peak condition by the Cruover machine, and the choice is second to none. Menus are produced daily, with an accent on fresh fish. Our experience suggests that the simpler dishes are the best bet, which seems at the time of writing largely to be the result of an overworked kitchen scarcely keeping pace with demand. Minor quibbles apart, though, the selection from the keenly-priced bar meals list or fixed price restaurant menu (£12.75 for two courses, £14.75 for three) is peerless. Start with cream of watercress soup (£1.75), fritto misto de mer (£4.50) with mustard dip, or steamed green-lipped mussels "oriental", and proceed to a North Sea fish gratin (£7), half guinea fowl with lime and ginger (£6.95), spinach tortellini with tomato and basil sauce (£5.75) or, on Sundays, simple old-fashioned roast beef and Yorkshire pudding (£6.75). Substantial and satisfying puddings include hot banana fritters with a honey nut sauce (£2.75), or pear and apple crumble served with custard. The dozen well-equipped bedrooms are similarly tasteful and all have private bathrooms, though three are not strictly en suite. Free-standing furniture is antique or decent quality reproduction, and both fabrics and furnishings are conducive to a restful stay. Pleasant staff take care of the rest, by offering a warm welcome, good but informal service, and a light breakfast promptly served in one's bedroom along with the morning paper.

Bar Meals: 12.30-1.45, 7.30-9.45   *Restaurant:* 12.30-1.30, 7.30-9.30   *Typical Dishes BAR:* leek and potato soup £1.75, pan-fried herring roes in fresh herbs £3.95, beef and Adnams ale casserole £6.90, North Sea fish chowder £7, whole grilled Dover sole £7.90, fresh mixed fruit crumble £2.75   *RESTAURANT dinner menu £17.75:* carrot and coriander soup, smoked fish platter, magret of duck with apricot sauce, tenderloin of pork, fillet of turbot   *Vegetarian Meals:* spiced vegetable strudel   *Children's Portions*   **Beer** Adnams   **Whisky**   Patio/terrace   Outdoor Eating   *Accommodation:* 12 bedrooms, all en suite, from £52 (single £33)   Children Welcome Overnight   Cots Available   Check-in: by arrangement   *Credit Cards:* Access, Amex, Visa

SOUTHWOLD Kings Head, South Green: Friendly local; children welcome; seafood specials.   **Red Lion**, South Green: Seafood good here too; nautical atmosphere, fine views; family room and garden.   **Swan Inn**, Market Place: Refurbished Adnams hotel bar; fresh bar food available lunch and evening.

SPROUGHTON   Beagle

Old Hadleigh Road IP8 3AR
Tel: (0473) 86455
Open: 11-2.30, 5-11
Licensee: W M Freeth

Tucked away out of the main village (get directions), the Beagle opened in 1987, converted from four farm cottages. There's now also a conservatory built on the side of the lounge bar. Reliably good food and a splendid sheltered garden.

Bar Meals: 12-2.15 (not Sun)   *Typical Dishes:* oxtail soup £1.50, Parma ham and melon £2.90, sausage and liver casserole £4.25, sweet and sour pork £4.25, chicken and mushroom pie £4.90, coffee and brandy gateau   *Vegetarian Meals:* macaroni bake £3.50   **Beer** Adnams; Bass; Greene King; Mauldon   Family Room (minimum age 5)   Garden   Outdoor Eating   *Credit Cards:* Access, Visa

---

STOKE-BY-NAYLAND   Angel Inn

near Colchester CO6 4SA
Tel: (0206) 263245
Open: 11-2.30, 6-11
Licensee: Peter Smith

Soft lamplight glows in the windows of this solid, beautifully restored old inn. Inside, the bar divides into two: a comfortable lounge bar with a brick fireplace, log-burning stove, exposed timbers and wooden furnishings, and a real sitting room with deep sofas, wing chairs and a grandfather clock. Fresh fish features prominently on the menu; reliably delicious food. Bedrooms are also recommended. Three original house rooms are reached via a small gallery above the restaurant, the others housed in an annexe, but all decent-sized and furnished with a strong sense of style. No children indoors; they're not keen on children overnight either, but if you should insist, a minimum age of ten applies.

Bar Meals: 12-2.30, 6.30 (7 Sun)-9   *Restaurant:* 12-2 (not Tue), 7.30-9; restaurant closed all day Sun/Mon   *Typical Dishes BAR:* gazpacho £2, skewered prawns and bacon £3.85, rack of English lamb £7.95, supreme of salmon £7.75, griddled fresh skate wings £7.50, brown bread ice-cream £2.50   *RESTAURANT:* wild mushroom consommé £2.95, smoked duckling with marinated vegetables £5.50, escalope of veal with Parma ham £12.75, venison cutlets £15.50, seafood parcels in crab sauce £10.50, tuile basket of fresh fruits £3   *Vegetarian Meals:* mushrooms in Malmsey wine £4.95   **Beer** Adnams;

*Greene King; Nethergate   Patio/terrace   Outdoor Eating   **Accommodation:** 6 bedrooms, all en suite, from £51.25 (single £38.50)   Check-in: all day   **Credit Cards:** Access, Amex, Diners, Visa*

STRADBROKE Ivy House, Wilby Road (B1117) Tel: (0379) 84634. Thatched and charming pub with various rooms, dining area and family garden. Bar menu includes home cooked daily casseroles and pies; modest bedrooms. Adnams, Marston, Whitbread beers.

SUDBURY   Waggon & Horses

Acton Square, Church Walk CO10 6HG   ¶
Tel: (0787) 312147
Open: 11-3, 6.30-11
Licensee: N Irwin

Revitalised town-centre back-street turn of the century pub, popular with local families and tourists. Public bar, games room, snug and dining room, in an architecturally diverse, attractive building reached through a courtyard.

Bar Meals: 11.30-2, 6.30-9.30; bar snacks lunchtime   ***Typical Dishes:*** *home-made soup £1.20, hot garlic prawns £2.50, mixed grill £6, steak £6.75, trout £5, cheesecake £1.75 Vegetarian Meals: vegetable bake   Children's Portions*   Beer   *Greene King*   Whisky *Family Room   Outdoor Play Area   Patio/terrace   Outdoor Eating   Summer Barbecue **Credit Cards:** Access, Amex, Visa*

SUDBURY Saracens Head, Newton Green: Interesting food in bar and restaurant; pub next to golf course.

WALBERSWICK Bell Ferry Road Tel: (0502) 723109. Atmospheric old fishing pub in quaint village; character furnishings and locals; lovely garden; five bedrooms overlooking the sea; fresh fish specials. Adnams beers. Open: 11-3.30, 6.30-11.

WETHERINGSETT   Cat & Mouse

Pages Green   ☼
Tel: (0728) 860765   ☺
Open: 11-3, 5-11
Licensees: Roy and Ann Booth

Roy and Ann Booth's 'Cat and Mouse' is one of those rare pubs which defies all conventions and threatens to survive against all odds – despite breaking most of the usual rules. Here we have a staunchly traditional pride of leonine publicans who truly believe that too much food can only get in the way of the proper enjoyment of one's pint. When it comes to real ale, read several pints, unalloyed – they hope – by stodgy pies or soggy chips. Sandwiches, or bread and cheese, may logically be called the alternative here, and these are available on request. By prior arrangement, more substantial catering can be provided; otherwise, there are multifarious proprietary crisps and nibbles. But the beer is the thing. Landlord Roy runs off up to a dozen names in a single breath, each pulled straight from the casks in full view, and, greatly to his credit (though, surely, also to his own cost?) takes the greatest possible pleasure in recommending which of the brews is in prime condition that day. He and Ann bought this closed, non-trading and generally written-off pub some six years ago from a national brewer. "Flying in the face of all advice", says she, they set it up then, and run it still as a vehicle for serving prime cask-conditioned ales, plus the "odd bit of food" for those requesting it. The reason that they have succeeded is not so much a mystery as it is self-evident to the Cat's devotees. Geographically, you'll find the pub at Pages Green, at a fork in the road no more than a couple of miles from Wetheringsett. Without directions from those with local knowledge, you'll maybe never find it. We should leave it that way: for to do otherwise would only spoil the romance of it all.

Bar Meals: lunchtime;   bar snacks   *Vegetarian Meals*   **Beer**   Adnams; Brakspears; Marston; Mauldons; Nethergate   **Cider**   Garden

SURREY

ALBURY HEATH   King William IV

Little London GU5 9DB
Tel: (048 641) 2685
Open: 11-3, 5.30-11
Licensees: Michael and Helen Davids

A surprisingly old-fashioned pub for generally improved-to-death Surrey; cottagey little rooms, rustic furnishings, and attractive odd bits of bric-a-brac. Decent food too.

Bar Meals: 12-2.30, 7-10; bar snacks lunchtime   *Restaurant:* 7.30-10   *Typical Dishes BAR:* stilton and celery soup £1.60, avocado and tomato £2, beef and venison pie £4.20, pigeon casserole £4, cod mornay £3.80, treacle tart £1.85   *RESTAURANT:* soup £2, quails on toast £3.50, salmon roll with prawns £3.50, beef Wellington £8.95, wild salmon and hollandaise sauce £8.95   *Vegetarian Meals:* home-made pizza   *Children's Menu*   **Beer**   Courage; Greene King; Samuel Smith   Children Allowed in Bar to Eat   Garden   *No Credit Cards*

BLACKBROOK   Plough

Blackbrook Road (off A24)   ♛
Tel: (0306) 886603
Open: 11-2.30 (12-2.30 Sun), 6-11 (10.30 winter Mon-Thur)
Licensee: Robin Squire

Nice views through large windows in the spacious, no-smoking saloon bar; traditional public bar with sewing machine tables and a vast collection of ties; the large garden is popular for barbecues in summer. Indoors, meanwhile, the bar menu is largely routine, with scampi, lasagne, fried fish and steaks, but also home-cooked daily specials.

Bar Meals: lunch and evening (not Mon eve);   bar snacks both sessions   *Typical Dishes:* tomato and coriander soup, swordfish in ginger, pork goulash, prawn curry, fruit crumbles (main courses average £4)   *Vegetarian Meals*   **Beer**   King & Barnes   Garden

CHERTSEY Golden Grove, Ruxbury Road, St Anns Hill. Traditional, old-fashioned dining pub on the edge of woods; decent lunchtime home cooking; enormous garden.

CHIDDINGFOLD   Crown

The Green, Petworth Road GU8 4TX
Tel: (0428) 682255
Open: all day
Licensees: S T Williams and T Buchanan-Munro

New licensees at this village green-set medieval inn since our last edition; superbly characterful bars have survived intact. Still recommended for bed and breakfast, too: the rooms dividing equally between the traditional, with timbers, sloping floors and four-poster beds, and the modern, with floral patterns and contemporary wooden fittings. All have smart en suite bathrooms, and all the usual comforts.

Bar Meals: 12-2.30, 7-9.30; bar snacks both sessions **Restaurant:** *12-3, 7-11* **Typical Dishes BAR:** *chicken and asparagus soup £1.85, paté £1.95, steak and kidney pie £5.40, sausage and mash £3.95, seafood crepe in lobster sauce £4.20, chocolate profiteroles £1.95* **RESTAURANT:** *seafood bisque £2.80, smoked mackerel and apple slices with lemon mayonnaise £4.40, breast of chicken £8.20, chateaubriand (for 2) £23.50, Dover sole £18.60, white chocolate marquise with orange curacao and dark sauce £4.05 Vegetarian Meals Children's Portions* **Beer** *Hall & Woodhouse; Shepherd Neame; Wadworth; Wells Children Allowed in Bar to Eat Patio/terrace Summer Barbecue* **Accommodation:** *8 bedrooms, all en suite, from £57 (single £47) Children Welcome Overnight Cot Available Check-in: all day* **Credit Cards:** *Access, Amex, Diners, Visa*

CLAYGATE   Swan Inn

2 Hare Lane KT10 9BT   ♟
Tel: (0372) 62582
Licensees: Derek Swift and Sara Harris

In summer the unofficial pavilion HQ of the local cricket team; its verandah handily overlooks the village green. The interior is charmingly Edwardian in style, and books and prints abound. Food is unpretentious and appetising.

Bar Meals: 12-2.30, 6.30-9.30; bar snacks both sessions **Typical Dishes:** *home-made steak and mushroom pie, liver and bacon, lamb stew, fish pie (main courses around £3.50)* **Beer** *Ruddles, Webster's Patio/terrace* **Credit Cards:** *Access, Amex, Diners, Visa*

COMPTON   Harrow Inn

The Street GU3 1EG
Tel: (0483) 810379
Licensees: Roger and Susan Seaman

Four bedrooms were planned, permission pending, as we went to press, at this well-heeled commuter-belt village dining pub. Bar meals are certainly in the upper price range, but all come with fresh vegetables at least. Outdoor dining by the car park.

Bar Meals: 12-3, 6-10; bar snacks both sessions **Typical Dishes:** *stilton and vegetable soup £2.75, giant prawns with garlic and chilli £5.75, steak and kidney pie £7, fillet steak kebab £7.50, whole lemon sole with prawn and mushroom sauce £7.50, treacle tart Vegetarian Meals: curry Children's Portions* **Beer** *Ind Coope Burton Ale, Tetley Bitter Children Allowed in Bar to Eat Patio/terrace Outdoor Eating* **Credit Cards:** *Access, Visa*

COMPTON Withies Inn, Withies Lane Tel: (04868) 21158. Friendly and old-fashioned, and often very busy: good light meals in the bar, more substantial fare in the restaurant; homely cooking (12-2, 7.30-9.30). Bass beers; all credit cards.

DUNSFOLD   Sun

The Common GU8 4LE
Tel: (048 649) 242
Open: 11-3, 6-11
Licensee: Judith Dunne

Charmingly village green-set Georgian-fronted pub with a 17th century barn interior.

Bar Meals: 12-2.15, 7-10 (12-2, 7-9.30 Sun)   *Typical Dishes: leek and potato soup £2, deep-fried brie £3.50, home-made steak and kidney pie, lamb noisettes in mint and cream, grilled New Zealand green-lipped mussels (main courses from £4.50), banoffee pie Vegetarian Meals: aubergine loaf with spicy tomato sauce   Children's Portions* ▉Beer▉ *Harveys; Ind Coope   Children Allowed in Bar to Eat   Garden   Outdoor Eating   Summer Barbecue   Credit Cards: Access, Amex, Diners, Visa*

EFFINGHAM   Plough

Orestan Lane KT24 5SW
Tel: (0372) 458121
Open: 11-3, 6-11
Licensee: Roderick Sutherland

Smartly rustic, family-run pub with reliable food.

Bar Meals: 12-2, 7-9.15 (not Sun eve); bar snacks both sessions   *Typical Dishes: cauliflower and sweet pepper soup, Arbroath smokie, bacon and mushroom au gratin, cod and prawn mornay, ratatouille and feta cheese bake (main courses £3-£4), treacle tart Vegetarian Meals: mushroom, pepper and tomato pasta   Children's Portions* ▉Beer▉ *Outdoor Play Area   Garden   Outdoor Eating   No Credit Cards*

ELSTEAD   Woolpack

The Green GU8 6HD   ☀
Tel: (0252) 703106   ☺
Open: 11-2.30, 6-11   ❢
Licensees: Kevin and Jill Macready

On an old wool trading route, the tile-hung Woolpack was in fact originally built as a wool-bale store in the 18th century, and only later developed into a hostelry. Now comfortably countrified, various artefacts dotted about the place still hint at the pub's previous use: bobbins and spindles of yarn, a lamb's fleece, an ancient pair of scales and a partly woven rug. Today folk flock here (no pun intended) to enjoy the notably, famously generous portions of home-cooked dishes chosen from a long blackboard menu, which ranges from baked goat's cheese on toast with garlic and mango sauce to steak and kidney pie. The pie in question is noteworthy for featuring properly cooked on-top-of-the-pie pastry, and not a pre-cooked square stuck on top as the pie leaves the kitchen, a practice all too common in pubs these days. Not everything is what is seems though; a green pea and vegetable soup turned up full of chunks of ham, for example, which is fine so long as you're not a vegetarian. Genuinely home-made puddings are something of a cottage industry here, with the landlord's mother-in-law and other local ladies contributing to the selection, which might include apple strudel, lemon meringue pie or a nectarine, coffee and hazelnut sponge, all served with suspiciously fluffy cream. Children can have smaller portions at smaller prices, or opt for baked beans and tinned spaghetti on toast. A children's room has nursery rhyme murals on the walls and bunches of flowers hung up to dry from the ceiling; there's also a slide in the pretty garden. Jill Macready looks after the food side whilst husband Kevin, who used to work as an area manager for a brewery, takes good care of the beers, which are drawn directly from barrels racked behind the bar.

Bar Meals: 12-2, 7-10.45 (7.30-9 Sun) *Typical Dishes: pea and ham soup £2, goats cheese on toast with garlic and mango sauce £4.25, chicken tikka £6.50, pork steak in cider and sage sauce £7.50, beef groundnut stew £6.50, puff pastry banoffee pie £2.50 Vegetarian Meals: spicy mixed bean casserole £5 Children's Menu/Portions* ▊Beer▊ *Ind Coope; Shepherd Neame Family Room Outdoor Play Area Garden Outdoor Eating* **Credit Cards:** *Access, Visa*

ESHER Albert Arms, 82 High Street. Victorian bistro-style pub with light paté/cheese lunches, and more substantial meals.

FELBRIDGE   Woodcock

Woodcock Hill (A22)   ▼
Open: 11-2.30, 6-11
Licensees: Peter and Valerie Jones

Leaded windows and original beams in the original bar, a handsome lounge leading off, elegantly decorated, and a chaise-longue strewn Victorian parlour. Upstairs, meanwhile, is a smart restaurant, candle-lit in the evenings; the fish speciality here is echoed in the downstairs specials. Altogether a stylish, individual pub, with reliably good food.

Bar Meals: 12.30-2, 7-10 *Typical Dishes: home-made soup £1.60, roast beef £4.95, langoustines £6.95, fresh fish of the day, steaks (from £6) home-made puddings from £1.95 Vegetarian Meals Children's Portions* ▊Beer▊ *Harveys; King & Barnes; Ruddles Family Room Patio/terrace Credit Cards*

FOREST GREEN Parrot Inn. Parrot-themed, popular dining pub; meals lunch and evening; restaurant; garden; families welcome; Courage beers.

GOMSHALL Black Horse On A25 Tel: (048 641) 2242. Handsome three-storey village inn, originally a brewery. Attractively furnished; good summer garden; routine bar food; four bedrooms. Youngs beers.

HASCOMBE   White Horse

near Godalming GU8 4JA   ▼
Tel: (048 632) 258
Licensees: James Ward and Susan Barnett

Grade II listed, 16th century pub in a beautiful corner of Surrey.

Bar Meals: 12-2.20, 7-10.15; bar snacks both sessions *Typical Dishes: leek and potato soup £2, taramasalata £3, home-made burger £4.50, poussin Dijonnaise £4.95, fish pie £4.85, banoffee pie £2.75 Vegetarian Meals: spinach and mushroom lasagne Children's Portions* ▊Beer▊ *Fullers London Pride; Ind Coope Burton Ale Family Room Children Allowed in Bar to Eat Garden Outdoor Eating* **Credit Cards:** *Access, Amex, Visa*

HASLEMERE   Crowns

4 Wey Hill GU27 2PD
Tel: (0428) 653363
Licensee: Mr Goodchild

Previously star-rated but the menu's changed; it's steak and scampi-led, topped up
by hot home-made daily specials. The bar's attractive, with its shelves of books,
rattan furniture and attractive prints. No children indoors.

Bar Meals and Restaurant: 12-2, 7-10 (no food Sun);   bar snacks both sessions
Childrens Portions   **Beer**   *Ind Coope Burton Ale, Tetley Bitter; Gales HSB   Outdoor*
Play Area   Garden   Outdoor Eating   Summer Barbecue   **Credit Cards:** *Access, Visa*

HORSELL COMMON   Bleak House

Chertsey Road GU21 5NL
Tel: (0483) 760717
Open: 11-2.30, 6-11 (11-3, 6.30-11 Sat)

Well-known and exceedingly lively village local in good walking country; live jazz
or blues on Monday evenings; famous visitors have included the Bedser twins, John
McCarthy, and Martians from outer space, who landed their craft outside (during
the filming of War of the Worlds).

Bar Meals: 12-2, 7-9.30 (not Sun/Mon eve); bar snacks both sessions   **Typical Dishes:**
home-made soup £1.30, garlic loaf £1.30, steak, gammon, cottage pie, trout (main courses
from £4) Vegetarian Meals: cracked wheat and walnut casserole   Children's Menu
  Beer   *Ind Coope, Tetley; Youngs   Children Allowed in Bar to Eat   Outdoor Play Area*
Garden   Outdoor Eating   Summer Barbecue   **Credit Cards:** *Access, Visa*

HURTMORE   Squirrel

Hurtmore Road GU7 2RN
Tel: (0483) 860223
Open: 11-3, 6-11
Licensees: David and Jane Barnes

Attractive, well-run pub with non-smoking restaurant and bedrooms in converted
cottages.

Bar Meals: 12-2.30, 6.30-10 (7-9.30 Sun);   bar snacks both sessions   **Typical Dishes:**
stilton and celery soup £1.95, giant stuffed mushrooms £3.95, sirloin Madagascar £9.95,
tarragon chicken £6.95, lamb and sweet potato pie £6.95, treacle tart £2.50   Vegetarian
Meals: stir-fried vegetable pancakes £4.95   Children's Portions   **Beer**   *Ruddles,*
Webster's   Family Room   Outdoor Play Area   Garden   Outdoor Eating
Accommodation: *13 bedrooms, all en suite, from £45 (single £35)   Children Welcome*
Overnight   Cots Available   **Credit Cards:** *Access, Amex, Diners, Visa*

KENLEY   Wattenden Arms

Old Lodge Lane
Tel: (081) 660 8638
Open: all day
Licensee: Ron Coulston

The Coulstons have been at this splendid village pub for almost 30 years now, and offer appetising bar meals as traditionally British as the portraits of Royals past and present crowding the panelled walls.

Bar Meals: 12-2.30, 7.30-9 (not Sun); bar snacks both sessions   **Typical Dishes:** *home-made soup £1.50, prawn cocktail £2, home-made steak pie £4.50, roast beef £5, ham, eggs and chips £4.50, bread pudding   Vegetarian Meals: vegetarian pie   Children's Portions*
Beer *Bass   Outdoor Play Area   Garden   Outdoor Eating*   **No Credit Cards**

LALEHAM Feathers, The Broadway. Café-style at lunchtimes, with red check tablecloths; good light snacks; tables outside.

LEIGH Plough Church Road Tel: (030 678) 348. Traditional country inn by the green; decent lunch and evening meals in the separate restaurant (not Sun, nor Mon eve).

MICKLEHAM   King William IV

Byttom Hill (off southbound A24 between Leatherhead   ▼
and Dorking) RH5 6EL
Tel: (0372) 372590
Open: 11-2.30 (12-2.30 Sun), 6-11; 12-2.30, 7-10.30 winter
Licensee: J E Benyon

Late 18th century alehouse, built originally for Lord Beaverbrook's estate staff; the large terraced beer garden has splendid views across the Mole valley. Very much a traditional family-run concern, keen on good beer and priding themselves on noteworthy home cooking. Recently they've become vegetarian dish specialists, with at least five hot meatless options daily, in addition to a more meaty menu. Evening meals may be introduced for 1992.

Bar Meals: 12-2 (7 days a week)   **Typical Dishes:** *home-made steak, kidney and Guinness pie £4.65, pasta with prawns £4.45, king-size stuffed mushrooms £4.25, chocolate and walnut fudge cake £1.95   Vegetarian Meals: menu of specials £3.95 Children's Portions*   **Beer** *Adnams; Hall & Woodhouse; Wadworth; Whitbread Children Allowed in Bar to Eat   Garden   Outdoor Eating*   **No Credit Cards**

OATLANDS Prince of Wales Anderson Road, Oatlands Park Tel: (0392) 852082. Freshly cooked, daily changing bar food, always decent, often imaginative (especially in the evening); can get packed with local rowing types. Good range of beers; open all day.

OUTWOOD Bell Inn. Antique-furnished dining pub just across from the village green and its landmark old windmill; robustly traditional English food in civilised surroundings. Nice garden.

REDHILL Plough Inn 11 Church Road, St Johns Tel: (0737) 766686. 17th century pub in conservation area next to Earlswood Common; very popular for lunch and evening bar food (not Sundays). Gales, Ind Coope beers.

RIPLEY   Seven Stars

Newark Lane GU23 6DL
Tel: (0483) 225128
Open: 11-3, 5.30-11
Licensee: Rodney Dean

Pleasant pebbledash pub on the B367, just to the north of Ripley itself. Food is informal and reliable, a list of around a dozen home-baked pizzas central to the menu. Real fire.

Bar Meals: 12-2.30, 7-9.30; bar snacks both sessions **Typical Dishes:** *French onion soup £1.20, Ardennes paté £2, rainbow trout £5.80, garlic Pacific prawns £6.50, pizzas £4.50, treacle tart £1.50* *Vegetarian Meals: celery, cheese and almond bake £3.60* Beer *Ind Coope Burton Ale, Tetley Bitter; Ringwood Bitter* *Children Allowed in Bar to Eat* *Outdoor Play Area* *Garden* *Outdoor Eating* *Summer Barbecue*

SHAMLEY GREEN   Red Lion

Shamley Green GU5 0UB
Tel: (0483) 892202
Open: 11-11
Licensee: Ben Heath

Reliably good, homely food in the bar and Doll's House carvery (complete with appropriate toys); fresh, chintzy, antique-furnished bedrooms upstairs. The splendid Victorian bathroom has been usurped by new en suite facilities. Restaurant dishes feature main courses like salmon with lemon and chive cream sauce (£7.95).

Bar Meals: 11.30-2.30, 6-10; bar snacks both sessions **Typical Dishes:** *courgette and brie soup, grilled brie-stuffed mushrooms, chicken breast with cream and tarragon, spaghetti with basil, mozzarella and bacon £4.45, fresh lemon sole (main courses from £4.50), sticky toffee pudding with home-made ice-cream* *Vegetarian Meals: vegetable curry* *Children's Menu/Portions* Beer *Ind Coope; Morlands; Shepherd Neame* *Children Allowed in Bar to Eat* *Outdoor Play Area* *Garden* *Outdoor Eating* **Accommodation:** *4 bedrooms, all en suite, from £45 (single £30)* *Children Welcome Overnight* *Cot Available* *Check-in: all day* **Credit Cards:** *Access, Amex, Diners, Visa*

THAMES DITTON   Albany

Queens Road KT7 0QY
Tel: (081) 398 7031
Open: 11-3, 5.30-11 (all day Thur-Sat)
Licensees: Brian O'Connor and Mark Frost

Spacious Victorian pub with a splendid riverside terrace, from which to admire Hampton Court Palace on a summer's day. There are new licensees since our last edition; the menu has changed, and a refurbishment is in progress as we go to press.

Bar Meals: 12-2.30, 6-9 (Wed-Sat eve); bar snacks lunchtime **Typical Dishes:** *cawl cennin £1.95, chicken liver and paté £2.95, chicken and tarragon casserole £4.25, beef and ale pie £4.35, lamb stew with dumplings £4.25, treacle tart £1.40* *Vegetarian Meals: leek and mushroom pancakes* *Children's Portions* Beer *Bass* *Children Allowed in Bar to Eat* *Outdoor Play Area* *Riverside Garden* *Outdoor Eating* *Summer Barbecue* **Credit Cards:** *Access, Amex, Visa*

THURSLEY Three Horseshoes Tel: (0252) 703268. Elegant but informal, tile-hung and stone-built pub, with a lovely front lawn; simple home cooking by the landlady, changing daily. Gales beers. Open: 11-3, 6-11.

WEYBRIDGE Farnell Arms Thames Street. Popular Victorian pub with hearty helpings of home-cooked food; large separate restaurant.

WINDLESHAM Brickmakers Arms Chertsey Road. Cosy little country pub, thoughtfully run; bar meals lunchtime and evening (children allowed); garden; outdoor eating; summer barbecue. Courage, Fullers, Wadworth beer. Access, Amex, Visa. Open: 10.30-3, 5-11.

WOTTON Wotton Hatch Guildford Road (A25) Tel: (0306) 885665. Former Surrey Trust House, with crowded low-ceilinged front bar, cocktail lounge, noisy tap room, and restaurant. Fullers beers. Open: 11-2.30 (3 Sat), 5.30-11.

EAST SUSSEX

ALCISTON	Rose Cottage

near Polegate BN22 6UW
Tel: (0323) 870377
Open: 11.30-2.30 (12-2 Sun), 6.30-11
Licensee: Ian Lewis

Cosy, rambling cottage pub with old pews, interesting bric-a-brac, cased stuffed birds and real fires. Children are allowed in the restaurant area at lunchtimes, which bar meal diners generally also spill over into; reliable home-made food, and the pies are particularly popular.

*Bar Meals: 12-2, 7-10 (12-1.30, 7-9.30 Sun); bar snacks both sessions   **Restaurant:** 7-9 (not Sun)   **Typical Dishes BAR:** home-made soup £1.75, avocado with prawns £3.50, home-made pie £4.10, barbecued spare ribs £5.25, home-made curry £4.95, peach crumble £1.95   Vegetarian Meals: curried nut loaf £4.75   Children's Portions   Beer Harveys; Ruddles   Outdoor Play Area   Garden   Outdoor Eating   **No Credit Cards***

ALFRISTON	George Inn

High Street BN26 5SY
Tel: (0323) 870319
Licensee: M Gregory

Tourists love this friendly, well-run little place, so overnight guests are advised to book well ahead. Outwardly appealing, flint and timber-built, it's also charming inside, with heavy dark timbers aplenty and an enormous inglenook fireplace. Recommended for bed and breakfast: the best room has a splendid four-poster bed and some carefully preserved original plaster; some of the others are more ordinary.

*Bar Meals: lunch and evening   Beer   Ruddles, Webster's   **Accommodation:** 8 bedrooms, 6 en suite, from £50   Check-in: all day   **Credit Cards:** Access, Amex, Diners, Visa*

ALFRISTON Market Cross, Waterloo Square: Atmospheric old inn, conservatory and garden; families welcome; bar food lunch and evening.

ALFRISTON Wingrove Inn, High Street Tel: (0323) 870276. Victorian colonial architecture, decent bar food, separate restaurant, three bedrooms.

BERWICK Sussex Ox Milton Street. Attractive country pub at the foot of the Downs, rustic furniture and homely cooking; good family garden.

BLACKBOYS   Blackboys Inn

on B2192
Tel: (0825) 890283
Open: all day
Licensee: Patrick Russell

Lots of interesting bric-a-brac, and a ramble of delightfully old-fashioned little rooms in this partly medieval old inn. Seats at the front of the building overlook the pond; seats at the rear in the orchard.

Bar Meals: lunch and evening; bar snacks both sessions   ***Typical Dishes:*** *home-made soup £1.60, garlic mussels £3.40, chicken Calabria £6, crab salad £6, home-made puddings £1.95   Vegetarian Meals*   **Beer** *Harveys   Outdoor Play Area   Garden Outdoor Eating*

BODLE STREET GREEN   White Horse Inn

Herstmonceux BN27 4RE
Tel: (0323) 833243
Open: 12-2.30, 7-10.30 (11 Sat); closed Mon
Licensee: R Tiney

Bright, cheerful pub run by a bright and cheerful couple. They pride themselves on producing properly pubby, informal but honest fare, rather than developing into a licensed restaurant business.

Bar Meals: lunch and evening Tue-Sun; bar snacks both sessions   ***Typical Dishes:*** *home-made soup £1.10, deep-fried mushrooms £2.50, steak and kidney pie £4.75, chicken curry £3.75, seafood provencale £5.50, spotted dick £1.65   Vegetarian Meals: spinach and mushroom lasagne £4.50*   **Beer** *Harveys Best Bitter*   **Whisky** *Patio/terrace   Outdoor Eating*   **No Credit Cards**

BRIGHTON   Greys

105 Southover Street BN2 2UA
Tel: (0273) 680734
Licensees: Mike Lance and Jackie Fitzgerald

Jackie Fitzgerald's splendid cooking draws the lunchtime crowds to this lively, popular little pub.

Bar Meals: 12.15-2 (not Sun); bar snacks   ***Typical Dishes:*** *Mediterranean fish stew £3.75, lamb brochette £4.75, feta and spinach filo parcels, apple and Calvados pancakes   Vegetarian Meals*   **Cheese**   **Beer** *Marston; Whitbread*

BURWASH   Bell Inn

High Street
Tel: (0435) 882304
Open: 11-2.30 (3 Sat), 6-11
Licensees: David and Dee Mizel

Heavy carved wooden pews set off rich red walls in the bar, where a log fire, beams
and yellowing plasterwork all add to the superb traditional character of this early
17th century inn; it's also friendly, well-run and clean. Recommended for bed and
breakfast: a couple of the rooms have ancient beams and sloping floors; all have old-
fashioned furniture, and share a neat, functional bathroom. No telephones or
televisions.

Bar Meals: *lunch and Mon-Sat eve; bar snacks both sessions   Vegetarian Meals*
Children's Portions   **Beer**   *Harveys;Whitbread   Family Room   Garden*
Accommodation: *5 bedrooms, sharing a bathroom, from £30 (single £20)   Check-in: by*
arrangement   **Credit Cards:** *Access, Visa*

CHIDDINGLY   Six Bells

near Lewes BN8 6HE
Tel: (0825) 872227
Open: 11-2.30, 6-11
Licensee: Paul Newman

Highly atmospheric, old-fashioned pub with attractive simple furnishings, a pianola
in the back bar, and a barn of an overflow bar cum function room. Extremely busy
at weekends.

Bar Meals: *12-2, 6-10; bar snacks both sessions*   **Typical Dishes:** *home-made soup 60p,*
buttered crab £2.25, spare ribs £3.25, Mexican spicy prawns £3.25, chilli £3   Vegetarian
Meals: lasagne   **Beer**   *Courage; Harveys   Family Room   Garden   Outdoor Eating*

COUSLEYWOOD   Old Vine

near Wadhurst TN5 6ER   ▼
Tel: (089 288) 2271
Open: 11.30-2.30 (12-2.30 Sun), 6-11
Licensee: A Peel

Long a favourite, this popular old dining pub has benches, farmhouse chairs, and a
bar menu which appears to be going up in the world – it's certainly not the
predictable choice of curries and fried fish, as described in our last edition, any
longer. Monday night is music night (a live trio), with a £10.50 set menu
throughout the pub.

Bar Meals: *12-2, 6.45-9.30 (music night menu only on Mon)*   **Restaurant:** *7-9.30*
Typical Dishes BAR: *duck, orange and brandy soup 95p, soft roes on toast £1.50, steak*
and kidney pie £4, peppered chicken in cream £4.75, poached salmon and prawn en croute
£5.25, raspberry and chocolate roulade   **RESTAURANT:** *set menus from £10.50: leek*
and potato soup, seafood risotto, chicken caprice, sirloin topped with stilton mousse, poached
halibut, strawberry pavlova   Vegetarian Meals: stuffed green peppers   Children's Portions
Beer   *Marston; Whitbread   Children Allowed in Bar to Eat   Garden   Outdoor Eating*
Credit Cards: *Access, Diners, Visa*

DITCHLING   Bull Hotel

2 High Street
Tel: (0273) 843147
Open: 11-2.30, 6-11
Licensee: R G Forty

Wonderfully atmospheric, historic old pub, with lots of original tavern features, handsome furnishings, and good value overnight accommodation.

Bar Meals: 12-2, 7-9.30; bar snacks both sessions   *Typical Dishes:* fresh vegetable soup, avocado, home-made steak and kidney pie, roast of the day, braised steak (main courses around £5)   Vegetarian Meals: macaroni cheese   Children's Portions   `Beer`   Whitbread Family Room   Riverside Garden   Outdoor Eating   Summer Barbecue   *Accommodation:* 3 bedrooms, sharing 3 bathrooms, from £42.50 (single £30.50)   Children Welcome Overnight   Cot Available   Check-in: all day   *Credit Cards:* Access, Visa

FIRLE   Ram Inn

West Firle, near Lewes BN8 6NS   `B&B`
Tel: (0273) 858222   ☼
Open: 11.30-2.30, 7-11 (11.30-3, 6-11 summer Sat)   ❢
Licensees: Michael Wooller and Margaret Sharp

The road runs out once it eventually reaches Firle village at the foot of the Downs. It's a quiet backwater now, but this, almost unbelievably, was one a main stage coach route and the Ram an important staging post. Built of brick and flint and partly tile-hung, the inn displays a fascinating mixture of periods. The restaurant is in the Georgian bit and was once the local courthouse. This is perhaps the smartest part of the building, with Regency striped wallpaper and little brass chandeliers. Other parts are older, and the kitchen dates back nearly 500 years. The main bar is a simple, unpretentious affair with a motley collection of tables and chairs on a red lino floor, and old photos dotted around the walls. A 'no smoking' snug bar is similarly modest. Michael Wooller had spent 20 years as a farm management consultant when the tenancy of the Ram, his local, came up a couple of years ago, and he leapt at the chance to indulge his interest in food a little closer to the consumer. Helped by his son Keith and daughter-in-law Christine, he concentrates on fresh local produce as much as possible – vegetables from a nearby market garden, game from the Firle estate – and uses organic produce when it can be had. Vegetarians are routinely well catered for here and fish is always fresh rather than frozen. Around six wines are available by the glass, including Berwick Glebe from the local vineyard and an organic white Burgundy, and a charming walled garden with rustic tables makes an idyllic spot for summer drinking. Simple bedrooms are bright and fresh, with a variety of antique furniture and new beds topped by duvets. The largest room features a shower cabinet and en suite toilet; the remaining four share a neat shower room. All rooms have tea and coffee making kits but, as a matter of policy, no televisions or radios. No children under 14 overnight.

Bar Meals: 12-2, 7-9; bar snacks lunchtime   *Restaurant:* 12-2 (Sun only), 7-9 (Wed-Sat)   *Typical Dishes BAR:* watercress soup £2.25, venison paté £3.35, pork provencale £4.45, beef and Guinness pudding £6.95, hand-raised ham and egg pie £6.95, fresh plum crumble £2.75   *RESTAURANT:* set-price dinners £16.95: game soup, fresh calamari, Barnsley chops, honey-roast crispy duck, bass in tarragon and wine, mint water ice Vegetarian Meals: spicy bean and vegetable pasties £6.15   Children's Portions   `Cheese` `Beer`   Bass Charrington; Harveys   Family Room   Garden   Outdoor Eating *Accommodation:* 5 bedrooms, 1 en suite, from £45 (single £25)   Check-in: all day *Credit Cards:* Access, Visa

| **FLETCHING** | **Griffin** |

near Uckfield TN22 3SS

Tel: (082 572) 2890

Open: 11.30-3, 6-11

Licensees: Nigel and David Pullan

FOOD
B&B

The last real excitement in this sleepy Sussex village was in 1264 when Simon de Montfort's army camped outside the church prior to the Battle of Lewes. These days visitors with a more peaceful intent are made more than welcome at the 16th century Griffin Inn, which is at the heart of Saxon Fletching's picturesque high street, and is everything a village local should be. The main bar has old beams, wainscot walls, a copper hooded brick fireplace and a motley collection of old pews and wheelback chairs; the public bar provides a pool table and fruit machine for the amusement of the local youth and there's a pretty Laura Ashley decorated restaurant. Good home-made food is a major attraction, with one daily-changing menu, written out at night, with a shorter version available at lunchtime, applying to both the bar and restaurant. An eclectic choice ranges from spicy cottage pie or pizza, through stir-fry beef marinated in ginger, to a terrine of duck and foie gras, or turbot en croute with lemon and dill. There are also char-grills, homely puddings and ploughperson's lunches large enough to cope with the sharpest appetite. Gourmet evenings offer a regular sample of the food and wines of different countries and regions, including a Beaujolais Nouveau dinner the weekend after Nouveau Day. Children are made very much at home, with suitably sized portions of adult dishes from the menu, and in summer the garden offers an outstanding view of the South Downs, as well as tables for al fresco eating. An excellent wine list, featuring some invigorating examples from the burgeoning Sussex vineyard scene, owes a good deal to family connections with the Ebury Wine Bar in London. There are three charming, beamed bedrooms, each with a fourposter bed, purpose-built to counteract the sloping floors and so ensure a level night's rest. Two of the rooms are on the small side, each with en suite showers, but sharing a toilet; the third, just £10 more expensive, is larger with its own en suite bathroom proper. Tea and coffee making kits are provided, and the substantial breakfasts are worth getting up for. An excellent stopover on the way to Newhaven, some sixteen miles distant, and the Dieppe ferry.

Bar Meals: 12-2.30, 7-9.30; bar snacks lunchtime   *Restaurant:* 12-2 (2.30 Sun), 7.30-9.15   *Typical Dishes BAR:* Scotch Broth £2.25, Sussex smokie £2.95, spicy ham loaf with fresh tomato sauce £4.25, salmon fishcakes with lemon mayonnaise £5.25, chicken and tarragon pancakes £4.95, treacle tart £2.95   *RESTAURANT:* spiced apple and parsnip soup £2.95, honey bags of crab with saffron, duck breast en croute with tarragon and orange sauce £8.95, salmon koulibiac with watercress sauce £7.95, calves liver with wine and sage £8.25, chocolate marquise with orange crème anglaise £2.95   *Vegetarian Meals:* ratatouille and cheese crumble £3.25   Children's Menu   **Beer**   Hall & Woodhouse; Harveys; King & Barnes   Family Room   Garden   Outdoor Eating   Summer Barbecue   *Accommodation:* 3 bedrooms, 1 fully en suite, from £40 (single £30)   Children Welcome Overnight   Check-in: all day   *Credit Cards:* Access, Amex, Visa

| **FRANT** | **Abergavenny Arms** |

Frant Road

Tel: (0892) 75233

Open: 11.30-2.30, 6-11

Licensee: Richard Bradley

Pleasant pub on Tunbridge Wells to Eastbourne road, in pretty village of Frant; competent, mainly traditional dishes appreciated by locals as well as those with the drive to the coast ahead of them.

Bar Meals: *12-2.30, 7-10 (not Sun/Mon eve); bar snacks both sessions*   **Typical Dishes:** *home-made soup £1.50, garlic prawns £2.50, home-made steak and ale pie £4.95, half shoulder of lamb £6.95, tuna, prawn and pasta bake £4.95   Vegetarian Meals: home-made vegetable bake   Children's Portions*   Beer   *Fullers; Harveys; Hopback; Charles Wells   Family Room   Patio/terrace   Outdoor Eating*   **Credit Cards:** *Access, Visa*

HASTINGS Dolphin Inn Old Harbour. Tables outside on terrace overlooking the harbour; fresh local fish on the otherwise routine bar menu.

JEVINGTON Eight Bells High Street. Enterprising, popular pub with fresh vegetables for sale as well as on the menu; good home-made pies; atmospheric medieval interior; nice garden; children allowed in to eat. Courage beers. Open: 11-2.30 (12-2.30 Sun), 6-11.

KINGSTON NEAR LEWES   Juggs

The Street BN7 3NT
Tel: (0273) 472523
Open: 11-2.30 (12-2.30 Sun), 6-11
Licensee: Andrew Browne

Picturesque little 15th century inn made from two tiny cottages. The main bar is particularly characterful with its low ceilings, rough black timbers, rustic benches and yellowing walls; there's also a small no-smoking dining area (same menu).

Bar Meals: *12-2, 6-9.30; bar snacks both sessions*   **Typical Dishes:** *vegetable soup £1.95, home-made mackerel paté £2.75, home-made steak and kidney pudding £7.95, Juggs special toasted pitta £3.75, Sussex bangers and chips £2.95, hot chocolate fudge brownie £1.95   Vegetarian Meals: vegetable savoury*   Beer   *Harveys Best Bitter; King & Barnes Broadwood, Festive   Family Room   Outdoor Play Area   Garden   Outdoor Eating*   **No Credit Cards**

MAYFIELD   Rose & Crown

Fletching Street TN20 6TE   ▼
Tel: (0435) 872200
Open: 11-3, 6-11
Licensee: Peter Seely

Delightful 16th century pub in a historic village, alongside what was the original London–Brighton road, now a quiet village lane. Unspoilt bars, particularly the two small front ones, have ochre walls, beams, an inglenook fireplace, two log fires, and an atmosphere in which shove ha'penny and cribbage are still keenly played. Strong traditions have now been matched by forward-looking ambitions: there's a new licensee since our last edition, and a host of plans for the pub in progress. A new car park, refurbished restaurant and newly landscaped gardens to front and rear should be completed for 1992. Bedrooms may also be further upgraded and extended.

Bar Meals and Restaurant: *12-2, 7-9.30; bar snacks both sessions*   **Typical Dishes:** *home-made soup £1.95, Florida prawns £2.95, Yorkshire beef in real ale £4.95, tarragon spring chicken £5.75, salmon and scallops £6.95, banoffee pie £2.25   Vegetarian Meals: mushroom stroganoff £4.75*   Beer   *Adnams; Gales; Harveys; Ringwood*   Whisky   *Children Allowed in Bar to Eat   Garden   Outdoor Eating   Summer Barbecue*   **Accommodation:** *3 bedrooms, all en suite, from £48 (single £38)   Children Welcome Overnight (minimum age 7)   Check-in: all day*   **No Credit Cards**

OXLEYS GREEN   Jack Fuller's

near Brightling (crossroads 3 miles from Robertsbridge   ⚑
on back road) TN32 5HD
Tel: (042 482) 212
Open: 12-3 (4 Sun), 7-11.30; closed Mon
Licensee: Roger Berman

Star-rated in our last edition, and still radiating star quality, but now very much a
restaurant, rather than a pub.

Restaurant: during all opening hours   **Typical Dishes:** *gammon and onion pudding*
£5.75, chicken casserole £5.75, prawn and halibut pie £5.75, banana and walnut pudding
£2.50   Vegetarian Meals: cashew, spinach and aubergine bake £5.75   Children's Portions
`Beer` *Brakspears; Harveys; Taylor; Wadworth   Family Room   Outdoor Play Area*
Garden   Outdoor Eating   Summer Barbecue   **Credit Cards:** *Access, Visa*

SEAFORD   White Lion

74 Claremont Road BN25 2BJ
Tel: (0323) 892473
Open: 11-3, 6-11
Licensee: Terence W Tidy

Comfortable, popular pub, locally liked for its bar and restaurant food, which ranges
from the homely to the dinnerish; children allowed in the restaurant. The two single
bedrooms will be converted into a double/family room for 1992. Big car park.

Bar Meals: 12-2, 6.30-9   Restaurant: 12-2, 7-9.30   Typical Dishes BAR: home-
made soup £1.20, whitebait, liver and bacon, poached salmon, steak and kidney pie (main
courses around £5), bread and butter pudding   Vegetarian Meals (restaurant)   Children's
Portions `Beer` *Brakspears; Courage; Harveys   Outdoor Play Area   Patio/terrace*
Outdoor Eating   **Accommodation:** *6 bedrooms, 1 en suite, from £40 (single £20)*
Children Welcome Overnight   Cot Available   **Credit Cards:** *Access, Visa*

TICEHURST Bull Inn Three Legged Cross. Genuinely unspoilt medieval local,
friendly to strangers. Lots of charm, a relaxing atmosphere, and decent bar food,
ranging from the mundane to delicious home-cooked specials (casseroles worth a
try); good puddings. Children welcome. Harveys, Shepherd Neame beers. Open:
11-3, 6-11 (no food Sun eve).

WARBLETON   War-Bill-in-Tun Inn

Heathfield TN21 9BD   ⚑
Tel: (0435) 830636
Open: 11-3, 7-11
Licensees: Bryan and Valerie Whitton

Attractive and well-kept old roadside dining pub with licensees who care about
good food from fresh produce; tables in the carpeted, pleasantly modernised low-
beamed bar areas are often at a premium. Friendly service.

Bar Meals and Restaurant: 12-1.45, 7-9.30 (not Sat eve in bar); bar snacks lunchtime
Typical Dishes BAR: home-made soup £1.40, home-made fish paté £2.05, steak and
kidney £4.55, pork chop £5.65, scampi £5.95, home-made puddings £2.60
RESTAURANT: similar starters and puddings, fillet steak £12.75, poached salmon

£10.45, Dover sole £14.50 Vegetarian Meals: fruit and nut pilaf £4.95 Children's Portions **Beer** *Harveys; Whitbread Children Allowed in Bar to Eat Outdoor Play Area Garden Outdoor Eating* ***Credit Cards:*** *Access, Visa*

WINCHELSEA — New Inn

German Street TN36 4EN
Tel: (0797) 226252
Open: 11-2.30, 6-11
Licensee: Richard Joyce

A strong specials selection, featuring the pie of the day, anything from wild boar to steak and oyster, enlivens an otherwise fairly routine printed menu, in a characterful, spacious 18th century inn with three rambling lounge rooms, nice old furniture, hop bines aplenty and good log fires. There's also a separate public bar. Some of the comfortable but simple bedrooms have delightful views.

Bar Meals: *12-2.30, 6.30 (7 Sun)-9.30; bar snacks lunch and Sun-Thur eve* ***Typical Dishes:*** *home-made soup £1.95, home-made paté £2.95, lamb cutlets with apricot sauce £5.95, home-made goulash £5.50, fresh local Dover sole £7.95, sherry trifle £1.75 Vegetarian Meals: lentil crumble Children's Menu/Portions* **Beer** *Courage Best; King & Barnes Sussex Bitter; Shepherd Neame Master Brew Bitter; Wadworth 6X* **Whisky** *Family Room Outdoor Play Area Garden Outdoor Eating* ***Accommodation:*** *6 bedrooms, sharing 1 bathroom, from £29 Children Welcome Overnight Check-in: by arrangement* ***Credit Cards:*** *Access, Amex, Diners, Visa*

WITHYHAM Dorset Arms on B2110: Cheering, traditional pub set well back from the road; fresh fish and daily specials of a homely simple kind enliven an otherwise routine bar menu. Children inside to eat at lunchtime only. Harveys beers. Open: all day (11-3, 6-11 Sat).

WEST SUSSEX

ASHURST Fountain Inn on B2135. Charming original bar, with flagged floor, handsome country furniture, and an inglenook fireplace; also modernised dining lounge, with a woodburning stove; large gardens with play area; interesting bar food (not Sunday, nor Wednesday evening). Batemans, Whitbread beers. Open: 11-2.30, 6-11.

BINSTED Black Horse Binsted Lane Tel: (0243) 551213. Secluded old inn, with splendid views, and decent bar meals lunch and Mon-Sat evenings. Real fire; no music; garden; bedrooms. Gales beers. Open: 11-2.30, 6-11 (all day Fri/Sat).

BUCKS GREEN — Queens Head

Guildford Road, Rudgwick RH12 3JF
Tel: (0403) 822202
Open: 11-2.20, 6-11
Licensee: Darrell Grainger

Well-kept, well-loved 17th century pub with log fires (some of them cheating ones), non-smoking areas, a long-standing landlord, and a mix of bought-in and home-cooked food, in generous portions.

Bar Meals: *11.30-2, 6.30 (7 Sun)-10; bar snacks lunchtime* ***Typical Dishes:*** *steak and kidney pie £4.50, chicken, ham and mushroom pie £4.50, fishermans pie £6, apple pie*

£1.75   Vegetarian Meals: lasagne   Children's Menu/Portions   **Beer**   *Courage   Family Room   Outdoor Play Area   Patio/terrace   Outdoor Eating*   **No Credit Cards**

BURPHAM   George & Dragon

near Arundel BN18 9RR   ♟

Tel: (0903) 883131

Open: 11-2.30, 6-11

Licensees: George and Marianne Walker

A delightful hillside village position on the outside, and a roomy, opened–out lounge bar within. New owners have taken the bar menu upmarket a little, and the Swiss landlady has influenced the style of the cooking.

*Bar Meals: 12-2, 7-10 (not Sun eve); bar snacks both sessions   **Restaurant:** 12-1.30 (Sun only), 7.30-9.30   **Typical Dishes BAR:** home-made soup £2.25, avocado and crab £4.30, tagliatelle bolognese £4.45, garlic chicken £6.95, fillet steak £12.25, fresh skate with capers £6.95, banoffee pie £2.35   **RESTAURANT:** fresh scallops £5.90, breast of duck £13.50, German style strips of veal £13.20, calves liver £12.90, chocolate roulade £3.25   Vegetarian Meals: rosti with herbs, tomatoes and mushrooms*   **Beer**   *Courage; Harveys; Ruddles   Children Allowed in Bar to Eat   Patio/terrace   Outdoor Eating*   **Credit Cards:** *Access, Amex, Visa*

CHILGROVE   White Horse

near Chichester PO18 9HX   ♟

Tel: (024 359) 219

Open: 11-2.30, 6-11 (closed Sun eve and all day Mon)

Licensee: Barry Phillips

Restauranty public house with an upmarket bar meal and wine list and a smart atmosphere: a business lunching favourite. No children indoors.

*Bar Meals: 12-2 (not Mon), 6-10 (Tue-Fri); bar snacks both sessions   **Restaurant:** 12-1.45, 7-9.30 (closed all day Sun/Mon)   **Typical Dishes BAR:** braised oxtail £6.50, coq au vin £6.50, lobster thermidor £14.95, treacle tart £2.75   **RESTAURANT:** set lunch menu £16.50, dinner £23: chicken and avocado salad, vegetable terrine, home-cured beef on a bed of leeks, escalope of veal with a parmesan crust, fish of the day, home-made ice-cream   Vegetarian Meals: baked aubergine with tomato and basil*   **Cheese**   **Beer**   *Courage Directors; King & Barnes Festive Bitter*   **Whisky**   *Outdoor Play Area   Garden   Outdoor Eating*   **Credit Cards:** *Access, Visa*

COMPTON   Coach & Horses

The Square PO18 9HA

Tel: (0705) 631228

Licensees: David and Christiane Butler, and John Jenner

Village local with a licensee–cook and seasonally changing menus. Table-top mini barbecues of a superior kind are the house speciality.

*Bar Meals and Restaurant: 12-2 (1.30 restaurant), 6-9.30; bar snacks both sessions   **Typical Dishes BAR:** broth £1.45, garlic mussels £3.10, lasagne £4.60, steak and kidney pie £4.60, skate with black butter £5.80, toffee pudding £2.25   **RESTAURANT:** mussel and saffron soup £4.15, duck liver and artichoke salad £4.15, saddle of hare £11.85, chicken breast with sweetbreads £10.15, fillet of halibut with black olives £11.55, apple and cinnamon cheesecake £3.65   Vegetarian Meals: bean and*

vegetable casserole £4.60 **Beer** *Bass; Fullers; Theakston; Whitbread   Garden
Outdoor Eating*   **Credit Cards:** *Access, Visa*

CUCKFIELD   Kings Head

South Street RH17 5JY
Tel: (0444) 454006
Open: noon-11pm
Licensees: Peter Tolhurst and J C Young

Popular and unspoilt village meeting place; banknotes of every kind adorn one
intimate, low-ceilinged bar, while the spacious, panelled public leads out to the beer
garden. Simple bar food is honestly prepared, but the big attraction here is the
excellent menu in the rustic, beamed restaurant; booking essential. Simply furnished,
good-sized bedrooms are warm and welcoming; all the usual little comforts.

Bar Meals: all day;   bar snacks both sessions **Restaurant:** *12.30-2, 7.30-9.30 (Tue-Fri
only)* **Typical Dishes BAR:** *steak and kidney pie £3.20, cottage pie £2.50, fish pie
£2.80, apple pie £1* **RESTAURANT:** *asparagus salad £3.75, wild duck £9.95,
guinea fowl £10.50, curried lamb £9.60, chocolate tart £3   Vegetarian Meals (bar)*
Beer *Harveys; King & Barnes; Morlands   Family Room (weekends)   Garden*
Accommodation: *9 bedrooms, 8 en suite, from £55 (single £42)   Cot Available   Check-
in: all day*   **Credit Cards:** *Access, Amex, Visa*

DONNINGTON Blacksmiths Arms, Selsey Road Tel: (0243) 783999.
Revitalised since being secured from the hands of big brewery ownership; now
earning itself a local reputation for good home cooking; weekly curry night; family
room; garden. Bass, Hall & Woodhouse, Ringwood beers. Open: 11.30-2.30, 6-11.

EASTBOURNE   Olde White Horse

Easebourne Street, Midhurst (on A272) GU29 0AL   ❢
Tel: (0730) 813521
Open: 11-2.30, 6-11
Licensee: Alan Hollidge

A modernised, comfortable lounge, bigger public bar and locals' tap room. In the
evenings, the restaurant menu applies throughout the pub; bar menu at lunchtimes
only. Children are allowed in the restaurant. The whole is run with great enthusiasm
and interest, and the food's worth a try.

Bar Meals: 12-2, 7-9; bar snacks lunchtime **Restaurant:** *7-9* **Typical Dishes BAR:**
*mushroom and madeira soup £1.95, lamb in red wine and orange £4.50, steak and kidney
pie £4.75, Selsey soufflé omelette £5.25, apple tart with pear sorbet £1.95*
RESTAURANT: *Mediterranean fish soup £2.25, chicken satay £2.75, steak in ale and
cream £6.50, jambalaya £8.85, chocolate rum pancakes £1.95   Vegetarian Meals:
ratatouille in home-made cheese pastry   Children's Portions* **Cheese** **Beer** *Greene
King   Garden   Outdoor Eating*   **No Credit Cards**

EASTERGATE   Wilkes Head

Church Lane PO20 6UT
Tel: (0243) 543380
Open: 11-2.30, 5.30 (5 Fri)-11 (11-3, 6-11 Sat)
Licensees: David and Christine Morris

A useful stopping place en route to Goodwood or Fontwell races, an 18th century
flagstone-floored pub with two well-worn bars, homely and relaxing. Simple,
honest home cooking by the landlady: the ground beef lasagne is recommended; eat
in the riverside garden in fine weather. Steaks and fish dominate the straightforward
restaurant menu.

*Bar Meals: 12-2, 7-9.30 (not Sun; 8.30 winter)   bar snacks lunchtime   **Typical Dishes:***
prawn cocktail £2.25, Yorkshire pudding with steak and kidney £4.50, cottage pie £3.35,
cheese and onion jackets with salad £2.50, home-made puddings £1.60   Vegetarian Meals
Children's Menu **Beer** *Ballards; Gales; Ind Coope, Tetleys   Family Room   Outdoor*
*Play Area   Garden   **Credit Cards:** Access, Visa*

EDBURTON   Tottington Manor Hotel

Tel: (0903) 815757
Open: 11-3, 6-11 (closed Sun eve Jan-Easter)
Licensees: David and Kate Miller

A Grade II listed 17th century inn-cum-hotel in its own grounds at the foot of the
South Downs, with lovely views. The bar is simple and properly pubby, with
country furniture and an open fire hogged by an assortment of animals. Good bar
food; prices are just a little higher in the restaurant. Bedrooms are pretty, with
soothing colours and good sturdy furniture, and en suite bathrooms have proper
guest toiletries. The residents' lounge is also rather fine.

*Bar Meals: 12-2.15, 7-9; bar snacks both sessions   **Restaurant:** 12-1.30, 7-9.30*
***Typical Dishes BAR:** wild mushroom soup £1.95, fresh salmon mousse with prawns*
£4.50, home-made sausages with red cabbage £5.15, home-made lamb and apricot pie
£5.25, fresh fish of the day, rum and raisin cheesecake £3   Vegetarian Meals: baked Sussex
mushrooms   Children's Portions **Cheese** **Beer** *Adnams; Batemans; Fullers; Greene*
King **Whisky** *Family Room   Outdoor Play Area   Garden   Outdoor Eating*
***Accommodation:** 6 bedrooms, all en suite, from £60 (single £40)   Children Welcome*
*Overnight   Cot Available   Check-in: all day   **Credit Cards:** Access, Amex, Diners, Visa*

ELSTED   Three Horseshoes

near Midhurst SU29 0JX
Tel: (073 085) 746
Open: 10-3, 6-11 (all day weekend summer)
Licensee: Ann and Tony Burdfield

Bowed walls, terracotta-tiled floors, gnarled beams and mellow stained plasterwork
all create an atmosphere of genuinely unspoilt charm in this popular Tudor inn,
romantically candle-lit at night. Food is as hearty and rustic as the surroundings, and
fish is a speciality, particularly at weekends – try the fried clams if available.

*Bar Meals: 12-2, 6.30-9.30; bar snacks both sessions   **Typical Dishes:** carrot soup*
£1.50, Lancashire hotpot £3.85, steak and kidney pie in Guinness £4.85, fresh local
plaice £5.25, treacle tart   Vegetarian Meals   Children's Portions **Cheese** **Beer**
Ballards; Batemans; Fullers; Ringwood **Cider** *Children Allowed in Bar to Eat   Garden*

ELSTED   Elsted Inn

Elsted Marsh, Midhurst GU29 0JT
Tel: (0730) 813662
Open: 11-3, 5.30-11
Licensees: Barry Horton and Tweazle Jones

FOOD
✷
❢

It would be very easy to drive past this unprepossessing Victorian roadside pub, but that would be to miss out on some good food and a warm welcome. It was built to serve the railway in the steam age, when there was a station here, but was later left stranded by Dr Beeching's 'axe' in the 1950s. This explains the old railway photographs that adorn the thankfully unmodernised and unpretentious bars, in what is very much a local community pub, free of background music and electronic games but with plenty of traditional pub pastimes like shove h'apenny, darts, cards, dominoes and even conversation. There are two small bars with lots of original wood in evidence, original shutters and open fires. A small dining room, candlelit in the evening, an old pine dresser and colourful cloths on a few dining tables surrounded by a motley collection of old chairs. Tweazle Jones and her partner Barry Horton have between them a varied catering background, including cooking in a Scottish school, chefing on luxury liners and working in directors' dining rooms in the city; Tweazle even spent a period as an inspector for Egon Ronay (who else!). The result is a globetrotting menu – always home-made and based on good local produce – with the likes of osso buco from Italy, coq au vin from France or Mexican tacos. England is also well represented though, with dishes like braised oxtail, mutton with caper sauce and sandwiches closely resembling doorsteps; vegetarians are well served, too, with lentil bakes and vegetable roulades. Children can have half portions at half price, and there's a car tyre hanging from a plum tree in the shady garden to keep them amused, plus petanque for the adults. Dogs are welcome, or at least tolerated by the house hounds, Truffle and Sam, and an area of the garden is fenced off to keep dogs and children apart. The pub is no longer owned by the local brewers, Ballards, but their Best, Trotton and Wassail ales are still served here along with Marston Pedigree and various guest beers.

Bar Meals: 12-2.30, 7-10 (9.30 Sun); bar snacks both sessions **Typical Dishes:** *spinach and sorrel soup £2, bressan de champignons £2.50, Sussex bacon pudding £5, venison fillet with green peppercorn sauce £7, pork and rabbit pie £5, Marlborough tart £2.25 Vegetarian Meals: garlic lentils in cream £5 Children's Portions* **Cheese** **Beer** *Adnams; Ballards; Batemans; Mitchells Family Room Outdoor Play Area Garden Outdoor Eating Summer Barbecue* **No Credit Cards**

FULKING   Shepherd & Dog

near Henfield BN5 9LU
Tel: (079 156) 382
Open: 11-2.30 (3 Sat), 6-11
Licensee: A Bradley-Hole

Attractive pub in a truly glorious setting. One long bar with polished tables and fresh flowers inside, and a good, varied selection of bar meals; there's usually a queue at the food servery (though the food's not as good as it used to be); hot specials in the evening, with lighter food at lunch.

Bar Meals: 12-2, 7-9.30 (not Sun eve); bar snacks both sessions **Typical Dishes:** *stuffed mushrooms, rack of lamb, seafood gratin, beef and Guinness pie (main courses from £4; £6 in the evening) Vegetarian Meals* **Beer** *Harveys; Ruddles, Webster's Outdoor Play Area Garden* **Credit Cards:** *Access, Visa*

HERMITAGE   Sussex Brewery

36 Main Road PO10 8AU   ❢
Tel: (0243) 371533
Open: 11-11
Licensees: Malcolm and Pat Roberts

A fresh carpet of sawdust is laid daily at this grade II listed pub-brewery, and open fires are continually alight from October to Easter. There's no jukebox or fruit machine, not even a cigarette machine. The former family room is being turned into a restaurant decorated on the theme of the old brewery. Speciality sausages are a popular new addition to the home-cooked dishes.

Bar Meals: *12-2, 7.30-9; bar snacks both sessions*   **Typical Dishes:** *mushroom soup £1.50, speciality sausages from £3.25, home-made curry £3.35, apple and rhubarb crumble £1.30   Vegetarian Meals: wholefood lasagne   Children's Portions*   **Beer**   *Eldridge Pope; Hall & Woodhouse; Morlands; Sussex Brewery   Children Allowed in Bar to Eat Garden   Outdoor Eating   Summer Barbecue*   **No Credit Cards**

LICKFOLD   Lickfold Inn

near Petworth GU28 9EY
Tel: (0798) 5285
Open: 11-3, 6-11
Licensees: Ron and Kath Chambers

Splendid interior with a vast open fire, handsome furnishings and a rug-strewn floor. Unusual and attractive gardens. No children.

Bar Meals: *12-2, 7-9.30; bar snacks both sessions*   **Typical Dishes:** *French onion soup £1.50, Oriental prawns £3.50, half shoulder of lamb, steak and kidney pie, red mullet with garlic and tarragon (main courses £4.50-£7), ginger pear dumpling £1.95   Vegetarian Meals: broccoli and cheese bake*   **Beer**   *Adnams; Ballards; Fullers; Hall & Woodhouse Garden   Outdoor Eating   Summer Barbecue*   **Credit Cards:** *Access, Visa*

LODSWORTH   Halfway Bridge Inn

on A272
Tel: (07985) 281
Open: 11-2.30 (12-2 winter Sun), 6-10.30 (closed winter Sun eve)
Licensees: Edric and Sheila Hawkins

This stylishly simple old country inn has got new licensees since our last edition, and the food's looking promising, if not exactly cheap. A marvellously relaxing venue for lunch, though, with its staunchly traditional and pretty interior, warmed by log fires in chilly weather. The same menu applies in the separate dining room, where children over 10 are permitted. A new outdoor patio has seating for 25.

Bar Meals: *12-2, 7-10; bar snacks lunchtime*   **Typical Dishes:** *home-made soup £2.25, steak, kidney and Guinness pie £5.95, lamb in red wine, rosemary and redcurrant £5.95, salmon with mint and cucumber mayonnaise £8.25, pear and ginger crumble   Vegetarian Meals: vegetable curry*   **Beer**   *Marston; Wadworth; Whitbread Boddingtons Bitter Garden   Outdoor Eating*   **Credit Cards:** *Access, Visa*

LURGASHALL   Noah's Ark

near Petworth GU28 9ET
Tel: (0428) 78346
Open: 11-2.30 (3 Sat), 6-11
Licensee: Ted Swannell

450 year old pub right on the village green which doubles up as a cricket pitch.
Inglenook fireplaces in both bars; 90 hanging baskets in summer.

Bar Meals: 12-2, 7-10; no food Sun; bar snacks both sessions   **Restaurant:** *7-10 (not*
Sun)   **Typical Dishes BAR:** *watercress soup £1.10, paté £2, calves liver and bacon*
£4.75, English lamb cutlets £4.50, moussaka £3.25, home-made apple pie £1.75
Vegetarian Meals: lasagne Children's Portions `Cheese` `Beer` *Greene King IPA,*
Abbot Ale `Wine` *Family Room Garden Outdoor Eating* **No Credit Cards**

MIDHURST Swan Inn Red Lion Street. Sensitively renovated town centre pub
with split-level bars, real fires, a 15th century mural, and home cooked food lunch
and evening. Harveys beers. Open all day.

PETWORTH   Welldiggers Arms

Pulborough Road GU28 0HG   ¶
Tel: (0798) 42287
Licensees: Mr and Mrs Whitcomb

Very much a dining pub, usually very busy in both bar and snug. Excellent seafood
and properly hung steaks.

Bar Meals: 12-2, 6 (7 Sun)-10   **Typical Dishes:** *crab soup, red mullet, roast duck with*
apple sauce, courgette casserole, home-made puddings (main courses from £5) Vegetarian
Meals `Cheese` `Beer` *Ruddles; Youngs* **Credit Cards:** *Access, Amex, Diners, Visa*

ROWHOOK   Chequers Inn

near Horsham RH12 3PY   ¶
Tel: (0403) 790480
Open: 11-2.30 (3 Sat), 6-11
Licensee: Gyles Culver

Agreeable 15th century pub, much modernised, but least so in the Flagstone Bar.
The thriving food trade exists alongside a loyal local following, and cooking is
reliable. A pretty garden has play equipment, animals and a petanque pitch.

Bar Meals: 12-2, 7-10; bar snacks both sessions   **Typical Dishes:** *home-made soup*
£1.75, garlic shrimps with crispy bacon £3.95, mushrooms and bacon au gratin £4.75,
baked chicken breast stuffed with avocado, cream cheese and garlic £5.25, fresh salmon
fishcakes with lemon mayonnaise £5.25, bread and butter pudding £1.95 Vegetarian
Meals: leek and potato au gratin £4.25 Children's Menu/Portions `Beer` *Marston;*
Whitbread Family Room Outdoor Play Area Garden Outdoor Eating Summer
Barbecue **Credit Cards:** *Access, Visa*

SOUTH HARTING   Ship Inn

South Harting GU31 5PZ
Tel: (0730) 825302
Open: 11.30-3, 6-11
Licensee: M B Oban-Palmer

Colourful flower baskets adorn the outside of this white-painted mid–17th century inn in the centre of the village, and a wisteria is just beginning to get established. Mind your head once through the door, as the beams are rather low. The interior furnishings are a mixture of varnished rustic tables, banquettes and wheelback chairs. Hunting prints around the walls reflect one of the interests of owners Michael and Juno; another is owning racehorses. When each of their horses won a race on the same day, it was free beer all round. The main bar is largely given over to eating, with an extensive menu of mostly home-made dishes; a watercress soup is just bursting with flavour, and the steak and kidney pie combines beautifully tender chunks of lean beef with a crisp pastry lid. Oysters are something of a feature in season too. Leave room for splendidly traditional puddings like spotted dick to round things off. It's usually wise to book for meals but at lunchtimes snacks are also offered, like sandwiches and jacket potatoes. A small public bar has a dartboard, fruit machine and a range of real ales, including the local Ballards beer. Children under 14 years are not allowed inside, but in fine weather are welcome in the small garden, which boasts an aviary with cockatiel and quail amongst other birds.

Bar Meals: 12-2.30, 7-9.30 (9 Sun eve); bar snacks lunchtime   **Typical Dishes:** *soup of the day £2.25, potted shrimps £3.30, steak and kidney pie £4.85, Hungarian goulash £5.95, chicken en croute £6.85, apple pie £2.30*   ■ Beer ■ *Ruddles   Garden*   **Credit Cards**: *Access, Visa*

SOUTH HARTING   White Hart

High Street GU31 5QB
Tel: (0730) 825355
Open: 11-3, 6-11
Licensees: Allan and Angie Hayter

Pleasant village pub with wooden tables, log fires and a decent choice of plain, fresh food. Veal, venison and lemon chicken are among the smarter restaurant dishes.

Bar Meals: 11-2, 7-10; bar snacks both sessions   **Restaurant:** *6.30-10.30*   **Typical Dishes:** *home-made soup £1, garlic mushrooms, toad in the hole, lamb cobbler, lasagne (main courses £4.50), home-made puddings £1.80   Vegetarian Meals: vegetarian chapatis   Children's Menu/Portions*   ■ Beer ■ *Gales; Ind Coope   Family Room   Garden   Outdoor Eating*   **No Credit Cards**

STOPHAM BRIDGE   White Hart

Pulborough RH20 1DS   ▼
Tel: (0798) 873321
Open: 11-3, 6.30-11
Licensee: Bill Bryce

· Neat, simple roadside stone built pub, a rambling assortment of bright, attractive carpeted bars with a dining area leading off down some steps: the resulting style is modern but relaxingly cottagey. Aside from the good hot bar meals listed here, there are lots of cold ploughman-ish platters and other snacks.

Bar Meals: 12-2.30, 7-9.30; *bar snacks both sessions* **Restaurant:** 12-2.15, 7-9
Typical Dishes BAR: *carrot and courgette soup £1.45, hot Loch Fyne kipper £2.95, home-made spicy sausages £2.95, fresh spinach ravioli £3.75, home-made fish pie £4.25, fresh fruit crumble £1.75* **RESTAURANT:** *lobster bisque £2.60, Arbroath smokie £2.95, swordfish with tarragon sauce £7.95, red snapper Cantonese £8.50, pan-fried tuna £8.50, banoffee pie* *Vegetarian Meals: lentil and vegetable curry* *Children's Menu/Portions* `Cheese` `Beer` *Marston; Whitbread* `Whisky` *Family Room Outdoor Play Area Riverside Garden Outdoor Eating Summer Barbecue* **Credit Cards:** *Access, Visa*

WARNHAM   Greets Inn

45 Friday Street RH12 3QY
Tel: (0403) 65047
Open: 11-2.30, 6-11
Licensees: Trevor and Pamela Chaplin

Popular and promising food pub, about to be thoroughly smartened up. Traditional features; 15th century origins; open fires. All home-made food – no boil in the bag, no bought-in specials, no convenience puddings. Fresh vegetables too. Same menu in the dining room.

Bar Meals: 12-2, 7-10; *bar snacks both sessions* **Typical Dishes:** *home-made madeira and mushroom soup £1.95, potato skins £2.95, half shoulder of lamb £7.50, chicken teriyaki £7.45, fresh salmon £7.70, home-made chocolate roulade* *Vegetarian Meals: vegetable bake* *Children's Portions* `Beer` *Whitbread beers* *Family Room Garden* **Credit Cards:** *Access, Amex, Diners, Visa*

WASHINGTON Frankland Arms Tel: (0903) 892220. The original Sussex Pieman pub, and offers home-cooked pies of every imaginable kind, featuring some unusual combinations, like rabbit and gooseberry. A la carte is more conventional in the evening. Children allowed in to eat; Gales, Wadworth, Whitbread beers.

WEST MARDEN   Victoria Inn

on B2146 PO18 9EN
Tel: (0705) 631330
Open: 11.30-3, 6-11
Licensee: James Neville

Popular food pub (book weekend evenings), roadside but country style. A separate dining room has the same menu; children are permitted to dine in here.

Bar Meals: 12-2, 7-9.30; *bar snacks both sessions* **Typical Dishes:** *spinach soup £1.80, Parma ham with melon £3.95, garlic chicken supreme en croute £7.20, stilton steakburger £6.60, seafood lasagne £5.60, vanilla cheesecake £1.70* *Vegetarian Meals: ratatouille £3.30* `Beer` *Gibbs Mew beers* *Outdoor Play Area Garden Outdoor Eating Summer Barbecue* **Credit Cards:** *Access, Visa*

WISBOROUGH GREEN   Three Crowns

Billingshurst Road RH14 0DX
Tel: (0403) 700207
Open: 11-3, 6-11
Licensees: Brian and Sandie Yeo

New tenants of four years ago have now bought the freehold of this comfortable, attractive pub, and are engaged in a total refurbishment programme. The food's beginning to look very interesting, too. One to watch.

Bar Meals and Restaurant: 12-2, 7-9 (9.30 Sat, not Mon)   **Typical Dishes:** *carrot and ginger soup £1.20, hand-breaded shrimps with home-made garlic dip £3.15, prime Scotch sirloin steak platter £8.25, home-cooked steak and kidney pie £4.50, home-cooked lasagne £4.50, treacle sponge pudding £1.90   Vegetarian Meals: potato, cheese and spinach pie £4.30   Children's Menu/Portions* Beer *Ind Coope, King & Barnes* Cider *Addlestones   Family Room   Outdoor Play Area   Garden   Outdoor Eating* **Credit Cards:** *Access, Visa*

TYNE AND WEAR

BIRTLEY Coach & Horses Durham Road: Cheap and cheerful roadhouse with popular restaurant. Bass beers. Open all day.

EIGHTON BANKS Lambton Arms, Rockcliff Way, Gateshead. Stone-built single-bar little local, partitioned up into four distinct areas; decent home cooking lunch and evening; children welcome; Whitbread beers. Open: 11-3, 5.30(6 Sat)-11.

NEWCASTLE UPON TYNE   Cooperage

32 The Close, Quayside NE1 3RF
Tel: (091) 232 8286
Open: 11-11
Licensee: Michael Westwell

A handsome Tudor ex-barrel making shop, a city landmark and a popular meeting place. Inside is comfortable rather than distinctively furnished or styled; modern machines and the juke box don't help. The food's cheap and cheerful though.

Bar Meals: 11-3.30; bar snacks lunchtime   **Restaurant:** 12-3   **Typical Dishes:** *ham and lentil soup 95p, beer and ale pie, stir-fried beef in black pepper sauce, smoked fish kedgeree (main courses from £3), bread and butter pudding   Vegetarian Meals   Children's Portions* Beer *Ind Coope; Marston* Cider *Addlestones, Coates* **Credit Cards:** *Access, Amex, Visa*

NEWCASTLE UPON TYNE Old George, Cloth Market. City centre wood-panelled old local, popular for lunchtime food; vegetarians and children catered for; real fire; garden; Bass beers. Open all day.

NEW YORK   Shiremoor House Farm

Middle Engine Lane NE29 8DZ   **FOOD**
Tel: (091) 257 6302
Open: all day
Licensees: H W Garrett and W Kerridge

This imaginative conversion of derelict farm buildings stands in open ground at the
edge of a small industrial estate in a new town suburb five minutes from the Tyne
tunnel. Courage and vision in unlikely circumstances have paid off, and in just three
short years the pub has won many friends; it's very rarely quiet. Lunchtimes bring
local trade from the industrial estate, while, in the evening, it's more of a drive-out-
from-Newcastle crowd. Inside this mellow stone building, a large open-plan bar,
(its counter under the original gin gang), is subtly lit, with stripped walls, decorative
old farming bric-a-brac and blown-up photographs of agricultural folk. Polished
flagstones are topped with a mix of tables and chairs, wicker, upholstered, wing,
country and banquette style. The only modern intruder in an otherwise jukebox and
fruit machine-free zone is the computerised till. Bravely, a conscious decision was
taken at the start to exclude chips from the Farm's menu; consequently, the
restaurant, in the old cow byre, is always full, and bar meal trade always busy.
Blackboard-listed dishes feature mostly fresh produce, like a tasty pork casserole in a
Dijon mustard flavoured cream sauce, accompanied by a generous array of fresh,
crisp vegetables. Old favourites from the English tavern repertoire, like liver and
bacon casserole, and steak and kidney pie, appear alongside re-interpreted classics:
poached haddock in a prawn and dill sauce, or chicken with mushrooms and
sweetcorn perhaps. It's honest, capable cooking at very competitive prices. Smartly
uniformed staff can appear on the mechanical side of efficiency.

Bar Meals and Restaurant: 11.30-2.30, 6 (7 restaurant)-9.30   *Typical Dishes BAR:*
chicken broth £1.10, garlic mushrooms £1.80, steak and kidney pie £3.85, chilli £3.45,
poached cod in prawn and dill sauce £3.95   RESTAURANT: deep-fried camembert
£3.10, beef olives £9.50, chicken American £8.75, sole paupiettes £8.75   Children's
Portions **Beer** *Bass; Taylor; Theakston   Family Room   Patio/terrace   Outdoor Eating*
Summer Barbecue   Credit Cards: Access, Amex, Visa

NORTH HYLTON Shipwrights Arms Ferryboat Lane. Refurbished in
traditional tavern style, and much extended, by original ferry landing (before the
A19 swooped by). Attractive first floor restaurant; food lunch and evening. Vaux,
Wards beers. Open: 11-3, 7-11.

NORTH SHIELDS   Chain Locker

Dyke Street, Ferry Landing NE29 6LQ
Tel: (091) 258 0147
Open: 11.30-3.30, 6-11 (11-11 Fri/Sat)
Licensee: Wilfred Kelly

A useful stopping-off point for those using the ferry. The licensee-cook produces
simple, fresh, good value food, strong on fresh fish; more fish, seafood and steak in
the restaurant. The decor is low key and genuinely nautical.

Bar Meals and Restaurant: 12-2.30, 6-9.30; bar snacks both sessions   *Typical Dishes:*
beef and vegetable soup £1.10, crab, steak cooked in ale, deep-fried cod or haddock, daily fish
dish (main courses from £3), home-made apple pie   Vegetarian Meals   Children's
Menu/Portions **Beer** *Ind Coope; Marston; Taylor   Children Allowed in Bar to Eat*
Riverside patio/terrace   Outdoor Eating   Credit Cards: Access, Visa

WALLSEND   Rose Inn

Rosehill Bank, Willington Quay NE28 6TR
Tel: (091) 263 4545
Open: 11-11
Licensees: J A and M B O'Keefe

A large Victorian roadside pub with a busy local bar meal and restaurant trade. No music.

Bar Meals: 12-2, 6-8; bar snacks both sessions **Restaurant:** *7-9* **Typical dishes BAR:** *beef and tomato soup 80p, mild curry pancake £1.50, chilli con carne £2.80, gammon steak with pineapple £3.60, baked trout provencale £4.20, apple and raspberry crumble 95p* **RESTAURANT:** *chicken and sweetcorn soup £1.50, prawn salad £2.80, lamb cutlets with rum sauce £8.20, strips of beef in whisky and cream sauce £7.80, T-bone steak £12.50, Scotch trifle £2.20 Vegetarian Meals: mushroom stroganoff Children's Menu/Portions* **Beer** *Marston; Ruddles; Theakston; Whitbread Children Allowed in Bar to Eat* **No Credit Cards**

WHITBURN Jolly Sailor East Street. Visit in the hope that one of the local whoppers (fish, that is) have made it to the menu. Real fire; no music; children welcome. Bass beers. Open all day.

WHITLEY BAY Briar Dene Inn Seafront. Decent food, making use of fresh local fish; comfortably refurbished pub, low prices.

WARWICKSHIRE

ALDERMINSTER   Bell

near Stratford-upon-Avon CV37 8NX   FOOD
Tel: (0789) 450414
Open: 12-2.30 (inc Sun), 7-11
Licensees: Keith and Vanessa Brewer

Food is very much the thing at the Bell, an old coaching inn standing alongside the A34 a few miles south of Stratford. It advertises itself as a Bistro and Bar, and the description is an apt one: the interior of this much-refurbished pub is now mainly given over to dining. The small bar area, with its exposed brickwork, wood and flagstone floors, sets the tone, and the main room features splendid polished flagstones, original wall and ceiling timbers, and farmhouse-style tables, each bearing a small vase of flowers and surrounded by rustic chairs, while a brick inglenook fireplace complete with stove features a number of polished brasses. Half the dining area has been designated non-smoking. The bar food is certainly above average, and so are the prices, though not excessively so. Only fresh produce, as much of it locally grown as possible, is used on a regularly changing blackboard menu, on which fresh crab paté, creamed mushrooms on toast and French onion soup are typical starters, perhaps followed by a generous portion of veal and pork ragout with rice, a cod steak with an unusual stilton sauce or a venison pie. A sampled mini rack of lamb was cooked pink, its meat tender and flavoursome, and partnered by a madeira sauce. Vegetables are good and fresh, and there's always a decent vegetarian alternative, like a hazelnut loaf. Puddings, which are listed on a separate blackboard brought to your table, are also an appealing bunch, featuring perhaps banoffiee pie or a chocolate fudge tart, both guaranteed to be oozing with calories. Service is well practised and efficient on the whole, but a little rushed at times. The atmosphere of the pub is light and informal, and although there's no official dress code, shorts would probably be frowned upon.

Bar Meals: *12-1.45, 7-9.30 (12-1.30, 7-9 Sun); bar snacks lunchtime* ***Typical Dishes BAR:*** *carrot and orange soup £2.25, haddock and mushroom au gratin £4.50, lamb and date casserole £7.50, bobotie £5.95, marinated cod steak £7.25, peach and almond tart £2.95 Vegetarian Meals: hazelnut roast with spicy tomato sauce Children's Portions* **Beer** *Whitbread Family Room Children Allowed in Bar to Eat Garden Outdoor Eating* ***Credit Cards:*** *Access, Visa*

ALVESTON — Ferry Inn

off B4089, Alveston CV37 7QX FOOD
Tel: (0789) 269883
Open: 11-2.30, 6-11
Licensee: D G Russon

Overlooking a small green at the centre of a quiet village only three miles from Stratford-upon-Avon, the well-run Ferry Inn is cream-painted and hung with large, hugely colourful baskets; the peaceful countrified atmosphere of both village and pub a welcome contrast to the commercially-oriented "plastic" pubs that predominate in Shakespeare's town. It's run by David and Sarah Russon, who were previously Guide recommended at the Howard Arms at Ilmington, on the other side of Stratford. The move to new premises certainly hasn't dampened their ambition; highly accomplished bar meals are attracting a growing number of customers, and on Friday and Saturday evenings, the pub is frequently packed to the gunnels. A large blackboard at the end of the lounge bar lists a menu strong on the fresh and local. While not exhaustive, the choice is interesting and well handled, from the simplest York ham and cheddar ploughmans to starters (or snacks) like crisply deep-fried courgette, cauliflower and mushrooms with a blue cheese dressing. More substantial meals might include spaghetti carbonara, a large Yorkshire pudding with a filling of steak and kidney, char-grilled Cotswold sausage or a vegetable and nut bake topped with crispy cheese. A dish of fresh salmon pieces and prawns in a light but full-flavoured lobster sauce comes on a bed of pasta verdi, accompanied by garlic bread (as are many dishes), as well as a rather miserly side salad. The Ferry's interior is neat and uncluttered, one large room broken up by large columns, with false-beamed ceilings and plain painted walls, hung with fishy pictures. Upholstered benches and round-back chairs – some arranged in one of the bay windows – red brick fireplaces and dry flower displays complete the picture. Besides a selection of well kept beers, some nine quality wines are served by the glass. A patio, complete with white garden furniture, comes into its own in fine weather.

Bar Meals: *11.45 (12 Sun)-2, 6-9 (not Sun); bar snacks lunchtime* ***Typical Dishes;*** *minestrone £1.60, deep-fried vegetables with blue cheese dip £2.50, Yorkshire pudding filled with steak and Guinness £4.95, lambs kidneys Turbigo £4.95, salmon and prawns in lobster sauce on tagliatelle £5.50, rich chocolate rum torte Vegetarian Meals: broccoli provencale £3.75* **Beer** *Marston; Whitbread Children Allowed in Bar to Eat (minimum age 7) Patio/terrace Outdoor Eating* ***Credit Cards:*** *Access, Diners, Visa*

ASTON CANTLOW Kings Head Bearley Road. Listed for its atmosphere, half-timbered without, stone-floored and settle-furnished within, with open fires, fresh flowers, and a little snug. Shakespeare's parents apparently held their wedding breakfast here. Garden. Whitbread beers.

BIDFORD ON AVON — White Lion Hotel

High Street B50 4BQ
Tel: (0789) 773309
Licensees: Mr and Mrs Lilley

In a pretty setting beside an old stone bridge on the banks of the Avon, an attractively refurbished hotel with lovely bedrooms: all have good dark wood furnishings (one with a four-poster), and prettily co-ordinated decor, plus neat modern bathrooms. The smartened-up bar contrasts bamboo style furnishings with original beams.

Bar Meals: lunchtime and evening ▬Beer▬ *Youngers* **Accommodation:** *10 bedrooms, all en suite, from £60   Children Welcome Overnight* **Credit Cards:** *Access, Amex, Diners, Visa*

BINLEY WOODS Cocked Hat Tel: (0203) 63767. Popular with business-lunchers; decent business-lunch food; bedrooms.

BROOM   Broom Tavern

High Street B50 4HL   ♟
Tel: (0789) 773656
Open: 11-3 (12-2 Sun), 6-11
Licensee: E Zdanko

Timbered 16th century village pub, still very much a local despite its popularity for food, which is reliably good.

Bar Meals and Restaurant: 12-2, 6.30 (7 restaurant)-10; bar snacks both sessions **Typical Dishes:** *home-made soup £1.55, steak and kidney pie £5.50, salmon, cod and prawn pie £5.75, simply grilled/poached salmon £7.25, chocolate rum crunch £2.50 Vegetarian Meals: lasagne* ▬Beer▬ *Bass; Marston; Whitbread   Family Room   Outdoor Play Area   Garden   Outdoor Eating* **Credit Cards:** *Access, Visa*

DUNCHURCH   Dun Cow Hotel

The Green CV22 6NJ
Tel: (0788) 810233
Open: all day
Licensee: Richard Ryan

At a crossroads in the town centre, a Georgian coaching inn with lots of charm; open fires warm the heavily beamed Smoke Room and cosy little oak-panelled cocktail bar, and there's an intimate lounge with wooden settles and winged armchairs. Spacious bedrooms, six of them cottagey, all with fine old furnishings (two four-posters); well-equipped bath or shower rooms.

Bar Meals: 12-2.15, 7-9; bar snacks both sessions **Restaurant:** *12-2.30, 7-10 Vegetarian Meals   Children's Portions* ▬Beer▬ *Marston   Family Room   Garden Outdoor Eating* **Accommodation:** *20 bedrooms, all en suite, from £38 (single £35) Children Welcome Overnight   Cots Available   Check-in: all day* **Credit Cards:** *Access, Amex, Diners, Visa*

ETTINGTON   Houndshill

Banbury Road CV37 7NS   ♟
Tel: (0789) 740267
Open: 12-3, 6 (7 Sat)-11
Licensee: A Martin

A pubby little bar and plain but bright dining room feature in this handsome white hotel on the A422. Bar food is routine stuff (higher prices in the dining room), but the bedrooms are light and attractive, with lemony cream walls, fitted grey carpets, pretty fabrics and pine furniture. All have excellent bath/shower rooms, too.

Bar Meals: 12-2, 7-10; bar snacks both sessions   Typical Dishes: beef and vegetable soup £1.25, deep-fried breaded mushrooms £2.25, steak and kidney pie £4, lasagne £4.75, sirloin steak £7.50, Bakewell tart £1.50   Vegetarian Meals: pizza   Children's Menu/Portions   Beer   *Theakston   Family Room   Children Allowed in Bar to Eat Outdoor Play Area   Garden   Outdoor Eating   Accommodation: 8 bedrooms, all en suite, from £48 (single £29)   Children Welcome Overnight   Cot Available   Check-in: all day   Credit Cards: Access, Visa*

ETTINGTON Chequers Inn Main Road (A422). A promising new entry,with an imaginative selection on the menu; fresh fish and game, home-made pies, French and other cuisines represented; food lunch and evening; Adnams, Marston beers. Garden; children allowed for meals.

GREAT WOLFORD   Fox & Hounds

Shipston on Stour CV36 5NQ
Tel: (0608) 74220
Open: 12-2.30 (not Mon), 7-11
Licensees: David and Joan Hawker

Cotswold stone pub, traditionally run by the proprietors, with traditional public bar games and discreet piped music in the main room. Furnishings are simple and various, and there's a log fire. All food is home-made; the weekday dining room (where children are permitted) becomes more restauranty at weekends.

Bar Meals: 12-2, 7-9.30 (9 Sun); bar snacks lunchtime   Typical Dishes: field mushroom soup £1.75, garlic mushrooms £2.50, beef bourguignon £5.95, roast duck in orange sauce £7.75, salmon steak with lemon butter £6.95, sticky toffee pudding £2   Vegetarian Meals: tagliatelle with ratatouille sauce £4.75   Children's Portions   Beer   *Marston; Wadworth; Whitbread*   Whisky   *Patio/terrace   Outdoor Eating   No Credit Cards*

HATTON   Waterman Inn

Birmingham Road CV35 7JJ
Tel: (0926) 492427
Open: 11-11
Licensees: Diane and Arturo Volpe

'Restaurant and traditional country inn' is the self-description here and it's very much a dining pub; eat in the bar or in the Gallery Restaurant proper (same menu). The printed menu is backed by often interesting daily specials, and a cold buffet of roasts and salads is popular at £5.25. Located by the Hatton locks on the Grand Union Canal.

Bar Meals: 12-2, 7-10; bar snacks both sessions   Typical Dishes: home-made soup of the day £1.30, prawns and mushrooms in garlic £2.95, chicken Neptune £9.95, gammon and egg £6.45, sirloin steak £9.95, apple pie £1.75   Vegetarian Meals: home-made curry £5.25   Children's Menu   Beer   *Greenalls   Family Room   Outdoor Play Area Riverside   Garden   Outdoor Eating   Summer Barbecue   Credit Cards: Access, Visa*

ILMINGTON Howard Arms

Lower Green CV36 4LN
FOOD
Tel: (060 882) 226
Open: 11-2.30, 7-11
Licensees: David and Melanie Smart

Ilmington is typical of the small local villages which delight visiting tourists, and the mellow Cotswold-stone Howard Arms, a rambling building overlooking the village green, is equally admired. Outside, there are five arched and bay windows and large hanging baskets, brimming with flowers in summer. Inside is immaculately maintained and full of period character. Splendid flagstone floors are covered with colourful rugs, rustic oak tables, settles and round-back chairs. There are huge, heavily-beamed ceilings and a wall of exposed stone. Other walls are hung with hunting and sporting prints. The Russons have now left, but new licensees are continuing the Howard Arms tradition of providing good quality food from fresh produce. The blackboard menu includes unambitious dishes like steak and Guinness pie, crispy cod, and chicken cordon bleu, but also a couple of more interesting things. Good quality rump or sirloin steak comes with a robust green peppercorn sauce; a lovely piece of fresh salmon was nicely poached, served with a well-flavoured cream and fresh basil sauce, and a pretty, crisp panaché of fresh vegetables. Good puddings. Then there's the restaurant, up a couple of steps from the bar, recently refurbished, with light-painted walls, and tablecloths. Regularly changing menus here show a good deal of thought and effort at a reasonable set price (currently £16 for three courses and coffee). Typical starters might include a leek and stilton mousse in puff pastry, with a vinaigrette of red and green peppers; to follow, red mullet with lemon and chive butter sauce, or noisettes of lamb with tomato and tarragon. Sundays see a traditional Sunday roast menu. There's nice service and a quiet civilised atmosphere throughout, but at times it gets very busy. It's best to book for the restaurant.

Bar Meals: 12-1.30, 7-9 (9.30 Fri/Sat) **Restaurant:** *7-9 (9.30 Fri/Sat): bar snacks both sessions* **Typical Dishes BAR:** *tomato and thyme soup £1.50, deep-fried butterfly prawns £2.25, steak and Guinness pie £5, poached salmon with basil cream £6.75, bread and butter pudding £2.50* **RESTAURANT:** *set-price £16 dinners: timbale of smoked salmon, chicken liver parfait, supreme of duck with blackberry glaze, roast turbot, artichoke hearts with oyster mushrooms in a herb cream, chocolate truffle cake* **Children's Portions** **Beer** *Marston; Whitbread Children Allowed in Bar to Eat Outdoor Play Area Garden Outdoor Eating* **Accommodation:** *2 bedrooms, both en suite, from £40 (single £25) Children Welcome Overnight Cots Available Check-in: by arrangement* **Credit Cards:** *Access, Visa*

KENILWORTH Clarendon Arms 44 Castle Hill. Routine bar menu, but interesting specials; good casseroles and creamy curries; even fresh lobster. Nicely renovated town-centre pub, getting increasingly foodie; family room; garden. Courage beers. Open: 11-3, 5.30-11.

LITTLE COMPTON Red Lion

Moreton-in-Marsh GL56 0RT
FOOD
Tel: (060 874) 397
B&B
Open: 11-2.30 (12-2 Sun), 6-11
Licensees: David and Sarah Smith

Honest and unassuming bar food at the Red Lion features some very well regarded steaks, which are cut from the joint to individual specifications, cooked to order and doused in the sauce of your choice or just served plain if preferred. The largest consumed in the pub to date was some 48 oz. Fish has recently increased its presence on the menu, dishes like grilled Dover sole, marinated and char-grilled swordfish steak, or poached halibut with a white wine, crab and prawn sauce. In addition, daily specials might include rack of lamb with a port, redcurrant and orange sauce. Licensees David and Sarah Smith are constantly on the lookout for new suppliers, the latest being a local butcher who produces some wonderful (and huge) pork sausages for the pub. Cooking is homely and competent throughout. The pub itself is a charming 16th century building of mellow local Cotswold stone, standing at the edge of the village, just off the A44. Its interior consists of two rooms, a simple public bar with exposed stone walls, modest furniture, a fruit machine and juke box (which can intrude into the other bar), and various other pub games. The lounge is unfussy but characterful, with exposed stone, low beamed ceilings and rustic style furnishings, some of its tables tucked neatly into alcoves. To the rear of the pub is a pretty, well planted garden, a nice spot in fine weather, despite the disappointment of white plastic furniture. You can eat outside, but be warned that if you do, full payment for your meal will be requested on ordering, as the pub has suffered a number of eat-and-runners. Three neat, unfussy bedrooms overlooking the garden provide comfortable, if understated, accommodation. Two have beamed ceilings and exposed stone walls, as well as double beds. The third is a twin. All have duvets, and their own washbasins. They share a well-kept, carpeted bathroom.

Bar Meals: 12-2 (1.30 Sat), 7-8.45 (9.30 Sat); bar snacks both sessions   **Typical Dishes:** celery, apple and prawn salad £3.60, home-made beef curry £4.85, breast of chicken with sherry, mushroom and asparagus sauce £5.65, rack of lamb in redcurrant, port and orange sauce £8.95, raspberry meringue £2   Vegetarian Meals: lasagne £4.85 Children's Menu/Portions   Beer   Donnington   Cider   Children Allowed in Bar to Eat   Outdoor Play Area   Garden   Summer Barbecue   **Accommodation:** 3 bedrooms, sharing a bathroom, from £32 (single £20)   Children Welcome Overnight (minumum age 8)   Check-in: by arrangement   **Credit Cards:** Access, Visa

NAPTON The Folly. Recently re-opened canalside pub in pleasant rural area; unpretentious and homely; the menu dominated by around a dozen pies, as well as other hot home-cooked dishes.

SHIPSTON ON STOUR   White Bear

High Street CV36 4AJ   FOOD
Tel: (0608) 61558
Open: 11-3, 6-11
Licensee: Suzanne Roberts   B&B

Just a few years ago, the White Bear was seriously in the running for Egon Ronay's Pub of the Year, and finished the contest a worthy runner-up. Later, licensees Hugh and Suzanne Roberts also took on the Fossebridge Inn, where they spent most of their time, and as a result standards began to slip alarmingly at the White Bear. Following the death of her husband, Suzanne Roberts moved back to Shipston, where she is now concentrating all her efforts on lifting the pub back to its former glory, and it's satisfying to be able to report that the White Bear is once more most definitely on the up. It's a fine old coaching inn, partly 16th century, overlooking the market place. The public bar has a large fireplace, log-burning stove, solid wood furniture and the obligatory fruit machine, while in the narrower and more characterful lounge there's a part red-tiled, part carpeted floor, fine stripped wood tables, roundback chairs, massive settles and some original beams. Rag-rolled walls are covered with a variety of pictures, including cartoons referring to regulars, old photographs of Shipston as it was in times past, and the daily newspapers are left out for customers to browse through, always a thoughtful touch. There's also a restaurant, to the rear of the bar, a more spartan room enlivened with large, colourful prints. Bar food is beginning to look well-conceived and skilfully cooked again: chilled cucumber and mint soup, salmon trout in aspic with Chinese spices, or plump fresh moules marinière with a light creamy sauce are typical of starters on the blackboard menu, and main dishes might include pork chop with apple and cider, chicken breast with avocado and garlic, or tender noisettes of lamb, cooked pink and served with redcurrant sauce. There's a good fresh selection of vegetables and potatoes, and to follow perhaps a traditional and delicious bread and butter pudding. It gets very busy, especially at lunchtimes, when service can appear on the harassed side, though managing to stay good-humoured; the whole pub has a lively and relaxed atmosphere in which locals mix easily with the business and holiday traffic. Meanwhile, up the narrow staircase, the White Bear continues to provide comfortable lodgings in its ten individually styled, though by no means large, bedrooms. The period of neglect is evident in the distinct datedness of the decor, though all have been well-maintained; refurbishment will no doubt follow in time. There's a mixture of period, pine and stripped wood furnishings, duvets and old televisions in each room, and all are en suite, seven having compact shower cubicles, the rest baths.

*Bar Meals: 12-2, 6.30-9.30 (10 Fri/Sat); bar snacks lunchtime   **Typical Dishes:** mushroom and coriander soup £2, warm salad of smoked chicken and ginger £3.95, chicken breast with wild mushrooms £7.25, tagliatelle with pesto £3.95, ragout of Cornish fishes £8.95, bread and butter pudding £2.50   Vegetarian Meals: field mushroom puffs with grain mustard   Children's Portions*   Beer   *Bass*   Whisky   *Children Allowed in Bar to Eat   Patio/terrace   Outdoor Eating   **Accommodation:** 9 bedrooms, all en suite, from £47 (single £35)   Children Welcome Overnight   Cots Available   Check-in: all day   **Credit Cards:** Access, Amex, Diners, Visa*

SOUTHAM Old Mint Coventry Street (A423).   Medieval pub with lots of armorial and other bric-a-brac, heavy beams, old furniture, and lasagne/cottage pie type bar food. Gets very busy. Good range of beers. Open: 11-2.30, 6.30-11 (11-3, 6-11 Sat).

STRATFORD-UPON-AVON   Lamplighter Inn

42 Rother Street CV37 6LP
Tel: (0789) 293071
Open: 11-11
Licensee: Paul Lumbers

16th century free house, less busy than some others, with a newish landlord, and a menu that at least avoids the scampi and chips routine. No chips, in fact: sauté potatoes and seasonal vegetables are offered with main courses instead.

*Bar Meals: 12-2.30, 6.30-9; bar snacks both sessions   **Typical Dishes:** orange and carrot soup £1.30, paté, chicken supreme in garlic and tomato sauce, mixed grills, fishermans pie (main courses from £4)   Vegetarian Meals: pan haggerty*   Beer   *Ansells, Tetley; Courage Family Room   Patio/terrace   Outdoor Eating   **No Credit Cards***

STRATFORD-UPON-AVON   Slug & Lettuce

38 Guild Street CV37 6QY   FOOD
Tel: (0789) 299700   ☻
Open: all day   ❢
Licensee: Steve Sartori

Occupying a corner site adjacent to the Birmingham road, close to the town centre, the Slug & Lettuce is one of Stratford's places to be seen. With more than a hint of wine bar/bistro atmosphere, the pub is a particular haven for the young and trendy; it's lively and informal, and usually packed to the gunnels at weekends. Walls are light wood-panelled, floors a mixture of flagstones and polished boards, strewn with rugs, and furniture is stripped pine country kitchen style, the sturdy tables topped with flowers and candles in old champagne bottles; clever evening lighting creates a splendid atmosphere. Civilised touches include a newspaper rack. The food at the Slug & Lettuce remains as good and popular as ever. Large blackboards display the day's choice of imaginative and well-handled dishes. Starters include good soups like tomato, orange and basil, and meatballs with mint, honey and lemon. There are light meals like stir-fried chicken wings or tagliatelle of salmon and prawns, and a main meal selection no less interesting, perhaps poached darne of salmon with a mushroom and basil sauce, honeyed lamb kebabs, or a tender breast of duck grilled and served with a rich game sauce flavoured with peach brandy and garnished with fresh peach and half a fanned nectarine. All main dishes come with a side dish of crisp fresh vegetables. Puddings are nice, there's a good choice of coffees too. Drinks are chosen from a blackboard wine list, real ale handpumps, or from a range of the designer lagers presently so fashionable. Staff are young and cheerful, but service would be quicker if they didn't spend so much time chatting up customers. Outside, a small paved patio, floodlit at night, is a nice spot for a summer drink.

Bar Meals: 12-2, 5.30-9 **Typical Dishes:** *fresh Cornish crab bisque £2, sliced marinated Scotch salmon, chicken breast stuffed with avocado and garlic, Barnsley lamb chop with port and spring onion sauce, poached lemon sole with dill and mango, banoffee pie Vegetarian Meals: vegetable bake* `Cheese` `Beer` *Ansells, Ind Coope Burton Ale, Tetley Bitter   Children Allowed in Bar to Eat   Patio/terrace   Outdoor Eating* **Credit Cards:** *Access, Visa*

TEMPLE GRAFTON   Blue Boar

near Alcester
Tel: (0789) 750010
Open: 11-3, 6-11
Licensee: Adrian Parkes

Country pub with old and new sections; exposed stone, log fire, and dining area proper. Well-heeled bar food (the restaurant even more so) comes with nicely-cooked vegetables.

Bar Meals: 12-2, 6.30-10 (9.30 Sun); bar snacks both sessions **Typical Dishes BAR:** *stilton and celery soup £1.50, devilled herring roes £2.75, lambs kidneys au poivre £5.50, beef in stilton £9.65, monkfish provencale £8.75, chocolate whisky pudding   Vegetarian Meals: spaghetti gardiniere £3.75   Children's Portions* `Beer` *Marston; Whitbread Family Room   Patio/terrace   Outdoor Eating* **Credit Cards:** *Access, Amex, Visa*

WARMINGTON   Wobbly Wheel

Warwick Road OX17 1JJ
Tel: (029 589) 214
Open: 11-3, 6-11
Licensee: Michael Hayden

Attractive pub with welcoming atmosphere.

Bar Meals and Restaurant: 12-2, 6.30-10; bar snacks both sessions **Typical Dishes BAR:** *mustard and mushroom soup £2.25, paté maison £2.95, steak and kidney pie £5.95, rump steak £8,95, saute of mussels £5.50, sherry trifle* **RESTAURANT:** *avocado Chollerford £4.50, tournedos Rossini £12.95, scampi provencale £11.50, Lady McLean's cake   Vegetarian Meals: vegetable and mushroom pancake   Children's Portions* `Beer` *Wadworth; Youngers   Children Allowed in Bar to Eat   Garden* **Accommodation:** *6 bedrooms, all en suite, from £62 (single £52)   Children Welcome Overnight   Cot Available   Check-in: all day* **Credit Cards:** *Access, Amex, Visa*

WELFORD ON AVON   Shakespeare Inn

Chapel Street CV37 8PX   ❦
Tel: (0789) 750443
Licensees: Mike and Jan Shaw

The menu looks ordinary, but everything is fresh and tasty here, testified to by a
loyal local following. Pies and pizzas on the main list, with recommended daily
specials lifting the standards at a stroke. The evening menu brings a conventional
steaks/chicken/grills choice.

*Bar Meals: 12-2, 7-9.30 (not Sun eve)   bar snacks lunchtime   **Typical Dishes:** tagliatelle
with ham, quiche, steak and ale pie, treacle tart (main courses from around £3.50)
Vegetarian Meals*   Beer   *Whitbread*   **Credit Cards:** *Access, Visa*

WHATCOTE   Royal Oak

near Shipston on Stour CV36 5EF   ❦
Tel: (0295) 88319
Open: 10.30-2.30, 6-11
Licensee: Catherine Matthews

Highly atmospheric ancient alehouse, with a romantic history: the inglenook
features rungs leading up to a secret chamber. Beams are very low, furnishings
various, and there's a miscellaneous array of bric-a-brac. Food is secondary, and the
usual menu routine, but the specials might be worth trying.

*Bar Meals: 12-2, 6-10.30 (12-2.30, 7-10 Sun); bar snacks both sessions   **Typical
Dishes:** devils brew soup £1.45, deep-fried mushrooms £2, steak and kidney pie £4.95,
pork chop £4.95, haddock fillets £3.50   Vegetarian Meals: vegetable and pasta bake
Children's Portions*   Beer   *Marston; Whitbread   Children Allowed in Bar to Eat
Garden   Outdoor Eating   **No Credit Cards***

WILMCOTE   Masons Arms

Stratford-upon-Avon CV37 9XX   ❦
Tel: (0789) 297416
Open: 11-2.30, 6-11
Licensee: Keith Snow

A short drive from Stratford on the A34 (in fact Wilmcote was the home of
Shakespeare's mother), the Masons is popular for its reliable bar food and smarter
restaurant fare (children allowed here).

*Bar Meals and Restaurant: 12-2, 6-9.30; bar snacks both sessions   **Typical Dishes**
BAR: chicken and leek soup, squid rings, steak and kidney pie, gammon steak, apple and
blackberry crumble   **Restaurant:** carrot and orange soup, smoked salmon, pork loin in
Calvados, entrecote bordelaise, poached salmon in vermouth and prawn sauce, bread and butter
pudding   Vegetarian Meals: lasagne   Children's Portions*   Beer   *Bass; Marston;
Whitbread   Outdoor Play Area   Garden   **Credit Cards:** Access, Visa*

WEST MIDLANDS

COVENTRY   William IV

1059 Foleshill Road (A444)   `FOOD`
Tel: (0203) 686394
Open: 11-2.30, 6-11 (11-3, 5-11 Fri/Sat)
Licensee: Perminder Bains

About three miles from the city centre, on the Nuneaton road, the William IV looks extremely ordinary, a mock timbered, red brick, typical roadside city pub, and the distinctly unassuming interior, with its light modern wallpaper hung with prints, plush banquette seating and the obligatory fruit machine, do nothing to belie this view. But open the front door and the aromas that greet you are unmistakable, for the food here is authentic Indian, though there are also English dishes for the less adventurous. A printed menu – if you can get one – offers a wide-ranging choice of competitively priced dishes, including the house specials, Kadhai dishes, biriyani and thalis, accompanied by the usual side dishes. A fashionable addition to the menu is the marking out of some options as healthy, or rather, healthier, with the Look After Your Heart symbol; though as most of the dishes on the menu seem to have been awarded this honour, including all the puddings, it might be wise to treat the symbol with a pinch of Lo Salt. The food itself is well spiced and flavoursome, though the cooking can be rather uneven on occasion. It's extremely busy, with a varied clientele; be prepared to share your table, and be prepared for a wait, as everything is cooked to order. On the whole the wait's worthwhile. A Mughlai biriyani, marinated chicken steamed with saffron rice, mixed spices and vegetables, was hot and flavoursome, though the vegetable samosa on one occasion was not as fresh as it might have been. Service is on the whole friendly, if occasionally abrupt.

Bar Meals: 12-2.30, 6 (5 Fri/Sat) – 10.30; no food Sun   *Typical Dishes:* shami kebab £1, chicken tikka £1.75, chicken rogan josh £3.10, lamb gosht pukht biriyani £4, badshani zafrani £4.50, kulfi ice-cream £1.40 Vegetarian Meals   Children's Portions
`Beer`   M&B Mild, Brew XI   Children Allowed in the Bar to Eat   Garden   Outdoor Eating   **No Credit Cards**

COVENTRY   Greyhound

Sutton Stop, Hawkesbury Junction CY6 6UF
Tel: (0203) 363046
Open: 11-2.30 (12-2.30 Sun), 6-11
Licensee: R A Hoare

Originally a farmhouse, the Greyhound's been a pub since 1822, when the North Oxford and Coventry canals were installed – they meet right outside the premises. The pub's well-known for its pies, which are instantly delivered after ordering and, in our experience, pretty ordinary. Nice atmosphere though.

Bar Meals: 12-2, 6.30-9 (not Sun/Mon eves); bar snacks both sessions   *Typical Dishes:* home-made soup £1.35, Whispering Smith pie (beef in ale and stilton) £4.85, Wellington pie £5.20, piscatorial pie (fish in provencale sauce) £6.20, bread and butter pudding Vegetarian Meals: chilli   `Beer`   Banks's; Bass   `Whisky`   Outdoor Play Area   Riverside Garden   Outdoor Eating   *Credit Cards:* Access, Visa

CRADLEY HEATH Sausage Works St Annes Road, Five Ways. Another of the Little Pub Co. Chain; this time devoted to the great British banger; their usual subtle style, but well-run with well-kept beers including their own.

| **HIMLEY** | **Crooked House** |

Coppice Mill (off B4176 to the east of Himley) DY3 4DA
Tel: (0384) 238583
Open: 11-11 (11.30-2.30, 6-11 winter weekdays)
Licensee: Gary Ensor

In keeping with the name, heavy mining subsidence has left the Crooked House sloping alarmingly away from right to left. And you haven't had anything to drink yet. The interior is Victorian rustic, half-panelled, red-tiled with an imposing brick fireplace and another of cast iron, plus lots of period decoratives. The two original bars are joined by a newer extension, prettily done with exposed bricks, country paper and fine antique pieces. Food is very secondary; you may be feeling a little too queasy to eat anyway.

Bar Meals: 12-2; bar snacks   ***Typical Dishes:*** *home-made steak and kidney pie £3.30, home-made faggots and peas £2.55, scampi £2.75, home-made apple pie 95p Children's Menu* `Beer` *Banks's Mild, Bitter Children Allowed in Bar to Eat (minimum age 3) Patio/terrace Outdoor Eating Summer Barbecue* ***No Credit Cards***

LYE Shovel Inn Pedmore Road. Steak and Guinness, fisherman's or chicken and mushroom pie among the popular, simple bar menu here; vegetarians catered for; children welcome for meals; good range of beers. Open: 11.30-3, 6.30-11.

OLDBURY Waggon & Horses Church Street. Submerged by the new civic centre, but a finely preserved Victorian town pub nonetheless; tiled walls; real fire; outdoor drinking; food lunch and evening. Good beers. Open: 12-2.30, 5.30-11.

QUARRY BANK Church Tavern High Street (A4100) Tel: (0384) 68757. Authentic Black Country cuisine at this popular High Victorian pub: faggots with peas included, plus home-made soups, pies and casseroles, simple and homely. Meals lunch and evening; children allowed in to eat; Holts beers. Open: 10-2.30, 5 (6 winter)-11 (all day Sat).

SEDGLEY Beacon Hotel Bilston Street. Unprepossessing roadside pub, which once inside turns into a Victorian treasure trove, with a maze of little rooms, and a 19th century approach to life; try the Sarah Hughes Dark Ruby Mild, made in the little brewery at the back. Families welcome; lunchtime food. Open: 12-2.30, 5.30-10.30 (11.30-3, 5.30-11 Fri/Sat).

TIPTON Mad O'Rourke's Pie Factory Hurst Lane, Dudley Road. Yet another of the Little Pub Co. chain, a cheery, buzzing pub,with frequent live music, the famous Desperate Dan pie, and tongue-in-cheek oddities like black pudding thermidor. Good beers, including their own.

WEST BROMWICH Manor House Hallgreen Road. Moated medieval manor house, carefully restored, and makes an unusually atmospheric pub. Food 12-2, 6-10 from a help-yourself servery, is hit and miss in character – we've enjoyed a chicken curry here in the past, but recently found meals overcooked and weary from their long sojourn on the hotplate. Take your chances. Banks's beers.

WOLVERHAMPTON Great Western Sun Street. Very popular, revitalised local next to the station, and full of railway memorabilia; pleasant garden and patio area, simple and cheap snacks of the pie and peas sort; good sandwiches, good beer: Bathams and Holdens. Open: all day (11-2.30, 6.30-11 Sat).

WILTSHIRE

AMESBURY Antrobus Arms, 15 Church Street. Attractive, antique-furnished pub in the heart of Salisbury Plain, not far from Stonehenge. Decent bar and restaurant food; 21 bedrooms (around £50 a double), and delightful garden. Open: 10.30-2.30, 6-11.

BARFORD ST MARTIN   Barford Inn

Junction A30/B3089, 2 miles from Wilton SP3 4AB
Tel: (0722) 742242
Open: 11-2.30 (12-2.30 Sun), 6.30-11
Licensee: Philip Stansfield

As well as dishes of the sort listed here, they offer plenty of starters or light snack options and a selection of 'ploughmen' including an oak-smoked lamb variety (£3.20), plus humbler fare of the scampi and chips sort. Blackboards carry a daily specials list. The present owners (Marcelle Stansfield does the cooking) have developed the original old inn, but old beams, natural brick, a log fire and a music, machine and pool table-free environment are maintained with justifiable pride. There may be overnight accommodation by 1992.

Bar Meals: 12-2, 7-9.30; bar snacks both sessions   **Typical Dishes:** *cauliflower and broccoli soup £1.45, Fjordling paté £2.85, rabbit casserole in cider and honey £5.85, tenderloin of lamb stuffed with figs £6.15, plaice in shrimp and brandy sauce £5.95, Dorset applecake £1.85 Vegetarian Meals   Children's Portions* Beer *Hall & Woodhouse Badger Best Bitter   Children Allowed in Bar to Eat   Patio/terrace   Outdoor Eating* **Credit Cards:** *Access, Visa*

BIDDESTONE   White Horse

The Green SN14 7DG
Tel: (0249) 713305
Open: 11-2.30, 6-11
Licensees: Gordon and Pat Taylor

Unassuming village local in delightfully quaint village, overlooking duck pond. Traditional multi-room layout retained; friendly atmosphere.

Bar Meals: 12-2, 7-10; bar snacks both sessions   **Typical Dishes:** *spicy tomato soup £1.30, garlic mushrooms £2.75, ham, egg and chips £2.95, barbecued spare ribs £4.25, mixed grill £8.95, spotted dick £1.25   Vegetarian Meals   Children's Portions* Beer *Courage; Wadworth   Children Allowed in Bar to Eat   Outdoor Play Area   Garden Outdoor Eating* **No Credit Cards**

BRADFORD ON AVON   Bunch of Grapes

14 Silver Street BA15 1JY   FOOD
Tel: (02216) 3877
Open: 11-2.30, 6.30-11
Licensee: Clive Crocker

Appropriately, given its name, but somewhat incongruously for a town-centre pub, there is a grapevine clinging to the outside of the Bunch of Grapes. The pub was once a shop, and has a little bow window which now houses a copy of the blackboard menu and also, more often than not, the pub cat having a doze in the sunshine. Old enough that its true age is shrouded in mystery, an old indenture records that the Grapes changed hands in 1846 for £300. It's long and narrow with red hessian walls above dark brown dado panelling, and the decor is unpretentiously old rather than of the style known as olde worlde. Convivial landlord Clive Crocker strives to keep the balance firmly that of a pub which also serves food, rather than becoming a dining pub, and stocks recherché beers with wonderful names like Summer Lightning, Lifeboat and Ash Vine, drawn up from the cellar by a genuine 1890s brass and porcelain beer engine. Just four beers are on the go at any one time, but are rotated from a repertoire of over 30 brands. A short list of about half a dozen wines changes almost as frequently, depending upon Clive's fancy, but might include the likes of Chateau Musar from the Lebanon, Marques de Caceres and Ricasoli Chianti, all available by the glass. The blackboard food menu lists whatever wife Chris has decided to cook that day. Steak and kidney pie, perhaps, with melt-in-the-mouth shortcrust pastry covering a rich dark filling and, if your luck is in, her bananarama – a sort of fluffy banana flan with a layer of soft caramel.

Bar Meals: 12-2, 6.45-8.45; no food Sun; bar snacks lunchtime **Typical Dishes:** *ham and vegetable soup £1.10, smoked trout paté £2.95, steak and kidney pie £3.55, lamb and apricot casserole £3.95, stilton, cauliflower and walnut quiche £3.10, strawberry crumble with Cointreau £1.12 Vegetarian Meals   Children's Portions* `Cheese` `Beer` *Ash Vine; Batemans; Burton Bridge; Smiles* `Cider` *Thatchers   Children Allowed in Bar to Eat* **No Credit Cards**

BRINKWORTH   Three Crowns

near Chippenham SN15 5AF
Tel: (066 641) 366
Open: 10-2.30, 6-11
Licensee: Anthony Windle

Huge ploughman's lunches and good jacket potatoes at lunchtime help balance an otherwise rather smart, restauranty menu. The rambling, cosy interior offers quiet corners for tete-a-tetes; two of the tables are 18th century former bellows. Nice setting on village green by church. Conservatory extension to seat 50, enlargement to car park and garden landscaping imminent.

Bar Meals: 12-2, 6.30-9.30; bar snacks both sessions **Typical Dishes:** *venison medallions £8.75, beef and Guinness pie £6.95, monkfish and salmon plate £9.95, home-made ice-cream £2   Vegetarian Meals: vegetarian crepe £6.95   Children's Menu/Portions* `Beer` *Archers Village Bitter; Wadworth 6X; Whitbread Flowers Original   Children Allowed in Bar to Eat   Outdoor Play Area   Garden   Outdoor Eating* **Credit Cards:** *Access, Visa*

BROMHAM   Greyhound Inn

near Chippenham SN15 2HA
Tel: (0380) 850241
Open: 11-2.30 (12-2.30 Sun), 7 (6.30 Fri/Sat)-11
Licensees: George and Morag Todd

Lively pub run with enthusiasm and verve. Menu often ingenious, featuring fine Malaysian dishes. Tons of atmosphere, thanks largely to bric-a-brac festooned walls and ceilings in both bars. Cosy, intimate dining room (same menu). Parents can get extra plates for informal children's portions.

Bar Meals: all open hours; bar snacks lunchtime **Typical Dishes:** *home-made soup £1.80, crab and mushroom bake £3.40, pork things £5.90, chicken verluccio £5.20, sambal udang £6.40, chocolate and brandy cheesecake £2.30   Vegetarian Meals: vegetarian bake £5.20* `Beer` *Wadworth IPA, 6X* `Whisky` *Children Allowed in Bar to Eat Garden   Outdoor Eating* **No Credit Cards**

BURTON   Old House At Home

near Chippenham SN14 7LT
Tel: (0454) 218227
Open: 11.30-2.30 (not Tue), 7-11
Licensees: Sally and David Warburton

Old standards and more interesting dishes on a printed menu; expensive though, starting at around £6 even for a humble bowl of chilli. Pleasant dining area; log fire.

Bar Meals: 12-2, 7-10.30 **Typical Dishes:** *home-made soup £2.10, home-made paté £2.80, oriental chicken £8.90, fillet cordon bleu £13.50, plaice Antoinette £9.30 Vegetarian Meals: chef's stir-fry £6.20* **Beer** *Draught Bass; Butcombe Bitter; Smiles Bitter; Wadworth 6X Outdoor Play Area Garden Outdoor Eating* **No Credit Cards**

CASTLE COMBE   Castle Hotel

near Chippenham SN14 7HN
Tel: (0249) 782461
Licensees: Mr and Mrs Baker-Joy

Splendid pub in picturesque village, with a fine medieval market cross and church. Brick-lined cellars are a cosy venue for decent bar meals; more than decent when chef Ivan Reid is present. Bedrooms are neat and clean, some with sloping floors and creaky character, and period furnishings. Front bedrooms are biggest, attic rooms the most romantic.

Bar Meals: 12-2.15, 7-9.45 **Typical Dishes:** *stilton and avocado soup, smoked venison with apricot chutney, poached sole with crab sauce, chicken breast in watercress sauce (main courses from £5) Vegetarian Meals* **Beer** *Bass; Eldridge Pope; Wadworth Children Allowed in Bar to Eat* **Accommodation:** *11 bedrooms, all en suite, from £65 Children Welcome Overnight Cots Available Check-in: all day* **Credit Cards:** *Access, Amex, Visa*

CHARLTON   Horse and Groom

near Malmesbury SN16 9DL   ❢
Tel: (0666) 823904
Open: 12-3, 7-11 (closed Sun eve, all day Mon winter)
Licensee: David Hall

Eminently civilised Grade II listed Cotswold stone pub, set well back from the main road. Open log fires, no music, small saloon bar and larger public. Well-heeled, and well-loved – booking advised for restaurant (same menu; closed Sun eve). All food is home cooked by landlady Virginia Hall.

Bar Meals: 12-2, 7-9.30; bar snacks both sessions **Typical Dishes:** *carrot and coriander soup £1.85, half-pint of prawns with garlic mayonnaise £3.20, stir-fry chicken £7.25, home-made steak pie £6.65, plaice Virginia £8.50, banoffee pie £2.30 Vegetarian Meals: fruity vegetable curry £4.85 Children's Portions* **Beer** *Archers; Moles; Tetley; Wadworth* **Cider** *Blands Children Allowed in Bar to Eat Outdoor Play Area Garden Outdoor Eating* **Credit Cards:** *Access, Visa*

CHICKSGROVE   Compasses

Tisbury SP3 6NB   ▼
Tel: (072 270) 318
Open: 12-3, 7-11.30
Licensees: Linda and Andrew Moore

Grade II listed pretty inn with a charmingly unspoilt bar: flagstones, inglenook, loads of old timber, and discreet modernisation. Owners are earning local fans with their food. Planning permission was being sought for six en suite bedrooms in the grounds as we went to press; they hope to be completed building for the 1992 season.

Bar Meals: 12-2, 7-9.30; bar snacks both sessions **Typical Dishes:** *home-made soup £1.95, gravadlax, beef or duck oriental £6.95, mixed grill £7.25, seafood platter £6.95, meringue nest £2.50 Vegetarian Meals: mushroom, nut and claret pie £4.95 Children's Portions* **Beer** *Adnams; Bass; Fullers; Wadworth Children Allowed in Bar to Eat Outdoor Play Area Garden Outdoor Eating* **No Credit Cards**

CHIPPENHAM   Nettleton Arms

Nettleton SN14 7NP
Tel: (0249) 782783
Open: 12-2.30, 7-11
Licensees: Les and Lesley Cox, Jim and Cynthia Harvey

Attractive old Cotswold stone inn, much modernised, but with a simple tap room style (that is, spartan and masculine) bar; the loudly carpeted Coddrington Room is the main dining area; sit-down Sunday lunches in here. Four comfortable, plainly furnished bedrooms in the barn conversion – the two upstairs with some old rafters.

Bar Meals: 12-2, 7-9 (10 Fri/Sat); bar snacks both sessions **Typical Dishes:** *vegetable soup £1.85, garlic mushrooms £3, steak and kidney pie, pork fillet in mustard sauce, chicken stuffed with smoked salmon and mozzarella (main courses from £4), treacle tart Children's Menu/Portions* **Beer** *Ind Coope Burton Ale, Tetley Bitter; Wadworth 6X Family Room Outdoor Play Area Garden Outdoor Eating* **Accommodation:** *4 bedrooms, all en suite, from £43.50 (single £27) Children Welcome Overnight Check-in: all day* **Credit Cards:** *Access, Amex, Visa*

CORSELY HEATH Royal Oak on A362 Tel: (037 388) 238. Busy pub near the Longleat Estate, with home-made simple bar meals (lunch and evening) including good pies; fresh vegetables; ambitious restaurant. Family room; garden; Wadworth beers.

CORTON   Dove Inn

near Warminster BA12 0SZ
Tel: (0985) 50378
Open: 11-3.30, 6-11 (all day Sat)
Licensee: Stuart Broadhurst

This delightful Victorian country pub has got new licensees since our last edition, and the menu has changed. It's still unusually stylish and well-kept, and the doves still coo in the rustic garden, too.

Bar Meals: 12-3, 7-10 (not Sun eve); bar snacks both sessions **Typical Dishes:** *home-made soup £1.40, paté £1.95, fish pie £3.95, Indonesian beef £4.95, roast quail £3.95,*

home made puddings   Vegetarian Meals   Children's Portions   `Beer`   *Ruddles, Ushers*
Outdoor Play Area   Garden   **Credit Cards:** *Access, Visa*

DEVIZES   Bear Hotel

Market Place SN10 1HS
Tel: (0380) 722444
Open: 10-3, 6-11 (all day Thur-Sat)
Licensee: Keith Dickenson

Famous old town-centre coaching inn with an old-fashioned air, civilised, rambling
and busy in typical market town style – hotelly rather than pubby, with a main
lounge slightly reminiscent of an ocean liner bar. The parquet-floored Lawrence
Room is smart and relaxing, and there's a splendid pea green sitting room. Good log
fires in winter. Bedrooms are floral, comfortable and well-equipped, with proper
sturdy furniture. Three have four-poster beds. Bar food is reliable, as is the beer, in
the home town of Wadworth brewery.

Bar Meals: *10-2.30, 7-9*   **Restaurant:** *12-2 (2.30 Sun), 7-9*   **Typical Dishes BAR:**
*Devizes pie with pickled egg £2.25, beef in real ale £3.95, mixed grill £4.25, Bear Club
triple decker £2.95, sticky toffee pudding £1.50*   **RESTAURANT:** *langoustine tails
poached in pastis £3.95, fillet of beef stroganoff £12,75, red mullet with Cornish brill
£11.75, pan-fried calves liver and bacon £12.25, chocolate brandy truffle torte   Vegetarian
Meals: parsnips Molly Parkin £1.95   Children's Portions*   `Beer`   *Wadworth   Family
Room   Children Allowed in Bar to Eat   Patio/terrace*   **Accommodation:** *24 bedrooms, all
en suite, from £55 (single £35)   Children Welcome Overnight   Cots Available   Check-
in: all day*   **Credit Cards:** *Access, Visa*

FONTHILL GIFFORD   Beckford Arms

Tisbury SP3 6PX
Tel: (0747) 870385
Open: 11-3, 6-11
Licensees: Bob Miles and Peter Harrison

Relaxing 18th century country pub, recently completely refurbished, next door to
Fonthill Vineyard. Nice log fire in winter. Children can choose from the bar snacks
menu in the restaurant.

Bar Meals: *12-2.30, 7-10; bar snacks both sessions*   **Restaurant:** *12-3, 7.30-11*
Typical Dishes BAR: *leek and stilton soup £1.50, ham, leek and cheese bake £2.75,*
RESTAURANT: *sole stuffed with crab and scallops £2.95, duckling in port and redcurrant
£7.50, Wiltshire trout stuffed with celery and apple £6.95, Beckford ghost £3.50
Vegetarian Meals: tagliatelle*   `Beer`   *Courage Best, John Smith's Bitter; Wadworth 6X
Family Room   Garden   Summer Barbecue*   **Accommodation:** *7 bedrooms, all en suite,
from £45 (single £27.50)   Children Welcome Overnight   Cot Available   Check-in: by
arrangement*   **Credit Cards:** *Access, Visa*

FOVANT   Cross Keys

Salisbury SP3 5JH
Tel: (0722) 70284
Open: 11-2.30, 5-11 (10.30 winter)
Licensee: Pauline Storey

13th century coaching inn by the A30 road, standing beneath the Fovant Emblems,
regimental badges carved into the hillside by first world war soldiers. Handsome

furnishings, low ceilings, nice fire, grandfather clock and friendly atmosphere. Bedrooms are warm and cottagey, with rough white-washed walls.

Bar Meals: 11.30-2, 6.30-9; *bar snacks both sessions*   *Restaurant:* 6.30-9   **Typical Dishes BAR:** *home-made soup £1, steak and kidney pie £5, roast gammon £5.25, cottage pie £5, steak £10, lemon meringue pie*   **RESTAURANT:** *whitebait £2.75, half honey-roasted duck £9, whole lemon sole £8, damson fool   Vegetarian Meals: lasagne £4 Children's Menu*   **Beer**   *Adnams; Wadworth   Family Room   Garden   Outdoor Eating* **Accommodation:** *4 bedrooms, sharing 2 bathrooms, from £35 (single £17.50)   Children Welcome Overnight   Check-in: by arrangement*   **Credit Cards:** *Access, Visa*

HINDON   Lamb Inn

High Street   ❢
Tel: (0747) 89573
Open: 11-11
Licensees: A J Morrison and J Croft

Wisteria clings to one corner of this mellow 17th century coaching inn. At its height, 300 post horses were kept here to supply the great number of coaches going to and from London and the West Country. Prime Minister William Pitt was apparently most put out to find no fresh horses available when he stopped off here in 1786. But there have also been less reputable visitors. Silas White, a notorious smuggler said to be leader of the Wiltshire Moonrakers, used the Lamb as the centre of his nefarious activities. These days, things in Hindon are rather more peaceful and the Lamb limits itself to providing honest hospitality to modern travellers who bring their own horsepower in four-wheeled form. The bar is slightly disappointing, a less characterful room than the build-up suggests, although there is a splendid old stone inglenook fireplace, and the atmosphere is enhanced by an ever-changing collection of paintings by local artists both here and in the rather smarter restaurant, which features splendid dark green tartan curtains. The blackboard bar menu is sensibly not over-long, but still manages to offer a reasonable choice. The ham, chicken and mushroom pie had succulent chicken and chunks of good ham, though a little more of the creamy sauce would make it even better; there might also be grilled sea bass, and a nut and vegetable bake. The emphasis is fishy on Tuesdays and Fridays, when the fishmonger calls, and in winter there's also plenty of game, from the estate of the local landowner who bought the inn just a couple of years ago. Overnight accommodation is also offered but, sadly, on our visit we found standards of housekeeping poor; our room hadn't had a good clean for some time.

Bar Meals and Restaurant: 12-2, 7-9.30; *bar snacks both sessions*   **Typical Dishes BAR:** *ham and leek soup £1.85, creamy fish pie £4.95, steak and kidney puie £4.95, venison and game casserole £5.50, chocolate mousse £1.85*   **RESTAURANT:** *set-price £18.95 menu   Vegetarian meals   Children's portions*   **Beer**   *Oakhill; Wadworth; Wiltshire; Youngs   Family room   Patio/terrace   Outdoor eating*   **Accommodation:** *15 rooms, 13 en suite, from £65 (single £55)   Children welcome overnight   Check-in: all day* **Credit Cards:** *Access, Amex, Diners, Visa*

HINDON Grosvenor Arms, High Street: Part-flagstoned original bar, enormous open fire and nicely chosen bits and pieces in a rambling old coaching inn, with decent bar food lunch and evening; live piano on Sundays; Bass, Wadworth, Whitbread beers. Open: 11-2.30, 6-11.

HOLT   Old Ham Tree

near Trowbridge BA14 6PY   `FOOD`
Tel: (0225) 782581
Open: 11.15-2.30 (12-2.30 Sun), 6.30-11
Licensee: John Francis

Cleanly modernised, beamed and pleasant 18th century inn overlooking the village green. Reliably good, simple food. Bedrooms are centrally heated, clean and airy, white-painted with matching furniture, pretty floral fabrics, and a modern shared bathroom. Residents' television lounge above the bar.

Bar Meals and Restaurant: 12-2, 7-10 (not Sun eve); bar snacks both sessions   *Typical Dishes BAR:* lentil and ham soup, spicy lamb with apricots and almonds, steak and Guinness pie, spicy pork ragout, poached salmon with watercress sauce (main courses from £4), rum, nut and raisin tart   *Vegetarian Meals:* broccoli, cheddar and walnut bake   *Children's Menu/Portions*   `Beer` Adnams; Wadworths; Youngs   *Family Room Children Allowed in Bar to Eat   Outdoor Play Area   Garden   Outdoor Eating Accommodation:* 5 bedrooms, 1 en suite, from £31 (single £21)   *Children Welcome Overnight   Check-in: by arrangement   Credit Cards:* Access, Amex, Diners, Visa

HORNINGSHAM   Bath Arms

Longleat BA12 7LY
Tel: (09853) 308
Open: all day
Licensee: Joseph Lovatt

Splendid country hotel close to Longleat, in a 'best-kept' village.

Bar Meals and Restaurant: 12-2, 6-10 (7-9.30 restaurant);   bar snacks both sessions   *Typical Dishes:* steak and kidney pie, smoked goose breast, rack of lamb, beef Wellington, raspberry pudding (bar main courses from £5, restaurant £8)   *Vegetarian Meals:* pasta   *Children's Menu/Portions*   `Beer` Bass; Eldridge Pope; Wadworth   `Whisky`   *Children Allowed in Bar to Eat   Garden   Outdoor Eating   Accommodation:* 7 bedrooms, all en suite, from £57.50 (single £35)   *Children Welcome Overnight   Cots Available   Check-in: all day   Credit Cards:* Access, Diners, Visa

LACOCK   Red Lion

High Street SN15 2LQ   ▼
Tel: (0249) 730456
Open: 11-3, 6-11
Licensees: Clive and Caroline Hurrell

Imposing redbrick Georgian inn at the centre of a National Trust village. The rambling bar is broken up by large pieces of agricultural memorabilia into smaller, cosier areas; smaller pieces, plates and prints litter the walls, and there's quite a collection of stuffed birds and animals. Nice old furniture, log fires, low beams, and Turkey rugs complete the picture. New licensees since our last edition may have changes to make, though probably not many. The food still looks interesting. There are plans for two more bedrooms, previously described by this guide as 'modest but comfortable'; all three existing rooms should be en suite for 1992. Prices may rise.

Bar Meals: 12.15-2.15, 6.30-9.45; bar snacks lunchtime   *Typical Dishes:* home-made soup £2.05, barbecued spare ribs £3.45, beef pie £5.50, pork chops in cream and cider £5.75, giant sausages £4.65, meringues £2.85   *Vegetarian Meals:* moussaka   *Children's*

Menu/Portions `Cheese` `Beer` *Wadworth   Children Allowed in Bar to Eat   Garden
Outdoor Eating   Summer Barbecue   Accommodation: 3 bedrooms, 1 en suite, around
£50   Children Welcome Overnight   Cot Available   Check-in: all day   Credit Cards:
Access, Visa*

LACOCK Rising Sun Bowden Hill: Characterful, busy pub, recently extended,
about a mile east of Lacock; lovely views from pretty garden; decent home-cooked
lunches. Moles, Wadworth beers. Open: 12-3, 7-11.

LITTLE BEDWYN   Harrow Inn

Marlborough SN8 3JL   ▼
Tel: (0672) 870871
Open: 11-3, 5.30-10.30 (11 Sat)
Licensees: Louize and Sean Juniper, Derek Waite

This little village local closed its doors in autumn 1990, but rose from the ashes in
August 1991 when an enterprising group of locals, two trained cooks among them,
joined forces to relaunch the place as a dining pub of some style. It's very early days,
but the menus – tapas style in the bar, more formal in the dining room – are
showing some promise, and there are plans to offer accommodation from summer
1992.

*Bar Meals: 12-2 (2.30 Sat), 12.30-2.30 Sun, 6-9 (not Sun eve); bar snacks both sessions
Restaurant: 12.30-2.30, 7-9.30 (not Sun eve)   Typical Dishes BAR: home-made
minestrone £1.75, stuffed mussels £3.75, meat balls in almond sauce £4, marinaded
vegetable shaslik £3.25, rice noodles with coriander mushrooms   RESTAURANT:
watercress and orange soup £2, stuffed soufflé omelettes £2.50, whole local trout stuffed with
spinach and feta cheese £7.50, home-made puddings   Vegetarian Meals: nut-stuffed
spaghetti marrow   Children's Portions* `Beer` *Arkells; Wadworth   Children Allowed in
Bar to Eat   Outdoor Play Area   Garden   Outdoor Eating   Credit Cards: Access, Visa*

MELKSHAM   Kings Arms Hotel

Market Place SN12 6EX   ▼
Tel: (0225) 707272
Open: 11-2.30, 5.30-11
Licensee: David Dodd

Substantial, pretty, L-shaped country inn set in attractive village at the heart of
prosperous Wiltshire. Hotelly, with some pubbiness, and gentrified in parts: most
attractive dining room/restaurant. A few tables out on the cobbled forecourt-cum-
square.

*Bar Meals: 12-2.15, 6.30-9; bar snacks both sessions   Restaurant: 12.30-2.15, 7-9
Typical Dishes BAR: carrot and orange soup £1.45, avocado with prawns £2.50,
Wiltshire gammon steak £5.50, T-bone steak £8.50, smoked salmon omelette £4.95,
sticky date pudding £2.10   RESTAURANT: baked egg on asparagus £2.85, chicken
with spiced apricots £8.50, sirloin steak platter £8.75, local trout £8.75, lemon cheesecake
£2   Vegetarian Meals: moussaka   Children's Portions* `Beer` *Wadworth 6X* `Whisky`
*Children Allowed in Bar to Eat   Patio/terrace   Accommodation: 14 bedrooms, 10 en
suite, from £51.25 (single £30.75)   Children Welcome Overnight   Cot Available
Check-in: all day   Credit Cards: Access, Amex, Diners, Visa*

MERE   Old Ship Hotel

Castle Street BA12 6JE
Tel: (0747) 860258
Licensee: Philip Johnson

Until 1682 the home of Sir John Coventry, MP, whose banishment from court led
to the expression "sent to Coventry", this sturdy coaching inn exudes old-world
charm. Winter log fires warm the beamed bar and there is a snug, peaceful residents'
lounge. Annexe bedrooms have practical units and modern bathrooms, while those
in the main building are more traditional in style, one boasting a four-poster bed. All
offer the usual little comforts.

Bar Meals: lunch and evening **Beer** *Hall & Woodhouse   Children Allowed in Bar to
Eat   **Accommodation:** 24 bedrooms, 16 en suite, from £47 (single £34)   Children
Welcome Overnight   Cots Available   Check-in: all day*   **Credit Cards:** *Access, Visa*

NUNTON   Radnor Arms

near Salisbury SP5 4HS
Tel: (0722) 329722
Open: 11-2.30, 6-11
Licensee: Richard Penny

Unpretentious little ivy-clad pub with honest, hearty home-made food on offer.
The 'restaurant' list below is in fact a selection of dishes from the evening à la carte,
also served in the bar.

*Bar Meals: 12-2, 7-9.30; bar snacks both sessions   **Typical Dishes BAR:** lovage and
potato soup £1.75, avocado and stilton bake £2.75, bacon and mushroom tagliatelle £4.95,
beef and oyster pie £5.50, fresh grilled/fried plaice £5.50, chocoholic flan £2.25
RESTAURANT: seafood bisque £1.75, duck breast in pink peppercorn sauce £7.95, pork
fillet in apple cream sauce £6.95, skate wings with caper sauce £7.25, apple and blackcurrant
pie £1.85   Vegetarian Meals: macaroni with tomato and ginger sauce £4.25   Children's
Menu/Portions* **Beer** *Hall & Woodhouse; Charles Wells* **Whisky** *Family Room
Outdoor Play Area   Garden   Outdoor Eating   Summer Barbecue   **No Credit Cards***

PEWSHAM   Lysley Arms

near Chippenham SN15 3RU
Tel: (0249) 652864
Licensees: Geoff and Ann Needham

Stone-roofed, flower-bedecked pub, equally attractive inside, with beams, chintzy
furnishings, and winter log fires. The blackboard menu mixes the familiar and
uncommon; good vegetables and puddings.

*Bar Meals: 12-2, 6.30-10 (12-1.30, 6.30-9.30 Sun)   **Typical Dishes:** home-made
soup, country chicken, medallions of pork with plums, vegetable gratin, chocolate roulade (main
courses from £5)   Vegetarian Meals   Children's Menu* **Beer** *Bass; Wadworth   Family
Room   Outdoor Play Area   Garden   **Credit Cards:** Access, Amex, Diners, Visa*

PITTON   Silver Plough

Salisbury SP5 1DZ   `FOOD`
Tel: (072 272) 266
Open: 11-3, 6-11
Licensees: Michael Beckett, Paul Parnell and Charles Mankelow

The Silver Plough was a farmhouse until after the second world war. Everything
about it is neat and well-kept: the lawns at the front, full of white plastic tables and
chairs for summer drinking, and the main bar with its dust-free jugs, bottles and
curios hanging from the ceiling timbers. Very much an eating pub, part of this bar
has some clothed tables, spilling over from the restaurant in the next room. There's
also a snug, with old settles and an extraordinary thatched roof over its bar counter,
off which is a skittle alley, available to the casual player when not booked by a
private party. At lunchtime the menu is set out on various blackboards, backed by an
additional printed menu at night. The choice is wide and the cookery adventurous:
fillet of shark with soy sauce, poached chicken wrapped in olive bread, or a ragout
of lambs' kidneys and snails in balsamic sauce typify the style. Even the ploughmans,
lunchtime only, offers a choice of seven different cheeses. Cooking is generally
sound, although the mussels would be better with their beards removed. The
selection of drinks is equally wide. There are real ales, of course, but also more
exotic brews from Czechoslovakia and Thailand, no less than ten wines offered by
the glass, from an excellent, wide-ranging list of bottles, and a whole raft of country
wines, from elderberry and damson to ginger and parsnip. Although not setting out
to attract children especially, they are happy to produce smaller portions of suitable
dishes and can always come up with a plateful of chips for philistine toddler tastes.

Bar Meals and Restaurant: 12-2, 7-10 (9.30 Sun) **Typical Dishes:** *mushroom and
stilton soup £2.35, avocado, melon and strawberry £4.25, breast of duck with field
mushrooms and lemon butter £14.25, best end of lamb £12.95, escalope of salmon
£13.25, strawberry meringue £3.25; 3-course dinners £19.45 Vegetarian Meals:
ratatouille au gratin £4.50 Children's Portions* `Cheese` `Beer` *Courage; Eldridge
Pope; Wadworth Family Room (skittle alley) Garden Outdoor Eating* **Credit Cards:**
Access, Amex, Diners, Visa

RAMSBURY   Bell

near Marlborough SN8 2PE
Tel: (0672) 20230
Open: 11.30-3, 6-11
Licensees: Graham and Julia Dawes

Star-rated in our last edition, the Bell has now got new licensees, who from the look
of their menu are keen to take up the challenge. It's an unassuming white cottage
pub in the middle of Ramsbury, convivial inside, and with a smart little restaurant.

Bar Meals: 12-2.30, 6.30-9.30; bar snacks both sessions **Restaurant:** *12-2.30, 7-10*
Typical Dishes BAR: *carrot and orange soup £1.80, taramasalata and Greek salad
£3.25, chicken satay £4.50, beef and ale pie £5.95, fresh grilled sardines £3.50, spotted
dick £2.50* **RESTAURANT** *set price £15.45: potato and leek soup, smoked cheese
gougère, venison with port and prunes, calves' liver in sage sauce, scallops in sorrel and cream,
brandy snap basket with fresh fruit Vegetarian Meals: stuffed aubergines Children's
Portions* `Beer` *Fullers London Pride; Ind Coope Burton Ale; Wadworth IPA, 6X*
`Whisky` *Family Room Outdoor Play Area Garden Outdoor Eating* **Credit Cards:**
Access, Amex, Diners, Visa

SALISBURY   Coach & Horses

Winchester Street SP1 1HG
Tel: (0722) 336254
Open: 11-11
Licensees: Martin and Angie Cooper

City's oldest inn, with delightful timbered and gabled exterior, refurbished interior, and dining emphasis. Lots of simple, appetising, snackish dishes on a long printed menu which is divided into sections, each named after a staging post town on the old A30 London-Penzance coaching route. They cater well for families, offering the children venison burgers for a change.

Bar Meals and snacks all day   *Typical Dishes:* home-made soup £1.45, chicken and vegetable terrine £2.75, farmer's feast £5.95, smoked haddock bake £3.25, Scotch salmon fillet oriental £6.75, bread and butter pudding with blackcurrants £1.75   *Vegetarian Meals:* spinach and celeriac bake   Children's Menu   `Cheese`   `Beer`   Ruddles County; Ushers Best Bitter   Family Room   Outdoor Play Area   Garden   Outdoor Eating
Accommodation: 2 bedrooms, both en suite, from £47.40 (single £37.50)   Children Welcome Overnight   Cot Available   Check-in: all day   *Credit Cards:* Access, Visa

SALISBURY   Haunch of Venison

1 Minster Street
Tel: (0722) 22024
Open: all day
Licensees: Antony and Victoria Leroy

A pub of great antiquity and genuinely unspoilt character, and consequently very popular with tourists, who crowd into the tiny bar and chop house above. Carved oak benches jut out of blackened stone walls, alongside beer barrel tables; watch out for the very low beams upstairs. Cheap and cheerful food, scarcely the point of a visit here (too busy, for one thing) is of the pies, casserole and curry sort.

Bar Meals: lunch and Mon-Sat evening   *Vegetarian Meals*   `Beer`   Courage   Children Allowed in Bar to Eat   *Credit Cards:* Access, Amex, Diners, Visa

SHERSTON   Rattlebone Inn

Church Street SN16 0LR   ▼
Tel: (0666) 840871
Open: 12-2.30 (inc Sun), 5.30-11 (12-11 Sat)
Licensees: D M and I H Rees

Busy old Cotswold stone pub with its original stone roof intact, and lots more exposed stone inside, oak beams and open fires. No music. Boules pitch in the garden. Disabled access ramps for 1992.

Bar Meals and Restaurant: 12-2, 7-10; bar snacks lunchtime   *Typical Dishes BAR:* stilton and celery soup £1.95, smoked salmon paté £2.95, lasagne £4.25, steak and kidney pie £5.25, breaded plaice £4.25, lemon syllabub   *RESTAURANT:* carrot and orange soup £1.95, local quails eggs £1.95, pork with stilton £7.25, chicken Kiev £6.95, salmon with dill and lime £8.25   *Vegetarian Meals:* fresh vegetable bake   Children's Portions   `Beer`   Butcombe; Moorhouse's; Wadworth   `Whisky`   Children Allowed in Bar to Eat   Garden   Outdoor Eating   *Credit Cards:* Access, Visa

UPAVON   Antelope Inn

3 High Street SN9 6AE
Tel: (0980) 630206
Open: 11-2.30 (3 Sat), 6-11
Licensees: Mervyn and Sandy Parrish

Still fairly new licensees at the Antelope and winning friends with their interesting bar food, which transforms this pleasant but unexceptional pub into something special.

Bar Meals and Restaurant: *daily lunchtime and evening; bar snacks both sessions* **Typical Dishes BAR:** *tomato and mint soup £1.95, garlic mushrooms £2.45, pork, apple and cider pie £4.45, pheasant and venison pie £4.45, fresh fish and prawn pie £4.45, bread and butter pudding £1.95 Vegetarian Meals: mushroom stroganoff Children's Menu/Portions* **Beer** *Bass; Wadworth Family Room Children Allowed in Bar to Eat Outdoor Play Area Garden Outdoor Eating Summer Barbecue* **Accommodation:** *4 bedrooms, sharing 2 bathrooms, from £32.50 (single £20) Children Welcome Overnight Cot Available Check-in: all day* **Credit Cards:** *Access, Amex*

WARMINSTER   Old Bell Hotel

42 Market Place BA12 9AN
Tel: (0985) 216611
Open: 10-3, 5.30-11
Licensee: Howard Astbury

Town–centre old coaching inn which dominates the market place. Outdoor eating in the handsome inner courtyard, or indoors in the foody Chimes Bar, a dining room with a cold buffet table, and cheap, cheerful hot dishes. There's also a pubbier drinkers' bar. Bedrooms are neat and simply furnished, functional rather than luxurious in style; front rooms have double glazing.

Bar Meals and Restaurant: *12-2 (2.30 restaurant), 6-10.30; bar snacks both sessions* **Typical Dishes BAR:** *steak and kidney pie £2.90, chilli £3.15, sweet and sour pork £3.15* **RESTAURANT:** *salmon mousse £2.25, fresh duckling £9, chicken Kiev £6.75, whole rainbow trout £7.50 Vegetarian Meals (bar): vegetable lasagne Children's Menu* **Beer** *Bass; Wadworth Children Allowed in Bar to Eat Patio/terrace Outdoor Eating* **Accommodation:** *20 bedrooms, 14 en suite, from £54 (single £39) Children Welcome Overnight Cots Available Check-in: all day* **Credit Cards:** *Access, Amex, Diners, Visa*

WOOTTON RIVERS   Royal Oak

near Marlborough SN8 4NQ
Tel: (0672) 810322
Open: 11-3, 6-11
Licensees: Rosa and John Jones

Very much an eating pub, though there's also a noisy public bar, the thatched and charmingly rustic Royal Oak is often packed with diners; tables can be booked, and people seem to dress up in the evenings. The same menu, encompassing traditional bar food (if not exactly at old-fashioned prices) and restaurant fare, applies throughout in bar and dining room. Jugs of Lone Island Iced Tea, Pimms, and freshly squeezed orange juice are summer favourites. Bed and breakfast, in the house next door, is of the 'help-yourself' kind.

Bar Meals: *12-2, 7-9.30; bar snacks lunchtime* **Typical Dishes:** *leek and potato soup £1.75, smoked prawns £3.50, home-made steak and kidney pie £6, grilled chicken breast* *with rosemary and lemon £8.50, pan-fried red mullet £8.50, home-made crème caramel £2.50   Vegetarian Meals: courgette provencale   Children's Portions* ▐ Beer ▐ *Hall & Woodhouse; Wadworth* ▐ Cider ▐ *Weston's   Children Allowed in Bar to Eat   Patio/terrace Outdoor Eating   **Accommodation:** 6 bedrooms, 2 en suite, from £30 (single £20) Children Welcome Overnight   Cot Available   Check-in: by arrangement   **Credit Cards:** Access, Visa*

WYLYE   Bell Inn

High Street (junction A306 and A36) BA12 0PQ   ▾
Tel: (09856) 338
Open: 11 (11.30 winter)-2.30 (12-2.30 Sun), 6-11
Licensees: Steve and Ann Locke

Purpose-built as an inn in 1373, and superbly set in the village centre, by a church of the same period. Low beams, cosy and comfortable, logs burning in large inglenook fireplace, walled garden and patio.

*Bar Meals: 12-2, 7-9 (9.30 summer, 10 weekends all year)   **Typical Dishes:** celery and stilton soup £1.25, grilled Portuguese sardines £2.25, home-made steak and kidney pie £4.25, Barnsley chop £5.50, Japanese prawns £5.10, fruit crumble £1.65   Vegetarian Meals: celery and walnut roast   Children's Menu* ▐ Beer ▐ *Gibbs; Hall & Woodhouse; Wadworth   Family Room   Garden   Outdoor Eating   **Accommodation:** 5 bedrooms, 2 en suite, from £30 (single £16.50)   Children Welcome Overnight   Check-in: by arrangement* **No Credit Cards**

NORTH YORKSHIRE

APPLETREEWICK   Craven Arms

Burnsall BD23 6DA
Tel: (075 672) 270
Open: 11.30-3, 6.60-11
Licensee: J Nicholson

Fairly routine bar food (steaks are popular) in a delightful stone-built National Park pub, with good views over Wharfedale from the garden. Log fires and a Yorkshire range, oak beams and bridle bits.

*Bar Meals: 12-2, 7-9.30; bar snacks both sessions   **Typical Dishes:** chicken and leek soup £1, garlic mussels £2, steak and kidney pie £3.60, Cumberland sausage £3.50, mixed grill special £7.40, fruit pie £1.50   Vegetarian Meals: cheese and broccoli flan* ▐ Beer ▐ *Tetley; Theakston* ▐ Whisky ▐ *Family Room   Outdoor Play Area   Garden   **No Credit Cards***

ASKRIGG   Kings Arms

Market Place DL8 3HQ   ▾
Tel: (0969) 50256
Open: 11-5 (3 winter), 6.30-11
Licensee: Raymond Hopwood

There's been more than a little tweaking with facilities at the Kings Arms since our last edition: a new hotel entrance, reception and foyer, two new residents' lounges, a 40 seat grill room, a private dining room, the addition of three suites and new off-street parking are all under way. Underneath it all is a listed former manor house, an inn since 1800, once used as a base by Turner when painting the Dales, more recently used for filming bits of All Creatures Great and Small. High ceilinged parlour bar, cosy low-beamed front bar, and juke box public bar. Country house-style bedrooms with draped beds. The Grill Room is intended to be an upmarket affair in a pub-hotel showing definite signs of aspiration.

Bar Meals: 12-2, 6.30-9; *bar snacks both sessions* *Restaurant:* 12-3, 7-10 **Typical Dishes BAR:** *home-made soup £1.75, moules marinière £3.25, steak and kidney pie £4.75, chicken, ham and mushroom pie £4.75, grilled Dales lamb cutlets £4.95, sticky toffee pudding with butterscotch sauce £2.25* *Children's Menu* `Cheese` `Beer` *Ind Coope, Tetley; McEwan, Youngers* `Whisky` *Family Room Patio/terrace* **Accommodation:** *9 bedrooms, all en suite, from £60 (single £40) Children Welcome Overnight (minimum age: 12) Check-in: all day* **Credit Cards:** *Access, Visa*

BAINBRIDGE — Rose & Crown

Wensleydale DL8 3EE
Tel: (0969) 50225
Open: 11-3, 6-11
Licensee: P H Collins

Pristine long white-painted early coaching inn, prettily set on the large village green. Traditional features remain – beams, panelling and the like in the mellow front bar, refurbished public and cosy snug, but there are also modern intrusions of the fruit machine and juke box sort. A new licensee since our last edition: the bar menu's looking more interesting, and bedrooms still are recommendable, though prices have risen.

Bar Meals: 12-2, 6-9; *bar snacks both sessions* *Restaurant:* 12-2 (Sun only), 7-9.30 **Typical Dishes BAR:** *country vegetable soup £1.70, cottage cheese with fruit and nuts £2.65, sausage and black pudding with pickled cabbage £4.35, chicken and sweetcorn in curry mayonnaise £3.85, chicken, ham and mushroom pie £4.95, apple and blackberry pie £1.75* **RESTAURANT:** *tomato, celery and apple soup £2.45, smoked haddock mousse £2.95, lamb chops with rosemary, redcurrant and mint sauce £8.75, sirloin steak with ham, onions and red wine sauce £10.95, local fresh trout stuffed with onions, tomatoes and herbs £8.75, profiteroles with banana cream £2.45* **Vegetarian Meals:** *avocado with chestnuts and mint sauce £3.25* *Children's Menu/Portions* `Cheese` `Beer` *John Smith, Younger* `Whisky` *Children Allowed in Bar to Eat Outdoor Play Area Patio/terrace Outdoor Eating* **Accommodation:** *12 bedrooms, all en suite, from £68 (single £43) Children Welcome Overnight Cot Available Check-in: all day* **Credit Cards:** *Access, Visa*

BREARTON — Malt Shovel

Harrogate HG3 3BX
Tel: (0423) 862929
Open: 12-3, 6.45-11; closed Mon
Licensee: Leigh Trafford Parsons

`FOOD`

The quiet country village of Brearton, just a short drive from the B6165, has a splendid pub in the Malt Shovel. Standing on the village's main street (it only has one!), it is a 16th century cream-painted building with colourful hanging baskets. The interior, reached through a recently added porch, has a relaxed and civilised air to it, and is pleasingly unpretentious in its decor and fittings. The bar counter has some fine old woodwork, and half oak panelling lines the rough white-painted and stripped stone walls. Red cushioned seating graces the benches and simple spindle-back chairs which surround the solid wood tables; hunting prints, old bottles, highly polished brass plates and other ornaments also feature. The smaller room has a dartboard, although this isn't really a locals' pub. It's a real family business: Marilyn Parsons owns the pub and does the cooking, along with daughter Joanne, while son Leigh is in charge of the cellar and front of house. Mother's and daughter's cooking has won many admirers, some coming surprisingly far to eat here. The lunchtime trade tends to be dominated by the retired age group, while evenings bring a more varied crowd. The day's dishes, all freshly prepared, are written up on the blackboard; the choice isn't exhaustive but should suit most tastes. Fresh produce is well handled in dishes like roast ham with parsley sauce, Trinidad prawn curry (always popular) and pork chop with apple sauce. Beautifully fresh haddock comes in a light crisp batter and with proper home-made chips; the size of the fillet will take your breath away. Vegetarians aren't forgotten either: perhaps a nut roast, spinach and mushroom lasagne or vegetable samosas. And you shouldn't leave without trying the desserts: lemon flan, banana fudge flan or a gooseberry and apple crumble, all home-produced. Service is informal, friendly and helpful. To the rear, a paved terrace has white tables and garden chairs, while at the end of the car park there's a small lawned area and discreet little caravan site. A real country village pub this, run by charming people.

Bar Meals: 12-2, 7-9 (not Sun eve) *Typical Dishes:* *fresh salmon with cucumber mayonnaise £6.10, fresh battered haddock £4.75, Trinidad prawn curry £5.10, fresh lemon flan Vegetarian Meals: leek and mushroom quiche £3.95 Children's Portions* ▣ Beer *Big End; Old Mill; Tetley; Theakston* ▣ Whisky *Children Allowed in Bar to Eat Outdoor Play Area Patio/terrace* **No Credit Cards**

BROMPTON-ON-SWALE   Crown

Richmond Road DL10 7UE
Tel: (0748) 811666
Open: 11-3, 6-11 (all day Sat)
Licensee: Maurizio Pastorello

A strong Italian influence here, and fresh pasta available every day.

Bar Meals and Restaurant: 12-2, 7-9.30; bar snacks lunchtime *Typical Dishes BAR:* *home-made soup £1.25, garlic mushrooms £1.85, home-made pies £3.75, scampi £4.25, hot crusty sandwiches £1.80 **RESTAURANT:** tagliatelle £2.50, veal £6.95, steaks £6.50, plaice mornay £5.25 Vegetarian Meals: vegetable lasagne £2.50 Children's Portions Children Allowed in Bar to Eat Outdoor Play Area Garden Outdoor Eating* **Credit Cards:** *Access, Visa*

BYLAND ABBEY   Abbey Inn

Coxwold YO6 4BL   ▼
Tel: (03476) 204
Open: 11-2.30, 6.30-11
Licensees: Peter and Gerd Handley

In an isolated spot, but signposted as a tourist attraction from the A170, this is a rambling, pleasingly old-fashioned pub, sited opposite the popular abbey ruins themselves. Handsome furnishings, flag and board floors, attractive decorative pieces, and home-cooked food prepared by the landlady.

Bar Meals: 12-2.30, 6.30-9.30 (not Sun eve, nor all day Mon); bar snacks both sessions *Typical Dishes:* *home-made soup £1.40, home-made paté £3.60, lamb rogan josh £4.75, breast of chicken with lemon and tarragon £5.50, steak and mushroom pie £4.75, sticky toffee pudding Vegetarian Meals: vegetable bake Children's Portions* ▣ Beer *Tetley; Theakston* ▣ Whisky *Family Room Outdoor Play Area Garden Outdoor Eating* **No Credit Cards**

CARLTON Foresters Arms Wensleydale. Popular for its atmosphere, service, and good home cooking; bar meals lunch and evening; Theakstons beers.

CARTHORPE   Fox & Hounds

Bedale DL8 2LG
Tel: (0845) 567433
Open: 12-2.30, 7-11; closed Mon
Licensees: Howard and Bernadette Fitzgerald

Very popular dining pub in a delightful village ex-blacksmith's, with an attractively modernised L-shaped bar and high ceilinged dining room with exposed rafters. The same menu, fairly restauranty in style and price, applies in both.

Bar Meals: 12-2, 7-10; bar snacks lunchtime **Restaurant:** *12-2 (Sun only), 7-9.30*
Typical Dishes BAR: stilton, cheese and onion soup £1.85, whole fresh dressed crab £4.95, chicken breast stuffed with Coverdale cheese £6.95, roulade of fresh salmon and halibut £6.95, lemon sole filled with salmon and prawns £6.95, choux pastry swans with hot chocolate sauce £2.25 Children's Portions `Cheese` `Beer` *John Smith's Bitter Children Allowed in Bar to Eat* **No Credit Cards**

COXWOLD   Fauconberg Arms

Main Street TO6 4AD   ❢
Tel: (03476) 214
Open: 11-3, 6-11
Licensees: Robin and Nicky Jaques

New licensees at this well-loved Yorkshire perennial have installed a more ambitious bar (and restaurant) menu here; hopefully the character of the inn will not change – it's a charmingly civilised, if invariably busy, place, with handsome old furnishings and an open fire. Bedrooms have long been popular here too, and still look like good value. The setting is delightful, in a peaceful (despite the traffic) straggling village, and the church across the road is worth a look; Lawrence Sterne is buried there.

Bar Meals and Restaurant: 12-2, 7-9; bar snacks both sessions **Typical Dishes BAR:** *white turnip and pear soup £1.75, garlic mushroom pastry puffs £2.95, steak, kidney and oyster pie £4.95, chicken in curried pineapple and coconut sauce £4.95, halibut in lemon yogurt £6.95, lemon treacle pudding £2.50* **RESTAURANT:** *cucumber and strawberry soup £1.95, smoked salmon and watercress mousse £3.50, breast of duck with apricot and walnut gravy £10.25, pan-fried lamb with apple-mint and rosemary gravy £9.75, salmon steak £10.25, home-made cheesecake £2.75 Vegetarian Meals: stuffed aubergines £4.95 Children's Menu/Portions* `Cheese` `Beer` *Tetley; Theakston Children Allowed in Bar to Eat Patio/terrace Outdoor Eating Summer Barbecue* **Accommodation:** *4 bedrooms, one with shower, from £40 (single £24) Children Welcome Overnight Check-in: all day* **Credit Cards:** *Access, Visa*

CRAY   White Lion

Skipton BD23 5JB
Tel: (0756) 760262
Open: all day
Licensee: Frank Day

Characterful stone-built Dales pub, popular with walkers. Beamed ceilings, stone floors and a warming open fire in the main bar, which also has farming bric-a-brac and a Ring the Bull game; separate small dining room, with plain homely food (more choice in the evening).

Bar Meals: 12-2, 6.30-9; bar snacks lunchtime   **Typical Dishes BAR:** *asparagus and stilton soup, paté, beef in ale, home-made steak and mushroom pie, Cumberland sausage (main courses from £3.50)   Vegetarian Meals: lasagne   Children's Menu*   `Beer` *Moorhouses; Theakston; Youngers   Family Room   Outdoor Play Area   Riverside Garden   Outdoor Eating*   **Accommodation:** *5 bedrooms, all en suite, from £40 (single £25.50) Children Welcome Overnight   Cots Available   Check-in: all day*   **Credit Cards:** *Access, Amex, Diners, Visa*

DALTON Jolly Farmers of Olden Times   Tel: (0845) 577359. Cosy country inn of real charm, a warm welcome, well-kept beer, and decent bar meals, all from fresh local ingredients; plain in the bar, fancier in the dining room (book). Booking essential for Sunday lunch. Cheap bed and breakfast. Ruddles, Webster's beers. Open: 11-2.30 (4 Sat; closed Thur), 7.30-11.

EAST LAYTON Fox Hall Inn   on A66   Tel: (0325) 718262. Imposing roadside inn with an attractive bar, decent bar food (especially the daily specials); children welcome; rear terrace; good value bed and breakfast. Theakstons beers. Open: 12-3, 7-11 (all day summer).

EAST WITTON   Cover Bridge Inn

Leyburn DL8 4SQ
Tel: (0969) 23250
Open: 10.30-11
Licensee: James Carter

Old, proprietor-run country inn, a good base for Dales visits, though the menu looks fairly routine.

Bar Meals: 12-2, 6.30-10; bar snacks both sessions   **Typical Dishes:** *vegetable soup £1.75, chicken, ham and mushroom pie £4.75, home-made steak pie £4.75, lasagne £4.75, banoffee pie £2   Vegetarian Meals: macaroni bake £3.95   Children's Portions*   `Beer` *John Smith; Theakston   Children Allowed in Bar to Eat   Outdoor Play Area Riverside Garden   Outdoor Eating   Summer Barbecue*   **Accommodation:** *3 bedrooms, all en suite, from £36 (single £20)   Children Welcome Overnight   Cot Available   Check-in: all day*   **Credit Cards:** *Access, Visa*

EGTON BRIDGE   Horseshoe Hotel

Whitby YO21 1XE   ▼
Tel: (0947) 85245
Open: 11-3.30, 6.30-11

Delightful old stone pub in pretty Esk-side spot. Lots of black panelling, simple wood furniture, and 'public end'; dining room (same menu) a little more feminine. Residents have their own riverside garden. Wines by the glass include the English Lamberhurst.

Bar Meals: 12-2, 6.45-9; bar snacks lunchtime   **Typical Dishes:** *home-made soup £1.70, rabbit pie £4.85, bacon chops in peach sauce £4.90, fresh local fish £4.90, sticky toffee pudding £1.95   Vegetarian Meals: vegetarian lasagne   Children's Menu*   `Beer` *Courage; Taylor; Tetley; Theakston   Family Room   Outdoor Play Area   Riverside Garden   Outdoor Eating*   **Accommodation:** *6 bedrooms, 3 en suite, from £36 (single £28) Children Welcome Overnight (no infants)   Check-in: all day*   **Credit Cards:** *Access, Amex, Visa*

ELSLACK   Tempest Arms

near Skipton BD23 3AY
Tel: (0282) 842450
Open: 11.30-3, 6.30 (7 Sat)-11
Licensee: Francis Pierre Boulongne

Traditional stone roadside inn with simple traditionally furnished bar and other civilised areas leading off, plus Bonaparte Restaurant; despite the location, this is a French-run establishment. Ambitious, appetising bar menu with deft Gallic touches. Fish fresh from Manchester market. Extension houses ten compact pretty bedrooms.

Bar Meals and Restaurant: 11.30 (12 Sun)-2.15, 6.30 (7 weekends)-10 (9.30 restaurant); bar snacks both sessions **Typical Dishes BAR:** *tomato and basil soup £1.60, home-cured gravadlax £3.75, home-made steak, kidney and mushroom pie £5.60, chicken breast with watercress sauce £6.25, venison casserole with noodles £5.25, apple and ginger crisp* **RESTAURANT:** *Bonaparte set dinner menu £14.50 (fish course £2.50 extra) Vegetarian Meals: aubergine parmesana* *Children's Menu* Beer *Tetley; Thwaites; Younger* *Family Room* *Outdoor Play Area* *Riverside Garden* *Outdoor Eating* **Accommodation:** *10 bedrooms, all en suite, from £47 (single £39.50)* *Children Welcome Overnight* *Cot Available* *Check-in: all day* **Credit Cards:** *Access, Amex, Diners, Visa*

FLIXTON   Foxhound Inn

Flixton YO11 3UB
Tel: (0723) 890301
Open: 11.30-2.30, 7-11

Large roadside white-painted inn, much extended and modernised, with a 100-seater dining room.

Bar Meals: 12-2, 7-9.30; bar snacks both sessions **Typical Dishes:** *home-made soup £1.95, hot mushrooms £2.95, roast of the day £5.75, steak and kidney pie £4.95, roast loin of pork £8.75* *Vegetarian Meals: nut roast* *Children's Portions* Beer *Tetley; Theakston; Youngers* *Family Room* **Credit Cards:** *Access, Amex, Diners, Visa*

GANTON   Greyhound

Main Street YO12 4NX
Tel: (0944) 70116
Open: 11-3, 7-11
Licensee: Neil Oliver

Popular dining pub on the A64, not far from the championship golf course.

Bar Meals:: 12-2, 7-10; bar snacks lunchtime **Typical Dishes:** *home-made soup £1.10, prawn cocktail £2.75, home-made steak and kidney pie £4, Highland chicken (stuffed with smoked salmon paté, cooked in whisky sauce) £5.75, 32 oz rump steak £15, fruit crumble £1.50* *Vegetarian Meals: broccoli and cream cheese bake £4.75* *Children's Portions* Beer *McEwan; Tetley* *Children Allowed in Bar to Eat* *Garden* *Outdoor Eating* **No Credit Cards**

GOATHLAND   Mallyan Spout Hotel

near Whitby YO22 5AN
Tel: (0947) 86206
Open: 11-3, 6.30-11
Licensee: Judith Ann Heslop

Splendid old hotel built of local stone, overlooking the green in remote, romantic moorland village. Modernised, rather smart interior. Lots of fish from nearby Whitby; pleasing list of local suppliers on set menu. Good walks nearby; lovely view from garden.

Bar Meals: 12-2, 6.30-9   *Restaurant: 12-1.45 (Sun only), 7-8.30*   **Typical Dishes** *BAR: pea and ham soup £1.65, toasted Grosmont goats cheese salad £2.95, steak, kidney and porter pie £4.60, Whitby cod £4.10, huge Yorkshire pudding £3.25, icky sticky toffee pudding £2.25*   **RESTAURANT:** *oxtail and butterbean soup £3.50, home-cured beef £5.50, casserole of duck legs and olives £10.50, poached skate with nut butter and capers £10.50, sautéed monkfish in a lobster and pink peppercorn sauce £13.50, summer pudding £3.50*   *Vegetarian Meals: vegetables au gratin*   *Children's Menu*   Cheese   Beer *Malton Double Chance*   Whisky *Ardmore, Banff*   *Family Room*   *Outdoor Play Area Patio/terrace*   *Outdoor Eating*   **Accommodation:** *24 bedrooms, all en suite, from £60 (single £40)*   *Children Welcome Overnight*   *Cot Available*   *Check-in: all day*   **Credit Cards:** *Access, Amex, Visa*

HAROME   Star Inn

Main Street YO6 5JE
Tel: (0439) 70397
Open: 11.45-3, 5.45-11
Licensee: T E Blackburn

Delightful thatched pub in a peaceful backwater. Stylishly unpretentious bar, pretty garden, and a new licensee, who has taken over the reins without instituting too many changes; in fact, the Star's much the same as ever. Lunchtime food consists mainly of interesting sandwiches, like the favourite curried chicken, good soup, and a hot daily special (around £5); you can take coffee up in the loft. Evening food is smarter altogether.

Bar Meals: 12-2   *Children's Portions*   Beer *Camerons; Taylor; Tetley; Theakston Family Room*   *Garden*

HARROGATE William and Victoria 6 Cold Bath Road. Cellar wine bar style pub worth knowing for interesting bar meals, good prices and atmosphere.

HELMSLEY   Feathers Hotel

Market Place YO6 5BH
Tel: (0439) 70275
Open: 10.30-2.30, 6-11 (all day Fri/Sat)
Licensee: Jack Feather

On the handsome market square of this most typical of North Yorkshire's affluent small market towns. It's part 15th century cottage – the venue for the traditional little bar – and part elegant 18th century house. Bedrooms are simply appointed, and en suite facilities functional.

Bar Meals: 12-2, 6.30 (7 Sun)-9; bar snacks both sessions   **Typical Dishes:** *home-made soup £1.50, deep-fried potato skins with dip £2.75, steak pie £5, lasagne £4.25, battered* *haddock £4.95, fruit crumble £2   Vegetarian Meals: nut cutlets £4.25   Children's Menu/Portions* `Beer` *Tetley; Theakston   Family Room   Garden   **Accommodation:** 17 bedrooms, 13 en suite, from £53 (single £31.50)   Children Welcome Overnight   Cots Available   Check-in: all day   **Credit Cards:** Access, Amex, Diners, Visa*

HELMSLEY   Feversham Arms Hotel

1 High Street YO6 5AG   ❢
Tel: (0439) 70766
Open: 10.30-2.30 (12-2.30 Sun), 6.30-11
Licensee: Rowan Bowie de Aragues

Golden stone building by the church, much modernised inside, and rather garishly decorated. Good facilities: tennis, heated outdoor pool for residents.

***Bar Meals:** 12-2; bar snacks   **Restaurant:** 12.30-2 (Sun only), 7-9   **Typical Dishes BAR:** home-made soup £1.75, snails in garlic butter £3.50, spaghetti bolognese £4, venison steak £9, lobster thermidor £14, chocolate mousse £2   **Restaurant:** set dinner price £18   Vegetarian Meals: aparagus omelette £4   Children's Portions* `Whisky`
***Accommodation:** 19 bedrooms, all en suite, from £60 (single £50)   Check-in: all day   **Credit Cards:** Access, Amex, Diners, Visa*

HETTON   Angel Inn

near Skipton, off B6265 BD23 6LT   ❢
Tel: (075 673) 263
Open: 12-2.30, 6-10.30 (10 winter)
Licensee: Denis Watkins

Best be early for a seat at this increasingly popular dining pub, whose fame has spread since our last edition. There are four interconnected rooms, full of 16th century nooks, crannies and beams, comfortably furnished, and overrun by diners at mealtimes; fresh flowers, attractive pictures and sepia photographs add charm, and it's immaculately kept. The menu is extensive, and reliably good; fresh seafood and fish is now a daily speciality.

***Bar Meals:** 12-2.30, 6 (7 Sun)-10; bar snacks both sessions   **Restaurant:** 12-2 (Sun only), 7-9.30 (not Sun)   **Typical Dishes BAR:** provencale fish soup £2.35, queen scallops baked with gruyère and garlic £3.85, duck with orange sauce £6.25, poached salmon £5.95, local goats cheese in filo pastry £4.25, summer pudding   **RESTAURANT** inclusive dinner price £18.80: charlotte of provencale vegetables, guinea fowl with tarragon sauce, roast monkfish with leek spaghetti, contrefilet of beef with horseradish mousse, sticky toffee pudding   Vegetarian Meals: fresh spinach noodles, basil and parmesan sauce* `Cheese`
`Beer` *McEwan; Theakston; Taylor* `Whisky` *Children Allowed in Bar to Eat Patio/terrace   Outdoor Eating   **Credit Cards:** Access, Visa*

HOVINGHAM   Malt Shovel

Main Street YO6 4LF
Tel: (0653) 628264
Open: 12-2.30 (inc Sun), 7 (6.30 Fri/Sat)-11
Licensees: Mike and Jenny Handley

Likeable village pub, locally popular, now possessed of a small, no-smoking dining room in which to serve evening 'restaurant' dishes. Fresh vegetables.

***Bar Meals:** 12-1.30; bar snacks lunchtime   **Restaurant:** 7-9.30 (bookings)   **Typical Dishes BAR:** black pudding and chutney £2.95, Hawaiian gammon £4.95, battered* *haddock £4, treacle sponge £1.50*   **RESTAURANT:** *Danish salad £2.95, Kentish lamb casserole £5.95, haunch of venison £9.50, trout with hazelnut and Cointreau £6.25, Athol Brose £2   Vegetarian Meals: courgette and tomato gougère   Children's Menu (lunch)*   **Beer** *Camerons Traditional Bitter*   **Whisky** *Children Allowed in Bar to Eat (lunch) Outdoor Play Area   Garden   Outdoor Eating*   **No Credit Cards**

HUBBERHOLME   George Inn

Kirk Gill BD23 5JE   **B&B**
Tel: (075 676) 223
Open: 11.30-3, 7 (6.30 Sat)-11
Licensees: John Fredrick and Marjorie Forster

Ruggedly beautiful countryside, much loved by walkers, surrounds the George, a rough whitewashed stone building formerly owned by the Church opposite. It stands in a wonderfully peaceful setting on the banks of the Wharfe, at the very heart of the Yorkshire Dales national park. Inside, it's a haven of unspoilt character. The bar and adjoining room, one level up, have splendid flagstoned floors and copper-topped tables with heavy cast iron legs. Seating is either on attractively upholstered cushioned benches or round-backed chairs. Stripped stone walls and blackened beamed ceilings also feature, while the second room has two tree trunks supporting the ceiling! An open kitchen range fireplace adds warmth in inclement weather. Bar food is basic and simple, with the likes of steak and kidney pie, steaks, gammon or roasted chicken legs appearing. It can get busy early evening when the unfussy dining room is often opened to cope with the numbers. The pub has three bedrooms to let above the bar and restaurant. These have plain white-painted walls, modest modern furniture and duvets. There's no call for modern amenities like television (can't get a picture anyway – too many hills) or telephone. None are en suite, but all have washbasins and plenty of towels. They have one functional bathroom and a separate toilet. Though modest in appointments, rooms are clean and well kept, and serve as a good base for those touring (or walking) in the area, whilst perhaps a little overpriced for what they are. A huge fry-up starts the day and should satisfy the heartiest rambler's appetite. While there's generally a friendly atmosphere in the bars, locals can be rather anti-grockles (tourists); there are a few picnic tables on a paved area to the rear, should you find the atmosphere too unfriendly. STOP PRESS: we've heard that the George is up for sale.

Bar Meals: *lunch and evening; bar snacks lunchtime*   ***Restaurant:*** *eves only*   **Typical Dishes BAR:** *home-made soup £1.30, chicken liver paté, venison in red wine, steak and kidney pudding, turkey and mushroom pie (main courses from £4), home-made apple pie Vegetarian Meals: lasagne*   **Beer** *Youngers No. 3, Scotch*   **Whisky** *Family Room Outdoor Play Area   Riverside Garden   Outdoor Eating*   ***Accommodation:*** *3 bedrooms, sharing a bathroom, from £36   Children Welcome Overnight (minimum age 8)   Check-in: all day*   **No Credit Cards**

LINTON IN CRAVEN Fountaine Inn on B6265. Attractive, well-run pub in charming hamlet; bar meals lunch and evening, a mix of scampi-style basket meals and smarter specials under the newish regime; family room; Theakstons beers. Open: 11.30-3, 5.30-11.

LITTON Queens Arms Tel: (075 677) 208: Ancient, simply modernised inn in good walking country; decent bar meals lunch and evening; family room; modest, cheap bedrooms. Youngers beers. Open: 11-3, 6.30-11 (all day Sat; closed winter Mon eve).

MALTON   Cornucopia

87 Commercial Street, Norton YO17 9HY
Tel: (0653) 693456
Open: 11-2.30, 6.30-11; closed Mon/Tue
Licensee: Harold St Quinton

Proprietor-run (he also does the cooking), foody pub enterprise. The same menu applies at Harold St Quinton's other pub, the Copper Horse in Seamer (q.v.).

Bar Meals: 12-2, 6.30-10; bar snacks lunchtime **Typical Dishes:** *home-made chunky mushroom soup £1.35, crunchy salad with bacon, apple and cheese £7.75, beef in ale with mushrooms and herb dumplings, pork in cider with crispy apple fritters £6.95, crisp boned half duck with apricot compote £8.95, hazelnut meringue Vegetarian Meals: cheese-stuffed deep-fried mushrooms £5.95 Children's Portions Children Allowed in Bar to Eat Patio/terrace Outdoor Eating* **Credit Cards:** *Access, Visa*

MASHAM   Kings Head Hotel

Market Place HG4 4EF
Tel: (0765) 689295
Open: 11-11
Licensee: Colin Jones

Popular bed and breakfast inn with an imposing facade and position. A modernised, opened-up lounge bar interior. Genuinely home-cooked chicken Kiev. Machines and pop music.

Bar Meals: 12-2.30, 6-8 (7-8.30 Sun); bar snacks lunchtime **Restaurant:** *12-2 (Sun only), 7-9 (9.30 Sat)* **Typical Dishes BAR:** *home-made soup £1.20, prawn cocktail £2.50, chicken Kiev £3.95, steak and kidney pie £3.25, grilled trout £3.25, banoffee pie £1.50* **RESTAURANT:** *grilled scallops £3.95, rack of lamb £7.25, breast of duck £7.75, fillet stilton £9.50, tarte tatin £1.75 Vegetarian Meals: felafel* Beer *Theakston Children Allowed in Bar to Eat Patio/terrace Outdoor Eating* **Accommodation:** *10 bedrooms, all en suite, from £55 (single £38.50) Children Welcome Overnight Cot Available Check-in: all day* **Credit Cards:** *Access, Amex, Diners, Visa*

MASHAM White Bear Brewery Yard Tel: (0765) 89319. Attractive, busy pub in part of the old Theakstons Brewery offices; characterful public bar stuffed full of bric-a-brac, simple modernised lounge, terrace seating, families welcome; bar meals (not weekend evenings) homely and home cooked; no chips. Two modest bedrooms. Theakstons beers. Open all day.

MIDDLEHAM   Black Swan

Market Place DL8 4NP
Tel: (0969) 22221
Open: 11-3, 7-11 (all day summer)
Licensees: George and Susan Munday

New licensees here, and changes afoot as we go to press: a general revamp, redecoration, re-upholstering, new bedroom furniture, new carpeting in the hotel area, and upgrading of the restaurant. Hopefully the atmosphere at this nicely higgledy-piggledy pub will remain unchanged. Bedrooms are neatly squeezed in, up odd staircases and down passageways in the modernised back section. It's a delightful, racehorse-training village.

Bar Meals: 12-2, 7-9; bar snacks lunchtime Restaurant: 12-2.30, 7-9.30 **Typical Dishes BAR:** *Wensleydale cheese soup £1.30, smoked mackerel paté, sirloin steak, salmon,* *beef in Old Peculier casserole (main courses from £4)   Vegetarian Meals   Children's Menu/Portions* **Cheese** **Beer** *Courage; Theakston   Family Room   Outdoor Play Area   Garden   Outdoor Eating* **Accommodation:** *7 bedrooms, all en suite, from £36 (single £25)   Children Welcome Overnight   Cot Available   Check-in: by arrangement* **Credit Cards:** *Access, Visa*

MOULTON   Black Bull

Richmond DL10 6QJ
Tel: (0325) 377289
Open: 12-2.30 (2 Sun), 6-10.30 (11 Fri/Sat)
Licensee: Audrey Pagendam

A stone's throw from Scotch Corner, this usually very busy retreat from the A1 is as popular as ever for its bar food. The lunchtime meals venue is the characterful, relaxing bar, warmed by a roaring fire in winter. A side room has become an informal seafood bar; there's also an attractive conservatory and converted Pullman coach for the evening trade, when the pub becomes a fish and seafood restaurant proper. No children in the bars.

Bar Meals: *12-2; also snacks* **Restaurant:** *12-2, 6.45-10.15* **Typical dishes BAR**: *carrot soup £1.75, garlic mushrooms £2, spare ribs £4.25, Welsh rarebit £4.25, tarte alsacienne £3.75, brandy snaps £1.75* **RESTAURANT:** *asparagus soup £2, soufflé £4.25, fillet steak £12, salmon £13.50, Dover sole £12.75, French apple tart £3* **Cheese** *(restaurant)* **Whisky** *Patio/terrace   Outdoor Eating* **Credit Cards:** *Access, Amex, Visa*

OSMOTHERLEY   Three Tuns

Northallerton DL6 3BN   **FOOD**
Tel: (0609) 83301   ☼
Open: 12-3.30, 7-11   ❢
Licensees: Hugh and Juliet Dyson

The Three Tuns sits amongst a row of solid stone cottages in the centre of the village, just two minutes' drive from the A19. Its frontage is greatly enhanced by some colourful hanging baskets and flower displays. Inside, three connecting rooms are served by a central bar, simply yet effectively furnished with solid bench-style seating softened by comfortable padded upholstery, and simple wooden tables. The walls are hung with sporting prints and, in the top bar, a display of framed deeds to the building, dating back to the 1700s. Plants and dried flower displays also feature. But it's the food that makes the Three Tuns stand out; the cooking is in the joint hands of licensees Hugh and Juliet Dyson, who create some extremely innovative and enjoyable dishes, and pride themselves on only using fresh produce, as much of it local as possible. Fish is especially strong, coming from Whitby. A printed menu is supplemented by a regularly changing specials board: perhaps scallops wrapped in bacon with spinach, a parcel of salmon and plaice with crab sauce, or fried goujons of Whitby sole. Meat dishes, too, show an imaginative touch, like Juliet's chicken – a breast of free-range chicken filled with cream cheese and nuts, served on an asparagus sauce – while a deceptively titled mini rack of lamb (actually rather large), which was rather too fatty, was served pink with an unusual sauce of strawberries and mint. Each meal is accompanied by a bread board bearing a generous hunk of good quality granary bread, and a selection of fresh vegetables is competently handled. Desserts are good: at the time of our visit, warm weather delights like summer pudding and strawberry trifle made decisive choices difficult. The main dining area is at the top of the pub, where neatly clothed tables provide a more formal setting. It is wise to be early: once tables there are all taken, diners eat in the bar areas, but when the pub is busy (which is fairly often), a hold might be put on meals served in this area. As everything is cooked to order, a short delay can occur between courses, which on busy nights might turn into a somewhat irritating wait, but the quality of the food generally makes the wait worthwhile. Prices are deliberately kept down and are really very reasonable; a competitively priced Sunday lunch is proving very popular indeed. Service can seem a little sombre, but is usually friendly enough. To the rear, a small garden has rustic furniture and, at the front, a couple of benches make an ideal venue for watching village life go by.

Bar Meals: 12-2.30, 7-9.30   Typical Dishes: Coble stew £1.65, deep-fried camembert with fresh raspberry sauce, steak in the hole with real ale sauce, chicken stuffed with cream cheese and pine nuts, salmon and Whitby plaice parcel in crab sauce, bread and butter pudding Vegetarian Meals: vegetable and nut parcel with tomato and basil sauce   Children's Portions Cheese   Beer *McEwan; Theakston   Family Room   Garden   Outdoor Eating   **No Credit Cards***

OSWALDKIRK   Malt Shovel

near Helmsley Y06 5XT
Tel: (04393) 461
Open: 11.30-2.30, 6.30-11
Licensees: P A Poole and N J Danford

There are new licensees (again) at this early 17th century manor house conversion, splendidly re-fashioned into a pub of real character. The tap room boasts a huge inglenook and lofty ceiling, and roaring log fires warm the two little bars. The menu's still worth a look, and this is a fine bed and breakfasting pub, its three decent-sized, creaky, sloping-floored bedrooms reached via a fine oak staircase. Redecoration is planned for spring 1992.

Bar Meals: 12-2, 7-9   Typical Dishes: courgette and mushroom soup £1.30, deep-fried brie with cranberry £2.95, beef in ale with horseradish dumplings £4.25, grilled dabs with parsley and lemon butter £4.50, local lamb with minted butter £4.95, jam roly poly 95p Vegetarian Meals   Children's Menu/Portions Beer *Sam Smiths Museum Ale, Old Brewery Bitter   Family Room   Outdoor Play Area   Garden   Outdoor Eating   Summer Barbecue   **Accommodation:** 3 bedrooms, sharing a bathroom, from £37 (single £18.50) Check-in: by arrangement   **No Credit Cards***

PICKHILL   Nags Head

Thirsk YO7 4JT   B&B
Open: 11-11
Licensees: Raymond and Edward Boynton

Both the village of Pickhill and the Nags Head are posted off the A1. In the centre of the village, just up from the village green, this former coaching inn, much extended and improved over the years, has been owned and run by brothers Raymond and Edward Boynton since 1972. Outside the cream-painted, part creeper-clad building, is the Boyntons' Infallible Weather Stone, basically a large stone on a chain with humorous explanations as to how it predicts the weather. The flagstoned porchway is also the inn's reception area, while a narrow corridor leads into the very lively public bar, which is extremely popular with locals and always a hive of noise and conversation. There are beamed ceilings, part-carpeted floors, red upholstered banquette seating, walls covered with photos of aircraft from local and visiting RAF stations, aerial photos of the pub, and a huge collection of ties hung around the whole bar – it's as if every male visitor to the pub had his tie pinched, so beware! The adjoining lounge bar is dimly lit, with the same banquette seating in dark green, fake beamed ceilings and a central fireplace. Walls are hung with a number of framed pictures, many of which are offered for sale. Two blackboards are in each bar, showing the day's choice of bar food (described as "informal eating"). The choice depends on what's fresh at the markets, and the cooking, though not without its faults (over-seasoning, thick sauces, overcooked meat in a stroganoff), is certainly of passable standard. It's an interesting selection, with dishes like osso bucco, smoked pork chop with sauerkraut, kromeskis (ham and chicken), fresh goujons of cod, and game pie. A longer restaurant menu has a more varied choice, with dishes priced a pound or two higher than in the bar. The restaurant itself is decorated in tones of green and salmon pink, with clothed tables and a more contemporary style. Bedrooms are split between the main building, the next-door house and a cottage, which can also be let in its entirety. Main building rooms have darker shades of decor, pine furniture and matching duvets. The house next door is more modern, with pastel pink walls, contrasting green borders and co-ordinated fabrics. Hairdryers and fresh fruit make useful extras, even if the chair provided is rather uncomfortable. En suite bathrooms (3 with shower only) are all carpeted, and those with baths also have good showers fitted over them.

Bar Meals: 12-2.30 (2 Sun), 6-10; bar snacks both sessions *Restaurant:* 12-2, 7-9.30 *Typical Dishes BAR:* pea and ham soup £1.50, green-lipped mussels £3.50, steak and kidney pie £5.75, chilli con carne £4.95, pork chop with apple and cider sauce £6.25 *RESTAURANT:* French onion soup £1.75, lambs kidneys with whisky and ginger £3.45, osso bucco £7.95, Barnsley chop £8.25, fillet steak Mont d'Or £10.25, summer pudding *Vegetarian Meals:* lasagne `Cheese` `Beer` Theakston; Younger `Whisky` Children Allowed in Bar to Eat Outdoor Play Area Garden Outdoor Eating *Accommodation:* 15 bedrooms, all en suite, from £42 (single £29.50) Children Welcome Overnight Cots Available Check-in: all day *Credit Cards:* Access, Visa

ROBIN HOODS BAY Dolphin Hotel King Street. 18th century inn with decent bar meals; fresh local fish specials.

ROSEDALE ABBEY   Milburn Arms

near Pickering YO18 8RA
Tel: (07515) 312
Open: 11.30-3, 6.30-11
Licensee: Terence Bentley

There's a new licensee at this charming inn-hotel in the centre of Rosedale Abbey, previously highly recommended for both bar food and accommodation. The bar is long and low with beams and an open fire, with an attractive family/function room leading off. Bedrooms divide between the main building and new extension.

Bar Meals: 12-2.15, 7-9.30; bar snacks both sessions *Restaurant:* 12-2 Sun only, 7-8.45 *Typical Dishes BAR:* carrot and coriander soup £1.50, game terrine £3, rabbit pie £5.25, game pie £6.25, local rainbow trout £5.50, sticky toffee pudding £1.95 Vegetarian Meals: hazelnut and brown rice bake Children's Portions `Beer` Fullers; Taylor; Theakston `Whisky` Children Allowed in Bar to Eat Garden Outdoor Eating *Accommodation:* 11 bedrooms, all en suite, from £57 (single £36) Children Welcome Overnight Cots Available Check-in: all day *Credit Cards:* Access, Diners, Visa

---

ROSEDALE ABBEY   White Horse Farm Hotel

near Pickering YO18 8SE
Tel: (07515) 239
Open: 12-3, 6.30-11 (11-11 Sat)
Licensee: Howard J Proctor

Lovely position, on a hillside with glorious views. Farm origins still evident in cosy beamed bar. Long menu of some 30 or so items.

Bar Meals: 12-2.30,6.30-9.45; bar snacks both sessions   **Restaurant:** 12-1.30 (Sun only), 7-8.45   **Typical Dishes BAR:** home-made soup £1.55, mussel ragout £3.95, home-made pies £4.95, Cropton stoggies (woodpigeon) £6.60, vegetable lasagne £2.99, brandy biscuit cake £1.65   **RESTAURANT:** set price, 4 courses from £16   Vegetarian Meals: stuffed mushrooms £3.60   Children's Menu   ▮Beer▮   Tetleys; Theakston Best ▮Whisky▮   Children Allowed in Bar to Eat   Garden   Outdoor Eating   **Accommodation:** 15 bedrooms, all en suite, from £60 (single £30)   Children Welcome Overnight   Cots Available   Check-in: all day   **Credit Cards:** Access, Amex, Diners, Visa

SAWLEY   Sawley Arms

Fountains Abbey HG4 3EQ
Tel: (0765) 620642
Open: 11.30-3, 6-11; closed Mon
Licensee: June Hawes

The landlady cook has been here for well over 20 years, and built up a strong local reputation for her bar food. A carpeted ramble of little rooms is pleasantly simple in style, with a mix of modern and old-fashioned furnishings and real fires. There's also a plain white-walled dining area. The pub is a Britain in Bloom winner. No children indoors.

Bar Meals: 12-2, 7-9 (not Sun eve; no food Mon); bar snacks both sessions   **Typical Dishes:** home-made soup £1.75, salmon mousse £3.50, chicken in mushroom sauce £4.95, roast boned duckling £9.50, plaice mornay with julienne of leek £4.90, amaretti schokoladentorte £3.50   Vegetarian Meals: cheese and spinach deep-fried pancakes   Garden **Accommodation:** 1 bedroom, en suite, £35   Check-in: by arrangement   **Credit Cards:** Access, Visa

SEAMER   Copper Horse

15 Main Street YO12 4BF
Tel: (0723) 862029
Open: 11-3, 6.30-11; closed Mon/Tue
Licensee: Harold St Quinton

See Cornucopia, Malton.

Bar Meals: 12-2, 6.30-10; bar snacks lunchtime   **Restaurant:** 12-2, 6.30-9.30 **Typical Dishes BAR:** minestrone £1.35, garlic mushrooms with bacon and mini sausages £2.85, roast pork joint rolled in thyme £7.50, pork fillet provencale £7.50, halibut, salmon and prawns on rice £6.95, chocolate brandy cake   Vegetarian Meals: vegetarian crepe £5.95 Children's Portions   ▮Beer▮   Youngers   Children Allowed in Bar to Eat   **Credit Cards:** Access, Visa

STAPLETON Bridge Inn The Green Tel: (0325) 350106. Mixed grill (£9.90), chicken satay (£5.70) and Indonesian mixed platter (£8.60) are among the bar meals offered 12-2.30, 6.30-10 here. Family room; garden; Vaux beers. Open all day.

STARBOTTON Fox & Hounds near Kettlewell, Upper Wharfedale Tel: (075 676) 269. Listed for atmosphere, a classic Yorkshire village pub with stone floors, rough walls, simple wooden tables and chairs and open fires in both bars. Lovely local walks in pretty countryside. Now also two bedrooms; bar meals routine, but good home-made soups. Patio. Youngers beers. Open: 12-3, 7-11 (closed all Mon/Tue lunch Nov-May).

STUTTON   Hare & Hounds

Manor Road SL24 9BS
Tel: (0937) 833164
Open: 11.30-3, 6.30-11
Licensee: Mr Chiswick

Getting a reputation for excellent quality bar meals in the York area, and regular pilgrimages are made from the city. The low-ceilinged lounge interior is decorated in good taste in that style known as Olde Worlde, with lots of beams, pictures, brass, fresh flowers, small windows and a general air of being very well cared-for. It's generally busy with diners, many of them regulars, even by 7pm at weekends. A second bar has now become a dining room proper. All dishes are listed on blackboards (no menus), so the choice is ever-changing. Good steaks and vegetables; disappointing puddings.

Bar Meals: 11.30-2. 6.45-9.30 (12-2 Sun, no food Sun eve) **Typical Dishes:** *chicken and mushroom soup £1.45, baked mushrooms £2.85, deep-fried haddock £4.50, steak and mushroom pie £4.75, medallion of beef fillet in cream and stilton sauce £8.95, treacle tart £2.25 Vegetarian Meals   Children's Portions   Children Allowed in Bar to Eat   Outdoor Play Area   Garden   Outdoor Eating* **Credit Cards:** *Access, Visa*

SUTTON HOWGRAVE   White Dog

Bedale DL8 2NS
Tel: (0765) 640404
Open: 12-2.30, 7-11; closed Sun eve and all day Mon
Licensees: Pat and Basil Bagnall

Quaint converted village cottage by delightful old green, with simply furnished, cosy interior featuring working kitchen range. Lovely in summer when the clematis and window boxes bloom, though you can't eat out of doors. Not a pub to bring the children to. Vegetarians catered for 'by request' in the restaurant.

Bar Meals: 12-1.45, 7-8.30; bar snacks lunchtime **Typical Dishes:** *French onion soup £1.50, smoked duck breast with melon £4.15, chicken casserole £4.75, venison pie £5.50, lamb casserole £5.10, puddings from £1.95 Vegetarian Meals (bar)   Garden* **No Credit Cards**

THORNTON WATLASS   Buck Inn

near Bedale HG4 4AH
Tel: (0677) 422461
Open: 11-2.30, 6-11 (perhaps all day summer)
Licensees: Michael and Margaret Fox

Next to the village green cricket pitch – it's a four if the ball hits the pub wall, a six if it clears the roof – this is a refurbished but traditional, well-run, friendly village institution. Eat in the bar or adjoining dining room, recently knocked through, so better to deal with the huge numbers of hungry people who beat a path to their door. To residents (good value B&B) they offer guided walks and fly fishing on the Urr; quoits in the garden on Wednesday evenings is open to all.

Bar Meals: 12-2, 6.45 (7 Sun)-9.30, bar snacks both sessions **Typical Dishes:** *pea and ham soup £1.40, salmon mousse £2.35, pork fillet with creamed mushrooms £6.25, steak and kidney pie £4.50, home-baked lasagne £4.50, home-made apple pie £1.50 Vegetarian Meals: baked aubergine and tomato £4.25   Children's Menu/Portions* **Beer** *Tetley; Theakston* **Whisky** *Family Room   Outdoor Play Area   Garden*

Outdoor Eating   **Accommodation:** *5 bedrooms, all en suite, from £40 (single £25)*
Children Welcome Overnight   Cot Available   Check-in: all day   **Credit Cards:** *Access,*
Amex, Visa

THRESHFIELD   Old Hall

Grassington Road BD23 5HB
Open: 11-3, 5.30-11
Licensee: Ian Taylor

Attractively simple, very popular pub, the rear room of which is Tudor, hence the
name. Reliably good bar meals; be early.

Bar Meals: *12-2, 6.30-9.30; bar snacks lunchtime*   **Typical Dishes:** *home-made soup
£1.50, mushrooms stuffed with ham and stilton £2.75, steak and mushroom pie £5, pan-
fried chicken breast in tarragon cream £6.45, halibut, salmon and king prawn bake £6.45,
pear and stilton pie £1.75   Vegetarian Meals: mushroom pasta bake £4.95   Children's
Menu/Portions* Beer *Timothy Taylor; Theakston; Younger* Whisky *Family Room
Outdoor Play Area   Garden   Outdoor Eating* **No Credit Cards**

WASS   ★ Wombwell Arms

Wass YO6 4BE   FOOD
Tel: (03476) 280
Open: 12-2.30, 7-11; closed Mon   B&B
Licensees: Lynda and Alan Evans

Having run pubs for some 10 years, but always for someone else, Lynda and Alan
Evans decided it was time they did it for themselves. They took a six month
busman's holiday, touring the country to find their ideal pub. The result is the
Wombwell Arms – though at the time they found it, it didn't look like much! This
whitewashed village inn dates from the 18th century and sits in the shadow of the
Hambleton hills, just a couple of miles from the A170, east of Thirsk. The pub was
in such a state when they found it that they decided to close completely for three
months and totally refurbish. The results are impressive, a happy marriage of
traditional country image and the 20th century, with stylish fabrics and furnishings.
The interior consists of four connecting rooms. The first room to the left of the
entrance has light wood floorboards, stripped pine tables and chairs, and half-
panelling. This room is especially good for families. The bar and its adjoining dining
area have a mix of flagstone and red-tiled flooring, some exposed stone walls, more
panelling and original beams. Some walls have attractive Laura Ashley wallpapers,
while farmhouse kitchen style tables are covered with colourfully designed cloths.
The final room is similarly appointed. Throughout the pub, there are splendid fresh
and dried flower displays, watercolours of chickens, foxes and other country
subjects, magazines and books. Over the bar is an original drawing of TV's Captain
Pugwash, drawn for the landlord by its creator John Ryan, an old boy of nearby
Ampleforth College. A huge blackboard displays the day's choice of interesting bar
food. Rather bistro in style, this is the preserve of Lynda Evans, who is a more than
competent cook. Only fresh, mostly local produce is used, and the choice is
extensive and varied: perhaps scampi and prawn provencale, venison casserole with
redcurrants, Haitian chicken with pineapple and ginger, or beef with orange and
brandy. A dish of paprika lamb featured tender pieces of local lamb in a creamy
paprika sauce, served with wholegrain rice. There are good vegetarian dishes too,
like cauliflower and three cheese quiche, or brandy creamed mushrooms. Desserts
are well up to standard, with a fine summer pudding, orange mousse or a hot cherry
sundae. There's also a selection of lighter lunch dishes. The three bedrooms are
equally impressive. Two doubles and a twin are kitted out in colourful Laura Ashley

wallpapers, with matching curtains and duvet covers, and stripped pine furniture. They're impeccably kept and offer a selection of magazines as well as televisions and radio alarms. Each room is en suite, one with a shower, two with baths. To immaculate housekeeping is added a sense of fun: plastic ducks are provided. Alan Evans looks after the bar and is an extremely jovial host. A quite exceptional country pub, well worth a detour.

Bar Meals: 12-2, 7-10; bar snacks lunchtime   ***Typical Dishes:*** *cauliflower soup £1.75, half-pint of prawns £3.75, venison sausages on red cabbage £4.50, casseroled beef in orange and brandy £6.15, scampi and prawn provencale, steamed syrup sponge £2.25   Vegetarian Meals: brandy cream mushrooms   Children's Portions* Cheese   Beer *Camerons; Everards   Children Allowed in Bar to Eat   **Accommodation:** 3 bedrooms, all en suite, from £39 (single £19.50)   Children Welcome Overnight (minimum age 8)   Check-in: by arrangement   **Credit Cards:** Access, Visa*

WATH-IN-NIDDERDALE   Sportsmans Arms

Pateley Bridge HG3 5PP   FOOD
Tel: (0423) 711306   ❢ ⊝
Open: 12-2.30, 7-11   B&B
Licensee: Ray Carter

Follow the signs for Wath from the centre of Pateley Bridge and after a couple of miles you'll see a sign to the pub itself. Once over a narrow bridge crossing the River Nidd, you'll see the mellow-stoned 17th century Sportsmans Arms, just back from the river bank in its own grounds, in beautiful moorland surroundings. Just up the road (quarter of a mile) is Gouthwaite Reservoir, a favourite spot with ornithologists. The Sportsmans has two cosy lounges, used by residents and diners alike. Each has a good assortment of armchairs and well-used couches, as well as antique furniture and a lot of parlour plants. The bar to the rear of the building is rather plush and most comfortably decorated in soft tones of salmon pink with blue upholstered banquette seating. Food, served in the bar every lunchtime, is interesting, fresh and skilfully produced under the watchful eye of owner Ray Carter. A printed menu is supplemented by a blackboard which offers an array of super seafood, exceptionally fresh and carefully handled: Scarborough woof with capers, prawns and lemon, baby plaice plain-grilled to retain all its natural flavour and moisture, or salmon served with a herb and prawn butter. Meat eaters aren't neglected: Ray Carter is constantly striving to find the best meat in the area for dishes like loin of pork in a delicious creamy mushroom sauce, or venison with juniper and cream. Excellent puddings might include a fine summer pudding or classic crème brulée. Very good coffee too. Prices are reasonable, with main items around the £6 mark. In the evenings (and at Sunday lunchtimes), the attractive restaurant comes into its own. The menus, both à la carte and fixed price, are more extensive and allow more scope for ambition in dishes like a trio of seafood with two sauces, or breast of duck in a lavender and vodka jus with raspberries. Expect to pay about £50 for two, although fixed price menus work out cheaper. It's worth it: cooking here is of a notably high standard and shows real flair. The seven bedrooms (five double, two twin) are light, airy and neatly maintained. All have smart light wood furniture, contemporary style wallcoverings in soft colours and bright soft furnishings. Two rooms have their own en suite shower rooms and toilet; the remainder share two good-sized bathrooms and two separate toilets. Front-facing rooms have fine country views. This is a hotel constantly undergoing improvements and serving first-rate food in a lovely peaceful spot. It also boasts fishing rights on the River Nidd, rich in trout.

Bar Meals: 12-2; bar snacks   ***Restaurant:*** 12-2.30 (Sun only), 7-9.30 (not Sun)
Typical Dishes *BAR: home-made soup £2.30, scallops in garlic butter £3.90, loin of pork in mushroom and mustard sauce £5.95, Scottish salmon with orange hollandaise £6.50, fresh lobster grilled with garlic, or thermidor £9.50, summer pudding £2.50*

RESTAURANT: quenelles of salmon mousseline £6.20, best end of lamb with asparagus, spring onions, garlic and beetroot £12.50, traditional Nidderdale grouse £14.50, fresh seafood £14.50, raspberry sablés £3.50   Vegetarian Meals: filo parcel of fresh vegetables   Children's Portions   `Cheese`   `Whisky`   Children Allowed in Bar to Eat   Garden   Outdoor Eating   **Accommodation:** 7 bedrooms, 2 en suite, from £45 (single £27)   Children Welcome Overnight   Cots Available   Check-in: all day   **Credit Cards:** Access, Visa

---

WEAVERTHORPE   Star Inn

near Malton YO17 8EY
Tel: (09443) 273
Open: 12-2.30 (weekends only), 7-11
Licensee: Susan Richardson

Well run, well kept, two bar Wolds village pub, outstanding for fresh local game in season, and with a pleasing philosophy geared towards regional foods and recipes all year round. Overnight accommodation is cheap and unassuming. A general, overall refurbishment, inside and out, is planned in readiness for 1992.

Bar Meals: weekend lunches, Wed-Mon eves; bar snacks evening   **Restaurant:** Sunday lunch, Wed-Mon eves   **Typical Dishes BAR:** home-made soup £1.95, mariners mix £3.50, pigeon breasts in red wine sauce £6.25, chicken stuffed with cheese and asparagus £7.50, mixed seafood pie £6, profiteroles with butterscotch sauce £2.50   Vegetarian Meals: peanut and celery risotto £6.25   Children's Portions   `Cheese`   `Beer`   Old Mill; Taylor, Tetley; Webster's   Family Room   Children Allowed in Bar to Eat   Outdoor Eating   **Accommodation** (closed Feb): 5 bedrooms, 3 en suite, from £25 (single £14.50)   Children Welcome Overnight (minimum age 5)   Check-in: by arrangement   **Credit Cards:** Access, Visa

---

WEST WITTON   Wensleydale Heifer

near Leyburn DL8 4LS
Tel: (0969) 22322
Open: 11-3, 6-11
Licensee: J A Sharp

Well kept, pleasant 17th century inn with chintzy furniture (perhaps more hotelly than strictly pubby in style), lounge and two further bars; good log fire in winter. Pretty bedrooms, half of them in adjacent cottages; three with four posters. On main A684 Leyburn-Hawes road, in attractive countryside.

Bar Meals: 12-2, 6.30-9; bar snacks lunchtime   **Restaurant:** 12-2 (summer Suns), 7-9   **Typical Dishes BAR:** home-made soup £1.60, stilton and quince paté £2.95, steak and kidney pie £5.50, Yorkshire ham and eggs £6.50, Dover sole £7.95, puddings £1.95   **RESTAURANT:** 5 course dinner £19.50   Vegetarian Meals: vegetable lasagne   Children's Portions   `Beer`   Theakston   `Whisky`   Family Room   **Accommodation:** 19 bedrooms, all en suite, from £62 (single £46)   Children Welcome Overnight   Cots Available   Check-in: all day   **Credit Cards:** Access, Diners, Visa

WHITBY Dolphin By the Bridge, Old Whitby: Decent home cooking, simple pies, occasionally local seafood; thriving, busy local.

WIGGLESWORTH   Plough Inn

Skipton BD23 4RJ
Tel: (07294) 243
Open: (9 am for coffee), 11.30-2.30, 7-11
Licensee: Brian Goodall

Five new en suite bedrooms and a huge, cane furnished pink and mint conservatory restaurant are the newest innovations at this fine old country inn with landscaped garden.

Bar Meals: 12-2, 7-9.30; bar snacks both sessions **Typical Dishes:** *home-made soup £1.60, mushrooms in garlic butter £2.60, charcoal-grilled minute steak £5.40, roast shoulder of lamb £6.90, seafood pancakes £4.50, sticky toffee pudding Vegetarian Meals: aubergine and tomato bake Children's Menu/Portions* Beer *Tetley; Whitbread* Whisky *Family Room Patio/terrace Outdoor Eating* **Accommodation:** *12 bedrooms, all en suite, from £49 (single £32.70) Children Welcome Overnight Cots Available Check-in: all day* **Credit Cards:** *Access, Amex, Diners, Visa*

WIGHILL White Swan: Warmly welcoming York commuter village pub, invariably busy, with a traditional, characterful ramble of rooms, open fires, attractive dining room, attentive, kindly landlady (very nice to babies), fairly routine food, more adventurous in the evening. Tetley, Theakston beers. Open: 12-3, 6-11.

WINKSLEY Countryman Inn: 18th century pub, busy with visitors to nearby Fountains Abbey in summer, a local off-season; decent and often imaginative bar meals; pool table in family room; front terrace. Ruddles, Webster's beers. Open: 12-3 (not Mon), 6.30-11.

YORK   Royal Oak

18 Goodramgate YO1 2LG
Tel: (0904) 653856
Open: 11-11
Licensee: David Smith

Regarded as one of the best pubs for bar food in this venerable old city centre; unfortunately that doesn't mean much. Food is generally competent, though a recent steak pie greatly disappointed. Usually busy, as it's close by the back entrance to the Minster, the pub can look overstretched at times and in need of a good dusting. Toilets aren't first rate either.

Bar Meals: 11.30-7.30 (12-2.30, 7-8.30 Sun); bar snacks both sessions **Typical Dishes:** *leek and potato soup with home-baked bread £1.20, roast beef and Yorkshire pudding £4.25, real ale, steak and kidney pie £3.75, tandoori chicken with pitta bread £3.40, bread and butter pudding £1.25 Vegetarian Meals: broccoli crepes in stilton sauce £3.20 Children's Portions* Beer *Camerons; Everards Family Room*

SOUTH YORKSHIRE

BAWTRY Turnpike 28-30 High Street. Converted wine bar premises, stylishly furnished in old alehouse style; good-value, varied bar menu lunch and Mon-Thur evenings. Try the local Stocks beers. Open: 11-3, 6-11.

CADEBY   Cadeby Inn

Main Street DN5 7SW
Tel: (0709) 864009
Open: 11-3, 5-11 (all day Sat)
Licensee: W W Ward

Stone-built ex-farmhouse pub with a cricket-mad main lounge, comfortable with one or two old pieces and a good open fire. Another little room, to the front, is usually quieter, and there's a separate darts room/public bar. No music. The bar menu is routine enough but quality is good. They sell 184 whiskies.

Bar Meals: 12-2, 6-10; bar snacks both sessions **Typical Dishes:** *vegetable soup £1, Yorkshire pudding with gravy £1.05, steak and kidney pie £3.45, gammon steak £4.25, mixed grill £5.25, rhubarb crumble £1.50 Vegetarian Meals: four-cheese lasagne £3.95 Children's Menu/Portions* Beer *John Smith; Samuel Smith; Tetley* Whisky *Family Room Outdoor Play Area Garden Outdoor Eating Summer Barbecue* **Credit Cards:** *Access, Visa*

KILNHURST   Ship

1 Hooton Road (B6090) S62 5TA
Tel: (0709) 584322
Open: 11.30-2.30, 6-11
Licensee: Terence Harper

Built in 1752, the oldest building in the village, close to railway and canal; a homely country inn boxed in by the urban landscape. Home-cooking by licensees. Set Sunday lunches. Bar room entertainment most evenings.

Bar Meals and Restaurant: 12-2, 7.30-10; bar snacks both sessions **Typical Dishes** *BAR: country vegetable soup 90p, smoked mackerel £1.75, home-made meat and potato pie £3, chilli £2.50, Yorkshire pudding with beef gravy £2.15, home-made apple pie Restaurant: mushroom soup 90p, garlic prawns £1.75, Tex Mex £6.95, surf and turf £6.95, mixed grill £6.50, apple crumble Vegetarian Meals: lasagne Children's Menu/Portions* Beer *Marston Pedigree; Whitbread Boddingtons Bitter, Castle Eden Ale Family Room Outdoor Play Area Garden Outdoor Eating* **No Credit Cards**

LANGSETT Waggon & Horses Tel: (0226) 763147. Traditional, music and electronics-free stone pub by the reservoir. Home cooked food 12-2, 7-9.30, interesting soups; pies, lasagne, with chips or new potatoes. Garden; family room; Bass, Theakston beers. Bedrooms are planned. Open: 12-3, 7-11.

PENISTONE   Cubley Hall

Mortimer Road, Cubley S30 6AW
Tel: (0226) 766086
Open: 11-3, 6-11
Licensee: John Wigfield

Converted from a rather grand Edwardian villa in 1983, and lots of Edwardian style survives the transformation, despite the fruit machines and piped music.

Bar Meals: 12-2, 6.30-10; bar snacks both sessions **Typical Dishes:** *soup £1.05, home-made paté £1.50, sirloin steak £6.50, home-made beef and vegetable pie £4.50, fillet of haddock £4.50, jam roly poly £1.50 Vegetarian Meals: lasagne Children's Menu/Portions* Beer *Ind Coope, Tetley; Marston Family Room Outdoor Play Area Garden Outdoor Eating* **Credit Cards:** *Access, Visa*

SHEFFIELD Devonshire Arms 118 Eccleshall Road Tel: (0742) 722202. Now in the empire of locally popular pub caterers the Stanaways; very cheap, cheerful bar food lunchtime and evening; filled Yorkshire puddings a speciality. The Wards brewery tap. Open all day.

SPROTBOROUGH Boat Inn Nursery Lane, Lower Sprotborough. Converted farmhouse pub on the banks of the Don; extensive terrace seating; the interior is plain and comfortable rather than characterful. Choose the local and home-made from the mixed menu. Music can be intrusive. Courage beers. Open: 11-3, 6-11 (all day summer Sat).

SUTTON   Anne Arms

Suttonfield Road DN6 9JK   `FOOD`
Tel: (0302) 700500   ☼
Open: 11-3, 6-11   ☺
Licensees: John and Irene Sims

The village of Sutton is signposted off the A19 about five miles north of Doncaster. At its heart is the ever-popular Anne Arms, a mellow stone building covered in creepers and colourful flower boxes. Its garden, which leads from an attractive conservatory (fitted with white cast iron furniture and featuring caged budgies and other birds) is full of children's play equipment and picnic tables. The interior of the main pub is bursting with character: in the main bar area, old wooden beams and panelling and polished wooden tables surrounded by floral upholstered chairs and bench seating. Glass display cabinets placed around the room hold a splendid collection of porcelain figurines and glassware. The ceiling, bar counter and window sills are adorned with a large collection of colourful Toby jugs as well as some Bavarian drinking steins. A small snug with bench seating and copper-topped tables has a number of stuffed birds, and the final lounge area has lace clothed tables and a host of highly polished brass and copperware. The pub appears to be especially popular with the retired and o.a.p. community, who flock here in droves. The queue to the food servery starts forming at about 11.50 am, and often stretches right back through the bar. The menu (rather oddly displayed at the front door) features a short selection of dishes like rabbit pie, braised steak with Yorkshire pudding, Barnsley chop, fresh salmon and a daily roast such as roast pork or stuffed breast of chicken. They cook the food in bulk (such is the turnover), then display and serve it quickly from a hot cabinet servery. Portions and prices – £3 for each dish with vegetables and potatoes – are very fair, but the quality can obviously decline the later you arrive; no doubt that's why it's so busy as soon as it opens. You may find it difficult to find a table anywhere if you arrive after 12! Staff are well-rehearsed but can at times appear rather abrupt. A waitress in blue overall, carrying a collecting bowl of dirty dishes, is rather at odds with the pleasant atmosphere that generally prevails. Don't expect wonders, but for good, cheap, honest home-made food, the Anne Arms is well worth a visit. Children are welcome in the conservatory or snug.

Bar Meals: 12-2, 7-9; no food Sun   ***Typical Dishes:*** *rabbit pie, Barnsley chop, braised steak and Yorkshire pudding (all £3), spotted dick £1.10*   *Children's Portions*   `Beer`   *Courage*   *Family Room (over 5 years)*   *Outdoor Play Area*   *Garden*   *Outdoor Eating*   ***No Credit Cards***

WATH UPON DEARNE Sandygate Inn Sandygate. Large hotel converted from an old hospital premises; decent lunch and evening bar meals; good facilities and family room. Theakston, Youngers beers. Open all day.

WENTWORTH George & Dragon Main Street Tel: (0226) 742440. Vigorously traditional village local, with a good range of beers; bar food is secondary. Open: 12-3 (12-2.30 Sun), 7-11.

WORSBOROUGH Edmunds Arms 25 Worsborough Village. Charming setting, opposite the village church, and a rather splendid little pub, very popular for food, served lunch and evening (not Sun, nor Mon eve). Sam Smith beers. Open: 11-3 (4 Fri/Sat), 7-11.

WEST YORKSHIRE

BARDSEY Bingley Arms Tel: (0937) 72462. Another of "Britain's oldest", but with apparently strong evidence in this case. Don't miss a glimpse at least of the beautiful dining hall. Interesting bar food including game sausages, smoked chicken salad, rabbit pie, all at keen prices. Meals lunchtime and evening; children allowed in to eat. Tetleys beers.

BRADFORD   Shoulder of Mutton

28 Kirkgate BD1 1QL
Tel: (0274) 726038
Open: 11-11 (12-2, 7-10.30 Sun)
Licensee: Peter Blackburn

Unprepossessing city centre Sam Smiths pub with a real oasis of a garden, which can take 200 people if pressed (and often is). Exceedingly busy at lunchtime with office workers and shoppers. 'Fast food, but not junk food' (their description); no starters or puddings, and vegetarians must put up with cheese flan or ploughman's lunch. Good daily specials. Children welcome in the garden.

Bar Meals: 11.30-2.15 (not Sun)   ***Typical Dishes:*** *home-made steak and kidney pie £2.50, curries £2.60, chicken chasseur £2.60*   Beer   *Sam Smith Old Brewery Bitter Garden   Outdoor Eating*   **No Credit Cards**

CRIDLING STUBBS Ancient Shepherd Inn near Knottingley. Worth trying for its winter game specials; decent bar meals all year (12-2, 7-10, no food Sun/Mon, nor Sat lunch). Tetleys beers.

ELLAND Barge & Barrel, Park Road. Victorian pub with lots of mahogany and etched glass; good family room; good beers; bar meals lunch and evening. Open: 12-11.

GRANGE MOOR   Kaye Arms

29 Wakefield Road WF4 4BG
Tel: (0942) 848385
Open: 11.30-3 (not Mon), 7-11
Licensee: Stuart Coldwell

Run by the same family for over 20 years, and recently bought from Tetley Brewery, the Kaye Arms is now blossoming into an interesting foodie pub, with all the cooking and serving done by various Coldwells. The evening brasserie style operation has a smarter menu; main courses around £7 then.

Bar Meals: 12-2, 7.30-10; bar snacks both sessions   ***Typical Dishes*** *(lunch): home-made soup £1.60, chicken liver paté with pickled oranges £2.30, steak and kidney pie £4.95, sausage, lambs kidney and bacon skewer £4.50, fresh salmon fishcake £3.70, praline parfait with mango sauce £2.05*   Whisky   *Children Allowed in Bar to Eat*   **Credit Cards:** *Access, Visa*

HARTSHEAD   Gray Ox

15 Hartshead Lane, Liversedge WF15 8AL
Tel: (0274) 872845
Open: 12-3 (not Mon), 7-11
Licensee: Jane Foster

Isolated, comfortable brick-built pub, with a very popular restaurant. This is one for
lovers of formidably large portions; steak-lovers come from far and wide. Not a
spelling mistake, incidentally: 'Gray' is correct, in this case.

*Bar Meals: 12-3, bar snacks lunchtime   Restaurant: 7-10.30 (10 Sun); no food in bar or
restaurant Mon eve   Typical Dishes BAR: tomato soup £1.40, breaded prawns Creole
£2.90, steak pie £2.60, 5 oz steak sandwich £2.95, 1 pint prawns £4.20
RESTAURANT: mushroom soup £1.40, garlic mushrooms £2.60, 32 oz rump steak
£15.50, chicken bel paese £6.60, pizza della casa £3.95, raspberry royale £1.75
Vegetarian Meals: tagliatelle   Children's Menu/Portions* ▉Beer▉ *Ruddles; Webster's
Children Allowed in Bar to Eat   Outdoor Play Area   Garden   Outdoor Eating   Summer
Barbecue* **No Credit Cards**

HAWORTH   Old White Lion Hotel

Main Street BD22 8DU
Tel: (0535) 642313
Open: 11 (11.30 winter)-3, 6-11
Licensee: J K Bradford

Brontë village hotel with a pleasant modernised bar. Ordinary bar food, better in the
restaurant. Good views from the rather small, modern bedrooms.

*Bar Meals: 11.30-2.30, 6.30-9.30; bar snacks both sessions   Restaurant: 12-2.30 (Sun
only), 7-9.30   Typical Dishes BAR: mushroom soup £1.20, home-made paté £1.50,
home-made steak pie £3.30, gammon £4, home-made lasagne £3.20, fruit pie £1.20
RESTAURANT: tomato, apple and celery soup £1.40, mussels in cream and brandy
£2.75, beef Americaine £9.25, game in season from £7.50, Dover sole from £8.95. black
cherries jubilee £2.95 Vegetarian Meals   Children's Portions* ▉Beer▉ *Ruddles; Webster's
Children Allowed in Bar to Eat   Accommodation: 14 bedrooms, all en suite, from £43.50
(single £30.50)   Children Welcome Overnight   Cot Available   Check-in: all day* **Credit
Cards:** *Access, Amex, Diners, Visa*

HEATH   King's Arms

Heath Common WF1 5SL
Tel: (0924) 377527
Open: 11.30-3, 6-11
Licensee: John Radley

Part of the five-pub-strong Clark's brewery empire, a stone-flagged gaslit 18th
century pub full of unspoilt character, surrounded by a hundred acres of common
grassland, yet only five minutes from the motorway. Oak settles, cast-iron framed
tables and a working kitchen range in the main bar, and a sympathetic modern
extension, plus three further rooms. Nice to vegetarians and children.

*Bar Meals and Restaurant: 12-2, 7-9.30 (not Sun/Mon eve); bar snacks both sessions
Typical Dishes BAR: carrot and onion soup £1.60, Yorkshire puddings £1.20, roast of
the day £3.50, lasagne £3, cod fillet with parsley butter £3.50, gateau £1.50
RESTAURANT: chicken and celery soup £1.50, asparagus and mushroom gratiné
£3.25, beef Wellington £9.25, T-bone steaks £9.50, lobster thermidor £16.25, Italian*

trifle £2.50   Vegetarian Meals: risotto £3.25   Children's Menu/Portions   `Beer`
Clark's Traditional Bitter, Rams Revenge; Taylor Landlord; Tetley Bitter   `Whisky`
*Family Room   Garden   Outdoor Eating   Summer Barbecue   **Credit Cards:** Access, Visa*

ILKLEY Wharf Cottage Inn Leeds Road Tel: (0943) 607323. Tiny, friendly
Dales-style pub on the edge of this now rather well-heeled town; homely home
cooking (strong on filled Yorkshire puddings) at lunchtime; garden; Ruddles,
Webster's, Theakstons beers. Open: 12 (11 Sat)-3, 6.30-11; closed Mon lunch.

JACKSON BRIDGE   Red Lion

New Mill, Holmfirth HD7 7HS   ☻
Tel: (0484) 683499
Open: 11.30-3, 5-11
Licensee: Stephen Oscroft

Nice pub in "Last of The Summer Wine" country.

Bar Meals: *12-2 Tue-Sat, 5.30-8.30 weekdays; bar snacks both sessions*   **Typical
Dishes:** *pea and mint soup £1.25, calamari, steak Diane £5.95, lamb chops £5.45, cod
with broccoli £4.50, pear belle Helene £1.35   Vegetarian Meals: mixed zucchini £3.95
Children's Portions*   `Beer`   *Marston; Tetley; Wadworth; Whitbread*   `Whisky`   *Children
Allowed in Bar to Eat   Garden   Outdoor Eating   **Accommodation:** 6 bedrooms, 3 en
suite, from £35 (single £22.50)   Children Welcome Overnight   Check-in: all day   **No
Credit Cards***

LEDSHAM   Chequers Inn

South Milford LS25 5LP
Tel: (0977) 683135
Open: 11-3, 5.30-11 (all day Sat); closed Sun
Licensee: Chris Wraith

Old-fashioned village pub with lots of little rooms leading off a central panelled
servery; real fires, low beams, cosy corners, and lots of customers, many of whom
come for the food. No music.

Bar Meals: *12-2, 6.30-8.30 (not Sat eve); bar snacks both sessions   **Restaurant:** 7.30-
9.30 Tue-Sat   **Typical Dishes BAR:** vegetable soup £1.05, paté £1.75, Yorkshire ham
£4.70, steak pie £4.75, lasagne £3.60, chocolate roulade £1.50   **RESTAURANT:**
onion soup £2, prawn scramble £3.35, gooseberry chicken £5.95, roast duckling £8.45,
tournedos Rossini £9.70, trifle £2.30   Vegetarian Meals: lasagne   Children's Portions*
`Beer`   *John Smith; Theakston, Younger   Garden   Outdoor Eating   **Credit Cards:**
Access, Visa*

LEEDS   Whitelocks

Turks Head Yard, Briggate LS1 6HB
Tel: (0532) 453950
Open: 11-11
Licensees: Fred and Julie Cliff

A real Yorkshire institution, tucked away in an alley off the shopping area. The
original bar is long and narrow, with an unspoilt Edwardian atmosphere; the popular
dining area with linen-laid tables opens out at one end. Good service and the sort of
prices which make a sit-down lunch an affordable luxury. Reliable cooking: good
Yorkshire puddings come with proper onion gravy. The less exciting overspill bar

further along the yard has been kitted out in Victorian style.

Bar Meals: 11-7.30; bar snacks both sessions   **Restaurant:** 12-2.30, 5.30-8   **Typical Dishes BAR:** *thick vegetable soup 80p, Yorkshire pudding £1, meat and potato pie £2, home-made pasty 85p, sausages, bubble and squeak £2, jam roly poly 95p*
RESTAURANT: *asparagus soup 85p, paté £1.50, roast beef £4.95, Scotch pot £4.65, seafood pie £4.65   Vegetarian Meals: cheese and onion quiche £1.20   Children's Portions*
Beer   *Youngers beers   Children Allowed in Bar to Eat   Patio/terrace*   **Credit Cards:** *Access, Amex, Visa*

LEES MOOR   Quarry House Inn

Bingley Road BD21 5QE
Tel: (0535) 642239
Open: 12-3, 7-12
Licensees: C M and J M Smith

Family-run ex-farmhouse high above Keighley, with superb views of the Worth valley and its famous steam railway. Cricket ground next door. 'Barn' function room, often in use. Eight bedrooms planned for late '92.

Bar Meals and Restaurant: 12-2, 7.30-10.30   **Typical Dishes BAR:** *home-made soup £1.60, Cumberland sausage £3.85, broccoli and cream cheese pie £4.15, steak sandwich £4   **RESTAURANT:** smoked bacon and chestnut soup £1.60, smoked Tay trout mousse £5.25, supreme of chicken in filo pastry £9.25, escalope of local pork £9.75, fillet steak stuffed with paté in a port sauce £11.25   Vegetarian Meals: creamy devilled mushrooms £4.65   Children's Portions*   **Beer**   *Ind Coope Burton Ale, Tetley Bitter; Taylor Landlord   Family Room   Garden   Outdoor Eating*   **Credit Cards:** *Access, Amex, Visa*

LINTHWAITE   Bulls Head

Blackmoorfoot, near Huddersfield HD7 5TR   **FOOD**
Tel: (0484) 842715
Open: 11-11 (11-4, 6-11 Sat)
Licensee: Stephen Head

The Bulls Head is a sombre stone free house standing high above Linthwaite on a wild and wuthering hillside. There's no easy way to find it, but having reached the village on the A62, look for signs to Blackmoorfoot (if you can find any) and proceed up the hill towards the Moors. If lost, flag down a passing local. To the front of the pub is a paved area with wooden tables. A stained-glassed door leads you into the main bar area, which has been decorated in contemporary style with two-tone wallcoverings. Cast iron legged tables are well spaced, surrounded by stools and smartly upholstered bench and banquette seating. A smaller seating area to the right of the entrance has a fine iron fireplace. Large parlour plants and some exposed stonework also feature, and a collection of old irons is displayed in the main bar. Blackboards display the day's choice of interesting, regularly changing bar food, for which the pub is well known. You order from the bar and pay the waitress when she appears. The local speciality, Yorkshire pudding, features prominently, along with roast topside of beef and leg of lamb, both served with fresh vegetables and roast potatoes. There's also a fine choice for vegetarians, with dishes like aubergine, mushroom and butterbean bake. Bakes are another house speciality: try the tuna, pasta and sweetcorn variety, or cauliflower, ham and courgette croustade. Lighter meals include roast beef and Yorkshire pudding sandwiches, and bean and bacon soup, while daily specials might include a chicken and apple crumble. The food, which is competently prepared, appears at such speed that it's obvious the bulk of it is cooked in advance. This doesn't affect the quality too much, but vegetables can lack colour and the roast lamb can look a bit anaemic. It can get very busy, and service is friendly and efficient. A separate dessert list features mainly home-made items. There's a fruit machine and piped music.

Bar Meals: 11-10; bar snacks all day   *Typical Dishes:* summer green soup £1, stir-fried king prawns £2.50, chicken breast in orange and watercress sauce £4, braised steak with gingered peppers £3.90, fresh salmon with a fresh herb crust £4, dark chocolate and hazelnut tart £1.60   Vegetarian Meals: blue cheese and apple filo parcels £3.50   Children's Menu/Portions   Cheese   Beer   Stones; Whitbread   Whisky   Family Room Patio/terrace   Outdoor Eating   **No Credit Cards**

MELTHAM   Will's O' Nat's

Blackmoorfoot Road, near Huddersfield HD7 3PS
Tel: (0484) 850078
Open: 11.30-3, 6 (6.30 Sat)-11
Licensee: Kim Waring Schofield

Busy moorland pub with enthusiastic management, lovely views, a large garden and an intriguing selection of malt whiskies. The dining room has the same menu.

Bar Meals: 11.30 (12 Sun)-2, opening time-10; bar snacks both sessions   *Typical Dishes:* home-made vegetable soup 85p, spare ribs £2.95, half a fresh roasted chicken £3.75, tagliatelle £2.95, grilled fresh fish £2.85-£5.50   Vegetarian Meals: spicy bean casserole £2.95   Children's Portions   Beer   Tetley Bitter; Theakston Best Bitter   Whisky   Milburn 1966   Children Allowed in Bar to Eat   Outdoor Play Area   Garden **Credit Cards:** Access, Amex, Visa

NEWALL Spite Inn Newall Carr Side. Well-loved hillside pub; the neighbouring pub, now long gone, was nicknamed the Malice (such was the rivalry between the two). Traditional and welcoming, with open fires and nice furnishings; good lunchtime snacks and an interesting (busy) little restaurant; no food Sun eve, nor all day Mon. Lovely summer garden. Webster's beers.

RIPPONDEN   Old Bridge Inn

Priest Lane HX6 4DF   ❢
Tel: (0422) 822595
Open: 11.30-4, 5.30-11 (all day Sat)
Licensee: Ian Hargreaves Beaumont (manager Tim Walker)

Ancient pub with medieval character, enormously thick stone walls and some nice old furniture in its three connecting bars. Probably originally a 14th century monastic guest house (a priest hole has been uncovered). The licensee, who bought the pub in 1963, has done a good deal of renovation work. The modern world intrudes little into the finished interior: no machines, music, pool table, and pump clips are only tolerated for guest beers. There isn't even an inn sign. The separate restaurant is across the bridge.

Bar Meals: 12-2 (cold buffet) weekdays only, 7-10   *Restaurant:* from 7 pm   *Typical Dishes BAR:* lunchtime buffet, set price £6.75; Sat lunch and evenings: home-made soup £1.45, deep-fried camembert £2.75, steak and kidney pie £3.95, ham shank with mushy peas £2.50, seafood crumble £3.25, sticky toffee pudding £1.75   *RESTAURANT* (separate): set dinner £20.50   Vegetarian Meals (bar): vegetarian hotpot £2.95   Beer Ruddles; Taylor; Whitbread   Children Allowed in Bar to Eat   Riverside Patio/terrace **Credit Cards:** Access, Amex, Visa (restaurant);   **No Credit Cards** in Bar

SHELF   Duke of York

West Street (A644), Stone Chair HX3 7LN
Tel: (0422) 202056
Open: 11.30-11

Amidst the scampi, chilli and so forth, there's also a list of six home-made Indian meals (rice or chips), the house specialities, and two or three other unexpected dishes. The bar is cosy, with a vast array of bric a brac. The Calderdale Way passes the front door.

Bar Meals: 12-2, 5-9 (8 Sat); 12-2.30, 7-9 Sun; bar snacks both sessions   ***Typical Dishes:*** *leek and potato soup £1.40, black pudding and mustard sauce £1.95, butter chicken £5.45, braised steak and Yorkshire pudding £4.95, fillet steak chasseur £7.95, knickerbocker glory £1.75   Vegetarian Meals: lasagne £4.95   Children's Portions* **Beer** *Marston; Taylor; Whitbread* **Whisky** *Children Allowed in Bar to Eat Patio/terrace   Outdoor Eating* ***Accommodation:*** *11 bedrooms, all en suite, from £35 (single £25)   Children Welcome Overnight (minimum age 5)   Check-in: all day* **Credit Cards:** *Access, Amex, Visa*

SHELLEY   ★   Three Acres Inn

Roydhouse HD8 8LR   `FOOD`
Tel: (0484) 602606   `B&B`
Open: 12-3 (not Sat), 7-11   ❢
Licensees: Neil Truelove and Brian Orme

The Emley Moor television mast, red-lit at night, makes a useful guiding emblem when heading towards this unassuming roadside greystone inn, set high in the Pennines above Huddersfield – it's just a couple of fields away and towers over Roydhouse. Inside, the bar is civilised rather than characterful, plain and modernised, but with lots of dark wood panelling around the bar counter, and in the ceiling beams. There's a patterned carpet, but otherwise few decorations; good solid wood dining height tables are partnered by cushioned country chairs, and the open fire is copper hooded. An attractive dining area, linen laid, leads off at one end, and there's a separate restaurant proper. All is clean and professionally run (in the same hands for over 20 years); its inn-meets-small-hotel style emphasised by the eleven extra bedrooms which were developed in adjacent cottages in '89. Bar food – served at lunchtime only, note – is still worth a detour here, for its quality, simplicity and presentation. It's a fairly short list, just four starters, nine mains, various daily puddings, and an appetising range of some 15 sandwiches, perhaps ox tongue with tomato and piccalilli, or smoked mackerel with apple and horseradish, from £2 to just under £5. Soups are excellent, ranging from a richly satisfying fish to a perfectly balanced potato and watercress, uncommonly good; and among the main course list, the likes of liver and onions, and sausages and mash unselfconsciously rub shoulders with smarter modern fare in the shape of three imaginative warm salads. The star of these features chicken livers, smoked bacon and croutons dressed with nutmeg cream on a generous base of fresh French leaves. Puddings tend to be wickedly rich: look out for our favourite, a chocolate and rum mousse. Bedrooms are light, nicely furnished and immaculately kept, those in the newer wing styled similarly to the originals. Old beams and occasional open fireplaces add age and character to otherwise smartly modern decor, with pretty pastels, nice carpets, pine furniture and beds, comfortable chairs or sofas, well-placed mirrors, and contemporary fabrics. Some of the neat, cream-carpeted en suite bathrooms have showers only. Prices are lower at weekends.

Bar Meals: 12-1.45; bar snacks   ***Restaurant:*** *12-1.45, 7-9.45* ***Typical Dishes BAR:*** *celery and stilton soup £2.35, warm chicken liver and bacon salad £5.15, steak and kidney pie £6.20, lambs liver and onions £6, roast of the day £6.55, home-made puddings*

RESTAURANT set lunches £7.95, à la carte dinners: fish soup £2.35, Galia melon with berries in cassis £3.95, breast of chicken in filo £6.95, pot-roast gammon hock £7.25, fresh seafood platter £12.95   *Vegetarian Meals (restaurant)*: baby vegetables in filo   *Children's Portions*   Beer   Taylor; Tetley; Theakston   Whisky   *Children Allowed in Bar to Eat Patio/terrace   Outdoor Eating   Accommodation:* 20 bedrooms, 18 en suite, from £57.50 (single £47.50)   *Children Welcome Overnight   Cots Available   Check-in: all day Credit Cards:* Access, Amex, Visa

---

SOWERBY BRIDGE   Moorings

No. 1 Warehouse, Canal Basin HX6 2AG
Tel: (0422) 833940
Open: 11.30-3, 5.30 (7 Sun/Mon)-11
Licensees: Ian Clay and Andrew Armstrong

Converted 1790 canalside warehouse, refitted in light, modern, if rather functional, style with lots of exposed stone and pine. Large windows overlook canal basin; good, balconied family room plus waterside patio. Light meals downstairs, more restauranty menu on 'upper deck'. Appetising range of about 100 bottled beers, including many fine Belgians.

Bar Meals: 12-2, 6.30 (7 Sun/Mon)-9.30; bar snacks both sessions   *Typical Dishes BAR:* home-made soup £1.10, spinach pancake £2.80, duck breast with a honey and lemon glaze £7.50, reef and beef £7.75, Murphy's pie £4.95, fruit pies £1.50 *Vegetarian Meals:* hot chilli crunch £5.50   *Children's Menu/Portions*   Cheese   Beer Moorhouse's; Theakston, Younger   Whisky   *Family Room   Outdoor Play Area Patio/terrace   Outdoor Eating   Credit Cards:* Access, Visa

SOYLAND Blue Ball Blue Ball Lane. Atmospheric old drovers inn, with fine views, well-kept beers, decent lunchtime and evening bar food (not Tue lunch); live music Friday nights. Children welcome. Marston, Taylor, Theakston beers.

THORNTON   Ring O' Bells

Hill Top Road BD13 3QL
Tel: (0274) 832296
Open: 11.30-3, 7-11
Licensee: Jack Bentley

Converted chapel with modern extension, in a windy spot above Thornton. Cooking by the licensee's son encompasses comforting old English supper specials and fussier modern restaurant fare. Children are allowed in the restaurant.

Bar Meals: 12-2, 7-10; bar snacks both sessions   *Typical Dishes:* chicken and leek soup £1.40, wild mushrooms in a creamy sauce with pasta £2.95, sirloin steak in cream, ham and garlic sauce with a julienne of spring vegetables £8.25, salmon and halibut in lobster sauce £6.75, haddock in prawn and cheese sauce £4.25, frangipane pancakes £2.25 *Vegetarian Meals:* home-made pasta dishes £4.95   *Children's Portions*   Beer   Old Mill; Ruddles; Webster's   *Outdoor Play Area   Patio/terrace   Credit Cards:* Access, Amex, Diners, Visa

TODMORDEN   Staff of Life

550 Burnley Road OL14 8JF
Tel: (0706) 812929
Open: 12-3 (not Mon), 7-11
Licensee: Freddie Sleap

By the A646 Burnley Road, just to the north of Todmarden and overlooked by a
steep hillside, the Staff of Life was created from a row of 19th century cottages. It's
an unusual pub insofar as its owners also own the brewery that supplies the beer,
Robinwood. The interior is full of that particular brand of atmosphere some might
describe as seedy, the well-worn appearance of a well-frequented local. Its three
adjoining rooms feature solid stripped stone walls and flagstone floors, with
upholstered settles (complete with ripped covers) and well-used tables. The walls are
hung with a large variety of objects, including a fine collection of pottery bedpans,
some horrendous-looking mounted spiders, horse tackle and deer horns. Rock
music is often blasted from the juke box. The bar food choice is short and simple.
Steaks, mixed grill, lasagne, chilli or, most interestingly, curries like chicken or lamb
bhuna, dopiaza or vindaloo. There's nothing spectacular about the cooking, but the
prices are extremely reasonable. Above the bar are two splendid double bedrooms
which are centrally heated and immaculately kept. Each has free-standing pine
furniture and beds; the attic room even has a sloping pine ceiling. Both have small
tiled shower rooms, though getting hot water through the shower proved a bit
difficult on our stay. Despite the roadside location, the rooms don't suffer too badly
from traffic noise. In the morning, a splendid fry-up of black pudding, sausages,
bacon, mushrooms, fried bread, tomato and egg does away with plans for lunch.
NB: we've heard the pub is up for sale. The owners, who are now to concentrate
solely on the brewery, think they have found a buyer who will keep the pub as it is,
but this has yet to be confirmed.

*Bar Meals: 12-2, 7-10; bar snacks both sessions   **Typical Dishes:** garlic bread 95p, 10 oz
rump steak £5.95, lasagne £2.75, chicken and spinach curry £2.95   Vegetarian Meals:
lentil cheese bake £2.45   Children's Portions   Beer   Robinwood Best Bitter, XB, Old
Fart; Taylor Landlord   Whisky   Cider   Coombes   Children Allowed in Bar to Eat
Patio/terrace   Outdoor Eating   **Accommodation:** 2 bedrooms, both en suite, from £30
(single £18)   Children Welcome Overnight   Check-in: by arrangement   **Credit Cards:**
Access, Diners, Visa*

Scotland

BORDERS

AUCHENCROW Craw Inn. Cosy, friendly English–style pub in a tiny hamlet just off the A1, near Eyemouth. Genuinely home–made food, and good local fish, in bar and restaurant. Idyllic front tables for a summer evening. Putting green/garden across the lane. Open: 11.30-3, 6-12 (12.30-11 Sun).

GREENLAW	**Castle Inn**

Greenlaw TD10 6UR   `FOOD`
Tel: (03616) 217   ☺
Open: 12-2.30, 6.30-11.30   ▼
Licensee: A W Appleton

Greenlaw is a small town on a major road; though not far from Hume castle and other attractions, there is not a lot of reason to stop at Greenlaw other than passing through to other places. Except, that is, for the handsome Georgian Castle Inn, which is the sort of place you could take a variety of people for lunch and feel confident that they would find something to their taste. It is expensive for bar meals, by local standards, and falls into the middle ground of bar meal and restaurant. The Mirror Room, where drinking and dining take place, is large and splendid; a large mirror on top of a marble fireplace transforming what would otherwise be a hall into a splendid room, with a comfortable sitting area by the fireplace, and ruffled curtains framing elegant Georgian windows, through which there's a view to well kept gardens. The octagonal room is a superb feature room to take coffee in, whilst a small library also makes an excellent coffee shop, and the bar itself is popular with the locals on Friday nights and weekend lunchtimes. The welcome is friendly but not intrusive. Children are welcome, and family facilities excellent: high chairs, baby foods, a Freddy Fox children's menu, and cheerful, tolerant staff. "Where you haste to the welcome, and prolong the goodbyes", their rather contrived catch phrase, appears with monotonous regularity in case you forget it. The rather downmarket-looking printed menu, supplemented by blackboard specials, is certainly very varied, with Indian, Chinese, Italian, Spanish and French elements, as well as steakhouse food, some seafood and a vegetarian selection. Bread is crusty and fresh (mini-baguettes are used for sandwiches), butter comes in pots, tables are laid with mats rather than cloths, and puddings are displayed in a chill cabinet. Tables are pleasantly spaced out, and service assured and friendly. Garlicky duxelles mushrooms were good and nicely presented, and a delicious piece of melon came with a proper spoon to attack it with. A huge piece of home-made lasagne (£3.95) was meaty and well sauced, though the noisettes of lamb Shrewsbury were disappointingly fatty; they did, however, come with a superb sloe-flavoured sauce. The local cheese is good, although served too cold, and house wine very drinkable.

Bar Meals: during all opening hours **Typical Dishes:** *carrot soup £1.60, Japanese prawns £3.25, noisettes of lamb Shrewsbury £7.35, paupiettes of pork Romano £7.35 Vegetarian Meals: curry Children's Menu* `Beer` *Belhaven; Caledonian* `Whisky` *Children Allowed in Bar to Eat* **Accommodation:** *6 bedrooms, 2 en suite (for 1992 season), from £40 (single £20) Children Welcome Check-in: all day* **Credit Cards:** *Access, Amex, Diners, Visa*

INNERLEITHEN   Traquair Arms

Traquair Road EH44 6PD   `FOOD`
Tel: (0896) 830229   `B&B`
Open: 11am-midnight (12.30-midnight Sun)   ☀
Licensee: Hugh Anderson   ☺

Hidden down a side street off the main road (well signposted) which runs through Innerleithen is the Traquair Arms Hotel, a handsome stone built hotel on the road leading to St Mary's Loch, which is, incidentally, a delightful journey across sheep-infested roads to one of the most picturesque parts of the Borders. The bar leads off the hotel reception area; dine here, or in the more comfortable dining room, or, if weather permits,in the garden. A choice of dining areas and a wide choice of freshly prepared meals is typical of the admirable flexibility of the Traquair Arms, where children are positively welcomed, even the most boisterous. For adults, a well-stocked bar features the Traquair's own Bear Ale, with a teddy bear clad pump. Food-wise, our lunchtime visit yielded a pakora starter of superb texture, with a good spicy sauce; smoked salmon was also first rate, while a main course of Traquair ale and steak pie came in a generous portion, with fresh and tasty meat, entirely superior to the usual pub offering, though vegetables were distinctly unmemorable by comparison. A courgette and minced beef layered pie came in its own pot and was surprisingly delicious; the accompanying salad varied and fresh. Cheese and coffee disappointed. Service, however, is genuine and informal, the atmosphere convivial. One benefit of dining in the bar is that glass doors lead off into the garden, which is enclosed and safe for energetic children. The bar is mysteriously enhanced by its slight shabbiness, though bar tables are rather too cramped for dining on; the linen-laid dining room proper, though pleasant in the evenings, is rather too formal for lunchtime. Bed and breakfast is recommended – particularly the handsome Scottish morning meal, complete with superb kippers. Traquair House, next door, is well worth a visit too, a romantic old house with pretty grounds and its own ancient brewhouse; the front gates of Traquair are firmly shut, and will never open again until a Stuart returns to the throne of Scotland.

Bar Meals: 12-9   *Restaurant:* 7-9   *Typical Dishes BAR:* curried apple soup £1.15, spiced lentil paté £2.30, Traquair steak and Bear Ale pie £4.25, Finnan savoury £4.05, courgette layer pie £3.95, Eve's pudding £1.55   *RESTAURANT* £15.50 menu: cauliflower and stilton soup, smoked salmon parcels, roast duckling with raspberry sauce, lamb cutlets with fresh ginger and lemon sauce, chicken with honey, cinnamon and tomatoes *Vegetarian Meals:* rice and vegetable cutlets   *Children's Portions*   `Cheese`   `Beer` *Broughton Greenmantle Ale; Traquair Bear Ale* `Whisky` *Family Room   Garden Outdoor Eating* **Accommodation:** 10 bedrooms, all en suite, from £52 (single £29) *Children Welcome Overnight   Cots Available   Check-in: all day* **Credit Cards:** Access, Visa

---

JEDBURGH   Carters Rest

Abbey Place TD8 6BE
Tel: (0835) 63414
Open: 11-11 (closed winter Sun)
Licensee: Michael Wares

Well-known central Borders pub-restaurant, much used for functions. 18th century origins – built of old abbey stones – but now cheerfully modernised; bustling and friendly.

Bar Meals and Restaurant: 12-2, 6-9 (10 Fri/Sat); bar snacks both sessions   *Typical Dishes BAR:* Scotch broth 85p, home-made chicken liver paté £2.50, home-made steak pie £4.20, chicken Kiev £4.95, fresh fried haddock £4.20   *RESTAURANT:* Scotch broth

£1.50, filet mignon £10.50, stir-fry chicken £8.25, veal au citron £8.75, sole Walewska £9.95, home-made Ballochmyllie trifle   Vegetarian Meals: cheese and nut croquettes £5.50   Children's Menu/Portions **Cheese** **Whisky** *Family Room   Patio/terrace   Outdoor Eating   Credit Cards: Access, Amex, Visa*

KELSO Sunlaws House Hotel. Book-lined extremely civilised bar of some 9 or 10 tables in grand country mansion house hotel in its own grounds, 7 miles from Kelso. Not a pub by any definition, but they do offer bar lunches, very reasonably priced at £7 for 2 courses and £9.50 for 3. Food is hit and miss, but the crockery fine, the silver real and toilets of exceptional quality. The conservatory is more suited to family dining; children are nicely treated. Some would find the atmosphere intimidatingly formal.

LEADBURN   Leadburn Inn

West Linton EH46 7BE
Tel: (0968) 72952
Open: all day
Licensee: Linda Thomson

Owned by the same people who have the Tattler in Edinburgh (see report), a smartly carpeted, attractively modernised 18th century inn, its atmosphere bordering on the genteel.

Bar Meals: 12-10; bar snacks all day   Restaurant: 6-10   Typical Dishes BAR: home-made soup £1.20, haggis £2.50, venison casserole £4.50, liver and onions £4.25, smoked haddock crumble £4.25, bread and butter pudding   RESTAURANT dinner menu £16: baked crab provencale, trout stuffed with melon, chicken supreme in rum and ginger, braised beef in red wine and pickled walnuts, Eve's pudding   Vegetarian Meals: stroganoff   Children's Portions **Beer** *Broughton Greenmantle Ale; Caledonian 80/-   Family Room* **Accommodation:** *5 bedrooms, 2 en suite, from £40   Children Welcome Overnight Cot Available   Check-in: all day   Credit Cards: Access, Amex, Diners, Visa*

MELROSE   Burts Hotel

Market Square TD6 9PN   ▼
Tel: (089 682) 2285
Open: 11-2.30, 5-11 (12.30-2.30, 6.30-11 Sun)
Licensee: Graham Henderson

Imposing 18th century inn at the heart of still-fairly-sleepy, affluent Melrose. Bar food shows an appetising balance of the comfortingly traditional and modern aspirational, and this philosophy could be said to sum up the whole hotel. The bar is comfortable rather than quaint, the bedrooms light, contemporary and in pristine order. Good Scottish produce in the rather smart restaurant includes quails' eggs, grouse, venison and scallops.

Bar Meals: 12-2, 6-9.30 (10.30 Fri/Sat); bar snacks both sessions   Restaurant: 12.30-2, 7-9.30   Typical Dishes BAR: game broth £1.40, roulade of trout and salmon, lamb casserole with honey and grapes, game casserole, haddock and mushroom bake (main courses from £4), jam roly poly   Vegetarian Meals: broccoli and egg bake   Children's Portions **Cheese** **Beer** **Whisky** *Children Allowed in Bar to Eat   Outdoor Play Area Garden   Outdoor Eating   Accommodation: 21 bedrooms, all en suite, from £64 (single £40)   Children Welcome Overnight   Cots Available   Check-in: all day   Credit Cards: Access, Amex, Diners, Visa*

MELROSE George & Abbotsford Hotel High Street Tel: (089 682) 2308. Clean, simple overnight accommodation; rooms divided between the main building (traditionally styled), to more modern ones in the extension. All have basic, clean en suite facilities. Residents lounge; pleasant public lounge bar; bar meals lunch and evening. 31 bedrooms, from £60.

PEEBLES   Kingsmuir Hotel

Springhill Road EH45 9EP
Tel: (0721) 20151
Open: 11-11 (12 Fri/Sat)
Licensee: Elizabeth Kerr

Handsome Victorian stone-built, gabled hotel on the quiet side of this attractive market town. Functional, spartan locals bar; modern dining room; comfortable residents' lounge with pretty views, clean simple bedrooms. Decent bar food.

Bar Meals and Restaurant: 12-2, 7-9.30; bar snacks lunchtime **Typical Dishes BAR:** *lentil soup 90p, salmon mousse £2.20, steak pie £4.20, turkey breast in tarragon sauce £4.60, trout Rob Roy £4.30, lemon delicious pudding £1.70* **RESTAURANT** *3-course dinner £12.50: Cullen skink, Aberdeen ramekin, roast venison, sirloin stuffed with haggis steeped in whisky, haddock fillet in pineapple sauce, raspberry mousse Vegetarian Meals: country-style mushrooms Children's Menu/Portions* `Beer` *Broughton Family Room Outdoor Play Area Garden Outdoor Eating* **Accommodation** *(closed 1st week Jan): 10 bedrooms, all en suite, from £53 (single £31) Children Welcome Overnight Cots Available Check-in: all day* **Credit Cards:** *Access, Amex, Visa*

ST BOSWELLS   Buccleuch Arms Hotel

The Green TD6 0EW
Tel: (0835) 22243
Open: all day (12.30-11 Sun)
Licensee: Lucy Agnew

Large, plain, Victorian corner site hotel near the village green. Panelled but oddly characterless lounge bar with log fires, and peachy, modern Garden Room restaurant. Modernised, neat bedrooms; country house-ish residents' lounge; ex public bar now the Salmon Room and reserved for functions. Good Border estate contacts for huntin', shootin' and fishin' enthusiasts, a recurrent decorative theme. Bar food list changes every month.

Bar Meals: 12-2, 6-9 (10 Fri/Sat); 12.30-2.15, 6.30-9 Sun; bar snacks both sessions **Restaurant:** *12-1.45, 6-8.45 (9.45 Fri/Sat); 12.30-2, 6.30-8.45 Sun* **Typical Dishes BAR:** *cauliflower soup £1.10, leek and stilton terrine £1.95, lambs liver with orange sauce £4.50, beef bobotie £4.25, pear fool* **RESTAURANT:** *Cullen skink £3.55, melon and pink grapefruit £3.65, beef fillet stuffed with scampi £11.25, mignons of venison £9.45, scallops in watercress sauce £7.45 Vegetarian Meals: pasta Children's Menu/Portions* `Cheese` `Beer` *Broughton Greenmantle Ale* `Whisky` *Children Allowed in Bar to Eat Garden Outdoor Eating* **Accommodation:** *19 bedrooms, 17 en suite, from £62 (single £34) Children Welcome Overnight Cots Available Check-in: all day* **Credit Cards:** *Access, Amex, Diners, Visa*

ST MARY'S LOCH   Tibbie Shiels Inn

St Mary's Loch TD7 5NE
Tel: (0750) 42231
Open: 11-11 (12 Fri/Sat); 12.30-11 Sun; closed winter Mon
Licensees: Jack and Jill Brown

There's a statue of Hogg at the turn-off in this wild romantic place, and the whole
area is steeped in Scots literary history, not least the Tibbie Shiels Inn itself, a lovely
white-washed single storey cottage with add-ons, on the shore of St Mary's Loch, in
the glorious Ettrick valley. Given this build-up, expectations may well be too high.
The Tibbie Shiels, famous throughout the Borders and elsewhere, is a disappointing
place to spend the night. But it can be recommended for three other things: first, the
atmospheric bar, busy with friendly locals and fishing and sailing types, second the
quality of the meat dishes, and third the situation of the inn itself: the large dining
room overlooks the beautiful loch and surrounding hills in this utterly remote and
enchanting place. Meat dishes are exceptional: both a char-grilled fillet steak and a
fine piece of venison were of excellent flavour and freshness. The copy book is
extremely blotted, however, by their accompanying vegetables, extremely over-
boiled, and a multitude of things in paper or foil packets, together with stark
overhead lighting, which almost cancelled out the charm of the view. Perhaps our
experience of an overnight stop was unusual; perhaps we were unlucky to stay in
the least attractive room, but judging by one recent experience, bedrooms are
uninviting, shabby and spartan, beds uncomfortable, a kettle and coffee sachets
balanced on a narrow shelf within reach of childish hands, and the shower room and
toilet, two corridors away, distinctly functional, with a lino floor and view directly
into the kitchen. The residents' lounge offers little solace, too, being something of a
1970s timewarp, complete with uncomfortably hard white leather couch and vivid
orange carpet. But worse than all this, our inspector found the atmosphere (other
than in the warm and jolly locals' bar) positively unfriendly and unwelcoming. The
moral of the tale? Don't judge by appearances. But the Tibbie is still an excellent
place to stop after a sojourn on the Southern Upland Way – for lunch and a drink in
the bar, at least.

Bar Meals: 12.30-2.30 (high tea 3.30-6.30), 6.30-8.30; bar snacks both sessions
Restaurant: 6.30-8.30 **Typical Dishes BAR:** *leek and oatmeal soup £1.20, spicy
chicken £3,. holy mole chilli £4, trout £4, clootie dumpling £1.40* **RESTAURANT:**
*similar starters and puddings, marinated trout with mustard sauce £2.10, escalope of veal with
cream and ginger sauce £7.25, poacher's pouch (stuffed sirloin steak) £8, scallops with bacon
and cream sauce £7.25* *Vegetarian Meals: cashew nut loaf* *Children's Menu/Portions*
Beer *Belhaven; Broughton* **Whisky** *Children Allowed in Bar to Eat* *Patio/terrace
Outdoor Eating* **Accommodation:** *5 bedrooms, sharing 2 bathrooms, from £32 (single
£20)* *Children Welcome Overnight* *Cots Available* *Check-in: all day* **Credit Cards:**
Access, Visa

STOW   Manorhead Hotel

168 Galashiels Road (A7)
Tel: (05783) 201

Victorian coaching inn with splendid grounds; decent bar meals lunch and evening;
real ale; 6 bedrooms.

SWINTON   Wheatsheaf

Main Street TD11 3JJ   `FOOD`
Tel: (089 086) 275
Open: 11-3, 5.30 (6 winter)-11 (11.30 Sat); closed Mon
Licensees: Alan and Julie Reid

The village of Swinton is six miles north of Coldstream, on the way to nowhere, and is easy to miss. The Wheatsheaf, dominating this simple Scots farming hamlet, overlooks the plain little village green and has very limited parking; at busy periods, the main street is chock a block with cars. Once through the front door, there's a small formal dining room to the right, with dark wooden tables and chairs, wine coloured linen, silver cutlery, fresh flowers and crystal glasses. To the left, a small bar rather overcrammed with lower seats and tables, a stone fireplace and wood-panelled bar counter, and leading off from here, a light and airy sun lounge extension, with a towering wood-panelled ceiling and lots of sunlight. Furniture is lighter here, too, with cane tables and chairs and upholstered cushions. This is very much a dining pub, (drinking goes on in the pool-tabled, fruit-machined public bar at the back, so separate from the food operation that most visitors aren't even aware it exists) with a very well-regarded restaurant, the Four Seasons, and it's wise to book even for bar meals, such is the reputation of the pub in the Borders. The emphasis is very much on fresh food: a printed-handwritten menu reproduced on one blackboard, daily specials listed on another. Tables are laid with cloths and place mats; freshly baked wheaten rolls are presented as a matter of course, and butter comes in a slab on a saucer, with no foil packets or sauce sachets in sight. We found a cream of courgette and leek soup (£1.75) gelatinous and bland, but the beef in ale was hard to fault, and a dish of cold Tweed salmon generously cut, although in truth rather tasteless and over-liberally sprinkled with paprika. A fillet of brill, however, was superbly fresh and beautifully cooked (brill in fact). Vegetables came in a separate dish, but had suffered from rapid reheating – beans were dried out and the dish too hot to touch. Salads, however, are imaginative and fresh. The house white was, similarly, excellent, and the summer pudding, a house speciality, of memorable quality and beautifully presented. Cheeses are good, and come with a mini-bottle of Leith port. Service is assured, if a little over-attentive, with frequent bouts of "everything alright?" from the uniformed waitresses. But this is still the best bar meal in the Borders. Good value bed and breakfast, too.

Bar Meals: 12-2.15, 6.30-9.30; bar snacks both sessions   **Typical Dishes BAR:** *chicken and vegetable broth £1.25, hot baked avocado with seafood £3.70, lambs liver with onions and bacon £4.95, braised beef in real ale £4.95, cold Tweed salmon £6.45, summer pudding £2.15   Vegetarian Meals: vegetarian stroganoff with saffron rice   Children's Portions* `Cheese`   `Beer` *Broughton Greenmantle Ale* `Whisky` *Family Room Outdoor Play Area   Garden   Outdoor Eating* **Accommodation** *(closed Nov-March): 3 bedrooms, 2 en suite, from £35 (single £22.75)   Children Welcome Overnight   Cot Available Check-in: all day* **Credit Cards:** *Access, Visa*

TWEEDSMUIR   Crook Inn

Tweeddale ML12 6QN
Tel: (08997) 272
Open: all day
Licensee: Stuart Reid

Famous old drovers' inn in glorious Tweed valley countryside. A strange but winning amalgam of old stone-flagged farmers' bar and 1930s ocean liner style lounges in the airy modern extension. Bar food is hit or miss, usually dependable, but watch out for peculiar combinations of accompanying vegetables, like chips with boiled sprouts.

Bar Meals: 12-2.30 (12-10 weekends), 6-9; bar snacks lunchtime *Restaurant:* 12-2
(Sun only), 7-8.15 *Typical Dishes BAR:* lentil soup £1.25, home-made paté £2.95,
home-made steak and kidney pie £4.95, chicken supreme with herb sauce £5.25, apple tart
£2.50 *RESTAURANT* £12.50-£15: chicken liver paté, entrecote Balmoral, Norfolk
duck, Tweed salmon in seafood sauce, chocolate cup Jamaica *Vegetarian Meals:* broccoli,
stilton and mushroom flan *Children's Portions* **Cheese** **Beer** Broughton
Greenmantle Ale **Whisky** *Family Room* *Outdoor Play Area* *Garden* *Outdoor Eating*
Accommodation: 8 bedrooms, all en suite, from £52 (single £26) *Children Welcome
Overnight (minimum age 3)* *Check-in: all day* *Credit Cards:* Access, Visa

WESTRUTHER Old Thistle Inn on B6456 Tel: (05784) 275. Isolated
moorland village pub, popular with local farmers, with a charming original little bar
and various other rooms; routine bar food but excellent steaks. Family room; cheap
bedrooms. Open: 11-2.30, 5-11 (all day summer).

YARROW   Gordon Arms

Mountbenger, Yarrow Valley TD7 5LE
Tel: (0750) 82232
**Open: 10-3, 7-11 (all day weekends; closed Mon); 10-11 summer
(12.30-11 Sun)**

Beautifully placed old inn, close by the Southern Upland Way, and popular with
walkers (youth hostel style bunkhouse available). The bar menu is largely scampi and
chips-ish, with three or four more appetising dishes. Pleasant, simple Scottish bar;
live folk music twice a month.

Bar Meals: 12-2.30, 7-9; bar snacks lunchtime *Typical Dishes:* home-made soup
£1.25, home-made steak pie £5.10, grilled lamb chops £5.10, fresh local trout £5.60
Children's Menu **Beer** Broughton; Jennings **Whisky** *Children Allowed in Bar to
Eat* *Accommodation:* 6 bedrooms, sharing 2 bathrooms, from £32 (single £18)
Children Welcome Overnight *Cot Available* *Check-in: all day* *No Credit Cards*

CENTRAL

ARDEONAIG Ardeonaig Hotel: Delightfully set lochside hotel with a
cheeringly pubby non-residents' bar and decent, informal food lunch and evening.

BRIG O' TURK   Byre Inn

By Callander FK17 8HT   ❢
Tel: (08776) 292
Open: Dec-Easter open Thur-Sun; 7 days summer; closed Nov 11-Dec 11
Licensee: John Park

Converted 18th century cow byre on the A821. Unusual interior, informal, airy and
relaxed, clean and well-run.

Bar Meals and Restaurant: 12-2.30, 6-9.30 (9 restaurant) *Vegetarian Meals* *BAR:*
home-made soup £1.15, haggis £2.15, home-baked gammon £4.45, chicken and bacon
£4.65, loin of pork £4.65, cheesecake £2.15 *RESTAURANT:* red snapper and trout
parfait £4.50, stuffed garlic and chive mushrooms £3.15, saddle of lamb £9.50, stuffed
quail Rossini £9.80, monkfish in lime sauce £11.20, choux swans with chocolate sauce

£2.95   Vegetarian Meals: stir-fried vegetables £5   Children's Portions **Beer**
Broughton Greenmantle Ale **Whisky**   *Children Allowed in Bar to Eat   Garden* **Credit**
Cards: *Access, Amex, Visa*

CALLANDER Myrtle Inn: Unusual bar food by Scottish standards. Usually busy.

DOLLAR Kings Seat 19 Bridge Street. Traditional Scots cooking, including the
national dish, mince and tatties, and other homely home-cooked dishes at this
popular, cosy pub on the Fife border; also à la carte evening menu. Belhaven,
Courage beers. Open: 11-2.30, 5.30-11.

DRYMEN   Winnock Hotel

The Square G63 0BL   ▼
Tel: (0360) 60245
Open: 11 am-midnight (1 am Fri/Sat)
Licensee: David Warnes

Large, attractively situated hotel with plans for even more bedroome – 32 will
become 38 by January 1992. They specialise in good Scottish cheeses and interesting
malts, the latter a 57-strong list.

Bar Meals and Restaurant: *12-2.30, 6-9.30; all day weekends; bar snacks both sessions*
Typical Dishes BAR: *home-made soup £1.15, salmon paté £1.95, breast of chicken Kiev
£5.75, tagliatelle carbonara £3.75, deep-fried haddock £3.95, blackcurrant and apple
crumble £1.85* **RESTAURANT:** *avocado and crab £3.45, fillet of venison £11.75,
whole grilled lemon sole £9.75, steamed seafood platter £10.45, chocolate soufflé £2.65
Vegetarian Meals: vegetable and nut cutlet   Children's Menu/Portions* **Cheese** **Beer**
Broughton; Ruddles, Theakston **Whisky** *Family Room   Outdoor Play Area   Garden
Outdoor Eating* **Accommodation:** *38 bedrooms, all en suite, from £56 (single £39)
Children Welcome Overnight   Cots Available   Check-in: all day* **Credit Cards:** *Access,
Amex, Diners, Visa*

Salmon Leap Inn, Main Street. Lots of fresh salmon and some exotic specials on a
regularly-changing menu, at an 18th century hotel near the famous salmon leaps at
Pots of Gartness. Food lunch and evening; families welcome; Belhaven beers.

KILLIN   Clachaig Hotel

Falls of Dochart FK21 8SL
Tel: (05672) 270
Open: 11 am- midnight
Licensees: John and Maureen Mallinson

18th century ex-smithy and coaching inn, once closely linked with the McNab clan,
and beautifully set overlooking the spectacular Falls of Dochart; very Richard
Hannayish. Rather basic inside, though, its bar usurped by juke box and pool table,
but bar food is plain and decently cooked, and clean, modest bedrooms are good
value for the area. The best of them have dramatic views over the Falls.

Bar Meals: *12-2.30, 5.30-9.30 (all day spring weekends and daily summer); bar snacks
both sessions* **Restaurant:** *6.30-9.30* **Typical Dishes BAR:** *Scotch broth 85p, prawn
cocktail £2.25, steak pie £3.75, haggis £2.75, kippers £3.75, Highland crumble £1.25*
RESTAURANT: *minestrone £1.25, Clachaig paté £2.75, Highland venison £7.95,
trout Rob Roy £7.95, Loch Tay salmon £8.25, apple and raspberry pie £1.65
Vegetarian Meals: broccoli quiche   Children's Menu/Portions* **Beer** *McEwan* **Whisky**
Family Room   Riverside Garden   Outdoor Eating **Accommodation:** *9 bedrooms, 8 en
suite, from £35 (single £17.50)   Children Welcome   Overnight   Check-in: all day*
Credit Cards: *Access, Visa*

KILMAHOG   Lade Inn

By Callander FK17 8HD
Tel: (0877) 30152
Open: 12-2.30, 5.30-11 (12 Fri); all day Sun; closed winter Mon/Tue
Licensee: David Stirrop

Tremendously popular stone-built single storey pub with a two storey addition. One bar to the left of the entrance hall has panelling, pine tables and chairs; there's another bar to the right. The dining area has large windows and leads out into the garden. The walls are mainly exposed stone and what looks like mock beams; bars are carpeted throughout, while prints and whisky boxes adorn the walls; the whole effect is clean, fresh and spacious. Tables are only set when food is ordered. Quiet and relaxing at 12.30, the lunch trade in summer is such that by 1 o'clock the Lade is usually packed with people. They come for the good, honest home-cooking, like a delicious mushroom soup, a meaty lasagne or good fresh fish; main courses come with the inevitable chips (fairly inevitable in Scotland anyway), though you can opt for a jacket potato instead; help yourself salads are good quality. Coffee comes with packets of sugar and UHT cream. Service is good and friendly, but informal, of the jeans and T-shirt-wearing kind. The Lade Inn is worth knowing about as a genuine, good value oasis in the often tourism-blighted Callander area.

Bar Meals: 12-2, 6-9.30 (all day Sun); bar snacks lunchtime *Typical Dishes (lunch):* cullen skink £1.95, chicken liver paté £1.95, Ruddles County steak pie £4.95, venison sausages £4.75, apple strudel £1.95 (evening): chicken satay £2.50, sirloin Rob Roy £7.95, pork spare ribs £4.95, cajun chicken £7.35, baked alaska £2.50 Children's Menu **Beer** Ruddles, Webster's **Whisky** Family Room Garden Outdoor Eating *Credit Cards:* Access, Visa

KIPPEN   Cross Keys

Main Street FK8 3DN
Tel: (078 687) 293
Open: 12-2.30, 5.30-12
Licensee: Angus Watt

A simple, welcoming Scottish pub with rooms, rather than an inn proper, set in a pleasant rural village not far from Stirling. The locals' public bar is large and basic, with pool table, fruit machine and television; a smaller, long and narrow lounge is where most of the food is served, and a larger family room has high-chairs primed and ready for use; there's also a small restaurant with seating for about 20. Most of the walls are of exposed stone, colour-washed white, and the furnishings a collection of old, polished tables and chairs. The restaurant is more modern. Bar food, which is well cooked rather than exciting, is chosen from a standard enough printed menu, enhanced by daily specials: poached salmon (£5.25) was delicious, though disappointingly accompanied by a rather standard issue salad, as well as chips. Home-made beefburgers (£3.30), meaty and moreish, came with good crunchy buttered cabbage, as well as the inevitable chips, which were, however, fresh-cut and home-made. Home-made soups are thick and warming. If staying the night, ask for one of the rooms under the eaves, which have sloping ceilings and fine views. Bedrooms are simple and homely, with the usual tea and coffee kits, and wash handbasins. Towels of good quality are provided, and there are extra blankets in the wardrobe. Housekeeping in the rooms is good, but the narrow stairway to the bedrooms and the small first floor hallway do not create a good impression – the stair carpet was threadbare and redecoration wouldn't go amiss; overnight stays are obviously a secondary part of the business. There is no residents' lounge, just the main bars downstairs, even midweek busy with diners and locals. Breakfasts, served on linen-laid tables in the restaurant, are hearty traditional fry-ups, but not too greasy, and service is pleasant and helpful. There's a beer garden at the rear with access from both the public and lounge bars.

Bar Meals: 12 (12.30 Sun)-2, 5.30-9.30; bar snacks both sessions   *Restaurant:* 12 (12.30 Sun)-2, 7-8.45   *Typical Dishes BAR:* lentil soup, crispy mushrooms with garlic mayonnaise, home-made steak pie, home-made lasagne, fresh fried haddock, apple pie (main courses from around £3.50)   *RESTAURANT:* spinach and pear soup, bramble and pork liver paté, roast venison in raspberry and red wine sauce, peppered fillet steak in brandy sauce, salmon in lime and ginger sauce, vanilla cheesecake with blackcurrant sauce   Vegetarian Meals: vegetarian flan   Children's Portions   Beer   Broughton Greenmantle Ale; Youngers No. 3   Whisky   Family Room   Outdoor Play Area   Garden   Outdoor Eating   *Accommodation:* 3 bedrooms, sharing a bathroom, from £39.50 (single £19.50) Children Welcome Overnight   Check-in: by arrangement   *Credit Cards:* Access, Visa

---

SHERIFFMUIR   Sheriffmuir Inn

Dunblane FK15 0LH
Tel: (0786) 823285
Open: 12-2.30, 5.30-11 (12-11 weekends and daily July/Aug)
Licensee: Peter Colley

A real oasis in a wild moorland location, a pub more of the English than Scots sort, with plush upholstered banquettes and prettifying touches. Good value bedrooms.

Bar Meals: 12-2 (2.30 weekends), 6-9 (9.30 Sat); bar snacks lunchtime   *Typical Dishes:* home-made soup £1.15, prawn cocktail £2.65, steak and Guinness pie £4.25, chicken Kiev £5.70, sirloin Sheriffmuir £8.45, apple pie £1.80   Vegetarian Meals: lasagne   Children's Menu/Portions   Beer   Arrols 80/-, Ind Coope Burton Ale   Family Room   Outdoor Play Area   Garden   Outdoor Eating   *Accommodation* (closed Jan/Feb): 2 bedrooms, sharing a bathroom, from £35 (single £29)   Children Welcome Overnight (minimum age 5)   Check-in: all day   *Credit Cards:* Access, Visa

---

STIRLING   Birds & The Bees

Easter Cornton Road, Causewayhead FK9 5PB
Tel: (0786) 73663
Open: 11 am-midnight (1 am Fri/Sat)
Licensee: R Henderson

Converted farmhouse with a striking interior, its open plan bar adorned with eccentric bits of agricultural equipment. Extremely popular for its decent, often imaginative bar food. Petanque is keenly played in the garden.

Bar Meals: 12-2.30, 5-11; bar snacks both sessions   *Typical Dishes:* cauliflower soup £1, mussels £2.30, chicken breast masala £5.50, beef with mushrooms and wine £5.90, freshly baked pizzas £2.90, banana and yoghurt tart £1.80   Vegetarian Meals: vegetable stroganoff   Children's Menu/Portions   Beer   Broughton; Caledonian; Tetley   Whisky   Family Room   Outdoor Play Area   Patio/terrace   Outdoor Eating   Summer Barbecue   *Credit Cards:* Access, Amex, Visa

THORNHILL Lion & Unicorn on A873 Tel: (078 685) 204. Traditional pub with its own bowling green; routine bar meals and one or two more interesting hot daily specials; good casseroles, low prices. Family room; children's portions; Broughton beers. Modest bedrooms. Open all day.

DUMFRIES AND GALLOWAY

AUCHENCAIRN	Balcary Bay Hotel

The Shore DG7 1QZ
Tel: (055 664) 217
Open: 12-2, 7-9
Licensee: Graeme Lamb

Distinguished white-painted 17th century hotel, with a strikingly simple yet elegant interior, and a welcome to non-residents for simple bar meals. Romantically set, almost on the beach in glorious isolation. Good post-lunch walks.

Bar Meals: 12-2; bar snacks   Restaurant: 12-2, 7-9   Typical Dishes BAR: home-made soup £1.50, paté £2.50, steak pie £4.70, lasagne £4, fresh salmon £6   Children's Portions (bar)   Children Allowed in Bar to Eat   Garden   Accommodation (closed Dec-Feb): 17 bedrooms, all en suite, from £80 (single £45)   Children Welcome Overnight   Cot Available   Check-in: all day   Credit Cards: Access, Visa (dinner only)

BARGRENNAN House o'Hill: Stunning scenery in the Galloway Forest Park, where sightings of buzzards and red deer are virtually two a penny. Decent meals in hotel bar, good to retire to after a morning walk.

CANONBIE	Riverside Inn

off A7 DG14 0UX   `FOOD`
Tel: (0383) 71512   ❗ ☕
Open: 11-2.30, 6.30-11   `B&B`
Licensee: Robert Phillips

This pristine white-painted Georgian country inn is in a quiet spot overlooking the river Esk, just over the Scottish border, some twelve miles off the top of the M6. Within, it's authentically rural rather than rustic in style, neat, clean and simple with a definite and individual charm which is, however, not the nicotine-stained creaky timbered gloom of the classic English alehouse. The carpeted bar has simple country chairs, some cushioned, some not, around sewing machine tables, and a stone fireplace and bar front; a few discreet decorations line the plain cream walls, framed fishing flies, the odd old cider jar, but there are otherwise few frills. The dining room is similar, but with proper eating height tables and chairs, and the small, cosy residents' lounge, which has the air of a private house sitting room, has a chintzy three-piece suite and a few other chairs arranged around a log-effect fire. Bedrooms are the prettiest feature of the inn, two of them with draped bedheads, another with a four-poster bed, and all individually styled with good quality fabrics and thoughtful little extras, electric blankets among them. Bathrooms are spotless, with decent toiletries. Bar food is never less than satisfactory, occasionally excellent, and takes particular care with first-rate fresh ingredients – local fish (some of it from the river only yards away), local suppliers, an increasing use of organic and farm produce, vegetables from their own garden, and a delicious range of cheeses. The long-standing hosts share the cooking duties, and are making good use of their new char-grill. Home-made soups are often intriguing combinations, like apricot and lentil; terrines and patés are light but well-flavoured – especially the fishy ones, a creamy smoked mackerel with just a hint of horseradish, a subtle herring roe mousse, or luxurious potted salmon. Main courses offer both modern dishes like calves liver with smoked bacon, and more homely country fare: a properly made quiche, a moreish chicken and mushroom pie, proper fish and chips, and the home-made duck sausages are always worth a try. Gorgeous and often unusual puddings too;

they use their own ice-cream in the profiteroles. There's also a daily changing restaurant menu. Satisfying hearty breakfasts.

Bar Meals: *12-2, 7-9; bar snacks both sessions*   **Restaurant:** *7.30-8.30*   **Typical Dishes BAR:** *home-made soup £1.55, chicken and bacon terrine £4.55, calves liver with smoked bacon £5.95, langoustines £5.25, fresh haddock and fat chips £4.55, nectarine split £2.25   Vegetarian Meals: mushroom stroganoff £4.55   Children's Portions* `Cheese` `Beer` *Adnams; Hook Norton; Yates* `Whisky` `Cider` *Thatchers   Children Allowed in Bar to Eat   Garden   Outdoor Eating* **Accommodation:** *6 bedrooms, all en suite, from £70 (single £60)   Children Welcome Overnight   Check-in: all day* **Credit Cards:** *Access, Visa*

DALBEATTIE   Pheasant Hotel

1 Maxwell Street DG5 4AH
Tel: (0556) 610345
Open: 11am-midnight
Licensee: Bill Windsor

Cheap bar food in upstairs lounge of popular hotel/local in plain little town. Look out for fresh local specials like salmon; vegetarians must make do with pineapple and cheese salad.

Bar Meals: *12-2, 6-9 bar snacks both sessions   Children's Portions   Children Allowed in Bar to Eat* **Accommodation:** *9 bedrooms, 2 en suite, from £28 (single £18)   Children Welcome Overnight   Cots Available   Check in: all day* **No Credit Cards**.

DUMFRIES Mabie House. A short drive out of the town, in Mabie Forest (good walks, and cycles for hire), a welcoming dining bar in an old country house, and a curious hybrid of cafe and Scots Baronial. Some unusual dishes on the very long menu. Good value. Nice to babies. McEwans beers.

ESKDALEMUIR   Hart Manor Hotel

By Langholm DG13 0QQ
Tel: (03873) 73217
Open: 11-2.30, 6.30-11 (12-2, 6.30-11 Sun)
Licensee: Pamela Medcalf

Remote hilltop hotel in lovely countryside. Decent, good value bar meals.

Bar Meals: *12 (12.30 Sun)-2, 6.30-9.30; bar snacks lunchtime*   **Restaurant:** *7.30-8.30* **Typical Dishes BAR:** *home-made soup £1, home-made paté £2.25, lamb cutlets £4.85, home-baked ham £4, rainbow trout £4.75, home-made puddings* **RESTAURANT** *dinner menu £15-£17.50: shrimp and tomato vinaigrette, steak Buccleuch, venison, pork fillet, chocolate and chestnut tart   Children's Portions* `Beer` *Broughton* `Whisky` *Children Allowed in Bar to Eat* **Accommodation:** *7 bedrooms, 5 en suite, from £40 (single £23)   Children Welcome Overnight   Cot Available   Check-in: all day* **No Credit Cards**

GATEHOUSE OF FLEET   Murray Arms Hotel

Gatehouse of Fleet DG7 2HY
Tel: (0557) 814207
Open: 11-2.30, 5-11 (12.30-2.30, 6.30-11 Sun)

Unsurprising bar food in charming old town centre hotel with Burns connections
(he wrote Scots Wha' Hae' here). Nice, if expensive, bedrooms. Lovely little town
in rich green Galloway countryside.

*Bar Meals: 12-9,45; bar snacks   **Restaurant:** 7.30-8.45   **Typical Dishes BAR:** home-
made soup £1.10, garlic mushrooms £1.95, lasagne £4.45, sirloin steak £7.95, haddock
£4.45   **Restaurant:** table d'hote £15.50   Vegetarian Meals: mushroom stroganoff
Children's Menu/Portions* `Cheese` ▪ `Beer` ▪ *Youngers No. 3* `Whisky` *Family Room
Children Allowed in Bar to Eat   Garden   Outdoor Eating   **Accommodation:** 13
bedrooms, all en suite, from £80 (single £40)   Children Welcome Overnight   Cots
Available   Check-in: all day   **Credit Cards:** Access, Amex, Diners, Visa*

GATEHOUSE Angel Hotel, High Street: Another Gatehouse favourite; popular
for bar lunches.

GRETNA Solway Lodge Hotel, Annan Road Tel: (0461) 38266: Only just in
Scotland. Decent bar food in comfy lounge; evening restaurant; good value en suite
bed and breakfast.

ISLE OF WHITHORN   Steam Packet Hotel

Harbour Row DG5 8HZ
Tel: (09885) 334
Open: 11-11 (11-2.30, 5.30-11 winter Mon-Thur)

Listed for its position, in this quaintly beautiful harbour, and good value bed and
breakfast – an excellent weekend haven. Ask for a room at the front. Lovely views,
too, from picture windows in the plush, attractively modernised bar; cosy downstairs
dining room. Cheap and cheerful bar food is enlivened by occasionally wonderful
fish and seafood specials. Boat trips from the harbour.

*Bar Meals and Restaurant: 12-2, 7-9.30; bar snacks both sessions   **Typical Dishes
BAR:** home-made soup 75p, prawn cocktail £1.75, steak pie £2.75, chicken curry £2.50,
fish and chips £2.75   **RESTAURANT:** paté £2, sirloin steak £8.50, whole grilled sole
£9.50, fruits of the sea £8.50   Children's Menu/Portions   Children Allowed in Bar to
Eat   Outdoor Play Area   Garden   Outdoor Eating   **Accommodation:** 5 bedrooms, all en
suite, from £42 (single £21)   Children Welcome Overnight   Cots Available   Check-in:
all day   **Credit Cards:** Access, Visa*

KIPPFORD   Anchor Hotel

Quayside DG5 4LN
Tel: (055 662) 205
Open: 11-2.30, 6-11 (10.30 am-midnight summer)
Licensee: Simon Greig

Prettily set, harbourside pub, with a plush modern dining lounge (be early for a
window seat) and much more characterful, rambling drinking bar. Predictable and
limited bar meal choice on laminated menu, but specials are often good, though
they might run out early at busy times. Young, casual staff are friendly and tolerant
of toddlers; one high chair.

*Bar Meals: 12-2, 6-9 (all day summer); bar snacks both sessions   **Typical Dishes:** home-*

made soup 95p, garlic and brandy paté £2.05, steak pie £3.55, sirloin steak £7.65, shellfish mornay £4.25, American fudge cake £1.65 Vegetarian Meals Children's Menu/Portions Beer *McEwans, Theakston* Whisky *Family Room (games room) Patio/terrace Outdoor Eating* **No Credit Cards**

KIRKCUDBRIGHT   Selkirk Arms

High Street DG6 4JG
Tel: (0557) 30402
Open: 11 am–midnight
Licensee: E J Morris

Modernised but characterful sleepy town hotel, its simple public bar popular with locals. Go on a sunny day and have lunch under the trees in the pretty little garden; they'll even carry out a high chair for babies. Bar meals are always decent, and occasionally shine – try the creamy seafood tagliatelle. Good choice on the à la carte, including local scallops, game and Galloway steaks, main course prices £7–£13.

Bar Meals: *12-2, 6.30-9.30; bar snacks lunchtime* **Typical Dishes:** *carrot and tarragon soup £1, queen scallops in white wine and smoked bacon £4.35, steak and Guinness pie £4.25, lasagne £4.50, fresh haddock in crispy batter £3.75 Vegetarian Meals: pasta bake Children's Menu/Portions* Whisky *Children Allowed in Bar to Eat Garden Outdoor Eating* **Accommodation:** *15 bedrooms, all en suite, from £65 (single £38) Children Welcome Overnight Cots Available Check-in: all day* **Credit Cards:** *Access, Amex, Diners, Visa*

LOCKERBIE Somerton House Hotel, 35 Carlisle Road Tel: (05762) 2583: Listed red sandstone Victorian hotel, with simple bar meals and fishy, gamey Taste of Scotland restaurant menu. Reasonably priced bed and breakfast. Tetley Bitter; Credit Cards.

MOFFAT   Black Bull

Churchgate DG10 9EG
Tel: (0683) 20206
Open: 11-11
Licensee: Jim Hughes

Modernised 16th century street-side local in this curiously old-fashioned, isolated little spa town, whose life blood is coach party tourism. Recently refurbished, but the proper local bar survives. Modestly priced, recommendable accommodation.

Bar Meals and Restaurant: *1.30-2.15, 6.30-9 (restaurant Fri/Sat only Jan-March); bar snacks both sessions* **Typical Dishes** *home-made soup 95p, whitebait £1.75, steak pie £3.45, sirloin steak £7.45, cheese hotpot £3.45, trifle £1.50 Vegetarian Meals: macaroni Children's Menu/Portions* Beer *Theakston* Whisky *Family Room Patio/terrace Outdoor Eating* **Accommodation:** *6 bedrooms, 2 en suite, from £36 (single £24) Children Welcome Overnight Cots Available Check-in: all day* **Credit Cards:** *Access, Visa*

MOFFAT Balmoral High Street: Also popular for bar food, and smart evening à la carte.

NEW GALLOWAY Cross Keys Tel: (06442) 494. One of several pub-hotels on the pretty terraced main street of this little village. Pleasant bar and dining room - head for the latter, for decent, fresh food (main courses £6-£9), iced water provided, but also sliced bread. Decent vegetables, nice puddings, excellent Galloway steaks. Lunch and evening.

NEWTON STEWART   Creebridge House Hotel

Minnigaff DG8 6NP
Tel: (0671) 2121
Open: 12-2.30, 6-11
Licensee: Christopher Walker

Charming and pleasingly pubby bar in delightful country house set in its own pretty grounds, just before the bridge on the Minnigaff-approach to Newton Stewart. Very popular with locals for good, often interesting bar food and very good value. Tolerant and helpful towards parents with young children, too.

Bar Meals: 12 (12.30 Sun)-2, 6-9 (10 Sat); bar snacks both sessions   *Restaurant:* 7-9
Typical Dishes   **BAR:** *home-made soup £1.25, deep-fried camembert £2.50, Galloway beef with mushrooms £4.50, steak and kidney pie £4.95, fillet of local salmon £5.25, Ecclefechan butter tart £1.50*   **RESTAURANT:** *garlic mushrooms £2.95, half-dozen oysters £6.50, fillet of beef Creebridge £9.10, roast breast of goose £8.95, lobster thermidor £15.25, banoffee pie £2.10*   *Vegetarian Meals: cracked wheat and walnut casserole Children's Menu/Portions*   `Cheese`   `Beer`   *Belhaven 80/-; Theakston Best Bitter, XB*   `Whisky`   *Family room*   *Garden*   *Outdoor Eating*   *Summer Barbecue*
Accommodation: 18 bedrooms, all en suite, from £61 (single £34)   Children Welcome Overnight   Cots Available   Check-in: all day   *Credit Cards: Access, Visa*

PORT LOGAN Port Logan Hotel: Bar meals and good atmosphere; particularly the Sunday night live Scots music sessions.

ST JOHNS TOWN OF DALRY Clachan Inn Tel (06443) 241. On main street of charming village, locally shortened to plain 'Dalry'. Welcoming, traditional bar, with real fire and a tolerance of walkers (Southern Upland Way). Routine printed menu and more interesting specials: good soup, nice home-made paté, decent steak and mushroom pie, mostly fresh vegetables. Children allowed until 8pm.

FIFE

ABERDOUR Aberdour Hotel High Street Tel: (0383) 860325. 17th century coaching inn close to two beaches. Fresh ingredients in lunch and evening bar meals: their own honey, eggs, herbs; good game specials. Family room; bedrooms; Belhaven beers.

ANSTRUTHER   Craw's Nest

Bankwell Road KY10 3DA
Tel: (0333) 310691
Open: all day
Licensee: Ian Birrell

Decent enough bar food, though the bar itself is rather functional in style. Modernised, uniformly decorated bedrooms divide between the main house and annexe. Residents' television lounge.

Bar Meals: 12.15-2, 6.15-9.30; bar snacks both sessions   *Restaurant:* 12.30-2, 7-9
Typical Dishes BAR: yellow split pea soup £1.05, potted hough salad £2.30, roast Aberdeen Angus beef £4.50, beefsteak pie £3.90, deep-fried Pittenweem haddock £4.50 Vegetarian Meals: lasagne Children's Portions   `Whisky`   *Children Allowed in Bar to Eat Garden*   *Accommodation: 50 bedrooms, all en suite, from £55 (single £35)   Children Welcome Overnight   Cots Available   Check-in: all day*   *Credit Cards: Access, Amex, Diners, Visa*

ANSTRUTHER   Dreel Tavern

16 High Street KY10 5DL
Tel: (0333) 310727
Open: 11-2.30, 5.30-11 (11-midnight Sat, 12.30-11 Sun)
Licensee: Barry Scarsbrook

Attractive, traditional three storey 16th century stone pub, popular for lunch. Real fires.

Bar Meals: 12 (12.30 Sun)-2, 6.30-9.30; bar snacks both sessions   *Typical Dishes:* home-made soup 95p, garlic mushrooms in cream £2, chicken and sweetcorn pie £3.95, ham with leek sauce £4.25, smoked fish pie £3.95, treacle and nut tart £1.20   Vegetarian Meals: broccoli quiche   Children's Menu/Portions   **Beer**   Children Allowed in Bar to Eat   Garden   Outdoor Eating   Summer Barbecue   *No Credit Cards*

CARNOCK   Old Inn

Main Street KY12 9JQ
Tel: (0383) 850381
Open: 11-3, 5-11 (11-11 Fri/Sat, 12.30-11 Sun)

Carpeted dining bar with roughcast cream painted walls and copper-top tables, set with Old Inn mats. Single storey restaurant extension. Food is acceptable rather than exciting.

Bar Meals and Restaurant: 12-2.30 (2 restaurant), 5.30 (6.30 restaurant)-9.30; bar snacks both sessions   *Typical Dishes BAR:* potato and leek soup 95p, deep-fried mushrooms in beer batter £2.85, beef, ale and mushroom pie £3.85, lasagne bolognese £3.85, minced beef and skirlie £3.50, baked apple crumble £1.80   *Restaurant:* stilton and port soup £1.25, funghi farcitti £3.85, sirloin steak Balmoral £10.95, chicken princess £8.95, salmon supreme Gairloch style £9.95   Vegetarian Meals: stuffed peppers £3.90   Children's Menu/Portions   **Beer**   Maclays   **Whisky**   Children Allowed in Bar to Eat   Outdoor Play Area   Garden   Outdoor Eating   *No Credit Cards*

CRAIL   Golf Hotel

4 High Street KY10 3TB   ❢
Tel: (0333) 50206
Open: all day
Licensee: Graham Guthrie

Busy inn in beautiful East Neuk fishing village; lively public bar, plain lounge, decent bar food, very good value bed and breakfast.

Bar Meals and Restaurant: 12-2, 6.30-9; bar snacks lunchtime   *Typical Dishes BAR:* lentil soup 95p, lamb and apricot pie £3.75, chicken and mushroom pie £3.75, seafood vol-au-vent £3.75, queen of puddings £1.50   *RESTAURANT:* cauliflower soup £1.25, prawn cocktail £2.75, home-made lasagne £4.85, pan-fried lemon sole £5.25, home-made apple crumble £1.50   Vegetarian Meals: lasagne   Children's Menu/Portions   **Whisky**   Family Room   Children Allowed in Bar to Eat   *Accommodation:* 5 bedrooms, all en suite, from £36 (single £24)   Children Welcome Overnight   Cots Available   Check-in: all day   *No Credit Cards*

DYSART   Old Rectory Inn

West Quality Street KY1 2TA   `FOOD`
Tel: (0592) 51211   ❄
Open: 12-2, 6.30-9.30 (12.30-2.30 Sun); closed Mon
Licensee: David North

Just a few hundred yards off the main road from Kirkcaldy to Leven, in the pretty
village of Dysart, is the imposing single storey Rectory Inn, resplendent on its
corner site perched above the harbour, and with a delightful walled garden. The
main bar is beamed, while a second room is served by a large hatch, and there's a
third small room through the dining area. Furnishings are a mixture of old solid
wood tables and chairs and more modern upholstered bench seating. Dining is very
much the thing, and tables are pre-set with mats (no cloths). Fresh flowers and free-
range butter (not encased in foil, that is) are plus points. An extensive menu is
supplemented by daily specials listed on a blackboard in the main bar: home-made
minestrone was tasty and filling, and a Continental salad starter of various cold meats
and chicken excellent. There was slight disappointment to come – the steak pie,
though crammed with tender beef, had a pie crust unmistakably of the separately
cooked kind. A delicious salmon and fish risotto, with proper risotto rice, made up
for it though. Salads are of the help yourself sort, from around 8 different selections
at the serving hatch. Home-made carrot cake was good; real coffee with
accompanying cream in a proper jug was a bonus, and of the bottomless sort (£1.76
for two people). Many fellow-lunchers were evidently regulars, on first name terms
with the owner-licensees, who are, however, commendably uncliquey and friendly
to strangers. It's also a popular business lunch venue in a small local way. The
menu's quite different in the evening, with lots more meat and fish dishes, some of
which are listed under Restaurant below. Vegetarians are not obviously provided
for, but can have something rustled up on the spot. There are high-chairs for
children.

Bar Meals and Restaurant: 12-2.30, 6.30-9.30 **Typical Dishes BAR:** *home-made
soup £1.15, mussel and onion stew £2.35, Spanish pork £4.40, venison and beef casserole
£4, tortellini £4.15, bread and butter pudding £1.25* **RESTAURANT:** *sweetbreads £5,
guinea fowl £9.50, peppered fillet steak £15, turbot £10, crepes Suzette £5 (for 2)
Vegetarian Meals: black-eyed bean casserole £3.85 Children's Portions* `Whisky` *Children
Allowed in Bar to Eat   Garden   Outdoor Eating* **Credit Cards:** *Access, Amex, Visa*

ELIE   Ship Inn

The Toft KY0 1DT
Tel: (0333) 330246
Open: 11 am-midnight (12.30-11 Sun)
Licensees: Richard and Jill Philip

Really wonderful little pub in unspoilt, old-fashioned little village, down by the
harbourside; lazy atmosphere, fishermen and locals, coal fire and various dogs.
Friendly new owners are making changes, including renovations, installing a kitchen
(no food previously) and dining area: the pub will be closed between January and
mid-April 1992. Menus are still in the planning stage; no prices yet, but bound to be
reasonable. The little waterside bar garden, over the quiet lane, has its own bar and
July/August barbecue.

Bar Meals: 12 (12.30 Sun)-2.30, 6.30-9.30; bar snacks both sessions **Typical Dishes:**
*meaty lentil soup, prawn, bacon and cream cheese paté, chilli pie, fillet of pork in cream sauce,
fresh fish, apple and mincemeat meringue pie   Vegetarian Meals: spinach pasties   Children's
Menu/Portions* `Beer` *Belhaven; Courage* `Whisky` *Family Room   Seaside
Patio/terrace   Summer Barbecue*

FALKLAND   Covenanter Hotel

High Street, The Square KY7 7BU
Tel: (0337) 57542
Open: 12-2, 6-9.30; closed Mon
Licensee: George Menzies

Pleasant old hotel in pretty village, just finished upgrading its bedrooms to business class; also own self-catering cottages nearby. Apart from printed bar food and restaurant menu, on which steaks feature prominently, fresh daily specials dependent on local produce.

Bar Meals and Restaurant: 12-2, 6-9.30 (7-9 restaurant) **Typical Dishes BAR:** *lentil soup 70p, mushroom dip £1.50, Cajun beef £4, lasagne £3.15, chicken tikka £3.25, bread and butter pudding £1.50* **RESTAURANT:** *minestrone £1.25, scampi dip £4, Alliance steak £10, lamb cutlets £5, chicken Diane £7.50, raspberry strudel £2 Vegetarian Meals: nut cutlet   Children's Portions*

KIRKCALDY   ★ Hoffmans

435 High Street KW1 2SG   `FOOD`
Tel: (0592) 204584   ❗
Open: 11am-midnight (closed Sun)   ☺
Licensees: Paul and Vince Hoffman

Hoffmans is an extraordinary place. Situated to the east of the town centre (don't be confused by the High Street address), it's an unlikely looking venue for a pub serving imaginative food, but first impressions can deceive. Owned in partnership by Vince and Paul Hoffman, it opened in March 1990, after Vince, who had worked in a variety of Scottish hotels – including Airds at Port Appin – returned to his home town and set up at a previous pub just down the road. The building they subsequently decided on to set up on their own was unpromisingly seedy; the interior was smartened up, with subtly toned wall coverings, brown upholstered bench seating, polished tables, a large central ceiling fan, angled mirrors and fake greenery. The attractive seascape and still life oils are courtesy of Hoffman sisters, and rather fine colour photographs by a couple of regulars. But the food is the thing here, and so popular that booking's advised for lunch as well as dinner. And rightly so. Vince Hoffman is so confident in the quality of his raw ingredients that local suppliers are listed at the front of the menu, which is handwritten and changes daily. Often it's not even decided on until just before opening time, when suppliers and fishmongers have been visited and produce assessed. Fish is a particular interest of Vince's, from a traditional deep-fried haddock to an elaborately modern salmon and monkfish dish in lobster sauce. The raw materials are first class, the handling first rate, and the prices remarkable: at lunchtime, main courses like Chicago pepperpot, poached haddock with Norwegian prawn sauce, pasta Toscana or roast stuffed lamb cost just over £3. Start with a creamy carrot soup and finish with delicious sticky toffee pudding, and a three course lunch can be had for as little as £5.90! In the evening, the room is partitioned, half the space reserved for drinkers, the other run as an à la carte restaurant Wednesday to Saturday, when tables are laid and candle-lit, and there's waitress service. Expect to pay around £32 for two then, for smart evening food of a more complex kind: venison with redcurrants, veal cutlet with green peppercorn sauce, or grilled salmon with a warm tomato sauce. Capable service is also genuinely friendly, thanks to the Hoffman teamwork: Vince and wife Jan look after the kitchen, Paul and wife Janette run the front of house.

Bar Meals: all day   Restaurant: 12-2, 7.30-10   Typical Dishes BAR: *Polish ham soup 80p, linguine carbonara £3.25, deep-fried haddock £3.25, braised ham in cherry sauce £3.25, bakewell tart £1.20* **RESTAURANT:** *roast guinea fowl £10.75, peppered*

steak £10.25, escalope of seafood thermidor £10.25, Mississippi mud pie £2.50
Vegetarian Meals   Children's Portions   `Beer`   McEwan, Youngers   `Whisky`   Children
Allowed in Bar to Eat   No Credit Cards

KIRKCALDY Harbour Inn: Overshadowed by the achievements of Hoffmans, but liked for simple home cooking. On the coast road.

PITTENWEEM Larrochmhor Hotel: Local seafood on otherwise routine bar menu, served in pleasant little dining room.

ST ANDREWS   Grange Inn

Grange Road KY16 8LJ   ♥
Tel: (0334) 72670
Licensee: Peter Aretz

Isolated pub on quiet road a mile and a half out of town. Restaurant well-regarded locally; bar meals decent too, with one or two really interesting things and excellent puddings. The nicest, pubbiest bar for miles around, particularly in winter, with its dark wood and glowing fire; unspoilt and very civilised. What a pity there's no decent beer! The bedroom is clean but modestly furnished.

Bar Meals: 12.30-2.30, 7-10   Restaurant: 12.30-2.30 (weekends), 7-9.30 (not Mon)
Typical Dishes BAR: vegetable soup £1.50, avocado with prawns £2.50, beef stroganoff
£4.50, marinated tongue £4.25, fresh salmon salad £5, sticky toffee pudding £1.75
RESTAURANT £20 menu: soup of the day, asparagus and orange salad, marinated breast
of chicken, grilled lamb cutlets with minted pear, stir-fried king prawns with vegetables and
ginger, white chocolate mousse   Vegetarian Meals: quiche   Children's Portions   Children
Allowed in Bar to Eat   Garden   Outdoor Eating   Accommodation: 1 bedroom, with own
bathroom, £60   Children Welcome Overnight   Check-in: all day   Credit Cards: Access,
Amex, Diners, Visa

STRATHMIGLO Strathmiglo Inn, 61 High Street Tel: (03376) 252: Village coaching inn with public bar, lounge and restaurant. Decent home cooking, with fresh vegetables. Bedrooms. Belhaven, Taylor beers. Open: 11-2.30, 5-11 (midnight Thur-Sun; opens 1½ hours later Sun).

GRAMPIAN

ABERDEEN   Craighaar Hotel

Waterton Road, Bucksburn AB2 9HS   ♥
Tel: (0224) 712275
Open: 11-11
Licensee: R M Simpson

Very simple bar food, Taste of Scotland restaurant, in suburban Aberdeen hotel.

Bar Meals: 12-2, 6.30-10; bar snacks lunchtime   Restaurant: 12-2, 7-9.30   Typical
Dishes BAR: Cullen skink £1.20, garlic bread 85p, steak and mushroom pie £3.50, roast
of the day £4.95, filled jacket potatoes £2.25   RESTAURANT: cauliflower soup
£1.25, crab claws in garlic and lemon butter £5.50, supreme of chicken with noodles £6.95,
deep-fried scampi with lemon £5.95, escalope of salmon with avocado coulis £5.95, sticky
toffee pudding   Vegetarian Meals: roast nut cutlets   Children's Portions   `Cheese`   `Beer`
Bass; Whitbread   `Whisky`   Family Room   Outdoor Play Area   Accommodation: 53
bedrooms, all en suite, from £65.50 (single £59.50)   Children Welcome Overnight   Cots
Available   Check-in: all day   Credit Cards: Access, Amex, Diners, Visa

ABERDEEN   Prince of Wales

7 St Nicholas Lane AB1 1HF
Tel: (0224) 640597
Open: 11-11 (12.30-11 Sun)
Licensee: Peter Birnie

An essential stop-off in any visit to the granite city. An atmospheric, usually very busy old tavern, located down a cobbled alley underneath the city centre, with the longest bar counter in town, winding round several distinctly styled drinking areas. Beer reliably good. No children under 14.

Bar Meals: 11.45-2; bar snacks lunchtime **Typical Dishes:** *home-made soup 90p, home-made pies £2.90, beef olives £2.90, pork chops £2.70* *Vegetarian Meals: lasagne* **Beer** *Bass; Caledonian; Theakston, Youngers* **No Credit Cards**

ABERDEEN Brentwood Hotel, 101 Crown Street: Modern hotel, simple home-made food in Carriages Brasserie. 62 bedrooms. Whitbread beers. Open: 11-2.30, 5-11.

BANCHORY Tor Na Coille, Inchmarlo Road (A9) Tel: (03302) 2242: Large hotel in own grounds on west side of town; good, unusual bar lunches. Family room. Theakstons beers. Open all day.

ELGIN Thunderton House Hotel Thunderton Place. Stylishly restored Victorian building, now a family-oriented pub, with good facilities and decent bar food lunch and evening. Belhaven, Broughton, Caledonian beers. Open: all day.

FETTERCAIRN   Ramsay Arms Hotel

Junction B966/B974 AB30 1XX
Tel: (05614) 334
Open: 11 (12 Sun)-11
Licensee: Kathleen Evans

Strikingly ugly roadside village inn, a lot older than it looks; Queen Victoria stayed here in 1861. Cheery homely lounge within, though.

Bar Meals and Restaurant: 12-2, 6-9 (10 Sat) (5.30-8.30 Sun); bar snacks both sessions **Typical Dishes BAR:** *soup of the day 85p, stuffed mushrooms £2, home-made mince pie £4.10, raised game pie £4.10, fresh haddock £4.15, clootie dumpling £1.75* **RESTAURANT:** *Finnan crepes £3, sirloin steak Bonny Prince Charlie £10.75, venison with maraschino cherry sauce £9.75, salmon in raspberry sauce £6.70, crunchy grape meringue flan £2.85 Vegetarian Meals (restaurant): green spring fraze £5.25* *Children's Menu/Portions* **Beer** *Theakston, Youngers* **Whisky** *Family Room* *Outdoor Play Area* *Garden* *Outdoor Eating* **Accommodation:** *12 bedrooms, all en suite, from £45 (single £31)* *Children Welcome Overnight* *Cots Available* *Check-in: all day* **Credit Cards:** *Access, Visa*

FINDHORN Crown and Anchor opposite Yacht Club Tel: (0309) 30243. Busy old stone-built inn with good beers, including a huge bottled foreign range, ciders and whiskies; go for local fish on the bar menu. Modest bedrooms. Good beach walks. Open all day.

FOCHABERS Gordon Arms High Street Tel: (0343) 820508. Former coaching inn alongside the A96; fishing trophies in the public bar. Simple overnight accommodation, clean and well-equipped (from £60); children welcome.

INVERURIE   Thainstone House Hotel

Inverurie Road AB5 9NT   ❢
Tel: (0467) 21643
Open: 11-11 (12.30-11 Sun)
Licensee: Edith Lovie

Country house hotel with a friendly non-residents bar, popular with locals, and splendid barbecues on summer Sundays. But big changes are afoot: from May 1992 the cosy 8 bedroomed operation will be radically extended, with a 42 bedroom extension, leisure club, pool and conference centre. Hopefully bar food will remain a reliable bargain. Restaurant main courses start at around £8.50.

Bar Meals and Restaurant: 12-2 (12.30-2.30 Sun), 6.30-9.30; bar snacks lunchtime
Typical Dishes BAR: cock a leekie soup, seafood marinade, skewers of beef and peppers, chicken in sesame seeds, fresh brill and prawns with crab claws and cashews (main courses from £4.75), ginger and lemon gateau   Vegetarian Meals: fettuccine   Children's Menu/Portions
Beer Courage; Orkney; Tetley; Whitbread **Whisky** Family Room   Children Allowed in Bar to Eat   Outdoor Play Area   Garden   Outdoor Eating   Summer Barbecue
Accommodation: 50 bedrooms, all en suite, from £85 (single £69)   Children Welcome Overnight   Cots Available   Check-in: all day   **Credit Cards:** Access, Amex, Diners, Visa

KINCARDINE O'NEIL   Gordon Arms Hotel

38 North Deeside Road AB34 5AA   ❢
Tel: (03398) 84236   **B&B**
Open: 11 am-midnight
Licensee: Bryn Wayte

An early 19th century coaching inn of sombre grey stone, the Gordon Arms stands alongside the busy A93, almost opposite the derelict 13th century village church. Behind a rather anonymous exterior is an inn of warm and informal atmosphere. The main bar area is spacious, sparsely furnished and utterly unpretentious, its high ceiling creating echoes on quiet days, plain painted walls minimally dotted with pictures, and the part bare-floorboard, part modestly-carpeted floor topped with varying sizes of tables and a motley crew of cushioned chairs. A large rough stone fireplace is decorated with old cider jars, and the wall above hung with a couple of fishing rods (this is a rich fishing area); there's a piano and splendid antique sideboard. A separate public bar has part panelled walls, old black and white photographs of the area, a television set and electronic games. There are two separate menus: a short bar choice with standard items like steak pie, chicken curry and deep-fried haddock, and a more interesting and enterprising dinner menu with an unusually wide choice of inventive vegetarian dishes (some suitable for vegans), like stir-fried tofu and peanuts, broccoli and mushroom pie, and fettuccine di funghetto. Carnivores aren't forgotten, though. Game pie, chicken Lochnagar and a choice of steaks are typical: the house special, steak Highland, is a sirloin (rather fatty, yet good flavoursome meat) topped with a Drambuie cream sauce (on the thick side) and a slice of haggis. An unusual combination which doesn't really work. Accompanying main courses come welcome fresh vegetables, but also frozen chips! Bread is baked on the premises, and there's a fair selection of organic wines. They also do a very popular Scottish high tea, in which tea, toast, scones and cakes are included in the price of a main course. The seven bedrooms are comfortable and unfussy. Care has been taken to keep decor and furnishing in keeping with the building's age, and all are of useful size. Some fine pieces of antique furniture are partnered by a worn, but very comfortable armchair. Two of the en suite rooms have compact shower rooms, the third a slightly larger bath/shower. The remaining rooms share two bathrooms located down a flight of stairs. There are plans to make two more rooms en suite ready for the '92 season.

Bar Meals and Restaurant: 12-2 (bar weekends only), 5-9.30; bar snacks both sessions
Typical Dishes BAR: Scotch broth 80p, garlic mushrooms £1.90, home-made steak pie
£2.75, home-made lasagne £3.70, deep-fried haddock £2.75, apple pie £1.25
RESTAURANT: chicken and leek soup £1.10, deep-fried brie £2.95, chicken Lochnagar
£6.25, game pie £5.75, sirloin Highlander £8.95, Kincar pancakes £1.95   Vegetarian
Meals: lasagne £3.70   Children's Menu/Portions   **Beer**   Theakston, Youngers
Whisky   Family Room Outdoor Play Area   *Accommodation:* 7 bedrooms, 3 en suite,
from £32 (single £20)   Children Welcome Overnight   Cot Available   Check-in: all day
Credit Cards: Access, Amex, Visa

MONYMUSK   Grant Arms Hotel

Signposted from B993
Tel: (04677) 226
Open: 11-2.30, 5-11 (12-11 Sun)
Licensee: C O Hart

18th century coaching inn in picturesque village, modernised but attractive inside
with its comfortable lounge, and fruit-machine and space-game public bar. Look out
for local seafood and game. Excellent fishing on 10 miles of the river Don. Ghillies
available at reasonable rates.

Bar Meals: 12-2.15, 6.30-9.15; bar snacks both sessions   *Restaurant:* 7-9.30   *Typical
Dishes BAR:* home-made soup £1.25, venison pie £3.95, king prawns £7.50,
salmon/sea trout £5.50, sticky toffee pudding £1.75 *RESTAURANT* dinner menu
£18.50   Vegetarian Meals: mushroom stroganoff   Children's Menu/Portions   **Beer**
McEwan   **Whisky**   Family Room   Outdoor Play Area   Patio/terrace   Outdoor Eating
Summer Barbecue   *Accommodation:* 15 bedrooms, 7 en suite, from £54 (single £31)
Children Welcome Overnight   Cots Available   Check-in: all day   *Credit Cards:* Access,
Amex, Diners, Visa

NETHERLEY   Lairhillock Inn

Netherley AB3 2QS   **FOOD**
Tel: (0569) 30001   ☻
Open: 12-2.30, 6-11   ▼

Despite standing alone surrounded by fields, the Lairhillock is easily spotted from the
B979, thanks to the large white INN daubed on its roof. The closest major village to
the inn is Peterculter, some four miles to the north; Netherley's a mile to the south.
Formerly a farmhouse, the original building is 17th century, with careful extensions,
and the interior is full of old rustic atmosphere. The large lounge is dominated by a
central log-burning fireplace; walls are half-panelled, and exposed floorboards
covered with numerous rugs. Heavy, iron-legged tables are surrounded by solid
wooden chairs of various sorts; polished brass plates and bedwarmers hang on the
wall. The public bar, in the oldest part, is by far the most characterful room, with its
exposed stone, panelling, open fire, old settles and bench seating, every kind of
horse tack, polished brasses and numerous other bits and pieces. One wall is covered
with postcards, some of them in dubious taste. But bar food is certainly taken
seriously at the Lairhillock, where only fresh produce is used, cooked to order. The
lunchtime menu, more limited than in the evening, still carries a fair choice,
changing daily. Typically there might be wild boar terrine, fettuccine al pepa,
fisherman's pie Aberdonian style, or chicken liandoise, thin strips of chicken breast
lightly sautéed and served with a creamy sauce finished with chanterelles – delicious,
with good crisp fresh vegetables, and potatoes. Puddings like St Honoré gateau and
mango cheesecake are changed daily. It gets extremely busy, especially on Friday
and Saturday evenings when a wait of up to an hour for a table isn't unheard of.

There's no booking at present, though this may come. Across from the main building, in the old stables, is the evening restaurant, with its high beamed ceiling, stone walls, red tiled flooring and solid polished tables. There's candlelight, and a pianist plays nightly from the first floor terrace, the small diners' lounge. There's a wide and interesting choice of dishes here too (from £20.75 table d'hote). Having undergone some periods of uncertainty (including a period in liquidation), the Lairhillock is back in the hands of a previous owner, who has brought back his former chef. They appear to be back on track. Service is pleasantly informal but always efficient.

Bar Meals: 12-2, 6-9.30 (10 weekends); bar snacks lunchtime   *Restaurant:* 12-2 (Sun only), 7.30-9.30   *Typical Dishes BAR:* asparagus soup £1.15, venison and blueberry paté £2.95, wild boar goulash with chanterelles £7.75, grilled lamb chops £7.40, whole grilled haddock with pepper butter £5.25, home-made meringues with butterscotch sauce £1.95   *RESTAURANT* dinner menu £20.75: guinea fowl terrine, smoked fish platter, steaks, chicken with smoked salmon, fish of the day, home-made puddings   Vegetarian Meals: chanterelle crepes   Children's Portions   `Cheese`   `Beer`   Courage; Felinfoel; McEwan; Whitbread   `Whisky`   Patio/terrace   *Credit Cards:* Access, Amex, Diners

---

NEWBURGH   Udny Arms Hotel

Main Street AB41 0BL   `FOOD`
Tel: (03586) 89444   `B&B`
Licensee: J D Craig   ♥ 🍴

This small, family-run hotel at the heart of the village, overlooking the main street, enjoys fine rear views over a 9 hole golf course and the Ythan estuary to a nature reserve on the northern bank of the river. The front, main house bar is small and cosy, furnished with sturdy stripped-pine tables and pine-board cushioned settles, the walls decorated with fishing flies and bird prints. An interesting menu (only served at lunchtime in this bar) is, naturally enough, strong on seafood: fresh mussels perhaps, or salmon with coriander, or char-grilled king prawns. There's good meat, too, like a good piece of steak with red wine and shallot sauce, or escalope of chicken Cadiz. This menu also applies in the Bistro at lunchtime, a split-level room with fine views over the estuary, stripped pine furniture, pretty floral curtains and a lot of greenery. In the evening, this is the venue for a more extensive, elaborate menu, again strong on fish. Expect to pay about £40 for two for 3 courses, not outlandish for dishes like salmon and scallops with coriander butter, or the Udny Creel, which brings together salmon, scallops, mussels, squid, prawns and crab in a lobster and cream stock. Service is both friendly and efficient. Added to all of this is a third hotel bar, down in the basement, very simply furnished and decorated in café style, where simpler food like minute steak and scampi is on offer. The hotel's 24 letting bedrooms have undergone some refurbishment, with new carpets and soft fabrics. Sizes, styles and furnishings vary, but all are neat and well maintained, with all the usual modern facilities: television, direct dial telephones, hair dryers and trouser presses. All, too, are en suite, with well-lit, tiled facilities, but the best and most sought-after rooms overlook the picturesque estuary. There's a rear lawn complete with garden furniture for sunny weather.

Bar Meals and Restaurant: 12.30-2, 6-9.3; bar snacks both sessions   *Typical Dishes BAR:* garlic and tomato soup £1.35, Orkney mussels in wine and cream £3.85, steak in shallot and wine sauce £3.95, chicken schnitzel £4.65, mixed game pie £3.95, sticky toffee pudding £2.95   *RESTAURANT:* stilton and broccoli soup £1.85, squid and crab salad nicoise £4.15, barbecued baby leg of lamb £10.95, char-grilled duck with mango £10.95, the Udny creel £11.85, five little treats £3.95   Vegetarian Meals: nutty rissoles £3.95   Children's Menu/Portions   `Beer`   McEwan, Theakston   `Whisky`   Family Room   Outdoor Play Area   Garden   Outdoor Eating   *Accommodation:* 26 bedrooms, all en suite, from £60 (single £48)   Children Welcome Overnight   Cots Available   Check-in: all day   *Credit Cards:* Access, Amex, Visa

STONEHAVEN   Marine Hotel

Shorehead AB3 2DY
Tel: (0569) 62155
Open: 11 am-midnight
Licensee: P Duncan

Lively, atmospheric harbourside pub-hotel, very much a local pub downstairs;
dining room upstairs. Good views from most bedrooms. Decent bar food; look out
for fresh local fish.

Bar Meals: 12-2, 5-10; bar snacks both sessions   **Typical Dishes:** *broccoli and cheese soup*
£1, local rollmop herring salad, beef olives in rich gravy, tandoori chicken, herring in oatmeal
(main courses from £4)   Vegetarian Meals: mushroom stroganoff   Children's Menu/Portions
█ Beer █ *Bass; Taylor* █ Whisky █ *Family Room   Outdoor Play Area   Outdoor Eating*
Accommodation: 7 bedrooms, sharing 2 bathrooms, from £25 (single £20)   Children
Welcome Overnight   Cot Available   Check-in: all day   Credit Cards: Access, Amex,
Visa

STONEHAVEN Heugh Hotel Westfield Road: Simple cheap bar food including
stovies; more interesting restaurant with good local beef, seafood, game, in attractive
listed old inn by the harbour. Tennents beer.

TURRIFF   Towie Tavern

Auchterless AB53 8EP
Tel: (08884) 201
Open: 11-2.30, 6-11 (12.30-2.30, 5-11 Sun)
Licensee: Douglas Pearson

A favourite for its satisfying, wholesome food, this is a roadside pebbledash pub on
the A497, some five miles south of Turriff. Smartly rustic decor and a new children's
play area; no smoking or music in the dining room. 50 whiskies.

Bar Meals and Restaurant: 12-2, 6-9 (later Sat, 5-8 Sun); bar snacks both sessions
Typical Dishes BAR: leek and potato soup £1.10, pate £2.95, Buchan beef lasagne
£4.40, skippers macaroni £4.30, fishermans crumble £4.30, sticky toffee pudding £1.95
RESTAURANT: cauliflower soup £1.80, mussels and prawns au gratin £3.40, supreme
of chicken Martinique £8.95, fillet of beef Towie Barclay £10.95, fresh king scallops and
monkfish mornay £10.50, crème bruleé £2.30   Vegetarian Meals   Children's Menu/Portions
█ Cheese █ █ Whisky █ *Children Allowed in Bar to Eat   Patio/terrace   Outdoor Eating*
Credit Cards: Access, Visa

UDNY GREEN Udny Green Hotel near Ellon. Good meals and snacks at
reasonable prices in a very pretty village; the hotel overlooks the green.

HIGHLAND

ACHILTIBUIE Am Fuaran: Welcoming but spartan Scots bar with views
towards Summer Isles; local seafood on specials board.

ACHILTIBUIE Summer Isles Hotel: This celebrated hotel also does bar meals
in its café at lunchtime. Extremely good. Down a 15 mile single track road, but
worth it.

APPLECROSS   Applecross Inn

Shore Street IV54 8LR
Tel: (05204) 262
Open: 11-2.30, 5-11 (12-2.30, 6-11 Sun); 11-11 daily Easter-Nov
Licensee: Judith Fish

In the word of the licensees, who've been here two years, Applecross is a "unique, mystical place"; it's certainly dramatic, reached via the Bealach na Ba, the highest mountain pass in Britain. Inspiring views of Skye. Inside, a staunchly traditional Scots inn, lots of photographs and memorabilia and a lively local atmosphere. Reliably good food, and the dinner menu's excellent value. Local lobsters, prawns, crabs, oysters and scallops arrive daily; booking essential. Beachside drinking.

Bar Meals: all day until 9 pm; bar snacks both sessions   **Restaurant:** *7-9*   **Typical Dishes BAR:** *vegetable soup £1.50, half pint prawns £4.75, sirloin steak garni £8.95, grilled wild salmon £5.95, queen scallops in sauce £5.25, blackcurrant and apple crumble* **RESTAURANT** *dinner menu £10.95: seafood soup, haggis in Drambuie, local lamb chops grilled in honey, crab and king prawns, squat lobster and queen scallops in cream sauce, raspberry cranachan   Vegetarian Meals: pasta bake   Children's Menu/Portions*   Whisky *Children Allowed in Bar to Eat   Outdoor Eating*   **Accommodation:** *5 bedrooms, sharing 2 bathrooms, from £30   Children Welcome Overnight   Cot Available   Check-in: all day* **No Credit Cards**

BEAULY   Priory Hotel

The Square IV4 7BX
Tel: (0463) 782309
Open: 11 (12.20 Sun)-11
Licensee: Stuart Hutton

Bustling, friendly local hotel in the main square, close to the ancient priory ruins. Restaurant meals similar to bar, at slightly higher prices.

Bar Meals and Restaurant: 12-2.15, 5.30-9 (9.30 restaurant); bar snacks both sessions **Typical Dishes BAR:** *home-made soup 75p, egg and prawns £2.50, roast rib of beef £4.25, deep-fried haddock £3.95, raspberry ice-cream £1.10 Vegetarian Meals: lasagne Children's Menu/Portions*   Whisky   *Family Room   Outdoor Play Area   Patio/terrace Outdoor Eating*   **Accommodation:** *24 bedrooms, all en suite, from £49.50 (single £31.50) Children Welcome Overnight   Cots Available' Check-in: all day*   **Credit Cards:** *Access, Amex, Diners, Visa*

CARRBRIDGE Dalrachney Lodge Hotel: Decent bar meals in cosy lounge with splendid fireplace.

CROMARTY   Royal Hotel

Marine Terrace IV11 8YN
Tel: (03817) 217
Open: 11 (12.30 Sun)-11
Licensee: Stewart Morrison

White harbourside hotel overlooking the Cromarty Firth and Ross-shire mountains. Bar food in lounge and bars, more formal meals in dining room. "Our girls are the best in the highlands", promises the shocking-pink, salmon-in-a-kilt-adorned menu. Individual menu prices not offered, but certainly not excessive. Bedrooms have views.

Bar Meals: 12-2, 5.30-9; *bar snacks both sessions* *Restaurant:* 12-2, 7-8.30 **Typical Dishes BAR:** *Scottish vegetable soup, mussel and onion stew, farmhouse pancake, whole local prawns Vegetarian Meals Children's Menu* **Whisky** *Family Room Outdoor Play Area Garden Outdoor Eating* **Accommodation:** *10 bedrooms, all en suite, from £45 (single £23.50) Children Welcome Overnight Cots Available Check-in: all day* **Credit Cards:** *Access, Amex, Visa*

DALWHINNIE Loch Ericht Hotel: Swedish lodge type modern hotel with decent bar food.

DULNAIN BRIDGE Muckrach Lodge Hotel Tel: (047 985) 257. Grilled wild salmon at just £4.50 features on the interesting bar menu at this popular hotel; good soups and puddings, and smarter restaurant; both daily lunch and evening. Children and vegetarians catered for. Bedrooms. Open: 11-3, 6-11 (12-2.30, 7-11 Sun).

GAIRLOCH Old Inn The Harbour Tel: (0445) 2006: Coaching inn in quiet glen with lovely views. Typically Scots, refurbished bar with copper-top tables, but more interesting bar meals, lunch and evening; vegetarian dishes, children's portions, family room, garden. Bedrooms. Belhaven, Tennents beers. Open all day and from 12.30 Sunday.

GLENCOE Clachaig Hotel Tel: (08552) 252. Remote walkers and climbers favourite, appropriately spartan but welcoming in style; lively folk evenings; routine bar meals. Family room; Youngers beers. Open all day.

GLENELG   Glenelg Inn

By Kyle of Lochalsh IV40 8AG
Tel: (059 982) 273
Open: Mon-Sat

Tucked away old beachside inn at the end of a gloriously scenic drive. Attractive old-fashioned interior and stylish restaurant,where the bar menu also applies at lunchtime. Afternoon teas until 4pm; no food October-Easter.

Bar Meals and Restaurant: 12.30-2, 7-8.30 (9 restaurant) **Typical Dishes BAR:** *tomato and orange soup £1.10, paté with cognac £1.75, tandoori chicken £4, beef goulash £4, sweet and sour pork £4, chocolate mousse £1.25* **RESTAURANT** *dinner menu £17.50: all local produce Vegetarian Meals: risotto Children's Menu/Portions* **Whisky** *Children Allowed in Bar to Eat Outdoor Play Area Garden Outdoor Eating Summer Barbecue* **Accommodation** *(closed Oct-Easter): 6 bedrooms, all en suite, from £40 (single £25) Children Welcome Overnight Cot Available Check-in: all day* **Credit Cards:** *Access, Visa*

GLENFINNAN   Stage House

on A830 PH37 4LT
Tel: (0397) 83246
Open: all day; closed Jan-March
Licensee: R Hawkes

Recommended in our last edition for its bed and breakfast accommodation, the Stage House has since changed hands; bar meals under the new regime feature fresh local produce. It's a prettily set late 17th century pub alongside the main road near Loch Shiel (where it has extensive fishing rights and several boats).

Bar Meals: 12-2.30, 5-6.30; *bar snacks lunchtime* *Restaurant:* 6.30-8.30 **Typical Dishes BAR:** *chicken broth £1.09, prawn cocktail £2.85, lamb cutlets £4.75, chilli con carne £4.90, langoustines £5.25, apple pie £1.75* **RESTAURANT:** *stilton and onion soup £2.60, goat's cheese £3.25, duckling £11.75, steak £11.45, salmon £11.75, carrot cake*

£2.95   *Vegetarian Meals: mushroom stroganoff*   *Children's Menu/Portions*   `Beer`   *Ind Coope Burton Ale*   `Whisky`   *Children Allowed in Bar to Eat*   *Patio/terrace* **Accommodation** *(closed Jan-March): 9 bedrooms, all en suite, from £51 (single £25.50)*   *Children Welcome Overnight (minimum age 5)*   *Check-in: all day*   **Credit Cards:** *Access, Visa*

INVERMORISTON   Glenmoriston Arms Hotel

near Inverness IV3 6YA   ♥
Tel: (0320) 51206
Open: 11 (12.30 Sun)-11
Licensee: Alan Draper

Pleasant white-painted hotel in an attractive spot on the A82 by Loch Ness. The public bar, the 'Glenmoriston Tavern', is a rather spartan brown room – as is the hotel dining room, though huntin', shootin' and fishin' paraphernalia cheer up some of the public areas. A huge selection of malts. Bedrooms are modern and light, well-kept rather than stylish.

Bar Meals: *12-2.15, 5.30-9; bar snacks both sessions*   **Restaurant:** *12-2, 6.30-8.30* **Typical Dishes BAR:** *carrot and turnip soup £1.20, chicken liver paté £1.55, home-made chicken and mushroom pie £4, chilli con carne £3.30, home-made lasagne £3.70, Scots trifle £1.60*   **RESTAURANT:** *leek and potato soup £1.55, haggis with whisky and chive sauce £2.50, sautéed guinea fowl in lobster and pink peppercorn sauce £9.75, fillet steak £10.75, sole and fresh salmon in orange herb butter £8.95*   *Vegetarian Meals: filo pastry tartlet with vegetables £3.60*   *Children's Portions*   `Cheese`   `Beer`   *McEwan 80/-*   `Whisky`   *Garden*   *Outdoor Eating*   **Accommodation** *(closed Jan/Feb): 8 bedrooms, all en suite, from £45 (single £29)*   *Children Welcome Overnight*   *Cots Available*   *Check-in: all day*   **Credit Cards:** *Access, Visa*

INVERNESS   Coach House Inn

Stoneyfield, Nairn Road IV1 2PA
Tel: (0463) 230244
Open: all day
Licensee: A Torrance

Solid white-painted inn near Culloden Field. It's changed hands since our last edition, in which we recommended the bed and breakfast. Modernised but attractive bars: the simple but incongruously carpeted Ostlers (public), and hotelly, armchair-filled Lairdshall Lounge. Nice views from the terrace.

Bar Meals: *12-2, 5-9; bar snacks all day*   **Typical Dishes:** *home-made soup £1.05, fishermans delight £2.75, pork chop en croute £4.75, poachers pie £4.25, deep-fried haddock £4.75*   *Vegetarian Meals: lasagne*   *Children's Menu/Portions*   `Whisky`   *Family Room*   *Outdoor Play Area*   *Patio/terrace*   *Outdoor Eating*   *Summer Barbecue* **Accommodation:** *5 bedrooms, all en suite, from £40 (single £27.50)*   *Children Welcome Overnight*   *Cots Available*   *Check-in: all day*   **Credit Cards:** *Access, Visa*

INVERNESS   Glen Mhor Hotel

Ness Bank IV2 4SG
Tel: (0463) 234308
Open: 11-2.30, 5-11 (all day Sat, 12.30-11 Sun)

Modernised hotel of great contrasts. Atmospheric, unspoilt Nicky Tams bar, and garish pizzaland style Nico's Bar. Comfortable rather than stylish bedrooms. Bar food has its fans though.

Bar Meals: 12-2, 5-9.30; bar snacks both sessions   *Restaurant:* 12.30-2 Sun only, 6.30-9.30   *Typical Dishes BAR:* Scotch broth £1, marinated Kessock herring £2.15, venison casserole £5.25, lasagne with gorgonzola £4.85, Arbroath smokies £5.30, sherry trifle £2.25   *RESTAURANT:* haggis in filo £3.75, gravadlax of wild salmon £6.65, Lisbon-style fillet steak £14.75, a purse of chicken breast £8.50, rendezvous of seafood £13.95, fresh lime soufflé £3.50   Vegetarian Meals: bean and vegetable casserole £3.85 Children's Menu/Portions   **Beer** Caledonian; Ind Coope Burton Ale **Whisky** Children Allowed in Bar to Eat   Patio/terrace   Outdoor Eating   *Accommodation:* 30 bedrooms, all en suite, from £60 (single £50)   Children Welcome Overnight   Cots Available   Check-in: all day   *Credit Cards:* Access, Amex, Diners, Visa

---

KYLESKU   Kylesku Hotel

Kylesku IV27 4HW
Tel: (0971) 2231
Open: 11-2.30, 5-11
Licensee: Marcel Klein

On the south side of the old ferry crossing, close to the spectacular new bridge, the Kylesku, more inn than hotel, has marvellous views of mountain and water, and is close to deserted beaches. Guaranteed peace.

Bar Meals: 12-2.15, 6-9; bar snacks both sessions   *Restaurant:* 7-9   *Typical Dishes BAR:* chicken and tarragon soup £1.75, baked mussels and prawns £2.50, chicken tikka £5.60, grilled salmon in lobster sauce £5.60, grilled langoustines £5.95 Restaurant dinner menu £15: smoked salmon soup, venison terrine, steak Café de Paris, lobster thermidor, salmon in puff pastry with beurre blanc   Vegetarian Meals: avocado and orange salad Children's Portions   **Whisky** Children Allowed in Bar to Eat   Lochside Patio/terrace Outdoor Eating   *Accommodation* (closed Dec-end April, apart from weekends): 7 bedrooms, sharing 2 bathrooms (3 showers), from £35 (single £18)   Children Welcome Overnight Cot Available   Check-in: all day   *Credit Cards:* Access, Visa

LAIRG Crask Inn on A836: In fact 13 miles north of Lairg, a quiet, unspoilt, refurbished inn with a log fire and local seafood in season.

LEWISTON   Lewiston Arms Hotel

Drumnadrochit IV3 6UN
Tel: (04562) 225
Open: 11-2.30, 5-11 (1 am Thur/Fri); all day Sat, 12.30-11 Sun
Licensee: N J Quinn

All bedrooms are now en suite at this homely old inn; half are in an adjoining converted farmhouse. The spacious, relaxing interior has a comfortable lounge bar and residents lounge.

Bar Meals: 12.30-2.30, 6.30-8; bar snacks lunchtime   *Restaurant:* 7-9   *Typical Dishes BAR:* Scotch broth £1, home-made paté £3, chicken, ham and leek pie £3.50, lasagne £3.50, lemon meringue pie £1.25   *RESTAURANT:* smoked salmon £4, roast Scotch beef £6.50, pan-fried sirloin steak £8.50, fresh salmon steak £7, harvest crumble slice £1.75 Vegetarian Meals (bar): broccoli and brie parcels £6   Children's Portions **Cheese** Outdoor Play Area   Garden   Outdoor Eating   *Accommodation:* 9 bedrooms, all en suite, from £45 (single £22.50)   Children Welcome Overnight   Cot Available Check-in: all day   *Credit Cards:* Visa

LYBSTER Portland Arms Hotel Tel: (05932) 208. Modernised old hotel with good value bedrooms (£45 en suite double), and decent bar and restaurant meals, with pleasing use of local game and Thurso salmon in season. Family room, patio, no real ales.

MUIR OF ORD   Ord House Hotel

Muir of Ord IV6 7UH   ▼
Tel: (0463) 870492
Licensee: John Allen

Charming country house hotel dating from 1602 in grounds of 25 acres. Nice
bedrooms with antique furniture and garden views. They grow their own
vegetables.

*Bar Meals: 12.30-2; bar snacks   Restaurant: 7.30-9   Typical Dishes BAR: smoked
chicken soup £1.65, smoked salmon paté £4.05, steak and kidney pie £3.95, shepherds pie
£3.75, chicken and bacon lasagne £3.95, chocolate mousse £3.05   RESTAURANT:
asparagus soup £2.50, gruyère salad roulade £3.50, char-grilled venison steak £11.15,
roast breast of duck £11.20, salmon in whisky and mushroom sauce £10.90, raspberry
millefeuille £3.45   Vegetarian Meals: tagliatelle carbonara   Children's Portions* Cheese
Whisky   *Family Room   Outdoor Play Area   Garden   Outdoor Eating
Accommodation (closed mid Oct-end April): 12 bedrooms, all en suite, from £54 (single
£30)   Children Welcome Overnight   Cots Available   Check-in: all day   Credit Cards:
Access, Amex, Visa*

NAIRN   Clifton House

Viewfield Street IV12 4HW   ▼
Tel: (0667) 53119
Open: 11.30-2.30, 6-11

Extraordinary, some would say eccentric Victorian hotel, its whole interior an
extended objet d'art, with exquisite furniture, ceramics, pictures, opulent colours
and fabrics. Not a pub of course, but they do offer light bar lunches to non-
residents.

*Bar Meals: 12-2; bar snacks both sessions   Restaurant: 7.30-9.30   Typical Dishes
BAR: home-made soup £1.50, chicken salad £5.50, omelette £5   Vegetarian Meals:
cashew nut stew* Cheese Whisky *Family Room   Garden   Accommodation (closed
mid-Dec to mid-Jan): 16 bedrooms, all en suite, from £91 (single £54)   Children Welcome
Overnight   Check-in: all day   Credit Cards: Access, Amex, Diners, Visa*

PLOCKTON Plockton Hotel Tel: (059 984) 250. Attractive, friendly inn at the
centre of a glorious coastal village, complete with gulf stream palm trees along the
shore. Routine bar food includes exquisite local seafood. McEwans beers.
Bedrooms. Open: 11-2.30, 5-12.

SHEILDAIGH   Tigh an Eilean

By Strathcarron IV54 8XN
Tel: (05205) 251
Open: 11-2.30, 5-11 (all day summer)
Licensee: Elizabeth Stewart

Beautifully set at the head of the loch, with soothing views and stunning sunsets.
Spartan locals' public bar, but homely and comfortable residents lounges; routine bar
food is enlivened by home-made pies, fresh salmon and local game (low prices),
when available. Ask for a front bedroom – a room with a view.

*Bar Meals: 12-2 (2.15 summer and Sun), 6-8 (8.30 summer;no food Sun eve)
Restaurant: 7-8.30   Vegetarian Meals: lasagne   Childrens Portions   Children Allowed
in Bar to Eat   Accommodation (closed late October – Easter): 12 bedrooms, sharing*

*4 bathrooms, from £54.70 (single £28.50)   Children Welcome Overnight   Cot Available
Check-in: after 2pm   **Credit Cards:** Access, Visa*

SPEAN BRIDGE   Letterfinlay Lodge Hotel

7 miles north of Spean Bridge PH34 4DZ
Tel: (039 781) 622
Open: 11 am-midnight (11.30-11.30 Sun); closed mid Nov-mid Feb
Licensee: Ian Forsyth

Sturdy 19th century hotel, overlooking Loch Lochy, seven miles north of Spean
Bridge. Run by the Forsyth family for well over 25 years. Comfortable bar with
banknote-adorned beams, good views from the sun lounge. Modestly furnished
bedrooms, some compact and modern, others old and spacious. Public bathrooms
have original Victorian fittings.

Bar Meals: *12-2.30; bar snacks* **Restaurant:** *7-9* **Typical Dishes BAR:** *home-made
soup £1.30, roast sirloin of Aberdeen Angus beef £4.25, sirloin steak £8.75, poached wild
salmon salad £5.50, home-made apple tart £1.75   Vegetarian Meals: nut roast £3.25
Children's Menu/Portions* Whisky *Family Room   Outdoor Play Area* **Accommodation**
*(closed mid Nov-mid Feb): 13 bedrooms, 9 en suite, from £53 (single £26.50)   Children
Welcome Overnight   Cots Available   Check-in: all day* **Credit Cards:** *Access, Amex,
Diners, Visa*

TAIN   Morangie House Hotel

Morangie Road IV19 1PY
Tel: (0862) 892281
Open: 12.15-2.30, 5-10.30 (12.30-2.30, 6-10.30 Sun)
Licensee: John Wynne

Civilised 19th century mansion house hotel with nice bar and pretty, light dining
room; very popular with Ross-shire eaters out.

Bar Meals: *12.15-2.30, 5-9.30; bar snacks both sessions* **Restaurant:** *12.30-2, 7-9.30*
Typical Dishes BAR: *cock a leekie soup £1.50, home-made paté £1.80, home-made
steak pie £4.20, roast sirloin of Ross-shire beef £4.70, grilled salmon steak £4.40, apple
and sultana pie £1.80* **RESTAURANT:** *mussel and onion stew £2.40, avocado
Singapore £3.80, tournedos Rossini £9.50, coquilles St Jacques £7.90, lobster thermidor
£16, cranachan with Drambuie £2.80   Vegetarian Meals: vegetarian lasagne   Children's
Menu/Portions* Beer *McEwan* Whisky *Family Room* **Accommodation:** *13
bedrooms, all en suite, from £60 (single £35)   Children Welcome Overnight   Cots
Available   Check-in: all day* **Credit Cards:** *Access, Amex, Diners, Visa*

ULLAPOOL   Ceilidh Place

West Argyle Street IV26 2TY
Tel: (0854) 612103
Open: 11-11 (12.30-2.30, 6.30-11 Sun)
Licensee: Jean Urquart

Celebrated northern community centre, which started as a coffee shop, and, like
Topsy, just growed. Extremely informal and friendly; live music, exhibition space,
and smart "ally carte". Unique.

Bar Meals: *all day until 7 pm; bar snacks lunchtime* **Restaurant:** *7-9* **Typical Dishes
BAR:** *home-made soup £1.20, stovies £2.50, roulades £4, haggis pie £3.75, curries*

£3.75, fish and chips £3.85   **RESTAURANT** dinner menu £17.50, or à la carte: venison £12.50, pan-fried salmon £12.50, prawns provencale £14   Vegetarian Meals: vegetarian stew and dumplings £3.50   Children's Portions   Children Allowed in Bar to Eat   Outdoor Play Area   Patio/terrace   Outdoor Eating   **Accommodation** (closed 8-22 Jan): 15 bedrooms, 8 en suite, from £56 (single £30)   Children Welcome Overnight   Cots Available   Check-in: all day   **Credit Cards:** Access, Amex, Diners, Visa

---

ULLAPOOL   Morefield Motel

North Road IV26 2TH   `FOOD`
Tel: (0854) 612161
Licensee: David Smyrl

Most of the specials at the Morefield, on one particular evening visit, appeared to involve scallops in some form or another; it's the week's recurrent leitmotif. There are sound reasons for what in other contexts might be labelled repetitive: they're very much dependent on what's in season and in the catch at this remote north western venue. There are personal reasons for the scallop's pre-eminence here too: the co-owners, including resident licensee, David Smyrl, were previously skippers of a pair of fishing and diving boats, scallop hunters par excellence, who diversified into activity holidays and ploughed all their profits into buying the Morefield Motel. That was 10 years ago, and their expertise has built an international reputation for genuinely sea-fresh fish and seafood. A sneaky glimpse of the visitors' book reveals fan messages from all over the world, but particularly Germany, for some reason - and it's especially revealing that so many of their remarks declare (in a tone of some astonishment) that they were unable to finish their meal. Portion control is a foreign language up here; when something's in season, it's generally piled high, and the seafood platter is particularly unfinishable (£32.50 for two in the restaurant; £14 each in the bar), to the point of notoriety. Aside from the Steak Plaice restaurant (vile name, fab food, and booking essential in summer), you can eat in the lounge bar or beer garden, and enjoy superb bar food at value for money prices. The printed broadsheet menu offers meat and fish in about equal proportions – this may be the king of seafood bars, but the Aberdeen Angus steaks are also praiseworthy – perhaps a venison bourguignon, beef stroganoff, or double lamb cutlet (£5-£7), or one of five sorts of steak, plain or well sauced. The strong fish list ranges from simple, fresh fried haddock (£4.40) to a whole lobster, from a vast dish of mussels to a homely haddock and cheese bake. House wine by the carafe keeps things nicely informal. This is a pub-hotel to visit for its food, and its glorious situation, on the shore of Loch Broom, but decidedly not for a quaintly romantic old-fashioned getaway. It's a rather starkly modern building, aptly named Motel, its bedrooms rather masculine and functional in style.

Bar Meals: 12-2, 5.30-9.30; bar snacks lunchtime   **Restaurant:** 6-9.15   **Typical Dishes BAR:** West Coast mussels £2.50, home-made chicken liver paté £1.95, Ross-shire steak pie £4.50, salmon with local prawn tails £8.75, monkfish kebabs £6.95, whole orange sorbet £1.95   **RESTAURANT:** haggis fritters £2.25, garlic local prawns £4.95, carpetbagger: Aberdeen Angus steak with scallops £14.50, halibut mornay £10.50, baked whole Lochinver sole £8.25, home-made puddings from £2   Vegetarian Meals: mushroom and aubergine bake   Children's Menu/Portions   `Whisky`   Family Room   Outdoor Play Area   Patio/terrace   Outdoor Eating   **Accommodation** (closed Nov-March): 11 bedrooms, all en suite, from £40 (single £25)   Children Welcome Overnight   Cots Available   Check-in: all day   **Credit Cards:** Access, Amex, Visa

WICK Rosebank Hotel: ordinary public drinking bars, but more interesting for fresh fish on the menu.

LOTHIAN

BLACKNESS Blackness Inn The Square Tel: (0506) 834252. Waterside inn close to the castle; good fresh fried haddock and chips, and other plain dishes; their own raspberries in summer. Children welcome; garden; bedrooms. Arrols beer.

CRAMOND   Cramond Inn

Cramond Glebe Road EH4 6NU
Tel: (031) 336 2035
Open: 11-2.30, 5-11 (all day Sat)
Licensee: Andrew Dobson

Popular old pub at the heart of a delightful village by the Firth of Forth, busy with Edinburghers at weekends; there are good walks along the shore in both directions, and the labrador count is high in all weathers. The pub itself is attractively modernised, with fairly routine bar meals of the lasagne/chilli sort (from £3), and more interesting restaurant menu, with dishes like chicken in red wine casserole, and good puddings.

Bar Meals: 12-2.15, 6-9.30 (12.30-2, 6-9 Sun) *Restaurant:* 12-1.45, 7-9.30 (not Sun eve) Beer *Caledonian; Marston; Thwaites Children Allowed in Bar to Eat Patio/terrace **Credit Cards:** Access, Visa*

DIRLETON Castle Inn off A198 Tel: (062 085) 221: Village green local opposite castle ruins. Bar with games room leading off; decent home-cooked lunches; real fire; no music. Open: 11–2.30, 5–11 (12.30–2.30, 6.30–11 Sun).

DIRLETON Open Arms: Tel: (062 085) 241: Smart pub with ambitious menu and expensive bedrooms.

EDINBURGH   Doric Tavern

Market Street
Tel: (031) 225 1084
Open: all day from noon; closed Sun
Licensee: Mr Voss

Wine bar style upstairs, particularly as the first encounter is with the little bistro-style eating area; the separate little bar is at the back, often crammed with students and other trendy types. But there's no mistaking it's a pub downstairs, in the spartan public bar, complete with dartboard by the door (watch out when entering). Snacks are available in the cosy, packed little drinking area upstairs, but the main emphasis is on the bistro; not-at-all-bad food, if a little overpriced (go for the set menu); service can be casual; interesting wine list. Tremendous atmosphere in the evenings, though, with its atmospheric deep reds and blues, and candlelight; looks a little scruffy in daylight.

Bar Snacks: all day *Restaurant:* 12-2.30, 6-10.30 *BAR SNACKS:* aubergine caviar £2.95, smoked salmon £4.25 *RESTAURANT:* £13.50 set menu (£9.50 lunch): mussels provencale, haggis with neeps and tatties, scallops in bacon and vermouth, crème caramel Vegetarian Meals Beer Bass; Caledonian; Maclays; McEwans Whisky **Credit Cards:** Access, Amex, Visa*

EDINBURGH   Fishers

1 The Shore, Leith   `FOOD`
Tel: (031) 554 5666   ❢
Open: 11 am-1 am (12.30 pm-1 am Sun)
Licensee: Jane McCrone

Fishers is a jewel cast up from the sea, an outstanding new seafood - speciality bar which serves full meals all day, noon-10.30 pm. Even in an area of previous neglect and notoriety like Leith, where trendy seafood bars are now becoming somewhat commonplace, this is an outstanding new arrival, opened in summer 1991. It's taken root in a renovated corner building at the end of The Shore, at the foot of what looks like an ancient bell-tower or lighthouse. The bar area, in which you can also eat, groups high stools around higher-still tables. Up a short flight of steps, the main eating area features light-wood panelling with night-sky blue tables and chairs, windows half of frosted glass, half giving a view to the harbour and beyond, and all presided over from a great height by a bejewelled mermaid figure. The pricing structure and the variety of food on offer are admirably suited to most appetites and pockets, whether for serious eating or quick snacking. It's worth going the full three rounds from starter to pudding, and make an evening of it, when it's also wise to book; word is spreading. In addition to the photocopied-handwritten menu, a blackboard of daily specials offers a host of starters and main courses which should appeal to more than fish fans alone: perhaps a fine piece of roast beef with shallot gravy (£5.50). The creamiest, most deeply delicious salmon soup (small £1.70, large £2.20) competes for attention with fish patés and oatcakes (£2.60), mussels in white wine, garlic, tomato and herbs (£2.50/£3.60), or one of the day's specials, a sheep's cheese and olive salad (£2.80). A large basket of brown and white baguette accompanies, and fresh butter comes in individual pots. The fish comes big. A whole lemon sole (£6.40) in a creamy sauce filled a whole platter, with little room left for the smooth and perfect new potatoes which came piled high in a separate bowl, garnished with mint. Salads are crunchy, fresh and in plenty – endive, Chinese leaves, tomatoes, radishes, mange-touts and spring onions. Choose your dressing from a piquant selection of onion, hazelnut or raspberry vinaigrettes, or mix your own combination from the bottles of Spanish olive oil and French champagne vinegar thoughtfully provided on each table. If any room remains, clean and simple desserts follow – fresh fruit salad with cream or yoghurt, or various popular local-brand ice-creams. Altogether excellent quality and value for money.

Bar Meals and Restaurant: 12 noon-10.30; bar snacks **Typical Dishes:** *Fishers'*
seafood soup, herring in dill and cucumber, lobster with pink champagne cream, monkfish tarts
with tomato and basil, grilled halibut with sour cream and chives, lemon meringue pie
Vegetarian Meals: harvest pie *Children's Menu/Portions* `Cheese` `Beer` *Caledonian*
80/-, IPA *Riverside* *Outdoor Eating* **Credit Cards:** *Access, Amex, Visa*

EDINBURGH   Magnum

Albany Street EH1 3PY   `FOOD`
Tel: (031) 557 4366

The Magnum disproves the warning that you shouldn't mix business with pleasure. In the heart of the city's business and law office district, and so discreet a venue as to be almost invisible, its intimate atmosphere is highly conducive to lunchtime entertaining, a private bit of gossip, or simply unwinding after work. In its dark-wood interior, an occasional spotlight highlights the high polish of tables, a glitter of gold lettering on a frieze around the walls names famous malts, stuffed pheasants stand mournfully to attention, and prints depicting glories of days gone by complete the genteel atmosphere. The bar itself curves between two adjoining rooms; drink and eat in either, or up a few steps in the dining area proper, as intimate and sophisticated a venue as any city restaurant. Book a table and this is where you are likely to dine, with candlelight and fresh flowers, and by floor to ceiling windows which look out onto one of the quieter corners of Edinburgh's New Town. The same full menu is offered both at lunch and in the evening. It's the details which turn a meal in the Magnum into an occasion and make it such a pleasant place to eat – new napkins at almost every course, flowers on every table, attentive staff, clean and polished tables, a blessed freedom from muzak, and well-presented food. Try the meltingly-soft chef's paté (£2) or the rich leek and potato soup (£1.35). Vegetarian and fish options are also tasty – deep-fried courgette (£3.60), tuna-fish pie (£4.75), seafood platter (£8.25), and roast joints of meat are a regular daily feature. Accompanying vegetables retain all their taste and bite. Alternatively, pop in just for sandwiches (£1.25) and coffee (85p). It tends to be busiest at lunchtime during the week and after 5 pm on a Friday.

EDINBURGH   Stockbridge Bar

44 St Stephens Street EH3 5AL   ❢
Tel: (031) 220 3774
Open: 11 am-12.30pm (10.30 am-11pm Sun)
Licensee: Michael Judge

A well-known pub in a trendy part of town which, on Sunday mornings, becomes a bolt-hole for morning-after blues and can usually provide a friendly opinion on the day's rugby and golfing prospects. The two-part eating area sits 18 comfortably in appropriately relaxed surroundings. Don't be put off by the numerous framed rugby pictures decorating the walls: scrumming is only necessary for the bar stools. Service is casual but prompt, and ever-respectful of the sanctity of your Sunday paper. This is a place for big, filling breakfasts: the full, traditional line-up of bacon, eggs, sausages, beans, black pudding and potato scones, all remarkably low on the grease and black bits so often expected from a good fry-up. Practically everything on the menu (even the toast and marmalade) could be prefixed with "mansize" and is, at £3.75, including tea or coffee, exceedingly good value for money.

Bar Meals: 12-2.30 (10.30-1.30 Sun brunch); bar snacks **Typical Dishes:** *Scotch broth 75p, mushrooms on toast 95p, home-made steak pie £3.20, lamb chop hotpot £2.95, chicken or beef curry £2.95, apple crumble 95p Vegetarian Meals: vegetable lasagne £2.95 Children's Portions* **Beer** *Caledonian; McEwan; Taylors* **Whisky** *Children Allowed in Bar to Eat* **No Credit Cards**

EDINBURGH   Tattler

23 Commercial Street, Leith EH6 6JA   **FOOD**
Tel: (031) 554 9999
Open: 11-11 (12 Fri/Sat); 12.30-11 Sun
Licensee: Linda Thomson

To step into the Tattler is to step several decades back into the subdued splendour of Scottish Victoriana – fringed table lamps, some of smoked glass, a bird cage in the window, green velvet bar stools, a chaise longue by the bar and, most charming of all, attentive and old-fashioned courtesy from the bar staff. The bar is popular itself – a gentlemanly local for unhurried chat – but most come to eat. The main room divides into three zones, the area by the bar, a snug to one side, and another level, up a few steps, plus a separate parlour at the back which opens when things get busy. The Tattler restaurant, another creature altogether, is reached through the snug and has a different menu, though there are a few overlaps. Music is speakeasy 1920s, with live piano some evenings. The walls are adorned with humorous antique prints and an intricately-carved dark wood fireplace with inset tiles completes the picture, only to be spoilt by incongruous Tennents salt and pepper pots on each table. A mulligatawny soup (90p) was flavoursome but not fiery, with lentils and vegetables coming through; a portion of paté (£1.95) rich and smooth. The main course list strikes a good balance between fish and meat dishes. A Dunbar crab salad (£3.95) was on offer alongside the more exotic grilled swordfish steak (£4.25), but the more homely seafood haddie (£4.25) is an enduring favourite, combining smoked haddock and prawns in an egg and cheese cream sauce topped with piping-hot potato. Portions are generous. Likewise, a doorstep-thick braised pork chop à l'orange (£4.25) assumed hunger of a serious kind, and came with huge helpings of potatoes and salad. Little room left to indulge the huge coupes of ice-cream (£2.95). Blackboard specials change daily; it's a pity that, unlike other Leith pioneers, they refuse to offer main courses also in starter sizes. But this is to nit-pick. It's truly first-class value for money: an opportunity to over-indulge without overspending.

Bar Meals and Restaurant: 12-2.30, 6-10; bar snacks both sessions   *Typical Dishes* BAR: *home-made soup 90p, Orkney herring fillets £2.25, spare ribs £4.25, spicy beef casserole £4.25, savoury haddock crumble £3.75, apple tart £1.95* RESTAURANT: *Dunsyre blue cheese croquettes £4.25, Lothian lamb rosettes £8.25, half roast duck New Orleans £8.50, grilled Scotch salmon £7.95, fresh fruit flan £1.95* Vegetarian Meals: *crispy fried vegetables Indienne £3.75* Children's Portions [Beer] *Draught Bass; Caledonian 70/- Family Room* Credit Cards: *Access, Amex, Diners, Visa*

EDINBURGH   Waterfront Wine Bar

Dock Place, Leith EH6 6LU   [FOOD]
Tel: (031) 554 7427   ❢
Open: 12-11 (midnight Fri/Sat); 12.30-4.30 Sun
Licensee: Ian Ruthven

The Waterfront's plain, red-brick exterior gives little indication of what lies within – this is one of Edinburgh's favourite food and drink spots. By the entrance there are wooden seats, some under a large sail, and at the bar a huge blackboard listing dozens of wines served by the glass, as well as unusual beers. Through the first doorway is a low-ceilinged room lit by low lamps, nautical maps and wine-crate panels doubling as wallpaper. Further back, the romantically-sited conservatory ("always fully booked") is attractively overhung by a growing vine, and looks out over the water; beyond this, a narrow "gangplank" seats a few brave summer tipplers. Service is casual but friendly, waiters often identifiable only by the speed at which they move; music is low and classical. Ashtrays are changed with unfailing regularity. There are no fixed or printed menus, and the dishes of the day are all listed on a blackboard. The fish soup (£1.50) is rich and creamy with plenty of chunky bread; chicken wings with coconut and lemon sauce (£2.60) tangy and up to expectations, with lots of colourful side salad and a fine vinaigrette, and Polish stuffed cabbage with caraway sauce (£2.60) makes a substantial starter in winter weather. A piece of wild salmon (£8), firm but yielding, is perfectly balanced by its tarragon sauce, while pan-fried duck breast with cherry sauce (£7.80) has a fine bitter edge. To finish, a raspberry cheesecake (£2), bearing little relation to the usual pub pudding of that name, somehow contrives to be both intensely fruity and light. Coffee is fresh and good, although surprisingly they don't offer cappuccino. Book well in advance for a weekend evening.

Bar Meals: 12-2.30, 6-9.30 (12-3, 6-10 Fri/Sat)   *Typical Dishes:* beef and tomato broth £1.30, baby squid stuffed with samphire mousseline £2.80, fillet of mackerel with ginger sauce £5, aubergine, sweet pepper and mozzarella filo bake £4.50, poached local seatrout with sorrel mayonnaise £6, fresh local raspberry cheesecake £2 Vegetarian Meals: *melanzane parmigiano £4.50* [Cheese] [Beer] *Caledonian* [Whisky] *Children Allowed in Bar to Eat (minimum age 5) Riverside Patio/terrace Outdoor Eating* **Credit Cards:** *Access, Visa*

GIFFORD   Tweeddale Arms

High Street
Tel: (062 081) 240
Open: 11.30-11 (midnight Fri/Sat)
Licensee: Chris Crook

Civilised, prettily set old white-painted inn, modernised and loungey, with a particularly splendid hotel sitting room. Bar meals are of the scampi/steak and kidney pie sort, though there are also more appetising daily specials (around £4.50), and cold poached salmon. Home made puddings. The elegant dining room has a smarter evening menu.

Bar Meals: lunchtime daily Vegetarian Meals   Childrens Portions ▮ Beer ▮ *McEwan 80/-Family Room* **Accommodation:** *Bedrooms, all en suite, from £60   Children Welcome Overnight   Cots Available Check in: by arrangement*

GIFFORD Goblin Ha': Large and popular local, friendly and well-run. Simple but genuine home cooking. Boules.

HOWGATE Old Howgate Inn Tel: (0968) 74244. Choose from an appetising and comprehensive selection of Danish open sandwiches in the bar, or opt for the dining room menu: a wide selection, from haggis in malt whisky and onion sauce to beef stroganoff; main courses from around £7. Wood-panelled, dimly-lit lounge; bright, large dining room; families catered for. Belhaven, Taylor beers. Garden. Open: 11-2.30, 5-12 (all day Sat).

LINLITHGOW   Four Marys

65 High Street EH49 7ED   ▮
Tel: (0506) 842171
Open: 12-2.30, 5-11 (all day Sat; 12.30-2.30, 7-11 Sun)
Licensee: Gordon Scott

High street old coaching inn near the famous palace where Mary Queen of Scots was born; the bars are full of Mary-obilia. Handsomely refurbished lounge, waitress-served bar food.

Bar Meals: 12-2, 6-9 **Typical Dishes:** *spinach soup 90p, paté £2.35, beef goulash £4, chicken basquaise £4.35, haggis and neeps £3   Vegetarian Meals: baked avocado £3.75 Children's Portions* ▮ Beer ▮ *Belhaven; Fullers; Harviestoun; Mitchells* ▮ Whisky ▮ *Family Room* **Credit Cards:** *Access, Amex, Visa*

QUEENSFERRY Morrings Inn, Hopetoun Road: Forth Bridge views and popular home cooked lunches. Family room.

RATHO   Bridge Inn

27 Baird Road EH28 8RA   ▮
Tel: (031) 333 1320
Open: 11-10.30 (12 Fri)
Licensee: Ronnie Rusack

Part of the Edinburgh Canal Centre, which also features two canalboat restaurants. A well-run, popular, family-oriented pub, winner of awards for its child facilities; also disabled-friendly premises. Huge variety of play equipment includes a putting green. Food's not bad either.

Bar Meals: 12-2, 6.30-9 (8 Sun); 12-9.30 summer; bar snacks both sessions
Restaurant: 12-2, 7-9 **Typical Dishes BAR:** *home-made chicken liver paté with brandy*

£2.30, melon with strawberries and mint £2.30, char-grilled home-made beefburger £4.35, home-made steak and mushroom pie £5.05, Loch Inver salmon and broccoli pie £4.35, apple, sultana and cinnamon pie £2.30 **RESTAURANT:** *wood-smoked Tweed salmon, crispy butterfly prawns £3.60, venison in whisky and port wine £10.75, steak Diane with Drambuie £12, Port Seton sole and scampi £10.15, cranachan £2.80* **Vegetarian Meals:** *savoury stuffed pancakes £6.90* **Children's Menu/Portions** `Beer` *Belhaven 80/- Family Room   Outdoor Play Area   Canalside Patio/terrace   Outdoor Eating   Summer Barbecue* **Credit Cards:** *Access, Amex, Diners, Visa*

WEST BARNS Battleblent Hotel. Converted country house set back from the A6094; small public bar on ground floor to the rear, leading into tiny dining area. Printed menu enlivened by good home made specials, perhaps chicken casserole (£3.95); decent steak and chips; home made apple pie. Also hotel restaurant. They cater for tourists, as their cartoon kilted highlander motif suggests. Belhaven beers. Open: 11.30-2.30, 5-11.

STRATHCLYDE

AIRDRIE   Staging Post

8/10 Anderson Street ML6 0AA
Tel: (0236) 67525
Licensee: David Barr

There are not many places to stay in Airdrie, so the Staging Post, in a quiet street near the centre, definitely has its uses. The accent is on convenience rather than luxury, bedrooms being on the small side, but there is room for an easy chair and a good-sized wardrobe, and there are shower rooms in all but two. The lounge bar has more appeal than the rather down-at-heel Highwayman Bar. No real ale.

Bar Meals: *lunch and evening   Childrens Menu* **Accommodation:** *9 bedrooms, 7 with shower, from £45   Children Welcome Overnight   Check-in: all day* **Credit Cards:** *Access, Amex, Diners, Visa*

ARDENTINNY   Ardentinny Hotel

Loch Long, near Dunoon PA23 8TR   ♥
Tel: (036 981) 209
Open: all day March-Nov
Licensee: John Horn

Old west coast droving inn by Loch Long in the Argyll Forest Park. Buttery, two popular public bars with loch views, and hotel dining room. Lots of local produce, particularly strong on venison and seafood. Good wine list. Popular with Clyde yachtsmen at weekends.

Bar Meals: *12-2.30, 6.30-9.30; bar snacks lunchtime* **Restaurant:** *7.30-9* **Typical Dishes BAR:** *orange and carrot soup £1.50, mussels £3.75, venison sausage £3.75, Musselburgh pie £6.25, prawn-stuffed croissant £4.75, bread and butter pudding £1.55* **RESTAURANT** *set menu £17.95: seafood bisque, crab cakes, pheasant Loch Eil, wild salmon, lobster thermidor, Highland bonnet* **Vegetarian Meals:** *lasagne* **Children's Menu/Portions** `Whisky` *Children Allowed in Bar to Eat   Outdoor Play Area   Seaside Garden   Outdoor Eating* **Accommodation** *(closed 1 Nov-14 Mar): 11 bedrooms, all en suite, from £40 (single £20)   Children Welcome Overnight   Cots Available   Check-in: all day* **Credit Cards:** *Access, Amex, Diners, Visa*

ARDUAINE   Loch Melfort Hotel

on A816, by Oban PA34 4XG
Tel: (08522) 233
Open: 11-11 (11-2.30, 6-11 winter)
Licensee: Philip Lewis

Well-known, high-class hotel, secluded from the busy road by its own splendid
grounds. The simple, brightly lit, subtly nautical non-residents' bar is popular with
locals and tourists: delicious food, wonderful views, good walks.

Bar Meals: 12-2.30, 6.30-9 (all day summer); bar snacks both sessions   **Restaurant:**
7.30-9   **Typical Dishes BAR:** *French onion soup £1.55, home-cured gravadlax £3.95,
spare ribs £4.15, venison pie £6.50, grilled lobster £12.50   Vegetarian Meals: spinach
and cream cheese pancake   Children's Menu* Cheese Whisky *Children Allowed in Bar
to Eat Outdoor Play Area   Patio/terrace   Outdoor Eating* **Accommodation** *(closed
Jan/Feb): 27 bedrooms, all en suite, from £80 (single £45)   Children Welcome Overnight
Cots Available   Check-in: after midday* **Credit Cards:** *Access, Diners*

AYR   Old Racecourse Hotel

2 Victoria Park
Tel: (0292) 262873
Open: 11am-midnight
Licensee: John Nichol

Imposing seaside sandstone Georgian townhouse. The popular, friendly lounge bar
has a huge central fireplace. Tolerant of families. Local fish and one or two other
interesting things on the bar menu. Restaurant.

Bar Meals: 12-2.30, 5-9.30 bar snacks both sessions   Children's Menu Beer
McEwan, Youngers   Family Room   Garden **Accommodation:** *12 bedrooms, 7 en suite,
from £55   Children Welcome Overnight   Check-in: by arrangement* **Credit Cards:**
Amex, Visa

AYR Chestnuts Hotel, 52 Racecourse Road (A719): Small lounge bar with
vaulted ceiling; lunch and evening bar meals. Family room, garden. Broughton,
Tennents beers. Open: 11am-midnight

CASTLECARY   Castlecary House Hotel

Castlecary Road, Cumbernauld G68 0HD
Tel: (0324) 840233
Open: 11-11 (11.30 Thur-Sat); 12.30-11 Sun
Licensee: K McMillan

Decent bar food in splendidly old-fashioned public bars at this popular hotel. The
large cottage annexe has very smart modern bedrooms.

Bar Meals: 12-2, 6-9 (12.30-9 Sun); bar snacks both sessions   **Restaurant:** *12 (12.30
Sun)-2, 7-10; high teas 4-7 Sun*   **Typical Dishes BAR:** *Scotch broth £1, Mexican
mushrooms £1.80, home-made steak pie £3.45, haggis in spicy batter £3.10, poached
salmon £4.50, sticky toffee pudding £1.60*   **RESTAURANT:** *cream of herb soup £2,
trout quenelles £3.60, brace of quail Caledonia £9.20, venison with mixed pepper £9.10,
Dover sole with scrumpy £10, Drambuie crepes £2   Vegetarian Meals: baked stuffed
marrow   Children's Menu/Portions* Beer *Belhaven 80/-; Broughton Greenmantle Ale;
Jennings Bitter; Maclays 70/-* Whisky *Children Allowed in Bar to Eat   Patio/terrace*

Outdoor Eating   **Accommodation:** *35 bedrooms, 31 en suite, from £51 (single £41)*
*Children Welcome Overnight   Check-in: all day   **Credit Cards:** Access, Amex, Diners,*
Visa

CRINAN   Crinan Hotel

The Harbourside PA31 8SR   ▼
Tel: (054683) 261
Open: 11-11
Licensee: N A Ryan

Very smart, large white hotel by the harbourside, with a famous seafood restaurant
upstairs, but also a piney, civilised café-bar where excellent light meals can be had
for a fraction of Lock 16 prices. The restaurant takes it name, incidentally, from the
fact that lock number 16 on the Crinan Canal, which guides boats into open sea, is
right outside the hotel. You can watch them from the small paved terrace at one
side of the Crinan Bar.

Bar Meals: *12.30-2; bar snacks*   **Restaurant:** *7-9*   **Typical Dishes BAR:** *home-made*
soup £1.50, Loch Sween mussels £4.95, Loch Crinan seafood platter £10.50, grilled fillet
of Loch Awe trout £4.95, baked fresh wild salmon £7.50, treacle tart £2.25   Vegetarian
Meals: hot vegetarian pasties   Children's Portions   Beer   *Broughton Greenmantle Ale;*
Maclays 80/-; Tennents 80/-   Whisky   *Children Allowed in Bar to Eat Outdoor Play*
*Area   Riverside Garden   Outdoor Eating   Summer Barbecue   **Accommodation:** 22*
bedrooms, all en suite, from £100 (single £75)   Children Welcome Overnight   Cots
*Available   Check-in: all day   **Credit Cards:** Access, Visa*

EAGLESHAM   Eglinton Arms Hotel

Gilmour Street G16 0LG   ▼
Tel: (03553) 2631
Open: all day
Licensee: Trevor Patterson

Village hotel, once a coaching inn, with real ale and popular food in its lounge, a
games-playing, real-fire lit snug, and the Postillion Restaurant.

Bar Meals: *12-2.15, 5-9; bar snacks both sessions*   **Restaurant:** *12-2.15, 7-9.30*
Typical Dishes BAR: *fried cheese plate £1.75, barbecued chicken £4.95, lamb kebab*
£4.25, fish bake £4.95, bread and butter pudding £1.75   **RESTAURANT:** *chicken*
masala £2.35, veal chop £8.45, lamb cutlets £6.50, shrimp bowl £5.95   Vegetarian
Meals   Children's Menu/Portions   Beer   *Youngers Scotch, No. 3   Children Allowed in*
*Bar to Eat   **Accommodation:** 13 bedrooms, all en suite, from £57 (single £27)   Children*
*Welcome Overnight   Cots Available   Check-in: all day   **Credit Cards:** Access, Amex,*
Diners, Visa

GILMERTON Bow Butts Tel: (0357) 40333: Modern rather characterless lounge
and old-fashioned public bar, in popular pub in tiny hamlet. Very busy with diners;
food until 8.30pm. Belhaven beers. Open: 11am-midnight (closed until 5pm
Tuesday).

GLASGOW   Babbity Bowster

16/18 Blackfriars Street G1 1PE
Tel: (041) 552 5055
Open: 11 am-midnight
Licensee: Fraser Laurie

A renovated Robert Adam town house in the city's business district is the setting for the splendidly informal and convivial Babbity Bowster, which is not exactly a pub, rather, a light and stylish café-bar, with a restaurant and hotel attached. Euro-café style, food of all kinds, from delicious light snacks to delicious full meals, are available all day.The restaurant is on the first floor, and there's a charming outdoor drinking area. Bedrooms have neat fitted furniture, duvets and shower rooms. Assured parking.

Bar Meals: 12-9; bar snacks **Restaurant:** *12-3, 6.30-11.30* **Typical Dishes BAR:** *Scotch broth £1.25, mussels with tomato and basil £3.65, spiced chicken stovies £3.85, Perthshire game pie £4.75, home-made puddings* *Vegetarian Meals: vegetarian haggis* **Beer** *Maclays Patio/terrace Outdoor Eating* **Accommodation:** *6 bedrooms, all en suite, from £56 (single £36) Check-in: all day* **Credit Cards:** *Access, Amex, Visa*

GLASGOW   Ubiquitous Chip

12 Ashton Lane G12
Tel: (041) 334 5007
Open: 11-11 (12.30-2.30, 6.30-11 Sun)

Busy bar above famous Glasgow restaurant; famously trendy, and dead bohemian. Impressive bar food of a resolutely simple kind. Eating here is largely a vehicle for some serious people-watching.

Bar Meals and Restaurant: 12-11 **Typical Dishes:** *cock a leekie soup 95p, peat-smoked haddie paté £2.30, smoked ham houghs £3.95, tattie pot £3.75, whole fish stew £5.95, bread pudding £1.95* *Vegetarian Meals: vegetarian bridie £3.20* *Children's Portions* **Beer** **Whisky** **Cider** *Addlestones Family Room* **Credit Cards:** *Access, Amex, Diners, Visa*

GLASGOW Baby Grand India Street: Continental café-bar with a lively young buzz and excellent hot lunchtime specials. **Horseshoe Bar,** Drury Street: Famous Glasgow landmark, an unspoilt Victorian tavern with the longest bar counter in Britain, at some 104 feet. Spectacularly ornate interior. Women usually head upstairs to the lounge, away from the masculine downstairs bar. School food in vast portions at bargain prices. An ethnic experience. **Maltman** Renfield Street: Main bar non-smoking, addicts segregated at the rear. Good value bar food, and trendy (pricey) downstairs restaurant.

HOUSTON   Fox & Hounds

South Street PA6 7EN
Tel: (0505) 612448
Open: 11 am-midnight (11.45 Sat); 12.30-11 Sun
Licensees: Hilary and Ronald Wengel

Modernised but attractive village inn with public 'Stables' bar, smarter Fox and Vixen lounge, and Huntsman restaurant, where bar food is also available. Nice to families.

Bar Meals and Restaurant: 12.30-2.30, 5.30-10 (all day Sat/Sun); bar snacks both sessions **Typical Dishes:** *home-made soup £1.50, smoked salmon and scrambled egg*

£3.75, home-made steak, kidney and mushroom pie £5.95, roast haunch of venison £6.95, fresh herrings in oatmeal £3.45, crème caramel Vegetarian Meals: creamed vegetable pie Children's Menu/Portions **Beer** *Broughton Greenmantle Ale; McEwans* **Whisky** *Family Room* **Credit Cards:** *Access, Visa*

KILBERRY ★ Kilberry Inn

Kilberry PA29 6YD `FOOD`
Tel: (08803) 223
Open: 11-2, 5-9 Easter-mid October (closed Sun all year)
Licensees: John and Kath Leadbeater

This one storey white cottage in an isolated, pretty little hamlet is close to glorious coastline, and reached by an invigorating drive down a winding, hilly road from the north, with superb views of Jura and other islands. A large sign on the front of the Kilberry Inn declares it to be "the only pub in Scotland with an Egon Ronay star", which indeed it was, until this year at least. John and Kath Leadbeater, English chef-proprietors, are vigorously interested in good food, and justifiably proud of their achievements here, in an out of the way spot where the vegetables come via van and taxi, and fresh fish is peculiarly hard to get. It's very much a dining pub, though locals and others are equally welcome to drop in for a drink. The building was originally a crofting house, and the snugly comfortable little bar, with a peat fire at one end, a wood-burning stove at the other, still has an unpretentious rural style. Leading off at the left, the brighter, plainer dining and family room has good-sized pine dining tables and a genuine welcome for children; John's Donald Duck impression certainly breaks the ice. The daily blackboard-listed short menu (perhaps only four or five main courses at lunchtime), genuinely home-made and morning-planned, is cheerfully annotated for ditherers with lively accounts of how each was made, and what's particularly recommended that day. This is very much John's role, circulating, chatting, advising, gossiping and occasionally quacking, in between stints in the kitchen and bar; Kath is very much behind the scenes, doing the hard work at the stove! The house speciality is home-made meat dishes of an old-fashioned country sort, often with a modern re-interpretation, but nevertheless delicious: perhaps a hearty sausage pie, beef in Old Peculier casserole, or pork in cider with apples; Kath has a famously light hand and the pastry is superb. She also makes the bread, and jars of pickle, jam and chutney on sale at the bar. Fish isn't really their interest, but the salmon fish pie, layered with sliced potato, is creamy and satisfying, though perhaps a little underseasoned. Whatever you do, if the lemon meringue pie is on the menu, make sure you leave room for it; probably the finest in the land, it's light and delicate yet intensely tangy, with a perfect fluffy top. Though there's no real ale, the Greenmantle range from Broughton Brewery in the Borders is available by the bottle, and the wine list includes a few offered by the glass. Note that the pub closes in the winter and never opens on Sundays.

Bar Meals: *12.15-2, 6.30-9; bar snacks lunchtime* **Typical Dishes:** *tomato and rice soup £1.75, smoked haddock mousse £3.50, pork fillet in cider with apples £9.50, rump steak and kidney pie £8.95, salmon fish pie £7.95, lemon meringue pie £2.50 Vegetarian Meals: fresh vegetable pie £6.95 Children's Portions* **Cheese** **Whisky** *Family Room* **Credit Cards:** *Access, Visa*

KILCHRENAN Taychreggan Hotel

On B845
Tel: (08663) 211
Open: 12-2.30, 6-11 (closed Nov-March)
Licensee: John Tyrrell

Gracious large white hotel on lochside in own splendid grounds. Decent, but not cheap, bar meals in modernised, unpubby bar, which has wall seating upholstered in red, a few chintzy cushions,and too-low-for-eating-on glass topped tables. The menu can promise rather more than it delivers: 'Chef's three-leaf salad with Scottish blue cheese' sounds grand, but the resulting dish looked like a cluster simply of oak leaf lettuce with the cheese crumbled over the top; we were tempted to make a sandwich with it. If it's fine, eat in the pretty enclosed courtyard. The large, airy dining room, in the modern extension, is for residents' use only, except for Sunday lunches.

Bar Meals: lunchtime **Typical Dishes BAR:** *camembert with cranberry sauce £3.25, smoked salmon £3.75, smoked fish platter £7.50, meat platter £6.95, poached salmon salad £6.95, lemon gateau* *Children Allowed in Bar to Eat* *Patio/terrace* *Outdoor Eating* **Accommodation:** *Bedrooms from £70 (single £35)* *Children Welcome Overnight* *Check-in: all day* **Credit Cards**

Kilchrenan Inn. White cottage inn on quiet country crossroads, charming without, totally modernised within, in a clean, simple pine and banquette style, open-plan, with a woodburning stove. Genuine home cooking – a very short blackboard menu offers three courses for under £10; perhaps cream of green pepper soup, vegetable quiche and pineapple meringues. Worth a try.

KILFINAN   Kilfinan Hotel

near Tighnabruaich PA21 2EP   ♥
Tel: (070 082) 201
Licensee: Tony Wignell

White-stoned coaching inn, a popular haven for travellers between Strachur and Tighnabruaich for over 100 years. Rural tranquillity, fine views of Loch Fyne and the coastal hills, and modern comforts blended successfully with traditional character. There are two bars, neither of them a lounge, but one with intricate Kashmir curtains. Bedrooms are either antique-furnished, or fitted out with modern units; all the usual little luxuries, including good quality toiletries in the carpeted en suite bathrooms.

Bar Meals: 12-2.30, 5-8.30 **Restaurant:** *12-2.30, 7.30-8.30* **Typical Dishes BAR:** *fresh tomato soup, home-made paté, home-made fish cakes, chicken tarragon, steak and stout pie, bread and butter pudding (main courses from £4)* *Vegetarian Meals: curry* *Childrens Menu/Portions* `Cheese` `Beer` *Theakston* *Family Room Outdoor Play Area* *Garden* *Outdoor Eating* *Summer Barbecue* **Accommodation:** *11 bedrooms, all en suite, from £68 (£45 single)* *Children Welcome Overnight* *Cot Available* *Check-in: all day* **Credit Cards:** *Access, Amex, Visa*

KILMARTIN   Kilmartin Hotel

By Lochgilphead   `B&B`
Tel: (05465) 244
Open: all day
Licensees: Keith and Heather Parkinson

A fire in March 1991 forced a total revamp of the bedrooms at this delightful little inn-hotel, and smart new fittings include carpets so new that bedroom doors on the top floor wouldn't close on our last visit. But this is easily forgiven; first floor rooms, called Spring and Summer, are perfectly decent (though perhaps a little cramped) but the second floor attic doubles are spacious and charming, and represent great value for money in a busy tourist area. Winter and Autumn, one looking out over the green at the front of the inn, the other over the less inspiring rear, don't have bathrooms but share an adjacent, spruce and attractive public one, and the third room, All Seasons, is a gracious family room (one double bed, one single) with a nice little en suite bathroom, free-standing antique furniture, including an attractive old bed, pretty fabrics, twin bedside tables and a dressing table. A cot can also be provided – but watch out on the top floor if you have toddlers or crawlers in tow – there are alarmingly wide gaps in the banister; it's very quiet up here though. Downstairs, the cosy, rambling bar, very popular with locals and buzzing with traditional pub atmosphere, has bar stools, a lovely stone fireplace (coal fire in winter) an ochre panelled ceiling at one end, by the bar counter, and a little square sitting area with lovely old spindle-backed and carved oak settles, a piano, and lots of Burns memorabilia and other kitsch Scots pictures. There's fiddle music at weekends. Leading off, a plushly comfortable little residents' lounge can be used for non-resident family visits, and has piped music ranging from Simon and Garfunkel to invigorating Russian operas. The licensees are charming and personable, often coming through to the lounge to socialise. The dining room is a wonderfully romantic venue for dinner and breakfast – but particularly so at night, with its midnight blue panelling, lovely old china, lace tablecloths and candlelight. Unfortunately the food isn't quite up to scratch, though a piece of wild salmon (provided by the local laird) was absolutely delicious. Starters and side vegetables disappointed, however, bread was strictly supermarket style, white wine served tepid (by one terribly overworked, sweet-natured waitress), and main courses suffer from pub garnish syndrome: coleslaw, lettuce and tomato, for colour rather than flavour. Puddings are hit and miss – go for the obviously home-made: bramble crumble was well put together, though the fruit was over-acidic. A little garden at the back has white patio furniture, but suffers from its proximity to the kitchen (and boisterous seasonal staff!), and a rather alarming amount of dog doings; parents take note.

Bar Meals: *all day*   ***Restaurant:*** *12-2, 6-9*   ***Typical Dishes***   RESTAURANT: *cauliflower and cheese soup £1.20, stilton and walnut paté £2.25, venison in red wine and blackberries £8.95, salmon steak in lime, chive and mushroom sauce £7.95, haggis with neeps and tatties £4.25, bread and butter pudding £1.75*   *Vegetarian Meals: mushroom and butter bean stroganoff £5.50*   *Children's Menu*   Beer   *Caledonian*   Whisky   *Family Room   Garden   Outdoor Eating*   ***Accommodation:*** *6 bedrooms, 4 en suite, from £50 (single £30)   Children Welcome Overnight   Cot Available   Check-in: all day*   **No Credit Cards**

KILMELFORD   Cuilfail Hotel

By Oban PA34 4XA
Tel: (08522) 274
Open: 11-2.30, 5-11
Licensee: D S Birrell

Handsome high-ceilinged roadside inn-hotel, which changed hands early in 1991. Renovations are in progress, and downstairs is a fetching blend of cosy bars and enormous, gracious public areas. Bedrooms are now being tackled; rather scruffy previously, with creaky floors, furniture a mix of antique and cheap modern pieces, and little discomforts like a lack of early morning hot water. But all this may change. Eat in modern little bistro or more formal dining room; very ordinary food on last visit. B&B cautiously recommended though.

Bar Meals: *12-2.30, 6.30-9.30; bar snacks lunchtime*   ***Restaurant:*** *6.30-9.30*   ***Typical Dishes***   BAR: *home-made soup £1.35, specialise in freshly cooked pastry dishes from £4.50, home-made pudding £1.65*   RESTAURANT *dinner menu £10-£15*   *Vegetarian Meals: risotto   Children's Portions*   Beer   *Younger's No. 3*   Whisky   *Family Room   Outdoor Play Area   Riverside Garden   Outdoor Eating*   ***Accommodation:*** *12 bedrooms, all en suite, from £60 (single £30)   Children Welcome Overnight   Cots Available*   **Credit Cards:** *Access, Visa*

LOCH ECK   Coylet Inn

Kilmun PA23 8SG
Tel: (036 984) 626
Open: 11-2.30, 5-11 (12 Fri/Sat); 10.30-2.30, 6.30-11 Sun
Licensee: Richard Addis

It's the setting that makes the Coylet really special: just the west coast road to
Dunoon, shrouded in trees, separates this pretty white building from the glorious
beauty of Loch Eck and the hills beyond. Not another house can be seen in any
direction; be early for a window seat in the bar or dining room. Inside it charms in
an unaffected way: a square entrance hall whets the appetite with its elegant old
furnishings and pictorial Victoriana. The public bar, on the left, is handsome and
cosy, and friendly local ghillies and others gather on bar stools to pass the time of
day. The beer's good too. Back through the hall is an attractively simple small dining
bar, where families (even tiny babies) are welcome. Plain oak tables and chairs line
the walls, and smaller tables flanked by old barrel seats fill the bright bay window
spaces. Through into the dining room proper are half a dozen dining tables (one,
large group size, in the prize bay window spot), wheelback chairs and a piano. The
food is a mix of standard bar menu stuff, from sandwiches (even in the evening) and
ploughmans to vast well-cooked platefuls of haddock and chips, or sizzling steaks;
the quality draws both locals and tourists. But it's worth waiting for the specials
board, a daily changing short blackboard list which applies from 7 pm. It might
typically feature local oak-smoked mackerel, home-made liver paté and Scotch
broth, local game in season, grilled local salmon or trout, and langoustine risotto. If
the risotto is on, you should order it and enjoy a generous pile of tender, fresh Loch
Fyne langoustines in a delicious sauce with garlic, cream, wine and herbs: a true and
memorable bargain at £7.25. Vegetables are also exceptional: crisp mange-tout,
perfect new potatoes, tender carrots; all included in the main course price. Puddings,
all home-made, are also good, and come in hefty portions: chocolate roulade,
pineapple cheesecake or a real apple pie are typical of the choice. Pity about the
Rombouts coffee. Upstairs are three tiny little bedrooms, which suffer from a lack of
facilities because of their size (no radiators, nowhere to hang damp towels, nowhere
to hang anything other than on the back of the door), but are quickly forgiven for
their charming decor and simple comfort. All have sash windows with views over
the loch, and pretty cottagey print paper and fabrics. The twin is a bit bigger than
the two doubles. The shared bathrooms, a very attractive, immaculately clean,
carpeted and pine panelled room, is bigger than any of them. Breakfasts are ungreasy
and commendably accommodating of personal preferences. Finally, a word about
the service, which is genuine and friendly from both the resident owners and their
few, able staff.

Bar Meals: *11.30-2, 5.30-10; bar snacks both sessions*   **Restaurant:** *12-2, 7-9*
Typical Dishes BAR: *marinated herring, smoked mussels, steak, lamb, game, chicken
specials, langoustine risotto, local salmon (main courses from £4), hazelnut and raspberry
meringue   Vegetarian Meals: broccoli and cheese flan   Children's Portions   Beer
Younger's No. 3   Whisky   Family Room   Outdoor Play Area   Garden   Outdoor Eating*
Accommodation: *3 bedrooms, sharing a bathroom, from £34 (single £17) Children
Welcome Overnight   Cot Available   Check-in: by arrangement   No Credit Cards*

LOCH ECK Whistlefield Inn Tel: (036 986) 250: Not far from the Coylet Inn,
up on the hill behind the lochside road. Good rural atmosphere, simple bar food
plus specials, lots of whiskies. McEwan 80/- beer. Bedrooms. Open: 11-2.30,
4-midnight (12-2.30, 6-midnight Sunday and quieter days).

LOCHGAIR Lochgair Hotel: Sleepy hospitable inn, popular for bar meals.

LUSS   Inverbeg Inn

Inverbeg, by Loch Lomond G83 8PD   ❢
Tel: (043 686) 678
Open: all day
Licensee: J A Bisset

Very popular white-painted inn set back a little from the extremely busy road
alongside Loch Lomond (A82). Rather dated modern interior; lovely garden at the
rear.

Bar Meals: all day; bar snacks   *Restaurant:* 12-2.30, 6.30-9.30   *Typical Dishes*
BAR: home-made soup £1.45, prawn cocktail £3.85, mixed grill £9.95, haggis, neeps
and mash £4.35, herby smoked mackerel £3.70   *RESTAURANT:* west coast fish bowl
£3.25, saddle of venison £13.75, lamb en croute £11.60, fillet steak Glen Douglas
£15.20   Vegetarian Meals: bean and chilli hotpot £4.10   Children's Menu   Whisky
Family Room   Outdoor Play Area   Patio/terrace   Outdoor Eating   *Accommodation:* 14
bedrooms, 7 en suite, from £50 (single £28)   Children Welcome Overnight   Cots
Available   Check-in: all day   *Credit Cards:* Access, Amex, Visa

PORT APPIN Airds Hotel: Well-loved, smart hotel, once an inn but now a
hotel proper, though it still welcomes non-residents for bar meals. Exceptional food.

STRACHUR Creggans Hotel on A815 Tel: (036 986) 279. Well-placed for
touring, and a charming little inn-hotel, with good loch and hillside views.
Promising bar food, too; try the fresh local seafood. Altogether rather smart. Fishing
and stalking can be arranged, on licensee Sir Fitzroy Maclean's land. £75 a double
room; children welcome; McEwans beers. Open all day.

TARBERT Columba Hotel, East Pier Road: Bar food popular in summer
Tarbert Hotel Tel (0880) 820204: Prettily set by the little harbour, decent food,
noisy in summer (light sleepers beware) when the yachting types move in, but
otherwise, best local B&B.

TAYVALLICH   Tayvallich Inn

By Lochgilphead pA31 8PR
Tel: (05467) 282
Open: 11-2.30, 5-12 (12.30-2.30, 6.30-11 Sun); closed Mon winter
Licensee: John Graffon

This simple white-painted dining pub – though it's fine to pop in for a drink, most
people come for the food – is in a marvellously pretty location at the centre of a
strung-along-the-road, scattered village stretching around the top of Loch Sween. Sit
outside, on the front terrace, at one of the five parasolled picnic tables, and enjoy the
view of a dozen little boats, and low wooded hills fringing the lochside; the word
Tayvallich means "the house in the pass". Aside from the odd car passing, perfect
peace, unless Elton John's Greatest Hits are full volume from the kitchen. Inside, the
Tayvallich is surprisingly modern – smartly pine-clad, with a little bar and larger
adjoining dining room proper. The bar is tiled-floored, with raffia back chairs and little
wood tables, the dining room similar, but spacious and relaxing, with a woodburning
stove, attractive dresser, and bentwood chairs around scrubbed pine dining tables. The
star of the handwritten menu is the freshest local seafood; so local that oysters come
from just yards away in Loch Sween itself, and clams from the Sound of Jura just
round the coast. Langoustines are local and meltingly fresh; mussels plump, salads
imaginative and crisp, with unusual touches like Cape gooseberries. Finger bowls are
provided, and clean napkins with each course. Portions are generous, and the whole
atmosphere very informal and relaxed. Holidaymakers turn up in shorts, and babies are
commendably tolerantly treated, with clip-on chairs and specially rustled up toddler

food – they'll even find chips for philistine youngsters. Puddings are of the chocolate nut slab and banoffee pie sort; few dedicated seafood lovers, having munched through two courses already, get that far though! Expect to pay about £30 for a three course lunch for two, including a half litre of house wine. Cracking good value.

Bar Meals and Restaurant: 12-2, 6 (7 restaurant)-9; bar snacks both sessions **Typical Dishes BAR:** *home-made soup £1.25, mussels £2, burger £3.75, smoked haddock pasta £4, breaded haddock £3.50, chocolate nut slab* **RESTAURANT:** *half dozen oysters £3.75, chicken £7.75, local scallops £9.50, turbot and capers £9.50, bannoffee pie £1.95 Vegetarian Meals: bean casserole   Children's Portions   Outdoor Play Area   Patio/terrace Outdoor Eating* **Credit Cards:** *Access, Visa*

TROON   Clubhouse

22 Ayr Street KA10 6EB
Tel: (0292) 317918
Open: 10 am-midnight (12.30-11 Sun)
Licensee: A H Adam

Atmospheric upstairs bar with golfing links – so to speak – and interesting bar food. The lunchtime list is represented here; evenings bring a smarter menu, steak, chicken and seafood-led (main courses around £7).

Bar Meals: 12-2.30, 6-9.30; bar snacks lunchtime **Typical Dishes:** *Scotch broth £1.25, garlic mushrooms £2.75, steak and kidney pie £4.50, grilled haggis with bacon £4.25, fried fillet of sole £4.50, home-made fruit puddings   Vegetarian Meals: vegetable stir-fry with provencale sauce   Children's Portions   Children Allowed in Bar to Eat* **Credit Cards:** *Access, Visa*

UPLAWMOOR   Uplawmoor Hotel

Neilston Road G78 4AF
Tel: (050 585) 565
Open: 11 (12.30 Sun)-2.30, 5-11
Licensees: R and P Smith

Rural village former coaching inn, now a modernised, rather ordinary-looking hotel. Almost all the dishes, they say, are home-made "apart from the ubiquitous scampi and chips". The £11.50 table d'hote (short choice) menu, which changes fortnightly, is a three course bargain. Lots of fresh local produce. Scottish high teas between 5 pm and 7 pm.

Bar Meals: 12 (12.30 Sun)-2.30, 5-9.30; bar snacks both sessions **Restaurant:** *5-9.30* **Typical Dishes BAR:** *home-made soup £1, home-made paté £1.65, chilli con carne £1.95, roast of the day £4.50, trout almondine £4.50* **RESTAURANT:** *minestrone soup £1.75, tartlet of quails eggs and smoked salmon £5.95, supreme of chicken Victor £9.75, escalope of venison £12.50, steak stuffed with oysters £12.95, sorbets £1.95 Vegetarian Meals: spinach and almond mornay £2.95   Children's Menu/Portions* **Beer** *Theakston Best Bitter, Youngers No. 3* **Whisky** *Children Allowed in Bar to Eat Patio/terrace   Outdoor Eating* **Accommodation:** *13 bedrooms, all en suite, from £59, (single £48)   Children Welcome Overnight   Cot Available   Check-in: all day* **Credit Cards:** *Access, Visa*

TAYSIDE

ALMONDBANK   Almondbank Inn

Main Street PH1 3NJ
Tel: (0738) 83242
Open: 11-2.30, 5-11 (11-11.45 Fri/Sat; 12.30-11 Sun)
Licensee: Charles Lindsay

Just off the A85 to the west of Perth, on the village main street, the whitewashed
Almondbank Inn enjoys fine views over the River Almond from its small well-kept
rear garden. Inside there are two adjoining rooms, similarly sized and decorated. The
predominant colour is green, made greener still with plants, both real and fake, and the
garden theme continues in florally-upholstered banquette seating and wooden chairs,
which surround solid wood tables almost all laid for dining. On the walls are a couple
of oil paintings and product mirrors. It's not a quiet pub: a juke box regularly pumps
out the latest hits, and there's a pool table on the first floor. Food is taken fairly
seriously, however, and the Birdcage Bistro, despite some rather gimmicky, tacky
descriptions (a "galaxy of titbits", "salad days are here again") produces generally
pleasing food, the majority of it from fresh produce , including some first rate home-
made chips. All the beef used is Aberdeen Angus from a local butcher, and even the
scampi is fresh and crumbed on the premises. The menu itself is long, running from
first courses like "name that tuna" and deep-fried camembert with cranberry sauce, to
main courses such as steak and onion pie, chicken in a creamy curry sauce, and a
whole list of Angus minute steaks with a variety of sauces. All come with fresh
vegetables, as well as the aforementioned chips. Puddings are largely ice-cream based,
but there's good cappuccino and espresso coffee. On Friday and Saturday evenings, a
slightly different menu is heavy on steak and chicken dishes, and prices throughout are
very reasonable. The uniformed staff are friendly and approachable and the locals,
gathered on stools at the bar, are also only too willing to chat.

*Bar Meals: 12 (12.30 Sun)-2.15, 5-8.30 (6.30-10 Fri/Sat); not Mon eve; bar snacks
both sessions* **Typical Dishes:** *cream of courgette soup 95p, breaded mushrooms in garlic
sauce £2.65, roast beef and Yorkshire pudding, oriental chicken with peaches, grilled minute
steak and Mexican sauce, apple tart (main courses from £4.50)* *Vegetarian Meals: samosas
Children's Menu* `Cheese` `Beer` *Broughton Greenmantle Ale* *Family Room
Riverside Garden* *Outdoor Eating* **Credit Cards:** *Access, Visa*

BROUGHTY FERRY Fishermans Tavern 12 Fort Street Tel: (0382) 75941.
Attractively modernised little pub, fairly routine bar food of the chilli/curry/scampi
sort, but also three more interesting hot daily specials; very cheap. Bass, Belhaven,
Whitbread beers. Modest bedrooms. Open all day.

BURRELTON   Burrelton Park Hotel

High Street PH13 9NX
Tel: (08287) 207
Open: 11-11
Licensee: Malcolm Weaving

A lot less grand than it sounds, but nonetheless rather smart, this attractive
proprietor-run roadside inn has a formidable local reputation for high class bar food,
from a multi-chef kitchen supplying both bar and restaurant. Only fresh produce is
used, including vegetables and mayonnaise; meat is butchered on the premises and
properly hung before use.

Bar Meals: 11-11; bar snacks **Restaurant:** *6.30-10.30* **Typical Dishes BAR:** *lentil
soup £1, paté with onion marmélade £2.30, Lancashire hotpot £3.95, pork schnitzels in*

cider and cream £5.65, half a crispy roast duckling £6.95, syrup sponge and custard £2
RESTAURANT: *French onion soup, tortellini carbonara, Barnsley chop £10.75, roast*
local pheasant £7.75, steak Diane £8.95, fruit-filled brandy snap basket £3.60
Vegetarian Meals: oven-baked aubergine Children's Menu ▮Beer▮ *Theakston* ▮Whisky▮
*Children Allowed in Bar to Eat **Accommodation:** 6 bedrooms, all en suite, from £45*
*(single £30) Children Welcome Overnight Cot Available Check-in: all day **Credit***
Cards: *Visa*

CLEISH Nivingstone House Hotel. Delicious lunchtime food, quite out of the
ordinary, in a splendid country house hotel not far from junction five of the M90.
Main courses around £4; very good value. Children welcome. Belhaven beers.
Open: 12-3, 6-11.

DUNDEE   Mercantile Bar

100-108 Commercial Street
Tel: (0382) 25500
Open: 10 am-11 pm (midnight Thur-Sat); 7-11 Sun
Licensee: A B Morrison

Reconstructed Victorian bar in an old warehouse setting, with a commendably
interesting bar menu: main courses accompanied by rice, salad or fresh vegetables,
rather than chips, and bargain Dundee prices throughout.

Bar Meals: *12-2, 5-7 (8 Thur-Sat); bar snacks lunchtime* **Typical Dishes:** *potato and*
leek soup 72p, melon and mandarin cocktail, chicken and mango curry £2.85, beef olive
chasseur £2.80, chicken breast with coriander £3, pear and cinnamon sponge £1.25
Vegetarian Meals: tagliatelle ▮Beer▮ *Draught Bass; Ind Coope Burton Ale; Maclays*
80/-; McEwan 80/- ▮Whisky▮ *Family Room **Credit Cards:** Access, Diners, Visa*

GLENCARSE   Newton House Hotel

near Perth PH2 7LX
Tel: (073 886) 250
Open: 12-2.30, 5-11
Licensees: Geoffrey and Carol Tallis

Former dower house built circa 1840, in its own grounds, just six miles from Perth,
catering to tourist and business trade. Inside, a cross between country house and
modernised Scottish inn, though it has just undergone total refurbishment, probably
further into country house style. Bar food in Cawley's Bar.

Bar Meals and Restaurant: *12-2, 5 (6.30 restaurant)-9; bar snacks both sessions*
Typical Dishes BAR: *cream of broccoli soup, garlic mushrooms, chicken Gowrie, steak and*
Guinness pie, sole Veronique, rhubarb pie (main courses from around £4.50)
RESTAURANT: *Arbroath smokie, Ogen melon, entrecote Glenisla, oak-smoked trout,*
fresh halibut, lemon soufflé Vegetarian Meals: home-made lasagne Children's
Menu/Portions Family Room Outdoor Play Area Garden Outdoor Eating
Accommodation: *10 bedrooms, all en suite, from £72 (single £50) Children Welcome*
*Overnight Check-in: all day **Credit Cards:** Access, Amex, Diners, Visa*

GLENDEVON   Tormaukin Hotel

By Dollar FK14 7JY   `FOOD`
Tel: (025 981) 252   `B&B`
Open: 11-11
Licensee: Marianne Worthy

Just south of Gleneagles, on the A823, and surrounded by glorious hill country, this
ruggedly handsome old white-painted inn sits on the bank of the river Devon, and is
remarkably peaceful, except when it's busy, which is apparently often. The warm and
welcoming interior consists of several communicating rooms, all with lots of exposed
stone, rough whitewashed walls and ceiling beams. Old settles (one of them beautifully
carved), upholstered stools and roundback chairs surround heavy iron-legged tables.
Old black and white photographs, colourful plates and pictures adorn the walls, and a
splendid open fire makes the Tormaukin an ideal retreat from the chill Scottish winter.
Food's a major attraction, to the extent that the bar menu makes a plea for patience at
busy times; this printed list is supplemented by a daily specials board. Begin, perhaps,
with potato skins, or a naturally-flavoured smoked fish paté, followed by venison
sausages in port wine sauce, stir-fried chicken-chilli with egg noodles, salmon en
croute, or a spicy lamb curry. Cooking is competent, if unspectacular; fresh local
produce makes all the difference. To the other side of the entrance, an exposed stone
and beam-laden restaurant features smartly laid polished tables, candle-lit in the
evening. The printed menu isn't wide in its scope – half the space is taken up by
various steaks – but not without interest; a duo of local venison and loin of hare
cooked in whisky and wild mushrooms stands out from the list, and prices are a good
deal higher than the bar menu, with starters at around £5, main courses averaging
£13. Recently refurbished bedrooms are extremely comfortable and appropriately
styled in keeping with the inn's age. Original features include yet more exposed stone
and a generous sprinkling of beams. Floral fabrics match with pretty wallcoverings,
furniture is pine and free-standing, beds are comfortable, sheets crisp. They have
showers only; nice local toiletries and plenty of towels compensate for slightly cramped
sizes. Four of the rooms, in a converted stable block, are more contemporary in style,
and all the bedrooms are named after whiskies. Service is admirably efficient and
friendly from a young, mostly female staff, who take most things in their stride.

Bar Meals: 12-2, 5.30-9.30 (12-9.30 Sun); bar snacks both sessions **Restaurant:** *6.30-
9.30* **Typical Dishes BAR:** *leek and potato soup £1.40, smoked fish paté £2, venison
sausages £4.25, stir-fry chicken with chillies £4.65, salmon en croute £6.75*
RESTAURANT: *celery and apple soup, warm tossed salad of quail livers, baby chicken
stuffed with haggis in Drambuie sauce, fresh halibut on samphire with strawberry sauce
Vegetarian Meals: bean and vegetable hotpot £4.40   Children's Menu/Portions* `Cheese`
`Beer` *Ind Coope Burton Ale; Tetley Bitter* `Whisky` *Family Room   Patio/terrace
Outdoor Eating* **Accommodation** *(closed 2nd/3rd week Jan): 10 bedrooms, all en suite,
from £58 (single £44)   Children Welcome Overnight   Cot Available   Check-in: all day*
Credit Cards: *Access, Amex, Visa*

GLENFARG   Bein Inn

Glenfarg PH2 9PY   `B&B`
Tel: (05773) 216
Licensees: Michael, Elsa and Stephen Thompson

By the A912 to the south of Perth, this pebble-dash ex-drovers' inn gets a mention
on many old maps. Actually just to the north-east of Glenfarg, it stands on its own

just five minutes from Junction 9 of the M90. Inside has an unfussy and homely feel. The entrance is decorated in deep tones of salmon pink, its walls hung with a variety of pictures. There are old, well-worn wing chairs aplenty and a grandfather clock in one corner. The small uncluttered bar has red plastic upholstered banquettes, wooden chairs and walls littered with clan coat of arms plaques, a large map of Scotland, rugby cartoons, golf prints and a few pieces of horse tackle. On the food side, evenings see a concentration on the restaurant and its à la carte menu. This is nothing special, but offers a selection of tried and trusted favourites, capably and unspectacularly handled. Typical of the choice are lemon sole Veronique, duckling à l'orange, beef stroganoff or tournedos Rossini – served in the rather quaint (and not often seen these days) silver service style. The lunchtime bar menu includes savoury chicken pancake, fried herring in oatmeal, and steak and mushroom pie with ale, again competently handled. Good overnight accommodation is provided in eleven bedrooms, 9 of them housed in converted garages, the upper floors of which connect with the main building courtesy of a walkway. Ground floor rooms are the largest, upper rooms very compact. All are furnished in unpretentious fashion with fitted units, matching curtains and duvets, with fully-tiled bathrooms (showers over the bath). However, extractor fans are rather noisy and go on for some time. The remaining two rooms are in the main house, neither of them en suite, but sharing a well-maintained bathroom. A reasonable Scottish breakfast starts the day (especially good bacon), but beware of less than helpful teapots!

Bar Meals: 12-2, 5-7; *bar snacks both sessions* *Restaurant:* 12-2.30, 7-9.30
Typical Dishes BAR: parsnip soup 80p, chicken liver paté £1.95, goujons of plaice £3.85, steak and mushroom pie £4.20, fried herring in oatmeal £4.30, hot apple pie £1.40 *RESTAURANT:* Holland game and whisky soup £2.50, deep-fried camembert £3.75, halibut steak dugléré £12.25, chicken tarragon £10.20, fillet of pork in stilton sauce £15.95, cloutie dumpling £2 *Vegetarian Meals* *Children's Menu* `Cheese` `Beer` Theakston, Youngers `Whisky` *Family Room* *Accommodation:* 14 bedrooms, all en suite, from £46 (single £34) *Children Welcome Overnight* *Cots Available* *Check-in:* all day *Credit Cards:* Access, Visa

---

KENMORE   Kenmore Hotel

Kenmore PH15 2NU
Tel: (08873) 205
Open: all day
Licensee: Philip Wain

The Kenmore claims to be Scotland's oldest inn, dating from 1572, in a lovely Perthshire village at the eastern tip of Loch Tay. The Poet's Parlour bar, devoted to Burns, is cosy, with green tartan seats; Archie's Bar is simpler, with glorious views of the river. Try to get a window table in the River View Restaurant. Excellent salmon fishing.

Bar Meals: 12-2.30, 7-9; *bar snacks both sessions* *Restaurant:* 7-9.15 (8.30 winter)
Typical Dishes BAR: white onion soup £1.65, hot button mushrooms £2.75, home-made lasagne £4.25, roast sirloin with Yorkshire pudding (Sundays) £6.50, omelette £3.15, raspberry pavlova £1.75 *RESTAURANT:* table d'hote menu £18.50: watercress and almond soup, locally smoked salmon, roast guinea fowl and redcurrants in red wine sauce, sirloin steak Café de Paris, poached fillets of lemon sole, profiteroles *Vegetarian Meals* (restaurant): nut cutlets with Cumberland sauce *Children's Portions* `Whisky` *Family Room* *Outdoor Play Area* *Riverside Garden* *Outdoor Eating* *Summer Barbecue* *Accommodation:* 38 bedrooms, all en suite, from £49.50 (single £27.50) *Children Welcome Overnight* *Cots Available* *Check-in: all day*

KILLIECRANKIE   Killiecrankie Hotel

By Pitlochry PH16 5LG   ❢
Tel: (0796) 3220 (473220 from May '92)
Open: 11-2.30 (12-2.30 Sun), 6-11
Licensee: Colin Anderson

The Andersons, having refurbished the bar and conservatory in a smart, traditional
country hotel style, with mahogany panelling and furnishings in the former, and
beech tables instead of the old copper-tops in the latter, have now turned their
attentions to the hotel accommodation. All bedrooms are now en suite, and have
been given the once over; the hotel has been recarpeted, and an open fireplace
installed in the dining room to cheer up winter evenings. It's a fine white-painted
old property, a former dower house, in its own grounds at the northern end of the
famous pass, in glorious central Scotland scenery.

*Bar Meals: 12.30-2, 6.30-9.30; bar snacks lunchtime   Restaurant: 7-8.30   Typical
Dishes: home-made soup £1.35, paté £2, game casserole £6.25, fresh pasta £6.25, fresh
fillets of fish £5.25, banoffee pie £1.90   Vegetarian Meals: fresh ravioli   Children's
Menu/Portions* Cheese Whisky *Children Allowed in Bar to Eat   Outdoor Play Area
Accommodation (closed Jan/Feb): 11 bedrooms, all en suite, from £77.20 (single £40)
Children Welcome   Overnight Cot Available   Check-in: all day   Credit Cards: Access,
Amex, Visa*

KINNESSWOOD   Lomond Country Inn

Kinnesswood KY13 7HN
Tel: (0592) 84253
Open: 11-11 (midnight Fri/Sat); 12-11 Sun)
Licensee: David Adams

Dramatically set, proprietor-run, attractive 19th century inn close to Loch Leven.
Fresh food including local produce in season.

*Bar Meals and Restaurant: 12-2, 6.30-9; bar snacks both sessions   Typical Dishes
BAR: home-made soup £1.25, chicken liver paté £2, steak pie £4.50, rib steak (for 2)
£15, Loch Leven trout £5, sticky toffee pudding £2.50   Vegetarian Meals: mushroom
stroganoff   Children's Menu/Portions* Beer *Jennings; Tetley* Whisky *Family Room
Outdoor Play Area   Patio/terrace   Accommodation: 12 bedrooms, all en suite, from £39
(single £24.50)   Children Welcome Overnight   Cot Available   Check-in: all day   Credit
Cards: Access, Amex, Visa*

PERTH   Greyfriars

15 South Street PH2 8PG
Tel: (0738) 33036
Open: 11-2.30, 5-11 (11 am-11.45 Fri/Sat; 12.30-11 Sun)
Licensee: Bryan Whyte

Friendly little city pub with upstairs dining room; routine stuff on the printed menu,
plus two hot specials a day, and lots of foreign bottled beers.

*Bar Meals: 11.30-2.30, 5-9 (9.30 dining room); bar snacks both sessions   Typical Dishes:
soup of the day 65p, home-made steak pie £3.20, home-cooked gammon steak £3.20, bread
and butter pudding   Vegetarian Meals: lasagne   Children's Menu/Portions* Beer
Caledonian; Ind Coope Burton Ale; Orkney Raven Ale   Family Room   No Credit Cards

PITLOCHRY   East Haugh House

off A9, south of Pitlochry PH16 5JS   ❢
Tel: (0796) 3121
Open: 11-2.30, 6-11
Licensee: Neil McGown

Handsome 17th century turreted stone house in two acres of grounds. All fresh local seasonal produce, some of it shot or caught by the proprietor. Non-residents are welcome: interesting bar food in the Conservatory Bar, or in the gardens in summer. Recommended for a pre- or post-Pitlochry Theatre supper (from 6pm).

Bar Meals: 12-2, 6-10.30 (10 winter); bar snacks both sessions **Restaurant:** *7-10* **Typical Dishes BAR:** *home-made soup £1.10, warm salad of smoked chicken and peppers £4.50, sautéed red deer liver £7.95, fresh haddock or plaice £5.95, fresh poached Tay salmon £9.95, summer pudding £2.95* **RESTAURANT:** *dinner menu £18.50: broccoli and lentil soup, lambs sweetbreads provencale, rack of Perthshire lamb, Scotch sirloin steak, escalope of fresh salmon, dark and white chocolate mousse* **Vegetarian Meals:** *warm vegetable terrine* **Children's Menu/Portions** `Cheese` `Whisky` *Children Allowed in Bar to Eat* **Outdoor Play Area** **Garden** **Outdoor Eating** **Accommodation** *(closed end Jan-early March): 6 bedrooms, all en suite, from £50 (single £20)* **Children Welcome Overnight** **Cots Available** **Check-in:** *all day* **Credit Cards:** *Access, Visa*

ST FILLANS   Achray House Hotel

Loch Earn PH6 2NF   ❢
Tel: (0764) 85231
Closed Nov-Feb
Licensee: Tony and Jane Ross

Family-run hotel by the lochside in pretty countryside. Interior typically Scottish – pine panelling, tartan carpet in dining room; bar rather garishly modernised. Famous for its home-made puddings.

Bar Meals: 12-2.30, 6.30-9.30 **Restaurant:** *6.30-9.30* **Typical Dishes BAR:** *cream of cauliflower soup £1.20, salade Nicoise £1.85, grilled venison burgers £3.90, ham, leek and cheese pancakes £3.90, rainbow trout fillet £5.45, apricot and brandy trifle £1.85* **RESTAURANT:** *home-made soup £1.80, sweet herring salad £3.95, chicken supreme Marengo £6.95, Aberdeen Angus fillet steak £11.70, baked trout with prawns and capers £7.50, coffee liqueur mousse with hazelnut shortbread £2.20* **Vegetarian Meals** `Cheese` `Whisky` *Deanston; Tullibardine* **Children Allowed in Bar to Eat** **Accommodation:** *10 bedrooms, 7 en suite, from £42 (single £27)* **Children Welcome Overnight** **Cot Available** **Check-in:** *all day* **Credit Cards:** *Access, Amex, Visa*

WEEM   Ailean Chraggan Hotel

By Aberfeldy PH15 2LD
Tel: (0887) 20346
Open: 11-11
Licensee: Alastair Gillespie

Delightful little cottage inn, beautifully located against a steep woodland backdrop, and with two acres of gardens overlooking the Tay valley. The bright, sunny, well-kept bar has a central log-burning stove, with a dining area beside the picture windows. Simple well-cooked food, the list enlivened by superb local seafood; try the Loch Etive mussels, served in huge steaming portions with garlic bread. There are special set menu seafood nights. Bedrooms are also recommended: spacious and light with nice pieces of old furniture, armchairs, and, in two rooms, small dressing areas. Ask for one of the front bedrooms, which have inspiring views to wake up to.

Bar Meals and Restaurant: 12-2, 6.30-10 (9 winter); bar snacks both sessions   **Typical Dishes:** *soup of the day £1.55, duck liver and Grand Marnier paté £3.85, beef and walnut casserole £5.95, grilled sirloin steak garni £10.50, Sound of Jura prawn platter £9.50, hot fruit crumble £2.65   Children's Portions*   Whisky   *Children Allowed in Bar to Eat Outdoor Play Area   Garden   Outdoor Eating   Summer Barbecue   **Accommodation:** 3 bedrooms, all en suite, from £47.30 (single £23.65)   Children Welcome Overnight   Cots Available   Check-in: all day   **No Credit Cards***

THE ISLANDS

ARRAN

BRODICK   Ormidale Hotel

Brodick KA27 8BY
Tel: (0770) 2293
Open: 12-2.30 (Easter-end Sept only), 4.30-12 (12-12 Sat/Sun)
Licensee: Tommy Gilmore

An appetising menu of fine malts by the glass is just one of the attractions at this sandstone hotel overlooking the golf course. The cosy bar is popular with locals; there's also a conservatory. Real fire; no music.

Bar Meals: 12.30-2 (summer only), 6-8 all year; bar snacks   **Typical Dishes:** *Arran cheese and bacon soup 95p, home-made liver pate £2.15, casserole of venison £4.95, home-made lasagne £4.45, Arran clams mornay £6.95, apple pie £1.25   Vegetarian Meals: cheese and lentils au gratin £4.25   Children's Portions*   Beer   *McEwan 70/-*   Whisky   *Children Allowed in Bar to Eat   Children Allowed in Bar to Eat   Outdoor Play Area Garden   Outdoor Eating   **Accommodation** (closed Oct-Easter): 9 bedrooms, sharing 2 bathrooms, from £39 (single £19.50)   Children Welcome Overnight   Check-in: all day* **No Credit Cards**

BRODICK Duncans Bar, Kingsley Hotel, Shore Road: Lovely views from the beer garden across the bay; large comfortable hotel bar; jazz and folk in summer; bar meals lunch and evening. McEwans beer. Open all day.

CATACOL Catacol Bay Hotel: Home-made pizzas and other bar meals almost all day; family room; garden; Tennents beer. Open all day.

SEIL

CLACHAN SEIL   Tigh-an-Truish

By Oban PA34 4QZ   ☂
Tel: (08523) 242
Open: 12-2.30, 5-11 (11-11 summer; 12.30-11 Sun all year)
Licensee: M H Brunner

18th century inn by the Atlantic Bridge. Boarded nicotine yellow ceiling, old pine bar counter and twin dartboards; popular with locals. Limited winter menu (perhaps only soup and sandwiches), but recommended for high season bar food, and for bed and breakfast, in two good sized bedrooms, one with bath, the other shower only.

Recent improvements have come in the shape of hairdryers and phones, but breakfast is still a self service affair.

Bar Meals: 12-2.15, 6-8.30; bar snacks both sessions **Typical Dishes:** *home-made soup £1.20, herring in mustard sauce £2.20, venison in Drambuie and cream £5.80, beef and Guinness pie £4, locally caught prawns £5.50, sticky toffee pudding £1.50 Vegetarian Meals: home-made nutburger £3 Children's Portions* `Beer` *McEwan 80/-* `Whisky` *Family Room Outdoor Play Area Garden Outdoor Eating* **Accommodation** *(closed Dec/Jan): 2 bedrooms, both en suite, from £40 (room rate, no singles reduction) Children Welcome Overnight Cot Available Check-in: all day* **No Credit Cards**

CLACHAN SEIL   Willowburn Hotel

Clachan Seil PA34 4TD
Tel: (08523) 276
Open: 12.30-2.30, 6-11 (closed Nov-Easter)
Licensee: A M Todd

Low cottage hotel in two acres on the sheltered south east shore; a peaceful haven with an imaginative bar menu.

Bar Meals: 12.30-2, 6-8.30; bar snacks lunchtime **Restaurant:** *7-8* **Typical Dishes BAR:** *smoky ham and lentil soup £1.25, lobster platter £5.45, chicken and broccoli crumble £4.80, house-baked ham £5.40, Atlantic salmon and dill cream quiche £3.75, rum and apple sponge £1.60* **RESTAURANT** *set dinner menu: £13: cream of watercress soup, crab with tomato salad, herb-roast chicken with Drambuie stuffing, popes eye steak with Glayva sauce, seafood au gratin, fresh fruit pavlova Vegetarian Meals (bar): spicy bean and vegetable hotpot Children's Portions* `Cheese` *(restaurant)* `Whisky` *Children Allowed in Bar to Eat Outdoor Play Area Riverside Garden* **Accommodation** *(closed end Oct-Easter): 6 bedrooms, all en suite, from £72 (single £36) (includes dinner) Children Welcome Overnight Check-in: all day* **Credit Cards:** *Access, Visa*

SHETLAND

BUSTA   Busta House Hotel

Brae ZE2 9QN
Tel: (080 622) 506
Open: 12-2.30, 6-11; (12.30-2.30, 6.30-11 Sun) closed 22 Dec-3 Jan
Licensee: Peter Jones

Tremendously civilised hotel in a wild place. A 16th century former laird's home overlooking the sea, simply furnished in Scottish rural style and, beyond its rather formidable exterior, open to non-residents for good home-cooked bar lunches and suppers. All fresh vegetables, and Raven Ale from 'nearby' Orkney. 136 malt whiskies on offer! Four acres of walled garden, small private sea harbour, and holiday packages of the fly/sail and drive kind, too.

Bar Meals: 12 (12.30 Sun)-2, 7-9 **Restaurant:** *7-9* **Typical Dishes BAR:** *leek and potato soup £1.30, marinated Shetland herring and oatcakes £2.05, steak, red wine and mushroom pie £4.85, grilled Shetland lamb cutlets, honey and mint glazed £4.55, home-breaded local fried haddock £4.40, home-grown rhubarb crumble* **RESTAURANT** *set price menus £17.75-£19.50 Vegetarian Meals: bean and vegetable stew Children's Portions* `Beer` *Orkney Raven Ale* `Whisky` *Kinclaith 1967; Mortlach 1936 Family Room Garden Outdoor Eating* **Accommodation** *(closed 22 Dec-3 Jan): 20 bedrooms, all en suite, from £70 (sngle £56) Children Welcome Overnight Cots Available Check-in: until 11 pm* **Credit Cards:** *Access, Amex, Diners, Visa*

SKYE

ARDVASAR   Ardvasar Hotel

near Armadale Ferry IV45 8RS
Tel: (04714) 223
Open: 11-2.30, 5-11
Licensee: Bill and Gretta Fowler

Handsome 18th century inn, not far from the shore, with superb views across the Sound of Sleat to the mountains beyond. A mix of the familiar and more interesting daily specials from the young chef proprietor; good local seafood and fish. Cocktail bar style lounge, simple public bar, and residents sitting room with open fire.

Bar Meals: 12-2, 5-7 (bar snacks to 9.30)   *Typical Dishes:* home-made soup £1.20, crab salad, steak and kidney pie, spaghetti bolognese, seafood au gratin (main courses from £3.50), Ecclefechan butter tart   *Vegetarian Meals:* potato and lentil spicy bake   *Children's Portions*   Cheese   Beer   *Tennent's*   Whisky   *Children Allowed in Bar to Eat Patio/terrace   Outdoor Eating   **Accommodation** (closed Jan/Feb): 10 bedrooms, all en suite, from £52 (single £26)   Children Welcome Overnight   Check-in: all day   **Credit Cards:** Access, Visa*

CARBOST   The Old Inn

Carbost IV47 8SR
Tel: (047 842) 205
Open: 11-2.30, 5-12 (11.30 Sat); 12.30-2.30, 6.30-11 Sun
Licensee: Deirdre Cooper

Next to the loch, and near the Talisker distillery, a charming, chatty little island cottage, popular as a good cheap walkers' base. Food is somewhat secondary; home-made fishy specials and puddings.

Bar Meals: 12-2, 6-10   *Typical Dishes:* lentil soup £1, paté £1.50, 8 oz sirloin steak with mushrooms and ratatouille £6.50, scampi and chips £3.85, herrings in oatmeal £3.95, home-made apple crumble £1.60   *Vegetarian Meals:* vegetable quiche with ratatouille   Children's Menu   Whisky   Family Room   Outdoor Play Area   Lochside Patio/terrace   Outdoor Eating   **Accommodation** (closed Oct-March): 3 bedrooms, sharing 2 bathrooms, from £27 (single £13.50)   Children Welcome Overnight   Check-in: by arrangement   **No Credit Cards***

PORTREE   Portree House

Home Farm Road IV51 9LX
Tel: (0478) 2796
Open: 11-2.30, 5-11 (all day summer and Sat all year); 12.30-4, 6 (6.30 winter)-11 Sun
Licensee: N G Wilson

Interesting bar food in comfortable lounge bar; self-catering accommodation in one and two bedroomed cottages.

Bar Meals: 12-2.30 (4.30 Sat and summer), 5.30-10; 12.30-3.45, 6.30 (6 summer)-10 Sun   *Typical Dishes:* minestrone 85p, gigot of lamb £7.40, Skye cod £6.95, fresh Skye salmon £9.10 (main courses evening), real ice-creams   *Vegetarian Meals   Children's Portions*   Whisky   Family Room   Outdoor Play Area   Garden   **Credit Cards:** Access, Visa*

Wales

CLWYD

BABELL   Black Lion Inn

near Holywell CH8 8PZ   ❦
Tel: (0352) 720239
Licensees: Mr and Mrs Foster

A recent American letter warmly endorsed our last edition's recommendation of the
Black Lion thus: "the meal was delicious, and the Fosters are the friendliest hosts we
have ever encountered". It's a peaceful country pub, in the same hands for almost
30 years.

Bar Meals: 12.15-2 (not weekends);   bar snacks **Restaurant:** *evenings (set menu)*
*Typical Dishes BAR: paté, prawn cocktail, veal in cream sauce, fillet of plaice with lemon
butter, ham in mustard sauce (main courses around £5)   Vegetarian Meals* ▮Cheese▮ *Credit
Cards: Amex, Diners, Visa*

BETWS-YN-RHOS   Ffarm Hotel

near Abergele LL22 8AR
Tel: (049 260) 287
Open: weekday evenings; weekends summer
Licensees: Lomax family

Eating is the main event at this discreet venue, hiding, signless, behind an impressive
crenellated stone facade. White-walled bars, comfortably modernised; printed menu
and blackboard specials; smiling service.

Bar Meals: 7-10 **Typical Dishes:** *liver and garlic paté, prawn cocktail, rack of lamb,
seafood gratin, chicken Creole (main courses from £5)   Vegetarian Meals* ▮Beer▮ *Ind
Coope, Tetley* **No Credit Cards**

BODFARI   Dinorben Arms

near Denbigh LL16 4DA
Tel: (074575) 309
Open: 12-3, 6-11
Licensee: Gilbert Hopwood

Heavily timbered 17th century inn transformed into a diverse and shipshape dining
pub: various bars and restaurants within offer decent bar meals, smorgasbord,
carvery, buffets (two new salad bars this year), and a family room; children genuinely
welcome. Amazing gardens too, with terraces, a verandah, fountains, a covered
terrace, pretty flowers, and a children's play area beyond the huge tiered car park.

Bar Meals and Restaurant: 12-2.30, 6 (7 Sun)-10; bar snacks lunchtime **Typical
Dishes BAR:** *home-made soup £1.45, steak and kidney pie £4.45, chicken, ham and
mushroom pie £4.45, poached salmon £5.45, home-made apple pie £1.40*
RESTAURANT: *smorgasbord lunch £5.95, farmhouse buffet (Wed/Thur eves) £8.95,
carverboard buffet (Fri/Sat) £12.95   Vegetarian Meals   Children's Menu/Portions*
▮Beer▮ *Thwaites* ▮Whisky▮ *Family Room   Outdoor Play Area/Garden   Outdoor
Eating* *Credit Cards: Access, Visa*

BRYNTRILLYN Sportsmans Arms on A543: 16th century local, and the
highest pub in Wales, in glorious isolation, with lovely country views. Decent bar

food, particularly the home-made pies, lunch and evening; children welcome for meals; Lees beers. Open: 11-3 (not Mon/Tue), 7-11.

BURTON ROSSETT   Golden Grove

Llyndir Lane, Burton Green LL12 0AS
Tel: (0244) 570445
Open: all day
Licensee: C D Rowlands

Remote black and white old Border inn, without even a pub sign (the scattered array of timbered buildings and big car park are a clue), but traditionally pubby within: low ceilings, a mix of old furniture, open fires, and decent food in both bar and restaurant; there's also an evening carvery. Vegetables from their own garden. Excellent family facilities.

Bar Meals and Restaurant: 12-2.30, 6 (7 restaurant)-10.30; bar snacks both sessions *Typical Dishes BAR: cauliflower and stilton soup £1, home-made steak and Guinness pie £3.50, steak and cider pie £3.50, pork Mexican £3.95, home-made puddings RESTAURANT: smoked salmon with Glenlivet £6.50, chicken Marengo £8.95, scampi Pernod £9.95, fresh, very large Dover sole £19.50   Children's Portions* `Cheese` `Beer` *Marston beers* `Whisky` *Family Room   Garden   Outdoor Eating   Summer Barbecue   Credit Cards: Access, Amex, Diners, Visa*

CILCAIN   White Horse

near Mold CH7 5NN
Tel: (0352) 740142
Open: 12-2.30, 7-11
Licensee: Peter Jeory

Classic Welsh village pub, partly 14th century, popular with walkers (Moel Fammau is nearby). Delightful lounge with original beams, brasses, an inglenook and very low seating; other intimate drinking areas leading off, plus old-fashioned quarry tiled public bar. Acts as local newsagency on Sundays. Aside from the dishes listed here, famous for its (local) ham and eggs; all good home cooking. Four real fires in winter. No children.

Bar Meals: 12-2, 7.30-9.30 (10 Fri/Sat); bar snacks both sessions *Typical Dishes: beef and barley soup £1.20, stilton and Guinness paté £2.40, chicken and herb pie £4.80, steak and kidney pie £4.30, Madras curried prawns £4.30, treacle tart £1.85   Vegetarian Meals: mushroom stroganoff £4.20* `Beer` *Ansells, Ind Coope; Sam Powell* `Cider` *Addlestones   Patio/terrace   Credit Cards: Access, Visa*

CYFFYLLIOG Red Lion Tel: (08246) 664: Charming little pub in glorious countryside; good value bar meals lunch and evening, and accommodation. Real fires, family room, garden; Lees Bitter. Open: 12-3, 6.30-11.

GLYN CEIRIOG   Golden Pheasant

near Llangollen LL20 8BB
Tel: (069 172) 281
Open: 11-11
Licensee: J T Gibourg

Routine bar meals, more interesting restaurant at this prettily set, comfortable country hotel.

Bar Meals and Restaurant: 12-3 (2 restaurant), 7-9; bar snacks both sessions   **Typical Dishes BAR:** *home-made soup £1.75, home-made lasagne £3.95, chilli £3.95, steak and kidney pie £3.95, apple pie*   **RESTAURANT** *set menu £17.95: pheasant in red wine, roast Welsh lamb, Ceiriog trout   Vegetarian Meals: lasagne   Children's Menu/Portions   Family Room   Outdoor Play Area   Garden   Outdoor Eating   **Accommodation:** 18 bedrooms, all en suite, from £59.80 (single £32)   Children Welcome Overnight   Cots Available   Check-in: all day   **Credit Cards:** Access, Amex, Diners, Visa*

GRAIGFECHAN Three Pigeons on B5429 Tel: (08242) 3178: Popular country pub, full of walkers in summer, and recently extended to accommodate more diners (including children). Home cooking of a plain and homely kind, from fresh local ingredients. Draught Bass. Open: 12-3 (summer only), 6.30-11.

HANMER   Hanmer Arms

near Whitchurch SY13 3DE
Tel: (094 874) 640
Open: 11.30-11 (12-3, 6-10.30 Sun)

Reasonable bar food – look out for obviously local meat and fish specials – and popular cobbled courtyard accommodation, complete with conferencing facilities.

Bar Meals: 12-2.30, 6.15-10.15; bar snacks both sessions   **Restaurant:** 12-2.30 (weekends only), 7-10   **Typical Dishes BAR:** *home-made soup £1, egg mayonnaise £1.30, spit-roasted half chicken £4.30, gammon £4.50, 12 oz rump steak £6.60, apple pie £1.60   **RESTAURANT:** cod goujons £2.20, chicken chasseur £7, steak Diane £8.90, Dover sole £11.20   Vegetarian Meals: moussaka   Children's Menu/Portions*   Beer *Ansells, Ind Coope, Tetley*   Whisky   *Children Allowed in Bar to Eat   Outdoor Play Area   Garden   Outdoor Eating   **Accommodation:** 20 bedrooms, all en suite, from £50 (single £25)   Children Welcome Overnight   Cot Available   Check-in: all day*   **Credit Cards:** *Access, Amex, Visa*

LLANARMON DYFFRYN CEIRIOG   West Arms Hotel

near Llangollen LL20 7LD
Tel: (069 176) 665
Open: 11-11
Licensee: T Alexander

Jigsaw puzzle-pretty, roadside pub in lovely valley, with a marvellous interior, stylish yet traditional, with stone floors, lots of heavy dark timbers, inglenook fireplaces, and daring deeply coloured paintwork, offset by pretty chintzes, and in the dining room, white linens; all very smart but balanced by a separate no-frills locals' public. Recommended for overnight accommodation.

Bar Meals: 12-2.30, 6.30-9.30; bar snacks both sessions   **Restaurant:** 12-2.30 (Sun only), 7.30-9.30   **Typical Dishes BAR:** *vegetable and lamb soup £1.75, herbed mushrooms with garlic mayonnaise £2.75, Welsh lamb cutlets £4.95, tagliatelle verdi with salmon and brie £5.50, grilled Ceiriog trout £5.25, summer pudding £2.25   **RESTAURANT** table d'hote £19.50: watercress and potato soup, chilled melon with summer fruit sorbet, breast of duck with apple, cider and sage; mignon of beef with stilton, red wine and rosemary; grilled salmon steak with anchovy and parsley butter; filo pastry basket with caramelised pineapple   Vegetarian Meals   Children's Portions   Family Room   Outdoor Play Area   Riverside Garden   **Accommodation:** 14 bedrooms, all en suite, from £78 (single £49.50)   Children Welcome Overnight   Cots Available   Check-in: all day*   **Credit Cards:** *Access, Amex, Diners, Visa*

LLANARMON DYFFRYN CEIRIOG Hand: owned by the same people, an equally civilised little inn.

LLANBEDR DYFFRYN CLWYD   Griffin Inn

Ruthin LL15 1UP
Tel: (08242) 2792
Open: 12-3, 6.30-11
Licensee: Menai Edwards (Mrs)

Comfortable bedrooms at very reasonable prices in this popular old inn, once an important coaching stage on the old turnpike road from Mold to Ruthin. Rambling interior, with a public bar, restaurant, and smallish lounge warmed by an open fire, but beyond the lounge a larger, plain extension, and then a cosy little sitting area complete with piano. Good views from the terrace.

Bar Meals and Restaurant: 12-2.30, 6.30-10; bar snacks both sessions **Typical Dishes** **BAR:** *leek and potato soup £1.25, marinated herrings in dill £2.85, steak and kidney pie £4.75, lasagne £4.75, asparagus and sweetcorn quiche £4.95, fresh fruit flan £2.25* **RESTAURANT**: *avocado with prawns £3.25, fillet steak with black pepper sauce £10.95, lamb with honey, rosemary, garlic and wine sauce £8.25, lemon sole with prawns £8.95, meringues £2.25   Vegetarian Meals: leek and gruyère pithiviers   Children's Menu Children's Portions (some)* ■ **Beer** *Hartleys Fellrunners, XB; Robinsons Best* ■ **Whisky** *Children Allowed in Bar to Eat   Patio/terrace   Outdoor Eating* **Accommodation:** *5 bedrooms, sharing 2 bathrooms, from £35 (single £20)   Check-in: all day* **Credit Cards:** *Access, Diners, Visa*

LLANFERRES   Druid Inn

Ruthin Road (A494), near Mold CH7 5SQ
Tel: (035 285) 225
Open: 11.30-3, 5.30-11
Licensees: Colin and Rosemary Carney

Family-owned and run, attractive white-painted roadside inn with charming views and mountain walks, overlooking the Alyn river. Plain, modernised interior decor. Home-made food favours fresh local produce.

Bar Meals and Restaurant: 12-2.30, 7-9.30; bar snacks both sessions **Typical Dishes:** *pea and ham soup £1.15, black pudding with apple sauce £1.90, chicken Lausanne £6.90, noisettes of Welsh lamb with mint and redcurrant jelly £6.10, baked plaice with prawn stuffing £5.90, lemon flan   Vegetarian Meals: fresh vegetable crumble   Children's Menu* ■ **Beer** *Burtonwood Bitter   Children Allowed in Bar to Eat   Patio/terrace   Outdoor Eating* **Accommodation:** *4 bedrooms, sharing a bathroom, from £32 (single £18.50) Children Welcome Overnight   Cot Available   Check-in: all day* **Credit Cards:** *Access, Visa*

LLANFWROG Cross Keys: Cosy country inn in a useful spot. Real fires, no music, lunchtime and evening meals (locally popular), Banks's beers. Open: 11.30-3.30, 6.30-11.

LLANGOLLEN   Britannia Inn

Horseshoe Pass LL20 8DW
Tel: (0978) 860144
Open: 11-3, 7-11
Licensee: M J Callaghan

A recent refurbishment by local craftsmen has brought traditional Welsh furnishings in local elm to both the characterful old bars at this popular holiday inn. All bedrooms have four poster beds. Dishes like pork Normande and duckling in the evening restaurant.

Bar Meals: *11.30-2.30, 7-10; bar snacks both sessions*   **Restaurant:** *7.30-9.30*   **Typical Dishes BAR:** *home-made soup £1.50, home-made steak pie, chicken tikka, peppered pork (main courses from £4), home-made apple pie   Vegetarian Meals (bar): leek crumble   Children's Portions* ▆Beer▆ *Whitbread beers   Children Allowed in Bar to Eat   Garden   Outdoor Eating*   **Accommodation:** *7 bedrooms, all en suite, from £40 (single £25)   Children Welcome Overnight   Check-in: all day*   **Credit Cards:** *Access, Diners, Visa*

LLANGOLLEN Wynnstay Arms Bridge Street Tel: (0978) 860710: Splendid old inn, rambling and cosy; real fires; family room; garden; bedrooms. Bar meals lunch and summer evenings. Ind Coope and Tetley beers. Open: 12-3, 7(6 summer)-11.

MOLD   We Three Loggerheads

Ruthin Road, Loggerheads CH7 5PG
Tel: (035 285) 337
Open: 12-3, 5.30-11 (7.30-10.30 Sun); 11-11 Fri/Sat
Licensee: Gary Willard

Well-run, busy old pub, with a characterful original little bar, bigger, pool-table dominated locals' bar, and modern, attractive high-raftered upper lounge, venue for most of the eating. A decent menu is enlivened by often imaginative daily specials; good special occasion feasts, especially the Welsh menu during Eisteddfod. Watch out for the juke box. Nature trails and good walks in the surrounding country park.

Bar Meals: *12-2.30, 6-10; bar snacks both sessions*   **Typical Dishes:** *cauliflower and stilton soup £1.65, lamb samosas £2.75, Thai green chicken curry in coconut shell £6.95, old-fashioned meatloaf in herb crust £5.25, trout with salmon soufflé filling £6.95, toffee and banana tart £1.95   Vegetarian Meals: broccoli and brie crepes £5.25   Children's Portions* ▆Beer▆ *Draught Bass   Children Allowed in Bar to Eat   Riverside Patio/terrace   Outdoor Eating*   **Credit Cards:** *Access, Visa*

OLD COLWYN Plough Inn, 282 Abergele Road: Attractively refurbished and relaxing village pub, popular for lunchtime and evening bar food. Greenalls beers. Open: 11.30-3, 5.30-11.

PONTBLYDDYN   New Inn

near Mold CH7 4HR
Tel: (0352) 771459
Open: 12-11
Licensee: James Elliott

Routine bar food except for an excellent home-made steak and kidney pie, but a useful stop-off and a typical country pub, with its own working cooperage.

Bar Meals: *12-9.45 (12-2.30, 7-9.45 Sun); bar snacks both sessions*   **Typical Dishes:** *home-made vegetable soup 80p, paté £1.80, home-made individual steak and kidney pie £3.30, home-cooked ham £3.30, fillet steak £7.25, lemon meringue £1.20   Vegetarian Meals: mushroom and butterbean stroganoff   Children's Menu* ▆Beer▆ *Ruddles   Family Room   Outdoor Play Area   Riverside Garden   Outdoor Eating*   **No Credit Cards**

RHEWL   Drovers Arms

near Ruthin LL15 2UD
Tel: (08242) 3163
Open: 11.30-3 (12-2.30 Sun), 6 (7 winter)-11
Licensee: Mike Mellor

18th century cottage pub; guest beers always on offer.

Bar Meals: 12-2.30, 6-9.45; bar snacks both sessions **Typical Dishes:** *beef and vegetable soup £1, garlic mushrooms £2.25, home-made steak pie £3.60, chicken Maryland £6.50, local fresh trout £5.25, home-made apple pie £1.25* *Vegetarian Meals: cannelloni verdi £3.65* *Children's Menu* █ Beer █ *Ruddles* *Children Allowed in Bar to Eat* *Outdoor Play Area* *Garden* *Outdoor Eating* **No Credit Cards**

TREMEIRCHION   Salusbury Arms

St Asaph LL17 0UN
Tel: (074 575) 262
Open: 12-3, 7-11; closed Mon
Licensees: Iain and Catherine Craze

No juke box, no pool table, no fruit machines or similar, at this staunchly traditional, attractively modernised old pub, with decent home-made bar food.

Bar Meals: 12-1.45, 7-9.45 (9.15 Sun); bar snacks both sessions **Typical Dishes:** *home-made soup £1.65, mussels in cream and wine £2.95, chicken with cream and tarragon £4.35, sausages wrapped in bacon £3.95, fillet steak stuffed with stilton in red wine sauce £10.50, raspberry tipsy pudding £2* *Vegetarian Meals: fettuccine in mushroom sauce £3.75* *Children's Menu* *Children's Portions (some)* █ Beer █ *John Smith's Bitter* *Children Allowed in Bar to Eat* *Garden* *Outdoor Eating* **Credit Cards:** *Access, Amex, Diners, Visa*

DYFED

ABERGORLECH   Black Lion

Carmarthen SA32 7SN
Tel: (0558) 685271
Open: 12-3, 7-11 (11-11 summer)
Licensee: Brenda Entwistle

High back settles, oak furnishings, flagstones and a woodburning stove in this 16th century timbered pub, which also has trout and salmon fishing rights on the river. Good afternoon teas in summer. They also offer one modest twin bedroom.

Bar Meals: 11.30-2.30, 7-10; bar snacks both sessions **Restaurant:** *12-2, 7-9.30* **Typical Dishes BAR:** *home-made soup £1.25, ham and mushroom tagliatelle £3.20, 10 oz gammon steak £4.20, seafood platter £4.20, apple pie* **RESTAURANT:** *frogs' legs £2.75, steak au poivre £7.95, scampi provencale £6.25, whole grilled Dover sole £8.75* *Vegetarian Meals* *Children's Menu/Portions* █ Beer █ *Felinfoel Double Dragon* *Children Allowed in Bar to Eat* *Outdoor Play Area* *Riverside Garden* *Outdoor Eating* *Summer Barbecue* **Credit Cards:** *Access, Visa*

BRYNHOFFNANT Brynhoffnant Inn on A487: Attractive Victorian building, opened-out inside, but with three distinct areas, a pool room at one end, dining area at the other. Bar meals lunch and evening; families welcome; garden. Bass, Buckleys beers. Open: 11-3, 5.30-11.

CAIO Brunant Arms off A482: Restaurant upstairs from attractive bar. Real fire; no music; garden. Fullers, Marston beers. Open all day.

CARDIGAN   Black Lion Hotel
High Street
Tel: (0239) 612532
Licensee: Anthony Antoniazzi

Much enlarged, but originally medieval town centre inn, with a characterful beamed interior, complete with linenfold panelling in one of the bars. Pine-furnished bedrooms, and a comfortable upstairs television lounge, as well as a quaint little writing room.

Bar Meals: lunch and evening   `Beer`   *Bass*   *Accommodation: 11 bedrooms, all en suite (some with shower only), from £45   Children Welcome Overnight   Check-in: all day* **Credit Cards:** *Access, Visa*

CENARTH   White Hart
Newcastle Emlyn SA38 9JP
Tel: (0239) 710305
Open: 11-3, 5.30-11
Licensees: Terry and Linda Parsons

Unpretentious, homely but recommendable food at a characterful old village pub with low beamed ceilings, carved wooden pews and a wood-burning stove.

Bar Meals: 12-2.30, 7-9; bar snacks both sessions   **Typical Dishes:** *traditional cawl with cheese £2.50, Anglesey eggs £2, steak and kidney pie £4.25, home-cooked ham £4, rainbow trout £5.50, sherry trifle £4   Vegetarian Meals: lasagne   Children's Menu* `Beer`   *Draught Bass; Buckleys Bitter   Family Room   Outdoor Play Area   Garden Outdoor Eating* **No Credit Cards**

FELINDRE FARCHOG   Salutation Inn
on A487 SA41 3UY
Tel: (0239) 820564
Open: 12-3, 6-11
Licensees: Richard and Valerie Harden

Pleasant, modernised, well-kept old inn at the centre of the Preseli National Park. 'Olde worlde' lounge, games room cum public bar, and overflow Garden Room leading off, with patio doors to riverside garden. Good bedrooms in modern wing are well-equipped and maintained; bright, good-sized residents' lounge. Dishes in the restaurant are of the fresh salmon, chicken Kiev and steak au poivre sort.

Bar Meals: 12-2, 6-9; bar snacks both sessions   **Restaurant:** *6.30-9.30*   **Typical Dishes BAR:** *home-made soup £1.70, home-made lasagne £4.40, home-made steak and kidney pie £4.40, home-made chilli £4.40, cheesecake £1.70   Vegetarian Meals: mushroom stroganoff   Children's Menu*   `Beer`   *Ind Coope Burton Ale   Family Room*

*Outdoor Play Area   Riverside Garden   Outdoor Eating   **Accommodation:** 9 bedrooms,
all en suite, from £48 (single £32)   Children Welcome Overnight   Cots Available
Check-in: all day   **Credit Cards** (restaurant/B&B only): Access, Visa*

FELINGWM UCHAF   Plough Inn

Nantgaredig SA32 7PR
Tel: (0267) 290220
Open: daily except Sun eve
Licensee: Leon Hickman

16th century coaching inn on a steep hill, now divided into a bar-bistro on one side,
the well-regarded Hickmans Restaurant at the other. The bar itself remains
pleasantly rustic, with a long bar, stone floors, beamed ceilings and an open fire.
Both bar food and bedrooms are recommended: the latter housed in a cottage over
the road, all fairly newly done, smart and immaculately kept, with an excellent
public bathroom.

Bar Meals and Restaurant: *12-2 (bookings only), 7-9.30 (10 Sat); bar snacks both
sessions   **Typical Dishes BAR:** leek and potato soup £2, melon and Parma ham £3.25,
home-made steak and kidney pie £4.75, Wiener schnitzel £7.50, spaghetti bolognese
£3.95, cappuccino cake £1.95   **RESTAURANT:** watercress and saffron soup £2.50,
cockles and bacon in wine £3.95, beef Wellington (for 2) £26, veal zurichoise £10.25,
salmon hollandaise £9.75, lemon and mint sorbet £2.25   Vegetarian Meals: stuffed peppers
£3.95   Children's Portions   Beer   Draught Bass   Children Allowed in Bar to Eat
Garden   Outdoor Eating   **Accommodation:** 5 bedrooms, 2 en suite, from £40 (single
£28)   Children Welcome Overnight   Check-in: by arrangement   **Credit Cards:** Access,
Amex, Diners, Visa*

LANDSHIPPING   Stanley Arms

Narberth SA67 8BE
Tel: (0834) 891227
Open: 12-3, 6-11

Just 200 yards from the estuary, and moorings are available there for customer use.
Nice interior includes 18th century public bar with original slate floor; live music
Fridays in summer, Saturdays in winter. Look for fresh local fish on the otherwise
routine bar menu. No under 14s overnight.

Bar Meals: *12-2, 7-9.30 (not winter Mon eve); bar snacks lunchtime   **Typical Dishes:**
vegetable soup £1.30, peppered mackerel £1.75, horseshoe gammon £4.25, lasagne
£4.25, local trout £4.05   Vegetarian Meals: cauliflower and kidney bean bake   Children's
Menu/Portions   Beer   Bass Worthington BB; Crown SBB   Family Room   Garden
Outdoor Eating   **Accommodation:** 2 bedrooms, sharing a bathroom, from £23   Check-in:
all day   **No Credit Cards***

LITTLE HAVEN Swan Inn off B4341 Tel: (0437) 781256: Interesting food
cooked by the enthusiastic chef-proprietor, both traditional and exotic, with lots of
fresh local fish; simpler food in bar; smarter in evening restaurant. Garden. Felinfoel
beers. Open: 11-3, 6.30-11. Delightfully set in rocky cove.

LLANDDAROG   Butchers Arms

near Carmarthen SE32 8NS   `FOOD`
Tel: (026 727) 5330   ❦
Open: 11-3 (not Sun), 5.30-12   ☼
Licensee: David James

This tiny pub stands by the 19th century stone-built St Tarog's church, and the old village street runs down to where the old A40 once thundered by. We say hooray today for the new by-pass which makes this such a sleepy spot, and say another as the low, flower-bedecked exterior of the pub gives way to a splendidly atmospheric interior. The single, central bar servery leads through into two dining rooms which radiate on either side; for male visitors, there's less of a treat in store when journeying to and from the primitive outside toilet. Felinfoel ales take their rightful place at the bar, as Welsh is widely spoken here, though this in no way detracts from the warm welcome and friendly service of Mavis James and her staff. A word to the wise: if you have decided to eat, then book ahead and side-step the queue. Take time, however, to admire the Toby jug collection hanging in the bar, and the shining collection of miniature brass lamps and candleholders on the mantel, under which the dog-grate glows in winter and flower vases add a blaze of summer colour. In addition to the regular menu, on which the prime steaks offer particularly good value, look for the specials board, which is strong on fresh fish and seafood: king prawns, fillets of river salmon with lemon butter, and a herby stuffed trout are typical examples. Otherwise, you might start with smoked venison, or avocado and bacon salad, followed by duck breast with orange and ginger, pork fillet with garlic and mushroom sauce, or a casserole of lamb in sweet Cumberland sauce. Garlic potatoes are so good as to be obligatory. Equally desirable for drivers and lunchtime generally are the 25cl bottles of Bordeaux; the white version cools neatly in a pint mug of iced water.

Bar Meals and Restaurant: 11-3, 5.30-10; *bar snacks both sessions* **Typical Dishes**
BAR: *beef and vegetable soup £1.30, garlic king prawns £3.60, mixed grill £5, smoked mackerel £3.80, home-cured ham and chips £4.50, lemon meringue pie £2.30*
RESTAURANT: *Hungarian chicken £5.50, seafood platter £10.50, pork fillet in garlic and mushrooms £7 Vegetarian Meals Children's Menu* `Beer` *Felinfoel Children Allowed in Bar to Eat Patio/terrace Outdoor Eating*

LLANDISSILIO   Bush Inn

near Clynderwen SA66 7TS
Tel: (09916) 626
Licensees: Ken and Joyce Honeker

Tiny, characterful little bar in cosy old pub. Polished tables, plants and dressers crammed with plates and ornaments provide a cosy background in the bright dining room, where help-yourself salads are laid out for the choosing; try them with turkey, ham or quiche, or choose a simple hot dish like steak and kidney pie. Good local cheeses and puddings. They also let bedrooms.

Bar Meals: 11-2.30, 6.30-10.30 (12-1.30, 7-10 Sun) *bar snacks both sessions*
Vegetarian Meals `Cheese` `Beer` *Bass; Pembrokeshire's Own Ales Garden* **Credit Cards:** *Visa*

LLANDYBIE   Red Lion

Ammanford SA18 3JA
Tel: (0269) 851202
Open: 11.30-3, 6-11 (closed Sun eve)
Licensees: Timothy Morgan and Sara Morgan Priestland

Renovated in 1987 after three years of gradual dereliction, a Grade II listed 18th
century pub run by a brother and sister team. Comfortable series of individual
rooms, old mirrors, local pictures, and separate restaurant. Sunday lunches popular.

Bar Meals and Restaurant: 12-2, 6.30 (7 restaurant)-10; bar snacks both sessions
Typical Dishes BAR: home-made soup £1.60, stuffed mushrooms £2.25, meatballs in
tomato and garlic sauce £4.25, chicken Kiev £5.50, lobster au gratin £12, orange and
hazelnut pavlova   RESTAURANT: hot seafood salad £2.95, pork fillet in honey and
cider £8.50, chicken supreme £8.25, salmon beurre blanc £9.50 Vegetarian Meals: stuffed
peppers £4.50   Children's Menu/Portions **Cheese** **Beer** *Whitbread Boddingtons,*
Flowers; Marston Pedigree Bitter   Family Room   Outdoor Play Area   Garden   Outdoor
Eating   Accommodation: 4 bedrooms, 1 en suite, 3 with separate bathrooms, from £35
(single £19.50)   Children Welcome Overnight   Cot Available   Check-in: by arrangement
Credit Cards: Access, Visa

LLANGADOG Castle Hotel Queens Square Tel: (0550) 777377: 15th century
inn in a Black Mountains village; decent home-made food including local
specialities; good-value bed and breakfast.

LLANGRANNOG   Ship Inn

Llangrannog SA44 6SL
Tel: (0239) 654423
Open: 12-3, 6-10
Licensees: Kevin and De Brown, Richard and Lynne Box

Beach-side pub in beautiful fishing village. Good atmosphere, revitalised under new
regime – now run by two energetic couples. Busy in summer.

Bar Meals: 12-3, 6-10; bar snacks both sessions   Typical Dishes: broccoli and orange
soup £1.20, stuffed mushrooms £2.65, pork fillet in sherry £4.95, tandoori chicken masala
£4.95, Dijon kidneys £4.10, strawberry pavlova £1.95   Vegetarian Meals: mixed bean
goulash £3.75   Children's Menu/Portions **Beer** *Ind Coope, Tetley; Marston;*
Whitbread   Family Room   Patio/terrace   Outdoor Eating   Accommodation (mid-May to
end September): 3 bedrooms, sharing a bathroom, from £30 (single £15)   Children
Welcome Overnight   Cot Available   Check-in: all day   No Credit Cards

LLWYNDAFYDD   Crown Inn

near New Quay SA44 6FU
Tel: (0545) 560396
Open: 12-3, 6-11
Licensees: K and A Soar

Modernised but comfortable 18th century inn, in a wooded valley a mile and a half
from the sea; a side lane by the pub leads down to a little cove. Huge patio seats 90
people, prettily landscaped garden and extensive play area. Very popular for its
decent, simple bar food.

Bar Meals: 12-2, 6-9; bar snacks lunchtime   *Restaurant:* 7-9   **Typical Dishes BAR:**
leek and potato soup £1.65, garlic mushrooms £2.45, home-made steak and kidney pie
£4.75, home-made lamb pie £4.75, grilled local trout £5.75, fruit crumble £1.30
RESTAURANT: carrot and coriander soup £1.85, mushrooms Andalucia £2.95,
supreme of chicken £8.45, loin of lamb with ginger and spring onion £8.95, grilled salmon
£7.95, profiteroles £2.45   *Vegetarian Meals:* home-made lasagne £4.75   *Children's
Menu*   Beer   *Draught Bass; Whitbread Flowers IPA, Original   Family Room   Garden
Outdoor Eating*   **Credit Cards:** *Access*

NEWPORT   Golden Lion

East Street SA42 0SY
Tel: (0239) 820321
Open: 11-3, 5.30-11
Licensees: A G and P A Rees

Routine bar food, but well-cooked in generous portions, and with good local fish,
in this pleasant rambling pub on the east side of the town,

Bar Meals: 12-2.30, 7-9.30; bar snacks lunchtime   *Restaurant:* 1-2, 7-9.30   **Typical
Dishes:** home-made soup £1, garlic mushrooms £1.85, steak and kidney pie £3.50,
chicken curry £3.25, fresh plaice £3.30, apple pie £1.75   *Vegetarian Meals: vegetable
curry   Children's Menu/Portions*   Beer   *Buckleys Bitter; Whitbread Boddingtons Bitter
Children Allowed in Bar to Eat   Outdoor Play Area   Garden   Outdoor Eating*
Accommodation: 10 bedrooms, 9 en suite, from £30 (single £18)   *Children Welcome
Overnight   Cot Available   Check-in: all day*   **Credit Cards:** *Access, Visa*

PELCOMB BRIDGE Rising Sun Inn   on A478   Tel: (0437) 765171:
Refurbished and characterful old country inn, proprietor-run; routine bar menu and
more interesting daily specials, lunch and evening. Bedrooms. Ind Coope, Tetley
beers. Open: 11.30-3, 7(6 summer)-11.

PEMBROKE FERRY   Ferry Inn

Pembroke Dock SA72 6UD
Tel: (0646) 682947
Open: 11.30-2.45 (12-2.45 Sun), 6.30 (7 Mon)-11
Licensees: Pat and David Henderson

Fresh fish and shellfish a speciality at a charming old waterside pub. Sunday carvery.
Children allowed in small restaurant at lunchtime.

Bar Meals: 12-2, 7-10 (12-1.30, 7-9.30 Sun); bar snacks lunchtime   *Restaurant:*
lunchtime Sun only, 7.15-9.15 (not Sun/Mon)   **Typical Dishes BAR:** pint of prawns
£2.75, pork schnitzel with mushroom sauce £4.95, sirloin steak garni £6.95, whole fresh
brill or turbot, from £5.95, meringues £1.75   **RESTAURANT:** seafood medley £5.25,
sliced duck's breast in orange and Cointreau £7.25, noisettes of local lamb in redcurrant and
lemon £6.50, surf and turf £9.95   *Vegetarian Meals: mushroom stroganoff   Children's
Portions*   Beer   *Draught Bass, Hancocks HB   Riverside Patio/terrace   Outdoor Eating*
Credit Cards: *Access, Visa*

PISGAH   Halfway Inn

Devil's Bridge Road (A4120) SY23 4NE   ♟
Tel: (097 084) 631
Open: 11-3, 6-11 (11-11 summer and winter Sats)
Licensees: Raywood and Sally Roger

We're losing count of the changes of hands at this marvellous country pub, but its character has survived the upheaval pretty well intact. Lovely setting, 650 feet up, with magnificent views, and well-known as a beer-lovers' favourite, with its choice of six beers, three of which are self-served. Food's looking more ambitious than it has for a while, and the good-value bedrooms have just been refurbished.

Bar Meals: 12-2, 7-9; bar snacks both sessions **Typical Dishes:** *chicken and celery soup £1.50, leek and cheese filo tartlet £2.50, chicken and ham pie £6.50, gammon steak £6.50, brie and broccoli pithiviers £4.50, hot treacle tart £2* *Vegetarian Meals: mushroom and garlic paté* *Children's Menu/Portions* `Cheese` `Beer` *Felinfoel; Wadworth; Whitbread* `Cider` *Weston's* *Family Room* *Outdoor Play Area* *Garden* *Outdoor Eating* **Accommodation:** *2 bedrooms, both en suite, from £35 (single £25)* *Check-in: all day* **Credit Cards:** *Access, Visa*

PONTARGOTHI   Cresselly Arms

Nantgaredig (on A40)
Tel: (0267) 290221
Open: 11-3, 6 (6.30 winter)-11
Licensee: Clifford Rees-Davies

The restaurant is popular, as much for its view as its food, and it's a good pub for family expeditions; fun play equipment in the garden.

Bar Meals: 12-2.30, 6.30-9.45; bar snacks both sessions **Restaurant:** *12-1.30, 7-9.30* **Typical Dishes BAR:** *leek and potato soup £1.25, mushroom and bacon pot £2.10, steak and kidney pie £3.35, chicken curry £3.35, salmon cutlet £5.74, lemon meringue pie £1.50* **RESTAURANT:** *cockles £2.50, medallions of venison £10.95, Sewin cutlet £9.15, chicken Tante Louise £9.15* *Vegetarian Meals: curry* *Children's Menu/Portions* `Beer` *Marston; Whitbread* *Family Room* *Outdoor Play Area* *Riverside Garden* *Outdoor Eating* **Credit Cards:** *Access, Visa*

PONTARGOTHI   Salutation Inn

Nantgaredig SA32 7NG   ♟
Tel: (0267) 290336
Open: 11-3, 6-12 (11.30 Sun eve)
Licensee: Bernard Kindred

Home-made specials on the daily board, as well as fresh fish and game in season, in attractive roadside pub.

Bar Meals and Restaurant: 12-2, 6-10 (7-9.30 Sun); bar snacks both sessions **Typical Dishes BAR:** *home-made soup £1.30, whitebait £2.75, home-made steak and kidney pie £5.50, chicken curry £4.50, seafood platter £4.75, fruit tarts £1.50* **RESTAURANT:** *deep-fried camembert £2.75, steak £7.50-£9.75, noisettes of lamb £6.50, lobster £9.50* *Vegetarian Meals: mushroom stroganoff £4.75* *Children's Menu/Portions* `Beer` *Felinfoel* *Family Room* *Patio/terrace* *Outdoor Eating* **Credit Cards:** *Access, Visa*

ST DAVIDS Farmers Arms Goat Street, off Cross Square: Original stone floors, beams and fireplaces in this unspoilt Victorian fisherman's local, plus a glorious view of the cathedral and countryside from the little terrace. Home cooked food lunch and evening. Welsh Bass beers. Open all day.

ST DOGMAELS — Ferry Inn

Take the Poppit Sands road from the village SA43 3LF
Tel: (0239) 615172
Open: 12-3, 6 (7 winter)-11
Licensees: Michael Clark and David Kendall

Riverside inn with a nautical theme; 'quarterdeck' and 'lower deck' bars, waterside gardens and views; welcoming to young families, very much geared to dining. Local sea trout and salmon in season. Petanque and quoits in garden.

Bar Meals: *12-2, 7-9.30 (6-10 summer); bar snacks both sessions* ***Typical Dishes:*** *courgette and cheese soup £1.45, ferryman's paté £2.45, mushroom chicken £4.95, moules marinière £4.25, sole fillets St Michel £10.25, Preseli toffee pudding £1.65 Vegetarian Meals: mushroom stroganoff £4.75 Children's Menu/Portions* **Beer** *Brains SA; Felinfoel Double Dragon; Ind Coope Burton Ale; Wadworth 6X Family Room Outdoor Play Area Riverside Garden Outdoor Eating* ***Credit Cards:*** *Access, Visa*

SOLVA Ship Inn Main Street: Handy for the coastal path, a 17th century village pub with decent home cooking, and good local fish; meals lunch and evening; family room; garden. Bass, Felinfoel beers. Open all day.

WOLF'S CASTLE — Wolfe Inn

near Haverfordwest SA26 5LS
Tel: (043 787) 662
Open: 11-3, 6-11
Licensees: Jack and Pamela Sandell

New owner-licensees have recently taken oven this popular little inn on the A40 road. Bars are cosy and inviting, the public stone-walled and traditional, the lounge plushly refurbished, and the attractive restaurant has polished tables and soft lighting. The bedrooms have trebled in number, from one to three (one a family room), and were recently redecorated; we previously warmly recommended the original room, located in a converted outhouse.

Bar Meals: *12-2.30, 6.30-9.30; bar snacks both sessions* ***Typical Dishes:*** *vegetable soup £1.50, avocado prawns £3.50, steak au poivre £9.95, chicken kiev £7.95, Dover sole £11.50, profiteroles £1.95 Vegetarian Meals Children's Menu* **Beer** *Ind Coope, Tetley Family Room Garden Outdoor Eating* ***Accommodation:*** *3 bedrooms, sharing a bathroom, from £30 (single £20) Children Welcome Overnight Cot Available Check-in: all day* ***Credit Cards:*** *Access, Visa*

GLAMORGAN

ALLTWEN, West Glamorgan   Butchers Arms

Pontardawe SA8 3BP
Tel: (0792) 863100
Open: 12-4, 6.30-11
Licensees: Patrick and Jolanta Swords

Traditional pub overlooking the Swansea valley. No juke box, no games machines, and all food is home-made on the premises, with fresh local produce, including the vegetables – interesting side-dishes include delicious garlic potatoes. Home-made rolls and puddings too. They specialise in saucy steaks.

Bar Meals: 12-2.30, 6.30-9; no food Sun eve; bar snacks lunchtime **Typical Dishes**
BAR: *French onion soup, garlic prawns, steak and kidney pie £4.25, beef Borgino £4.25, bread and butter pudding* **RESTAURANT:** *laverbread, cockles and bacon, chicken £8.95, salmon and prawns £7.25 Vegetarian Meals: fettuccine Children's Portions* Beer
Courage Directors; Everards Old Original; Fullers London Pride; Wadworth 6X Whisky
Children Allowed in Bar to Eat Patio/terrace Outdoor Eating **Credit Cards:** *Access, Visa*

CAERPHILLY, Mid Glamorgan **Courthouse**, Cardiff Road. Medieval pub with a splendid view of the castle from the rear café-bar and terrace drinking area. Bar food, lunch and evening, is a mix of the familiar and imaginative. They make their own cheese. Courage beers. Open all day.

CARDIFF, South Glamorgan   Fox & Hounds

Chapel Row, St Mellons CF3 9UB
Tel: (0222) 777046
Open: all day

On the eastern outskirts of the city, off the B4487 Newport road; the standard menu is cheered up by home-made daily specials. Good beer too.

Bar Meals: 11.30-2.45; bar snacks **Typical Dishes:** *French onion soup, prawn cocktail, steak and kidney pie, chicken curry, lasagne Vegetarian Meals: lasagne Children's Portions*
Beer *Brains Children Allowed in Lounge to Eat Outdoor Play Area Garden Outdoor Eating* **Credit Cards:** *Access, Visa*

CARDIFF Old Cottage, Cherry Orchard Road, Thornhill: Converted a couple of years ago; downstairs bar and upstairs restaurant, lunch and evening meals. Ansells, Ind Coope, Tetley beers. Open: 11.30-3, 5.30-11. **Ty Mawr Arms** Craig Road, Lisvane: Charming ex-farmhouse pub tucked away in a rural spot, just a short drive from the city. Routine bar meals, more interesting restaurant; food lunch and evening. Huge range of beers. Open 12-3, 6-11.

DINAS POWIS, South Glamorgan **Star Inn** Station Road. Lively village local with genuine home cooking, lunchtime and evening (no food Sunday); children allowed in for lunches; live jazz on Sundays. Brains beers. Open: 11.30-3.30, 5.30 (5 Fri)-11 (all day Sat).

EAST ABERTHAW, South Glamorgan ★ Blue Anchor

near Barry CF6 9DD
Tel: (0446) 750329
Open: 11-11
Licensee: Jeremy Coleman

FOOD

There's a full six centuries of history to the splendid Blue Anchor, and the old cliché about stepping back in time is truer here than usually. Entering this quaint thatched cottage through the black oak door, under hanging ivy that appears to be holding the old stone walls together, visitors are taken by way of tiny nooks and crannies into a smugglers' den which includes an internal doorway little more than four feet high. Fifty years now in ownership of the Coleman family, and administered day-to-day by the urbane Jeremy, the pub has gone from strength to strength since the opening last year of its new restaurant. A nearly hidden, almost cavernous stairway leads to a dining room of surprising spaciousness, presided over by brilliant young chef, Andrew Lawrence. The output of his young team, producing bar lunches daily (except Sunday), a six-night restaurant menu (not Sunday), and comprehensive Sunday lunch, is little short of prodigious. The Coleman vegetable garden weighs in with onions and fresh vegetables, garden fruits and herbs, and local suppliers add the fish, free-range meats and eggs, as well as a commendable list of Welsh cheeses. From a regularly changing restaurant menu, choose the Cenarth-smoked Wye salmon or 'aigrettes' of Welsh cheeses and laverbread in choux buns; followed perhaps by pan-fried veal kidneys en croute, or Brecon lamb cutlets with rosemary and garlic butter. Bar lunches are equally varied, offering spicy chicken pittas, roasts or curries of the day, while the blackboard serves as a market place for predominantly fishy specials – perhaps a rendezvous of white fish and shellfish – varying daily. Yet downstairs, the Blue Anchor remains a historic pub, chock-full of interest and atmosphere, an equal draw for history buffs and real ale aficionados, its regular beer list supplemented by often interesting guest names.

Bar Meals: 12-2 (not Sun); bar snacks lunchtime *Restaurant:* lunchtime Sun, 7-9.30 (not Sun eve) *Typical Dishes BAR:* home-made soup of the day £1.60, garlic mushrooms £1.80, home-made steak and kidney pie £3.50, cauliflower cheese with bacon £3.50, baked fish cocotte £3.50, home-made puddings £1.75 *RESTAURANT:* chicken and sweetcorn moneybag £3.25, noisettes of Brecon lamb £9.65, brochette of veal offal £10.75, baked fillet of Towy sewin £10.25 Vegetarian Meals: Glamorgan cheese sausages Children's Menu/Portions **Cheese** **Beer** Buckleys; Marston; Theakston; Wadworth **Whisky** Family Room Patio/terrace Outdoor Eating *Credit Cards:* Access, Visa

GOWERTON, West Glamorgan **Berthlwydd Inn.** Popular pub overlooking estuary; characterful interior and interesting lunch and evening meals. Courage, Felinfoel beers. Open: 12-3.30, 6-11.

KENFIG, Mid Glamorgan **Prince of Wales.** The only pub in Britain to hold the local Sunday school upstairs. Historic pub in formerly important port, long since deserted by the sea. Cheap and ordinary bar food. Huge range of beers. Open: 11.30-4, 6-11.

LLANCADLE, South Glamorgan **Green Dragon Inn.** Lovely old thatched pub, recently extended, and imaginatively run, with interesting bar menu (lunch and evening); family room; Bass beers; Open: 11-3.30, 7-11 (all day Fri/Sat).

LLANGYNWYD, Mid Glamorgan **Old House Inn**. Modernised but still characterful ancient thatched pub, tucked away behind the church. Fresh fish specials, good steaks. Conservatory; garden; children welcome; Whitbread beers. Open: 11-4, 6-11 (all day summer).

OGMORE, Mid Glamorgan **Pelican**. Rather smart country pub overlooking the castle ruins. Simple home-cooked food; garden; children allowed in for lunch. Courage beers. Open: 11.30-4, 6.30-11 (all day Fri/Sat).

OLD WALLS, West Glamorgan — Greyhound Inn

North Gower, Swansea SA3 1HA
Tel: (0792) 390146
Open: 11-11
Licensee: Peter Green

Attractive, well-run freehouse in the middle of the unspoilt Gower peninsula. Decent bar food – look out particularly for freshest local fish, interestingly cooked at reasonable prices – good local cheeses, and a commendable variety of beers (plus occasional farmhouse ciders). Go down to the astonishingly dramatic Rhossili beach for a walk after lunch.

Bar Meals: 12-3, 6.30-10; bar snacks both sessions **Typical Dishes:** *Welsh lamb broth £1.50, marinated Welsh lamb steak £5, Chinese style chicken and mushroom stir-fry £4.50, cockles, laverbread and bacon £3, apple pie £1.75 Vegetarian Meals: tortellini ricotta £3.95 Children's Menu/Portions* Cheese Beer *Bullmastiff; Robinsons; Wadworth; Whitbread Family Room Outdoor Play Area Garden Outdoor Eating* **Credit Cards:** *Access, Visa*

PARKMILL, West Glamorgan — Gower Inn

Swansea SA3 2EQ
Tel: (044 128) 3116
Open: 11.30-3, 6-11 (11-11 summer)
Licensee: Alan Pritchard

Art deco interior, spacious and airy; big car park.

Bar Meals: 12-2.30, 6.30-9.30; bar snacks both sessions **Typical Dishes:** *home-made soup (winter) £1.40, ham and chicken longboat £2.25, home-made steak and kidney pie £4.10, carbonara twirls £3.90, beef Madras £4.35 Vegetarian Meals: spring vegetables £4.35 Children's Menu* Beer *Draught Bass, Hancocks HB Family Room Garden Outdoor Eating Summer Barbecue* **Credit Cards:** *Access, Visa*

PENLLYN, South Glamorgan **Fox Inn**. Old favourite, recently changed hands, and been "redeveloped" (some would say ruined), in a ubiquitous pub style, with carpets in, restaurant out. Short menu at the time of our visit: grilled sardines, chicken kiev, steaks and so on.

SIGINISTONE, South Glamorgan — Victoria Inn

Cowbridge CF7 7LP
Tel: (0446) 773943
Open: 11.30-3, 7-11
Licensee: Graham Williams

Fairly routine bar and restaurant menus, but much more interesting home-cooked specials, old-fashioned casseroles and saucy fish bakes, in a delightfully atmospheric old pub, always busy despite its fairly remote location.

Bar Meals: 11.30-2, 7-10 **Restaurant:** *7-11* **Typical Dishes BAR:** *home-made steak and kidney pie, gammon and egg, deep-fried seafood platter (all £4.50), apple pie £1.80* **RESTAURANT:** *home-made soup £1.75, fisherman's delight £3.25, 9 oz fillet steak £9, pork tenderloins £8, fresh Scotch salmon £8 Vegetarian Meals: lasagne Children's Portions* Beer *Draught Bass, Worthington BB* Whisky *Children Allowed in Bar to Eat Patio/terrace* **Credit Cards:** *Access, Visa*

TAFF'S WELL, Mid Glamorgan **Anchor** Cardiff Road. Nautical-themed Whitbread pub, with good fishy bar snacks; separate restaurant; garden. Open all day.

GWENT

ABERGAVENNY   Llanwenarth Arms Hotel

Brecon Road NP8 1EP
Tel: (0873) 810550
Open: 11-3 (12-2 Sun), 6-11
Licensee: D'Arcy McGregor

If you think Llanwenarth is tough to pronounce, try Pantrhiwgoch, its former name.
Much extended Usk-side inn with two friendly bars and attractive conservatory.
Home-made food in both bar and restaurant (same menu). Two stretches of good
fishing available to residents. Compact modern bedrooms in three storey annexe, all
with splendid views.

Bar Meals and Restaurant: 12-1.45, 6-9.45; bar snacks both sessions **Typical Dishes:**
*smoked ham and cauliflower soup £2.25, Malmsey mushrooms £4.95, steak and kidney pie
£7.50, guinea fowl in port wine sauce £10.95, salmon, prawn and asparagus in cheese sauce
£6.25, waffles with maple syrup £3.50   Vegetarian Meals: vegetable bake £7.25
Children's Menu* **Beer** *Draught Bass; Wadworth 6X   Family Room   Riverside
Patio/terrace   Outdoor Eating* **Accommodation:** *18 bedrooms, all en suite, from £50
(single £49)   Children Welcome Overnight   Cots Available   Check-in: all day* **Credit
Cards:** *Access, Amex, Diners, Visa*

CAERLEON   Bell

Bullmoor Road NP6 1QQ
Tel: (0633) 420613
Open: 11.30-3, 5.30-11 (all day Sat)
Licensees: Brian and Sally Shannon

450 years old, a former coaching inn, in the famous Roman settlement of Caerleon:
baths, amphitheatre, and many finds in the local museum.

Bar Meals: 12-2, 7-10; bar snacks both sessions **Typical Dishes:** *home-made soup
£1.40, 10 oz sirloin steak £8.95, haddock and prawn pie £5.40, prawn and fresh
pineapple curry £6.40, banoffee pie   Vegetarian Meals: lasagne £5.20   Children's Portions*
Beer *Marston; Whitbread   Children Allowed in Bar to Eat   Patio/terrace   Outdoor
Eating* **No Credit Cards**

CHEPSTOW   Castle View Hotel

16 Bridge Street NP6 5EZ
Tel: (02912) 70349
Licensees: Martin and Vicky Cardale

Attractive white-painted 18th century former private house with rather dated aspects
to its interior style. Two bedrooms are in a modern annexe. Lovely garden.

Bar Meals and Restaurant: 12-2, 6.30-9.30; bar snacks lunchtime **Typical Dishes**
*BAR: celery and stilton soup £1.95, steak, ale and mushroom pie £5.95, stir-fried fresh
prawns £5.45, salmon and prawn flan £4.85, bread and butter pudding £2.50
RESTAURANT: mushroom and madeira soup £2.15, devilled crab £3.95, chicken
stuffed with stilton £10.45, carbonade of beef £8.45, rack of Welsh lamb £11.45, crème
brulée £2.85   Vegetarian Meals: curry £4.25* **Beer** *Allied or Butcombe   Family*

Room *Outdoor Play Area* Garden *Outdoor Eating* **Accommodation:** *11 bedrooms, all en suite, from £57.50 (single £39.50) Children Welcome Overnight Cots Available Check-in: all day* **Credit Cards:** *Access, Amex, Diners, Visa*

CLYDACH Rock & Fountain, Old Black Rock Road Tel: (0893) 830393. A newish chef-proprietor has rejuvenated this secluded little pub into an attractive and foodie oasis; smart food at moderate prices, but also a busy local and gets very lively; children welcome; Ruddles beers. Three bedrooms (£40 a double). Open: 12-3, 7-11 (all day Sat).

LLANDEWI SKIRRID   Walnut Tree Inn

Abergavenny NP7 8AW
Tel: (0873) 852797
Open: 12-4, 7-12; closed Sun/Mon and 2 weeks Feb
Licensee: Ann Taruschio

To call the Walnut Tree a pub these days is stretching the definition just about as far as it will go, as main course prices listed below confirm, but this is still a pub in licensing terms, and it is theoretically possible to roll up just for a drink. The food is terrific.

Bar Meals and Restaurant: *12-3, 7-10* **Typical Dishes:** *zucchini soup £5, crispy crab pancake £5.45, suckling pig £16.35, Gressingham duck with kumquats £16.35, panaché of fish with balsamic vinegar £15.85, trio of chocolate desserts £6.15 Children's Portions* `Cheese` `Whisky` *Patio/terrace Outdoor Eating* **No Credit Cards**

LLANDOGO   Sloop Inn

near Monmouth NP5 4TW
Tel: (0594) 530291
Open: 11-11 (11-3, 4.30-11 winter)
Licensees: G Evans and G Morgan

18th century inn, a mix of ancient and modern. Bedrooms include a suite with a French window leading out onto a private balcony.

Bar Meals: *during all opening hours until about 9.30; bar snacks* **Typical Dishes:** *home-made soup £1.40, paté £1.60, 8 oz rump steak £6.50, chilli £3.95, rainbow trout £5.45, chocolate fudge cake £1.60 Vegetarian Meals Children's Portions* `Beer` *Hook Norton; Smiles Children Allowed in Bar to Eat Outdoor Play Area Garden Outdoor Eating* **Accommodation:** *4 bedrooms, all en suite, from £37 (single £25.50) Check-in: all day* **Credit Cards:** *Access, Amex, Visa*

LLANTHONY Abbey Hotel off A465 Tel: (08732) 487: Ancient inn set in Norman priory ruins, formerly partly the prior's lodge. Stone-flagged, vaulted bar and dining room with handsome old furnishings; bedrooms via a spooky stone staircase (from £45 a double). Routine bar meals. Brains, Ruddles, Whitbread beers.

LLANVETHERINE   Kings Arms

near Abergavenny NP7 8RG
Tel: (0873) 821221
Open: 11 am-midnight (11-3, 6-12 winter)
Licensees: Steve and Janice Coop

17th century coaching inn on the B4521, within 400 yards of the Offa's Dyke footpath. One new feature: the Stable Restaurant, in the old converted stables. Seven real ales.

Bar Meals: 11-10 (12-2.30, 6-10 winter); bar snacks both sessions **Restaurant:** *12-2.30, 6-10* **Typical Dishes BAR:** *French onion soup £1.50, mushrooms with garlic dip £2.55, steak and Guinness pie £4.50, liver, bacon and onions £4.75, gammon, egg and pineapple £4.95, summer pudding* **RESTAURANT:** *potato and herb soup £1.50, home-made chicken liver paté £2.75, 16 oz T-bone steak £9.95, supreme of chicken £7.95, poached salmon hollandaise £7.95* *Vegetarian Meals: vegetables au gratin Children's Menu/Portions* **Beer** *Draught Bass; Felinfoel; Morlands; Taylor* *Family Room* *Outdoor Play Area* *Garden* *Outdoor Eating* *Summer Barbecue* **Credit Cards:** *Access, Visa*

LYDART   Gockett Inn

near Monmouth NP5 4AD   `FOOD`
Tel: (0600) 860486
Open: 11-3, 5-11
Licensees: Mr and Mrs Short

This former staging post on the St David's to London route stands atop the escarpment (now the B4293) three miles outside Monmouth; "Gockett" was the local name for the black grouse which inhabited these heathlands until their extinction a century or so ago. Central to the inn's modern attractions are Hazel Short's daily selected menus, wherein brevity is made a virtue by careful buying of top quality foodstuffs, and by her innovative approach to traditional recipes. Thus the beef pie today may be cooked with Guinness and mushrooms; tomorrow's chock full of smoked oysters. Equally popular are the rabbit pie with mustard and rosemary, and a creamy chicken and mushroom variety with herbs. Home-made soups are thick and flavourful, alongside the likes of garlic mushrooms, duck liver paté, local salmon mayonnaise, or tagliatelle Alfredo. Though all are officially starters, a light lunch of two of them is equally acceptable, except on Sundays, when bookings should be made for the fixed price lunch. Alongside the hefty pies, other main courses are equally substantial: excellent beef sirloins with peppered sauce, salmon steaks with lemon butter sauce, and vegetarian alternatives like a stuffed aubergine or potato and hazelnut roast. To accompany, expect a generous side plate of assorted fresh vegetables and potatoes. The pudding list which follows is simple but commendable in scope: bread and butter pudding, apple and blackberry crumble, hot chocolate sponge, lemon meringue pie, and sherry trifle. Leather banquettes, silk flowers and gathered drapes lend a bright, cottagey feel to the original dining room, where tables are neatly spaced in front of a smoky, stone fireplace hung with horse brasses and copper bed-warmers. A more recent extension to the bar has increased the space – though not perhaps enhanced the character – and leads to an enclosed rear patio and a neat garden still in its infancy, for al fresco eating in fine weather.

Bar Meals and Restaurant: 12-2, 7-10; bar snacks lunchtime **Typical Dishes:** **BAR:** *home-made soup £2.25, crab mousse £3.50, navarin of lamb £3.95, rabbit pie £6.25, bread and butter pudding £2.50* *Vegetarian Meals: stroganoff £5.95* *Children's Portions* **Beer** *Bass; Felinfoel* *Children Allowed in Bar to Eat* *Outdoor Play Area* *Garden*

Outdoor Eating   **Accommodation:** *2 bedrooms, 1 en suite, from £36 (single £20)*
Children Welcome Overnight   *Check-in: all day*   **Credit Cards:** *Access, Visa*

MACHEN White Hart   off A468   Tel: (0633) 441005: Attractive old wood-panelled pub with decent home cooking lunch and evening (Tue–Sat in restaurant). Brains and guest beers.

MAMHILAD Horseshoe Inn: Quiet former mailing coach stop, in pretty rural area. Bar meals lunch and evening; garden; Felinfoel, Marston and Whitbread beers. Open: 11–3.30, 6.30–11 (all day summer).

MONMOUTH   Punch House

Agincourt Square NP5 3BT   ♥
Tel: (0600) 713855
Open: 11-11 (11-3, 5-11 winter Mon-Thur)
Licensee: W J L Wills

Historic, pristine old inn dominating the market square; pretty cobbled drinking area. Popular upstairs restaurant; vegetarian meals to order only.

Bar Meals: *11.30-2.30, 6-9.30; bar snacks lunchtime*   **Restaurant:** *12-2, 7-9*   **Typical Dishes BAR:** *turkey and vegetable soup £1.50, paté maison £2.25, steak and kidney pie £5, rack of Welsh lamb £6, seafood curry £5*   **RESTAURANT:** *home-made soup £2.25, fresh haddock mornay £4, pork Agincourt £14.50, tournedos Saint Crispin £15, halibut meunière £13.25, gateaux £2.50*   `Beer`   *Bass; Wadworth*   *Children Allowed in Bar to Eat*   *Patio/terrace*   *Outdoor Eating*   **Credit Cards:** *Access, Visa*

PENALLT   Boat Inn

Lone Lane NP5 4AJ
Tel: (0600) 712615
Open: 11-3, 6-11
Licensee: Steffan Rowlands

Live folk music on Tuesday evenings, and jazz on Thursdays are a popular local attraction at this classic riverside pub. All hot meals are home-cooked, from an enormous menu featuring 18 main courses; a huge selection of real ales, too.

Bar Meals: *12-2.30, 6-9.30; bar snacks both sessions*   **Typical Dishes:** *tomato and courgette soup £1.25, stuffed mushrooms £1.40, rogan josh and rice £3.40, turkey and mushroom crumble £3.40, pan haggerty £3, bread and butter pudding £1.30*   *Vegetarian Meals*   *Children's Portions (some)*   `Beer`   *Greene King; Hook Norton; Theakston; Wadworth*   `Cider`   *Family Room*   *Riverside Garden*   *Outdoor Eating*   *Summer Barbecue*   **No Credit Cards**

PONTHIR   Star Inn

near Newport   `FOOD`
Tel: (0633) 420582   ✳
Licensee: Neil Danbury   ☺

Just two miles up the B4236 from historic Roman Caerleon, Neil Danbury runs an immaculate pub, earning numerous plaudits from Ansells brewery for his cellar; both the session bitter and prize-winning Burton Ale are served in prime condition here. The building is faced in stone, with carriage lamps at the entrance, and splendid floral displays in tubs and hanging baskets signalling its presence to passers-by on the main road. The small public bar is plainly set with tub chairs and Britannia tables, while to the rear a small garden boasts half a dozen picnic tables and stands handily adjacent to Ponthir's municipal children's playground. The Kiln lounge is unusually decorated with panels of local Cambrian bricks, illustrating a dozen different types of colour and finish. Buttoned dralon banquettes partition ten or so tables, often scarcely sufficient to accommodate the many fans of Mrs Danbury's excellent value home-cooked food. As everything is freshly prepared, she keeps the menu sensibly short, and the day's extra dishes are posted on the nearby blackboard. Typically, these might include boozy pie – steak and mushrooms cooked in Guinness – a smoked gammon grill, or turkey biryani, and the good news is that, with generous chips and freshly cooked (though not always fresh) vegetables, they never run to more than £5. Main dishes on the regular menu don't even break the £4 barrier, for which choices are from roast chicken, corned beef pie, home-made lasagne, or ridiculously starchy combinations like chicken curry with rice and chips and mango chutney. Puddings are rather less adventurous: chocolate fudge or walnut cakes served hot with cream or ice-cream, and apple and blackberry pancakes.

Bar Meals: 11.30-2, 5.30-9; bar snacks both sessions   **Typical Dishes**: *lasagne £3.50, boozy pie £3.95, beef/chicken curry £3.95, hot chocoloate fudge cake £1.20   Vegetarian Meals: lasagne   Children's portions*   Beer   *Ansells, Ind Coope   Garden   Outdoor eating* **No Credit Cards.**

PONTYPOOL Open Hearth Inn The Wern, Griffithstown. Modernised, tidy dining pub, with decent, simple food lunch and evening, a popular restaurant, and a good range of beers. Children allowed in to eat. Open: 11.30-3 (4 Sat), 6-11.

RAGLAN   Beaufort Arms Hotel

High Street NP5 2DY
Tel: (0291) 690412
Open: daily
Licensees: Mr and Mrs Dorey

Spotlessly maintained both inside and out, a smart, whitewashed village inn, built in the 15th century: exposed stonework and Tudor timbers survive in the Castle Country Bar. Bar food is wholesome and home-made; good daily specials in generous portions. £11.50 table d'hote available in the restaurant. Bedrooms have multiplied since our last edition; bright, comfortable and attractively decorated.

Bar Meals: 12-2, 6-10; bar snacks both sessions   **Restaurant:** *7-9.30*   **Typical Dishes** **BAR:** *home-made soup £1.50, deep-fried mushrooms in garlic £2.50, steak pie £5.50, half roast chicken £5.50, poached salmon £7.50*   **RESTAURANT:** *tournedos Rossini £12.50, duckling with Grand Marnier £10.50, veal with lemon and chive sauce £10.95   Vegetarian Meals: nut cutlets   Children's Portions*   Beer   *Brains; Courage   Children Allowed in Bar to Eat   Patio/terrace   Outdoor Eating*   **Accommodation:** *15 bedrooms, all en suite, from £45 (single £35)   Children Welcome Overnight   Cot Available   Check-in: all day*   **Credit Cards:** *Access, Amex, Diners, Visa*

SHIRENEWTON   Carpenters Arms

near Chepstow NP6 6BU   ❋
Tel: (02917) 231
Open: 11-3, 6-11
Licensee: James Bennett

Arguably one of Gwent's most characterful pubs, the Carpenters stands hard by the B4235, a row of low, white-painted 17th century cottages which once housed a smithy and wheelwright's, as well as the local carpenter's workshop. There are many unique reminders within, among them the original foot-operated bellows, suspended from the ceiling of the Smithy bar, itself framed in several places by aged wagon wheels set into the stone. Echoing the seven phases of the moon and seven ages of man (not to mention the seven deadly sins), landlord James Bennett promotes his business as offering seven rooms, seven real ales and seven-day opening, in a location exactly seven miles from the Severn bridge. A high-backed settle partitions an entrance lobby area in which hang the blackboard menus, while, to one side, a central three-legged brazier warms two of the rooms from beneath its copper-hooded open chimney. The central bar servery is unique, facing four different ways at three levels, with service counters reconstructed from ornate church dado panels. On any one day, Courage, Hook Norton, Ruddles, Marston, Wadworth and Charles Wells breweries might be represented on the handpumps here. More suitable for quiet snacking is a carpeted lounge with gas fire and central heating, and with direct access to half a dozen roadside picnic tables in a setting embellished by flower pots and hanging baskets. In this context, the menu is largely popular by design, led by a profusion of filled baguettes and baked potatoes, and quite a lot from the fryer besides. Nonetheless, smoked salmon (£2.95) to start, steak and mushroom pie (£4.95), and apple pie (£1.95) or fresh strawberries to finish won't upset more discerning diners, nor offend their pockets. Grills include gammon (£4.50), with egg or pineapple, sirloin steaks (£5.75), lamb chops (£5.50) served with real gravy, and grilled spicy sausages (£3.50), which go down particularly well with the youngsters.

Bar Meals: 12-2, 7-9.30; bar snacks both sessions   **Typical Dishes:** *home-made soup £1.75, Japanese prawns £2.75, rabbit casserole £3.75, lasagne £3.95, steak and mushroom pie £4.25, bread and butter pudding £1.75   Vegetarian Meals   Children's Menu* [Cheese] [Beer] *Bass; Hook Norton; Ruddles; Wadworth   Family Room Patio/terrace   Outdoor Eating* **No Credit Cards**

TRELLECK Lion Inn: New licensees have introduced a fish-dominated menu, featuring Wye salmon and 'Welsh style' trout (£5.50–£10.75) in this otherwise unassuming local pub.

USK   Royal Hotel
New Market Street NP5 1AT
Tel: (02913) 2931
Open: 11-3, 7-11
Licensees: Anthony Lyons and Sylvia Casey

Grade II listed Georgian market town inn, with pleasingly traditional atmosphere.

Bar Meals: 12-2, 7-9.30; bar snacks lunchtime   **Typical Dishes:** *chicken béarnaise £4.50, beef in red wine £4.50, grilled steaks from £7.25, toffee apple tart £1.75 Vegetarian Meals: Llandenny bake £4.50   Children's Menu* [Beer] *Draught Bass; Hancocks PA; Felinfoel Double Dragon   Children Allowed in Bar to Eat   Patio/terrace* **No Credit Cards**

WHITEBROOK   Crown at Whitebrook
Monmouth NP5 4TX   [FOOD]
Tel: (0600) 860254   ⊟
Open: 12-2, 7-10.30 (closed Sun night/Mon lunchtime)   ▼
Licensees: Roger and Sandra Bates   [B&B]

Scarcely the archetypal Welsh pub, scarcely, in fact, a pub at all, the Crown's uniqueness lies in the successful re-creation of a French style auberge deep in the Wye valley. Don't be deterred by the road: Whitebrook may be signposted as a mile from the A466 at the river bridge, but the inn is at least two, through a doubt-inducing farmyard crossing; keep going. Once safely within, a welcoming lounge, mixing deep sofas and coffee tables, leads to an almost rustic dining room of a dozen or so tables, and a gingham-clothed extension which serves as a breakfast room. For lunch or dinner (the latter menu also optional at lunchtime), the accent of Sandra Bates' menus is firmly set in France, yet remains in harmony with the rural Welsh setting. Dinner is prix fixe (£24): soufflé de fromage de chevre, or tartelette Alsacienne (with cheese, smoked ham and onions) preceding mousse de brochet et homard, or carré d'agneau en croute, with perhaps a vacherin aux fruits or crepes Normande to follow. The £14.50 lunch menu is a little simpler: perhaps a terrine of chicken breast, strips of salmon with a wine, vermouth and cream sauce, and hazelnut meringue with chocolate and coffee ice. Bar meals are somewhat secondary by comparison, though equal in quality and imagination. Goat's cheese soufflé (£4.50), and a tartlet of Llanboydie cheese and laverbread (£4.50), ficelles bretonne with ham, gruyère and mushrooms (£4.75), or ficelles de mer stuffed with crab and prawns (£4.95), are typical of the light main courses, with a tartelette Normande (£4.25) or pineapple slices in rum (£3.95) to follow. Splendid accompaniments include a 100-bottle wine list with, in addition, 30 half bottles; and a fine selection of mostly Welsh cheeses. Residents are particularly rewarded by their journey up the valley; this is a delightful refuge from the world. A dozen pastel-coloured bedrooms feature up-to-date fittings, cosy, carpeted bathrooms, and peace undisturbed by anything other than whispering trees and the dawn chorus. Morning brings a commendably un-Gallic tradition: full English (or is it Welsh?) breakfast in bed.

Bar Meals: 12-2 Tue-Sat; bar snacks   *Restaurant:* 12-2, 7-9.30   *Typical Dishes*
BAR: cauliflower soup with stilton crepe £2.50, terrine of pigeon breast and liver £3.95, seafood pancakes £4.95, gruyère and prawn pastries £5.25, tarte Alsacienne £4.50, Normandy apple tart £4.25   RESTAURANT lunch menu £14.50, dinner £24: celery and roquefort soup, trout paté, guinea fowl with red wine and wild mushrooms, chicken in vermouth and saffron with mussels, rack of lamb en croute, baked Alaska   Vegetarian Meals Children's Portions   Cheese   Beer   Newquay Steam Bitter   Whisky   Children Allowed in Bar to Eat   Patio/terrace   Outdoor Eating   *Accommodation (closed 2 weeks Jan, 2 weeks Aug): 12 bedrooms, all en suite, from £76 (single £48)   Children Welcome Overnight   Cots Available   Check-in: all day   Credit Cards: Access, Amex, Diners, Visa*

GWYNEDD

ABERDOVEY	**Penhelig Arms**
Aberdovey LL35 0LT	FOOD
Tel: (0654) 767215	▮
Open: 11-3, 6-11	B&B
Licensees: Robert and Sally Hughes	☀

"On the main road by the railway bridge" are directions which might usually strike fear into the hearts of prospective customers. But here are also unrivalled views across the Dyfi estuary to Ynyslas, making a splendid setting for Robert and Sally Hughes' smart black and white painted pub by the A493. Some disadvantages are inherent in a situation where no pavement exists 'twixt front door and double yellow lines, nor greater space, almost, between the single rail line at Penhelig halt and the hotel's gable end. Road noise and BR's occasional arrivals notwithstanding, the sea wall opposite makes a marvellous spot at any state of the tide to enjoy a leisurely al fresco lunch, while the tiny Fisherman's Bar provides a relaxing, and shady, alternative. Fan-cooled on the hottest summer days, and heated by two open fires in winter (set back-to-back beneath a central stone chimney), here's an ideal place to enjoy a pint of good beer and catch up on some local gossip. The bar's the focal point of lunches from Monday to Saturday, and, when the weather's inclement, eaters soon overflow into the restaurant next door. Bar food features smoked haddock chowder with granary bread, and bacon and mushroom vol-au-vents served with salad, besides more substantial meals served with vegetables or chips, perhaps minted lamb cutlets, minute steak with mushrooms, or a brandy-flamed chicken supreme with apricots and cream. By night, bar meals are suspended in favour of a set-price dinner offering diverse daily choice: stilton, onion and celery soup; dressed crab or seafood salad; salmon hollandaise or hake with lemon butter; rack of Welsh lamb or Barbary duck with redcurrant and juniper sauce. Sunday lunch, rather more economically priced, has a more limited choice, but brings cooking of equally consistent quality: roast beef, loin of lamb, cutlets of salmon or fillets of plaice. Booking is advised. Plump for a room with a view: in fact, only two of the bedrooms lack a seascape. All have a cottagey feel and benefit from an individual approach to decor which makes the best of their higgledy-piggledy layout. Private bathroom, television and radio, and beverage trays, are included throughout, but for a truly special occasion ask for one of the three superior rooms, whose balconies and sea views are worth every inch of the extra mile.

Bar Meals and Restaurant: 12-2 *(restaurant Sun only)*, 7-9; *bar snacks lunchtime* *Typical Dishes BAR:* *stilton, onion and parsley soup £1.50, chicken liver, apple and walnut paté £2.95, fresh chicken with brandy and apricots £4.50, whole lemon sole with parsley butter £5.75, steamed fillet of local salmon £5.95, chocolate cheesecake £1.75* *RESTAURANT* *3-course menu £14.95: smoked haddock chowder, warm sea trout with lime and dill mayonnaise, rack of local lamb with honey, local salmon or turbot, lime soufflé* Cheese Beer *Ind Coope, Tetley; Marston* Whisky *Family Room Patio/terrace Outdoor Eating* *Accommodation:* *11 bedrooms, all en suite, from £58 (single £34) Children Welcome Overnight Check-in: all day Access, Visa*

ABERSOCH St Tudwals Hotel, Main Street Tel: (075 881) 2539: Smartened up old pub with plush lounge, rear locals' bar, restaurant and spacious patio. Open fires; families welcome; bar meals; modestly priced bedrooms; good local walks. Robinsons beers.

BANGOR Union Garth Road Tel: (0248) 362462: Old-fashioned town pub overlooking the bay, with one bar and lots of little bric-a-brac packed rooms. Decent lunchtime bar meals; garden; bedrooms. Burtonwood beers. Open all day.

BEAUMARIS   Olde Bulls Head

Castle Street LL58 8AP
Tel: (0248) 810329
Open: 11-11
Licensee: David Robertson

A highly promising new entry: the licensees used to be at the well-regarded Seahorse Restaurant, and the atmospheric downstairs bar offers some delicous, good value bar lunches here. Smarter food at smarter prices in the restaurant, strong on meat dishes. Bedrooms are named after Dickens characters; he stayed here in 1859.

Bar Meals: 12-2.30 *Mon-Sat; bar snacks lunchtime* *Restaurant:* 12-1.30 *(Sun only)*, 7.30-9.30 *Typical Dishes BAR:* *smoked chicken and lentil soup £1.70, pastrami and artichoke salad £2.50, braised lamb with leeks and coarse-grain mustard £4.25, chicken korma with yogurt and spring onions £4.25, fresh grilled local plaice with herb butter £4.50, almond frangipane tart £1.50* *RESTAURANT* *wild mushroom and walnut soup £3.25, warm smoked salmon with cream and saffron £4.95, stuffed breast of guinea fowl £10.95, roast canon of Welsh lamb £11.75, cassolette of local seafood £12.50, passion fruit délice with tropical fruit coulis £3* *Vegetarian Meals: marinated vegetable kebabs with cumin Children's Portions (some)* Cheese Beer *Bass Children Allowed in Bar to Eat Outdoor Eating* *Accommodation:* *11 bedrooms, all en suite, from £68 (single £40) Children Welcome Overnight Cots Available Check-in: all day* *Credit Cards: Access, Visa*

BEDDGELERT Prince Llewellyn Smith Street Tel: (076 686) 242: Handsome three storey riverside pub, in a soothingly rural area. Warm and welcoming, decent bar food, good-value bed and breakfast. Robinsons beers.

BETWS-Y-COED   Ty Gwyn Hotel

Betws-y-Coed LL24 0SG   ♥
Tel: (0690) 710383
Open: 12-2, 7-11
Licensees: James and Shelagh Ratcliffe

The license here involves customers either having a meal or staying the night, or both; just a drink is not allowed, and the obvious benefit of this is that it's a rare example of a delightfully unspoilt inn further unruined by overcrowding. Antique furnished and civilised interior.

Bar Meals and Restaurant: 12-2, 7-9 (9.30 Fri/Sat); bar snacks lunchtime **Typical Dishes:** *borscht £1.60, mushrooms stuffed with fresh crab £3.95, breast of quail stuffed with oysters £9.95, fillet mignon roulade stuffed with spinach £10.25, seafood symphony £9.75, coffee and nut meringue £1.95* *Vegetarian Meals: mushroom and sunflower seed stroganoff £7.25* *Children's Menu/Portions* `Cheese` `Beer` *McEwans 80/- Children Allowed in Bar to Eat* **Accommodation:** *13 bedrooms, 9 en suite, from £35 (single £18) Children Welcome Overnight Cots Available Check-in: all day* **Credit Cards:** *Access, Visa*

CAPEL CURIG   Cobden's Hotel

on A5 LL24 0EE   ♥
Tel: (06904) 243
Open: daily
Licensee: Craig Goodall

Smart country hotel with plush lounge and muddy-boots public bar, in the Snowdonia National Park.

Bar Meals: 12-2.30, 6.30-9.30; bar snacks both sessions *Restaurant: 7-9* **Typical Dishes:** *home-made soup £1.95, grilled goat's cheese £2, toad in the hole £4.25, chicken escalope £5.50, spaghetti carbonara £4.50, spicy bread pudding £1.75* *Vegetarian Meals: vegetarian stroganoff £4.50* *Children's Portions* `Beer` *Courage Directors* `Whisky` *Children Allowed in Bar to Eat Patio/terrace* **Accommodation:** *16 bedrooms, all en suite, from £50 (single £25) Children Welcome Overnight Cot Available Check-in: all day* **Credit Cards:** *Access, Amex, Visa*

CRICCIETH   Prince of Wales

High Street LL52 0HB
Tel: (0766) 522556
Open: 11-3, 6-11 (closed Sun)
Licensee: Chris Johnson

Busy pub, right on the square, and a lively local: live music on Tuesday nights, and a piano in the bar (impromptu performances encouraged). Family-oriented: children are positively welcomed, not just tolerated. Extensive, wide-ranging menu.

Bar Meals: 12-2.30, 6-8.30; bar snacks lunchtime **Typical Dishes:** *prawn cocktail £3.75, ham and leek crumble £3.50, grilled sirloin steak £6.75, chicken cordon bleu £5.25, apple and cider sponge pudding* *Vegetarian Meals: lasagne* *Children's Menu* `Cheese` `Beer` *Whitbread Family Room* **No Credit Cards**

DULAS — Pilot Boat

Amlwch, Anglesey LL70 9EX
Tel: (0248) 88205
Open: 11-3.30, 6 (7 winter)-11; all day Sat
Licensees: Duncan and Rose Knight

A smithy in the 19th century, and now a popular pub within view of the sea.

Bar Meals: 12-2, 6-8.30; bar snacks both sessions   ***Typical Dishes:*** *steak and kidney pie £3.25, vegetable curry £2.99, stuffed plaice £3.80, raspberry flan £1   Vegetarian Meals: vegetable casserole   Children's Menu* Beer *Robinsons beers   Family Room (until 8.30) Outdoor Play Area   Garden   Outdoor Eating   **No Credit Cards***

FAIRBOURNE Fairbourne Hotel off A493 Tel: (0341) 250203: Spacious, gracious hotel in its own grounds, with lovely views out over the estuary. Good value, tasty bar food; real fire; families welcome; McEwans beers. Open: 11-3, 6-11.

GLANWYDDAN — Queens Head

Llandudno Junction LL31 9JP
Tel: (0492) 546570
Open: 11-3.30, 6.30-11.30
Licensee: R F W Cureton

Interesting bar food is on offer in this well-run pub; look out especially for local seafood and fish. Original front public bar and modern, attractive dining lounge behind; gets very busy in summer.

Bar Meals: 12-2.15, 6.30-9; bar snacks both sessions   ***Typical Dishes:*** *mushroom and hazelnut soup £1.50, local potted seafood £2.50, braised oxtail, pickled walnut and Guinness pie (winter), Conway mussels, Arbroath smokies (main courses from around £4), bread and butter pudding £1.95   Vegetarian Meals: mushroom and cheese vol-au-vent Children's Portions (some)* Beer *Benskins, Ind Coope, Tetley   Children over 7 Allowed in Bar to Eat   **Credit Cards:** Access, Visa*

GLYN GARTH — Gazelle Hotel

Menai Bridge, Anglesey LL59 5PD
Tel: (0248) 713364
Open: all day
Licensee: Kenneth Moulton

Attractive white-painted country hotel on the edge of the Menai Straits, directly opposite Bangor Pier.

Bar Meals and Restaurant: 12-2, 6-9.30 (9 restaurant); bar snacks both sessions ***Typical Dishes*** *BAR: broccoli and almond soup £1.30, paté £3.25, steak pie £4.25, gammon and pineapple £4.95, lamb chops £5.20, fruit pie £2   **RESTAURANT:** home-made soup £1.75, egg mayonnaise £2.25, beef Wellington £11.50, roast duck £9.25, halibut steak £9.50   Vegetarian Meals: nut cutlet   Children's Menu/Portions* Beer *Robinsons   Family Room   Riverside Garden   Outdoor Eating   **Accommodation:** 12 bedrooms, 7 en suite, from £43.50 (single £28.50) Children Welcome Overnight   Cot Available   Check-in: all day   **Credit Cards:** Access, Visa*

LLANBEDR Y CENNIN Olde Bull Inn off B5106 Tel: (049 269) 508: 16th century local in a pretty spot in the Conwy Valley: homely cooking by the landlady in bar; seafood and steaks on restaurant menu; cheap. Children allowed in to eat. Bedrooms. Garden. Lees beers. Open:12-3, 6.30-11.

LLANBEDROG   Glyn-y-Weddw Arms

Abersoch Road LL53 7TH
Tel: (0758) 740212
Open: 11-11 (11-3, 6-11 winter); closed Sun
Licensee: Geoffrey Hope-Whitney

Attractive, popular pub close to a delightful beach; the garden can get very hectic in nice summer weather, when the whole village is a sheltered sun-trap. A varied menu keeps tourists, families and locals happy; good daily specials. Renovations are planned for early 1992 subject to brewery consent.

Bar Meals: 12-10 (12-2.30, 6-10 winter); bar snacks both sessions **Typical Dishes:** *home-made soup £1, chicken liver paté £2, liver and gammon casserole £3.50, 16-18 oz rump steak £9.75, whole lobster salad £12.50, sherry trifle £1.50 Vegetarian Meals: lasagne £4.20 Children's Menu* ■Beer■ *Robinsons Family Room Outdoor Play Area Garden* **Credit Cards:** *Access, Visa*

LLANBEDROG   Ship Inn

Bryn-y-Gro LL53 7PE
Tel: (0758) 740270
Open: 12-3, 6-11 (11-11 summer); closed Sun
Licensees: Brian and Pat Ward

Cosy and traditional alternative to the above; extensive menu, very popular.

Bar Meals: 12-2.45, 5.30-10 (12-2.30, 6-10 winter); bar snacks both sessions **Typical Dishes:** *home-made soup £1.20, crab mornay £2.50, home-made steak and kidney pie £4.90, steak au poivre £7.70, roast chicken breast £4.20 Vegetarian Meals: lasagne Children's Menu/Portions* ■Beer■ *Burtonwood Family Room Patio/terrace Outdoor Eating* **No Credit Cards**

LLANDUDNO   Cottage Loaf

Market Street LL30 2SR
Tel: (0492) 870762
Open: 11-11 (11-3, 5.30-11 winter)
Licensee: W T Rowlands

Smartly styled newish conversion from the old bakery.

Bar Meals: 11-2.15; bar snacks **Typical Dishes:** *fresh vegetable soup 95p, Ardennes paté £1.75, chicken, ham and mushroom pie £3.25, beef espagnole £3.25, liver and onions £3, bread and butter pudding Vegetarian Meals: vegetarian chilli Children's Portions* ■Beer■ *Ruddles, Webster's Children Allowed in Bar to Eat Garden Outdoor Eating* **No Credit Cards**

LLANDUDNO   Kings Head

Old Road Tram Station LL30 2NB
Tel: (0492) 877993
Open: 11-11 (11-3, 6.30-11 winter)
Licensees: Alan Dunton and Marcus Farrington

Two fresh fish specials a day and a selection of entirely Welsh cheeses are the main culinary attractions here. Three family areas; dogs welcome in quarry-tiled areas; log fires all winter.

Bar Meals: 12-2.30, 6-10 (all day Sat July/Aug); bar snacks both sessions   **Typical Dishes:** *asparagus soup 95p, spare ribs £1.95, Lancashire hotpot with red cabbage £3.50, megamix grill £6.50, 8 oz salmon steak in cheese and prawn sauce £4.95, bread and butter pudding £1.95   Vegetarian Meals: vegetable cobbler £3.50   Children's Menu/Portions* `Cheese` `Beer` *Ind Coope, Tetley; Whitbread   Family Room   Garden   Outdoor Eating*   **Credit Cards:** *Access, Visa*

LLANENGAN   Sun Inn

Abersoch LL53 7LG
Tel: (075 881) 2660
Open: 11-11 (closed Sun)
Licensee: J M C Evans

Traditional pub by Hells Mouth beach on the edge of the Lyn. No juke boxes, no pool table; locally very popular for food.

Bar Meals: 12-2, 6-9; bar snacks lunchtime   **Typical Dishes:** *crab soup £1.25, paté, 20 oz rump steak £12.95, Welsh gammon with cheese £5.50, fish in home-made beer batter £5.25, summer pudding £2.75   Vegetarian Meals: stuffed peppers £4.75   Children's Menu/Portions* `Cheese` `Beer` *Ind Coope Burton Ale, Tetley Bitter   Children Allowed in Bar to Eat   Outdoor Play Area   Garden   Outdoor Eating   Summer Barbecue* **No Credit Cards**

LLANWNDA   Goat Inn

off A499 LL54 5SD
Tel: (0286) 830256
Open: 11-4, 5.30 (6 Sat)-11; closed Sun
Licensee: Ann Griffith

In the Griffith family for over 150 years; Ann's father and grandfather were here before her. The main dining emphasis is on the excellent lunchtime buffets, of unusually good quality.

Bar Meals: 12.15-2.15; bar snacks   **Typical Dishes:** *potato and leek soup £1.50, unlimited cold table lunches £5; also farmhouse grill, home-made ham rissoles, fresh fish   Vegetarian Meals: macaroni cheese   Children's Portions* `Cheese` `Beer` *Bass; Whitbread   Family Room   Outdoor Play Area   Garden   Outdoor Eating*   **Accommodation:** *3 bedrooms, sharing a bathroom, from £30 (single £15)   Children Welcome Overnight   Cot Available   Check-in: all day* **No Credit Cards**

LLWYNGWRIL Garthangharad Inn on A493 Tel: (0341) 250484: Characterful three-roomed coastal village pub; no music; family room; lunchtime and evening bar food; bedrooms. Banks's beers. Open: 12-3, 7-11.

MAENTWROG   Grapes Hotel

Blaenau Ffestiniog LL41 4HN   ▼
Tel: (076 685) 208/365
Open: 11-11
Licensee: Brian Tarbox

Most attractive, stone-built 19th century inn, with a lovely old bar, unspoilt by progress. Food is beginning to look interesting, too. Children are allowed in the dining room or on the verandah. A new restaurant entrance and the refurbishment of two of the bedrooms in the old oast house are planned for the 1992 season.

Bar Meals: 12-2.15, 6-9.30; bar snacks both sessions   **Typical Dishes BAR:** *broccoli and stilton soup £1.25, escargots £3.25, spare ribs £4.50, 10 oz home-made 'au poivre' burger £3.75, chicken korma £5, strawberry and rhubarb pie £1.75*   **RESTAURANT:** *spring onion and mint soup £1.75, seafood mille feuilles £3.75, pork in apricot and brandy sauce, local fillet of lamb, local poached salmon, main courses from raspberry crowdie Vegetarian Meals: stilton and mushroom bake £4.75   Children's Menu/Portions* `Cheese` `Beer` *Draught Bass; Theakston Best* `Whisky` *Patio/terrace   Outdoor Eating* **Accommodation:** *8 bedrooms, all en suite, from £46 (single £23)   Children Welcome Overnight   Cots Available   Check-in: all day* **Credit Cards:** *Access, Visa*

MENAI BRIDGE   Liverpool Arms

St George's Pier, Anglesey LL59 5EY
Tel: (0248) 712453
Open: 11-3.30, 5.30-11
Licensee: Tony Thickett

Presently there's a mews flat available for family holiday lets at this nautically atmospheric, rambling old pub, with a 15 bedroom development to follow in late 1992. Try the pies – all cooked on the premises.

Bar Meals: 12-2, 6-8.30 (no food Sun eve); bar snacks lunchtime   **Restaurant:** 12-2, 6 till as late as business warrants   **Typical Dishes:** *tomato and basil soup £1.30, home-made chicken liver paté £3, leek and ham mornay £3.30, steak, mushroom and potato pie £3.80, gammon and eggs £5.30, home-made apple pie   Vegetarian Meals: lasagne   Children's Portions* `Beer` *Greenalls   Family Room   Patio/terrace   Outdoor Eating* **Accommodation** *(MEWS FLAT): 3 bedrooms, from £27.50 per person Children Welcome Overnight* **Credit Cards:** *Access, Amex, Diners, Visa*

MORFA NEFYN Bryncynan Inn: At the junction of the A497 and B4412; good local seafood in season; good home-made puddings. Children allowed in for meals until 9pm. Ind Coope, Tetley beers. Open: 11-3, 5.30-11.

NANT PERIS Vaynol Arms on A4086: Listed for its unique position, a traditional, whitewashed old inn, totally overshadowed by the foothills of Mount Snowdon, rising steeply behind. Lunchtime and evening bar food. Robinsons beers. Open: 11-3, 6-11.

PENMAENPOOL   George III Hotel

Dolgellau LL40 1YI
Tel: (0341) 422525
Open: 11-3, 6-11
Licensee: Gail Hall

Handsome old inn at the head of the Mawddach estuary; bedrooms divide between the original building and the converted railway house – trains used to pass along the waterside here. The bar counter is fashioned from an antique Welsh dresser, and there are fishing nets in the atmospheric first floor bar, while in the cellar is a locals' bar, with beams overhead and slate under foot. Bedrooms have Stag furniture and carpeted bathrooms. There's a huge variation in room prices; a double can cost twice the price listed here.

Bar Meals: 12.15-2 Mon-Sat; bar snacks lunchtime   **Restaurant:** 12.15-2 (Sun only), 7.15-8.45   **Typical Dishes BAR:** *home-made soup £1.20, home-made liver paté £2.75, home-made steak and kidney pie £4.45, spare ribs with barbecue sauce £4.60, fresh salmon* *with mayonnaise £5.50, home-made gooseberry pie £1.60* **RESTAURANT:** *fresh mango with peeled prawns £4.80, roast rare duck breast with tomato and black olives £10.90, fresh fillet of brill in ginger and lime £9.90, poached local salmon in aniseed and saffron sauce £11.25, orange and curacao crème £2.25* Vegetarian Meals: *avocado, apple and cheese bake £6* Children's Portions Riverside Patio/terrace **Accommodation:** 12 bedrooms, 10 en suite, from £43 (single £31) Children Welcome Overnight Cot Available Check-in: all day **Credit Cards:** *Access, Amex, Visa*

PORTHNADOG   Ship

Lombard Street LL49 9AP
Tel: (0766) 512990
Open: 11-11 (closed Sun)
Licensees: Robert and Nia Jones

Authentic Thai/Malaysian cuisine in the first floor restaurant is a major draw at this simple, unassuming terraced pub, built in 1824. Everything is cooked fresh to order, chosen from a full menu of around 100 items, especially helpful in its instructions to novices. A full Thai or Malaysian banquet can be had for £15 a head. The pub itself has been nicely done, has comfortable seating, an enormous open fire, and a friendly atmosphere. The restaurant can get very busy.

Bar Meals: *12-2.15, 6.30-9.30; bar snacks lunchtime* **Restaurant:** *6.30-10.30* **Typical Dishes BAR:** *spicy tomato soup £1.10, home-made paté £1.25, steak and onion pie £3.95, chicken and vegetable pie £3.95, local salmon steak with cucumber sauce £6.20* **RESTAURANT:** *hot and sour chicken soup £3, Thai squid salad £4.50, stir-fried beef with basil £4.50, shrimp soup with vermicelli £4, diced chicken with peanut sauce £5, bananas in coconut milk and syrup £1.80* Vegetarian Meals: *vegetable stroganoff £3.95* **Beer** *Ind Coope, Tetley* Family Room **Credit Cards:** *Access, Visa*

RED WHARF BAY   Ship Inn

Anglesey LO75 4RJ   FOOD
Tel: (0248) 852568
Open: 11-3, 7-11 (all day July-Sept)
Licensee: Andrew Kenneally

Right on the shore at Traeth Coch and overlooking the sweep of the bay, the low white-painted limestone Ship Inn is fronted by hanging baskets and sports a fine pair of Lloyd and Trouncer cast iron street lamps at its entrance. A depiction of SS Royal Charter is inlaid in the upper wall, and a Silver Jubilee replica of the royal yacht Britannia's wheel is mounted in the bar. Customers come early at mealtimes, so at busy summer peak times delays are unavoidable, yet the menu remains sensibly short and with it comes a guarantee of freshness. Stick around a while and see the local fishermen delivering their catch. The menu includes a selection of light meals, described as snacks: paté and toast, smoked salmon trout, mushrooms in batter with a garlic dip, and cheese and onion quiche, all of which come with salad and are under £5. Main meals, accompanied by chips or baked potato, start with cottage pie, ham and broccoli mornay and mussels in garlic (topped with cheese) at under £4.50, progressing to gammon and pineapple, turkey steak in a cream and mushroom sauce, or the grilled catch of the day in the £7-£9 range. The board may change at a moment's notice, the likes of lasagne and chilli con carne regularly moving in to fill the gaps. Desserts show rather less variety: coffee mandarin gateau, pecan pie, fresh raspberry meringue, and lemon mousse cake are a typical selection. Quarry-tiled floors, genuine exposed beams and stonework, plus a mish-mash of maritime memorabilia and chiming clocks all make for an interesting interior; look too for the Tom Browne snooker cartoons and the fine Toby jug collection, whose rarest specimens are glass-encased. Beer drinkers fare well on well-kept Tetleys and Marston, and wine drinkers are offered a fair selection: Entre Deux Mers, Vouvray, Jacobs Creek Red and Cape Blush (by the bottle) among them. Children can enjoy their own menu in the little back family room, or, while parents keep a constant eye on the treacherous tide, they can romp in the garden right on the shore line.

Bar Meals: *12-2.15, 7-9.15   bar snacks both sessions*   **Restaurant:** *7-9.15*   **Typical Dishes BAR:** *carrot and caraway soup £1.75, ham and mushrooms £3.50, beef olives £4.95, garlic chicken £4.45, fish stew £4.65, autumn pudding £2.20   Vegetarian Meals Children's Menu*   Beer   *Marston; Tetley*   Whisky   *Family Room   Outdoor Play Area Garden   Outdoor Eating*   **Credit Cards:** *Access, Visa*

TY-CROES Queens Head, Bryn Du Tel: (0407) 810806: Unspoilt and cosy wood-panelled local, its various little rooms leading off a central hatch servery. Home cooked lunchtime and evening food; real fires; no music. Burtonwood beer. Open all day.

TYN-Y-GROES	**Groes Inn**

near Conwy LL32 8TN
Tel: (0492) 650545
Open: 12-3 (2.30 winter weekdays), 7 (6.30 summer)-11
Licensee: Dawn Humphreys

14th century free house with old beams, log fires, and a collection of antique tins, as well as jugs, hats, carnival glassware and portraits. Lovely river Conwy views from the pretty summer garden.

Bar Meals and Restaurant: *12-2, 6.30 (7 winter)-9; bar snacks lunchtime*   **Typical Dishes BAR:** *home-made soup £1.65, home-made paté £3.50, home-made game pie £5.50, stuffed whole local pigeon £5.50, Indian haddock with prawns £4.95, treacle tart*   **RESTAURANT:** *Arbroath smokie £4.25, local lamb with honey and rosemary £6.95, roasted boned half duck £7.50, Anglesey gammon and eggs £6.95   Vegetarian Meals: vegetable stroganoff   Children's Portions*   Beer   *Ind Coope, Tetley   Children Allowed in Bar to Eat   Outdoor Play Area   Garden   Outdoor Eating*   **Credit Cards:** *Access, Visa*

POWYS

BLEDDFA Hundred House Inn on A488 Tel: (054 781) 225: Comfortable village pub with various rooms, mainly home-cooked food in bar and restaurant; real fire; no music; garden; Marston, Ruddles, Whitbread beers. Bedrooms. Open: 11-3, 6-11 (all day summer)

BRECON	**Wellington Hotel**

The Bulwark LD3 7AD
Tel: (0874) 5225
Licensee: Ian Blair and Anne Thomas

Converted from a well-heeled merchant town house, a Georgian-fronted hotel standing opposite the Iron Duke's statue in the market square. Recent modernisation has brought up-to-date hotel facilities but kept the informality of a popular local; the former courtyard and stables are now a shopping arcade, with a coffee shop and pub access. Diverse food choices: a wide variety of snacks, stuffed pancakes, grills, 'house-special' jumbo-sized vol-au-vents; the residents' breakfast room is coffee-shop by day, candle-lit restaurant by night, with strong showings for both traditional Welsh and modern vegetarian cooking. There's also Bacchus, an intimate wine bar, which offers charcoal grills and self-served salads. Neatly-kept, plainly-furnished bedrooms; first floor residents' lounge.

Bar Meals: 11am (noon Sun)-10.30pm   *Restaurant:* evenings   *Vegetarian Meals* *Children's Portions*   **Beer**   Bass   Children Allowed in Bar to Eat   *Accommodation:* 18 bedrooms, all en suite, from £59 (single £39)   Children Welcome Overnight   Cots Available   Check-in: all day   *Credit Cards:* Access, Amex, Diners, Visa

BRECON George Hotel George Street Tel: (0874) 3422: Pubby hotel popular for its wide bar meals menu, from pizzas to seafood (available all day); conventional steaks and duckling menu in the restaurant. Children allowed for meals. Bedrooms. Garden. Bass, Marston, Wadworth beers. Open all day.

CRICKHOWELL	Bear Hotel

Brecon Road (A40) NP8 1BW   **FOOD**
Tel: (0873) 810408   ♈
Open: 10.30-3, 6-11   **B&B**
Licensee: Judith Hindmarsh

As late as the year 1852 there were a dozen daily coach departures from the Bear, the London coach heading for Gloucester at 4.50 pm and the North Mail leaving for Brecon at midnight. Vehicular access today is through the same cobbled archway, and the probable former waiting rooms, the bars of today, are still evocative of those romantic days, with open fires, blackened oak beams, ponderous Welsh dressers and Victorian farmhouse furniture. Further inside in a maze of rooms and recesses, the original layout, with its various levels, has been mercifully preserved in three tiers of restaurant and function rooms which share the tranquillity of rear views across the garden. Where the old now meets the new is virtually impossible to detect. Eating arrangements are similarly two-tiered. Aged-looking bar menus offer starters and light snacks like soups, home-made paté (£2.50), Arbroath smokie (£2.95), mushroom terrine (£3.50) and deep-fried plaice goujons (£2.95). More substantial and eclectic dishes include vegetable and chicken stir-fries (£5.85), sausage jambalaya (£5.75) and lamb with cumin and cardamom (£5.95); house specials might feature baked sea trout (£6.95), or turkey Cymraig, done in onions, mustard and garlic and served with sauté potatoes. Typical of the pudding list are raspberry sablé, lemon crunch pie, bread and butter pudding with rum-soaked raisins, and the cautionary "chocoholics anonymous". Some modernism and complication sets in à la carte. Timbale of leeks and pistachio in a mushroom sauce, a salmon-wrapped oyster baked in a pastry case – these are the stuff of discerning diners and require a competent kitchen. Both emerge pretty much unscathed. Candlelight and lacy Victorian tablecloths are appropriate and welcome; piped music and paper napkins rather less so. Attractive main house bedrooms are approached overlooking the Bear's wondrous interior on stairs with antique gnarled oak balustrades; the curve of the main road, less enchantingly, brings modern traffic within inches of the windows, a disadvantage of the front rooms. The inn's extension successfully echoes the balconied theme, with access to the neatly appointed new bedrooms looking inward over the brick paving and flower beds of the courtyard. There is also a splendid honeymoon suite with four-poster bed and whirlpool bath.

Bar Meals: 12-2, 6.30-10 (7-9.30 Sun); bar snacks lunchtime   *Restaurant:* 7-9.30 *Typical Dishes BAR:* leek and potato soup £1.50, dhal popovers £2.95, turkey Cymraeg £6.25, lasagne £5.75, salmon bechamel pie £6.50, bread and butter pudding £2.50 *RESTAURANT:* lightly curried mussels £2, leek timbale £3.95, rack of Welsh lamb £10.95, pigeon en croute £10.95, panache of seafood £10.95, chocoholics anonymous £2.50   Vegetarian Meals: parsnip and cashew nut bake   Children's Portions   **Beer** Bass; Ruddles   **Whisky**   Family Room   Garden   Outdoor Eating   *Accommodation:* 24 bedrooms, all en suite, from £48 (single £33)   Children Welcome Overnight   Cots Available   Check-in: all day   *Credit Cards:* Access, Amex, Visa

CRICKHOWELL   Nantyffin Cider Mill

Crickhowell NP8 1LG
Tel: (0873) 810775
Licensees; G Bridgeman and S Gerrard

Under new licensees, who also happen to be keen cooks, and carefully remodelled within; there's now a dining room proper in the restored mill, complete with original granite mill wheel. Looking very promising.

Bar Meals: 12-2, 6-10; bar snacks both sessions **Typical Dishes:** *celery, stilton and pear soup £1.95, avocado, bacon and scallop salad £3.95, steak and kidney pie with stout £5.80, rack of lamb with parsley crust £9.25, smoked haddock with egg sauce £5.60, sticky toffee pudding Vegetarian Meals: filo parcel with stilton, nuts and leeks £6.75 Children's Menu/Portions* `Cheese` `Beer` *Felinfoel Double Dragon; Marston Pedigree* `Cider` *Stonehouse Devon Cider Family Room Outdoor Play Area Garden Outdoor Eating* **Credit Cards:** *Access, Visa*

GLASBURY ON WYE Harp Inn Tel: (04974) 373: Popular, busy riverside inn; cheery atmosphere, families welcome. Real fires, music-free corners, garden; decent lunch and evening bar meals; bedrooms. Robinsons, Whitbread beers. Open: 11-3, 6-11.

HAY-ON-WYE   Old Black Lion

26 Lion Street HR3 5AD
Tel: (0497) 820841
Open: 11-3, 6-11
Licensees: John and Joan Collins

Hay-on-Wye, the bookshop (and tourist) town, is in fact in Wales, though often listed under Hereford & Worcester. But only just in Wales, and with a half-English, typically Welsh Marches atmosphere. This fine old town-centre inn is not idyllically quiet by any means, but does have plenty of unspoilt charm and a gregarious welcome, as well as low ceilings, steep stairs to bed, creaky floors, and painted furniture. The olde worlde pubbish restaurant has plates on the walls, black beams, dark wood tables, and candlelight. There are three possible breakfasts: the standard, the fisherman's special (salmon anglers abound) and the romantic, which offers caviar and a glass of champagne for a £4.50 supplement. Bedrooms include the Cromwell, where Oliver is said to have spent the night. Very popular as a meeting and eating place with locals.

Bar Meals: 12-2, 7-9; bar snacks both sessions **Restaurant:** *12-2 (Sun only), 7-9* **Typical Dishes BAR:** *lentil and tomato soup £2, smoked haddock mousse £3.20, steak and kidney pudding £5.60, Mediterranean seafood pasta £6.10, stuffed green peppers £5.85, treacle and walnut pie £2.65* **RESTAURANT:** *broccoli soup £2.10, lavercakes and bacon £3.20, Kashmiri lamb £9.20, chicken in Calvados £8.70, guinea fowl with black cherry sauce £9.95, Tia Maria meringue Vegetarian Meals: lentil bolognese £5.35 Children's Portions (some)* `Cheese` `Beer` *Draught Bass; Whitbread Flowers Original Children Allowed in Bar to Eat Patio/terrace Outdoor Eating* **Accommodation:** *10 bedrooms, 9 en suite, from £39.90 (single £16.95) Children Welcome Overnight Cot Available Check-in: all day* **Credit Cards:** *Access, Visa*

HOWEY   Drovers Arms

Llandrindod Wells LD1 5PT   ♥
Tel: (0597) 822508
Open: 11.45-3, 6.45-11 (12-2.30, 7-11 winter); closed Tue lunchtime
Licensees: David and Janet Day

Characterful Victorian pub; piano in the public bar; woodcarving in the lounge;
getting itself a reputation for good home cooking.

Bar Meals: 12-1.45, 7-9.30; bar snacks both sessions **Typical Dishes:** *minestrone with
parmesan £1.75, garlic prawns £2.75, lamb noisettes with cream, brandy and tarragon sauce
£6.50, steaks from £7.95, Oriental pork chop £6.50, treacle and lemon tart Vegetarian
Meals: home-made pasta Children's Menu/Portions* Beer *Marston; Whitbread
Children Allowed in Bar to Eat Outdoor Play Area Patio/terrace Outdoor Eating*
Accommodation: *3 bedrooms, 1 en suite, from £26 (single £14) Children Welcome
Overnight Check-in: by arrangement* **No Credit Cards**

LLANDRINDOD WELLS   Llanerch Inn

Llanerch Lane, off Waterloo Road LD1 5BG
Tel: (0597) 822086
Open: 11.30-3, 6-11
Licensee: John Leach

Welcoming and attractive 16th century inn; good summer garden, where boules is
keenly played.

Bar Meals: 12-2.15, 6 (7 Sun)-9; bar snacks both sessions **Restaurant:** *12-2 (Sun
only), 6-9.30* **Typical Dishes BAR:** *home-made broth £1.25, steak and kidney pie
£3.75, mixed grill £7.50, fishermans pie £2.75* **RESTAURANT:** *French onion soup
£1.50, carbonade of beef, coq au vin, seafood casserole (main courses all £5) Vegetarian
Meals: lasagne Children's Menu Children's Portions (some)* Beer *Bass; Robinsons
Family Room Outdoor Play Area Garden* **Accommodation:** *bedrooms from £35
(single £20)*

LLANFAIR CAEREINION   Goat Hotel

High Street SY21 0QS
Tel: (0938) 810428
Open: 11-11
Licensee: Richard Argument

18th century coaching inn. Romantically gloomy bedrooms with lots of original
features; all have TVs. Interesting home-made vegetarian selection.

Bar Meals: 12-2, 7-9; bar snacks both sessions **Restaurant:** *7-9 (weekends only)*
Typical Dishes BAR: *home-made soup of the day £1.50, paté £1.75, ham, cheese and
broccoli pie £3.50, home-made chicken dhansak £3, sugar-baked ham £3.25, chocolate
chiffon pie £1.25* **RESTAURANT:** *home-made chicken liver paté £1.75, grilled 12 oz
rump steak £7, Welsh lamb cutlets £5.25, duck breast with cream and Grand Marnier sauce
£7, summer fruit compote £1.25 Vegetarian Meals: barley bourguignon £3.25
Children's Portions* Cheese Beer *Felinfoel Dougle Dragon; Hancocks HB Family
Room Garden Outdoor Eating* **Accommodation:** *6 bedrooms, 4 en suite, from £30
(single £18) Children Welcome Overnight Cot Available Check-in: all day* **Credit
Cards:** *Access, Visa*

LLANFRYNACH   White Swan

Llanfrynach LD3 7BZ
Tel: (0874) 86276
Open: 12-3 (2.30 winter, closed Mon), 7-11; closed last 3 weeks Jan
Licensees: Mr and Mrs Bell

Externally looking a bit dowdy, but inside is as fascinating as ever, with its stone floors, rough stone walls, original timbers and a vast inglenook fireplace. Extension into a neighbouring cottage is apparently under way. Hearty, carefully prepared bar food, from an overlong, rather mixed menu; go for the obviously home-made.

Bar Meals: 12-2, 7-10 (12-1.30, 7-9 Sun; no food Mon); bar snacks both sessions
Typical Dishes: *French onion soup £1.95, smoked mackerel paté £3.50, chicken curry £4.85, beef and mushroom pie £6.90, fishermans pie £5.60, chocolate cream mousse £2.10   Vegetarian Meals: ratatouille au gratin £3.90   Children's Menu* `Beer`
*Brain's; Whitbread   Children Allowed in Bar to Eat   Garden   Outdoor Eating   **No Credit Cards***

LLANGATTOCK Vine Tree on A4077: Very busy in summer, separated from Crickhowell by the pretty river Usk and old bridge; good views from pub terrace. Decent snacks, sound, often ambitious bar meals; children allowed in for meals. Whitbread beers. Open: 11-3, 6-11.

LLANGENNY Dragon's Head: Delightful summer pub in pretty area; genuinely welcoming to allcomers; decent, often imaginative food (not Sun eve, nor all day Mon); children allowed in to eat. Garden. Bass, Brains beers. Open: 12-3.30, 6-11.

LLANGORSE   Castle Inn

Brecon LD3 7UB
Tel: (0874) 84225
Open: 11.30-3, 6-11 (all day if busy)
Licensees: Jan Bristow and Ian Little

17th century cottage pub with flagstoned bar and open fireplace; bar meals in the separate buttery.

*Bar Meals: 12-2, 6-9.30 (7-9 Sun); bar snacks both sessions   **Typical Dishes:** carrot and orange soup £1.40, garlic mushrooms £2.50, home-made chicken Kiev £5.50, beef, mushroom and red wine casserole £4.35, home-made chicken provencale, home-made apricot pie £1.40   Vegetarian Meals: lasagne £3.95   Children's Menu/Portions* `Beer`
*Brains; Hancocks; Whitbread   Family Room   Patio/terrace   Outdoor Eating   **Credit Cards:** Access, Visa*

LLANGORSE Red Lion Tel: (087 484) 238: Recommended for bed and breakfast, a pleasant village pub with ten homely, immaculately clean bedrooms at very reasonable prices. Cosy, stone-walled bars; children welcome overnight. Marston, Whitbread beers.

LLANGURIG Blue Bell Inn Tel: (05515) 254: Recommended for bed and breakfast, a welcoming, charming fishing inn, in the highest village in Wales. Slate-floored, simple bar; homely residents' lounge; compact, rustic bedrooms with modern units. Children welcome overnight. Powell, Whitbread beers. Open: 11-2.30, 6-11.

LLANWRTYD WELLS   Neuadd Arms Hotel

The Square LD5 4RB
Tel: (05913) 236
Open: 11-3, 6-11
Licensee: Gordon Green

Imposing riverside hotel at the centre of Britain's smallest town. The landlord is a great organiser of walks, cycling (hire) and the mid-Wales Beer Festival (November). Traditional Welsh back bar with traditional Welsh singing at weekends; more sedate lounge. Very friendly.

Bar Meals: 12-2.30, 6-8.30; bar snacks both sessions   *Restaurant:* 7.30-8.30   **Typical Dishes BAR:** *leek broth £1.90, smoked mackerel, double Welsh lamb cutlets £4.80, prime Welsh sirloin steak with mushrooms £7.20, Madras chicken curry £3.70, chocolate meringue chantilly*   **RESTAURANT** *table d'hote £9.50: roast Welsh lamb with apricot stuffing, beef carbonade, chicken Basquaise, Grand Marnier soufflé   Vegetarian Meals: vegetarian chilli £3.20   Children's Menu* ▮Beer▮ *Bass; Felinfoel   Children Allowed in Bar to Eat Patio/terrace   Outdoor Eating* **Accommodation:** *18 bedrooms, 8 en suite, from £37 (single £18.50)   Children Welcome Overnight   Cots Available   Check-in: all day* **Credit Cards:** *Access, Visa*

LLOWES   Radnor Arms

Llowes HR3 5JA   ▮FOOD▮
Tel: (04974) 460   ☺
Open: 11-3, 6.30-11.30 (closed Sun eve, all Mon)   ☼
Licensee: Brian Gorringe

Developed over the years from its original identity as the old village school to its current state of culinary refinement, the Radnor Arms nevertheless still remains more a pub for eating in than a restaurant-with-bar. Few restaurants, in fact, would be so ambitious in their menu selection, and the rod which proprietor Brian Gorringe makes for his own back is arguably the pub's biggest downfall. With only a dozen tables and no more than forty seats, it's all the more surprising to encounter 99 starters, snacks and main dishes from which to choose! Despite the useful summer overflow to several picnic tables in the garden, still the pub's so tiny that both gents' and ladies' toilets are relegated to the outhouse. Inside, the Radnor Arms divides by means of heavy pine panels into the bar area proper, popular by day, and a more spacious, lofty-beamed garden side for more leisurely evening enjoyment, and for which you ought to book. Either way, there's good beer from the bar – with Flowers IPA and Felinfoel Double Dragon on handpump – and a modest selection of house wines. Now to the menu, where the soup choice might include carrot and orange (£2), French onion, watercress or game; meat dishes might include lamb's liver and bacon, breaded sweetbreads (£6.30) or steak and oyster pie (£6.80); the fish choice haddock mornay (£6.85), whole grilled place (£9.40) or trout (£6.75); more exotically, perhaps, goujons of Hoki fish (£5.50), paella Valenciana (£7.35), Wiener schnitzel (£7.40) or Louisiana Cajun fish (£6.30), while the spinach and stilton quiche (£4.25), savoyarde omelette (£4.50) and spaghetti milanese (£3.95) are guaranteed meat-free. Puddings include banana fritters, compote of summer fruits (£2.70), boozy rum babas piled with cream and strawberries, or a scarcely less exotic range of ice-cream sundaes (£1.95). Some homely touches help to extend a warm Welsh welcome. Cruets and coffee sets are of hand-made Black Mountain pottery, and there are woolly dolls and framed three-dimensional paper découpages for sale alongside souvenir Rugby World Cup Wine, the latter bottled in Bordeaux yet commemorative of Cardiff.

Bar Meals and Restaurant: lunch and evening;   bar snacks both sessions   *Vegetarian Meals* ▮Beer▮ *Felinfoel; Whitbread* ▮Whisky▮ *Garden/Outdoor Eating* **No Credit Cards**

LLYSWEN ★ Griffin Inn

On A470 LD3 0UR
Tel: (0874) 754241
Open: 12-3 (2.30 winter), 7-11
Licensees: Richard and Di Stockton

FOOD
B&B

Mythically speaking, the griffin is a creature of vast proportions, half lion, half dragon, its whole being considerably less awesome than its constituent parts. No such problems exist for Richard and Di Stockton, for their Griffin is nothing short of splendid in all departments and so conspicuously well-run as to have been voted the most welcoming pub in Britain. That locally-caught salmon and brook trout feature so regularly on the menu is scarcely surprising as the Griffin employs its own ghillie, and fishing stories abound in the bar, which is the centre of village life. It's hung with framed displays of fishing flies and maps of the upper and lower reaches of the Wye valley, and dominated by a splendid inglenook fire. Good beer is also taken seriously and kept in tip-top condition, summer Boddingtons and Flowers IPA likely giving way in winter to sturdier brews like Brains and Bass. In the adjacent lounge, low tables, high-backed Windsor chairs, and window seats make a comfy setting for either a light snack or one of the daily-changing hot dishes, perhaps ratatouille pasta au gratin, jugged beef and kidneys in port, ragout of lamb with tarragon, or simply grilled fresh plaice. Evening meals provide a wider choice of more substantial fare, either in the no smoking restaurant or the bars, as space allows. Here, duck liver paté, marinated seafood or grilled sardines precede wild pigeon in cider, poached salmon with Glanwye sauce, or roast Welsh lamb, followed by treacle tart, passion fruit mousse and crème brulée, or a scrummy home-made ice-cream or sorbet. Bedrooms, recently increased to eight and all but one with en suite facilities, revert to the fishing theme: Alexander Durham Ranger and Green Highlander, for instance, being named after fishing flies. To say that they are cottagey is not to decry the pretty floral curtains and bed-covers; they are also wonderfully tranquil, and though there are telephones, television is considered superfluous. The splendid new residents' lounge on the upper floor of the inn's oldest part is dramatically set under original rafters dating, it is thought, from 1467.

Bar Meals: 12-2, 7-9; bar snacks lunchtime   *Restaurant:* 12 (1 winter)-2 (Sun only), 7-9 (not Sun)   *Typical Dishes:* home-made soup £2.35, hot chicken liver and bacon salad £3.35, jugged venison and beef £7.85, Griffin curry £5.35, fresh salmon with Glanwye sauce £9.75, treacle tart £2.55   Vegetarian Meals: ratatouille pasta £5.10   Children's Portions   Cheese   Beer   Whitbread Boddingtons Bitter, Flowers IPA   Children Allowed in Bar to Eat   Patio/terrace   Outdoor Eating   *Accommodation:* 8 bedrooms, 7 en suite, from £50 (single £28.50)   Cots Available   Check-in: all day   *Credit Cards:* Access, Amex, Diners, Visa

MONTGOMERY Dragon Inn

Montgomery SY15 6AA
Tel: (0686) 668359
Open: 11-11
Licensees: Mark and Sue Michaels

Timbered 17th century coaching inn, modernised and with a brand new indoor heated pool, freely available to diners; perhaps a dip before dinner?

Bar Meals and Restaurant: 12-2 (restaurant Sun only), 7-9; bar snacks both sessions except Sat eve   *Typical Dishes BAR:* home-made soup £1.50, prawn cocktail £2.75, steak and Guinness pie £4.95, fresh salmon salad £6.85, deep-fried vegetables with garlic dip £4.95, sherry trifle £1.75   *RESTAURANT:* whole prawns in garlic and crabmeat sauce £5, rack of lamb £11.55, grilled red mullet with lemon cream £11.25, stuffed mushrooms au gratin

£8.25, chocolate and whisky mousse £2.50   Vegetarian Meals   Children's Menu/Portions
Beer *Felinfoel; Sam Powell; Wood's   Family Room   Garden   Outdoor Eating*
Accommodation: *15 bedrooms, all en suite, from £58.75 (single £35.75)   Children*
Welcome Overnight   Cots Available   Check-in: all day **Credit Cards:** *Access, Amex, Visa*

OLD RADNOR   Harp Inn

Presteigne LD8 2RH   ▼
Tel: (054 421) 655
Open: 12-2.30 (not Tue), 7-11
Licensees: Robert and Shirley Pritchard

Friendly, welcoming, comfortable, a good place to spend a weekend; traditional bars
of real character, and chatty hosts. The troublesome gander has now been segregated
from visitors, and the "antique landlady refurbished", apparently. Delightfully
peaceful, with seats on the large common overlooking the valley.

Bar Meals and Restaurant: *12-1.30 (restaurant Sun only), 7-9 (not Sun eves); bar snacks
both sessions* **Typical Dishes BAR:** *home-made chicken soup £1.50, prawn cocktail
£2.55, lasagne £4, chicken curry £5.50, faggots £3.75, apple pie £1.75*
RESTAURANT: *similar starters and puddings; sirloin steak £8, gammon and egg £6,
trout £8   Vegetarian Meals: lasagne   Children's Menu (limited)   Children's Portions*
Beer *Hook Norton; Whitbread; Wood's; Wye Valley   Family Room   Children
Allowed in Bar to Eat   Outdoor Play Area   Garden   Outdoor Eating* **Accommodation:**
*3 bedrooms, all en suite, from £40 (single £25)   Children Welcome Overnight   Cot
Available Check-in: all day* **No Credit Cards**

PRESTEIGNE   Royal Oak

High Street LD8 2BA
Tel: (0544) 267510
Open: 11.30-3, 6-11
Licensees: Alan and Alison Leach

Tiny bar and larger restaurant area; the kitchen has recently been entirely
refurbished.

Bar Meals: *11.30-2.30, 6.30-9.30; bar snacks both sessions* **Restaurant:** *6.30-9.30*
Typical Dishes BAR: *minestrone £1.20, garlic mushrooms £2.25, home-made steak and
kidney pie £3.65, home-made lasagne £3.75, late breakfast £3.50, chocolate brandy crunch
£1.50* **RESTAURANT:** *mushroom soup £1.40, home-made paté £1.95, steaks from
£8.50, lamb flambé £8.95, scampi provencale £8.50   Vegetarian Meals: moussaka
Children's Menu* **Beer** *Draught Bass   Children Allowed in Bar to Eat   Patio/terrace
Outdoor Eating   Summer Barbecue* **No Credit Cards**

TRECASTLE   Castle Hotel

Trecastle LD3 8UH   ▼
Tel: (0874) 636354
Open: 12-2.30, 7-11.30 (inc. Sun)
Licensees: Clive and Corinne Marshall

Imposing Georgian hotel, a former coaching halt, with lots of character surviving.
Bar meals in the cosy hotel bar – open fire, long wooden tables, benches and
window seats; also elegantly proportioned restaurant. Individually decorated
bedrooms vary in size from small to spacious; B&B good value.

Bar Meals: *12-2, 7-9; bar snacks both sessions*   **Restaurant:** *12-2 (Sun only), 7.30-9 (not Sun)*   **Typical Dishes BAR:** *broccoli and stilton soup £2.20, deep-fried crispy vegetables £2.75, steak and ale pie £5.20, tandoori chicken £5.45, grilled gammon £5.95, summer pudding £2.20*   **RESTAURANT:** *avocado and prawns £3.95, honey glazed lamb steak £7.50, peppered fillet steak £11.50, whole lemon sole Bretonne £9.75*   Vegetarian Meals: *celery and cashew nut risotto*   Children's Menu/Portions   `Cheese`   `Beer`   Courage   Children Allowed in Bar to Eat   Patio/terrace   Outdoor Eating   **Accommodation:** *9 bedrooms, 5 en suite, from £36 (single £26)*   Children Welcome Overnight   Cots Available   Check-in: all day   **Credit Cards:** *Access, Visa*

Channel Islands and Isle of Man

CHANNEL ISLANDS

ALDERNEY

ST ANNE   Georgian House

Victoria Street   ♥
Tel: (0481) 822471
Open: 10-3, 6.30-12
Licensee: Stephen Hope

Attractive whitewashed Georgian town house on a picturesque cobbled street.
Convivial hosts, and a characterful bar, with reliably good food; good daily fish
specials. Refurbishment of the bedrooms (curiously reduced in number from four to
two), means no overnight accommodation until (probably) late spring 1992. Bed
and breakfast was previously warmly recommended in this guide.

Bar Meals: 12-3; bar snacks   *Restaurant:* 12-3 (bar menu), 7.30-12   **Typical Dishes**
BAR: *home-made soup of the day £1.50, melon and sorbet £2.50, curry of the day £4,*
fillet steak £11.50, king prawn tails with garlic £6.50   **RESTAURANT** *(around £15 a*
head): home-made chicken liver and brandy paté, sautéed scallops, rack of lamb with
Cumberland sauce, spring chicken, char-grilled fillet steak, home-made puddings   Vegetarian
Meals   Children's Menu/Portions ▆Cheese▆ ▆Beer▆ *Ringwood Best   Children Allowed*
in Bar to Eat   Garden   Outdoor Eating   Summer Barbecue   Accommodation (closed for
refurbishment until spring '92): 2 bedrooms, both en suite; no prices available   Credit
Cards: Access, Amex, Diners, Visa

ST ANNE Moorings Hotel Braye Harbour Tel: (0481 824221) Decent bar meals;
children welcome; garden. Bedrooms. Guernsey beers. Open all day.

GUERNSEY

FOREST   Deerhound Inn

Le Bourg
Tel: (0481) 38585
Open: 11 am-11.45 pm (12-2.30, 7-11 Sun, if eating)
Licensee: Brian Stone

Cosy, friendly country inn, popular for bar meals.

Bar Meals: 12-1.45, 7-9.30; bar snacks both sessions   **Typical Dishes:** *celery and stilton*
soup £1.25, poacher's hot smokie £2.25, steak and mushroom pie £3.95, supreme of
chicken Dijonnaise £4.75, fresh Guernsey whiting £3.95, lemon apple pie £1.25
Vegetarian Meals: cauliflower cheese   Children's Menu/Portions ▆Beer▆ *Guernsey*
Brewery Bitter   Family Room   Outdoor Play Area   Garden   Outdoor Eating
Accommodation: 10 bedrooms, 2 en suite, from £32 (single £16)   Children Welcome
Overnight   Cot Available   Check-in: all day   Credit Cards: Diners, Visa

ST MARTINS   La Trelade Hotel

Forest Road
Tel: (0481) 35454
Open: 11.30-2.30 (12-2 Sun), 5.30-11.30

Comfortably if not stylishly modernised; good fresh fish specials.

Bar Meals: 12-2, 6-8.30   **Restaurant:** *7-8.30*   **Typical Dishes BAR:** *vegetable soup £1.25, avocado with prawns £2.80, supreme of chicken £4.50, curry of the day £3.80* **RESTAURANT:** *steak au poivre £4.50, scallops £7, half lobster salad £6.50 Vegetarian Meals: avocado cheese bake   Children's Menu/Portions   Family Room Outdoor Play Area   Garden   Outdoor Eating   Summer Barbecue* **Accommodation:** *45 bedrooms, all en suite, from £48 (single £34)   Children Welcome Overnight   Cots Available   Check-in: all day*   **Credit Cards:** *Access, Visa*

ST PETER PORT   Ship & Crown

Pier Steps
Tel: (0481) 721368
Open: 10.30 am-11 pm (closed Sun)
Licensee: Glen Pontin

Usually-buzzing yachting pub opposite marina. Lots of maritime pictures and memorabilia, in simply furnished busy main bar and quieter back drinking area. Fresh, unfussy, fishy food. This was the Germans' naval HQ during the World War II island occupation. No children.

Bar Meals: 11-3 (2 Sat); bar snacks   **Typical Dishes:** *fresh local crab salad £7, fresh local fish and chips £4.20, home-made pies £3.50*   `Beer` *Guernsey Bitter* `Whisky` *No* **Credit Cards**

JERSEY

ST AUBIN   Old Court House Inn

Tel: (0534) 46433   ▼
Open: 11-11 (11-1, 4.30-11 Sun)
Licensee: Jonty Sharp

A splendid position overlooking the characterful harbour is enjoyed by this tall, white-painted 15th century inn. Simple but appetising lunchtime snacks are served in the lively, atmospheric cellar bars, with their exposed stone walls and low oak-beamed ceilings. A second, quieter bar upstairs is shaped like a ship's cabin and panelled throughout in teak; there's also a relaxing little lounge. Bedrooms are a tasteful combination of old pine furnishings and pretty, co-ordinating wallpapers and fabrics. All the usual little comforts, and excellent, stylishly tiled bathrooms. Many (including the penthouse suite) have the bonus of fine sea views.

Bar Meals: 12.30-2.15, 7.30-9.30 (eves Nov-Mar only)   **Restaurant:** *12.30-2.30, 7.30-11*   **Typical Dishes BAR:** *crab bisque £2.50, moules marinière £4.25, fillet of pork Calvados £6.50, monkfish in filo pastry £8.75, poached turbot Américaine £12, hot rum baba   Vegetarian Meals: lasagne   Children's Menu/Portions   Family Room   Garden Outdoor Eating*   **Accommodation:** *10 bedrooms, all en suite, from £50 (single £25) Check-in: all day*   **Credit Cards:** *Access, Visa*

ST BRELADE   La Pulente Hotel

Tel: (0534) 41760
Open: all day (11-1, 4.30-11 Sun)

Dramatically set above rocky cove; cleanly modernised inside, pretty terrace, piped music can be intrusive.

Bar Meals: 12-2, 6.30-8 (Wed-Sat eves winter); no food Sun; bar snacks lunchtime
Typical Dishes: home-made soup (winter) £1, rump steak garni, spare ribs, gambas in garlic
Vegetarian Meals: vegetable moussaka **Beer** *Draught Bass   Family Room*
Patio/terrace Outdoor Eating **No Credit Cards**

ST BRELADE   Smugglers Inn

Ouaisne Bay
Tel: (0534) 41510
Open: 11-11 (11-1, 4.30-11 Sun)
Licensee: N Godfray

Food is routine, but good traditional atmosphere in the stone and timber bars, close to beach.

Bar Meals: 12-2, 6-8.30; bar snacks lunchtime   *Typical Dishes: home-made soup £1,*
potato wedges £1.70, lasagne £3.50, 8 oz real beefburger £3.50, Jersey plaice £4.80,
apple pie £1.50   Vegetarian Meals: vegetable pasta bake £3.75 **Beer** *Draught Bass*
Family Room **No Credit Cards**

ISLE OF MAN

PEEL   Creek Inn

Tel: (062 484) 2216
Open: 11-10.45 (12-1.30, 8-10 Sun)
Licensees: Robert and Jean McAleer

Bustling, quaintly situated quayside pub with views of working fishing boats. Large, bright, unpretentious bar with real fire. Well-known for its seafood and fishy menu; queenies are Manx scallops.

Bar Meals: throughout opening hours.   *Typical Dishes BAR: vegetable soup 85p, smoked*
salmon or kipper paté £2.95, home-made lasagne £3.95, fresh Manx kippers £2.95,
queenies mornay £4.20, lemon meringue pie £1.20   Vegetarian Meals: rigatoni and
vegetable bake £3.95   Children's Menu/Portions **Beer** *Okells Mild, Bitter* **Whisky**
Children Allowed in Bar to Eat   Riverside Patio/terrace **No Credit Cards**

READERS' COMMENTS

Please use this sheet, and the continuation overleaf, to recommend pubs of really **outstanding quality.**

Complaints about any of the Guide's entries will be treated seriously and passed on to our inspectorate, but we would like to remind you that you should always take up your complaint with the management at the time.

We regret that owing to the volume of readers' communications received each year, we will be unable to acknowledge these forms, but your comments will certainly be seriously considered.

Please post to:
Egon Ronay's Guides, 35 Tadema Road, London SW10 0PZ
Please use an up-to-date Guide. (Pub Guide 1992)

Name and address of establishment	*Your recommendation or complaint*

Readers' Comments Continued

Name and address of establishment	Your recommendation or complaint

Your Name _____
(BLOCK LETTERS PLEASE)

Address _____

READERS' COMMENTS

Please use this sheet, and the continuation overleaf, to recommend pubs of really
outstanding quality.

Complaints about any of the Guide's entries will be treated seriously and passed on
to our inspectorate, but we would like to remind you that you should always take up
your complaint with the management at the time.

We regret that owing to the volume of readers' communications received each year, we
will be unable to acknowledge these forms, but your comments will certainly be
seriously considered.

Please post to:
Egon Ronay's Guides, 35 Tadema Road, London SW10 0PZ
Please use an up-to-date Guide. (Pub Guide 1992)

Name and address of establishment	Your recommendation or complaint

READERS' COMMENTS CONTINUED

Name and address of establishment	Your recommendation or complaint

Your Name _____
(BLOCK LETTERS PLEASE)

Address _____

READERS' COMMENTS

Please use this sheet, and the continuation overleaf, to recommend pubs of really
outstanding quality.

Complaints about any of the Guide's entries will be treated seriously and passed on
to our inspectorate, but we would like to remind you that you should always take up
your complaint with the management at the time.

We regret that owing to the volume of readers' communications received each year, we
will be unable to acknowledge these forms, but your comments will certainly be
seriously considered.

Please post to:
Egon Ronay's Guides, 35 Tadema Road, London SW10 0PZ
Please use an up-to-date Guide. (Pub Guide 1992)

Name and address of establishment	*Your recommendation or complaint*

READERS' COMMENTS CONTINUED

Name and address of establishment	*Your recommendation or complaint*

Your Name _____
(BLOCK LETTERS PLEASE)

Address _____

_____

_____

_____

READERS' COMMENTS

Please use this sheet, and the continuation overleaf, to recommend pubs of really
outstanding quality.

Complaints about any of the Guide's entries will be treated seriously and passed on
to our inspectorate, but we would like to remind you that you should always take up
your complaint with the management at the time.

We regret that owing to the volume of readers' communications received each year, we
will be unable to acknowledge these forms, but your comments will certainly be
seriously considered.

Please post to:
Egon Ronay's Guides, 35 Tadema Road, London SW10 0PZ
Please use an up-to-date Guide. (Pub Guide 1992)

Name and address of establishment	*Your recommendation or complaint*

READERS' COMMENTS CONTINUED

Name and address of establishment	Your recommendation or complaint

Your Name _____
(BLOCK LETTERS PLEASE)

Address _____

_____

_____

_____

READERS' COMMENTS

Please use this sheet, and the continuation overleaf, to recommend pubs of really
outstanding quality.

Complaints about any of the Guide's entries will be treated seriously and passed on
to our inspectorate, but we would like to remind you that you should always take up
your complaint with the management at the time.

We regret that owing to the volume of readers' communications received each year, we
will be unable to acknowledge these forms, but your comments will certainly be
seriously considered.

Please post to:
Egon Ronay's Guides, 35 Tadema Road, London SW10 0PZ
Please use an up-to-date Guide. (Pub Guide 1992)

Name and address of establishment	*Your recommendation or complaint*

READERS' COMMENTS CONTINUED

Name and address of establishment	Your recommendation or complaint

Your Name _____
(BLOCK LETTERS PLEASE)

Address _____